Review Annual

Evaluation Studies

Review Annual

Volume 10   1985

Edited by
Linda H. Aiken
and
Barbara H. Kehrer

 **SAGE** PUBLICATIONS   Beverly Hills   London   New Delhi

For information address:

SAGE Publications, Inc.
275 South Beverly Drive
Beverly Hills, California 90212

SAGE Publications India Pvt. Ltd.
M-32 Market
Greater Kailash I
New Delhi 110 048 India

SAGE Publications Ltd
28 Banner Street
London EC1Y 8QE
England

Printed in the United States of America

International Standard Book Number 0-8039-2506-9

International Standard Series Number 0364-7390

Library of Congress Catalog Card No. 76-15865

FIRST PRINTING

CONTENTS

About the Editors

LINDA H. AIKEN is Vice President of The Robert Wood Johnson Foundation in Princeton, New Jersey. The foundation, a national philanthropy devoted to improving health care in the United States, has devoted a substantial portion of its resources to large-scale multiple site demonstration and evaluations. Dr. Aiken is a sociologist and nurse, a member of the Institute of Medicine of the National Academy of Sciences, past chair of the American Sociological Association's Medical Sociology Section, and past president of the American Academy of Nursing. Dr. Aiken was a member of the recent national Advisory Council on Social Security. She is editor of three books on nursing and public policy, is co-editor (with David Mechanic) of *Applications of Social Science to Clinical Medicine and Health Policy*, and has published papers on health policy and evaluation research issues.

BARBARA H. KEHRER is Vice President of the Henry J. Kaiser Family Foundation in Menlo Park, California. An economist who has specialized in health policy research, Dr. Kehrer joined the Kaiser Family Foundation in 1984, after spending two years as senior program officer at The Robert Wood Johnson Foundation. From 1975 to 1982, she was a senior economist at Mathematica Policy Research (MPR) in Princeton, New Jersey. At MPR, Dr. Kehrer directed several research projects for the U.S. Department of Health and Human Services, including an evaluation of the National Health Service Corps, an evaluation of the department's Health Manpower Shortage Area criteria, two research projects on the impact of income maintenance on infant health status, and a study of the temporary nursing services industry. Previously Dr. Kehrer was Director, Department of Economic Research, American Medical Association (1971-1975) and a member of the Economics Department faculty of Fisk University in Nashville, Tennessee (1968-1971).

Introduction

Linda H. Aiken and Barbara H. Kehrer

Twenty years ago President Johnson joined former President Truman in signing the historic Medicare and Medicaid programs into law. These programs were part of a ten-point strategy outlined in the 1964 *Economic Report of the President* to eradicate poverty in the United States. The ten-point strategy, which was to become known as the War on Poverty, included, in addition to improving access to medical care for the poor and the elderly, the ambitious objectives of expanding educational opportunity, eliminating racial discrimination, improving the work opportunities of disadvantaged youth, eliminating hunger, improving housing conditions, and providing financial help for the disabled and the poor elderly.

The programs of the War on Poverty were launched with bipartisan enthusiasm. Many policymakers and academics viewed the social and economic problems facing the nation in the early 1960s as solvable given the right interventions. In some areas, such as health, major new programs—particularly Medicaid and Medicare—were enacted and launched rather quickly. In other areas, such as income maintenance and housing, experimental approaches were designed and tested on a scale never before experienced. The needs of policymakers for practical information on program outcomes spawned a large and vigorous evaluation research enterprise.

In the 20 years since the launching of the War on Poverty, the mood of the nation has changed. The widespread confidence of the 1960s that the nation's complex social problems could be solved—particularly by government intervention—has given way to skepticism and a general assessment that change has been too slow and that the gains do not justify the nation's investment to date.

The social policy debate in 1985 is substantially different from that of twenty years ago. The nation is emerging from a serious economic recession. The public's concerns focus more on their own economic well-being than on solving complex social problems. In an era of huge federal budget deficits, there is almost no support for new major initiatives to combat poverty or to eliminate social injustice. Those policies that *are* on the agenda represent incremental changes or efforts to reduce spending for existing programs.

Evaluation research, however, has not faded from the scene in this changing environment. In fact, evaluation studies—particularly those of large-scale experiments and national demonstrations—have assumed a surprisingly central role in the current heated debate over reductions in domestic spending. Two recent controversial books provide good illustrations of how the accumulated body of evidence on program effectiveness derived from two decades of evaluation research is marshalled to argue for two entirely different points of view on the success of social programs of the past two decades. Both books have weaknesses that have been noted in numerous reviews. We find them interesting, however, as illustrations of how evaluation research findings are being used in current policy debates.

Charles Murray's *Losing Ground* (1984) has gained considerable attention from ideological conservatives. However, independent of his ideological perspective, the volume is a tribute to the diversity of evaluation studies and the wealth of statistics gathered under federal sponsorship over the past 20 years. Murray marshalls these data to support the thesis that federal social welfare programs launched between 1950 and 1980 failed to eliminate poverty despite huge expenditures, which increased twenty-fold in constant dollars over the period. Rather, he argues, many of the programs initiated in the areas of welfare, education, job training, and criminal justice made matters worse by rewarding failure rather than encouraging productive problem-solving behaviors that eventually led most of us to economic independence. Thus Murray effectively uses the studies commissioned in a different era by advocates of social change to provide grist for the mills of those favoring dismantling the nation's social welfare programs.

In contrast, Schwarz in *America's Hidden Success* (1983) uses the same body of research to reach a very different set of conclusions. Schwarz argues that the programs of the past 20 years have been much more successful in reducing poverty than has been generally acknowledged. He notes that when government cash benefits and in-kind transfers are considered, poverty has declined substantially. Schwarz contends further that most social welfare spending is devoted to groups that are outside the labor market and are therefore unlikely to be affected by vigorous economic growth. These groups include the elderly, the disabled, and single women with small children. Moreover, in reviewing evaluation studies from many of the programs Murray dismisses as failures, Schwarz interprets the sometimes inconclusive results as failures in implementation rather than concept.

A key difference between Schwarz and Murray, and between the opposing sides of the current policy debate over social spending, is the definition of poverty used. Figure 1 illustrates three different definitions of poverty. The official definition used by the Census Bureau is based only on cash income. However, many of the federal antipoverty programs provided benefits instead of or in

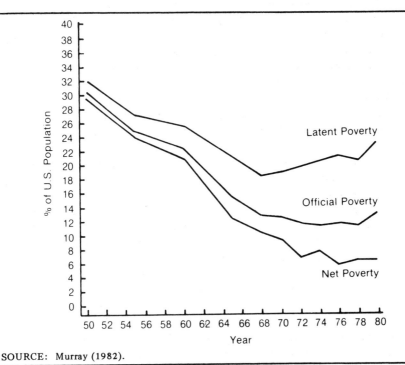

SOURCE: Murray (1982).

Figure 1   Three Measures of Poverty 1950-1980

addition to cash payments. Such "in-kind transfers" include Medicare, Medicaid, food stamps, subsidized housing, subsidized day care, and job training. In-kind transfers represent 40 percent of all social welfare spending and constitute the fastest-growing segment of the social welfare system. In 1980, the Bureau of the Census calculated a new poverty definition—"net poverty"—which takes into account both cash income and in-kind transfers. The third measure of poverty—"latent poverty"—represents the number of people who would be poor in the absence of federal assistance.

A major objective of the War on Poverty was to decrease the proportion of Americans who were dependent on some form of public support. Using this criterion, Murray argues that latent poverty has increased, showing that Americans have become more dependent on public support, not less. Schwarz, taking the opposite view, argues that the continuing decline in net poverty is conclusive evidence that our social welfare system is working.

The debate over the successes and failures of social welfare programs promises to continue as pressures to reduce domestic spending escalate. Although advocates and opponents of particular programs continue to use and perhaps even abuse the substantial body of evaluation research derived from the past two decades, researchers still have not written the final chapters on many of the programs at issue.

We have chosen as the unifying theme of this volume an exploration of what we now know from major evaluations of large-scale national demonstrations and social experiments. In reviewing the evaluation research literature for the past 18 months, we placed highest priority on the selection of recent studies of major multisite demonstrations that have potentially important implications for public policy. In most cases, the papers were chosen because they exemplify well-designed and well-executed evaluation research. However, we have also tried to portray honestly the difficulties, dilemmas, and trade-offs inherent in evaluation research. Thus where possible we have included published data and commentary representing different perspectives on the research findings from important studies.

In addition to selecting studies evaluating recent large-scale demonstrations, we have included continuing work on large and important social experiments such as the Seattle and Denver Income Maintenance Experiments, the Health Insurance Study, and the Experimental Housing Allowance Program that remain a source of continuing public policy debate. We have also included secondary analyses that shed additional light on controversial studies with major policy implications, such as the Coleman report comparing the effectiveness of public and private schools.

The composition of the volume represents the focus and themes of evaluation research from 1983 to mid-1985. We have tried to represent the literature of this period across a broad range of social policy concerns. The level of evaluation research activity varies tremendously across social policy areas, reflecting current rates of public investment. Health care has been the most active area for evaluation research. The Health Insurance Study is the major remaining large-scale social experiment of the 1970s on which initial findings are still emerging. A number of other evaluations of multisite demonstrations in health care have recently been completed as a result of the infusion of private foundation funds. Thus although our own backgrounds are in health policy, what may seem to be an overrepresentation of health research is simply indicative of the far greater evaluation research activity in health care at this time.

The themes of the period we reviewed are well characterized by David Greenberg and Philip Robins in Chapter 1 on the changing role of social experiments in policy analysis. The papers included in the volume show the transition in evaluation research that has necessarily followed the shift in public policy from broad, comprehensive social interventions aimed at accomplishing multiple goals—such as welfare reform and national health insurance—to more recent efforts representing incremental changes in existing programs to accomplish specific targeted outcomes—such as motor vehicle inspection to reduce accidental death and injury, and modifying the Medicare program to permit coverage of hospice services.

Evaluation research design, methodology, and statistical methods have continued to advance during the 1980s. We have included a sample of papers on topics of design and methods. In some cases we have chosen papers that discuss the implications of methodological and statistical advances rather than the original papers themselves due to the highly technical nature of the latter papers. We hope interested readers will pursue the original sources.

We are grateful to the authors and publishers who made it possible for us to include their work in this volume. We also wish to acknowledge the substantial contributions of Katherine Parker, who managed the project from its inception to its completion.

REFERENCES

Murray, C. A. (1982). Two wars against poverty: Economic growth and the Great Society. *The Public Interest, 69* (Fall), 3-16.
Murray, C. A. (1984). *Losing ground: American social policy 1950-1980.* New York: Basic Books.
Schwarz, J. E. (1983). *America's hidden success: A reassessment of twenty years of public policy.* New York: Norton.

1

The Changing Role of Social
Experiments in Policy Analysis

David Greenberg
University of Maryland—Baltimore County

Philip Robins
University of Miami

From the perspective of the social sciences, the 1970s might be called "The Decade of the Social Experiments." During this decade, close to $1 billion of federal tax revenue (in current prices) was expended to pilot test the workability and implications of proposed changes in social policy within a controlled experimental setting. The distinguishing characteristic of these social experiments was the random assignment of individuals or families to two types of groups: experimental groups and control groups. Members of the experimental groups were subjected to the change in social policy being tested—the "experimental treatment"—but members of the control groups were not. Because the characteristics of these two groups were typically similar, effects of the tested programs could be measured by comparing the behavior of persons in the experimental group with the behavior of individuals in the control group.[1]

Social experimentation can be usefully contrasted with other techniques that are frequently used to measure policy outcomes. For example, evaluations are often made of ongoing programs by comparing data gathered on a group of program participants with data on a group of nonparticipants.[2] Ideally, these two groups should be identical in all essential respects except their exposure to the program. Unfortunately, this ideal is seldom attained in the case of an ongoing program, because individuals are randomly assigned between the two groups but instead can usually select for themselves whether or not to participate. Consequently, evaluations of ongoing programs are often plagued by mis-

Authors' Note: A version of the paper is published in the *Journal of Policy Analysis and Management,* Summer 1985. Copyright © 1985 by the Association for Public Policy Analysis and Management. Reprinted by permission of John Wiley & Sons, Inc.

matches between program and comparison groups that can only be partially controlled for statistically.

There have also been numerous pilot tests of proposed policy changes that, unlike social experiments, have not used randomization. Important examples of such nonrandomized pilot tests, which are often referred to as "demonstrations," include the Public School Voucher Demonstration and the National Tenant Management Demonstration. In many pilot tests of social programs, random assignments is simply not feasible because all members of the target group at the site of the demonstration are eligible to participate in the tested program. Such demonstration projects are sometimes referred to as "saturation experiments." In some saturation experiments—the Youth Incentive Entitlement Pilot Project and the Minnesota Work Equity Project are two prominent examples—a comparison group is obtained by use of a "quasi-experimental" approach in which comparison sites are carefully matched to program sites and data are collected on target group members in both.

Because social experiments allow comparisons to be made between individuals who have been randomly assigned to experimental and control groups, they are widely believed to provide measures of program outcomes that are superior to those obtained through other evaluation techniques. Moreover, they allow a policy to be tested prior to a decision on whether it is to be generally adopted. Thus, beginning with the New Jersey Income Maintenance Experiment, which was initiated in 1968 by the Office of Economic Opportunity, experimental techniques were used during the 1970s to test basic changes in welfare, health, housing, and employment and training policy.[3] The use of experimentation to evaluate alternative social welfare policies has not ended; several social experiments are currently being conducted. However, social experiments initiated after the first half of the 1970s have tended to be more modest than earlier social experiments, in terms of both scale of operation and scope of the policy change being tested.

The large-scale experiments of the 1970s and the analysis of the data they generated have now been largely completed. Massive numbers of papers have been written concerning their methodology and results and numerous conferences have taken place in which the policies tested were discussed and debated. This appears to be a good point in time, therefore, to step back and take general stock of the social experiments.

PREVIOUS AND CURRENT SOCIAL EXPERIMENTS

Since 1968, more than 35 social experiments involving about 120,000 families (60 percent of which received an experimental treatment) have been conducted in the United States. A summary of these experiments, in chronological order, is presented in Parts A and B of the appendix table found at the end of the paper. In interpreting this table, the reader should keep in mind several points. First, we have used fairly rigorous criteria in defining what constitutes a "social experiment," limiting the research projects listed in the table to those in which some sort of randomization process was used in assigning persons from the target population to program and comparison groups. This rather narrow definition, which excludes most demonstration projects,[4] appears consistent with the methodological ideas of those who first introduced the concept of social experimentation (see Orcutt and Orcutt, 1968). Second, the information provided on the dates of the experiments pertains to the time periods over which the field work was conducted. Preliminary planning and data analysis often encompass a considerably longer period of time than the field work alone. Third, we have not only provided information in the table on total project costs, but whenever possible we have attempted to indicate how total costs are allocated across project components. These components typically include payments to members of the experimental groups, costs incurred in administrating the experimental program, and "pure" research costs (data collection, data analysis, and the like). However, information is often available on only one of these components or on the aggregate of all three components.

The information provided in the appendix table suggests that from a chronological perspective social experiments in the United States might roughly, but usefully, be divided into three separate groups: experiments initiated prior to the end of 1975 (Era I experiments), experiments begun between 1976 and 1982 (Era II experiments), and experiments launched since the end of 1982 (Era III experiments). Each of these eras differs substantially in terms of levels of expenditures on social experimentation and, more fundamentally, in terms of the types of policy measures tested through social experiments.

Differences Among Eras

Table 1 identifies the main features of each era. Table 1 suggests, for example, that Era I social experiments were launched to test the feasibility of major reform measures. Thus, these experiments attempted to measure the effects of such policies as replacing existing welfare programs with a noncategorical negative income tax program, pilot testing a new national housing allowance system for the low income population, providing information needed in the development of national health insurance legislation, and measuring the cost-effectiveness of a major new innovative type of manpower program. As the appendix table indicates, the amount of resources spent to support these major reform experiments was considerable (about $813 million in 1983 dollars). Era II experiments, in contrast, tended to be considerably smaller in scale and much less costly and, perhaps more importantly, the policy reforms they were designed to test were decidedly more incremental in scope.[5] That is, rather than test major new policy initiatives, as did the Era I social experiments, the Era II experiments were more likely to focus instead on testing relatively small new programs that would be confined to narrowly defined subsets of the population or on testing modifications of existing programs designed to enhance their performance efficiency.

TABLE 1
Main Features of Three Eras of Social Experiments

	Era I	Era II	Era III
Period initiated	1968-1975	1975-1983	1983-
Scale	large	small	moderate
Programs tested	major new programs	small new programs or incremental changes in existing programs	incremental changes in existing programs
Group responsible for field operations	experimenters	state agencies	stage agencies
Duration of experiment	relatively long (3-10 years)	relatively short (1-3 years)	medium length (3-5 years)

Another important difference between Era I and Era II experiments is that the Era I experiments tested what were for the most part conceptually simple policies (such as the negative income tax). Era II experiments, on the other hand, tended to test relatively more complex policies (such as job training programs). Moreover, Era I experiments tended to test policies having parameters that may be characterized as continuous (e.g., tax rates and income guarantee levels), whereas the Era II experiments tended to test policies that may be described as discrete (e.g., a package of training program services). However, the design models used in the Era I experiments were considerably more complex than the design models used in the Era II experiments. Hence, Era I may be loosely characterized as consisting of complicated experiments testing simple policies that could be reasonably extrapolated to nontested variants of the same policy, whereas Era II may be characterized as simple experiments testing complicated policies that could not be easily extrapolated to other types of similar policies.

It is still too early to determine for certain whether 1983 really marked the beginning of a new experimental period, Era III. However, several of the social experiments listed in the appendix table as having been launched during 1983 are distinctive in several respects from those begun earlier. They are, for example, much larger than the experiments characterizing Era II. Yet, unlike the Era I experiments (and to a large extent the Era II experiments), they are not tests of new social programs. Instead, they represent attempts to test the feasibility of effectuating major improvements in existing programs. Indeed, the treatments being tested in the Era III experiments are being administered by existing state and local government agencies, unlike the treatments tested in the Era I experiments, which were usually administered by field operations that were specifically set up by government contractors for that purpose.[6]

The transition from Era I to Era III has involved a considerable loss in scientific structure. The Era III experiments tend to be more "black box" in nature, with the treatments less precisely defined. This is because the programs tested are to a large extent determined by the agency conducting the experiment. Hence, even though the experimental designs in Era III are fairly straight-forward, the nature of the programs tested are much more difficult to characterize.

Reasons for the Differences

What is behind the trends that appear to be occurring in social experimenta-tion? There are several fairly obvious explanations of why large-scale experi-mental tests of major new social programs, such as those run during Era I, are no longer being conducted. First, in terms of federal funds that have historically been available for social science research, expenditures on the early social experiments were enormous. Given the current competition for these resources, it is not surprising the funding available for social experiments has diminished.[7]

Second, there appears to be much less current interest in implementing, and, hence, in testing major new social initiatives than was the case 10 or 15 years ago. The current political climate is clearly more conservative than that of the late 1960s and early 1970s. Furthermore, there has been an enormous growth in public expenditures on social welfare programs since this earlier period and the number of persons with a vested interest in protecting existing government social programs and the bureaucracy that runs them has also almost certainly increased. Consequently, there is considerable pressure to see if existing programs can be improved and made more cost effective. As would be anticipated, more recently implemented social experiments tend to reflect this pressure.

Third, and perhaps most important, the usefulness of the expensive Era I major reform experiments as vehicles for bringing about social reform may be seriously questioned. It is at least possible that experimental tests of incremental modifications in existing programs—which in any event are usually relatively less expensive to conduct—are more likely to result in desirable changes in social policy than are tests of more fundamental reforms. It is to this topic that we turn next.

IMPACT OF ERA I EXPERIMENTS ON THE REFORM PROCESS

An important characteristic of the large-scale Era I social experiments listed in the appendix table is that none of the innovative social programs they tested has yet been implemented, although at least preliminary results from all these experiments have been available for some time. Of course, there are many reasons why new social reform measures have not been adopted in the United States in recent years, including an increasingly conservative political climate, and social experiments constitute only one of many inputs into the overall policymaking process—often a very minor one. In this section, we attempt to assess the impact of the Era I experiments on the overall policymaking process.

We argue that even though hundreds of millions of dollars have been spent on the Era I experiments, for a variety of reasons they often have had only a negligible effect on the policymaking process. Moreover, to the extent there has been any impact, various limitations to which the Era I experiments are subject have systematically acted to reduce the chances that the tested policy measures will ever be implemented on a nationwide basis. Although it is probably too early to know whether the policies tested in the Era II and III experiments are more likely to be implemented than those tested in the Era I experiments, it appears that the ability of the Era II and Era III experiments to facilitate the policymaking process will depend to a large degree on the extent to which they can overcome these limitations.

Before we begin our discussion of the specific reasons why the Era I experiments have, if anything, reduced the chances that the policies they tested will be implemented, it is important to emphasize two things. First, the impact of social experiments on the policy process is not the only basis on which to judge such experiments. From a purely scientific point of view, for example, social experiments have made major methodological contributions.[8] Even more important, as compared to alternative nonexperimental approaches, experiments probably provide the most reliable information about the potential workability of proposed policy reforms. Nonetheless, given the size of society's investment in the Era I experiments, it seems reasonable to assess their impact on the policy process. For reasons detailed below, we believe this impact is nonneutral. That is, there appears to be little evidence that large-scale experiments of the Era I type can substantially enhance the probability that the tested policies will be implemented—almost regardless of actual experimental outcomes. Instead, findings from such experiments tend either to be largely ignored or have an inhibiting effect on the policymaking process.

Second, we do not wish to imply by our discussion that we necessarily believe the policies tested in the Era I experiments are "good" policies that deserve to be enacted, or that policymakers have been wrong in rejecting these policies. Rather, as indicated above, our contention is that the probability of enactment of these policies is reduced as a direct consequence of experimentally testing them and that this reduced probability occurs regardless of the initial (pretested) probability of enactment or the inherent superiority or inferiority of the tested policy in comparison to possible alternatives (including the status quo).[9]

Reasons for the Nonneutrality of the Era I Experiments

Social Experiments as a Conservative Force. One important reason for the nonneutrality of social experiments in the policy process is that research and evaluation (both experimental and nonexperimental) tends to be a generally conservative force.[10] In the absence of scientific evidence about the costs and behavioral impacts of a particular proposed program, policymakers tend to focus attention on moral issues. Consequently, successful enactment of the program depends on the extent to which proponents of the program are committed to achieving reform and their ability to persuade Congress and the general public. The availability of scientific evidence shifts attention to methodological issues that are complex in nature and generally have no clearcut solutions. Controversy then ensues about the merits of the proposed program, creating a cautionary environment that ultimately reduces the probability of eventual enactment of the program.

To some extent, experimental research is a more conservative force than nonexperimental research because it is frequently easier to dismiss nonexperimental evidence as inappropriate or irrelevant, thereby lessening the impact of scientific evidence on the policy debate. Furthermore, it appears that the more significant the social experiment (and the underlying reform), the more likely it is to be a conservative force. For example, the smaller-scale social experiments initiated during Era II typically had more limited objectives than the large-scale experiments initiated during Era I, and consequently were less likely to create controversy or be subjected to careful methodological scrutiny. However, as we indicate below, small-scale experiments are subject to many of the same methodological limitations as large-scale experiments, particularly those pertaining to experimental design and research methods used to evaluate the experimental data. Although few would argue that less knowledge is better than more, it is not difficult to envision the uncomfortable possibility that the policies most likely to be adopted on a nationwide basis in the future are those for which the least evidence exists regarding their impacts on human behavior.

As a case in point, consider the legislative change contained in the Omnibus Reconciliation Act of 1981 that reestablished a 100 percent benefit reduction rate on earnings under the AFDC program (applicable after 4 months of employment). The income maintenance experiments tested a variety of benefit reduction rates, but all of them were well under 100 percent. Despite the fact that economic theory predicts drastic reductions in labor supply for individuals subjected to a 100 percent benefit reduction rate, the lack of experimental evidence on this issue precluded credible discussion of potential labor supply effects.[11] Perhaps, if experimental evidence had existed regarding the labor supply effects for individuals subjected to 100 percent benefit reduction rates, the legislation might not so easily have passed Congress.

Time Lags. Another reason for the limited impact of social experiments on social reform is time lags. James Coleman has argued that the greatest source of incompatibility between research and policy may be the fact that policy decisions have time schedules that are often in serious conflict with the time schedules of research (Coleman, 1979). This was especially true of the large-scale Era I social experiments. One of the most important reasons why Era I experiments may have had relatively little policy impact is that they simply lasted too long. By the time their results became available, interest in the specific policy being tested often had waned and the policies of current interest tended to incorporate major features not included in the tested treatments. It is difficult for experimental designers to guess what specific policies will be of greatest interest five or ten years in the future and, even if they could, it would usually be impossible for them to obtain the public resources necessary to mount a social experiment testing those policies.

Consider, for example, the income maintenance experiments. Interest in a negative income tax (NIT) surfaced in the early 1960s and became more intense during the late 1960s. One consequence of this interest was that four major NIT experiments were launched by 1971. However, as the idea evolved during the 1970s and results from the experiments began to trickle in, it became clear that an NIT would not be enacted without some sort of work requirement. However, because this design feature did not seem important at the time the NIT experiments were launched, none of them tested a work requirement. Consequently, evidence on the impact of such a policy was not available. Thus, although the NIT experiments provided valuable information for the design of alternative pure cash transfer schemes, time lags prevented the testing and evaluation of the specific policy that was of current policy interest.

Although still present for the smaller-scale experiments, time lags may be much less important. Because the policy issues tested by small-scale experiments are typically of less intense interest to the policy community than those tested by the large-scale experiments, time lags, even if present, may not seriously jeopardize the possibility of eventual adoption.

Communicating Results to Policymakers. Though often ignored, the ability to effectively communicate the results of social experiments to policymakers is of critical importance in determining the experiments' overall impact on policy. Some observers, such as the General Accounting Office (GAO), believe, in fact, that development of an effective communications network for social experiments should be given top priority (see U.S. General Accounting Office, 1981).

There are two layers to an effective communications network. The first layer consists of the research team (usually a private consulting firm or a university) and the sponsoring agency. The second layer consists of the sponsoring agency and the general policy community (other governmental agencies, Congress, the administration, and the general public).

Communication within the first layer has been somewhat spotty across the social experiments. In many instances, for example, researchers have been unable or unwilling to provide simplified discussions of the experimental design and the evaluation methodology, consequently causing general confusion as to what was tested and what was found. Indeed, sometimes, the researchers appear to have been more concerned with methodological issues than with policy issues. This is partially a reflection of the fact that scientific journals place more emphasis on articles having innovative methodological content than on articles merely reporting results using standard evaluation techniques. As we discuss below, this preoccupation with methodology not only creates problems in communicating results, but also in convincing policymakers of the usefulness of the results.

Communication within the second layer has sometimes been almost non-existent. Indeed, the General Accounting Office has suggested that lack of effective communication concerning the results of the NIT experiments may have been partially responsible for the quick demise of the 1977 Carter Welfare Reform proposal. They suggest that had HHS disseminated the findings earlier and in a more organized fashion, Congress might not have been so confused by the results and the proposal might have been better received. As a consequence, GAO made specific recommendations to Congress and the Department of Health and Human Services (the sponsoring agency) for improving communication of the findings. For example, GAO recommended to HHS that (1) the experimental results be summarized in layperson's terms and distributed to all interested and affected Federal legislators and executive branch program managers and (2) lessons learned about the conduct of the experiments be summarized and shared with other agencies. GAO recommended to Congress, that (1) end-users be identified, (2) procedures for monitoring and coordinating the experiments be established, and (3) procedures for disseminating results to end-users be developed.

Although GAO recommendations have merit, it would probably be extremely difficult to implement them fully. Furthermore, it is not clear that a more organized dissemination of the findings from the NIT experiments would have resulted in a more favorable public reception of the Carter Plan. Nevertheless, better planning and organization on the part of policymakers is likely to remove part of the confusion and uncertainty surrounding communication of the policy findings of social experiments to Congress and the general public.

Convincing Policymakers. Establishing an effective communications network does not, of course, ensure that social experiments will have a positive impact on policy. Policymakers must also be convinced of the usefulness of the results. Here, in fact, is where social experimenters face their biggest challenge. These difficulties are engendered by methodological weaknesses in the design and evaluation methodologies of the experiments.

Although a full discussion of the various methodological problems associated with the social experiments is far beyond the scope of this paper,[12] some of the more important ones are briefly enumerated in this subsection. We then discuss how these problems affect policymakers' acceptance of the experimental findings. Before we begin, it is important to emphasize that evaluations of ongoing programs and demonstration projects are subject to far more severe methodological problems than evaluations of social experiments. Nevertheless, because social experiments are conducted in the "real world," the analogy with laboratory experiments in the physical sciences that is sometimes made in the case of social experimentation breaks down somewhat, and important problems do arise. As in the case of nonexperimental evaluations, the very process of scientific inquiry that results from attempts to deal with these problems affects the way in which findings from the social experiments are perceived by policymakers and the extent to which they are utilized.

Some of the methodological weaknesses of the social experiments are potentially correctable in future experiments (although the corrections may not always be practical), some are uncontrollable within an experimental setting, and still others are the result of random events that cannot be anticipated by the experiment designers. Several of the correctable weaknesses result from the fact that social experimentation is a relatively new research tool and experimenters are still undergoing a sizable learning process. One example of such a weakness is the particular complex design model used in all four of the NIT experiments and in the housing allowance demand experiment. A number of researchers have suggested that this model, which assigned participants to various types of experimental treatments on the basis of certain characteristics such as income levels, causes major problems, both in the evaluation of the experiments and in communicating the results to policymakers and that some form of pure randomization is preferable (see Morris et al., 1977; Keeley and Robins, 1980; Hausman and Wise, 1983).

Another weakness, which is correctable but only at considerable costs, has been the small sample sizes of many of the experiments. The 20-year Denver Income Maintenance Experiment, for example, could have provided definitive evidence on the potential biases resulting from the limited duration of social experiments, but the sample size (roughly 170 families initially) was simply too small to provide reliable estimates.[13] Interesting to note, the Era II and III pilot tests of incremental changes in policy may be even more subject to this problem than the major changes in social policy tested in the Era I social experiments because the experimental impacts may be smaller, and consequently, larger samples may be required to estimate them precisely. However, sufficiently large samples are not always feasible because of their high associated cost.

A related problem has been the frequently large number of treatments tested. For example, the Health Insurance Study tested 16 experimental treatments, the housing allowance demand experiment tested 17 treatments, and the Seattle-Denver Income Maintenance Experiments tested 58 treatments. This has made it difficult to obtain reliable estimates of the impacts of each separate treatment because relatively few persons could be assigned to each treatment. After studying the problem, Hausman and Wise concluded that precise estimation of a smaller number of treatments should be one of the top priorities of future experiments (see Hausman and Wise, 1983). Of course, this limits the ability to extrapolate the results to other similar policies.

Several weaknesses of the experimental approach that probably cannot be fully corrected result from the fact that the tested programs differ in important respects from programs that might easily be implemented. One important such weakness is the inability of experiments to measure the marketwide effects of the tested policy. For example, a nationwide housing allowance program could generate responses on the part of housing suppliers. The magnitude of such marketwide responses cannot be easily ascertained, but could be potentially substantial. One approach to estimating marketwide effects is to conduct a saturation experiment, an approach that was used in the case of the housing allowance experiment. However, saturation experiments are inherently expensive to conduct and may suffer from lack of an appropriate control group.

Indeed, a saturation experiment is not really a true experiment because control group members must be obtained from "matched" nonexperimental sites, a procedure that may greatly reduce their comparability to members of the experimental group and make evaluation very difficult.

A possible alternative to saturation experiments for estimating marketwide effects is the use of microsimulation. This technique, which can make use of behavioral response estimates derived from experimental data to predict the nationwide effects of implementing specific policy proposals, was used extensively in conjunction with findings from the NIT experiments to aid in the design of the Carter welfare reform proposal (Betson et al., 1980; Aaron and Todd, 1978). One study suggests that by using microsimulation methods, it may be possible to set bounds on potential marketwide effects (Greenberg, 1983). These bounds may be so broad, however, as to be of little practical use in designing programs.

Other potential sources of bias that are difficult to correct include the limited duration of the experimental treatments, systematic misreporting by experimental participants when interviewed, changes in community attitudes, lengthy periods of adjustment to the experimental treatments, sample attrition, and self-determination of participation.[14] Although econometric methods have been developed to help correct for some of these potential biases, their very existence limits the ability of researchers to convince policymakers of the validity and usefulness of findings from social experiments.

Random real world events can also seriously hamper evaluation of a social experiment. The most commonly cited example of such an event is the adoption of a statewide welfare program for two parent families just after the New Jersey income maintenance experiment was launched. To a lesser extent, the massive layoff of aerospace workers in Seattle during the Seattle Income Maintenance Experiment may also have hampered evaluation. The possibility of random events occurring in the control environment is one major factor that distinguishes social experiments from laboratory experiments.

A major consequence of the methodological problems just discussed is that by making it more difficult to evaluate social experiments, they tend to reduce their credibility in the eyes of the policymaker. A related consequence is that social experiments—especially large-scale ones—inevitably tend to generate competing sets of results. Important examples may be cited from the NIT experiments with respect to their impacts on labor supply and marital stability. With regard to labor supply, for example, one study concludes that in the New Jersey experiment "the overall responses to tax rates that (on average) cut net wages in half and to income guarantees that were equal to a substantial fraction of preexperimental income are barely detectable, and could be interpreted as being so minor that further analysis is unwarranted" (Watts and Horner, 1977). Using the same experimental data, but an alternative methodology, another study concludes "the central finding of an analysis of the labor supply response of white male heads of household in the New Jersey-Pennsylvania Negative Income Tax

Experiment is a large, statistically significant labor supply withdrawal" (Cogan, 1978). Similarly, in the Seattle-Denver experiment, two studies argue that the labor supply responses are large (Keeley and Wai, 1980; Bishop, 1980), another study implies that they are moderate (Robins and West, 1983), still another study argues that they are fairly small (Greenberg and Halsey, 1983), and finally another study suggests that the size of the response ultimately depends on how one frames the question to be asked of the data (Burtless and Greenberg, 1983). With respect to marital stability, only the Seattle-Denver experiment produced significant findings (marital dissolutions increased for all groups except Hispanics), but the pattern of results by treatment plan is perplexing and many outside researchers appear to have placed little credence in them (see U.S. Department of Health and Human Services, 1978).

In light of such controversy among the researchers, what are the policymakers to believe? Most simply do not have the technical expertise, time, or patience to evaluate the various methodologies. Often, it takes several years for the scientific community to reach a consensus, if indeed it ever does, but by then interest in the experiment results may well have waned.

The process of scientific inquiry almost ensures that competing sets of results will be obtained, at least in the case of large-scale, highly publicized experiments. Once the first set of findings are published, other researchers eager to make a name for themselves must come up with different approaches and results to get their studies published. And because of the methodological problems associated with social experimentation they almost certainly will.

Both advocates and opponents of the tested policy are now provided with "scientific" ammunition for their position (see U.S. Finance Committee, 1978). Unfortunately, one set of "negative" results is often all that is required to create significant public concern about the desirability of the program, even if other experimental results reflect favorably upon it. For example, Senator Daniel Patrick Moynihan of New York, whose support of the Carter Welfare Reform plan was necessary if the plan was to have any chance of passage, originally called the plan "superbly crafted" (*Washington Star*, August 7, 1977), but later reversed his position, calling the plan "calamitous," when "negative" findings from the Seattle-Denver experiment were made available (Moynihan, 1978; *Fortune*, 1978). Hence, the social experiment served to identify potential weaknesses in the Carter Plan that probably contributed to its demise.[15]

Smaller-scale experiments seem less likely to produce competing sets of results than larger-scale ones because they engender less interest on the part of the research community and, hence, less scientific inquiry. Consequently, their findings may be more readily accepted by policymakers. For example, although Era II monthly reporting experiments are less known and have been less scrutinized than any of the considerably larger Era I social experiments, the policy they tested, which involves incremental revisions in welfare program administration, has actually been adopted nationally for purposes of administering both the AFDC and Food Stamp Programs. Interesting to note, however, although initial analysis of data from the monthly reporting experiments implied positive policy outcomes, since implementation of monthly reporting on a national basis, there has been further analysis of data from these experiments suggesting that monthly reporting performs no better than the old system of prospective reporting and may actually be more costly.[16] Hence, it appears that smaller-scale experiments, like their large-scale counterparts, are not immune to generating competing sets of findings.

A further problem with the small-scale experiments is that the absence of more general research interest in them may increase the likelihood that their evaluation methodologies contain serious flaws that go undetected. This implies that the quality of the research performed from these experiments may be lower than from the larger earlier experiments and that the likelihood of making erroneous policy decisions may be greater.

Increasing Awareness of Policymakers. The final reason we suggest for why the Era I social experiments may have inhibited social reform is that they appear to have produced increased awareness among policymakers of the full complexity of implementing the very programs they tested. Of course, this is a desirable effect of social experimentation because it raises the level of the debate and leads to more informed decision making.[17] However, policymakers have tended to let the existence of complex issues thwart the decision-making process. Thus, unless a social experiment provides clear evidence that adoption of the tested policy will bring about a social improvement—and for reasons already discussed this appears unlikely to occur very often—the experiment may well reduce the possibility that the policy is ever implemented.

CONCLUSIONS

A review of almost any important research tool is likely to highlight its limitations, and the discussion in this paper is certainly no exception. A final assessment of the use of social experimentation for policy analysis, however, must consider the alternatives. With this in mind, we would like to emphasize our basic agreement with the following comment made near the end of the Era I period by Alice Rivlin (1974: 353):

> The cautionary tone of this paper should emphatically not be construed as a rejection of experimentation as a tool for finding answers to policy questions. Experiments may be expensive compared with traditional forms of social research, but even the costs of major experiments are small compared with the costs of social policies that do not work or that might have been significantly more effective if experimental results had been available. . . . Ever fancier statistical manipulation of inadequate data from traditional sources is unlikely to improve knowledge about policy choices significantly.

Even if, as Rivlin asserts, social experimentation is often more cost effective than analysis of nonexperimental data or no analysis at all, the question still remains as to how social experiments can best be structured to produce socially optimal policy decisions. This question has no easy answer, although obviously, as suggested earlier, weaknesses in experimental methodology should be corrected whenever possible and improvements in communication should be made among researchers conducting experiments, agencies sponsoring them, and the general policy community.

Nonetheless, the lessons provided so far by previous social experiments are not especially encouraging. On the one hand, there is evidence that almost regardless of actual experimental outcomes or the inherent desirability of the policy tested, large-scale Era I-type testing of new innovative social programs is more likely than not to reduce the chances of the program ever being adopted. On the other hand, small-scale Era II-type testing of rather modest incremental policy changes may command little attention on the part of the research community at large, resulting in insufficient quality control and possible acceptance by policymakers of erroneous findings. Perhaps, the new Era III social experiments will provide a workable middle ground. As noted earlier, these experiments test major modifications of existing social programs. Consequently, the policy changes they test may be more easy to implement than those tested in the Era I experiments. Furthermore, these experiments are sufficiently large and important that they should generate a reasonable amount of outside professional review.

APPENDIX TABLE
Part A
Selected Characteristics of Major Social Experiments Conducted in the United States

Experiment	Period of Study	Major Target Group(s)	Sample Size	Experimental Treatments	Major Outcomes of Interest
ERA I					
New Jersey/Pennsylvania Income Maintenance Experiment	1968-1972	Low income, 2-parent families	725 experimentals 632 controls	Negative Income Tax plans	Labor supply responses, effects on consumption patterns
Rural Income Maintenance Experiment	1969-1973	Low income, 2-parent families	372 experimentals 437 controls	Negative Income Tax plans	Labor supply responses
Gary Income Maintenance Experiment	1971-1974	Low income, 1- and 2-parent black families	1,028 experimentals 771 controls	Negative Income Tax plans, day care subsidies	Labor supply responses, utilization of day care
Seattle/Denver Income Maintenance Experiment	1971-1978	Low income, 1- and 2-parent families	2,747 experimentals 2,053 controls	Negative Income Tax plans, employment counseling, subsidies of educational expenditures	Labor supply responses, effects on marital stability, effects on earnings
Wildcat Supported Work Program	1972-1974	Ex-addicts with records of unemployment	194 experimentals 207 controls	Temporarily subsidized jobs in a highly supportive work environment	Effects on post-program earnings, criminal activity, and drug abuse; program operating costs
Living Insurance for Ex-Offenders	1972-1974	Repeat theft offenders (excluding drug addicts) who were released from Maryland prisons and returning to Baltimore	216 experimentals 216 controls	Provision of weekly cash transfers for up to 13 weeks and job placement services	Effects on earnings and on criminal activity
Carbondale Job Finding Club	1973	Unemployed persons not receiving unemployment benefits	60 experimentals 60 controls	Group job search training, supervised job search	Job finding rate, starting wage

(continued)

Experiment	Period of Study	Major Target Group(s)	Sample Size	Experimental Treatments	Major Outcomes of Interest
Experimental Housing Allowance Program					
a. Demand (Consumer Experiment)	1973-1977	Low-income renter households	2,466 experimentals 1,100 controls	Cash Housing Allowance Payments	Household utilization of housing allowances, effects on housing quality
b. Supply (Market) Experiment (Random Assignment not used)	1973-1976	Low-income renter households	open enrollment	Cash Housing Allowance Payments	Impacts on supply and cost of housing
c. Administrative Experiment (Random Assignment not used)	1973-1976	Low-income renter households	6,400 participating households	Cash Housing Allowance Payments	Cost and effectiveness of alternative means of administrating housing allowances
Health Insurance Study	1974-1981	Households with annual incomes under $25,000 and member under 65 years of age	2,823 experimentals 0 controls	Alternative fee-for-service health insurance plans with different coinsurance rates and deductibles. In addition, a prepaid group health insurance plan was tested	Effects on demand for health care and on health status
Carbondale Handicapped Job Finding Club	1974-1975	Job seekers with severe employment handicaps	80 experimentals 74 controls	Group job search training, supervised job search	Job finding rate, starting wage
Supported Work Demonstration Project	1975-1979	Women on AFDC, ex-addicts, ex-offenders, young (17-20) school dropouts	3,214 experimentals 3,402 controls	Temporary subsidized jobs in a highly supportive work environment	Operating costs; changes in earnings, criminal activity, welfare dependency, and drug abuse

ERA II

Study	Year	Target group	Sample	Treatment	Effects measured
Effectiveness of Counseling in the U.S. Employment Service Pilot Study	1975	Employment Service applicants identified	486 experimentals 459 controls	Vocational counseling	Effects on earnings and duration of unemployment
Colorado Monthly Reporting Experiment and Pretest	1976-1978	AFDC recipients	1,825 experimentals 1,841 controls	Monthly reporting of income and household composition; retrospective accounting system for computing AFDC payments	Impact on case load size and transfer payment costs; administrative cost and feasibility
WIN Job Finding Clubs	1976-1978	WIN registrants	487 experimentals 490 controls	Group job search training, supervised job search	Job finding rate, starting wage
Transition Aid Research Project	1976	Released prisoners from Georgia and Texas	1,551 experimentals 400 controls (arrest records of an additional 2,031 controls followed through computer records)	Provision of weekly cash transfers while unemployed for up to 13 or 26 weeks; provision of enhanced job placement services through the Employment Service	Effects on arrests, employment, and earnings
Massachusetts Work Experience Program	1978-1979	Male heads of families receiving AFDC-U	754 experimentals 279 controls	Waiver of the AFDC-U 100 hour limitation on work; 13 weeks of mandatory work experience	Effects on employment; effects on costs of AFDC-U program
Louisville Individual Job Search Experiment	1978-1980	Female AFDC recipients registered in the WIN program	811 experimentals 800 controls	Staff provision of job leads on a daily basis for up to 6 weeks	Effects on earnings, AFDC payments, types of jobs held
Denver Volunteer Services Experiments	1978-1980	Female volunteer WIN registrants with child under six	1,117 experimentals 1,113 controls	Special recruitement effort, training, child care, work-related counseling	Effects on earning and AFDC payments
Madison and Racine Quality Employment Program	1978-1980	New female WIN registrants who were over 18, not in school, and unemployed	316 experimentals 317 controls	On-the-job training reimbursements to employers for jobs paying at least $4 per hour	Effects on employment status and AFDC payments

(continued)

APPENDIX TABLE A (Continued)

Experiment	Period of Study	Major Target Group(s)	Sample Size	Experimental Treatments	Major Outcomes of Interest
Career Advancement Voucher Demonstration Project	1979-1981	CETA-eligible youth	500 experimentals 200 controls	Full financial support for two-year full time college program plus counseling	Effects on college attendance and subsequent employment
Employment Opportunity Pilot Projects	1979-1981	Heads of households receiving public assistance	Enrollment never completed	Mandatory job search followed, if necessary, by mandatory training or employment in subsidized public service jobs	Participation rate, impact on public assistance caseload size, impact on private sector labor markets, effects on costs of public assistance programs, operational feasibility, effect on participant earnings
Cambridge Job Factory for Youth	1979-1980	CETA - eligible unemployment youth	203 experimentals 165 controls	Group job search training for 1-week followed by 3-weeks of supervised job search; CETA stipends and bonus	Job finding rate, starting wage
Summer Experimental Youth Training Project	1980	Graduating low-income high school seniors	285 experimentals 100 controls	Various combination of group job search training and supervised and individual job search	Job finding rate
Ex-Offenders Research Project	1980-1981	Men just released from prison	179 experiments 134 controls	Provision of public service employment jobs and counseling	Effects on subsidized and non-subsidized employment; effects on recidivism
Transition Project	1980-1982	Former drug users	146 experimentals 78 controls	Preparation of employment through a cooperative effort of private corporations and treatment programs	Effects on employment, continuation of recommended treatment, and use of welfare programs. Program cost-effectiveness

Education Improvement Effort	1980-1981	Job Corps participants	1,100 experimentals 1,100 controls	Alternative teaching approaches; including computer-assisted, instruction and self-paced learning	Effects on reading and mathematical competencies
Louisville Group Job Search Experiment	1980-1981	Female AFDC recipients registered in the WIN Program	376 experimentals 374 controls	Provision of up to six weeks of groups job search assistance	Effects on earnings, AFDC payments, and types of jobs held
Denver Post-Employment Services Experiment	1980-1981	Female mandatory WIN registrants entering employment	270 experimentals 281 controls	Provision of post-placement services to increase job retention (e.g., scheduled telephone contacts, special emergency funds)	Effects on employment status and on AFDC payments
Illinois Monthly Retrospective Reporting Demonstration	1981-1982	AFDC and food stamp recipients	6,000 experimentals 3,000 controls	Monthly reporting of income and household composition; retrospective accounting for computing AFDC payments	Impact on caseload size, transfer payment costs, and error rates; administrative costs and feasibility
Massachusetts Monthly Retrospective Reporting Demonstration	1981-1982	AFDC recipients	3,500 experimentals 3,500 controls	Monthly reporting of income and household composition; retrospective accounting for computing AFDC payments	Impact on caseload size, transfer payment costs, and error rates; administrative costs and feasibility
Food Stamp Work Registration and Job Search Demonstration	1981-1984	Work registrants in the Non-Public Assistance Food Stamp Population	8,839 experimentals 5,500 controls	Various combinations of work registration procedures, job search techniques, and agency administration approaches	Effects on Food Stamp benefit amounts, effects on job finding rate
Structured Training in Employment Transitional Services Demonstration	1982-1983	Moderately retarded persons (I.Q. generally between 40 and 80), 18-24 years of age	250 experimentals 250 controls	Placement in subsidized low-stress jobs for 3 months, followed by placement in (sometimes subsidized) private sector jobs. Close supportive supervision provided throughout the 12 month period of program participation	Effects on post-program earnings, job stability, use of social services, and reliance on transfer programs; program operating costs

(continued)

37

APPENDIX TABLE A (Continued)

Experiment	Period of Study	Major Target Group(s)	Sample Size	Experimental Treatments	Major Outcomes of Interest
National Long-Term Care Demonstration (The Chaneling Demonstration	1982-1985	Severely disabled elderly	2,500 experimentals 2,400 controls	Expansion of community-based, non-institutional care care services; expenditure cost-control of services; assessment and case management	Cost effectiveness of treatment; reductions in hospital and nursing home utilization; effects on health status and well-being; utilization of provided services
Claimant Placement and Work Test Demonstration	1983	Unemployment Insurance Recipients	4,500 experimentals 1,500 controls	Alternative combination of the following 3 treatments: 1) 3 hour job search workshop 2) enhanced job placement assistance 3) more stringent work test requirement for receipt of unemployment insurance	Effects on duration of unemployment and on unemployment insurance benefit levels
Retaining Delaware's Dislocated Workers	1983	Persons receiving Unemployment Insurance for 7 to 12 consecutive weeks	65 experimentals 116 controls	Special job development efforts, employability skill development through a 16 hour job search workshop	Effects on unemployment insurance benefit levels and on post-employment earnings

38

ERA III

AFDC Homemaker-Home Health Aide Demonstrations	1983-1985	Trainees: Female AFDC recipients Clients: Persons at risk of institutionalization (primarily the aged and disabled)	Trainee sample: 3,000 experimentals 3,000 controls	Trainee: Training as home-maker–home health aides, up to one year of sub-sidized employment as an aide Clients: Provision of home-maker–home health aide services of up to 100	Trainees: Increases in un-subsidized employment, reductions in welfare costs, costs of training and sub-sidization participation rates Clients: Effects on health status and probability of institutionalization, par-
MDRC Work/Welfare Demonstration	1983-1987	Adult AFDC recipients and, in some sites, AFDC-U recipients	18,680 experimentals 13,806 controls	Treatments vary considerably among sites and treatment groups, but usually involve mandatory job search activ-ities and public sector work experience in exchange for receipt of a public assistance grant. In some sites, training and other employment services are also provided.	Administrative feasibility, operating costs, welfare savings, impacts on earn-ings and employment, impact on welfare case-load size

APPENDIX TABLE
Part B
Selected Characteristics of Major Social Experiments Conducted in the United States

Experiment	Sites	Major Funding Agency	Major Contractor(s)	Total Cost [Costs in 1983 Dollars Appear in Brackets]
ERA I				
New Jersey/Pennsylvania Income Maintenance Experiment	Trenton, Jersey City, & Paterson-Passaic, N.J.: Scranton, Pa.	Office of Economic Opportunity, HEW	Institute of Research on Poverty, Mathematica	$7.8 million [$22.2 million] (payments to participants: $2.4 million [$6.8 million]
Rural Income Maintenance Experiment	Rural Iowa, Rural North Carolina	Office of Economic Opportunity, HEW	Institute for Research on Poverty	$6.1 million [$15.6 million] (payments to participants: $2.4 million [$6.1 million])
Gary Income Maintenance Experiment	Gary, Indiana	Department of Health & Human Services	Mathematica Policy Research Poverty	$20.3 million [$45.2 million] (payments to participants: $5.5 million [$12.2 million])
Seattle/Denver Income Maintenance Experiment	Seattle and Denver	Department of Health & Human Services	SRI International	$77.5 million [$132.7 million] (payments to participants: $20.4 million [$34.9 million])
Wildcat Supported Work Program	New York, N.Y. Expe	National Institute of Drug Abuse, New York City, Ford Foundation, Department of Labor	Vera Institute of Justice Ford Founda	Research Component only: $1.4 million [$2.9 million]
Living Insurance for Ex-offenders	Baltimore, Md.	Department of Labor	American Bar Association	Approximate operating costs: $200,000 [$421,000] Approximate research costs: $30,000 [$63,000]
Carbondale Job Finding Club	Carbondale, Ill.	Illinois Department of Mental Health	Anna Mental Health Center	Under $20,000 [Under $50,000]
Experimental Housing Allowance Program a. Demand (Consumer) Experiment	Pittsburgh and Phoenix	Department of Housing & Urban Development	Abt Associates, Inc.	Total for 3 components: $ $205.7 million [$352.2 million] (payments to participants:
b. Supply (Market) Experiment	Green Bay and South Bend	Department of Housing & Urban Development	Rand Corporation	$112 million [$191.8 million])

Study	Location	Sponsor	Contractor	Cost
c. Administrative Experiment	Salem, Peoria, Tulsa, Bismark, Springfield, San Bernardino, Durham, Jacksonville	Department of Housing	Abt Associates, Inc.	
Health Insurance Study	Dayton, Ohio; Seattle, Washington; Fitchberg and Franklin Counties, Mass.: Charleston and Georgetown Counties, S.C.	Department of Health & Human Services	Rand Corporation	$75 million [$115 million] (payment to participants: $14.7 million [$22.6 million])
Carbondale Handicapped Job Finding Club	Carbondale, Ill.	Illinois Department of Mental Health	Anna Mental Health Center	Under $20,000 [under $50,000]
Supported Work Demonstration Project	Atlanta, Chicago, Hartford, Jersey City, Newark, New York, Oakland, Philadelphia, San Francisco, Wisconsin (Fond due Lac & Winnebargo Counties)	Department of Labor	Manpower Demonstration	$82.4 million [$126.8 million] (research component: $11 million [$16.9 million])
ERA II				
Effectiveness of Counseling in the U.S. Employment Service Pilot Study	Minneapolis, Minn.; Salt Lake City, Utah; West Palm Beach, Fla.	Department of Labor	SRI International	Operating costs: $0 Research costs: $250,000 [$428,000]
Colorado Monthly Reporting Experiment and Pretest	Denver and Boulder Counties, Colorado (Random assignment only used in Denver)	Department of Health & Human Services	Mathematica Policy Research	Operating costs: about $2 million [about $3 million] Research costs: about $1.5 million [about $2.3 million]
WIN Job Finding Clubs	Milwaukee, Wisc.; New York, N.Y.; New Brunswick, N.J.; Tacoma, Wash.; Wichita, Kans.	Department of Labor	Anna Mental Health Center	Around $100,000 [around $150,000]

(continued)

APPENDIX TABLE B (Continued)

Experiment	Sites	Major Funding Agency	Major Contractor(s)	Total Cost [Costs in 1983 Dollars Appear in Brackets]
Transitional Aid Research Program	Georgia and Texas	Department of Labor; Department of Justice, Texas, Georgia	University of Massachusetts; University of California, Santa Barbara	$3.4 million [$5.6 million] Research cost: $2.3 million [$3.8 million]
Massachusetts Work Experience Program	Massachusetts	Department of Labor	Brandeis University	Operating costs: $270,000 [$390,000] Research costs: approximately $300,000 [$435,000]
Louisville Individual Job Search Experiment	Louisville, Kentucky	Department of Labor	Manpower Demonstration Research Corporation	Not available[a]
Denver Volunteer Services Experiment	Denver, Colorado	Department of Labor	Manpower Demonstration Research Corporation; University of Denver	Not available[a]
Madison and Racine Quality Employment Program	Madison and Racine, Wisconsin	Department of Labor	Manpower Demonstration Research Corporation; University of Wisconsin, Milwaukee	Not available[a]
Career Advancement Voucher Demonstration Project	Washington, D.C., El Paso, Pittsburgh, Atlanta, Little Rock	Department of Labor	Clark, Phipps, Clark and Harris, Inc.	Operating costs: approximately $1.8 million [approximately $2.2 million] Research costs: approximately $.5 million [approximately $.6 million]
Employment Opportunity Pilot Projects	14 different communities, with random assignment only used in Philadelphia (matched comparison sites were provided for the other 13 experimental sites)	Department of Labor	Mathematica Policy Research	$200 million [$246 million] [b]

Project	Location	Funding Agency	Research Organization	Cost
Cambridge Job Factory for Youth	Cambridge, Mass.	Department of Labor	Brandeis Center for Employment and Income Studies	$328,000 [$450,000]
Summer Experimental Youth Transition Project	Baltimore, Md.	Department of Labor	City of Baltimore	Not available
Ex-Offender Research Project	Baltimore	Department of Labor	Blackstone Associates	Operating costs: $2.5 million [$2.7 million] Research costs: $.3 million [$.32 million]
Transition Project	New York City	Department of Labor	National Association on Drug Abuse Problems, Inc.	Research component only: $186,631 [$203,081]
Education Improvement Effort	11 different job corps centers	Department of Labor	TEAM Associates	Approximately $2.5 million [approximately $3.1 million]
Louisville Group Job Search Experiment	Louisville, Kentucky	Department of Labor	Manpower Demonstration Research Corporation	Not available[a]
Denver Post-Employment Services Experiment	Denver, Colorado	Department of Labor	Manpower Demonstration Research Corporation, University of Denver	Not available[a]
Illinois Monthly Retrospective Accounting Demonstration	Cook County, Ill.	Department of Health and Human Services, Department of Agriculture	Abt Associates, Inc.	Operating costs: $3 million [$3.2 million] Research costs: $2 million [$2.1 million]
Massachusetts Monthly Retrospective Accounting Demonstration	Boston, Mass.	Department of Health and Human Services	Abt Associates, Inc.	Operating costs: $2.5 million [$2.7 million] Research costs: $1 million [$1.1 million]
Food Stamp Work Registration and Job Search Demonstration	18 different communities located throughout the country	U.S. Department of Agriculture	Brandeis University's Heller Graduate School and Abt Associates, Inc.	$9.5 million (projected)
Structured Training in Employment Transitional Services Demonstration	Minneapolis-St. Paul, Los Angeles, Tucson, Cincinnati, New York City	Department of Labor	Manpower Demonstration Research Corporation, Mathematica Policy Research	Not available

(continued)

APPENDIX TABLE B (Continued)

Experiment	Sites	Major Funding Agency	Major Contractor(s)	Total Cost [Costs in 1983 Dollars Appear in Brackets]
National Long Term Care Demonstration (The Channeling Demonstration	Southern Maine; Lynn, Mass., Cleveland; Rans- selaer, N.Y.; Phila- delphia, Middlesex County, N.J.; Baltimore; Eastern Kentucky; Miami; Houston	Department of Health and Human Services	Mathematica Policy Research, Brandeis University, Arthur Young and Company, Temple University	Operating cost: $20 million Research cost: $12 million
Claimant Placement and Work Test Demonstration	Charleston, S.C.	Department of Labor	SRI International; Mathematica Policy Research	Operating cost: $25,000 Research cost: $260,000
Retraining Delaware's Dislocated Workers	Delaware	Delaware State Department of Labor	Bloom Associates	Research component only: $10,000
ERA III				
AFDC Homemaker - Home Health Aide Demonstra- tions	Arkansas, Kentucky, New Jersey, New York, Ohio, South Carolina, Texas	Department of Health and Human Services	Abt Associates, Inc.	Research component only: $9,000,000 (projected)

| MDRC Work/Welfare Demonstration | San Diego and San Mateo Counties, Ca.; Cook County, Ill.; 8 counties in Arkansas; State of Maine; Baltimore, Md.; Md.; 11 cities and/or counties in Virginia; 21 counties in West Virginia | The Ford Foundation and participating states | Manpower Demonstration Research Corporation | Research component only: approximately $7 million (projected) |

a. The research, design, and management components of the following experiments and demonstrations totaled approximately $2.5 million: Louisville Individual Job Search Experiment, Denver Volunteer Services Experiment, Madison and Racine Quality Employment Program, Louisville Group Job Search Experiment, Denver Post-Employment Services Experiment.

b. Originally allocated costs; project terminated substantially before completion.

NOTES

1. A "true" controlled experiment should be designed in such a way as to allow behavioral effects to be estimated precisely using theory-free analysis of variance methods. Many of the experiments, particularly the earlier ones, did not possess this desirable characteristic because complicated design models were used to assign subjects to treatments (see Keeley and Robins, 1980).

2. One excellent example of an evaluation of an ongoing program can be found in Long et al. (1981).

3. Experimental techniques have also been used to examine the potential effects of other types of policy changes—for example, variations in electricity rates and in military personnel policy. The discussion in this chapter, however, is limited to experimental tests of proposed changes in social welfare policy.

4. A few projects that have had both an experimental component and a demonstration component are listed in the table. For example, the demand component of the Experimental Housing Allowance Program (which constituted about one-quarter of the total project cost) was a true social experiment, and the supply and administrative components were essentially demonstrations. Similarly, the Denver segment of the Colorado Monthly Reporting Experiment (which was mainly concerned with AFDC client responses to the experimental treatment) utilized random assignment techniques, and the segment based in Boulder (which was concerned with administrative costs and feasibility) was actually a demonstration project.

5. The major exception to this characterization of the Era II period is the Employment Opportunities Pilot Projects (EOPP), which were designed to test a guaranteed employment program for primary earners in low-income families with children. If carried to completion, EOPP would have cost about $200 million. However, the EOPP project utilized random assignment procedures in only 2 of the 14 demonstration sites (1 of which never got off the ground) and was consequently more of a demonstration than an experiment. EOPP was terminated in the early days of the Reagan Administration.

6. Era II experiments were also for the most part administered by existing state and local government agencies. Judged by this criterion, the distinction between Era II and Era III is not as great as the distinction between Era I and Era II. In fact, Orr (1983) differentiates between "experiments" and "demonstrations" on the basis of this criterion and, hence, would probably consider many Era II and Era III experiments "demonstrations."

7. Interesting to note, although the Era II MDRC Work/Welfare Demonstration is a relatively large-scale social experiment, it is not being supported by federal funds.

8. See Abt et al. (1978) for a general discussion of the methodological contributions of social experiments.

9. There is no particular reason to believe that the policies tested in the Era I experiments are either inherently good or bad. Perhaps, however, a case could be made that policymakers are unlikely to test policies that are obviously so good or bad that a political consensus exists. It is difficult to envision why policymakers would devote such large resources to testing policies unless there is an absence of such a consensus.

10. The conservative nature of research and evaluation is forcefully delineated in Aaron (1978).

11. Although theory predicts that the labor supply of individuals whose benefit reduction rate is increased to 100 percent will decline, this increase in the benefit reduction rate will not necessarily cause the aggregate labor supply to fall. The reason for this is that as the benefit reduction rate rises, fewer persons qualify for program benefits. However, experimental evidence does not exist on the effects of a 100 percent benefit reduction rate on either individual or aggregate labor supply.

12. See Moffitt and Kehrer (1981) for a comprehensive discussion of the methodological weaknesses of social experiments.

13. It should be noted that as a cost-saving measure, the government elected to terminate this experiment only 6 years after it began, despite the ethical issues this raised about proper treatment of human subjects. For a discussion of the labor supply response to this experiment, see Robins (1984).

14. For a discussion of the self-determination bias and the circumstances under which it occurs, see Burtless and Greenberg (1983).

15. We do not wish to imply that the policymakers should have ignored the "negative" findings. Our point is that the process of scientific inquiry inevitably generates negative findings that provide strong political ammunition for opponents of the program. Whether these negative findings are overemphasized is difficult to determine and depends on the nature of the findings and the context in which the findings are debated in the political arena.

16. Experience with the national implementation of monthly reporting appears much more consistent with this later experimental analysis than with the earlier analysis.

17. That social experiments improve the quality of the debate has been pointed out by several authors including Abt et al. (1978).

REFERENCES

AARON, H. J. (1978) Politics and the Professors: The Great Society in Perspective. Washington, DC: Brookings Institute.

———and J. E. TODD (1978) "The use of income maintenance experiment findings in public policy 1977-1978." Proceedings of the 31st Annual Meeting of the Industrial Relations Research Association, August 29-31.

ABT, C. C. et al. (1978) "An overview of cost-benefit evaluation of applied social research," pp. 1-19 in C. C. Abt (ed.) Perspective on Costs and Benefits of Applied Social Research. Cambridge, MA: Council for Applied Social Research.

BETSON, D., D. GREENBERG, and R. KASTEN (1980) "A micro-simulation model for analyzing alternative welfare reform proposals: an application to the program for better jobs and income," pp. 153-188 in R. Haveman and K. Hollenbeck (eds.) Microeconomic Simulation. New York: Academic Press.

BISHOP, J. (1980) "My reactions to the latest SIME/DIME labor supply results." (memorandum, unpublished)

BURTLESS, G. and D. GREENBERG (1983) "Measuring the impact of NIT experiments on work effort." Industrial and Labor Relations Rev. 36(July): 592-605.

———(1983) "Inappropriate comparisons as a basis for policy: two recent examples from the social experiments." J. of Public Policy 1(October): 381-399.

COGAN, J. F. (1978) Negative Income Taxation and Labor Supply: New Evidence from the New Jersey-Pennsylvania Experiment (R-2155-HEW). Santa Monica, CA: Rand.

COLEMAN, J. (1979) "The use of social science in the development of public policy." (unpublished)

Fortune (1978) Interview with Daniel Patrick Moynihan, December 4.

GREENBERG, D. H. (1983) "Some labor markets effects of labor supply responses to transfer programs." Socio-Economic Planning Sciences 17(Fall): 141-151.

———and H. H. HALSEY (1983) "Systematic misreporting and experimental effects on work effort: the Seattle-Denver income maintenance experiment." J. of Labor Economics 1(October): 380-407.

HAUSMAN, J. A. and D. A. WISE (1983) Technical Problems in Social Experimentation: Cost Versus Ease of Analysis (Working Paper No. 1061). Cambridge, MA: National Bureau of Economic Research.

KEELEY, M. C. (1981) Labor Supply and Public Policy: A Critical Review. New York: Academic Press.

———and P. K. ROBINS (1980) "The design of social experiments: a critique of the Conlisk-Watts model and its application to the Seattle and Denver income maintenance experiments," pp. 293-333 in R. Ehrenberg (ed.) Research in Labor Economics. Greenwich, CT: JAI Press.

KEELEY, M. C. and H. S. WAI (1980) "Labor supply response to a permanent negative income tax program." SRI International. (unpublished)

LONG, D. A., C. D. MALLAR, and C.V.D. THORNTON (1981) "Evaluating the benefits and costs of the job corps." J. of Policy Analysis and Management 1(Fall): 55-76.

MOFFITT, R. and K. KEHRER (1981) "The effect of tax and transfer programs on labor supply: the evidence from the income maintenance experiments," in R. Ehrenberg (ed.) Research in Labor Economics. Greenwich, CT: JAI Press.

MORRIS, C., J. NEWHOUSE, and R. ARCHIBALD (1977) On the Theory and Practice of Obtaining Unbiased and Efficient Samples in Social Surveys and Experiments (R-2173-HEW). Santa Monica, CA: Rand.

MOYNIHAN, D. P. (1978) Letter to *National Review*, September 29.

ORCUTT, G. H. and A. G. ORCUTT (1968) "Incentive and disincentive experimentation for income maintenance policy purposes." Amer. Econ. Rev. 58(September): 754-772.

ORR, L. (1983) "The use of experimental methods to evaluate demonstration products." (unpublished)

ROBINS, P. K. (1984) "The labor supply response of twenty-year families in the Denver income maintenance experiment." Rev. of Economics and Statistics 66(December): 491-495.

———and R. W. WEST (1983) "Labor supply response to the Seattle and Denver income maintenance experiments," pp. 91-198 in Final Report of the Seattle-Denver Income Maintenance Experiments. Washington, DC: Government Printing Office.

RIVLIN, A. M. (1974) "How can experiments be more useful?" Amer. Econ. Association Papers and Proceedings 64(May): 346-354.

U.S. Department of Health and Human Services (1978) Comments on SRI Research Reports on Marital Stability. Washington, DC: Government Printing Office.

U.S. General Accounting Office (1981) Income Maintenance Experiments: Need to Summarize Results and Communicate the Lessons Learned (Report No. HRD 81-46). Washington, DC: Government Printing Office.

U.S. Senate Finance Committee (1978) Hearings on Welfare Research and Experimentation. Washington, DC: Government Printing Office.

WATTS, H. W. and D. HORNER (1977) "Labor supply response of husbands," pp. 57-114 in The New Jersey Income-Maintenance Experiment, Volume 11, Labor-Supply Responses. New York: Academic Press.

I

HEALTH CARE

In 1963, half the elderly had no private health insurance. Commercial insurance companies were reluctant to offer individual coverage to the elderly due to their high risk of serious illness, and most employers did not provide group coverage to retirees. The few policies offered were prohibitively expensive when compared to the modest incomes of most elderly people. As a result of lack of insurance coverage, many of the elderly were rendered indigent by the high costs of serious illness. To ameliorate this widespread problem, the Social Security Act was amended in 1965 to create the Medicare Program, which provided health insurance coverage to virtually all of the nation's elderly 65 years of age and over.

Broad bipartisan support of the Medicare program for the elderly provided the political momentum to enact a health insurance program for the poor. Improving access to medical care for the poor was part of the overall strategy of the War on Poverty the help the disadvantaged help themselves. The poor have historically had a higher burden of illness than the nonpoor. It was hoped that the Medicaid program, by facilitating access to mainstream medical care, would result in improved health, enabling the poor to compete more effectively in the larger society. Its implementation, however, was tied to state welfare eligibility requirements, which resulted in the program serving primarily poor single mothers and their children, groups that are generally outside the labor force.

Within 20 years, Medicare and Medicaid grew to pay for most of the health care provided to one in five Americans, including over 25 million elderly, 5 million disabled people, 9 million poor children, and 4 million single, low-income parents. In 1965, as the nation embarked on these two programs, national health expenditures totalled $42 billion, which accounted for 6 percent of the nation's gross national product (GNP). In 1985, close to $400 billion will be spent on health care, which is expected to account for 10.5 percent of GNP. Public sources now provide 42 percent of total national expenditures for health. Escalating public expenditures have resulted in close scrutiny of the cost-effectiveness of health services, a concern that has generated continuing activity in evaluation research.

In the 1960s and early '70s, the primary emphasis in health policy and evaluation research was how to extend access to medical care to those having difficulty obtaining needed services. After the passage of Medicare and Medicaid there was renewed interest in the enactment of national health insurance for all Americans, an idea that actually predated the Social Security Program. The Health Insurance Study, the largest single study of health services ever conducted, was initiated to test various options for implementing a national health insurance plan.

The Health Insurance Study, a controlled trial of health care financing and organization, was conducted between 1974 and 1982 at an estimated cost of over $70 million. A total of 2756 families consisting of 7706 persons in six sites were randomized to one of 14 different insurance plans or to a Health Maintenance Organization. The insurance plans varied the cost of care to the families. Originally the study results were meant to guide policymakers in the design of national health insurance. By the time the study was completed, national health insurance had faded from the public agenda and had been replaced with concerns as to how the nation could restructure its existing insurance programs to be less costly without adversely affecting health outcomes. Chapters 2, 3, and 4 are results to date from the health insurance study. The study is important because of its sheer magnitude and complexity, its randomized design, its contributions to the state of the art of measuring health status, and the importance of the findings for national health policy.

Chapter 2 by Newhouse and associates is an evaluation of the impact of different levels of health insurance cost-sharing on beneficiaries' use of services. A key concern in the design of all insurance programs is to encourage the insured to use medical care in a timely fashion when care is likely to improve their health and well-being, but not to overutilize medical services so that costs far exceed benefits. Newhouse and his associates report that persons fully covered for medical services spend about 50 percent more on health services than do persons who must pay more of their health bills themselves. Both ambulatory services and hospital admissions increase when patients do not have to pay part of the bill themselves. Although national health insurance is no longer on the public agenda, these findings have been widely cited as encouraging employers to increase coinsurance and deductibles on health insurance packages provided to their employees. Some states have added small copayments for ambulatory visits for Medicaid patients. And even though the Health Insurance Study included no elderly, the findings on coinsurance have been used by advocates of more cost-sharing in the Medicare program.

Having documented that increasing cost-sharing discourages the use of services and therefore saves money, the critical question is whether cost-sharing has an adverse impact on health status. Chapter 3 by Brook and his associates examines whether patients receiving "free care"—that is, they were fully insured—experienced improvement in health compared to similar patients who had to pay part of their health bill and thus used fewer services. Measurement of changes in health status over time is difficult. The methodologies developed by researchers at the Rand Corporation have made a significant contribution to health status outcome measurement. The study reports that free care was associated with some improvement in vision and blood pressure control. No significant effects were detected on eight other measures of health status and health habits.

Chapter 4 by Manning and associates compares utilization and costs of patients randomized to a Health Maintenance Organization compared to those receiving free care from a fee-for-service physician of their choice. The study reports the rate of hospital admissions was about 40 percent less and that expenditures were 25 percent less for the HMO group than the fee-for-service group. This finding is consistent with other studies of savings achieved by HMOs over fee-for-service arrangements. Because of its randomized design, the Health Insurance Study demonstrated that cost savings were not due to selection bias of healthier patients choosing to enroll in HMOs, which had been a frequent criticism of past studies. The randomized design of the Health Insurance Study offers strong evidence that HMOs do indeed have high savings potential. Subsequent papers from this study will examine whether health outcomes are comparable for patients in the HMO despite their much lower use of hospital care.

Chapters 5 and 6 present the results of two large-scale demonstrations to improve access to medical care. The regionalized perinatal services program reported in Chapter 5 was undertaken to demonstrate the impact on infant mortality and morbidity of improving access to appropriate specialty services for high-risk pregnant women and newborns. The evaluation by McCormick, Shapiro, and Starfield is notable in its design for following the surviving infants to age one year to determine whether increasing survival rates were associated with increased rates of functional impairment and disability. This evaluation illustrates a problem common to health demonstrations: diffusion of the interventions to the comparison communities making it difficult to discern program effects.

The aim of the Hospital-Sponsored Primary Care Services Program (Chapter 6) was to improve access to health services for a cross section of community residents, particularly for those who were having problems obtaining medical care, by encouraging community hospitals to expand their ambulatory services. The program evaluation was two-dimensional. The evaluation by Aday, Andersen, and associates was designed to ascertain whether the new program succeeded in reaching previously underserved people and, if so, at what cost. The evaluation findings reported by Shortell, Wickizer, and Wheeler explore organizational and fiscal issues related to long-term program viability.

Two evaluations of hospice programs follow in Chapters 7 and 8. In Chapter 7, Greer and associates report the findings from a nonexperimental evaluation of the costs and outcomes of care for patients treated in 26 hospices in 16 states compared with terminally ill cancer patients receiving care from cancer centers. Some hospices, through special waivers, received Medicare reimbursement for certain services not routinely covered. Chapter 8 by Kane and associates is a single-site randomized trial of a Veterans' Administration hospice in which patients received care in a hospice or conventional care in the VA medical system. Both evaluations focused on the costs and benefits of hospices compared with conventional care for terminally ill cancer patients. Because of the lack of randomization in the Medicare demonstration, the evaluators had the difficult task of attempting to control for significant differences in the types of patients using hospices and conventional care. We have included both studies to illustrate the potential trade-offs between nonexperimental versus randomized experimental designs.

Chapter 9 is an evaluation of an ongoing federally funded program in Massachusetts that provides nutritional supplements and medical examinations to poor pregnant and nursing women and their children. A primary objective of the WIC (Women-Infant-Children) Program is improving pregnancy outcomes. The report of the study and the related commentary typify the dilemmas of evaluating operational programs in which randomization is not feasible and the difficulties of identifying an appropriate control group are substantial.

Chapters 10 and 11 by Klein, Bohannan, Stamm and associates are reports from a multisite demonstration to test the efficacy of preventive dental regimens in school settings. The findings contradicted a substantial body of previous research. The explanation of why this occurred will be of interest to evaluation researchers. First, dental decay rates have been falling substantially in the general population. The average school-aged child has few caries to prevent. Thus from a public health standpoint, given that the potential for prevention is so small, only inexpensive techniques such as fluoridating water supplies are cost-effective. Much of the previous research on fluoride mouthrinses was conducted during a period when caries rates were much higher and thus the potential for prevention was much larger than is currently the case. In addition, much of the research on the efficacy of preventive techniques used pre- and posttest designs without longitudinal comparison groups. Because the rate of caries was declining rapidly in the general population, evaluators, in the absence of comparison groups, overestimated the treatment effects of preventive techniques.

2

Some Interim Results from a Controlled Trial of Cost Sharing in Health Insurance

Joseph P. Newhouse, Willard G. Manning, Carl N. Morris,
Larry L. Orr, Naihua Duan, Emmett B. Keeler,
Arleen Leibowitz, Kent H. Marquis, M. Susan Marquis,
Charles E. Phelps, and Robert H. Brook

I. INTRODUCTION

The controversy over the desirability of cost sharing in health insurance policies has simmered for decades and occasionally boiled
over, in part because of the meager quantitative evidence about the
effects of cost sharing on health status and on the demand for medical
services. The limited information available prompted the federal government to sponsor a social experiment, or controlled trial, of the effects of cost sharing. The experiment, which was intended to be as
definitive as possible, began in the first site in late 1974 and will end
in the last site in early 1982. Results concerning the effects of cost
sharing on health status are not yet available, and we have only interim results on the use of medical services. But in light of the ongoing debate over the appropriate role—if any—of cost sharing in health
insurance plans, we consider it useful to release these preliminary
results now.

From Joseph P. Newhouse et al., "Some Interim Results from a Controlled Trial of Cost Sharing in
Health Insurance," Rand Corporation Publication No. R-2847-HHS, prepared under a grant from
the U.S. Department of Health and Human Services, January 1982. Reprinted by permission of The
Rand Corporation.

II. PRIOR STUDIES

Even as late as 1971, a leading authority, testifying before the Senate Subcommittee on Health, could cite no evidence that cost sharing methods, such as deductibles and coinsurance, led to lower use of health services (Fein, 1971). Subsequently, a number of studies, each with its own limitations, suggested that the extent of cost sharing did affect use;* the quantitative sensitivity of use to cost sharing has, however, remained quite uncertain. The estimates in these studies differed by a factor of three or more in how much the use of health services would increase if an average uninsured person became fully insured. And some argued that fully insuring ambulatory services would *reduce* total expenditure by encouraging preventive care and more appropriate use of the hospital (Roemer et al., 1975), although other evidence suggested the contrary (Hill and Veney, 1970; Lewis and Keairnes, 1970).

The uncertainty about the effects of cost sharing on particular types of individuals exceeds the uncertainty about its effect, on average, on the population as a whole. For example, some believe that cost sharing affects primarily the poor and has very little, if any, effect on the middle class. Evidence from Canada suggests that the poor and those with larger families respond relatively more to cost sharing (Beck, 1974), but one study in the United States did not detect any marked difference in the response of different income groups (Newhouse and Phelps, 1976). In another instance, lower-income groups did respond more, percentagewise, to coinsurance, but absolute changes were similar (Phelps and Newhouse, 1972; Scitovsky and Snyder, 1972).

Still others believe that for children, the demand for health care is less sensitive to cost sharing than for adults, maintaining that much of children's demand for medical services is predictable (Marmor, 1977). They use this predictability to support the argument that cost sharing should be eliminated for children's medical services. At the same time, the rate at which children visit physicians has been notably more sensitive to income than has the rate for adults (NCHS, 1972), suggesting that children's use of medical services may, on average, be more discretionary than that by adults. (In more recent data, however, this trend is not nearly so apparent (NCHS, 1979).)

---

*See Beck, 1974; Enterline et al., 1973; Feldstein, 1978; Newhouse, 1978a; Newhouse and Phelps, 1976; Newhouse, Phelps, and Schwartz, 1974; Phelps and Newhouse, 1972, 1974; Rosett and Huang, 1973; Scitovsky and McCall, 1977; Scitovsky and Snyder, 1972.

In sum, nonexperimental data suggest that use will vary with the amount of cost sharing, but are inconclusive about the magnitude of this effect and its possible variation among different types of people.

III. METHODS

SELECTION OF FAMILIES AND SITES

A total of 2756 families, consisting of 7706 persons, have been enrolled in one of several different health insurance plans, 70 percent of them for 3 years and the rest for 5 years. The details of the experimental design as of late 1973 are given in Newhouse (1974), but are briefly reviewed and updated here. The families come from six areas of the country (listed by size): Seattle, Washington; Dayton, Ohio; Charleston, South Carolina; Fitchburg-Leominster, Massachusetts; Franklin County, Massachusetts; and Georgetown County, South Carolina. Families who moved after enrollment were kept in the study as long as they remained within the United States.*

Within these six sites, families were selected at random, subject to the following restrictions: Families were excluded in which heads were eligible for Medicare at the beginning of the study (or who would become so by virtue of age before the end of the study). Hence, our results do not necessarily apply to the aged population. Families participating in the Supplemental Security Income (SSI) program, including those participating in the Disability Medicare program, were ineligible. So, too, were families eligible for the military medical care system, veterans with total disability that was service-connected, and persons residing in institutions that assumed responsibility for medical care (e.g., prisons, mental institutions). Families with incomes in excess of $25,000 (1973 dollars) were ineligible; this rule excluded so few people (approximately the upper 5 percent of the income distribution) that it should not materially affect our results. Persons over 62 at the time of enrollment in otherwise eligible families were excluded, but the remainder of the family was eligible. Finally, low-income families within each site were mildly oversampled.

The sites were selected as follows. First we calculated the optimal number of sites for a given budget. This implied balancing the effect of additional dollars spent to reduce between-site variance by adding more sites with that of additional dollars spent to reduce within-site

---

*Except for families enrolled in the control group at the Health Maintenance Organization. These participants are not included in the analysis described in this report.

variance by adding more families. Our estimates showed that the optimal number of sites for our budget was between four and nine. We settled on six.

It remained to determine the exact sites. The six sites were selected (a) to represent all four census regions and thus account for any regional variation in responsiveness of demand to cost sharing; (b) to obtain a spectrum of city sizes, because the complexity of the medical care delivery system (and hence the response to insurance) could vary with city size; (c) to achieve variation in waiting times for an appointment and the proportion of primary care physicians accepting new patients, since response to demand could vary according to the amount of excess demand for ambulatory services; (d) to include participants from both Northern and Southern rural areas, because these areas tend to differ in economic and racial characteristics; and (e) to ensure that one site had a well-established, prepaid group practice.

The actual sites chosen satisfied these criteria (Table 1). We have not yet reweighted the sample to represent a national probability sample, because any weights would change with each new increment of data. But the characteristics of the unweighted sample, when averaged across the sites, do not markedly differ from those of the nation, save for the intentional departures, such as the exclusion of the aged.

ASSIGNMENT OF FAMILIES TO EXPERIMENTAL INSURANCE PLANS

The families selected to enroll in the experiment were assigned to an insurance plan by an unbiased method, the Finite Selection Model (Morris, 1979). The model retains some randomization, but improves upon simple and stratified random assignments by making the distribution of the several family and individual characteristics represented in each insurance plan as similar as a limited number of families permit. The characteristics taken into account are described in Morris (1979).

Fifteen percent of the families contacted were not enrolled because they refused a screening or baseline interview (Table 2). There is no way of knowing whether these families would behave differently from those who ultimately enrolled. Another 20 percent of the families refused a subsequent enrollment interview or the offer of enrollment in the experimental plan. If they refused, they could not participate in the experiment at all. Because the characteristics and the prior use of medical services of families who ultimately enrolled in the experiment do not differ significantly from those of eligible families who completed baseline interviews, refusal of this 20 percent should not bias the results.

Table 1

CHARACTERISTICS OF SITES

Site	Census Region	Population of Urbanized Area or County (1970)	Primary Care Physicians per 100,000 Population (1972)[a]	Days Spent Waiting for an Appointment with a Primary Care Physician,[b] New Patient (1973, 1974)	Median Family Income (1969)	Percent Over Age 24 with Less Than 5 Years of Education (1970)	Percent Black (1970)	Number of Enrollees
Seattle, WA	West	1,200,000	59	4.1	11,800	1.8	3	1,220[c]
Dayton, OH	North Central	690,000	41	7.5	11,400	3.3	13	1,140
Charleston, SC	South	230,000	33	15.9	8,300	6.2	25	780
Fitchburg-Leominster, MA	North East	78,000	30	25.0	10,000	4.3	1	724
Franklin County, MA	North East	59,000	46	9.2	9,900	2.8	1	891
Georgetown County, SC	South	34,000	44	0	6,400	20.6	48	1,061
United States	—	—	46	7.1	9,600	5.5	11	—

[a]Includes general practitioners, family practitioners, internists, and pediatricians.

[b]Physicians who do not use appointment systems and take patients on a first-come, first-served basis are valued as having zero wait time. All physicians sampled in Georgetown County at the time of the survey accepted patients on this basis. For other sites, the values are negligibly changed if only physicians using appointment systems are included.

[c]An additional 1892 participants were enrolled in the Group Health Cooperative of Puget Sound.

Table 2

PROPORTION OF SAMPLE REMAINING AFTER ACCOUNTING
FOR REFUSALS AT VARIOUS STAGES
(Percentage/100)

Enrollment Criteria	Dayton	Seattle[a]	Massachusetts	South Carolina	Total
Initial sample	1.0	1.0	1.0	1.0	1.0
Did not refuse screening interview	.88	.85	1.0[b]	1.0[b]	.94
Did not refuse baseline interview	.74	.78	.88	.95	.85
Did not refuse enrollment interview	.73	.70	.76	.84	.76
Did not refuse offer of enrollment	.68	.59	.62	.71	.65
Number of families enrolled	390	484	566	568	2008

NOTE: These numbers do not account for families who moved prior to enrollment, could not be located, were chronically not at home, or other losses from the sample not due to refusal.

[a]Excludes 752 families enrolled in the Group Health Cooperative of Puget Sound.

[b]There was no screening interview in Massachusetts or South Carolina.

DESCRIPTION OF INSURANCE PLANS

The insurance plans that were offered to the families varied along two dimensions: the coinsurance rate (fraction of the bill paid by the family) and the Maximum Dollar Expenditure (an upper limit on annual family out-of-pocket expenditure). The coinsurance rates were 0 (free care), 25, 50, or 95 percent. The Maximum Dollar Expenditure varied as a fraction of family income, either 5, 10, or 15 percent, to a maximum of $1000.* The 95-percent coinsurance plan, together with the limit on the family's expenditure, approximates an income-related catastrophe plan.

The following example illustrates how the experimental plan operated. A family assigned to a plan with a 25-percent coinsurance rate and a $1000 Maximum Dollar Expenditure would pay 25 percent of all medical and dental bills in each year until the total of all of these bills reached $4000. At that point it would have spent $1000 out-of-pocket, after which all further expenditure during that year would be fully paid (or reimbursed) by the experimental plan. At the beginning of the next year, the family would again pay the 25-percent coinsurance until the $1000 limit was reached.

One plan differed somewhat from all the others in that its ceiling on out-of-pocket expenditure was not related to income. This plan had a 95-percent coinsurance rate, but the maximum out-of-pocket expenditure was limited to $150 for each person or, alternatively, to $450 for the family. Thus, this plan approximates one with a $150-per-person annual deductible, with a provision that no more than three people in the family must satisfy the "deductible." We refer to this plan as the Individual Deductible Plan.

Most enrolled families were permitted to seek care from any provider. Some families in Seattle, however, were assigned to a prepaid group practice, the Group Health Cooperative of Puget Sound in Seattle; their medical care was free as long as it was received at the Cooperative. In addition, some families were included who were already members of the Cooperative. Results on families enrolled in the Cooperative are not yet available.

A wide variety of services were covered in all plans, including hospital, physician, dental, mental health, visual, and auditory services, drugs (including over-the-counter drugs for certain chronic conditions), and supplies. Services of nonphysician providers, such as audiologists, chiropractors, clinical psychologists, optometrists, physical therapists, and speech therapists, were also covered. The only noteworthy exclusions from coverage were nonpreventive orthodontic ser-

---

*In the 25-percent coinsurance plans, the maximum was $750 in most site-years.

vices, cosmetic surgery for pre-existing conditions, and outpatient mental health visits exceeding 52 per year.

Each policy covered all services at a single coinsurance rate with two exceptions. First, three plans required 50-percent coinsurance for dental and outpatient mental health services, but only 25 percent for all other services. These plans are grouped with the 25-percent coinsurance plans below. Second, the Individual Deductible Plan applied cost sharing to *outpatient* services only; inpatient services were free to the family. The Individual Deductible Plan thus approximated the situation of many families who have complete or nearly complete insurance coverage for inpatient services but incomplete coverage for outpatient services. It was designed to test the hypothesis that failure to provide full coverage for outpatient services inflates total medical expenditures by inducing additional hospitalization (Roemer et al., 1975).

A number of minor changes in the insurance plans were made after the plans had been in operation for a year in the first site (Dayton). In the first year in Dayton, dental services for adults were not covered in plans with nonzero coinsurance rates, but were covered thereafter like any other service. Also during the first year in Dayton, expenditures for outpatient mental health services were covered at the coinsurance rate specified in the policy. Such expenditures did not count toward the Maximum Dollar Expenditure during the first year, but subsequently they did. Finally, in the first year in Dayton, there were plans with 100-percent coinsurance rather than 95 percent; at the beginning of the second year in Dayton, the plans with 100-percent coinsurance were changed to 95-percent coinsurance. The change from 100 to 95 percent is ignored for simplicity in the following analysis, but because of the different treatment in the first year in Dayton, we will omit dental and outpatient mental health services from the analysis.

Upon enrollment, families signed over (assigned) the benefits from any existing health insurance coverage to the experiment; such policies were kept in force so that the families could return to them at the end of the experiment. Any family whose existing coverage was such that participation in the experiment could make it potentially worse off financially was paid, over the course of the experiment, an amount at least equal to its maximum possible loss. (This payment was made irrespective of the family's actual use of medical services.) For example, if the family had been assigned to an experimental plan with a $450 Maximum Dollar Expenditure and had an existing policy with a $100 deductible and a 20-percent coinsurance above the deductible, it was paid at least $280 per year (280 = 450 − 100 − .2(450 − 100)). Thus, a family always gained financially by enrolling.

ARTIFACTS OF THE EXPERIMENT

Our analyses are designed to control for several methodological artifacts of the experiment, including the "hold-harmless" payments just described, possible transitory effects from the limited duration of the experiment, the frequency of questionnaire administration, and the initial screening examination. The methods used to adjust for any effects that these artifacts may have had are described in Appendix A.

SAMPLE ANALYZED

The sample analyzed below includes individuals who participated in the experiment for the entire year in question and decedents who had participated during the year in which they died. (If, for example, a person withdrew sometime during the second year, data for that person are included in the analysis of the first year's experience only.) The inpatient expenditures for newborns are included with those of their mothers. The resulting sample includes roughly 95 percent of the individuals initially enrolled in the experiment. Attrition has been minimal—on the order of 2 or 3 percent per year—and no adjustment has been made for any bias that may have been introduced by attrition.

Our results include data from all sites except the two in South Carolina. The 3-year South Carolina sample was not enrolled until late 1978 and early 1979; consequently, the data now available are too few to merit analysis. The sample analyzed comprises data from the first 3 years of the Dayton site and the first 2 years of the Seattle and Massachusetts sites. Overall, these data constitute about 40 percent of the ultimate number of person-years.

METHOD OF ANALYSIS

One can, of course, analyze data from this experiment by computing means and standard deviations by plan (simple analysis of variance). Because plan was designed to be unrelated to any known covariates, differences in mean values by plan will yield unbiased estimates of differences among plans. Although such a procedure is satisfactory for ambulatory expenditure, the standard errors associated with per person total expenditure by plan are unacceptably large. The imprecision results from rare, very large claims that make the sample mean a relatively unreliable estimate of the population mean. For these reasons, we have augmented our analysis with more sophisticated methods. These methods consist of four estimated equations that predict expenditure. The equations are sketched in Appendix A and are described at greater length by Duan et al. (forthcoming).

In addition to its greater precision, the four-equation analysis permits a more reliable estimate of standard errors. When one is computing standard errors of differences among plan means (i.e., using analysis of variance), it is difficult to account for intrafamily and intertemporal correlation. We have made two different estimates of these correlations: a maximum likelihood estimate and a method of moments estimate. Unfortunately these methods yield different results for the estimated standard errors of the plan means. When the maximum likelihood method is used, the estimated correlations are sufficiently small that their effect on the standard errors is negligible (relative to assuming the correlation to be zero). When the method of moments is used, the correlation is such that the estimated standard errors are increased about 25 percent (above what they would have been had the correlation been zero). Because of the uncertainty about the magnitude of this correlation, we have not corrected the standard errors of the simple means for intrafamily and intertemporal correlation (i.e., standard errors for simple means assume no intrafamily or intertemporal correlation). The standard errors for values predicted by the four equations are corrected for intrafamily correlation, but are not corrected for intertemporal correlation. If intertemporal correlation were accounted for, the standard errors would increase by at most 7 percent (Duan et al., forthcoming).

IV. RESULTS

OVERALL EXPENDITURE

Per capita total expenditure (inpatient plus ambulatory, excluding dental and outpatient mental health services) rises steadily as coinsurance falls (Table 3). Expenditure per person in the plan with no coinsurance (the most generous plan) is about 60-percent greater than in the plan with 95-percent coinsurance, which approximates income-related catastrophe coverage $(0.6 = (401 - 254)/(254))$. Expenditure in the other plans falls between these two extremes. Differences among plans with different Maximum Dollar Expenditures were small; therefore, for clarity, all plans with the same coinsurance rate have been combined.

It is difficult to compare the figures in Table 3 with national data. Appendix B shows that the average expenditure in the country, adjusted for comparability, is around $350. As it should, this value lies within the range of our plans.

Precision for ambulatory expenditure is sufficiently good to permit disaggregation by site and year. In each site and year analyzed to date, per person expenditure on ambulatory services rises as coinsurance falls, save for a few insignificant exceptions (Table 4).

Although the simple arithmetic mean provides acceptable precision for analyzing ambulatory expenditure, it does not do so for plan-related differences in total expenditure (given the sample size available to date in this experiment). Even ignoring intrafamily and intertemporal correlation, the differences in total expenditure between any two plans shown in Table 3 are mostly insignificant at the 5-percent level (although the differences between the free care plan and the family deductible plan and between the 25-percent coinsurance plan and the 95-percent (family deductible) plan are significant at the 1-percent level). This lack of precision occurs because a few large medical expenditures account for a substantial portion of all expenditures on a given plan and can therefore affect the average quite dramatically; e.g., over the 9 site-years, 1 percent of the individuals in the sample accounted for 28 percent of the total expenditure.

Application of techniques better suited to such data yields a somewhat different, but probably more reliable, estimate of what per person expenditure would be if a larger number of families had been enrolled. The resulting estimates show narrower but more significant differences among plans than the actual per person expenditure presented in Table 3. Averaged across all sites, predicted expenditure per person in the 95-percent coinsurance plan is 69 percent of that in the free care plan; in other words, free care causes expenditure to increase by nearly 50 percent (Table 5). The predicted difference in dollars for the two plans is $132; a 95-percent confidence interval around this difference is ±$44. In some site-years, the predicted expenditure for the 50-percent coinsurance plan was smaller than that for the 95-percent coinsurance plan, but the difference is statistically insignificant. This misordering appears to be attributable to the sampling error, given the relatively few participants enrolled in the 50-percent coinsurance plan.

The estimated effects of experimental artifacts are uniformly small and insignificant at the 5-percent level. Any transitory effects associated with the limited duration of the experiment appear negligible. Responsiveness in Dayton was relatively constant across 3 years (Table 5). Failure of the response to decline over time suggests that any initial surge in the free care plan was unimportant. End-of-ex-

Table 3

Actual Annual Total and Ambulatory Expenditure Per Person, by Plan: Nine Site-Years

Plan	Total Expenditure	Ambulatory Expenditure	Number of Person-Years for Total Expenditure	Number of Person-Years for Ambulatory Expenditure[a]
Free care	$401 (±52)	$186 (±9)	2825	2834
25-percent coinsurance	346 (±58)	149 (±10)	1787	1792
50-percent coinsurance	328 (±149)	120 (±12)	766	766
Family Deductible, 95-percent coinsurance	254 (±37)	114 (±10)	1763	1764
Individual Deductible,[b] 95-percent coinsurance	333 (±74)	140 (±11)	1605	1609

NOTE: 95-percent confidence intervals are shown in parentheses. Dollars are current dollars, beginning in late 1974 and extending through late 1978. The figures are uncorrected for site price-level differences or for small differences in allocation to plan by site. Confidence intervals are uncorrected for intertemporal and intrafamily correlation; such a correction cannot be made without imposing strong assumptions about the nature of the correlation. Ignoring intertemporal and intrafamily correlation, the F-value to test the null hypothesis of no differences among the plans in total expenditure with 4,8741 degrees of freedom is 3.14, significant at the 5-percent level. The F-value to test the null hypothesis of no differences among the plans in ambulatory expenditure is 33.4, significant at well under the 1-percent level.

[a]The sample for ambulatory expenditure includes 19 individuals with a known hospital admission for whom the amount of inpatient expenditure is missing.

[b]Coinsurance in this plan applies to outpatient care only; inpatient care is free.

Table 4

Expenditure on Ambulatory Care Per Person, by Plan, Site, and Year

Plan	Dayton			Seattle		Fitchburg		Franklin County	
	Year 1	Year 2	Year 3	Year 1	Year 2	Year 1	Year 2	Year 1	Year 2
Free care	$180 (±25)	$188 (±25)	$235 (±37)	$192 (±21)	$192 (±24)	$168 (±27)	$205 (±46)	$153 (±21)	$159 (±30)
25-percent coinsurance	84%†	78%*	68%	77%	88%†	96%†	63%	79%*	83%†
50-percent coinsurance	69	59	58	—	—	72*	51	72*	75†
95-percent coinsurance	55	68	51	60	72*	80†	56	51	59
Individual Deductible, 95-percent coinsurance	83†	67	60	86†	78*	64	68*	86†	82†
Total number of persons	1110	1103	1092	1171	1146	704	693	875	871

NOTE: 95-percent confidence intervals for the free plan are shown in parentheses. If no symbol appears to the right of the number, the difference from the free plan is significant at the 1-percent level. An asterisk (*) to the right of the number indicates that the difference from the free plan is significant at the 5-percent level; a dagger (†) indicates that the difference is not significant at the 5-percent level. (All tests are one-tail tests.) No persons were assigned to the 50-percent coinsurance plan in Seattle. The 19 individuals with a known hospital admission but missing hospital expenditures have been included in the sample for this table (see note a in Table 1). Standard errors are not corrected for intrafamily correlation.

TABLE 5

PREDICTED TOTAL EXPENDITURE PER PERSON, BY PLAN, SITE, AND YEAR

(Dollars for free plan; percentage of free plan elsewhere)

Plan	Dayton			Seattle		Fitchburg		Franklin County		All Site-Years
	Year 1	Year 2	Year 3	Year 1	Year 2	Year 1	Year 2	Year 1	Year 2	
Free care	$414 (±65)	$472 (±77)	$514 (±83)	$382 (±56)	$442 (±70)	$376 (±65)	$477 (±91)	$374 (±63)	$399 (±73)	$430 (±50)
25-percent coinsurance	75%	79%	72%	85%*	81%	90%†	81%*	83%*	91%†	81%
50-percent coinsurance	64	61	63	—	—	71	59	78*	71	67
95-percent coinsurance	69	73	62	73	72	76	67	66	66	69
Individual Deductible, 95-percent coinsurance[a]	76	70	67	86*	81	81*	75	82*	80	77

NOTE: 95-percent confidence intervals for the free plan are shown in parentheses. If no symbol appears to the right of the number, the value is significantly different from the free plan value for that site-year at the 1-percent level (one-tail test). An asterisk (*) indicates that the value is significantly different at the 5-percent level. A dagger (†) indicates that the value is not significantly different at the 5-percent level; in the two instances in which this occurs, the t-statistic exceeds one. The dollars are current dollars, beginning in late 1974 and extending through late 1978; they are uncorrected for site price-level differences. The sample is the same as that in Table 2 except that the 19 individuals with missing inpatient expenditures, who were excluded from Table 1, are also excluded here. Standard errors are corrected for intrafamily correlation.

[a]Coinsurance applies to outpatient care only; inpatient care is free.

periment effects also appear minimal. There is only an insignificant difference in the predicted per person expenditure between the 3- and 5-year groups during the third year in Dayton (data not shown). The estimated effect of the hold-harmless payment is also negligible. That its effect should be negligible is plausible—it is as if an employer increased the cost sharing in the health insurance plan, passed on the savings in premiums to employees, and added a general wage increase that averaged less than 10 percent. It does not seem likely that the use of medical services would be much affected by a wage increase of this magnitude. This matter is discussed further in Appendix A.

DIFFERENCES IN USE AMONG PLANS

Expressing differences among plans in dollars is a natural method of aggregating various services. But it does not indicate whether observed differences in expenditure reflect differences in the actual amount of services consumed or in the price per unit of service. Which of these two factors predominates clearly affects one's interpretation of expenditure differences.

In fact, variation in the quantities of services consumed appears to account for most of the differences among plans. Using plan means from the four site-years for which both expenditure and visit data are now available (Year 2 in each site), we find that the correlation between visits per person and ambulatory expenditure per person is 0.94. As an example, in the second year in Dayton, physician visit rates varied across plans by almost the same percentage as ambulatory expenditure rates, suggesting that price per visit varied little (Table 6). The misordering between the 50- and 95-percent coinsurance plans is insignificant and appears to reflect random fluctuation.

The likelihood of a physician visit or a hospital admission during a year also differs markedly across plans (Table 7), further demonstrating that differences in expenditure result from variation in actual amounts of services consumed. The admission likelihood in the zero coinsurance plan is 13 to 42 percent above the rates in other plans. The admission likelihood in the Individual Deductible Plan, in which inpatient services are fully covered, lies between the likelihood in the zero coinsurance plan and that in the 25-, 50-, and 95-percent coinsurance plans, suggesting that both the price of outpatient services and the price of inpatient services determine hospital admissions. By contrast with the likelihood of admission, annual expenditure per hospi-

TABLE 6

AMBULATORY EXPENDITURE RATES AND OFFICE VISIT RATES
PER PERSON, BY PLAN: DAYTON, YEAR 2

Plan	Ambulatory Expenditure Rates (Free plan = 100)	Office Visit Rates[a] (Free plan = 100)
Free care	$188 (100)	5.4 visits (100)
25-percent coinsurance	(78)	4.4 visits (81)
50-percent coinsurance	(59)	3.2 visits (59)
95-percent coinsurance	(68)	3.7 visits (69)
Individual Deductible, 95-percent coinsurance	(67)	3.7 visits (68)

NOTE: All differences in expenditure and visits between the free plan and other plans are significant at the 1-percent level except the differences between the free and 25-percent coinsurance plans for ambulatory expenditures, which are significant at the 5-percent level using a one-tail test. Standard errors are corrected for intrafamily correlation.

[a]Visits are defined from claims. A visit is any outpatient service performed by an M.D. or D.O. or his staff for a given patient on a single day. Nonbilled services such as telephone visits or visits to industrial clinics are not counted as visits by this definition.

tal stay shows no consistent pattern with respect to plan, and we cannot reject the null hypothesis of no relationship between plan and expenditure per stay at the 5-percent level of significance (F with 4,735 d.f. = 2.03, P-value approximately 0.1).

Differences in expenditure among plans can be disaggregated into differences in the number of participants in each plan who use any medical services during a year and differences in the amount of expenditure among those who use any services. The number of participants who use any service rises from 75 percent or somewhat more in the family deductible plan to 90 percent in the plan in which all services are free (Table 8). This difference in the number of users accounts for approximately one-third to one-half of the difference in overall expenditure among plans, depending on the site and year.

Although price per unit of service does not differ much across the plans, one should not infer that treatment intensity does not respond to coinsurance. Because the fraction of users increases as coinsurance falls, users in the plan with lower coinsurance may be, on average,

TABLE 7

ANNUAL PROBABILITY OF ONE OR MORE PHYSICIAN
VISITS OR HOSPITAL ADMISSIONS,
NINE SITE-YEARS

Plan	Physician Visits	Hospital Admissions
Free care	.84 (±.02)	.102 (±.013)
25-percent coinsurance	.78 (±.03)	.081 (±.014)
50-percent coinsurance	.75 (±.05)	.072 (±.021)
95-percent coinsurance	.69 (±.04)	.076 (±.014)
Individual Deductible, 95-percent coinsurance[a]	.73 (±.04)	.090 (±.016)

NOTE: 95-percent confidence intervals are shown in parentheses. The differences in the likelihood of a physician visit between the free plan and the other plans are significant at well under the 1-percent level; the differences in hospital admissions between the free care plan and the other plans are also significant at the 1-percent level, except for the free-care 25-percent coinsurance difference, which is significant at the 5-percent level, and the free-care individual-deductible difference, which is not significant at the 5-percent level. All tests are one-tail tests. Standard errors are corrected for intrafamily and intertemporal correlations.

[a]This plan has zero coinsurance (free care) for inpatient services.

less sick, thereby offsetting the possible tendency for persons with a given illness to be treated more intensively as the coinsurance rate falls.

The values in Tables 6 and 7 are consistent with national data, implying that the choice of sites, the package of covered services, the administrative procedures used, and the transitory nature of the experiment do not distort the results. Because coverage of hospital services in the nation is quite high, the national likelihood of admission should lie between that found in the free plan and those found in the other plans. In fact, it does; the national rate in 1977 for the under-65 population was 0.095 (NCHS, 1977). This value is also close to that found in the Individual Deductible Plan, as it should be. The national likelihood of visiting a physician, 0.75 in 1977, lies at the value for the 50-percent coinsurance plan, consistent with the partial existing coverage of ambulatory services (Newhouse, Phelps, and Schwartz,

TABLE 8

PREDICTED EXPENDITURE, BY PLAN AND AGE GROUP: YEAR 1

(Dollars for free plan; percentage of free plan elsewhere)

Plan	Dayton Adult	Dayton Child	Seattle Adult	Seattle Child	Fitchburg Adult	Fitchburg Child	Franklin County Adult	Franklin County Child
Free care	$555 (±91)	$196 (±32)	$500 (±76)	$174 (±27)	$521 (±95)	$185 (±34)	$507 (±92)	$186 (±32)
25-percent coinsurance	75%	77%	84%*	91%†	88%†	98%†	81%*	89%†
50-percent coinsurance	62	71	—	—	68	82†	74*	93†
95-percent coinsurance	69	69	72	75	75	78*	66	69
Individual Deductible, 95-percent coinsurance[a]	76	75	85*	89†	81*	83†	81*	86*

NOTE: 95-percent confidence intervals are shown in parentheses. If no symbol appears to the right of the number, the difference from the free plan is significant at the 1-percent level (one-tail test). An asterisk (*) indicates that the value is significant at the 5-percent level; a dagger (†) indicates that the value is not significant at the 5-percent level.

[a] Coinsurance applies to outpatient care only; inpatient care is free.

1974; NCHS, 1977). Finally, the visit rates appear consistent with the national rate of 3.9 office, home, and clinic visits per person (NCHS, 1979). Across the four sites in the second year for which data are available, the visit rate in the free plan was above this value, in the 25-percent plan it equalled it, and in the other plans it was below it.

USE BY SUBGROUPS

An important objective of the experiment is to judge the effect of cost sharing on various subgroups of the population. Of special interest is whether cost sharing has a different effect on adults and children, poor and nonpoor, and blacks and whites. Expenditure by adults shows greater responsiveness to variation in cost sharing than does expenditure by children (Table 8), largely because the likelihood of at least one hospital admission for children shows no significant response to plan (observed differences for children are insignificant), whereas the likelihood for adults is markedly higher in the free care plan (Table 9).

Different income groups have relatively similar responses (Table 10). In Dayton, families in the lower third of the income distribution show somewhat more responsiveness to coinsurance than those in the upper third, but in the other three sites the two groups respond almost identically. Even in Dayton the apparent greater responsiveness admits of a different interpretation; the absolute decline in actual dollars as coinsurance rises is very similar between the two income groups. (This is also true in the two subsequent years in Dayton, which are not shown.) In all cases, the income measure is average family income for the 2 years before enrollment; more current income data now being processed should yield more precise estimates.

Blacks in Dayton spend about 20 percent less than whites, holding a variety of characteristics constant, including plan, pre-enrollment self-assessed health status, and income; the difference is significant at the 1-percent level. Values for blacks in other sites and for other minorities are not presented because of insufficient representation in our sample (Table 1). Why blacks in Dayton spent less is not clear. Whether this result will continue to hold in the two South Carolina sites, where the proportion of blacks is markedly higher, is not known.

TABLE 9

ANNUAL PROBABILITY OF ONE OR MORE HOSPITAL ADMISSIONS,
BY PLAN AND AGE GROUP

Plan	Child (17 years or under)[a]	Adult (Over 17 years)
Free care	.056 (±.015)	.133 (±.018)
25-percent coinsurance	.047 (±.017)	.104 (±.020)
50-percent coinsurance	.057 (±.029)	.082 (±.028)
95-percent coinsurance	.045 (±.017)	.095 (±.020)
Individual Deductible, 95-percent coinsurance[b]	.065 (±.023)	.104 (±.019)

NOTE: 95-percent confidence intervals are shown in parentheses.
For adults, 50- and 95-percent coinsurance values are significantly different from the free plan value at the 1-percent level, and the 25-percent
and Individual Deductible values are significantly different at the 5-per-
cent level. For children, no plan difference is significant at conventional
levels. All tests are one-tail tests. Standard errors are corrected for intrafamily and intertemporal correlations.

[a]The mean for children in our plans is .054 (±.008); the national
mean is .050 (±.004) (Newhouse, 1974).

[b]This plan has zero coinsurance (free care) for inpatient services.

V. DISCUSSION

Our results clearly show that the use of medical services responds
to cost sharing; demand in an insurance plan with full coverage appears to be about 50 percent above that in an income-related catastrophe insurance plan. The fragmentary evidence now in the
literature is roughly consistent with this value; e.g., the 25-percent
decline in visits observed in a natural experiment among Stanford
University employees when their coinsurance rate was changed from
zero to 25 percent (Scitovsky and McCall, 1977; Scitovsky and Snyder,
1972) is similar to the 20-percent decline in ambulatory expenditure
observed between the zero and 25-percent coinsurance plans (Table 3).
And the magnitude of differences in insurance premiums for policies
with 10-, 15-, 20-, and 25-percent coinsurance is consistent with the
differences in total use between the zero and 25-percent coinsurance
plans (Phelps and Newhouse, 1974).

TABLE 10

PREDICTED EXPENDITURE, BY INCOME TERTILE AND PLAN: YEAR 1

(Dollars for free plan; percentage of free plan elsewhere)

Plan	Dayton Low	Dayton High	Seattle Low	Seattle High	Fitchburg Low	Fitchburg High	Franklin County Low	Franklin County High
Free care	$395 (±67)	$446 (±69)	$384 (±59)	$381 (±57)	$403 (±73)	$367 (±65)	$391 (±69)	$368 (±64)
25-percent coinsurance	71%	78%	85%*	85%*	89%†	90%†	82%*	83%*
50-percent coinsurance	60	67	—	—	71	71	77*	78*
95-percent coinsurance	65	72	72	73	75	76	65	67
Individual Deductible, 95-percent coinsurance[a]	73	78	86*	86*	81*	82*	81	82*

NOTE: 95-percent confidence intervals are shown in parentheses. Comparisons do not hold factors constant other than income; they simply compare predictions for actual families with incomes below $9548 and above $15,264 (1972 dollars) in Dayton; below $8222 and above $13,882 (1973 dollars) in Seattle; below $9548 and above $13,033 (1973 dollars) in Fitchburg; and below $9374 and above $13,155 (1973 dollars), in Franklin County. These values define the lower third and upper third of the income distribution for the site. If no symbol appears to the right of the number, the difference from the free plan is significant at the 1-percent level. An asterisk (*) indicates that the difference is significant at the 5-percent level; a dagger (†) indicates that the difference is not significant at the 5-percent level. All tests are one-tail tests. Standard errors are corrected for intrafamily correlations.

[a]Coinsurance applies to outpatient care only; inpatient care is free.

The response to the experimental plans by families at different income levels was similar. In Dayton, the response among the lower third of the income distribution somewhat exceeded that among the upper third in percentage terms (although not in absolute terms); but in Seattle and the two Massachusetts sites, responsiveness was virtually identical between the lower third and upper third of the income distribution.

As others have conjectured, expenditure for children depends less on coinsurance than does expenditure for adults.

THE POLICY DEBATE OVER COST SHARING

Many arguments have been advanced about the desirability and shortcomings of cost sharing. One alleged shortcoming is that cost sharing, especially for ambulatory services, raises overall costs by inducing individuals to delay seeking care and physicians to hospitalize patients who could be treated as outpatients (Roemer et al., 1975). The results from the Individual Deductible Plan tend to refute this argument. Under that plan the incentives for inappropriate use of the hospital are stronger than in other plans because inpatient services are free. Physicians thus have a greater incentive to perform procedures in the hospital that could be performed in the office. But the probability of hospitalization in the Individual Deductible Plan is lower than in the free care plan, significantly so for adults (Table 9). Evidently, given the reduced use of outpatient services under the Individual Deductible Plan, physicians less frequently see illness that leads to hospitalization. The medical consequences of the decreased hospital use in the Individual Deductible Plan are not clear.

Any increase in total expenditure resulting from delay in seeking care because of cost sharing is outweighed by other forces. The 95-percent coinsurance and free care plans probably differ most in the incentive to delay, yet total expenditure in the free care plan is well above that in the 95-percent coinsurance plan, and the difference is significant at the 1-percent level in each site and year studied (Table 5).

Another negative argument about cost sharing is its alleged promotion of an inequitable distribution of services. This argument is difficult to address because no consensus exists on an operational measure of equity. If, in fact, the poor responded more to cost sharing than did middle-income groups, some might argue that the proportion of services going to the poor when care is free is the equitable amount —and that the proportion going to the poor when services are not free is, by implication, too low.

Our interim results indicate that the poor are not more responsive to cost sharing if, as in the experiment, the cost sharing is less for low-income families. But our results do suggest that cost sharing unrelated to income would differentially affect lower-income families. Because, in the experiment, the Maximum Dollar Expenditure was less for poor families, they were more likely to exceed it and not face cost sharing for any additional use. Thus, they faced less cost sharing on the average. Because cost sharing affects use, and because income-related cost sharing affects income groups equally, cost sharing not related to income would have caused disproportionate reductions in use among the poor.

Another definition of equity requires minimal variation of utilization with income (Andersen, 1975). In three of the four sites for which we have results, the estimated relationship between expenditure and income is small and insignificant. In the fourth (Dayton), a 1-percent increase in income, other factors equal, elicits approximately a 0.2-percent increase in expenditure in each of the 3 years, and the relation is significant at the 1-percent level. We cannot, however, detect any difference among the plans in this relation; thus, providing free care does not appear to eliminate the variation of use with income in Dayton.

Perhaps the most frequently made argument for eliminating cost sharing is that medical services are a right for all and ought not to be rationed by price. Although this argument is philosophical, it may be based on the premise that full coverage improves health, or that cost instrument for affecting costs once patients are admitted. Potentially more effective instruments include regulation, an example of which was the Carter Administration's hospital cost containment proposal, and greater competition in medical care (Enthoven, 1978; Newhouse and Taylor, 1971).

CAN THE RESULTS BE GENERALIZED?

The Health Insurance Experiment has measured how the demands of a small number of consumers increased as cost sharing fell, i.e., how many more services the participants sought and their physicians delivered as coinsurance decreased. Will the experimental results generalize to a widespread health insurance plan of a similar nature? The consistency of the results with national averages suggests they will, but certain circumstances could cause behavior to differ.

First, if insurance for ambulatory services were suddenly expanded, the resulting increase in the entire population's demand could exceed the short-run capacity of the medical care delivery system. If so, the additional demand could be rationed in several possible ways (Newhouse et al., 1974). Most likely, longer waits for an appointment would occur, as happened in Montreal when cost sharing was eliminated (Enterline et al., 1973). We do not yet have a good understanding of which services would not be delivered if appointment times lengthened.

Second, the delivery system might not be allowed to expand to meet any new demand; it could, for example, be constrained by budget limits or rate and fee controls so that only a certain proportion of the demand would be met. The experimental plan, in general, reimbursed billed fees or charges, but regulations or fee schedules might not permit such a procedure. We cannot predict from experimental data who might receive what services if budgets were so constrained that not all the demand could be met.

Third, if present cost sharing levels increased so that demand fell, some argue that physicians would create additional demand to offset the decline (Barer et al., 1979). The evidence supporting this argument, however, has been sharply questioned (Sloan and Feldman, 1978; Bureau of Health Manpower, 1980). Moreover, recent evidence on physician location behavior suggests that physicians cannot fully offset a decline in demand per physician (Schwartz et al., 1980).

In sum, unless budget limits or other regulations constrain the response, a reduction in cost sharing will expand the total volume of resources in medical care and conversely. Would such expansion be instrument for affecting costs once patients are admitted. Potentially more effective instruments include regulation, an example of which was the Carter Administration's hospital cost containment proposal, and greater competition in medical care (Enthoven, 1978; Newhouse and Taylor, 1971).

CAN THE RESULTS BE GENERALIZED?

The Health Insurance Experiment has measured how the demands of a small number of consumers increased as cost sharing fell, i.e., how many more services the participants sought and their physicians delivered as coinsurance decreased. Will the experimental results generalize to a widespread health insurance plan of a similar nature? The consistency of the results with national averages suggests they will, but certain circumstances could cause behavior to differ.

First, if insurance for ambulatory services were suddenly expanded, the resulting increase in the entire population's demand could exceed

JOSEPH P. NEWHOUSE et al.   77

the short-run capacity of the medical care delivery system. If so, the additional demand could be rationed in several possible ways (Newhouse et al., 1974). Most likely, longer waits for an appointment would occur, as happened in Montreal when cost sharing was eliminated (Enterline et al., 1973). We do not yet have a good understanding of which services would not be delivered if appointment times lengthened.

Second, the delivery system might not be allowed to expand to meet any new demand; it could, for example, be constrained by budget limits or rate and fee controls so that only a certain proportion of the demand would be met. The experimental plan, in general, reimbursed billed fees or charges, but regulations or fee schedules might not permit such a procedure. We cannot predict from experimental data who might receive what services if budgets were so constrained that not all the demand could be met.

Third, if present cost sharing levels increased so that demand fell, some argue that physicians would create additional demand to offset the decline (Barer et al., 1979). The evidence supporting this argument, however, has been sharply questioned (Sloan and Feldman, 1978; Bureau of Health Manpower, 1980). Moreover, recent evidence on physician location behavior suggests that physicians cannot fully offset a decline in demand per physician (Schwartz et al., 1980).

In sum, unless budget limits or other regulations constrain the response, a reduction in cost sharing will expand the total volume of resources in medical care and conversely. Would such expansion be worth the foregone opportunities for other desired goods and services? One may wish to reserve judgment on that issue until more is known about how the additional medical services affect health and well-being.

REFERENCES

American Hospital Association, *Guide to the Health Care Field,* 1979 Edition, American Hospital Association, Chicago, Illinois, 1979, Table 1.
Andersen, R., "Health Service Distribution and Equity," in R. Andersen, J. Kravits, and O. Anderson (eds.), *Equity in Health Services,* Ballinger Press, Cambridge, Massachusetts, 1975.

Barer, M. L., R. G. Evans, and G. Stoddart, *Controlling Health Care Costs by Direct Charges to Patients: Snare or Delusion?* Economic Council, Toronto, Ontario, 1979.

Beck, R. G., "The Effects of Co-payment on the Poor," *J. Hum. Resour.,* 9:129-142, 1974.

Brook, R. H., J. E. Ware, A. Davies-Avery, A. L. Stewart, C. A. Donald, W. H. Rogers, et al., "Overview of Adult Health Status Measures Fielded in Rand's Health Insurance Study," *Med. Care,* 17(7), Special Supplement, 1979, pp. 1-131.

Bureau of Health Manpower, *The Target Income Hypothesis and Related Issues in Health Manpower Policy,* DHEW Publication No. (HRA) 80-27, Government Printing Office, Washington, D.C., 1980.

Duan, N., W. G. Manning, C. N. Morris, and J. P. Newhouse, "A Comparison of Alternative Models of the Demand for Medical Care," paper presented at the Annual Meeting of the Econometric Society, Denver, Colorado, September 6, 1980; to be published as Rand Report R-2754-HHS (forthcoming).

Eisen, M., C. A. Donald, J. E. Ware, and R. H. Brook, *Conceptualization and Measurement of Health for Children in the Health Insurance Study,* The Rand Corporation, R-2313-HEW, May 1980.

Enterline, P. E., V. Salter, A. D. McDonald, and J. C. McDonald, "The Distribution of Medical Services Before and After 'Free' Medical Care—The Quebec Experience," *N. Engl. J. Med.,* 289:1174-1178, 1973.

Enthoven, A. C., "Consumer Choice Health Plan," *N. Engl. J. Med.,* 298:650-658, 709-720, 1978.

Fein, R., Testimony, *Health Care Crisis in America, 1971,* Hearings Before the Subcommittee on Health of the Committee on Labor and Public Welfare, United States Senate, February 22 and 23, 1971, Part 1. 92nd Cong., 1st sess., Washington, D.C., Government Printing Office, p. 146.

Feldstein, M. S., "Quality Change and the Demand for Hospital Care," *Econometrica,* 45:1681-1702, 1977.

Hill, D. B., and J. E. Veney, "Kansas Blue Cross/Blue Shield Outpatient Benefits Experiment," *Med. Care,* 8:143-158, 1970.

Gibson, R. M., and C. R. Fisher, "Age Differences in Health Care Spending, Fiscal Year 1977," *Soc. Secur. Bull.,* 42:(1):5, 10, 1979.

Health Care Financing Administration, *Medicare, 1976, Reimbursement by State and County,* HCFA Publication No. 018 (6-78), Government Printing Office, Washington, D.C., 1978.

Hogg, R. V., "Statistical Robustness: One View of Its Use in Applications Today," *Amer. Statistician,* 33:108-115, 1979.

Lewis, C. E., and H. Keairnes, "Controlling Costs of Medical Care by Expanding Insurance Coverage," *N. Engl. J. Med.*, 282:1405-1412, 1970.

Marmor, T. R., "Rethinking National Health Insurance," *Public Interest*, 46:73-94, 1977.

Morris, C. N., "A Finite Selection Model for Experimental Design of the Health Insurance Study," *J. Econometrics*, 11:43-61, 1979.

NCHS (National Center for Health Statistics), *Physician Visits: Volume and Interval Since Last Visit, United States, 1969*, Vital and Health Statistics Series 10, No. 75, DHEW Publication No. (HSM) 72-1064, Government Printing Office, Washington, D.C., 1972.

NCHS, *Hospital and Surgical Insurance Coverage*, Vital and Health Statistics Series 10, No. 117, DHEW Publication No. HR-77-1545, U.S. Government Printing Office, Washington, D.C., 1977.

NCHS, *Physician Visits: Volume and Interval Since Last Visit, United States, 1975*, Vital and Health Statistics Series 10, No. 128, DHEW Publication No. (PHS) 79-1556, Government Printing Office, Washington, D.C. 1979.

Newhouse, J. P., "A Design for a Health Insurance Experiment," *Inquiry*, 11:5-27, 1974.

Newhouse, J. P., "Insurance Benefits, Out-of-Pocket Payments, and the Demand for Medical Care: A Review of the Literature," *Hlth. Med. Care Serv. Rev.*, 1(4):1, 3-15, 1978a.

Newhouse, J. P., "The Structure of Health Insurance and the Erosion of Competition in the Medical Marketplace," in W. Greenberg (ed.), *Competition in the Health Care Sector: Past, Present, and Future*, Aspen Systems Corporation, Germantown, Maryland, 1978b.

Newhouse, J. P., and C. E. Phelps, "New Estimates of Price and Income Elasticities," *The Role of Health Insurance in the Health Services Sector*, National Bureau of Economic Research, New York, 1976.

Newhouse, J. P., C. E. Phelps, and W. B. Schwartz, "Policy Options and the Impact of National Health Insurance," *N. Engl. J. Med.*, 290:1345-1359, 1974.

Newhouse, J. P., and V. Taylor, "How Shall We Pay for Hospital Care?" *Public Interest*, 23:78-92, 1971.

Phelps, C. E., and J. P. Newhouse, "Effects of Coinsurance: A Multivariate Analysis," *Soc. Secur. Bull.*, 35(6):20-29, 1972.

Phelps, C. E., and J. P. Newhouse, "Coinsurance, the Price of Time, and the Demand for Medical Services," *Rev. Econ. Statist.*, 56:334-342, 1974.

Roemer, M. I., C. E. Hopkins, L. Carr, and F. Gartside, "Copayments for Ambulatory Care: Penny-wise and Pound-foolish," *Med. Care,* 13:457-466, 1975.

Rogers, W. H., K. N. Williams, and R. H. Brook, *Power Analysis of Health Status Measures,* The Rand Corporation, R-1987/7-HEW, March 1979.

Rosett, R. N., and L. F. Huang, "The Effect of Health Insurance on the Demand for Medical Care," *J. Polit. Econ.,* 81:281-305, 1973.

Schwartz, W. B., J. P. Newhouse, B. Bennett, and A. P. Williams, "The Changing Geographic Distribution of Board-Certified Physicians," *N. Engl. J. Med.,* 303:1032-1038, 1980.

Scitovsky, A. A., and N. McCall, "Coinsurance and the Demand for Physician Services: Four Years Later," *Soc. Secur. Bull.,* 40(5):19-27, 1977.

Scitovsky, A. A., and N. M. Snyder, "Effect of Coinsurance on Use of Physician Services, *Soc. Secur. Bull.,* 35(6):3-19, 1972.

Sloan, F. A., and R. Feldman, "Competition Among Physicians," in W. Greenberg (ed.), *Competition in the Health Care Sector: Past, Present, and Future,* Aspen Systems Corporation, Germantown, Maryland, 1978.

U.S. Bureau of the Census, *Statistical Abstract, 1979,* Government Printing Office, Washington, D.C., 1980a.

U.S. Bureau of the Census, *Statistical Abstract, 1980,* Government Printing Office, Washington, D.C., 1980b.

Various authors, *Conceptualization and Measurement of Physiologic Health for Adults* (various volumes), The Rand Corporation, R-2262-HHS, various dates.

3

The Effect of Coinsurance on the Health of Adults
Results from the Rand Health Insurance Experiment

Robert H. Brook, John E. Ware, Jr., William H. Rogers,
Emmett B. Keeler, Allyson R. Davies, Cathy D. Sherbourne,
George A. Goldberg, Kathleen N. Lohr, Patricia Camp,
and Joseph P. Newhouse

SUMMARY

METHODS OF THE EXPERIMENT

Sample

The Rand Health Insurance Experiment was carried out to answer the question (among others), "Does free medical care lead to better health than insurance plans that require the patient to shoulder part of the cost?" It ran from November 1974 through January 1982 in six sites (Dayton, Ohio; Seattle, Washington; Fitchburg and Franklin County, Massachusetts; and Charleston and Georgetown County, South Carolina). Altogether, 3958 individuals between the ages of 14 and 61 were enrolled; they belonged to 2005 families and were free of disability serious enough to have made them eligible for the Medicare program (i.e., public Disability Insurance).

From Robert H. Brook et al., "The Effect of Coinsurance on the Health of Adults," Rand Corporation Publication No. R-3055-HHS, prepared under a grant from the U.S. Department of Health and Human Services, December 1984. Reprinted by permission of The Rand Corporation.

Insurance Plans and Benefits

Families were randomly assigned to one of several insurance plans for three (70 percent) or five years. One plan provided *free* care; the others required that enrollees pay a share of their health bills. On the *individual deductible* plan, the family paid 95 percent of the cost of all outpatient care up to an annual out-of-pocket expenditure of $150 per person ($450 per family); all outpatient care beyond that amount, as well as all inpatient care, was free. On the *intermediate coinsurance* plans, the family paid 25 or 50 percent of all health bills each year, inpatient and outpatient, until it had spent 5, 10, or 15 percent of its income or $1000 (whichever was less). On the *income-related catastrophic* plans, the family paid 95 percent of its health bills up to the same ceiling as in the intermediate plans. All plans covered ambulatory and hospital care, preventive services, most dental services other than orthodontia, psychiatric and psychological services up to 52 visits per person per year, prescription drugs, and nonprescription drugs for certain chronic conditions.

Health Status Measures

We developed or adapted several measures to evaluate the effect of cost-sharing on health in four distinct categories: general health, health habits, physiologic health, and the risk of dying from any cause. This monograph reports on 11 measures from these categories: physical health, role functioning, mental health, social contacts, and general health ratings (collectively referred to as the general health measures); smoking behavior; weight; cholesterol level; diastolic blood pressure level; visual acuity; and an index of the risk of dying related to specific risk factors (systolic blood pressure, cholesterol, and smoking habits).

Plan of Analysis

For these analyses, we adopted a three-step analytic strategy. We first identified important variables that might explain differences in the dependent health status measures just named, such as the family's experimental insurance plan, family income adjusted for size and composition of the family, and initial state of health. Then we used regression methods to estimate the influence of these explanatory variables on the various measures of health status at the experiment's end. To interpret these results, we employed the results of the regression equations to predict the exit health status of people who had a given set of entry characteristics, including the "average" participant and participants in certain subgroups that differed by income and by level of initial health.

Possible Artifacts and Biases

We also undertook extensive analyses to detect and counteract any problems that might lead to biased estimates or erroneous inferences. For example, we compared health status values at enrollment (a) for participants in each plan and (b) for persons who accepted the offer to enroll in the experiment versus those who did not. By including initial health status values in the regression analyses, we also controlled for any effect of nonrandom composition of the sample. Further, we collected longitudinal information on several measures for persons who had left the experiment prematurely and included information about most of these dropouts in the analyses. Finally, we imputed scores on certain variables to persons with missing enrollment data and included them in the analysis.

RESULTS

Threats to Validity

Steps taken to overcome possible problems of bias or erroneous inference were successful. Our analyses showed that different acceptance rates were unlikely to have affected any conclusions; the same was true of differences among plans in retention of participants until the end of the study. In addition, enrollment health status values in the actual sample used for each analysis did not differ by plan.

Effects on Health Status

For the *average* person enrolled in the experiment, we observed two significant positive effects of free care relative to cost-sharing: corrected far vision (i.e., when the enrollee was wearing his or her usual glasses or contact lenses) was better by 0.1 Snellen lines ($p = 0.001$) and diastolic blood pressure was lower by 0.8 mm Hg ($p = 0.03$). For the remaining measures, confidence limits for the differences between the free and cost-sharing plans were sufficiently narrow to conclude that, for the average participant, any true differences would be clinically and socially negligible.

For the five general health measures, we could detect no significant positive effect of free care for persons who differed by income (high versus low income) and by initial health status (good versus ill health). Because the confidence intervals around differences between free and cost-sharing plans were larger in these subgroup analyses, however, we could be less certain that *clinically* important effects did not occur.

Among participants who were judged to be at elevated risk with respect to smoking habits, cholesterol levels, and weight, free care had no detectable effect.

Among individuals whose uncorrected far vision was worse than 20/20, corrected far vision was 0.2 Snellen lines better (p = 0.001) on the free than on the other plans. For persons who were in the upper quartile of the distribution of risk factors included in the risk of dying index, the risk of dying was 10 percent lower on the free than the cost-sharing plans (p = 0.02). Improvements in vision and the risk of dying, as well as in blood pressure, were largest among persons with low incomes. Poor people at elevated risk apparently benefited from receiving free care, although we cannot draw any firm conclusion about persons of higher incomes at elevated risk.

CONCLUSIONS

We drew three main conclusions about the influence of free care on the health status of HIE adults. First, free care did not affect the major health habits associated with cardiovascular disease and many types of cancer, even though those habits (especially smoking) were at levels where substantial health benefit from behavior change was possible. Second, free care had at most a small effect on any of five general health measures for the average enrollee. Confidence intervals were wider for subgroups of persons with low income or initially in poor health; therefore, we cannot rule out clinically meaningful changes in particular subgroups. Third, people having specific conditions with well-established diagnostic and therapeutic procedures (myopia, hypertension) benefited from free care, and these improvements appeared to be greater among the poor.

Chapter 1

INTRODUCTION

Spending at least some money on medical care is indisputably worthwhile. But does spending yet more buy still better health? In individual cases, the answer may be an obvious yes or no, but in the population as a whole the point of diminishing (or absent) returns has been difficult to identify.[1]

Critics of the existing system have contended that developed countries spend too much on medicine; they argue that this practice increases iatrogenic illness (Carlson, 1975; Illich, 1977). The extreme versions of this argument, a kind of "therapeutic nihilism," have been cogently criticized (Starr, 1976; Rogers and Blendon, 1977), and in this country public policy has proceeded for more than five decades on the assumption that if some medical care is good, more would be better. A main instrument of this policy has been increased insurance coverage, both public and private. While this policy has been in effect, the national outlay on medical care has steadily increased and has now reached a level that causes concern in many quarters. One of the few potential ways to reduce expenditures appears to be to raise the proportion of costs borne by the individuals who are consuming medical care.

What fraction of their costs, if any, patients should be required to pay is thus a central and serious question of policy. Proponents of cost-sharing argue that it curtails frank abuse and restrains the purchase of care that yields little or no benefit. Opponents counter that if people must pay out of pocket for medical care, their access to appropriate levels of care will decrease and they will suffer accordingly. Data in support of either position have been all but nonexistent.

This dearth of information prompted the federal government to support a controlled trial, known as the Rand Health Insurance Experiment. The project randomly assigned a sample of families to a variety of different insurance plans; one group received all their medical care free of charge, whereas others paid some percentage of their health bills up to a stipulated maximum. We have already reported that when

---

[1]See, for example, Benham and Benham (1975); Rice and Wilson (1976); Cochrane et al. (1978); Miller and Stokes (1978); Newhouse and Friedlander (1980); Miller and Miller (1981); and Hadley (1982).

cost-sharing was higher, use of medical care (visits to physicians, adult hospitalizations) and, accordingly, total expenditures, were lower (Newhouse et al., 1981). To illustrate, people enrolled in cost-sharing plans made only about two-thirds as many outpatient visits as those receiving free care (Keeler and Rolph, 1983).

These earlier analyses left an important question unanswered: Were the people who received free medical care, and thus used more of it, *healthier* as a result? Without being able to remove all doubt on this score, we can now reduce the uncertainty. Here we report what happened to health status among a group of adults under age 65 who received free care, as compared with a similar group required to share in the cost of care.

Chapter 2

EXPERIMENTAL DESIGN AND ANALYTIC METHODS

SAMPLE AND SITES

The experiment, which ran from November 1974 through January 1982, enrolled 3958 persons between the ages of 14 and 61 who belonged to 2005 families. Included in the study but not in this analysis (or the above numbers) were children under the age of 14 and families enrolled in a prepaid group practice; they are the subjects of separate analyses. Families who moved stayed in the experiment as long as they remained in the United States, except for those enrolled in a control group in the prepaid group practice. Seventy percent of the sample participated for three years, the remainder for five.

Families lived in six sites: Dayton, Ohio; Seattle, Washington; Fitchburg and Franklin County, Massachusetts; and Charleston and Georgetown County, South Carolina. To select sites, we first calculated the optimal number of sites for our budget, which turned out to be between four and nine. We decided to use six sites, chosen according to several criteria: (a) to represent all four census regions and thus account for any regional variation in the responsiveness of demand for medical care to cost-sharing; (b) to obtain a spectrum of city size, because the complexity of the medical care delivery system (and hence the response to insurance) could vary with city size; (c) to achieve variation in waiting times for an appointment and in the proportion of primary care physicians accepting new patients, because response to demand could vary according to the amount of excess demand for ambulatory services; (d) to include participation from both Northern and Southern rural areas, because these areas differ in economic and racial characteristics; and (e) to ensure that one site had a well-established prepaid group practice.

Enrolled families represented the general populations where they lived except for several intentional differences. The experiment excluded families with annual incomes exceeding $54,000 (1982 dollars), or about 3 percent of the families initially contacted. Families participating in the Supplemental Security Income (SSI) program, persons who were so disabled that they were eligible for Medicare, and family members over the age of 61 at entry to the study also were excluded. Low-income families were slightly oversampled. Major demographic characteristics of the HIE sample (averaged across our sites) do not differ markedly from those of the nation as a whole, save for the intentional departures such as those relating to age.

INSURANCE PLANS AND BENEFITS

Families were assigned to one of 14 experimental insurance plans by a random sampling technique, the Finite Selection Model, that made the distribution of over 25 family and individual characteristics as similar as possible across plans (Morris, 1979). We offered families only the plan to which we randomly assigned them because we judged that explaining all the plans before asking a family to join the experiment would be confusing and might make the enrollment process difficult to complete.

For this report, the 14 insurance plans are grouped into four categories (one providing free care, the other three requiring cost-sharing):

- The "free-care" plan, in which the family received all its care without charge (i.e., 0-percent coinsurance).
- The "individual deductible" plan, which imposed a 95-percent coinsurance rate on *outpatient* expenditures only, up to a maximum out-of-pocket expenditure of $150 per person ($450 per family) per year; all outpatient care beyond that amount, and all inpatient care, was free.
- The "intermediate coinsurance" plans, consisting of nine plans with either a 25-percent or a 50-percent coinsurance rate. On these plans, the family paid 25 or 50 percent of its medical bills each year up to a maximum dollar expenditure of $1000 (in 1973 dollars) or 5, 10, or 15 percent of family income, whichever was less. In three of these nine plans, the family paid 50 percent of the cost of its mental and dental services; in some sites and years, the maximum expenditure was held to $750.
- The "income-related catastrophic" plans, which included three plans with a 95-percent coinsurance rate and the same income-related limitations on maximum dollar expenditure as the intermediate coinsurance plans.

The following example illustrates how the experimental plans operated. A family assigned to a plan with a 25-percent coinsurance rate and a $1000 maximum dollar expenditure would pay 25 percent of all medical and dental bills in each year until the total of all of these bills reached $4000. At that point it would have spent $1000 out of pocket, after which all further expenditures during that year would be fully paid (or reimbursed) by the plan. At the beginning of the next year, the family would again pay the 25-percent coinsurance until the $1000 limit was reached.

For all cost-sharing plans, the $150 individual deductible and the $1000 (or $750) cap on family out-of-pocket expenditure remained constant during the entire experiment; these caps were not modified to reflect inflation, which was considerable. At the end of the experiment (1982), nearly $2000 was required to purchase the amount of medical care that $1000 had bought at the beginning (1974). Subject to the $1000 cap, the family's maximum expenditure ceiling would be adjusted each year to reflect any change in family income.

Families assigned to an experimental plan that was less generous than their current insurance were paid an amount (in installments every four weeks) that was sufficient to prevent their ever becoming worse off financially by enrolling (i.e., was equal to their highest possible loss). This money was paid irrespective of actual use of medical services; its intent was to help ensure that acceptance and retention rates would be high and independent of both the plan to which the family was assigned and the family's health status. For example, if the family had been assigned to an experimental plan whose maximum dollar expenditure turned out to be $425 and the family had had an existing policy with a $100 deductible and a 20-percent coinsurance above the deductible, it would have been paid $260 a year, that is (260 = 425 − 100 − 0.2 (425 − 100), or about $20 every four weeks. Such payments had a negligible effect on use (Newhouse et al., 1981).

All plans were administered by the Family Health Protection Plan (FHPP) through a fiscal intermediary with considerable experience in the insurance industry. All plans had an identical, very comprehensive definition of covered services. These included hospital, physician, dental, mental health, vision, and hearing services; drugs (including over-the-counter drugs for certain chronic conditions); and supplies. Services of nonphysician providers, such as audiologists, chiropractors, clinical psychologists, optometrists, physical therapists, and speech therapists, were also covered. The only noteworthy exclusions from coverage were nonpreventive orthodontic services, cosmetic surgery for pre-existing conditions, and outpatient mental health visits exceeding 52 per year. Appendix A gives a detailed accounting of the FHPP benefits; Clasquin and Brown (1977) and Brown (1984) present more information on operations and administration of the FHPP and the HIE.

In many analyses reported in Chapter 3, we grouped the cost-sharing plans and compared them with the free-care plan. In these instances, the total cost-sharing plan represents an equally weighted average of the three types of cost-sharing plans.

HEALTH STATUS VARIABLES

Starting with the World Health Organization (1948) definition of health, we developed or adapted measures to evaluate the effect of cost-sharing on health status. This comprehensive set comprised four distinct categories: general health, health habits, physiologic health, and the risk of dying from any cause related to various risk factors. Appendix B lists the health status variables studied and describes the main data collection procedures.

In this report we analyze 11 measures from these four categories; these measures are described in Tables 1 and 2. Appendixes C and D give more detail about the ways these health measures were defined and assessed. A number of other physiologic measures, as well as measures of dental health, remain to be examined. Data on the general health measures (such as physical functioning, role functioning, and health perceptions) and health habits (such as smoking) were collected from a medical history questionnaire (MHQ) that was self-administered at the beginning of the experiment (enrollment) and three or five years later (exit). The reliability, validity, and other psychometric properties of the five general health measures are reported elsewhere and summarized in Appendix C.[1]

Serum cholesterol, blood pressure, and visual acuity were measured at medical screening examinations that were given at enrollment to a randomly selected 60 percent of the sample and at exit to the entire sample (see Appendix D for citations to works that describe these measures). The random sample was used to estimate the effect of the screening examination itself on the use of medical services and subsequent health status. Technicians who collected data at the entrance and exit screening examinations did not know the insurance plan to which the family belonged.

Because actual deaths in our experimental population (about 40 adults in all the fee-for-service plans) were too infrequent to allow

---

[1]Physical functioning was measured by the Personal Functioning Index, role functioning by the Role Limitation Index, mental health by the Mental Health Inventory, social contacts by the Social Contacts Scale, and health perceptions by the General Health Ratings Index. See Davies et al. (forthcoming) for rules on scoring these measures, and Appendix C for citations to individual volumes describing their development.

meaningful analysis, we calculated an index that would predict the extent to which longevity would be affected by specified risk factors (systolic blood pressure, smoking behavior, and serum cholesterol level (McGee and Gordon, 1976)). Data for the index came from both the screening examination and the MHQ.

METHODS OF ANALYSIS

To answer the question "Did the free plan improve health more than the cost-sharing plans?" we began by identifying certain variables that could be expected to affect the results and could be used to develop health care policy. We then employed regression methods to estimate the influence of the "explanatory" variables on the "dependent" variable—namely, health status at exit.

Explanatory variables in the regression models included: insurance plan; other experimental variables (whether the subject took the enrollment screening examination; length of enrollment period); site; family income adjusted for size and composition of the family; the subject's initial value for the dependent (health status) variable; and other variables that helped explain health status at exit. Details of these models can be found in Appendixes E and F.

To interpret these effects we then used the results from the regression equations to predict the exit health status of people with any given set of entry characteristics. In particular, using the coefficients for the explanatory variables from the main regression equations, we calculated values for health status at exit for the average participant and for those in certain subgroups with relatively high or low incomes, good or poor health.

Because we especially wanted to know the effect of cost-sharing on persons with poor health or low income, we measured all interactions between health and income and the various insurance plans. A score on each of the five general health measures was determined for a person who was initially "ill" or in "good" health with respect to the specific dependent variable under consideration. We defined "ill" as the mean value of persons in the lowest one-fifth of the distribution at enrollment and "good" as the mean in the highest two-fifths (Table 1). The effect of "low" or "high" income at enrollment was also tested. A "low" income was the mean for the lowest one-fifth of the income distribution (for a family of four, about $7,300 in 1982 dollars), and "high" the mean for the highest two-fifths ($40,000). To generate the predic-

Table 1

OPERATIONAL DEFINITIONS AND ENROLLMENT VALUES OF HEALTH STATUS MEASURES USED
TO DEFINE SUBGROUPS FOR PREDICTION ANALYSES: FIVE GENERAL HEALTH MEASURES

Health Measure and Operational Definition	Typical Item	Mean Value of Persons at Enrollment		Interpretation of Effect Size
		"Good" Health[a]	"Ill" Health[b]	
PHYSICAL FUNCTIONING: A standardized (0-100) scale (21 items) that indicates the degree to which the person has limitations in personal self-care, mobility, or physical activities. A high score means greater capacity for physical activity.	"Do you have any trouble either walking one block or climbing one flight of stairs because of your health?"	100	44.8	A 10-point difference = effect of having chronic, mild osteoarthritis.[c,d]
ROLE FUNCTIONING: A dichotomous measure (2 items) that indicates whether the person can do work, school, or housework activities free of limitations because of poor health. A high score means a higher probability of role functioning. Mean probabilities are expressed as percentages.	"Does your health keep you from working at a job, doing work around the house, or going to school?"	100	0	A 1-point difference = 1-percentage-point higher probability of being limited in the performance of one's major role.
MENTAL HEALTH: A standardized (0-100) scale (38 items) that measures anxiety, depression, emotional ties, behavioral/emotional control, and psychological well-being during the past month. A high score reflects higher or more positive levels of mental health.	"How much of the time, during the past month, have you felt down-hearted and blue?"	86.4	53.0	A 3-point difference = impact of being fired or laid off from a job.

Table 1 (continued)

Health Measure and Operational Definition	Typical Item	Mean Value of Persons at Enrollment		Interpretation of Effect Size
		"Good" Health[a]	"Ill" Health[b]	
SOCIAL CONTACTS: A standardized (0-100) scale (3 items) that measures contacts with friends and relatives during the past month or year. A high score reflects higher levels of social activity.	"About how often have you visited with friends and relatives at their homes during the past month?"	94.3	29.1	A 10-point difference = a 2-percentage-point increase in the probability of being psychiatrically impaired.
HEALTH PERCEPTIONS: A standardized (0-100) scale (22 items) that measures the person's perceptions of past, present, and future health, susceptibility to illness, and worry about health. A high score reflects better perceptions of one's health status.	"My health is excellent."	83.6	47.8	A 5-point difference = effect of having been diagnosed as hypertensive.[e]

[a]Mean of the healthiest 40 percent of the distribution.
[b]Mean of the sickest 20 percent of the distribution.
[c]Among participants in the experiment, adjusted for age and sex.
[d]Classification based on the person's responding yes to questions about ever having acute or chronic pain, aching, swelling, or stiffness in fingers, hip, or knee.
[e]Classification based on the person's responding yes to a question about ever being diagnosed as having high blood pressure and yes to a question about being so diagnosed more than once or to a question about having been prescribed pills or medicines for high blood pressure.

93

Table 2

OPERATIONAL DEFINITIONS AND VALUES OF HEALTH STATUS VARIABLES
USED TO DEFINE SUBGROUPS FOR PREDICTION ANALYSES:
HEALTH HABITS AND PHYSIOLOGIC MEASURES

Health Variable and Operational Definition	Mean Value of Persons at Elevated Risk[a]	Specific Scoring
SMOKING: A six-level measure of the risk of death from smoking compared to not smoking.	1.89	Never smoked/ex-smoker: 1.00 Pipe/cigar smoker only: 1.06 Cigarette smoker: <1 pack/day 1.57 1 pack/day 1.79 2 packs/day 2.07 >2 packs/day 2.20
WEIGHT (kg):[b]	88.5	Standardized for height (in meters) by multiplying by $(1.75/\text{height}^2)$ for men and by $(1.65/\text{height}^{1.5})$ for women. Standardized for sex by summing 0.5 (average value for men) and 0.5 (average value for women).
SERUM CHOLESTEROL (mg/dl):	242	
DIASTOLIC BLOOD PRESSURE (mm Hg):	87	
FUNCTIONAL FAR VISION: Measured in Snellen lines. Functional means with whatever correction (if any) was used by the individual to improve vision.	2.95[c]	Line 2 = 20/20 Line 3 = 20/25 Line 4 = 20/30 Line 5 = 20/40
RISK OF DYING: The risk of dying from any cause compared to persons with average values of major risk factors: 100 exp(Index)/(1 + exp(Index)). Index = 1.28 smoking scale + 0.0023 cholesterol + 0.023 systolic blood pressure − 4.92.	2.02	The coefficients of the risk factors are median values of the coefficients in the logistic regressions for death from any cause in five studies of heart disease in middle-aged men.

[a]Mean of the sickest 25 percent of the distribution except for functional far vision. For smoking and weight, these are enrollment values. For cholesterol, blood pressure, vision, and risk of dying, these are predicted exit values.

[b]Excludes those 14-17 at enrollment and pregnant women.

[c]Mean corrected vision of those whose uncorrected vision in the better eye was worse than 20/20; i.e., mean of the worst 53 percent of the distribution.

tions, we used mean population values for all remaining explanatory variables.

Medical care could be expected to benefit most those people who have a health problem, but the effects of cost-sharing might be obscured were data on this subsample pooled with the whole. Accordingly, for each indicator of physiologic health (blood pressure, vision), health habits (smoking, weight, and cholesterol), and risk of dying (Table 2) we divided our sample into those likely, by exit, to have abnormal or normal values. The division was based on data from the initial examination and responses to pertinent items on the MHQ for each measure separately. Appendix F describes how the elevated-risk groups were defined in more detail, and the possible effects of alternative definitions on our conclusions can be found in Appendix G.

We detected few important effects of plan on values for the group expected to exit with normal values, so we focused the analysis on the group expected to be least healthy or at elevated risk of dying. The least healthy one-quarter of the sample for five of these six measures was arbitrarily designated a priori as the elevated-risk group. For visual problems, we defined "high risk" as an acuity at exit worse than 20/20 in the better eye without glasses (roughly half the sample). Because the "best" results might have been obtained had the elevated-risk groups been more (or less) inclusive, we performed additional analyses to clarify how size of the group might have influenced our findings. This work is discussed in Appendix G.

We had no prior expectations of positive or negative effects of cost-sharing, so we used two-tailed tests of significance throughout. All statistical tests were corrected for correlation of the error term within each family and for the nonconstant variance of the error term (Huber, 1967). The corrections were generally small.

We followed the convention of labeling a result "significant" were it likely to occur by chance no more often than one time in 20 (i.e., $p \leqslant 0.05$). Nonetheless, results falling short of this criterion should not be dismissed. In some cases, the confidence intervals may indicate that the result's actual value could plausibly have some clinical importance; that is, the range of values having 95-percent likelihood of bracketing the real one could include some that are medically important. For this reason, we have generally given a probability value if that value is close to the 5-percent level.

POSSIBLE ARTIFACTS AND BIASES

We anticipated three problems that may have led to biased estimates or erroneous inferences. First, the various plan offerings might have been accepted by different kinds of people whose health or other characteristics would have biased the outcome. Second, participants may have dropped out of the various plans at different rates as a function of their current health. Either factor could distort our picture of the actual effects of a particular plan. Third, certain data were missing: Some gaps were "unplanned" (for example, participants occasionally did not complete all questions on the exit questionnaire), and some were "planned" (certain participants, for instance, were not asked to take an enrollment screening examination). Only the unplanned loss of data carried the potential for bias, because the planned gaps were distributed randomly.

We adopted several strategies to counter the potential for bias. First, we compared health status values at enrollment for participants in each plan, and we compared selected characteristics of people who refused the offer with those of people who accepted. If these groups had similar values, we would have little reason to suspect bias.

Second, our regression models included initial values of the health status variables and of other variables known to influence the response variable under study. (For example, high blood pressure at entry predicts high blood pressure at exit.) We thereby controlled statistically for any effect of nonrandom composition of the sample with respect to these explanatory variables.

Third, we obtained longitudinal information on the general health measures and smoking for people who voluntarily withdrew from the experiment and for those who did not complete the experiment for other reasons. These data came from an abbreviated medical history questionnaire completed after they left the experiment or from an annual health questionnaire filled out during the experiment. Thus, the analyses included information on many of the dropouts. We did not attempt to recover information on physiologic measures from participants who left the sample prematurely; results for these measures are based only on those who completed the experiment.

Missing data from unplanned nonresponses never amounted to more than 2 percent for any one question, so bias from this source should be negligible. Nevertheless, to include people with missing data in the analysis, we imputed scores to them. For the questionnaire-based measures we estimated a value from that individual's responses to related questions or used values from questionnaires completed in the previous year. For the physiologic measures and risk of dying, persons who by design did not receive the initial screening examination were imputed an enrollment value from a prediction equation based on age, sex, and MHQ data. They were included in the analysis but given less weight (Dagenais, 1971).

To determine whether various factors such as site, sample loss, or missing data biased our results, we carried out several special analyses. Appendix H examines whether findings on the general health ratings index, diastolic blood pressure, and vision differed by study site. Appendix I gives additional information on sample loss, and Appendixes J and K deal with the effects of including or excluding from the analytic sample persons who were missing enrollment or exit data. Appendix J in particular shows that, for the health measures based on screening examination information, not including persons who were missing such data because they left the study prematurely had only negligible effects on our findings.

Most of our measures are continuous, not categorical, but often the medical profession views people as being in one of two categories, sick or well. We investigated whether our main results on the effects of the plan would persist when enrollees were classified as "sick" (diastolic blood pressure 90 mm Hg or higher or corrected vision 20/40 or worse) or "well" (all others). Findings based on the proportion hypertensive or myopic by plan are discussed in Appendix L.

Chapter 3

RESULTS OF DESIGN AND HEALTH STATUS ANALYSES

THREATS TO VALIDITY

Acceptance of the Enrollment Offer

Acceptance rates varied by plan: 92 percent of the families accepted the offer to join the free plan, 83 percent the individual deductible plan, 89 percent the intermediate plans, and 75 percent the catastrophic plans. To determine whether these different acceptance rates might have biased our results, we examined the health status of all enrollees at the start of the experiment and detected no significant differences among plans in any enrollment health measure or in family income, education, or age (Table 3). Only the proportion of females differed slightly by plan, and one significant difference would be expected by chance alone among the 20 comparisons made.

We also compared people who refused the enrollment offer with those who accepted. Results of this comparison (Rogers and Camp, forthcoming) established that the different acceptance rates were unlikely to have affected our conclusions.

Retention in the Experiment

During the experiment, each plan lost some of its participants owing to voluntary withdrawal (including joining the military), involuntary factors (such as incarceration), health reasons (mainly by becoming eligible for disability Medicare), or death. The latter two health-related factors did not differ materially by plan (Table 4). In all, 95 percent of those on the free plan completed the experiment and exited normally by completing the MHQ and going through the final screening examination, as did 88 percent of those on the individual deductible plan, 90 percent on the intermediate plans, and 85 percent on the catastrophic plans.

To test whether these differences affected our results, we collected data on general health measures and smoking behavior of people who had terminated for various reasons. Our findings were not altered by

Table 3

VALUES ON DEMOGRAPHIC, STUDY, AND HEALTH STATUS MEASURES AT
ENROLLMENT, BY TYPE OF EXPERIMENTAL INSURANCE PLAN[a]

Variable and Brief Description[b]	Cost-Sharing Plans				Free Plan	t-Test Value[d] for Difference Between Free and Cost-Sharing Plans
	Cata- strophic	Inter- med.	Ind. Deduct.	Total Cost- Sharing[c]		
No. of enrollees ≥14 years of age	759	1024	881	2664	1294	
Mean age (yr)	32.8	33.8	33.6	33.4	33.3	−0.0
Sex (% female)	56.1	53.5	53.8	54.4	52.2	−2.1
Race (% nonwhite)	20.8	17.4	18.3	18.9	16.6	−0.5
Mean family income adjusted for family size ($ 1982 thousands)	21.5	22.8	23.3	22.5	22.1	−0.5
% Hospitalized in year before enrollment	11.5	11.2	12.0	11.6	11.7	0.1
Mean no. of physician visits in year before enrollment	4.49	4.23	4.80	4.51	4.55	0.2
Mean education (yr)	11.9	12.0	12.0	12.0	11.8	−1.4
% Taking enrollment screening examination	59.1	57.8	58.6	58.5	62.5	1.6
% Enrolled for 3 years	69.8	67.4	71.3	69.5	68.9	−0.3
Physical functioning (mean score, 0–100)						
Enrollees	89.6	88.7	89.1	89.1	88.9	−0.2
Analytic sample	89.6	89.0	89.6	89.4	89.0	−0.5
Role functioning (mean score, %)						
Enrollees	94.8	91.9	91.8	92.8	93.1	0.3
Analytic sample	94.8	92.1	92.5	93.1	93.0	−0.2
Mental health (mean score, 0–100)						
Enrollees	73.8	75.0	73.7	74.2	74.7	0.9
Analytic sample	73.8	75.1	73.9	74.3	74.7	0.8
Social contacts (mean score, 0–100)						
Enrollees	72.8	72.1	72.3	72.4	72.5	0.1
Analytic sample	72.6	72.2	72.0	72.2	72.5	0.3

Table 3 (continued)

Variable and Brief Description[b]	Cost-Sharing Plans				Free Plan	t-Test Value[d] for Difference Between Free and Cost-Sharing Plans
	Cata-strophic	Inter-med.	Ind. Deduct.	Total Cost-Sharing[c]		
Health perceptions (mean score, 0–100)						
Enrollees	70.5	71.1	69.4	70.4	69.7	−1.2
Analytic sample	70.4	71.2	69.7	70.4	69.8	−1.2
Smoking scale (mean score, 1–2.20)						
Enrollees	1.29	1.30	1.32	1.30	1.29	−0.7
Analytic sample	1.28	1.29	1.30	1.29	1.29	−0.3
Mean standardized weight (kg)						
Enrollees	71.5	71.3	71.0	71.3	71.3	0.0
Analytic sample	71.6	71.3	71.6	71.5	71.6	0.2
Mean cholesterol level (mg/dl)						
Enrollees	207	205	206	206	202	−1.9
Analytic sample	208	205	207	207	204	−1.5
Mean diastolic blood pressure (mm Hg)						
Enrollees	75.2	75.3	75.4	75.3	74.6	−1.4
Analytic sample	76.0	75.4	75.7	75.7	74.7	−1.9
Functional far vision (mean no. of lines)						
Enrollees	2.28	2.39	2.42	2.37	2.33	−0.9
Analytic sample	2.28	2.37	2.41	2.35	2.32	−0.9
Risk of dying (mean score)						
Enrollees	0.99	1.05	1.12	1.05	1.04	−0.6
Analytic sample	1.00	1.06	1.13	1.06	1.03	−0.8

[a]Values are adjusted for differences according to site.

[b]For demographic data, table entries include everyone with valid enrollment data. For health measures, the mean score for enrollees excludes persons who did not have valid enrollment data owing to the study design (e.g., they were not assigned to an initial screening examination) or to missing data, and the mean score for analytic samples excludes the same persons plus those who did not have valid exit data.

[c]Values represent equally weighted averages of the three types of cost-sharing plans.

[d]Value shown is for the difference between free and total cost-sharing plans.

Table 4

NUMBERS OF ADULT ENROLLEES, ACCORDING TO CATEGORY OF
PARTICIPATION IN EXPERIMENT AND PLAN

Category of Participation	Cost-Sharing Plans								Free Plan		Grand Total	
	Cata-strophic		Inter-med.		Ind. Deduct.		Total					
	No.	%	No.	%	No.	%	No.	%	No.	%	No.	%
Total enrolled	759	100.0	1024	100.0	881	100.0	2664	100.0	1294	100.0	3958	100.0
Completed enrollment and exited normally	642	84.6	926	90.4	772	87.6	2340	87.8	1225	94.7	3565[a]	90.1
Left experiment voluntarily	83	10.9	43	4.2	53	6.0	179	6.7	5	0.4	184	4.7
Terminated for health reasons[b]	3	0.4	13	1.3	11	1.3	27	1.0	15	1.2	42	1.1
Terminated for nonhealth reasons[b]	24	3.2	31	3.0	34	3.9	89	3.3	38	2.9	127	3.2
Died	7	0.9	11	1.1	11	1.3	29	1.1	11	0.9	40	1.0
Recovered for analysis[c]	94	80.3[d]	84	85.7	69	63.3	247	76.2	54	78.3	301	76.6

[a]The actual analyses were based on a slightly smaller sample, because forms were not available for under 1 percent of this sample.

[b]Participation ended because the person no longer fulfilled criteria for eligibility. Health reasons included becoming eligible for disability Medicare and being institutionalized; nonhealth reasons included joining the military and failure to complete data-collection forms.

[c]Form nonresponse not included. The number analyzed equals the number completed plus the number recovered minus the number of nonresponses.

[d]Percentages in this row are based on the number of enrollees in each plan who did not complete enrollment.

including or excluding these data, which were obtained from 73 percent of those who withdrew voluntarily, 83 percent of those terminated for health reasons, 82 percent of those terminated for nonhealth reasons, and 78 percent of those who were reported to have died. Thus, reported results include data from these individuals, and the final sample for the questionnaire-based analyses comprises 99 percent of the participants on the free and intermediate plans, 97 percent of those on the catastrophic plan, and 95 percent of those on the individual deductible plan. The percentages with complete data on physiologic measures (as well as weight) are lower because no post-enrollment screening examination was administered to the participants who left the experiment early.

As a further check for possible bias, we examined the values for health status at enrollment in the actual sample used for each analysis. We detected no significant differences by plan (Table 3).

EFFECTS ON HEALTH STATUS

Exit Values, by Plan

For the *average* person enrolled in the experiment, the only significant positive effects of free care ($p < 0.05$) were for corrected far vision and diastolic blood pressure (Table 5). Corrected vision of enrollees in the free plan was better (2.4 versus 2.5 Snellen lines, or an acuity of about 20/22 versus 20/22.5). Blood pressure was lower in the free plan by 0.8 mm Hg.[1]

For any individual, of course, a change of 0.1 Snellen line seems small. As discussed in Appendix L, for the dichotomous analyses we classified these same enrollees as "having impaired vision even with correction" when their measured vision was 20/40 or worse (Snellen line 5 or higher) at exit. With this definition of impairment, 9.6 per-

---

[1]This figure differs from those we reported earlier (Brook et al., 1983), which did not show a significant difference for the average enrollee ($p = 0.06$ in that analysis). The new results come from analyses that differed in three respects from the earlier one. First, we were able to include an additional 207 people from the South Carolina site on whom data had not been previously available. Second, we include the 58 people with incomplete MHQ enrollment data but complete exit data, after imputing to them an enrollment value based on site, sex, and age. They had been included in the other physiologic analyses but inadvertently omitted in blood pressure studies. Finally, in the earlier analyses, we had mistakenly used the first of two exit blood pressure readings in much of the sample; for this report, we used the second (and typically lower) reading in all cases. Appendix D explains when the two blood pressure measurements were taken during the screening examinations.

cent of persons on the free plan had a deficit in their corrected vision, contrasted with 12.0 percent on the cost-sharing plans.

A drop in blood pressure of 0.8 mm Hg translates into about a 2-percent decrease in the risk of dying, about the amount of decrease shown in Table 5. When the same sample is classified as hypertensive or not (i.e., at or above 90 mm Hg diastolic blood pressure), 14.1 percent of persons in the free plan and 16.9 percent of those on the cost-sharing plans would be hypertensive at exit (see Appendix L.)

No other health measure showed a significant difference between the free and cost-sharing plans. Furthermore, only for the risk of dying and role functioning did the direction of the overall (main) effect appear to favor the free plan (see the column for predicted mean differences in Table 5).[2] For the remaining measures, the direction of the main effect favored the cost-sharing plans or was neutral.[3]

Confidence limits for the differences between the free and the other plans were relatively narrow in all cases; thus, it is unlikely that our conclusion of little or no effect is far off the mark. To verify that this conclusion does not depend on our method of prediction, we compared the predicted differences with the differences between the raw means of the two groups. The predicted differences and the differences in the raw means scarcely diverged (see the two rightmost columns of Table 5), although precision is better for the predicted values.

Outcomes were more similar among the cost-sharing plans than between the free care plan and the cost-sharing plans. Such a finding is not surprising because utilization differences were greater between the free plan and the cost-sharing plans than within the cost-sharing group (Newhouse et al., 1981).

The Influence of Income and Health Status on General Health

In addition to detecting no significant effect on five general measures of health for the average individual, we were unable to detect any significant differences among subgroups who differed in income and initial health status (Table 6). Confidence intervals for subgroup

---

[2]In the earlier analyses (Brook et al., 1983), the first of two exit systolic blood pressure readings (rather than the second) was used to calculate the risk of dying index. Analyses were revised to use the second measurement in all cases, but because blood pressure is only one of three components in this index, changes in results were negligible. For example, the predicted mean difference fell from -0.018 to -0.014. The difference for the elevated-risk group (Table 7) fell from -0.21 to -0.19. Consequently, the results shown here are those already published.

[3]As explained in Appendix M, we could detect no meaningful effect on our results of including or excluding pregnant women in the physical and role functioning analyses, so they were left in these reported findings.

Table 5

PREDICTED EXIT VALUES AND RAW MEAN DIFFERENCES OF HEALTH STATUS MEASURES FOR AN AVERAGE PERSON, ACCORDING TO MEASURE AND PLAN

Health Status Measures	No.[a]	Cost-Sharing Plans				Free Plan	Predicted Mean Difference (Free Minus Cost-Sharing)[b]	Raw Mean Difference (Free Minus Cost-Sharing)
		Cata-strophic	Inter-med.	Ind. Deduct.	Total			
General Health (score, 1–100)								
Physical functioning	3862	86.0	85.0	84.9	85.3	85.3	0.0(−1.6,1.5)	−0.3(−2.3,1.7)
Role functioning	3861	95.5	95.0	94.7	95.1	95.4	0.3(−0.6,1.2)	−0.3(−2.2,1.6)
Mental health	3862	75.6	75.5	75.8	75.6	75.5	−0.2(−1.1,0.8)	−0.1(−1.1,1.0)
Social contacts	3827	69.3	70.2	69.8	69.8	69.4	−0.3(−2.3,1.6)	−0.2(−2.4,2.0)
Health perceptions	3843	68.1	68.0	67.9	68.0	67.4	−0.6(−1.5,0.3)	−0.9(−2.1,0.3)
Health Habits								
Smoking (scale, 1–2.20)	3758	1.28	1.29	1.29	1.29	1.29	0.0(−0.02,0.02)	−0.00(−0.03,0.03)
Weight (kg)	2804	72.8	72.6	73.1	72.8	72.8	0.0(−0.5,0.5)	0.0(−1.0,1.0)
Cholesterol level (mg/dl)	3381	202	200	204	202	203	1.0(−1.0,3.0)	−1.3(−4.5,1.9)
Physiologic Health								
Diastolic blood pressure (mm Hg)	3495	79.0	78.5	78.8	78.8	78.0	−0.8(−1.5,−0.1)[c]	−0.9(−1.8,−0.1)[d]
Functional far vision (no. of Snellen lines)	3477	2.55	2.50	2.51	2.52	2.42	−0.1(−0.16,−0.04)[e]	−0.13(−0.21,−0.05)[f]
Risk of dying (score)	3317	1.01	0.98	1.03	1.01	0.99	−0.02(−0.05,0.02)	−0.03(−0.08,0.02)

[a]Numbers of persons in various parts of the analysis are dissimilar because noncompleters were not included for physiologic health, weight, or cholesterol level and because of differences among measures in the number of persons with valid enrollment or exit data. Teenagers 14–17 at enrollment and pregnant women were excluded from analyses of weight.

[b]Numbers in parentheses are 95-percent confidence intervals; an approximate confidence interval is given for role functioning.

[c]t = 2.21; p = 0.03.
[d]t = 2.20; p = 0.03.
[e]t = 3.29; p = 0.001. Persons with normal vision were included and given a value of 2.0.
[f]t = 3.18; p = 0.001.

104

Table 6

PREDICTED EXIT VALUES OF FIVE GENERAL HEALTH MEASURES,
ACCORDING TO MEASURE, PLAN, INCOME, AND
INITIAL HEALTH STATUS[a]

General Health Status Measure	Total Cost-Sharing	Free Plan	Free Minus Cost-Sharing[b]	Total Cost Sharing	Free Plan	Free Minus Cost-Sharing[b]
	Low Inc. and Initial Ill Health			*Low Inc. and Initial Good Health*		
Physical functioning	60.3	65.9	5.6(−2.9,14.0)	89.8	91.2	1.4(−1.6,4.4)
Role functioning	69.0	46.3	−22.7(−53.2,7.8)	95.0	96.1	1.1(−1.8,4.0)
Mental health	65.6	67.0	1.4(−1.8,4.7)	81.1	79.3	−1.8(−4.1,0.6)
Social contacts	51.8	55.3	3.5(−5.2,12.2)	77.7	77.9	0.2(−4.1,4.5)
Health perceptions	54.2	54.6	0.3(−3.0,3.7)	74.7	72.4	−2.3(−4.8,0.1)
	High Inc. and Initial Ill Health			*High Inc. and Initial Good Health*		
Physical functioning	59.9	55.6	−4.3(−9.8,1.2)	92.6	91.9	−0.6(−2.8,1.6)
Role functioning	60.3	56.0	−4.3(−24.1,15.5)	96.3	96.3	0.0(−2.0,2.0)
Mental health	63.3	64.5	1.3(−1.6,4.1)	82.7	82.1	−0.6(−1.9,0.7)
Social contacts	47.3	47.6	−0.3(−5.0,5.5)	82.2	80.1	−2.1(−5.1,1.0)
Health perceptions	52.8	52.1	−0.7(−3.1,1.7)	77.7	77.8	0.1(−1.4,1.6)

[a]Initial health status is defined with respect to the individual health measure denoted in each row.
[b]Numbers in parentheses are 95-percent confidence intervals; approximate confidence intervals are given for role functioning.

analyses were, of course, wider than for the sample as a whole. Hence, we cannot be as certain as with the entire sample that clinically important effects did not occur in these subgroups.

The Elevated-Risk Groups

At the end of the experiment, smoking, cholesterol, weight, and blood pressure did not differ significantly as a function of plan among participants judged to be at elevated risk on these measures at the study's outset (Table 7). Among those whose uncorrected far vision was worse than 20/20, corrected vision was, collectively, about 0.2

Table 7

PREDICTED EXIT VALUES FOR HEALTH HABITS AND PHYSIOLOGIC VARIABLES
IN ELEVATED-RISK GROUPS, ACCORDING TO VARIABLE AND PLAN

Health Habits and Physiologic Variables	Definition of Elevated-Risk Group[a]	Total Cost-Sharing	Free Plan	Free Minus Cost-Sharing[b]
Smoking	≥1.79 (≥1 pack per day)	1.75	1.73	−0.02(−0.06,0.03)
Weight	20% over ideal weight (kg)	89.1	89.4	0.3(−1.1,1.7)
Cholesterol level	≥220 mg/dl	243	244	2(−3,7)
Diastolic blood pressure	>83 mm Hg or taking hypertension drugs at enrollment	88.4	87.6	−0.7(−2.2,0.8)
Functional far vision	Line 3 (20/25) or worse for better eye	2.98	2.78	−0.2(−0.3,−0.1)[c]
Risk of dying	Risk >1.42	2.11	1.90	−0.21(−0.39,−0.04)[d]

[a]Elevated-risk groups are the least healthy 25 percent of the people as defined with respect to the individual health measure denoted in each row. For functional far vision, all persons with uncorrected natural vision worse than 20/20 are included.
[b]Numbers in parentheses are 95-percent confidence intervals.
[c]$t = 3.29$; $p = 0.001$.
[d]$t = 2.41$; $p = 0.02$.

Snellen lines better, an improvement in visual acuity from 20/25 to 20/24 ($p = 0.001$).

For the average person at exit, the risk of dying from any cause (based on smoking habits, cholesterol level, and systolic blood pressure) was set arbitrarily at 1.0. By comparison, the relative risk of dying for someone in the elevated-risk group at enrollment (generally the upper quartile of the distribution of risk factors) was, on average, 2.02; a member of this group would be twice as likely to die during the next year as the average person of the same age and sex. For high-risk members on the free-care plan, the relative risk of dying was 1.90 at exit, as contrasted with 2.11 for those in the cost-sharing plans (Table 7). This 10-percent difference favoring free care was significant ($p =$

0.02) and was principally attributable to the improved control of high blood pressure among those on the free plan.[4]

Improvements in vision, blood pressure, and risk of dying were largest in the group with low income and elevated risk (see the first column of Table 8). For them, the differences between the free and cost-sharing plans were substantial for blood pressure and significant for the risk of dying; neither difference was significant in the higher income group. For instance, diastolic blood pressure for persons of low income judged initially to be at increased risk of hypertension was 2.3 mm Hg lower in the free plan (p = 0.08); for such persons of high income it was 0.1 mm Hg higher in the free plan.[5]

At this point, it is tempting to infer that free care improved the health of the sick poor but not the sick rich. Unfortunately, our data do not permit quite such a firm conclusion. If we begin with the hypothesis that free care makes *no* difference to the poor who are at elevated risk, our findings permit us to reject it: Free care *did* make a difference especially for the risk of dying measure, as shown by the values in Table 8. On the other hand, we did not demonstrate that free care benefited people with a high income and high risk; here we cannot reject the equivalent null hypothesis. Given the conditions of our experiment, free care made no *detectable* difference to this group. Now, however, a paradox emerges. If we start with another null hypothesis—that the two income groups responded in the same way to the various plans—we would expect to see it rejected, but because the differences between the two groups are not significant, we cannot reject this hypothesis.

Apparently, poor people at elevated risk benefited from receiving free care, but we cannot draw any conclusion about the higher-income group. We cannot say that they benefited from receiving free care, but we also cannot show that they responded differently from the lower-income group, which did benefit.

---

[4] Qualitatively, the systolic blood pressure results were very similar to those for diastolic blood pressure.

[5] Again, the findings for blood pressure differ somewhat from those reported in Brook et al. (1983). In particular, the results for the low income group had been significant at the p < 0.05 level in favor of the free-care plan.

Table 8

PREDICTED EXIT VALUES OF BLOOD PRESSURE, VISION,
AND RISK OF DYING IN ELEVATED-RISK GROUPS,
FOR LOW AND HIGH INCOME GROUPS

Physiologic Measure	Total Cost-Sharing	Free Plan	Free Minus Cost-Sharing
Elevated Risk and Low Income[a]			
Diastolic blood pressure	89.3	87.0	−2.3 (−4.9,+0.3)[b,c]
Functional far vision	3.61	3.30	−0.3 (−0.6,+0.02)
Risk of dying	2.13	1.83	−0.30[d] (−0.6,−0.04)
Elevated Risk and High Income			
Diastolic blood pressure	88.0	88.1	+0.1 (−2.0,+2.2)
Functional far vision	3.21	3.14	−0.07 (−0.4,+0.2)
Risk of dying	2.09	1.96	−0.13 (−0.4,+0.1)

[a]For definitions of elevated risk for diastolic blood pressure and risk of dying, see Table 7. For functional far vision, elevated risk in this table refers *only* to the upper one-quarter of the distribution of values for uncorrected natural vision. Predictions in these two columns were made with use of the mean value of the elevated-risk group.
[b]Numbers in parentheses are 95-percent confidence intervals.
[c]$t = 1.72$; $p = 0.08$.
[d]$t = 2.23$; $p = 0.03$.

Chapter 4

DISCUSSION OF THE HEALTH STATUS RESULTS

A central purpose of the HIE was to learn whether varying the amount of cost-sharing in medical care, including imposing no cost-sharing, affects the health of a general, nonaged population. Cost-sharing, or for that matter providing free care, is not a targeted or disease-specific approach to curtailing or expanding the use of medical services, in contrast to a program such as hypertension detection and follow-up.

Participants in the experiment received one of a graded set of insurance plans; for some, medical care was absolutely free, whereas for others the annual cost could range up to the lesser of 15 percent of family income or $1000. The experiment was designed to be as "realistic" as possible. The sample was typical of a general population of adults with two major exceptions: It excluded severely disabled individuals eligible for public Disability Insurance (and hence Medicare) and those over age 65. (The disabled eligible for Medicare constitute 1 percent of the population.) Moreover, the study was conducted at sites representing a cross-section of American medicine; participants could, and did, choose their own physicians.

We found that under these circumstances the more people had to pay for medical care, the less they used. Adults who had to share the cost of care made about a third fewer ambulatory visits and were hospitalized about a third less often (Newhouse et al., 1981). Such reductions involve decisions both on the part of the patient to seek care and on the part of the physician to order services; they might well be expected to affect health status.

From our data, we can draw three conclusions about how such large differences in use affected health. We can therefore narrow the range of speculation about the relationship between cost-sharing and health status.

First, free care had *no* effect on the major health habits associated with cardiovascular disease and many types of cancer. More generous insurance, which prompted an average of one to two more encounters with a physician each year for several years, had no impact on smoking, on the weight of either the average or the overweight enrollee, or on cholesterol levels (either average or elevated). Moreover, these habits, especially smoking, were at levels where substantial health benefit from behavior change was possible.

Second, we detected no effects of free care for the average enrollee on any of five general health measures (physical health, role functioning, mental health, social contacts, or health perceptions), and the confidence intervals rule out the possibility of anything beyond a modest effect. With respect to subgroups differing in income and initial health status, we can be less certain that this interpretation is correct, because the smaller samples yield wider intervals. Nonetheless, persons who scored low on these measures at enrollment exhibited substantial impairment in their health, and a more noticeable benefit from free care might have been anticipated for them.

Third, people who have certain conditions that are easy to diagnose and have well-established treatments (myopia, hypertension) benefited from free care. At the end of the experiment, enrollees with free care had better visual acuity and lower blood pressure. From the latter improvement, we infer that their risk of early death had been diminished. Although differences between income groups were insignificant, the improvements appear greater among the poor.

To illustrate the magnitude of the gains we did observe, consider the following examples. An average 50-year-old man in the late 1970s had approximately a 5-percent chance of dying within five years (U.S. Public Health Service, 1980). A 50-year-old man at elevated risk had approximately double that chance of dying. If 1000 50-year-old men at elevated risk were enrolled on a free rather than a cost-sharing plan, then we would anticipate that about 11 of them, who would otherwise have died, would be alive five years later ($1000 \times 0.05 \times (2.11 - 1.90)$ = 10.5). An average 39-year-old woman, on the other hand, had a 1-percent chance of dying over the five-year period (U.S. Public Health Service, 1980); free care given to 1000 high-risk women of that age could be expected to keep only two more women alive than would care provided under cost-sharing arrangements.

These mortality reductions, in and of themselves, are not sufficient to justify free care for all adults. Investment in more targeted programs, such as hypertension detection and screening, represents a more cost-effective method for saving lives (Berwick et al., 1980). If free care yielded other life-saving benefits, for example a reduction in cancer deaths because of increased or more appropriate screening, such a conclusion could change.

Precisely how the various health benefits occurred is not yet known. We can comfortably conclude that free care did not prevent the occurrence of hypertension or visual impairments but rather ameliorated their consequences. Future analyses based on data collected during the experiment, which examine both the use of services and the quality of medical care provided to patients with these conditions, will shed light on how the benefits—or lack thereof—came about.

Certainly, our results should prompt further examination of how, in the context of the fee-for-service system, people use services and physicians render care, and what the medical profession sees as its responsibility for improving the health of the nation. The questions prompted by our results are myriad: Why, when the levels of ambulatory care and hospital admissions were on average one-quarter to one-half again as high on the free as on the cost-sharing plans, were there so few positive effects on health status? Why was there no effect on health habits? Why was more physician contact seemingly of little or no benefit for many people, especially for those who reported themselves in poor health at the beginning of the study?

In view of other ways for improving health, we conclude that providing all medical services free to the nonaged public at large is not justified by the health benefits realized. A case for free care could be made, however, on other grounds. Cost-sharing plans could be inequitable to the poor or to those who have or will develop a chronic problem that demands continuing treatment. The latter group will clearly bear less of the medical bill, the less the cost-sharing. In addition, some may feel that free medical care, at least for some services, is necessary for a just society.

Our results must be used with caution to derive policies for special groups in the population. Poor families were protected by an income-related ceiling on their out-of-pocket medical expenses. The aged and those too disabled to work were not included in the experiment. Additional medical care for such persons may well provide benefits that a young, relatively healthy population does not experience.

The findings presented here may well disappoint those physicians who believe that reducing financial barriers to their care will dramatically improve patients' health. Some of these physicians might now contend that their apparent inability to influence patients' health habits argues for improved medical training and postgraduate education. Others may say it is evidence that such concerns should not fall within the purview of medicine, but rather are the obligation of lay groups or individuals themselves. One can only speculate whether professional training or the nature of the help that society seeks from physicians and other health care professionals could be sufficiently altered so that, if this experiment were to be repeated in the coming decades, its outcomes would be appreciably different.

Future studies will evaluate the benefits of free care already observed, as well as other possible benefits, relative to their costs. At this juncture, we conclude that although free care did not improve health status across the entire range of measures or income groups examined, it did confer demonstrable benefits for patients with selected conditions that physicians are trained to manage.

REFERENCES

Aitchison, J., and J.A.C. Brown, *The Lognormal Distribution, with Special Reference to its Uses in Economics*, Cambridge University Press, Cambridge, Massachusetts, 1957.

Beck, A. T., *Depression—Causes and Treatment*, University of Pennsylvania Press, Philadelphia, 1967.

Benham, L., and A. Benham, "The Impact of Incremental Medical Services on Health Status, 1963–1970," in R. Andersen, J. Kravit, and O. W. Anderson (eds.), *Equity in Health Services: Empirical Analyses in Social Policy*, Ballinger Publishing Company, Cambridge, Massachusetts, 1975.

Berwick, D., S. Cretin, and E. Keeler, *Children, Cholesterol, and Heart Disease: An Analysis of Alternatives*, Oxford University Press, New York, 1980, Table 7.1.

Brook, R. H., D. M. Berman, K. N. Lohr, et al., *Conceptualization and Measurement of Physiologic Health for Adults: Vol. 3, Hypertension*, The Rand Corporation, R-2262/3-HHS, August 1980.

Brook, R. H., K. N. Lohr, E. B. Keeler, et al., *Conceptualization and Measurement of Physiologic Health for Adults: Vol. 11, Hypercholesterolemia*, The Rand Corporation, R-2262/11-HHS, September 1981.

Brook, R. H., J. E. Ware, Jr., W. H. Rogers, et al., "Does Free Care Improve Adults' Health? Results from a Randomized Controlled Trial," *The New England Journal of Medicine*, Vol. 309, 1983, pp. 1426-1434.

Brown, M., *Lessons Learned from the Administration of the Rand Health Insurance Experiment*, The Rand Corporation, R-3095-HHS, May 1984.

Carlson, R. J., *The End of Medicine*, John Wiley & Sons, New York, 1975.

Clasquin, L., and M. E. Brown, *Rules of Operation for the Rand Health Insurance Study*, The Rand Corporation, R-1602-HEW, May 1977.

Cochrane, A. L., A. S. St. Leger, and F. Moore, "Health Service 'Input' and Mortality 'Output' in Developed Countries," *Journal of Epidemiology and Community Health*, Vol. 32, 1978, pp. 200-205.

Comrey, A. L., *Comrey Personality Scales*, Educational and Industrial Testing Services, San Diego, California, 1970.

Costello, C. G., and A. L. Comrey, "Scales for Measuring Depression and Anxiety," *The Journal of Psychology*, Vol. 66, 1967, pp. 303-313.

Dagenais, M. G., "Further Suggestions Concerning the Utilization of Incomplete Observations in Regression Analysis," *Journal of The American Statistical Association*, Vol. 66, 1971, pp. 93-98.

Davies, A. R., and J. E. Ware, Jr., *Measuring Health Perceptions in the Health Insurance Experiment*, The Rand Corporation, R-2711-HHS, October 1981.

Davies, A. R., C. D. Sherbourne, J. R. Peterson, and J. E. Ware, Jr. (eds.), *Scoring Manual: Adult Health Status and Patient Satisfaction Measure Used in Rand's Health Insurance Experiment*, The Rand Corporation, N-2190-HHS, forthcoming.

Dohrenwend, B. S., B. P. Dohrenwend, and D. Cook, "Ability and Disability in Role Functioning in Psychiatric Patient and Non-Patient Groups," in J. D. Wing and H. Hafner (eds.), *Roots of Evaluation*, Oxford University Press, London, 1973, pp. 337-360.

Dohrenwend, B. P., P. E. Shrout, G. Egri, and F. S. Mendelsohn, "Nonspecific Psychological Distress and Other Dimensions of Psychopathology," *Archives of General Psychiatry*, Vol. 37, 1980, pp. 1229-1236.

Donald, C. A., and J. E. Ware, Jr., *The Quantification of Social Contacts and Resources*, The Rand Corporation, R-2937-HHS, October 1982.

Donald, C. A., and J. E., Ware, Jr., "The Measurement of Social Support," in J. F. Greenley (ed.), *Research in Community and Mental Health*, Jai Press, Greenwich, Connecticut, 1984 (in press).

Donald, C. A., J. E. Ware, Jr., R. H. Brook, et al., *Conceptualization and Measurement of Health for Adults in the Health Insurance Study: Vol. IV, Social Health*, The Rand Corporation, R-1987/4-HEW, August 1978.

Hadley, J., *More Medical Care, Better Health?* The Urban Institute, Washington, D.C., 1982.

Huber, P. J., *The Behavior of Maximum Likelihood Estimates Under Nonstandard Conditions. Fifth Berkeley Symposium, 1965*, University of California Press, Berkeley, California, 1967, pp. 221-233.

Hulka, B. S., and J. C. Cassel, "The AAFP-UNC Study of the Organization, Utilization, and Assessment of Primary Medical Care," *American Journal of Public Health*, Vol. 63, 1973, pp. 494-501.

Illich, I., *Medical Nemesis: The Expropriation of Health*, Pantheon Books, New York, 1977.

Keeler, E. B., and J. E. Rolph, "How Cost Sharing Reduced Medical Spending of Participants in the Health Insurance Experiment," *Journal of the American Medical Association*, Vol. 249, 1983, pp. 2220-2222.

Manning, W. G., Jr., J. P. Newhouse, and J. E. Ware, Jr., "The Status of Health in Demand Estimation: Beyond Excellent, Good, Fair, and Poor," in V. R. Fuchs (ed.) *Economic Aspects of Health*, The University of Chicago Press, Chicago, 1982, pp. 143–184.

McGee, D., and T. Gordon, "Section 31. The Results of the Framingham Study Applied to Four Other US-Based Epidemiologic Studies of Cardiovascular Disease," in W. B. Kannel and T. Gordon (eds.), *The Framingham Study: An Investigation of Cardiovascular Disease* (DHEW Publication No. (NIH) 76–1083), National Heart and Lung Institute, National Institutes of Health, Bethesda, Maryland, April 1976.

Miller, A. E., and M. G. Miller, *Options for Health and Health Care. The Coming of Post-Clinical Medicine*, John Wiley & Sons, New York, 1981.

Miller, M. K., and C. S. Stokes, "Health Status, Health Resources, and Consolidated Structural Parameters: Implications for Public Health Care Policy," *Journal of Health and Social Behavior*, Vol. 19, 1978, pp. 263–379.

Morris, C. N., "A Finite Selection Model for Experimental Design of the Health Insurance Study," *Journal of Econometrics*, Vol. 11, 1979, pp. 43–61.

Myers, J. K., J. J. Lindenthal, M. P. Pepper, et al., "Life Events and Mental Status: A Longitudinal Study," *Journal of Health and Social Behavior*, Vol. 13, 1972, pp. 398–406.

National Center for Health Statistics, *Limitations of Activity and Mobility Due to Chronic Conditions: United States, 1972*, (DHEW Publication No. (HRA) 75–1523), National Center for Health Statistics, Rockville, Maryland, 1974.

Newhouse, J. P., "A Design for a Health Insurance Experiment," *Inquiry*, Vol. 11, 1974, pp. 5–27.

Newhouse, J. P., and L. Friedlander, "The Relationship Between Medical Resources and Measures of Health: Some Additional Evidence," *Journal of Human Resources*, Vol. 15, 1980, pp. 200–218.

Newhouse, J. P., W. G. Manning, C. N. Morris, et al., "Some Interim Results from a Controlled Trial of Cost Sharing in Health

Insurance," *New England Journal of Medicine,* Vol. 305, 1981, pp. 1501–1507. (Also published as R-2847-HHS, The Rand Corporation, January 1982).

Patrick, D. L., J. W. Bush, and M. M. Chen, "Toward an Operational Definition of Health," *Journal of Health and Social Behavior,* Vol. 14, 1973, pp. 6–23.

Rice, D. P., and D. Wilson, "The American Medical Economy: Problems and Perspectives," *Journal of Health Politics, Policy, Law,* Vol. 1, 1976, pp. 151–172.

Rogers, D. E., and R. J. Blendon, "Special Communication. The Changing American Health Scene. Sometimes Things Get Better," *Journal of the American Medical Association,* Vol. 237, 1977, pp. 1710–1714.

Rogers, W. H., and P. Camp, *Refusal and Attrition in the Health Insurance Experiment,* The Rand Corporation, N-2195-HHS, forthcoming.

Rubenstein, R. S., K. N. Lohr, R. H. Brook, et al., *Conceptualization and Measurement of Physiologic Health for Adults: Vol. 12. Vision Impairments,* The Rand Corporation, R-2262/12-HHS, July 1982.

Smith, L. H., G. A. Goldberg, R. H. Brook, et al., *The Health Insurance Study Screening Examination Procedures Manual,* The Rand Corporation, R-2101-HEW, September 1978.

Starr, P., "The Politics of Therapeutic Nihilism," *Working Papers,* Vol. IV, No. 2, 1976, pp. 48–55.

Stewart, A. L., "The Reliability and Validity of Self-Reported Weight and Height," *Journal of Chronic Diseases,* Vol. 35, 1982, pp. 295–309.

Stewart, A. L., R. H. Brook, and R. L. Kane, *Conceptualization and Measurement of Health Habits for Adults in the Health Insurance Study: Smoking,* The Rand Corporation, R-2374/1-HEW, June 1979.

Stewart, A. L., R. H. Brook, and R. L. Kane, *Conceptualization and Measurement of Health Habits for Adults in the Health Insurance Study: Overweight,* The Rand Corporation, R-2374/2-HEW, July 1980.

Stewart, A., J. E. Ware, Jr., and R. H. Brook, "The Meaning of Health: Understanding Functional Limitations," *Medical Care,* Vol. 15, 1977, pp. 939–952.,

Stewart, A. L., J. E. Ware, Jr., and R. H. Brook, "Advances in the Measurement of Functional Status: Construction of Aggregate Indexes," *Medical Care,* Vol. 19, 1981, pp. 473–488.

Stewart, A. L., J. E. Ware, Jr., and R. H. Brook, *Construction and Scoring of Aggregate Functional Status Indexes*, The Rand Corporation, R-2551-1-HHS, August 1982a.

Stewart, A. L., J. E. Ware, Jr., and R. H. Brook, *Construction and Scoring of Aggregate Functional Status Indexes: Appendixes*, The Rand Corporation, N-1706-1-HHS, August 1982b.

Stewart, A. L., J. E. Ware, Jr., R. H. Brook, et al., *Conceptualization and Measurement of Health for Adults in the Health Insurance Study: Vol II, Physical Health in Terms of Functioning*, The Rand Corporation, R-1987/2-HEW, July 1978.

U.S. Public Health Service, "Life Tables," *Vital Statistics of the United States, Vol. II, Sec. 5-2* (DHHS Publication No. (PHS) 81-1104), U.S. Government Printing Office, Hyattsville, Maryland, 1980.

Veit, C., and J. E. Ware, Jr., "The Structure of Psychological Distress and Well-Being in General Populations," *Journal of Consulting and Clinical Psychology*, Vol. 51, 1983, pp. 730-742.

Ware, J. E., Jr., "Scales for Measuring General Health Perceptions," *Health Services Research*, Vol. 11, 1976, pp. 396-415.

Ware, J. E., Jr. "The General Health Rating Index," in N. K. Wenger, M. E. Mattson, C. D. Furberg, and J. Elinson (eds.), *Assessment of Quality of Life in Clinical Trials of Cardiovascular Disease*, Le Jacq Publishing Co., New York, 1984 (in press).

Ware, J. E., Jr., and A. H. Karmos, *Development and Validation of Scales to Measure Perceived Health and Patient Role Propensity: Vol. II of a Final Report*, NTIS Publication No. PB 288-331, National Technical Information Service, Springfield, Virginia, 1976.

Ware, J. E., Jr., A. Davies-Avery, and C. A. Donald, *Conceptualization and Measurement of Health for Adults in the Health Insurance Study: Vol. V, General Health Perceptions*, The Rand Corporation, R-1987/5-HEW, September 1978.

Ware, J. E., Jr., A. Davies-Avery, and R. H. Brook, *Conceptualization and Measurement of Health for Adults in the Health Insurance Study: Vol. VI, Analysis of Relationships Among Health Status Measures*, The Rand Corporation, R-1987/6-HEW, November 1980.

Ware, J. E., Jr., R. H. Brook, A. R. Davies, et al., *Choosing Measures of Health Status for Individuals in General Populations*, The Rand Corporation, N-1642-HHS, January 1981.

Ware, J. E., Jr., S. A. Johnston, A. Davies-Avery, et al., *Conceptualization and Measurement of Health for Adults in the Health Insurance Study: Vol. III, Mental Health*, The Rand Corporation, R-1987/3-HEW, December 1979.

Ware, J. E., W. G. Manning, N. Duan, et al., "Health Status and the Use of Outpatient Mental Health Services," *American Psychologist*, Vol. 39, No. 10, 1984a (in press).

Ware, J. E., Jr., C. T. Veit, and C. A. Donald, *Refinements in the Measurement of Mental Health for Adults in the Health Insurance Experiment*, The Rand Corporation, R-2737-HHS, 1984b (forthcoming).

Williams, A. W., C. A. Donald, and J. E. Ware, Jr., *The Effects of Life Events and Social Supports on the Psychological Well-Being of Women and Men*, The Rand Corporation, 1984 (forthcoming).

Williams, A. W., J. E. Ware, Jr., and C. A. Donald, "A Model of Mental Health, Life Events, and Social Supports Applicable to General Populations," *Journal of Health and Social Behavior*, Vol. 22, No. 4, 1981, pp. 324–336.

World Health Organization, "Constitution of the World Health Organization," in *Basic Documents*, Geneva, 1948.

Zung, W. K., "A Self-Rating Depression Scale," *Archives of General Psychiatry*, Vol. 12, 1965, pp. 63–70.

4

A Controlled Trial of the Effect of
a Prepaid Group Practice on Use of Services

Willard G. Manning, Arleen Leibowitz, George A. Goldberg, William H. Rogers, and Joseph P. Newhouse

Abstract Does a prepaid group practice deliver less care than the fee-for-service system when both serve comparable populations with comparable benefits? To answer this question, we randomly assigned a group of 1580 persons to receive care free of charge from either a fee-for-service physician of their choice (431 persons) or the Group Health Cooperative of Puget Sound (1149 persons). In addition, 733 prior enrollees of the Cooperative were studied as a control group.

The rate of hospital admissions in both groups at the Cooperative was about 40 per cent less than in the fee-for-service group (P<0.01), although ambulatory-visit rates were similar. The calculated expenditure rate for all serv-

ices was about 25 per cent less in the two Cooperative groups (P<0.01 for the experimental group, P<0.05 for the control group). The number of preventive visits was higher in the prepaid groups, but this difference does not explain the reduced hospitalization. The similarity of use between the two prepaid groups suggests that the mix of health risks at the Cooperative was similar to that in the fee-for-service system. The lower rate of use that we observed, along with comparable reductions found in non-controlled studies by others, suggests that the style of medicine at prepaid group practices is markedly less "hospital-intensive" and, consequently, less expensive. (N Engl J Med 1984; 310:1505-10.)

HEALTH-maintenance organizations (HMOs) have been advocated for many years as an important innovation in medical-care delivery; indeed, for a decade, federal legislation and subsidies have encouraged their formation. Previous studies played a large part in persuading the Congress and the executive branch to promote enrollment in HMOs. They indicated that the prepaid-group-practice variant of HMOs has ambulatory-visit rates similar to those in fee-for-service medicine but has hospital-admission rates that are as much as 40 per cent lower[1-4] — a prospect with wide appeal.

However, a cloud of doubt has lingered concerning the ability of HMOs to keep the promise of reduced cost. Virtually all studies comparing HMOs with fee-for-service medicine have used a self-selected sample — that is, they compared persons who had voluntarily chosen an HMO with those who either had opted for fee-for-service medicine or had had no choice. If persons choosing an HMO were healthier than those choosing the fee-for-service system, the observed reduced use of HMOs could simply have been an artifact. Indeed, the single previous randomized study found that one prepaid group practice did lower hospital use but had sufficiently higher use of ambulatory care to make it significantly more expensive overall.[5] This finding, however, has not dimmed enthusiasm for prepaid group practices, perhaps because the particular plan studied was small and just beginning.

To isolate the relation between prepayment and use of services, we have conducted a controlled trial in one well-established prepaid group practice. Specifically, we sought to answer two questions. First, when persons previously receiving care from fee-for-service physicians are randomly assigned to receive care at a prepaid group practice, how does their use differ from that of persons who remain with fee-for-service physi-

From the Health Sciences Program, The Rand Corporation, 1700 Main St., Santa Monica, CA 90406, where reprint requests should be addressed to Dr. Manning.

Supported by the Health Insurance Study grant (016B80) from the Department of Health and Human Services. The views expressed are those of the authors and do not necessarily represent the views of the Department of Health and Human Services or The Rand Corporation.

cians? Second, when persons previously receiving care from fee-for-service providers are randomly assigned to receive care at a prepaid group practice, how does their use differ from the use of persons who are already enrolled in the prepaid plan?

The prepaid group practice that we studied, Group Health Cooperative of Puget Sound (GHC), is located in Seattle, Washington. It was established in 1947 and currently has an enrollment of 324,000 people — about 15 per cent of the Seattle-area population. Its history has been described elsewhere.[6] In 1976, at the beginning of our study, GHC owned its own hospital; in 1977 it opened a second hospital.

METHODS

Design of the Trial

We compared four groups. The first three were samples of the Seattle-area population who were not enrolled in GHC in 1976 but who were otherwise eligible for the trial. Ineligible persons included those over 62 years of age at the time of enrollment, Seattle-area families with incomes of more than $56,000 in 1983 dollars (this excluded 1 per cent of the families contacted), those who were institutionalized, members of the military and their dependents, veterans with service-connected disabilities, and those eligible for Medicare disability or the end-stage renal-dialysis programs.

Participants in the first two groups were assigned to plans that covered virtually all health services from fee-for-service physicians and ancillary personnel, such as speech therapists. In the first group the services were provided at no cost to the participant; this plan is referred to as the "free fee-for-service plan." In the second sample, participants had to share the costs of their medical care. They paid 25 or 95 per cent of their medical bills, subject in most cases to a limit on out-of-pocket expenditure of up to $1,000 per family (less for the poor). In the individual-deductible plan, however, participants paid 95 per cent of outpatient bills, up to $150 per person or $450 per family per year; all inpatient services were free. Participants in these first two groups formed part of the sample we had studied previously to assess the effects of cost sharing on use of services and health outcomes.[7,8]

Participants in the third group, the GHC experimental group, received free services at GHC. If the Cooperative did not provide a service (e.g., chiropractic), the plan offered full coverage for provision of the service outside GHC. If participants, on their own, sought outside care for a service that GHC provided, they were reimbursed only 5 per cent of the cost. However, referrals that GHC made to fee-for-service providers, as well as emergency out-of-area care, were fully covered. Except for the restriction to GHC providers and facilities, the benefits received by the GHC experimental group were identical to those received by the free fee-for-service group.

Although there was an element of randomization in the assignment of families to the fee-for-service and GHC experimental groups, a statistical method analogous to stratification was used to obtain greater comparability among the three groups than would be expected if simple random assignment were used.[9]

The fourth group used in our analysis was a random sample of GHC members in 1976 who otherwise met the eligibility requirements described above and had been enrolled in the Cooperative for at least one year. Hereafter, we refer to this group as the GHC controls. Participants in this group remained in whatever benefit plan they were enrolled in at the start of the experiment. Although control participants received most services free of charge, some involved moderate cost sharing (see the Appendix).*

*See NAPS document no. 04193 for 10 pages of supplementary material. Order from NAPS c/o Microfiche Publications, P.O. Box 3513, Grand Central Station, New York, NY 10163. Remit in advance (in U.S. funds only) $7.75 for photocopies or $4 for microfiche. Outside the U.S. and Canada add postage of $4.50 ($1.50 for microfiche postage). This material is presented in more detail in a forthcoming report by Rand.[10]

At enrollment the free fee-for-service group consisted of 431 persons (162 families), the cost-sharing fee-for-service group consisted of 782 persons (319 families), the GHC experimental group consisted of 1149 persons (448 families), and the GHC control group consisted of 733 persons (301 families). Refusals to participate and sample loss after enrollment, although differing by group, did not appear to affect any of our qualitative conclusions (see Appendix).

The GHC control group was enrolled in the study for five years; half the GHC experimental group was enrolled for five years, and the remainder for three years; and 25 per cent of the fee-for-service sample was enrolled for five years, and the remainder for three years. Assignment to three- or five-year participation was made at random. In analyses not shown in this paper we have found that use rates did not differ significantly between the three- and five-year groups, so we have combined them in the analyses presented here.[10] The sample used in our analyses consisted of originally enrolled participants while they remained in the experiment and in the Seattle area.

Measurement of Use

Data on use at GHC are from abstracted GHC records.[11] Data on out-of-plan use, in the case of the GHC groups, as well as all data on use by the fee-for-service participants, come from claim forms filed with the experiment, which functioned as the participants' insurance company.

We compared the number of visits and the number of admissions, but such a partial comparison does not detect any differential intensity of service per visit or per admission between GHC and fee-for-service participants. Therefore, we constructed a measure of intensity, which we call "imputed expenditure." Our method for calculating imputed expenditure differed for hospital services and physician services. For admissions at the GHC hospitals, we used the dollar figure that GHC would have charged, had it billed the services to a payer outside the Cooperative. (GHC does bill for some admissions; two common instances are emergency admissions of nonenrollees and Workman's Compensation cases.) For admissions at fee-for-service hospitals, we used the hospital's actual billed charges.

In the case of physician services, we compared the number of California Relative Value Studies units that GHC and fee-for-service physicians delivered.[12] To arrive at an imputed-expenditure figure, we valued units in both systems at the same dollar figure. Further details can be found in the Appendix.

In addition to comparing the rates at which the participants saw physicians, we compared the rates of preventive-care visits in the various plans. Preventive care included any "well-care" service other than vision, hearing, and prenatal care. Well-care services were defined by the physician's diagnosis, by the use of certain procedures (e.g., immunizations), or by a preventive-treatment-history code, in conjunction with the patient's indication that the reason for the visit was preventive care. We used the patient's reason for the visit because we feared that some fee-for-service physicians might fail to label some visits as preventive (because many standard health-insurance plans, although not ours, do not reimburse for preventive services). Any such failure in labeling would bias a comparison of the amount of preventive care the various groups received.

Analytical Methods

We generally calculated sample means (analysis of variance) for each of the four groups. Work reported elsewhere shows that adjustment for participant characteristics did not qualitatively affect any of our conclusions.[10]

In the estimation of imputed expenditure, however, we have obtained a worthwhile gain in precision by including age and sex as covariates; the Appendix discusses this point in more detail. The values for imputed expenditure in Table 1, however, are not corrected for any age and sex differences among the four groups. In particular, any effects from the control group's slightly higher mean age and number of female subjects (Appendix Table A-1) are reflected in the values in Table 1. We have corrected all standard errors for intertemporal and intrafamilial correlation.[10]

Table 1. Comparison of Likelihood of Using any Service, Likelihood of Hospitalization, and Imputed Annual Expenditure among the Group Health Cooperative (GHC) and Fee-for-Service Plans.*

PLAN	USE OF INPATIENT OR OUTPATIENT SERVICE IN YEAR	ONE OR MORE HOSPITALIZATIONS IN YEAR	IMPUTED ANNUAL EXPENDITURE PER PARTICIPANT (1983 DOLLARS) †
	% of participants		
GHC experimental	86.8 (1.0)	7.1 (0.50)	439 (25)
GHC control	91.0 (0.8)	6.4 (0.55)	469 (44)
Fee-for-service			
Free	85.3 (1.6)	11.1 (1.17)	609 (66)
25%	76.1 (2.7)	8.8 (1.37)	620 (103)
95%	68.4 (3.4)	8.5 (1.18)	459 (72)
Individual deductible	73.9 (2.4)	7.9 (0.96)	413 (51)

*The sample consists of all participants present at enrollment, while they remained in the Seattle area. Except for decedents, observations on partial years of participation have been deleted. Standard errors are in parentheses.

†Values include both in-plan and out-of-plan use by GHC participants. The method of imputing expenditure is described in the text and in the Appendix. The t statistics for the difference in expenditure between the GHC experimental group and the five groups listed below it are 0.87, 3.22, 2.22, 0.30, and −0.56, respectively. Because of the inclusion of age and sex as covariates, these t statistics are larger than those that would be calculated from the standard errors shown in the table.

RESULTS

Although the GHC experimental and control groups differed little with respect to imputed expenditure on medical services, they both differed markedly from the free fee-for-service group (Table 1). Imputed expenditures were 28 per cent lower in the GHC experimental group than in the free fee-for-service group (P<0.01) and about 23 per cent lower in the GHC control group (P<0.05).

The magnitude of the expenditure reduction at GHC was comparable to that achieved by 95 per cent coinsurance in the fee-for-service system, although the means by which expenditure was reduced were considerably different. The percentage of GHC enrollees seeking care was comparable to or even exceeded the percentage in the free fee-for-service plan; GHC had a lower expenditure than the free fee-for-service plan because fewer GHC enrollees were admitted to the hospital. With 95 per cent coinsurance, the percentage of enrollees seeking care, as well as the percentage admitted to the hospital, was notably lower than the percentage of participants in the free fee-for-service plan. The reduction in use appears to have been largest in the individual-deductible plan, even though inpatient services were free in this plan. However, the difference in expenditure between the individual-deductible plan and the other two cost-sharing plans was not significant and could well have reflected random variation; if data from three other sites are combined with these data, enrollees in the individual-deductible plan spent more (but not significantly more) than those enrolled in the 95 per cent coinsurance plan.[7]

The differences between GHC and the fee-for-service plans come even more sharply into focus when we examine admissions, hospital days, and visit rates (Table 2). There were 40 per cent fewer admissions (P<0.01) and hospital days in the two GHC groups than in the free fee-for-service plan, but face-to-face visits occurred at the same rate in all three plans. In contrast, all the cost-sharing plans had both lower admission rates and lower visit rates than the free fee-for-service plan. The differences in total expenditure and admission rates between the 95 per cent coinsurance plan and the two GHC groups were not significant at the 5 per cent level, but the differences in the rate of face-to-face visits were significant at this level.

Although the overall rates of face-to-face visits were similar for the two GHC groups and the free fee-for-service plan, the number of preventive visits was significantly higher in the two GHC groups; cost sharing further reduced preventive visits, to a level below the values in the free fee-for-service plan (Table 2).

Use of non-GHC services by the two GHC groups was relatively limited (Table 3). Not surprisingly, participants in the experimental group were more likely than controls to seek care outside GHC. About 2 per cent of the experimental group sought care each year exclusively from ancillary providers, such as speech therapists, chiropractors, Christian Science practitioners, and podiatrists. Half the out-of-plan admissions were related to accidents or to psychiatric diagnoses.

DISCUSSION

The Literature on Prepaid Group Practice

Our results show minor and generally insignificant differences between the two GHC groups, suggesting that results from noncontrolled studies may not be seriously contaminated by selection effects. In particular, imputed expenditures were 6 per cent lower in the experimental group than in the control group. In view of the standard errors for these expenditure figures, which were between 5 and 10 per cent of the mean, it is unlikely that there was a large difference between the groups.

The validity of our results is strengthened by their general consistency with the results in the literature regarding prepaid group practices. Luft's review of several noncontrolled studies found that such practices had 10 to 40 per cent fewer hospitalizations than fee-for-service practices.[3,4] In our study, GHC controls were 40 per cent less likely to go into the hospital than those in the free fee-for-service group and about 5 to 20 per cent less likely to be admitted than those in the cost-sharing groups.

It is plausible that the difference in admission rates between the GHC control group and the free fee-for-service group should be as large as differences observed in the literature. The free fee-for-service plan had better ambulatory benefits than virtually all fee-for-service plans described in the literature, and more

Table 2. Annual Rates of Admission and Face-to-Face Visits.*

Plan	Admission Rate †	Hospital Days	Face-to-Face Visits ‡	Preventive Visits §
	per 100 persons		per person	
GHC experimental	8.4	49	4.3	0.55
	(0.67)	(9.6)	(0.14)	(0.02)
GHC control	8.3	38	4.7	0.60
	(1.01)	(9.0)	(0.17)	(0.02)
Fee-for-service				
Free	13.8	83	4.2	0.41
	(1.51)	(26)	(0.25)	(0.03)
25%	10.0	87	3.5	0.32
	(1.43)	(28)	(0.35)	(0.03)
95%	10.5	46	2.9	0.29
	(1.68)	(9.9)	(0.34)	(0.04)
Individual deductible	8.8	28	3.3	0.27
	(1.20)	(5.1)	(0.33)	(0.03)

*The sample includes all participants present at enrollment, while they remained in the Seattle area. For GHC control and experimental groups the data include both in- and out-of-plan use. Standard errors are in parentheses.

†A count of all continuous periods of inpatient treatment.

‡Includes all visits involving face-to-face contact with health providers for which a separate charge would have been made in the fee-for-service system. Excludes radiology, pathology, prenatal and postnatal care, speech therapy, psychotherapy, dental care, chiropractic, podiatry, Christian Science healing, and telephone contacts.

§Includes well-child care, immunizations, screening examinations, routine physical and gynecologic examinations, and visits involving Pap smears (other than for an established diagnosis of cancer). Excludes visits for prenatal care, vision, and hearing. In the case of GHC, includes in-plan and out-of-plan visits.

extensive coverage of ambulatory services leads to more hospitalization among those using fee-for-service physicians.[7] For the same reason, the difference between the admission rates in the GHC control group and in the cost-sharing plans should be near the low end of Luft's range.

Outpatient-visit rates among GHC controls were not significantly higher than rates in the free fee-for-service plan but were higher than those in the cost-sharing plans (P<0.01). Luft found roughly similar results among a variety of studies he reviewed.[3] Thus, the comparison of use in the GHC control group with use in the fee-for-service groups resembles comparisons in the literature and lends support to the validity of the findings for the GHC experimental group.

The Lower Hospitalization Rate at GHC

Services delivered in the hospital account for about half of all U.S. expenditures on personal health services.[13] That GHC could lower the hospitalization rate so markedly relative to the free fee-for-service group invites closer scrutiny. What could be the explanation? In order to achieve sharply lower hospitalization rates, GHC may have been providing more preventive care or treating more cases on an outpatient basis and avoiding hospitalization. The data examined to date do not provide any clear explanation for the lower hospitalization rate at GHC. Although preventive visits were more numerous at GHC than in the fee-for-service plans, the hospitalization rates were not significantly different from those in the fee-for-service cost-sharing plans, which had only about half as many preventive visits as the GHC groups. Moreover, about two thirds of the preventive visits were for well-child

care or gynecologic examinations. Because gynecologic and pediatric admissions represent a minority of hospitalizations, it seems unlikely that preventive care accounted for much of the large difference in hospitalization rates. Indeed, despite the concentration of preventive care among children, the percentage reduction in admission rates among children was similar to the percentage reduction among adults ($\chi^2_5 = 3.83$, P>0.50, Table 4).

Outpatient-visit rates in the two GHC groups were similar to those in the free fee-for-service group; if some problems for which fee-for-service participants were hospitalized were being managed on an outpatient basis at GHC, one might expect such rates to be higher. Of course, the similar outpatient-visit rates at GHC could have been the result of more intensive outpatient treatment of those whom fee-for-service physicians would have hospitalized, combined with less intensive treatment of those who would not have been admitted in any event. Further investigation will be required to address this possibility.

How Many Dollars Would Be Saved If HMO Enrollment Increased?

The 28 per cent difference in imputed expenditure between the GHC experimental plan and the free fee-for-service plan is striking (Table 1). However, one can ask how much error the imputation process might have introduced. Although a more detailed analysis could yield a more precise figure, it seems unlikely that the true difference could have been much less than 25 per cent. Both admissions and total hospital days were 40 per cent lower at GHC than in the free fee-for-service plan (Table 2), and ambulatory-visit rates

Table 3. Annual Use of Services Outside GHC.*

Type of Use	GHC Experimental Group	GHC Control Group
Hospital admissions (per 100 persons) †	0.74 (0.26)	0.21 (0.09)
Hospital-days (per 100 persons)	15 ¶ (9)	1.4 (0.8)
Ambulatory face-to-face visits (per person) ‡	0.14 (0.02)	0.08 (0.02)
Visits to chiropractors, podiatrists, Christian Science practitioners (per person)	0.72 (0.12)	0.12 (0.06)
Visits to speech therapists (per person) §	0.0002 (0.0002)	0.007 (0.006)
Expenditures per person (1983 dollars) §	63 (13)	15 (5)

*The sample includes all participants present at enrollment, while they remained in the Seattle area. Standard errors are in parentheses.

†Comparison significant at P<0.05.

‡A face-to-face visit was one for which a separate charge would have been made in the fee-for-service system. Excludes radiology and pathology and visits involving pregnancy, speech therapy, psychotherapy, chiropractic, podiatry, and Christian Science healing. Comparison significant at P<0.05.

§Comparison significant at P<0.01.

¶One case accounts for two thirds of this mean; inpatient psychiatric cases account for one sixth of it.

Table 4. Likelihood of One or More Admissions per Year among Children and Adults.*

PLAN	CHILDREN (<18 YR)	ADULTS (≥18 YR)
	per cent	
GHC experimental	3.5 (0.56)	9.2 (0.68)
GHC control	3.6 (0.70)	7.8 (0.73)
Fee-for-service		
Free	6.2 (1.13)	13.7 (1.71)
25%	5.8 (1.92)	10.6 (1.62)
95%	3.2 (1.08)	11.6 (1.62)
Individual deductible	6.0 (1.64)	8.7 (1.26)

*The sample consists of all participants present at enrollment, while they remained in the Seattle area. Except for decedents, observations on partial years of participation have been deleted. A chi-squared value for comparability of response is 3.8 with 5 df, P>0.50. Standard errors are in parentheses.

were similar. How many dollars might such a reduction in use save? First of all, suppose the reduction in admissions was random. In that case inpatient expenditure, which accounted for somewhat over half the total expenditure,[7] would fall by 40 per cent. If ambulatory expenditure in the two systems was similar, the total expenditure would fall by about a quarter, as our imputed figures indicate.

But suppose the 40 per cent reduction in admissions was not random but rather was disproportionately made up of short-stay admissions. This would suggest that GHC also reduced the length of stay among patients it admitted. Otherwise, the reduction in hospital days would have been less than 40 per cent. A combination of reduced admissions and reduced length of stay that together yielded a 40 per cent reduction in hospital days could certainly have caused a true reduction in expenditure by approximately 25 per cent.

Moreover, our method does not account for any efficiencies GHC may have enjoyed in the delivery of physician services, such as greater substitution of paramedical personnel. To estimate the magnitude of such efficiencies, if there are any, would require a study of costs within each system — something we did not attempt. Nonetheless, it is difficult to escape the conclusion that the true expenditure was substantially lower in the two GHC groups than in the free fee-for-service group.

One might question whether the free fee-for-service plan is a relevant reference group. Few individuals in the population who use fee-for-service physicians do so without sharing the cost; therefore, one might adopt the cost-sharing plans as a standard of comparison. In the case of the 95 per cent coinsurance plans, the differences between GHC and the fee-for-service system narrow sharply.

Does this mean that if the current proportion of the population enrolled in prepaid group practices (5 per

cent) were to increase markedly, use of the hospital would not change much? In fact, one might expect considerably less hospitalization as the HMO market share grows, because the national hospitalization rate is not far from the free-plan value. In a previous analysis of fee-for-service data from four sites (including Seattle), we found that the annual likelihood of one or more hospitalizations among average Americans under age 65 was 9.5 per cent, which is close to the free-plan value of 10.2 per cent, whereas the values in the cost-sharing plans ranged from 7.2 to 9.0 per cent.[7] Because the national average appears to be close to the free-plan rate, our data suggest the potential for a substantial drop in use of inpatient services.

On the other hand, the reduced cost of prepaid group practices that is due to lower use of inpatient services will be partially offset by the increased use of ambulatory services, as compared with current levels of use in fee-for-service cost-sharing plans. National ambulatory-visit rates fall between the rates observed in the 25 per cent and 95 per cent fee-for-service plans.[7] On balance, the net effect from increased enrollment in prepaid group practices would still be a saving, unless cost sharing in the fee-for-service system were to increase above present levels.

Policy Implications

Plainly, there was much less hospitalization among study participants receiving care at GHC than among those with similar benefits (i.e., no cost sharing) who received care from fee-for-service physicians. Because of our experimental design, we can virtually rule out population characteristics as an explanation of the lower hospitalization rate at GHC. We conclude that GHC physicians were simply practicing a different style of medicine from that of fee-for-service physicians. Although our study was limited to a single, not necessarily typical prepaid group practice, the general consistency between our results and those in the literature indicates that a less "hospital-intensive" style of medicine than that practiced by the average physician is possible.[3,14]

But is such a style desirable? The results presented above shed little light on this question. We have obtained extensive measures of the health status of our participants,[8,15-18] and future analysis of these data should detect any pronounced effects of the different style of medical treatment on health status. Nonetheless, prepaid group practices have existed for decades, and it seems unlikely that there can be large deleterious health effects from their style of medicine.

In contrast, the different style could well affect patient satisfaction. Indeed, because many persons choose not to enroll in a prepaid group practice, it seems almost certain that their expected level of satisfaction, were they to join, would be lower than in fee-for-service medicine. To be sure, some may decline the option to join because they receive no cost advantage (e.g., the employer pays the entire health-insurance premium). However, others pay more to receive their care from the fee-for-service system, and one can surmise that they believe they receive something in return.

Whatever the motivation of those choosing the fee-for-service system, many observers argue that such persons ought to pay all the additional costs.[19,20] For this to occur, employers (or the government) would have to pay an equal sum for each available health-plan option instead of paying more for a fee-for-service plan than an HMO plan, as many do now. If employers did pay an equal sum, price competition between HMOs and fee-for-service insurance plans could well increase.

Some fear that increased price competition without regulation of benefit packages will bring risk selection — that is, better risks in one plan than in another.[19] We found no appreciable difference in use between the GHC experimental and control groups, suggesting that there was no risk selection in this case. Nonetheless, this result may not be generalizable. Economic theory suggests that risk selection can occur if individuals know more about their future health demands than do insuring organizations or HMOs,[21-23] and other studies have found evidence of risk selection.[3,24]

In sum, GHC delivered a different, less-expensive style of medicine than did fee-for-service practitioners in the Seattle area when both treated comparable groups receiving free care. Adding cost sharing to the fee-for-service insurance plans brought expenditures more closely into line with those of GHC but appeared to result in yet another style of care, one with markedly fewer ambulatory contacts. How the GHC style fares on dimensions other then expense remains an open question, but the lower expense at GHC cannot be explained by differences in the population that it treats.

We are indebted to our Rand colleagues Rae Archibald, Robert Brook, Marie Brown, Maureen Carney, Allyson Davies, Naihua Duan, Emmett Keeler, and Ken Krug, to our former colleagues Carl Morris and Marshall Rockwell, Jr., to William Schwartz of Tufts University, and to our past and present DHHS project officers Larry Orr and James Schuttinga for helpful advice and assistance over the years and for assistance in implementing the project; to Glen Slaughter, Cliff Wingo, Marilyn Hecox, Lauron Lindstrom, Judi Wilson, Tom Weston, and their colleagues at Glen Slaughter and Associates for processing claims and maintaining the status of the sample during the experiment; to Bernadette Benjamin and Jack Seinfeld for their meticulous programming and data management; and to the Group Health Cooperative of Puget Sound for agreeing to participate in the study and especially to Richard Handschin, its director of research during the study period, for assistance in the trial's implementation and comments on this manuscript. Neither the Cooperative nor any of the above individuals necessarily agrees with or endorses the findings reported here.

REFERENCES

1. Gaus CR, Cooper BS, Hirschman CG. Contrasts in HMO and fee-for-service performance. Soc Secur Bull 1976; 39(5):3-14.
2. Luft HS. Assessing the evidence on HMO performance. Milbank Mem Fund Q 1980; 58:501-36.
3. Idem. Health maintenance organizations: dimensions of performance. New York: John Wiley, 1981.
4. Idem. How do health-maintenance organizations achieve their "savings"?: rhetoric and evidence. N Engl J Med 1978; 298:1336-43.
5. Perkoff GT, Kahn L, Haas PJ. The effects of an experimental prepaid group practice on medical care utilization and cost. Med Care 1976; 14:432-49.
6. MacColl WA. Group practice and prepayment of medical care. Washington, D.C.: Public Affairs Press, 1966.
7. Newhouse JP, Manning WG, Morris CN, et al. Some interim results from a controlled trial of cost sharing in health insurance. N Engl J Med 1981; 305:1501-7.
8. Brook RH, Ware JE Jr, Rogers WH, et al. Does free care improve adults' health? Results from a randomized controlled trial. N Engl J Med 1983; 309:1426-34.
9. Morris CN. A finite selection model for experimental design of the health insurance study. J Econometrics 1979; 11:43-61.
10. Manning WG, Leibowitz A, Goldberg GA, Rogers WH, Newhouse JP. A controlled trial of the effect of a prepaid group practice on utilization. Santa Monica, Calif.: Rand Corporation (in press).
11. Goldberg GA. The health insurance experiment's guidelines for abstracting health services rendered by Group Health Cooperative of Puget Sound. Santa Monica, Calif.: Rand Corporation, 1983. (Rand publication no. N-1948-HHS).
12. Committee on Relative Value Studies, California Medical Association. 1974 Revision of the 1969 California relative value studies. San Francisco: California Medical Association, Sutter Publications, 1975.
13. Waldo DR, Gibson RM. National health expenditures, 1981. Health Care Financ Rev 1982; 4(1):1-35.
14. Nobrega FT, Krishan I, Smoldt RK, et al. Hospital use in a fee-for-service system. JAMA 1982; 247:806-10.
15. Brook RH, Ware JE Jr, Davies-Avery A, et al. Overview of adult health status measures fielded in Rand's Health Insurance Study. Med Care 1979; 17(7): Suppl:1-131.
16. Eisen M, Donald CA, Ware JE, Brook RH. Conceptualization and measurement of health for children in the health insurance study. Santa Monica, Calif.: Rand Corporation, 1980. (Rand publication no. R-2313-HEW).
17. Conceptualization and measurement of physiologic health for adults. Santa Monica, Calif.: Rand Corporation. (Rand publication no. R-2262-HHS).
18. Measurement of physiologic health for children. Santa Monica, Calif.: Rand Corporation. (Rand publication no. R-2898-HHS).
19. Enthoven A. Health plan: the only practical solution to the soaring cost of medical care. Reading, Mass.: Addison-Wesley, 1980:70-92.
20. McClure W. Implementing a competitive medical care system through public policy. J Health Polit Policy Law 1982; 7:2-44.
21. Arnott R, Stiglitz J. Equilibrium in competitive insurance markets — the welfare economics of moral hazard. I. Basic analytics. Kingston, Ontario: Queens University, 1982. (Discussion paper 465).
22. Cave JAK. Equilibrium in insurance markets with incomplete information: adverse selection under asymmetric information. Santa Monica, Calif.: Rand Corporation, April 1984. (Rand publication no. R-3015-HHS).
23. Rothschild M, Stiglitz J. Equilibrium in competitive insurance markets: an essay on the economics of imperfect information. Q J Econ 1976; 90:629-50.
24. Eggers P, Prihoda R. Pre-enrollment reimbursement patterns of Medicare beneficiaries enrolled in 'at-risk' HMOs. Health Care Financ Rev 1982; 4(1):55-73.

5

The Regionalization of Perinatal Services
Summary of the Evaluation of a National Demonstration Program

Marie C. McCormick, Sam Shapiro, and Barbara H. Starfield

● The success of modern perinatal management techniques has led to the recommendation of the regional organization of perinatal services. This report summarizes the evaluation of a national demonstration program of such regionalization that was funded by the Robert Wood Johnson Foundation (RWJF) in 1975. In both funded regions and comparison areas, the neonatal mortality rates decreased sharply over the decade of the 1970s. This decline was linked to shifts in the hospital of delivery that indicated antepartum risk identification and transfer of management of high-risk pregnancies to tertiary centers for delivery, a change in service pattern consistent with some aspects of regionalization. The centralization of high-risk deliveries appeared so widespread that the special effect of the RWJF program could not be detected. Surveys of surviving 1-year-old infants showed that the decrease in neonatal mortality was accompanied by a decrease in selected morbidity.

(*JAMA* 1985;253:799-804)

THE APPARENT success of modern perinatal management techniques has led to the recommendation of regional organization and coordination of perinatal services.[1,2] The intent

For editorial comment see p 826.

of such recommendations is to assure pregnant women and their newborn infants prompt access to the level of care appropriate to the degree of obstetric or neonatal risk to improve

From the Health Services Research and Development Center, Johns Hopkins School of Hygiene and Public Health, Baltimore. Dr McCormick is now with the Departments of Pediatrics and Medicine, University of Pennsylvania Medical School of Children's Hospital of Philadelphia.
Reprint requests to Health Services Research and Development Center, Johns Hopkins School of Hygiene and Public Health, Baltimore, MD 21205 (Mr Shapiro).

pregnancy outcome.[3] A regionwide organization of perinatal services would be expected to contribute to a reduction in adverse pregnancy outcome through the provision of risk assessment of pregnant women and infants and the development of mechanisms for facilitating the movement of patients within a graded system of care, with the delivery of the highest-risk patients being centralized in tertiary (usually university) medical centers.[2] Indirect support for such regional models has come from a variety of observations,[1,4-7] particularly those that demonstrate improvements in neonatal outcome in high-risk infants born in hospitals with intensive care units as compared with similar infants born in hospitals without such units.[8]

Direct support for the effectiveness

of the regional organization of medical services such as perinatal services is not strong, however. The effectiveness of the regional organization of perinatal services has been assessed for only a limited number of settings,[1,7,9] and the evidence is not considered conclusive.[10] Studies of the regionalization of other services have produced mixed conclusions concerning its effectiveness in changing health status.[11,12] Finally, questions have been raised concerning the feasibility of a regionalization model involving the movement of patients among different levels of care,[13] a concern reinforced by its unknown effect on the continuity of care[14] and the availability of local services.[15]

To address the question of the effect of the regionalization of perinatal services, the Robert Wood Johnson Foundation (RWJF) in 1975 launched a major demonstration program to determine whether the early promising results in the regionalization of perinatal services could be duplicated on a much larger scale and in heterogeneous populations. Eight sites received funding to promote coordinated systems of perinatal care for entire geographically defined regions. The elements appropriate to regionalized perinatal care were specified, but the program regions emphasized different elements according to local conditions. Residents of the eight funded regions accounted for 200,000 births annually, or about 6%

From "The Regionalization of Perinatal Services: Summary of the Evaluation of a National Demonstration Program," *JAMA, The Journal of the American Medical Association*, 1985, 253(6), 799-804. Copyright 1985 by the American Medical Association. Reprinted by permission.

of all births in the United States.

At the same time, an independent evaluation of this program by the Health Services Research and Development Center at Johns Hopkins School of Hygiene and Public Health, Baltimore, was initiated. The major questions addressed by this evaluation were as follows:

1. To what extent did the neonatal mortality rates decline in these regions, and what was the major factor in the decline: a decrease in the proportion of low-birth-weight (LBW) infants or increased survival of these high-risk infants? (Examination of the changes in fetal mortality rates and mortality among multiple births forms a separate analysis. Preliminary results, however, parallel the results for neonatal mortality, but data are less complete.)

2. Was the decline in neonatal mortality accompanied by shifts in the site of service indicative of regionalization? In particular, if the decline was due to a decrease in birth weight–specific mortality and increased survival of LBW infants, was this associated with movement of these high-risk deliveries to hospitals capable of intensive management, such as tertiary or university medical centers?

3. If evidence of regionalization was observed, did the RWJF program accelerate this process as compared with the period before the funding and with the progress observed in similar areas without such funding?

4. If the decline in neonatal mortality resulted from an increased survival of LBW infants, was there evidence that this was accompanied by an increase in the proportion of impaired survivors?

METHODS

This analysis involves eight regions selected for funding and eight comparison regions (Table 1). The eight RWJF regions were selected after a national solicitation. The basis of selection was an assessment by consultants to the foundation of the feasibility of the introduction of a regionalization program after review of a standardized application and site visits. Comparison areas were identified by the evaluation project staff on the basis of similarity in demographic distributions and, where possible, location in the same state.

The data on LBW rates, place of delivery, and neonatal mortality were derived

Table 1.—Geographically Defined Regions in RWJF* Program and Selected Comparison Areas

RWJF Regions	Comparison Areas
Syracuse, NY	15 counties around Syracuse (Broome, Cayuga, Chenango, Cortland, Herkimer, Jefferson, Lewis, Madison, Oneida, Onandago, Oswego, Otsego, St Lawrence, Tioga, and Tompkins)
Albany, NY	18 counties around Albany (Albany, Clinton, Columbia, Delaware, Essex, Franklin, Fulton, Greene, Hamilton, Montgomery, Rensselaer, Saratoga, Schenectady, Sullivan, Troy, Ulster, Warren, and Washington)
Buffalo	6 counties around Buffalo (Allegheny, Cattargus, Chautauga, Erie, Niagara, and Wyoming)
Rochester, NY	11 counties around Rochester (Chemung, Genesee, Livingston, Monroe, Ontario, Orleans, Schuyler, Seneca, Steuben, Wayne, and Yates)
Upper West Side of Manhattan	3 health districts in Manhattan, New York City (Riverside, Washington Heights, and central Harlem)
Brooklyn, NY	6 health districts in Brooklyn (Williamsburg-Greenpoint, Redhook-Gowanus, Fort Green, Brownsville, Bushwick, and Bedford-Stuyvesant)
Arizona	Arizona
Cleveland	Cleveland
Wayne County, Michigan (including Detroit)	Wayne County
Southeastern Los Angeles County	1 health region in Los Angeles County (including Watts)
Central Los Angeles and San Gabriel Valley	2 health regions in Los Angeles County (including Los Angeles and eastern suburbs)
Coastal Los Angeles County	1 health region in southern Los Angeles County along Pacific Coast
San Diego	San Diego County
Dallas County	Dallas County
Harris County, Texas	Harris County (including Houston)
Tarrant County, Texas	Tarrant County (including Fort Worth)

*RWJF indicates Robert Wood Johnson Foundation.

from reproduced computer tapes of births and matched infant death and birth certificates for the years 1970 through 1979 obtained from state and local health offices. The lack of availability for matched infant death/birth tapes for the entire decade placed some restrictions on the analysis, such as the number of comparison areas for the Los Angeles regions. In addition, such data could be obtained for only half the decade for the comparison area selected for Arizona (Oklahoma) and for a portion of one of the RWJF regions (the part of Cuyahoga County outside the city of Cleveland). The analysis was restricted to single live births to residents of the region. Rates are reported for two-year periods combined: 1970 and 1971, 1974 and 1975, and 1978 and 1979.

Three variables obtained from the vital statistics data were used in this report: (1) birth weight, which was coded as 1,500 g or less, 1,501 to 2,500 g, and more than 2,500 g ($\leq$1,500 g was designated as very low birth weight [VLBW]; $\leq$2,500 g [including the VLBW group], LBW; and >2,500 g, normal birth weight); (2) neonatal mortality rate, ie, the number of infant deaths up to 27 days of age per 1,000 single live births; and (3) tertiary center, ie, hospital of birth, located in the region, averaging

more than 1,000 deliveries annually over the decade as indicated in the American Hospital Association (AHA) guide issues,[16-18] and noted to have a neonatal intensive care unit in the *AHA Guide* of 1980[16] and/or in the list of such units compiled by Ross Laboratories.[19]

Infant morbidity information was obtained only for the RWJF regions. Changes in health problems, medical care use, and developmental status of surviving infants were assessed for a sample of infants born to residents of the region in a six-month period in 1976 (early in the program) as compared with another sample of infants born in the same six-month period in either 1978 or 1979. Infants for the survey were selected at random from the birth certificate file to include almost all infants weighing 2,500 g or less and 3% of infants weighing more than 2,500 g, all regions combined. Both survey methods[20] and results[21] have been published elsewhere and will only be summarized briefly herein.

The focus of this report was in the proportion of infants with a combination of congenital anomalies and/or developmental delay (CA/delay): severe, moderate, and mild. (*Severe CA/delay* was defined as the presence of a congenital anomaly likely to shorten life or affect functioning severely and/or gross motor delay corresponding to a developmental quotient [DQ] of <70; *moderate CA/delay*, a congenital anomaly likely to affect functioning moderately and/or gross motor performance corresponding to a DQ of 70 to 79; and *mild congenital anomaly*, a congenital anomaly likely to have minor effect on functioning.) This type of morbidity was of interest because previous studies indicated an association between CA/delay and factors, including birth weight, that affect the risk of neonatal mortality,[22] and because description of potential changes in the burden of morbidity from all conditions associated with antenatal and intrapartum events, rather than selected conditions such as neurodevelopmental outcomes, was considered important in assessing the impact of changes in neonatal mortality on infant health.

The association between the rates of decline of the neonatal mortality rates and the rate of change in place of delivery was assessed using Kendall's T̂. Because of the small number of observations (N=13), such a nonparametric measure of the independence of two variables in a single sample was considered desirable.[23] Kendall's T̂ is interpreted in a way similar to a correlation coefficient. The greater the deviation of T̂ from zero in either the positive or negative direction (and the smaller the accompanying α-level, an indication of statistical significance), the greater the likelihood that the variables are associated.[23]

RESULTS

Changes in Neonatal Mortality and LBW Rates

The RWJF and comparison regions varied substantially in annual number of births to residents, from 7,000 in the Upper West Side of Manhattan to more than 40,000 in central Los Angeles and Wayne County. Almost all regions, with the exception of Arizona, experienced a decline in the number of births in the early part of the decade, with an increase toward the end of the period of observation. This increase was generally more prominent in the southwestern regions. The number of births in the RWJF regions and the comparison areas was comparable (Table 2).

The proportion of LBW infants also varied, from more than 10% in the New York City areas to under 6% in several areas. When the RWJF regions were combined, 6.4% of the births in 1974 and 1975 were LBW, an 8% relative decrease from 1970 and

Table 2.—Single Births, Total and by Birth Weight, in RWJF* and Comparison Regions

	1970/1971	1974/1975	1978/1979
Total			
RWJF regions combined	424,952	371,352	407,353
Comparison regions combined	454,031	370,430	392,830
% of infants weighing ≤2,500 g			
RWJF regions combined	6.94	6.37	6.04
Comparison regions combined	7.78	7.35	6.96
% of infants weighing ≤1,500 g			
RWJF regions combined	0.96	0.92	0.99
Comparison regions combined	1.15	1.16	1.17

*RWJF indicates Robert Wood Johnson Foundation.

Table 3.—Neonatal Mortality Rates, Total and by Birth Weight, in RWJF* and Comparison Regions

	1970/1971	1974/1975	1978/1979
Total			
RWJF regions combined	11.53	9.51	7.66
Comparison regions combined	13.12	11.05	8.24
Infants weighing ≤2,500 g			
RWJF regions combined	116.51	102.11	87.34
Comparison regions combined	122.18	109.22	88.30
Infants weighing ≤1,500 g			
RWJF regions combined	559.39	509.43	421.12
Comparison regions combined	555.73	523.83	402.82

*RWJF indicates Robert Wood Johnson Foundation.

1971. During the program period, a further decrease of 6% was observed, for a total of 13% relative decrease over the decade. The proportion of LBW infants in the comparison areas was higher than that seen in the RWJF regions throughout the decade due to a slightly higher proportion of nonwhite births, but similar modest declines were observed. (This difference does not affect the interpretation of these results, which rely on birth weight-specific rates.)

Although the total proportion of LBW infants declined over the decade in both RWJF and comparison regions, the proportion weighing 1,500 g or less increased slightly. Thus, by the end of the decade, the composition of the LBW group was more heavily weighted by the highest-risk infants.

In contrast to the rather modest changes in birth weight, neonatal mortality rates declined sharply in both RWJF and comparison areas (Table 3). In the RWJF regions, the neonatal mortality declined by 34% during the 1970s; the decline was the same in the funded period as before (19% v 17%, respectively). A comparable decline was observed in comparison areas, 37% over the dec-

ade. In these regions, the decline was greater in the latter part of the decade as compared with the period before 1974 and 1975 (25% v 16%, respectively).

Increased survival of LBW infants was a major factor in the decline in neonatal mortality. Further analysis (not shown) disclosed that more than two thirds of the change in neonatal mortality could be accounted for by reductions in mortality for LBW infants. Neonatal mortality for LBW infants decreased by 25% in the RWJF regions and 28% in the comparison areas (Table 3). The rate of decline in the LBW group accelerated after 1974 and 1975 in all regions, a trend more noticeable for the VLBW group than for the entire group of LBW infants.

Changes in Place of Delivery

The pattern of sharp decrease in neonatal mortality with only modest declines in the proportion of LBW infants suggested changes in the hospital-based management of high-risk infants once they are born to increase their chances of survival, including intensive-care management of very-high-risk infants. In the regionalized

Table 4. — Single Live Births Delivered in Tertiary Centers,* Total and by Birth Weight, in RWJF† and Comparison Regions‡

	1970/1971	1974/1975	1978/1979
% of total			
RWJF regions combined	32.04	35.97	43.32
Comparison regions combined	26.13	28.38	30.58
% of infants weighing ≤2,500 g			
RWJF regions combined	36.27	42.35	50.39
Comparison regions combined	29.00	32.71	39.79
% of infants weighing ≤1,500 g			
RWJF regions combined	35.72	47.30	59.40
Comparison regions combined	29.67	34.18	47.19

*A tertiary center was a hospital averaging more than 1,000 deliveries annually over the decade and reported as having a neonatal intensive care unit in 1979 and 1980.
†RWJF indicates Robert Wood Johnson Foundation.
‡Texas regions not included; hospital of delivery not recorded on birth certificates.

model described earlier, the process of care for high-risk deliveries included early assessment of obstetrical risk and transfer of the management of high-risk deliveries to tertiary centers, either in the form of an antenatal referral or maternal transfer. In either case, if this regionalized model were operating, a change in the place of delivery would have occurred such that higher-risk infants would have been more likely to be born in tertiary centers. The alternative, an increased survival of LBW infants without a shift in place of delivery, would have suggested a diffusion of intensive-care techniques to community hospitals. To address these questions, the proportion of infants of different birth weights born in the tertiary centers was examined.

As indicated in Table 4, about one third of the births in the RWJF regions were occurring in tertiary centers, regardless of birth weight at the beginning of the 1970 decade. By the end of the decade, a clear gradient by birth weight had emerged, such that about 40% of all births, 50% of LBW births, and 60% of VLBW births were occurring in tertiary centers. Similar changes were seen in the comparison areas, although the percentage of births in tertiary centers was generally lower than that in the RWJF regions. In all areas, this difference in hospital of birth by birth weight by 1978 and 1979 was seen among white and nonwhite births. The degree to which changes in neonatal mortality were associated with these shifts in the proportion of births in tertiary centers was then examined (Table 5). A general pattern emerged that those regions with

greater increases in the proportion of infants born in tertiary centers experienced greater declines in neonatal mortality rates, expressed as a positive ↑. The association between these two changes was particularly strong for LBW and VLBW infants early in the decade (1970 and 1971 through 1974 and 1975). Potential reasons for some of the variation in these associations are noted in a later section. In summary, however, the results showed changes in the site of delivery consistent with regionalization, and these changes were associated with decreases in neonatal mortality.

Effect of RWJF Program

The results provide little evidence of a special effect of the RWJF program, as measured by comparisons in the changes in neonatal outcome and site delivery. For example, while the decline in neonatal mortality rates, especially among LBW and VLBW infants, accelerated during the period of funding, these changes were no greater than those observed in the comparison areas for the same period. Also, the rate of centralization of high-risk deliveries in tertiary centers was not strikingly greater than 1974 and 1975 in the RWJF regions as compared with the remaining areas.

Changes in Morbidity Among Surviving Infants

The similarity in the changes in pregnancy outcome and perinatal services between the RWJF and the comparison areas suggested that changes in morbidity associated with antenatal and perinatal events among the surviving infants observed in the RWJF regions would be of broader

significance. In the 1976 cohort, the proportion of all infants with CA/delay of all types was 15.5%; with severe CA/delay, 1.7%. This varied with birth weight, however, from 15.0% of those weighing more than 2,500 g to 49.3% of those weighing 1,500 g or less. Infants with severe CA/delay ranged from 1.6% of those weighing more than 2,500 g to 14.2% of those weighing 1,500 g or less.

Near the end of the funding period in 1978 and 1979, neonatal mortality in the sample cohort was 18% lower than in the 1976 cohort. The proportion of infants with CA/delay had decreased relatively by 16%, from 15.5% to 13.1%. This change was seen in all birth-weight groups, ranging from a 15% relative decrease for those weighing more than 2,500 g (down to 12.7%) to 22% in the group weighing 1,500 g or less (down to 38.7%). No statistically significant change in the proportion with severe CA/delay was seen. The proportion for all single live births was 2.0%; for those weighing more than 2,500 g, 1.8%; and for those weighing 1,500 g or less, 12.3%. (Detailed analysis of changes in morbidity have been published elsewhere.[21])

COMMENT

The pattern of changes in birth-weight distribution and neonatal mortality, ie, modest declines in the proportion of LBW infants accompanied by sharp declines in neonatal mortality rates, parallels and extends the observations of others,[4,5] thereby reinforcing the conclusion of a broad national trend. More important, our results offer some insights into how these changes might be occurring.

By 1978 and 1979, in most regions in the study, there had been a large increase in the proportion of those infants at highest risk of mortality by virtue of their VLBW who were being born in tertiary centers. This change indicates that some antenatal assessment of risk is occurring and that the management of high-risk pregnancies is being transferred to the tertiary centers at some point before delivery. Moreover, this centralization of high-risk deliveries can be linked to the decrease in neonatal mortality experienced by these regions. These findings are consistent with what would be expected with regionalized perina-

Table 5.—Association* Between Changes in Neonatal Mortality and Delivery in Tertiary Hospitals

% Increase of Births in Tertiary Hospitals v % Decrease in Neonatal Mortality					
All Infants		Low-Birth-Weight Infants		Very-Low-Birth-Weight Infants	
Years	$\hat{T}$ (α)	Years	$\hat{T}$ (α)	Years	$\hat{T}$ (α)
1970/1971-1974/1975	0.051 (0.338)	1970/1971-1974/1975	0.385 (0.038)	1970/1971-1974/1975	0.436 (0.021)
1974/1975-1978/1979	0.128 (0.273)	1974/1975-1978/1979	0.308 (0.082)	1974/1975-1978/1979	−0.128 (0.273)
1970/1971-1978/1979	0.179 (0.218)	1970/1971-1978/1979	0.000 (0.500)	1970/1971-1978/1979	0.051 (0.338)

*Association expressed as Kendall's $\hat{T}$ with associated α-level for n= 13. Texas regions were eliminated from this analysis because the hospital of birth is not coded on the birth certificate file.

al services as described by Merkatz and Johnson,[2] and provide some evidence that regionalization has contributed to the improvement in pregancy outcome in these regions.

The lack of difference between the RWJF regions and the comparison regions in this regard is not altogether unexpected. Local conditions and priorities led to considerable heterogeneity in the focus and pace of activities in the RWJF regions. Although the degree of change in the comparison areas would not have been predicted at the start of the program, subsequent events may have increased the attention paid to the identification of obstetric risk and referral of high-risk patients. In paricular, the publication of the National Foundation-March of Dimes recommendations[1] and the recognion given to RWJF program particibants[24] may have encouraged regionalization in the absence of specific 'unding. The result of these factors would have been to diminish the lifference between the RWJF and comparison areas.

While the effect of these events makes the detection of a program effect difficult, it acts to enhance the generalizability of the findings concerning morbidity in the surviving infants in the RWJF regions. In this period of rapid decline in neonatal mortality, the risk of CA/delay of all types combined has declined, and no change has occurred in the proportion severely affected. These changes are seen in every birth-weight group, including the VLBW infants, a subgroup with especially high mortality and morbidity. These results argue that the declines in neonatal mortality are not being accompanied by increases in infant morbidity related to antenatal and intrapartum events.

The broad level at which the analysis in this report is being conducted should be recognized. At this level, many issues of importance in the organization of perinatal services cannot be addressed. For example, the degree to which access to tertiary services varies within regions among different subgroups in the population is difficult to determine, especially in densely populated, urban regions, although the experience in large regions such as Upstate New York and Arizona suggest that the tertiary centers are receiving referrals from providers throughout the region. In addition, the contribution of transport systems to the shift in site of delivery and to increased access after delivery for high-risk neonates cannot be assessed. Finally, since the analysis is restricted to hospital of birth in the defined regions, tertiary care that may be received by residents of the region in hospitals outside the region would not be reflected in the analysis.

Besides questions of access to tertiary services, the lack of detailed clinical information on the birth certificate does not permit the determination of the obstetric problems that were more likely to be recognized early enough for antepartum referral and the changes in perinatal services that contributed to the decline in adverse outcome. It should be noted that, although most of the hospitals classified as tertiary centers by the criteria in this report are readily recognizable as university teaching hospitals, this fact does not preclude variation in the content and volume of perinatal services from one part of the decade to the next. Since VLBW infants would be more likely to require the most sophisticated technology, potential disparities in service would be most likely to affect this group, and this might account for the relatively weaker relationship between neonatal mortality and

changes in hospital of birth for this group after 1974 and 1975.

The success of many of these regions in achieving a high degree of centralization of high-risk deliveries might itself act to weaken the relationship between changes in site of delivery and mortality. In regions where the majority of such infants were alreay being delivered in tertiary centers, the opportunity of further substantially increasing the proportion born in such centers is limited. Continued decreases in neonatal mortality for these infants would require improvements in management both at the tertiary and community hospital level, rather than further changes in the hospital of birth. This factor may be particularly relevant to changes in mortality in the latter part of the decade.

Among the services that would contribute to further decreases in the neonatal mortality rates for these regions, services directed to the acceleration in the decline of the proportion of LBW and VLBW in infants assume special importance. Although the results of this and other studies support the conclusion that a major factor in the current declines in neonatal mortality in the United States has been the increased survival of LBW infants, in part through the application of more intensive management techniques such as those available in tertiary centers, the costs associated with this type of management are high, especially for the VLBW group. Furthermore, while our inquiry in the RWJF regions found a decrease in the proportion of surviving infants with CA/delay, the LBW, and particularly VLBW, infants remain at relatively high risk for these conditions. Thus, services that might reduce neonatal mortality through decreasing the proportion of such high-risk infants would also contribute to a decrease in the morbidity among survivors.

In summary, in the regions in this study, the neonatal mortality rates have decreased sharply despite only relatively modest declines in the proportion of LBW infants. Concomitant with the declines in neonatal mortality, changes in the site of delivery are occurring that are consistent with antepartum identification of obstetric risk and transfer of management of high-risk pregnancies to tertiary centers for delivery. These changes in service pattern can be linked to the decreases in neonatal mortality. This

phenomenon does not appear to be an isolated event as similar changes have occurred in regions quite heterogeneous with respect to geography, size, and medical care, and are sufficiently widespread so that the effects of a program funded by the RWJF to accelerate regionalization could not be detected. Moreover, although these changes in mortality have resulted in the increased survival of LBW and VLBW infants, no increases in the proportion of surviving infants with morbidity related to antepartum and intrapartum events has been seen. In view of the high degree of concentra-

tion of high-risk deliveries alrea reached in many of these region further reductions in neonatal mo tality will require the implementati of other services on a regionwi basis—especially services direct toward the reduction of LBW births

This investigation was supported by a gr from the Robert Wood Johnson Foundati Princeton, NJ.

State and local health departments provid access to reproduced statistical birth and dea record information, and the morbidity surve staff also participated in this study. Barba Crawley and Marcia Sass provided techni assistance. Dianne Greer provided cleri assistance in the preparation of the mar script.

References

1. Usher R: Clinical implications of perinatal mortality statistics. *Clin Obstet Gynecol* 1971; 14:885-925.

2. Merkatz IR, Johnson KG: Regionalization of perinatal care for the United States. *Clin Perinatol* 1976;3:371-376.

3. *Toward Improving the Outcome of Pregnancy*. White Plains, NY, The National Foundation-March of Dimes, 1976.

4. Kleinman JC, Kovar MG, Feldman JJ, et al: A comparison of 1960 and 1973-1974 early neonatal mortality in selected states. *Am J Epidemiol* 1978;108:454-469.

5. Lee KS, Paneth N, Gartner LM, et al: Neonatal mortality: An analysis of the recent improvements in the United States. *Am J Public Health* 1980;70:15-21.

6. Budetti P, McManus P, Barrand N, et al: *The Implications of Cost-Effectiveness Analysis of Technology: Background Paper #2: Case-Studies of Medical Technologies (Neonatal Intensive Care)*, publication DTA-BP-H-9 (10). Washington, DC, Congress of the United States, Office of Technology Assessment, 1980.

7. Horwood SP, Boyle MH, Torrance GW, et al: Mortality and morbidity of 500- to 1,499-gram birthweight infants live-born to residents of a defined geographic region before and after neonatal intensive care. *Pediatrics* 1982;69:613-620.

8. Paneth N, Kiely JL, Wallenstein S, et al: Newborn intensive care and neonatal mortality in low-birthweight infants. *N Engl J Med* 1982;

307:149-155.

9. Swyer PR: The regional organization of special care for the neonate. *Pediatr Clin North Am* 1970;17:761-775.

10. Sinclair JC, Torrance GW, Boyle MH, et al: Evaluation of neonatal intensive-care programs. *N Engl J Med* 1981;305:489-494.

11. Luft HS, Bunker JP, Enthoven AC: Should operations be regionalized?: The empirical relationship between surgical volume and mortality. *N Engl J Med* 1979;301:1364-1369.

12. Finkler SA: Cost-effectiveness of regionalizations: The heart surgery example. *Inquiry* 1979;16:264-270.

13. Ginzburg E: The many meanings of regionalization, in Ginzburg E (ed): *Regionalization and Health Policy*, publication (HRS) 77-623. Dept of Health, Education, and Welfare, 1977.

14. Klein MC, Papageorgiu AN: Can perinatal regionalization be reconciled with family centered maternal care. *J Fam Pract* 1977;5:969-974.

15. Ryan GM, Fielden JG: The impact of regionalization on patterns of perinatal care. *Obstet Gynecol* 1979;53:187-189.

16. *American Hospital Association Guide to the Health Care Field, 1980 Edition*. Chicago, American Hospital Association, 1980.

17. *American Hospital Association Guide to the Health Care Field, 1970 Edition*. Chicago, American Hospital Association, 1970.

18. *American Hospital Association Guide the Health Care Field, 1975 Edition*. Americ Hospital Association, 1975.

19. *1979 Guide to Referral Centers Providi Perinatal and Neonatal Care*. Columbus, Oh Ross Planning Associates, 1979.

20. McCormick MC, Wessel KW, Krischer et al: Preliminary analysis of development observations in a survey of morbidity in infan *Early Hum Dev* 1981;5:377-393.

21. Shapiro S, McCormick MC, Starfield B et al: Changes in infant morbidity associat with decreases in neonatal mortality. *Pediatr* 1983;72:408-415.

22. Shapiro S, McCormick MC, Starfield B, al: Relevance of correlates of infant deaths f significant morbidity at one year. *Am J Obs Gynecol* 1980;136:363-373.

23. Hollander M, Wolfe DA: *Non-parametri Statistical Methods*. New York, John Wiley Sons Inc, 1973.

24. Merkatz IR, Hobel CJ: A functioni regional perinatal system. Presented as a scie tific exhibition at the 25th annual meeting of t American College of Obstetrics and Gynecolog Chicago, May 1977.

25. Boyle MH, Torrance GW, Sinclair JC, et Economic evaluation of neonatal intensive ca of very-low-birthweight infants. *N Engl J M* 1983;308:1330-1337.

6

Hospital-Sponsored Primary Care
I. Organizational and Financial Effects

Stephen M. Shortell, Thomas M. Wickizer, and John R.C. Wheeler

Abstract: Findings are presented from a seven-year (1976–83) evaluation of the Community Hospital Program (CHP), a national demonstration program sponsored by the Robert Wood Johnson Foundation to assist 54 community hospitals in improving the organization of access to primary care. Upon grant expiration, 66 per cent of hospital-sponsored group practices continued under some form of hospital sponsorship; over 90 per cent developed or were planning to develop spin-off programs; and new physicians were recruited and retained in the community. About 9 per cent of hospital admissions were accounted for by group physicians and grantee hospitals experienced a greater annual increase in their market share of admissions than competing hospitals in the area.

While only three of the groups generated sufficient revenue to cover expenses during the grant period, 21 additional groups broke even during the first post-grant year. Productivity and cost per visit compared favorably with most other forms of care. Hospitalization rates from the hospital-sponsored practices were somewhat lower than those for other forms of care. Medical director leadership and involvement and the organization design of the practice were among several key factors associated with higher performing practices. The ability of such joint hospital-physician ventures to meet the needs of the poor and elderly in a time of Medicare and Medicaid cutbacks is discussed along with suggestions for targeting future initiatives in primary care. (Am J Public Health 1984; 74:784–791.)

Introduction

This is the first of two articles which summarize the major findings from an independent evaluation of the Community Hospital Program (CHP), a national demonstration program sponsored by the Robert Wood Johnson Foundation to assist community hospitals in improving the organization of primary care in their areas. The Foundation provided approximately $27 million in grants to 54 hospitals* for a period of up to four years and in an amount up to $500,000 per hospital. Awards were made over a three year period beginning May, 1976 for purposes of program planning and development including salary support for physicians and other professional/clerical staff and funds for equipment and supplies.[1,2] Hospitals were expected to assure the availability of appropriate facilities. It was expected that the groups would continue under hospital sponsorship upon grant expiration and would obtain continuing financial support (from the hospital or other sources) if their revenues did not cover their operating expenses.

While the original idea of hospital-sponsored or affiliated group practices can be traced to the Committee on the Costs of Medical Care[3] in 1932, the more immediate impetus for the CHP were concerns about access to primary care which had developed in many American communities in the early 1970s. These included:

● Access problems in low income rural and urban inner-city areas and in many parts of more middle class urban and suburban areas, as evidenced by increasing demands for community hospitals to provide front-line primary care;[4–7]
● There were thought to be too many specialists and not enough generalists available to provide primary care;[5–8]
● The existing system of care was fragmented and poorly integrated, resulting in inappropriate use of services, discontinuity, and considerable consumer dissatisfaction;[5–7] and
● It was assumed that many of these problems could be addressed by a rational reorganization of hospital primary care services.[5–7,9,10]

The Community Hospital Program (CHP) was intended to correct these deficiencies by forging partnerships between hospitals and physicians to provide front-line primary care. These partnerships were to build in the following elements: linkages of patients with one particular physician whom they would see regularly for care; 24-hour coverage; comprehensive, continuous care for the entire family in a single setting; and the benefit of an organized referral system to assure the accessibility of both specialty and inpatient hospital services.[11]

As a group, the 53 grantees were generally similar to community hospitals nationwide, being located in all regions of the country and ranging in bed size from 38 to 800 beds. However, more of the grantees were religion-affiliated hospitals (40 per cent) than is true for community hospitals nationwide, and grantee hospitals tended to have somewhat higher cost per adjusted patient day ($133.43 in 1975—the base year before funding) than community hospitals who did not apply for funding ($118.61). Twenty-four sites were located in urban areas, 17 in rural areas, and 12 in suburban areas; 29 were located on hospital grounds and 24 off grounds; 31 were single specialty (i.e., family medicine) practices while 22 were multi-specialty. Most of the practices represented newly developed groups, employed physicians on a straight salary, and had their own on-site laboratory. Slightly over one-third of the groups used nurse practitioners and/or physician assistants, about one-fourth had some on-site radiology exam capability, and approximately one-fifth had a residency program affiliation.

Methods

The organizational evaluation was designed to answer four major questions. First, could hospitals and their medical

---

* Awards were made to 54 grantees, one of which was returned. One award was made jointly to two hospitals. Thus there were 53 grantees and 54 hospitals involved in the program.

Address reprint requests to Stephen M. Shortell, PhD, A.C. Buehler Distinguished Professor of Hospital and Health Services Management, and Professor of Organization Behavior, J.L. Kellogg Graduate School of Management, and Center for Health Services and Policy Research, Northwestern University, Evanston, IL 60201. Mr. Wickizer was Research Associate and Project Director, Department of Health Services, School of Public Health and Community Medicine, University of Washington, Seattle and is currently a doctoral student in the Health Services Organization and Policy Program at the School of Public Health at the University of Michigan; Dr. Wheeler is Associate Professor, Program in Hospital Administration, School of Public Health, University of Michigan, Ann Arbor. This paper, submitted to the Journal November 1, 1983, was revised and accepted for publication February 14, 1984.

Editor's Note: See also related article p 792 and editorial p 759 this issue.

staffs become committed to providing primary care on an ongoing basis? Second, could such involvement result in improved organization of access to care through recruitment and retention of new physicians to the community? Third, could such a program have positive effects on the financial viability of the hospital? Fourth, could hospital-sponsored group practices break even financially upon grant expiration or within a reasonable time period thereafter? The first two questions, involving ongoing commitment and improving the organization of access, address "social efficiency" issues; the latter two questions, involving the financial impact on the hospital and the break-even status of the group itself, address "managerial efficiency" issues. Due to resource constraints, it was not possible to compare over time the grantees with those applicants who were not funded but went ahead with practices anyway. Limited first year comparisons are reported elsewhere.[12] It is important to note that the CHP represents only one generic model of providing primary care and the evaluation is limited to this model and not a comparison of alternative models. The absence of explicit comparison groups or models limits the degree to which the outcomes observed can be attributed solely to the influence of the CHP. It is possible that other factors were operating to produce these outcomes and it is also possible that other forms of primary care might achieve equivalent or better results. However, some of the possible alternative explanations are at least partially controlled for through the multivariate statistical analysis, and 13 longitudinal comparative case studies provided further insights into the effects of the program versus other factors.

Data collection included review of application proposals; collection of financial, operational, and organizational data on an annual basis through specially designed report forms; and detailed information obtained through yearly on-site interviews with 13 groups (12 randomly selected) constituting a longitudinal comparative case study analysis.** This multiple methods approach permitted not only examination of the statistical relationships among the data but also, primarily through the 13 case studies, a more detailed and refined understanding of the factors involved in implementing the program. The present article focuses primarily on the results for all 53 grantees. The findings pertaining to the case studies are reported elsewhere.[14]

Data collection was guided by the framework shown in Figure 1 which indicates the main set of variables of interest. In brief, hospitals and their medical staffs needed to consider community demand and supply factors, and hospital background characteristics which would affect how the group practices were designed and managed. These factors would influence group productivity and physician retention which, in turn, would affect the outcome objectives of interest pertaining to ongoing commitment, improved organization of access to care, financial impact on the hospital, and financial viability of the group itself. The specific variables

examined under each set of factors are described in the Appendix.

The relationships suggested in Figure 1 were tested through ordinary least squares regression and logistic regression[15,16] when the assumptions of ordinary least squares regression were not met.

Results

Achievement of Program Objectives

Findings pertaining to the degree to which program objectives were met are shown in Table 1 and discussed below. Unless otherwise indicated, they are based on each grantee's experience as of the end of the grant period.

Hospital Ongoing Commitment to Primary Care

Sixty-six per cent of the grantees (35/53) continued under some form of hospital sponsorship upon termination of the grant. Sponsorship ranged from a relatively loose affiliation such as leasing of facilities (four groups) to more formal arrangements involving ongoing contractual relationships between the group physicians and the hospital (3 groups). Eleven additional groups terminated their relationship with the hospital after grant funds expired, but continued as independent group practices in the community. Seven of the 53 groups discontinued operations before grant funds expired.

Ongoing commitment to primary care was also evidenced by the number of "spin-off" programs developed by the hospitals. Three-fourths of the grantees developed at least one such initiative while an additional 17 per cent were planning to develop such initiatives. In addition, both the group practices and the hospitals provided an average of nearly one additional organized innovative service over the course of the grant (see Table 1).

Improving Organization of Access to Primary Care

Upon grant expiration, 57 per cent of the groups (29/51)*** had three or more full-time equivalent (FTE) physicians with an overall average of 3.51 full-time equivalent (FTE) physicians per group. As shown in Table 1, an average of 3.2 new FTE physicians were brought into the community. These included those practicing with the groups as well as others who left the group but who were still practicing in the community. The majority of physicians recruited were board-certified with many being recent graduates of family medicine residency programs. Annual average physician turnover was 10.6 per cent (12.1 per cent multispecialty, 9.5 per cent single specialty, no differences by location of site). This is as low or lower than that reported elsewhere.[17] In addition to the regular hours offered by group practices, the main attractions to physicians were: the ability to build a practice quickly with relatively little risk involved; the ability to practice medicine as they were trained during their residency program; the ease of integrating primary, secondary, and tertiary services; and, for some, involvement in larger hospital policy-making and health delivery issues. Primary disadvantages involved what was perceived to be overly tight hospital supervision and control (lack of autonomy) in a number of cases, and the inability to build equity in the practice.

** The 12 case study sites were randomly selected from among the first 42 grantees funded as of July 1, 1977. Five of the 42 were eliminated from consideration because they were judged to be poor candidates for long-run survival and a sixth case which was outside the continental US was deleted due to high data collection costs. The remaining 36 sites were stratified on their likely effect on improving access to primary care (high, medium, and low) and on their likely organizational ability to implement the program (high, medium, and low). Sites were randomly selected within each of the strata. Those grantees served as case study sites for both the organizational analysis and the household-interview based access analysis.[13]

*** Two groups left the program in very early stages and thus had no opportunity to develop a stable group.

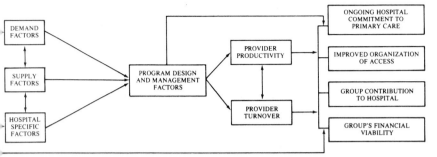

FIGURE 1—Framework for Community Hospital Program Evaluation

Sixty per cent of the groups provided after hours (evening and weekend) care. Overall, an average of five additional hours of care was provided per week beyond the usual 9 to 5 office hours.

The data also indicate that the groups were attracting some patients (approximately 9 per cent) from their hospitals' emergency rooms. Twenty-three of the grantees indicated that a major reason for entering the program was to reorganize their outpatient department and/or transfer non-emergent and non-urgent patients from their emergency room to the primary care group practices. These grantees had a significantly higher volume of emergency room visits in 1976 (the beginning of grant awards for most groups) than other grantees and were also more likely to locate their practices on hospital grounds. However, the percentage of their patient visits coming from the emergency room was no higher than that for other grantees. Case study findings suggest two reasons for the lack of a greater shift in non-emergent and non-urgent emergency room patients. First, faced with close medical staff scrutiny, if not opposition, most grantees followed strict emergency room on-call procedures for referrals and were careful not to show any favoritism to the hospital-sponsored group. Second, during the period 1976–82, a number of grantees, following a national trend, contracted with physician groups to provide emergency room care. It was usually in the economic interest of these groups to serve even the non-urgent patients rather than refer them to other physicians.

The case study analyses also suggest that in some cases hospital-sponsored primary care groups may be an effective way of providing comprehensive, coordinated medical care to underserved populations. A number of the inner-city grantees built modern well-equipped facilities staffing them with recent residency program graduates and offering a comprehensive range of services and a different type of care than was previously available from the hospitals' emergency room or outpatient department.

Data also indicate that the groups were reaching their target populations. For example, for the low-income urban sites, 32 per cent of their revenue was from Medicaid patients, a percentage that compares favorably with 39.6 per cent Medicaid reported in a study of a small private urban

hospital emergency room,[18] 36 per cent in a study of 135 hospital clinics in New York[19] and 19.4 per cent in a study of the outpatient department at Beth Israel in Boston.[20]† The fact that the group practices received a relatively small percentage of their patient visits from the hospital emergency room or outpatient department suggests that many of the Medicaid patients were new to the hospital rather than simply a re-distribution of patients from the emergency room or outpatient department.

Financial Impact on the Sponsoring Hospital

Group practice patients accounted for an average of 9 per cent of all hospital admissions (Table 1). As expected, this figure was higher for smaller hospitals and for practices located on hospital grounds. However, several larger hospitals (400–500 beds) also benefited greatly with group physicians accounting for between 20 and 30 per cent of all admissions. This is similar to other findings reported in the literature.[22]

It has been suggested that physicians practicing in such groups might hospitalize patients more frequently than other physicians in the community and thus increase costs.[23] The average number of admissions per FTE physician per month among grantees was 10. While national data are not available, this figure compares favorably with a derived figure of 12 admissions per physician per month†† reported in a study of Washington state family practitioners providing care in a variety of settings.[24] Overall, group patients averaged 3.5 admissions per 100 office visits. Assuming a national average of approximately 3.5 office visits per person per year this amounts to 12.25 admissions per 100 people which is somewhat less than the national average of 14.2/100.[25] Further, Aday, et al, in their companion study of utilization in 12 of the CHP communities found that inpatient use was comparable to that of other sources of care.[13] While the above data

———————
† Overall, the CHP grantees may be providing a slightly higher percentage of Medicaid services (15.7 per cent of revenue) than community hospital outpatient departments nationally (11 per cent of expenses).[21]

†† Three admissions per 100 office visits per physician were reported. Assuming 20 visits per day, 100 office visits constitute one week. Multiplying three admissions per week by four yields 12 admissions per month.

TABLE 1—Summary of Performance Measures (n = 53) at Expiration of Grant

Concept and Measure	Mean or Per Cent (Standard Deviation)	Range
1. Ongoing Commitment to Primary Care		
Continued hospital sponsorship	66%	
Mean number of hospital spinoff programs developed*	2.47 (1.53)	0 to 6
Growth in innovative services provided by group**	.961 (1.75)	−1.98 to 5.30
Growth in innovative services provided by hospital**	.881 (2.04)	−3.78 to 6.40
2. Improving Organization of Access to Primary Care		
Number of group FTE physicians upon grant expiration	3.51 (1.93)	1 to 11.5
Number of new FTE primary care physicians brought to the community***	3.20 (2.44)	0 to 12
Number of after-hours care provided per week	4.80 (7.25)	0 to 36
Per cent patients received for initial care from emergency room	4.10% (6.53%)	0 to 40%
Per cent patients received for follow-up care from emergency room	4.50% (4.32%)	0 to 21%
3. Financial Impact on Sponsoring Hospital		
Per cent total hospital admissions accounted for by group physicians	9.1% (19.1%)	0 to 88%
Change in annual market share of admissions†	1.3% (5.5%)	−9.2 to 29.7%
Group laboratory tests per total hospital admissions	.55 (1.10)	0 to 5.20
Group radiology exams per total hospital admissions	.21 (.33)	0 to 1.71
4. Group Financial Indicators		
Operating Margin††	−.29 (.19)	−.673 to .085
Visits per FTE physician per year‡	4,568 (1,392)	2,194 to 8,375
Direct cost per visit‡‡	$28.04 ($7.36)	$12.40 to $45.87

*Examples of "spin-off" programs include developing a new clinic, health center, ambulatory surgery unit, or becoming involved in a health maintenance organization.
**A service was defined as innovative if it represented a specifically designated program offered by the group or hospital beyond the usual provision of care and usually with a specific individual in charge. Examples include organized health screening programs, health education classes, and school health exams. An index of innovativeness was constructed for each grantee based on the formula: $1 - \frac{n}{N}$ where n = the number of grantees offering a specific service and N = 53, representing the total number of grantees.
***Includes physicians who left the group practice but stayed in the community.
†Measures the degree to which the grantee hospitals average annual percentage increase in admissions exceeds that of competing hospitals over the period 1976–81.
††Operating Margin = Net operating revenue minus direct expenses divided by direct expenses. A negative figure indicates a deficit, zero indicates the break-even point, and a positive figure indicates a surplus.
‡The number of visits are based on an average working year of 47 weeks and includes both office and hospital visits.
‡‡None of the groups allocated indirect costs to the group using any of the conventional cost allocation methods. Most of these costs were directly incorporated as part of the budget for the group and paid for under the terms of the grant. Space costs and hospital administrative overhead costs are not included.

and comparisons do not reflect adjustments for age, sex, case severity, or health status, they do not provide support for the belief that physicians associated with hospital-sponsored groups hospitalize patients more frequently than physicians associated with other forms of practice or more frequently than the national average.

Grantees' average annual market share of inpatient admissions increased slightly over that of its perceived competitors (Table 1). Overall, approximately two-thirds of the grantees showed some increase in average annual market share of admissions. In the absence of a true experiment, it not possible to attribute this increase to the effects of the CHP, but it is important to note that both the grantee hospitals and their perceived competitors were subject to the same external market, legal, regulatory, and political forces operating in their respective areas.

In addition to admissions, groups also contributed ancillary revenue to the hospital through use of the hospital laboratory and radiology services. Over the course of the grant, hospitals experienced an average annual inflation adjusted increase of 5 per cent in laboratory and radiology revenues—some of which can be attributed to the volume generated by group physicians. In addition to their direct impact on hospital use, 6.7 per cent of patient visits to the group practice physicians resulted in referrals to specialists in the community. There were no differences in regard to practice location, whether the practice was multi-specialty or single specialty, or whether or not an incentive payment arrangement existed.

Group Financial Status, Productivity, and Costs

Generating sufficient revenues to cover expenses was the most difficult criterion for the groups to meet. Only three of the groups were able to break even or generate revenue in excess of expenses by the time the grant expired. However, an additional 21 of the 39 groups followed over the subsequent year did break even. Of the remaining 18 groups 14 were still under some form of hospital sponsorship, all of which continued to receive financial support from the hospital or, in one case, from a hospital foundation. One additional site was an independent practice supported by a nearby medical school for residency purposes. Three additional sites had subsequently dissolved although one of these became a family practice residency training program with the hospital supporting the deficit. The average monthly estimated deficit for those sites not breaking even was approximately $3,100/month ($37,320 per year).

The groups averaged approximately 4,600 patient visits per FTE physician per year, which is comparable to that reported elsewhere for both subsidized and nonsubsidized ambulatory care programs,[26,27] but lower than the approximately 5,400 visits/FTE physician/year reported for primary care fee-for-service physicians in private practice.[28–30] Productivity was more closely related to practice volume than to internal efficiencies achieved within the practices themselves.

The average cost per visit of $28.04 (based on 1981 prices) was lower than that reported for hospital outpatient departments and emergency rooms,[22,31] and when inflation adjusted was lower than that reported for neighborhood health centers.[32] Cost per visit was comparable to or only slightly higher than that reported for private practices[26,30,3] and inner-city ambulatory care programs.[31] There was no difference in the cost per visit between practices located on hospital grounds versus those located off grounds. Care must be taken in evaluating these comparisons because the CHP data include all direct costs and many indirect costs, but not hospital administrative expenses or space costs. These comparisons must also be interpreted cautiously as they do not reflect possible differences in patient case mix or health status.

There are strong functional relationships among these measures of group financial performance. In particular hose groups able to achieve satisfactory levels of physician productivity are the groups with the lowest direct cost per isit. And, those groups with the lowest cost are typically he ones closer to achieving break-even status. Break-even tatus is also strongly affected by the revenue-generating apacity of the group, which depends on the net price per isit that the group is able to charge. This net price depends, n turn, on the levels of insurance coverage and income in he service population and prices being charged by competi-ors. Therefore, the key questions in assessing whether a group practice is likely to become financially viable are whether the group will be able to attract a sufficient volume of patients and whether these patients have the means to pay or their services. The question of operational efficiency is also important, but somewhat less so than these other considerations.

Correlates of Successful Performance

Table 2 summarizes the variables most strongly and consistently associated with achievement of program objec-ives. The major lessons and their implications are discussed below.

Hospital Ongoing Commitment to Primary Care

The stronger the degree of initial hospital commitment, the more likely the group was to remain under sponsorship. This was particularly true where the group was seen as central to the hospital's overall mission and long-run strate-gic plan. For example, one hospital developed the idea of satellite ambulatory care practices in the late 1960s as a way of attracting a more balanced mix of paying and non-paying patients and to provide additional services to outlying com-

TABLE 2—Variables Significantly Associated with Better Performance

	Regression Coefficients
A. *Ongoing Commitment to Primary Care*†	
Strong initial hospital commitment (positive)	.69**
Hospital committee involvement of group medical director (positive)	.14*
Similarity of physician ages (positive)	.39*
B. *Improving Organization of Access to Primary Care*††	
Professional organization design (positive)	.49*
Use of residents (positive)	6.15*
Suburban site location (positive)	5.81*
High volume of visits per FTE physician (positive)	.0002***
C. *Financial Impact on Sponsoring Hospital*‡	
Number of FTE physicians per hospital bed (positive)	.71***
Low physician turnover (positive)	.14**
Rural or suburban site location (positive)	.06**
D. *Group Financial Performance*‡‡	
Percentage of commercially insured patients (positive)	.19*
Price of an intermediate exam (positive)	.004*
Volume of visits per FTE physician (positive)	.001*
Multi-specialty practices (positive)	.05**
Use of nurse practitioners and/or physician assistants (positive)	.09***
Incentive compensation (positive)	.004***

*p ≤ .01.
**p ≤ .05.
***p ≤ .10.
†Between 7 and 27 per cent of the variation in Ongoing Commitment to Primary Care was explained by the variables in the model. The first coefficient shown is the maximum likelihood coefficient based on logistic regression.
††Forty per cent of the variation was explained by the variables in the model.
‡Forty-six percent of the variation was explained by the variables in the model. These results are based on pooling the data across all operational years.
‡‡Between 58 and 78 per cent of the variation was explained by the variables in the model. These results are based on pooling the data across all operational years.

munities. In this case, the Community Hospital Program was seen as central to the overall direction in which the hospital had been moving for over 10 years. In another case, an inner-city hospital made an explicit decision in the late 1970s to stay in the central city area rather than move to the suburbs. A key factor in this decision was the commitment to develop more ambulatory care and community outreach initiatives which would help establish a referral base to attract additional specialists. The Community Hospital Pro-gram represented a cornerstone of this thrust.

Group medical director involvement in hospital commit-tees and decision-making forums was also associated with ongoing commitment to primary care. Relevant committees included the hospitals' ambulatory care committee, family practice committee, management policy committee, and management executive committee. Such involvement pro-vided group medical directors with an important forum for educating others about the purposes, activities, and achieve-ments of the group, for learning about the constantly shifting hospital policies and priorities, and for influencing these future policies, plans, and priorities as they related to the delivery of primary care. Through this means, group medical directors were able to "institutionalize" primary care as an ongoing commitment of the hospital.

Similarity or homogeneity of physician ages was partic-ularly related to increases in organized innovative services provided by the group practices over the course of the program. This overall finding was further supported by the in-depth case studies which indicated that physicians of similar ages shared relatively similar practice styles and philosophies. Stronger medical directors would often "hand pick" physicians to join the group based on similarity in age, practice style, and philosophy.

In addition to the above variables, organizing the prac-tice along professional rather than bureaucratic lines[34,35] was generally associated with greater ongoing commitment to primary care. A professional design is characterized by greater involvement of physicians in administrative as well as clinical oversight of the practice, fewer bureaucratic reporting requirements, and direct access to the chief execu-tive officer of the hospital. Group practices organized this way also tended to have a considerable degree of autonomy in developing their own personnel, purchasing, and budget-ing policies and had generally strong medical director leader-ship. These characteristics greatly facilitated the likelihood that the groups would remain under hospital sponsorship by meeting physician needs of independence and a high degree of self-governance.

In addition, these characteristics reflect the reality that the needs of primary care groups differ from those of inpatient acute care institutions. Group practices require personnel who can perform generalist functions, rather than the more specialized personnel needed in hospitals. Also, group practices need to have the flexibility to purchase items quickly and usually in smaller quantities than hospitals. Thus, it was important for groups to develop their own personnel policies and job descriptions and to purchase from non-hospital vendors and commercial laboratories where prices were often cheaper. In brief, the greater the degree to which the groups could function like small independent group practices without overly bureaucratic administration, the more likely they were to maintain an ongoing relation-ship with the hospital upon expiration of program funds.

On one dimension of ongoing commitment—namely the likelihood of developing "spin-off" programs—hospital location was important. Specifically, hospitals located in suburban and urban areas were more likely to develop "spin-off" programs than those located in rural areas—primarily because for the smaller size hospitals in rural areas the group practice was meeting many of the community's needs, and also because rural hospitals lacked the resources to develop additional initiatives.

Improving Organization of Access to Primary Care

Organizing the group along professional lines also facilitated physician recruitment and retention, thus improving the overall organization of access to primary care in the communities involved (Table 2). As expected, productivity as measured by the volume of visits per FTE physician per year was also associated with improvements in the organization of access to care, primarily reflecting the existence of stable groups.

Sites using residents and sites located in suburban areas were most likely to offer after-hours care.

None of the variables in the model was significantly associated with the transfer of emergency room patients to the group practice. As previously noted, other factors were operating to dilute this effect.

Financial Impact on the Sponsoring Hospital

The size of the group in terms of FTE physicians relative to hospital bed size was strongly associated with a positive financial impact on the hospital, in terms of both admissions and ancillary services.[†††] This was as expected with the underlying variable of interest being successful physician recruitment and retention. This is further supported by the finding that low physician turnover was also associated with a positive effect on growth in hospital market share of admissions and ancillary services. Sites located in rural and suburban areas were also more likely to show increases in market share than those located in urban areas.

Group Financial Viability, Productivity and Costs

Groups with lower direct cost per visit were more likely to approach break-even status during the grant period. Direct cost per visit was influenced by the productivity of the group which was higher in rural areas and by sites using nurse practitioners and/or physician assistants. These findings are consistent with existing literature.[27,36,37] In addition, the percentage of commercially insured-patients served, the fees charged, being a multi-specialty practice, and having a physician incentive compensation plan were each positively associated with better operating margins.

A common factor associated with many of the above variables was strong medical director leadership. Such leadership facilitated physician recruitment which, in turn, helped to build volume and productivity. Strong medical directors were also able to work effectively with hospital administration and mitigate medical staff opposition through equitable referral practices and appealing largely to patients not being served by other staff members. Effective medical

---

[†††] Group practices seen as central to the hospital's mission also tended to have a positive effect on sponsoring hospitals, particularly in regard to ancillary services use. But this effect was overwhelmed by the number of FTE physicians relative to hospital bed size. In brief, a key way in which centrality to mission was expressed was through the willingness and ability to recruit and retain a stable group of primary care physicians. Smaller hospitals which were able to do this enjoyed distinct financial benefits, although several larger hospitals managed to recruit a larger number of physicians, and these hospitals also enjoyed such advantages.`

directors were generally older, highly respected members of the hospital staff or highly regarded family practice residency graduates with leadership qualities.

Other Factors

Multi-specialty practices admitted no more patients than single specialty family medicine practices, because most of the multi-specialty groups were small and often had only one internist or pediatrician in addition to a family practitioner.

A number of practices experienced problems due either to physicians moving into the area over the course of the program or to nearby hospitals starting similar programs. However, overall the competitive factors were not as important in explaining the performance outcomes as the factors described above.

Three Models

In many ways, each group practice was unique, having its own set of distinctive characteristics, history, and experience. Nonetheless, it was possible to identify three relatively distinct practice models. These included a "hospital service" model, a "hospital teaching" model, and a "private practice" model.

• The hospital service model representing 18 grantees tended to be fairly closely linked to the hospital but with an emphasis on services, rather than teaching. Specifically it was characterized by being a pre-existing group or transformed outpatient department, having greater utilization of the hospital laboratory and radiology facilities, being located on hospital grounds, and serving a higher percentage of Medicaid and low-income patients.

• The hospital teaching model representing seven grantees was also closely linked to the hospital but with greater emphasis given to teaching activities. Like the hospital service model, it tended to be a pre-existing group or reorganized outpatient department but was more likely to use residents, provided more after-hours care, served a somewhat higher income area, and had strong medical director leadership.

• The private practice model representing 26 grantees tended to be more loosely linked to the hospital. It was characterized by a high degree of operating autonomy, and a relatively low degree of linkage between the group administrator and the hospital.

None of the three models was any more likely to continue under hospital sponsorship upon grant expiration. But the hospital teaching model was more likely to show increases in the number of organized innovative services provided by the group than the other two models ($F = 4.92$; $p \le .011$) and both the hospital teaching and hospital service models were more likely to have developed spin-off programs than the private practice model ($F = 3.44$; $p \le .04$). The teaching model (because of residents) was much more likely to offer after-hours service ($F = 5.14$; $p \le .009$) and both the service and teaching models had a greater percentage of patient visits coming from the hospital emergency room than the private practice model ($F = 3.21$; $p \le .049$). There were no significant differences among the models in regard to financial impact on the hospital, although there was a tendency for the service model to have a somewhat greater impact. Finally, while there were no significant differences among the models in productivity or direct cost per visit, both the teaching and private practice models had better operating margins than the service model ($F = 6.44$; $p \le$

03), due seemingly to their ability to charge somewhat gher fees and collect a higher percentage of their revenue. rom a public policy and institutional perspective, these esults suggest that the hospital teaching and hospital service nodels are more likely to meet social efficiency objectives involving commitment to and improvement in organization f access to care while the private practice model is more kely to meet management efficiency objectives—at least elative to the financial status of the practice.

ummary

ublic Policy and Managerial Implications

The original intent of the CHP—to provide better organized primary care than that usually available in hospital outpatient departments and emergency rooms—takes on dded importance today. Cutbacks in the Medicare and Medicaid programs along with prospective payment on a xed rate per case basis are likely to impact most significant-y on the poor and elderly.[38] There is national concern that a wo-tier system of medical care will emerge with private aying patients receiving higher quality and more comprehensive care than publicly sponsored patients. The question rises as to whether new forms of hospital-physician linkges, such as hospital-medical staff sponsored group practices, can provide a more stable base for meeting the needs of the disadvantaged through pooling of human and financial resources. At the same time, hospitals and physicians are aced with increased regulatory and competitive pressures[39-41] and are actively searching for new ways of expanding patient referral bases and increasing market share. The challenge for both hospitals and physicians is to balance the social and managerial issues. Hospital-physician joint ventures are a growing response to this challenge and the findings from the present evaluation offer some insight as to heir likely success.

As a whole, our findings suggest that hospitals with a strong initial commitment to primary care, and which take into account physician needs for autonomy while at the same ime providing needed integration through active medical director involvement in key hospital committees, are more likely to show a longer run commitment to primary care. Recognizing physicians' autonomy needs is also positively associated with physician recruitment and retention helping o improve the organization of access to primary care. Successful physician recruitment and retention, in turn, is associated with a positive financial impact on the hospital through admissions and ancillary services use, particularly for smaller hospitals. The financial status of the group practice itself is primarily associated with its cost per visit which, in turn, is a function of the group's productivity, the use of nurse practitioners and/or physician assistants, a higher percentage of commercially insured patients, its fee structure, and being a multi-specialty practice. Strong medical director leadership was frequently found to be associated with these characteristics.

Given the subsidy inherent in the CHP, it is not possible to determine whether four years or more of development time is necessary for most group practices to achieve financial viability. It may be that a grant subsidy period of two to three years is sufficient to allow practices to develop sufficient physician recruitment, marketing, and service production activities, and that removal of the subsidy after this shorter period would stimulate operating efficiencies resulting in earlier attainment of financial viability. Alternatively,

a loan program tied to achievement of short-run and long-run performance objectives could be developed.

Numbers aside, perhaps the most significant contribution of the Community Hospital Program was to help clarify and demonstrate the hospital's role as a catalyst and organizer for the delivery of relatively broad-based primary health care services. Targeted federal or foundation support may be needed for selected inner-city hospitals possessing desirable characteristics. Financially weak hospitals with little capacity for ongoing support, hospitals lacking medical staff and administrative leadership, and hospitals who do not see primary care as a central part of their mission are not likely to be good candidates for hospital-physician joint ventures.

ACKNOWLEDGMENTS

This research was supported by research grants (#4106, #4189 and #7558) from the Robert Wood Johnson Foundation, Princeton, New Jersey. Appreciation is expressed to LuAnn Aday, Linda Aiken, Ronald Andersen, Robert Blendon, Howard Freeman and to reviewers for their comments and suggestions. Appreciation is also expressed to Stephen Williams, Nicole Urban, William Dowling, Betty Gilson, Scott McStravic, John Geyman, Ira Moscovice, William Richardson, Austin Ross, Ruth Riedel, Linda Curtis, Richard Holladay, Sandra Matthews, Susan Krock, Brad Miller, and Jim Wolfe for their contributions to the study over the seven-year period.

Portions of this paper were presented at the American Public Health Association 111th Annual Meeting, Dallas, Texas, November 1983.

REFERENCES

1. Block JA, Bourque D, Froh R, Lear J: Physicians and hospitals: providing primary care. Med Group Manage 1978; 25:34–38.
2. Block JA, et al: Hospital sponsored primary care: the community hospital program. J Amb Care Mgt 1980; 3:1–13.
3. Committee on the Cost of Medical Care for the American People. Chicago: University of Chicago Press, 1932.
4. Piore N: Ambulatory care issues in the United States today. In: Bryant JH, Ginsberg AS, Goldsmith SB, Olendzki MC, Piore N (eds): Community Hospitals and Primary Care. Cambridge, MA: Ballinger, 1976; 3–26.
5. Somers AR: Health Care in Transition: Directions for the Future. Chicago: HRET, 1971.
6. Aiken LH, Blendon RJ, Rogers DE, Freeman HE: Evaluating a private foundation's health program. Eval Program Plan 1980; 3:119–129.
7. Rogers DE: Shattuck Lecture—The American health-care scene. N Engl J Med 1973; 288:1377–1383.
8. Citizens Commission on Graduate Medical Education: The Graduate Education of Physicians. Chicago: AMA, 1966.
9. Bryant JH, Ginsberg AS, Goldsmith SB, Olendzki MC, Piore N: Community Hospitals and Primary Care. Cambridge, MA: Ballinger, 1976.
10. Goldsmith SB: A look at the issues in hospital-based ambulatory care. Trustee 1977; 30:40–42.
11. Robert Wood Johnson Foundation: Community Hospital-Medical Staff Sponsored Primary Care Group Practice Program. Princeton, NJ: The Foundation, 1974.
12. Williams SJ, Wickizer TM, Shortell SM: Hospital-based ambulatory care: a national survey. Hosp Health Serv Admin 1981; 26:66–80.
13. Aday LA, Andersen R, Loevy SS, Kremer B: Hospital-sponsored primary care: II. impact on patient access. Am J Public Health 1984; 74:792–798.
14. Wickizer TM, Shortell SM: Organizational and management issues in the development of a hospital-sponsored primary care group practice: findings from the community hospital program. J Amb Care Mgt 1983, 25–42.
15. Press J, Wilson S: Choosing between logistic regression and discriminant analysis. J Am Stat Assoc 1978; 73:699–705.
16. Cox DR: The Analysis of Binary Data. London: Methune, 1970.
17. Vayda E: Stability of the medical group in a new prepaid medical care program. Med Care 1970; 8:161–168.
18. Gavaler JS, Van Thiel DH: The nonemergency in the emergency room. JAMA 1980; 72:33–36.
19. Cugliana A: Patterns of hospital based ambulatory care. Soc Sci Med 1978; 12:55–58.
20. Beraducci AA, Del Banco TL, Rabkin MJ: The teaching hospital in primary care: closing down the clinic. N Engl J Med 1975; 292:615–620.
21. Davis CK: An update from HCFA. Hlth Care Fin Mgt 1983; 12:35–37.
22. Katz G, Hollander FL: From clinic to group practice. Hospitals 1975; 49:67–71.

23. Gold M: Hospital-based versus free-standing primary care costs. J Amb Care Mgt 1979; 2:1–20.
24. Rosenblatt RA, Moscovice IS: The physician as gatekeeper: factors influencing the decision to hospitalize. Med Care 1983.
25. Current Estimates from the National Health Interview Survey, United States, 1981. Series 10, No. 141. DHHS Pub. No. DHS, 82-1569. Washington, DC: Govt Printing Office, 1982.
26. Brecher C, Forman M: Financial viability of community health centers. J Hlth Pol Polit Law 1981; 5:742–767.
27. Moscovice IS, Rosenblatt RA: Rural health delivery amidst federal retrenchment: lessons from the Robert Wood Johnson Foundation's rural practice project. Am J Public Health 1982; 72:1380–1385.
28. Kimball L, Lorant J: Physician productivity and returns to scale. Health Serv Res 1977; 12:367–379.
29. Reinhardt U: A production function for physicians' services. Rev Econ Stat 1972; 54:55–56.
30. Medical Group Management Association: Production Survey and Cost Survey. Denver: The Association, 1983.
31. Campbell B, Hudson E: Transformation of a hospital clinic to a private office practice. J Amb Care Mgt 1978; 1:1–8.

32. Sparer G, Anderson A: Costs of services at neighborhood health centers. N Engl J Med 1972; 286:1241–1245.
33. Lyle CB, Citron DS, Sugg WC, Williams OC: Cost of medical care in practice of internal medicine. Ann Int Med 1974; 81:1–6.
34. Mintzberg H: The Structure of Organizations. Englewood Cliffs, N.J.: Prentice-Hall, 1979.
35. Kaluzny AD, Konrad TR: Organization design and the management of primary care services. In: Bisbee GE. Jr (ed): Management of Rural Primary Care—Concepts and Cases. Chicago: HRET, 1982: 33–67.
36. Wallack S, Kretz S: Rural Medicine: Obstacles and Solutions for Self Sufficiency. Lexington, MA: Lexington, 1981.
37. LeRoy L: The cost effectiveness of nurse practitioners. In: Aiken LH (ed): Nursing in the 1980s. Philadelphia: J.B. Lippincott, 1982: 295–314.
38. Rogers DE, Blendon RJ, Moloney TW: Who needs Medicaid? N Engl J Med 1982; 307:13–18.
39. Christianson JB, McClure W: Competition in the delivery of medical care. N Engl J Med 1979; 301:812–818.
40. McNerney WJ: Control of health care costs in the 1980s. N Engl J Med 1980; 303:1088–1095.
41. Ginzberg E: Competition in cost containment: N Engl J Med 1980; 303:1112–1115.

APPENDIX
Examples of Specific Variables Associated with Each Set of Factors Shown in Figure 1

A. Community Demand
1. Per cent Medicaid in target area.
2. Per cent low income in target area.

B. Community Supply
1. Number of primary care physicians per capita in target area.
2. Number of competing hospitals.

C. Hospital Characteristics
1. Degree to which group was seen as central to hospital's mission* (high, medium, low based on ratings by the evaluation team).
2. Original degree of hospital commitment* (1 to 5 scale based on ratings by evaluation team and CHP staff).
3. Degree of medical staff opposition* (1 to 5 scale based on ratings by evaluation team and project staff).

D. Practice Design
1. Multi-specialty vs. single-specialty practice.
2. Professional organization design (characterized by little hierarchy, easy access to hospital administration, and high physician participation in managing the group) vs. bureaucratic design.
3. Group practice autonomy (e.g. group could decide its own budgeting, purchasing, and personnel policies).
4. Differences in physician ages.
5. Use of residents.
6. Use of nurse practitioners and/or physician assistants.
7. Size (number of FTE physicians).
8. Physician incentive compensation based on productivity.
9. Fees charged for different types of exams (routine, intermediate, etc.).

E. Management
1. Degree of medical director leadership* (high, medium, low as rated by the evaluation team).
2. Degree to which medical director was integrated into committee structure of hospital (number and type of committees of which the medical director was a member).

F. Intermediate Outcomes
1. Productivity (volume of physician visits per FTE physician).
2. Physician turnover (# of MDs who left divided by # of MDs at beginning of year plus those added during the year).

---

*There was approximately 80 per cent agreement among the raters on all of these variables.

Hospital-Sponsored Primary Care
II. Impact on Patient Access

Lu Ann Aday, Ronald Andersen, Sara Segal Loevy, and Barbara Kremer

Abstract: This article, the second of two, considers the impact of a nationwide demonstration of 53 community hospital sponsored group practices (CHPs). Surveys of a sample of the communities in which the CHPs were introduced suggest that about half of the communities were socioeconomically and, to some extent, medically disadvantaged. The CHPs tended to attract people who had previously not had a regular source of care or who used hospital outpatient departments or emergency rooms, as well as patients of established primary care physicians. Access to care and satisfaction appeared to be as good or better for CHP patients compared to regular patients of physicians in the target areas. The programs did not increase the use of inpatient services, emergency rooms, or hospital outpatient departments. The findings suggest that at present community hospital sponsored group practices would not have a profound effect on access to care if adopted nationally, but that targeted implementation by hospitals in lower income and minority communities can improve patient opportunities for appropriate primary care services. (*Am J Public Health* 1984; 74:792–798.)

Introduction

The University of Chicago Access Impact Study of the Community Hospital Program (CHP) sponsored by the Robert Wood Johnson Foundation, described in the preceding article by Shortell, *et al*,[1] was charged with evaluating the success of the CHP groups in improving access to medical care in the communities they served. The initial design work for this evaluation began in 1976. As is often the case in long-term evaluations, policy and programmatic changes during the course of the study and the availability of new data served to challenge the assumptions on which the demonstration was based originally.[2]

For example, with respect to the assumptions cited in the previous paper regarding access, new data now suggest that "things have changed" since the early 1970s, when hospitals were increasingly considering ways to rationalize their role in the delivery of primary care.

• There have been substantial improvements in access to medical care for all types of individuals and communities over the past decade;[3]

• There is substantial evidence that there is a "hidden system" of primary care provided by medical specialists[4] and, contrary to fears of physician shortages expressed in the late 1960s, the Graduate Medical Education National Advisory Committee (GMENAC) report released at the beginning of this decade shows that there will, in fact, be a considerable surplus of physicians by the 1990s;[5]

• Most American consumers express satisfaction with the medical care they receive and, through Medicaid and Medicare coverage, the traditionally disadvantaged groups are better able to "buy their way" into the private provider system;[3,6]

• There is competition between hospitals and private physicians for the primary care business in some markets, which may alter considerably the traditional availability of services to consumers. For example, non-hospital based primary providers have opened their own emergency and urgent care centers, birthing centers, and outpatient surgery units.[7]

Some researchers have argued that hospital-sponsored primary care group practices may have negative, rather than positive, impact on patient access and cost, reasoning that close hospital affiliations on the part of ambulatory care providers may increase the use of costly inpatient services,[8–10] and that more bureaucratic settings may lead to greater, rather than less, patient dissatisfaction and discontinuity.[11,12] Others express doubts that institutionally-sponsored practices can attract paying middle class patients and establish a high quality, humanitarian primary care alternative.[13]

The changes and developments in the organization of primary care in the United States and, in particular, the hypothesized successes and shortcomings of community hospital-sponsored primary care group practices provide the context in which the results of the University of Chicago Access Evaluation of the Robert Wood Johnson Foundation Community Hospital Program (CHP) will be presented.

These issues will be addressed in the context of three major evaluation questions:

• Did the sponsoring hospitals establish group practices in communities with a demonstrated need for additional organized primary care services?

• Are hospital-sponsored group practices able to attract a cross-section of the community as well as more disadvantaged groups?

• Did the group practices improve access to a regular family doctor, the availability and convenience of services, the appropriateness of ambulatory and inpatient utilization, and overall patient satisfaction?

Methods

Twelve of the 53 Community Hospital Program sites eventually funded were sampled for inclusion in the Access Impact Evaluation. The method of sampling these practices is described in some detail in the previous paper.[1]

Of the 12 programs selected initially, one group (Site 09) withdrew from the Program. Consequently, Time 2 data were not collected for this group practice. In addition, the original Site 08 was involved in a hospital merger. We could not be sure where it would eventually be located at the time we commenced the evaluation. It was, therefore, dropped from the sample. A new, not randomly selected, site (08) was chosen to replace it.

Address reprint requests to Lu Ann Aday, Senior Research Associate and Associate Director for Research, Center for Health Administration Studies, Graduate School of Business, University of Chicago, 5720 South Woodlawn Avenue, Chicago, IL 60637. Dr. Andersen is Professor of Sociology and Director, CHAS and Graduate Program in Health Administration, at the University; Dr. Loevy is Assistant Professor, Department of Health Systems Management, Rush University; Dr. Kremer is Project Director, American Academy of Pediatrics. This paper, submitted to the Journal November 1, 1983, was revised and accepted for publication February 14, 1984.
Editor's Note: See also related article p 784 and editorial p 759 this issue.

139

TABLE 1—Selected Characteristics of the Community Hospital Program Access Impact Evaluation Sites, Time 2

CHP Sites	Service Area	% CHP Penetration Rate	Group Practice
01	Northeastern Central City of 138,000, Minority, Low Socioeconomic Status	4.1	Multi-specialty Satellite, Reorganized OPD, 530+ bed hospital
02	Southern Central City of 18,400, White, Low Socioeconomic Status	26.2	Multi-specialty Satellite, Existing clinic, 320+ bed hospital
03	Western Rural Area of 53,500, White, Lower Middle Class	7.7	Single specialty Family Practice Satellite, New practice, 90+ bed hospital
04	North Central Suburb of 426,000, White, Middle Class	2.6	Multi-specialty Hospital-based, Reorganized OPD, 710+ bed hospital
05	Southern Small Town of 22,900, White, Middle Class	17.1	Multi-specialty Satellite, New practice, 380+ bed hospital
06	North Central Mid-sized City of 72,600, White, Middle Class	5.3	Single specialty Family Practice Satellite, New practice, 500+ bed hospital
07	Northeastern Rural Area of 22,300, White, Low Socioeconomic Status	13.2	Single specialty Family Practice Satellite, New practice, 70+ bed hospital
08	Southern Small Town of 41,600, White, Lower Middle Class	3.6	Single specialty Family Practice Satellite, New practice, 560+ bed hospital
09	Western Suburb of 222,000, White, Middle Class	—	Multi-specialty Satellite, New practice, 270+ bed hospital
10	Northeastern Suburb of 24,900, White, Middle Class	7.0	Single specialty Family Practice Satellite, New practice, 190+ bed hospital
11	Southern Central City of 78,000, Black, Low Socioeconomic Status	4.3	Multi-specialty Hospital-based, Reorganized OPD, 160+ bed hospital
12	Western Central City of 629,000, Minority, Low Socioeconomic Status	0.1	Multi-specialty Hospital-based, Reorganized OPD, 380+ bed hospital

Analyses comparing the 12 study sites included in the evaluation with the universe from which the sample was chosen suggest that the sampled sites are relatively similar to the original universe of 36 programs.[1] They do differ in more respects from the 17 sites not included, however. The latter were more apt to be sponsored by smaller hospitals, had smaller volumes of outpatient visits, were more likely to be located in rural rather than suburban areas, had less experience with primary care, and were more apt to have hospital-based (rather than satellite) groups.

Once the sites were chosen, considerable attention was given to determining the prospective service areas for the programs, based on patient origin studies, initial proposals, and conversations with program administrators and physicians. Of the sampled sites, the service areas in major urban and suburban areas (01, 04, 09, 12) tended to encompass larger numbers of people than did those in small town or rural areas (05, 07) (Table 1).

Penetration rates were computed to reflect the proportion the CHP patient load represents of the entire population in the area served by the program. These rates at Time 2 ranged from a high of 26.2 per cent (Site 02) to a low of 0.1 per cent (Site 12), as shown in Table 1. These rates tend to be lower for sites that have larger market areas or for which patient load growth rates have been slower.

The organizational characteristics of the CHPs in the selected sites tend to vary, as well, by size of sponsoring hospital (from 70 to 700+ beds), single or multi-specialty status, whether they represent new or reorganized practices, or are satellites or hospital-based.

Community (area sample) surveys were conducted at the 1978–79 baseline (Time 1) and at follow-up (Time 2) some two years later.* One randomly selected adult and one randomly selected child (if there were one in the family)

were selected for intensive interview in the community surveys. The adult in the family best-informed about the child's health served as the proxy for the child. In those sites that were already seeing patients at Time 1, we also drew samples of patients to be interviewed. Both adults and children were eligible for inclusion. Patient surveys were conducted in all the sites at the follow-up time period. A subset of the same households surveyed at Time 1 were resampled at Time 2 in the community surveys and, similarly, a subsample of patients were reinterviewed.

The response rates in both the community and patient samples were 80% or higher in most sites.** The response rates for Time 2 tended to parallel the Time 1 rates. The respondents appear to be representative of the communities and patients surveyed. A small methodological study in one site indicated that there were no substantial differences between CHP patients who participated in the study and those who did not do so.

Personal face-to-face interviews were the primary mode of data collection. In some instances, phone interviews were conducted with hard-to-reach respondents. The questionnaire was modeled upon a 1976 national medical access survey conducted by the Center for Health Administration Studies and the National Opinion Research Center, University of Chicago.[3] Indicators of both potential and realized access to medical care and characteristics of the individuals that might be correlated with these indicators were operationalized in the survey instrument.[14]

Central to the analyses of the data collected in the community and patient surveys is a determination of who are the "users" of the CHP. It is CHP "users" who represent

---
* Site 09, as noted, withdrew from the program.

** Site 12 had the lowest response rates at both Time 1 and Time 2 for community and patient surveys (72 per cent and 54 per cent, respectively, at Time 1, and 68 per cent and 65 per cent at Time 2). There may, therefore, be significant biases in the estimates for this site.

e "experimental" group of most relevance in directly valuating program impact. For the purposes of the analy-s, users were defined as community residents or patients ho consider the CHP site their regular source of care or the ace they would go and have, in fact, been. Nonusers were ea residents who claimed some other place as their regular ource of care.

Considerable attention was devoted in the analyses to nderstanding the differences between users and nonusers or the purpose of estimating and controlling for selection ffect differences between the two groups, such as age, sex, ace, income, or health status.

Three modes of analyses were applied in estimating rogram effects. First, traditional tests of the significance of ifferences between users and nonusers on key access idicators were carried out in which standardizing weights ere applied to the CHP users' data to make them compara-le to nonusers on the key selection effect variables. In the econd approach, the original analysis was essentially repli-ated using logistic regression or Analysis of Variance-1ultiple Classification Analysis (ANOVA-MCA), instead of tandardizing weights, to control for the major selection ifferences between users and nonusers. In the third meth-d, synthetic T1 user and nonuser scores were constructed y assigning the T1 community sample data two different weights to reflect the adjustment of the T1 area sample to the 2 user and nonuser selection effect characteristics, respec-vely. Aggregate gain scores were then constructed as ollows: (U2-U1)-(NU2-NU1). Differences in access be-

tween T2 users (U) compared to their (synthetically estimat-ed) pre-program (T1) access levels were then compared to the same differences for nonusers (NU). A positive program effect would be that users change in a more "favorable" direction than do nonusers.

All hypotheses were tested at p LE .05. A program for which there was a significant difference between users and nonusers using one or more of the analytic methods de-scribed above is reported to perform better (or worse, as appropriate) than other regular care providers.

Results

Did the Target Communities Need Additional Primary Care Services?

Table 2 compares baseline access profiles for the CHP communities relative to the national average based on a 1976 national access survey conducted by the Center for Health Administration Studies at the University of Chicago.[3]

One of the primary objectives of the community hospi-tal-sponsored practices was to ensure linkages of patients with a regular family physician. According to the baseline survey data in the study sites, the proportion of the commu-nity without a regular source of care was about the same as the national average in two-thirds of the communities. In only one of the sites was a hospital emergency room or outpatient department reported as the regular source of care more often than was true on average nationally.

TABLE 2—Comparison of CHP Communities to National Average on Selected Measures of Access, Time 1

Access	US Average, 1976	Compared to the National Average, in What Proportion of CHP Communities Is Access Better (a), About the Same, Worse (a)(b) (n = 12)			Range for CHP Communities
Regular Source					
Percent medically disadvantaged that is, with:					
• No regular source	12%	.00	.67	.33	10–31%
• Hospital OPD or ER as regular source	7	.58	.33	.08	1–45%
Per cent seeing a particular doctor	89	.33	.50	.17	60–96%
Per cent with regular source that is primary care specialty	80	.67	.25	.08	69–93%
Convenience					
Availability of regular source (Per cent):					
• Evening coverage	30	.42	.08	.50	7–73%
• Saturday morning coverage	65	.17	.25	.58	34–81%
• Other weekend coverage	11	.50	.33	.17	4–30%
• Home visits	26	.17	.08	.75	1–44%
• Emergency care after hours	92	.08	.42	.50	70–96%
Per cent with office waiting time of 30 minutes or less	64	.50	.33	.17	55–82%
Utilization					
Per cent seeing a doctor in the year	76	.25	.67	.08	71–81%
Mean number of doctor visits in the year for those seeing a doctor	5.4	.17	.83	.00	4.7–7.6
Rate of hospital inpatient services to total services	.62	.00	1.00	.00	.48–.66
Rate of hospital ER and OPD use to total non-inpatient use	.15	.25	.50	.25	.06–.42
Per cent having a general exam in the year	52	.42	.58	.00	45–64%
Appropriate Use					
Per cent seeing a doctor more (+) or less (−) often for symptoms than physicians thought appropriate (Symptoms Response Ratio)	−5	.08	.75	.17	−17–+17%
Satisfaction					
Per cent satisfied with:					
• Office waiting time	75	.25	.58	.17	67–84%
• Out-of-pocket cost	65	.50	.50	.00	61–83%
• Physician interaction overall	93	.08	.92	.00	90–98%

(a) Better and worse indicate statistical significance, p ≤ .05.
(b) An access score "worse" than the national average generally means the community average is lower than the U.S. average except for the following indicators, in which a higher score for the community means poorer access performance: percent medically disadvantaged, rate of hospital inpatient services to total services, and rate of hospital ER and OPD use to total non-inpatient use.

Contrary to the assumptions at the time the Community Hospital Program was initiated, the majority of the CHP communities were not ones in which large numbers of residents had no established linkages with primary care providers. In about a third of the sites, however, the proportion of patients without a regular source or who used hospital OPDs or ERs as their regular source did tend to be high. These communities best fit the initial assumptions about the need for better linkages between patients and providers.

Another access goal expressed in the initial formulation of the community hospital-sponsored groups was to enhance the availability of 24-hour a day coverage.[1] In a number of the communities the availability of evening, weekend, home visit, or after-hours emergency care coverage does not compare favorably to the national average. Although the majority of residents may have regular family doctors—as was suggested in originally formulating the program—the existing system of primary care does not necessarily provide comprehensive, well-integrated after-hours and emergency care in many communities.

According to another measure of convenience—the average amount of time patients in the CHP communities waited to see a physician, once in the office—community averages were as good as or better than the national average in over 80 per cent of the sites. In most communities, patients experienced fairly average waiting times before getting to see their doctor.

Realized access—in contrast to the potential access indicators just examined—is expressed in terms of the rates at which people actually use services and their satisfaction with the care they receive.[3] On these realized access indicators, the vast majority of CHP communities seemed to fare as well or better than the national average. In 25 per cent of the sites the rates of hospital emergency room and outpatient department care were higher than the national average, however. These communities and the ones noted earlier in which there were relatively higher rates of residents with no regular source of care or who used hospital OPDs or ERs best fit the assumptions about primary care underserved communities most likely to benefit from community hospital-sponsored primary care alternatives.

The results of the baseline needs assessments in the target communities for the groups then did not support some of the early assumptions about the need for such a program in many American communities. Some communities seem to fit the profile upon which the assumptions for initiating hospital-sponsored group practices were based. For others, the present system of care appeared to be performing quite well.

Who Uses Community Hospital Sponsored-Group Practices?

Table 3 compares characteristics of patients of the community hospital-sponsored groups to those of the general population in the communities included in the final Access Evaluation (n = 11). On many characteristics the patients of the CHPs appeared to be similar to other community residents. In almost half the sites, however, the poor were disproportionately represented among CHP patients. These programs tended to be located in inner-city areas with high concentrations of low-income and minority populations. They were the same programs which were the best candidates for hospital-sponsored primary care alternatives due to the higher proportions of people with no regular source of

TABLE 3—Percentage Comparison of CHP Patients to the Community on Social Characteristics, Time 2

Social Characteristic	Proportion of Sites in Which Social Characteristics of CHP Patients Compare to the Community (n = 11)			Range for CHP Patients
	More Likely to be:	About the Same:	Less Likely to be:	
				%
Under 6 years	.09	.82	.09	4–17
Poor	.45	.55	.00	4–72
Black	.09	.91	.00	0–100
Hispanic	.18	.73	.09	1–39
Less than High School Graduate	.09	.82	.09	8–71
Uninsured	.27	.55	.18	4–19

NOTE: More and less likely indicate statistical significance, p ≤ .05.

care or with high rates of OPD or ER use in the community relative to national norms.

Results from a panel analysis of patients who became users of the CHP in seven sites for which panel data are available are summarized in Table 4. In the urban inner-city (02, 11) and rural (07) sites, the CHPs did capture a large number of people who did not have a previous regular source of care or who used hospital outpatient departments and emergency rooms. The CHPs tended to attract a substantial proportion of patients from the private physician sector as well. This was particularly true in the more advantaged small town or suburban communities (05, 06, 08, 10). In these sites also, however, the CHPs attracted some people who previously had no regular source of care.

The loyalty of CHP patients varied by site, particularly in the inner-city areas. Many people did not necessarily consider the CHP as their regular source of care or dropped out of the program over time. These retention rates were considerably influenced by the length of time the practice had been operational and the overall physician turnover during the development of the plan. High patient turnover was strongly associated with high physician turnover in a practice.

In summary, CHPs, contrary to the critics, may be a "provider of choice" for middle class patients, as well as meeting the needs of the poor and underserved. Patient attrition results, as it does in the private, non-institutionally affiliated primary care sector, when a patient's "provider of choice" leaves the practice.

What Impact Do Community Hospital-Sponsored Group Practices Have on Access?

Table 5 shows that, in almost half of the communities, CHP users were as likely as non-users in the same community to see a particular physician. The remainder of the communities were equally divided between those in which CHP users were more likely and those in which they were less likely to see a particular physician. CHP users who were less likely to have an established linkage were in programs in disadvantaged communities.

The majority of community hospital-sponsored groups did not improve 24-hour coverage over that available from existing providers, perhaps because they were still "young". Some programs established institutionally-affiliated walk-in clinics as alternatives to such coverage, however.

TABLE 4—Per Cent Distribution of Time 1 Regular Source of Care for CHP Joiners

Site	Physician Office, Clinic	Group	Government Clinic	Hospital ER/OPD	Other	None	Total
02	50.0	1.3	9.0	24.4	1.3	14.1	100.0
	(39)	(1)	(7)	(19)	(1)	(11)	(78)
05	28.2	56.4	0.9	0.0	2.7	11.8	100.0
	(31)	(62)	(1)	(0)	(3)	(13)	(110)
06	65.0	20.0	0.0	0.0	0.0	15.0	100.0
	(13)	(4)	(0)	(0)	(0)	(3)	(20)
07	59.5	0.0	0.0	2.4	0.0	38.1	100.0
	(25)	(0)	(0)	(1)	(0)	(16)	(42)
08	63.2	17.5	0.0	0.0	0.0	19.3	100.0
	(36)	(10)	(0)	(0)	(0)	(11)	(57)
10	23.8	53.3	0.0	1.6	11.5	9.8	100.0
	(29)	(65)	(0)	(2)	(14)	(12)	(122)
11	22.2	11.1	11.1	37.8	0.0	17.8	100.0
	(10)	(5)	(5)	(17)	(0)	(8)	(45)

For the vast majority of programs, office waiting times for CHP users were better than that of other sources of care.

The proportion of CHP users who had seen a physician at least once in the year was higher in about half of the programs. Once a physician was contacted, there was no evidence of overutilization on the part of CHP patients.

For the majority of sites, there were no differences between CHP users and regular users of other sources of care on other utilization indicators, including rates of emergency room and outpatient department use, general exams, use of physician services in response to symptoms of illness and (Table 5).

TABLE 5—Comparison of CHP Users to Users of Other Sources of Care in the Community on Selected Measures of Access, Time 2

Access (a)	Compared to Other Users, in What Proportion of Sites Do CHP Users Have Access That Is:			Range for CHP Users
	Better	About the Same (n = 11)	Worse (b)	
Regular Source				
Per cent seeing a particular doctor	.27	.45	.27	27–100%
Convenience				
Availability of regular source (%):				
● Evening coverage	.09	.45	.45	2–76%
● Saturday morning coverage	.09	.36	.55	12–82%
● Other weekend coverage	.18	.36	.45	0–39%
● Home visits	.09	.64	.27	0–25%
● Emergency care after hours	.00	.73	.27	61–93%
Per cent with office waiting time of 30 minutes or less	.82	.18	.00	69–99%
Utilization				
Per cent seeing a doctor in the year	.45	.55	.00	72–96%
Mean number of doctor visits in the year for those seeing a doctor	.00	1.00	.00	3.6–9.9
Rate of hospital inpatient services to total services	.00	1.00	.00	.34–.72
Rate of hospital ER and OPD use to total non-inpatient use	.27	.73	.00	.06–.24
Per cent having a general exam in the year	.27	.73	.00	51–83%
Appropriate use				
Per cent seeing a doctor more (+) or less (−) often for symptoms than physicians thought appropriate (Symptoms Response Ratio)	.09	.91	.00	−26–+36%
Satisfaction				
Per cent satisfied with:				
● Office waiting time	.36	.55	.09	61–95%
● Out-of-pocket cost	.00	1.00	.00	38–86%
● Physician interaction	.18	.73	.09	76–98%

(a) These tests of significance were made after adjusting for differences in demographic and health status characteristics between CHP patients and other patients in the community. For detailed discussion of these adjustments, see Aday LA, Andersen R, Loevy SS, Kremer B. Hospital Sponsored Primary Care: A Study of Impact on Community Access. Unpublished manuscript submitted for publication. Chicago: Center for Health Administration Studies, The University of Chicago, 1983.

(b) An access score "worse" for CHP users compared to nonusers generally means the user average is lower than the nonuser average except for the following indicators, in which a higher score for CHP users means poorer access performance: rate of hospital inpatient services to total services and rate of hospital ER and OPD use to total non-inpatient use.

TABLE 6—Comparison of Hospital Utilization of CHP Users and Users of Other Sources of Care in the Community, Time 2

Hospital Utilization (a)	CHP Sites											US Average
	01	02	03	04	05	06	07	08	10	11	12	
Per cent hospitalized in the year												11
CHP Users	18	11	8	8	10	12	8	9	8	12	12	
Other Users	9	13	11	9	10	13	12	11	10	13	8	
Mean hospital admissions (those with 1+)												1.2
CHP Users	1.5	1.5	1.3	1.3	1.4	1.0	1.2	1.3	1.2	1.3	1.2	
Other Users	1.6	1.4	1.5	1.2	1.2	1.2	1.4	1.2	1.1	1.1	3.7	
Mean hospital days in the year (those with 1+)												11.3
CHP Users	28.2	10.6	7.7	10.6	10.0	4.5	17.3	9.9	5.3	15.9	7.0	
Other Users	9.9	16.8	8.3	12.2	11.6	8.4	13.9	10.9	5.7	16.5	21.5	

(a) These estimates reflect adjustments for differences in demographic and health status characteristics between CHP patients and other patients in the community.

Contrary to the critics' expectations, there were no statistically significant differences between hospital inpatient service volume for CHP users compared to regular users of other sources of care. On average, in fact, CHP users tend to use less inpatient care. Table 6 provides detailed site-specific hospital utilization data. In the vast majority of sites, hospitalization rates were either very similar or less for CHP users. Any differences found were not statistically significant because of the large standard errors associated with the respective estimates.

Contrary to criticisms of these more institutionalized modes of practice, CHP users in the vast majority of sites appear to be as satisfied or more satisfied with their care than are regular users of other sources.

Discussion

Most of the funded CHPs were not found in communities with demonstrated needs for additional primary care services, as originally planned. Nevertheless, in those that were so located (inner-city and rural areas), the poor and underserved were heavy users of the CHP. These CHPs were also able to attract other sections of the community—that is, they did not serve the poor alone. Services provided by CHPs were more or less equivalent to those provided to non-CHP users in the same communities. Clearly, for poor communities which were underserved, the CHPs performed a needed and valuable service.

The high physician turnover in several of the newly developing practices and the greater use by some of nurse practitioners help explain why some groups failed to link patients with a single family care physician. Providing after-hours coverage in some of the practices was exacerbated by multi-specialty staffing patterns, the small relative size of some of the groups, and the fact that some of the sponsoring hospitals encouraged the development of alternative after-hours arrangements in which linkages with the group practice were not always apparent.

The full impact of community hospital-sponsored group practices on the overall availability and convenience of front-line primary care in American communities should ideally be measured after their maturation as well-established and integral providers of care in the communities they serve.

Some preliminary implications for national health policy may be drawn from this national evaluation, however. Given the current levels of access nationally and the de-emphasis on federal support for access programs in general, it appears unlikely that community hospitals can be counted on consistently to establish group practices in communities with serious access problems. Once established, these hospital sponsored practices do, however, have the capacity to promote primary care without increasing inpatient or emergency room services. Policies that provide loans or grants to committed institutions to establish such groups seem warranted by the findings reported here. In particular, targeted implementation by hospitals in lower income and minority communities would seem to offer the greatest promise for improving patient opportunities for appropriate primary care services among those groups most in need of improved primary care alternatives.

ACKNOWLEDGMENTS

The authors gratefully acknowledge the constructive response and suggestions on this paper from Linda Aiken, Robert Blendon, and Catherine McCaslin of the Robert Wood Johnson Foundation; Howard Freeman, University of California at Los Angeles; and Stephen Shortell, Northwestern University.

The research on which this paper was based was supported by grants from the Robert Wood Johnson Foundation (Princeton, New Jersey).

REFERENCES

1. Shortell SM, Wickizer TM, Wheeler JRC: Hospital-sponsored primary care: I. organizational and financial effects. Am J Public Health 1984; 74:784–791.
2. Rossi PH, Freeman HE, Wright SR: Evaluation: A Systematic Approach. Beverly Hills: Sage, 1982.
3. Aday LA, Andersen R, Fleming GV: Health Care in the US: Equitable for Whom? Beverly Hills: Sage, 1980.
4. Aiken L, Lewis CE, Craig J, Mendenhall RC, Blendon RJ, Rogers DE: The contribution of specialists to the delivery of primary care. N Engl J Med 1979; 300:1363–1370.
5. Graduate Medical Education National Advisory Committee: Report of the Graduation Medical Education National Advisory Committee. Washington, DC: Department of Health and Human Services, Office of Graduate Medical Education, 1980.
6. Lou Harris and Associates: Access to Health Care Services in the United States: 1982. New York: Lou Harris and Associates, Inc, 1982.
7. Friedman E: Slicing the pie thinner: hospitals and physicians square-off over primary care services. Hospitals 1982; 56:62–74.

8. Elnicki RA: Substitution of outpatient for inpatient hospital care: a cost analysis. Inquiry 1976; 13:245–261.
9. Gold M: Hospital-based versus free-standing primary care costs. J Amb Care Manage 1979; 2:1–20.
10. Gold M, Greenlick M: Effect of hospital-based primary care setting on internists' use of inpatient hospital resources. Med Care 1981; 19:160–171.
11. Mechanic D: The Growth of Bureaucratic Medicine. New York: John Wiley, 1976.

12. Richardson W, Boscha M, Diehr P, et al: The Seattle Prepaid Health Care Project. A Comparison of Health Services Delivery. Seattle: University of Washington Press, 1976.
13. Donmell WE: Ambulatory patients don't belong in hospitals. Med Econ 1974; 51.
14. Aday LA, Andersen R, Fleming GV, Chiu G, Daughety V, Banks MJ: Overview of a design to evaluate the impact of community hospital-sponsored primary care group practices. Med Group Manage 1978; 25:42–46.

7

An Alternative in Terminal Care
Results of the National Hospice Study

David S. Greer, Vincent Mor, John N. Morris,
Sylvia Sherwood, David Kidder, and Howard Birnbaum

Hospice is both a philosophy and a system of terminal care. As a philosophy it reflects late twentieth-century western cultural and social values. It confronts the dying process openly and prepares people to experience dying as an inevitable, natural phase in the life cycle (Lack, 1977; Stoddard, 1978; National Hospice Organization, 1979). Hospice stresses personal autonomy and, at least by implication, is critical of perceived paternalism and authoritarianism within the medical profession (Twycross, 1980; Dubois, 1980; Mount, 1980). In the United States, the hospice preference is for home care and family support as opposed to institutional care and professional intervention; institutions are perceived as relatively cold and impersonal, and professionals as often insensitive to basic human needs (Stoddard, 1978).

In less than a decade since its arrival on American shores, hospice has evolved from a mission into a major movement encompassing more than one thousand heterogeneous organizations (General Accounting Office, 1979; JCAH, 1981). The remarkable growth of the hospice movement within barely a decade (Lack and Buckingham, 1978) includes small volunteer-dominated community programs caring for a handful of patients as well as large institutions and agencies with major commitments to hospice care (National Hospice Organization, 1982). Hospice has become a significant segment of the health care system and a potent

Authors' Note: We would like to acknowledge gratefully Spike Duzor and Richard Yaffe of the Health Care Financing Administration as well as Dr. Sidney Katz and National Hospice Study staff analysts for their helpful comments on earlier drafts of this manuscript. Gratitude is also expressed to Dr. Martita Marx and the late Dr. Michael Pozen whose contributions to the development of the study were invaluable.

political force, as evidenced by the recent addition of hospice benefits to the Medicare Program as part of the Tax Equity and Fiscal Responsibility Act (TEFRA) (Federal Register, 1982).

Hospice claims to provide better pain relief than conventional care (Twycross, 1978; Saunders, 1979) and to improve the quality of life of terminal patients and their families while maximizing time spent at home and minimizing aggressive traumatic intervention (Mount, 1980; Lack and Buckingham, 1978). Hospice prepares patients and their families emotionally and spiritually for death (Twycross, 1980; Saunders, 1979) and thereby anticipates better adjustment during the premortem and bereavement periods (Stoddard, 1978; National Hospice Organization, 1982; Dubois, 1980). Finally, hospice promises to cost less than conventional care (Amado et al., 1979; Van Buren, 1980; Hansen and Evashwick, 1981).

The National Hospice Study (NHS) emerged in response to Congressional and Department of Health and Human Service interest in hospice (Congressional Record, 1978). The study examined a wide range of issues pertaining to hospice. The present report addresses the three major research questions posed in the NHS:

(1) What is the difference between hospice and conventional care?
(2) What is the comparative impact of hospice and conventional care on the quality of life of patients and their families?
(3) What is the impact of hospice on the health care costs incurred by terminal cancer patients?

METHODS

Sites and Samples

Data for the current report were assembled on hospice and conventional care patients who were selected by predetermined criteria from a population of over 12,000 terminal cancer patients and identified in 40 hospices and 14 conventional oncological care (CC) settings distributed nationally. A total of 26 of the hospices received special Medicare demonstration waivers allowing payment for normally noncovered services. Study sites could not be randomly selected because the demonstration hospices had been chosen competitively by the Health Care Financing Administration (HCFA) from a pool of 233 applicants; nondemonstration hospices were therefore selected by the evaluators to resemble demonstration sites organizationally. The results in the demonstration and nondemonstration hospices did not differ significantly, so they were aggregated. American hospices vary greatly in organizational structure. After careful review of both behavior and structure, hospices were classified as those with beds, usually hospital-connected (Bedded, B) and those without beds, usually home health agency or independently sponsored (Unbedded, UB). Conventional care settings were selected by the evaluators based on willingness to cooperate and ability, as judged by the investigators, to provide quality oncological care.

The sample considered in this report consisted of cancer patients and their families served in B or UB hospices or in CC settings who consented to participate in a "follow-up" study. Follow-up study eligibility was based upon: (a) cancer confirmed by tissue diagnosis (except for brain and pancreatic cancer); (b) remote metastasis (except for lung, brain, and pancreatic cancer); (c) presence of a primary care person (PCP), generally a family member in the household; (d) age 21 or older; (e) for CC patients only, a Karnofsky Performance Status (KPS) (Karnofsky et al., 1948) of 50 or less, that is, requiring assistance in daily activities. These criteria were based upon a review of modal hospice patient characteristics: 90 percent have cancer, over 95 percent have a PCP, almost all are over age 21, and over 90 percent require assistance with personal care at the time of hospice admission.

A total of 1,754 patients (833 B hospice, 624 UB hospice, and 297 CC) were included in the follow-up sample (Table 1). Trained and tested interviewers assessed patient eligibility from available records. The refusal rate of patients and PCPs (both had to give written consent) was 3.4 percent in hospice and 20.6 percent in CC settings; dropout among those signing consent forms was 4.4 percent, with no significant difference among settings. Only patients who died during the study period were included in the final analytic samples because outcomes were assessed in relation to proximity to death.

Data Gathering Methods

The NHS data collection methodology has been described in detail elsewhere (Greer et al., 1983). Personal interviews with the patient and PCP were conducted at study entry. A first follow-up contact occurred 7 days later and was repeated every 14 days thereafter until the patient's death. About 90-120 days after the patient's death, a bereavement interview with the PCP was conducted. In addition to the patient interviews, at each contact the PCP provided data on his own condition and attitudes, presented a record of all health services utilized by the patient, and reported on the patient's condition. Information on primary site, histology, metastases, date of disease onset, and prior treatment was obtained from medical records.

Outcome Variables

Measures were adapted or developed to evaluate the impact of the hospice model of care in four areas: pattern of care, patient outcome, family outcome, and cost and utilization. Within each outcome area multiple domains and measures were used, many of which were based upon established scales (Karnofsky et al., 1948; Spitzer et al., 1981; Melzack, 1975; Oleson and Bresler, 1979; Wolf et al., 1978; McNair et al., 1981; Saunders et al., 1979). Many of the patient outcome measures were based upon PCP reports because most of the

TABLE 1
Distribution of Demographic, Medical, Functional, and
Support Characteristics of the Patient Followup Sample
(in percents)

		Unbedded Hospice (N = 833)	Bedded Hospice (N = 624)	Conventional Care (N = 297)
Age*	21-64	31.8	23.6	57.2
	65+	68.2	76.4	42.8
Female		51.3	51.8	52.7
Married		62.4	58.3	62.4
Nonwhite		7.5	4.7	8.1
Patient family income under $10,000*		46.0	55.8	45.1
Patient lives alone*		6.7	16.1	16.6
PCP is spouse or child		83.8	82.7	78.0
PCP is employed*		29.2	38.7	41.2
Karnofsky Performance Status at study entry*				
leave functional (10-30)		45.8	49.8	67.7
most functional (40 and over)		54.2	50.2	32.3

*p < 0.05

patients could not be interviewed in the weeks just prior to death (Table 3). Family outcomes focused on the PCP and were measured both prior to and following the patient's death (Table 4).

Service utilization data, from which costs were derived, were obtained from the PCP and checked with Medicare and other reimbursement records whenever feasible. Unit cost coefficients were developed utilizing the national and demonstration data obtained from HCFA. Total costs included "charges" when only charges were available, for example, physician services, drugs, supplies, and equipment purchased at home. The details of the adjustment procedures have been reported elsewhere (Birnbaum and Kidder, 1984).

Because measures of patient outcome were relatively stable until five weeks prior to death and nearly 20 percent of the patients survived only one week in hospice, the analyses focused on the period just prior to death. The last measure occurred, on average, 7 days before death and the penultimate measure occurred approximately 21 days predeath with no significant differences among settings. To compare the experiences of nonrandomized hospice and conventional care samples in purposefully selected sites, multivariate statistical adjustment models were developed (Draper and Smith, 1981; Klienbaum, 1982). These have been described previously (Greer et al., 1983). Statistical significance was determined at the $p < 0.05$ level.

RESULTS

Hospice claims to serve patients in the last six months of life, but in our study, over 50 percent of the population had lengths of stay less than 35 days, and 20

TABLE 2

Hospice and Nonhospice Patients' Pattern of Care:
Percentage Receiving Medical and Social Service Interventions
in the Last Weeks of Life Adjusted for Sample Differences

	3 Weeks Premortem			1 Week Premortem		
	Unbedded Hospice	Bedded Hospice	Conventional Care	Unbedded Hospice	Bedded Hospice	Conventional Care
Intensive medical services	13	21	32*	10	11	19*
Diagnostic tests	34	37	64*	35	36 6	62*
Oxygen or respiratory therapy	21	24	19	29	26	35
Social services (last week of life)	–	–	–	61	65	49*

*p < 0.05; see text for direction of significant paired contrast(s).

percent survived less than one week in hospice. However, 8 percent stayed more than 210 days, and more than 10 percent were discharged alive, mostly long-stay patients. The population of patients served by hospices with inpatient units (B) had shorter lengths of stay and were more functionally impaired upon admission than those in hospices without inpatient units (UB). Even after adjusting for these differences in patient mix, patients served by hospices without beds were nearly twice as likely to die at home (Mor and Hiris, 1983), one of the major objectives of American hospices.

Patient Sample Description

Table 1 presents selected demographic, medical, and functional characteristics of the follow-up patients served in the three settings. Conventional care patients were younger and more functionally impaired, but patient awareness and ability to respond to the interview were comparable in the three groups. There were no significant differences among the groups in sex, marital status, race, primary cancer site, or duration of disease.

Interventions

Table 2 compares the medical and social service interventions patients received in their last weeks of life, adjusting for sample differences. Patients in hospice were significantly less likely than CC patients to experience one of the aggressive interventions. Hospice patients were also significantly less likely to have diagnostic blood tests or X-rays. There were no differences in the probability of receiving oxygen or respiratory therapy. Social service use was more prevalent among hospice patients throughout the course of the study. Intravenous therapy in patients with liver metastases and either weight loss or hemorrhage was more prevalent in the CC system than in hospice; the difference was greatest in the least functional patient group as measured by the KPS and increased as death approached (data not shown).

Patient Outcome

There were similar decreases in functional performance as measured by the Karnofsky Performance Status and "Uniscale." Other measures such as the HRCA Quality of Life Index, Emotional Quality of Life, and Patient Awareness were also comparable. Table 3 compares patient outcomes at the last measure, but comparisons for earlier periods were also performed.

Three weeks prior to death, patients in UB hospices received significantly more hours of social visiting than CC patients from persons other than their PCPs, principally because they spent more time at home (data not shown). Patients in UB hospices also had significantly higher levels of direct care help from their PCPs than either B hospice or CC patients (Table 3). Although ratings were very high in all three samples, PCP judgment of patients' Social Quality of Life at the measure closest to death was significantly higher among CC patients than in either type of hospice.

Pain and Other Symptoms

Because patients, particularly those experiencing high levels of pain, frequently could not be interviewed during the last few weeks of life, it was necessary to use the PCP's evaluation of the patient's pain to ensure complete data. B hospice patients were reported to have less pain than comparable UB or CC patients.[1] A "pain index" incorporating aspects of symptom severity revealed a similar pattern (Table 3), though statistically significant only for the penultimate measure. Similarly, patients in B hospices were likely to experience fewer symptoms[2] than comparable patients in either UB hospice or CC. Subgroup analyses revealed that significant differences persisted regardless of the level of symptoms at intake.

Detailed data on analgesic utilization were assembled for a subset of patients (N = 181) in both hospice and conventional care settings. Comparison of the prevalence of analgesic prescription and consumption among the three groups revealed that 91.3 percent of B hospice patients, 69.7 percent of UB patients, and 66.1 percent of CC patients had an analgesic prescribed ($p < 0.01$); B hospice patients were also significantly more likely to have actually consumed analgesics in the last weeks of life.

Satisfaction With Care

Patients in both hospice and CC reported similarly high levels of satisfaction. However, the primary care persons of B hospice patients were more satisfied with the patient's care than those of UB hospice or CC patients. Despite marked differences in the percentage of patients dying at home (62 percent, 27 percent, and 13 percent of UB hospice, B hospice, and CC patients, respectively), PCPs in both types of hospices were satisfied with where the patient died, but both

TABLE 3

Patient Outcomes Experienced by Terminal Cancer Patients
at Last Measure Premortem, Adjusted for Sample Differences

Quality of Life Domain (Score Range and Direction)	Unbedded Hospice	Bedded Hospice	Conventional Care
Overall Quality of Life			
HRCA Quality of Life Index[a] (0-10; 0 = worst)	2.99	3.04	3.24
Karnofsky Performance Status[f] (0-100; 0 = worst)	23.72	25.39	23.88
"Uniscale" a unidimensional Q-L[a] (0-14; 0 = worst)	2.92	3.10	3.09
Patient awareness (judged by PCP)[a] (1-4; 4 = worst)	2.28	2.18	2.23
Emotional quality of life (judged by PCP)[a] (0-14; 0 = worst)	5.63	6.12	6.00
Social Quality of Life			
Hours of direct care help from PCP[b] (0-6; 0 = least)	4.16	3.02	2.82*
Hours of social visiting from other than PCP[b] (0-4; 0 = least)	2.61	2.55	2.41
Overall social quality of life as judged by PCP[a] (1-7; 1 = lowest)	5.03	5.09	5.62*
Pain and Symptoms			
Proportion in persistent pain (0-1; 0 = none)	.13	.05	.22*
Composite Pain Index[a] (0-4; 0 = none)	1.61	1.48	1.65
Composite Symptom Severity Scale[c] (0-7; 0 = none)	3.05	2.78	3.38*
Satisfaction with Health Care			
Patient satisfaction with care: self report[d,e] (1-5; 5 = most)	4.87	3.76	4.20
	One-Time Measures		
satisfaction reported by PCP while patient alive[e] (1-5; 5 = most)	4.39	4.54	4.38*
satisfaction reported by PCP after patient death[e] (1-5; 5 = most)	4.36	4.48	4.33*

a. Modified from Spitzer et al. (1981).
b. Study-specific measure.
c. Modified from Melzack (1975) and Oleson and Bresler (1979).
d. First patient interview after study entry rather than that closest to death; most patients were unable to communicate later.
e. Modified from Wolf et al. (1978).
f. Modified from Karnofsky et al. (1948).
*$p < 0.05$; see text for direction of significant paired contrast(s).

TABLE 4
Family Outcomes Before and After Patient's Death
Adjusted for Sample Differences

	Unbedded Hospice	Bedded Hospice	Conventional Care
Before Patient's Death			
Anxiety/depression (POMS)[a] (0-5; 0 = worst)	2.96	2.98	3.01
Perceived caretaking burden[b] (0-6; 0 = least)	3.32	2.91	3.13*
Reported increased drinking	2%	2%	4%
Used medication for anxiety, depression	11%	10%	14%
After Patient's Death			
Reported increased drinking	4%	5%	6%
Used medication for anxiety, depression	16%	12%	15%
Overall emotional distress[c] (0-10; 0 = least)	5.06	4.49	4.82*
Morbidity During Bereavement Period			
Hospitalized within 90-120 days after patient's death	6%	6%	5%
Physician visits during 90-120 days after patient's death (0-4+; 0 = none)	1.35	1.25	.95

a. Modified from McNair et al. (1981).
b. Study-specific measure.
c. Modified from Saunders et al. (1979).
*p < 0.05; see text for direction of significant paired contrast(s).

hospice PCP groups were more satisfied with where the patient died than were CC PCPs (data not shown).

Family Outcomes

When the patient was alive there were no significant differences among the PCP groups on a modified mood state scale measuring anxiety and depression. Similarly, no significant difference among the groups was observed in use of medications for anxiety or depression, and there was no reported increased use of alcohol (Table 4). At this time PCPs of UB patients reported a significantly higher caretaking burden.

The bereavement interview that occurred about four months after the patient's death suggested generally better PCP adjustment postmortem than expected from the literature (Clayton, 1974; Klerman and Izen, 1977; Parkes and Brown, 1972). Few PCPs reported increased absenteeism from work (4 percent) or regret concerning the medical treatment the patient had received (11 percent), with no significant differences among settings. Annualized estimates of age-sex

TABLE 5
Costs per Study Day Adjusted for Sample Differences
(in dollars)

Service Category	Unbedded Hospice	Bedded Hospice	Conventional Care
Inpatient costs	46	99	135*
Home care costs	54	46	6*
Physician visit costs	9	8	18*
Outpatient clinic costs	1.8	1.2	3.0*
Personal, drug, supplies, and equipment expenditures	1.8	.7	.1
Total costs	101	146	149*

*$p < 0.05$; see text for direction of significant paired contrast(s).

adjusted hospitalization rates for the PCPs were lower than the national average. Age-sex adjusted physical visit rates were higher than the national annual average (U.S. National Center for Health Statistics, 1983), but comparison of PCPs drawn from the hospice and CC samples showed no difference in hospitalizations, physician visits, use of medications for depression, or increased alcohol use during the bereavement period. PCPs of UB hospice patients reported significantly greater emotional distress postmortem than B hospice PCPs, possibly because they had experienced the greater burden of home care.

Cost and Service Utilization Outcomes

Hospice cost comparisons revealed that costs per study day were higher in B than in UB hospices (Table 5). This was principally the result of greater inpatient utilization by B hospice patients (Table 6). UB hospice patients had more home visits than B patients, but the difference in home care costs per day was not large enough to counterbalance the large inpatient cost difference. Physician and outpatient clinic costs per study day were very similar in both types of hospice.

Hospice and conventional care costs were compared (Table 5). Total cost per study day was substantially lower in UB than in B hospice or CC; total costs were comparable for the B hospice and CC groups. Inpatient and physician costs per study day were significantly higher in CC than in either type of hospice. These differences between settings appeared to be related to utilization patterns. CC patients spent more time in inpatient settings than hospice patients and used very few home care services (Table 6). UB hospices substituted home care for inpatient services more frequently than B hospices.

Inpatient utilization increased as death approached in all of the systems of care (Figure 1). Home service use increased dramatically in the last week of life only in the UB hospice sample. Higher costs were associated with increased inpatient utilization.

TABLE 6
Health Service Utilization per Patient
Adjusted for Sample Differences and Study Duration

Service Category	Unbedded Hospice	Bedded Hospice	Conventional Care
Inpatient days	8.0	18.0	23.0*
Home nursing visits	15.5	11.0	3.5*
Home health/homemaker visits	18.0	10.5	4.0*
Social service/other therapies visits	2.5	1.0	.2*
Physician and outpatient clinic visits	9.0	13.0	20.0*

*p < 0.05; see text for direction of significant paired contrast(s).

DISCUSSION

The results of this multisite study confirm that hospice care is different from conventional care. Hospice patients were less likely to receive diagnostic tests, X-rays, and aggressive antitumor therapy in the terminal period, and they were more likely to receive social service support than CC patients. Despite the substantial variation in the pattern of care, we were unable to detect significant improvement in patient quality of life attributable to hospice, with the exception of somewhat better pain and symptom control in bedded (B) hospices than in unbedded (UB) hospices or CC, which was associated with more liberal use of analgesics, both prescribed and consumed. CC providers did not use analgesics as regularly or liberally, and there was reluctance on the part of both patients and providers to treat symptoms as aggressively at home as in the inpatient setting. Physical functioning and a wide variety of quality of life indices were not significantly better in hospice than in conventional care in the last weeks of life.

Because UB hospice patients spent more time at home, they received more direct care and social visiting from family and friends. All patients appeared to maintain social interactions, and their social quality of life was rated highly by the PCPs in all systems.

Families appeared to tolerate the stress of terminal illness and bereavement better than expected. Despite the burden of patient care during the terminal illness, the PCPs reported little social dislocation. Both patients and families reported high levels of satisfaction with the care received in all of the service models. Some of this may, of course, reflect self-selection, but it also could be the result of the extremely high level of support from family and friends that is mobilized in the presence of terminal illness and may leave little room for incremental improvement from professional sources.

Hospice care is less costly than conventional terminal care during the last weeks of life but longer stays erode these economies. UB hospices are more economical than B hospices or CC, largely because the latter two utilize more inpatient care. The economies attributable to hospice progressively decrease with increasing length of stay, but unbedded hospices remain the most economical.

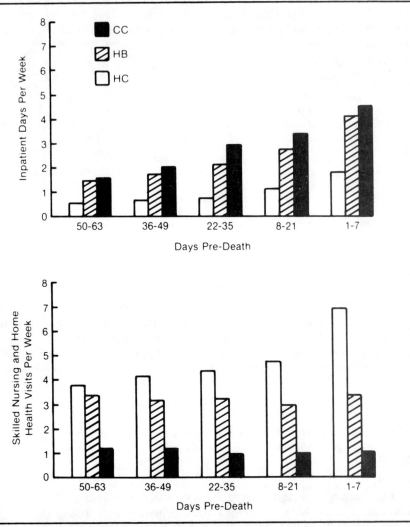

Figure 1   Inpatient and Homecare Utilization Patterns of Follow-Up Sample Members as Death
Approaches by Treatment Setting

These findings conform to preliminary analyses based on a larger Medicare sample of hospice and CC patients (Birnbaum and Kidder, 1984).

In summary, hospice care in the NHS did not consistently improve the quality of life of patients and families when compared to conventional terminal care. Comparable patient/family outcomes were achieved in hospice, however, despite significant reductions in the use of invasive therapeutic and diagnostic procedures, many of which are costly and traumatic. In the last few weeks of life, when conventional care providers liberally utilized inpatient facilities, ancillary services, and invasive procedures, hospice care was less costly. Hospices without their own inpatient facilities were more economical than hospices with such facilities because they were more inclined to keep patients at home, and home care, even when used extensively, was less expensive than inpatient care. Hospice is a viable alternative to conventional terminal care for some patients but is not consistently superior in either outcome or cost.

NOTES

1. Patient self-report utilizing the Melzack Scale failed to confirm these findings, but 50 percent of the patients at two weeks prior to death, and 80 percent at one week, could not report.
2. Nausea, dry mouth, constipation, dizziness, feverishness, dyspnea.

REFERENCES

AMADO, A., B. CRONK, and R. MILEO (1979) "Costs of terminal care: home hospice vs. hospital." Nursing Outlook 27: 522-526.
BIRNBAUM, H. G. and D. KIDDER (1984) "What does hospice cost?" Amer. J. of Public Health (July).
CLAYTON, P. (1974) "Mortality and morbidity in the first year of widowhood." Archives of General Psychiatry 30: 747-750.
Congressional Record (1978) House Resolutions 12358 and 14324.
DRAPER, N. and H. SMITH (1981) Applied Regression Analysis. New York: John Wiley.
DUBOIS, P. M. (1980) The Hospice Way of Death. New York: Human Science Press.
Federal Register (1982) September 29, 47: 42904-09.
General Accounting Office (1979) Hospice Care—A Growing Concept in the United States. Washington, DC: U.S.G.A.O. HRD-79-50.
GREER, D. S., V. MOR, S. SHERWOOD, J. N. MORRIS, and H. BIRNBAUM (1983) "National Hospice Study analysis plan." J. of Chronic Diseases 36: 737-780.
HANSEN, M. and C. EVASHWICK (1981) "Staffing and cost implications for home health agencies." Home Health Care Services Q. 2: 61-81.
JCAH (Joint Commission on the Accreditation of Hospitals) (1981) JCAH Hospice Project Interim Report, Phase I. Chicago, IL: JCAH.
KARNOFSKY, D. A., W. H. ABELMAN, L. F. CRAVER, and J. H. BURCHENAL (1948) "The use of nitrogen mustards in palliative treatments of carcinoma." Cancer 1: 634-656.
KLERMAN, G. and J. IZEN (1977) "The effects of bereavement and grief on physical health and general well-being." Psychosomatic Medicine 9: 1-41.
KLIENBAUM, D. G., L. L. KUPPER, and H. MORGENTERN (1982) Epidemiologic Research. Belmont, CA: Lifetime Learning Publications.
LACK, S. A. (1977) "The hospices concept—the adult with advanced cancer." Proceedings of the American Cancer Society Second National Conference on Human Values and Cancer: 160-166.
———and R. W. BUCKINGHAM (1978) First American Hospice: Three Years of Home Care. New Haven, CT: Hospice Inc.
McNAIR, D. M., M. LORR, and L. F. DROPPLEMAN (1981) EITS manual for the profile of mood states. San Diego, CA: Educational and Industrial Testing Services.
MELZACK, R. (1975) "The McGill pain questionnaire: major properties and scoring methods." Pain 1: 277-299.

MOR, V. and J. HIRIS (1983) "Determinants of the site of death among hospice cancer patients." J. of Health and Social Behavior 24: 375-385.

MOUNT, B. M. (1980) "Hospice care." J. of the Royal Society of Medicine 73: 471-473.

National Hospice Organization (1982) Locator Directory of Hospices in America, 1981-82. McLean, VA: Author.

———(1979) Standards of a Hospice Program of Care. McLean, VA: Author.

OLESON, T. D. and D. E. BRESLER (1979) "California pain assessment profile," in T. D. Oleson and R. Turbo (eds.) Free Yourself from Pain. New York: Simon & Schuster.

PARKES, C. M. and R. BROWN (1972) "Health after bereavement: a controlled study of young Boston widows and widowers." Psychosomatic Medicine 34: 449-461.

SAUNDERS, C. (1979) "The nature of terminal pain and the hospice concept," in J. J. Bonica and V. Ventafridda (eds.) Advances in Pain Research and Therapy. New York: Raven Press.

———P. MAUGER, and P. STRONG (1979) A Manual for the Grief Experience Inventory. University of Southern Florida, Loss and Bereavement Resource Center.

SPITZER, W. O., A. J. DOBSON, J. HALL, et al. (1981) "Measuring the quality of life of cancer patients: a concise QL index for use by physicians." J. of Chronic Diseases 34: 585-597.

STODDARD, S. (1978) The Hospice Movement: A Better Way of Caring for the Dying. New York: Random House.

TWYCROSS, R. G. (1980) "Hospice care—redressing the balance in medicine." J. of the Royal Society of Medicine 73: 475-481.

———(1978) "The assessment of pain in advanced cancer." J. of Medical Ethics 4: 112-116.

U.S. National Center for Health Statistics (1983) "Sex differences in health and use of medical care: United States, 1979." Vital & Health Statistics 3(24).

VAN BUREN, L. (1981) "Hospice home care: a cost analysis of a sample of patients seen during 1980." Home Health Rev. 4: 10-13.

WOLF, M. H., S. M. PUTNAME, S. A. JAMES, and W. B. STILES (1978) "The medical interview satisfaction scale: development of a scale to measure patient perceptions of physician behavior." J. of Behavioral Medicine 1: 391.

8

A Randomised Controlled Trial of Hospice Care

Robert L. Kane, Jeffrey Wales, Leslie Bernstein, Arleen Leibowitz, and Stevan Kaplan

Summary Terminally ill cancer patients at a Veterans Administration hospital were randomly assigned to receive hospice or conventional care. The hospice care was provided both in a special inpatient unit and at home. 137 hospice patients and 110 control patients and their familial care givers (FCGs) were followed until the patient's death. No significant differences were noted between the patient groups in measures of pain, symptoms, activities of daily living, or affect. Hospice patients expressed more satisfaction with the care they received; and hospice patients' FCGs showed somewhat more satisfaction and less anxiety than did those of controls. Hospice care was not associated with a reduced use of hospital inpatient days or therapeutic procedures and was at least as expensive as conventional care.

INTRODUCTION

MEDICINE has undergone a profound change in the way it cares for the dying. Spurred by the work of thanatologists, medical personnel have become more concerned about the quality of patients' last days of life. This transition has resulted in the evolution of the hospice.[1] Pioneered in the United Kingdom in the late 1960s, this institution represents a commitment to palliative and supportive care for those patients whose terminal status can be forecast, usually cancer patients. In the United States there has been intense interest in the hospice.[2] A General Accounting Office study in 1979 identified 59 organisations providing hospice-type care, with 73 more in the planning stages.[3] A survey by the Joint Commission on Accreditation of Hospitals indicated that in early 1983 there were 1100–1200 hospice programmes in the United States (National Hospice Organization, personal communication). These programmes may be either hospital-based or free-standing and may use home care, institutional care, or some combination of the two.

The enthusiasm for hospice care, stimulated by the growing recognition of the importance of care for the dying and a parallel concern about the costs of terminal care,[4] is based primarily on anecdotal data. Claims have been made for benefits including better pain control, fewer symptoms, improved affect, and greater satisfaction with care.[5,6] The early attempts to evaluate hospice care were limited essentially to descriptive studies.[7,8] A large national quasi-

Multicampus Division of Geriatric Medicine,
UCLA School of Medicine, Los Angeles, California 90024, USA

From Robert L. Kane et al., "A Randomised Controlled Trial of Hospice Care," *The Lancet,* 1984, April, 890-894. Copyright 1984 by The Lancet. Reprinted by permission.

experimental study of hospice care is underway to address the differences in outcomes achieved by different modes of hospice care associated with the various ways of funding such care.[9,10] Such investigations must contend with questions about self-selection of hospice patients and the difficulties of identifying comparable controls. Here we present data collected in a randomised controlled trial of hospice effectiveness in the treatment of terminal cancer patients. We examine several outcomes of hospice care that correspond to the stated goals of the hospice and estimate the costs of hospice and standard care.

METHODS

Setting

The hospice programme studied is based at the Veterans Administration (VA) Medical Center, West Los Angeles, Wadsworth Division, a university-affiliated teaching hospital. The hospice includes an 11-bed inpatient unit staffed by 2 physicians, 19 nurses, a social worker, a chaplain, and about 30 volunteers; a home-care programme serving about 25 patients at any given time; and a consultation service for patients awaiting admission to the hospice inpatient unit or needing emergency hospital care when no hospice inpatient beds are available. Although patients on the consultation service are regarded as hospice patients, they remain in the care of a conventional primary physician. Hospice staff provide limited help and advice for the patient and his familial care giver (FCG) during this time.

Patients

To ensure that all patients eligible for hospice care had an opportunity to receive such care, a complete register of cancer patients was developed by continual monitoring of patients in relevant services. For each hospital admission, the primary physician of each patient on the roster was consulted to ascertain whether the patient's condition was terminal. When the physician believed that the patient had a terminal prognosis of two weeks to six months and the patient had been informed of this prognosis, the patient was invited to participate in the study. Each potential subject was told about the nature of hospice care and the conditions of random assignment. An eligible patient was asked to name a person (FCG) to whom he felt close and who helped care for him. When available, the FCG was also asked to participate.

After informed consent was received from patients and their FCGs, patients were randomly assigned to receive hospice or conventional care; the sampling proportion was deliberately weighted to favour hospice care. Baseline interviews were then conducted. Hospice patients were referred to the hospice programme, which conducted its own assessment and developed a treatment plan. Control patients continued under their current care. During the study, no subjects were admitted to the hospice programme except through this process of informed consent and randomisation.

Both hospice and control patients and their FCGs were interviewed according to a fixed schedule until the patient's death or until a preestablished number of interviews of each type had been conducted. The intervals between interviews varied with different questionnaires, and generally became longer over time so as to avoid burdening respondents. The methods have been reported in detail elsewhere.[11]

Measures

The outcome variables selected for measurement were based on tenets of quality outlined by the National Hospice Organization and numerous individual hospices. These include controlling pain and symptoms, providing the necessary support to allow for death at home (if desired), slowing deterioration of functional abilities, lessening depression and anxiety, and increasing patient and FCG satisfaction with patient care, the environment, and their involvement in care decisions. These tenets were endorsed by the hospice staff.

Previously validated measures of these outcome variables were adapted from other studies. Pain scores were based on the work of Melzak.[12] Data are reported in terms of both the presence or absence of pain and the intensity of the pain. The symptom scale was adapted from the California Pain Assessment Profile.[13] It reflects the number and frequency of symptoms reported. The depression scale was adapted from the National Institute of Mental Health's Center for Epidemiologic Studies' scale;[14] previous studies suggest that a score above 13 represents significant depression. Anxiety measures were derived from a section of the General Well-Being Measure used in the Rand Health Insurance Study;[15] a score of 21 or more suggests anxiety. Satisfaction measures included the interpersonal care scale adapted from the Ware scale,[15] a physical environment scale based on that of McCaffree and Harkins,[16] and involvement-in-care questions adapted from the National Cancer Institute's Hospice Study.[17] The involvement-in-care scale yielded a range of scores from 4 to 7; for interpersonal care, the range was 40–50. In both cases, higher scores indicated greater satisfaction. Functional status was assessed by the Katz Activities of Daily Living scale; it was scored as a Guttman scale, and scores ranged from 0 to 6, with higher scores indicating greater disability.[18] These measures have been shown to be reliable and valid for terminal cancer patients and their FCGs.[11]

Analysis

Because the analysis involved comparison of changes in each measure over time in a population continually depleted by death, testing of statistical significance was of special concern. Comparisons at any time-point between the experimental and control groups were confounded by repeated measure bias, which tends to overestimate the significance of differences.

t-tests on baseline data revealed no significant differences between hospice and control subjects on any measures. Because subjects were interviewed according to a fixed schedule until their deaths, there was a wide range in the number of interviews completed. There were, however, no significant differences in the survival patterns of hospice and control patients (see figure) or in the mean number of interviews per subject.

Two measures of pain were evaluated—a dichotomous response variable (present/absent); and, for patients experiencing pain, the score resulting from the administration of the McGill Pain Scale.[12] We first performed t-tests for group differences in the proportions of patients experiencing pain at *each* scheduled interview. To assess whether there were group differences in the proportions of subjects experiencing pain *across* interviews (over time), a likelihood ratio

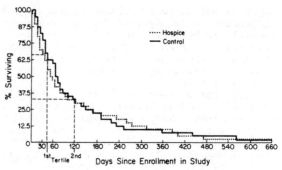

Survival of hospice and control patients.

test was developed. We also computed the percentage of interviews in which each subject experienced pain and made group comparisons based on this measure, evaluating all subjects and subgroups of subjects completing a given number of interviews. *t*-tests at each scheduled interview were performed to determine whether there were group differences in the level of pain experienced by patients in pain.

Repeated-measures analyses of covariance, with baseline score as a covariate, were performed for symptoms, affect, satisfaction, activities of daily living, and involvement-with-care measures to determine whether there were differences between hospice and control subjects. Because repeated-measures analyses require the same number of repeated measurements on each subject, it was necessary to define "cohorts" of subjects according to the minimum number of interviews completed. Five such cohorts were defined as all subjects completing at least 3, 4, 5, 6, and 7 interviews including the baseline interview. Further cohorts were not defined because less than one-third of the original sample of subjects survived beyond seven interviews (about eighteen weeks).

Costs

Costs of care were calculated for each subject in the study for whom a complete file could be assembled. Because the VA does not bill its patients for medical services, we estimated what a non-VA hospital would have billed by ascertaining the services provided and assigning prices charged during the same period at a comparable hospital, the UCLA Medical Center. UCLA is about one mile from the Wadsworth VA and many of the medical staff have appointments in both institutions.

The number of hospital days the patient spent in the hospice ward, the intermediate care ward, a general medical ward, or an intensive care unit was obtained from the charts of each patient who died. For the 23 patients who had inpatient stays in other hospitals, we obtained the total number of hospital days, but we were often unable to obtain the breakdown of days between intensive care unit and other wards. A logit regression indicated that control patients were more likely to be admitted to hospital out of the area than were hospice patients ($p = 0 \cdot 02$). However, because the total number of inpatient days did not differ significantly between the control patients admitted to hospital only in the area and those with at least one out-of-area admission ($p = 0 \cdot 56$), we restricted our detailed analyses to the patients who had all their hospital admissions in the area.

In the cost study we obtained utilisation data from completed inpatient charts. A total of 144 patients had complete data for all cost elements, but bed-day calculations were made on a larger sample of 230 patients. A logit regression revealed no significant differences between patients who were included in the cost substudy and those not included, in terms of hospice or control status, age, race, or diagnosis group at entry.

Completed inpatient charts were abstracted to obtain records of the patient's use of drugs, laboratory, radiology, surgical, and diagnostic procedures, chemotherapy, radiation therapy, nuclear medicine, and consultation services. Each of these was assigned a price. The number of times each drug was administered was summed and multiplied by the unit price of the drug to obtain the total drug costs for a given patient over all hospital stays.

We were able to obtain prices for drugs, major surgical procedures, pathology, and chemotherapy, as well as the cost of a bed in a general medical or intensive-care unit. However, the VA operates two classes of beds for which there was no ready equivalent at UCLA. Wadsworth VA operates an intermediate-care ward for patients not requiring treatment as intensive as that given in a general medical bed. We used the VA cost accounting estimates that an intermediate-care bed costs 70% as much as a general medical bed. For hospice per diem costs, we used two alternate assumptions—(1) equal to intermediate care; and (2) equal to a general medical bed.

RESULTS

Utilisation

Of the 263 patients eligible for the study, only 17 (6%) declined to participate. Another 10 patients withdrew after enrolment. 73% of the patients had someone whom they identified as a primary source of assistance, and 95% of these FCGs agreed to participate (6% dropping out after enrolment). Table I summarises salient features of the experimental and control groups. The mean age in both groups was about 64, with a range of 34–92. Because the study was based at a VA hospital, patients were almost all male. Most subjects were or had been employed, usually in

TABLE I—CHARACTERISTICS OF EXPERIMENTAL
AND CONTROL GROUPS

Characteristic	Hospice (N = 137)	Control (N = 110)
Mean age	63·3	64·0
Male	97·8%	97·2%
White	59·1%	63·6%
Occupation (current or former):		
Operatives	51·8%	51·8%
Professional/technical	14·6%	20·8%
Clerical	10·2%	9·1%
Craftsman	8·0%	6·4%
Unknown	15·3%	12·7%
Primary cancer site:		
Lung	36·5%	35·5%
Prostate	11·0%	10·0%
Ear, nose, throat	9·5%	10·9%
Brain	7·3%	7·3%
Other	35·8%	36·4%

blue-collar activities. The primary cancer sites were similarly distributed in the two groups, lung being the most common site.

The survival curves for the hospice and control groups were essentially the same. Despite the hospice philosophy of eschewing heroic efforts to extend the life of a dying patient, hospice patients died no sooner than did the controls. As shown in the figure, one-third of the group died within 45 days after enrolment, the second third within 120 days. The analysis of outcomes was based on data from this period when at least one-third of the subjects were available. The remaining subjects lived for as long as two years.

Hospice patients who went home were assured direct admission to the hospital at any time. Almost 60% of the hospice patients who died during the study period expired in the hospice, and another third died elsewhere in the hospital. Only 3% died at home. Of controls, almost 80% died in the hospital and 7% died at home. The rest of the deaths for both groups occurred at other institutions, usually nursing homes. These differences are not statistically significant.

Table II shows the total number of inpatient days and their distribution among hospital services for patients assigned to hospice or control group. Hospice patients spent an average of 51 days as inpatients, control patients an average of 47·5 days. There were no statistically significant differences in the total number of days spent in the hospital by hospice and control patients, either in the entire sample or in the sample without out-of-area hospital admission.

The data do not generally indicate less intensive treatment for hospice inpatients. The average number of intensive-care-unit days for hospice and control patients was only 0·2 and 0·3, respectively, and did differ significantly. For control patients, the remaining inpatient days were spent either in general medical beds or in the intermediate-care ward.

Hospice patients were generally treated on the hospice ward. However, if space was not available there, they were admitted to either a general medical ward or an intermediate-care ward. Table II reflects this pattern. Hospice patients spent significantly less time on a general medical ward than did control patients and had fewer days of intermediate care. Another component of institutional care is the use of nursing homes; the control patients had significantly longer average stays in nursing homes.

Because hospice attempts to improve the patient's last days by reducing or eliminating invasive diagnostic procedures and curtailing treatments such as radiation, chemotherapy, and surgery, one would expect to find fewer of these procedures among hospice patients. Table II reveals only two significant differences between hospice and control groups—major surgical procedures and chemotherapy treatments—for both of which hospice patients had significantly more than controls. The majority of both groups had no treatment. Of hospice patients, 74% had no surgery, 62% no radiation, and 84% no chemotherapy. The

TABLE II—UTILISATION OF SERVICES

Service	Mean no per subject*	
	Hospice (N = 128)	Control (N = 102)
Total inpatient days	51·0	47·5
General medical†	13·2	20·7
Hospice	29·2	—
Intensive care unit	0·2	0·3
Intermediate care†	8·3	26·5
Nursing home days†	1·0	11·4
Days at home	44·8	37·9
Surgical procedures	0·51	0·31
Major surgical procedures†	0·09	0·01
Minor surgical procedures	0·42	0·30
Radiation treatments‡	7·4	7·7
Chemotherapy treatments§	1·3	0·49

*Based on chart review for those patients who died before study conclusion.
†p = <0·05.
‡Over 80% of both hospice and control patients had no radiation treatments. However, those few who did had as many as 48 treatments, hence the large number.
§p = 0·03.

corresponding proportions for controls were 82%, 52%, and 84%. The differences in proportions were not statistically significant for any treatment category.

Hospice patients did receive a different style of care. They were treated by a special team in a unit with a heavier staffing ratio than that on the rest of the general hospital wards. This team sought to spend more time with the patient and his family to help them cope more effectively with impending death.

Outcomes

What was the effect of this added effort? At baseline, only 41% of hospice patients and 38% of controls reported pain. Over the course of the study, 34% of hospice and 31% of control subjects *never* reported pain. Neither of these differences was statistically significant. There was no significant difference between the groups in the proportion of subjects with pain over time. Comparison of means for the individually computed percentages of interviews with pain showed no significant differences between groups. For patients experiencing pain, there were no differences in mean pain score at any interview time-point.

Table III summarises the results of the repeated-measures analyses of covariance on cohorts. No differences were found for symptom scores, whether one looked at all symptoms or only those most closely related to cancer. No significant differences in activities-of-daily-living scores were observed between the groups. For depression, control patients had consistently higher scores (ie, were more depressed) than hospice patients, but none of the cohorts showed a statistically significant treatment effect for either depression or anxiety.

TABLE III—EFFECT OF STUDY GROUP, DETERMINED BY
ANALYSIS OF COVARIANCE

Measure	Cohort*				
	3	4	5	6	7
Symptoms	NS	NS	NS	NS	NS
Activities of daily living	NS	NS	NS	NS	NS
Anxiety	NS	NS	NS	NS	NS
Depression	NS	NS	NS	NS	NS
Satisfaction with interpersonal care	<0·02	<0·001	<0·003	<0·002	<0·004
Involvement in care	NS	<0·02	<0·05	<0·003	<0·003

*Minimum number of interviews completed.
NS = p>0·05.

Significant differences do emerge in satisfaction scores. In two of the three areas examined, hospice patients expressed more satisfaction than did control patients. For interpersonal care, all five cohort analyses showed significant differences ($p<0·01$); for involvement in care, four of five were significant ($p<0·01$). Because the physical-environment-satisfaction scale was applicable only to patients who were in hospital, the numbers of respondents at each administration are less than for the other satisfaction measures, and cohorts could not be constructed. t-tests at each of seven time-points revealed no differences in satisfaction with the physical environment between hospice and control groups.

The effects of hospice care on measures of affect and the satisfaction scores of the patients' FCGs are presented in table IV. For anxiety, significant differences favouring hospice were found in three of five cohorts and, for satisfaction with involvement in care, in two of five cohorts.

Costs

To assess how differences in utilisation affect total costs, we assigned prices to the various inpatient and nursing-home services. When we equate the cost of a day in the hospice ward with that of a day in an intermediate-care ward, total mean inpatient cost per hospice patient is about the same as for

TABLE IV—FAMILIAL CARE GIVER RESULTS: EFFECT OF STUDY GROUP,
DETERMINED BY ANALYSIS OF COVARIANCE

Measure	Cohort*				
	3	4	5	6	7
Anxiety	<0·03	<0·02	<0·04	NS	NS
Depression	NS	NS	NS	NS	NS
Satisfaction with interpersonal care	NS	NS	NS	NS	NS
Involvement in care	NS	NS	<0·003	<0·002	NS

*Minimum number of interviews completed.
NS = p>0·05.

TABLE V—ESTIMATED MEAN EXPENDITURE PER PATIENT

Item	Hospice (N=80)	Control (N=64)
Drugs	$1192	$724
Laboratory	692	826
Diagnostic testing	319	366
Major surgery and procedures	364	313
Chemotherapy	70	13
Radiation therapy	953	1249
Nursing-home costs	55	388
Inpatient costs		
Assumption 1 (hospice per diem cost=intermediate care)	11 618	11 614
Assumption 2 (hospice per diem cost=general medical)	14 125	11 614
Total covered costs		
Assumption 1	15 263	15 493
Assumption 2	17 770	15 493

controls ($11 618 *vs* $11 614). The alternative assumption, that hospice per diem costs equal those of a general medical ward, gives hospice costs about $2500 higher ($14 125).

Table V presents average expenditures on main categories of services. There are no significant differences between hospice and control groups for any of these. When costs for hospital days are added, totals per patient are $15 262–17 770 for hospice and $15 493 for controls.

DISCUSSION

Intensive hospice care did not yield the expected benefits in pain or symptom relief or in alleviation of psychological distress when compared with conventional care in a university-affiliated hospital. The differences in satisfaction suggest that both patients and their families appreciated the qualitative differences in hospice care. The pattern of service utilisation suggests that care in this type of hospice is not cheaper than conventional care. Since our findings suggest no substantial difference in cost or effectiveness, we suggest that hospice care should be available as a matter of choice. Some people will want such care; others will opt for more traditional management.

The model of hospice care studied represents a comprehensive approach. Patients received both inpatient and home-care services, often both. It is thus impossible to link a given outcome with a given pattern of care. Questions may be raised about the influence of the hospice consultation service patients on the results. Hospice consultation patients are regarded as hospice patients although they are not under direct hospice control at the time. Reasons for this include being on the waiting list for a hospice inpatient bed, receiving special treatment elsewhere in the hospital such as palliative surgery or radiation, and returning from the hospice home-care programme and awaiting a hospice inpatient bed. During the time that a consultation patient is waiting to enter or re-enter the hospice programme, he is seen by hospice staff but is under the direct care of non-hospice physicians.

We examined the effect of excluding data on these consultation patients. Although no formal statistical analyses could be performed because patient status was not consistent throughout the study, the plots of data did not suggest any significant differences. The exclusion of hospice consultation patients did affect comparison of medical procedures between the hospice and control groups. When the hospice consultations were included, hospice patients had significantly more major surgical procedures than did control patients. When the consultations are removed, the opposite is true. We include the hospice consultations as part of total hospice care because, in practice, a hospital-based hospice may not be able to accommodate in its allotted beds all patients returning from home care on a particular day and because consultation status did not arise randomly but resulted in part from referrals for surgery by the hospice staff.

The lack of significant differences is unlikely to be attributable to small numbers of subjects. The sample sizes were selected to provide a power of $0·8$ to detect a medium effect by t-tests and to account for 5–10% of the variability in general linear models.[19] In the analyses of proportions of patients with pain, power calculations (at the $0·05$ level of significance) based on the number of patients randomised to each group indicated that the power to detect a difference between proportions $0·4$ and $0·25$ was $0·77$, and to detect a difference between the proportions $0·4$ and $0·2$ was $0·95$.[20]

Absence of differences in pain and symptom frequency between hospice and control patients suggests that the hospice may have a lesser role in this technical area than has been suggested. Alternatively, the explanation may be not that hospice care is less effective but that conventional care has become more effective. Better management of pain and symptoms is a medical skill that can be propagated by education. The hospice movement may have made its contribution by sensitising practitioners to their inadequacies.

The randomised control design surmounts one of the major obstacles to hospice research by ensuring that onset of care is comparable for the different groups. (Other hospice investigators have had to work backwards from the date of death to assign a hospice-eligible status to the controls.) However, the randomisation comes at a cost. Only one hospice has been studied. We cannot be sure that our findings are of wide applicability, especially since the VA clientele are atypical of the general population. The VA facility is also part of a large university teaching centre, and may therefore have been early to adopt the hospice philosophy. This study is thus best viewed as part of the evolving picture of hospice care and its consequences. The data from the quasi-experimental study of US hospice care should provide other important dimensions with regard to the effects of different systems on different clients.

This work was supported by grants from the California chapter of the American Cancer Society and the Henry J. Kaiser Family Foundation and by direct assistance from the VA Medical Center, Wadsworth. We thank John Beck, Robert Brook, Bradford Gray, and David Solomon for their comments on an earlier version of this paper.

Correspondence should be addressed to R. L. K., The Rand Corporation, 1700 Main St, Santa Monica, CA 90406, USA.

REFERENCES

1. Cohen KP. Hospice: Prescription for terminal care. Germantown, MD: Aspen Systems Corporation, 1979.
2. Osterweis M, Champagne DS. The U.S. hospice movement: Issues in development. *Am J Publ Health* 1979; **26:** 492–96.
3. U.S. Comptroller General. Hospice care—A growing concept in the United States. Washington, DC: General Accounting Office, 1979 (HRD 79-50).
4. Lubitz J, Prihoda R. Use and costs of Medicare services in the last years of life. In: Health United States 1983. Washington, DC: Public Health Service (in press).
5. Krant MJ. The hospice movement. *N Engl J Med* 1978; **299:** 546–49.
6. Mount BM, Scott JF. Whither hospice evaluation. *J Chron Dis* 1983; **36:** 731–36.
7. Barzelai L. Evaluation of home-based hospice. *J Fam Prac* 1981; **12:** 241–45.
8. Vande Creek L. A home-care hospice profile: Description, evaluation, and cost analysis. *J Fam Prac* 1982; **14:** 53–58.
9. Greer DS, Mor V, Sherwood S, Morris JN, Birnbaum H. National hospice analysis plan. *J Chron Dis* 1983; **36:** 737–80.
10. Mor V, Birnbaum H. Medicare legislation for hospice care: Implications of national hospice study data. *Health Affairs* 1983; 2: 80–90.
11. Wales J, Kane RL, Robbins S, Bernstein L, Krasnow R. The UCLA hospice evaluation study: Methodology and instrumentation. *Med Care* 1983; **27:** 734–44.
12. Melzak R. McGill pain questionnaire: Major properties and scoring methods. *Pain* 1975; **1:** 277–99.
13. Oleson TD, Bresler DE. California pain assessment profile. In: Oleson TD, Turbo R, eds. Free yourself from pain. New York: Simon and Schuster, 1979.
14. Radloff LS. The CES-D scale: A self-report depression scale for research in the general population. *Appl Psychol Meas* 1977; **1:** 385–406.
15. Ware JE Jr, Johnston SA, Davies-Avery A, Brook RH. Conceptualization and measurement of health status for adults in the health insurance study. Vol. 3. Mental Health. Santa Monica: Rand Corporation, 1979 (R-1987/3-HEW).
16. McCaffree KM, Harkins EM. Final report for evaluation of nursing home care. Seattle: Battelle Human Affairs Research Centers, 1976.
17. Baker TH. A cost analysis of three hospice programs. Los Angeles: Kaiser Permanente Medical Care Program, 1981.
18. Katz S, Ford A, Moskowitz R, Jackson B, Jaffe M, Cleveland MA. The Index of ADL: A standardized measure of biological and psychosocial function. *JAMA* 1963; **185:** 914–19.
19. Cohen J. Statistical power analysis for the behavioral sciences. New York: Academic Press, 1977.
20. Casagrande JT, Pike MC, Smith PG. The power function of the exact test for comparing two binomial distributions. *Appl Stat* 1978; **27:** 176–80.

9

WIC Participation and Pregnancy Outcomes
Massachusetts Statewide Evaluation Project

Milton Kotelchuck, Janet B. Schwartz, Marlene T. Anderka, and Karl S. Finison

Abstract: The effects of WIC prenatal participation were examined using data from the Massachusetts Birth and Death Registry. The birth outcomes of 4,126 pregnant women who participated in the WIC program and gave birth in 1978 were compared to those of 4,126 women individually matched on maternal age, race, parity, education, and marital status who did not participate in WIC. WIC prenatal participants are at greater demographic risk for poor pregnancy outcomes compare to all women in the same community. WIC participation is associated with improved pregnancy outcomes, including, a decrease in low birthweight (LBW) incidence (6.9 per cent vs 8.7 per cent) and neonatal mortality (12 vs 35 deaths), an increase in gestational age (40.0 vs 39.7 weeks), and a reduction in inadequate prenatal care (3.8 per cent vs 7.0 per cent). Stratification by demographic subpopulations indicates that subpopulations at higher risk (teenage, unmarried, and Hispanic origin women) have more enhanced pregnancy outcomes associated with WIC participation. Stratification by duration of participation indicates that increased participation is associated with enhanced pregnancy outcomes. While these findings suggest that birth outcome differences are a function of WIC participation, other factors which might distinguish between the two groups could also serve as the basis for alternative explanations. (*Am J Public Health* 1984; 74:1086–1092.)

Introduction

Efforts to improve the health status of pregnant women and their young children through nutritional supplementation and education have long been a part of public health programs in the United States. The Special Supplemental Food Program for Women, Infants and Children (WIC), established in 1972, is the largest and most specifically targeted public health nutrition program in the United States today. The WIC program is designed to reach high-risk pregnant and lactating women, infants, and children up to 5 years of age with supplemental foods and nutrition education, as an adjunct to good health care.[1]

WIC is the first federal nutrition program to use identifiable nutritional risk, in addition to low income, as a criterion for eligibility. Since its inception, WIC has grown to provide benefits to 2.9 million persons monthly, at a cost of $1.36 billion in fiscal year 1983. An estimated 500,000 pregnant women now participate in the WIC program.

Eligible participants receive a monthly set of food vouchers redeemable at local grocers for specific foods tailored to individual needs. Allowable foods include: milk, cheese, iron-fortified cereal, 100% fruit juices, eggs, dried beans, peanut butter, and iron-fortified formula for infants. The cost of the food package is approximately $30 per month, provided at no cost to the participants. Nutrition education is also provided. A more complete description of the WIC program appears elsewhere.[2]

The WIC program, despite its magnitude and its clearly stated public health goals, has not been extensively examined. The lack of research may be the result of a moral acceptance of the virtues of feeding high-risk women or of the methodological difficulties of conducting quality research in a large, decentralized nutrition program. The latter include the difficulty of obtaining a proper comparison sample, the lack of data collected uniformly across program sites, and the need for large sample sizes to show stable

From the Division of Family Health Services, Massachusetts Department of Public Health. Address reprint requests to Milton Kotelchuck, PhD, MPH, Department of Social Medicine and Health Policy, Harvard Medical School, 25 Shattuck Street, Boston, MA 02115. This paper, submitted to the Journal June 27, 1983, was revised and accepted for publication March 21, 1984. Editor's Note: See also Different Views, pp 1145–1149 this issue.

program effects. To date, only two evaluations of prenatal participation in WIC based on perinatal outcomes have been published. Despite quite divergent methodologies, Edozien, *et al*,[3] and Kennedy, *et al*,[4] both reported that WIC participation is positively associated with maternal weight gain, infant birthweight, and gestational age, and that the WIC programs' effectiveness is enhanced by increasing duration of participation. Others maintain that the value of WIC is unproven.[5]

This paper reports the results of the Massachusetts WIC Statewide Evaluation Project, which examined the association between maternal participation in the WIC Program in 1978 and the outcomes of pregnancy. Specifically, four questions were addressed:

- Does the WIC Program reach its target population?
- Is WIC participation associated with more positive outcomes of pregnancy?
- Are the effects of WIC participation similar across all high-risk subpopulations?
- Are the effects of the WIC program enhanced with increased duration of participation?

The Massachusetts WIC Program

The Massachusetts WIC program is similar to WIC programs nationally. In 1978, it operated through 23 non-profit local health centers and social service agencies under contract with the State Department of Public Health. Approximately 22,000 persons participated monthly, of whom over 4,000 were pregnant women. At the time of the study, geographic eligibility, in addition to income guidelines and nutritional risk, was a criterion for WIC participation.

In Massachusetts, the issuance and redemption of all WIC food vouchers is centrally monitored through a single computerized bank control system. This system allows for an accurate documentation of the names, duration of participation, and number of vouchers redeemed for all prenatal WIC participants.

Methodology

Study Population

The basic design of the study is a direct comparison of the pregnancy outcomes of two groups of Massachusetts women who gave birth in 1978: those who participated in the WIC prenatal program, and a matched control group of non-WIC women. The derivation of the study population and

TABLE 1—Selected Maternal Demographic Characteristics, 1978: WIC Participants, Catchment Area Residents and All Massachusetts Residents

Characteristics	% WIC Participants	% Catchment Area Residents	% All Massachusetts Residents	% WIC Saturation of Catchment Area
Age				
≤17 years	12.2	6.0	3.8	36.4
≤19 years	28.6	16.9	11.5	30.4
Education				
≤9 years	14.9	10.5	5.1	25.4
<12 years	49.2	31.5	19.0	28.0
Marital Status				
Unmarried	40.7	23.9	13.7	30.6
Married	59.3	76.1	86.3	14.0
Race				
Black	23.8	16.0	6.2	27.0
White	73.6	81.6	91.8	16.2
Parity				
1	44.9	45.9	44.6	17.6
5+	6.5	4.1	3.3	28.4
TOTAL (N)	(4,126)	(22,995)	(67,187)	

study data results from the linkage of two computerized data systems: the WIC bank voucher system, and the State Birth and Death Registry. Appendix A summarizes the three steps were involved.*

First, the names of all women who registered as a WIC prenatal participant were drawn from the WIC computerized participant voucher reports (N = 4,898). Data on the duration and number of vouchers cashed per month were also extracted. Failure to pick up vouchers for two consecutive months resulted in administrative termination from the program. Administrative termination codes were noted on 525 names. Specific causes for termination were known for 172 of the names, while 353 names remained unaccounted for. As this was a study of women who actively participated in WIC, all 525 women with termination codes were excluded from the study, leaving 4,373 eligible participants.

Second, each mother's name (plus town of residence, race, and expected date of delivery) obtained from the WIC reports was linked, by hand, to the corresponding infant's birth certificate record listed in the state's computerized Birth Registry file. Twin births (46) and know fetal deaths (15) were excluded, as were 191 names which could not be positively linked.

Third, each WIC participant was individually matched to a control subject on the basis of five maternal characteristics available on the birth certificates: age, race, parity, educational level, and marital status (Appendix B). Controls were selected from the pool of 64,000 remaining non-WIC births in the computerized State Birth Registry (68,000 total 1978 resident births minus the approximately 4,000 WIC births). Matching was performed by hand with the aid of computer-derived lists. Efforts were made to facilitate geographic similarity of the WIC and control subjects; matching was attempted first within the same catchment area, then within similar types of towns, and finally anywhere within the state. The first eligible woman meeting all five study criteria was chosen. All matching was exact.** Five subjects who could not be matched were excluded.

The final sample, composed of 4,126 matched pairs of

* Detailed procedure manual available from authors upon request.
** Since the computerized birth registry is sequenced by date of birth, the control subjects tend to be born earlier in the year. Given the expansion of the WIC program in Massachusetts during 1978, the WIC subjects tend to be born later in the year. No seasonality bias in birth outcomes was noticed.

WIC and non-WIC mothers, included 95 per cent of all eligible 1978 prenatal WIC participants in Massachusetts.

Derivation of Study Data

Once the WIC cases and matched controls were selected, all data from their birth certificates were extracted for analysis. The Massachusetts birth certificate provides data on maternal demographic characteristics, prenatal care, and pregnancy outcomes.[6] The State Death Registry file provides information on all neonatal deaths between birth and 28 days.

Data Analysis

The demographic characteristics of WIC participants were contrasted with the characteristics of all pregnant women residing in the same catchment area and statewide in 1978. WIC participants were then compared directly to their matched non-WIC controls on the birth outcome measures. Differences were statistically examined by use of paired T-test comparisons for continuous data items and by McNemar Chi-square comparisons for ordinal data items. Pairwise deletions were used for any subject pair having missing data. The women in the WIC sample and their matched controls were then stratified into a number of subpopulations for separate analyses of birth outcome differences. These subgroups were defined on the basis of demographic characteristics or duration of WIC participation and are not statistically independent of each other.

Results

WIC Population Characteristics—The comparison of selected demographic characteristics (Table 1) suggests that the WIC population comes from demographic groups at higher risk for poor pregnancy outcomes. The WIC prenatal population is younger and less educated, contains more unmarried and minority women, and has a larger number of high parity births compared to all women who reside in the same WIC catchment area or statewide and gave birth in 1978. The Massachusetts WIC program sites in 1978 were located in more disadvantaged areas of the state and, within the program, the higher risk subpopulations were proportionally more heavily represented. Almost 18 per cent of all women who gave birth in 1978 in WIC catchment areas were WIC prenatal participants.

Overall WIC and Control Group Comparison—The

TABLE 2—Comparison of WIC and Control Birth Outcomes

Findings	N	WIC	Control	Difference	95% Confidence Interval
Birthweight					
Birthweight (in grams)	4121	3281	3260	+21*	±23.4
Per Cent Low Birthweight	4121	6.9	8.7	−1.8**	±1.1
Per Cent Small for Gestational Age†	3615	5.0	5.0	0.0	±1.0
Gestation Adjusted Birthweight (in grams)††	4121	−52.0	−48.4	−3.6	±21.9
Gestation					
Gestational Age (in weeks)	3722	40.0	39.7	+0.3***	±.1
Per Cent Premature (<37 weeks)	3722	8.5	9.8	−1.3*	±1.3
Morbidity					
Per Cent with Complications of Pregnancy, Delivery and Labor	4115	20.2	21.1	−0.9	±1.7
Per Cent with Congenital Malformations	4126	1.7	1.7	0.0	±0.6
Per Cent Low (≤5) Apgar Score (one minute)	3732	5.1	5.7	−0.6	±1.0
Per Cent Low (≤5) Apgar Score (five minute)	3716	.5	1.0	−0.5*	±0.4
Mortality					
Number of Neonatal Deaths	4126	12	35	−23**	±13
Prenatal Care					
Number of Prenatal Visits	3721	11.2	10.8	+0.4***	±0.2
Month Prenatal Care Began	3721	2.7	2.9	−0.2***	±0.1
Adequacy of Prenatal Care Index†††	3675	1.34	1.41	−0.07***	±0.03
Per Cent with Inadequate Care	—	3.9	7.0	−3.1***	±1.0
Per Cent with Intermediate Care	—	26.7	26.7	0.0	±2.0
Per Cent with Adequate Care	—	69.4	66.3	+3.1**	±2.1

* = p < .10.
** = p < .05.
*** = p < .01.
**** = p < .001.

†Small for gestational ages is defined as an infant weighing below the 10th percentile for their gestational age at birth. Figures derived from Battaglia and Lubchecno.[7]

††The gestational correction for birthweight is determined by subtracting the observed birthweight from the mean Massachusetts birthweight for that gestational age.

†††The Institute of Medicine adequacy of prenatal care index is a 3-point index combining the number of prenatal visits and month prenatal care began, with an adjustment for gestational age. Adequate care assumes that the first prenatal care visit occurs in 1st trimester, with one additional visit per month of pregnancy.[8]

overall results are presented in Table 2. WIC participation is associated with improved pregnancy outcomes: small improvements in overall mean birth characteristics (gestational age and birthweight) and larger reductions for some of the low frequency and marginal pregnancy outcomes (low birthweight, low 5 minute Apgar scores, neonatal mortality, and prematurity). There is a 21 per cent decrease in the incidence of low birthweight (283 WIC vs 360 control infants). The reduction in prematurity associated with WIC participation reaches statistical significance if prematurity is defined below 36 weeks gestational age (5.7 per cent vs 7.0 per cent). The mean 1 minute and 5 minute Apgar scores were not significantly different.

WIC participation is also associated with better prenatal care; there is a 44 per cent decrease in the number of women receiving inadequate care.

High Risk Subpopulations—Teenage mothers, as a group, show increased birthweight, increased gestational age, decreased LBW status, and improved prenatal care (Table 3). In general, there is an inverse relationship between age of mother and the impact of WIC on birth outcome. The youngest mothers, age 15 and under, had the largest pregnancy benefits and biggest decline in inadequate prenatal care (6.1 per cent WIC vs 18.7 per cent non-WIC).

WIC participation is associated with positive birth outcomes for Black, White, and Hispanic origin women.***

*** For this analysis, Hispanic status is defined solely on the basis of maternal birth site and includes women born in Latin America, Puerto Rico, or other Caribbean Islands. Hispanics born in the US are not included. Matched controls for Hispanic origin women are not necessarily of Hispanic origin.

Improved birth outcomes appear strongest for women of Hispanic origin, with significant improvements in birthweight, gestational age, and LBW status, but with no changes in prenatal care. In general, the positive association of WIC participation and birth outcomes seems stronger for Blacks than for the White population, and even stronger when the Hispanic population is removed. Significant benefits are associated with WIC participation for unmarried women: improvements in birthweight, gestational age, LBW status, and adequacy of prenatal care. The trends appear similar to those for teenage women, many of whom also fall into this category. An inverse relation between maternal education and improved birth outcomes is evident. Women with less than a high school education show significant improvements in birthweight, LBW status, and adequacy of prenatal care. Stratification of the sample by birth parity revealed no consistent pattern.

Increased Duration of WIC Participation—Duration of prenatal participation in WIC is based on the number of months between the month of the first redemption of a voucher and the month of delivery. The mean duration of prenatal participation in WIC in 1978 was 4.6 months.

The cumulative impact of WIC participation on birth outcomes was examined in two ways. First, WIC participants and their matched controls were stratified into three groups based on absolute number of months in the WIC program: 33 per cent participated for one to three months; 45 per cent for four to six months; and 22 per cent for seven to nine months. Second, to compensate partially for differing lengths of gestation, participants were also stratified into four groups based on percentage of pregnancy in the WIC

TABLE 3—Selected Birth Outcome Differences by Demographic Subpopulations (WIC Minus Control)

Subpopulation	N	Birthweight Difference	LBW Difference	Gestation Difference	Inadequate Care Difference
Maternal Age (years)					
≤15	95	98	−3.2	.5	−11.6
≤17	504	57	−3.2°	.5*	−7.3***
≤19	1178	38°	−3.0*	.4***	−5.2***
20–34	2781	16	−3.2°	.1	−2.3***
34+	162	−10	−4.9	.2	−0.6
Race/Ethnicity					
Hispanic origin	906	65*	−2.4*	.3*	0.8
Black	978	37	−2.1	.3**	−4.6***
White	3010	14	−1.7**	.2***	−2.6***
White—Hispanic	2298	8	−1.3	.2**	−2.7***
Marital Status					
Unmarried	1677	35°	−2.5**	.3***	−6.7***
Married	2445	14	−1.2	.1	−0.5
Education (years)					
<12	2033	36*	−2.5	.2	−4.4***
12	1498	2	−1.4	.3**	−4.0***
>12	468	10	−1.0	.1	−1.3
Parity					
1	1852	14	−1.6°	.3**	−4.0***
2–3	1956	12	−1.6	.2	−1.5*
4+	520	20	−3.3°	.1	−4.8*

° = p < .10.
* = p < .05.
** = p < .01.
*** = p < .001.

rogram: 32 per cent participated for 0–40 per cent of their regnancy; 40 per cent participated for 41–70 per cent; 20 per ent participated for 71–100 per cent; and 8 per cent had nknown gestations.

The results for duration in the WIC prenatal program by umber of months are presented in Table 4. Increased uration in WIC is associated with enhanced pregnancy utcomes. In particular, increased duration is significantly

associated with increases in mean birthweight and gestational age, and decreases in the incidence of low birthweight, prematurity, small for gestational age (SGA), and neonatal deaths. The findings are strongest for the 7–9 month participants. It would appear that the reduction in the incidence of some of the poorer marginal pregnancy outcomes (LBW and neonatal mortality) is significant from 4–6 months of participation, while enhancement of mean birth characteristics

TABLE 4—Selected Birth Outcome Measures by Duration WIC Participation

Birth Outcome	Months WIC Participation			Per Cent of Pregnancy WIC Participation			
	1–3	4–6	7–9	Unknown	0–40%	41–70%	71–100%
Birthweight (grams)							
WIC	3236	3264	3385***	3272	3260	3269	3341*
Control	3260	3253	3274	3245	3254	3252	3291
Low Brithweight %							
WIC	8.2	7.6*	3.4***	7.7	8.0	7.6*	5.9*
Control	7.8	9.5	8.6	10.8	8.7	10.5	8.6
Gestational Age (weeks)							
WIC	39.8	39.8	40.4***	39.8	40.1**	39.9**	39.8
Control	39.8	39.8	39.7	39.9	39.8	39.7	39.8
Premature (<37 weeks)							
WIC	10.7	9.1	4.3***	12.9	10.5	8.5	9.5
Control	9.5	9.4	9.5	9.7	11.5	11.2	9.7
Small for Gestational Age %			✓				
WIC	5.3	5.2	2.6*	8.2	6.2	6.4	4.8
Control	4.5	5.4	4.7	6.5	5.2	5.9	5.2
Neonatal Mortality (#)							
WIC	7	5*	0*	1	4	5	2
Control	12	15	8	4	13	11	7
Inadequate Prenatal Care %							
WIC	7.7	2.6***	0.6***	8.8	7.4	2.7***	0.6***
Control	6.8	7.7	5.6	8.6	6.8	8.7	5.8
Total (N)	(1365)	(1848)	(909)	(308)	(1307)	(1664)	(844)

° = p < .10.
* = p < .05.
** = p < .01.
*** = p < .001.

(birthweight and gestational age) are significant only for the 7–9 month participants.

Improved prenatal care is also associated with increased duration in WIC. Significant improvements are noted for the 4–6 month participants, and even more strongly for 7–9 month participants. However, the 1–3 month WIC participants have received less adequate prenatal care than their matched controls.

The results for percentage of pregnancy in the WIC program are also presented in Table 4. Mean birthweights and mean birthweight differences increase in a positive direction with increasing percentage of pregnancy in WIC. Both the moderate and highest percentage duration groups show decreases in LBW. The relative incidence of LBW (the WIC/control ratio) decreases with increasing percentage of pregnancy on WIC (91 per cent, 72 per cent, 68 per cent).

Gestationally based measures do not follow the prior pattern. Since the stratifying factor—percentage of pregnancy in WIC—controls in part for differing length gestations, no duration trends would be expected for gestationally based measures; none are seen for percentage premature or SGA. However, for short and moderate length percentage of pregnancies, WIC participants have significantly longer mean gestations than their matched controls. This may be an artifact, however; this stratification will bias WIC women with the longest gestations into the lower percentile categories.

Prenatal care measures are the least influenced by the two methods of analysis for duration effects. Improved prenatal care is associated with increased percentage of pregnancy in WIC. The incidence of inadequate prenatal care declines rapidly with increasing duration.

Discussion

The present study design overcomes, in part, the difficulty of establishing an adequate comparison sample for WIC evaluations·by using well defined individually matched controls available from the State Birth Registry. Standardized birth outcome information collected uniformly on all births, independent of WIC participation status, should eliminate any ascertainment bias between WIC and non-WIC subjects. The inclusion of virtually the entire 1978 Massachusetts prenatal WIC population should make the results more robust than studies based on smaller samples and more limited numbers of WIC sites. The larger sample size and the matched pair study design allows for analyses of subpopulations and low frequency birth events, neither of which were accessible to earlier studies.

Presumably, if WIC is properly targeted, demographic groups that are expected to have a higher percentage of poorly nourished women[9] will be more heavily represented in the WIC population. Massachusetts WIC program sites are located in more disadvantaged areas of the state and, within the WIC program itself, the higher risk subgroups are more heavily represented. Although appropriately targeted, there are many more women eligible for the WIC prenatal program who did not or could not participate; in 1980, the federal government estimated that only 21 per cent of eligible women in Massachusetts were enrolled in WIC.[10]

Our results indicate that participation in WIC is associated with enhanced pregnancy outcomes. The direction and the magnitude of the results are in general accord with earlier WIC evaluation studies.[3,4] The small birthweight gain (21 grams) and gestational age gain (two days) suggest that overall mean birth characteristics may not be easily shifted by public health nutrition supplementation and education programs in industrialized countries. Even the gains associated with the lengthier WIC participation (+111 grams birthweight and +5 days gestational age) are relatively small representing no more than 2–3 per cent of the total pregnancy weight gain and gestation.

The larger reductions in the incidence of low birth weight, prematurity, and neonatal mortality suggest that nutrition intervention programs may be more effective in impacting on the poorer outcomes of pregnancy. Those at the lowest end of the birth outcome distribution seem to have benefited most from the WIC participation. It is these high risk births that public health programs such as WIC are trying to reduce; these are the births associated with late childhood morbidity, developmental delays, and higher use of health and special education services.[11] The magnitude of the decrease in LBW infants (21 per cent) seen in this study is consistent with the prior WIC studies by Edozien, et al,[3] and Kennedy, et al,[4] which noted 23 per cent and 32 per cent LBW reductions, respectively.

The observed decrease in neonatal mortality has not been noted in earlier WIC evaluations. Approximately 50 per cent of the improvement in neonatal mortality (12.08 deaths) appears to be due to the better WIC birthweight distribution compared to the control population. The remaining improvements must therefore reflect enhanced birthweight specific mortality, although any WIC-associated causes for this cannot be determined by the present study. While prenatal care differed between the two study groups, approximately equal numbers of WIC and control births and neonatal deaths were born in level III hospitals with neonatal intensive care units and in small hospitals with under 1,000 deliveries annually. Causes of death revealed no distinctive patterns.

One must consider the possibility of neonatal death being undercounted. Information on neonatal deaths is derived from a different data source than all other birth outcomes measures in the study—the annual neonatal matched birth and death file from the State Death Registry. When all WIC, control excluded, and unlinked names were carefully re-examined with names in this file, no additional deaths were found. (The absence of birth certificates for the excluded and unlinked names increases the possibility of their being undercounted.) Potential undercounting notwithstanding, from the moment of viability, defined by the existence of a birth certificate, the WIC and control samples looked different in terms of subsequent neonatal mortality. Nevertheless, some caution must be used in interpreting the magnitude of the mortality findings. Further research confirmation is needed before extrapolations to other high-risk populations are warranted.

Comparative information on all fetal deaths was not available to this study; the non-WIC control sample was selected from a population of viable births (e.g., infants having a birth certificate). Thus the WIC and control populations could not be compared over the full range of fetal outcomes.

The improvement in prenatal care among WIC participants, especially the decrease in the per cent of women with inadequate prenatal care, has not been demonstrated previously. Whether WIC participation encourages more subsequent utilization of health care, as some researchers have noted,[12] or whether better prenatal care leads to increased WIC enrollments cannot be determined from this study. All enatal WIC participants must document their pregnancy atus, an act that encourages a formal prenatal care visit and ereby increases the likelihood of being drawn at an early age into a prenatal care health network. Improved prenatal are is both an important goal and an achievement of the 'IC program.

Benefits associated with WIC participation do not appear limited to any particular population group, but are seen cross a wide spectrum of subpopulations. Subpopulations higher nutritional risk for poor pregnancy outcomes, owever, appear to benefit more strongly, especially teenage, unmarried, and Hispanic origin women. In general, the eediest populations seem to benefit the most from the WIC rogram.

Increased duration of participation in the WIC program ppears to be associated with enhanced birth outcomes, in eneral accord with prior WIC research.[3,4] The birth outomes for the longest duration WIC participants reach or urpass the State's overall mean birthweight (3343 grams) nd incidence of LBW (6.55 per cent).

Estimating the exact magnitude of the cumulative beneits associated with increased duration of participation in WIC is methodologically complicated. Duration of participaion and gestational age are, in part, confounded. WIC enefits may be mediated through increased gestational age ut in turn, increased gestational age allows for increased luration in WIC. Any grouping of subjects for statistical analysis on the basis of extensive absolute duration of participation in WIC virtually assures that they have longer gestations and higher birthweight; while any statistical corrections for length of gestation will eliminate the benefits associated with the program's enhancement of gestational age.

Since no ideal analytic solution exists,[13] we used two alternative methods: absolute duration in WIC, and percentage of pregnancy in WIC. Since the absolute duration measure may be an over-estimation and the percentage of pregnancy may be an under-estimation, we suggest that the magnitude of the cumulative benefits associated with WIC should fall between these two estimates. Both methods of analyses imply that more extensive WIC participation is associated with more beneficial birth outcomes. The absolute duration analysis would indicate that the benefits are not simply linear; WIC participation greater than six months would appear maximally beneficial.

It is not only chance or self-motivation that determines if a person enters WIC early or late. Barriers and incentives to early participation exist. Haddad and Willis[14] have shown that the probability of women entering WIC in their first three months of pregnancy is significantly enhanced if the WIC program site has been open a long time, delivers it supplementation through retail stores, and uses public service announcements. The potential benefits associated with the WIC program are not yet being reached; only 22 per cent of the WIC prenatal participants participated for more than six months.

The comprehensiveness of the case population is an important element in assessing the validity and generalizability of the present study. The names of 525 women administratively excluded from the WIC prenatal program were omitted from this study. Unfortunately, very little demographic or motivational information is available about them from the WIC computerized records. The 353 names, which had no reason specified for their exclusion, were similar racially to the WIC study population (68.6 per cent White

excluded group vs 73.6 per cent study group). We are doubtful that most of these 353 names led to an actual Massachusetts birth. Less than 10 per cent of these women had locatable birth certificates. Abortions, fraud, computer errors, and out-of-state moves are the more likely unrecorded realities for these names.† Women do not always inform the WIC program of their reasons for discontinuance. Nevertheless, one cannot rule out the possibility that the administratively excluded names may have had specific characteristics which would bias the overall study results.

The birth certificates for 191 women who were in the WIC program prenatally could not be located. Again, little epidemiologic information is available about these women. Racially (based on their WIC records) they are similar; their duration of participation in WIC is essentially the same as the WIC group. No fetal deaths were located among this group. One can not rule out the possibility that they may have had specific characteristics which would bias the overall results. Five WIC women with birth certificates were not matched to controls.

Overall, we estimate that at least 95 per cent of the WIC prenatal participant population were included in the study which represents the largest and most comprehensive series on WIC prenatal participants to date.

Establishing the existence and magnitude of a WIC program effect also depends critically on the comparability of the WIC and matched control groups. Unfortunately, there are inherent limitations to the conclusions that can be drawn from a retrospective cohort study in which the exposure (WIC) group is self-selected and the control group is derived by a post-hoc matching procedure. A more ideal randomized case control study would pose serious ethical dilemmas. Since many known confounding factors have been controlled, we believe that the statistical differences between the WIC and control groups are a function of WIC participation; however, additional confounding factors may also be characteristic of the WIC or control populations and account for any birth outcome differences noted.

The Massachusetts birth certificates do not provide specific information on maternal pre-pregnancy weight or height, maternal weight gain, maternal smoking habits, or maternal morbidity. Any of these factors, if unevenly distributed, may be sufficient to distort the overall outcomes. WIC participants may be more strongly motivated to improve the prenatal health of their future offspring than are the control women. Such a motivational difference could cause both an improvement in pregnancy outcome and a desire to enroll in the WIC program. The findings of earlier and more frequent prenatal care visits may be supportive of this view. The increase in prenatal care may also be the cause of the improved birth outcomes, and not simply another consequence of WIC participation. The lack of prenatal care improvements among Hispanic origin women who show enhanced birth outcomes argues somewhat against this interpretation. The present study design does not lend itself to a study of prenatal care, nutrition supplementation, or nutrition counseling independently of each other.

Although these alternative explanations for the birth outcome differences tend to suggest that the attributed WIC program effects may be over-estimated, an under-estimation may be just as likely. The WIC population could be financial-

---

† Women who delivered prematurely, even shortly after joining the WIC program, would not be administratively excluded; these women would be switched to the WIC postpartum program and their birth records included in this study.

ly poorer and at greater obstetric risk than their matched controls. All WIC participants must have an income under 195 per cent of the poverty level, while the controls have no restrictions on income, and presumably some have higher incomes. Post-hoc analyses reveal that there were more women of Hispanic origin in the WIC than the control sample (906 vs 509). And WIC participants are selected, in part, on the basis of poor prior obstetrical histories, while no such criteria exists for the control group. These potential confounding factors in a matched study design would decrease the likelihood of showing positive birth outcomes associated with WIC participation.

In summary, the Massachusetts WIC Statewide Evaluation Project compared the birth outcomes of 4,126 WIC prenatal participants and 4,126 individually matched controls, utilizing public birth and death certificates. Results showed that the WIC program appears to be targeted to women at high demographic risk for poor pregnancy outcomes; that overall WIC participation is associated with small improvements in mean birth characteristics, larger reductions in marginal pregnancy outcomes, and enhanced prenatal care; and, that these benefits are observed more strongly in higher risk subpopulations and are enhanced with increased duration of participation. Based on the information available to this study, we conclude that participation in the WIC prenatal program is associated with improved pregnancy outcomes for women at high nutritional and financial risk.

REFERENCES

1. Public Law 94-105, USC 1786, Section 14, 1975.
2. Berkenfield J, Schwartz JB: Nutrition intervention in the community—the "WIC" program. N Engl J Med 1980; 302:579–581.
3. Edozien JC, Switzer BR, Bryan RB. Medical evaluation of the Special Supplemental Food Program for Women, Infants and Children. Am J Clin Nutr 1979; 32:677–682.
4. Kennedy ET, Gershoff S, Reed RB, Austin JE. Evaluation of the effect of WIC supplemental feeding on birth weight. J Am Dietet Assoc 1982; 80:220–227.
5. Rush D: Is WIC worthwhile? (editorial) Am J Public Health 1982; 72:1101–1103.
6. US Dept of Health and Human Services: The 1978 Revision of the US Standard Certificates. DHHS Pub. No. PHS 83-1460, Series 4, No. 23. Washington, DC: Govt Printing Office, 1983.
7. Battaglia FC, Lubchenco LO: A practical classification of newborn infants by weight and gestational age. J Pediatr 1967; 71:159–163.
8. Kessner DM, Singer J, Kalk CE, Schlesinger ER: Infant Death: An Analysis of Maternal Risk and Health Care. Washington DC: Institute of Medicine, National Academy of Sciences, 1973.
9. US Dept of Health, Education, and Welfare: Caloric and Selected Nutrient Values for Persons 1–74 years of Age, First Health and Nutrition Examination Survey, United States, 1971–74. DHEW Pub. No. PHS 73–1311, Series 11, No. 209. Washington DC: Govt Printing Office, 1976.
10. US Dept of Health and Human Services: Better Health for our Children: A National Strategy. DHHS Pub. No. PHS 79-55071, Vol III. Washington, DC: Govt Printing Office, 1981.
11. Fitzhardinge PM: Follow-up studies of the low birthweight infants. Clin Perinatol 1976; 3:503–516.
12. Kotch JB, Whiteman D: Effect of a WIC program on children's clinic activity in a local health department. Med Care 1982; 20:691–698.
13. Harris JE: Prenatal medical care and infant mortality. In Fuchs VR (ed) Economic Aspects of Health. Chicago: University of Chicago Press 1982.
14. Haddad LJ, Willis CE: An analysis of factors leading to early enrollment in the Massachusetts Special Supplemental Feeding Program for Women Infants and Children. Amherst: Massachusetts Experimental Station Research Bulletin, University of Massachusetts, 1983; No. 682.

Acknowledgments

This study was conducted with the support of the US Department of Agriculture, Grant #593198974. Preparation of this text was supported, in part, by funds granted by the Jane Hilder Harris Foundation and the Robert Wood Johnson Foundation to the Harvard Medical School. The authors wish to thank the staffs of the WIC Program and the Divisions of Family Health Services and Health Statistics and Research at the Massachusetts Department of Public Health for their support of this study; Barbara Bullock, Barbara Hayes, and Eleanor Stagliola for the preparation of the data and manuscript; and Kathleen DesMaisons, Bernard Guyer, Eileen Kennedy, Pearl Russo, and Linda Jo Stern for their critical comments on the earlier drafts of this paper. An earlier version of this paper was presented at the Annual Meeting of the American Public Health Association, Los Angeles, October 1981.

APPENDIX A

Derivation of Study Population: Massachusetts WIC Evaluation Project

Number of Names of Eligible WIC Prenatal Participants		4,898
Number of Excluded Names	525	
Known moved out-of-state		18
Known abortions and miscarriages		62
Computer errors		82
Terminated for cause from program*		353
Number of Names Eligible for Study		4,373
Number of Omitted and Unlinked Names	252	
Twins omitted		46
Stillbirths omitted (no birth certificates)		15
Unlinked (no birth certificate found)**		191
Number of Unmatched Names	5	
No control found		5
Number of WIC Prenatal Participants Linked to their Infant's Birth Certificate and Matched to a Control		4,126
Per Cent Study Cases of Eligible WIC Names		95%

*Causes for administrative termination include: non-use of issued vouchers, no longer at nutritional risk, violations of regulations, no longer income eligible, possible fraud.
**Reasons include: out-of-state move, name changes, possible fraud.

APPENDIX B

Matching Criteria between WIC and Control Samples

Age (years): 15 & under, 16–17, 18–19, 20–24, 25–29, 30–34, 35+
Race*: Black, White, Oriental, Other
Parity: 1, 2, 3, 4, 5+
Years of Education: 8 and under, 9–11, 12, 13–16, 17 or more
Marital Status: Married, Unmarried

*Hispanic ethnicity is coded racially as White on birth certificates following the NCHS convention.

Some Comments on the Massachusetts WIC Evaluation

David Rush

The Special Supplemental Food Program for Women, Infants and Children (WIC) is a pathfinding nationwide effort aimed to improve the health and nutrition of pregnant women, and children up to the age of five, in families of low income, deemed to be at great risk of ill health due to marginal or deficient nutrition. There have been numerous efforts to assess the impact of the WIC program on its recipients; we have recently reviewed some 46 studies.[1] Many of these studies were small, or of relatively unsophisticated design or execution. It is therefore of great importance to have as many studies as possible that will help us to specify the value of the WIC program.

Unfortunately, despite hard work and the highest of motives, the study published in this issue of the journal by Kotelchuck, et al,[2] needs some additional work before it can contribute to the specification of the effects of the WIC program during pregnancy on perinatal outcome. There is one problem of study design, and another of analysis, that suggest that it would be wise to defer drawing conclusions from this work until supplemental information and analyses are available.

The Fate of Women Who Were Terminated from the WIC Program

The initial sample included 4,898 women who were known to have been enrolled in the WIC program during pregnancy and then delivered infants in Massachusetts in 1978. Five hundred twenty-five women were immediately excluded from the study group, 353 of whom had been terminated from the program. Kotelchuck, et al, state in Appendix A that "Causes for termination include: non-use of issued vouchers, no longer at nutritional risk, violations of regulations, no longer income eligible, possible fraud."[2] When joining the WIC program in Massachusetts, the participant signs an agreement, which states that "If you do not pick up your vouchers two months in a row, you will be terminated from the program." Thus, a woman might have used her issued vouchers, returned for a second set, used those, but if she did not return a second time for a further supply of vouchers, she was terminated from the program. What sort of bias might be introduced into the study by the exclusion of this group (of indeterminant size, since the 353 include women who were those terminated for all reasons)? It seems obvious that one of the reasons for not returning could have been premature delivery. Thus, among these 353, we must hypothesize that there might have been a higher frequency of preterm delivery, and consequent low birth-

weight, than among the residuum of women who, by definition, had to have returned to pick up vouchers at least twice. How might this have affected the results reported by Kotelchuck, et al? Among their major findings were a much lower frequency of neonatal death in the WIC group. There were 35 neonatal deaths in the control group and 12 in the WIC group. Given that women in the WIC group were of low income, at moderately high medical and nutritional risk, and frequently of minority ethnic status, this rate of neonatal death (in 1978) of 2.9 per 1,000 is remarkably low, lower than that among the most privileged populations in the world at that time. Also, there was a greater difference in frequency of birthweight under 1500 grams between the WIC group and controls than in any other birthweight category (not reported in this paper, but reported in their reports submitted to the Department of Agriculture): more than twice as many infants under 1500 grams were born in the control group (n = 43) as in the WIC group (n = 20).

Given such low rates of neonatal death and very low birthweight, we must be concerned that some confounding factor may be responsible for these results. The one which appears most likely is that the terminated cases may have included a subgroup of very early deliveries that were excluded from the WIC but not from the control group, and that the proper comparison would have been between all women recruited into the WIC program (including those terminated) and matched controls. Until the authors are able to trace the fate of the 353 terminated women, the results for both neonatal death and frequency of low birthweight remain problematical.

Effects of Duration of WIC Benefits on Outcome

In their Table 4, the authors compare the outcomes of WIC recipients with their matched controls, stratified by the recipient's number of months of participation in the WIC program. The results as presented cannot be interpreted as effects of greater duration of participation in the WIC program. The numbers of months of participation are surely strongly correlated with the duration of pregnancy and the analysis is confounded by duration of gestation. Thus, in order to have had seven to nine months participation, the duration of gestation would have had to have passed, at minimum, seven and a half or eight months. A woman who enrolled relatively early in pregnancy would not meet this seven-month criterion if she delivered very prematurely. On the other hand, this restriction is not present for controls: they will have an array of durations of gestation independent of the duration of WIC participation of the woman to whom they were matched. Since short duration of WIC participation (one to three months) is likely to be correlated with short duration of gestation, and thus with low birthweight, we might expect controls to have higher birthweight than

Address reprint requests to Dr. David Rush, Department of Pediatrics, Albert Einstein College of Medicine and Yeshiva University, Rose F. Kennedy Center, Bronx, NY 10461.
Editor's Note: See also related article p 1086 this issue.

short-term WIC participants, and lower birthweight than long-term WIC participants, independent of any program effect. This is, in fact, what happened. Compared to those with short duration of WIC participation, infants of controls weighed more, while, compared to those with long duration of WIC participation, controls weighed less. Until this confounding with duration of gestation is removed from the analysis, no conclusions are possible from this table. In prior versions of this work, where birthweight was adjusted for duration of gestation, no significant relationships persisted between duration of WIC benefits and birthweight.

Matching by Geographic Area

In the final report to the funding agency[3] of this research, the authors stated that each WIC infant was matched to a control on six maternal characteristics (the sixth was geographic location, which was defined as urban, suburban, or rural). In the current version, it is stated that matching was for five characteristics, but "efforts were made to facilitate geographic similarity of the WIC and control populations; matching was attempted first within the same catchment area, then within similar types of towns, and finally anywhere within the state."[2] These definitions are not identical, nor are we told what proportion of women could be matched within the catchment area, or in the other geographic categories.

Adequacy of Matching

Matching was on age, race, parity, educational level, and marital status. These variables are available on the birth certificate, and were used to attempt to select women comparable to those recruited into the WIC program. On the other hand, the WIC group is further defined by both low income and additional health and nutritional risk. It is likely, therefore, that WIC women are at higher risk of poorer perinatal outcome than controls, even after matching. Therefore, all other things being equal, it is likely that observed differences were an *underestimate* of WIC effect, since the WIC group would, in all likelihood, be at higher health and nutritional risk, and of lower income, than controls.

In summary, there are two biases in this research working in opposite directions: on one hand, the exclusion of terminated cases probably inflates observed differences; on the other hand, to whatever extent matching was imperfect, differences were underestimated. Unfortunately, while the bias associated with exclusion of terminated cases can—at least theoretically—be corrected, it is less easy to contend with bias associated with undermatching. One possible approach would be to assess other characteristics of the cases and controls which were not matched, such as the economic status of the census tract of residence, past pregnancy loss, or past frequency of low birthweight. It would be reassuring to know that cases and controls were indeed comparable on some measures of social or health status not used for matching. If these were not different across study groups, the security of the results would be increased.

I am hopeful that Dr. Kotelchuck and his colleagues may be able to supply us some of the additional information which would allow more secure conclusions to be drawn from their generally careful and hard work.

REFERENCES

1. Rush D, Alvir JM, Garbowski GC, Leighton J, Sloan NL: Review of past studies of health effects of the Special Supplemental Food Program for Women, Infants, and Children (WIC). Submitted to the Food and Nutrition Service, US Department of Agriculture, Washington, DC, 1984.
2. Kotelchuck M, Schwartz JB, Anderka MT, Finison KS: WIC participation and pregnancy outcomes: Massachusetts statewide evaluation project. Am J Public Health 1984; 74:1086–1092.
3. Kotelchuck M, Schwartz JB, Anderka M, Finison K: The Massachusetts special supplement food program for women, infants, and children (WIC) evaluation project; The Massachusetts Department of Public Health, Boston, Massachusetts. Final report to the food and nutrition service, US Department of Agriculture, Washington, DC, 1981.

Response to David Rush's Comments

Milton Kotelchuck, Janet B. Schwartz, Marlene T. Anderka, and Karl S. Finison

Perhaps because of the highly politicized nature of the debates in recent years in Washington, DC over the funding and reauthorization of WIC—the Special Supplemental Food Program for Women, Infants and Children—scientific evaluations of the effectiveness of WIC have come to play a more important role than usual in assessing the continued utility of this public health program.[1] Evaluation of the WIC program is not an easy task. Participation is based on voluntary enrollment; comparison populations are not readily accessible; and utilization of random assignment for scientific evaluation is ethically dubious. Debates over the validity of evaluation studies will likely be a permanent feature of this program. Dr. Rush's different view[2] cautions that it would be wise to defer drawing conclusions from the Massachusetts Statewide WIC Evaluation Program.[3] We believe that the results indicate a more positive evaluation of WIC prenatal participation than implied by Dr. Rush's review. Several of his points deserve rebuttal.

Dr. Rush suggests that we may have inappropriately defined our WIC population by excluding a special high-risk population (women administratively terminated by the WIC program), thereby distorting the results in a direction favorable to WIC. We believe that our decision defining a WIC participant is appropriate and that the exclusion of names does not seriously distort our results.

The definition of a WIC participant has not been formally addressed in any prior WIC evaluation. It is not as obvious as it may seem. Participation can be defined along a continuum: being referred to WIC by a health care worker, being screened for eligibility, being enrolled on an acceptance/waiting list, redeeming the first WIC voucher, obtaining WIC vouchers and counseling regularly, redeeming 50 per cent of the vouchers, redeeming 100 per cent of the vouchers. We have defined a prenatal WIC participant as an enrolled woman who redeems at least one WIC voucher and who is regarded as an active participant by the state's WIC program. Our definition is based on the Massachusetts WIC program's statewide administrative participant rule, which excludes an enrollee after she has failed to pick up her food vouchers for two consecutive months—a rule made necessary by the existence of eligible persons on waiting lists. The large majority of prenatal WIC participants (78 per cent) made extensive use of the program, redeeming more than 90 per cent of their issued vouchers.

The definition of a WIC participant does make a difference in program outcomes. If we stratify our sample by participants who redeem 90 per cent or more of their vouchers (N = 3,128) versus participants who redeem less (N = 908), significant positive birth outcome benefits are associated only with the high utilizers (birthweight = +34 gms (p < .05); LBW = −1.7 per cent (p < .01), and gestational age = +2.1 days (p < .001)), while no such trends are detected for low utilizers (birthweight −24 grams, +1.0 per cent LBW, and +0.3 days gestational age, respectively). The further along on the definition continuum (i.e., the more active the level of WIC involvement), the stronger the benefits of the program appear to be.

Address reprint requests to Milton Kotelchuck, MPH, Department of Social Medicine and Health Policy, Harvard Medical School, 25 Shattuck Street Boston, MA 02115.

Dr. Rush is incorrect when he states that all 4,898 Massachusetts women enrolled in WIC in 1978 actually delivered in Massachusetts in 1978. The 4,898 are *names* of enrollees and do not necessarily represent subsequent Massachusetts births. As stated in the article,[3] we were only able to locate subsequent birth records for less than 10 per cent of the 353 names of women who were administratively excluded without a specific cause noted. Given the retrospective nature of the study design and the use of WIC and vital statistics records only, it is impossible to confirm directly what happened to these names of women. We believe that most of the 353 names did not result in a subsequent Massachusetts birth, but in abortions, out-of-state births, or reregistrations under new names.

The authors share Dr. Rush's concern over possible confounding factors which might have inadvertently decreased the number of poor WIC outcomes. The 353 names may be one source of the confounding; however, Dr. Rush's hypothesis that substantial numbers of these names subsequently had undetected premature births and were excluded from the study population seems unlikely. His hypothetical scenario shows a misunderstanding of how the WIC program operates in the field. First, Dr. Rush incorrectly implies that two consecutive visits must occur to be included in the WIC program, rather than two visits consecutively missed must occur to be excluded. Second, he seems to imply that premature births might be treated differently than any other births. After a WIC participant gives birth (premature or term), she contacts the local WIC site and is automatically placed either in a six-week postpartum program or in a six-month lactation program if breast-feeding. Neither prematurity status nor duration of prior participation affects this shift. In fact, many of the study women prior to their deliveries were on WIC prenatally only one month (N = 216) or two months (N = 508), or gave birth prematurely (N = 239). The linkage of a WIC enrollee's name to a subsequent birth or death certificate should be equivalent for all names, independent of study inclusion status or prematurity status. It is, therefore, highly unlikely that a premature birth would result in both administrative termination and failure to detect a birth or death certificate, and hence, be lost to the study population.

By contrast to the above concerns, Dr. Rush believes that our matching procedures may have produced a control group at less risk than our WIC group, such that we are underestimating the WIC benefits. We agree with him. Like Dr. Rush, we speculated in the article that differences in income and obstetric status (the WIC eligibility criteria) may be present despite the strong matching procedure based on five sociodemographic and biologic factors. Post-hoc analyses noted some non-comparable characteristics, such as Hispanic status. Further new analyses show that the spouses of WIC participants were slightly less educated (10.9 vs 11.4 years of education) and that WIC women had shorter interconceptual periods (28.9 vs 31.7 months), although no differences in episodes of prior birth fatalities. While the WIC and control groups are demographically quite similar, all sources of non-comparability point to the WIC group being at slightly higher risk. Perhaps, this explains the smaller mean birthweight gains associated with WIC participation detected in this study than in prior WIC studies.[4,5]

To increase the similarity of the WIC and control populations, we proposed in our initial grant application that we would attempt to match on town of residence (geographic similarity). This proved impractical as the study proceeded; insufficient matches existed when the percentage of participants in a town was high. Nonetheless, such matching efforts did characterize this study. In our sample, 81 per cent were matched within the same catchment area, 15 per cent within similar type of towns (urban, suburban, rural), and 4 per cent anywhere throughout the state; 69 per cent were specifically matched on the same town of residence.

Dr. Rush also seems concerned over our analysis of duration of WIC on birth outcome. As clearly stated in the article, the confounding of duration of participation and duration of gestation make the evaluation of increased participation methodologically complicated. To address this issue, we choose to present two alternative methods for estimating cumulative benefits; absolute duration on WIC, which we (and Dr. Rush) seem to feel overestimates the benefits, and percentage of pregnancy on WIC, which we believe underestimates the benefits. We suggested the cumulative benefits would lie between the two estimates. Dr. Rush does not comment on our general approach, or on the second estimate which would seem to answer directly his specific concerns for a gestational control. Regardless of the approach, the results are basically the same—increased participation in WIC is associated with increased birthweight benefits.

Dr. Rush notes that, in our final report to the US Department of Agriculture,[6] the analysis of birthweight completely adjusted for gestational age showed no significant duration benefits. We chose not to include this analysis in our paper, since it only measures fetal size independent of gestation and ignores any birthweight benefits due to the overall WIC-associated increases in gestational age. Nonetheless, even this restricted analysis shows a general pattern similar to the overall trend of enhanced birth outcomes associated with increased duration; e.g., the differences in mean birthweight are -28 gms, -3 gms, $+34$ gms, and in the

incidence of small for gestational age birthweight are $+.8$ per cent, -0.3 per cent, and -1.6 per cent ($p < .10$), stratified at 1–3, 4–6, 7–9 months of participation, respectively.

We believe that the results of our study are supportive of our conclusion that WIC prenatal participation is associated with improved pregnancy outcomes. We have been mindful of the limitations of our study and tried to describe them in the paper. Dr. Rush's criticisms seem to reflect more concern with early drafts of our analyses rather than with our final paper. No single study will "prove conclusively" that WIC or any other voluntary public health program produces positive results. Our study, however, supports a growing body of WIC evaluations[4,5,7,8] that indicate WIC prenatal participation is associated with improved outcomes of pregnancy.

REFERENCES

1. GAO: WIC Evaluations Provide Some Favorable But No Conclusive Evidence on the Effects Expected for the Special Supplemental Program for Women, Infants, and Children. General Accounting Office PEMD 84-4. Washington, DC: Government Printing Office, 1984.
2. Rush D: Some comments on the Massachusetts WIC evaluation (Different View). Am J Public Health 1984; 74:1145–1146.
3. Kotelchuck M, Schwartz JB, Anderka MT, Finison KS: WIC participation and pregnancy outcomes: Massachusetts Statewide Evaluation Project. Am J Public Health 1984; 74:1086–1092.
4. Edozien JC, Switzer BR, Bryan RB: Medical evaluation of the Special Supplemental Food Program for Women, Infants and Children. Am J Clin Nutr 1979; 32:677–682.
5. Kennedy ET, Gershoff S, Reed R, Austin JE: Evaluation of the effect of WIC supplemental feeding on birthweight. J Am Diet Assoc 1982; 80:220–227.
6. Kotelchuck M, Schwartz JB, Anderka MT, Finison KS: Final Report: 1980 Massachusetts Special Supplemental Food Program for Women, Infants and Children (WIC) Evaluation Project. Final Report submitted to Food and Nutrition Services, US Department of Agriculture, Washington, DC, 1981.
7. Metcoff J, et al: Nutrition in Pregnancy. Final Report submitted to Food and Nutrition Service, US Department of Agriculture, Washington, DC, 1982.
8. Kennedy ET, Kotelchuck M: The effects of WIC supplemental feedings on birthweight: a case-control analysis. Am J Clin Nutr 1984; 40:580–586.

Science and Social Policy

Alfred Yankauer

If WIC* program research is looked upon as an effort to explore scientific issues about the relationship of nutrition to infant health, the purpose and importance of the research can be justified. Readers have the opportunity to form their own judgments about this relationship by reading the preceding communications.[1-3] The comments I wish to make are directed at another issue which is raised by this type of research.

The WIC program—like Head Start, Improved Pregnancy Outcome (IPO), and other large child health and welfare programs—was sold to legislators by advocacy groups on the grounds that the services provided would achieve gains in health that could be measured by specific health indicators. The scientific evidence for such claims in the United States was debatable at best, and particularly uncertain for a large scale national program in which execution of the intermediate steps as planned could never be guaranteed.[4] The strategy by which these programs were promoted and sold to legislators thus left their advocates in a vulnerable position if evaluation failed to show that measurable outcomes had been achieved as promised, or that the program costs exceeded their benefits by a substantial margin.

If looked at from a different vantage point, however, Head Start, WIC, IPO, and comparable programs can and should be justified on stronger grounds. The United States is virtually unique among its peer countries in failing to provide family allowances and in regarding many child health and welfare services—which consensus considers basic to life in a complex industrial society—as amenities to be purchased only by those who can afford them. Instead of squarely facing the issue of government responsibilities to support a floor of equity in access to essential services, we seem to need other reasons before taking action. Thus when these services, which other countries provide to all their citizens, are extended with tax dollars to those whom we define as unable to afford them, we seem forced to justify the extension in other terms.

Why is the United States so unique among the developed nations of the world? It is not as if our systems of health and welfare are more efficient or less costly than those of other countries. In point of fact the reverse seems to be true; thus the reason must be sought elsewhere. Perhaps it resides in a belief in human nature that is rarely expressed as frankly as in the remarks of a recent Counselor to President Reagan: the Counselor asserted that those who lined up at soup kitchens were free-loaders rather than in need of food.

Other reasons advanced for our nation's singularity include the inefficiency of government operations and the high costs of the services themselves. Efficiency, however, is not an issue here. Even the reactionary Republican Administration has not proposed to do away with tax-supported education; it merely wants to substitute vouchers for direct subsidies, which is exactly what the WIC program already does. The costs of extending benefits to all citizens is another matter. First we must look more closely at how our health and welfare funds are spent. Billions of dollars support an end-stage renal disease program whose benefits are available without charge to all who want to receive them; coronary by-pass operations are funded under Medicare and Medicaid. Paradoxically, our generosity of heart relative to very costly services is the reverse of.our position in relation to basic and less costly services. Second, if we examine all government expenditures rather than just those allocated to health care and are guided by the principle of preserving life instead of destroying it, we can surely afford to pay for health care of all kinds to all our citizens.

Whatever the reason for our singularity, the very conceptualization of the WIC program was a reflection of our distrust of human nature as well as a distortion of logic and ethics. We could have provided eligible women with the funds to purchase food or to use the money for other items to which they assigned higher priority. Clearly we did not trust them to use the money wisely, although distribution of money would have been far more efficient than the current system. Of course, we still have no control over whether vouchers are redeemed or food is consumed.

Logically, if we do not trust women to feed themselves and their children the "right food" we should have eliminated the income-eligibility criterion and provided food or vouchers to all pregnant women and infants. Otherwise the eligibility criterion only reflects discrimination against a class that happens to be characterized by low income and, often enough, minority group membership as well.

The existence of programs such as WIC and IPO did indeed provide an opportunity for large scale scientific research that might have helped us identify interventions in the form of health services, educational activities, or nutritional supplementation that led to healthier reproductive outcomes. Many types of research can be planned as part of the introduction of a new program that cannot be planned at a later date. Furthermore, the research can be entirely ethical. The fact that advantage was not taken of these opportunities accounts for the paucity and poor quality of WIC and IPO program-related research. From a purely scientific point of view, the claims which were used to sell these programs to legislators remain as debatable today as they were before the programs were initiated.

Given the nature of the political process, perhaps these programs would never have received congressional and presidential approval if they had been promoted on the basis of logic and equity rather than on the questionable achievement of measurable objective benefits. This is a possibility that might be profitably explored in scientific rather than intuitive fashion by the advocates of such programs before they decide on strategy. In the long run, a Machiavellian approach which makes assertions on manifestly weak grounds in order to gain a broader social objective may be a poor strategy.

However deeply we feel about equity and the need to do all we can to assure access to essential services to all our citizens, scientific objectivity must be kept separate from social advocacy. There are many areas in health and welfare where science can strengthen advocacy; but where science is distorted to serve the advocate, the social goal itself becomes contaminated and the advocate suspect.

*The special supplemental food program for women, infants, and children.

Address reprint requests to Dr. Alfred Yankauer, Department of Community and Family Medicine, University of Massachusetts Medical Center, Worcester, MA 01605.

REFERENCES

1. Kotelchuck M, Schwartz JB, Anderka MT, Finison KS: WIC participation and prenancy outcomes: Massachusetts Statewide Evaluation Project. Am J Public Health 1984; 74:1086–1092.
2. Rush D: Some comments on the Massachusetts WIC evaluation. (Different View) Am J Public Health 1984; 74:1145–1146:
3. Kotelchuck M, et al: Response to David Rush's comments. (Different View) Am J Public Health 1984; 74:1146–1148.
4. Strobino DM: Is it possible to evaluate the IPO project? (editorial) Am J Public Health 1984; 74:541–542.

10

The Cost and Effectiveness of
School-Based Preventive Dental Care

Stephen P. Klein, Harry M. Bohannan, Robert M. Bell,
Judith A. Disney, Craig B. Foch, and Richard C. Graves

SUMMARY

The National Preventive Dentistry Demonstration Program assessed the cost and effectiveness of various types and combinations of school-based preventive dental care procedures. The program involved 20,052 first, second, and fifth graders from five fluoridated and five nonfluoridated communities. These children were examined at baseline and assigned to one of six treatment regimens. Four years later, 9,566 members of this group were examined again. Analyses of their dental examination data showed that dental health lessons, brushing and flossing, fluoride tablets and mouthrinsing, and professionally applied topical fluorides were not effective in reducing a substantial amount of dental decay, even when all of these procedures were used together. Occlusal sealants prevented one to two carious surfaces in four years. Children who were especially susceptible to decay did not benefit appreciably more from any of the preventive measures than did children in general. Annual direct per capita costs were $23.00 for sealant or fluoride prophy/gel applications and $3.29 for fluoride mouthrinsing. Communal water fluoridation was reaffirmed as the most cost-effective means of reducing tooth decay in children.

I. INTRODUCTION

Numerous articles published over the past thirty years have reported that systemic fluorides, obtained through fluoridated water supplies and tablets, are very effective in preventing dental decay in children.[1,2] Fluoride protection also can be obtained topically, through toothpaste, mouthrinse, and professionally applied fluoride treatments.[1-5]

The application of a resin coating, called "pit and fissure sealant," to the occlusal surfaces of the posterior teeth also has been shown to be very successful in preventing decay.[6,7]

From Stephen P. Klein et al., "The Cost and Effectiveness of School-Based Preventive Dental Care," Rand Publication No. R-3203-RJW, prepared under a grant from The Robert Wood Johnson Foundation, April 1985. Reprinted by permission of The Rand Corporation.

Because fluorides are most effective in preventing dental caries on smooth tooth surfaces[8] whereas sealants are applied primarily to occlusal surfaces, it has been assumed that the *combination* of systemic fluorides, topical fluorides, and sealants would virtually eliminate all dental decay in children.

Arguments in favor of preventive dental care are often supported by comparisons between the estimated costs of the preventive procedures and the costs of restoring (through fillings) the tooth surfaces that would otherwise have been affected by decay.[9] Several articles have ascribed relatively low costs for these procedures when they are delivered to children in their schools.[10-12] For example, it has been estimated that the annual costs of a school-based topical fluoride mouthrinse program ranges from $0.71 to $9.27 per child,[13] whereas the cost in 1981 dollars of restoring a surface (through the placement of an amalgam filling) is about $19.92.[14]

The National Preventive Dentistry Demonstration Program was undertaken to test two hypotheses: 1) The combination of fluorides and sealants would eliminate almost all dental caries in children; and 2) the cost of school-based preventive dental care would be quite low, especially in comparison with the costs of restoring the surfaces that would have become decayed if this care had not been provided.

II. METHODS

PROGRAM SITES

Announcements about the study were sent to dental schools, dental associations, health departments, and education agencies throughout the United States.[15] These announcements described the study's procedures and requirements for participation, such as a high student retention rate, no previous involvement in a school-based preventive dental health program, and a willingness on the part of teachers and school district staff to participate. From the 120 sites that applied, 10 were selected that satisfied the requirements and varied on factors that were known to be related to dental decay.

Table 1 lists the 10 sites. Five of them reportedly had optimally fluoridated water supplies for their region (0.8 or 1.0 ppm F ion); the other five were designated as "nonfluoridated" (less than 0.2 ppm F ion). It was discovered shortly after the program began, however, that one of the reportedly nonfluoridated sites (Wichita, Kansas) actually had about 0.4 ppm F ion in its water supply, whereas one of the supposedly fluoridated sites (Hayward, California) had intermittent fluoridation during the 10-year period before the program started. The sites varied in urbanization, average socioeconomic status, percent of children in four racial/ethnic groups (Anglo, Black, Hispanic, and Asian), prevalence of dental decay, and type of local sponsoring agency (e.g., school district and health department).

SAMPLE

Of the children who were eligible to enroll in the study, 82 percent obtained their parents' written consent to receive annual dental examinations and to participate in any one of the project's six treatment regimens.[15,16] Our study population consisted of the 20,052 first, second, and fifth graders in this group who also received a baseline dental exam between September 1977 and March 1978. The study's four longitudinal cohorts consisted of children in grades 1+2 and 5 at fluoridated sites and grades 1+2 and 5 at nonfluoridated sites. Children who began the study in grade 1 or 2 at a site were combined into one group because of the similarity of their data. The children in all four cohorts received annual dental examinations for four years after baseline, provided they were still enrolled in the study.

The sample used to measure the effectiveness of the preventive procedures consisted of the 9,566 children who received both the baseline and the final examination. The loss of 52 percent of the baseline population in 48 months yielded a relatively low attrition rate per month compared with other studies of school-based preventive dental care.[4,17] Discontinuing the New York site after the third year accounted for 10 percent of the attrition. The remaining 42 percent of the attrition was due mainly to children leaving their site during the course of the study, not obtaining parental consent to participate in the fourth year (the initial consents were for three years), or having braces placed on their teeth. There was no systematic relationship between attrition rate and treatment group across sites in any of the four cohorts; and there was essentially no difference in average baseline dental decay level between the children who did and did not complete the program.

Table 1

NUMBER OF CHILDREN AT BASELINE AND AT THE END OF THE PROGRAM,
BY SITE AND BASELINE GRADE LEVEL

Site	Baseline		End	
	Cohort 1+2	Cohort 5	Cohort 1+2	Cohort 5
Nonfluoridated				
Billerica, Massachusetts	1449	728	1006	423
Tallahassee, Florida	1647	727	816	335
Wichita, Kansas[a]	1259	524	607	287
Monroe, Louisiana	1194	523	750	332
Pierce County, Washington	1351	617	781	311
Total nonfluoridated	6900	3119	3960	1688
Fluoridated				
Chattanooga, Tennessee	1329	576	607	181
New York, New York	1359	628	(b)	(b)
Minneapolis, Minnesota	1510	739	935	394
El Paso, Texas	1409	673	693	346
Hayward, California[a]	1240	570	542	220
Total fluoridated	6847	3186	2777	1141

[a]Wichita had 0.4 ppm fluoride ion in its water supply, and Hayward had intermittent water fluoridation during the 10-year period before the program began.

[b]The program was discontinued at the New York site after three years of operation primarily because of the extremely high cost of running the study at this site.

Table 1 shows the distribution of children in the baseline population and in the analysis sample by baseline grade level and site. The samples used to assess the costs of the preventive procedures consisted of all the children who received these procedures and were thereby consuming project resources.

Two other groups of children were examined to provide cross-sectional comparison data. The children in one group received only a baseline examination; those in the other group were seen only at the end of the program. The 4,320 children in the first group were drawn from grades 3, 4, 6, 7, and 8 at the same schools as those who were assigned to the program's treatment regimens. The 4,746 children in the second group also attended these schools, but they did not receive any preventive care from the program. These children were in grades 1 through 9 at the time they were examined.

EXAMINATIONS

Annual clinical (visual-tactile) examinations were performed by 31 specially trained dentists, although only 16 members of this group participated after baseline. Usually, six to eight examiners visited a site each year and in most cases, a given examiner went to the same sites each year. Standard examination criteria were used.[18]

The examiners were very consistent with themselves and each other in their evaluations of whether a tooth surface was affected by decay.[19] Examination errors (as measured by a surface being classified as carious or filled one year and as sound the next) were not related to whether examiner/child pairings were or were not maintained across years.

Bitewing radiographs were taken at the beginning and again at the end of the study by trained technicians using a mobile X-ray van. Analyses indicated that adding the radiograph data to the clinical results did not change the study's findings. Most of the previous studies on the efficacy of preventive procedures do not include radiographs. Thus, in order to facilitate comparisons with this literature, radiograph results are not presented here, but they may be found in other reports.[19,20]

RESEARCH DESIGN

Table 2 shows the six treatment regimens used at each site. Each of the first five regimens contained one or more preventive procedures. Two procedures, sealants and fluoride prophy/gel treatments, were provided by a clinic team of dental hygienists and assistants who moved from school to school within a site. This team delivered these services under the general supervision of a dentist. The remaining procedures were administered by classroom teachers or aides.

The treatment regimens differed slightly between fluoridated and nonfluoridated sites. Fluoride tablets were not given at fluoridated sites, and regimen 2 at these sites provided sealants instead of prophy/gel applications. This planned variation in protocol was designed to reflect differences in the types of programs that might be adopted eventually by the two kinds of communities. The children in regimen 6 did not receive any of the preventive measures, but they received the same examinations as the children in the other five regimens. The regimen 6 children therefore served as a longitudinal control group for the other five regimens.

Schools within a site were assigned to regimens in a way that balanced baseline decay level, numbers of children, and racial mix across treatment regimens.[15] Schools, rather than individual children, were assigned to regimens because some of the procedures, such as fluoride

Table 2

ASSIGNMENT OF PREVENTIVE PROCEDURES TO THE SIX TREATMENT
REGIMENS AT NONFLUORIDATED AND FLUORIDATED SITES

	Preventive Procedure				
Regimen	Delton sealant applied and, if needed, reapplied up to 3 times	Acidulated paste prophylaxis and 1.23% F ion gel (2 times/year)	0.2% neutral sodium F mouthrinse (1 time/week)	1 mg F in 2.2 mg of neutral sodium F tablet (5 times/week)	Biweekly brushing and flossing, 10 health lessons per year, and home supply of F dentifrice
Nonfluoridated					
1	X	X	X	X	X
2	-	X	X	X	X
3	X	X	-	-	-
4	-	-	X	X	X
5	-	-	-	-	X
6	-	-	-	-	-
Fluoridated					
1	X	X	X	/	X
2	X	-	X	/	X
3	X	X	-	-	-
4	-	-	X	-	X
5	-	-	-	-	X
6	-	-	-	-	-
Persons providing procedure	Clinic team	Clinic team	Classroom teachers	Classroom teachers	Classroom teachers

NOTE: F = fluoride. An X indicates that the regimen included the procedure. Children in all six regimens received annual dental examinations. All teacher-provided classroom procedures were discontinued after two years in Cohort 5.

mouthrinsing, were delivered more efficiently to children when they were in classroom groups. Table 3 shows the number of children in the four-year continuous residence sample in each regimen.

ANALYSIS OF TREATMENT EFFECTS

The analysis of treatment effectiveness focused on the number of decayed, missing due to decay, and filled permanent tooth surfaces that a child acquired between baseline and the end of the study (about a 48-month period), hereafter referred to as the child's DMFS increment score.

Only 1 to 3 percent of the variation among children in DMFS increment scores was uniquely associated with the school they attended.[20] This finding, and the fact that each school in a site-regimen combination tended to enroll about the same number of children, meant that regimen means were not sensitive to the choice of the child or school as the unit of analysis. For example, in 20 of the 24 cohort/regimen combinations, the mean four-year DMFS increment score computed using the school as the unit was within 0.09 surfaces of the mean

Table 3

NUMBER OF CHILDREN IN THE FOUR-YEAR CONTINUOUS
RESIDENCE SAMPLE, BY TREATMENT
REGIMEN AND COHORT

Regimen	Nonfluoridated		Fluoridated	
	Cohort 1+2	Cohort 5	Cohort 1+2	Cohort 5
1	666	279	498	201
2	565	260	487	192
3	677	312	432	199
4	692	258	537	195
5	620	284	393	154
6	740	295	430	200
Total	3960	1688	2777	1141

computed using the child as the unit (see App. A). The average difference was 0.05 surfaces. We chose the child as the unit because it allowed us to study whether the treatment procedures were especially effective with children who were unusually susceptible to decay, and it allowed us to control for differences in the background characteristics of children in different schools.

Differences in mean DMFS increment scores between treatment and control regimens were explored through a series of analyses of covariance. This technique allowed us to estimate what the mean DMFS increment score in a regimen would have been if: each regimen had half boys and half girls; each regimen had an equal number of children from each site; there were no differences among regimens in their children's average age, baseline DMFS scores, or socioeconomic status; and the racial/ethnic mix was the same in all six regimens. Thus, differences among regimens do not reflect artificial differences caused by imbalances in the children's background characteristics. Appendix B shows the effects of these adjustments.

Separate analyses were run for four groups of children. Groups were defined on the basis of their site's water supply (fluoridated or nonfluoridated) and baseline grade level (first + second graders or fifth graders). In order to increase the sensitivity of statistical tests, a preventive procedure's effectiveness was assessed with data from all the regimens that used it.[20] For example, information on the set of classroom components was provided by comparisons between regimens 1 and 3, and between 4 and 6. Because the results of these comparisons did not differ significantly from each other, the reported classroom effect is the average of these two estimates.

Although using the child rather than the school as the unit of analysis had little effect on regimen means, it could bias tests for differences between means. The standard errors generated in the analyses of covariance (and presented in a previous report[20]) were therefore rescaled to control for the small (0.00 to 0.02) intraschool correlations in the covariate-adjusted DMFS increment scores. The rescaling, using a procedure described by Scott and Holt,[21] involved multiplying all of a cohort's analysis of covariance standard errors by a constant. The constants were 1.14, 1.29, 1.45, and 1.00 for cohorts 1+2 and 5 at nonfluoridated sites and cohorts 1+2 and 5 at fluoridated sites, respectively.

COST ANALYSIS PROCEDURES

The resources required to provide the treatment regimens were measured conservatively using the following procedures:

Labor: All the members of a site's dental team (coordinator, dentist, hygienists, dental assistants, and clerk) indicated how they spent each 30-minute interval of each workday (i.e., type of activity and in which regimen the activity was conducted). The cost of this time was computed initially on the basis of hourly wage rates.

Direct labor costs excluded time spent by teachers, volunteers, and other school personnel; site staff downtime (such as when children were not available for care), vacation time, and other necessary indirect expenses; and time spent in conducting administrative and research activities, such as the annual dental examinations. Research staff time, such as in providing computer support and in hiring and training site staff, also were not considered in computing direct labor costs.

Capital: This category included the amortized cost of the equipment, such as portable dental chairs and lights, that were used to provide the preventive procedures. These costs were allocated to procedures and then to regimens in proportion to their use of this equipment.

Materials: Essentially all consumable supplies were purchased centrally in bulk for the study and then shipped to the sites. The costs of these materials were allocated to the preventive procedures and then to regimens in proportion to the number of children who consumed them.

III. RESULTS

PROGRAM IMPLEMENTATION

Examination data indicated that sealants were provided to 96 percent of the children scheduled to receive them. Almost all of the remaining 4 percent did not have teeth that were suitable for sealing. Treatment records showed that 79 percent of the children scheduled to receive a total of four gel applications during the middle 24 months of the study received all four, whereas 7 percent received fewer than three, 12 percent received three, and 2 percent received more than four.[20] The primary reason some children did not receive their full set of gel applications was that they were absent on the days the clinic team visited their school. Questionnaire surveys of teachers and principals conducted during the study, monitoring visits by program staff, and analyses of the quantities of supplies used indicated that school personnel generally understood and followed the protocols for administering the dental health lessons and the brushing, flossing, mouthrinse, and tablet components.[20,22]

Almost 50 percent of the teachers complained about the amount of time it took to provide the classroom procedures. They estimated that the total number of minutes spent in a typical week was 16 to 30 for biweekly brushing and flossing, 6 to 11 for weekly mouthrinse, and 20 to 25 for daily tablets. Complaints about the time required to administer these procedures were less common at the lower grade levels, even though the procedures took longer for younger children than for older children. Throughout the program, teachers of grades 1, 2, and 3 were more willing to continue to use the classroom procedures than were teachers at the upper grade levels.

TREATMENT EFFECTS

All the children who received both a baseline and a final examination were included in the analysis of treatment effects regardless of whether they received all their scheduled treatments. This approach was adopted in order to assess the effectiveness of the procedures under actual field conditions. Our results may therefore differ from those obtained under the special requirements of a randomized clinical trial.

Table 4 shows the number of surfaces saved from decay by each regimen in four years in comparison with its longitudinal control group. For instance, at fluoridated sites, the mean DMFS increment in cohort 5's longitudinal control group was 3.07 as compared with 1.05 in regimen 1. This 2.02 surface difference corresponds to a 66-percent reduction in decay. It is evident from these data that the children in the sealant regimens (1, 2, and 3 at fluoridated sites, and 1 and 3 at nonfluoridated sites) developed consistently less decay than their respective control groups. There were only two instances in which a nonsealant regimen had a statistically significantly lower mean increment score than its control group: regimens 2 and 4 with cohort 1+2 children at nonfluoridated sites.

Table 5 shows the amount of decay prevented in four years by each procedure, the combination of all of the clinic procedures, and the combination of all of the classroom procedures. The methods used to compute these effects are described by Bell,[20] and on the basis of preliminary analyses, assume there are no interactions among procedures.

Table 4

DIFFERENCE BETWEEN EACH REGIMEN AND ITS LONGITUDINAL CONTROL GROUP IN THE MEAN NUMBER OF SURFACES THAT BECAME DECAYED IN FOUR YEARS

| | Nonfluoridated | | Fluoridated | |
Regimen	Cohort 1+2	Cohort 5	Cohort 1+2	Cohort 5
1 Rinse (tablets) + lessons + brushing + sealants + prophy/gel	1.90**	1.91**	1.29**	2.02**
2 Rinse + lessons + brushing + sealants	(a)	(a)	1.00**	1.62**
2 Rinse + tablets + lessons + brushing + prophy/gel	0.68*	0.65	(a)	(a)
3 Sealants + prophy/gel	1.68**	1.83**	1.24**	1.74**
4 Rinse (tablets) + lessons + brushing	0.67*	-0.55	0.04	-0.61
5 Lessons + brushing	0.12	-0.60	-0.25	-0.42

NOTE: Fluoride tablets were given at nonfluoridated sites only. The four-year DMFS increments in decay in the longitudinal control group (regimen 6) at nonfluoridated sites were 3.13 and 4.75 surfaces for cohorts 1+2 and 5, respectively; corresponding values at fluoridated sites were 2.19 and 3.07. A negative value in this table indicates that a treatment group had a larger increment in decay than its longitudinal control group.

*Differs from regimen 6 mean at the 0.01 level.
**Differs from regimen 6 mean at the 0.001 level.
None of the other comparisons with regimen 6 differed at the 0.05 level.
aRegimen 2 included prophy/gel at nonfluoridated sites and sealants at fluoridated sites.

Table 5

REDUCTIONS IN FOUR-YEAR DMFS INCREMENTS, BY TREATMENT PROCEDURE,
COHORT, AND FLUORIDATION STATUS

	Nonfluoridated		Fluoridated	
Procedure	Cohort 1+2	Cohort 5	Cohort 1+2	Cohort 5
Clinic				
Sealants	1.33**	1.11*	0.96**	2.00**
Prophy/gel	0.12	1.04	0.29	0.18
Total clinic	1.46**	2.15**	1.25**	2.18**
Classroom				
Mouthrinse/tabletsa	0.44*	0.21	0.29	0.03
Health lessonsb	0.01	-0.44	-0.24	-0.20
Total classroom	0.45**	-0.24	0.05	-0.16

NOTE: The analysis of a procedure's effect involved children from several regimens; e.g., only regimen 2's data were excluded from the measurement of the mouthrinse effect.

*Differs significantly from zero at 0.05 level.

**Differs significantly from zero at 0.001 level.

aFluoride tablets were offered only at nonfluoridated sites.

bIncludes biweekly brushing and flossing plus home supply of fluoride dentifrice.

Table 5 shows that sealants saved 1 to 2 surfaces from decay in four years. The fluoride prophy/gel applications reduced decay by one surface in four years only in the most caries-prone group, cohort 5 at nonfluoridated sites. Figure 1 shows that in this group, the chances are 95 in 100 that the combination of sealants and fluoride prophy/gel applications saved between 1.36 and 2.94 surfaces in four years. The highest average annual benefit of the fluoride mouthrinse was only 0.11 surfaces, and this reduction was obtained with only cohort 1+2 at nonfluoridated sites. The education program, which included biweekly brushing in the classroom without a dentifrice, did not prevent any decay.

A procedure prevented about as much decay in the first two years of the program as it did during the last two.[20] The two exceptions to this trend were in cohort 5, where the additional reductions in the last two years of the study over the first two were 0.54 surfaces for sealants at fluoridated sites and 0.90 surfaces for prophy/gel at nonfluoridated sites. However, only the latter difference was statistically significant (p = 0.05). Although the rinse/tablet component ran for only 1.5 years in cohort 5, the reductions attributable to this component at the end of the first two years were about the same as those observed during the last two years.

The two-year results at the New York site were essentially the same as those at the other four fluoridated sites. The four-year effectiveness of a procedure at one site paralleled very

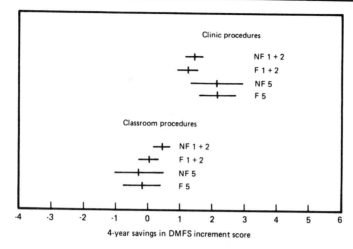

Fig. 1—95 percent confidence interval for clinic and classroom
effects by cohort and fluoridation type

closely its effectiveness at the other sites with similar water supplies. Figure 2 illustrates this consistency by showing the 95-percent confidence intervals by site for the combination of prophy/gel and sealant applications. Figure 3 shows the intervals for the combination of all the classroom procedures.

TREATMENT COSTS

Direct treatment costs were calculated for school years 2 and 3.[23] These two years were chosen in order to eliminate possible biases due to start-up or close-down activities. The two years had very similar costs for a given regimen. There were no differences in the average costs of regimen 2 that were systematically related to fluoridation status even though this regimen involved sealants at fluoridated sites and prophy/gel treatments at nonfluoridated sites. Thus, the data for this regimen were combined across site types. Similarly, the incremental cost of providing fluoride tablets was so negligible that it did not require separate cost analyses for fluoridated and nonfluoridated sites. All costs are reported in 1981 dollars in order to facilitate comparisons with other studies.

There was considerable variation among sites in the direct costs of each regimen. This variation occurred because 1) the sites differed in mean cost of living and thereby local wage rates, 2) state laws at three sites required that a dentist be present to perform or supervise certain tasks, 3) El Paso had high costs for just the regimens that involved classroom procedures because its staff devoted considerable time to developing instructional materials that were shared with the other sites, and 4) New York had atypically high costs for all regimens.

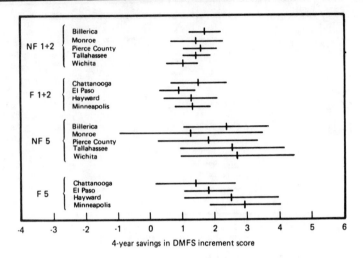

Fig. 2—95 percent confidence intervals for clinic effect,
by site and fluoridation status

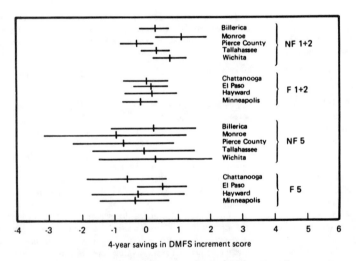

Fig. 3—95 percent confidence intervals for classroom effect,
by site and fluoridation status

The intersite variation in actual costs was reduced substantially by spreading the El Paso educational development costs across all 10 sites, eliminating New York's data from the cost analysis, and then adjusting for the other two factors listed above. For example, the following hourly wage rates were assigned to all sites: dentist, $20; site coordinator, $13; hygienist, $10; dental assistant, $6.50; and clerk, $6. These rates were very close to the nine-site averages for these job classifications.

Table 6 shows the adjusted annual direct costs per child in each regimen, the nine-site standard deviation, and the cost at New York. This table indicates that it was almost as expensive to provide regimen 1 ($54.92), which involved all the clinic and classroom procedures, as it was to provide these two groups of procedures separately (regimen 3 @ $40.02 + regimen 4 @ $15.15 = $55.17).

Because there is no real cost-sharing between clinic and classroom procedures, the annual average direct cost of maintaining a child in a sealant or prophy/gel program can be estimated by the difference in cost between regimens 2 and 4 ($37.97 - $15.15 = $22.82). This estimate, in comparison to regimen 3's cost of $40.02, suggests that a $5.62 annual savings was obtained by combining sealants and prophy/gel into one regimen (because 2 × $22.82 = $45.64). A child could have from 0 to 16 teeth sealed, depending upon the number of erupted teeth that had pits and fissures but were not carious or filled. About 10 teeth were sealed per child in four years. Thus, it cost about $8 to $9 to seal a tooth and maintain that seal.

The cost of adding fluoride mouthrinsing to a supervised dental health program that already included lessons and brushing was estimated in two ways: a) regimen 4 - regimen 5 = $3.41 and b) regimen 1 - (regimens 3 + 5) = $3.16. The average of these two estimates is $3.29.

Table 6

ADJUSTED ANNUAL DIRECT COSTS PER CHILD

(In $ 1981)

Regimen	9-Site Average				9-Site Standard Deviation	Average Cost at New York
	Labor	Capital	Supplies	Total		
1 All class & clinic	39.92	4.11	10.89	54.92	7.14	92.55
2 All class + 1 clinic	26.69	2.35	8.92	37.97	5.08	64.01
3 All clinic	31.80	4.26	3.95	40.02	7.25	56.36
4 All class	8.21	--	6.94	15.15	3.57	30.22
5 Lessons + brushing	7.36	--	4.38	11.74	2.22	20.85

NOTE: Regimen 5 included all the classroom procedures with the exception of fluoride (F) mouthrinse at all sites and F tablets at nonfluoridated sites.

IV. DISCUSSION

DECREASING PREVALENCE OF DECAY

The study's most caries-prone children, the cohort 5 longitudinal control group at non-fluoridated sites, averaged fewer than 1.25 newly affected surfaces per year. The mean in each of the other three longitudinal control groups was much less than one surface per year.

These small increases in decay level are consistent with prevalence data that have recently been reported by others.[24] For example, in the national surveys conducted between 1963 and 1973,[25-28] 12-year-olds had about 6.6 surfaces affected by decay whereas in the 1979-1980 survey,[29] 12-year-olds had only 4.2 affected surfaces. This large decline has been found in both nonfluoridated and fluoridated communities and is probably due to several factors, including the increased prevalence of fluorides "in the food chain, especially from the use of fluoridated water in food processing, increased use of infant formulas with measurable fluoride content, and even unintentional ingestion of fluoride dentifrices."[30]

The study's cross-sectional data also suggest there has been a significant decline in decay level.[20] For example, the program's 12-year-olds had a mean DMFS score of 6.6 at baseline,[31] whereas four years later, another group of 12-year-olds at these same schools had a mean of only 5.1 surfaces.[20] Since the latter group did not participate in any school-based preventive dental care program, this 1.5 surface decline must be due to other causes.

EFFECTIVENESS

The children in the end of program cross-sectional control group (as well as the children in the program's longitudinal control and treatment groups) could have received preventive care from their family dentist and/or used fluoride mouthrinse or tablets at home. However, several results suggest that if such non-program care occurred, it did not significantly bias our estimates of treatment effects. Specifically, 1) only a small percentage of children in the cross-sectional and longitudinal control groups had sealants; 2) there was a high degree of consistency in the size and pattern of treatment effects across sites despite the considerable variation among sites on factors that are correlated with DMFS increment scores and/or the amount of professional dental care received; and 3) if non-program preventive care had had a significant impact, we would not have been able to detect the large sealant effect that was obtained.

Our finding that fluoride mouthrinsing prevented only slightly more than one tenth of a decayed surface per year in cohort 1+2 is consistent with the results obtained with children of comparable age in the only randomized clinical trial of weekly sodium fluoride rinse that has been conducted in a nonfluoridated community in the United States in the past 15 years.[32] Our results with cohort 1+2 also are consistent with those obtained in the only other large-scale study of fluoride rinsing—the study conducted by the National Institute of Dental Research (NIDR) in 17 nonfluoridated communities across the United States.[13] NIDR reported that children in grades 1-8 in 1975 who had not rinsed in school had an average of one more carious surface than children in grades 1-8 at these same schools in 1979-1980 who had rinsed for three years—an apparent preventive effect of 0.33 surfaces per year.

If the program had used this same type of historical comparison, we would have attributed a reduction of 0.34 surfaces per year to the rinse. The average DMFS score of 10-to-11-year-olds at our nonfluoridated sites in 1977–1978 who had not rinsed was 1.34 surfaces higher than that of the 10-to-11-year-olds in 1981–1982 who had rinsed for four years. Thus, because of the secular decline in decay, a cross-sectional comparison indicates a reduction of 0.23 surfaces per year greater than the 0.11 reduction that was actually obtained when a longitudinal control group was used. If the NIDR data are corrected for this bias (by subtracting 0.23 surfaces per year from its reported annual reduction), then both the program and NIDR studies attribute a 0.10 to 0.11 reduction per year to fluoride mouthrinsing. The two studies also reported almost identical average costs for a mouthrinse program.

The data from cohort 1+2 provide the most realistic estimate of the size of the mouthrinse effect in an operational program because most of the children who rinse in public schools today are in elementary school. It is simply not feasible to continue the rinse after the sixth grade in most school districts because of difficulties in obtaining student and teacher compliance at the upper grade levels.[33] If it were possible to continue a rinse program to the ninth grade, then our four-year data would underestimate the size of the benefit derived from the rinse in cohort 5 because this cohort only rinsed for 1.5 years. No such bias existed for the fluoride prophy/gel component, because almost all of the children in both cohorts 1+2 and 5 who were scheduled to receive eight fluoride prophy/gel applications did receive them.

COSTS

Several factors cause the large differences among studies in their estimates of the cost per child for a given preventive procedure. For example, the estimates depend on whether standard accounting techniques are used to assess costs and report them in a particular year's dollars, whether estimates are based on the actual costs of providing the procedure under realistic field conditions, the number of children treated, whether estimates include indirect expenses, and whether all necessary direct expenses are measured.[12,34–36] Because such factors have a major impact on estimated costs, they must be considered in determining the utility of a given procedure. For example, the usually cited estimate of $1 per child per year for mouthrinsing[10] does not include many direct expenses, such as the necessary cost of training and supervising classroom teachers to make sure they dispense the rinse properly.[37]

Recent empirical studies[13,35] as well as a U.S. General Accounting Office report[38] show that when most direct expenses are considered, the cost of rinsing (in 1981 dollars) is about $3.50 per child per year. However, these estimates do not include necessary indirect costs, which tend to be about 50 percent of direct costs.[23,35] Readers are therefore cautioned that average total costs of a preventive procedure in an operational school program are likely to be substantially higher than those presented in Table 6.

COSTS VERSUS EFFECTIVENESS

The application of sealants was the only school-based procedure that was consistently effective in reducing decay. However, the average *direct* cost of providing sealants as part of a school-based program (about $23 per child per year if not provided in conjunction with fluoride prophy/gel applications) was far more than the *total* cost of restoring the 0.25 to 0.50 surfaces that sealants prevented from becoming decayed per year (@ $19.92 per restoration).

The study strongly reaffirmed the value of communal water fluoridation. The cohort 1+2 longitudinal control group at nonfluoridated sites experienced 0.94 more DMF surfaces in four years than the comparable group at fluoridated sites. There was a 1.68 surface savings due to water fluoridation with the cohort 5 children. The reductions in decay attributable to water fluoridation in both cohorts are therefore almost the same as those obtained in these cohorts with sealants. However, in contrast to the $23 per year cost of maintaining a child in a sealant program, the annual per capita cost (in 1981 dollars) of water fluoridation in five United States communities ranged from $0.06 in Denver, Colorado, to $0.80 in rural West Virginia.[39]

A comparison of the costs of a school-based sealant program with the cost of restoring the surfaces that would have become decayed without such a program would have to consider several variables that were not quantified in the present research, such as the perceived value of a sound tooth relative to one that has been restored, the discounted value of funds spent to prevent a future problem, and the expected life of a restoration and a sealant. Such a comparison also would have to come to grips with the fact that our bare-bones estimate of the direct cost for a school-based sealant program is about $40 to $80 per surface saved from decay when sealants are provided to all children regardless of their susceptibility to tooth decay.

TARGETING PREVENTIVE PROGRAMS

Analyses of the study's baseline data and DMFS increment scores indicated that a small number of children accounted for a disproportionally large amount of the decay.[31] For example, the 20 percent of the cohort 5 children at fluoridated sites in regimen 6 who had the highest DMFS score increments accounted for 55 percent of all the new decay in that group. These findings, together with the high cost of the preventive procedures, led to a preliminary investigation of the utility of targeting preventive care on high-risk children.

The targeting study used data on the children in regimen 5 to construct a multiple regression equation to predict their DMFS increment scores. Separate equations were constructed for each combination of water supply type and cohort. The variables in each equation included such factors as socioeconomic status, site, and the number of erupted and decayed permanent teeth at baseline.

The regression equations constructed with regimen 5 children were able to predict only 6 to 10 percent of the variance in regimen 6 DMFS increment scores. This finding is consistent with previous attempts to predict DMFS increments.[40] Despite this low predictability for individual children, the 25 percent who were estimated to have the largest DMFS increments had twice the mean increment of children in general at nonfluoridated sites and three to four times as many at fluoridated sites.[20] Table 7 shows that the group predicted to have the largest increments benefited only slightly more from the preventive measures than did children in general. The difference was never more than 0.75 surfaces in four years.

It must be noted that the program was not designed to identify children likely to have the highest DMFS score increments. If it had been so designed, we would have gathered data on other variables such as the amount of decay on primary teeth that might have improved the prediction system. Nevertheless, even if a much more successful prediction system were available, several factors would still have to be considered in assessing the utility of a school-based targeting program. Such factors would include: the cost of identifying high-risk children, the relative effectiveness of the preventive procedures with high-risk versus typical-risk children, and the difficulties of reaching the targeted children during the school day. There may also be ethical problems about delivering preventive care to only a small segment of the eligible population.

Table 7

REDUCTIONS IN FOUR-YEAR DMFS INCREMENTS DUE TO THE CLINIC
PROCEDURES BY RISK GROUP, COHORT, AND
FLUORIDATION STATUS

	Risk Group			All Children	Difference Between High and All
Group	Low	Medium	High		
NF 1+2	1.04	1.46	1.54	1.46	0.08
NF 5	1.46	2.31	2.90	2.15	0.75
F 1+2	0.73	1.36	1.59	1.25	0.34
F 5	1.25	2.55	2.75	2.18	0.57

NOTE: NF and F refer to nonfluoridated and fluoridated sites. Children whose predicted DMFS increment
fell in the lowest and highest quartiles of the distribution of predicted increment scores constituted
the low- and high-risk groups, respectively.

V. CONCLUSIONS AND IMPLICATIONS

School-based weekly fluoride mouthrinsing, daily fluoride tablets, biannual fluoride paste prophylaxis and gel applications, dental health lessons, and biweekly brushing and flossing were not consistently effective in preventing clinically significant amounts of tooth decay beyond that already prevented by typical home and dental office care. These results, obtained when the procedures were used singly and in combination, were consistent across age groups and sites.

Sealant application was the only procedure that was effective in reducing decay in all four study groups. Although sealants prevented 23 to 65 percent of the decay that occurred in the longitudinal control group, this percentage translated to merely one to two carious surfaces prevented in four years. This is about the same amount of decay that was prevented by community water fluoridation, although sealants only affected pit and fissure surfaces. Because of the considerable difference in costs between sealants and water fluoridation, the latter procedure will continue to play the primary role in preventing dental decay.

The small preventive effect of several of the school-based procedures used in this study appears to have been due in part to the precipitous decline in the prevalence of tooth decay. Nevertheless, most children are still experiencing some decay. It will therefore be important to determine the reasons for the recent decline and its long-range impact in order to plan what types of school and nonschool preventive programs will be needed in the future. The limited resources available for preventive care and the finding that a small percentage of children have most of the decay suggest that research also is needed to assess the feasibility of developing a program that could accurately identify high-risk children and effectively target care on them.

REFERENCES

1. Newbrun E: Fluorides and Dental Caries, 2d ed. Springfield, IL: Charles C. Thomas, 1975.
2. Driscoll WS: The use of fluoride tablets for the prevention of dental caries. In: Forrester DJ, Schutz EM (eds.): International Workshop on Fluorides and Dental Caries Reduction. Baltimore, MD: University of Maryland Press, 1974; 25–93.
3. Glass RL: The use of fluoride dentifrices: a public health measure. Community Dent Oral Epidemiol 1980; 8:272–282.
4. Driscoll WS, et al.: Caries-preventive effects of daily and weekly fluoride mouthrinsing in a fluoridated community: final results after 30 months. J Am Dent Assoc 1982; 105:1010–1013.
5. Wei SHY: The potential benefits to be derived from topical fluorides in fluoridated communities. In: Forrester DJ, Schutz EM (eds.): International Workshop on Fluorides and Dental Caries Reduction. Baltimore, MD: University of Maryland Press, 1974, 178–240.
6. Ripa LW: Occlusal sealants: rationale and review of clinical trials. Intern Dent J 1980; 30:127–139.
7. Silverstone LM: The current status of adhesive fissure sealants. In: Horowitz AM, Thomas HB (eds.): Dental Caries Prevention in Public Health Programs. NIH Pub. No. 81-2235. Bethesda, MD: National Institutes of Health, 1981; 83–118.
8. Russell AL: The inhibition of approximal caries in adults with lifelong fluoride exposure. J Dent Res 1953; 32:138.
9. Cuzacq G, Glass RL: The projected financial savings in dental restorative treatment: the results of consuming fluoridated water. J Public Health Dent 1972; 32:2–57.
10. Heifetz SB: Cost-effectiveness of topically applied fluorides. In: Burt BA (ed.): The Relative Efficiency of Methods of Caries Prevention in Dental Public Health. Ann Arbor: University of Michigan, 1978.
11. Davies GN: Cost and Benefit of Fluoride in the Prevention of Dental Caries. Geneva: World Health Organization, WHO Offset Pub. No. 9. 1974.
12. Foch CB: The Costs and Benefits of Preventive Dental Care: A Literature Review. The Rand Corporation, N-1732-RWJ, 1981.
13. Miller AJ, Brunelle JA: A summary of the NIDR community caries prevention demonstration program. J Am Dent Assoc 1983; 107:265–269.
14. Wall TP: Dental fees charged by general practitioners and selected specialists in the United States, 1982. J Am Dent Assoc 1984; 108:83–87.
15. Klein SP, Bohannan HM: The First Year of Field Activities in the National Preventive Dentistry Demonstration Program. The Rand Corporation, R-2536/1&2-RWJ, 1979.
16. Leone FH, Klein SP, Bohannan HM: A profile of non-participants in a school-based preventive dentistry program. Paper presented at International Association of Dental Research, Chicago, March 1981.
17. Heifetz SB, Meyers RJ, Kingman A: A comparison of the anticaries effectiveness of daily and weekly rinsing with sodium fluoride solutions: final results after three years. Pediatr Dent 1982; 4:22–26.
18. Radike AW: Criteria for diagnosis of dental caries. Proceedings of the Conference on the Clinical Testing of Cariostatic Agents, held by the American Dental Association, October 14–16, 1968. Chicago, IL: ADA, 1972.

19. Klein SP, Bell RM, Bohannan HM, et al.: The Reliability of Clinical and Radiographic Examinations in the National Preventive Dentistry Demonstration Program. The Rand Corporation, R-3138-RWJ, 1984

20. Bell RM, et al.: Treatment Effects in the National Preventive Dentistry Demonstration Program. The Rand Corporation, R-3072-RWJ, 1984.

21. Scott AJ, Holt D: The effect of two-stage sampling on ordinary least squares methods. J Am Stat Assoc 1982; 77:848–854.

22. Klein SP, et al.: Teacher and Principal Survey Results in the National Preventive Dentistry Demonstration Program. The Rand Corporation, N-1921-RWJ, 1984.

23. Foch CB, et al.: Costs of Treatment Procedures in the National Preventive Dentistry Demonstration Program. The Rand Corporation, R-3034-RWJ, 1984.

24. Glass RL (ed.): First International Conference on the Declining Prevalence of Dental Caries. J Dent Res (Special Issue) 1962; 61:1304–1383.

25. Harvey C, Kelly JE: Decayed, Missing, and Filled Teeth Among Persons 1–74 Years, National Health Survey, 1971–74, USDHHS, Series 11, No. 223. Washington, DC: Govt Printing Office, August 1981.

26. Kelly JE, Harvey CR: Basic Dental Examination Findings of Persons 1–74 Years, National Health Survey, 1971–74, USDHEW, Series 11, No. 214. Washington, DC: Govt Printing Office, May 1979.

27. Kelly JE, Harvey CR: Decayed, Missing, and Filled Teeth Among Youths 12–17 Years, National Health Survey, 1966–70, USDHEW, Series 11, No. 144. Washington, DC: Govt Printing Office, October 1974.

28. Kelly JE, Scanlon JV: Decayed, Missing, and Filled Teeth Among Children, National Health Survey, 1963-65, USDHEW, Series 11, No. 106. Washington, DC: Govt Printing Office, August 1971.

29. Miller AJ, et al.: The Prevalence of Dental Caries in United States Children. USDHHS, NIH Pub. No. 82-2245. Washington, DC: Govt Printing Office, 1981.

30. Leverett DH: Fluorides and the changing prevalence of dental caries. Science 1982; 217:26–30.

31. Bell RM, et al.: Results of Baseline Dental Exams in the National Preventive Dentistry Demonstration Program. The Rand Corporation, R-2862-RWJ, 1982.

32. Horowitz HS, Creighton WE, McLendon BJ: The effect on human dental caries of weekly oral rinsing with a sodium fluoride mouthwash: a final report. Arch Oral Biol 1971; 16:609–616.

33. Eckhaus B, et al.: Enrollment in and compliance with a community demonstration program of caries prevention for grades kindergarten through 12. J Public Health Dent 1982; 42:142–154.

34. Foch CB: A Cost Analysis Plan for the National Preventive Dentistry Demonstration Program. The Rand Corporation, N-1670-RWJ, 1981.

35. Doherty NJG, et al.: Costs of school based mouthrinsing in 14 demonstration programs in USA. Community Dent Oral Epidemiol 1984; 12:35–38.

36. Doherty NJG, Powell EA: Clinical Field Trial to Assess the Cost-Effectiveness of Various Caries Preventive Agents. Bethesda, MD: National Institute of Dental Research, July 1980.

37. Coombs J, et al.: The transfer of preventive health technologies to schools: a focus on implementation. Soc Sci Med 1981; 15A:789–791.

38. GAO: Reducing Tooth Decay—More Emphasis on Fluoridation Needed. Report to the Congress of the United States. US General Accounting Office, HRD-79-3, Washington, DC: April 13, 1979.

39. Young WO, Striffler DF, Burt BA: The prevention and control of dental caries: fluoridation. In: Dentistry, Dental Practice, and the Community, 3d ed. Philadelphia: W.B. Saunders, 1983; 155–200.

40. Bibby BG, Shern RJ: Methods of Caries Prediction. Washington, DC: Information Retrieval, Inc, 1978.

41. Bohannan HM, et al.: Examination Procedures in the National Preventive Dentistry Demonstration Program. The Rand Corporation, N-2187-RWJ, 1984.

11

The Efficiency of Caries Prevention with Weekly Fluoride Mouthrinses

John W. Stamm, Harry M. Bohannan, Richard C. Graves, and Judith A. Disney

In the health field, the urgency with which different preventive programs are pursued will vary depending upon the extent and severity of the specific problem and the effectiveness of the preventive program. Furthermore, a given health problem does not remain immutable over time; rather, its impact on society tends to rise or fall depending on circumstances. For example, a disease such as smallpox has been eradicated and tuberculosis is now a relatively minor problem in the developed world. On the other hand, lung cancer and occupational diseases appear to be rising health problems.[1,2] Not surprisingly, the resources allocated to preventive programs take into account these shifts in disease burdens.

A review of the history of prevention in dentistry indicates a number of significant milestones. Most important was the discovery by Dean and his collaborators that fluoride in the drinking water is effective in the reduction of dental caries.[3] This finding spawned much research and a host of subsequent preventive methods based on the use of both systemic and topical fluorides. Second, beginning around 1950 there was a considerable increase in publicly administered preventive dental programs.[4] This expansion was related to the relatively high levels of dental caries among schoolchildren and coincided with the increasing awareness of childrens' dentistry as a specialized field of dental care. The third significant marker occurred in the late 1960s when the prevention movement captured private dental practice.[5] This was an important milestone in the evolution of dental care, one that has enhanced the stature of the dental profession and probably has exerted an appreciable impact on the oral health status of the public.

In the past five years it has become increasingly evident that caries attack among children has diminished appreciably in most developed countries. The causes for this decline are not fully determined, but in large part increased fluoride in the food chain, the widespread use of efficacious fluoride dentifrices, and better personal and professional dental care are most likely to

Dr. Stamm is chairman, Department of Community Dentistry, McGill University, Montreal. Dr. Bohannan is research professor and Dr. Graves is associate professor, Department of Dental Ecology, University of North Carolina at Chapel Hill, North Carolina. Dr. Disney is graduate research assistant, Department of Biostatistics, School of Public Health, University of North Carolina at Chapel Hill.

be responsible. Consequently, it is necessary and desirable to reexamine the current usefulness of various caries preventives, including those involving fluorides. Such an evaluation would enable dental professionals to reinforce the most effective preventive technologies while placing reduced emphasis on the less effective methods.

With that background as the point of departure, this paper seeks to reappraise school-based weekly fluoride mouthrinse programs (FMR) for the prevention of dental caries in nonfluoridated communities in the United States. To attain this goal the analysis will make use of economic evaluation to answer the question: "Is this procedure worth doing compared to other things that could be done with these same resources?"

The Rationale for Economic Evaluation of Prevention

An economic appraisal of prevention is best visualized as the fourth stage in a series of procedures that constitute health program evaluation. The four evaluation stages answer the following questions:

1. **Can the procedure work?** Does the preventive technique reduce disease occurrence in subjects who use the procedure precisely as prescribed? In other words, how well does the specific preventive measure work under ideal conditions? The impact of a preventive technique associated with a high percentage of compliance is often termed efficacy. This is the object of most caries randomized clinical trials, which report findings and formulate conclusions based only on those subjects who successfully completed the study.

2. **Does the procedure work in practice?** Does the preventive technique reduce disease when the procedure is implemented in the community where reduced compliance and program slippage are factors to be reckoned with? The impact of a preventive procedure on persons to whom it was originally offered is called effectiveness. In the caries context, effectiveness is the practical or real-world caries reduction that may be expected across the whole population in a community-based caries prevention program. Significantly, while this is the information usually required by program planners, it is not provided by caries clinical trials for the reasons indicated above.

From J. W. Stamm, H. M. Bohannan, R. C. Graves, and J. A. Disney, "The Efficiency of Caries Prevention with Weekly Fluoride Mouthrinses," *Journal of Dental Education*, 1984, 48(11), 617-624.

3. Is the procedure reaching those who need it? Is the preventive procedure accessible to all those who could benefit from it? This type of evaluation concerns availability.

4. Is the procedure worth doing? Does the preventive technique provide an outcome such that society is satisfied that the required resources should be spent in this rather than in some other way? Appraisal of this type is referred to as efficiency or economic evaluation.

The general method of conducting efficacy, effectiveness, and availability evaluation in the health field has been described by Sackett and Chambers.[6] Appropriate methods for undertaking economic evaluations of preventive programs have been developed by Stoddart and Drummond,[7] from whom the above questions were drawn.

In focusing on an economic evaluation of fluoride mouthrinses in the United States, this paper first seeks to examine the efficacy and effectiveness of FMR. This evaluation is followed by an examination of costs associated with FMR. The evidence for effects and costs is then merged to provide information about the most probable cost effectiveness of FMR attainable in nonfluoridated communities. The paper concludes with a discussion of the most significant policy implications arising out of the analysis. No attempt is made to undertake an availability analysis for FMR programs in the United States.

Efficacy of Weekly Fluoride Mouthrinses

A determination of the efficacy of fluoride rinses requires that the data for the analysis possess certain characteristics.[8] First, the findings should derive from properly designed experiments. Nonexperimental evidence has its place and can provide important information about etiology (e.g., actinic radiation and oral cancer) and adverse treatment procedures (e.g., abrasive dentifrices). But those most familiar with nonexperimental research generally agree that it is not suitable for the demonstration of efficacy.[9] This position is also implicit in the criteria employed by the U.S. Food and Drug Administration and the American Dental Association's Council on Dental Therapeutics for the recognition of new drugs and therapeutic agents. In short, the efficacy of prevention techniques can best be determined by well-designed experiments, which in the health field are commonly known as randomized clinical trials (RCT).

A second consideration, one particularly necessary for economic evaluation, is that the preventive impact be expressed in an absolute metric rather than in percentage terms.[10] As Horowitz has stated in the context of caries clinical trials, using abstract percentage figures without reference to actual mean values can be highly misleading.[11]

The use of weekly FMR for caries prevention was first reported by Hagglund in 1969.[12] The first U.S. report,

by Horowitz et al., appeared in 1971.[13] A reasonably large number of FMR papers have appeared since then, but surprisingly, only seven represent U.S. randomized clinical trials that used longitudinal control groups for estimating the efficacy of weekly FMR in American nonfluoridated communites. Of these, only six report on sodium fluoride, the current agent of choice, and only four were conducted during the past ten years. Table 1 presents the empirical findings for each of these seven studies and expresses the efficacy of the fluoride rinse in terms of caries increment saved per year.[13-19]

With respect to children in grades one and two, the two revelant investigations[13,19] indicate that rinsing with 0.2 percent sodium fluoride for a period of between 20 to 46 months will lead to a savings in the dental caries increment of approximately 0.11 to 0.13 surfaces per year. It should be noted that in the study by Bell et al.[19] children were also on a regimen of 1.0 mg fluoride tablets administered during school days.

The data regarding older children are inconsistent. Examining just the neutral NaF results reveals that three studies obtained a savings in caries increment of between 0.5 and 0.76 surfaces per year,[13,14,19] while another three investigations were unable to show clinically or statistically significant results.[16,18,19] It is obvious that when confronted by such contradictory results the analyst finds himself in an unenviable situation. In the absence of more data for older children, a determination of the efficacy of weekly FMR in nonfluoridated communities involves educated guesswork. Exacerbating this uncertainty is the knowledge that the efficacy results are based on a higher degree of subject compliance than can be expected realistically in nonexperimental settings.

The variation in study results requires a method of permitting aggregation of the data into a best estimate of FMR efficacy. Whatever method is chosen, it should avoid reliances on hypothetical estimates or loosely supported opinions. Assuming that the studies are reasonably homogeneous in most of their principal characteristics, a technique based on weighted averaging, where weights are based on sample size and variance, can serve to generate acceptable empirical estimates of caries preventive efficacy.[20] Applying this approach to the neutral sodium fluoride results in Table 1 indicates that with a high degree of subject compliance, FMR in nonfluoridated communities can prevent 0.12 permanent tooth surfaces per year in children grades 1 and 2 and 0.28 surfaces per year in children grades 5 and 6. To the degree that FMR reduces the caries increment in the primary dentition, the estimate of efficacy in the younger age group is understated.

As a further perspective, it can be argued persuasively that the dental caries environment for the studies in Table 1 has changed significantly over time. By the early 1980s, the enamel caries incidence was appreciably lower than was the case 10 years previously. If one aggregates the four FMR studies conducted during the past ten years,[16-19] Table 1 indicates that, even with the advantage of full compliance, the efficacy of weekly fluoride rinses declines to approximately 0.21 surfaces per year in children grades 5 and 6.

Effectiveness of Weekly Fluoride Mouthrinse

From a practical and economic point of view, it is extremely important to know how fluoride mouthrinses will perform under conditions less controlled than those in a randomized clinical trial.[21,22] This question corresponds to effectiveness evaluation. What kinds of data would permit such an analysis? Ideally, the study would be designed as an RCT but would follow up all subjects to whom the treatment and control procedures were offered initially.[23] In other words, the data analysis would not focus exclusively on subjects who were continuous participants in the investigation; rather, it would analyze the preventive impact based on all who were offered the treatments. This approach implies that appropriate caries data from those who refused consent and those who dropped out during the study must be treated in the final statistical analysis. Understandably, such studies are virtually nonexistent for FMR.

For an alternative, though decidedly inferior, source of data, one may turn to nonexperimental, weekly 0.2

Table 1. Results from Randomized Clinical Trials of Weekly Fluoride Mouthrinse in Nonfluoridated Communities in the United States[a]

Investigator	Agent Tested	Study Location	Study Duration	Study Groups	Final Sample Size	DMFS Baseline	DMFS Final	DMFS Increment Saved Per Year
Horowitz et al.,[13] 1967-69	NaF 0.2%	Portland Ore.	20 mo.	Gr. 1	C = 135	.97	2.26	
					T = 125	.90	1.98	.13
				Gr. 5	C = 112	6.48	9.40	
					T = 117	6.97	8.62	.76
Heifetz et al.,[14] 1969-70	NaF 0.3% APF 0.3%	Portland, Ore.	24 mo.	10-12 yrs.	C = 154	9.28	15.01	
					NaF = 126	8.52	12.94	.65
					APF = 133	9.38	13.94	.58
Packer et al.,[15] 1969-72	APF 0.1%	Knoxville, Tenn.	28 mo.	8.6 yrs.	C = 97	6.48	9.13	
					T = 108	6.80	8.37	.46
Doherty and Powell,[16] 1975-79	NaF 0.2%	Springfield, Mass.	40 mo.[b]	11-13 yrs.	C = 536[c]	10.12	15.50	
					T = 525[d]	9.90	15.47	.26[e]
Heifetz et ak,[17] 1976-79	NaF 0.2%	Biddeford, Me.	30 mo.	10-12 yrs.	C = 204	6.56	10.64	
					T = 199	5.98	8.81	.50
Ringelberg et al.[18] 1978-80	NaF 0.2%	Polk Co., Fla.	20 mo.	12.5 yrs.	C = 249	4.93	8.27	
					T = 253	4.11	6.77	.41
Bell et al., 1977-78 to[19] 1981-82	NaF[f] 0.2%	Billerica, Mass. Monroe, La. Pierce Co., Wash.	46 mo.	Gr. 1 + 2	C = 2043[c]	1.11	3.80	
					T = 1365[d]	1.10	3.25	.11[e]
		Tallahassee, Fla. Wichita, Kan.		Gr. 5[g]	C = 893[c]	4.82	9.16	
					T = 543[d]	4.89	8.96	.05[e]

[a] Visual-tactile examinations only.
[b] Approximate mean interval between baseline and final examination. However, treatments only provided during first 30 months of the study.
[c] Study children receiving regimens without FMR.
[d] Study children receiving regimens in which FMR was all or part of treatment.
[e] DMFS increment saved determined by multivariate estimation technique based on study design.
[f] Children also obtained a daily fluoride supplement so that results reflect the combined effect of rinsing and F supplementation.
[g] The FMR/supplement regimen was provided for only 18 months though reported caries increment based on 46 months.

percent NaF mouthrinse programs or demonstration studies that have estimated effectiveness based on historical comparisons. Table 2 presents data from all such studies conducted in nonfluoridated communities in the United States.[24-29] Before dealing with the data themselves it is worth noting that, aside from the NIDR-sponsored demonstration studies,[24] only two other studies have used historical comparisons.[24,2b] As far as the NIDR-sponsored demonstrations are concerned, detailed findings have been reported only for the three programs directed by Eckhaus,[25] Ripa,[27] and Leverett.[28] A recent report on the aggregate findings relies on graphic displays but does not provide precise and detailed numerical findings, making it difficult to incorporate the results into the present paper.[29]

The consistency in DMFS increment saved per year in Table 2 might lead to the conclusion that weekly FMR in nonfluoridated communities results in 0.33 fewer carious surfaces per child per year. However, this would be an overestimation of FMR's effectiveness and, in fact, its efficacy as well. This overestimation arises because the historical comparison design cannot separate the unique contribution of FMR from the impact of the secular caries decline with respect to the overall reduction in caries increment in children. The

existence and nature of the secular decline in dental caries experience among children in the United States have been well documented.[30-32] Virtually all the FMR studies using historical comparisons were conducted during this period of falling caries attack rates.

It should also be noted that, unlike the RCT, the historical comparison design cannot assure an absence of examiner bias since the study does not incorporate the all-important double blind characteristic. This criticism does not imply that examination bias occurred. However, it must be understood that the burden of proof falls on the study to demonstrate that such biases did not occur. Generally, such evidence has not been provided. Thus, the results in Table 2 should be interpreted with great caution. Given the built-in deficiencies of historical comparison studies, the effectiveness of weekly 0.2 percent sodium fluoride mouthrinse in elementary schoolchildren must be estimated at less than 0.33 surfaces saved per child per year.

The Efficiency of Weekly Fluoride Mouthrinse Programs

Besides the variations in efficacy and effectiveness cited above, the recent literature on caries prevention with

Table 2. Results from Weekly Fluoride Mouthrinse Studies Conducted in Nonfluoridated Communities and Using Historical Comparisons in the United States[a]

Investigator	Agent Tested	Location	Duration	Group	Year	Mean DMFS	Year	Mean DMFS	Increment Saved Per Year
Ringelberg et al.,[24] 1973-75	NaF 0.2%	Alachua Co., Fla.	24 mo.	8-12 yrs.	1973	2.81	1975	2.19	.31
Eckhaus et al.,[25b] 1975-78	NaF 0.2%	Livermore, Calif.	36 mo.	Gr. 1-8	1975	4.10	1978	2.73	.46
Petchel and Mello,[2b] 1977-80	NaF 0.2%	Colorado City, Ariz.	40 mo.	Gr. 5	1977	3.0[c]	1980	2.3[c]	.24[c]
Ripa et al.[27b] 1975-81	NaF 0.2%	Three Villages, N. Y.	72 mo.	Gr. 1-6	1975	2.30	1981	1.03	.21
Leverett and Jensen[28b] 1975-82	NaF 0.2%	Schuyler Co., N. Y.	84 mo.	Gr. 1-8	1975	4.27	1982	1.68	.37
Miller and Brunelle,[29] 1975-76 to 1979-80	NaF 0.2%	17 Comm.	42 mo.	Gr. 1-6	1975-76	?	1979-80	?	.33 (est.)

[a] Visual-tactile examinations only.
[b] Included also in the Miller and Brunelle report.
[c] DMFT index.

FMR reveals that there are significant disparities in the estimated cost of rinsing programs. The most obvious outcome of such uncertainty is that it creates considerable confusion about the efficiency of FMR programs. Such a situation is not uncommon, however, and even large and prestigious agencies can be unclear about specific costs associated with disease prevention. For example, at one time the American Cancer Society endorsed a screening procedure of six sequential stool tests for detecting cancer of the bowel. It was obvious to many that the screening cost per case identified would rise appreciably with each test. However, the society never dreamed that the cost would reach $47 million per cancer detected by the sixth test in the sequence.[33] While this is an extreme example, it is apropos of the situation in caries prevention where, analogously, the interest revolves around the program cost per surface of caries prevented.

Cost of Weekly FMR Programs. Table 3 summarizes nominal cost estimates for U.S. FMR programs as reported in the literature.[13,29,34-41] From the perspective of a program planner, the great variation in cost figures causes confusion when determining whether or not to develop and implement (or to maintain) an FMR program. Overcoming this dilemma requires a closer look at how FMR costs per child per year are constructed.

The literature on costing FMR programs is somewhat obscure, in large part due to the varying terminology and definitions employed in expressing costs. In classical economic terms, total cost is the sum of fixed and variable costs with the latter broken down into direct and indirect cost components.[42,43] However, Leverett and Sveen define total cost as the sum of actual and contributed costs.[36] Doherty et al. equate total cost to the sum of explicit and implicit costs.[39] Foch et al. sum direct and overhead cost to determine total cost for FMR programs.[40] The latter authors explicitly exclude the cost of donated goods and services, a category apparently included by Leverett and Sveen[36] and by Doherty et al.[39]

Using the definition supplied by Foch et al.,[40] the total cost for a mouthrinse program is the sum of direct and overhead costs. Direct costs comprise the labor, materials, and capital costs incurred in operating the ongoing program. Overhead costs derive from legitimate activities occurring outside the program which nevertheless appear to contribute to the successful functioning of the program. Foch et al. give some examples of overhead activities, including meetings with school officials to discuss program schedules, recordkeeping, and built-in slack for times when children are unavailable for program activity.

With this position as background, it now becomes possible to form a reasonably accurate impression of the annual, per-child costs of an FMR program by focusing on those studies in Table 3 that report, at a minimum, what resembles the total direct costs as previously defined. Included in this group are the investigations by Brunelle and Miller,[35] Leverett and Sveen,[36] Miller and Brunelle,[29] Doherty et al.,[39] Foch et al.,[40] and Doherty and Powell.[41] Since these studies covered different time periods, the costs have been converted to 1981 dollars. Using the adjusted dollar figures, the lowest mean cost estimate comes to $3.41 while the highest reaches $9.64. In the case of the low estimate, it is assumed that an ongoing school dental health education program already exists so that the $3.41 figure represents an incremental cost. Further, no allowance is made for overhead such as administration or slack periods nor are donated goods and services included in the cost. In the case of the high cost, $9.64, this figure relates only to variable costs and does not include a fixed-cost component. In short, neither cost figure should be seen as inflated.

These comments on Table 3 should suggest to the program administrator that consideration of an FMR program for 10,000 children would require a minimum annual budget in the range of $50,000 (in 1981 terms). This estimate would have to be adjusted to local circumstances, including wage rates, and to variations in the cost of overhead as well as donated goods and services.

Cost Effectiveness of Weekly FMR Programs. The question of a preventive program's efficiency in comparison to other programs that attempt to achieve the same outcome may be addressed by cost-effectiveness

Table 3. Estimated Annual Costs Per Child of Fluoride Mouthrinse Programs in North America

Investigator	Year Reported	Estimated Cost Nominal	$1981[h]
Horowitz et al.[13]	1971	$ .31[a]	$ .81
Ripa et al.[34]	1977	.45[a]	.68
Brunelle and Miller[35]	1979	3.49[b]	5.24
Leverett and Sveen[36]	1980	2.35[c]	3.53
Doherty and Powell[41]	1980	6.01[d]	9.64
Heifetz[37]	1982	.75[a]	1.13
Driscoll et al.[38]	1982	.62[a]	.78
Miller and Brunelle[29]	1983	.71-9.27[e]	.99-12.93
Doherty et al.[39]	1983	4.70[f]	6.56
Foch et al.[40]	1984	3.41[g]	3.41

[a] Materials cost only.
[b] Mean of 17 NIDR-sponsored demonstration programs after 2 years.
[c] Reduces to $2.02 if contributed costs are excluded.
[d] Variable costs only. Fixed costs associated with program are excluded.
[e] Same set of studies as in b; suggests a mean somewhat over $3.49.
[f] Mean cost based on 14 of studies in b. Reduces to $3.18 if implicit costs are excluded.
[g] Incremental direct cost if an ongoing dental education program already exists in the school.
[h] Adjusted costs assume nominal costs apply to period of study rather than year study reported.

analysis. For caries prevention, an estimate of efficiency is often obtained by evaluating the costs various preventive techniques incur for preventing one surface of tooth decay per child.[44,45] To be meaningful, a cost-effectiveness analysis must have accurate effectiveness and cost data as inputs. The cost effectiveness of FMR in nonfluoridated areas appears to vary according to the age of the children involved. Assuming that in 6- to 7-year-old children FMR saves 0.12 surfaces a year, it is clear that over the first 3 to 4 years the procedure is not cost effective. Four years of rinsing at an annual cost of approximately $5.00 indicates that for a program expenditure of $20.00 less than one-half a surface of decay has been averted. Alternatively, two children in this age range would have to rinse for four years at a total cost of $40.00 to save one surface of decay. Given that the 1981 fee for a one-surface amalgam filling was approximately $19.92,[46] strong doubt is cast over the efficiency of school-based weekly FMR programs as a procedure for the younger age groups.

On the other hand, if the FMR program is aimed at children aged 10 and 11, and if full compliance can be assured for a four-year period (something far from certain), then the data suggest that an approximate annual savings of between 0.20 and 0.30 decayed surfaces is possible. Taking the lower estimate first, this implies that five children rinsing for four years at a total program cost of $100 would prevent four surfaces of decay. Using the amalgam surface fee as a reference, the program expended $100 to avert $79.67 in restorative costs. However, if 0.30 surfaces saved per child per year is the appropriate estimate of effectiveness, this means that the same five children would be spared a total of six surfaces of decay over a four-year period. In this case the $100 program cost would be offset by the $119.52 saved in first-time expenditures for amalgam fillings.

In short, the data compiled in this paper suggest that unless a weekly fluoride mouthrinse program can reduce the target population's mean caries increment by approximately 0.25 surfaces a year or more, the efficiency of the FMR program may be sufficiently low as to cast doubt on its economic viability.

Discussion

Perhaps the most striking outcome of the present evaluation is the reserve we attach to weekly FMR as a school-based dental public health measure. Since this position runs counter to conventional wisdom about mouthrinses,[47,48] it is useful to add some comment to the results already presented.

First, it is noteworthy how few studies actually exist on which a technically appropriate evaluation of FMR is possible. In this respect, review papers stating that "approximately 50 clinical trials have shown that mouthrinsing fortnightly, weekly, or daily with dilute solutions of fluoride will reduce the incidence of dental caries in children by about 35 percent" are too exuber-

ant.[49] It is simply not true that all the studies referred to qualify as clinical trials. In addition, the variety of agents studied, the differences in the ages of the children involved, and the aggregation of fluoridated and nonfluoridated communities inhibits the practical usefulness of such generalizations. In contrast to others, we believe there are very few studies to which program planners can turn when considering whether or not to launch FMR programs in the United States (see Table 1).

Second, the literature on FMR is replete with statements about percent caries reductions. As stated earlier, percentages provide an inappropriate basis on which to evaluate the potential contribution weekly FMR can make to dental public health programs. By themselves, expressions of percent caries reductions may be acceptable for public relations exercises but they are not suitable for program planning or evaluation.

The third issue we would like to emphasize is the distinction between the efficacy and effectiveness attainable by a given preventive measure. Persons experienced in the conduct of randomized clinical trials realize that the results obtained are not likely to be observable under the conditions of community programs. Hence a distinction must be drawn between efficacy, as determined by randomized clinical trials, and effectiveness, as observed in ongoing community programs. When assessing whether or not to implement FMR in a region or community, the planner must base his or her decision on effectiveness considerations as only these relate to the possible outcomes of the program. As pointed out earlier, true effectiveness data are rarely available for FMR programs. As a practical matter, therefore, the astute planner has little choice but to use discounted efficacy results in forming decisions about FMR programs.

A fourth consideration, and one related to the previous point, is that FMR programs suffer from problems with compliance. Randomized clinical trials, quite properly, circumvent this problem by basing the analysis of results only on those subjects who complete the study. All those to whom the FMR was offered but who dropped out along the way are ignored for the purpose of determining the impact of the rinse. In this way an RCT can cope with an attrition rate of, say, 50 percent, so long as treatment group imbalance does not become too severe. With ongoing community programs, however, a significant dropout rate from a school-based activity may well compromise its viability.

We feel the compliance issue is too often swept under the rug. On the one hand are periodic statements to the effect that 8-12 million U.S. schoolchildren are rinsing weekly with dilute fluoride solutions.[50,29] On the other hand are the acknowledged compliance problems as described by Eckhaus et al.,[25] Coombs et al.,[51,52] and Klein et al.[53] The clinical trials reported in Table 1 experienced attrition rates of 48 percent (grade 1, 20 months),[13] 45 percent (grade 5, 20 months),[13] 56 percent

10-12 year-olds, 24 months),[14] and 37 percent (10-12 year-olds, 30 months).[17] These rates do not include potential subjects who declined to participate at the outset. It is entirely likely that nonexperimental, community FMR programs run through public health departments would face similar or worse compliance, attrition, and enrollment difficulties, resulting in a substantial decrease in effectiveness. Indeed, a carefully conducted 1984 survey of state and local health departments could account for only 3.2 million children in state and/or local FMR programs.[54] The discrepancy between this figure and the numbers claimed above deserves more attention from both researchers and program planners.

Fifth, turning to a consideration of FMR program costs, our analysis suggests that commonly cited, informational estimates are too low. Suggestions that fluoride mouthrinse programs of any significant size can be implemented at a cost of less than a dollar per child per year lack realism. However, the disparity in cost estimates is understandable given different organizational frameworks and analytical perspectives. Costs take on different meanings depending on whether one takes the perspective of a budget officer, an accountant, or an economist. For example, if a dental program director uses dental hygienists already on the staff to implement and operate a school-based FMR program, it may be that the only new item in his or her budget would be the materials cost for the rinsing activity. From this view the program appears quite affordable. The accountant, on the other hand, would certainly add salaries to program expenditures, thereby raising the program cost appreciably. The economist, working under the principle of opportunity cost, would add the further cost of donated goods and services as might be supplied by volunteers or homeroom teachers. Indeed, one might speculate that one reason for the rather poor experience with FMR program compliance has been underinvestment in program operation based on the belief that FMR programs are inexpensive. Such beliefs may well have been nurtured by the hypothetical cost and cost-effectiveness exercises[43] which, at least by implication, suggest that FMR programs can be operated on the basis of materials cost alone.

Sixth, the future cost effectiveness of FMR programs will be linked to the changes in caries increment. If caries levels continue to decline due to fluorides in the food chain, the widespread use of fluoride dentifrices, better personal and professional dental care, and possibly other factors, then it follows that there will be less caries to prevent. Furthermore, among children caries attack is increasingly concentrated on the pit and fissure surfaces where fluorides generally exert a relatively lesser preventive effect. As the preventable increment declines, the average cost effectiveness of fluoride rinses will also decrease, as will the value of professionally applied topical fluorides and, to some extent, sealants and six-monthly diagnostic visits.

However, if the cost effectiveness of FMR is dependent on the caries attack level, this also implies that regional caries conditions may be such as to recommend an FMR program. Dental public health directors must determine the nature of the caries challenge in their areas in order to know whether a school-based rinsing procedure would be efficient. No general prescription for the use of FMR programs can be supplied.

Seventh, it is a fact that conventional economic appraisals of health care have relied on the human capital approach for the valuation of benefits. This is a relatively empty concept in the case of dental programs. As a result, the most common approach to evaluating preventive dental care has involved cost-effectiveness analysis. However, this approach has only sidestepped the problem of what a caries-free tooth surface is really worth. In this paper we too have followed the conventional but exceedingly narrow view that the value of a prevented carious surface is equivalent to the price of a one-surface amalgam restoration. There is some debate as to whether this represents an entirely satisfactory approach. It is conceivable, indeed logical, that society should place more value on a sound tooth surface than on a surface of amalgam. Such a perspective would serve to enhance the cost effectiveness of fluoride mouthrinses.

Conclusion

In conclusion, we offer the perspective that school-based, weekly FMR programs in nonfluoridated regions are less efficient than is commonly believed. An evaluation of FMR programs suggests that: (1) effectiveness claims are modestly overstated, (2) the caries increment in untreated children is frequently overestimated, (3) the problems with longer term compliance are generally disregarded, and (4) the true cost of operating a school-based FMR program is usually understated.

REFERENCES

1. McKeown, T. A Historical Appraisal of the Medical Task. In Medical History and Medical Care. Oxford University Press, 1971.
2. Lalonde, M. A New Perspective on the Health of Canadians: A Working Document. Ottawa: Government of Canada, 1974, pp. 76.
3. Dean, H. T., F. A. Arnold, and E. Elvove. Domestic Water and Dental Caries. Additional Studies of the Relation of Fluoride Domestic Waters to Dental Caries Experience in 4,425 White Children, Aged 12 to 14 Years, of 13 Cities in 4 States. Pub. Health. Rep. 57:1115-79, 1942.
4. Dunning, J. M. Principles of Dental Public Health. Second edition. Cambridge: Harvard University Press, 1970, pp. 598.
5. Katz, S., J. L. McDonald, and G. K. Stookey. Preventive Dentistry in Action. New Jersey: D.C.P. Publishing, 1972, pp. 324.
6. Sackett, D. L., and L. W. Chambers. Review of Health and Social Service Programs: Some Methodologic Criteria. Department of Clinical Epidemiology and Biostatistics, McMaster University, Hamilton, Ontario, 1980, pp. 26.
7. Stoddart, G. L., and M. F. Drummond. A User's Guide to Economic Evaluation of Health Services. Department of Clinical Epidemiology

and Biostatistics, McMaster University, Hamilton, Ontario, 1983, pp. 32.

8. Fletcher, R. H., S. W. Fletcher, and E. H. Wagner. Clinical Epidemiology: The Essentials. Baltimore: Williams and Wilkins, 1982, pp. 223.

9. Sartwell, P. E. Retrospective Studies: A Review for the Clinician. Ann. Intern. Med. 81:381, 1974.

10. Kaman, A., J. Schmee, and W. Meeker. Propriety of Using Percentages in Reporting Anticariogenic Studies. J. Dent. Res. 55:703, 1976.

11. Horowitz, H. S. Measurement and Expression of Treatment Effects in Caries Clinical Trials. J. Dent. Res. (in press).

12. Torell, P., and Y. Ericsson. The Potential Benefits to be Derived from Using Fluoride Mouth Rinses—State of the Art Paper. Paper presented at the International Workshop on Fluorides and Dental Caries Reductions, Baltimore, 1974.

13. Horowitz, H. S., W. E. Creighton, and B. J. McLendon. The Effect on Human Dental Caries of Weekly Oral Rinsing with a Sodium Fluoride Mouthwash: A Final Report. Arch. Oral Biol. 16:609-16, 1971.

14. Heifetz, S. B., W. S. Driscoll, and W. E. Creighton. The Effect on Dental Caries of Weekly Rinsing with a Neutral Sodium Fluoride or an Acidulated Phosphate-Fluoride Mouthwash. JADA 87:364-68, 1973.

15. Packer, M. W., H. R. Laswell, J. Doyle, H. H. Naff, and F. Brown. Cariostatic Effects of Fluoride Mouthrinses in a Non-Fluoridated Community. J. Tenn. Dent. Assoc. 55:22-26, 1975.

16. Doherty, N. J., and E. A. Powell. Clinical Field Trial to Assess the Cost-Effectiveness of Various Caries Preventives. Final report for the National Institute of Dental Research (Contract No. NO1-DE-52449), 1980.

17. Heifetz, S. B., R. J. Meyers, and A. Kingman. A Comparison of the Anticaries Effectiveness of Daily and Weekly Rinsing with Sodium Fluoride Solutions: Final Results After Three Years. Pediat. Dent. 4:300-03, 1981.

18. Ringelberg, M. L., A. J. Conti, C. B. Ward, B. Clark, and S. Lotzkar. Effectiveness of Different Concentrations and Frequencies of Sodium Fluoride Mouthrinse. Pediat. Dent. 4:305-08, 1982.

19. Bell, R. M., S. P. Klein, H. M. Bohannan, J. A. Disney, R. C. Graves, and R. Madison. Treatment Effects in the National Preventive Dentistry Demonstration Program. Publication No. R-3072-RWJ. Santa Monica, Calif: The Rand Corporation, 1984.

20. Clark, D. C., J. A. Hanley, P. L. Weinstein, and J. W. Stamm. An Empirically Based System to Estimate the Effectiveness of Caries Preventive Agents. Caries Res. (in press).

21. Schwartz, D., and J. Lellouch. Explanatory and Pragmatic Attitudes in Therapeutical Trials. J. Chron. Dis. 20:637-48, 1967.

22. O'Mullane, D. M. Efficiency in Clinical Trials of Caries Preventive Agents and Methods. Comm. Dent. Oral Epidemiol. 4:190-94, 1976.

23. Doherty, N. J. G. Economic Costs of Attrition in Clinical Trials. J. Dent. Res. 61:649-53, 1982.

24. Ringelberg, M. L., A. J. Conti, and D. B. Webster. An Evaluation of Single and Combined Self-Applied Fluoride Programs in Schools. J. Pub. Health Dent. 36:229-36, 1976.

25. Eckhaus, B., S. Silverstein, J. Fine, and J. Boriskin. Enrollment in and Compliance with a Community Demonstration Program of Caries Prevention for Grades Kindergarten through 12. J. Pub. Health Dent. 42:142-54, 1982.

26. Petchel, K. A., and A. F. Mello. A School Fluoride Mouth Rinse Program. J. Sch. Health 47:557-58, 1977.

27. Ripa, L. W., G. S. Leske, A. Sposato, and T. Rebich. Supervised Weekly Rinsing with 0.2 Percent Neutral NaF Solution: Final Results of a Demonstration Program after Six Years. J. Pub. Health Dent. 43:53-62, 1983.

28. Leverett, D., and O. E. Jensen. Weekly Rinsing with a Fluoride Mouthrinse in an Unfluoridated Community: Results after Seven Years. A. J. Pub. Health 73: Abstract, P-4, 1983.

29. Miller, A. J., and J. A. Brunelle. A Summary of the NIDR Community Caries Prevention Demonstration Program. JADA 107:265-69, 1983.

30. Brunelle, J. A., and J. P. Carlos. Changes in the Prevalence of Dental Caries in U.S. Schoolchildren, 1961-1980. J. Dent. Res. 61(Sp. Iss.): 1346-51, 1982.

31. Leverett, D. H. Fluorides and the Changing Prevalence of Dental Caries. Science 217:26-30, 1982.

32. Bell, R. M., S. P. Klein, H. M. Bohannan, R. C. Graves, and J. A. Disney. Results of Baseline Dental Examinations in the National Preventive Dentistry Demonstration Program. Publication number R-2862-RWJ. Santa Monica, Calif.: The Rand Corporation, 1982.

33. Neuhauser, D., and A. M. Lewicki. What Do We Gain from the Sixth Stool Guaiac? New Eng. J. Med. 293(5):226-28, 1975.

34. Ripa, L. W., G. S. Leske, and W. G. Lowey. Fluoride Rinsing: A School-based Dental Preventive Program. J. Prev. Dent. 4(5):25-30, 1977.

35. Brunelle, J. A., and A. J. Miller. Cost Analysis of School-based Mouthrinse Programs in 17 Communities in the U.S. and Guam. J. Dent. Res. 58(Sp. Iss. A):Abstract No. 1189, January 1979.

36. Leverett, D. H., and O. B. Sveen. Cost Effectiveness Considerations in Weekly Fluoride Mouthrinsing. Paper presented at 108th Annual Meeting, American Public Health Association. Detroit: 1980.

37. Heifetz, S. B. Self-applied Fluorides For Use at Home. Clin. Prev. Dent. 4(2):6-10, 1982.

38. Driscoll, W. S., P. A. Swango, A. M. Horowitz, and A. Kingman. Caries-Preventive Effects of Daily and Weekly Fluoride Mouthrinsing in an Optimally Fluoridated Community: Findings after Eighteen Months. Pediat. Dent. 3:316-20, 1982.

39. Doherty, N. J. G., J. A. Brunelle, A. J. Miller, and S. H. Li. Costs of School-based Mouthrinsing in 14 Demonstration Programs in USA. Commun. Dent. Oral Epidemiol. 12:35-38, 1984.

40. Foch, C. G., S. P. Klein, H. M. Bohannan, P. E. Anderson, F. H. Leone, J. A. Disney, and M. Oshiro. Cost of Treatment Procedures in the National Preventive Dentistry Demonstration Program. Publ. No. R-3034, RWJ. Santa Monica, Calif.: The Rand Corporation, 1984.

41. Doherty, N. J. G., and E. A. Powell. Costs and Effects of Various Caries Preventive Regimens in a Clinical Field Trial. Contract No. 1-DE-52449, National Institute of Health, Bethesda, July 1980.

42. Mansfield, E. Microeconomics: Theory and Applications. Third edition. New York, N.Y.: W. W. Norton & Co., 1979.

43. Asimakopulos, A. Microeconomics: An Introduction to Economic Theory. Oxford: Oxford University Press, 1978.

44. Heifetz, S. B. Cost-Effectiveness of Topically Applied Fluorides. Paper presented at a Workshop titled "The Relative Efficiency of Methods of Caries Prevention in Dental Public Health." University of Michigan, 1978.

45. Horowitz, H. S., and S. B. Heifetz. Methods for Assessing the Cost-Effectiveness of Caries Preventive Agents and Procedures. Internat. Dent J. 29:106-17, 1979.

46. Wall, T. P. Dental Fees Charged by General Practitioners and Selected Specialists in the United States, 1982. JADA 108:83-87, 1984.

47. Carlos, J. P. The Prevention of Dental Caries: Ten Years Later. JADA 104:193-97, 1982.

48. Mellberg, J. R., and L. W. Ripa. Self-Applied Topical Fluoride. Chapter 9 in Fluoride in Preventive Dentistry. Edited by J. R. Mellberg and L. W. Ripa. Chicago, Ill.: Quintessence Publishing Co. Inc., 1983, pp. 290.

49. Horowitz, H. S. Alternative Methods of Delivering Fluorides: An Update. Dental Hygiene May:37-43, 1983.

50. Burt, B. A. Other Methods for the Prevention and Control of Dental Caries. Chapter 8 in Dentistry, Dental Practice and the Community. Third edition. Edited by D. F. Striffler, W. O. Young, and B. A. Burt. Philadelphia, Penn.: W. B. Saunders Co., 1983, pp. 512.

51. Coombs, J. A., et al. The Transfer of Preventive Health Technologies to Schools: A Focus on Implementation. Social Science and Medicine 15(A): 789-91, 1981.

52. Coombs, J. A., J. B. Silversin, M. E. Drolette, et. al. A National Study of Fluoride Mouthrinse Adoption: Implications for School Health Personnel. J. Sch. Health 53:39-44, 1983.

53. Klein, S. P., H. M. Bohannan, R. M. Bell, J. A. Disney, C. B. Foch, and R. C. Graves. The Cost and Effectiveness of School-based Preventive Dental Care. Paper presented at the Annual Meeting of the American Public Health Association, Dallas, 1983.

54. Connolly, G. N., and H. Bednarsh. Preliminary Report on Fluoride Mouthrinse Programs of State and Local Health Departments. Mimeo, pp. 13, Massachusetts Department of Health, Boston, 1984.

II

EDUCATION

Government's long history of involvement in education, the nation's philosophy of public education as a citizen's right, the commonly held view of education's significance in determining an individual's ultimate intellectual and material achievement, and the frequent debates about the adequacies of public education, all join to make education a rich field of endeavor for evaluation researchers. The five chapters in this section provide a sample of recent work in evaluation research in the educational field, spanning the period from preschool to high school.

The study of High School and Beyond (HSB) is a major longitudinal evaluation research project of the National Center for Education Statistics (NCES). In the first wave of HSB (1980), data were collected by the National Opinion Research Center (NORC) under contract with NCES on 58,728 sophomores and seniors in 1,015 U.S. high schools. As detailed in NORC's final report by Coleman, Hoffer, and Kilgore (1981) and in their subsequent book (1982), the principal finding was that Catholic schools and non-Catholic private schools are more effective than public schools in enhancing students' cognitive skills. The so-called Coleman Report was publicized in the media and has been subject to a number of critiques; and the HSB database, which is publicly available from NCES, has been reanalyzed by many researchers.

The first two chapters in this section are part of the substantial and growing literature on HSB. Chapter 12, by Richard Murnane, is a review essay on the Coleman book and related research. The essay is in three parts: a discussion of unrecognized differences in conceptual perspectives underlying the methodological debates about the NORC research and its interpretation; neglected substantive findings; and the usefulness of the research in informing the policy process.

In Chapter 13, Murnane, with Stuart Newstead and Randall Olsen, reanalyze HSB to resolve differences between the NORC findings and those obtained in a reanalysis of the HSB data by Noell (1982). One criticism of the NORC research is that the results are contaminated by selectivity bias; Noell reanalyzed the HSB data using a model that took account of the selection process and found almost no statistically significant difference between the effectiveness of public and Catholic schools in raising their students' cognitive skills. In response, Coleman et al. analyzed the HSB data again, using a selectivity correction, and found an even greater estimated advantage of Catholic schools over public schools than their original analysis had suggested. A key finding from the economic analysis of Murnane and his colleagues is that the results of using selectivity models are extremely sensitive to a number of assumptions and that the NORC-Noell conflict is partly attributable to differences in the assumptions underlying the estimation strategies used. Another source of the conflict are differences in the proportion of minority students in the two studies. This was the result of differences in (1) the specific control variables used and hence in the observations included in the analysis and (2) the use of design weights to weight the observations in the sample. The authors also examine differences among ethnic groups in the direction of selectivity bias and in the estimated "Catholic school advantage."

Turning from high school to preschool, the next two chapters are studies of early childhood education; both suggest that such interventions are beneficial to participants. Chapter 14, by Martha Bronson, Donald Pierson, and Terrence Tivnan, presents findings from an evaluation of the Brookline Early Education Project (BEEP), an experimental program designed to reduce school problems through an intervention during the preschool years. BEEP provided education and health services beginning at a child's birth and continuing until entrance into kindergarten. Unlike many preschool intervention programs that focus exclusively on children from low-income families (such as the Perry Preschool Project described in Chapter 15), BEEP served children from a wide range of family backgrounds. The evaluation examined 169 second-grade children who had participated in BEEP and a comparison group of 169 children selected randomly from the same classrooms as the BEEP children. Trained observers collected data on the children's classroom behavior using outcome measures tailored to the program's objectives. Findings suggest the potential usefulness of early education for all children, not just for those from lower socioeconomic backgrounds, but that children of more educated parents benefit from even minimal services whereas children of less educated parents require more service-intensive programs.

Chapter 15 provides dramatic evidence of the benefits of early childhood education for low-income children from a longitudinal study that has examined a wide range of academic, social, and economic outcome measures over a more than 15-year follow-up period. The High/Scope Perry Preschool Project, which began in 1962, was an intervention targeted toward low-income children at risk of school failure and placement in special education. The treatment consisted of preschool education and weekly home visits. The evaluation used an experimental design with random assignment of subjects to treatment or control groups; the 123 subjects were followed through grade school, high school, and early adulthood. Study findings have been reported in a series of monographs; Chapter 15 is an excerpt from the most recent study report by Weikart, Berrueta-Clement, Schweinhart, Barnett, and Epstein that contains findings through the subjects' emergence into young adulthood at age 19.[1] The excerpt provides an overview of the study's findings; we urge interested readers to learn more about the study methods and its detailed findings by consulting the complete report. In short, findings were that program participants experienced greater academic achievement in both primary and high school, less unemployment and higher earnings by age 19, less delinquency and fewer encounters with the criminal justice system, fewer pregnancies and births, and a greater likelihood of attending church. The excerpt also includes a detailed cost-benefit analysis of the program, which demonstrates, the authors argue, that one year of preschool for children at risk of poor school performance appears to be a good investment for society, though not necessarily for the children's own families.

The related topic of day care is addressed in Chapter 16, which closes this section. Susan Rose-Ackerman provides an economist's policy analysis of some unintended effects of government regulations that impose high standards of quality on subsidized social services, using child day care as a paradigm. Secondary analyses of data from the National Day Care Study by Abt Associates and from other sources are used to examine the impact of high federal standards for subsidized day care. The analysis shows that although stringent regulations may improve the quality of services for those who qualify, they "may actually curtail the supply of services, promote segregation, and expand the role of large subsidized for-profit firms." Interested readers will find more on this subject in Chapter 39, which demonstrates how the interaction of various governmental social service programs—including tax law, food stamps, Aid to Families with Dependent Children, and block grants for social services—effectively determine the nation's day care policy.

NOTE

1. The editors caution that despite this study's dramatic findings and their apparent significance, we were unable to locate articles on the study in refereed professional journals. Hence these findings have not, to our knowledge, been subjected to the same degree of peer scrutiny as most of the other selections in this volume.

REFERENCES

Coleman, J. S., Hoffer, T., & Kilgore, S. (1981). *Public and private schools.* Report to the National Center of Education Statistics by the National Opinion Research Center. Chicago: University of Chicago Press.

Coleman, J. S., Hoffer, T., & Kilgore, S. (1982). *High school achievement: Public, Catholic, and private schools compared.* New York: Basic Books.

Noell, J. (1982). Public and Catholic schools: A reanalysis of "public and private schools." *Sociology of Education, 55* (April/July).

12

A Review Essay—
Comparisons of Public and Private Schools
Lessons from the Uproar*

Richard J. Murnane

On April 7, 1981, at a conference attended by 500 educators and the press, James Coleman announced the findings of research that he had conducted, with Thomas Hoffer and Sally Kilgore, on public and private high schools in the United States. Their principal finding was that Catholic schools and non-Catholic private schools are more effective than public schools in helping students to acquire cognitive skills.

Coming at a time of widespread criticism of public education and Presidential support for tuition tax credits for families who use private schools, this finding was widely reported in the press and evoked a range of spirited reactions. Critics and supporters responded to Coleman, Hoffer, and Kilgore's (henceforth CHK's) work with articles and editorials with lively titles such as "Coleman Goes Private (in Public)," "Lessons for the Public Schools," "Coleman's Bad Report," and "Private Schools Win a Public Vote."[1]

Over the succeeding months CHK's work remained visible as critiques of their research and reanalyses of the data they used appeared in a variety of journals, in some cases accompanied by lengthy responses by CHK. Another wave of interest was sparked by the publication and subsequent reviews of CHK's *High School Achievement: Public, Catholic, and Private Schools Compared* [6], in which they presented their final research findings. As a result of the wide range of responses to CHK's work and the numerous symposiums in which CHK have debated their

---

Editors' Note. The editors invited the author to write this review essay on the Coleman, Hoffer, and Kilgore book, *High School Achievement: Public, Catholic, and Private Schools Compared* (New York: Basic Books, 1982).

* Helpful comments on earlier drafts were provided by Anthony Bryk, David Cohen, Paul Dimaggio, Dan Levy, Richard Nelson, Barbara Newfeld, and Randall Olsen. I would particularly like to acknowledge the help of Edward Pauly, who read several drafts of this paper and provided many important ideas.

1 In order of appearance, the titles are from Goldberger [11], Keisling [15], Comer [8], and *Newsweek* [23].

critics in print, there is now ample material available to any reader interested in forming a judgment about the quality of the research that produced their main conclusion.[2] For this reason, this essay does not provide yet another critique of their methodology.

Indeed, the purpose of this essay is to attempt to clarify the meaning of CHK's central finding by tracing its roots in the conceptual and empirical issues that have been debated since the report's release. In doing so, I examine three kinds of significant, but neglected, lessons to be drawn from CHK's work and the critiques and reanalyses it provoked. The first set of lessons concerns unrecognized differences in perspectives that underlie debates about how the research on public and private schools should be conducted and how the results should be interpreted. The second set concerns neglected substantive findings, including findings about which all analysts agree, but the significance of which has been neglected, and anomalies and puzzles that have been relegated to asides or footnotes, but should not be. The third set of lessons concerns the strengths and weaknesses of the particular philosophy that has guided CHK's interpretation of their research findings.

Before turning to these lessons, I want to describe briefly the data base used to generate the recent public school–private school comparisons and to clarify the meaning of certain terms. The data base used by CHK and their critics is the first wave of data generated by the High School and Beyond (HSB) project, a longitudinal study of 58,728 U.S. high school students. The sample includes students who were either sophomores or seniors in 1980 in one of 893 public schools, 84 Catholic schools, or 38 non-Catholic private schools, of which 11 were selected as representatives of high performance private schools. The HSB data base has a stratified sample design with an oversampling of students in certain types of schools, including public and Catholic schools in which more than 30 percent of the students were minority group members. The data base includes design weights that in principle permit estimation of the characteristics of the U.S. high school student population.

The small number of non-Catholic private schools in the sample, and the wide variation across these schools in school characteristics, student characteristics, and student performance, has led most analysts to conclude that there is insufficient data to derive reliable conclusions about the population of such schools. As a result, attention has focused primarily on public school–Catholic school comparisons, especially on whether Catholic schools are more effective than public schools in imparting cognitive skills to students. I will refer to this as the question of whether there is a Catholic school advantage.

---

2 See, for example, the symposiums in *Harvard Educational Review,* November 1981, and *Sociology of Education,* April/July 1982.

I. UNSTATED DIFFERENCES IN PERSPECTIVES UNDERLIE METHODOLOGICAL DEBATES

Families' School Choices and School Effectiveness

Can CHK's research findings be used to predict the consequences of policies that would induce students to move from public to Catholic schools? This question has been ardently debated by CHK and their critics, with the discussion focused primarily on whether CHK's finding of a Catholic school advantage is contaminated by selectivity bias. The selectivity bias issue clearly merits attention because it influences the interpretation of CHK's central finding. However, preoccupation with this issue has diverted attention from another important issue, namely, whether the effectiveness of school programs is sensitive to the factors that influence families' schooling choices. This issue also influences in a critical way the interpretation of CHK's central finding.

Let me begin my explanation by summarizing briefly CHK's methodology. CHK used multiple regression analysis to estimate the impact of 17 student background variables on the achievement of students in public schools. In a separate regression, they estimated the impact of these same variables on the achievement of students in Catholic schools. They then used the regression results to predict the achievement that a hypothetical student with the characteristics of the average public school student would have if he or she attended a public school or a Catholic school. The predictions indicated that the hypothetical student would have higher achievement in a Catholic school; hence, the conclusion of a Catholic school advantage.[3]

Critics immediately pointed out that the 17 student background variables may not fully account for differences in the skill and motivation levels that Catholic school students and public school students bring to school. Consequently, CHK's finding may be contaminated by selectivity bias. In response to these criticisms, CHK and other analysts employed a variety of alternative techniques to investigate the selectivity bias question.[4] An explicit assumption common to all of these techniques is that the factors that influence family schooling choices, such as family incomes, schools' tuition, and schools' admission and dismissal policies, make it difficult to compare school programs because they result in non-random assignment of students to schools. Techniques for controlling selectivity bias attempt to control statistically for the differences in skills and motivations that students bring to different schools.

---

3   See Goldberger and Cain [12] for a more detailed explanation of CHK's methodology.

4   For example, see Alexander and Pallas [1], CHK [6], Fetters et al. [10], Murnane, Newstead, and Olsen [20], Noell [21], Page and Keith [22], and Willms [24].

There is a second assumption implicit in the strategies for controlling selectivity bias that has not received much attention, namely, that the factors affecting families' school choices do not themselves influence the effectiveness of school programs. In fact, it is the assumption of a conceptual distinction between the determinants of school effectiveness and the factors that influence families' schooling choices that justifies framing the evaluation question in terms of asking what the relative effectiveness of public schools and Catholic schools would be in educating randomly assigned samples of students.

An alternative view of the relationship between families' schooling choices and school effectiveness is that at least some of the factors that influence families' schooling choices also influence the effectiveness of school programs. For example, control over admission and dismissal policies not only may help a school to attract talented students, but also may improve a school's program by making it easier to attract high quality teachers, many of whom do not want to work with disruptive students (Antos and Rosen [2]). Similarly, charging tuition not only may result in a school's attracting primarily students from high income families, but also may strengthen a school's program by stimulating parental supervision of students' homework.

Viewed from this perspective, comparing the effectiveness of public and Catholic schools in educating randomly assigned students is not the appropriate conceptual experiment for learning about the consequences of policies that would induce students to move from public schools to Catholic schools. Instead, we must learn the extent to which each of the many factors that influence families' school choices also influence schools' effectiveness. This is necessary because policies designed to change families' school choices may themselves alter the relative effectiveness of different schools.

At several points in their book, CHK endorse the view that many of the factors that influence families' school choices also influence the effectiveness of school programs. For example, they discuss the impact that control over admissions and dismissals may have on the quality of school programs (p. 100). A weakness of CHK's book, however, is that they do not explain clearly the implications of this view for the interpretation of their results. I will try to provide this explanation.

CHK's research compares Catholic schools as a group with public schools as a group. They find that the package typically associated with Catholic schools (tuition charged, significant control over admission and dismissal of students) is associated with higher student achievement than is the package typically associated with public schools (no tuition, no control over admissions, limited control over dismissals). If one believes that CHK's methods eliminate selectivity bias, then one might predict from their findings that a public school that adopted the entire Catholic school package would be able to increase its effectiveness.

This is not the type of policy change that is currently being debated, however. Instead, the changes under discussion concern the introduction of policies such as tuition tax credits or education vouchers that would induce more students to attend private schools. To predict the consequences of these policies, we would need to know, first, exactly how they would impact on the incentives that influence family schooling choices and on the control that individual schools have over student admissions and dismissals. Then we would need to know how each of these changes in the determinants of families' school choices influences the effectiveness of school programs. CHK do not address either of these questions. In particular, they do not explore whether the variation among schools in the private sector in tuitions and in control over student admissions and dismissals explains the variation in the effectiveness of individual school programs. Since these are the types of variables that would be affected by policies designed to induce students to move to private schools, we need to know how these variables influence school effectiveness in order to evaluate how such policies would influence the distribution of student achievement.

School Policies

To what extent are school policies responsible for differences in the achievement of students attending public schools and Catholic schools? CHK claim that school policies, defined as "homework, curriculum, and disciplinary practices" (p. 205), do play a significant role in contributing to a Catholic school advantage. Moreover, they conclude,

> ... where such things as curriculum and disciplinary practices have effects on student behavior and achievement that are independent of school type and student background, we can institute changes in any school that would affect achievement. It is for this reason that the results in this chapter are as relevant to public schools as they are to private schools. (p. 207)

These findings and CHK's interpretation of them have been highlighted in articles with names like "How to Save Our Public Schools" (Keisling [14]), and have troubled many public school educators and left them wondering what the research really means.

How should we interpret CHK's statement that a school's homework and discipline practices have an effect on student achievement, independent of student body composition? Does this mean that the faculties of public schools could raise student achievement if they simply altered practices, and that these practices are unambiguously subject to their control? If this is the correct interpretation, then one must ask why these steps have not already been taken. Is the reason laziness? Lack of interest? A lack of awareness that these things matter? In effect, this interpretation implies an extraordinary indictment of teachers and administrators in public schools characterized by low student achievement. Do CHK intend such an indictment? At no point in their book do they directly criticize public school educators. But what other interpretation can there be?

I believe that the answer lies in alternative definitions of the term "school policy." To my mind a school policy should be defined as a set of instructions that tells the personnel responsible for carrying out the policy exactly what they should do. It is crucial that the mandated actions are actually subject to the control of those responsible for the policy's execution. An example of a school policy that would satisfy this definition is a rule that teachers must assign one hour of homework every night and that any student who does not complete the homework must be kept after school for a period of one hour. If CHK had found that clearly defined school policies such as this were systematically related to student achievement, then it would be appropriate, indeed important, to ask school personnel why such policies were not in effect in all schools.

CHK's results are not of this sort, however. They analyzed no variables that are school policies in the sense of the definition described above. Instead, CHK's analyses were directed at a somewhat different, more diffuse, objective. They wanted to investigate whether the difference between the average achievement of students attending public schools and Catholic schools was due in part to differences in what happened in these schools. In other words, they wanted to challenge the allegation that the Catholic school advantage was due solely to selectivity bias. To investigate this issue, they adopted the term "school functioning" to characterize what went on in schools. The evidence they collected on school functioning consisted of students' reports on such things as how much homework they completed and their perceptions of the quality of the disciplinary environment. CHK standardized these variables to account for observed differences in students' backgrounds.[5] They found that the standardized student reports, aggregated to the school level, explained part of the difference between the average achievement of students attending public schools and Catholic schools (pp. 166–75). These variables also explained part of the variation in the average achievement of students attending different public schools.[6] CHK rely heavily on this second set

5   CHK's methodology, which is based on regression analysis, is analogous to the methodology they used in calculating the relative effectiveness of public schools and Catholic schools in raising student achievement. See Macias [17] for other potential problems with the student reports.

6   These averages were computed from a sample that contained all sophomores in the HSB data base for whom test scores and basic demographic information were available.

of findings to support their conclusion that "we can institute changes in any school that would affect achievement" (p. 207).

But what are these changes? CHK do not tell us. Throughout much of the book CHK seem implicitly aware that they have presented no evidence about what clearly defined actions would improve schools. I presume that this explains their tendency to use the term "school functioning" rather than the term "school policies" to describe their homework and discipline variables. However, they do not consistently retain this distinction. For example, in describing their empirical work relating the homework and discipline variables to student achievement, CHK state, "This will allow us to identify school policies which increase achievement within each sector" (p. 159).

I believe that CHK's ambiguity about the meaning of the term "school policy" underlies the frustration that many public school educators feel toward their work. The experiences of many educators lead them to believe that there are no well-defined school policies that consistently produce high levels of homework and an orderly disciplinary environment. Had CHK made clear that these dimensions of school functioning are not policies, but rather intermediate outcomes that are consistently related to student achievement, then I believe that the reactions of educators to this work would have been more positive. Many educators would have embraced such findings as much-needed documentation of the importance to school effectiveness of struggling and searching for ways to improve school discipline and to increase the amount of homework students complete.

II. NEGLECTED FINDINGS

The publicity surrounding a few of CHK's findings has resulted in neglect of several patterns in the HSB data about which all analysts agree, but the significance of which has not been appreciated. The first of these is that there are important differences in the quality of education offered in different American schools. In light of the debate over the relative quality of public and private schools, this seems obvious and not worth emphasizing. However, recall the press reports following the publication of *Equality of Educational Opportunity* [4] in 1966 that might be summarized as: schools don't matter, families do.[7] The evidence from the HSB data is that differences among schools do matter.

The second finding concerns diversity among public schools and among private schools. While there is considerable disagreement about

---

7   It is important to distinguish between the findings that were published in *Equality of Educational Opportunity* [4] and the press reports describing and interpreting these findings. See Murnane [18] for a discussion of this distinction.

whether Catholic schools and other private schools are more effective on average than public schools, there is agreement that even the largest estimates of a private school advantage are small relative to the variation in quality among different public schools, among different Catholic schools, and among different non-Catholic private schools. Consequently, in predicting the quality of a student's education, it is less important to know whether the student attended a public school or a private school than it is to know which school within a particular sector the student attended.

A third set of findings about which analysts agree is that variables describing the composition of the student body in a school are systematically related to the achievement of individual students in the school (cf. CHK [6], Crain and Ferrer [9], Kilgore [16], Murnane [19]). To date, student body composition has been characterized in terms of the average values of demographic characteristics of the students in a school. However, no analyst has asserted that the averages themselves are the critical variables. One plausible interpretation for why variables describing student body composition matter is that they serve as proxies for the number of students in a school who do not want to be in school, who come to school without motivation to succeed in school, and who come without the parental support that typically accompanies academic success. I believe that an important interpretation of CHK's book is that it provides documentation of the paths through which such troubled and indifferent students influence the quality of education provided to their fellow students. As CHK explain, these students reduce the achievement of their peers through their impact on teacher morale, through their effects on the implementation of school policies, and through their effects on the behavior of other students.

Viewed in this light, CHK's research demonstrates the significant tension that exists in our society between honoring the commitment to educate all citizens and developing high quality educational programs. Finding ways to resolve this tension is perhaps the greatest challenge that public educators face.

CHK interpret some of the patterns in the HSB baseline data—public school students feel that discipline is less fair and teachers are less interested than Catholic school students feel—as indicating that the trends in public education over the past 15 years toward more state and federal regulation of schools and greater legal protection of student rights have not been an effective strategy for meeting this challenge (p. 100). CHK also speculate that alternative strategies would be more effective—in particular, strategies that "involve more choice by parents and students and more leverage for the school to make demands and exercise authority" (p. 193).

CHK's suggestions can be viewed only as untested hypotheses since their research does not examine the effect on student achievement of either state and federal regulations or student choice plans. However, these are interesting hypotheses, and it is important to ask how research might throw light on the consequences of policies that would increase student choice and/or increase the authority of schools to select and dismiss students.

In particular, it is important to learn whether such policies would bring about beneficial changes in the in-school behaviors of troubled and indifferent students or whether the policies would only make it easier for individual schools to avoid working with such students (thereby relegating them to another school whose effectiveness would suffer as a result). This distinction is not critical in predicting how the effectiveness of an *individual* school would be influenced by a policy change. However, the distinction is critical in evaluating whether a particular policy change would be a useful strategy for reforming a school *system* committed to educating all students. I believe there are three areas of research that might increase our knowledge of these issues.

The first explores the role of admission and dismissal policies in public high schools in explaining the variation in student achievement among schools. More than one-fourth of the public school districts in the U.S. provide students with some form of choice of school, including many programs that are as rich and distinctive as those of much admired private schools (Bridge and Blackman [3], p. v). Yet we know very little about the factors that influence the choices families make among alternative public schools. There also appears to be significant variation across schools concerning what happens to students who do not meet academic or disciplinary standards. Learning more about the variation in admission and dismissal policies of the schools in the HSB study and whether these policies serve only to allocate students among schools or whether they influence student behaviors may be a fruitful approach for learning about the extent to which organizational reforms can lead to improvements in the efficacy of public schools.

A second potentially fruitful area of research is to learn more about the practices of Catholic schools, which appear (on the basis of the cross-sectional data available from the HSB study) to be effective in helping many minority group students and students from low income families to acquire cognitive skills. In many respects—student-teacher ratios, income distribution of students' families—Catholic schools are more similar to public schools than to other private schools.

Of course, Catholic schools do have more control over the composition of their student bodies than public schools typically do. In the past this may have dissuaded researchers interested in improving public schools from examining Catholic schools. However, as public school districts explore the merits of a variety of plans—magnet schools, open enrollments, minischools within schools—that involve matching students with programs, the Catholic schools' experiences may be relevant. For example, it would be valuable to explore whether admissions interviews with students and parents, a common practice in Catholic schools, not only serve to select students, but also to inform families about how a particular school works, and as a first step in helping students to adopt behavior patterns that lead to high achievement for them and their peers.

Another area in which there may be important things to be learned from Catholic schools concerns the recruitment of teachers. How are Catholic schools able to attract teachers at modest salaries who demonstrate great interest in and commitment to students, as reflected in student responses to the HSB questionnaires? Is part of the answer a willingness among Catholic schools to hire new college graduates who are interested in teaching for a few years, but do not plan to make teaching a long-term career? Does control over student admissions make teaching in Catholic schools more satisfying than teaching in many public schools? Is it important that hiring of teachers is done by the individual Catholic school, while most public-sector hiring is done at the school district level, often without input from individual school administrators and without the applicants' knowledge of where he or she will be assigned? Learning the answers to these questions might provide ideas for making public schools more effective.

Finally, a third research approach for learning more about how schooling works in America is to explore the many puzzles and anomalies that analyses of the HSB data have produced. These puzzles are present both in CHK's book and in a book by Andrew Greeley [13] that uses the HSB data to examine the experiences of minority group students in Catholic schools and public schools. The logic underlying this approach is that, if we are going to take seriously the implications of CHK's most highly publicized findings, we should also examine the meaning of other statistically significant patterns in the data, puzzling as the patterns may appear. Two of these puzzles deal with the achievement of students in non-Catholic private schools and may possibly be artifacts of the small number of such schools in the HSB data base. However, I include them in the list because they suggest how different non-Catholic private schools are from Catholic schools.

The puzzles and anomalies include:

1. Although attendance is positively related to performance for students attending most schools in the HSB data base, students in high performance public schools have poorer attendance records than students attending any other type of school identified in the HSB data base (CHK [6], p. 108).

2. Although student reports of the quality of the disciplinary environment are positively related to student achievement in most schools, reports of the quality of the disciplinary environment in Catholic schools

are negatively related to the achievement of sophomores (CHK [6], pp. 171–72).

3. Although the education provided by different Catholic schools appears to be relatively homogeneous in quality (compared to public schools or non-Catholic private schools), students attending Catholic schools run by religious orders have higher achievement, controlling for student backgrounds, than do students attending Catholic schools run by dioceses and parishes (Greeley [13], p. 68).

4. Although Catholic schools appear to be more effective than public schools in educating many types of students (according to CHK and Greeley), students in Catholic schools who plan to graduate from college and whose fathers attended college have lower achievement than students with these same backgrounds and aspirations who attend public schools (Greeley [13], pp. 83–84).

5. The achievement of students in non-Catholic private schools is more dependent on family background than is the achievement of students in public schools. This is in contrast to CHK's finding that the achievement of students in Catholic schools is less dependent on family background than is the achievement of students in public schools (CHK [6], p. 195).

6. Although CHK emphasize the importance of the disciplinary environment and the amount of student homework completed in explaining the achievement of students attending different public schools, these variables explain an even larger part of the variation in achievement among students attending different non-Catholic private schools (CHK [6], p. 172).

7. Although black students in private schools in most parts of the country are less segregated into schools serving primarily black students than is the case for black students in public schools, minority students in private schools in the western part of the United States are more segregated into schools serving primarily minority students than are minority students in public schools in that part of the country (CHK [6], p. 220).

Understanding the sources of these statistically significant patterns in the HSB data may improve our understanding of the schooling options available to different American families, the choices families make, and the effects that different types of schools have on students from different backgrounds.

III. HOW DOES RESEARCH INFORM THE POLICY PROCESS?

In the last section of the final chapter of their book (pp. 220–27), CHK articulate their view of the role of research in informing public policy:

... Policy is the resultant of pressures from a multitude of interests. ...
The role of research is to inform these interests. ... The proper function
of policy research is to make it possible for each ... interested party to
better see the lines along which to pursue its interests. ... [R]esearch results
do not replace interest groups—they are used by interest groups. ... [R]esults
should be available to all and in full view, and ... the very openness of
the process will lead to disputes over what the research data really show.
(p. 221)

The debate concerning the interpretation of recent research comparing
public and private schools has been carried out very much along the lines
James Coleman and his associates advocate. To a large extent this is
because Coleman has been extraordinarily energetic in participating in
this debate, in publicizing the implications of his research, in responding
to critics at great length and in a variety of publications, and in facilitating
continuation of the debate by providing potential critics with data, computer printouts, and explanations of his statistical methods.

In concluding this essay, it may be useful to examine briefly the
strengths and weaknesses of the research philosophy that has shaped the
manner in which the debate about research on public and private schools
has been conducted.

One significant strength of this research philosophy is that it does
stimulate criticism and further research. In the two years since the April
1981 conference when Coleman first announced his research findings
concerning public and private schools, more than 30 articles have been
published that either criticize CHK's research or provide reanalyses of
the HSB data. Thus, only a short time after the first wave of HSB data
became available for analysis, sufficient research has been published to
support an essay such as this that tries to sort out the important lessons.

A second implication of this philosophy is that it does push researchers to emphasize the policy implications of their work since that
is, after all, what interest groups want to know about. To the extent that
there really are policy implications that stem from research, the fact that
they will receive attention is a strength.

At the same time, the emphasis on policy implications is a significant
weakness of this research philosophy. The reason is that research based
on data from a natural experiment, particularly cross-sectional data, rarely
provides reliable evidence about the effects of a policy change; CHK's
research is not an exception to this general rule. In my view, the weakest
parts of CHK's book are those that emphasize policy implications. One
example is the section emphasizing the importance of homework and
discipline, in which CHK's language implies that these attributes of schools
can be produced by policies, but no documentation of what these policies
are is presented.

Another example is a section that projects the effects on private school enrollment of providing families with an additional $1000 of income (pp. 65–71). The projections are based on income elasticities estimated from demand equations that contain no variables describing the availability or prices of alternative schooling options. If the omitted variables are correlated with family incomes, the estimates of the income elasticities will be inconsistent, and consequently the enrollment projections will be inaccurate.

Not all of CHK's book emphasizes policy implications. There are sections that have a very different emphasis, and a different tone. These sections try to educate the reader about the variation in school programs, student bodies, and student achievement that exists in an educational system requiring universal participation of students, but permitting extensive choice among schooling alternatives, with the range and quality of the options very sensitive to family income.

CHK show that the choices families make, as constrained by their incomes and locations, result in a large variation in the quality of education provided by different schools. There are many high quality schools, both public and private. Although there are exceptions, these schools tend to be attended by students from families with above-average incomes. There are also many schools that are not successful in helping students to acquire cognitive skills. These schools, again with exceptions, tend to be attended by students from families that either have below-average incomes, are of minority group status, or both.

CHK also show that life in high quality schools is characterized by an orderly disciplinary environment, by the presence of concerned teachers, and by high levels of student homework. This is true not only in the typical high quality schools that serve primarily students from affluent families, but also in the exceptional high quality schools attended by students from lower income families.

I find extremely interesting and informative the parts of CHK's book that emphasize the patterns present in U.S. schools today. To my mind, CHK's book would have been a stronger piece of social science research if the authors had explicated these patterns more completely and had made a clearer distinction between the statistical evidence documenting these patterns and their speculations, unsupported by evidence, about what should be done to improve American education.

I believe that such a redirection of emphasis is consistent with CHK's goal of informing the policy process. For example, their findings are rich in evidence supporting the notion that the consequences of any policy designed to increase the number of students attending private schools will be very sensitive to the details of the policy. Moreover, their findings suggest that there are tradeoffs in policy design between enhancing the options of families currently without good schooling options and protecting the freedom of action of private schools that is critical to their effectiveness. Making participants in the policy process aware of these tradeoffs may be important in producing good public policy.

CHK's findings also provide important lessons for school principals and teachers about improving school quality. The lessons include encouragement that schools can be improved and the significant suggestion that educators focus their attention on what they can do to improve discipline and to get students to do more homework.

Clearly, these lessons are modest, particularly when contrasted with predictions about the consequences of particular well-defined policies. However, the modest lessons are important. Moreover, I believe that they are the only kind of lessons stemming from analysis of cross-sectional data that have the potential for weathering well the test of time.

REFERENCES

1. Karl Alexander and Aaron M. Pallas. "Private Schools and Public Policy: New Evidence on Cognitive Achievement in Public and Private Schools." *Sociology of Education* (forthcoming).
2. Joseph R. Antos and Sherwin Rosen. "Discrimination in the Market for Public School Teachers." *Journal of Econometrics* 3 (May 1975): 123–50.
3. R. Gary Bridge and Julie Blackman. *A Study of Alternatives in American Education, Vol. IV: Family Choice in Schooling.* Santa Monica, Calif.: Rand Corporation, 1978.
4. James S. Coleman, Ernest C. Campbell, Carol J. Hobson, James McPartland, Alexander M. Mood, Frederic Weinfeld, and Robert L. York. *Equality of Educational Opportunity.* Washington: U.S. Government Printing Office, 1966.
5. James S. Coleman, Thomas Hoffer, and Sally Kilgore. "Cognitive Outcomes in Public and Private Schools." *Sociology of Education* 55 (April/July 1982): 65–76.
6. ———. *High School Achievement: Public, Catholic, and Private Schools.* New York: Basic Books, 1982.
7. ———. "Questions and Answers: Our Response." *Harvard Educational Review* 51 (November 1981): 526–45.
8. James P. Comer. "Coleman's Bad Report." *The New York Times,* April 19, 1981, p. E11.
9. Robert L. Crain and Robert L. Ferrer. "Achievement Prediction With School Level Equations: A Non-Technical Example Using the Public and Private Schools Data." Report No. 323, Center for Social Organization of Schools, Johns Hopkins University, March 1982.
10. William Fetters, F. Owings, S. Peng, and R. Takai. "Review of NORC Report, Public and Private Schools." National Center for Education Statistics, Memorandum, June 26, 1981.
11. Arthur S. Goldberger. "Coleman Goes Private (in Public)." Unpublished

paper cited by Albert Shanker, "Another Attack on the Coleman Report." *The New York Times*, July 26, 1981, p. E7.

12. Arthur S. Goldberger and Glen G. Cain. "The Causal Analysis of Cognitive Outcomes in the Coleman, Hoffer and Kilgore Report." *Sociology of Education* 55 (April/July 1982): 103–22.
13. Andrew M. Greeley. *Catholic High Schools and Minority Students.* New Brunswick, N.J.: Transaction Books, 1982.
14. Phil Keisling. "How to Save Our Public Schools." *Readers Digest* (February 1983): 181–88.
15. ————. "Lessons for the Public Schools." *New Republic* 187 (November 1, 1982): 27–32.
16. Sally Kilgore. "School Policy and Cognitive Growth in Public and Catholic Secondary Schools." Ph.D. dissertation, University of Chicago, 1982.
17. Cathaleen J. Macias. "Reactions to Coleman." *Private School Monitor* 4 (Quarters 1 and 2 1982): 1–11.
18. Richard J. Murnane. "Evidence, Analysis, and Unanswered Questions." *Harvard Educational Review* 51 (November 1981): 483–89.
19. ————. "How Clients' Characteristics Affect Organization Performance: Lessons from Education." *Journal of Policy Analysis and Management* 12 (Spring 1983): 403–17.
20. Richard J. Murnane. Stuart Newstead, and Randall J. Olsen. "Comparing Public and Private Schools: The Puzzling Role of Selectivity Bias." Programs on Non-Profit Organizations Working Paper 68, Institution for Social and Policy Studies, Yale University, June 1983.
21. Jay Noell. "Public and Catholic Schools: A Reanalysis of 'Public and Private Schools.'" *Sociology of Education* 55 (April/July 1982): 123–32.
22. Ellis B. Page and Timothy Z. Keith. "Effects of U.S. Private Schools: A Technical Analysis of Two Recent Claims." *Educational Researcher* 10 (August/September 1981): 7–17.
23. "Private Schools Win a Public Vote." *Newsweek*, April 13, 1981, p. 107.
24. J. Douglas Willms. "Do Private Schools Product Higher Levels of Academic Achievement? New Evidence for the Tuition Tax Credit Debate." In *Public Dollars for Private Schools: The Case for Tuition Tax Credits,* eds. T. James and H. Levin. Philadelphia: Temple University Press, 1983.

13

Comparing Public and Private Schools
The Puzzling Role of Selectivity Bias

Richard J. Murnane, Stuart Newstead, and Randall J. Olsen

Recent articles using the same data and variants of the same estimation technique report conflicting estimates of the relative quality of education provided by public and Catholic schools. This article explains the reasons for the conflict. In so doing, the article clarifies the assumptions underlying the increasingly popular two-step methods for controlling selectivity bias and highlights the hazards of using these methods when the assumptions are not satisfied. The article also illustrates an alternative method for detecting the presence of selectivity bias.

KEY WORDS: Selectivity bias; Public and private schools; High School and Beyond data base; Distribution of residuals.

1. INTRODUCTION

Research on the controversial question of whether private schools in the United States are more effective than public schools in enhancing student achievement has been hindered by a variety of conceptual problems and data limitations. At the center of the research difficulties is the problem of distinguishing student achievement differences due to the effectiveness of school programs from those due to the abilities of students. This problem is particularly difficult because the school choices made by American families, who are faced with varied schooling alternatives and financial constraints, result in significant selection of students with particular backgrounds and abilities to particular schools. Unless the influence of student ability on student achievement is controlled, the estimates of school program effects will be contaminated by what is known in the econometric literature as selectivity bias.

In recent years new techniques have been developed to deal with selectivity bias. These techniques could, in principle, help one develop reliable estimates of the relative effectiveness of public and private schools. Among the contributors to this new methodology are Goldberger (1972, 1980), Gronau (1973, 1974), Maddala and Lee (1976), Olsen (1980, 1982), and most important, Heckman (1974, 1976, 1978, 1979). These

techniques have quickly come into widespread use in evaluating education and manpower training programs (Farkas et al. 1980; Mallar et al. 1980) and in estimating demand equations (McGuire 1981; Willis and Rosen 1979) and production functions (Orazem 1983). For 1981 alone, the *Social Science Citation Index* lists 79 references to the Heckman articles.

Until 1981 lack of data prevented application of the new techniques to the issue of the relative effectiveness of public and private schools. In that year, however, a data set became available that provided information on the background and skill levels of large numbers of students attending public and private (predominantly Catholic) high schools. As of this writing, two sets of papers (Coleman, Hoffer, and Kilgore 1981b, 1982; Noell 1981, 1982) have applied the new techniques to the new data. The results have not clarified the relative school quality issue, however. In fact, the studies reported conflicting estimates of the relative effectiveness of public and Catholic high schools. Since both sets of papers were based on the same data and both used variants of the new techniques for controlling selectivity bias, the conflict between the results poses a significant puzzle.

The research described in this article was undertaken to solve the puzzle of the conflicting results. As the research progressed, a second theme developed—

rom Richard J. Murnane et al., "Comparing Public and Private Schools: The Puzzling Role of electivity Bias," *Journal of Business & Economic Statistics,* 1985, 3(1), 23-35. Copyright 1985 by merican Statistical Association. Reprinted by permission.

namely, that the results from the new techniques can be extremely sensitive to a number of assumptions, and consequently it is important to adopt an analysis strategy that permits investigation of these assumptions.

To the reader interested only in the substantive puzzle or only in selectivity bias methodology, the organization of this article may be initially frustrating because the two themes are interwoven. We believe, however, that this structure is necessary for two reasons. First, understanding the solution to the substantive puzzle requires a thorough understanding of the new methodology for controlling selectivity bias and the different ways in which this methodology can be applied. Second, the many assumptions involved in applying the selectivity bias methodology and the methods that can be used to investigate the validity of the assumptions can best be explained in the context of a substantive problem.

2. THE PUZZLE

In April 1981, Coleman, Hoffer, and Kilgore (henceforth CHK) completed a highly publicized study of the relative effectiveness of public and private high schools in the United States. Their report, "Public and Private Schools," used the baseline data from "High School and Beyond" (HSB), a federally funded longitudinal study of students who were in their sophomore or senior year in a United States high school in 1980. Of the 58,728 students in the sample, 87% attended public schools, 9% attended Catholic schools, and 3% attended other non-Catholic private schools. Since the non-Catholic private schools in the sample formed a very small yet exceedingly diverse group, attention has focused on differences between public schools and Catholic schools, and this article will address only the reported public school–Catholic school comparisons.

The most controversial aspect of CHK's report was the conclusion that Catholic schools are more effective than public schools in enhancing the cognitive skills of students (as measured by scores on tests of reading and mathematics). Critics attacked many aspects of the report, but perhaps the most common criticism concerned the methodology used to generate the public school–Catholic school achievement comparisons. CHK attempted to control for differences between the attributes of public and Catholic school students by including 17 background variables in equations predicting student achievement. These equations were estimated by using ordinary least squares. (See Goldberger and Cain 1982 for a detailed description of CHK's original methodology.)

The basic criticism of this methodology was that even the inclusion of a large number of family background variables in an equation predicting student achievement did not necessarily eliminate selectivity bias (Barnow et al. 1980). This criticism raised the issues of whether other techniques, such as those developed by Heckman were appropriate for examining differences in the effectiveness of public and Catholic schools and whether the use of such techniques would produce different results.

Later in 1981 and again in 1982, papers by Noell based on the HSB data, reported that the results were different when public–Catholic school differences were estimated in a framework that explicitly modeled the selection process. Noell's results, based on estimation of a Heckman-type model, indicated that contrary to CHK's original results, there were almost no statistically significant differences between the effectiveness of public and Catholic schools in developing the cognitive skills of their students.

CHK responded to the criticisms of their ordinary least squares methodology by also bringing the Heckman technique to bear on the HSB data. They reported, however, that this produced a *larger* estimated advantage of Catholic schools over public schools than ordinary least squares (CHK 1981b, pp. 529–530; 1982, pp. 213–214).

Individually, neither the CHK nor the Noell results are illogical, since the direction of bias in the estimated program effect produced by ordinary least squares is not known a priori (Barnow et al. 1980). The conflict, however, between the results of studies that apply the same general estimation strategy to the same data base is puzzling.

3. SUMMARY OF THE TWO-STEP TECHNIQUES FOR CONTROLLING SELECTIVITY BIAS

3.1 General Framework

This section (based on Barnow et al. 1980) provides a brief formal description of the selectivity bias problem in the context of public school–Catholic school comparisons. Sections 3.2 and 3.3 describe and compare the variants of the new methodology for controlling selectivity bias adopted by Noell and CHK.

For the ith child, ($i = 1, \ldots, n$), let y_i be the test score; z_i, the school type (1 = Catholic, 0 = public); w_i the unobserved ability; X_{1i}, the exogenous vector of l background variables, including 1; X_{2i}, the exogenous vector of m background variables, where X_{1i} is a subset of X_{2i}; and t_i, the unobserved continuous variable determining school type. The model that underlies Heckman's method for controlling for selectivity can be expressed as follows:

$$y_i = w_i + \alpha z_i + \epsilon_{0i} \qquad (3.1)$$

$$w_i = X'_{1i}\beta_1 + \epsilon_{1i} \qquad (3.2)$$

$$t_i = X'_{2i}\beta_2 + u_{2i}$$

$$z_i = 1, \quad \text{if } t_i \geq 0$$

$$= 0, \quad \text{if } t_i < 0. \qquad (3.3)$$

Substituting (3.2) into (3.1) produces (3.4), which is of central interest:

$$y_i = X'_{1i}\beta_1 + \alpha z_i + u_{1i}, \qquad (3.4)$$

where $u_{1i} = \epsilon_{0i} + \epsilon_{1i}$. It is assumed that u_{2i} is normally distributed and $E(u_{1i} \mid u_{2i})$ is a linear function of u_{2i} such that

$$E(u_{1i}) = E(u_{2i}) = 0,$$

$$\text{var}(u_{1i}) = \sigma_1^2, \qquad \text{var}(u_{2i}) = 1,$$

$$\text{cov}(u_{1i}, u_{2i}) = \rho\sigma_1,$$

$$\text{cov}(u_{1i}, u_{1j}) = \text{cov}(u_{2i}, u_{2j}) = \text{cov}(u_{1i}, u_{2j}) = 0,$$

$$\text{if } i \neq j.$$

The standardization of u_{2i} to have unit variance entails no loss of generality.

Now define $\theta_i = -X'_{2i}\beta_2$. Barnow et al. (1980) showed that

$$E(u_{2i} \mid \theta_i, z_i)$$
$$= z_i f(\theta_i)/(1 - F(\theta_i)) - (1 - z_i)f(\theta_i)/F(\theta_i)$$
$$= h_i(\theta_i, z_i), \text{ say.} \qquad (3.5)$$

$f(\cdot)$ and $F(\cdot)$ represent the standard normal density and distribution functions. For notational convenience, let $h_i = h_i(\theta_i, z_i)$. It follows that

$$E(u_{1i} \mid \theta_i, z_i) = \rho\sigma_1 h_i. \qquad (3.6)$$

Equation (3.6) shows that ordinary least squares applied to (3.4) will produce unbiased estimates of the parameters α and β_1 only if $\rho\sigma_1 h_i = 0$. Any of the following three conditions will satisfy this requirement:

1. Equation (3.3) predicts school sector choice without error ($u_{2i} = 0$ for all i).
2. Students are randomly assigned to Catholic and public schools [var(u_{1i}) $\neq 0$, var(u_{2i}) $\neq 0$, cov(w_i, t_i) = 0, and therefore cov(u_{1i}, u_{2i}) = 0].
3. Although ability and school choice are correlated in the population [cov(w_i, t_i) $\neq 0$], there is no correlation between ability and school choice after conditioning on observed X_2 [cov($w_i, t_i \mid X_2$) = cov(u_{1i}, u_{2i}) = 0 for all i].

Typically researchers justify the use of ordinary least squares to estimate Equation (3.4) by asserting that either the second or third condition is fulfilled. (Since w_i is unobserved, these two conditions cannot be distinguished in practice.) If this assertion is not justified, then ordinary least squares will produce an overestimate of the Catholic school advantage if ρ is positive (able students of a given background have a tendency to choose Catholic schools over public schools) or an underestimate if ρ is negative (able students are more likely to choose public schools).

3.2 Estimation Under the Assumption of One Student Population

If we assume that the student bodies of public and Catholic schools are drawn from a single population of students, all of whom attend either public or Catholic high schools and for whom the values of β_1 are independent of school choice, then consistent estimates of the parameters can be derived by the following two-step method.

First, use maximum likelihood probit analysis to estimate β_2 from the equation

$$\Pr[z_i = 1] = F(X'_{2i}\beta_2). \qquad (3.7)$$

Call this estimator $\hat{\beta}_2$, and employ either one of the following second steps: (a) Replace z_i in (3.4) by $\hat{z}_i = F(X'_{2i}\hat{\beta}_2)$, and estimate (3.8) by least squares,

$$y_i = X'_{1i}\beta_1 + \alpha\hat{z}_i + \omega_i. \qquad (3.8)$$

Or (b) calculate $\hat{\theta}_i = -X'_{2i}\hat{\beta}_2$ and

$$\hat{h}_i = z_i f(\hat{\theta}_i)/(1 - F(\hat{\theta}_i)) - (1 - z_i)f(\hat{\theta}_i)/F(\hat{\theta}_i),$$

add the auxiliary regressor $\hat{h}_i$ to (3.4), let $c = \rho\sigma_1$, and estimate (3.9) by least squares,

$$y_i = X'_{1i}\beta_1 + \alpha z_i + c\hat{h}_i + \eta_i. \qquad (3.9)$$

Noell (1982) chose the first of these two estimation strategies. (The two second steps produce the same results only if the assumptions underlying the model are correct. This point is often neglected in discussions of these techniques.)

Although the parameter estimates in (3.8) and (3.9) are consistent, the standard errors yielded by ordinary least squares are not, in general, correct because the errors ω_i and η_i are heteroscedastic unless $\rho = 0$ (Heckman 1976). Appendix A.1 describes a simple method for obtaining correct standard errors on the estimates of α, β_1, and c in (3.9).

3.3 Estimation Under the Assumption of Two Student Populations

The estimation strategy used by CHK is based on the premise that the structure of Equation (3.9), including the values of β_1 and c, is different for the public and Catholic school student populations. (See Muthen and Joreskog 1983 for another discussion of the distinction between one- and two-population models.) Consistent estimates of β_1 and c can be derived for each of the two populations by extending the methodology of the one-population model as follows:

First, as in the case of the one-population model, run maximum likelihood probit on all observations and construct $\hat{h}_i$ for each student. Thus $\hat{h}_i = -f(\hat{\theta}_i)/F(\hat{\theta}_i)$, for the ith public school student, and $\hat{h}_j = f(\hat{\theta}_j)/(1 - F(\hat{\theta}_j))$, for the jth Catholic school student.

Second, use least squares to estimate

$$y_i = X'_{1i}\beta^p_1 + c^p h_i + \eta^p_i, \qquad (3.10)$$

for the public school subsample, and

$$y_j = X'_{1j}\beta^c_1 + c^c h_j + \eta^c_j, \qquad (3.11)$$

for the Catholic school subsample. Correct standard errors can be calculated by a method very similar to that used in the one-population case.

From the estimates of (3.10) and (3.11), an estimate of the Catholic school advantage for a student with a particular k vector of characteristics, x^*, can be calculated as

$$\hat{y}^c - \hat{y}^p = x^{*'}\hat{\beta}^c_1 - x^{*'}\hat{\beta}^p_1,$$

with standard error $[x^{*'}(V^p + V^c)x^*]^{1/2}$, where V^p is the variance–covariance matrix of the estimated β^p coefficients and V^c is the variance–covariance matrix of the estimated β^c coefficients. In estimating the Catholic school advantage, CHK defined x^* to be the average characteristics of students attending public high schools. (Because of software peculiarities, CHK estimated the two-population selectivity bias model with a method slightly different from the method described in the text. The two methods, however, produce results that have the same interpretation and differ only in sign.)

There are two differences between the one- and two-population models that are important to recognize. First, since β^c and β^p are not constrained to be equal, the estimate of the Catholic school advantage may depend critically on x^*; second, since c^p and c^c are not constrained to be equal, a finding of "loss of cream" from the public school sample ($c^p > 0$) need not imply "extra cream" ($c^c > 0$) in the Catholic school sample.

The second difference would be implausible if all students of high school age attended either public or Catholic schools, but some teenagers choose non-Catholic private schools and others choose not to attend school at all. As a result, the nature and extent of student selection in the public and Catholic schools could be different.

As we show in Section 4, the choice of a one-population or two-population model plays a role in explaining the difference between Noell's and CHK's results. The differences between the one- and two-population models are emphasized here because many articles in the evaluation literature that discuss the application of the new techniques for controlling selectivity bias do not clarify the implicit assumptions involved in the choice of the one- or two-population model (e.g., Barnow et al. 1980).

4.   OUR RESEARCH STRATEGY

4.1   General Framework

One problem with the strategies used by CHK and Noell is that estimation of the selection equation (3.7)

by probit analysis is computationally expensive. Since our basic strategy for unraveling the puzzle of the conflicting results was to examine the sensitivity of the results to the many small differences distinguishing the two methodologies, it was important to adopt a low-cost estimation strategy. It is possible to develop computationally inexpensive techniques by assuming that instead of being normally distributed, u_{2i} is distributed uniformly over the interval $[0, 1]$ for each $i = 1, \ldots, n$.

4.2   Estimation Under the Assumption of One Student Population

As shown in Appendix A.2 consistent estimates of the parameters of Equation (3.4) for the one-population model can be derived by the following two-step method.

First, estimate $\hat{z}_i$, the probability that z_i is 1, for each observation, using the linear probability model

$$\hat{z}_i = \Pr[z_i = 1] = X'_{2i}\hat{\beta}_2. \qquad (4.1)$$

Second, add the auxiliary regressor $\hat{s}_i = z_i - \hat{z}_i$ to Equation (3.4) and estimate Equation (4.2) by least squares:

$$y_i = X'_{1i}\beta_1 + \alpha z_i + \delta \hat{s}_i + \nu_i \qquad (4.2)$$

As with (3.8) and (3.9), standard errors on the estimates of β_1, α, and δ will, in general, be incorrect if the ordinary least squares method is applied to (4.2). Appendix A.1 also shows how correct standard errors may be derived.

This technique, which we have called the "s method," yields consistent estimates of the coefficients. Appendix B shows that the estimates of β_1 and α produced by this method are identical to the estimates provided by the two-stage least squares method, in which the first stage consists of estimation of the linear probability model, Equation (4.1). The s method has the advantage, however, of providing a direct test of the null hypothesis of no selectivity bias [cov(u_{1i}, u_{2i}) = 0]. The null hypothesis will be rejected if the estimate of δ is significantly different from zero when compared to its standard error.

4.3   Estimation Under the Assumption of Two Student Populations

The only difference between our method for estimating the Catholic school advantage and the method developed by Heckman and used by CHK is that we estimate the selection equation with generalized least squares instead of probit analysis. Thus we replace $\hat{h}_i$ in (3.10) and (3.11) with $\hat{s}_i$ and estimate (4.3) for the public school subsample and (4.4) for the Catholic school subsample as follows:

$$y_i = X'_{1i}\beta^p_1 + \delta^p \hat{s}_i + \nu^p_i \qquad (4.3)$$

and

$$y_j = X'_{1j}\beta^c_1 + \delta^c \hat{s}_j + \nu^c_j. \qquad (4.4)$$

4.4 Comparison of Least Squares and Probit Methods

We found that the predicted probabilities of Catholic school attendance generated by least squares and probit methods were very close—the correlation coefficient exceeded .99 for most samples. As would be expected under these circumstances, the estimates of the Catholic school advantage generated by these alternative methods were very similar. Thus our methods provide a low-cost strategy for examining the sources of the puzzle posed by the conflict between CHK's and Noell's results.

The s method requires an exclusion restriction to identify the achievement equations—(4.2) in the one-population model and (4.3) and (4.4) in the two-population model. This is not, however, a serious disadvantage of the s method relative to the probit-based methods, since application of the latter often produces unstable results when identification is made solely through functional form (Olsen 1980). CHK reported this instability when they applied the Heckman methodology to the HSB data with no exclusion restriction (CHK 1981b, pp. 529–530). In further probit-based analyses, both CHK and Noell adopted the following identifying restriction: a student's religious status (1 = Catholic, 0 = other) influences choice of school type and is included in the X_2 vector, but does not influence achievement, and therefore is not included in the X_1 vector. We chose the same identifying restriction. [In addition to religious status, CHK (1982, p. 214) assumed that two other variables—educational expectations in the eight grade and family income—affected school choices but did not have a direct effect on achievement. We did not explore the influence of these additional restrictions on the results, in part because we found the exclusion of these variables from the achievement equation unconvincing and in part because our estimates using the single exclusion restriction replicated CHK's reported results.]

We conducted our work with 19,213 observations from the HSB sample, which included all sophomores in public and Catholic schools for whom complete data were available. Summary statistics describing the distributions of the variables used in the empirical work are presented in Table 1.

5. WHY CHK'S AND NOELL'S RESULTS DIFFER

5.1 Two Reasons

There are many differences between the specifications of CHK's and Noell's models, including the choice of background variables in the achievement and selection equations (X_{1i} and X_{2i}) and the choice of scale used to measure the dependent variable. These differences influence the results to some extent. Our sensitivity analysis, however, indicates that the conflict stems primarily from the following two factors, listed in decreasing order of importance:

Table 1. Means and Standard Deviations of Variables Used

Variable	Pooled	White	Black	Hispanic
YBMATHRT	19.27	20.64	14.51	15.55
	(7.28)	(7.17)	(5.55)	(6.14)
YBREADRT	9.43	10.08	7.35	7.58
	(3.83)	(3.78)	(3.19)	(3.40)
School	.11	.09	.13	.17
Black	.11			
Hispanic	.13			
Parents	.72	.76	.45	.72
Female	.54	.53	.57	.55
BBSESRAW	−.04	.09	−.40	−.47
	(.73)	(.69)	(.73)	(.73)
NEast	.21	.23	.19	.15
NCent	.30	.35	.19	.10
South	.31	.26	.54	.39
Cathrel	.39	.37	.12	.75

NOTE: Standard deviations are given in parentheses; standard deviations of 0–1 variables are not given. YBMATHRT is the sum of correct answers on two math tests (38 items); YBREADRT is the number of correct answers on reading test (20 items); and BBSESRAW is the composite SES measure constructed by the HSB sample designers. The other nine variables are 0–1 variables that take the value 1 according to these definitions: School = Catholic; Black = black but not Hispanic; Hispanic = Hispanic descent; Parents = both parents live at home; Female = female; NEast = resident in Northeast; NCent = resident in North Central; South = resident in South; Cathrel = Catholic. Black and Hispanic are defined following CHK (1981a, p. 39, footnote to Table 3.1.1). The variables Black, . . . , South constituted X_1. The variables Black, . . . , Cathrel constituted X_2. As explained in the text, the selection equation was estimated on subsamples of the observations in each ethnic group. The sizes of the subsamples (N) and percentage of students that attended Catholic schools in each subsample (mean of the variable School) are as follows: for Whites, N = 6,563 and School = .08; for Blacks, N = 886 and School = .04; and for Hispanics, N = 633 and School = .10. The group sample sizes used in estimating the achievement equation were: 19,213 for Pooled, 14,464 for Whites, 2,206 for Blacks, and 2,543 for Hispanics.

1. differences in the percentage of minority students in the two samples and
2. different choices about the use of a one- or a two-population model.

5.2 Why the Percentage of Minority Students Matters

Noell's sample contained a smaller percentage of minority group students than CHK's, one reason being that his model included a larger number of student background variables. Since data on student background tend to be missing more often for minority students than for white students, the extra data requirements of Noell's model, coupled with the decision to include in the sample only observations with complete data, left him with a smaller percentage of minority students.

A second reason concerns the weighting of individual observations in the HSB data base, which is a stratified random sample with an oversampling of black and Hispanic students. The data base includes design weights that, in principle, permit the creation of a weighted sample that reflects the U.S. high school student population in 1980. Noell used the design weights to weight the observations in his sample. In effect this reduced the weight given to the oversampled black and Hispanic students. CHK did not use the design weights and hence implicitly weighted every observation equally, including the oversampled black and Hispanic students. (CHK did use the weights in their original analysis, which employed least squares methods without explicit modeling of the school-selection process.) Thus the different weighting choices made by Noell and CHK contributed to the difference in the minority-group representation in their samples. (We do not report the percentages of black and Hispanic students present in CHK's and Noell's samples because CHK did not report this information in their published work. The reason for this omission was apparently that CHK estimated a model that specifically accounted for selectivity bias only in response to criticisms of their ordinary least squares analysis. When the results indicated a Catholic school advantage even larger than that present when ordinary least squares were used, CHK became skeptical of the applicability of this methodology.)

Clearly the percentages of black, Hispanic, and white students in a particular sample influence the results only if the structure of the model is different for these groups—something neither Noell nor CHK reported investigating. We examined this hypothesis by using the s method to estimate Equations (4.1) and (4.2) separately for white, black, and Hispanic students. Both reading scores and mathematics scores were used as dependent variables in the achievement equation (4.2). We weighted each observation equally (i.e., we did not use the design weights) in estimating this equation to preserve the homoscedastic properties of the error terms.

It was not appropriate to estimate the school selection equation (4.1) by using the same samples, however, since Catholic school students are overrepresented in the HSB data base. Since the choice of Catholic or public school is the dependent variable in the selection equation, use of these samples would have resulted in biased estimates of the relationship in the population between the student background variables (X_2) and

school choice. To form appropriate samples for estimation of (4.1), we used the information on the extent of oversampling provided by the design weights to produce simple random samples of the sophomores of each ethnic group in public and Catholic high schools in the United States. The sizes of these random samples and the percentages of students in Catholic schools are stated in Table 1. We estimated the school selection equation (4.1) by using these simple random samples. Then we used the estimated coefficients to construct values of $\hat{s}_i = z - \hat{z}_i$ for all sophomores of each ethnic group for whom complete data were available. These larger samples were then used to estimate the achievement equation (4.2).

F test results, which are reported in the last row of Table 2, indicate that there are significant differences in the structure of the achievement equation (4.2). Most important, the estimates of the Catholic school advantage, also presented in Table 2, differ across ethnic groups. For white students, there are no significant differences between Catholic and public schools in the reading and math scores. For black and Hispanic students, however, there are large, statistically significant Catholic school advantages.

The variation across ethnic groups in the estimated Catholic school advantage contributes to an explanation of the conflict between CHK's and Noell's results. The smaller percentage of minority students in Noell's sample meant that his estimates based on a sample pooled across ethnic groups gave less weight to the large Catholic school advantages for black and Hispanic students than did CHK's estimates.

Table 2 also presents estimates of the Catholic school advantage for each ethnic group derived from estimating (3.4) with ordinary least squares. Comparison of these estimates with those derived from (4.2), which

Table 2. Estimates of the Differences in the Reading and Math Skills of Students Attending Catholic and Public Schools, Using a One-Population Model

	Reading			Math		
	White	Black	Hispanic	White	Black	Hispanic
The Catholic school advantage (α) derived from estimating Equation (4.2) with the s method	−.28 (.35)	3.31* (1.05)	6.32* (1.24)	.69 (.66)	7.26* (1.72)	13.58* (2.39)
The extent of selectivity bias (δ)	.85* (.38)	−2.30* (1.12)	−5.05* (1.27)	.10 (.70)	−6.54* (1.83)	−11.36* (2.44)
R^2 from estimating Equation (4.1) with the s method	.10	.07	.11	.14	.07	.12
The Catholic school advantage (α) obtained by estimating Equation (3.4) with ordinary least squares	.14* (.03)	1.19* (.21)	1.47* (.18)	.78* (.19)	1.25* (.37)	2.67* (.32)
F (17, 19,196) statistic from testing null hypothesis that the structure of Equation (4.2) is the same for all ethnic groups[b]		9.40*			17.55*	

[a] Statistically significant at the .05 level.
[b] Separate intercepts for white students and minority students were included in the pooled regressions.
NOTE: Standard errors are given in parentheses. (The complete regression results are available upon request from the first author.)

explicitly attempts to control selectivity bias, reveals that the latter set of estimates differs much more across ethnic groups than do the former estimates. We will return later to the question of whether either set of estimates accurately reflects the relative efficacy of public and Catholic schools in providing education to students of different ethnic groups.

5.3 Why the Choice of a One- or Two-Population Model Matters

Table 3 presents estimates of the Catholic school advantage for each ethnic group based on the two-population model. The estimates were calculated for two sets of values of x^*: the average characteristics of students attending public schools (line 1) and the average characteristics of students attending Catholic schools (line 2). (The design weights were used in calculating the appropriate means but not in estimating the equations.) The estimates of the Catholic school advantage for black students are included for completeness but are extremely unstable because of the low explanatory power of the predicting equations.

The results in Table 3 show that for blacks and Hispanics, the Catholic school advantage estimated from a two-population model, with x^* assuming the values of the characteristics of the average public school student, is larger than the advantage estimated in a one-population model (see Table 2). The differences are

most striking—especially for Hispanic students—when math scores are used as the dependent variables, as in CHK's analysis. Thus CHK's choice of the two-population model and Noell's choice of the one-population model contributed to the difference in their results.

It is also interesting to note that the estimates of the Catholic school advantage obtained from a two-population model are somewhat sensitive to the choice of x^*. The results would be even more sensitive if the characteristics of the average public school student and the average Catholic school student of each ethnic group were less similar than they in fact are.

6. NEW PUZZLE AND A PROPOSED SOLUTION

6.1 The New Puzzle

The results of estimating both the one- and two-population models for the separate ethnic groups indicate that the direction of selectivity bias is different for white and minority students. In both models, the estimated value of $\text{cov}(u_1, u_2)$ is positive for white students, although in most cases the coefficient is not large enough relative to its standard error to reject the null hypothesis of no selectivity bias. The estimates of $\text{cov}(u_1, u_2)$, however, are consistently negative for black and Hispanic students. This implies that among black and Hispanic sophomores with the same background characteristics, students of relatively low ability are

Table 3. Estimates of the Differences in the Reading and Math Scores of Students in Catholic and Public Schools, Using a Two-Population Model

	Reading			Math		
	White	Black	Hispanic	White	Black	Hispanic
Catholic school advantage, based on predicting achievement in public schools [Eq. (4.3)] and Catholic schools [Eq. (4.4)] for:						
Average public school student	−2.02	3.56*	7.47	.14	7.71*	20.60*
	(1.61)	(1.82)	(5.15)	(2.94)	(3.26)	(8.80)
Average Catholic school student	−2.24	3.43*	7.11	−.79	6.78*	19.24*
	(1.58)	(1.73)	(4.89)	(2.88)	(3.10)	(8.80)
Extent of selectivity bias						
In public school sample (δ^p)	.77**	−2.18	−5.16*	.18	−6.97*	−11.58*
	(.38)	(1.42)	(1.23)	(.72)	(2.31)	(2.37)
In Catholic school sample (δ^c)	3.20	−2.43	−6.20	1.72	−5.81	−18.82
	(1.94)	(2.05)	(5.83)	(3.54)	(3.61)	(9.94)
R^2 from predicting achievement using the s method						
Public school sample [Eq. (4.3)]	.10	.04	.07	.14	.05	.09
Catholic school sample [Eq. (4.4)]	.06	.04	.07	.06	.07	.09
Catholic school advantage, based on a two-population model estimated by ordinary least squares without a selectivity bias correction for:						
Average public school student	.68*	1.38*	2.59*	1.57*	2.45*	3.09*
	(.12)	(.41)	(.23)	(.22)	(.72)	(.39)
Average Catholic school student	.43*	1.20*	1.39*	.63*	1.34*	2.14*
	(.10)	(.23)	(.23)	(.19)	(.40)	(.40)

* Statistically significant at the .05 level.
NOTE: Standard errors are given in parentheses.

more likely to attend Catholic schools than public schools. The negative covariances (which are statistically significant for both black and Hispanic students in the one-population model and for Hispanic students in the two-population model estimated with math scores as the dependent variable) are somewhat counterintuitive. Moreover, it is not apparent why the direction of selectivity bias for minority students should differ from that for white students.

6.2 An Alternative Test of Selectivity Bias

In an attempt to solve this new puzzle, we applied an alternative technique for investigating selectivity bias (Olsen 1982). Imagine that one knew what the population distribution of residuals from a regression of white students' test scores on their background characteristics would be if *all* white students attended Catholic school. Compare this distribution with the distribution of residuals of white students who *do* attend Catholic schools. If there is a correlation between ability and choice of school type, then the Catholic school residuals will not be a random sample from the underlying population, and these two distributions will therefore have different shapes. In particular, if $cov(u_1, u_2) > 0$, then the observed Catholic school residuals will underrepresent the left tail of the population distribution.

Unfortunately this strategy cannot usually be implemented directly because the population distribution of residuals is rarely known; however, an approximation is available. The achievement residuals of white Catholic school students who have a high estimated probability of attending a Catholic school, based on their background characteristics, should roughly represent the population distribution of whites' residuals. On the other hand, the achievement residuals of white Catholic school students who have a low estimated probability of attending a Catholic school, based on their background characteristics (unusually high value of u_{2i}), should be affected by any selectivity bias that is present. If these two distributions are sufficiently different, this

Table 4. $\chi^2(2)$ *Statistics for Testing Null Hypotheses of No Selectivity Bias*

Sector	White	Black	Hispanic
Public	86.956*	3.006	1.074
Catholic	1.776	.198	2.180
No. of students in sample used for χ^2			
Public schools	2,027	1,922	2,102
Catholic schools	1,346	284	441

* The null hypothesis of no selectivity bias is rejected at the .05 significance level
NOTE: To make the size of the sample of white public school students comparable to the sizes of the black and Hispanic public school student samples used in the χ^2 tests, 11,091 white students in public schools who had a medium probability of being in a public school were excluded from the test sample.

will be evidence of selectivity bias. For a more detailed exposition, see Olsen (1982).

We applied this technique to the samples of white, black, and Hispanic students in public and Catholic schools, producing six tests of selectivity bias. Math scores were used as the dependent variable in generating the distributions of residuals, since the differences across ethnic groups in the estimates of selectivity bias using the s method were more pronounced when math scores were used as the dependent variable than when reading scores were used. The results of the likelihood ratio tests are reported in Table 4.

One striking aspect of these results is that no selectivity bias was found among black or Hispanic student samples in either public or Catholic schools. This is in contrast to the results obtained from the s method and suggests that the conclusion of significant selection of the less able minority students to Catholic schools stems from a specification error—namely, the assumption that Catholic religious affiliation does not influence student achievement. In fact, the significant coefficient, δ, on the auxiliary regressor, $\hat{s}$, actually reflects the influence of Catholic religious status on the achievement of minority students.

To see this, compare Equation (6.1) below to Equations (4.1) and (4.2), which were estimated with the s method.

Table 5. The Relationship Between Selectivity Bias and Catholic Religious Status

	Whites	Blacks	Hispanics
Coefficients on Catholic religious status (r) in Equation (6.1) estimated by ordinary least squares	−.02 (.13)	1.26* (.39)	1.62* (.28)
Coefficient on Catholic religious status (ξ) in Equation (4.1) estimated by the linear probability model with generalized least squares[b]	.18* (.01)	.19* (.03)	.14* (.02)
Extent of selectivity bias (δ) in Equation (4.2) estimated by the s method	.10 (.70)	−6.54* (1.83)	−11.36* (2.44)
The Catholic school advantage derived from estimating Equation (6.1) by ordinary least squares	.78[c] (.21)	.72 (.40)	2.22* (.33)

* Statistically significant on a two-tailed .05 t test.
[b] As explained in the text, Equation (4.1) was estimated on a random sample of United States sophomores of a particular race/ethnic group.
[c] The evidence on selectivity bias indicates that the true Catholic school advantage is less than this point estimate.
NOTE: Standard errors are given in parentheses. The sample sizes were 14,464 for Whites, 2,206 for Blacks, and 2,543 for Hispanics. The results reported here used math scores as the dependent variable in Equations (4.2) and (6.1). (The complete regression results are available upon request from the first author.)

$$y_i = X'_{1i}\beta_1 + \alpha z_i + rR_i + e_i \qquad (6.1)$$

Let R denote Catholic religious status and ξ be the coefficient on R in the selection equation (4.1). It is easily shown that $\delta = -r/\xi$. Since ξ is positive for all ethnic groups, δ assumes the opposite sign from r. As shown in Table 5, the estimates of r are negative for whites and positive for blacks and Hispanics. This solves the puzzle posed in Section 6.1 concerning the difference in the direction of selectivity bias for white and minority students. [If the selection equation (4.1) had been estimated on the same sample used in estimating the achievement equations (4.2) and (6.1), then $\delta = -r/\xi$ would hold as an identity for each ethnic group. Since (4.1) was estimated, however, on a subset of the observations for each ethnic group used in estimating (4.2) and (6.1), the equality does not hold exactly.]

Thus one lesson from the Olsen test of selectivity bias is that the two-step methods developed by Heckman and others—which examine whether the *mean* of the least squares achievement residuals shifts with the probability of being in a particular sector—are sensitive to specification error. Use of these methods led to the inference that low ability minority group students were selected into Catholic schools. The distributions of residuals for minority students indicate that this inference is incorrect and that the negative values of δ stemmed from the improper exclusion restriction.

Taken at face value, the exclusion restriction chosen by Noell and CHK appears reasonable. This impression only points out the difficulty of properly specifying models of human behavior and the importance of finding ways to test the validity of any assumption made. [Stryker (1981) presented evidence that for some but not all ethnic groups, religious status is related to achievement, presumably because it serves as a proxy for unobserved attributes or resources.]

A second striking finding from the Olsen test is that the results indicate significant selectivity bias among white students in public schools. The nature of this bias is illustrated by Figure 1, which shows the theoretical densities of the residuals for white students who have a high or low probability of being in a public school. The distribution for high-probability students is skewed to the left, implying either that the distribution of residuals for the underlying population of all white students is nonnormal or that the sample distribution underrepresents low-achieving students who are absent from school on test days. The theoretical density of residuals for low-probability public school students is skewed to the right relative to the high-probability distribution, indicating underrepresentation of high-achieving students. The chi-squared test reveals that the distributions of the two sets of residuals are significantly different, indicating selectivity bias among white students in public schools. This finding—that high-achieving white students are underrepresented in public schools—implies that the population mean that would be observed if all whites attended public schools is underestimated

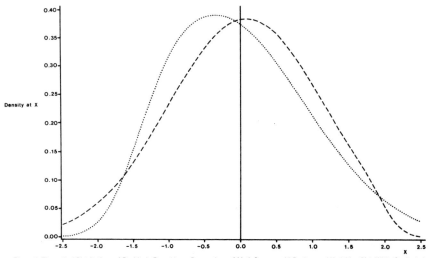

Figure 1. Theoretical Distributions of Residuals From Linear Regressions of Math Score on All Background Variables (X_2): White Students in Public Schools with a High or Low Estimated Probability of Attending a Public School. · · · ·, high estimated probability; – – –, low probability.

by the sample mean of whites who choose to attend public schools. Thus this finding allows us to infer the direction of selectivity bias, but not its size.

The reason that the significant selectivity bias among white students in public schools did not show up when the s method was used is that as was the case with minority students, the achievement equation was unidentified and the effect of selectivity bias was confounded with the impact of religious status on student achievement. Thus we see that an improper exclusion restriction can lead either to the conclusion of selectivity bias when there is in fact none or to the conclusion of no selection when in fact selection is present.

It is interesting to note that the result of the chi-squared test reveals no selectivity bias among white students in Catholic schools. This suggests that the high ability white students, who are underrepresented in public schools, have not chosen Catholic schools but, rather, have chosen to attend non-Catholic private schools. It also emphasizes that the assumption implicit in the use of the one-population model to compare the effectiveness of two programs—that "loss of cream" from one program implies "extra cream" in the other—should be examined carefully.

The presence of significant selectivity bias among white students in public schools means that the use of ordinary least squares will not produce consistent estimates of the relative efficacy of public and Catholic schools in educating white students. Is there an alternative methodology that will produce consistent estimates? The two-step method based on Heckman's and Olsen's work cannot be used unless an alternative exclusion restriction can be justified, and this is doubtful.

Maximum likelihood methods are another alternative; however, these methods require stronger assumptions about the population distributions of the achievement residuals. To illustrate this point, consider the case in which the only regressor in the school choice equation (3.7) is a constant. In this case the two-step methods collapse because the auxiliary regressor, h_i, is perfectly collinear with the constant in the achievement equation (3.9). Maximum likelihood methods, however, will still yield estimates of α and β_1 under these circumstances because identification is possible through the more complete specification of the residuals distribution. The results presented in this section indicate, however, that the most common distributional assumption—that u_{1i} and u_{2i} are distributed bivariate normal—is not justified.

7.   LESSONS

Perhaps the most significant lesson concerning comparisons of school quality is how difficult it is to make reliable estimates, in part because of the difficulty in controlling for student ability and in part because the quality of schools, both public and private, available to

students with different characteristics is itself so varied. With these caveats in mind, the results suggest that the best available estimates of the relative quality of the public and Catholic schools available to Hispanic and black students come from ordinary least squares estimation of an achievement equation that includes family religious status as an explanatory variable. Such estimates are presented in Table 5. These results indicate a modest (one-third of a standard deviation), statistically significant Catholic school advantage for Hispanic students but no statistically significant Catholic school advantage for black students. This pattern raises the interesting question of whether Hispanic and black students fare differently in the same public and Catholic schools or whether the schools available to these groups differ systematically.

Although the presence of selectivity bias among white students in public schools creates bias in the ordinary least squares estimate of the Catholic school advantage for white students, we do know from the inferred direction of selectivity bias for public school whites that the ordinary least squares estimate presented in Table 5 provides an upper bound on the true advantage in imparting math skills.

Among the lessons of this article relevant to the increasingly large number of users of the two-step methods for dealing with selectivity bias are the following:

1. Selection can work differently for different subgroups in the population (e.g., different ethnic groups). When this is the case, results can be extremely sensitive to the weights given to different groups in the sample used in empirical work.

2. In comparing the effectiveness of two alternative programs (e.g., public and Catholic school education), using a one-population model, one makes the implicit assumption that nonrandom selection of participants to one program (e.g., cream skimming) implies the complementary type of selection of participants to the other program (loss of cream). In fact, this may not be a valid assumption when there are alternatives to the two programs.

3. An improper exclusion restriction can lead to extremely misleading inferences about selectivity bias. Consequently it is important to evaluate carefully whether one really knows enough about the determinants of program choice to model the process *and* to identify a variable that affects program choice but not program outcome.

4. A method based on the distribution of residuals provides a useful test of the validity of exclusion restrictions.

ACKNOWLEDGMENTS

The research for this paper was supported by Grant NIE-G-79-0084 from the National Institute of Education and by grants from the Institution for Social and

Policy Studies and the Program on Nonprofit Organizations, Yale University. We thank John Bishop, Richard Nelson, Sharon Oster, Edward Pauly, Jon Peck, and Paul Schultz for helpful comments on earlier drafts.

APPENDIX A: STANDARD ERRORS FOR THE PARAMETERS OF THE SELECTIVITY BIAS MODELS

In this appendix it will be convenient in places to use vectors and matrices, rather than the subscripted scalars of Sections 3 and 4. To this end let $y = (y_1, \ldots, y_n)'$, and let the other variables be described by appropriate n vectors, except $X_1 = (X_{11}, \ldots, X_{1n})$, an $(n \times k)$ matrix, and $X_2 = (X_{21}, \ldots, X_{2n})'$, an $(n \times m)$ matrix.

A.1 Selectivity Bias and the Probit Model

u_{2i} is assumed to be standard normal and $E(u_{1i}/u_{2i}) = \rho \sigma_1 u_{2i}$. The arguments of this section parallel those of Heckman (1979) and Greene (1981).

$$\text{var}(u_{1i}/\theta_i, z_i) = 1 + \theta_i h_i - h_i^2,$$

so

$$\text{var}(u_{1i}/\theta_i, z_i) = \sigma_1^2((1 - \rho^2) + \rho^2(1 + \theta_i h_i - h_i^2)).$$

Combining this information with Equation (3.6), we can rewrite Equation (3.4) in vector form:

$$y = X_1\beta_1 + \alpha z + ch + v, \quad (A.1)$$

where $E(v/\theta, z) = 0$, $E(vv'/\theta, z) = M$, and $c = \rho \sigma_1$. 0 is the n vector of zeros, and M is an $(n \times n)$ diagonal matrix whose (i, i)th entry is

$$M_{ii} = \sigma_1^2 + c^2(\theta_i h_i - h_i^2).$$

Note that the error vector v does not have homoscedastic elements.

Since β_2 is unknown, we must replace h in (A.1) with $\hat{h}$, its estimate in Section 3.2. Equation (A.1) therefore becomes

$$y = A\gamma + \eta, \quad (A.2)$$

where

$A = (X_1, z, \hat{h})$, an $n \times (k + 2)$ matrix;

$\gamma = (\beta_1, \alpha, c)'$, a $(k + 2)$ vector;

$\eta = c(h - \hat{h}) + v$.

Performing ordinary least squares on (A.2) yields consistent estimates, $\hat{\gamma}$, of γ.

Under general conditions on the elements of z and X_2 (Amemiya 1973; Jennrich 1969),

$$n^{1/2}(\hat{\beta}_2 - \beta_2) \rightarrow N(0, \Omega)$$

as $n \rightarrow \infty$ for some positive definite $(m \times m)$ matrix Ω, and

$$n^{1/2}(\hat{h} - h) \rightarrow N(0, \Delta X_2 \Omega X_2' \Delta)$$

as $n \rightarrow \infty$, conditional on z and θ, where $\Delta = \partial h/\partial \theta$ is an $(n \times n)$ diagonal matrix such that

$$\Delta_{ii} = \partial h_i/\partial \theta_i = h_i^2 - \theta_i h_i.$$

To assign appropriate standard errors to the estimates of α, β_1, and c, we need to determine the asymptotic distribution of $n^{1/2}(\hat{\gamma} - \gamma)$:

$$n^{1/2}(\hat{\gamma} - \gamma) = n(A'A)^{-1} \cdot n^{-1/2}A'[c(h - \hat{h}) + v].$$

Now

$$\plim_{n \to \infty} n(A'A)^{-1} = \plim_{n \to \infty} n((X_1, z, h)'(X_1, z, h))^{-1} = B,$$

a positive definite symmetric $(k + 2) \times (k + 2)$ matrix, if the Amemiya–Jennrich conditions hold.

Then, $n^{1/2}(\hat{\gamma} - \gamma) \rightarrow N(0, B\psi B)$ as $n \rightarrow \infty$, where

$$\psi = \plim_{n \to \infty} (\psi_1 + \psi_2),$$

$$\psi_1 = n^{-1}A'MA,$$

and

$$\psi_2 = c^2 n^{-2}(A'\Delta X_2)\Omega(A'\Delta X_2)'.$$

An estimate for the variance–covariance matrix of $\hat{\gamma}$ is thus

$$(A'A)^{-1}[A'\hat{M}A + \hat{c}^2(A'\hat{\Delta}X_2)\hat{\Sigma}(X_2'\hat{\Delta}A)](A'A)^{-1} \quad (A.3)$$

Here $\hat{\Sigma}$ is the estimated variance–covariance matrix of $\hat{\beta}_2$ from the probit ($\lim_{n \to \infty} n\hat{\Sigma} = \Omega$), $\hat{c}$ is the estimated coefficient on $\hat{h}$ from regression equation (A.2), $\hat{\Delta}_{ii} = \hat{h}_i^2 - \hat{\theta}_i \hat{h}_i$, $\hat{M}_{ii} = \hat{\sigma}_1^2 - \hat{c}^2 \hat{\Delta}_{ii}$,

$$\hat{\sigma}_1^2 = n^{-1} \sum_{i=1}^{n} \hat{\eta}_i^2 + \hat{c}^2 n^{-1} \sum_{i=1}^{n} \hat{\Delta}_{ii},$$

and $\hat{\eta}$ is the vector of observed residuals from regression equation (A.2). The correlation between the achievement and selection errors (u_1 and u_2) can be estimated by $\hat{\rho} = \hat{c}/\hat{\sigma}_1$. $\hat{c}$, $\hat{M}$, $\hat{\Delta}$, $\hat{\rho}$, and $\hat{\sigma}_1^2$ are consistent estimators of c, M, Δ, ρ, and σ_1^2.

Heckman's censored sample model can be estimated with minor modifications of the methodology presented here. In that model, one only observes y for those individuals in the sample for whom $u_{2i} > \theta_i$. That is, z_i is 1 if y_i is observed. Suppose the first n_1 individuals have observations on y and the last $n - n_1$ do not. First, perform maximum likelihood probit for all n cases; then construct

$$\hat{h}_i = f(\hat{\theta}_i)/(1 - F(\hat{\theta}_i))$$

only for the first n_1 cases, and estimate (A.2) for these n_1 individuals, setting $X_1 = (X_{11}, \ldots, X_{1n_1})'$, $A = (X_1, \hat{h})$, and $\gamma = (\beta_1, c)'$. Finally, construct (A.3) with $X_2 = (X_{21}, \ldots, X_{2n_1})'$ and n replaced by n_1 in the estimation of M, Δ, and σ_1^2.

A.2 Selectivity Bias Controlled by the Linear Probability Model

We suppose that u_{2i} is uniform on $[0, 1]$ for each $i = 1, \ldots, n$, rather than being standard normal, so $E(u_{2i}) = \frac{1}{2}$, and $\text{var}(u_{2i}) = \frac{1}{12}$. We also assume that

$$E(u_{1i}/u_{2i}) = \rho\sigma_1(12)^{1/2}(u_{2i} - \tfrac{1}{2})$$

(Olsen 1980). Then

$$\Pr[z_i = 1] = X'_{2i}\tilde{B}_2. \tag{A.4}$$

Here $X'_{2i}\tilde{B}_2 = 1 - \theta_i$, where $\theta_i = -X'_{2i}\beta_2$, as defined in Section 3.1. Now

$$E(u_{2i}/\theta_i, z_i) = (\theta_i + z_i)/2$$

and

$$\text{var}(u_{2i}/\theta_i, z_i) = (\theta_i - z_i)^2/12.$$

Let $\delta = \rho\sigma_1\sqrt{3}$. Then $E(u_{1i}/\theta_i, z_i) = \delta(\theta_i + z_i - 1)$, $\text{var}(u_{1i}/\theta_i, z_i) = \sigma_1^2 - (\delta^2/3)(1 - (\theta_i - z_i))^2 = M_{ii}$, say.

Equation (3.4) therefore can be rewritten, in vector form,

$$y = X_1\beta_1 + \alpha z + \delta s + v, \tag{A.5}$$

where $s_i = z_i - (1 - \theta_i)$ (1 is the n vector of 1's); $E(v/\theta, z) = 0$ (0 is the n vector of 0's); and $E(vv'/\theta, z) = M$, a diagonal $(n \times n)$ matrix whose (i, i)th entry is M_{ii}.

It can be seen that s, the auxiliary regressor, has an ith component that is the difference between the actual value of z_i and the probability that z_i is 1. To avoid collinearity between X_1, z, and s in (A.5), we must identify at least one variable that is in X_2, but not in X_1, that is, a variable that affects school choice but does not directly affect achievement.

Use the fitted values, $\hat{z}$, from the regression of z on X_2 to construct $\hat{s} = z - \hat{z}$. Then

$$y = A\gamma = v. \tag{A.6}$$

In this specification, $A = (X_1, z, \hat{s})$, an $n \times (k + 2)$ matrix; $\gamma = (\beta_1, \alpha, \delta)'$, a $(k_1 + 2)$ vector; and $v = \delta(s - \hat{s}) + v$.

If the usual conditions hold on X_2 and z (Theil 1973),

$$\operatorname*{plim}_{n\to\infty} n(A'A)^{-1} = \operatorname*{plim}_{n\to\infty} n[(X_1zs)'(X_1zs)]^{-1} = B,$$

a positive definite symmetric $(k + 2) \times (k + 2)$ matrix, and $n^{1/2}(\hat{\beta}_2 - \beta_2) \to N(0, \Omega)$ as $n \to \infty$, for some positive definite $(m \times m)$ matrix Ω, which need not be the same as the Ω of Section A.1 above. Thus

$$n^{1/2}(\hat{s} - s) \to N(0, X_2\Omega X'_2)$$

as $n \to \infty$, and we can find the limiting distribution of $n^{1/2}(\hat{\gamma} - \gamma)$ in a manner similar to that demonstrated before:

$$n^{1/2}(\hat{\gamma} - \gamma) \to N(0, B\psi B)$$

as $n \to \infty$, where

$$\psi = \operatorname*{plim}_{n\to\infty}(\psi_1 + \psi_2),$$

$$\psi_1 = n^{-1}A'MA,$$

and

$$\psi_2 = \delta^2 n^{-2}(A'X_2)\Omega(A'X_2)'.$$

An estimate for the variance–covariance matrix of $\hat{\gamma}$ is then

$$(A'A)^{-1}[A'\hat{M}A + \hat{\sigma}^2(A'X_2)\hat{\Sigma}(X'_2A)](A'A)^{-1}. \tag{A.7}$$

Here $\hat{\Sigma}$ is the estimated variance–covariance matrix of the coefficients from the linear probability model $(\lim_{n\to\infty} n\hat{\Sigma} = \Omega)$, $\hat{\delta}$ is the estimated coefficient on $\hat{s}$ from regression Equation (A.6), $\hat{M}_{ii} = \hat{\sigma}_1^2 - \hat{q}_i$,

$$\hat{\sigma}_1^2 = n^{-1}\sum_{1=1}^{n}\hat{v}_i^2 + n^{-1}\sum_{1=1}^{n}\hat{q}_i,$$

$$\hat{q}_i = (\delta^2/3)(1 - (\hat{\theta}_i - z_i)^2)$$

$$= (\hat{\delta}^2/3)(1 - (\hat{z}_i - (1 - z_i))^2),$$

and

$$\hat{\rho} = \hat{\delta}/\sigma_1\sqrt{3}.$$

$\hat{v}$ is the vector of observed residuals from regression Equation (A.6); $\hat{\Delta}$, $\hat{M}$, $\hat{\rho}$, and $\hat{\sigma}_1^2$ are consistent estimators of the true parameter values.

The censored sample model of Olsen can be estimated by running the linear probability model on all n observations, using least squares on (A.6) for the n_1 individuals for whom y is observed, and then setting $\hat{s} = 1 - \hat{z}$, $X_1 = (X_{11}, \ldots, X_{1n_1})'$, $A = (X_1, \hat{s})$, and $\gamma = (\beta_1, \delta)'$. Finally, (A.7) is constructed with $X_2 = (X_{21}, \ldots, X_{2n_1})'$ and n replaced by n_1 in the estimation of σ_1^2, q, and M.

It is a fairly straightforward matter to compute the standard errors given by the diagonal elements of (A.3) or (A.7) once the achievement regression [Equation (A.2) or (A.6)] has been run. The matrix $(A'A)^{-1}$ is just the estimated variance–covariance matrix of the coefficients of this regression, multiplied by the estimated variance of the regression; $\hat{\Sigma}$ is the estimated variance–covariance matrix from the probit or least squares regression of z on X_2; and the other estimates are easily constructed.

One problem in finite samples is that there is no guarantee that σ_1^2 will be positive in either Section A.1 or A.2. This can result in negative diagonal elements in (A.3) (Greene 1981).

Once we condition on X_2, the ith residual from the linear probability model has variance $\theta_i(1 - \theta_i)$. One way to induce homoscedastic errors is to run the linear probability model using ordinary least squares, and then to run weighted least squares on the same equation, giving the ith observation a weight $[\hat{z}_i(1 - \hat{z}_i)]^{-1/2}$. Such a scheme requires each predicted probability, $\hat{z}_i$, to lie between 0 and 1.

APPENDIX B: TWO-STAGE LEAST SQUARES AND THE s METHOD

Recall that $\hat{s} = z - \hat{z}$, where $\hat{z}$ is the vector of fitted values from the regression of z on X_2. The application of ordinary least squares to the achievement equation,

$$y = X_1\beta_1 + \alpha z + \delta\hat{s} + v,$$

yields a vector of predicted scores, $\hat{y}$,

$$\hat{y} = X_1\hat{\beta}_1 + \hat{\alpha}z + \hat{\delta}\hat{s},$$

where $\hat{\beta}_1$, $\hat{\alpha}$, and $\hat{\delta}$ are the least squares estimates of β_1, α, and δ. Therefore

$$\hat{y} = X_1\hat{\beta}_1 + \hat{\alpha}z + \hat{\delta}(z - \hat{z})$$
$$= X_1\hat{\beta}_1 + \hat{\alpha}(\hat{z} + (z - \hat{z})) + \hat{\delta}(z - \hat{z})$$
$$= X_1\hat{\beta}_1 + \hat{\alpha}\hat{z} + (\hat{\alpha} + \hat{\delta})(z - \hat{z}).$$

But if we use ordinary least squares to regress z on X_2, then the residual vector, $z - \hat{z}$, is orthogonal to $\hat{z}$ and X_2, hence also to X_1, since X_2 contains all of the variables in X_1. Therefore the estimates of β_1 and α from the s method will be the same as those derived by applying two-stage least squares to the model,

$$y = X_1\beta_1 + \alpha z + u_1$$

and

$$z = X_2\beta_2 + u_2.$$

Moreover, if we use two-stage least squares, then the standard errors of the estimated coefficients will be correct; however, application of the two-stage least squares method does not permit an immediate test of selectivity bias.

[Received September 1983. Revised May 1984.]

REFERENCES

Amemiya, T. (1973), "Regression Analysis When the Dependent Variable Is Truncated Normal," *Econometrica*, 41, 997–1017.

Barnow, S. N., Cain, G. G., and Goldberger, A. S. (1980), "Issues in the Analysis of Selectivity Bias," in *Evaluation Studies* (Vol. 5) eds. E. W. Stromsdorfer and G. Farkas, Beverly Hills, CA: Sage Publications.

Coleman, J., Hoffer, S. N., and Kilgore, S. (1981a), "Public and Private Schools," report to the National Center for Education Statistics by the National Opinion Research Center.

————— (1981b), "Questions and Answers: Our Response," *Harvard Educational Review*, 51, 526–545.

————— (1982), *High School Achievement: Public, Catholic and Private Schools Compared*, New York: Basic Books.

Farkas, G., Olsen, R. J., and Stromsdorfer, E. W. (1980), "Reduced-Form and Structural Models in the Evaluation of the Youth Entitlement Demonstration," in *Evaluation Studies* (Vol. 5), eds. E. W. Stromsdorfer and G. Farkas, Beverly Hills, CA: Sage Publications.

Goldberger, A. S. (1972), "Selection Bias in Evaluating Treatment Effects: Some Formal Illustrations," Discussion Paper 123-172, University of Wisconsin, Institute for Research on Poverty.

————— (1980), "Abnormal Selection Bias," Discussion Paper 8006, University of Wisconsin, Social Systems Research Institute.

Goldberger, A. S., and Cain, G. G. (1982), "The Causal Analysis of Cognitive Outcomes in the Coleman, Hoffer and Kilgore Report," *Sociology of Education*, 55, 103–122.

Greene, W. H. (1981), "Sample Selection Bias as a Specification Error: Comment," *Econometrica*, 49, 795–798.

Gronau, R. (1973), "The Effect of Children on the Housewife's Value of Time," *Journal of Political Economy*, 81, S168–S201.

————— (1974), "Wage Comparisons—A Selectivity Bias," *Journal of Political Economy*, 82, 1119–1144.

Heckman, J. J. (1974), "Shadow Prices, Market Wages, and Labor Supply," *Econometrica*, 42, 679–694.

————— (1976), "The Common Structure of Statistical Models of Truncation, Sample Selection, and Limited Dependent Variables and a Simple Estimator for Such Models," *Annals of Economic and Social Measurement*, 5, 475–492.

————— (1978), "Dummy Endogenous Variables in a Simultaneous Equations System," *Econometrica*, 46, 931–960.

————— (1979), "Sample Bias as a Specification Error," *Econometrica*, 47, 153–162.

High School and Beyond: A National Longitudinal Study for the 1980's (1981), conducted for the National Center for Education Statistics, U.S. Dept. of Education, Chicago: National Opinion Research Center.

Jennrich, R. I. (1969), "Asymptotic Properties of Nonlinear Least Squares Estimators," *Annals of Mathematical Statistics*, 40, 633–643.

McGuire, T. B. (1981), *Financing Psychotherapy: Costs, Effects, and Public Policy*, Cambridge, MA: Ballinger.

Maddala, G. S., and Lee, L. (1976), "Recursive Models With Qualitative Endogenous Variables," *Annals of Economic and Social Measurement*, 5, 525–545.

Mallar, C. D., Kerachsky, S. H., and Thornton, C. V. D. (1980), "The Short-Term Economic Impact of the Job Corps Program," in *Evaluation Studies* (Vol. 5), eds. E. W. Stromsdorfer and G. Farkas, Beverly Hills, CA: Sage Publications.

Muthen, B., and Joreskog, K. G. (1983), "Selectivity Problems in Quasi-Experimental Studies," *Evaluation Review*, 7, 139–174.

Noell, J. (1981), "The Impact of Private Schools When Self-Selection Is Controlled: A Critique of Coleman's 'Public and Private Schools'," unpublished paper, Office of Planning, Budget, and Evaluation, U.S. Dept. of Education, Washington, DC.

————— (1982), "Public and Catholic Schools: A Reanalysis of 'Public and Private Schools'," *Sociology of Education*, 55, 123–132.

Olsen, R. J. (1980), "A Least Squares Correction for Selectivity Bias," *Econometrica*, 48, 1815–1820.

————— (1982), "Distributional Tests for Selectivity Bias and a More Robust Likelihood Estimator," *International Economic Review*, 23, 223–240.

Orazem, P. (1983), "Black–White Differences in Human Capital Investment and Earnings," unpublished Ph.D. dissertation, Yale University, Economics Dept.

Social Science Citation Index, Philadelphia: Institute for Scientific Information.

Stryker, R. (1981), "Religio-Ethnic Effects on Attainments in the Early Career," *American Sociological Review*, 46, 212–231.

Willis, R. J., and Rosen, S. (1979), "Education and Self-Selection," *Journal of Political Economy*, 87 (Suppl.), 7–36.

14

The Effects of Early Education on Children's Competence in Elementary School

Martha B. Bronson, Donald E. Pierson, and Terrence Tivnan

Programs of early education have focused primarily on low-income populations and on outcomes available from traditional assessments of children's intelligence or achievement. This evaluation used observations of children's behavior in elementary school classrooms several years after the program services had been delivered. Children from a wide range of family backgrounds were included. The results indicated that program participants benefited particularly in the area of mastery skills or academic learning behaviors. Children with highly educated mothers showed advantages regardless of program service level, but children whose mothers were less highly educated showed advantages only with relatively intensive service level.

O ver the past twenty years there have been a large number of early education programs designed to provide services to preschool children and their families. These programs have provided major challenges for evaluators because of the diversity of program goals, settings, and types of families for whom these programs are intended. Partly as a result of this diversity it has been difficult to come to any conclusions about the overall efficacy of such early interventions. It has only been relatively recently that any consistent evidence of long-term effects has emerged. The Consortium for Longitudinal

AUTHORS' NOTE: *This article is based in part on a presentation prepared for the Biennial Meeting of the Society for Research in Child Development, Detroit, Michigan, April, 1983. The work was made possible by funds granted by Carnegie Corporation of New York and The Robert Wood Johnson Foundation. The statements made and views expressed are solely the responsibility of the authors.*

Studies (Lazar and Darlington, 1982) has documented that early education programs for children from low-income families have important and lasting effects. The effects—evident several years after conclusion of the intervention—include fewer assignments to special education services and fewer retentions in grade. At the present time, however, neither the Consortium data nor other available studies (e.g., Gray·and Wandersman, 1980; Schweinhardt and Weikart, 1980) have determined adequately whether the effects of early education can be identified in elementary school classroom behaviors and, if so, whether such effects extend to children other than those from low-income backgrounds.

In developing measures to evaluate early education programs, many psychologists and educators have criticized the traditional reliance on intelligence tests (Zigler and Butterfield, 1968; McClelland, 1973; Seitz et al., 1975; Zigler et al., 1973). Others have stressed the importance of focusing on social or functional competence, including cognitive, social, and motivational components (Anderson and Messick, 1974; Zigler and Tricket, 1978; Gotts, 1979; Zigler and Seitz, 1980; Scarr, 1981). Despite these persuasive appeals to measure how children function within the classroom domain, the prekindergarten and elementary education evaluation literature has shown little response. The difficulties encountered in developing and implementing innovative methods for assessing effectiveness have limited most evaluations to more traditional measures.

In only very few instances have early education program evaluations been carried out on heterogeneous groups of participants. Fewer still have focused on children's behaviors in classrooms. Pierson et al. (1983) found significant behavioral advantages during fall and spring of the kindergarten year for a heterogeneous group of early education participants. The outcome measures were designed to assess the child's functional competence in social and learning situations in the classroom setting. These measures corresponded closely to the goals of the intervention and to the notions of competence held by the school system in which the children were enrolled. The study reported in this article extends the earlier work by following up on children when they were enrolled in second grade, using the same classroom observation instrument. Children who had been enrolled in an early education program were observed in their second grade classrooms. The observations focused on assessing their functional or educational competence.

Thus this study provides an approach to evaluation of early education programs that addresses several of the limitations of the available literature. First, the participants come from a wide range of family backgrounds, not just low-income families. Second, this study represents an opportunity for follow-up evaluation of a program that ended at the children's entry into kindergarten. Finally, the evaluation involves the use of classroom observations, focusing on behaviors considered important by the project as well as the local school system

METHOD

\

PROGRAM DESCRIPTION

The Brookline Early Education Project (BEEP) involved a combination of services: parent education, periodic monitoring of the children's health and development, and early childhood programs. The parent education services were administered at three levels to assess the cost effectiveness of different service packages. Families were assigned at random to one of three cost levels: Level A included home visits and meetings at least once per month as well as unlimited contacts with staff and some child care in the project Center; Level B offered home visits and meetings about once every six weeks as well as the Center options; Level C was restricted primarily to services available at the Center. BEEP staff were available to families at the Center but no home visits, meetings or child care services were scheduled. In working with parents, teachers followed curriculum goals that were oriented toward supporting the parents in the role of primary educators of their child.

The monitoring of health and development was intended to prevent or alleviate conditions that might interfere with learning during the first five years of life. A team of psychologists, pediatricians, and a nurse conducted the examinations of hearing, vision, neurologic status, and language, perceptual, and motor skills. Follow-up conferences and advocacy work were pursued by teachers and social workers as needed. These diagnostic services were available equally to all participants in the project.

The early childhood programs involved a weekly play group at age two years and a daily prekindergarten program at ages three and four years. These were held in the Center or at elementary schools and were focused on individually tailored educational goals (Hauser-Cram and Pierson, 1981). As with the exams, the children's educational programs were available to all families regardless of the parent education cost-level assignment.

The project's primary goal was to reduce or eliminate school problems. For this reason, the evaluation focuses on whether the program decreased the proportion of children who fell below certain minimal competencies defined as necessary for effective functioning in second grade.

SUBJECTS

The experimental subjects were 169 second grade children who participated from birth to kindergarten in BEEP. Enrollment was open to all residents of Brookline and to ethnic minority families from the adjacent city of Boston. Participants were recruited through the schools, health, and social service agencies, and neighborhood networks. Recruitment strategies were designed to locate and inform families who were expecting to have babies in the coming months and who ordinarily would not seek or hear about such a program. All participants in BEEP had the option of attending the public schools of Brookline either as town residents or through METCO, a state-funded desegregation program.

At second grade, 104 of the participants were enrolled in the Brookline public schools; another 65 children had moved to other schools, but were within commuting distance of Brookline and available to the study.

A comparison group of 169 children was selected from the same classrooms as the BEEP children. Each comparison child was matched with a BEEP participant by selecting a child at random from within the same classroom and sex group as the participant group child. The children were spread out over 82 classrooms in over 50 different elementary schools. Table 1 shows that demographic characteristics of the two groups are quite similar and that the children involved in this study represent a heterogeneous collection of families. For example, the education levels of the families range from those with less than a high school education to those with college and postcollege degrees. Over 10% of the families spoke first languages other than English.

MEASURE

The outcome measures in this study are taken from a classroom observation instrument. The instrument was developed in response to

TABLE 1
Distribution of Background Characteristics
for BEEP and Comparison Group

| | | Percentage Number of Children | |
Characteristics		BEEP (N = 169)	Comparison (N = 169)
Mother's education	College graduate	59	54
	High school graduate	33	37
	Not high school graduate	8	9
Father's education	College graduate	63	65
	High school graduate	29	29
	Not high school graduate	8	6
Number of parents in home	Two	83	81
	One	17	19
First language	English	87	82
	Spanish	9	4
	Chinese	4	2
	Russian	0	4
	Hebrew	0	2
	Other	0	6
Birth order	First	44	50
	Second	38	27
	Third	11	12
	Fourth or later	7	11
Gender	Female	48	48
	Male	52	52

the well-documented evidence that a dearth of adequate measures had hindered previous efforts to evaluate Head Start and other early education programs (Smith and Bissell, 1970; Walker et al., 1973; Butler, 1974; Raizen and Bobrow, 1974). Trained observers recorded the frequency of specific classroom behaviors. The instrument thus avoided the traditional reliance of educational evaluations on tests individually administered outside the classroom milieu. The instrument also focused on specific behaviors that reflected the project's position on what constitutes competent functioning in young school-age children.

The observation instrument, entitled the Executive Skill Profile (Bronson, 1975, 1978, 1981), provided a way of recording a child's performance in planning and organizing work, interacting with others, and carrying out social interactions and learning tasks. The concept of "executive skill" is applied to both social and learning activities in the sense of using effective strategies for choosing and reaching goals.

The trained observers followed and recorded the behavior of each child for six 10-minute periods in the spring of the second grade year. The modified time-sampling procedure required that three of the observations begin at the start of a social interaction and three at the start of academic work. The observers were instructed to make certain that at least one of the academic tasks be a language arts (reading/writing) task and at least one be a math activity. Each 10-minute observation was scheduled for a different day, spread out over no less than three and no more than six weeks. Sometimes children's absences from school or scheduling difficulties extended or compressed the observation period.

Behaviors were recorded on a sheet that allowed both the frequency and duration of specific behaviors to be collected. The duration of behaviors was measured either with a small timing device that clicked at 15-second intervals into an earphone worn by the observer (Leifer and Leifer, 1971) or with a stop watch (some observers found this easier). During a two-week training period observers studied a manual (Bronson, 1983) and were trained in classrooms to record each behavior variable to a criterion of 90% interobserver agreement with the observation supervisor. Observers were not informed about the specific purposes of the study and safeguards were employed to avoid divulging children's membership in the participant versus comparison group.

The observations covered eleven variables divided into three categories of behavior: mastery skills, social skills, and use of time. The mastery skills category included three variables designed to measure a child's success in planning and carrying out school learning tasks: resistance to distraction, use of appropriate task attack strategies, and successful completion of tasks.

The social skills category included four variables pertaining to interpersonal relations: cooperative interaction with peers, successfully influencing others, use of effective cooperative strategies and use of language rather than physical force to persuade and gain the attention of others.

The use of time category consisted of four variables related to a child's degree of involvement in activities within the classroom: proportion of time spent in social activities, proportion of time in mastery tasks (not necessarily mutually exclusive with social time), proportion of time spent without any focused activity (mutually exclusive with both preceeding variables) and rate of social acts. Each observation variable yielded a rate or percent score based on a full set of six 10-minute observations.

Taken as a whole, the observation procedures used in this study provide several important advantages for this evaluation. Information is collected on a wide range of important behaviors. Observation is directed at the behavior of individual children rather than on groups or classrooms or teacher behavior. The focus is on in-classroom behavior, rather than individualized, out-of-classroom assessment. In addition, the Executive Skill Profile has been successfully used in other settings (Bronson, 1975, 1978, 1981; Pierson et al., 1983), and it attempts to measure behaviors that are consistent with the goals of the local school system that is the setting for the evaluation. Thus is addresses some of the important limitations of more traditional evaluation instruments used in elementary schools.

A major goal of the Brookline Early Education Project was to prevent school problems—or, conversely, to increase the proportion of children attaining minimal competencies. Thus it was considered important to analyze the data by looking at the proportions of children who were having difficulty in school as well as by looking at average performance. Criteria for determining adequate performance versus "concerns" or "problems" were derived from clinical impressions of effective behavior and from analyses of data on non-BEEP children. The pivotal point for determining whether a given score should be regarded as "adequate" or "concern" always fell at least one standard deviation below the group mean score for that category. Concerns were considered to indicate a "problem" if scores for two or more variables in a given area (i.e., mastery skills, social skills, or use of time) fell below the criteria for "concern." The results of the comparison of mean scores and the comparisons of percentages of children showing problems will be presented separately.

RESULTS

Table 2 shows the differences between the category means of the BEEP participants and the randomly selected comparison group. The BEEP participants show significant advantages over the comparison group in both mastery and social skills, with the strongest effects in the mastery skills area. There is no difference between the two groups in the use of time area.

Another way of viewing the data is by focusing on the proportions who have problems. Table 3 shows the percentage of children with

TABLE 2
Differences Between the Means of BEEP and Comparison Children
in Second Grade Spring Classroom Observations

	BEEP (N = 169)		Comparison (N = 169)		Significance[a]
	Mean	SD	Mean	SD	
Mastery Skills Area					
Percentage tasks completed successfully	84	18	76	23	<.001
Rate task attack strategies	2.13	.86	1.82	.83	<.001
Percentage time attending, not distracted	94	6	91	12	<.001
Social Skills Area					
Percentage time in cooperative interaction	79	20	77	23	ns
Rate cooperative strategies	.50	.41	.41	.36	<.01
Percentage success in influencing others	97	4	96	5	<.05
Percentage use of language to influence	97	5	95	6	ns
Use of Time Area					
Percentage time in mastery tasks	54	13	53	13	ns
Percentage time in social activities	51	12	51	12	ns
Rate of social acts	5.34	1.29	5.34	1.32	ns
Percentage time involved	98	2	98	3	ns

a. Significance is based on t tests for matched pairs.

"concerns" (low scores in categories) or "problems" (two or more low scores in an area) in the BEEP and comparison groups. Again the BEEP group shows a significant advantage over the comparison group in both mastery and social skills with the strongest effect in the mastery skills area. The BEEP group has fewer overall problems and many fewer children with problems in more than one area.

The reduction in severity of difficulties for BEEP participants can also be seen in the numbers of children with low scores across several of the eleven categories. Figure 1 presents the frequency distributions, showing more children with multiple concerns in the comparison group than in BEEP.

TABLE 3

Percentage Number of Children with Concerns[a] or Problems[b]
for BEEP Participants and Randomly Selected Comparison Group
in Second Grade Classroom Observations

| | Percentage Number of Children Below Competence Criteria | | |
	BEEP (N = 169)	Comparison (N = 169)	Significance[c]
Mastery Skills Concerns			
Tasks not completed successfully	14	27	<.01
Inadequate rate of task attack strategies	18	32	.001
Time distracted	18	29	<.05
Social Skills Concerns			
Inadequate time in cooperative interaction	6	8	ns
Inadequate rate of cooperative strategies	18	21	ns
Unsuccessful in influencing othes	2	7	<.05
Ineffective use of language to influence	3	7	ns
Use of Time Concerns			
Inadequate time in mastery tasks	11	11	ns
Inadequate time in social activities	17	18	ns
Inadequate rate of social acts	2	2	ns
Time not involved	1	2	ns
Problem in Mastery Skills	12	25	<.01
Problem in Social Skills	2	8	<.05
Problem in Use of Time	2	1	ns
Overall Difficulty: Problems in One or More Areas	14	29	<.01

a. A "concern" is a score below the established criterion in any single category.
b. "Problems" are two or more scores below the criteria in an area.
c. McNemar's matched-pairs test.

Figure 2 shows the numbers of children in the BEEP and random comparison groups who met the criteria for competence in the observations (by having no problems in any of the three areas assessed) with distinctions for mother's education and program cost level. BEEP children with highly educated mothers (college graduates) show advantages over their counterparts. For these subgroups, even the minimal cost-level program resulted in significant ($p < .01$) advantages. However, for children whose mothers were not so highly educated (less than college graduates) a more substantial investment and outreach, represented by cost level A, was required to attain significant ($p < .01$) advantages over the comparison group.

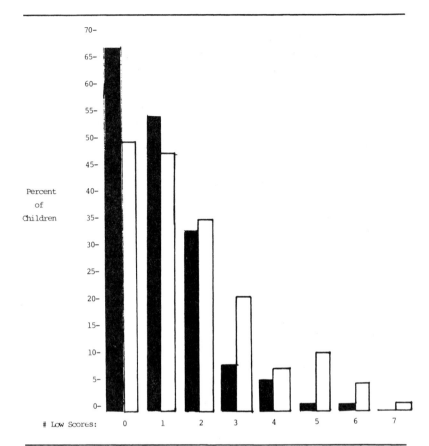

Figure 1:   Frequency Distribution of the Number of Low Scores Obtained by BEEP (solid bars) and Comparison (clear bars) Children on Eleven Observation Variables

Focusing on the cost levels within BEEP, we find that no significant overall differences across the three groups emerge. The only trend is for the Level A participants to be ahead of Levels B and C among the less educated families. These results are consistent with other analyses of the within-program differences.

CONCLUSIONS AND DISCUSSION

Children who participated in the Brookline Early Education Project showed several advantages in second-grade classroom behavior indices

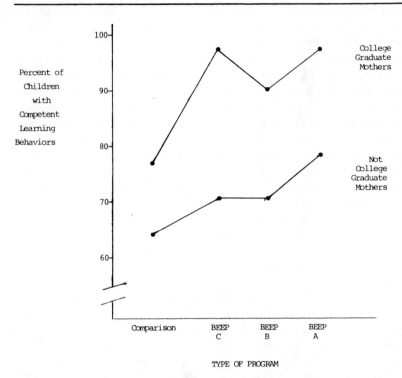

NOTE: Percentage of children with no difficulties in mastery skills, social skills, or use of time behaviors, analyzed by level of mother's education and type of program, is shown.

Figure 2: Overall Competencies Observed

over comparison children. Advantages for the BEEP participants were apparent both in mean differences in the behavior categories and in the relative numbers of children performing below competence criteria. The BEEP advantage was most pronounced in the mastery, or academic learning area. BEEP children with highly educated mothers showed significant advantages over comparison children regardless of program level, but children whose mothers were less highly educated showed significant advantages only with the relatively intensive level A program.

Observations of BEEP and comparison children in kindergarten (Pierson et al., 1983) with the same observation instrument showed significant advantages for the program group with the greatest differences appearing in the social and use of time areas. In the second grade observations the BEEP advantage is greatest in the mastery area. This shift in the pattern of BEEP advantages over comparison children is interesting. In the fall of kindergarten year classroom behavior differences favoring BEEP children were strongest in the social and use of time areas. In the spring of kindergarten year there was a shift in the pattern of BEEP advantages, with use of time behaviors being less important, mastery behaviors becoming more important, and social behaviors continuing to be strong discriminators between the two groups. By second grade, mastery behaviors are the strongest discriminators. The social behavior categories show a consistent but less strong BEEP advantage, and the use of time categories reveal no differences between the BEEP and comparison groups.

This shift in the pattern of the relative advantages of BEEP over comparison children seems to be related to the changing patterns of classroom demands at these three time periods. In the fall of kindergarten year, academic demands are few and the emphasis in classroom is on school adjustment and learning school routines. The behaviors in the social and use of time areas are those most likely to pick up differences in school-related competence under these circumstances. In the spring of kindergarten year some academic demands are being introduced—numbers, letters, printing, and so on—and most children have adapted to school routines. This shift in emphasis in the classroom away from routines and toward academic demands is reflected in the changing pattern of advantages of BEEP children, away from use of time categories and toward differences in mastery categories. By the second grade, the primary demands in the classroom are academic. There is less time for social interaction and less room for differences in use of time categories since children's involvement in various activities is much more controlled. The pattern of BEEP advantages reflects these shifts in classroom demands and constraints.

An additional finding that deserves some attention was the lack of strong main-effect differences across the three program service levels. For the highly educated families the least intensive level of service was as effective as the most intensive level. For the less highly educated, there were no differences between the moderate and lowest levels of service, and only the most intensive level showed a significant advantage over the comparison group. Of the three major service components that were part of BEEP—parent education, diagnostic monitoring of children's status, early childhood programs for children—only the parent education services were offered differentially; diagnostic and education programs for children were equally available to all. So it should not be surprising that in this study, focusing on outcomes for children some years after the provision of services, few differences among the service levels should be observed. Nevertheless, the search for interaction effects, or differential impact on different types of families, is important in evaluating and planning early education programs. The evidence here, although limited, suggests that service levels need to be more intensive when parents are less educated. More educated parents appear to benefit from even minimal services. This finding indicates the potential usefulness of early education for all children, not only the less educated or economically needy groups. The benefits may well vary across different types of families, and the types of services that will be helpful may also vary considerably. This issue deserves more attention from evaluators.

From the evaluation perspective, the results suggest the value of classroom observations as an evaluation technique and the importance of tailoring outcome measure to intervention goals. It is noteworthy, in this regard, that there were few differences between BEEP and comparison groups on a traditional measure of IQ or ability obtained at entry into kindergarten (see Pierson et al., 1983). So without the use of observations in the classrooms the impact of the early intervention would be very difficult to detect, and criticisms similar to those cited earlier concerning reliance on traditional tests (e.g., Zigler and Seitz, 1980; Scarr, 1981) would be relevant.

The reduction in classroom behavior problems also has significant practical implications for elementary schools. Even if behavior problems are not so severe as to require expensive special services, behavior problems in the classroom require teacher attention and reduce the amount of productive teacher time and energy available to all children. Fewer behavior problems in a classroom result in a more positive classroom atmosphere and more "learning time" for all children.

In summary, the results of this study suggest the importance of a carefully planned program like the Brookline Early Education Project for all school systems. Education and support services to parents of young children coupled with early education programs for the children should be recognized as an essential part of a high quality elementary school curriculum. Early detection and prevention of learning difficulties is more effective, and less expensive in the long run, than remediation.

REFERENCES

ANDERSON, S. and S. MESSICK (1974) "Social competence in young children." Developmental Psychology 10: 282-293.

BRONSON, M. B. (1975) "Executive competence in preschool children." Presented to the annual meeting of the American Educational Research Association, Washington, D.C., April. ERIC Document Reproduction Service ED 107 378.

BRONSON, M. B. (1978) "The development and pilot testing of an observational measure of school-related social and mastery skills for preschool and kindergarten children." Doctoral dissertation, Harvard Graduate School of Education.

BRONSON, M. B. (1981) "Naturalistic observation as a method of assessing problems at entry to school." Presented to the annual meeting of the Society for Research in Child Development, Boston, April.

BUTLER, J. A. (1974) Toward a new cognitive effects battery for Project Head Start. Santa Monica, CA: Rand Corp.

GOTTS, E. E. (1979) "Early childhood assessment." In D. A. Sabatino and T. L. Miller (Eds.) Describing learner characteristics of handicapped children and youth. New York: Grune & Stratton.

GRAY, S. W. and L. P. WANDERSMAN (1980) "The methodology of home-based intervention studies: Problems and promising strategies." Child Development 51: 993-1009.

HAUSER-CRAM, P. and D. E. PIERSON (1981) The BEEP Prekindergarten Curriculum: A Working Paper. Brookline, MA: Brookline Early Education Project.

LAZAR, I. and R. DARLINGTON (1982) "Lasting effects of early education: A report from the Consortium for Longitudinal Studies." Monographs of the Society for Research in Child Development 47 (2-3, Whole No. 195).

LEIFER, A. D. and L. J. LEIFER (1971) "An auditory prompting device for behavior observation." J. of Experimental Child Psychology 2: 376-378.

McCLELLAND, D. C. (1973) "Testing for competence rather than for 'intelligence'." Amer. Psychologist 28: 1-14.

PIERSON, D. E., M. B. BRONSON, E. DROMEY, J. P. SWARTZ, T. TIVNAN, and D. K. WALKER (1983) "The impact of early education as measured by classroom observations and teacher ratings of children in kindergarten." Evaluation Rev. 7: 191-216.

RAIZEN, S. and S. B. BOBROW (1974) Design for a National Evaluation of Social Competence in Head Start Children. Santa Monica, CA: Rand Corp.

SCARR, S. (1981) "Testing for children: Assessment and the many determinants of intellectual competence." Amer. Psychologist 36: 10 1159-1166.

SCHWEINHART, L. and D. P. WEIKART (1980) Young Children Grow Up. Ypsilanti: Monographs of the High/Scope Educational Research Foundation Seven.

SEITZ, V., W. D. ABELSON, E. LEVINE, and E. F. ZIGLER (1975) "Effects of place of testing on the Peabody Picture Vocabulary Test scores of disadvantaged Head Start and non-Head Start children." Child Development 45: 481-486.

SMITH, M. S. and J. S. BISSELL (1970) "Report analysis: the impact of Head Start." Harvard Educ. Rev. 40: 51-104.

WALKER, D. K., M. J. BANE, and A. S. BRYK (1973) The Quality of the Head Start Planned Variation Data (2 vols.) Cambridge, MA: Huron Institute.

YURCHAK, N.J.H. (1975) Infant Toddler Curriculum of the Brookline Early Education Project. Brookline, MA: Brookline Early Education Project.

ZIGLER, E. F. and E. C. BUTTERFIELD (1968) "Motivational aspects of changes in IQ test performance of culturally deprived nursery school children." Child Development 39: 1-14.

ZIGLER, E. F. and V. SEITZ (1980) "Early childhood intervention programs: A reanalysis." School Psychology Rev. 9(4): 354-368.

ZIGLER, E. F. and P. K. TRICKETT (1978) "I.Q., social competence, and evaluation of early childhood intervention programs." Amer. Psychologist 33: 789-798.

ZIGLER, E. F., W. D. ABELSON, and V. SIETZ (1973) "Motivational factors in the performance of economically disadvantaged children on the Peabody Picture Vocabulary Test." Child Development 44: 294-303.

Martha B. Bronson is an educational psychologist who specializes in observational research methods for studying young children's behavior in preschool and elementary school classrooms.

Donald E. Pierson was the director of the Brookline Early Education Project since the inception of the longitudinal study in 1972. He is currently Professor of Education at the University of Lowell in Massachusetts.

Terrence Tivnan is currently Assistant Professor at the Harvard Graduate School of Education, where he teaches courses in research methods and data analysis.

15

Changed Lives—
The Effects of the Perry Preschool Program
on Youths Through Age 19
Reviewing and Interpreting Study Outcomes Over Time

John R. Berrueta-Clement, W. Steven Barnett, and
David P. Weikart

Preface

Historically, education has been a means by which individuals improved their prospects for a more productive and personally satisfying life. Our society, investing in education, has reaped the benefits of meaningful progress in all aspects of our nation's development. Led by the report of the National Commission on Excellence in Education, public debate about education took on a new urgency in 1983. Today, people are seeking new ways to improve the quality of education and thereby improve the quality of life.

In this light, there is growing public recognition that early childhood education programs can help students to be more successful'throughout their school careers than would be possible without early education. The evidence generated by longitudinal research on the effectiveness of early childhood education programs of high quality strongly supports decisions by policymakers to use public funds to expand such programs.

In particular, research concerning the key importance of early childhood education to learning and success in life for low-income children began a few years before the advent of the national Head Start program, in a series of specially designed and controlled research projects. Later, evaluation studies were funded to study the impact of the national Head Start program. These two streams of work came to fruition recently with remarkable evidence of long-term effectiveness (Lazar, Darlington, Murray, Royce, & Snipper, 1982; Hubbell, 1983). The basic finding is that early childhood education of high quality can improve the lives of low-income children and their families; most important from the public viewpoint, it has payoffs for society as well in that it can enhance the quality of life for the community as a whole.

The High/Scope Perry Preschool Project, the subject of this monograph, is from that group of studies begun early in the 1960s. It is one of the principal studies supporting the value of early education.

From John R. Berrueta-Clement, Lawrence T. Schweinhart, W. Steven Barnett, Ann S. Epstein, and David P. Weikart, *Changed Lives: The Effects of the Perry Preschool Program on Youths Through Age 19*, Monograph Number Eight, pp. xiii-xvii, 77-92, 189-192. Copyright 1984 by the High/Scope Educational Research Foundation, Ypsilanti, Michigan. Reprinted by permission.

The Perry Preschool Study

The High/Scope Foundation's Perry Preschool study is a longitudinal study designed to answer the question, Can high quality early childhood education help to improve the lives of low-income children and their families and the quality of life of the community as a whole? The project has progressed through four of five phases. Each phase has examined issues that reflect the growth of the children as they move from family to school to the wider world of adulthood. As new phases begin, new variables gain central importance.

Phase One focused primarily on the operation of a high quality program of early childhood education, with extensive curriculum development and annual replication of program components. Importance was placed on the documentation of the curriculum and the home visits. The principal measurement concern was the early childhood development of intellectual ability. This phase coincided with the operation of the program from 1962 to 1967 (Weikart, Deloria, Lawser, & Wiegerink, 1970; Weikart, Rogers, Adcock, & McClelland, 1971).

Phase Two began the longitudinal follow-up of the project as the children and parents were tracked into elementary school through third grade or age 8. The principal measurement concerns of this phase were intellectual development, school achievement patterns, and social maturity. This phase also included an examination of parental attitudes and demographic information. The project's first "real-world" measures were introduced: scholastic placement and the first cost-benefit analysis (Weikart, Bond, & McNeil, 1978; Weber, Foster, & Weikart, 1978).

Phase Three extended the longitudinal study of children and families from age 8 to age 15. The emphasis continued to be on intellectual development, school achievement patterns, and family attitudes. The real-world measures grew in importance and included examinations of scholastic placement, delinquent behavior, after-school employment, and cost-benefit analysis (Schweinhart & Weikart, 1980).

Phase Four is reported in this volume. It continues the focus on the longitudinal development of the study participants, now young adults, through school departure and subsequent experience at age 19. The shift from psychological to real-world variables is all but complete by age 19. Instead of an intelligence or traditional achievement test, study participants took a test of functional competence that focused on information and skills used in the real world. Other measures focused on social behavior in the community at large, job training, college attendance, pregnancy rates, and patterns of crime. For the first time, the cost-benefit analysis is based on actual data from complete school records, police reports, and state records of welfare payments. Employment histories and birth records have been verified. While projections of lifetime earnings are still necessary, the basic patterns of the subjects' adult lives are beginning to unfold.

Phase Five, the next piece of work, will follow subjects into adulthood—through age 26. Their life patterns will have stabilized; they will have formed clear patterns of family functioning, employment, use of welfare assistance, crime, and social behavior. A cost-benefit analysis at that time will provide a final reckoning of the economic value of the preschool program, with a strong base in actual data for projections into the future.

Strengths of the Perry Preschool Study

The Perry Preschool study has become the cornerstone of a body of longitudinal research that permits definitive statements about the value of early childhood education for children from low-income families. This body of research is having major impact on federal policies as expressed, during the Reagan Administration, in steadily increasing funding for the national Head Start program. There are certain facts about the Perry Preschool study that support its strong position in this group of studies in influencing policy development.

First, the study was designed as a true experiment with random assignment of subjects to experimental or control groups. Rarely are social experiments established in such a fashion outside artificial laboratory settings. This experimental design was created during a simpler time: We had not yet learned how difficult experimental designs are in field research. Also, President Johnson's War on Poverty had yet to be conceived, and the old authoritarian institutional structures were still in place, allowing an experimental approach to service to be accepted by participants. Thus, the community accepted the project for what it was—a study of low-income children growing up and a school district trying to find ways to help them.

Second, the study repeated the experimental/control group design annually for five successive waves of children. This design pattern was natural to a special services division of a school system, to which each year brought a new group of students and renewed funding from state resources.

Third, while the study sample (123 subjects) is small compared to cross-sectional surveys, nearly all of the sample subjects are still available to the project. Such availability eliminates the problem of attrition that plagues so many longitudinal studies, even those that last only a few years.

Fourth, during follow-up, although both control-group and experimental-group children were sometimes recognized by teachers as participants in a child development study, there was no reason for teachers to attach importance to the fact that some children had attended a preschool program and some had not. At the time, early education was a rare occurrence for any child. Teacher bias toward one group or the other was essentially nonexistent. Further, beyond the reach of any potential bias are the important data on employment, pregnancy, welfare, crime, and postsecondary education.

Fifth, data from the study have been internally consistent over the years, no matter how or by whom the data were collected. There are no indications that the control group did better than the experimental group under any circumstances. Also important is the fact that the data collected from subjects' self-reports have been corroborated by data collected by outside agencies. Arrest records, documented on police blotters, corroborate self-reports of arrest. Official school records confirm the findings of testing and interviews of subjects by project staff. Computer files of the Department of Social Services agree with self-reported welfare findings.

Sixth, the study includes the most complete cost-benefit analysis of early childhood education yet undertaken. A first, rudimentary effort was undertaken in 1971, by looking at scholastic placement from a cost-savings orientation. A second, major effort was carried out under the direction of an economist, with data collected from the schools through 1973

(Weber et al., 1978). This monograph presents a new economic analysis based on data collected through 1982 from schools, police and courts, and social services.

Seventh, the study has focused on collecting variables meaningful to society rather than variables meaningful only to psychologists. The effort has focused on real success in school as well as on test scores. Thus, we have used special education placement, school attendance, retention in grade, remedial education placement, and school completion as guides to outcomes. Outside of school we have focused on labor force participation, crime and delinquency, and arrest rates.

Hence, the Perry Preschool study has a number of features that make it worthy of special attention—experimental design repeated over five years, lack of attrition, consistency of findings regardless of source of data, cost-benefit analysis, and variables meaningful to society.

How the Study Was Accomplished

An interesting component of effective longitudinal work in a social science field is its ability to survive the changing times. The Perry Preschool study is a good example. When the study began, it operated outside the bounds of general social popularity. The project began in the early 1960s as a local attempt to solve a local problem of school failure and delinquency on the part of the disadvantaged segment of the school population. At that time, the advice of several outside consultants was not to initiate the project, because it might be harmful to the children and their families. Of course, with the great social movement of the late 1960s coming to fruition in the War-on-Poverty legislation passed by Congress in 1965, preschool education suddenly became a national effort (through Head Start), and the public's attitude shifted dramatically to favor such programs. During the 1970s things gradually tightened up both economically and philosophically, early childhood education for low-income children became less popular, and it barely survived the early cuts in social programs introduced by the Reagan Administration. Nevertheless, evidence of the cost-effectiveness of such high quality preschool programs has enabled them to become part of the social "safety net." So, the Perry Preschool Project began as a "suspect" innovation, then became one of a multitude in a surge of public support for such efforts, and has played a major role in legitimating preschool education through the research evidence of its cost-effective nature as a social investment.

Impossible to plan for in advance, an accident of history finds that a small midwestern project, carefully designed and executed, has the right data at the right time 20 years after its inception to join with similar carefully designed studies and actually affect social policy at a national (and increasingly international) level.

It is worth mentioning a particular difficulty involved in carrying out longitudinal research. Such research receives praise more often than it receives funding. Both government agencies and private foundations admire such efforts, but are wary of making the long-term funding commitments that such studies require. Thus, the researcher must constantly seek funds from all possible resources. In the Perry Preschool Project we have found a wide range of funding sources for our work; fundraising is a recurring process that begins again and again when we hear, "Our agency policy has changed" or "We've done our share, now find others to help."

More than three years of the study were totally unfunded. So how did the data collection continue? Some data collection was delayed. Staff were asked to increase their workloads. Reports were delayed until new funding sources were found. Although the recurring funding difficulties sometimes impede our progress, the work continues.

The Perry Preschool Project data demonstrate that preschool education of high quality can alter the lives of children living in poverty. I believe that high quality early childhood education programs can contribute to solving the major social problems of our times; the data support this belief. Preschool programs are well worth the investment required even in times of limited resources, because they have long-term, positive outcomes that make them cost-effective. The challenge we face now is to develop systems of early education provision that are consistently of the highest quality so they can be widely disseminated and can guarantee delivery on their promise.

David P. Weikart
Principal Investigator
1984

In the first section of this chapter we summarize the outcomes of the Perry Preschool program, presenting the findings that have been reported in previous volumes in this series as well as in earlier chapters of this book. The next section presents a causal model that illustrates how these preschool effects developed over two decades and how outcomes relate to each other. The final section offers a summary of the economic analysis of the program and its outcomes.

Summary of Group Differences

The Perry Preschool study is based on a program of early intervention in the lives of low-income children who were at risk of school failure and placement in special education. The treatment consisted of either one or two years of preschool education and weekly home visits. To evaluate the program's effects, participants were selected for the study on the basis of their similar background characteristics and were assigned at random to an experimental (preschool) group and a control (no-preschool) group. Follow-up of study participants has occurred regularly since the project began in 1962.

Immediate Effects of Preschool on School Success

During and at the end of preschool, early education improved the performance of study participants on IQ tests. The IQ difference between treatment groups diminished over time, however, and by second grade was no longer statistically significant. Similar trends were found for other measures of academic aptitude.[29] Nevertheless, early education led the sub-

---

[29]The Arthur Adaptation of the Leiter International Performance Scale (Arthur, 1952); the Peabody Picture Vocabulary Test (Dunn, 1965); and the Illinois Test of Psycholinguistic Abilities (McCarthy & Kirk, 1961). For details of findings, see Weikart et al., 1978.

jects to increased academic achievement, as measured by standardized tests, throughout the elementary and middle-school grades. Teacher ratings of children's social and emotional maturity after kindergarten also showed significant overall trends favoring the group that had attended preschool (Weikart et al., 1978). By fourth grade, children who had attended preschool were less likely to have been placed in special education or retained in grade than those who had not attended preschool. Through the elementary years, preschool attendees also had fewer absences than their no-preschool counterparts. By age 15, youths who had attended preschool placed a higher value on schooling and had stronger commitments to school than did the no-preschool group (Schweinhart & Weikart, 1980).

Later Effects of Preschool on School Success

Through secondary school, youths who had attended preschool had fewer failing grades and better marks than the no-preschool subjects. Throughout their entire period of formal schooling, compared to the no-preschool subjects, preschool attendees spent fewer years in special education, were less likely to be classified as mentally retarded, and more frequently were assigned to remedial education. At age 19, persons who had attended preschool had higher scores than those with no preschool on a measure of competence in skills of everyday life (the Adult Performance Level Survey). They also expressed more favorable attitudes toward high school than did the other group.

Preschool's Effects on Early Socioeconomic Success

Early education led subjects to higher levels of employment, less unemployment, and higher earnings by age 19. Study participants were more likely to be employed at the time of their interview if they had attended preschool; since leaving school, those who had attended preschool had spent fewer months unemployed. In the calendar year in which they were 19, preschool attendees had been employed longer and had higher median incomes than the no-preschool group; they also reported being more satisfied with their jobs.

Subjects who had attended preschool were more likely to be supporting themselves on their own (or their spouses') earnings at the time they were interviewed; they also reported receiving less public assistance than the no-preschool subjects. Examination of official records also showed that preschool led to reduced use of at least certain kinds of welfare: Persons who had attended preschool less frequently received General Assistance funds. Compared to the no-preschool subjects, a higher percentage of subjects who had attended preschool reported that they saved money with some regularity.

Preschool's Effects on Social Responsibility Through Early Adulthood

Fewer of the preschool subjects had ever been arrested, and that group also had a lower total number of arrests. Youths who had attended preschool were less likely to come to the attention of juvenile authorities. Those with preschool had fewer offenses as adults than did those without preschool:

More of the preschool subjects had records of committing no offenses and fewer had records of five or more offenses. Preschool also led to reductions in some types of delinquent behavior as reported by the individuals themselves. Those who had attended preschool had lower median scores on a scale measuring delinquent-event frequencies weighted by seriousness.

Preschool education led the preschool group to fewer pregnancies and births than the no-preschool group as reported at age 19 by women in the study.

In their responses to the age-19 Young Adult Interview, persons who had attended preschool were more likely than their no-preschool counterparts to report "doing things to help" family and friends, but less likely to report doing volunteer work. Preschool subjects were also more likely than no-preschool subjects to report attending church sometimes or often.

This brief summary of group differences demonstrates that the children who attended the Perry Preschool were changed in ways that have had long-term, positive effects on their lives. To understand the role of early education in producing these long-term outcomes, however, we must move beyond the examination of group differences and look at the relations among study variables. We have developed a causal model for this purpose.

A Causal Model of Preschool's Effects

The Perry Preschool program has had long-term impact because the immediate program effects were the first links in a chain of cause and effects that permanently changed the lives of the preschool subjects. This chain of causes and effects is the basis of our causal model. Chapter 1 presented the conceptual framework for that model (p. 3). The statistical procedures of multiple regression analysis allow us to examine how well the model conforms to the data from the study. In what follows we present a causal model of the links connecting early childhood education to measures of adult success, in the context of some of the important effects of personal characteristics and family background. This is a rather modest attempt to elucidate the long-term effects of preschool, and not an effort to provide a complete explanation for differences among the study subjects in school and post-school success.

Figures 7 and 8 present a causal model of a dozen variables associated with the effects of preschool education, with Figure 7 isolating the chain of effects from preschool to adulthood. The variables in the model can be divided chronologically into three sets: variables in early childhood, school process variables in childhood and adolescence, and variables in early adulthood. The five early childhood variables are as follows: preschool, intellectual performance before preschool (as measured by Stanford-Binet IQ's), intellectual performance at school entry, family socioeconomic status, and gender. The four school process variables are as follows: social maturity and misbehavior[30] (representing commitment to

---

[30]Social maturity is a factor based on eight items: appears generally happy; social relationship with classmates; [not] withdrawn and uncommunicative, friendly and well-received by other pupils; degree of trust of total environment (suspicious, trusting); [does not] appear depressed; level of emotional adjustment; direction of interest (introversion, extroversion); and [not] isolated with few or no friends. Misbehavior is a factor based on seven items: disobedient, influences others towards troublemaking, resistant to teacher, lying or cheating, resentful of criticism or discipline, easily led into trouble. and swears or uses obscene words.

Figure 7

A CAUSAL MODEL FOR EFFECTS OF THE PERRY PRESCHOOL PROGRAM

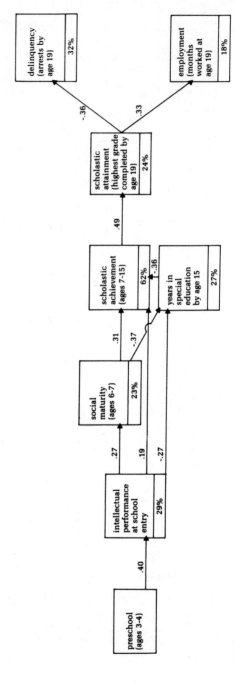

Note. Analyses are based on *n* = 112. Causal paths are indicated by arrows joining variables, with direction of the arrows from cause to effect. Path coefficients are beta weights in ordinary-least-squares regressions; arrows connect variables only if paths are significant (at *p* < .10, two-tailed). The directions of paths between oretical framework and should be interpreted with caution. The percent presented at the bottom of each variable is the percent of variance in that variable accounted for by statistically significant predictors. Figures 7 and 8 are based on the same analyses; variables are excluded from Figure 7 only for purposes of clarity in

A CAUSAL MODEL FOR EFFECTS OF THE PERRY PRESCHOOL PROGRAM IN THE CONTEXT
OF IMPORTANT BACKGROUND VARIABLES AND INTERRELATIONS

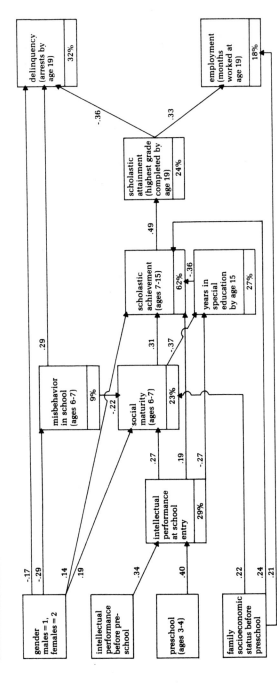

Note. Analyses are based on n = 112. Causal paths are indicated by arrows joining variables, with direction of the arrows from cause to effect. Path coefficients are beta weights in ordinary-least-squares regressions; arrows connect variables only if paths are significant (at p < .10, two-tailed). The directions of paths between variables measured at the same time points are dependent on the model's the-oretical framework and should be interpreted with caution. The percent presented at the bottom of each variable is the percent of variance in that variable accounted for by statistically significant predictors. Figures 7 and 8 are based on the same analyses; variables are excluded from Figure 7 only for purposes of clarity in presentation.

schooling), number of years in special education (representing scholastic placement), and scholastic achievement. The three early adulthood variables are as follows: scholastic attainment (years of schooling completed), delinquency (arrests), and employment (months worked).

In Figures 7 and 8, each arrow indicates a hypothesized path from cause to effect. Arrows appear only when the association between variables is statistically significant (two-tailed $p < .100$). If an arrow does not join two variables, there is no direct causal connection between them, although there may be an indirect connection between them through other variables. The path coefficient next to each arrow is the beta weight derived from ordinary least squares regression analysis; this number indicates the degree of change in an effect, given one unit of change in the cause. The coefficient of determination appears below a variable and indicates the percentage of variance accounted for by the hypothesized variables appearing in the figure. The goal for any dependent variable is to account for 100% of its variance.

Turning first to Figure 7, we examine in isolation the links between preschool and adult success. Preschool had an immediate positive effect on intellectual performance measured immediately before school entry. This improvement in performance is hypothesized to affect initial transactions with teachers and the school environment, leading to greater school commitment and better scholastic placement. These hypotheses are supported by the finding of significant effects of intellectual performance on teacher ratings of social maturity (which implies school commitment), on placement in special education, and on achievement. Both social maturity and special education placement also had their own effects on scholastic achievement. Achievement, in turn, is the only significant direct predictor of scholastic attainment at age 19. Finally, scholastic attainment is the principal predictor of adult success as measured by number of arrests and months worked.

In Figure 8 the effects of preschool are shown in the context of the effects of other important early childhood background variables. An additional measure of commitment to schooling—misbehavior—is also introduced. The effects of the background variables are much as one would expect. Comparing genders (with other variables "held constant"), females are judged by their teachers to be better behaved and more mature. Females also have higher scholastic achievement and are less likely to be arrested than are males. Intellectual performance measured prior to preschool affects only intellectual performance measured at school entry. Family socioeconomic status has direct positive effects on social maturity, scholastic achievement, and employment at age 19. Lastly, although teacher ratings of misbehavior were neither directly nor indirectly affected by preschool, it is interesting that they are significantly related to the number of arrests through age 19.

Several of the intermediate connections in the causal model shown in Figure 8 are also revealing. Intellectual performance at school entry directly affected social maturity, special education placement, and scholastic achievement, and indirectly affected scholastic attainment. Intellectual performance did not affect delinquency or employment except through these scholastic variables. Scholastic achievement was the gateway to scholastic attainment; none of the other school process variables affected scholastic attainment except through their effects on scholastic achievement. Similarly, scholastic attainment served as the gateway to early employment for the other school process variables.

In summary, the causal model confirms that preschool education provides poor children with a "head start" both intellectually and socially. It suggests that the initial effect of preschool on intellectual performance generates long-term effects through its intermediate effects on scholastic achievement directly, and on commitment to schooling and scholastic placement, which indirectly affect scholastic achievement. These intermediate effects are important in their own right—increasing subjects' maturity, reducing their need for special education services, enhancing their scholastic achievement, and eventually helping them to stay in school longer. Finally, the effects of preschool have extended beyond school into the adult world as these young people have found more employment and have experienced less involvement in delinquent activities than their no-preschool counterparts.

A Summary of the Economic Analysis

This section presents the overall results of cost-benefit analysis and consolidates the economic implications of the findings presented in earlier chapters.

The Costs of Early Education

Of the immediate effects of the preschool program, the most obvious is program cost. Compared to program cost, other immediate effects of preschool are much more difficult to measure and to assign a monetary value; insofar as they can be measured, they appear to be of less economic significance. The first step in the calculation of program cost is the estimation of explicit costs. Basic cost data were obtained from Ypsilanti Public School reports of budget data, much of it collected earlier by Weber for her initial study (Weber et al., 1978), and from Ypsilanti Public School accounting records. Explicit program costs are categorized as follows: instruction, administration and support staff, overhead, supplies, and psychological screening.

Instruction costs include teacher salaries, fringe benefits, and the employer's share of social security taxes. Administration and support staff costs represent the contribution of nonteaching special education staff to the preschool program, including the program's management by the Director of Special Education. Overhead costs include a share of the costs of general administrative and nonteaching staff of the school system, as well as maintenance, utilities, and other general school system costs. Supply costs represent the equipment required each year for the classroom. This category includes the costs of food for daily snacks, as well as materials used by the children. Finally, screening accounts for the costs of testing and interviewing to select a sample that was economically disadvantaged, with a relatively poor prognosis of educational success.

There are also implicit program costs that must be estimated to measure the Perry Preschool program's full economic cost to society: imputed interest and depreciation on fixed capital. Imputed interest on fixed capital is calculated to account for the income foregone when fixed assets were employed in the preschool program. It is assumed, in other words, that if these assets had not been used in the preschool program they would have been used in some other way that benefited society. The loss of these other benefits is a cost of the preschool program and it is accounted for by imputing interest on the fixed capital. Depreciation on fixed capital is calculated to account for the decrease in value of fixed assets due to wear, age, and other causes.[31]

Costs by major category for a typical school year (1963-1964) are presented below:

Explicit Costs

Instruction	$26,251
Administration and support staff	1,100
Overhead	1,600
Supplies	480
Screening	115

Implicit Costs

Interest and Depreciation	2,236
Total Program Costs	**$31,782**
Cost Per Child	**$ 1,589**

These costs are in 1963-1964 dollars. Total program costs by year and wave are listed in Table 25, in dollars actually spent in 1962-1967 as well as in constant 1981 dollars both undiscounted and discounted at 3 percent. The average present value of per-child cost for one year of preschool is $4,818 and for two years it is $9,289. Average undiscounted costs for one year and two years are, respectively, $4,963 and $9,708. Year-to-year variations in costs per child result primarily from variation in the teacher-child ratio; the number of children varied from one year to another, while the number of teachers remained fixed.

The cost-per-child figures presented above indicate that the Perry Preschool program was relatively expensive. This is not surprising, since it was a program of high quality for children whose educational prognosis was poor. However, the expensiveness of the Perry Preschool program relative to other programs may easily be exaggerated unless other factors are taken into consideration. One factor is that the Perry Preschool program cost figures are not simply budgeted expenses but upper-bound estimates of the full economic cost of the program to society. For example, the preschool program did not pay anything for the physical facilities it used (many preschool programs use space that is donated or provided at a below-market price), but we imputed a cost for these facilities because there was an opportunity cost to society, since the facilities could have been used for something else. Another factor is that the figures represent the actual costs of the program rather than the minimum cost of producing the program's results. This minimum would have been reached only if the Perry Preschool program was the most efficient possible, but it was an experimental program dealing with many unknowns. There was little knowledge about what was efficient. In addition, there is some evidence from the program that it could have been made more efficient. The student/teacher ratio, a major determinant of program cost, varied between 5

---

[31]This way of estimating the facility costs of the Perry Preschool program, while appropriate in estimating costs to society as a whole, may not be typical of the way educational administrators think about program costs.

Table 25

PERRY PRESCHOOL TOTAL PROGRAM COSTS

Costs	School Year				
	1962-63 $n = 21$	1963-64 $n = 20$	1964-65 $n = 25$	1965-66 $n = 25$	1966-67 $n = 12$
	Wave 0 $n = 13$	Wave 1 $n = 8$	Wave 2 $n = 12$	Wave 3 $n = 13$	Wave 4 $n = 12$
Total costs, current	$19,632	$12,665	$16,583	$19,135	$20,425
Per-child costs, current	1,510	1,583	1,381	1,472	1,702
Per-child costs, 1981	5,223	5,287	4,501	4,624	5,044
Present value[a]	5,071	4,984	4,243	4,359	4,754
	Wave 1 $n = 8$	Wave 2 $n = 12$	Wave 3 $n = 13$	Wave 4 $n = 12$	
Total costs, current	$12,129	$19,117	$18,068	$17,783	
Per-child costs, current	1,516	1,593	1,389	1,482	
Per-child costs, 1981	5,172	5,320	4,527	4,655	
Present value[a]	5,021	5,165	4,395	4,519	

[a]Present value is discounted at 3% per year from the start of the program for each study cohort; thus the first year of preschool is discounted at 3% and the second at 3% compounded for two years, or 6.09%.

to 1 and 6.25 to 1 with no perceptible influence on program results. More important, one year of preschool produced the same effects as two.

In addition to the program costs borne by the general public, there were immediate costs and benefits to the children attending preschool and to their families. There were no fees and all school supplies were provided by the program, so that explicit costs can be set at zero. The only resource required of participants in the preschool program was their time, which therefore constitutes an implicit cost. For the children, the net immediate effect of early education was positive (a benefit) rather than negative (a cost). The program was designed to be enjoyable and enriching; the level of cognitive ability of participants surged substantially ahead of that of the children who did not attend preschool. Thus we may conclude that pre-school attendance produced for the participating children substantial benefits that outweighed the opportunity cost of their time (considered as the satisfaction they would have received from their activities had they not attended preschool). Since it proved impossible to assign a monetary value to this net effect and it is assumed to be positive, we conservatively set it at zero.

The Perry Preschool program had two immediate effects on the parents of children attending preschool: It provided child care for part of the day and it involved home visits in which teachers worked with both children and parents. An exact value for child care (apart from any expected long-term benefits) cannot be determined; however, a lower-bound estimate can be derived from information on the amounts parents in similar populations paid for basically custodial child care. Our estimate is

$299 per child per year in constant 1981 dollars; the discounted present value is $290 for one year and $572 for two years. The home visits required parents to spend time—a cost—but also provided benefits. These benefits might include opportunities for positive social interactions with the teacher and their children during the home visit; services provided by the teacher in conjunction with the home visit (for example, providing information about social services and bringing educational materials to the home); and opportunities to generally interact more positively with their children and to better understand their children's development. Again, these kinds of benefits are nearly impossible to quantify and even more difficult to value monetarily. However, we can continue to assume that the net effect of the home visits was positive. Further, parents' participation in the home visits was voluntary; parents could, and sometimes did, choose not to receive a visitor. Parents' participation in home visits can therefore be interpreted as evidence that participation was (in the parents' own judgment) preferred to the best alternative use of their time.[32] The net effect of home visits for the parents is, for this reason, conservatively estimated to be zero, with immediate benefits left unquantified.

The immediate economic effects of the preschool program for the study are program costs (borne by the general public), opportunity costs of time for participating children and parents, child care and what can generally be described as a higher quality of life for both children and parents. Program costs are precisely estimated; a lower-bound estimate of the monetary value of child care is also produced. For the remaining effects, the value of benefits is determined to exceed time costs, but the amount of this positive net benefit is unknown. In summary, the net present value of the cost of one year of the preschool program is estimated at $4,818 (in 1981 dollars). The net present value of one year's part-time child care provided by the preschool program is $290. Comparable estimates for two years are $9,289 for program costs and $572 for part-time child care.

The Benefits Resulting from Program Outcomes

In previous chapters the effects of early education on school success, early socioeconomic success, and social responsibility have been extensively documented, and the economic consequences of these effects have been discussed. This section summarizes the effects noted above and takes a broader approach to the analysis of economic outcomes by exploring all of the significant costs and benefits, regardless of whether their monetary value can be estimated.

The economic consequences of increased school success can be divided into those accruing to program participants and those accruing to the general public. The general public receives benefits because costs of

---

[32] It can be questioned to what extent parents' willingness to participate in home visits results from the value placed on the immediate effects of the visits, as opposed to expectations of long-term benefits to the child. Here the question is not relevant, since we do not elsewhere measure benefits to the parents of assuring long-term benefits to their children. We would argue that the parents' concern for the long-term welfare of their children extends beyond, and is not substantially dependent on, the expectation of economic transfers from child to parent in the future.

elementary and secondary education are reduced; this cost reduction was discussed in Chapter 2, and its average value per student in the Perry Preschool study amounts to $7,082 (in 1981 dollars, undiscounted). The discounted (at 3 percent) present value is $5,113 for one year of preschool and $4,964 for two years. School success, paradoxically, also represents a cost to the general public, since students stay in school longer; this cost is already included in our calculations through grade 12. On the basis of age-19 interview data on college enrollment and national statistics on educational attainment, the preschool program's average effect on costs of higher education was estimated to be an increase of $1,168 (undiscounted) per person; discounted at 3 percent, the present value is a cost increase of $704 for one year of preschool and $684 for two years. Almost the entire cost is borne by the general public.[33]

Program participants benefit from increased school success by receiving an increased quantity (and possibly better quality) of education. These benefits can be categorized either as consumption benefits (yielding immediate satisfaction) or as investment benefits (yielding satisfaction over an entire lifetime). Some of the investment benefits of school success have been measured in the Perry Preschool study by age 19 and we discuss these when we consider social responsibility and early economic success. Other investment benefits can only be predicted from educational outcomes and will be considered later.

Immediate benefits raise participants' quality of life both in and out of school; there are several measures pointing to increased quality of life for persons who attended preschool: Their achievement scores were higher, as were their grades; they were less likely to be labelled as mentally retarded and placed in special education programs; and they had more positive attitudes toward high school. These results suggest that their school experiences were more worthwhile and enjoyable. Greater school success may also have increased the social status of preschool participants in their schools and communities. Finally, the experiences involved in attending college, apart from their longer-term implications, may themselves be considered benefits.

Investment benefits of school success were measured partially at age 19. Benefits in the area of social responsibility occur in the areas of reproductive events and of crime and delinquency. Women who attended preschool reported fewer pregnancies and births by age 19. This finding is consistent with evidence that the ability to obtain desired family size as well as desired timing and spacing of births increases with the level of education (Michael, 1975). We believe that delaying the onset of reproductive events for teen parents is of benefit both to the study participants and to the general public, but our data are too incomplete at this point to assign a monetary value.

---

[33] All study participants attending college were enrolled in public institutions; tuition at public institutions of higher education accounts for only about 13 percent of total revenues (National Center for Educational Statistics, 1980, p. 144). A number of students obtained subsidized loans for tuition payments, which shifts more of the costs to the general public; the same result occurs with scholarships offered to low-income students. There are unquestionably a number of private costs of school—books, supplies, and transportation, for instance. These are viewed as relatively minor and are not estimated here. Details of all calculations are provided in a technical report (Barnett, 1984).

Efforts to assign a monetary value to effects of preschool in reducing crime and delinquency were considerably more successful. Reasonably complete estimates could be obtained for criminal justice system costs. Costs to crime victims, however, could only be partially estimated.[34] Building on data for crime and its costs through age 20, an extrapolation for lifetime costs of crime was produced. The present value (discounted at 3 percent) of the preschool program's effect on crime costs through age 20 is $1,233 for one year of preschool and $1,197 for two years. Estimates of the effect beyond age 20 are presented later.

The final category in which effects were manifest by age 19 is that of economic success. Benefits were measured in these interrelated areas of economic success: employment, earnings, and economic independence. Compared to subjects with no preschool, those who attended preschool were more likely to be employed at the time of interview and had experienced fewer months unemployed since leaving high school. They had higher median annual earnings at age 19 and were more satisfied with their type of work. They were more likely to have some savings. In conjunction with their greater labor market success the preschool attendees were more likely to consider themselves self-supporting. In this regard they were also less likely to be receiving welfare and received lower payments, on average.

Even for these measures of economic success, we were not able to translate all benefits into monetary values. The benefits of labor market success are measured by the increase in earnings only, which through age 19 is $1,040 undiscounted, with a present value (discounted at 3 percent) of $642 for one year of preschool and $623 for two years. This earnings increase captures some of the benefits from increased employment, but not all of them, as there is some value beyond mere earnings to having more regular employment (and less uncertainty regarding income). In addition, we have no measure of the monetary value of the greater satisfaction with type of work reported. The primary beneficiaries of this labor market success are the preschool program participants and their families. However, a significant portion of earnings, about 25 percent, benefits the general public through increased tax payments. Turning to the participants' increased savings, we have no measure of the amount of increase and thus cannot estimate the monetary value to the participants or the general public. Likewise, the participants' increased economic self-sufficiency, though a widely held and highly prized goal, is a benefit for which we have no complete measure of monetary value. There is certainly some value to both participants and society from participants' avoiding the need for welfare payments. The cost of welfare payments to society as a whole is merely the administrative cost of these payments; the payment itself is not a cost but a transfer from the general public to welfare recipients. That is, although the general public benefits by the amount of the payment plus the administrative cost, the welfare recipients lose the amount of the payment (a loss offset by increased income). In Chapter 3 we found that the estimated decrease in annual payments was $876 undiscounted, with ad-

---

[34] No attempt was made to measure costs of crime and delinquency to those persons committing the acts, except insofar as costs of imprisonment or a criminal record are reflected in foregone earnings.

ministrative costs of 10 percent ($88). The present value (discounted at 3 percent) of the decrease in annual payments is $546 for one year of preschool and $530 for two years, with administrative costs of $55 and $53, respectively.

The effects of the preschool program are unlikely to have ended at the point of our last measurement. Indeed, theory and empirical evidence indicate that the effects observed through age 19 have permanently changed the lives of the preschool participants. These permanent changes can be predicted from the observed effects, and their benefits evaluated over the participants' lifetimes. Some of these changes can be predicted quantitatively, others only qualitatively. Where predictions are quantitative it is possible to estimate the monetary value of benefits. Where predictions are qualitative it is only possible to indicate that benefits are associated with the changes; dollar values cannot be estimated.

Changes in economic success, self-sufficiency, and social responsibility can be predicted quantitatively from observed effects at age 19. These changes have been partially measured at age 19, providing an empirical justification from the sample for their prediction beyond age 19. The benefits predicted are increased earnings, reduced crime costs, and reduced welfare costs. The estimation of monetary values for each of these benefits was described in earlier chapters. Increased earnings is the most important of these because of its magnitude. The present value (discounted at 3 percent) of increased earnings beyond age 19 (including wages, fringe benefits, and other employment-related benefits) is estimated to be $23,813 for one year of preschool, and $23,121 for two years. Reduced crime costs beyond age 20 are estimated to have a present value of $1,871 for one year of preschool and $1,816 for two years. Finally, the present value of reduced welfare costs (administrative costs only) is estimated to be $1,438 for one year of preschool and $1,396 for two years.

In addition to the benefits quantified above, there are a number of other benefits of early education that may be expected but have not been measured in the present study. These predicted benefits are based on the observed improvement in .educational outcomes and the empirical relationship between educational attainment and other important social and economic variables. They are related to such areas as family formation, personal and family health care, the quality of leisure, and consumer activities. It would have been premature to attempt their measurement at age 19; since they have not been measured, there are insufficient grounds for any predictive estimation of their magnitude. They are not considered here.

Summation of Costs and Benefits

To summarize all of the costs and benefits identified, Table 26 lists measured and predicted costs and benefits and the estimated present value of each. As shown in that table, summation of costs and benefits yields a sizeable positive net present value for both one and two years of preschool. Thus, judged simply on its overall return, the Perry Preschool program was a good investment for society. This general conclusion depends to some extent on predictions of costs and benefits beyond age 19.

However, even if the analysis is limited to costs and benefits directly observed through age 19, the data support a very strong conclusion. By age 19 it is clear that there is a positive net present value generated by one year of preschool. In other words, by age 19, fifteen years after the initial investment, the data demonstrate that one year of preschool is a good investment for society.

The degree of confidence that can be placed in the conclusion that preschool is a good investment depends on the margin for error allowed by the results and on the strength of the underlying statistical evidence. From the ratios in Table 26 it can be seen that the size of benefits relative to costs allows considerable margin for error. The present value of benefits exceeds seven times the present value of cost for one year of preschool. In earlier chapters, for each of the variables yielding economic benefits, we presented measures of the statistical confidence with which preschool's effect has been estimated. We also have such measures for preschool's overall effect on measured economic benefits per se through age 19 (age 20 for crime). Table 27 presents our best estimate of preschool's total measured economic benefits for society, and for taxpayers only, together with the estimated standard deviations and p-values. Total benefits to society include benefits for participants, taxpayers, and potential crime victims.

Table 26

SUMMARY OF COSTS AND BENEFITS[a]

Type of Benefit (or Cost)	Benefit or Cost[b] (in dollars)	
	1-yr Preschool	2-yr Preschool
Measured		
Preschool program	-4,818	-9,289
Child care	290	572
Education, K-12	5,113	4,964
Earnings, ages 16-19	642	623
Welfare at age 19	55	53
Crime through age 20	1,233	1,197
Predicted		
College	-704	-684
Earnings after age 19	23,813	23,121
Crime after age 20	1,871	1,816
Welfare after age 19	1,438	1,396
Net benefit[c] (dollars)	28,933	23,769
Benefit-cost ratio	7.01	3.56

[a]Table entries are present values in constant 1981 dollars, discounted at 3% annually.

[b]Costs are indicated as negative amounts.

[c]Column sums differ from net benefits because of rounding.

The information presented in Table 27 indicates that we can be quite confident that preschool has significant economic benefits. We are somewhat less confident that preschool's measured economic benefits through

Table 27

PRESCHOOL'S EFFECT ON MEASURED ECONOMIC BENEFITS[a]

Type of Benefit	Effect	Standard Deviation	p[b]
Taxpayers' and potential crime victims' benefit[c]	$6,544	$3,874	.094
Total social benefit[c]	6,846	4,045	.093

[a]n = 109
[b]The statistical test used is Student's t test; p-values are reported if less than .100.
[c]Present values discounted at 3% for one year of preschool.

Table 28

DISTRIBUTION OF COSTS AND BENEFITS[a]

	Benefit or Cost[b] (in dollars)			
	For Preschool Participants		For Taxpayers and Potential Crime Victims	
Type of Benefit or Cost	1-yr Preschool	2-yr Preschool	1-yr Preschool	2-yr Preschool
Measured				
Preschool program	0	0	-4,818	-9,289
Child care	290	572	0	0
Education, K-12	0	0	5,113	4,964
Earnings, ages 16-19	482	467	161[c]	156[c]
Welfare at age 19	-546	-530	601	583
Crime through age 20	0	0	1,233	1,197
Predicted				
College[d]	0	0	-704	-684
Earnings after age 19	19,233	18,674	4,580	4,446
Welfare after age 19	-14,377	-13,959	15,815	15,355
Crime after age 20	0	0	1,871	1,816
Net benefit[e] (dollars)	5,082	5,224	23,852	18,544

[a]Table entries are present values in constant 1981 dollars, discounted at 3% annually.
[b]Costs are indicated as negative amounts.
[c]Assumes 25% of estimated earnings is paid in taxes.
[d]Some college costs are undoubtedly borne by the participants and their families, but we have no estimate for the amount. The most conservative assumption toward increasing the relative benefits of participants was to assign all college costs to the taxpayers.
[e]Column figures may not sum to net benefits due to rounding.

age 19 alone exceed costs, although this is our best estimate of the outcome. If we also consider the predicted benefits beyond age 19, we can have considerably more confidence. Even if actual benefits through age 19 had fallen 1 standard deviation below the mean, the addition of only one-tenth of predicted later benefits would be sufficient for benefits to exceed the costs for one year of preschool.

The preschool program can be judged by another criterion in addition to that of its returns to society—the fairness of its distribution of costs and benefits. Table 28 offers some perspective on this issue. The estimated present value of net benefit is positive for both taxpayers (especially potential crime victims) and program participants. No one loses; taxpayers and participants both are better off with early education than without it. It should be noted that the program costs of early education were not borne by the participants. Indeed, from our analysis, it is clear that they should not bear these costs. If families of study participants had to pay for even one year of preschool, their returns through age 19 would be considerably lower than their costs. There is little hope that they would recover the cost of two years of preschool even over the entire lifetime of their child. Since taxpayers are the primary beneficiaries, taxpayers should bear the primary burden of financing early education for children from low-income families.

References

American College Testing Program. (1976). *User's guide: Adult APL Survey.* Iowa City, IA: Author.

Arthur, G. (1952). *The Arthur Adaptation of the Leiter International Performance Scale.* Beverly Hills, CA: Psychological Service Center Press.

Bachman, J. G., & Johnston, J. (1978). *The Monitoring the Future questionnaire.* Ann Arbor, MI: University of Michigan Institute for Social Research.

Barnett, W. S. (1984). *A benefit-cost analysis of the Perry Preschool program and its long-term effects.* Ypsilanti, MI: High/Scope Press.

Bissell, J. (1971). *Implementation of planned variation in Head Start.* Washington, DC: U.S. Office of Child Development, DHEW.

Blau, M., & Duncan, O. (1967). *The American occupational structure.* New York: John Wiley and Sons.

Bloom, B. S. (1964). *Stability and change in human characteristics.* New York: John Wiley & Sons.

Bronfenbrenner, U. (1974). *A report on longitudinal programs: (Vol.2). Is early intervention effective?* (DHEW Publication Number OHD 74 – 24). Washington, DC: U.S. Government Printing Office.

Chorvinsky, M. (1982). *Preprimary enrollment 1980.* Washington, DC: National Center for Education Statistics.

Consortium for Longitudinal Studies. (1978). *Lasting effects after preschool* (Final report, Grant No. 90C-1311, to the U.S. Administration for Children, Youth and Families, Office of Human Development Services, DHEW Publication No. OHDS 79-30178). Washington, DC: U.S. Government Printing Office.

Cronbach, L. J., Gleser, G. C., Nanda, H., & Rajaratnam, N. (1972). *The dependability of behavioral measurements: Theory of generalizability for scores and profiles.* New York: John Wiley & Sons.

Donaldson, M. C. (1978). *Children's minds.* New York: Norton.

Dropout rate falling here, statewide. (1982, July 18). *Ann Arbor News,* pp. A1, A3.

Dunn, L. M. (1965). *Peabody Picture Vocabulary Test manual.* Minneapolis, MN: American Guidance Service.

Elliott, D. S., Ageton, S. S., & Canter R. J. (1979). An integrated theoretical perspective on delinquent behavior. *Journal of Research in Crime and Delinquency, 16*(1), 3-27.

Espenshade, T. J. (1984). *Investing in children: New estimates of parental expenditures.* Baltimore, MD: Urban Institute Press.

Freeberg, N. E. (1974). *Development of assessment measure for use with youth-work training program enrollees, phase 2: Longitudinal validation* (Final Report, U.S. Department of Labor, Document No. ETS PR-74-1). Princeton, NJ: Educational Testing Service.

Freeberg, N. E. (1976). Criterion measures for youth-work training programs: The development of relevant performance dimensions. *Journal of Applied Psychology, 61*(5), 537-545.

Garber, H. L., & Heber, R. (1981). The efficacy of early intervention with family rehabilitation. In M. J. Begab, H. C. Haywood, & H. L. Garber (Eds.), *Psychosocial influences in retarded performance: Vol. II. Strategies for improving competence* (pp. 71-88). Baltimore, MD: University Park Press.

Gray, S. W., Ramsey, B. K., & Klaus, R. A. (1982). *From 3 to 20—The Early Training Project.* Baltimore, MD: University Park Press.

Haller, A. O., & Portes, A. (1973). Status attainment processes. *Sociology of Education, 46*(1), 51-91.

Hohmann, M., Banet, B., & Weikart, D. P. (1979). *Young children in action: A manual for preschool educators.* Ypsilanti, MI: High/Scope Press.

Howe, M. (1953). *The Negro in Ypsilanti.* Unpublished master's thesis, Eastern Michigan University, School of Education, Ypsilanti, MI.

Hubbell, R. (1983). *Head Start evaluation, synthesis, and utilization project* (DHHS Publication No. OHDS 83-31184). Washington, DC: U.S. Government Printing Office.

Hunt, J. McV. (1961). *Intelligence and experience.* New York: Ronald Press.

Irvine, D. J. (1982). *Evaluation of the New York State Experimental Prekindergarten Program.* Paper presented at the annual meeting of the American Educational Research Association, New York City.

Jencks, C. S., Bartlett, S., Corcoran, M., Crouse, J., Eaglesfield, D., Jackson, G., McClelland, K., Mueser, P., Olneck, M., Schwartz, J., Ward. S., & Williams, J. (1979). *Who gets ahead? The determinants of economic success in America.* New York: Basic Books.

Jencks, C. S., Smith, M., Acland, H., Bane, M. J., Cohen, D., Gintis, H., Heyns, B., & Michelson, S. (1972). *Inequality: A reassessment of the effect of family and schooling in America.* New York: Basic Books.

Kahn, G. (1982). *School enrollment of 3- and 4-year-olds by race/ethnic category.* Washington, DC: National Center for Education Statistics.

Karnes, M. B., Schwedel, A. M., & Williams, M. B. (1983). A comparison of five approaches for educating young children from low-income homes. In Consortium for Longitudinal Studies, *As the twig is bent...lasting effects of preschool programs* (pp. 133-170). Hillsdale, NJ: Lawrence Erlbaum Associates.

Klaus, R., & Gray, S. W. (1968). The early training project for disadvantaged children: A report after five years. *Monographs of the Society for Research in Child Development, 33*(4, Serial No. 120).

Kohen, A. I. (1973). *Determinants of labor market success among young men: Race, ability, quantity, and quality of schooling.* Columbus, OH: The State University Center for Human Resource Research.

Krech, D., Rosenzweig, M. R., & Bennett, E. L. (1960). Effects of environmental complexity and training on brain chemistry. *Journal of Comparative Physiological Psychology, 53*, 509-519.

Lazar, I., Darlington, R., Murray, H., Royce, J., & Snipper, A. (1982). Lasting effects of early education. *Monographs of the Society for Research in Child Development, 47*(1-2,Serial No. 194).

Levenstein, P., O'Hara, J., & Madden, J. (1983). The Mother-Child Home program of the verbal interaction project. In Consortium for Longitudinal Studies, *As the twig is bent...lasting effects of preschool programs* (pp. 237-264). Hillsdale, NJ: Lawrence Erlbaum Associates.

Levin, H. M. (1977). A decade of policy developments in improving education and training for low-income populations. In R. H. Haveman (Ed.), *A decade of federal antipoverty programs: Achievements, failures, and lessons* (pp. 521-570). New York: Academic Press.

Lindner, E. W., Mattis, M. C., & Rogers, J. R. (1983). *When churches mind the children.* Ypsilanti, MI: High/Scope Press.

Ludlow, J. R., & Allen, L. (1979). The effect of early intervention and preschool stimulus on the development of the Down's syndrome child. *Journal of Mental Deficiency Research, 23,* 29.

Maisto, A. A., & German, M. L. (1979). Variables related to progress in a parent-infant training program for high risk infants. *The Journal of Pediatric Psychology, 4,* 409-414.

Mallar, C., Kerachsky, S., Thornton, C., Long, D., Good, T., & Lapczynski, P. (1978). *Evaluation of the economic impact of the Job Corps Program* (First follow-up report 78-14). Princeton, NJ: Mathematica Policy Research, Inc.

McCarthy, J. J., & Kirk, S. A. (1961). *Examiner's manual: Illinois Test of Psycholinguistic Abilities, experimental version.* Urbana, IL: University of Illinois, Institute for Research on Exceptional Children.

Michael, R. T. (1975). Education and fertility. In F. T. Juster (Ed.), *Education, income, and human behavior.* New York: McGraw-Hill.

Miller, L. B., & Bizzell, R. P. (1983). The Louisville Experiment: A comparison of four programs. In Consortium for Longitudinal Studies, *As the twig is bent . . . lasting effects of preschool programs* (pp. 171-200). Hillsdale, NJ: Lawrence Erlbaum Associates.

Monroe, E., & McDonald, M. S. (1981). *Follow-up study of the 1966 Head Start program, Rome City Schools, Rome, Georgia.* Unpublished paper cited by Hubbell (1983).

Moore, M. G., Fredericks, H. D. B., & Baldwin, V. L. (1981). The long-range effects of early childhood education on a trainable mentally retarded population. *Journal of the Division for Early Childhood, 4,* 93-109.

Nam, C. B., LaRocque, J., Powers, M. G., & Holmberg, J. (1975). Occupational status scores: Stability and change. In *Proceedings of the American Statistical Association,* pp. 570-575.

National Association for the Education of Young Children. (1983). Progress report on the Center Accreditation Project. *Young Children, 39*(1), 35-46.

National Center for Education Statistics. (1980). *The condition of education—1980 edition.* Washington, DC: U.S. Government Printing Office.

National Center for Education Statistics. (1982). *The condition of education—1982 edition.* Washington, DC: U.S. Government Printing Office.

Nieman, R. H., & Gastright, J. F. (1981, November). The long-term effects of Title I preschool and all day kindergarten. *Phi Delta Kappan, 63*(3), 184-185.

Palmer, F. H. (1983). The Harlem Study: Effects by type of training, age of training, and social class. In Consortium for Longitudinal Studies, *As the twig is bent...lasting effects of preschool programs* (pp. 201-236). Hillsdale, NJ: Lawrence Erlbaum Associates.

Phillips, L., & Votey, H. L. (1981). *The economics of crime control* (Sage Library of Social Research, 132). Beverly Hills, CA: Sage Publications.

Piaget, J., & Inhelder, B. (1969). *The psychology of the child.* New York: Basic Books.

Ramey, C. T., Bryant, D. M., & Suarez, T. M. (1984). Preschool compensatory education and the modifiability of intelligence: A critical review. In D. Detterman (Ed.), *Current topics in human intelligence.* Norwood, NJ: Ablex Publishing Company.

Ramey, C. T., & Haskins, R. (1981). The causes and treatment of school failure: Insights from the Carolina Abecedarian Project. In M. J. Begab, H. C. Haywood, & H. L. Garber (Eds.), *Psychosocial influences in retarded performance: Vol. II. Strategies for improving competence* (pp. 89-112). Baltimore, MD: University Park Press.

Rosenberg, M. (1965). *Society and the adolescent self-image.* Princeton, NJ: Princeton University Press.

Sameroff, A., & Chandler, M. (1975). Reproductive risk and the continuum of caretaking casualty. In F. Horowitz (Ed.), *Review of child development research* (Vol. 4). Chicago: University of Chicago Press.

Schweinhart, L. J. (1981). Comment on Intelligence Research and Social Policy. *Phi Delta Kappan, 63*(3), 187.

Schweinhart, L. J., & Weikart, D. P. (1980). *Young children grow up: The effects of the Perry Preschool program on youths through age 15* (Monographs of the High/Scope Educational Research Foundation, 7). Ypsilanti, MI: High/Scope Press.

Scott, J. P. (1962). Critical periods in behavorial development. *Science, 138*(3544), 949-957.

Sellin, T., & Wolfgang, M., E. (1964). *The measurement of delinquency.* New York: John Wiley and Sons.

Simeonsson, R. J., Cooper, D. H., & Scheiner, A. P. (1982). A review and analysis of the effectiveness of early intervention programs. *Pediatrics, 69,* 635-641.

Smith, M. S. (1973). *Some short-term effects of Project Head Start: A preliminary report on the second year of planned variation, 1970-71.* Cambridge, MA: Huron Institute.

Steiner, G. Y. (1976). *The children's cause.* Washington, DC: Brookings Institution.

Tobias, T. N., Baker, M. W., & Fairfield, B. A. (1973). *The History of Ypsilanti—150 years.* Ypsilanti, MI: Ypsilanti Sesquicentennial Committee.

U.S. Administration for Children, Youth and Families (1983). *Ninth annual report to Congress on Head Start services.* Washington, DC: Author.

U.S. Bureau of the Census. (1982a). *Money income and poverty status of families and persons in the United States: 1981* (Current Population Reports: Consumer Income, Series P-60, No. 134). Washington, DC: U.S. Government Printing Office.

U.S. Bureau of the Census. (1982b). *Trends in child care arrangements of working mothers* (Current Population Reports: Special Studies, Series P-23, No. 117). Washington, DC: U.S. Government Printing Office.

U.S. Bureau of Education for the Handicapped. (1976). *A summary of the Handicapped Children's Early Education Program.* Washington, DC: Author.

U.S. Department of Justice, Federal Bureau of Investigation. (1980). *Uniform Crime Reports.* Washington, DC: U.S. Government Printing Office.

U.S. Office of Special Education and Rehabilitative Services. (1983). *Fifth annual report to Congress on special education services.* Washington, DC: Author.

Weber, C. U., Foster, P. W., & Weikart, D. P. (1978). *An economic analysis of the Ypsilanti Perry Preschool Project* (Monographs of the High/Scope Educational Research Foundation, 5). Ypsilanti, MI: High/Scope Press.

Weikart, D. P. (Ed.). (1967). *Preschool intervention: Preliminary results of the Perry Preschool Project.* Ann Arbor, MI: Campus Publishers.

Weikart, D. P., Bond, J. T., & McNeil J. T. (1978). *The Ypsilanti Perry Preschool Project: Preschool years and longitudinal results through fourth grade* (Monographs of the High/Scope Educational Research Foundation, 3). Ypsilanti, MI: High/Scope Press.

Weikart, D. P., Deloria, D., Lawser, S., & Wiegerink, R. (1970). *Longitudinal results of the Ypsilanti Perry Preschool Project* (Monographs of the High/Scope Educational Research Foundation, 1). Ypsilanti, MI: High/Scope Press.

Weikart, D. P., Epstein A. S., Schweinhart, L. J., & Bond, J. T. (1978) *The Ypsilanti Preschool Curriculum Demonstration Project: Preschool years and longitudinal results* (Monographs of the High/Scope Educational Research Foundation, 4). Ypsilanti, MI: High/Scope Press.

Weikart, D. P., Rogers, L., Adcock, C., & McClelland, D. (1971). *The Cognitively Oriented Curriculum: A framework for preschool teachers.* Urbana, IL: University of Illinois.

Weisberg, H. I. (1974). *Short-term cognitive effects of Head Start programs: A report on the third year of planned variation—1971-72.* Cambridge, MA: Huron Institute.

Westinghouse Learning Corporation. (1969). *The impact of Head Start: An evaluation of the effects of Head Start on children's cognitive and affective development* (Vols. I-II). Athens, OH: Ohio University.

Wolfgang, M. E., Figlio, R. M., & Sellin, T. (1972). *Delinquency in a birth cohort.* Chicago: University of Chicago Press.

Wylie, R. (1974). *The self-concept: Volume 1. A review of methodological considerations and measuring instruments* (revised ed.). Lincoln, NB: University of Nebraska Press.

16

Unintended Consequences
Regulating the Quality of Subsidized Day Care

Susan Rose-Ackerman

Abstract

Advocates for the poor frequently support uniform, high federal standards for subsidized social services. While such standards may improve the quality of services for those who qualify, they can also have unintended but important side effects. Stringent regulations may actually curtail the supply of services, promote segregation, and expand the role of large subsidized for-profit firms. All these possibilities are illustrated by the history of federal regulation in subsidizing child day care. The federal government's retreat from regulation in 1980 and 1981 may have had results that—even if unintended—were in many ways salutary.

Economists are fond of identifying the detrimental effects of government regulation on the organization and behavior of regulated industries. Their commentaries have mostly overlooked the case of federal rules that regulate the quality of subsidized services. If higher standards apply to suppliers that receive subsidies than to unsubsidized firms, the needy may end up segregated from other customers. If federal standards are expensive and reimbursement rates are inadequate, the supply of publicly supported services may be held down. If the federal government imposes uniform national rules, this policy may favor large, multistate firms over small, local providers. Each of these possibilities is cogently illustrated by the federal regulation and subsidy of child day care.

THE DAY CARE INDUSTRY

The "Informal" Sector

Only a small fraction of the country's children are cared for during the day by someone from outside the family. A Department of Commerce study for 1974 showed that 80% of children aged 3–13 years old were usually cared for by a parent when they were not in school.[1] Child care of this kind is little affected by state regulation. To be sure, mothers receiving welfare payments for themselves and their children may be given advice on child care by social workers. In a few instances, the state even removes children from their homes

From Susan Rose-Ackerman, "Unintended Consequences: Regulating the Quality of Subsidized Day Care," *Journal of Policy Analysis and Management*, 1983, 3(1), 14–30. Copyright © 1983 by the Association for Public Policy Analysis and Management. Reprinted by permission of John Wiley & Sons, Inc.

if parents physically abuse their offspring or are otherwise unable to care for them. But these are minor exceptions to the *laissez-faire* pattern.

In recent years, however, with the entry of more mothers into the labor force and the growth of single-parent families, the provision of day care by nonrelatives has grown. Considering only the preschool children of mothers who are employed full-time, the proportion cared for by nonfamily members increased from 31% in 1958 to 48% in 1977.[2] Almost three-quarters of the care by nonrelatives is provided by "informal" suppliers of child care services—babysitters who come to a child's home or women who look after a few children in their own homes. The services provided by these informal suppliers are largely unregulated and unreported. Although money may change hands, it is frequently not reported to the tax collector[3] and no organized "firm" exists to provide the service.[4] Exchange babysitting arrangements are also common. One study found that in 48% of the cases where children were cared for in the home of a nonrelative, payment took the form of services.[5] In another study researchers reported that many operators of unlicensed day care homes were afraid of income tax problems or were on welfare and were afraid of losing welfare benefits.[6]

Although most states do not regulate "babysitting" that takes place in the home, thirty-three states plus the District of Columbia do attempt to license family day care homes.[7] However, there is widespread agreement that, even in these states, most small providers escape the licensing net.[8]

The Regulated Sector In spite of the continuing importance of informal providers, organized centers have been playing an increasing role. Between 1960 and 1977, the number of organized centers rose from about 4400 to more than 18,300.[9] At the beginning of this period, the capacity of such centers was about 141,000 while at the end their enrollment was almost 898,000.[10] The percentage of preschool children of working mothers in day care centers rose from 8.2% in 1965 to 14.7% in 1977.[11]

All states require the licensing of these organized centers. The details of the regulations vary from state to state, but all except Mississippi and Connecticut specify maximum ratios of children to staff. Most also have some minimum educational requirements for staff, as well as limits on group size, minimum requirements for program content, and minimum standards for physical facilities.[12] Of course, even if no regulation existed, parental preferences would impose some constraints on center owners. However, unless the regulations perfectly mirror parental preferences, the state requirements limit the competitive advantages that licensed day care centers have over unlicensed alternatives.

Since state laws commonly impose educational requirements on staff, these standards may at first seem consistent with the conventional wisdom of economists, which assumes that suppliers lobby for regulations which give them monopoly profits.[13] However, not all parents believe that professional training is needed in order to provide high-quality child care. In any case, the large number of

persons with professional training in preschool education mean
that any efforts by day care professionals to develop monopoly
power face substantial obstacles.

Thus, state regulation seems to have benefitted neither child
development professionals relative to untrained workers, nor large
well-established firms relative to new entrants. However, the
restrictive effect of state regulations on firms is illustrated by a
recent study that I conducted of the organized day care industry
The study showed that wherever the maximum ratio of children to
staff was fixed by the state at relatively low levels, the number of
places provided by such centers was also relatively low, when compared with states that have weaker regulations.[14] Thus, regulation
appears to restrict entry by raising costs, but it gives no monopoly
power to qualifying firms.

The history of federal regulation of day care has been complex
and full of controversy.[15] However, for some years, federal regulation did subject some day care centers—those that elected to receive
subsidized children—to a fairly rigorous set of controls. The behavior of the day care industry during the period in which these controls applied offers a number of important lessons about the effects
of regulations imposed as a condition for receiving subsidies.

Federal Regulation and In 1968, a group composed of officials of various federal agencies
Subsidy proposed a set of day care regulations called the Federal Interagency Day Care Requirements (FIDCR). The group's proposals followed
the state pattern of regulating child-to-staff ratios, group sizes, and
safety and cleanliness, but the standards were generally more stringent than state rules. The child-to-staff ratios, in particular, were
very restrictive relative to most states' licensing laws. The FIDCR
also established requirements for food service, medical examinations, social service provision to families, parent conferences, and
parent advisory councils.[16]

The status of the FIDCR was initially unclear: Were they to be
viewed as recommendations or as legally binding regulations? In
1975 this question was largely resolved when Congress incorporated a modified version of the FIDCR into Title XX of the Social
Security Act. This act provided social service grants to the states but
gave them considerable freedom to decide how to spend the grants.
In general, about one-fifth of Title XX funds have been spent on the
day care of children. In fiscal year 1979, about $800 million of both
state and federal money went to subsidize day care.[17] About 78% of
these funds were used to subsidize care in organized centers,
although only 61% of the children receiving subsidies were in such
centers [18] The remaining children were cared for by individual
sitters or in day care homes. Thus, strict enforcement of the FIDCR
could have had an important impact on the quantity and quality of
subsidized care.

Almost immediately, however, those who provided day care services complained about the costliness of the FIDCR. In response,
Congress quickly suspended the controversial child-to-staff ratios
and ordered a study of the feasibility of the entire package of regulations.[19] While the study was going on, the remaining FIDCR provi-

sions were meant to be enforced. Although compliance with these other requirements varied from state to state, the FIDCR did seem to impose a set of more stringent requirements on centers that accepted subsidized children. A government-sponsored study of day care carried out by private consultants in 1976–1977 showed that subsidized centers were more likely than others to meet the federal requirements.[20] Even when federal child-to-staff ratios were not legally in force, the distinction between centers that accepted subsidized children and centers that did not continued to be evident; 67% of centers with subsidized children met the federal standards, as compared with only 38% for other centers.[21]

In July 1980 the Department of Health and Human Services issued new draft regulations[22] which took account of the results of the consultant's report.[23] The consultant recommended that the government relax its regulations limiting the number of children in relation to staff and that it pay more attention to limiting the overall number of children in each group or classroom. Shortly thereafter, Congress included a provision in the Omnibus Budget Reconciliation Act of 1980 that suspended the FIDCR.[24] The next year Congress altered Title XX to provide a more general block grant to the states and it eliminated the statutory authority on which the FIDCR had been based, a step which led to the total repeal of the suspended regulations.[25] The law now requires only that federally subsidized children be cared for in centers that comply with state and local regulations. Although one cannot say with certainty how the continued application of FIDCR standards would have affected the pattern of operations of day care centers, some plausible inferences can be made.

REGULATION AND INTEGRATION
It is difficult to achieve a high level of integration by race or income class in day care centers because most centers are relatively small, neighborhood-based organizations which can only be as integrated as local housing patterns. In a world with no subsidized day care, most poor children would be cared for in the informal portion of the market, and day care centers would serve mostly middle- and upper-income children. Those few poor children whose parents did choose centers would be enrolled in facilities near their homes or near their parents' jobs; accordingly, day care centers would have highly segregated clienteles.

The current system, which provides some subsidy for day care, has increased the number of poor children in centers. However, the level of segregation by race and class is high under existing programs. Using the consultant's report mentioned earlier, I calculated several segregation indices for both race and class, which are presented in Tables 1 and 2. In Table 1 the second column records statewide measures of a segregation index that was originally developed by Karl and Alma Taeuber for use in their studies of segregated housing patterns. The index measures the percent of black children who would have to change centers in order for each center to have the same proportion of black children as the proportion of black children in all centers. The numbers for the Taeuber

Table 1.   Indices of segregation by race in day care centers in the U.S., by states, 1976–1977.

	Proportion black[a]	Taeuber index[b]	"Exposure" index of blacks[c]	"Exposure" index of nonblacks[d]	Schnare index[e]
New England					
Maine	0.01	0.63	0.96	0.01	0.03
New Hampshire	0.01	0.64	0.95	0.01	0.04
Vermont	0.01	0.55	0.96	0.01	0.03
Massachusetts	0.18	0.58	0.54	0.12	0.34
Rhode Island	0.24	0.71	0.40	0.13	0.47
Connecticut	0.31	0.77	0.26	0.11	0.63
Middle Atlantic					
New York	0.47	0.58	0.30	0.27	0.43
New Jersey	0.39	0.63	0.29	0.19	0.52
Pennsylvania	0.39	0.77	0.19	0.12	0.69
East North Central					
Ohio	0.30	0.64	0.35	0.15	0.50
Illinois	0.35	0.79	0.19	0.10	0.70
Michigan	0.20	0.63	0.45	0.12	0.44
Wisconsin	0.26	0.76	0.12	0.04	0.84
Indiana	0.20	0.55	0.50	0.12	0.38
West North Central					
Minnesota	0.13	0.68	0.53	0.08	0.40
Iowa	0.13	0.50	0.66	0.10	0.24
Missouri	0.33	0.81	0.17	0.08	0.74
North Dakota	0.02	0.48	0.93	0.02	0.05
South Dakota	0.01	0.78	0.95	0.01	0.04
Nebraska	0.19	0.73	0.37	0.09	0.54
Kansas	0.19	0.73	0.29	0.07	0.64
South Atlantic					
Delaware	0.51	0.50	0.32	0.33	0.35
Maryland	0.44	0.67	0.25	0.20	0.55
District of Columbia	0.87	0.78	0.06	0.43	0.51
Virginia	0.38	0.67	0.27	0.17	0.56
West Virginia	0.20	0.67	0.42	0.10	0.48
North Carolina	0.32	0.76	0.26	0.12	0.62
South Carolina	0.45	0.73	0.21	0.17	0.63
Georgia	0.39	0.86	0.14	0.09	0.78
Florida	0.32	0.79	0.22	0.10	0.68
East South Central					
Kentucky	0.20	0.70	0.40	0.10	0.50
Tennessee	0.39	0.80	0.18	0.11	0.71
Alabama	0.37	0.83	0.16	0.09	0.75
Mississippi	0.54	0.89	0.07	0.09	0.84
West South Central					
Arkansas	0.20	0.73	0.33	0.08	0.58
Louisiana	0.34	0.81	0.16	0.08	0.75
Oklahoma	0.27	0.78	0.22	0.08	0.70
Texas	0.17	0.72	0.32	0.07	0.61

able 1. (*Continued*)

	Proportion black[a]	Taeuber index[b]	"Exposure" index of blacks[c]	"Exposure" index of nonblacks[d]	Schnare index[e]
Mountain					
Montana	0.02	0.60	0.93	0.02	0.06
Idaho	0.01	0.75	0.95	0.01	0.05
Wyoming	0.04	0.43	0.89	0.04	0.07
Colorado	0.09	0.64	0.53	0.05	0.42
New Mexico	0.04	0.47	0.90	0.04	0.06
Arizona	0.08	0.54	0.76	0.07	0.17
Utah	0.03	0.58	0.86	0.03	0.02
Nevada	0.11	0.66	0.39	0.05	0.56
Pacific[f]					
Washington	0.07	0.69	0.53	0.04	0.44
Oregon	0.02	0.69	0.79	0.02	0.20
California	0.20	0.69	0.37	0.09	0.54
Hawaii	0.01	0.54	0.95	0.01	0.04

Sources: The indices were calculated from data collected by Abt Associates as part of the National Day Care Study. The raw data are available on computer tape from Abt Associates. The segregation indices are discussed in Schnare, Ann, "Trends in Residential Segregation by Race: 1960–1970," *Journal of Urban Economics*, 7 (1980):293–301.
[a]Proportion of children in sample who are black.
[b]Taeuber index for blacks versus nonblacks (TB), where

$$TB = \frac{1}{2} \sum_{i=1}^{n} \left| \frac{B_i}{B} - \frac{NB_i}{NB} \right| ,$$

where B_i is the number of blacks in center i, B is the number of blacks in sample, NB_i is the number of nonblacks in center i, NB is the total number of nonblacks in sample, $i = 1, \ldots, n$, where n is the number of centers in sample for which this information was available.
[c]"Exposure" index for black children (BX), where

$$BX = \frac{1}{B} \sum_{i=1}^{n} B_i \left(\frac{NB_i}{B_i + NB_i} \right) .$$

[d]"Exposure" index for nonblack children (NBX),

$$NBX = \frac{1}{NB} \sum_{i=1}^{n} NB_i \left(\frac{B_i}{B_i + NB_i} \right) = BX \cdot \frac{B}{NB} .$$

[e]Schnare index:

$$SB = (Rb - NBX)/Rb, \text{ where } Rb = B/(B + NB).$$

[f]Alaska omitted.

Table 2.   Indices of segregation by income in day care centers in the U.S., by states, 1976–1977.

	Proportion poor[a]	Taeuber index[b]	"Exposure" index for poor[c]	"Exposure" index for nonpoor[d]	Schnare index[e]
New England					
Maine	0.54	0.56	0.27	0.32	0.42
New Hampshire	0.31	0.47	0.53	0.23	0.24
Vermont	0.47	0.36	0.41	0.37	0.21
Massachusetts	0.52	0.60	0.26	0.29	0.45
Rhode Island	0.52	0.53	0.31	0.33	0.36
Connecticut	0.29	0.56	0.46	0.19	0.35
Middle Atlantic					
New York	0.44	0.52	0.37	0.29	0.34
New Jersey	0.31	0.66	0.33	0.15	0.52
Pennsylvania	0.50	0.52	0.30	0.30	0.40
East North Central					
Ohio	0.33	0.71	0.29	0.15	0.56
Illinois	0.27	0.64	0.39	0.15	0.47
Michigan	0.26	0.60	0.38	0.13	0.49
Wisconsin	0.34	0.61	0.38	0.20	0.43
Indiana	0.36	0.52	0.41	0.23	0.36
West North Central					
Minnesota	0.18	0.58	0.49	0.11	0.40
Iowa	0.32	0.56	0.43	0.21	0.36
Missouri	0.40	0.63	0.33	0.22	0.46
North Dakota	0.41	0.55	0.35	0.24	0.41
South Dakota	0.37	0.50	0.43	0.25	0.32
Nebraska	0.51	0.63	0.26	0.27	0.47
Kansas	0.34	0.52	0.42	0.22	0.36
South Atlantic					
Delaware	0.45	0.82	0.16	0.12	0.72
Maryland	0.29	0.75	0.29	0.12	0.59
District of Columbia	0.35	0.65	0.33	0.18	0.49
Virginia	0.22	0.73	0.37	0.11	0.52
West Virginia	0.29	0.62	0.39	0.16	0.45
North Carolina	0.30	0.83	0.21	0.09	0.70
South Carolina	0.53	0.82	0.13	0.15	0.73
Georgia	0.37	0.75	0.24	0.14	0.62
Florida	0.35	0.77	0.23	0.12	0.65
East South Central					
Kentucky	0.34	0.67	0.32	0.16	0.51
Tennessee	0.45	0.70	0.22	0.18	0.60
Alabama	0.40	0.88	0.12	0.08	0.80
Mississippi	0.44	0.69	0.24	0.19	0.57
West South Central					
Arkansas	0.42	0.73	0.23	0.17	0.60
Louisiana	0.28	0.82	0.21	0.08	0.71
Oklahoma	0.46	0.58	0.30	0.26	0.45
Texas	0.23	0.79	0.29	0.09	0.62

ble 2. (*Continued*)

	Proportion black[a]	Taeuber index[b]	"Exposure" index of blacks[c]	"Exposure" index of nonblacks[d]	Schnare index[e]
ountain					
Montana	0.47	0.56	0.32	0.28	0.39
Idaho	0.14	0.49	0.64	0.11	0.25
Wyoming	0.23	0.56	0.48	0.14	0.38
Colorado	0.22	0.68	0.40	0.11	0.48
New Mexico	0.34	0.59	0.36	0.18	0.46
Arizona	0.26	0.57	0.47	0.17	0.37
Utah	0.46	0.57	0.32	0.27	0.41
Nevada	0.21	0.63	0.46	0.12	0.43
acific[f]					
Washington	0.36	0.62	0.34	0.19	0.47
Oregon	0.35	0.52	0.41	0.23	0.36
California	0.31	0.70	0.32	0.14	0.54
Hawaii	0.26	0.69	0.37	0.13	0.49

Sources: The indices were calculated from data collected by Abt Associates as part of the National Day Care tudy (NDCS). The raw data are available on computer tape from Abt Associates. The segregation indices are iscussed in Schnare, Ann, "Trends in Residential Segregation by Race: 1960–1970," *Journal of Urban Economics,* (1980):293–301.

[a]Proportion of children in sample who are poor. Poor children were defined by Abt as children from families rning under $6000 per year.

[b]Taeuber index for poverty. Defined in the same way as in Table 1 but with poor and nonpoor substituted for lack and nonblack.

[c]See footnote c to Table 1.

[d]See footnote d to Table 1.

[e]See footnote e to Table 1.

[f]Alaska omitted.

index are highest in Mississippi, Alabama, Louisiana, and Georgia; but the numbers for some northeast and midwestern states such as Connecticut, Pennsylvania, and Illinois are not much lower. In Table 2 similar indices for the poverty population, defined here as children from families earning under $6000 per year, also show a pronounced sorting.

The tables also show several other measures of segregation in day care centers which are consistent with the Taeuber indices. The "exposure" index for nonblack children measures the average proportion of blacks in each center weighted by the number of non-blacks in that center. It is obviously heavily influenced by the racial composition of day care centers. White children in North Dakota, for example, are not "exposed" to many black children. Ann Schnare developed an index which corrects the exposure index for the racial composition of the state. In states with high Schnare indices the racial composition of centers differs markedly from the racial composition of the children in day care. Under this measure, Mississippi remains the most racially segregated state, but it is tied with Wisconsin. For poverty, Alabama is most segregated, followed at a distance by South Carolina, Delaware, and Louisiana.

Although we have no way to measure the net effect of the public programs, the policies of the 1970s clearly did not produce a high degree of integration. Indeed, a little thought indicates that the program made increased segregation likely. The federal regulation were generally stricter than the corresponding state rules and most had to be applied to all children in a center; subsidized children could not be treated differently from other children in the same facility. Centers could have specialized either in providing care at breakeven prices to the children of cost-conscious parents or in serving some mixture of subsidized children and children whose parents were willing to pay for care that met federal standards. It is likely that some day care centers chose to accept subsidized children along with the restrictions that accompanied the subsidies while others refused subsidized children in order to be free of the restrictions. If the FIDCR child-to-staff ratios had been strictly enforced, the tendency toward segregated care would have been even higher.

I have no direct evidence for these propositions, but other data do suggest that the subsidy programs may have increased the degree of segregation. According to the available data, centers that accept subsidized children had a higher proportion of poor and black children than other centers.[26] In some cases the differences were very large, especially in the deep south.

Data on the percentage of enrollment paid for by government reimbursements not only suggests the specialization of centers but also points to important differences between nonprofit and for-profit centers. Forty percent of the nonprofit centers that accepted subsidized children had their entire budget paid by public subsidy,[27] whereas only 10% of the for-profits that were eligible to accept subsidized children were financed entirely by the government. In general, when a for-profit accepted subsidized children the subsidies were unlikely to account for a large share of the center's budget. This fact does not imply, however, that for-profits as a group were committed to integrating subsidized and unsubsidized children. Three-quarters of the for-profit providers did not even participate in the subsidy program.[28] And the for-profits that accepted subsidized children were more racially segregated than nonprofits.[29] For-profits that accepted subsidized children are less segregated by income class and more racially segregated than comparable nonprofits.[30]

Anecdotal evidence also supports the view that the subsidy program may have encouraged segregation by income level. Thus, a study done for the Department of Health, Education and Welfare claims that ". . . If parents are unwilling to pay the additional cost resulting from lower child–staff ratios, and if reimbursement rates are sufficient to cover the cost of meeting the FIDCR ratios, a center might choose to increase its staff to meet the ratio and serve only subsidized children."[31] In another study, the authors interviewed the director of a charitable nursery who reported: "The welfare department will pay $40 a week for every child which they send, but I have to prove I'm spending $40 on all my other children. The board can't see how we manage unless we take only welfare children. This will solve our financial problems, but we don't want to offer a segregated program."[32]

The point here is not that segregation would be absent without federal regulations, but that these regulations increased the incentives for segregation. Of course, the residential clustering of families by income leads centers to attract customers from similar socioeconomic backgrounds, and some wealthy people and whites prefer their children to be segregated from poor and black children. Nevertheless, federal regulatory requirements seemed to have exacerbated this tendency. If one of the objectives of the federal program was to reduce segregation in the delivery of day care services, then the suspension of the FIDCR appears to have fortuitously helped to further this objective.

UNDERSUPPLY   We have seen how high standards for subsidized care can produce segregated care. These same standards can also limit the number of children able to benefit from a public program. Making the plausible assumption that strict regulations are costly and assuming that reimbursement rates are set to cover the costs of marginal producers, a program with a fixed budget will benefit fewer children as regulations are made more stringent.

Some observers of the day care industry have tried to deny the seemingly obvious tradeoff between high standards and broad coverage. They point to the fact that some high-quality nonprofits seem to be able to break even with lower fees than lower-quality for-profits. The fallacy in this comparison rests on the different cost conditions facing the two types of firms. The high-quality nonprofits frequently do not have to pay the full opportunity costs of the resources they use. They often operate with donated inputs, low-rent space in churches and schools, and volunteer labor.[33] Firms without these benefits must charge higher prices in order to break even at the same quality level. In an effort to provide a high-quality, low-cost program, public authorities might set reimbursement rates at low levels so that only those nonprofit firms using donated inputs are willing to participate. However, such firms may be unwilling to expand in response to the introduction of a public subsidy. They may welcome the subsidy mainly because it permits more selective admission policies.[34] Furthermore, it may be difficult to establish nonprofits which rely on donated inputs, since there is no reason to suppose that increased donations are easily available. Therefore, a public policy that sets reimbursement rates too low to attract for-profits may be unable to find enough centers willing to accept subsidized children. The tradeoff between price and quality has not been eliminated.

Although only about 10% of subsidized children in centers were accommodated by for-profit firms,[35] in most states both for-profits and nonprofits with no donated inputs participated in the program. The presence of such suppliers indicates that the tradeoff has been resolved by keeping reimbursement rates high enough (and enrollment low enough) to permit all types of suppliers to at least break even on their subsidized children.

DAY CARE CHAINS   Stringency is only one aspect of federal regulatory standards. Th
other key characteristic is uniformity. Thus, under FIDCR the sa
set of rules was to be applied to subsidized centers throughout
country. This policy, if strictly enforced, could have favor
national firms over locally based day care centers.

Although chains represent only a little over 5% of all day c
centers in the industry, the sector recently has shown increas
signs of concentration and growth.[36] One chain, Kinder-Care,
emerged as the industry leader both by expanding internally and
purchasing other chain operations. By the end of 1980 it opera
over 700 centers in the United States and Canada and had annu
revenues of $87 million, three times its 1979 revenues. The n
largest firm had revenues of $14.4 million in 1980, followed by t
third-place supplier with revenues of $2 million in fiscal 1980.[37]

In spite of the entrepreneurial ambitions of Kinder-Care,[38] t
fundamental economics of the industry does not suggest that chai
will dominate the supply. Much of the quality of care depends on t
talents and commitment of workers in individual day care cente
rather than on economies of scale. Parents are unlikely to chan
suppliers frequently because of the costs imposed on children.
long as nonprofits have access to low-rent space and as long
people can start day care businesses in their homes, there are fe
benefits from being part of a nationwide organization. Neverth
less, chains do have some other benefits. They have enhanced ba
gaining power in purchasing supplies and financing operations
They can establish brand-name recognition through advertisi
and maintain a reputation for quality, especially with respect
equipment, food, and cleanliness.

They also can compete on the basis of price. More subtle, le
visible aspects of quality can be reduced in an attempt to redu
costs. This may be possible because, as one study claims: "Paren
. . . tend to inquire about costs and to form a general impressic
from the appearance of the center; few ask about program a
teacher qualifications."[40] Kinder-Care's presentation to the Ne
York Society of Security Analysts is quite explicit about the con
pany's attempts to keep tight control over personnel costs.[41] The
hire and fire people as enrollments change in order to keep child-t
staff ratios just below the state regulatory maximums. This strateg
is made possible by the existence of a large unemployed pool
female workers with some training in education, who are ordinari
paid only the minimum wage. The executives, however, blame th
high turnover not on the company's personnel policies but on "th
nature of the people we are employing"; they explain the turnove
as being due to pregnancies and to the female workers' need
follow their husbands' jobs.[42] It should be realized, however, tha
workers in the nonprofit sector are, on the whole, not much bett
paid than those in for-profits, and turnover rates, although lower i
nonprofit centers, are high in both sectors.[43] In any case, Kinde
Care's presentation makes it clear that nominal compliance wit
public standards will not always be synonomous with high-qualit
care.

The quantity of low-priced day care services that just meet stat standards will, of course, depend on how much leeway firms are offered by the state in which they propose to operate. These standards vary widely from state to state. In 1976–1977, for instance, the maximum permitted child-to-staff ratios in the various states ranged from 6.3 in New York to 17.8 in Hawaii.[44] These differences may have encouraged for-profit centers in states with relatively lax regulations, but the variation in standards from state to state may have inhibited the growth of franchises and chains. Standardized requirements for physical capital and materials are especially helpful to chains if there are economies from large-scale purchasing and from the centralized planning of facilities. Even standardization of personnel requirements may be helpful by permitting the firm to maintain a common personnel policy at its various locations. Therefore, the imposition of well-enforced uniform federal standards covering a large segment of the industry might be relatively favorable to chains. Although they would still face strong competition from nonprofits run by child care professionals who try to meet the FIDCR requirements even with no government oversight, chains could gain market share at the expense of small, marginal firms, whether nonprofits or for-profits. To be sure, under the FIDCR this possibility was not realized, because most for-profits did not participate in the subsidy program. The chain operators, along with most other for-profits, have concentrated on serving the children of middle-class working parents. However, an open-ended entitlement program for day care combined with uniform federal regulations could benefit chains so long as subsidy rates are set high enough to permit them to break even.

Another day care subsidy of an entirely different kind may also improve the position of chains. In 1981 Congress changed the income tax law to permit employees to receive employer-subsidized day care without incurring added tax liability.[45] The National Association for Child Care Management, the trade association of for-profit suppliers, supported this provision, believing it would help their members.[46] Some for-profit firms apparently are poised to enter the market that the new tax provision promises to create.[47] In order for employees to benefit from the new provision, however, employers need not supply the day care service directly to their employees. They can, instead, issue vouchers for use in facilities chosen by the employees. The relative attractiveness of vouchers versus on-site day care will depend, in part, upon the regulations written by the Internal Revenue Service. If the IRS requires employers to certify the quality of care, this will encourage the establishment of on-site centers that can be monitored closely. This strategy will favor for-profit chain operators who can provide package deals to large firms. If, as seems more likely,[48] no strict monitoring of quality will be required, voucher programs may be simpler for most firms to administer. The National Association for Child Care Management may have won only a minor victory.

On balance, it is impossible to determine whether a change in industry structure which gives chains a larger role would be desirable, undesirable, or irrelevant. In the absence of parental demands for high levels of quality, for-profit chains can be expected to pro-

vide the minimum quality of service permitted by the rules, in ord
to keep costs down. If the rules, in fact, bear only a rough relatic
ship to quality and if other factors are more important, the quali
of care may not be very high in spite of the regulations. Howev
more costly requirements alone are not the answer. They wou
simply drive marginal for-profit firms from the market and cou
produce a scarcity of day care services for both subsidized a
unsubsidized children. Therefore, the retreat of the feder
authorities in 1980 and 1981 from strong, uniform national regu
tions may well have had constructive results.

FINAL THOUGHTS Neither parents nor child development professionals nor pub
bureaucrats know how to measure accurately the quality of d
care being provided to children. Nevertheless, all three try. Difficu
ties arise if public standards for day care centers do not refle
either professionals' beliefs or parents' willingness to pay. Prof
sionals might abandon the sector to profit-maximizing manage
and parents might turn to the informal sector rather than pay f
regulated care. We have seen that when subsidy is combined wi
regulation another set of related problems can arise. Paying cu
tomers may end up segregated from the needy, not because they a
prejudiced, but because integrated care is costly. Uniform feder
regulations may encourage the growth of for-profit, nationwi
chains. This may be perfectly acceptable if the regulated chains
actually provide care of acceptable quality, but if the corr
spondence between formal regulation and quality is not very clos
it may be a cause for concern. Furthermore, if the regulation
subsidized care reflects the professionals' child care ideals, it
likely to prove costly. Therefore, if the subsidy program has a fix
budget, fewer children will be aided as standards rise. These co
cerns all suggest that unsubsidized and subsidized clients ought
face equivalent regulations. One solution, which is embodied
recent legislation, is simply to require that day care providers ne
only comply with state and local laws relating to day care. T
major disadvantage of this policy is the variation in standards l
location. Given the federal government's limited resources and t
desirability of encouraging the integration of children by incor
level, however, the policy of following state law appears to be
sensible second-best accommodation.

Nevertheless, more innovative strategies are possible. Two alte
natives—vouchers and "proxy" shopping—have been suggeste
Under the former, beneficiaries receive day care "tickets" and c
choose their own supplier, constrained only by the cash value of t
tickets.[49] Under proxy shopping, policymakers rely on the choices
unsubsidized customers to assure high-quality care for the needy
this is done by refusing to provide subsidy payments to a day ca
center unless that center is also selling services to unsubsidiz
clients. If plans such as these could be implemented, they mig
succeed in combining the goals of integration and quality contr
But their success would depend, in part, on whether middle-cla
customers are willing to patronize integrated facilities. It wou

also depend on parents' ability to evaluate day care quality, on whether they are willing to pay for these qualities when they find them, and on whether parents' preferences bear any relationship to the views of child development professionals.[51] On all these points, there is still a great deal to be learned.

Research support provided by the Yale Program on Non-Profit Organizations. I am grateful to Arnold Sheetz and Neil Briskman for extremely able research assistance. Dov Dublin generously shared his computer tape of the Abt Associates data on day care.

SUSAN ROSE-ACKERMAN is Professor of Law and Political Economy, Columbia University.

NOTES   1. U.S. Department of Commerce, Bureau of the Census, *Daytime Care of Children: October 1974 and February 1975,* Current Population Reports, Population Characteristics, P-20, No. 298 (Washington, DC: U.S.GPO, October 1976).
2. Calculated from data in U.S. Department of Commerce, Bureau of the Census, *Trends in Child Care Arrrangements of Working Mothers,* P-23, No. 117 (Washington, DC: U.S.GPO, 1982), Table A-3, p. 42.
3. Moore, Kristin, and Hofferth, Sandra L., "Women and Their Children," in *The Subtle Revolution: Women at Work,* Smith, Ralph, Ed. (Washington, DC:, The Urban Institute, 1981), p. 143.
4. For earlier studies of day care which emphasize the importance of the "informal" sector, see Woolsey, Suzanne, "Pied Piper Politics and the Child-Care Debate," *Daedalus, 106* (1977): 127 – 145; Young, Dennis, and Nelson, Richard, *Public Policy for Day Care of Young Children* (Lexington MA: D.C. Heath, 1973); and Strober, Myra, "Formal Extrafamily Child Care—Some Economic Observations," in *Sex, Discrimination, and the Division of Labor,* Lloyd, C., Ed. (New York: Columbia University Press, 1975), pp. 346 – 375.
5. Data in Bane, Mary J., Lein, Laura, O'Donnell, Lydia, Steuve, C. Ann, and Wells, Barbara, "Child-care Arrangements of Working Parents," *Monthly Labor Review, 102* (October 1979): 53.
6. Keyserling, M. D., *Windows on Day Care: A Report on the Findings of Members of the National Council of Jewish Women on Day Care Needs and Services in Their Communities* (New York: National Council of Jewish Women, 1972), pp. 130 – 132.
7. Gold, Jane Roosevelt, *Administration of the FIDCR: A Description and Analysis of the Federal Day Care Regulatory Role* (Washington, DC: U.S. Department of Health, Education, and Welfare, Office of the Assistant Secretary for Planning and Evaluation, 1980), p. 17.
8. See Keyserling and Moore and Hofferth, *op. cit.;* Prescott, Elizabeth, Milich, Cynthia, and Jones, Elizabeth, *The "Politics" of Day Care* (Washington, DC: National Association for the Education of Young Children, 1972); and Weiner, Samuel, "The Child Care Market in Seattle and Denver," in *Child Care and Public Policy,* Robins, Philip, and Weiner, Samuel, Eds. (Lexington, MA: D.C. Heath, 1978), pp. 43 – 85.
9. The 1960 figure is reported in Steiner, Gilbert, *The State of Welfare* (Washington, DC: Brookings Institution, 1971), p. 52; and the 1977 figure is from Coelen, C., Glantz, F., and Calore, D., *Day Care Centers in the U.S.,* Final Report of the National Day Care Study, Vol. III (Cambridge, MA: Abt Associates, 1979) (hereafter cited as Abt), Table 33, p. 83; The U.S. Department of Commerce, Bureau of the Census, *1977*

Census of Service Industries: Other Service Industries, SC77-A-53, Table Summary Statistics for the United States, 1977, pp. 53-1-2, 53-1 reported a total of 24,800 centers in 1977 using a less restrictive definition of day care center.

10. Source for 1960 is Steiner, *op. cit.*, p. 52, and for 1977 is Abt, *op. cit.*, Table 33, p. 83. The Abt data include both full-time and part-time children. Full-time equivalent enrollment was 791,000.

11. Calculated from U.S. Department of Commerce (fn. 2), Table A-3, p.

12. Gold, *op. cit.*, pp. 1–20. See, e.g., Connecticut State Department Health, Public Health Code Regulations for Child Day Care Centers a Group Day Care Homes (1978); Illinois Department of Children a Family Services, Licensing Standards for Day and Night Care Cente (1980); Commonwealth of Massachusetts, Office for Children, 102 CM 7.00: Standards for the Licensure or Approval of Group Day Care Ce ters (1978). In addition to such measurable requirements as child/st ratios, educational requirements for staff, and square feet of space p child, the states specify various intangible requirements. Thus, in Co necticut the staff must have "the personal qualities to work with ch dren, and to relate to other adults" (p. 3). In Illinois "meals shall relaxed and unhurried" (p. 32) and toys must be available in sufficie number and variety to prevent constant quarreling or waiting (p. 2 The Massachusetts standards require centers to provide "experienc which are in harmony with the life style and cultural background of t children enrolled" (p. 162).

13. Stigler, George, "The Theory of Economic Regulation," *Bell Journal Economics*, 2 (Spring 1971): 3–21.

14. Rose-Ackerman, Susan, "The Market for Lovingkindness: Day Care Cen ters and the Demand for Child Care," Columbia University, New Yor draft, May 1983.

15. The history of the FIDCR is outlined in Nelson, John R., Jr., *The Feder Interagency Day Care Requirements (FIDCR): A Case Study of Feder Regulatory Policymaking* (Washington, DC: National Research Counc 1981), mimeographed, p. 248; and U.S. Department of Health, Educa tion, and Welfare, *The Appropriateness of the Federal Interagency Da Care Requirements* (Washington, DC: U.S. GPO, 1978), Chap. 1 an Appendix B. The politics of day care subsidy and regulation in genera are discussed in Steiner, Gilbert, *The Children's Cause* (Washington, D(Brookings Institution, 1976) and *The Futility of Family Policy* (Wasł ington, DC: Brookings Institution, 1981), and Woolsey, *op. cit.* (fn. 4

16. U.S. Department of Health, Education, and Welfare (1978, Appendix A contains a complete text of the FIDCR. For three- and four-year-ol children the FIDCR required no more than 15 in a group, and a child-te adult ratio not greater than five to one. In a recent survey, only New Yor State had requirements as stringent as this. See Gold, *op. cit.*, p. 10.

17. The total of $803 million also includes two smaller programs admir istered by the Social Security Administration. U.S. Department Health and Human Services, Office of Human Development Service *Social Services U.S.A. FY'79*, No. (HDS) 81-02020 (Washington, DC: U.S GPO, 1981), II-19-25, III-15. The next largest day care program is Hea Start, but other government agencies also support some day car including the Department of Agriculture, the Appalachian Regiona Commission, the Community Services Administration. See U.S. Senate *Child Care: Data and Materials*, report prepared by the staff for th Senate Committee on Finance, 1977, and U.S. Congress, Congressiona Budget Office, *Child Care and Preschool: Options for Federal Suppore* 1978, pp. 23–32.

18. Calculated from U.S. Department of Health and Human Services, III-10-21, Q1-37, Q2-37, Q3-37, Q4-37.

19. Nelson, *op. cit.*

20. See Abt, *op. cit.* (fn. 9), p. 66 and Table 159, p. 176. Within each organizational form (i.e., nonprofit or for-profit), centers which accept subsidized children are generally more likely to comply. The one exception is group size where centers with subsidized children are slightly less likely to comply than those which do not *(ibid.*, p. 66).

21. *Ibid.*, pp. 62–63.

22. See U.S. Department of Health and Human Services, "Interim Regulations Guide: HHS Day Care Regulations," July 1980, mimeo. See also Nelson, *op. cit.*, pp. 256–265.

23. The results of this study are reported in Travers, Jeffry, and Goodson, Barbara Pillar, *Research Results of the National Day Care Study*, Vol. II (Cambridge, MA, Abt Associates, 1980).

24. P.L. No. 96-499, § 1001, 95 Stat. 2655.

25. Omnibus Budget Reconciliation Act of 1981, Pub. L. N. 97-35 §2352, 95 Stat. 357. The Department of Health and Human Services repeal of the FIDCR is found in 47 Fed. Reg. 7668 (February 22, 1982). A concise summary of the recent changes in the law and the regulations is in Zeitlin, J., and Campbell, N.D., "The Impact of the Economic Recovery Tax Act of 1981 and the Omnibus Budget Reconciliation Act of 1981 on the Availability of Child Care for Low-Income Families," *Clearinghouse Review, 16*(4) (1982): 297–301. The elimination of the FIDCR's statutory authority was supported by the National Association for Child Care Management (NACCM), the representative of the proprietary centers. See "News from NACCM," August 2, 1981; *NACCM NEWS*, April 1981.

26. Abt, *op. cit.* (fn. 9), Table 65, p. 107. In only two states (Michigan and Texas) do centers which accept subsidized children have a lower percentage of black children than centers which do not. The Texas result can probably be explained by the large Hispanic population.

27. Over half (57%) received 80% of their budget from subsidies. *Ibid.* p. 158.

28. *Ibid.*, p. 83.

29. *Ibid.*, Table 60, p. 102. Centers with no subsidized children are, however, even more racially segregated.

30. *Ibid.*, Tables 55–56, 60–61, pp. 98–99, 102–103.

31. See Conly, Sonia Rempel, *Cost Implications of the FIDCR* (Washington, DC: U.S. Department of Health, Education, and Welfare, Office of the Assistant Secretary for Planning and Evaluation, 1980), p. 26.

32. Prescott, Milich and Jones, *op. cit.* (fn. 8), p. 9.

33. Abt, *op. cit.* (fn. 9), Table 126, p. 152.

34. Jackson, Emma, "The Present System of Publicly Supported Day Care," in Young and Nelson, *op. cit.* (fn. 4), pp. 21–46, and Keyserling *op. cit.* (fn. 6), p. 93.

35. Abt *op. cit.* (fn. 9), p. 45 and Table 33, p. 83.

36. *Ibid.*, Table 34, p. 83. This category is called "group for-profits" in the table. Overall, for-profit firms cared for 37% of the children in centers and accounted for 41% of all centers. The 1977 Census of Service Industries, using a definition of day care center that differed from the Abt study, counted 10,641 nonprofits and 14,172 for-profits. The Census excluded publicly run centers. The for-profits accounted for 48% of total receipts of $829 thousand in 1977. U.S. Department of Commerce, Bureau of the Census, *1977 Census of Service Industries*, Geographic Area Series, Sc77-A-53 (Washington, DC: U.S. GPO, 1981). HEW figures from 1970 listed 1200 public centers, 5600 private nonprofits, 8400 for-profit, and 1400 not reported. Their capacities were 50,700, 234,000, 293,000, and 48,100, respectively (reported in Keyserling, *op. cit.* p. 73). For-profit centers not connected with chains are mainly small, marginal firms

37. The data on the firms in the industry were obtained from "Children's World, Inc.," *Moody's OTC Industrial Manual* (1981), p. 1194; "Kinder Care Learning Centers," *Moody's Investors' Fact Sheets —OTC, 4* (October 13, 1981): Sec. 31 File 04453; "Making Millions by Baby-Sitting," *Time*, July 3, 1978, p. 65, "Child Care Grows as a Benefit," *Business Week*, December 21, 1981, pp. 61, 63; Ling, Flora, "Baby-Sitting is Big Business," *Forbes*, July 24, 1978, pp. 80—84, and *Forbes*, June 25, 1979, pp. 67—69.

38. See Smith, Geoffrey, "Perry Mendel's Golden Diapers," *Forbes*, June, 1979, p. 69.

39. Forty percent of nonprofits and 2% of for-profits used donated space. Donated equipment was used by 35—40% and 10—15%, respectively. Nonprofits also made greater use of volunteer labor (Abt, *op. cit.* (fn. Table 126, p. 152).

40. Prescott, Milich, and Jones *op. cit.* (fn. 8), p. 46.

41. Mendel, Perry, and Grassgreen, Richard, "Kinder-Care Learning Centers, Inc.," presentation to the New York Society of Security Analysts, July 16, 1980, *Wall Street Transcript*, March 24, 1980, pp. 57-331—57-33

42. Mendel and Grassgreen, *ibid.*

43. Abt, *op. cit.* (fn. 9), pp. 141, 156.

44. *Ibid.*, p. 173. These are averages which combine the separate standards for each age group.

45. Economic Recovery Tax Act of 1981, P. L. 97-34 §124 (e), I.R.C. §129. The same act also changed the tax credit available when a child's parents work. Until 1981 this subsidy did not favor one kind of day care over another because it was not accompanied by any regulations that would affect the quality of care. In 1981, in addition to increasing the level of the credit for lower-income families, Congress also mandated that if children are cared for in centers which enroll more than six children then the center must comply with applicable state and local laws; this change may favor both larger centers and individual babysitters at the expense of unlicensed group homes. Economic Recovery Tax Act of 1981, P. L. 97-34, §124 (d): I.R.C. §44A (c)(2)(C), 129. See Zeitlin and Campbell, *op. cit.* (fn. 25), pp. 290—291.

46. "The Newest Fringe: Employer-Paid Child Care," *NACCM News*, October 1981.

47. "Child Care Grows as a Benefit," *Business Week*, December 21, 1981, pp. 60, 63.

48. Past practice suggests that the IRS will be unwilling to become an agency charged with determining the quality of day care. The IRS does not check the quality of day care provided under the individual child care deduction, and a tax law provision permitting the rapid write-off of employer-run centers that meet certain quality standards has not produced any IRS monitoring of quality.

49. For a discussion of the use of vouchers to provide day care for the needy see Young and Nelson, *op. cit.* (fn. 4). The vouchers can, of course, be issued by employers under the Economic Recovery Tax Act of 1981. See text.

50. For a fuller discussion of this idea, see Rose-Ackerman, Susan, "Social Services and the Market: Paying Customers, Vouchers and Quality Control," *Columbia Law Review, 83* (October 1983), forthcoming.

51. The National Day Care Study [Travers and Goodson *op. cit.* (fn. 23)] isolated determinants of high-quality day care, but failed to measure parental understanding of or willingness to pay for these characteristics.

III

INCOME MAINTENANCE
AND EMPLOYMENT

The 1970s were the era of the federal government's great social experiments in
elfare reform. These income maintenance experiments, in urban New Jersey
ad Pennsylvania, in rural North Carolina and Iowa, in Gary, Indiana and in
eattle and Denver, were designed to test the effects of changing the welfare
stem to a "negative income tax" (NIT).

The Seattle and Denver Income Maintenance Experiment (SIME/DIME),
hich began in 1970, was the largest and the last of the four experiments. Almost
)00 families in Seattle and Denver were randomly assigned to one of eleven
perimental NIT treatment plans or to no treatment (control group). Participa-
on in the experiment was for either three or five years. As was true for the other
ree NIT experiments, the primary emphasis of SIME/DIME was to examine
e work disincentive effects of the income maintenance program. SIME/DIME
dditionally paid special attention to the program's impact on marital stability.
hapter 17 is a nontechnical overview of the final report on the SIME/DIME
roject that was prepared by Felicity Skidmore for the U.S. Department of
Iealth and Human Services, based upon the technical reports prepared by SRI
iternational and Mathematica Policy Research.

In addition to Skidmore's excellent summary, the impact of SIME/DIME
ontinues to be examined by evaluation researchers in secondary analyses of the
xceptionally rich SIME/DIME database. Space constraints prohibited us from
ncluding other articles in this section, but we refer the interested reader to the
ontinuously growing corpus of technical literature spawned by SIME/DIME.
among this body of work are two interesting papers published in 1983 by Gary
urtless and David Greenberg and by Greenberg and Harlan Halsey.

Because the NIT would extend benefits to the working poor, a primary focus
f the income maintenance experiments was to examine the impact of
articipation in an NIT program on work incentives. In addition, a number of
ederal government program initiatives focused specifically on improving the
mployment potential of youth whose employment possibilities otherwise were
kely to be limited.

The Comprehensive Employment and Training Act (CETA) program,
stablished by Congress in 1972 and eliminated in 1982, provided training and
mployment opportunities for disadvantaged workers and hard-to-employ
ersons. In Chapter 18, Laurie Bassi presents findings from an analysis of
ETA's impact on the posttraining earnings of participants. CETA was an

actual program, not an experiment or demonstration, and so the problems c
selection bias and the selection of an appropriate comparison group are a majc
focus of Bassi's analysis. Data used for the study were obtained from th
Continuous Longitudinal Manpower Survey. Findings suggest that CETA ha
had a positive and often significant effect on participants' earnings and tha
women benefit more from the program than do men.

The Youth Employment and Demonstration Projects Act of 1977 (YEDPA
was designed to provide both jobs and future career-planning skills for youth
Two demonstration programs funded under YEDPA were the Youth Incentiv
Entitlement Pilot Projects (YIEPP) and the Public versus Private Sector Job
Demonstration Project.

Previous programs designed to increase the employment of teenagers typicall'
had not paid explicit attention to the problem that such programs might hav
negative school enrollment effects. The YIEPP was a demonstration of ;
subsidized employment program for teenagers accompanied by a requiremen
that participants continue in school. Specifically, the YIEPP offered a minimun
wage job, part-time during the school year and full-time during the summer, tc
low-income teenagers who were still enrolled in school.

In Chapter 19, Farkas, Smith, and Stromsdorfer present findings on th
impact of the YIEPP on youth employment and school enrollment as well as or
employment displacement, or YIEPP fundings of jobs that would have beer
available in the absence of the program. Because the YEDPA required that al
eligible youths who wished to participate be given a program job, randon
assignment could not be used to measure program effects. Thus, as was the cas
for Bassi's study of CETA, selection of an appropriate comparison group was a
major study design decision. Farkas et al. found large positive employmen
effects for the YIEPP participants, suggesting that the unemployment of these
youths is largely involuntary due to insufficient demand at the minimum wage.
They also found small positive school enrollment effects and an employment
displacement rate of 31.6 percent.

The Public versus Private Demonstration was designed to identify differences,
if any, between the two sectors' ability to improve work attitudes, skills, and
youths' chances to find and keep unsubsidized jobs. Like the YIEPP, this
demonstration provided minimum wage jobs to disadvantaged youth. Unlike the
YIEPP, however, the demonstration's target population had to be out of school,
and random assignment was used to allocate participants to jobs in the public or
private sector.

James Gilsinan's assessment of this demonstration (Chapter 20), however, is
concerned less with the policy questions addressed in the demonstration itself
than with an evaluation of the attainment of a more general YEDPA goal, that of
"knowledge development" concerning solutions to the meta-level problem of
youth unemployment. In Gilsinan's view, although the demonstration produced
much useful "information," it was not considered successful because it produced
little "knowledge." Suggestions are offered for making evaluations more useful

program operators and for improving evaluation design to facilitate greater ontributions to knowledge.

REFERENCES

urtless, G., & Greenberg, D. (1983). Measuring the impact of NIT experiments on work effort. *Industrial and Labor Relations Review, 38* (July), 592-605.

reenberg, D., & Halsey, H. (1983). Systematic misreporting and effects of income maintenance experiments on work effort: Evidence from the Seattle-Denver experiment. *Journal of Labor Economics, 1*, 380-407.

17

Overview of the Seattle-Denver Income Maintenance Experiment Final Report

Felicity Skidmore

The Seattle-Denver Income Maintenance Experiment (SIME/DIME) was the last in a series of four large-scale income maintenance experiments undertaken in the late 1960s and early 1970s to measure the disincentive effects of cash transfers on the market work of those eligible for them.

The purpose of this summary is to provide an overview of the rationale behind the income maintenance experiments in general and SIME/DIME in particular; a brief description of SIME/DIME experimental design; and a synopsis of the SIME/DIME research results.

THE POLICY CONTEXT

In the mid 1960s, a consensus emerged among policy analysts that there were potential problems with the existing set of transfer programs available to those in need. Programs were believed to be fragmented and characterized by variations in benefit levels and administrative access among different types of families. In particular, the working poor in two-parent families were largely excluded. In 1966, the Aid to Families with Dependent Children-Unemployed Father (AFDC–UF) program covered less than 100,000 families, although one-third of all the poor were in two-parent families where the husband worked full-time all year round. The existing set of transfer programs was also asserted to be antifamily. For example, one possible way a poor father could help his family would be to leave his wife and children—thus enabling them to apply for AFDC.

A variety of policy reform proposals were being developed during this period, such as the Heineman Commission's 1969 proposal for a federal negative income tax with universal eligibility. Since a major objective of such proposals was to extend coverage to the working poor, it was considered important to determine if the benefits of increased coverage would be offset by reductions in work. The major reason for the income maintenance experiments was to measure how strong the work disincentive of such a program might be.

Other policy concerns of the period also shaped the design of SIME/DIME. First, the 1960s and early 1970s saw a rapid increase in rates of divorce and separation, and hence, the proportion of female-headed families. This development focused attention on whether a negative income tax with universal eligibility would increase martial stability. Second, "Great Society" programs were not conceived primarily as income support, but rather as a way to increase the ability of the poor to be economically self-sufficient. This led to the question of whether a job counseling and education or training subsidy program administered simultaneously with a negative income tax could offset the reductions in work that might result from the negative income tax alone.

Four income maintenance experiments were undertaken, starting with the New Jersey Experiment in 1967, including the Rural (1968) and Gary (1971) Experiments, and ending with SIME/DIME, the subject of this overview. SIME/DIME was the largest of the four experiments—indeed larger than the other three combined—and lasted for the longest period of time. For this reason, its results can be viewed with the most confidence.

From Felicity Skidmore, "Overview of the Seattle-Denver Income Maintenance Experiment Final Report," Office of Income Security Policy, Office of the Assistant Secretary for Planning and Evaluation, U.S. Department of Health and Human Services, May 1983. Washington, DC: U.S. Government Printing Office.

The next section of the overview discusses the potential of social experimentation as a policy research tool. The third section describes the design and administration of SIME/DIME, and the rest of the overview presents the major research findings that resulted from the analysis of SIME/DIME data.

SOCIAL EXPERIMENTATION

A social experiment is a field test of one or more social programs—or, to use the phraseology of the natural sciences, a test of one or more "treatments." A social experiment is a field test in the sense that families or individuals are actually enrolled in a pilot social program offering some type of special benefit or service. It is "experimental" in the sense that families or individuals are enrolled in each of the tested programs on the basis of a random assignment process, for example, the flip of a coin. To draw conclusions about the effects of the treatments, it is necessary to collect information about the people who are enrolled in each experimental program and about those who receive no special treatment (called the control group), and then to compare them on the basis of the collected information. If the composition of each of the groups is determined by a random process and the groups are composed of similar families or individuals, any differences in measured behavior between the groups can be attributed to the effects of the programs being tested.

It is the random assignment procedure that gives social experimentation its advantage as a policy research tool. Most nonexperimental data sources are simply observations of behavior or situations resulting from a myriad of unspecified and indeterminate influences. With such nonexperimental data, one can observe factors that appear to change simultaneously or sequentially. However, at best, only tentative conclusions can be drawn about causality. Since experimentation can deliberately inject a new element into an environment, keeping everything else the same, subsequent changes can be attributed to the influence of the new element within known statistical confidence intervals.

This cause-effect characteristic does not, of course, guarantee that social experiments will produce definitive findings; the treatment may turn out to have no effect or to have an effect that is not precisely measurable. And even if there are definitive findings, there is no guarantee that these findings will be those that were expected by the designers of the experiment or will be useful for policy purposes. The scientific success of the experiment depends on several important factors:

—how precisely the propositions to be tested can be formulated;
—how the well experiment is designed to test those propositions;
—how large the experimental and control groups are and how long is the period over which they experience the treatment;
—how much difference the treatment makes to the environment faced by the experimental group compared to the otherwise identical environment faced by the control group—in other words, how strong the treatment is;
—the extent to which unforeseen or uncontrollable situations and events distort the observed experimental-control comparison.

It is worth expanding briefly on each of these factors.

The propositions to be tested. In order to test whether something is the cause of something else, it is important not only to define the treatment and the hypothesized effect clearly and unambiguously, but also to be able to spell out the logic of the mechanism connecting the treatment to the hypothesized effect. If the issue of policy interest cannot be given prior shape in this manner, the unique analytic strength of the experimental approach is not worth its expense.

The primary focus of SIME/DIME—the effect of income maintenance on work effort or labor supply—was a good subject for experimentation from this point of view. Economists had developed a rigorous and widely accepted theory of how changes in effective wage rates and unearned incomes caused changes in individual labor supply, i.e., the number of hours people worked. The direction of the expected experimental effect was clear and so was the expected cause-effect mechanism. An increase in unearned income or a decrease in the effective wage rate were hypothesized to lead to decreases in labor supply. By the late 1960s, analyses of nonexperimental survey data had yielded numerical estimates of the magnitude of such decreases. However, the wide range of available estimates suggested that social experimentation was an appropriate research strategy to improve the accuracy of the numerical estimates.

The design of the experiment. Given a well-defined treatment, an expected effect, and an expected cause-effect mechanism, the next step is to design an experiment that will clarify the cause-effect relationship. Developing such a design is complex. The basic aim, however, is straightforward: to introduce deliberate and systematic variations in the strength of the treatment and in the characteristics of those people exposed to it, so that the resulting pattern of behavorial responses permits identification of how the effects vary both as the treatment changes *and* as the characteristics of those exposed to the treatment change. If the number of treatment variations is numerous in comparison to the number of enrolled families or individuals, the experiment may fail to detect the impact of each of the tested variations with adequate precision. In this case the experiment will have failed in its basic purpose.

For this reason, experiments cannot be designed to test everything. While large-scale social experiments can and do collect a great deal of information on many issues, the most precise data collected will relate to the central issues motivating the experimental design. In the case of SIME/DIME, the experiment was in fact designed to test the effect of two different kinds of social programs on participant work effort. As has been noted, the two policies were a variety of cash transfer or negative income tax programs and several combinations of job counseling and education or training subsidy programs. Many other topics were examined in SIME/DIME—in particular, the relationship between cash transfers and marital stability—but it should be kept in mind that the statistical advantages of the experimentally generated data are somewhat greater for the labor supply analysis.

Size of sample and strength of treatment. Other things equal, the larger the sample size, the greater the ability of an experiment to detect treatment effects and the greater the statistical confidence that can be placed in the findings. Having a larger sample size than all the other income maintenance experiments combined, SIME/DIME produced the results to which one could attach the greatest degree of confidence.

The "strength" of the cash transfer treatment was greater in SIME/DIME than in the other experiments, both in terms of the generosity of the benefit levels and in terms of the length of the treatment period. The more generous the benefit levels, the greater the expected effects on behavior. Given this expectation, the more generous the benefit level, the smaller is the treatment group size required to detect the effect of the treatment at any given level of statistical confidence. In addition, to the extent that it takes time for families to learn what the treatment means and to make adjustments in behavior, longer treatment periods will also increase the likelihood of detectable response.

With respect to treatment generosity, however, a caveat is in order. Although a stronger treatment is more likely to advance scientific understanding of labor supply behavior, it will not yield better estimates of the probable labor supply response to a national cash transfer program if the benefits proposed in that program differ substantially from those in the experiment. Care must be exercised, therefore, in drawing policy implications from the experimental results.

The treatment-control comparison. We have been discussing random assignment of treatments to subjects in an experimental study. One "treatment" that is frequently tested is no treatment at all, in other words the "control" treatment. Families or individuals enrolled in the control group are not eligible for any special benefit or service, but provide the same information to the experimenters as that provided by the enrollees in the experimental treatments. The control families, of course, do not exist in a vacuum. They are eligible for and participate in ongoing programs similar to the experimental treatments. It is possible to imagine a situation in which, midway through an experiment, a regular government program is implemented that is exactly like the experimental treatment. In such a case, all the difference in behavior between the experimental and control groups might disappear. This is not to say that the treatment has lost its effect—merely that the difference in environments experienced by experimental and control families has disappeared. In the case of SIME/DIME, for example, the members of the control group were potentially eligible for the AFDC and AFDC-UF programs and Food Stamps as well as for a variety of job training programs. Any observed effects of the experiment, therefore, must be interpreted as the differential effects of the experimental treatment compared to existing government programs. Thus, an observed experimental-control differences in outcomes must be interpreted as estimates of the effect of replacing the early 1970s status quo with the experimental programs.

In addition to such external influences, certain occurrences within the experimental environment may pose problems for the interpretation of the results. Two that are inevitable in any experiment are sample attrition and mismeasurement of behavior. Attrition occurs when members of the experimental and control groups drop out of the sample and stop providing information to the experimenters. Mismeasurement occurs when information used to measure the effect of the treatments turns out to be inaccurate. Since most of the information used to evaluate SIME/DIME was supplied in personal interviews, the predominant form of mismeasurement here consisted of misreporting of income or hours worked and earnings information.

If we could guarantee that the incidence of attrition and misreporting are random and thus identical for the experimental as well as the control group, the observed experimental responses would provide undistorted estimates of treatment effects. But the incentives to drop out of the experiment and to report income incorrectly may differ for the two groups. With respect to the misreporting bias, experimentals might be expected to underreport in comparison with controls, because the less income they report the larger will be their benefit. Of course, controls receiving AFDC face a similar incentive *vis-a-vis* the welfare office, but less so with respect to the SIME/DIME interviewers. Controls' incentive to underreport earnings to the welfare office, however, may be relatively lower than experimentals', since AFDC benefit levels were lower than SIME/DIME benefit levels. If controls report to the interviewers a higher fraction of their earnings than do experimentals, then the effect of the misreporting bias is to overestimate the actual work reduction effect. Of course, if experimentals report a higher fraction of their earnings than controls the actual work reduction effect is underestimated. With respect to attrition, people in the control group and in low-benefit treatment might be expected to drop out with greater frequency than those on the high-benefit plans—because they have less to lose by leaving the experiment. But those on the high-benefit plans can be expected to have a larger behavorial response to the experiment. Therefore, attrition may cause the observed experimental-control difference to overestimate the actual effect, unless the difference in attrition rates can be explained by measureable family character-istics and these characteristics are controlled for in the analysis.

Additional difficulties in interpreting results may arise in an experiment like SIME/DIME, where different types of treatments were tested in combination. While SIME/DIME was designed so that the independent effects of the two dif-ferent types of treatment (cash transfers and job counseling/training subsidies) could be separately measured, the separation of effects introduces additional sta-tistical complexity, and thus, potential controversy into the analysis of the experi-mental data.

Finally, there are inherent limitations in social experiments regardless of design quality. Because experiments have finite durations, they may not com-pletely represent the conditions of a fully implemented, permanent national pro-gram. Participants may alter their behavior in response not only to the program options being tested, but to the experiment itself, a phenomenon known as the "Hawthorne effect". Furthermore, participants, knowing the experimental condi-tions are only temporary, may not respond in the same way they would to a per-manent program. For example, given the opportunity to participate in an income maintenance experiment, individuals may use it to increase their schooling; also a temporary activity.

THE DESIGN AND IMPLEMENTATION OF SIME/DIME

SIME/DIME was launched in Seattle, Washington, in 1970 and extended in 1972 to a second site in Denver, Colorado. The prime contractors for SIME/DIME were the States of Washington and Colorado, which subcontracted with SRI International for the design, operation, and research evaluation of the experi-ment. SRI International, in turn, subcontracted with Mathematica Policy Re-search (MPR) for the administration of the cash transfer or negative income tax (NIT) treatment and all the field data collection from both experimental and con-trol groups. For the administration of the job counseling/training subsidy treat-ment, SRI subcontracted with the Seattle Central Community College and the Community College of Denver.

The experiment involved almost 5,000 families. In order to test whether, and if so to what extent, behavioral responses varied by duration of treatment, the families in the experimental groups were also randomly assigned to a 3-year or 5-year treatment duration. The four basic treatment combinations were (a) NIT only, (b) counseling/training only, (c) NIT and counseling/training, (d) no treat-ment. The NIT and counseling treatments are described briefly below.

Cash transfer (NIT) treatments. The cash transfer treatment tested in SIME/DIME, as in the previous income maintenance experiments, consisted of a series of negative income tax plans. A negative income tax is simply a cash tranfer pro-gram in which there is (a) a maximum benefit (called the guarantee) for which a family is eligible if it has no other income and (b) a rate (called the benefit reduc-tion or tax rate) at which the maximum benefit is reduced as other income rises. The combination of a gruarantee and a tax rate defines an income level (called the breakeven level) at which the benefit falls to zero. Families whose incomes rise above this breakeven level no longer receive benefits, although they retain program eligibility and regain benefit entitlement should their income fall below the breakeven level at some future date.

In all the experiments, more than one version of the negative income tax treatment was tested. This was to provide information on how behavioral re-sponses might differ as program structure varied—making the results useful for predicting response to a wide range of cash transfer plans. Table 1 shows the plans tested: three guarantee levels and four tax rates, combined in such a way as to produce 11 negative income tax plans in all. The three guarantee levels for a family of four in 1971 dollars were $3,800, $4,800, and $5,600.[1] The dollar guarantee levels varied with family size (as does the poverty line) with larger families qualifying for higher guarantee levels under a given NIT plan. In the three earlier income maintenance experiments, only constant tax rates were tested (that is, tax rates that remained the same for every level of family income below the breakeven). SIME/DIME tested two constant tax rates: 50% and 70%. In addition to constant tax rates, however, SIME/DIME also testd two declining tax rate schedules. These rates were 80% and 70%, respectively, for the first $1,000 of nonexperimental income and then declined by 5 percentage points for each additional $1,000 of nonexperimental income.[2]

TABLE 1.—NEGATIVE INCOME TAX PLANS TESTED IN SIME/DIME

Initial guarantee [1]	Tax rate			
	50 percent	70 percent	70 percent (declining)	80 percent (declining)
$3,800	X	X	X	X
$4,800	X	X	X	X
$5,600	X	X		X

[1] 1971 dollars.

A major point to keep in mind about the cash transfer plans tested is that they constituted a rather generous benefit range compared with transfer programs now in place or contemplated in most policy proposals. The SIME/DIME treatments averaged out to a negative income tax plan with a maximum benefit for those with no other income of about 115% of the poverty line and an effective marginal tax rate of about 50%. (The effective marginal tax rate was this low because families assigned to the declining tax plans typically face rather low marginal rates). With respect to breakeven level (that is, the income level below which experimental families receive positive benefits), 88% of the two-parent families had breakeven levels above 150% of the poverty line, and 58% were above twice the poverty line. For female-headed families the proportions were 83% and 43% respectively.[3]

The relative generosity of the average benefit received by experimental families as compared with the average received by the control group can be seen in Table 2, which shows the average amount of experimental and other transfers received over the course of the experiment, expressed in 1971 dollars.[4] It should be noted that, over the life of the experiment, there was a rising income trend among the sample families independent of the experiment, leading to a decline for both groups in the percentage of families with incomes low enough to receive transfer benefits of any kind.

---

[1] These correspond to 95%, 120%, and 140% of the official poverty line for a family of four ($4,000 in 1971 dollars). The relationship of these levels to the poverty line was preserved throughout the experimental period by adjusting the dollar guarantee levels regularly according to increases in the Consumer Price Index, as is the poverty line itself.
[2] The last two variants were introduced because a declining tax rate schedule provides less of a work disincentive than a constant tax rate plan with the same guarantee and breakeven level and therefore needs a smaller cash transfer budget.
[3] Under the 1981 AFDC amendments, there is a limit on total non-AFDC income at 150% of the state needs standard. On the basis of the poverty lines and state needs standards of 1980, the breakeven level at 150% of the needs standard is below the poverty line in all but 15 states.
[4] All citations are to the *Final Report of the Seattle-Denver Income Maintenance Experiment* (denoted *Final Report*), Washington, D.C.: U.S. Government Printing Office, 1983.

TABLE 2.—AVERAGE TRANSFERS RECEIVED BY SIME/DIME FAMILIES

[In 1971 dollars]

	Experimental groups		Control groups	
	Sample size [1]	Average transfer	Sample size	Average transfer
Husbands:				
Year:				
1	1,393 (440)	$1,361	1,071	$263
2	1,294 (415)	1,296	990	220
3	1,183 (392)	1,276	851	210
4	(374)	1,233	804	195
5	(340)	990	562	165
Wives:				
Year:				
1	1,408 (445)	1,455	1,089	295
2	1,343 (427)	1,524	1,026	327
3	1,253 (416)	1,564	895	383
4	(406)	1,618	849	397
5	(372)	1,323	600	348
Single female heads:				
Year:				
1	1,102 (304)	2,105	699	1,171
2	1,066 (294)	2,185	649	1,089
3	997 (286)	2,032	562	1,014
4	(278)	1,908	525	932
5	(260)	1,776	381	748

[1] The sample sizes for the 5-year sample are in parentheses.

NOTE.—For experimental families the transfer total includes SIME/DIME payments plus AFDC, AFDC-UF, and bonus value of food stamps as reported in interviews. For control families the transfer total includes AFDC, AFDC-UF, and the Food Stamp bonus value as reported in interviews. The husband and wife sample sizes differ because of family splits.

Source: *Final Report*, Volume 1, Part III, Chapter 4, Tables 3.1 and 3.2.

Counseling/training subsidy treatments. There were three variants of the counseling/training subsidy treatments: counseling only, counseling combined with a 50% subsidy for approved education [5] or training courses, and counseling combined with a 100% subsidy for approved education or training. Within a family enrolled in the counseling/training subsidy programs, every family member aged 16 and older was eligible for the experimental counseling and training subsidies. The counseling component of the treatment can be characterized as voluntary, informational, and nondirective. Included in the training of the SIME/DIME counselors, all of whom had extensive previous counseling experience, was a special three-day workshop in nondirective counseling at the start of the experiment. Within this nondirective framework, the counseling had three main features: self-assessment, labor market assessment, and job search assistance.

Self-assessment consisted not only of getting sample members to evaluate their own employment records and work skills, if any, but also of encouraging them to explore their long-range hopes and unfulfilled expectations without regard to the feasibility of these goals. Feasibility was discussed at a later stage. Labor market assessment consisted of providing counselors with detailed reports on occupations of interest to clients including specific tasks involved, credentials and experience required, usual hiring channels, and career potential of the occupation. Although job openings were indicated in cases where that information happened to be available, such information was not usually provided to counsel-

---

[5] It is important to note that the subsidy was available for a wide range of training or education, including liberal arts courses. However, for simplicity, the remainder of the paper refers to this treatment as the counseling/training subsidy treatment.

ors. The job search assistance component did not involve direct job placement or referrals but, rather, general help in preparing resumes and in practicing job interview skills.

The culmination of the counseling process was the formulation of a "plan of action". Although the counselor did at this stage examine with the participants the obstacles in the way of successfully completing the proposed plan, the participant selected the goal and the counselor helped the participant assess the assets and liabilities of the participant's choice.

The training subsidy component of the treatment was also flexible and geared to providing maximum freedom of choice with respect to the type of education or training subsidized. Two subsidy plans were tested. In one, individuals who chose to receive job-related training were reimbursed for 50 percent of the direct costs of training (tuition, fees, materials, transportation, and child care expenses); in the other, clients were reimbursed for 100 percent of training costs. In both subsidy plans, the amount of training subsidized was limited to the cost of the least expensive local institution providing the desired training. Within that constraint, individuals were free to use the subsidy at the institution of their choice. The requirement that training be "job related" was liberally interpreted so that individuals could receive subsidized training that was required for ambitious career goals (like professional and managerial positions). There was no fixed limit on the amount of training that would be subsidized, either with respect to cost or duration, except that subsidies were limited to the three- or five-year period of experimental eligibility.

Administration of the treatments. The cash transfer treatment, as has been noted, was defined by a guarantee and a tax rate. The amount of payment actually received by a family was calculated according to information regarding nonexperimental income, assets, and expenses contained in a monthly Income Report Form submitted by the family to the SIME/DIME payments office. This information was used to calculate the benefit to be paid by check to the family in the subsequent month.

Such a reporting and payment system differed from what was then common state welfare policy, where benefits were calculated for a future period based on projected income and the expected expenses for that future period.[6] Another important difference between the payment calculations used in the income maintenance experiments and those still prevailing under state welfare policy is that, in the former, the underlying basis for experimental benefits was the income received over the previous year. This ensured that families with the same annual income received the same total benefit over the course of a year. For those families whose income remained below their breakeven level throughout the year (most of the sample), this constraint made no difference to the amounts received each month. For those whose incomes fluctuated around their breakeven levels—so that in some months they were above it and in some months below it—receipt of benefits in any month depended not only on whether the family income was below the breakeven level for the most recent month, but also on the family's nonexperimental income over the previous twelve-month period. A third important difference in SIME/DIME was the monthly Income Report Form. The conventional welfare system had no regular reporting form for clients.

Families were enrolled into the experiment in a face-to-face interview at which they were told about the guarantee level and tax rate of the negative income tax plan to which they had been assigned, how the benefit payments were calculated, and how long the experiment would last for them. The filing and record keeping responsibilities of the sample families, the specifics about

---

[6] Projected income and expected expenses were typically based on the most recently verified monthly data, which were assumed to hold true in future months.

what counted as income and what were deductible expenses, the details of the payment calculation formula, and the conditions under which the experiment could withhold benefit checks were all spelled out in considerable detail in a set of rules and regulations given each family. Penalties for misrepresentation were also specified, and appropriate audit and appeal procedures were set up. Although, as in any program, some cases of misreporting did occur, the incidence of deliberate fraud seems to have been low and repayments were usually achieved through appropriate deductions from future payment streams.

Throughout their period of experimental eligibility, families in the treatment group who were also eligible for AFDC or AFDC-UF were allowed to choose which program they wished to receive benefits from in any given month. They were not, however, allowed to receive checks from both SIME/DIME and AFDC simultaneously. A major part of the auditing functions thus involved making sure that families were not benefiting from both SIME/DIME and AFDC in the same payment period.

The administration of the counseling/training subsidy treatment involved informing families of their eligibility for the counseling/training subsidy program at the time of the enrollment interview mentioned above. A counselor then contacted them and arranged individual or group sessions for those individuals who desired counseling.

Data collection. The primary data for analysis of behavioral responses to the experiment came from a series of face-to-face interviews administered three times a year, for the duration of the treatment period and at least one year beyond. These took about forty minutes each, were administered in the families' homes by specially trained interviewers, and were identical for both experimental and control group families.

Detailed questions on every aspect of labor force participation, earnings, and job change for the period since the previous interview were included in each questionnaire. The database thus contained a continuous work history on each family member (age 16 and over) from two years prior to enrollment until at least one year after treatment ended. In addition to the regular labor force core questions, each questionnaire included modules covering other aspects of behavior. In all, 53 questionnaire modules were developed, covering additional economic information such as consumption and wealth as well as family functioning, education, and social and psychological attitudes.

In addition to the rich body of information from these periodic interviews, Social Security and Internal Revenue Service records were collected so that validation studies of the interview-reported earnings information could be conducted.

The sample. The composition of the SIME/DIME sample was defined partly with reference to the likely population to be included in any national negative income tax program and partly to assure that important questions about the magnitude of the overall work effort response and about possible differential responses by different population groups could be satisfactorily answered.

The sample was restricted to families with heads between 18 and 58 years of age at enrollment in order to focus on those at least potentially in the prime-aged labor force. For this reason, families with disabled heads were excluded. In addition, eligibility was limited to families with total earnings of less than $9,000 a year if one head was employed, or earnings of $11,000 a year if both husband and wife were employed. These earnings cutoffs were a compromise between the need to include those, although above their breakeven income level at enrollment, could be expected to fall below it during the period of the experiment, and the wish to exclude people whose incomes were so high that potential eligibility for cash transfers appeared highly unlikely. These earnings cutoffs do raise the potential problem of sample selection bias in the results.

To be able to detect differences by family type, both one-parent families with a dependent child present and couples were included in the sample. For convenience, the latter type of family is frequently referred to as two-parent, although there was no requirement that such families contain a dependent child. Nor was there a requirement that the two family heads be legally married, although for convenience they are often referred to as husbands and wives. Three ethnic groups were included in the SIME/DIME sample—blacks, whites, and (in Denver only) Chicanos. All enrolled families were residents of selected low-income Census tracts in Seattle and Denver.

The experimental sample was designed using a sophisticated mathematical procedure to yield the maximum amount of useful information within a fixed budget. To achieve this purpose, enrolled families were divided into a large number of different types or "strata." For example, families were divided into seven different income levels, depending on their average incomes over a number of years prior to the start of the experiment. They were further subdivided according to race and the number of family heads present (one or two). In addition to including a large number of family types or strata, the experiment tested a variety of treatment combinations: twelve NIT treatments (the eleven NIT plans tested plus the control treatment) combined with four counseling/training subsidy treatments (three experimental plans plus the control treatment), in combination with two different periods of experimental eligibility (three and five years). In the interests of economy, the experiment did not test every possible combination of these treatments, but a large number were tested.

After determination of the treatment combinations to be tested and family types to be enrolled, the essence of the sample design problem is to determine the number of families of each family type to be assigned to each treatment combination. For a particular family type and treatment combination, this number is known as the "cell size". Obviously, the average experimental cost of families in a given cell will depend both on the characteristics of the family and the generosity of the treatment combination. Low-income families, for example, will receive higher NIT benefits under a given plan than high-income families. Families assigned to high-guarantee NIT plans or to 100 percent training subsidy plans will cost more to enroll than families in the control group or in low-guarantee and less generous training subsidy plans. It should also be mentioned that not every treatment combination tested was of equal interest or importance. For example, certain guarantee/tax-rate combinations were considered more feasible than others (basically, those in the middle range were considered the more policy-relevant), and consequently the designers put greater emphasis on obtaining precise behavioral response estimates for these combinations.

Taking account of the cost differences of the various cells and their varying degrees of policy relevance as well as their relative contributions to statistically precise measurement of the response pattern, the mathematical procedure alluded to earlier was used to determine the cell sizes in SIME/DIME. A family of a given type which had been selected for the sample was then randomly assigned to a particular treatment combination on the basis of the cell sizes computed by this mathematical model. Since assignment to particular treatment combinations was completely random for all families of a given family type, the hoped-for result was that measured differences in the behavior of people subject to different treatment combinations measured the effect of the treatment differences.

In all, 4,800 families were enrolled in SIME/DIME including control families. The way the initial sample was distributed by family structure and race and by assignment to site, treatment, and treatment duration can be seen in Table 3. Note that the "pure" control group (that is, the group eligible for neither the cash transfer nor the counseling/training subsidy treatments) accounts for less than one quarter of the sample because the same comparison group can be used for all the treatment variants. The groups eligible for the cash transfer treatment only and the counseling/training subsidy treatment only were slightly smaller than the control group. The group eligible for both a cash transfer and a counseling/training subsidy treatment is about twice as large as either group receiving a single type of treatment.

TABLE 3.—THE DISTRIBUTION OF THE SIME/DIME SAMPLE AT ENROLLMENT

Site:	
Seattle	2,042
Denver	2,758
Family structure:	
2-parent families	2,769
1-parent families	2,031
Ethnic group:	
White	2,071
Black	1,862
Chicano	867
Treatment/control status:	
Negative income tax (NIT) only	946
Counseling/training subsidy only	1,012
NIT plus training/counseling	1,801
Control group	1,041
Treatment Duration:	
3 years	2,638
5 years	1,121
Control Group	1,041

Source: Murarka, B. A. and R. G. Spiegelman, "Sample Selection in the Seattle and Denver Income Maintenance Experiments," SRI International Technical Memorandum 1, July 1978, p. 53, as quoted in the *Final Report*, Volume 1, Part I.

Families were located through an intensive survey effort, which first identified the areas in Seattle and Denver that would be most fruitful in terms of the expected yield of eligible families and then canvassed those areas on an individual dwelling-unit basis.

During the period of the experiment, in spite of strenuous efforts to keep track of sample families and persuade them to continue in the experiment, some families dropped out. Over the first thirty months of the experiment, 20% of the originally enrolled husbands, 15% of originally enrolled wives, and 15% of single heads of families dropped out. The husband-wife differences are due to differential drop-out rates in the cases of couples that split up.

SIME/DIME RESULTS

Introduction

The major SIME/DIME results are presented under three headings. First, the effects of the experiment on work effort or labor supply are presented. The primary focus is the effect of eligibility for a negative income tax plan, but the analysis sample used to obtain these findings includes all families enrolled in the experiment, including those families enrolled only in the counseling/training subsidy treatments. Second, the effects on hours worked and earnings of the counseling/training subsidy treatments are discussed specifically. Third, the effects of the experiment treatments on "marital stability" are described. Recall that marital stability is not used in the literal sense here since couples were not required to be legally married. For the marital stability research, the analysis sample included those who were eligible for the negative income tax and counseling/training subsidy treatments alone plus those who were eligible for both, as well as those eligible for neither—the control group. Many other types of behavioral response to the experimental treatments have also been analyzed and are discussed in the *Final Report.* Tables of Contents for Volume I (the research findings) and Volume II (the administration of the experiment) are included at the end of this overview as a guide for readers wishing to pursue issues not covered here.

In all cases, unless otherwise noted, the results presented in this overview are experimental-control differences, adjusted by statistical methods to control for the variation in sample characteristics across treatment combinations.

Cash Transfer Effects on Labor Supply

The labor supply results for husbands, wives, female family heads, and youth will be summarized in turn. For each group, the overall response to the SIME/DIME negative income tax plans taken together is described first. A discussion of differences in response among the different NIT plans follows.

As mentioned above, the samples used for the labor supply analysis include families that were eligible for the counseling/training subsidy treatment. There is no statistically significant evidence that the counseling/training subsidy treatment altered the effect of the negative income tax treatment on labor supply behavior. Consequently, the labor supply analysis can statistically separate the effect of the two treatments, and the results described in this section can be interpreted as the effect of just the negative income tax plans on work effort.

The NIT treatment was administered for two different lengths of time (three and five years) to get some information both on how long the family members took to adjust their behavior to the change and on whether a long-term program might have a different effect from a short-term one. Obviously the experiment could not go on indefinitely. The hope was, however, that any differences between the responses of the three- and five-year sample would help predict long-term program effects. In addition, interview information was collected for at least one post-experimental year in order to measure any effects of the cessation of benefits.

Husbands. The results for husbands show that the combination of negative income tax plans tested in SIME/DIME—which, as already mentioned, represents on average a relatively generous cash transfer program with a guarantee of 115% of the poverty line and a tax rate of 50%—has a significant negative effect on hours worked per year. Table 4A shows the findings by experimental year and duration of treatment. The best measure of the overall labor supply effect for the combined three- and five-year samples is probably the disincentive effect as measured in the second year—after all the experimentals have had time to adjust to the treatment but before the three-year families start preparing for the treatment to end. This percentage reduction in hours of labor supplied for the three- and five-year families combined, as measured in the second experimental year, is about 9%. For the three-year sample, the maximum labor supply response is a 7.3% decline, occurring in both the second and third years. For the five-year sample, the maximum response is a 13.6% decline, occurring in the fourth year of the five-year treatment period. These maximum percentage responses represent in absolute terms a decline of about 133 and 234 hours of work per year, respectively.

TABLE 4.—LABOR SUPPLY RESPONSE OF HUSBANDS
A. *Overall NIT response* (percentage difference in annual hours worked)

	Year				
	1	2	3	4	5
3-yr sample	−1.6	−7.3	−7.3	−0.5	−0.2
5-yr sample	−5.9	−12.2	−13.2	−13.6	−12.3
Total sample	−3.1	−9.0	−9.3		

B. *Second year response, by NIT plan* (percentage difference in annual hours worked)

Guarantee	Tax rate			
	50 percent	70 percent	70 percent (declining)	80 percent (declining)
$3,800	−6.7	−5.6	−10.0	−8.9
$4,000	−8.8	−1.5	−14.5	−9.9
$5,600	−11.8	−10.4		−8.7

Source: Derived according to the formula in the *Final Report*, Volume 1, Part III, Chapter 5, footnote 3 and data in Tables 3.4 and 3.9.

The larger response for husbands enrolled in the five-year group suggests that the response to a long-term national program of comparable generosity might be higher than the response measured for the three-year sample, or even for the combined three- and five-year sample. It should be noted, however, that no general statement about the effect of treatment duration on response can be made, since this effect depends critically on the generosity (i.e., the guarantee/tax rate combination) of the NIT.

By the end of the first post-treament year, labor supply for NIT-eligible husbands had again returned essentially to the same level as that for controls, indicating strongly both that the observed response was indeed a result of the treatment and that husbands can adjust their labor supply fairly rapidly to changed incentives. Average work reductions were observed to be larger among black and chicano men than among white men. However, these results were not statistically significant. Similarly, work reductions were observed to be larger in Denver (which had a tight labor market during the experiment) than in Seattle which had high unemployment during most of the experiment). Again, these results failed to be statistically significant.

When the results for all 11 negative income tax plans are estimated separately, as shown in Table 4B, we begin to see how the pattern of response changes with changes in the negative income tax plan. As the guarantee becomes more generous, the labor supply response becomes generally more negative. Response does not, however, change in any clear pattern as the tax rate changes. This result may at first appear surprising. However, recall that plans with higher tax rates—and greater associated work disincentives for NIT recipients— also have lower breakeven levels. Consequently, higher tax plans will have fewer recipients, and a smaller fraction of the population will be affected by their work disincentives.

When the plans are grouped according to relative overall generosity as measured by the breakeven level (not shown), the magnitude of the labor supply reductions for husbands increases as the generosity of the plan increases. Findings by plan again indicate greater responses for the five-year sample than the three-year sample. In addition, although the response is uniformly greater for the five-year sample than the three-year sample, the difference between the two is less for the lower than for the higher generosity plans.

What form did the decrease in annual hours worked take? Was it mainly that people worked with the same regularity but for fewer hours each week, or was it that they spent more time not working at all—that is, unemployed or out of the labor force? Experimental husbands did work significantly fewer weeks than control husbands: annual weeks worked were 2.8 weeks less during the second year. Most of this reduction came about through a significant increase in unemployment.[7] Weeks unemployed for experimental husbands were on average 2.2 more than for controls. One interpretation of this result might be that the cash transfer program enabled husbands to take more time to find a better job. However, other findings from the experiment show that husbands in the experimental group did not find measurably better jobs than their control counterparts, at least as judged by the wage rate. Disregarding the distinction between unemployment and out of the labor force, a safer conclusion is that NIT eligibility induced men who were out of work to spend more time between jobs than men in the control sample. For a few men, the time spent out of employment was increased quite considerably. For example, during the second experimental year the proportion of men in the NIT-eligible group who worked at least one week during the year dropped by 7 percent in comparison to that observed in the control group. For those experimentals who did work, there was a significant reduction in the proportion who worked full time, but no significant impact on the proportion working overtime or only part time.

A question remains as to whether the missing observations of those who dropped out during the experiment and/or possible misreporting bias cause the estimates presented above to be distorted in any measurable way. This is, by its very nature, a difficult question to answer. Examination of other earnings records (particularly from Social Security, but also, on a more fragmentary basis, from the Washington and Colorado Departments of Employment Security) on both experimental and control families suggests that for husbands any attrition and misreporting bias is probably small.

Wives. The labor supply response of wives to the SIME/DIME negative income tax treatment was significantly negative and larger in percentage terms than the response for husbands, at least when that response is measured with SIME/DIME interview data. As shown in Table 5A, the average work reduction for the three- and five-year samples taken together, as measured in the second experimental year, is about 20%. For the three-year sample the maximum effect was a decrease in annual hours of 16.5% in hours worked, occurring in the second year. For the five-year sample, the maximum effect was a decrease in annual hours of approximately 27.1%, occurring in the fourth year. In absolute terms these decreases—just over 100 hours a year and just over 200 hours per year, respectively—are smaller than for husbands. The larger percentage decreases should be interpreted in the context of the smaller average hourly commitment of these women to market work than the average hourly commitment of their husbands. Wives readjusted at the end of the experiment as quickly as husbands, with the wives in the three-year sample even showing a tendency to work more than comparable control families during the second post-experiment year.

---

[7] Unemployed means out of work but looking for a job. Out of the labor force means not working and not looking for a job.

TABLE 5.—LABOR SUPPLY RESPONSE OF WIVES

A. *Overall NIT response* (percentage difference in annual hours worked)

	Year				
	1	2	3	4	5
3-yr sample	−4.0	−16.5	−15.2	−2.0	+13.4
5-yr sample	−15.1	−26.5	−21.6	−27.1	−24.0
Total sample	−8.1	−20.1	−17.4		

B. *Second year response, by NIT plan* (percentage difference in annual hours worked)

Guarantee	Tax rate			
	50 percent	70 percent	70 percent (declining)	80 percent (declining)
$3,800	−24.7	−13.2	−1.6	−19.7
$4,800	−29.3	−23.2	−20.7	−18.7
$5,600	−28.1	−40.1		−12.6

Source: Derived according to the formula in the *Final Report*, Volume 1, Part III, Chapter 5, footnote 3 and data in Tables 3.5 and 3.9.

When response is estimated separately for the eleven plans tested (see Table 5B), the response for wives, as for husbands, generally increased in magnitude as the guarantee became more generous and, again as for husbands, showed a somewhat inconsistent pattern with respect to the tax rate. When plans are arrayed by generosity of the breakeven level, wives show the expected pattern of generally increasing response magnitude as generosity increases. The five-year responses are uniformly although not significantly larger than the three-year responses for wives. The treatment duration differences that do exist are again smaller for less generous NIT plans than for plans with higher breakeven levels.

There are some interesting differences between the behavior of wives and husbands with respect to the form the decrease in work actually took. Weeks worked per year were about 3.8 less for experimental wives than for control wives in the second experimental year. Virtually all of this difference took the form of an increase in weeks out of the labor force (rather than weeks unemployed as was the case with husbands).[8] The probability of working at least one week during the year was also significantly less for experimental wives during the second experimental year. With respect to changes in the amount worked by those who did work, there was a significant reduction in the probability of both full-time and part-time work.

Analysts have investigated the importance of possible misreporting and attrition biases on the experimental results for wives. Employment and earnings checks with the same records used to validate the results for husbands suggest that both the attrition bias and the misreporting bias for wives may be substantial—with both working in the direction of exaggerating observed experimental-control differences. Once again, incomplete data make it impossible to come up with precise estimates of the magnitude of the biases, though examination of the Social Security and unemployment insurance records suggests that as much as half of the measured response may be attributable to differential attrition bias and that a large fraction of the remaining response may represent misreporting bias. The reader should therefore be cautioned that the observed labor supply response for wives might overstate the work reduction that actually occurred.

Female family heads. As with the previous two groups, female family heads responded to the SIME/DIME negative income tax treatment by reducing work effort significantly. The overall response of the three-year and five-year samples taken together, as measured in the second treatment year, was 14%. Their maxi-

---

[8] The difference, again, is whether they are looking for a job or not.

mum response was larger in absolute and percentage terms than that of either husbands or wives. For the three-year sample (see Table 6A) the maximum reduction was about 22%, occurring in the final treatment year; for the five-year sample the maximum response was about 32 percent, also occurring in the final treatment year. These correspond to absolute reductions of about 220 and 405 hours per year, respectively. These maximum responses, it should be noted, are about double the average response.

Unlike husbands and wives, female heads do not seem to have responded differently to the three- and five-year treatments, since the responses for the two samples measured over the same period of time are not significantly different. However, their adaptation both to the experiment and to its end appears to have been slower, suggesting that female heads adjust more slowly to changes in financial incentives than do husbands or wives. This suggests that the response observable in any brief-duration experiment, such as three or five years duration, will understate the work reduction of female family heads relative to a permanent program.

TABLE 6.—LABOR SUPPLY RESPONSE OF FEMALE HEADS

A. *Overall NIT response* (percentage difference in annual hours worked)

	Year				
	1	2	3	4	5
3-year sample	−5.5	−14.1	−21.6	−8.9	−7.7
5-year sample	−7.9	−15.0	−21.2	−28.3	−31.8
Total sample	−6.3	−14.3	−21.4		

B. *Second year response by NIT plan* (percentage difference in annual hours worked)

Guarantee	Tax rate			
	50 percent	70 percent	70 percent (declining)	80 percent (declining)
$3,800	−7.0	−19.4	−2.5	−16.0
$4,800	−21.7	−11.7	−20.9	−10.5
$5,600	−6.9	−23.7	−	−25.1

Source: Derived according to the formula in the *Final Report*. Volume 1, Part III, , Chapter 5, footnote 3 and data in Tables 3.6 and 3.9.

When the responses are calculated separately for the eleven plans tested (see Table 6B) no obvious pattern of variation between the labor supply response and either guarantee or tax rate is found.

How did the average reduction in annual hours worked manifest itself in patterns of employment for female family heads? First, as with the other two groups, there was a significant reduction in weeks worked. For female heads this reduction was higher than for husbands but lower than for wives. As with wives, but not husbands, this was accounted for by dropping out of the labor force rather than by being unemployed. The probability of working at all during the year also decreased significantly for female heads—again, the magnitude of the labor force participation decline is between those for husbands and for wives. With respect to changes in full-time, part-time, or overtime work by those who worked, female heads reacted more like the husbands than the wives. The only significant change for those that worked was a decrease in full-time work.

With respect to the question of possible misreporting and attrition bias in the observed responses, comparison with other data records suggests that there was no misreporting bias. There is, however, evidence of moderate attrition bias that goes in the other direction from that observed for wives. When interpreting the results for female heads, therefore, it should be kept in mind that the observed responses might underestimate slightly the actual reduction.

Youth. Based on their own interview-reported hours and earnings, both male and female youth (at least age 16 but under age 21) appeared to respond to the negative income tax plans tested in SIME/DIME by reducing their labor supply significantly. For the three- and five-year samples for males taken together, the observed reduction was substantial; reported hours worked per week decreased on average by about 24% and the proportion of the year during which they reported working decreased by about 17%. Although the proportional reductions in work effort are large for both young men and women, the absolute reductions are quite small, since average work effort among teenagers is low.

When the labor supply response of youth is estimated for the three- and five-year samples separately, the differences between the two are not generally significant. However, the fact that the observed effects for the five-year sample are larger (and, in the case of young men, sometimes much larger) than for the three-year sample suggests that the work effect of a permanent program might be larger than the observed response in this limited-duration experiment. Differentiating response by plan yields the same lack of tax rate effect as appeared for the other groups; and for youth there is no systematic guarantee effect either.

Labor supply response does vary in an important respect according to whether the youth remained dependents or set up separate households. For males who continued to live at home and for males who left their original family to form new, two-parent families (both eligible for continued payments), the observed work disincentive is substantial. By the second half of the third experimental year, hours worked by the new husbands had declined by about 33% (mainly accounted for by increased unemployment), and the hours worked by those continuing to live at home had declined by about 43% (about equally accounted for by increased unemployment and increased time out of the labor force). But for young men who left their parental family to live as single individuals, there is no significant work disincentive effect. For females there is a significant work disincentive (about a 42% decrease in hours worked) only for those who continue to live with their parental family. For none of the youth groups was the decrease in hours worked accompanied by an increase in time spent in school. The observed work reductions tend to be largest for those who are not in school, but labor supply declines are not restricted to youths in that group.

Generalizing to the national population. As emphasized earlier in this overview, the observed labor supply responses presented so far are effects that are specific to the population enrolled in SIME/DIME and relate only to NIT programs actually tested in that experiment. In order to predict from the observed SIME/DIME responses the effects of national programs of differing generosity, the SIME/DIME analysts developed a more general form of the work disincentive response.

The most noteworthy pattern they found is that, although the decrease in hours worked by participants gets larger the higher the tax rate (holding the guarantee constant), the work disincentive for the U.S. population as a whole gets smaller. This is because a higher tax rate implies a lower breakeven income level and a smaller number of participants. The positive labor supply response among those losing eligibility is big enough to offset the larger negative response among the program participants.

Counseling/training subsidy effects

A unique feature of SIME/DIME among the four NIT experiments was the testing of a labor market counseling and training subsidy program in addition to a negative income tax transfer program. The rationale for including these programs was to determine whether increased labor market information and increased education and training could offset the decline in work effort that was predicted to occur due to the negative income tax program. As described at the beginning of this overview, the SIME/DIME counseling treatment was informational and nondirective in nature, and types of training deemed appropriate for subsidization were very flexibly defined. The expectation was that the counseling would lead, at least eventually, to better labor market match of skills to jobs and thus higher wage rates, earnings and, possibly, job status. The training subsidy was expected to lead to the same general outcomes, possibly after a brief period of decreased labor market activity in the short run as the extra training was acquired.

Participation. There was substantial participation in the counseling and subsidized training programs, particularly among single women. Many of those who participated in the counseling program demonstrated interest in obtaining additional training, including even some who were not eligible for a training subsidy. There was marked diversity in the goals of those who planned to seek training. A majority chose relatively modest occupational and training objectives, but a substantial minority chose quite ambitious objectives that presumably held lower prospects for successful attainment.

Table 7 shows the proportions of the SIME/DIME sample that participated in the counseling and training subsidy programs. Participation rates for counseling rose consistently as the amount of subsidy offered increased. Husbands and wives participated at similar rates (nearly 40% for the counseling only group, just over 50% for the 50% subsidy group and about 60% for the 100% subsidy

TABLE 7.—RATES OF PARTICIPATION IN THE COUNSELING/ TRAINING SUBSIDY TREATMENTS

	Counseling only			Counseling and 50 percent subsidy			Counseling and 100 percent subsidy		
	H	W	FH	H	W	FH	H	W	FH
Number of eligibles...	510	510	374	671	670	481	391	392	313
Percent attending at least 1 counseling session....................	39.8	38.2	54.0	51.4	52.8	64.4	60.6	56.6	71.9
Of those participating: Average number of sessions...........	4.8	4.9	5.8	6.6	6.4	7.3	6.5	7.4	7.7
Percent receiving some subsidy......				21.0	21.3	34.9	36.3	36.5	46.6
Of those receiving subsidy: Average amount....				$363	$401	$650	$666	$954	$857
Average number of academic quarters subsidized..........				4.0	3.6	4.1	3.8	3.9	4.1

[1] Demographic groups are husbands(H), wives(W), and female heads(FH).

Source: *Final Report,* Volume 1, Part IV, Chapter 3, Table 4.1.

group). Female heads participated in counseling at uniformly higher rates (54% for the counseling only group, 64% for the 50% subsidy group, and 72% for the 100% subsidy group). A similar pattern emerges for participation in the training subsidy programs, though the percentages are lower. Just over 20% of husbands and wives chose to participate in the 50% subsidy option and 36% chose to participate in the 100% subsidy option. For female heads the figures are 35% and 47%, respectively.

For those who participated in counseling, the average number of sessions also increased as the amount of subsidy offered increased—from the 4.8-to-5.8 range for the counseling only group to the 6.5-to-7.7 range for the 100% subsidy group. The average amount of the subsidy for those who chose to participate ranged from a low of $363 for husbands on the 50% subsidy plan to a high of $954 for wives on the 100% subsidy plan. The average number of academic quarters subsidized ranged between 3.6 and 4.1.

With respect to the amount of schooling received, counseling-only did not make a difference. The subsidies did tend, however, to increase the amount of schooling received—mildly for husbands, more strongly for wives, and most strongly for female heads. For the latter two groups the effects on schooling were generally stronger the more generous the subsidy.

Impact on labor market performance. The counseling/training subsidy treatment did not have the expected positive effects for most groups. The effects on average annual earnings and hours of work are shown in Table 8. Earnings declined during the experimental period and, quite unexpectedly, the negative results tended to continue into the post-program period as well, through these post-program reductions were not statistically significant. Not all results for all groups are statistically significant, but the negative pattern shows clearly throughout the estimates—in earnings, hours worked, and wage rates.

TABLE 8.—EFFECT OF COUNSELING AND TRAINING SUBSIDIES ON ANNUAL EARNINGS AND HOURS OF WORK

	Experimental year					
	1		4		6	
	Earnings	Hours	Earnings	Hours	Earnings	Hours
Husbands						
Counseling only:						
3-year sample	+$6	−3.0	−$5	+24.1		
5-year sample	−31	−2.8	−185	−80.6	−$239	−115.6
Counseling and 50 pct subsidy:						
3-year sample	[2] −248	[2] −71.7	−101	+22.4		
5-year sample	[1] −398	[1] −105.6	−161	−73.7	−33	−18.7
Counseling and 100 pct subsidy:						
3-year sample	[2] −317	[1] −88.8	−245	−37.9		
Wives						
Counseling only:						
3-year sample	+21	−8.6	−215	−61.8		
5-year sample	[3] −187	[3] −77.1	[1] −534	[1] −197.9	[3] −430	−125.8

TABLE 8.—EFFECT OF COUNSELING AND TRAINING SUBSIDIES ON
ANNUAL EARNINGS AND HOURS OF WORK--Continued

| | Experimental year | | | | | |
| | 1 | | 4 | | 6 | |
	Earnings	Hours	Earnings	Hours	Earnings	Hours
Counseling and 50 pct subsidy:						
3-year sample	+ 6	– 14.9	– 199	– 63.9		
5-year sample	[1] – 255	[1] – 107.8	– 124	– 43.1	– 301	– 52.1
Counseling and 100 pct subsidy:						
3-year sample	– 37	– 10.0	[3] – 222	[3] – 96.1		
Female Heads						
Counseling only:						
3-year sample	+ 148	+ 36.1	+ 144	+ 13.2		
5-year sample	+ 123	+ 31.8	+ 184	+ 81.1	+ 426	[3] + 183.4
Counseling and 50 pct subsidy:						
3-year sample	– 32	– 4.6	– 207	– 98.1		
5-year sample	– 114	– 81.3	– 89	– 77.9	– 37	– 112.8
Counseling and 100 pct subsidy:						
3-year sample	– 11	– 20.7	– 45	– 35.7		

[1] Significant at the 1 percent level.
[2] Significant at the 5 percent level.
[3] Significant at the 10 percent level.
Source: *Final Report*, Volume 1, Part IV, Chapter 5, Table 4.5–4.7.

Table 8 shows the results for the three- and five-year samples for years 1, 4, and 6, to indicate both in-program and post-program effects. For husbands, the three-year counseling only program had virtually no impact on earnings. In contrast, the five-year counseling program had a predominantly negative impact on earnings, even in the sixth year when experimentals were no longer eligible for counseling. In addition, eligibility for counseling resulted, for those husbands who were working, in consistently lower wage rates than those of their control counterparts. The training subsidy programs led to substantial and significant first year decreases in earnings and hours. The 50% subsidy for example, led to a $248 decrease in annual earnings for the three-year sample and a $398 decrease for the five-year sample. The 100% subsidy, only administered to the three-year sample, led to a $317 decrease. In year 4 the decrease in earnings was smaller and not significant; in year 6 it had practically disappeared.

Wives show a similar pattern of response to the counseling-only program with even larger negative effects. Both the three-year and five-year counseling programs resulted in lower earnings and hours of work for wives in every year, and these effects are generally significant for the five-year program. For example, in the first post-program year, wives eligible for the five-year counseling treatment earned $430 less than did comparable controls, a 19% reduction. Wives eligible for the training subsidy programs also had lower earnings and worked fewer hours than did controls. These effects tend to be significant in the early years but are also large and negative in the later years.

For single female heads, the counseling only program probably did have positive results on earnings. Although not statistically significant, the effect on earnings is substantial: in the fifth year, female heads eligible for the counseling only program earned between $275 and $300 more per year than did controls, approximately a 10% increase. Furthermore, the counseling only program did have some significant post-program impacts on the wage rates and hours of work of female heads.

For the combined counseling/training subsidy program, in contrast, the effects were negative for female heads, as for the other groups. As for husbands and wives, female heads eligible for subsidies generally had lower earnings and worked fewer hours than did comparable controls even in the post-program period.

It would be instructive to be able to separate out the effects of the counseling from the effects of the training subsidies, to test the possibility that the counseling was the driving negative influence. While no definitive conclusion on this point can be drawn, because counseling was a prerequisite to the subsidy program, it is possible to infer the separate impact of subsidies when added to an existing counseling program. Here the results for female heads suggest strongly and those for husbands suggest weakly that the addition of a training subsidy program causes even larger earnings and hours reductions than counseling by itself. For wives, the negative impact of counseling plus subsidies is approximately equal to the impact of counseling by itself.

Possible reasons for the effects. How did programs intended to improve the employment and earnings experiences of eligibles actually lead to lower earnings? If the results had indicated no effects, one might be able to explain the results by hypothesizing that very little actually happened in the counseling and training programs. The finding of negative effects, however, cannot be so dismissed. Something did occur in counseling and in training that actually reduced the earnings prospects of participants.

Analysis of data gathered on the objectives of participants suggests that a substantial fraction of the subsidized training was oriented to achieving ambitious career goals. For an important fraction of participants, the goals were evidently overambitious, and the training did not translate into higher earnings even though it may have provided immediate satisfaction to the participants. Evidently, the SIME/DIME counseling/training subsidy program induced short-run reductions in earnings without supporting the type of training or education that would enable participants to secure better paying jobs, at least during the one to three year follow-up period. This "training ineffectiveness argument" would explain a zero treatment response, but it doesn't really offer an explanation of the observed negative response. Perhaps the counseling and training experiences of those with ambitious upward mobility goals actually made it more difficult to pursue a career consisting of a series of relatively low-paying jobs. In any case, a different type of counseling might have resulted in training and education decisions that were less ambitious, but this is entirely conjectural.

Effects on marital stability [9]

Although, as mentioned earlier, the experiment was not explicitly designed to test effects on marital stability, much attention was paid to the issue in terms of both data collection and analysis. To the extent that the effects of the experiment on marital dissolution were expected to depend on the guarantee and the tax rate, and to the extent that they were expected to differ according to income, ethnicity, and family type, the experimental design was well suited to the task of determining such effects. But to the extent that response might depend on other factors—such as presence or absence of children, degree of stigma attached to the program, or to some unanticipated combined effect of the cash benefit and counseling/training subsidy treatments—the design was not optimal for testing those hypotheses. This nonoptimality implies only that the response is measured with less statistical efficiency than with an optimal design, not that the design affects the validity of the response analysis.

---

[9] The reader is reminded that, for simplicity, the term "marital stability" is used in this overview, but legal marriage was not a condition of eligibility for SIME/DIME couples.

Expected effects. Previous research on the possible determinants of marital stability had not reached as well defined a consensus on the expected effects of cash transfers on marital dissolution and the chain of causation through which these effects might occur, as was the case with respect to labor supply. There was some theoretical basis in the literature for believing both that cash transfers would reduce marital dissolution and that they would increase it.

The "conventional wisdom" at the time the experiment began, however, was relatively unambiguous. The widely held view then was that the welfare system might be contributing to marital dissolution. AFDC was restricted largely to one-parent families. The AFDC–UF program for which two-parent families with children were eligible was not available in every state and, even where available, was so highly restrictive in its eligibility requirements that few two-parent families actually participated. The empirical evidence on whether AFDC increased marital dissolution was mixed, but the policy presumption was that, if it did, a negative income tax for which both one-parent and two-parent families were eligible would be a stabilizing influence. A negative income tax with universal eligibility would be available to all families as soon as their incomes fell below a certain level, regardless of who was part of the family. Therefore, the argument went, the incentive to leave one's family in order to make them eligible for cash transfers would no longer exist.

The analysis. As already noted, two-parent families with children did not have to be legally married, or even claim to be, in order to be eligible for SIME/DIME benefits. All they needed was to be living together on a continuing basis. Unmarried couples without children were ineligible for SIME/DIME. The SIME/DIME rules also permitted persons who had left their original partner to retain SIME/DIME eligibility and continue receiving negative income tax payments if their current incomes were below the breakeven level given their new family size. Thus, if an original two-parent family split up, the experiment permitted both halves of the original family to continue receiving (separate) NIT payments. If a member of the original couple formed a new continuing relationship, the new person was counted after a short waiting period as an eligible family member in computing SIME/DIME benefits.

During the first three years of SIME/DIME, roughly one in five of the couples married at enrollment were observed to break up. Table 9 shows the proportion of original marriages that dissolved during the first three payment years, broken down by duration of treatment and ethnic group.

The methodology used in the statistical analysis of the SIME/DIME data is complex and need not be spelled out in this overview. A number of points are worth keeping in mind as the analytical results are discussed below. First, the estimation methodology properly places substantial emphasis not only on the number of events but also on their timing.[10] Second, the analysts place more emphasis on their findings for the smaller number of families in the five-year treatment group than for the larger number of families in the three-year treatment group, arguing that the longer treatment more closely approximates a permanent program. In addition, as the raw data in Table 9 suggest, the statistical analysis demonstrates that the different ethnic groups react differently to the treatments, and hence need to be analyzed separately, thus reducing further the size of the samples used in the analysis.

Third, the treatment group on which the statistical results are based includes those who received both the negative income tax treatment and the counseling/

---

[10] Essentially, earlier marital dissolutions counted more heavily in the analysis than later dissolutions. For example, suppose two groups of families had the same proportion of dissolutions over the course of the experiment, but in one group all the dissolutions were observed near the beginning of the experiment, whereas in the other the dissolutions occurred toward the end. The estimation methodology correctly attributes to the first group a higher rate of marital dissolution.

training subsidy treatment, as well as those on the negative income tax treatment only. The statistical procedure used in the marital dissolution analysis to adjust for the counseling/training subsidy treatment is basically the same as that used in the labor supply analysis. Although the interaction between the NIT and counseling/training subsidy treatments is statistically significant for whites (but not for blacks or Chicanos), the analysts conclude that the unsystematic nature of the interaction is most plausibly explained by sampling variability. An additional finding that leads the authors to discount the importance of the interaction between the two types of treatments is that when they used their statistical methodology to reestimate rates of marital dissolution in the New Jersey income maintenance experiment, they found the NIT effects to be similar in New Jersey (where there was no counseling or training subsidy) and SIME/DIME.

TABLE 9.—PROPORTIONS OF ORIGINAL MARRIAGES OBSERVED TO END DURING THE FIRST 3 YEARS OF SIME/DIME [1]

	Blacks	Whites	Chicanos
Control group	0.205	0.145	0.185
	(435)	(608)	(200)
NIT treatment group	.278	.203	.222
	(504)	(691)	(338)
3-year sample	.270	.198	.223
	(333)	(479)	(238)
5-year sample	.292	.212	.220
	(171)	(212)	(100)

[1] The number of original couples is shown in parentheses.

Sources: *Final Report*, Volume 1, Part V, Chapter 5, Table 5.3.

The overall effect. Table 10 shows the estimated effect of the negative income tax treatment for the three-year treatment and five-year treatment families, by ethnic group. The rate of marital dissolutions among Chicanos is unaffected by the NIT. As can be seen, the overall effect on marital dissolution rates is positive and substantial for black and white families in both the three-year and five-year NIT treatment groups.

To confirm the observed effects for blacks and whites, the analysis differentiated the dissolution rates during the experiment from those occurring in the period after the treatments ended. For this analysis, three time periods were used—enrollment to three years later, three years after enrollment to five years after, and five years after enrollment to seven years after (i.e., the post-experimental years for the five-year treatment group). The impact of the NIT on marital dissolution was allowed to vary for each period. With this specification, the marital dissolution effects for both the three-year and five-year treatments are again positive and significant for blacks and whites but not for Chicanos. In the post-treatment period, the experimental-control difference disappears altogether for both the three-year and five-year treatment groups. Thus, the observed response in dissolution is clearly attributable to the experiment.

A separate analysis of the experimental effect on remarriage concludes that the NIT treatments did not affect remarriage rates for single white or black women, but did reduce the rate by over 60 percent for single Chicano women. Furthermore, after an analysis of how sample attrition may have biased estimates of the change in dissolution rates, the analysts concluded that the unadjusted esti-

TABLE 10.—ESTIMATED PERCENTAGE CHANGE IN MARITAL DIS-
SOLUTION RATES CAUSED BY THE NIT TREATMENTS: ALL
MARRIAGES [1]

	Blacks	Whites	Chicanos
3-year treatment sample	[2] +47	[2] +41	+19
5-year treatment sample	[2] +43	[2] +43	+2
Number of marriages	1,203	1,714	698

[1] Includes relationships entered into after the start of the experiment; 3-year treatment effect is estimated over a 3-year period and 5-year effect over 5 years.
[2] Significant at 1 percent level.

Source: *Final Report,* Volume 1, Part V, Chapter 5, Table 5.5.

mates for whites and blacks, which range in Table 11 from 40 percent to 50 percent, should be reduced about 10 percentage points for blacks and about 5 percentage points for whites.

Explanation of effects. What is the reason for the experimental effect on black and white marriages and single Chicano women, given that that this effect is the differential effect of the SIME/DIME NIT treatments compared to the effect of the public assistance (AFDC) option present in the control environment? The analysts begin explaining the increase in marital dissolution rates by noting a surprising general pattern of the experimental effects when estimated separately by NIT plan. There was no perfectly consistent pattern, but what pattern there was suggested the paradox that lower martial dissolution rates are associated with higher guarantees.

Grouping by guarantee confirms that the experimental effect tends to decrease as the generosity of the guarantee increases. In fact, for white couples the effect is statistically significant only for the low $3,800 guarantee (an 82 percent increase in the rate of martial dissolution), and for blacks the effect is statistically significant only for the $3,800 guarantee (a 60 percent increase) and the medium $4,800 guarantee (a 91 percent increase). For neither blacks nor whites is the effect significant for the high $5,600 guarantee. This pattern of effects is especially striking in view of the fact that the $3,800 guarantee most closely approximates the generosity of the AFDC and AFDC–UF programs available to the control group.

Recognition of two aspects of the situation may account for this pattern of findings. First, according to the existing literature, an increase in cash transfers can be expected to have two opposing effects on the martial dissolution rate. Increases in family income tend to stabilize marriages, giving rise to an *income effect;* but a cash transfer program that provides financial alternatives to marriage for low-income women also tends to destabilize marriage, causing an *independence effect.* Depending on the strength of the two effects, which are opposite in direction, a negative income tax reform may increase martial dissolution, decrease it, or leave it unchanged. Second, since the basic income support offered to low-guarantee experimentals is similar to that already available to controls with children, it is also clear that the relevant difference between the two environments must be nonpecuniary.

Three nonpecuniary differences between the NIT and existing welfare programs may be relevant. Knowledge of the availability of benefits in the event of marital dissolution is likely to be greater for experimentals under the SIME/DIME rules than for controls who would have to go to the local welfare office to apply for AFDC and Food Stamps. The time and nuisance cost of becoming eligible for benefits in the event of a dissolution is lower for the experimentals. Experimental families already had eligibility for SIME/DIME; the only change due to a dissolution would be noting a change in family composition and available family resources on the regular monthly income report form. The necessary procedure for applying for AFDC and Food Stamp benefits is more difficult and more time consuming. Finally, the social and psychological costs (or stigma) of applying for AFDC and using Food Stamps are likely to be higher. The SIME/DIME payments process was largely private. The use of Food Stamps or AFDC exposes applicants to public acknowledgment of dependence or to interaction with possibly condescending welfare workers. One way to sum up these nonpecuniary differences between the programs is to say that a dollar from welfare is less attractive than a dollar from SIME/DIME.

CONCLUSIONS SUGGESTED BY THE SIME/DIME RESULTS

Marital stability

How can the SIME/DIME results be used as a guide to the possible effects on family structure of new public policy initiatives? The analysts themselves "caution the reader against uncritically extrapolating from these or any other summary measures of the effects of SIME/DIME on marital dissolution."[11] They stress as reasons for this statement the following facts: the SIME/DIME sample is nationally unrepresentative, the relationship of the impact of a limited duration experiment to that of a permanent national program is ambiguous, nonpecuniary differences in programs (caused by different administrative procedures and/or work requirements, for example) seem to have important effects on the family structure impact, the social context of SIME/DIME and of a national program are likely to differ in important respects, the remarriage effects of a national program would probably differ because of the possible incentive to marry into the experiment, and the differences among ethnic groups in the treatment effects suggest strongly that the behavioral effects of SIME/DIME on family structure are not yet fully understood. Yet after discussing all these reasons, the analysts conclude: "We have discussed a number of factors that complicate any attempt to extrapolate from SIME/DIME to any other NIT program. None of these factors alter our qualitative conclusions. Given the magnitude of these findings, it is unlikely that any national NIT program would be neutral with respect to marital stability. Although the effects of a national NIT program are unlikely to be as dramatic as the experimental effects, the potential for such effects must not be ignored".[12]

Labor supply. The work responses to be expected from transfer programs of varying generosity are much more precisely known as a result of SIME/DIME than they were before. It is now possible, as a consequence of the SIME/DIME labor supply analysis, to predict with some confidence how much more or less people will work as a result of new policy initiatives and what the cost implications of new programs will be. The response to tax rate variations turn out to be smaller than was formerly thought, permitting the imposition of higher—and more cost saving—marginal tax rates. The responses to guarantee variations turn out to be systematic and predictable. The responses to *breakeven* variations turn out to be very important because (a) the income level at which benefits cease is the critical determinant of the size of the beneficiary population, and (b) the size of the beneficiary population is the most important determinant of program costs and aggregate work reductions.

---

[11] *Final Report.* Volume 1, Part V, Chapter 11.
[12] *Ibid.*

Counseling/training. With respect to the counseling/training subsidy results, two major points deserve emphasis. Participation in both the counseling and training-education programs was strongly related to the amount of the subsidy. Both the 50 percent and 100 percent subsidy plans induced statistically significant increases in formal schooling (although not work-related training). These increases provide a plausible explanation of the negative results—namely that hours worked and earnings both during and (to a lesser extent) after program participation tended to be reduced. While in formal schooling it is reasonable to expect employment to be reduced, and the employment records of participants to become less regular. The formal schooling was not, however, typically job-related. Therefore, the potentially deleterious effect of the reduced work history was not compensated for by any job-related skills acquired during the subsidy period.

18

The Effect of CETA on
the Postprogram Earnings of Participants*

Laurie J. Bassi

ABSTRACT

This paper is a report of a study of efforts to use the Continuous Longitudinal Manpower Survey to estimate the effect that CETA has had on the posttraining earnings of participants. Particular attention is given to developing estimates that are free of selection bias—whether it results from nonrandom self-selection or selection by program administrators. The results indicate that CETA has had a positive and often significant effect on the earnings of participants, and that women benefit more from participation than do men. Among the various program activities that have been available under CETA, no one program is clearly more beneficial than the others.

For almost a decade, the Comprehensive Employment and Training Act of 1973 (CETA) had major responsibility for the provision of federally funded training. The program was originally designed primarily to provide training for disadvantaged workers. With the recession of 1974–1975, the emphasis of the program shifted to providing employment opportunities in the public sector for the cyclically unemployed. By 1978 the program had reverted to a structural program—providing employment and training opportunities for only the most disadvantaged and hard-to-employ individuals. More recently the Reagan Administration cut CETA expenditures drastically by eliminating its Public Service Employment

The author is a member of the Economics faculty at Georgetown University.

* This research was supported by contract number B9M10505 from the Office of Assistant Secretary for Policy, Evaluation, and Research, U.S. Department of Labor, and by a grant from the Alfred P. Sloan Foundation to The Urban Institute. The opinions expressed are my own and do not represent the official position of the Department of Labor, the Sloan Foundation, The Urban Institute, or Georgetown University. I would like to thank O. Ashenfelter, J. Brown, F. Levy, P. Moss, I. Sawhill, and two anonymous referees for helpful comments.

component and maintaining only its training component. Finally, in late 1982 CETA was scrapped altogether to be replaced in 1983 by the Jobs Training Partnership Act (JTPA).

This paper reports a study of efforts to use the recently available Continuous Longitudinal Manpower Survey (CLMS) to estimate the effect that CETA has had on the posttraining earnings of participants. The analysis is based on the (fiscal year) 1976 cohort of participants. By redoing the analysis, using only those participants who would have met the eligibility criteria after 1978, it is possible to examine how the legislative and funding changes that CETA has undergone have affected its ultimate impact on participants. And since this group of participants is likely to be very similar to future JTPA participants, we are able to speculate about the earnings effects that we can expect from JTPA.

The plan of the paper is as follows: The conceptual framework for the analysis is discussed in the first section. Section II includes descriptions of both the data that are available from the CLMS and the comparison groups. The empirical results are presented in Section III, and the findings of the study are summarized in the final section.

I. THE ESTIMATION TECHNIQUE

The major difficulty in estimating the effect of education or training on earnings is the much discussed selection bias problem.[1] In the absence of an experimental design where individuals are randomly assigned between groups, it is likely that the decision to participate in the program is highly correlated with the unobservables in the earnings equation. As is well known, this correlation makes ordinary least squares estimators inconsistent.[2] If one is willing to impose a good deal of structure on the error term, methods are available for purging the error term of its correlation with the right-hand side regressors, even within cross-section data.[3] With longitudinal data, however, it is possible to achieve these same results with much less restrictive assumptions about the structure of the error term.

Random Effects Estimator

A general specification of the earnings function that is often used for this type of analysis with longitudinal data is given by

---

1   See, for instance, Griliches [7], Heckman [8, 9], or Willis and Rosen [15].
2   An alternative way of thinking of the problem is that the earnings and participation equations are part of a set of simultaneous equations. Unless their simultaneity is explicitly accounted for, all of the parameter estimates will be biased.
3   See Heckman [8, 9].

$$(1) \qquad Y_{it} = X_{it}\gamma + P_i\beta_t + \epsilon_i + \epsilon_t + \epsilon_{it}$$

where Y_{it} = earnings of individual i in period t; X_{it} = measured characteristics affecting earnings; P_i = a set of dummy variables measuring participation in the program by type of activity in which the individual was enrolled; ϵ_i = an error term specific to individual i, and constant over time; ϵ_t = an error term specific to year t, and constant across individuals; and ϵ_{it} = an error term specific to individual i at time t.

The most simple form of nonrandom participation in the program (from an econometrician's point of view) would be based on observable characteristics. Under these circumstances, estimation of equation (1) by ordinary least squares (a random effects estimator) would produce unbiased estimates provided that (1) all of the relevant observable characteristics were included as regressors (thereby eliminating any correlation between the error term and the participation dummy variable), and (2) the underlying earnings structure was the same between participants and nonparticipants.[4] So if the eligibility criteria were the only source of nonrandomness in CETA participation, this could easily be controlled for by including these variables on the right-hand side of equation (1).

Fixed Effects Estimator

The next most simple form of selection into the program is based on ϵ_i, the individual nonobservables that are constant over time. Innate ability or intelligence are examples of such an unobservable. If individuals either self-select into CETA or are selected by administrators on the basis of ϵ_i, there is correlation between the error term and the independent regressors in equation (1)—making OLS estimates inconsistent.

This correlation can be eliminated easily by differencing equation (1) over two time periods. Let s be the period prior to CETA participation and t be a postprogram period; this differencing yields

$$(2) \qquad Y_{it} - Y_{is} = (\epsilon_t - \epsilon_s) + (X_{it} - X_{is})\gamma + P_i\beta_t + (\epsilon_{it} - \epsilon_{is})$$

This is the fixed effects estimator used by Ashenfelter and Kiefer.

Ashenfelter has also used an autoregressive model where earnings are used as control variables in equation (1). In other words, lagged values of earnings are included on the right-hand side. The intuition behind this is that previous earnings levels capture ϵ_i, the fixed effect. Cain and Goldberger have shown that if selection in the program is determined solely on the basis of earnings in the preprogram period, then consistent estimates of program effects can be derived by including preprogram earnings

---

4   In fact, estimation of equation (1) by generalized least squares would produce maximum likelihood estimates.

as an independent variable in equation (1). The problem with either of these approaches is that they will produce biased and inconsistent results if the error term is autoregressive, as it almost surely is in earnings equations. Consequently, I have chosen the fixed effects estimator over the autoregressive estimator.

Application of OLS to equation (2) produces unbiased estimates provided that $Cov(\epsilon_{it} - \epsilon_{is}, P_i) = 0$.[5] There is some reason to expect that this condition may be violated. Since CETA administrators have been evaluated on the postprogram employment and earnings records of the individuals that participate in their program, they have an incentive to choose those individuals who are only temporarily eligible for the program because of bad luck. In other words, they would "cream" from the pool of eligible applicants, choosing only those individuals with the highest possible permanent income and the greatest negative transitory income, thereby creating correlation between ϵ_{is} and P_i.

"Creaming," in and of itself, does not create particularly difficult estimation problems. All that is needed is to use a fixed effects estimator, such as equation (2), where the base period is chosen to be a few years prior to program participation. The difficulty that creaming presents, however, is in detecting its presence. If the earnings structures are similar between participants and nonparticipants over several years prior to training and then diverge prior to training, we cannot tell if the difference is only transitory or if it is the beginning of a permanent difference between the groups. So it is necessary to bracket the estimates by using several different base periods in the estimation of equation (2).

If there is, indeed, widespread creaming, then fixed effects estimates that use the year immediately prior to training as the base will overestimate the true training effects. If, however, differences in earnings between participants and nonparticipants in the year prior to training reflect permanent declines in participants' earnings, then using a base period two years prior to training will underestimate the true training effects. By using both base periods, it is possible to determine the significance of these effects. It is not possible, however, to choose which set of fixed effects estimates is the true one.

*A Method of Choosing Among Estimation Techniques
and Comparison Groups*

As has already been mentioned, divergence of the earnings equations of

---

5   It is also necessary that $Cov(\epsilon_{it} - \epsilon_{is}, X_{it} - X_{is}) = 0$ and that the earnings structures be the same for participants and nonparticipants. Analysis of covariance would produce maximum likelihood estimates, but would fail to produce an estimate of β_t, the cumulative effect of the program.

participants relative to nonparticipants in the year immediately prior to training may be evidence of creaming. A simple method of testing for this is to include a dummy variable measuring program participation in equation (2) where earnings are differenced between periods s (the year prior to participation) and $s - 1$. This provides a test for whether or not the mean value of the error term in such an equation ($\epsilon_{is} - \epsilon_{is-1}$) is significantly different between participants and nonparticipants. If the coefficient on the dummy variable in this preprogram equation is significantly different from zero, then we must conclude that the error term is correlated with participation, violating a necessary condition for unbiased estimation. This test can be repeated, differencing over priors $s - 1$ and $s - 2$. If the coefficient on the dummy variable is significant in this regression, then it is likely that there are permanent differences between participants and nonparticipants that cannot be controlled for by a fixed effects estimator.

It is, of course, possible that the true preprogram differences between the two groups may be large but not statistically significant because of large standard errors. Consequently, an insignificant coefficient on the dummy variable in the preprogram earnings equation is a necessary (but not a sufficient) condition for unbiased estimation. Fortunately, in the data being examined here the coefficient on the dummy variable in the preprogram equations turned out to be small when the standard errors were large.

A final possibility is that the comparison groups have been so well chosen that there are no unobservable differences between participants and nonparticipants. This possibility can be checked by repeating the test outlined above in a preprogram random effects model, equation (1). If the coefficient on the dummy variable is insignificant in this equation, then the random effects estimator can be used.[6] This assumes, of course, that the relationship between the observable variables, X, and earnings is the same for both groups. This assumption is easily tested by doing Chow tests on the preprogram equations. These tests should be done for both the random and fixed effects estimators and for each of the available comparison groups.

If the results from both of these tests indicate that neither of these two necessary assumptions for unbiased estimation is violated by a random effects estimator, then it should also follow that they are not violated by a fixed effects estimator. This suggests that an appropriate procedure to follow is to sequentially test the validity of the assumptions—first using the random effects estimator and then the fixed effects estimator using two different base periods. While this testing technique is not completely

---

6 Once again, an insignificant coefficient is a necessary (but not sufficient) condition for unbiased estimation.

air-tight (because of reasons discussed above), it does represent a substantial improvement over earlier evaluations of this type which have simply *assumed* that the available comparison groups were adequate for unbiased estimation.

The results from these tests are reported in the next section, which begins with a description of the data available on CETA participants from the CLMS and on nonparticipants from the Current Population Survey (CPS).

II. THE CLMS AND ITS COMPARISON GROUPS

The Continuous Longitudinal Manpower Survey (CLMS) represents a major data development effort of the Department of Labor for evaluation of CETA-funded employment and training programs. The currently available public-use tapes contain representative samples of 6700 individuals who participated in the program during fiscal year 1975, and 13,300 who participated during fiscal year 1976. For each of these individuals, the CLMS included a four-year record of labor force experience beginning one year prior to CETA enrollment, the type of CETA program(s) in which the individual participated,[7] basic demographic characteristics, a history of public benefits received by the individual and/or the individual's family, and family-related variables. Although the CLMS is a far superior data base for evaluating training programs than has previously been available, it is still less than ideal. A number of variables that are often included in earnings equations (union status, geographic location, and work experience, for example) are not available. However, one of the unique features of the CLMS is that the March 1976 Current Population Survey (CPS) has been included in the public-use tapes for purposes of comparison. Both the CLMS and the CPS have been merged with the records from the Social Security Administration so that each observation also has a record of reported annual Social Security earnings for 1951–1978.

The Comparison Groups

The Bureau of the Census collected and prepared the data, while Westat, Inc., was responsible for data management (and preliminary analysis). In lieu of a true control group, Westat created a series of "match lists" from the CPS. These match lists are comparison groups generated by selecting individuals from the CPS that "match" a particular CETA participant on a variety of sociodemographic and past earnings variables.

---

7   CETA encompasses a variety of programs, including Public Service Employment, On-the-Job Training, Adult Work Experience, Youth Work Experience, Classroom Training, Summer Youth Programs, and direct referral services.

Westat constructed three comparison groups (nos. 11, 12, and 13) for the 1976 CETA sample by first dividing the sample into three income groups and then doing the matching separately for low, middle, and high income groups, respectively. The only available comparison group for the entire 1976 CLMS must be derived by pooling groups 11–13.

Both the particular procedures used in the matching process to create the comparison groups and the matching process itself have been subject to serious criticism. Many economists would argue that matching is unnecessary, as a comparison group could be generated by drawing a random sample from the CPS and using ordinary least squares to control for any differences between the comparison and treatment groups. Alternatively, an autoregression earnings equation could be used to control (directly through regression analysis) for the same things that the matching process does.

Nonetheless, I have used Westat's comparison groups, primarily to maintain comparability with previous research. In addition, I have drawn a random sample from the CPS to serve as an alternative comparison group.

An Analysis of the Comparison Groups

The first step toward choosing among the estimation techniques and the comparison groups is to specify the functional form of the random effects model. The following variables were included in the preprogram random effects estimator: age, age squared, age cubed, education (in years), and dummy variables measuring head of household status and program participation.

The empirical work will be done separately for four race/sex groups: white men, minority men, white women, and minority women. The specification of the functional form is, however, distressingly lean. Obviously, there are many other variables that affect earnings and should be included in the random effects estimator, but the specification given above incorporates all of the variables that are common to both the CLMS and CPS.

The meager specification that is available for a random effects estimator suggests that a fixed effects estimator should be tested even if nonrandom selection was not a concern, since many of the variables normally included in an earnings equation would be eliminated in the process of differencing. After differencing, the only variables left to be included in the fixed effects estimator are age, age squared, and program participation.[8] As was explained earlier, the program participation dummy

---

8 Differencing reduces the degree of any polynomial by a factor of one, so the cubic in age in the random effects estimator becomes a quadratic in the fixed effects estimator. Since head of household status is observed at only one point in time, it cannot be used in the fixed effects estimator.

variable remains in the fixed effects estimator (even after differencing) to test for correlation between it and the error term.

Both of the hypothesis tests described in the first section were done for each comparison group and for each of the estimation techniques—random effects (using the year immediately prior to training) and fixed effects with two different base periods, and each test was done separately for each race/sex group. All individuals under the age of 23 during the participation year were excluded from the sample since they do not have a long enough earnings history on which to base the hypothesis tests. Since CETA programs have generally served youth in large numbers, this exclusion substantially reduces the sample size. Even after this exclusion, the participants remaining in the sample are very young. Consequently, I have used only two years of preprogram data to avoid further sample shrinkage.

Table 1 reports the coefficients on the dummy variable in the preprogram earnings equation. Chow test results are not reported here since there was no case in which a comparison group or estimator was rejected because of the Chow test when it was not also rejected on the basis of Table 1 results. A number of interesting conclusions emerge from this table, the most obvious being that a random sample is a failure as a comparison group. This tells us that CETA participants are so different from randomly chosen members of the population that none of the estimation techniques used here can adequately control for these differences. Westat's nonrandom samples are vastly superior. Unfortunately, only one comparison group is available for the entire 1976 cohort,[9] so we will be unable to test the sensitivity of the estimated training effects to the choice of a comparison group.

In general, the comparison groups perform better for women than for men, and better for minorities than for whites, which is consistent with the fact that low wages are paid to CETA participants. Thus the program is more attractive to groups that typically earn low wages—women and minorities. This tells us that, in general, selection into the program of individuals in low-wage groups will be closer to random than for high-wage groups. Indeed, selection of white men into the program is so nonrandom that none of the estimators is adequate for unbiased estimation. Consequently, we do not present earnings effects for this group.

The only exception for white men is that the comparison group for low earners (no. 11) performs adequately. In general, this comparison group works much better than the comparison group for high earners (no. 13). Once again, this is in keeping with our expectation that non-

9   The only comparison group for the entire 1976 cohort must be derived by combining comparison groups 11–13.

TABLE 1
COEFFICIENTS ON DUMMY VARIABLE
IN PREPROGRAM EARNINGS EQUATION

Race/Sex Group	Estimation Technique	11	12	13	11–13 (Combined)	Random Sample
White	A	−7	−4	−40	−33	−1219*
women		(.2)	(0)	(.2)	(.3)	(8.0)
	B	−205*	−17	−185	−38	−1306*
		(3.0)	(.5)	(1.2)	(.6)	(6.5)
	C	29	−82	359	14	−1108*
		(.5)	(.7)	(.8)	(.2)	(5.3)
Minority	A	−70	−210	−65	−266*	−1486*
women		(1.2)	(1.1)	(.2)	(1.7)	(5.9)
	B	−53	−510*	−25	−244*	−1368*
		(.9)	(2.0)	(.1)	(2.2)	(4.9)
	C	−100	387*	−91	104	−1293*
		(.9)	(2.1)	(.6)	(1.0)	(4.7)
White men	A	−5	−60	−1314*	−1882*	−3661*
		(.1)	(.5)	(9.7)	(13.6)	(20.5)
	B	−92	−355*	−531*	−556*	−1942*
		(1.5)	(1.9)	(5.6)	(6.7)	(18.6)
	C	249*	158*	−180*	−347*	−2103*
		(1.8)	(2.4)	(2.0)	(4.8)	(19.2)
Minority men	A	83	158	−365	−670*	−2741*
		(1.0)	(.8)	(1.1)	(2.9)	(7.7)
	B	−122	188	−365	−93	−1792*
		(1.4)	(.6)	(1.5)	(.6)	(7.0)
	C	−151	−294	619*	−215	−1509*
		(.8)	(1.3)	(2.6)	(.9)	(5.6)

Note: Absolute *t*-values in parentheses
Notation: A—random effects; B—fixed effects, base period one year prior to training; C—fixed effects, base year two years prior to training.
* Indicates significance at the .05 level.

random selection into the program is a less severe problem among low-income individuals.

There does not seem to be a great deal of evidence indicating that creaming is a serious concern, for there is no systematic difference in the bias between the fixed effect estimators in the two preprogram years. Recall, however, that the negative coefficient on the dummy variable in the preprogram earnings equation could reflect either permanent or transitory differences between the participant and comparison groups.

There also has been a good deal of speculation that assignment of participants among the various programs within CETA has been non-random. It has been assumed that the most qualified participants were assigned to Public Service Employment (PSE) and On-the-Job Training (OJT) and the least qualified to Adult Work Experience (AWE). The same series of hypothesis tests that was used to test for nonrandom participation into CETA was used to test for nonrandom assignment among CETA activities.[10] The results from these tests (not reported in detail here) indicate that there has, indeed, been nonrandom assignment among the program activities since a random effects estimator fails the joint hypothesis test. As before, a fixed effects estimator is generally sufficient to control for nonrandom assignment. Again, the exception is for white men. For this group, both assignment into CETA and assignment among CETA activities seems to be hopelessly nonrandom. In general, these results show that the assignment process has been consistent with expectations. The coefficients on the dummy variables measuring program assignment in the preprogram earnings equations are generally positive and significant for PSE and OJT, and negative and significant for AWE.

III. ESTIMATED TRAINING EFFECTS

As the earlier discussion indicated, CETA has undergone several major legislative changes since it was first enacted in 1973. After its reauthorization in 1978, it was increasingly targeted on the most disadvantaged workers. This trend will be continued under JTPA, CETA's replacement.

Estimated Training Effects by Eligibility Criteria

The results reported here are based on fixed effects estimates (techniques B and C) using the comparison group for the entire 1976 cohort (groups 11–13 combined). Ideally, we would like to be able to estimate CETA's effect on more recent cohorts óf participants—those who were the most disadvantaged—since this is the group that will be served by JTPA. However, the 1976 cohort is the most recent one available on the public-use tapes.[11] To shed some light on how the targeting changes have affected CETA's impact, I have divided the sample of 1976 participants into two subsamples—those who would have met the tighter eligibility criteria after 1978, and those who would not have met the criteria. Roughly speaking, the eligibility criteria after 1978 required that an individual either be a member of a family receiving public assistance or have a family income

---

10   These tests were based on data for participants only, using the entire 1976 cohort.
11   After the writing of this article, the 1977 cohort has become available.

)elow the Office of Management and Budget poverty line. I will refer to this group as individuals who are economically disadvantaged, and the)ther group (those who did not meet the 1978 criteria) as being not economically disadvantaged. The comparison groups for this analysis were derived by dividing the comparison group for the 1976 cohort (groups 11–13 combined) according to the same criteria.

Table 2 reports the estimated effect of CETA participation on earnings of the 1976 cohort in the postprogram years 1977 and 1978.[12] The results, which are in nominal terms, are summarized separately by race/sex group for the entire 1976 cohort, those who were economically disadvantaged, and those who were not. As noted above, because we could find no unbiased method to estimate the training effects for white men, their results are not shown.

Nevertheless, we can draw a number of conclusions from the table. Despite our inability to produce any unbiased results for white men, it seems likely that women benefit more from CETA participation than do men. This is certainly the case for minority women at least. There is some indication that these benefits may actually increase in the first two years after leaving the program—results that are consistent with those of other studies of CETA participation (see Westat [11]) as well as studies based on earlier federally funded programs (see Ashenfelter [1]).

Table 2 also provides some evidence that the benefits to the economically disadvantaged do not become statistically significant until the second year after training. Unfortunately, there are not enough postprogram data for us to be able to see if the benefits continue to grow over time, stabilize, or deteriorate. At any rate, the benefits in the second postprogram year are impressive, particularly in light of the participants' very low average level of earnings. The jury is still out on whether the economically disadvantaged benefit more than those who are not disadvantaged. Certainly one could not reasonably argue on the basis of these estimates that the disadvantaged benefit less. Given binding resource constraints, one could argue, based on equity considerations (and perhaps efficiency as well), that the changes made in CETA's 1978 reauthorization increased its effectiveness in achieving its objectives of human capital development among the most disadvantaged.

On the basis of the available data, it is impossible to provide a rigorous explanation of why women benefit from the program more than men do. Perhaps what CETA does best is prepare participants for low-paying, entry-level jobs. This preparation seems to represent an improvement in the labor market status of women.

---

12 I have not included estimates of the effect of CETA on in-program year since the 1976 cohort is based on the fiscal year, not the calendar year, making it impossible to isolate an in-program effect.

TABLE 2

SUMMARY OF ESTIMATED TRAINING EFFECTS
FOR ADULTS WHO PARTICIPATED IN CETA DURING FISCAL YEAR 1976

Group	Dependent Variable Is Change in Earnings from:				Sample Size	
	1977–1974	1977–1973	1978–1974	1978–1973	Participants	Comparison
Entire cohort						
White women	778*	740*	1145*	1108*	1417	1491
	(5.50)	(5.31)	(6.89)	(6.61)		
Minority women	671*	426*	788*	431*	724	366
	(2.91)	(1.81)	(2.79)	(1.86)		
Minority men	211	117	113	27	783	317
	(.67)	(.37)	(.30)	(.07)		
Economically disadvantaged						
White women	263	130	679*	545*	705	355
	(1.22)	(.61)	(2.68)	(2.19)		
Minority women	944*	669*	1054*	776*	515	184
	(3.39)	(2.41)	(3.05)	(2.31)		
Minority men	309	133	−104	−264	448	117
	(.66)	(.29)	(.19)	(.48)		
Not economically disadvantaged						
White women	996*	1050*	1210*	1267*	712	1136
	(5.99)	(6.19)	(6.05)	(6.23)		
Minority women	236	169	461	375	209	182
	(.64)	(.43)	(1.04)	(.80)		
Minority men	−142	−246	8	−100	335	182
	(.36)	(.61)	(.02)	(.21)		

Note: Absolute t-values in parentheses.
* Indicates significance at the .05 level.

338

TABLE 3

ESTIMATED TRAINING EFFECTS BY PROGRAM ACTIVITY
FOR ECONOMICALLY DISADVANTAGED ADULTS WHO PARTICIPATED
IN CETA DURING FISCAL YEAR 1976[a]

Year	Group	Estimation Technique B					Estimation Technique C				
		PSE	AWE	CT	OJT	MUL[b]	PSE	AWE	CT	OJT	MUL[b]
1977	White women	701*	−120	205	382	602	614*	−293	63	80	433
		(2.11)	(.36)	(.77)	(.90)	(1.39)	(1.89)	(.90)	(.24)	(.19)	(1.02)
	Minority women	815*	1023*	633*	1549*	1599*	259	872*	426	1368*	1195*
		(1.81)	(2.54)	(2.13)	(2.91)	(2.92)	(.58)	(2.18)	(1.37)	(2.58)	(2.19)
	Minority men	−23	−310	773	2057*	−1654*	−213	−391	582	2053*	−2171*
		(.04)	(.47)	(1.46)	(2.16)	(1.87)	(.38)	(.61)	(1.11)	(2.64)	(2.49)
1978	White women	1660*	−115	752*	117	1043*	1573*	−288	610*	−185	873*
		(4.30)	(.30)	(2.44)	(.24)	(2.06)	(4.14)	(.76)	(2.01)	(.38)	(1.75)
	Minority women	1448*	869*	811*	1223*	1634*	894*	698	575	1044	1231*
		(2.59)	(1.73)	(2.09)	(1.85)	(2.40)	(1.64)	(1.42)	(1.52)	(1.62)	(1.85)
	Minority men	−557	−618	606	328	−1200	−739	654	427	333	−1706
		(.80)	(.78)	(.95)	(.34)	(1.13)	(1.08)	(.84)	(.68)	(.36)	(1.62)

a See Table 2 for relevant sample sizes.
b Multiple program activities.
* Indicates significance at the .05 level.

339

Estimated Training Effects by Program Activity

The Reagan Administration recently eliminated the Public Service Employment (PSE) component of CETA which typically had accounted for the lion's share of the program's budget. One of the justifications for this change—in addition to the obvious one of budget-cutting—was that the federal government can be of the most assistance to economically disadvantaged and hard-to-employ individuals by providing training rather than employment opportunities.

This assertion can be tested by estimating the postprogram effects separately, based on the type of CETA activity in which participants were enrolled. The results of this estimation, reported in Table 3, are based on only the 1976 participants who were economically disadvantaged, the group that comes closest to approximating the participants who were affected by the Reagan Administration's changes. One of the unfortunate consequences of dividing the sample in this way is that when it is further subdivided by program activity, we are less likely to be able to identify statistically significant relationships.[13] Nevertheless, the program activities considered include PSE, On-the-Job Training (OJT), Classroom Training (CT), Adult Work Experience (AWE), and a combination of these activities (MULTIPLE).

In general, the estimated training effects by program activity are consistent with the overall estimated effects that were reported in Table 2.[14] The estimated effects are usually positive for women, although generally not statistically significant for white women. The exception is for AWE which has consistently negative (albeit insignificant) estimated effects. The results for men are generally insignificant and sometimes negative, especially for minority men.

Minority women clearly benefit from participation in all of the programs, while PSE and multiple activities (which probably includes PSE) have the most decisive effect on white women's postprogram earnings. OJT is the only program for which it is possible to identify significant, positive postprogram effects for men. This general lack of significance makes it difficult to rank the program activities according to their effectiveness in increasing earnings of participants.

---

13 The results by program activity are derived by running a single regression for each race/sex group and replacing the dummy variable measuring program participation by a series of dummy variables that capture the various program activities. It is the small number of individuals within each of these cells that creates the problem.

14 Additional results (not shown here) indicate that the earnings across program activities during the in-program years (1975 and 1976) are consistent with our expectations. CT participants (who received no in-program stipend) had the lowest earnings, followed by Adult Work Experience (who generally received a small in-program stipend). OJT and PSE participants (who received in-program wages) had the highest earnings in 1975 and 1976.

The results from Table 3 do indicate, however, that it would be difficult to make a case for PSE being, in some sense, "best" for achieving this goal. This is particularly true when we consider the costs of the program. In fiscal year 1976, the average cost per CETA participant by program activity was $8231 for PSE, $2636 for OJT, $1418 for CT, and $5844 for AWE.[15] Even when these costs are adjusted downward to account for budgetary offsets created by reduced levels of transfer payments (which are particularly large for PSE), OJT and CT are clearly much less expensive programs.[16] Combining this information with the results from Table 3 leads us to conclude that the Reagan Administration was probably justified in its elimination of PSE. Training opportunities as opposed to employment opportunities seem to be a much more cost-effective means of increasing disadvantaged workers' employment and earnings prospects.

In all fairness to the PSE program, however, it should be noted that in 1976 the primary emphasis of the program was on reducing cyclical unemployment, not on increasing workers' long-term earnings. Thus it will not be possible to provide a completely fair test of PSE's effectiveness in increasing participants' earnings until more recent cohorts of the CLMS are available.

Another factor that has not been considered in the calculation of the cost-effectiveness of PSE is the value of the output produced by PSE participants. Since we are unable to estimate these benefits, we have underestimated the cost effectiveness of the program.[17]

Contamination Bias

In addition to nonrandom selection, a potentially serious difficulty in developing unbiased estimates of training effects results from unidentified CETA participants being chosen as members of the comparison group. Since the comparison group is drawn from the CPS, which is a representative sample of the entire U.S. population, it should contain the same percentage of CETA participants as does the population at large. In 1976,

15 These costs were derived from unpublished documents from the Department of Labor.
16 The adjusted cost of PSE is $4692. See Bassi [3]. It is not possible to calculate comparable adjusted costs for OJT, CT, and AWE.
17 A final bias in the cost-effectiveness of PSE (and AWE) is created by using Social Security earnings as the dependent variable. Social Security earnings are measured with error because not all workers are covered by the program. Although the vast majority of workers are covered, most uncovered workers are in the public sector. Since PSE and AWE participants are more likely to be employed in the public sector after leaving the program than are their nonparticipant counterparts, this creates a downward bias in the estimated postprogram earnings gains. I have investigated the magnitude of this bias (Bassi [2]) and found it to be very small.

approximately .8 percent of the population participated in CETA. However, the probability that individuals in the comparison group are actually unidentified CETA participants is greater than the same probability for a randomly chosen individual. This follows since the comparison groups are chosen to "match" the observable characteristics of CETA participants.

The weights assigned to each individual in the CPS and CLMS can be used to calculate the probability of contamination for the nonrandom comparison group. An examination of these weights indicates that between 4 and 5 percent of the individuals in the comparison group were enrolled in CETA during 1976.[18] A second source of contamination bias is that some members of the comparison groups have participated either before or after this period. This source of contamination bias accumulates over time and will be most significant in years when there were large numbers of program participants. By adjusting the 1976 contamination rate to account for contamination during other relevant years in which CETA was in operation, we arrive at the cumulative rates given in Table 4.[19]

The figures in this table can be roughly interpreted as the downward bias in the estimated training effects that results from contamination of the comparison groups.[20] Dividing the training effects in Table 2 by one minus the numbers in Table 4 would yield estimates that are (approximately) corrected for contamination bias.

IV. CONCLUSIONS

A number of interesting substantive and methodological results have emerged from this analysis. The first is that CETA has had positive and often significant effects on the earnings of participants. It seems clear that these effects are larger for women than for men, a result that has appeared with remarkable consistency through the manpower-training literature.

Although we can only speculate on why this is so, the most likely

---

18 Westat estimates a lower contamination rate of 2 to 3 percent. Their procedure, however, does not account for the fact that selection into the program is not random—even among the eligible population. Using the weights in the CPS and CLMS corrects for this oversight.

19 These rates have been derived by adjusting for the number of CETA participants in 1974, 1975, 1977, and 1978. These are the relevant years since the program was not operating prior to 1974 and 1978 is the most recent year for which data are available.

20 These numbers are only approximate because of possible interactions between the contamination ratios and other exogenous factors which may influence the estimated training effects. These interactions are probably less significant in a fixed effects model than in a random effects model because the former has fewer exogenous variables. A mathematical derivation of these principles is available from the author.

TABLE 4
ESTIMATED CUMULATIVE FRACTION OF UNIDENTIFIED CETA
PARTICIPANTS IN THE COMPARISON GROUP
FROM 1974–1978

Group	Age			
	23–29	30–44	Over 44	Over 23
White women	.183–.195	.187–.191	.183–.187	.183–.191
Minority women	.164–.172	.144–.152	.164–.176	.156–.164
White men	.179–.187	.199–.203	.195–.203	.187–.195
Minority men	.160–.172	.160–.187	.168–.179	.164–.172

explanation is that CETA has been relatively effective in training partic-ipants for entry-level jobs. While this training represents an improvement for female participants, it leaves male participants no better off.

Among the various program activities that have been available under CETA, no one of them is clearly more beneficial to participants than the others. This leads us to conclude (subject to the caveats already men-tioned) that, given the extremely high cost of the PSE program, the Re-agan Administration was justified in abandoning it for less expensive training options.

It is unfortunate that there are not enough years of postprogram data available to enable us to firmly conclude that economically disadvantaged participants experience substantially larger postprogram earnings gains than participants who are not economically disadvantaged. As more years of earnings data become available, it should be possible to detect a more consistent pattern in the estimated training effects. On the basis of the evidence presented here, however, one could not reasonably argue that the disadvantaged benefit less. Given binding resource constraints and equity considerations (and perhaps efficiency considerations as well), it seems likely that the changes in CETA at the time of the 1978 reau-thorization increased its effectiveness in achieving its objective of human capital development among the most disadvantaged. The fact that this is the group that will continue to be served under JPTA is encouraging.

Yet several questions remain unanswered. The empirical work pre-sented here does not provide overwhelming support for the conclusion that CETA has significant, long-term effects on participants' earnings. Nor does it provide significant evidence to the contrary. There simply are not yet enough years of postprogram data to make convincing ar-guments about long-term effects. And, unfortunately, the bias created by contamination of the comparison group will become increasingly worse over time.

Unbiased estimation of CETA's effect on the earnings of white men seems impossible unless a better set of comparison groups is found. Nevertheless, the nonrandom comparison groups drawn from the CPS are, in general, far superior to a comparison group that is created by drawing a random sample. Care must be used, however, in working with these comparison groups. Estimation techniques that account for non-random selection between the participants and the comparison group, as well as nonrandom selection within the group of participants, are essential.

REFERENCES

1. Orley Ashenfelter. "Estimating the Effect of Training Programs on Earnings." *Review of Economics and Statistics* 60 (February 1978): 47–57.
2. Laurie J. Bassi. "Estimating the Effect of Training Programs with Non-Random Selection." Ph.D. dissertation, Princeton University, October 1982.
3. ——. "CETA—Did It Work?" *Policy Studies Journal* (forthcoming).
4. Glen G. Cain. "Regression and Selection Models to Improve Nonexperimental Comparisons." In *Evaluation and Experiment*, eds. C. A. Bennett and A. A. Lumsdaine. New York: Academic Press, 1975.
5. Congressional Budget Office. "Effects of Eliminating Public Service Employment." Staff Working Paper. Washington: 1981.
6. Arthur Goldberger. "Selection Bias in Evaluating Treatment Effects." Discussion Paper 123–72. Institute for Research on Poverty, University of Wisconsin, 1972.
7. Zvi Griliches. "Estimating the Returns to Schooling: Some Econometric Problems." *Econometrica* 45 (January 1977): 1–22.
8. James J. Heckman. "Sample Selection Bias as a Specification Error." *Econometrica* 47 (January 1979): 153–61.
9. ——. "Shadow Prices, Market Wages, and Labor Supply." *Econometrica* 42 (July 1974): 679–94.
10. Nicholas M. Kiefer. "The Economic Benefits from Four Government Training Programs." In *Research in Labor Economics: Evaluating Manpower Training Programs*, ed. Farrell E. Bloch. Greenwich, Conn.: JAI Press, 1979.
11. U.S. Department of Labor and U.S. Department of Health, Education, and Welfare. *Employment and Training Report of the President*. Washington: U.S. Government Printing Office, 1976–1979.
12. Westat, Inc. "The Impact on 1977 Earnings of New FY 1976 CETA Enrollees in Selected Program Activities." Net Impact Report No. 1, November 1980.
13. ——. "The Impact of CETA on Participant Earnings." Working Paper #2, June 1980.
14. ——. "The Impact of CETA on Participant Earnings." Working Paper #1, January 1980.
15. Robert J. Willis and Sherwin Rosen. "Education and Self-Selection." *Journal of Political Economy* 87 (October 1979): S7–S36.

19

The Youth Entitlement Demonstration
Subsidized Employment with a Schooling Requirement*

George Farkas, D. Alton Smith, and Ernst W. Stromsdorfer

ABSTRACT

The YIEPP offered a minimum wage job, part-time during the school year and full-time during the summer, to 16–19-year-olds from low-income households who had not as yet graduated from high school and who were enrolled in school. Our finding of large positive employment effects for this population is strong evidence that the unemployment of these youths is largely involuntary, due to demand deficiency at the minimum wage. We also find small positive school enrollment effects, and an employment displacement rate of 31.6 percent—that is, 31.6 percent of subsidized employment would have been available for the target population even in the absence of the program.

I. INTRODUCTION

"These results suggest, however, that a successful policy to reduce unemployment among dropouts might well have the side effect of encouraging boys to drop out of school before high-school graduation." (Duncan [6, p. 134])

Thus, 17 years ago did Beverly Duncan identify the potential school enrollment disincentive of programs or policies designed to increase the

The authors' affiliations are, respectively, School of Social Sciences, University of Texas at Dallas; School of Social Sciences, U.S. Military Academy; and Abt Associates Inc.

* Portions of the work reported here were funded by Manpower Demonstration Research Corporation (MDRC) under contract to Abt Associates Inc. MDRC was, in turn, funded by the Employment and Training Administration, U.S. Department of Labor. The points of view or opinions stated in this paper do not necessarily represent the official position or policy of the supporting funding agencies. [Manuscript received August 1982; accepted March 1983.]

employment of teenagers. Since that time, two principal strategies have been considered to increase youth employment. The first, subsidized youth employment programs, typically (but not exclusively) at the federal minimum wage, have been implemented under many rubrics, and relatively continuously since the 1960s. Such programs have occasionally involved employment during the school year, but rarely with explicit attention to the potentially negative school enrollment effects of such employment.[1] The second, a youth subminimum wage, has been much discussed, but also rarely with attention to the potentially negative school enrollment effects of such a policy. A youth subminimum wage has never been successfully passed into law.

Recently two studies have found evidence for school enrollment disincentive effects of policies designed to increase employment demand for youths without regard to the school enrollment of these youths (Ehrenberg and Marcus [7, 8], Gustman and Steinmeier [14]). By contrast, a study of the Job Corps, a residential subsidized employment program for disadvantaged youths in which schooling is an integral part, found strong positive effects on both employment and high school graduation (Mallar et al. [17]). In this paper we report the during-program employment and school enrollment effects of the Youth Incentive Entitlement Pilot Projects (YIEPP). This demonstration, funded by the Youth Employment and Demonstration Project Act of 1977, offered a minimum-wage job, part-time during the school year and full-time during the summer, to 16–19-year-olds from low-income households who had not as yet graduated from high school, and who were enrolled in school and making satisfactory progress toward a degree. School dropouts were prohibited from entering YIEPP employment, as the aim of the program was to increase youth employment while requiring school enrollment. If program employment effects are large, we may conclude that target population youths do wish to work at the minimum wage, and that high youth unemployment rates are at least partially due to demand deficiency at this wage. If program school enrollment effects are positive, or at least not negative, we may conclude that the YIEPP model is at least one strategy by which youth work experience can be increased without decreasing human capital investment through schooling.[2]

---

1 Programs providing subsidized employment to youths during the school year include the Neighborhood Youth Corps, the Youth Conservation Corps, and the Youth Employment and Training Program.

2 The implicit model is one in which youths allocate their time between work, school, and leisure, with YIEPP providing an intervention which reduces the demand-side "distortions" (such as the minimum wage) for youths who are willing to be enrolled in school. For related models of youth labor markets, see Ehrenberg and Marcus [7] and Farkas, Olsen, and Stromsdorfer [11].

Net Job Creation

Even if program employment effects are large, we may ask whether these effects have been efficiently achieved. This question is closely related to the issue of displacement in public service employment programs, the magnitude of which has been recently debated and is still in some doubt (see, for example, Johnson [15], Johnson and Tomola [16], Borus and Hamermesh [3], Nathan et al. [18]).

In the case of YIEPP "job creation," we may well ask where the jobs to provide 76,051 youths with 45 million hours of work experience came from.[3] If these were all "new" jobs—jobs which would not have been available in the absence of the program—then employment in these jobs represents a net addition to previous employment, and the site-wide YIEPP employment effect is simply equal to total YIEPP employment. Unfortunately, this is unlikely to be the case. For YIEPP administrators, the need to find a large number of good quality jobs in a short time span provided a strong impetus to permit the shifting of preexisting jobs onto the YIEPP payroll. This might occur for previously unsubsidized jobs or for jobs that would have been paid for by a non-YIEPP subsidy program, and it could occur in either the public or private sector. From the employer's perspective, such displacement of a portion of his wage bill by YIEPP funds is desirable; there would be particularly strong incentives for such displacement in the private sector.

Figure 1 displays the relationship among YIEPP employment, the YIEPP effect on employment in the pilot site as a whole, and the magnitude of the displacement effect. The target population youths in a site's labor market may be thought of as a relatively homogeneous group of entry-level workers whose total labor supply exceeds the pre-YIEPP demand at the federal minimum wage.[4] In the figure, the effect of YIEPP is to provide a horizontal (infinitely elastic) demand curve at the minimum wage, permitting all target population youths who wish to work at this wage to do so. As a consequence, total employment shifts from its preprogram level of E_0 to its during-program level of E_1^T, the YIEPP effect on total site employment being $E_1^T - E_0$. The magnitude of this effect is independent of any displacement that may occur.

The effect of displacement is to shift the non-YIEPP labor demand curve to the left—that is, fewer non-YIEPP jobs are now available in the pilot site, the number of such jobs at the minimum wage now being E_1.

---

3 For a discussion of the magnitude of the demonstration and the non-makework nature of the jobs provided, see Diaz et al. [5].

4 High unemployment rates for the target population and high YIEPP participation rates are evidence for supply in excess of demand. For a discussion of these and related issues, see Farkas et al. [9, 10].

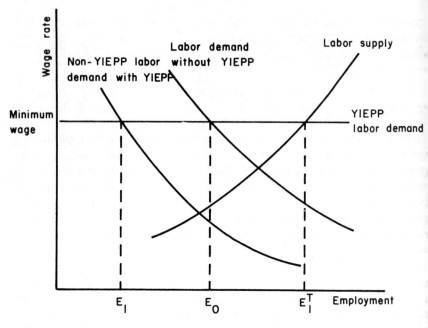

FIGURE 1
THE MECHANISM OF PROGRAM EFFECTS
ON TOTAL EMPLOYMENT FOR THE TARGET POPULATION
YIEPP effect on total employment $= E_1^T - E_0$
YIEPP employment $= E_1^T - E_1$
Displacement $= E_0 - E_1$
So, YIEPP effect = YIEPP employment − displacement

Since E_1^T youths still wish to work at the minimum wage, YIEPP employment equals $E_1^T - E_1$. Displacement—the number of non-YIEPP jobs transferred to the YIEPP payroll, is given by $E_0 - E_1$. Thus, YIEPP employment equals the YIEPP employment effect plus displacement, and the YIEPP employment effect equals YIEPP employment minus displacement. When a program such as YIEPP is put in place, total employment shifts out to E_1^T, youth labor supply at the minimum wage, whether or not displacement is present. However, the extent of displacement determines the number of program jobs which must be funded in order to achieve this effect. In this paper we present estimates of both quantitites, the YIEPP effect on the percent of time employed by program-site target population youths and net job creation rates—the ratio of the YIEPP employment effect to total YIEPP program employment rates for target population youths $(E_1^T - E_0)/(E_1^T - E_1)$. The former is the program effect, and the latter measures the efficiency with which this effect was created. Of course the resulting estimate is only a lower bound for the employment displacement attributable to the program since it does not account for nontarget population workers who may have been displaced as a result of YIEPP.

I. METHODOLOGY

Since the congressional act[5] mandating YIEPP required that all eligible youths who desired to participate be given a program job, it was not possible to measure program effects by randomly assigning youths to program and nonprogram groups. Therefore, an alternative strategy was chosen that used comparison sites matched to the program sites, and program effects are estimated by assuming that (regression-adjusted) comparison site behavior by eligibles during the program period represents what would have been observed in the program sites in the absence of the program. That is, the existence of YIEPP in a program site is considered an exogenous "treatment" administered to the eligible population in the site as a whole, and the program effect is measured by the extent to which school enrollment or employment rates for the entire site are altered. This site-wide program effect is a function of both the participation rate for YIEPP and the program's effect on participating youths. Since, however, participation rates are quite high (across four study sites, 40–80 percent of target population youths who aged into and through eligibility participated in YIEPP at some time[6]), sufficient statistical power is available to observe any program effects of practical policy importance.

The Data

YIEPP began in the spring of 1978, enrolling youths in 17 local labor markets. Four of these—Denver, Cincinnati, Baltimore, and eight rural counties in southern Mississippi—were chosen as study sites. The matched comparison sites chosen were, respectively, Phoenix, Louisville, Cleveland, and a group of counties in western and eastern Mississippi.

Between February and July 1978, a study sample was selected in the eight sites by the following procedure: First, household screening interviews were administered to a probability sample of about 130,000 households to determine the presence of program-eligible youths. Next, enumerators returned to each of the program-eligible households and secured baseline interviews with the eligible youths and their parents. The questionnaire was designed to elicit detailed information on the youth's school

---

5 YIEPP was created as part of the Youth Employment and Demonstration Project Act, PL 95-93, August 5, 1977.

6 For further discussion of YIEPP participation, see Farkas et al. [9, 10].

and work history in the preprogram period as well as other information regarding the household and family, income, and attitudes and aspirations. It was in no way identified with the YIEPP program.

Subsequently, wave II and wave III reinterviews captured information on behavior during the spring 1978 to summer 1980 period of full-scale program operations. In this paper we use the wave I–wave III merged data to estimate YIEPP program effects. (In subsequent analyses we will employ a fourth wave of interviews to estimate effects during the postprogram period.)

In this paper we present estimates calculated from the subset of the full sample, consisting of black youths aged 15–16 on June 1, 1978. This subsample selection on the basis of exogenous characteristics serves two analytic purposes. First, by restricting attention to youths who aged into program eligibility at approximately the time of program start-up (as opposed to having already passed through the earliest eligible ages prior to YIEPP implementation), we gain a view of individual longitudinal behavior in the presence of the program which most nearly approximates that which would be observed in an ongoing national program. And second, by focusing on black youths (generally residing in inner-city and rural poverty areas) we provide program-effect estimates for that population subgroup which was most effectively reached by the program. (Participation rates for blacks were far more than twice those for whites. See Farkas et al. [9, 10]). In addition, since the great majority of the study sample is black, and these young blacks are a relatively homogeneous group (many regressors became insignificant when attention is restricted to 15–16-year-old black youths), effects for this subgroup are both particularly accurate and meaningful.

School enrollment and employment rates were calculated as follows: Enrollment and employment time lines were elicited from each survey respondent by drawing lines on a calendar to indicate those periods when the individual was, respectively, enrolled and employed. Then, associated with each such period, a series of questions was asked about the nature of the school or work experience. The resulting three waves of information have been merged to create continous school and work histories for each individual, and these histories provide the basis for our analysis.

The preprogram period for each individual begins in January 1977 and ends with the date he turned 16 or March 1978 (the start of program operations), whichever is later. The during-program period stretches from the end of the preprogram period to the earliest date on which any of the following events occurred: the youth reached 20 years of age, the youth graduated from high school (or received an equivalency degree), or the program terminated full-scale operations (August 1980). For each individual, for each of these periods, we calculate the percent of days (a) enrolled in school and employed, (b) enrolled in school and not employed,

(c) not enrolled in school and employed, and (d) not enrolled in school and not employed. These rates are the basic outcome measures for this analysis.[7]

Estimating Program Effects

Program effects are the difference between actual program site rates and estimates of what the rates would have been in the absence of YIEPP. These estimates were obtained by fitting ordinary least squares regression models for the percentage of time spent in the school/work states. The models included as right-hand-side variables a dichotomous variable indicating residence in a program site, the percentages of time spent in each of the school/work states in the preprogram period, and a number of sociodemographic control variables.[8] Estimated rates in the absence of the program are fitted values from these models, setting the program variable to zero and using the program site means for the other variables.[9] Program effect estimates are reported in text Tables 1 and 2; means and regression coefficient estimates can be found in Appendix Tables A1 and A2.

It is important to recognize that the pilot site/matched control site

---

7   Potential bias might arise due to the endogeneity of the length of each period—the date of high school graduation is potentially affected by YIEPP. However, regression analysis with these data show no evidence of such a program effect.

8   Included in these variables were the following: age in months, a dichotomous variable for females, highest grade completed as of the summer of 1977, total 1977 (preprogram) family income, the average of the highest grades completed by the youth's parents, a dichotomous variable for preprogram health problems, variables indicating the presence of one or both of the youth's natural parents in the preprogram period, and a dichotomous variable for youths who were themselves parents in the preprogram period.

9   When ordinary least squares is used to estimate a system of equations with continuous, limited dependent variables which sum to one (i.e., a shares model), the coefficients on a particular variable in the different equations will sum to zero. In our case, this assures that the program effects on the proportion of time spent in each school/work state will add to zero, an attractive restriction. However, this analysis strategy raises two questions: (a) It does not restrict the predicted proportions for any one state from being less than zero or greater than one, and (b) it could possibly lead to biased coefficients or standard errors due to the limited nature of the dependent variables. We are able to eliminate concern on the first point by computing fitted values for each member of the sample on each of the dependent variables. The proportion of the sample with fitted values below zero or above one is as follows: enrolled and employed, 1.9 percent; enrolled and not employed, 0.1 percent; not enrolled and employed, 0.0 percent; not enrolled and not employed, 0.2 percent. As for the second point, we estimated tobit models with a lower truncation of zero (observations at zero were much more likely than at one) for each of the school/work states. Because of the nonlinearity of the tobit model, there is no guarantee that estimated program effects on the various proportions will sum to zero. Neither the estimated program effects obtained with the tobit nor the standard errors of those effects differed significantly from the results reported below.

TABLE 1

YIEPP PROGRAM EFFECTS ON THE PERCENTAGE OF PROGRAM-ELIGIBLE
TIME SPENT IN DIFFERENT SCHOOL AND EMPLOYMENT STATES

Percent of Program-Eligible Time Spent:	Program Site Percentages	Estimated Program Site Percentages in the Absence of the Program	Program Effect (*t*-statistic)	Program Effect as a Percent of Rate in the Absence of the Program
Enrolled in school and employed	28.0	9.4	18.6 (14.6)	197.6
Enrolled in school and not employed	35.1	51.9	−16.8 (12.1)	−32.4
Not enrolled in school and employed	12.2	8.7	3.5 (5.2)	40.2
Not enrolled in school and not employed	24.7	30.0	−5.3 (4.6)	−17.7
Total enrolled in school	63.1	61.3	1.8	2.9
Total employed	40.2	18.1	22.1	122.1

Note. Estimates for black youths in the YIEPP survey sample who were 15−16 years of age on June 1, 1978. See text for further description of data and methods.

methodology avoids the possibility of selection bias (Barnow, Cain, and Goldberger [1]) at the cost of possible bias due to site effects not removed by the regression adjustment. Despite matching on geographical region, population density, socioeconomic characteristics of the population, and labor market conditions, we can never be completely sure that the comparison sites constitute an adequate control group for the program sites. However, indirect evidence is available. We regressed proportions of time in each school/work state during the preprogram period on a constant, a pilot site dummy variable, age, and a female dummy variable. The coefficient on the pilot site variable was statistically significant in only one of the four regressions, and, for all of the school/work states, the pilot-comparison site difference was less than one percentage point. One might argue that these results could be expected in any case; youths in the sample for this study were 14 or 15 years old during the preprogram period and, therefore, likely to be in school and not employed. As a stronger test of preprogram pilot/control matching, we selected older cohorts (youths aged 16–17 and 17–18 at the same time sample youths were 15–16) and repeated the analysis. None of the pilot-comparison site differences was statistically significant or greater than two percentage points. Accordingly, we are reasonably confident that the program/comparison site strategy leads to at most small biases in YIEPP program effect estimates.

III. RESULTS

Table 1 presents estimated program effects on the percent of days spent in each of the school/work states. Reading across the first row, we find that YIEPP dramatically increased the site-wide average share of days that target population youths spent both enrolled in school and employed; in the absence of the program this is estiamted to be 9.4 percent of a youth's time, whereas during program operations the percentage increases to 28.0, an increase of 18.6 percentage points or almost 200 percent of the nonprogram rate. This effect is statistically significant and demonstrates that the program succeeded at its primary operational goal—to increase dramatically the joint school/employment experience of the target population.[10]

The second row of Table 1 reveals the source of much of the increase in joint school/work—it results from decreased time spent in school and

---

10 It should be kept in mind that these are site-wide effects which average together the program effect on participants with (presumably) no effect on nonparticipants. An estimate of the effect on participants can be constructed by inflating the reported site-wide effect by the program participation rate. See Farkas et al. [9], Tables A3.7 and A4.6.

not employed. As a consequence of YIEPP, time in this state decreased by 16.8 percentage points, or 32.4 percent of the level in the absence of the program, primarily because in-school youths who are not employed find the program most attractive,[11] but at least partly due to the fact that target population youths spend the majority of their time in this state in the absence of the program. These facts combine to circumscribe somewhat the magnitude of the school enrollment increase potentially attainable by the program.

The third row shows the YIEPP effect on the percent of time not enrolled in school and employed. These percentages combine summer employment with employment of dropouts during the school year. Those in the latter group are prohibited from YIEPP participation, a regulation that apparently was successfully enforced (see Farkas et al. [10], Table 3.6 for the evidence). Accordingly, the estimated program effect in increasing time in this state by 3.5 percentage points is almost entirely due to increased summer employment.[12] This increment is significantly smaller than that for the joint school/work state, a result that is consistent with other calculations showing that the YIEPP employment effect is much larger during the school year than during the summer. This may be due to the narrowed gap between summer minimum wage supply and demand in the absence of YIEPP (recall Figure 1) resulting from subsidized employment provided by the Summer Youth Employment Program and other federal programs in force during the summers of 1978, 1979, and 1980. Thus, it is possible that if a program like YIEPP were to be implemented in the years ahead, with the reduced funding that is likely to be available for other subsidized employment programs at that time, the resulting summer employment effects of YIEPP would more closely approximate those observed for the school year.

The fourth row of Table 1 shows that YIEPP decreases the share of days spent neither enrolled in school nor employed by 5.3 percentage points, which is 17.7 percent of the rate in the absence of the program. This positive effect of the program is important since it is just such time without school or work activity which is thought to be unproductive for the youths themselves and generative of antisocial activity whose effects are felt by others.[13]

---

11 Such youths have by far the highest program participation rates. See Farkas et al. [9, 10].
12 YIEPP summer employment was available to program eligibles who had been enrolled in school during the preceding spring. Such youths were not obligated to return to school in the fall.
13 We also estimated separate program effects (entirely separate regressions) for males and females. The estimated effects on both schooling and employment were higher for females, but not significantly so.

These effects are estimated for sample population members who completed all three survey waves. To test for the possibility of bias due to differential sample attrition in program and comparison sites, an attempt was made to find a subset of attritors from the wave II survey, and those who were found were administered both wave II and wave III time lines. These data were then used to estimate program effects. The results were similar in magnitude to those reported in Table 1 and in no case was there a statistically significant difference. (These calculations are available from the authors upon request.) Accordingly, we discount attrition as a potential source of bias in our estimates.

Net Job Creation

As discussed above and portrayed in Figure 1, the difference between YIEPP program employment and the effect of YIEPP in increasing site-wide employment is the extent of displacement—YIEPP funding of jobs which would have been available in the absence of the program. The net job-creation rate, defined as the ratio of the YIEPP employment effect to YIEPP program employment, measures the extent to which such displacement occurred, or the efficiency with which the YIEPP employment effect was achieved. When this rate is equal to its maximum attainable value, 1.0, every YIEPP job hour leads to a full one-hour increment for site-wide employment over the level such employment would have attained in the absence of the program. When this rate is equal to its minimum, 0.0, complete displacement has occurred with no net job creation, since YIEPP simply subsidized jobs that would have been available in any event. Between these extremes, the net job-creation rate measures the percent of each YIEPP employment hour that provided employment that would not have been otherwise available, and is a straightforward measure of program job-creation efficiency.

Table 2 reports these net job-creation rates for total and sectoral employment. The first panel of the table shows employment effects, separately by sector—17.0 percentage points for the public sector and 4.6 percentage points for the private sector or, respectively, 212.5 and 43.4 percent of the rates expected in the absence of the program.[14] We then computed the ratio of each of these effects to the sectoral YIEPP employment rate, which yielded the net job-creation rates shown in the second panel. They are 74.2 percent for public-sector YIEPP employment, 52.9 percent for private-sector YIEPP employment, and 68.4 percent for total employment. Higher private- than public-sector displacement as a result of subsidized employment programs is consistent with a more competitive environment in the private sector, but to the best of our knowl-

---

14   The regression analyses underlying these results are reported in the Appendix.

TABLE 2
YIEPP NET JOB CREATION RATES, BY SECTOR

	Percent of Program-Eligible Time Spent in:		
	Public-Sector Employment	Private-Sector Employment	Total Employment
YIEPP Employment Effects			
Program site percentages	25.0	15.2	40.2
Estimated program site percentages in the absence of the program	8.0	10.6	18.6
Program effect	17.0	4.6	
(*t*-statistic)	(12.2)	(4.0)	21.6
Program effect as a percent of rate in the absence of the program	212.5	43.4	116.1
Net Job Creation			
Program effect on percent of time employed	17.0	4.6	21.6
Percent of time on YIEPP subsidized employment	22.9	8.7	31.6
Net job-creation rate	74.2	52.9	68.4

edge such sectoral differences have not been previously reported. Overall, we find that the large YIEPP employment effects are due to two mutually reinforcing factors: first, the great majority of YIEPP jobs were in the public sector, and second, the net job-creation rate was higher in this sector than in the private sector.

The total displacement rate for eligible youths is calculated to be 31.6 percent (displacement = 1 − net job creation). Of course, displacement of ineligibles must be added to this in order to get displacement for the population as a whole. However, given the magnitude of the rate for eligibles reported here, it appears likely that displacement for the population as a whole fell somewhere between previous CETA displacement estimates, ranging from approximately 20 percent to close to 100 percent (Nathan et al. [18], Johnson and Tomola [16]).

IV. DISCUSSION

"Constant references to *the* youth employment problem, as if all or the majority of young persons had difficulty obtaining jobs, appear to misnterpret the nature of the difficulty. Youth joblessness is in fact concen-rated, by and large, among a small group who lack work for extended eriods of time. . . . The youths who make up [this group] . . . have distinct haracteristics. They are disproportionately black, disproportionately high chool dropouts, and disproportionately residents of poverty areas." Freeman and Wise [13, p. 2])

The YIEPP demonstration was reasonably well targeted on the group dentified by Freeman and Wise as being at greatest risk of extended oblessness. A unique feature of this program was its entitlement nature—ufficient funds were available to provide jobs to all eligibles who applied. Our finding of large positive employment effects for this population is trong evidence that the unemployment of these youths is largely invol-untary, due to demand deficiency at the minimum wage. This result is consistent with previous results in which we estimated an offered wage/asking wage model of youth labor supply with preprogram data (Farkas, Olsen, and Stromsdorfer [11]; Farkas and Stromsdorfer [12]), and pro-vides a useful adjunct to the findings presented in Freeman and Wise 13].

A second unique feature of the program was the school enrollment equired for participation. Other findings (Ehrenberg and Marcus [8], Gustman and Steinmeier [14]) suggest that attempts to increase employ-ment without reference to school enrollment among the YIEPP target population might have the undesired side-effect of decreasing schooling for this group. Thus, the small, but positive, YIEPP school enrollment effect indicates that program regulations were successfully enforced and did exert an effect in the desired direction. That this school enrollment effect was not large is due primarily to the fact that program participation was highest among those youths who would have been enrolled in school in any event. This appears to be an unavoidable feature of an entitlement program such as YIEPP.

Prior studies suggest that at least some displacement—less than 100 percent "job creation efficiency"—inevitably accompanies subsidized em-ployment programs, so that measurement of the magnitude of displace-ment is now a standard feature of evaluations of such programs (see, for example, Bishop et al. [2]). In the case of the YIEPP, subsidized em-ployment dramatically increased total employment for the target popu-lation, but with a displacement rate of 31.6 percent. That is, 31.6 percent of the employment that was subsidized would have been available for the target population in the absence of the program. Additionally, we found that public-sector displacement is lower than private-sector dis-placement. These effects occurred even though YIEPP, as a consequence of third-party monitoring, was better managed than the majority of public employment programs.[15] These displacement estimates must be an input into future benefit/cost calculations of program efficiency.[16]

Finally, it should be noted that the ultimate assessment of programs such as YIEPP depends not only upon during-program effects, but also upon the translation of these effects into postprogram effects on employment and earnings. The existence and magnitude of such postprogram effects will be examined in future analyses.

REFERENCES

1. Burt S. Barnow, Glen G. Cain, and Arthur S. Goldberger. "Issues in the Analysis of Selectivity Bias." In *Evaluation Studies Review Annual—Volume 5.* eds. Ernst W. Stromsdorfer and George Farkas. Beverly Hills, Calif.: Sage Publications, 1980.
2. John Bishop, George Farkas, Michael C. Keeley, C. Eric Munson, and Philip K. Robins. "A Research Design to Study the Labor Market Effects of the Employment Opportunity Pilot Projects." In *Evaluation Studies Review Annual—Volume 5.* eds. Ernst W. Stromsdorfer and George Farkas. Beverly Hills, Calif.: Sage Publications, 1980.
3. Michael E. Borus and Daniel S. Hamermesh. "Estimating Fiscal Substitution by Public Service Employment Programs." *Journal of Human Resources* 13 (Fall 1978): 561–65.
4. William S. Diaz, Joseph Ball, Nancy Jacobs, Loren Solnick, and Albert Widman. *The Youth Entitlement Demonstration: Second Interim Report on Program Implementation.* New York: Manpower Demonstration Research Corporation, 1980.
5. ———. *The Youth Entitlement Demonstration: Final Report on Program Implementation.* New York: Manpower Demonstration Research Corporation, 1982.
6. Beverly Duncan. "Dropouts and the Unemployed." *Journal of Political Economy* 73 (April 1965): 121–34.
7. Ronald G. Ehrenberg and Alan J. Marcus. "Minimum Wage Legislation and the Educational Outcomes of Youths." In *Research in Labor Economics,* Vol. 3, ed. Ronald G. Ehrenberg. Greenwich, Conn.: JAI Press, 1980.
8. ———. "Minimum Wages and Teenagers' Enrollment-Employment Outcomes: A Multinomial Logit Model." *Journal of Human Resources* 17 (Winter 1982): 39–58.
9. George Farkas, D. Alton Smith, Ernst W. Stromsdorfer, Christine Bottom, and Randall J. Olsen. *Early Impacts from the Youth Entitlement Demonstration.* New York: Manpower Demonstration Research Corporation, 1980.

---

15 Program administration by local CETA prime sponsors was coordinated with a very firm hand by Manpower Demonstration Research Corporation, a nonprofit organization in New York City. For discussion of program administration issues, see Diaz et al. [4, 5].

16 Such calculations must also allow for displacement of program ineligibles, the magnitude of which could not be estimated from our data.

10. ———. *Impacts from the Youth Incentive Entitlement Pilot Projects: Participation, Work, and Schooling over the Full Program Period.* New York: Manpower Demonstration Research Corporation, 1982.
11. George Farkas, Randall J. Olsen, and Ernst W. Stromsdorfer. "Youth Labor Supply During the Summer: Evidence for Youths from Low-Income Households." In *Research in Labor Economics,* Vol. 4, ed. Ronald G. Ehrenberg. Greenwich, Conn.: JAI Press, 1981.
12. George Farkas and Ernst W. Stromsdorfer. "Comment" on Albert Rees and Wayne Grey, "Family Effects in Youth Employment." In *The Youth Labor Market Problem: Its Nature, Causes, and Consequences,* eds. Richard B. Freeman and David A. Wise. Chicago: University of Chicago Press, 1982.
13. Richard B. Freeman and David A. Wise, eds. *The Youth Labor Market Problem: Its Nature, Causes, and Consequences,* Chicago: University of Chicago Press (for the National Bureau of Economic Research), 1982.
14. Alan L. Gustman and Thomas L. Steinmeier. "The Impact of Wages and Unemployment on Youth Enrollment and Labor Supply." *Review of Economics and Statistics* 63 (November 1981): 533–60.
15. George Johnson. "The Labor Market Displacement Effect in the Analysis of Net Impact of Manpower Training Programs." In *Evaluating Manpower Training Programs,* ed. Farrell Bloch. Greenwich, Conn.: JAI Press, 1979.
16. George Johnson and James Tomola. "The Fiscal Substitution Effect of Alternative Approaches to Public Service Employment Policy." *Journal of Human Resources* 12 (Winter 1977): 3–26.
17. Charles Mallar, Stuart Kerachsky, Craig Thornton, Michael Donihue, Carol Jones, David Long, Emmanuel Noggoh, and Jennifer Schore. *The Lasting Impacts of Job Corps Participation.* Princeton, N.J.: Mathematica Policy Research, 1980.
18. Richard Nathan, Robert F. Cook, V. Lane Rawlins, and Associates. *Public Service Employment: A Field Evaluation.* Washington: Brookings Institution, 1981.

TABLE A1
PROGRAM EFFECTS ON PERCENTAGE OF TIME
IN SCHOOL/WORK STATES: OLS COEFFICIENTS
AND PROGRAM SITE MEANS

| | Coefficient (t-statistic) | | | |
Variable	Proportion of Time Enrolled, Employed	Proportion of Time Enrolled, Not Employed	Proportion of Time Not Enrolled, Not Employed	Program Site Means
Program site	.186	−.168	−.052	1.00
	(14.6)	(12.1)	(4.55)	
Age in months	−.157	−.556	.478	1.94
(in hundreds)	(1.49)	(4.82)	(5.00)	
Female	.011	.003	.020	.538
	(.880)	(.261)	(1.80)	

TABLE A1 (*Continued*)

| Variable | Coefficient (*t*-statistic) | | | |
	Proportion of Time Enrolled, Employed	Proportion of Time Enrolled, Not Employed	Proportion of Time Not Enrolled, Not Employed	Program Site Means
Proportion of preprogram time				
Enrolled, employed	.151 (.757)	1.17 (5.34)	−.135 (.747)	.049
Enrolled, not employed	−.053 (.268)	1.41 (6.48)	−.096 (.535)	.699
Not enrolled, employed	.058 (.272)	.964 (4.10)	.168 (.864)	.048
Not enrolled, not employed	−.293 (1.47)	1.16 (5.31)	.439 (2.43)	.204
Highest grade completed, Summer 1977	.052 (7.57)	.036 (4..84)	−.078 (12.9)	6.93
Highest grade missing	.370 (6.25)	.248 (3.83)	−.534 (9.95)	.176
Parents' highest grade completed	.005 (2.17)	−.001 (.409)	−.004 (1.93)	8.96
Parents' grade missing	.064 (1.80)	−.009 (.239)	−.030 (.929)	.050
Family income, 1977 (in thousands)	−.0005 (.974)	.0005 (.911)	.0002 (.398)	10.9
Health problems	.008 (.275)	−.024 (.736)	.026 (.965)	.038
Living with:				
Natural mother only	.010 (.769)	−.018 (1.22)	.004 (.343)	.636
Natural father only	−.081 (1.83)	.025 (.521)	.063 (1.57)	.016
Neither natural parent	.026 (1.15)	−.043 (1.74)	.002 (.097)	.086
Has own children	−.009 (.333)	−.103 (3.59)	.118 (4.96)	.061
N	1611	1611	1611	
R^2	.198	.147	.265	

TABLE A2
PROGRAM EFFECTS ON PERCENTAGE OF TIME
IN EMPLOYMENT/SECTOR STATES: OLS COEFFICIENTS
AND PROGRAM SITE MEANS

| Variable | Coefficient (t-statistic) | | Program Site Means |
	Proportion of Time Employed in Public Sector	Proportion of Time Employed in Private Sector	
Program site	.170	.046	1.00
	(12.2)	(4.00)	
Age in months (in hundreds)	.372	−.026	1.94
	(3.37)	(.286)	
Female	.030	−.039	.538
	(2.32)	(3.63)	
Proportion of preprogram time:			
Employed in public sector	−.198	.202	.051
	(.906)	(1.13)	
Employed in private sector	−.786	.528	.047
	(3.58)	(2.93)	
Not employed	−.676	.158	.902
	(3.13)	(.897)	
Family income, 1977 (in thousands)	−.00009	−.00002	10.9
	(.159)	(.053)	
Health problems	.012	−.025	.038
	(.376)	(.961)	
Living with:			
Natural mother only	.003	.005	.636
	(.174)	(.411)	
Natural father only	−.096	.008	.016
	(1.96)	(.200)	
Neither natural parent	.028	−.005	.086
	(1.14)	(.267)	
Has own children	−.040	−.039	.061
	(.380)	(.369)	
N	1611	1611	
R^2	.079	.133	

20

Information and Knowledge Development Potential
The Public vs. Private Sector Jobs Demonstration Project

James F. Gilsinan

It seems clear from initial published reports and documents that the extent of knowledge development under the Youth Employment and Demonstration Projects Act of 1977 (YEDPA) has been disappointing. By presenting the findings from a specific YEDPA demonstration project, this article suggests that the rather limited success in meeting knowledge-development goals is due more to a misunderstanding of the phrase "knowledge development" than to an actual lack of important information. It illustrates the differential degrees of value of what was discovered concerning the ability of the private sector to improve work attitudes, skills, and youths' chances to find and keep unsubsidized jobs. It concludes with a discussion of the kinds of knowledge that can reasonably be expected from projects of this type.

*G*oldhaber (1974) notes that each word in the English language has, on the average, 28 different meanings. If this is true, the number of interpretations available when single words are strung together in phrases, sentences, paragraphs, and so on is truly staggering. The point becomes clear when one considers the guiding phrase of the Youth Employment and Demonstration Projects Act of 1977 (YEDPA). This 1.5 billion dollar bill sought to provide both jobs and future career-planning skills for youth. Innovative, experimental approaches with rigorous evaluation components were encouraged. "Knowledge

AUTHOR'S NOTE: *I wish to thank E. Allan Tomey, the codirector of the Public versus Private Sector Jobs Demonstration Project. He was responsible for helping with initial collection and analyses of some of the data reported here.*

From James F. Gilsinan, "Information and Knowledge Development Potential: The Public vs. Private Sector Jobs Demonstration Project," *Evaluation Review,* 1984, 8(3), 371-388. Copyright 1984 by Sage Publications, Inc.

development" was therefore the clarion call to CETA prime sponsors, community-based organizations, researchers, and others who desired participation in this massive effort.

By the late fall of 1982, most of the research and evaluation reports spawned by this knowledge-development thrust had been completed and submitted to the Department of Labor's Office of Youth Programs. In the meantime, however, the federal government had undergone a significant change in leadership, with consequent changes in philosophy, agendas, and the number of federal employees working in social programs. This last change has considerably slowed the release of much of the information gathered under the auspices of YEDPA. Nevertheless, it seems clear from initial published reports and documents that the extent of knowledge development has been disappointing (Hedrick et al., 1981; Osterman, 1981; Fuller, 1981). To understand why, researchers who were involved in this effort need to make available to a wider audience specific project findings, their analyses of project strengths and weaknesses, and any suggestions that they might have for improving the art of program evaluation. There is, however, a very real danger in such dissemination. Skeptics might too rapidly conclude that 1.5 billion dollars were wasted, since the amount of knowledge development may well appear to be miniscule. This article cautions against such a harsh judgment. By presenting the findings from a specific YEDPA demonstration project, it suggests that the rather limited success in meeting knowledge-development goals is due more to a misunderstanding of the phrase "knowledge development" than to an actual lack of important information. Borrowing the distinctions discussed by Meltsner and Bellavita (1983) among the terms "data," "information," and "knowledge," the article illustrates the differential degrees of value of what was discovered. It concludes with a discussion of the kinds of knowledge that can reasonably be expected from projects of this type and with suggestions for strengthening such knowledge components in the designs of similar evaluation efforts.

PROJECT OVERVIEW

The variety of programs established to improve the work readiness of youth had faced numerous criticisms. Particular concern had been expressed about the seeming overreliance on public-sector jobs for providing work experience. The Public versus Private Sector Jobs

Demonstration Project (a discretionary funded youth project under CETA, Title IV, part a, subpart 3-YEDPA) was undertaken to pinpoint what differences, if any, existed in the ability of either sector to improve work attitudes, skills, and youths' chances to find and keep unsubsidized jobs.

The demonstration focused on 16 to 21 year-old YEDPA-eligible youths who were out of school. It was conducted in five sites: Portland, Oregon; Saint Louis, Missouri; Philadelphia, Pennsylvania; New York, New York; and rural Minnesota. Each site was to place 320 youths, evenly divided between the public and private sectors (rural Minnesota's plan called for 240 youths). Once eligible youths had completed the necessary intake forms, their names, together with selected characteristics, were sent to Saint Louis University's Center for Urban Programs, the central research agent for the project. Here, youths from the same site were matched on the bases of age, race, sex, and a reading test (the SelectAble screener) score. They were then randomly assigned to either a public or a private-sector work-experience slot.

Employers participating in this demonstration were provided youths fully subsidized by the program at 100% of the minimum wage for 25 weeks. If a youth proved to be an acceptable employee, employers were encouraged to place him or her in an unsubsidized position at the program's end. Where this was not feasible, program operators attempted to develop an unsubsidized job for the youth at a different company or agency.

Data were gathered using two sets of instruments. Since this demonstration project was one of a number of efforts by the Department of Labor's Office of Youth Programs to develop a national data base, a standardized assessment system formulated by Educational Testing Services was used. The standardized package consisted of a series of pre-post assessment and follow-up instruments that sought to measure changes in work-related attitudes, knowledge, and the eventual employment outcomes of youths being served. Youths were pretested on world-of-work attitudes and knowledge on the first day of a three-day program orientation. They were posttested when they terminated from the program. Follow-ups on employment status occurred at 90 days after termination and at 240 days after the program ended. Further, a separate set of instrumentation, developed at Saint Louis University, was used to test some of the assumptions typically made about the private sector and its availability, benefits, and transitional opportunities for disadvantaged youths. These instruments measured the level of effort needed to develop work-experience slots and unsubsidized job opportunities in both the public and private sectors.

YEDPA projects seemed plagued by a failure to demonstrate robust programmatic effects. Some of these failures have been explained in terms of implementation problems (see, particularly, Hedrick et al., 1981). The Public versus Private Demonstration, while not altogether avoiding implementation difficulties, experienced relatively few problems in this regard. This was due to a Standard Grant Plan jointly developed by the Office of Youth Programs, Saint Louis University's Center for Urban Programs, and program operators. The plan specified the requirements that would be met by all operators in project organization, youth recruitment and selection, worksite development, worksite assignment and referral, program services, placement services, participant wage-payment processes, and research, record keeping, and reports. Each operator provided attachments to the standard items detailing how they would implement each specific phase of the demonstration. On-site monitors, Department of Labor personnel, and research staff continually assessed program compliance with the Standard Grant Plan.

A cogent argument has been made by Osterman (1981) and Fuller (1981) that correcting implementation procedures will not by itself improve the knowledge gained from such demonstration projects. At least as much attention has to be given to conceptual issues if knowledge development is to advance significantly. Failure here, regardless of the exactness of implementation, will still leave evaluators and policymakers with a dearth of robust programmatic effects. The research reported here lends credence to this argument. Although implementation problems were minimal, so too were the demonstrated program effects. As will be discussed, a greater focus on the conceptual dimensions of youth unemployment, meaningful work experience, and world-of-work socialization would probably have resulted in greater knowledge. Yet, even these substantive concerns are insufficient if policymakers are to maximize the utility of such research efforts. Knowledge, while desirable, is not always a possible outcome of evaluation, nor is it always needed by policymakers and researchers. At times, "information" or simply "data" are sufficient. Demonstrating the differences among these three terms with the findings of the Public versus Private Sector Project will illustrate the conditions under which each might be used to structure interventions and advance understanding.

PROJECT FINDINGS:
DATA, INFORMATION, AND KNOWLEDGE

Although the terms "data," "information," and "knowledge" are often used interchangeably (Meltsner and Bellavita, 1983), it is useful to distinguish them analytically to understand both the problems and prospects of YEDPA-like demonstrations. Data are simply observations about phenomena. Information is data that will make a difference. Knowledge is information that provides guidance for action by describing relationships between means and ends. Meltsner and Bellavita illustrate the differences among these terms by the example of student test scores. The scores themselves are data. Arrayed to show that minority students do worse than nonminority students, the data become information, particularly to those interested in minority achievement. Were further analyses to suggest what factors influence such achievement and how a manager might manipulate these factors, the information would achieve the status of knowledge.

Given the above distinctions, the phrase "knowledge development" may well have been an unfortunate one for guiding YEDPA projects. At least in the Public versus Private Sector Jobs Demonstration, the phrase raised the expectations of the researchers and Department of Labor personnel to unrealistic levels. Mostly, we discovered information. Since we were looking for knowledge, however, the information was not utilized as it should have been. Further, since it is the eye of the beholder that determines which is which, researchers and DOL personnel did not always agree on whether something was knowledge or whether it was simply data. Finally, pressures of time left much of what was discovered clearly in the data realm.

The following "information" highlights emerged from this project (Gilsinan and Tomey, 1981a):

- A much greater effort was needed in the private sector to develop worksites for the demonstration. Twice the number of private-sector employers had to be contacted in order to develop the required number of worksites, resulting in considerably lower participation rates and higher contact rates (Tables 1, 2, and 3).
- A smaller percentage of youths assigned to the private sector who started the program actually began a work experience. Moreover, close to one-half of the youths assigned to the public sector completed the program, while those in the private sector had a completion ratio of less than 40% (Table 4).

- Without considering the influence of demographics or psychometric variables, program completers are far more likely to be in an unsubsidized position at the program's end than are noncompleters (46.4% versus 16.8%, Table 5).
- When completers are compared by sector assignment, with no other variables controlled, those from the private sector are more likely to be in an unsubsidized position at the program's end than are those from the public sector (52.5% versus 39.2%, Table 5).
- Follow-up data need to be interpreted with a great deal of caution since approximately 60% of the overall sample of 2,126 youths could not be found at the 90-day follow-up. Of those that were interviewed, program completion and private-sector experience continued to be associated with full-time, unsubsidized employment (Table 6).
- At 240 days these trends continue to hold based on a sample of approximately 35% of the total (Table 7).

Nakamura and Smallwood (1980) describe the different types of linkages that can exist between the policymaker and the policy implementer. In situations where the policymaker supports abstract, vaguely defined goals, implementers are given rather broad discretion in refining and meeting policy ends. This "discretionary experimental" linkage develops when there is a lack of information on how to achieve a particular goal, but political pressure "to do something" (Nakamura and Smallwood, 1980: 128). Programs developed within this framework, therefore, take a step toward solving a problem while simultaneously gathering better information that will aid in directing future steps (Nakamura and Smallwood, 1980). YEDPA clearly represents a policy environment of this type. The legislation itself is filled with vague terms such as "meaningful work" and, of course, "knowledge development." But information rather than knowledge was both the more appropriate and more possible outcome of the YEDPA demonstrations.

TABLE 1
Total Number of Employers Contacted by Site, by Sector

City	Public*	Private	Total
New York	93	307	400
Philadelphia	486	1002	1488
St. Louis	92	158	250
Minnesota	225	505	730
Portland	129	340	469
Total	1025	2312	3337

*Includes private, not-for-profit businesses.

TABLE 2
Youth in Jobs Employer Participation Rate by Site, by Sector*
(percentages in parentheses)

City	Public	Private	Total
New York	66 (70.9)	147 (47.9)	213 (53.3)
Philadelphia	88 (18.1)	105 (10.5)	193 (13.0)
St. Louis	61 (66.3)	101 (63.9)	162 (64.8)
Minnesota	116 (51.5)	157 (31.1)	273 (37.4)
Portland	74 (57.4)	101 (29.7)	175 (37.3)
Total	405 (39.5)	611 (26.4)	1016 (30.2)

*Total number of employers providing at least one worksite/total number of employers contacted.

TABLE 3
Number of Contacts Needed to Develop One Job by Site, by Sector

City	Public	Private	Total
New York	.53	1.43	1.06
Philadelphia	3.66	8.97	5.93
St. Louis	.46	1.95	.71
Minnesota	2.49	4.25	3.41
Portland	1.12	3.10	2.07
Average (by sector)	1.67	3.40	2.57

Unfortunately, information such as that reported above was not used in a way that would have made it most effective. To maximize its utility, information should have been available to programs *as they operated*, thereby increasing their ability to take the next step. As it was, most steps were taken in the dark while researchers collected information that they hoped would produce knowledge. Specifically in the Public versus Private Demonstration, high dropout rates should have been addressed as a primary issue, with programs and evaluators continually assessing changes made in procedures to stem the outflow of participants. The

TABLE 4
Flow of Youth Through Program Phases, by Sector for Each Site

	Youth Matched		Youth Starting Program		Youth Starting Worksite		Early Program Terminators and Termination Rate (150 days or less)		Program Completers (151-180+ days) and Completion Rate	
	Public	Private	Public	Private	Public	Private	Public	Private	Public	Private
New York (% moving to next program phase)	256	268	230 (89.8)	234 (87.3)	202 (87.8)	205 (87.6)	88 (38.3)	106 (45.3)	142 (61.7)	128 (54.7)
Philadelphia	260	292	208 (80.0)	232 (79.5)	192 (92.3)	203 (87.5)	80 (38.5)	129 (55.6)	128 (61.5)	103 (44.4)
St. Louis	308	330	212 (68.8)	219 (66.4)	188 (88.3)	166 (76.5)	103 (48.6)	154 (70.3)	109 (51.4)	65 (29.7)
Rural Minnesota	248	281	188 (75.8)	202 (71.9)	165 (87.8)	173 (86.1)	114 (60.6)	118 (58.4)	74 (39.4)	84 (41.6)
Portland	294	299	196 (66.7)	205 (68.6)	145 (74.4)	132 (64.4)	144 (73.5)	167 (81.5)	52 (26.5)	38 (18.5)
Total	1366	1470	1034 (75.7)	1092 (74.3)	892 (86.3)	879 (80.7)	530 (51.1)	675 (61.8)	504 (48.9)	417 (38.2)

Source: Gilsinan and Tomey (1980).

TABLE 5
Percentage in Various Outcomes at Completion

	Total Group	Completers	Noncompleters	Completers Public/Private	
Unsubsidized employment	29.7 (615)	46.4 (419)	16.8 (196)	39.2 (199)	52.5 (220)
Other positive	10.3 (214)	9.6 (87)	10.9 (127)	12.6 (62)	5.1 (25)
Nonpositive	60.0 (1243)	44.0 (398)	72.4 (845)	47.1 (232)	40.4 (166)
Subtotal	100.0 (2072)	100.0 (904)	100.0 (1168)	100.0 (493)	100.0 (411)
Unknown	2.54 (54)	1.85 (17)	3.07 (37)	2.18 (11)	1.44 (6)
Total %	100.0	100.0	100.0	100.0	100.0
Total N	(2126)	(921)	(1205)	(504)	(417)

SOURCE: Gilsinan and Tomey (1981a).

TABLE 6
Percentage in Various Outcomes During 90-Day Follow-up Period

	Total Group	Completers	Noncompleters	Completers Public/Private	
Unsubsidized job (F-T)	51.8 (468)	56.0 (279)	46.7 (189)	50.2 (144)	64.0 (135)
Unsubsidized job (P-T)	18.1 (163)	16.3 (81)	20.3 (82)	16.0 (46)	16.6 (35)
Education training	23.2 (209)	22.3 (111)	24.2 (98)	25.6 (74)	17.5 (37)
Negative status	7.0 (63)	5.4 (27)	8.9 (36)	8.0 (23)	1.9 (4)
Subtotal	100.0 (903)	100.0 (498)	100.0 (405)	100.0 (287)	100.0 (211)
Unknown	57.5 (1223)	45.() (423)	66.4 (800)	43.1 (217)	41.4 (206)
Total %	100.0	100.0	100.0	100.0	100.0
Total N	(2126)	(921)	(1205)	(504)	(417)

SOURCE: Gilsinan and Tomey (1981a).

TABLE 7
Percentage in Various Outcomes During 240-Day Follow-up Period

	Total Group	Completers	Noncompleters	Completers Public/Private	
Unsubsidized job (F-T)	54.4 (403)	55.9 (218)	52.7 (185)	52.2 (119)	61.1 (99)
Unsubsidized job (P-T)	24.3 (180)	23.8 (93)	24.8 (87)	23.2 (53)	24.7 (40)
Education training	2.7 (20)	2.3 (9)	3.1 (11)	3.9 (9)	(−)
Negative status	18.6 (138)	17.9 (70)	19.4 (68)	20.6 (47)	14.2 (23)
Subtotal	100.0 (741)	100.0 (390)	100.0 (351)	100.0 (228)	100.0 (162)
Unknown	65.1 (1385)	57.6 (531)	70.9 (854)	54.8 (276)	61.1 (255)
Total %	100.0	100.0	100.0	100.0	100.0
Total N	(2126)	(921)	(1205)	(504)	(417)

SOURCE: Gilsinan and Tomey (1981a).

experimental culture of the demonstration, however, prevented programmatic tinkering since any changes would have added confounding
variables to account for in the quest for knowledge. Failure to utilize
such information correctly, though, is a major reason for the lack of
clear, robust program effects. The dropout rate obviously affects the
ability of researchers to state means-ends linkages unequivocally.

The importance of using information in an appropriate context can
be underscored also by noting the level of effort findings (Tables 1
through 3). While it is clear that the private sector required a much
greater level of effort to gain appropriate worksites, it is also apparent
that the St. Louis program had to expend less effort than other
locations. Fortunately, the researchers made an attempt to find out why
this might have been so (Gilsinan and Tomey, 1981b). The program
operator in St. Louis was a community-based organization (Urban-
League) that had had continuous contact with various private sector
"influentials" through its board of directors. By using these contacts and
experienced job developers, the St. Louis program was fairly successful
in obtaining private-sector work-experience slots for youth. Programs
that had to expend a significantly greater degree of effort relied more

heavily on "cold calls"—approaching businesses without the aid of intermediaries. Moreover, they tended to assign multiple tasks to job developers (such as initial intake and screening chores) or to use individuals who were either inexperienced in job development or more clearly committed to the counseling function. This is useful information and perhaps could even be considered knowledge. Had we been able to tinker with the worksite development procedures during the program, the benefits of a specialized worksite development role and use of informal community contacts within the private sector might have been verified.

The goal of the Public versus Private Demonstration was not, however, knowledge for the purpose of efficient program administration. It was far more grandiose. What was sought in this demonstration, and other YEDPA projects was the solution to a meta-level problem (Caplan, 1979)—youth unemployment. But, as Caplan notes, it is precisely such problems that need far more conceptual rigor in their definitions than is typically available through normal agency and bureaucratic sources. Conceptually, the definition of youth unemployment and the assumptions about its causes remained vague and/or unarticulated. Thus, issues considered central to the demonstration shifted as different actors explored the variety of policy implications flowing from the many-faceted policy areas of youth unemployment. These differing definitions of the problem not only emphasized different remedies, but they also pointed to different research techniques for gathering and analyzing data. For example, the Educational Testing Service's assessment package assumed that attitudinal and cognitive impediments were primary factors in youth unemployment. Improve these and youth employment would also improve. The Public versus Private Demonstration originally began with a different view of the problem—namely, that a great deal of youth unemployment could be explained by lack of access to appropriate jobs, particularly in the private sector. Therefore, the demonstration was not set up specifically to change attitudes and cognitions; Once ETS instruments were mandated for all YEDPA demonstrations, however, an after-the-fact rationale had to be provided for their use in the Public versus Private Project. This after-the-fact rationale postulated that private-sector work experience would have a more beneficial impact on attitudes and cognitions than public-sector work experience. "Why," was not articulated.

As noted, a pre-post survey with seven subscales was administered to youths prior to and at the end of their subsidized work experience. The seven subscales that formed the pre- and post-surveys were (1) Vocational Attitudes, (2) Job Knowledge, (3) Job Holding Skills, (4) Work Relevant Attitude Inventory, (5) Job Seeking Skills, (6) Sex Stereotyping of Adult Occupations, and (7) Self-esteem. An analysis of Table 8 shows that sector assignment had little impact on a variety of individual attitudes and cognitions that might affect the employment chances of youth. Moreover, the statistically significant differences that do emerge on Job Holding Skills and Sex Stereotyping favor the public sector. While such findings do not greatly advance knowledge development, they should not be surprising given the lack of a necessary precondition for knowledge discovery—conceptual clarity.

The difficulties created by a lack of conceptually anchored variables becomes even clearer when examining the results of regression runs used

TABLE 8
Program Completers by Sector

Variable	Group	N	Pretest Unadjusted Mean	Posttest Unadjusted Mean	Posttest Adjusted for Covariates Mean	F	p
VA	1	401	20.536	22.54	22.62	.824	.364
	2	316	20.722	22.51	22.41		
JK	1	408	22.568	21.56	21.62	.321	.571
	2	323	22.654	21.58	21.50		
JHS	1	403	31.101	30.96	30.96	3.907	.048*
	2	320	30.985	30.62	30.62		
WRAI	1	392	48.758	50.06	50.18	.454	.501
	2	312	49.362	50.06	50.91		
JSS	1	407	12.614	12.90	12.94	1.877	.171
	2	321	12.714	12.73	12.69		
SSAO	1	402	46.050	47.15	47.31	4.223	.040*
	2	318	46.480	46.62	46.43		
SE	1	394	36.796	37.30	37.27	3.580	.059
	2	318	36.894	36.81	36.84		

SOURCE: Gilsinan and Tomey (1981a).

NOTE: Group 1 = public; Group 2 = private. Covariates: pretest, race, sex, economic status, step.

*Significant at the .05 level.

TABLE 9
Transition Status Regressed on Participant Characteristics
and Sector Assignment

	Simple r	Beta
(A) Plusterm		
Variable		
Sector assignment	.10	.11*
Change in vocational attitude	.11	.14*
Sex	−.06	−.11*
$R^2 = .06670*$		
(B) Unsubsidized Employment		
Variable		
Change in vocational attitude	.16	.13
Sector assignment	.15	.14*
Sex	.06	−.14*
Race	.12	.13*
Age	.08	.14*
Change in sex stereotyping	.03	−.11
Job knowledge posttest	.08	.20
Change in job knowledge	−.04	−.17
$R^2 = .0981$		
(C) Other Positive		
Variable		
Sector assignment	−.10	−.11*
Job knowledge posttest	.07	.14
Change in job knowledge	.03	−.10
$R^2 = .0392*$		
(D) Nonpositive		
Variable		
Reading score	−.15	−.11*
Change in vocational attitude	−.11	−.14*
Sex	.06	.10*
Work-related attitudes inventory posttest	−.14	−.11
$R^2 = .06605*$		

SOURCE: Gilsinan and Tomey (1980).
*Significant at the .05 level.

to determine what factors appear most significant for determining employment outcomes. Table 9 is illustrative of the low level of explanation generated in the project.

Four outcome measures were used in the analysis of participant status at the program's termination. The first was "Plusterm," which constituted a summary measure combining all the possible positive outcomes into one variable. The second outcome measure was "Unsubsidized Employment," which included any unsubsidized job, full- or part-time, in either sector. "Other Positive Terminations" included entering a full-time academic or vocational school, entering a non-CETA funded manpower program, an intertitle transfer, completing program objectives not involving unsubsidized employment, and entering the armed forces. "Nonpositive Termination" included being laid off or an inability to work because of health problems, pregnancy, family care responsibilities, or transportation problems. Those individuals who moved from the area, refused to continue, had been administratively separated from the program, or could not be located were also included in this category.

At the program's end, among completers, the most powerful predictor of unsubsidized employment is private-sector assignment. Being an older white male also predicts unsubsidized employment at this point. Unfortunately, though, only 10% of the variation in unsubsidized employment is explained by the 8 factors displayed under B of Table 9. The single contribution of sector assignment to this outcome, while statistically significant, is quite small. Problems of interpretation of these kinds of data became even greater at the point of the 90-day and the 240-day follow up because of the extremely high attrition rates.

The frustration created by these types of findings for policymakers was underscored near the end of the research. Tables with percentage comparisons, statistical descriptions, and regressions made up the bulk of some of the interim reports. The researchers were convinced that they had some knowledge (at least if knowledge is defined as statistical significance). Policymakers were not convinced. One policymaker made the point quite forcefully: "Present your findings dramatically! Put the tables in the back." For this particular individual, the tables simply were data. Knowledge should have been made more evident. Given the nature of the demonstration, however, the best we could produce was information. Knowledge would have to await a more conceptually anchored project.

IMPROVING THE KNOWLEDGE
COMPONENTS OF DEMONSTRATIONS

The literature commenting on the current state of evaluation research makes it clear that, while technologically sophisticated, the field is woefully underdeveloped in terms of theory. For example, Daniel Glaser (1980) demonstrates that had the evaluations of various criminal offender programs been theory-based, the conclusion "nothing works" would not have been reached by numerous researchers. A theory-focused approach to evaluation can, as Glaser notes, more clearly answer the question of what works best for whom, avoiding or considerably lessening the problems of sampling, program application bias, and theoretical irrelevance of findings. In short, theory-based evaluations can provide conceptual clarity that, in turn, can produce knowledge for policymakers as they approach meta-problems.

Employment and training research, perhaps even more than research on crime and delinquency-prevention programs, suffers from a certain theoretical sterility. The findings reported above underscore a need for trying to focus such evaluations theoretically, lest those concerned with the impact of public policy too quickly arrive at the erroneous conclusions argued by some in criminal justice (that is, nothing works).

The diagram below, adopted from LaMar Empey's (1980) discussion of criminal justice evaluation, can pinpoint theoretically relevant issues when applied to employment and training data:

Problem Definition———Intervention Principle———Final Goal

The first step in theoretically reorienting an evaluation would be in terms of how a problem is defined. For the research reported here, the problem was defined as unemployed youths, an administrative category. On reflection, it was erroneous to assume that any one program could effectively address the variety of employment problems present in a large group of individuals described simply as young and unemployed. Presumably, individuals within this category are at different stages of employment readiness. Conceptually, therefore, the original problem can be cast in more theoretical terms. These terms should describe variations in the population being observed, variations that appear theoretically relevant to likely success in a work-experience program. Youths would then be matched and assigned to sectors based on similar theoretically derived characteristics rather than simply on similar demographic profiles. A theoretically differentiated population would indicate more clearly what type of program works best and for whom. This avoids treating unemployed youths as an undifferentiated mass against which the success or failure of any program can be gauged.

The problem addressed in this research and demonstration project had a second component. The second component focused on comparing two different types of "treatment"—namely, the supposedly different employment experiences available in two sectors of the economy. Again, however, the distinction public versus private sector has little if any theoretical anchor. What informed the researchers initially was the supposed superior tasks, supervision, and real-world experiences available in the private sector. It perhaps would have been more fruitful to define this second component in terms of sociology of work concepts, that is, acceptance or rejection into the work group, informal socialization, or the ability to learn the unspoken rules of the work place. Work experiences varying along these dimensions are probably more influential in determining a person's orientation toward the world of work than is the specific sector of the individual's work experience.

Theoretically focusing the research problem requires a somewhat different agenda for data gathering. Thus, the second element taken into consideration when theoretically refocusing evaluation, concerns those things that must be accomplished before a final goal is reached. These might be called "intervention principles" (Empey, 1980: 161). In the research described here, there were three intervention principles or intermediate goals thought to be necessary before the final goal could be reached. The first was an increase in cognitive or attitudinal skills. Again, however, the demonstration was not designed to precisely impact these characteristics nor was there a great deal of theoretical development as to why these particular skills should be expected to impact the ability to get and to keep a job.

The second intervention principle was in terms of program type. Private-sector experience was hypothesized as superior and therefore more likely to lead to an unsubsidized position. As discussed above, it is clear that differentiating work experiences simply by sector misses key elements in the work-experience process. It is, therefore, not surprising that very little variation in outcomes was explained by program type.

The third intervention principle dealt with the notion that any kind of structured program was superior to a nonprogram in trying to help unemployed youths. However, as with all field research, the high dropout rate clouds the issue of whether those who dropped out of the program and were never heard from again failed to gain meaningful employment. The problem of dropouts is less serious when the research is theoretically focused. One can theoretically predict those youths likely to drop out of a structured program and then test the results of the dropout pattern against such theoretical assumptions. In this way, even dropouts can be tied into a broader theoretical framework.

Finally, the ultimate goal of the program was to place youths in unsubsidized employment. While laudable, this goal again remains at the level of an atheoretical category. Such a category is subjected to the whims of the marketplace, and factors that are not controlled by the program can impact this ultimate outcome. Again, a more theoretical statement of the goal would help overcome this problem and give a clearer evaluation of program effects. Thus, the question needs to be asked whether the goal was simply employment or a commitment to the system. If the goal were framed in terms of some type of social commitment, then a wider variety of outcomes could be used as indicating program success.

This discussion is not meant to imply that the findings of YEDPA-like projects are useless or, perhaps worse, that there are no findings. Rather, it is meant to underscore the necessity for recognizing the type of results generated from different approaches and their usefulness, given particular policy environments. YEDPA generally, and the Public versus Private Demonstration specifically, were ideal vehicles for generating information. Had this been stressed, the information could have been put to better, more immediate use. Knowledge development requires less broad, more in-depth approaches. Formal theory should guide these types of efforts, recognizing, however, that only a relatively few, relatively narrow set of questions can be answered with such an approach.

REFERENCES

CAPLAN, N. (1979) "The two-communities theory and knowledge utilization." Amer. Behavioral Scientist 22 (January-February): 459-470.

EMPEY, L. (1980) "Field experimentation in criminal justice: rationale and design," in Klein and Teilmann (eds.) Handbook of Criminal Justice Evaluation. Beverly Hills, CA: Sage.

FULLER, B. (1981) "Educational evaluation and shifting youth policy." Evaluation Review 5 (April): 167-189.

GILSINAN, J. and A. TOMEY (1980) "Public v. private sector jobs demonstration project: an analysis of in-program effects and outcomes." Submitted to the Department of Labor, Office of Youth Programs, contract no. 99-9-2061-33-26.

———(1981a) "Public v. private sector jobs demonstration project: final report." Submitted to the Department of Labor, Office of Youth Programs, contract no. 99-9-2061-33-26.

———(1981b) "Developing private sector worksites." Submitted to the Department of Labor, Office of Youth Programs, contract no. 99-9-2061-33-26.

GLASER, D. (1980) "The interplay of theory, issues, policy, and data," in Klein and Teilmann (eds.) Handbook of Criminal Justice Evaluation. Beverly Hills, CA: Sage.

GOLDHABER, G. M. (1974) Organizational Communication. Dubuque, IA: W.C. Brown.

HEDRICK T. E., C. J. OROS, and G. SCHMUTTE (1981) "Two ceta youth employment programs: evaluation in a local setting." Evaluation Review 5 (December): 723-757.

MELTSNER, A. J. and C. BELLAVITA (1983) The Policy Organization. Beverly Hills, CA: Sage.

NAKAMURA, R. T. and F. SMALLWOOD (1980) The Politics of Policy Implementation. New York: St. Martin's.

OSTERMAN, P. (1981) "The politics and economics of ceta programs." APA Journal 47 (October): 434-446.

James F. Gilsinan is a Professor of Urban Sociology and Criminal Justice in the Center for Urban Programs at St. Louis University. He is also Criminal Justice Coordinator for the University. He has been involved in numerous evaluation efforts at the federal, state, and local levels. Besides contributing to professional journals, he has authored the book, Doing Justice: How the System Works as Seen by the Participants *(Englewood-Cliffs, NJ: Prentice Hall,, 1982).*

IV

HOUSING

The provision of affordable housing of reasonable quality for low-income families has been an important objective of the nation's domestic social programs over the past two decades. However, a shortage of low-cost housing, especially in large cities, persists. There are probably more than 1 million homeless people in our country; current estimates range from 250,000 to more than 3 million. Although lack of affordable housing is not the only reason for homelessness, it is certainly a major one. Moreover, the homeless are thought to represent a relatively small portion of a larger, less visible population of people living in substandard housing.

In part, the shortage of inexpensive housing in our cities is due to the success of urban renewal programs over the past 15 years in the rejuvenation of deteriorating neighborhoods. Successful housing rehabilitation programs have resulted in the conversion of many housing units from low- to high-cost properties. Thus the challenges of how to continue to revitalize our cities without displacing the poor by eliminating low-cost housing are as great today as they were when President Johnson declared war on poverty.

The three chapters in this section are evaluations of three different options for improving housing opportunities for the disadvantaged. The focus of Chapter 21 is the Experimental Housing Allowance Program (EHAP), the largest, longest, and most expensive of the social experiments undertaken by the federal government over the last two decades. EHAP falls within the Era 1 major social experiments discussed in Chapter 1. The experiment, which ran from 1973 to 1982, was intended to evaluate the impact of providing direct cash housing payments to low-income families in need of decent housing rather than providing subsidized housing built by or for the government. Three sets of questions were raised about housing allowances that were addressed by three different, though interrelated experiments: How do families respond to housing allowances? How are housing markets affected by allowances? How might a housing allowance program be administered, and what are its administrative costs?

The Experimental Housing Allowance Program consisted of three major experiments: the Demand (Consumer) Experiment, the Supply (Market) Experiment, and the Administrative Experiment. The design and objectives of each are described by Friedman and Weinberg in the history and overview portion of Chapter 21. All three evaluations are reported in the volume edited by Friedman and Weinberg, *The Great Housing Experiment* (1983). We have chosen to include an overview of the entire experiment and a more detailed report on the supply experiment assuming that interested readers will refer to the primary source volume for more information.

The Housing Allowance Program Experiment was a landmark study from methodological perspective. It contributed substantially to the art and science social experimentation as a form of evaluation research. However, question have been raised about whether the findings justify an expenditure of almo $160 million. Marc Bendick and Raymond Struyk suggest in *The Great Housir Experiment* (in a chapter not reproduced for this volume) that, in retrospect, combination of housing market simulation models plus some househol information could have provided the same answer provided by the Suppl Experiment at a much reduced expenditure.

The federal government has invested in only a handful of national soci experiments like the Experimental Housing Allowance Program. Rece evaluations of housing program initiatives are considerably more modest i scope and design. One of the few studies on housing to be completed this year the rental rehabilitation project described in Chapter 22 by Redburn.

The purpose of the rental rehabilitation study was to identify the benefits ove and above providing rent subsidies to families using public subsidies to stimulat rehabilitation of privately owned rental housing in areas where the supply standard rental housing is inadequate. Detailed information was collected by a in-house HUD research team on 350 properties rehabilitated with publi assistance in 18 communities. The cost to benefit ratios of four housin; rehabilitation strategies are compared using multivariate statistics. This evalua tion represents in scope and general design much of the recent research in th housing field.

An emerging area of concern in housing policy that promises to become o even greater importance in the future is how the nation can provide supportiv housing arrangements for the functionally dependent. Elderly Americans ove the age of 85 represent the nation's fastest-growing population subgroup. A larg proportion of the elderly live in large urban areas at some distance from thei families. In order to prevent premature institutionalization of the frail elderly, a combination of subsidized housing with a social services component is required. In addition, the deinstitutionalization of the chronically mentally ill and the mentally retarded places added burdens on communities to develop sheltered housing arrangements for thousands of people who in another era would have resided in special public institutions.

Chapter 23 by Sherwood, Morris, and Ruchlin presents findings from the Pennsylvania Domiciliary Care Experiment, a practical outcome evaluation of the use of board and care facilities for the aged, the mentally ill, and the mentally retarded. We believe that this evaluation will be of particular interest to evaluators working for state and local governments in light of the fact that many public agencies have initiated small demonstrations to house the functionally

...npaired, and the design used in this evaluation is modest enough to be widely ...plicated.

REFERENCE

...iedman, J., & Weinberg, D. (Eds.). (1983). *The great housing experiment*. Beverly Hills, CA: Sage.

21

Experimental Housing Allowance Program
History and Overview

Joseph Friedman and Daniel H. Weinberg

THE EVOLUTION OF HOUSING PROGRAMS:
FROM SUPPLY TO DEMAND SUBSIDIES

In the nineteenth century, public concern was concentrated on sanitation rather than directly on housing, and public intervention in the housing sector was limited to regulatory measures such as building and occupancy codes to assure minimum standards of safety and health. As cities became increasingly populated by poor immigrants, public officials became aware of the severe health problems in densely settled neighborhoods. They proceeded to install or improve water supply and sewage systems. This trend was reinforced in the late nineteenth century as the germ theory of disease gained prominence (Burns and Grebler, 1977: 75). Government requirements were extended to include sanitary and running water systems and improved ventilation in newly constructed buildings.

Housing conditions that may facilitate the spread of disease have been eliminated in the United States. Nevertheless, continuing large-scale public intervention in the housing sector demonstrates that there are additional reasons for public involvement. The two major contemporary rationales for government intervention in the housing sector are "merit goods" and housing market imperfections.

The basic argument for providing cash assistance to households to be used specifically for housing instead of general cash transfers is based on the belief that housing is a "merit good—a form of consumption which society views more important than allowed for by individual choices" (Musgrave, 1976: 215), coupled with the feeling that "the poorest people among us

AUTHORS' NOTE: *This chapter is based in part on descriptions of the Experimental Housing Allowance Program by Allen, Fitts, and Glatt (1981); Frieden (1980), Hamilton (1979), Struyk and Bendick (1980), and U.S. Department of Housing and Urban Development (1980).*

should live in better housing than they are able to afford, and that they should be assisted to do so" (Weicher, 1976: 182). In particular, the imposition of building codes to improve the quality of housing increases its cost and places a floor under the rents of such housing. This rent is typically higher than the share of income families at the lower end of the income scale would freely choose to allocate for housing. Housing subsidies could then be viewed as a way to compensate poor families for the government's actions in limiting their housing choices.

Imperfections in the housing market arise from "such factors as the fixed supply of land in urban settings, zoning and discrimination which reduce tenant mobility, linkages between location and job availability, lumpiness of housing outlays, credit risks, and so forth" (Musgrave, 1976: 215). Further, the existence of externalities in neighborhoods whereby the attributes and living conditions of one dwelling unit can affect the value and living conditions of another also argues for the government to attempt structural remedies for these imperfections.

The Housing Act of 1937 proclaimed the goal of decent, safe, and sanitary dwellings for low-income families. During the four decades that followed, various program approaches for meeting that policy goal have been either tried or debated. Beginning with the Public Housing program, which was established by the 1937 Act, these programs were usually directed at the production or supply of housing, with the subsidy permanently linked to housing units, not to families. As long as families remained eligible and lived in these particular units, subsidy benefits were passed on in the form of below-market rents.

In contrast, housing allowances (also called housing vouchers or rent certificates) link the subsidies to families and are directed toward stimulating demand for decent housing. Housing allowances are payments made directly to eligible households to help them pay the costs of living in housing of their choice. Such payments can vary, depending on what income limits or other household characteristics are used to establish eligibility; whether or not households receiving payments are required to live in housing that meets specific quality standards and, if so, the nature of those standards; and the method used to compute the size of the payment received by each household.

Housing allowances are not a new idea. The topic has been debated in Congress in some way for more than 40 years. Housing vouchers were considered but rejected in formulating the Housing Act of 1937. The favored approach was the public housing program that attempted to satisfy several objectives. These objectives included the housing-oriented goals of slum clearance and improved living conditions of low-income people, as well as anti-Depression goals of job creation and income generation through public spending.

The alternative of housing allowances or rent certificates was proposed by organizations like the U.S. Chamber of Commerce, the National Association of Real Estate Boards, and conservatives in both the House and Senate. Proponents of rent certificates argued that the program would operate through the private market and keep government out of the housing business, that it would be more manageable and less costly than building new housing, and that it would grant low-income households more choice.

On the other side of the debate, two of the nation's leading housing experts of that time—Catherine Bauer and Edith Elmer Wood—opposed rent certificates. Bauer argued that they would be administratively unworkable, while Wood held that such a program would not result in any additional housing being built for low-income families. The Senate Committee on Education and Labor finally concluded:

> In dealing with the housing of families of low income, systematic [construction of] low-rent housing should be substituted for [financial] relief [including rent certificates]. This procedure will be cheaper for the government, more beneficial to business, and infinitely more desirable to those of our citizens who are now living in slums and blighted areas, both in urban and rural parts of the country [Semer et al., 1976: 95].

Thus, Congress opted for a housing production approach, and the rent certificate approach was shelved.

Housing allowances were reconsidered in the Taft Subcommittee hearings on postwar housing policy in 1944. However, the final report of the subcommittee stated:

> It has been argued that families should be assisted by rent certificates just as grocery stamps have been furnished to needy families. The number of families entitled to rent certificates upon any such basis would be infinitely larger than those requiring other relief. It is not at all certain that such a plan would bring about improvements in the bad housing accommodations that now exist. In fact, the scheme might work to maintain the profitability of slum areas and, consequently, to retard their elimination. It would certainly require a detailed regulation of private rental quarters both as to condition and rent [Semer et al., 1976: 40].

The rent certificates idea was considered and rejected again in designing the Housing Act of 1949 and in the 1953 report by the President's Advisory Committee on Government Housing Policies and Programs.

A step toward a program of housing allowances was made in the Housing and Urban Development Act of 1965, which added two programs—the rent supplement program and the Section 23 leased housing program. Both moved in the direction of the housing allowance by giving participants more flexibility in choosing the places they could live and by making the value of the subsidy depend on a family's income. The Section 23 housing program allowed public housing authorities (PHAs) to lease existing private dwelling units and subsidize low-income households to live in them. One potential expansion of this program was to provide housing allowances—a direct payment to enable eligible households to purchase adequate housing in the private market. The households themselves would then be responsible for finding apartments and negotiating with landlords. One further step toward such an unrestricted system of housing subsidies was the 1974 revision of the Section 23 program, retitled Section 8. The revision took place after the initiation of the Experimental Housing Allowance Program and was obviously influenced by many features of the experiment's design. The Existing Housing portion of the Section 8 program focused on households as objects of the subsidy and permitted them to locate suitable units by themselves, but the government retained some control over location and assisted in lease negotiation, with payment going directly to the landlords.

During the 1960s, economists, housing specialists, and the public at large criticized most housing programs as inequitable and wasteful—inequitable because they served only a small fraction of the population eligible for housing assistance, and wasteful because the subsidized units were more expensive to build and maintain than similar units in the private housing market. Economists added an efficiency argument: that the housing subsidy received was as an in-kind benefit and was therefore valued by the recipients as worth less than its cost to the government.

The shift to demand-oriented programs was a response to widespread criticism of the production-oriented programs as either too costly, not working as desired, or not serving enough eligible families. These traditional programs had only a limited impact because they required deep subsidies. The Congressional Budget Office (1979) estimated that the cost of supply-oriented programs in 1980 dollars ranged from $2200 to 2530 per dwelling unit per year.

Because the cost per unit was so high, only a limited number of housing units could be built with the available housing funds each year. Consequently, only a small number of income-eligible households could be helped each year. Indeed, in recent years, less than 10% of income-eligible households were receiving housing assistance by occupying subsidized housing. The remaining often equally deserving 90% received nothing. National housing policy had thus created inequities within the low-income population by providing large and costly subsidies to relatively few and nothing to the rest.

A related problem is the high cost of construction programs relative to programs utilizing the existing housing stock. Mayo et al. (1980a, 1980b) estimated that the total annual program cost, including administration costs, required to provide a minimum standard unit by a new construction program was from 35% to 91% higher than the cost required to rent such a unit in the housing market. This much higher cost associated with new construction programs reflects construction, operation, and implementation inefficiencies.

Another problem with construction programs is that they restrict the locational choices of participants and tend to create high concentrations of the poor in racially segregated neighborhoods. The resulting problems were graphically illustrated by the colossal failure of the Pruitt-Igoe Public Housing Project in St. Louis.[1] Although the project should be considered an atypical extreme, its demolition in 1972 convinced many housing experts that a new approach to solving the housing problem was needed.

The research at the New York City Rand Institute lent some additional support to the housing allowance idea. Ira S. Lowry and his associates (Lowry, 1971) analyzed the New York City housing market during the 1960s. They discovered that from year to year, a large volume of sound housing was deteriorating in quality, and more than 30,000 units each year were being taken off the market through demolition, conversion to nonresidential use, or outright abandonment. Between 1965 and 1968, housing losses were greater than new construction by a substantial margin. The main reason for this rising volume of deterioration and abandonment was that a large number of the city's low-income population were unable to pay enough rent to cover the rising costs of operating and maintaining rental property. Landlords who were unable to earn a competitive return were cutting back on maintenance, and, in time, walking away from their buildings.

Lowry concluded from the Rand studies that the most effective way to meet the housing needs of low-income families in New York City was to raise the level of maintenance in existing buildings while they were still in good condition. He estimated that an annual rent increase of $400-$700 (in 1967 dollars) would be required to support moderate renovation and good maintenance in typical older apartments. Since low-income families cannot afford even these relatively small increases, Lowry proposed a housing allowance plan that would augment family income at an average cost of little more than $600 per family.

In 1968 the President's Committee on Urban Housing (the Kaiser Committee) had a mandate to analyze existing housing programs and their impacts on households and markets, focusing on low-income households. The committee's 1968 report argued in favor of a housing allowance and recommended that the government undertake an experiment to determine whether a housing allowance program would be feasible and worthwhile.

The Kaiser Committee's support of housing allowances stemmed largely from the increasing difficulty of the public housing program in finding decent sites for large housing projects and a concern for the consequence of segregating the poor and minorities in limited areas of cities. The committee also stressed that an

allowance system offers the opportunity for the free market to operate in its traditional fashion [and that] widespread distribution of housing allowances to poor families should reduce the economic dependence on slum housing and shift the demand upward for standard units. In response to this shift in demand, suppliers of housing would be induced to produce more standard housing, either by upgrading slum properties or through new construction [p. 11].

The committee recommended not a full-scale national program but rather an experimental one because of several concerns. First, the committee perceived a need in the short term to stimulate new construction and felt that the conventional project subsidy approach would best accomplish that result. Second, the committee was concerned that a massive allowance program "would be likely to inflate the costs of existing housing considerably, at least in the short run. . . . Consequently, any large-scale housing allowance system would have to be introduced gradually." Finally, the committee feared that without "strong programs of consumer education and vigorous attacks on racial discrimination" an allowance system could have adverse results (p. 71).

The publication of the Kaiser Committee's recommendations coincided with the change from the Democratic administration of Lyndon Johnson to the Republican administration of Richard Nixon. Incoming officials in the Office of Management and Budget and the Department of Housing and Urban Development (HUD) were interested in the idea of housing allowance as consistent with Republican goals of increased utilization of the private market in public programs (Struyk and Bendick, 1981: 29). In 1970 the first housing allowance demonstration program (under the auspices of the Model Cities program) was launched in Kansas City, Missouri and in Wilmington, Delaware. HUD began preliminary studies and designs for a systematic national experiment in 1970 and 1971, and then organized its Experimental Housing Allowance Program (EHAP).

In January 1973, the Nixon administration suspended almost all existing federal housing subsidies for the poor and announced its intention to search for more effective programs. The housing allowance experiment, then getting under way in 12 selected cities, took on special importance as part of that search.

As EHAP was being completed in 1981, the incoming Reagan administration established a new President's Commission on Housing in February 1981. Its mandate was to review existing programs and research on housing and recommend directions for U.S. housing policy by April 1982. Once again, housing allowances are a major focus of a presidential commission's recommendations.

THE EXPERIMENTAL HOUSING ALLOWANCE PROGRAM

To elicit empirical evidence about the concept of housing allowances, Congress directed HUD to establish EHAP in Title V, Section 504, of the 1970 Housing and Urban Development Act. It authorized $20 million for the program, called for its completion by the end of fiscal year 1973, limited the program to rental housing, and specified the payment formula. In 1974 Section 504 was amended to reflect the program design described below.[2]

The many issues raised about housing allowances defined three basic sets of questions:

(1) How do families respond to housing allowances?
(2) How are housing markets affected by allowances?
(3) How might a housing allowance program be administered, and what are its administrative costs?

These questions were addressed by three different, though interrelated, experiments—the Demand Experiment, the Supply Experiment, and the Administrative Agency Experiment.

THE DEMAND EXPERIMENT

The Demand Experiment focused on how families respond to housing allowances. The specific questions it addressed were as follows:

- Who participates, and how are participation rates affected by program features such as payment levels?
- Does a housing allowance program cause participants to move to new locations?
- What portion of the allowance payment is used for housing?
- Does the quality of housing improve for participating households?
- What are the major differences in household responses between a payment program constrained by housing requirements and a program of unconstrained allowances, such as welfare payments?
- How do housing allowances compare with other housing programs in terms of participation, housing quality attained, locational choices, and costs?

Answers to these questions depend partly on program rules, so the design systematically varied payment levels, housing requirements, and payment formulas to learn how outcomes would differ. The specific variations tested are described below.[3]

The Housing Allowance Demand Experiment (HADE) was the only one of the three to include a control group. To isolate the effects attributable solely to the housing allowances from changes that would have occurred in the absence of any program, HADE collected data on similar families (controls) that did not receive such payments. The difference between the changes in housing conditions of control families and those receiving housing allowances represents the *induced* effects of the program. The HADE design also included a comparison of the effects on similar families of receiving unconstrained payments (with no housing requirements to meet) and housing allowances.

HADE was conducted over a three-year period in two metropolitan areas: Allegheny County, Pennsylvania, the Pittsburgh Standard Metropolitan Statistical Area (SMSA); and Maricopa County, Arizona, the Phoenix SMSA. These sites were selected from among 31 SMSAs by applying a set of criteria that included vacancy rate and size of housing market area as key selection factors. Given the objectives of the experiment, both sites chosen had to be sufficiently large to prevent the allowances to experimental households from having any significant inflationary effect on market rents. Both sites had populations in excess of 500,000 and vacancy rates of about 6% in 1970. The other factors in the set of criteria reflected differences of interest to policymakers. Pittsburgh is a slowly growing, older city with a large black population; Phoenix is a rapidly growing, newer city with a large Hispanic population.

In each of these housing markets, about 50,000 families were surveyed. Representative samples of families eligible by income were selected to be offered participation in the various groups discussed above. In the two sites, approximately 950 control families were selected, and about 2500 families were enrolled in either constrained or unconstrained payment plans.

Through combinations of payment formulas and housing requirements, 17 experimental plans were tested. Two payment formulas were used. The *housing gap formula* can be expressed as $S = b_1C - b_2Y$, where S was the allowance payment; C was the cost of standard housing established for the program which varied by household size, site, and the experimental parameter b_1; b_2 was the rate at which the allowance is reduced as household income increases (or the implicit tax rate), also varied experimentally; and Y was net family income. Under the *percent of rent formula*, the payment, S, was a percentage of the family's rent, $S = aR$, where R was the rent and "a" was the fraction of the rent paid by the allowance. This formula was included to enable estimation of demand functions that describe the way in which expenditures on housing are related to income and the price of housing and other goods.

In combination with the primary payment formula (housing gap), four approaches to housing requirements were tested. Based on American Public Health Association criteria, a set of minimum housing standards was developed as the principal approach. They include 15 major categories of physical attributes that, when taken together, define a decent, safe, and sanitary housing unit. In addition, an occupancy standard limited occupants to two per acceptable bedroom. A second approach, the unconstrained plan, did not require participants to meet any housing standards. As a possible alternative for the physical standards, two other housing requirements were tested; "Minimum Rent High" and "Minimum Rent Low." In these plans, payments were made, regardless of the physical quality of the dwelling, if a household's rent was at or above a required minimum. (The minimum was 90% of C for Minimum Rent High plans and 70% of C for Minimum Rent Low plans.)

THE SUPPLY EXPERIMENT

The purpose of the Housing Assistance Supply Experiment (HASE) was to determine the effects of housing allowances on housing markets. Among the specific questions this experiment was designed to address were the following:

- When all eligible families are offered the opportunity to receive housing allowances, will landlords, developers, homeowners, mortgage lenders, real estate brokers, and others accommodate the recipients in their attempts to improve their housing conditions? Or, as some predicted, will the price of housing simply increase without a corresponding improvement in housing?
- To what extent will housing allowances stimulate repairs, substantial rehabilitation, or the construction of new units?
- As housing allowance recipients attempt to increase their housing consumption by moving, what neighborhoods will they seek and which ones will they succeed in entering? What is the impact on the neighborhoods they leave and enter? Will families move from the central city to the suburbs?

While some of the specific questions of HASE were similar to those of HADE, a different approach was required to answer these questions (see Lowry, 1973, for more details). In HASE, enrollment was open to all eligible families in two metropolitan housing markets. In addition, payments to households were promised for a period of 10 years, as long as the eligibility requirements were met. This long-term commitment was considered necessary to enable demand subsidies to induce supply response.

Both homeowners and renters were eligible to participate in the program. Only one housing allowance plan, a housing gap payment schedule with a minimum standards requirement, was used. The payment formula and standards were similar to those in the Demand Experiment (the standards were modified according to local housing codes of the supply experiment sites).

The two housing markets for HASE were Brown County, Wisconsin, whose central city is Green Bay; and St. Joseph County, Indiana, whose central city is South Bend. These locations were selected from all SMSAs. The housing markets chosen had to differ in certain ways, yet be typical of a substantial portion of markets throughout the nation. Brown County has a rapidly growing urban center, a relatively tight housing market, a good housing stock, and a very small minority population. St. Joseph County has a declining central city with a deteriorating housing stock, a minority population of average size but growing, and an excess supply of central-city housing.

THE ADMINISTRATIVE AGENCY EXPERIMENT

The objective of the Administrative Agency Experiment (AAE) was to gather information about the administration and costs of delivering housing allowances. The design and analysis, therefore, focused on those administrative functions considered of major importance for the administration, management, and operation of a national housing allowance program.[4]

The experiment consisted of experimental housing allowance programs administered by several different types of public agencies and an independent evaluation. The research firm and all agencies performed their roles under contract to and in consultation with HUD. The design provided for natural rather than systematic variations in administrative procedures. Agencies were encouraged to develop their own procedures for administering the allowance program within a set of broad guidelines developed by HUD.

The AAE was implemented as if it were a typical housing program. Eight agencies, which potentially could administer a national housing allowance program, were selected to operate the experiment. They consisted of two public housing authorities, two county agencies, two state community development agencies, and two welfare agencies. The eight agencies were the Salem (Oregon) Housing Authority; the Tulsa (Oklahoma) Housing Authority; the San Bernardino (California) County Board of Supervisors; the Jacksonville (Florida) Department of Housing and Urban Development; the Commonwealth of Massachusetts Department of Community Affairs; the State of Illinois Department of Local Government Affairs; the Social Services Board of North Dakota; and the Durham County (North Carolina) Department of Social Services.

In the eight agencies, the number of households to which payments could be made was limited to 900 in six cases, to 500 in one case, and to 400 in another. The payment formula was similar to the one used in the supply experiment and to one of the housing gap types in the demand experiment: the difference between the cost of modest standard housing and 25% of the family's preallowance income. Payments were made only to families that either lived in or moved to units that met the program's housing standards.

Figure 1.1 indicates the location of each of the 12 experimental sites and of the two housing allowance demonstration projects that were locally initiated and funded under the Model Cities program.

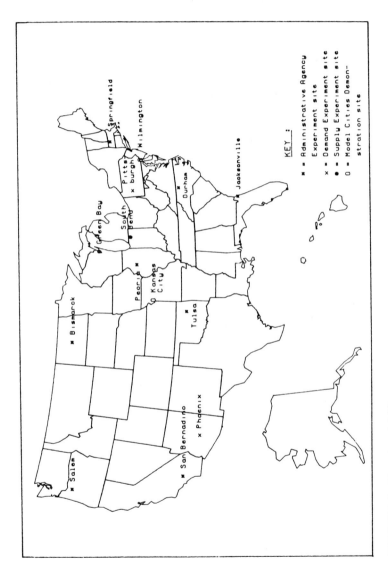

FIGURE 1.1   Experimental Sites

NOTES

1. The Pruitt-Igoe Project, completed in 1956, consisted of 43 buildings on 57 acres near St. Louis's city center. By 1970, the project was so ridden by crime and vandalism and had so deteriorated as a result of the inability of the St. Louis Housing Authority to keep up proper maintenance and repair that it became impossible to find tenants for the many vacant units in the project. At first, the housing authority responded by closing down more than half of the buildings. Eventually the entire project was vacated and demolished (Helbrun, 1981: 369).

2. The initial authorization of $20 million amounted to only one-eighth of the total cost of the experiment. By mid-1980, when most of the research had been completed, the total cost was $158 million. The distribution of this amount was (in millions):

Experiment	Payments to Households	Administration and Program Operation	Research and Monitoring	Total
Demand	$ 4	$ 2	$25	$ 31
Supply	40	18	41	99
Administrative agency	10	3	9	22
Integrated analysis	0	0	7	7
Total	$53	$23	$82	$158
Percentage	34	15	51	100

SOURCE: Struyk and Bendick (1981: 297; estimates as of April 1980).

3. See Abt Associates Inc. (1973) for a detailed description of the experimental design.
4. See Hamilton (1979) for a detailed description of the AAE.

Experimental Housing Allowance Program
The Supply Experiment

Ira S. Lowry

□ THE HOUSING ASSISTANCE SUPPLY EXPERIMENT (HASE) was designed to test the market and community effects of a full-scale allowance program. It was undertaken because many observers doubted the ability of low-income families to bargain effectively in local housing markets and feared that their allowances would be absorbed by rent increases that were not matched by housing improvements, to the detriment of both participants and others. For example, in 1968 the President's Committee on Urban Housing warned:

> The immediate adoption of a massive housing allowance system would be likely to inflate the cost of existing housing considerably, at least in the short run. The large infusion of new purchasing power would result in a bidding up of housing prices for the existing standard inventory. Consequently, any large-scale allowance system would have to be introduced gradually. Such a system might also require strong programs of consumer education and vigorous attacks on racial discrimination to work effectively [pp. 71-72].

Others were interested in or concerned about the neighborhood effects of such a program. Optimists foresaw rejuvenation of deteriorating neighborhoods as landlords repaired rental dwellings to attract allowance recipients and low-income homeowners obtained allowances that enabled them to improve their homes. Pessimists foresaw a general exodus of allowance recipients from deteriorated neighborhoods, leading to the collapse of property values there, and social tensions arising in better neighborhoods as allowance recipients sought housing there. How such a program would affect racial segregation was not clear to anyone; although it would provide minority participants with the means to pay for better housing and neighborhoods, it would not directly address exclusionary practices.

EXPERIMENTAL DESIGN

To explore these issues, HUD authorized ten-year allowance programs in two metropolitan areas: Brown County, Wisconsin (metropolitan Green Bay) and St. Joseph County, Indiana (metropolitan South Bend). The Rand Corporation supervised program operations for the first five years and monitored concurrent events in local housing markets by means of annual field surveys addressed to the owners and occupants of marketwide samples of residential properties. Whereas the Demand Experiment observed the effects on individual households of the "treatment" each received, the Supply Experiment's subjects were housing markets and the treatment was an allowance program.

The experimental strategy in HASE was to apply the same treatment to markets that differed in ways likely to affect outcomes. Because a full-scale allowance program would be expensive, only two sites were chosen—both small in size but contrasting as to market structure and initial condition.

Brown County (48,000 households) had a relatively new housing inventory, its population was growing, property values were high, and vacancy rates were low despite steady growth of the inventory. Less than 2% of the county's inhabitants belonged to racial minorities, so its housing market was unsegregated. St. Joseph County (76,000 households) had an older inventory, including much deteriorated housing in central South Bend; South Bend's population was decreasing, property values were low, and vacancy rates were high. Nineteen percent of the city's households were black or Latin, nearly all of them living in deteriorated neighborhoods where rental vacancy rates exceeded 12% and single-family houses often sold for under $10,000. In each site, we initially estimated that about a fifth of all households would be eligible for assistance.[1]

Identical allowance programs, open to nearly all low-income renters and owners, were operated in the two sites. By the end of the first three program years, enrollment had reached 3600 households in Brown County and 6500 in St. Joseph County. Thereafter, program growth was slow; about a third of all enrollees dropped out each year (usually because they became ineligible) and were replaced by others who were newly eligible. During this steady state, about 8% of all households (about 15% of all renter households) in each county were enrolled in the program.

The allowance programs offered eligible households monthly cash payments calculated on the "housing gap" principle. That is, a household's entitlement equaled the estimated local cost of adequate housing, less one-fourth of the household's adjusted gross income. In practice, this formula worked out to an average annual payment (in 1977) of about $1000 to renters whose gross incomes averaged $4000; and $800 to owners whose gross incomes averaged $4900. At that time, a well-maintained four-room dwelling rented for about $2150 annually, including utilities.[2]

Although enrollment was open to anyone whose allowance entitlement would exceed $120 annually, payments were made only to enrollees whose dwellings met detailed standards as to living space, domestic facilities, safety, and sanitation. These standards were enforced by initial and annual on-site inspections. An enrollee whose dwelling failed could either arrange for repairs or move to an adequate dwelling, and thereby qualify for payments. Recipients whose dwellings failed annual inspections or who moved to inadequate housing faced suspension of payments unless the housing defects were remedied.

The allowance program in each site was administered by a nonprofit corporation created for that purpose, called a housing allowance office (HAO).[3] The two HAOs publicized the program, inviting applications from all who thought they might be eligible. Applicants who passed the eligibility tests were enrolled and informed of their entitlements and of the housing requirements they had to meet in order to receive payments. Participants found their housing on the private market without help from the HAOs and could move or change tenure (renting or owning) without losing their allowances, provided always that their dwellings met program standards.

The HAOs did not set either minimum or maximum housing expenses for participants, and the amount of the allowance did not vary with actual expenses. Participants were entirely responsible for negotiating rents or home purchases, for arranging repairs, and for meeting their financial obligations. The HAOs had no dealings with or obligations to landlords, lenders, repair contractors, or others who might be involved in a participant's housing transactions.

EXPERIMENTAL FINDINGS[4]

During the first five years of program operations, a total of 25,000 households enrolled in the two sites and 20,000 received one or more payments. Four annual surveys of residential properties in each site produced nearly 8,400 records of interviews with landlords, 18,200 records of interviews with renters and homeowners, and 11,500 records of observations on residential buildings. Joint analysis of program and survey data yields the following findings:

- In the mature program, about one-third of those who were currently eligible were currently receiving payments. The main reasons for nonparticipation were the small entitlements of those who were only marginally or briefly eligible and the unwillingness of some whose dwellings were unacceptable to either repair them or move to better housing. The neediest were most likely to participate, but more of them would have participated in the absence of minimum housing standards. However, the standards did prompt considerable housing improvement, as noted below.

- About half of those who enrolled were then living in dwellings that did not meet the program's quality standards. Among those who had to repair or move in order to qualify for payments, about two-thirds did so and one-third dropped out. Overall, 80% of the enrollees eventually qualified for payments. Most of those who dropped out could have recovered repair costs from their first few allowance payments.

- Participation in the program increased the likelihood of occupying standard housing from about 50% to about 80%, and reduced preenrollment housing expense burdens from about 50% of gross income to about 30%. In addition to making required repairs, three-fourths of the owners voluntarily improved their dwellings each year and two-fifths of the renters moved to larger or better dwellings. However, the average participant increased his housing expenditures by only 8% over his estimated expenditures absent the program.

- Enrollees were able to meet program standards without much increase in expenditure because their housing defects were mostly minor health and safety hazards, rather than major structural defects or lack of basic domestic equipment. Repairs were generally made by the participants themselves, their friends, or their landlords, rather than by professional contractors. The average cost of repairing a failed dwelling was about $100, including an imputed wage for unpaid labor. Although allowances augmented the typical renter's income by about a fourth and the typical owner's income by a sixth, they chose to spend only a fifth of the extra money on housing. Thus, four-fifths of all allowance payments were allocated to nonhousing consumption.

- A full-scale open-enrollment allowance program had no perceptible effect on rents or property values in either a tight housing market (Green Bay) or a loose market (South Bend). One reason was that the program increased aggregate housing demand by less than 2%. Another was that it proved relatively easy and inexpensive to transform substandard to standard dwellings. When a renter joined the program without moving, his rent typically increased by less than 2%, even though his landlord may have made minor repairs to bring the dwelling up to program standards.

- The program had little effect on the physical appearance or social composition of residential neighborhoods. Even in neighborhoods where participants made up a fifth or more of all residents, the housing improvements were inconspicuous because program standards were not concerned with cosmetics. Though many renters moved, the origins and destinations of the moves were too diffuse to alter neighborhood populations. The degree of racial segregation did not change perceptibly because of the program.

- After three years of experience with the program, a majority of all household heads and 90% of all participants thought it was a "good idea." Landlords were less enthusiastic, but a majority of those whose tenants included recipients approved of the program. In general, the public approved of who got help, what the help was for, and how the program was run.

- The allowance programs in Green Bay and South Bend were administered by nonprofit corporations under the supervision of Rand and HUD. Hiring staff locally at prevailing wages, these housing allowance offices performed their functions promptly, equitably, and humanely at the surprisingly low cost of $163 per recipient-year. Many of the program's administrative features that contributed to this outcome are transferable to other federal programs.

Reflecting on the experimental evidence, and consulting available national data, we offer the following judgments about the effects of a national program that followed the same design as the experimental one.

(1) Some poor households live in inexpensive and inadequate dwellings; others are adequately housed by dint of spending half or more of their incomes for housing. Housing allowances are flexible enough to remedy whichever circumstances apply to a particular case and can serve homeowners as easily as renters. Nationally, as well as in the experimental sites, budgetary relief is probably a higher priority for low-income households than is better housing.

(2) The public cost per assisted household would be far below that entailed in programs that build new housing for the poor; moreover, we estimate that 85 cents of each program dollar would directly benefit participants. A comparable estimate for the Section 8 Existing Housing program is 57 cents; for the federal public housing program, 34 cents; and for an income maintenance program with no housing requirements, 89 cents.

(3) At most, 10% of all households (half of those eligible) would participate in a permanent national program, at an average public cost of about $1100 per recipient year (1976 dollars), including administration. About 30% of the participants would occupy safer and more sanitary dwellings than they otherwise would, and all would be able to spend more for nonhousing consumption.

(4) We judge that a national housing allowance program would affect only participants and their housing; the broader community would be unaffected for good or ill. Specifically, we think that a program open to all low-income renters is not at all likely to cause significant rent increases for either participants or others, even in moderately tight housing markets. On the other hand, we do not think that a full-scale program would much alter the appearance or social composition of low-income neighborhoods; nor would it much expedite the residential integration of racial minorities.

METHODOLOGICAL ISSUES

MARKET EFFECTS

HUD's Experimental Housing Allowance Program was planned in a period of great ferment in federal housing policy. Those plans were further shaped by a new sense of the possibilities of applying experimental science to the problems of government. Until the mid-1960s, experimentation in government essentially meant launching new national programs whose designs at best reflected theoretical analyses of probable effects but which sometimes provided for systematic evaluation after the programs were operating. The new idea was that the essential features of a contemplated national program could be tested by a carefully designed experiment conducted on a relatively small scale, the results of which would allow much more precise estimation of the effects of the full-scale counterpart and provide valuable guidance on program rules, administrative requirements, and costs if a national program were adopted.

The intellectual model for these social experiments, as they came to be called, was the clinical trial in medical research. In clinical trials, a therapy of unknown effectiveness is administered under controlled conditions to a carefully chosen sample of ailing persons; similar samples get alternative or no treatment. Even if detailed causal links between the treatment and the subject's response cannot be identified, clinical trials enable experimenters to assess the statistical effectiveness of the treatment as against alternative or no treatment of the same ailment.

The Demand Experiment followed this model quite closely. Screened samples of low-income households in two metropolitan areas were offered housing allowances on various terms and conditions. Their responses to those offers and the housing conditions, actions, and expenditures of those who accepted were analyzed as functions of the terms of the offers; and their experiences were compared to those of a control group of households in each site. Thanks to the attentiveness and imagination of a highly capable research team, the comparisons among treatment groups and between treatment and control groups forestalled many attractive but erroneous inferences. Response parameters were estimated with as much precision as sample sizes would support.

As guides to housing policy, these experimental findings were limited in several respects. First, because those treated comprised only small fractions of those in each site who would be eligible for a similar national program, their housing actions rarely impinged on each other and would not be generally noticed as market signals. Second, the housing market context of their actions was neither controlled nor deeply investigated; the analysts could only speculate about reasons for intersite differences in responses. Third, the recruitment of participants and subsequent transactions with them differed substantially from the modes likely to be employed in a national program. Fourth, the maximum term of participation was three years, of which only the first two were analyzed (to avoid misleading termination effects).

These limitations were foreseen and motivated HUD to commission the complementary Administrative Agency and Supply Experiments. The latter's mission was to estimate the market and community effects of a permanent full-scale program. After exploring various alternatives (computer simulation using nonexperimental data, analysis of naturally occurring analogues to the market stimulus expected from an allowance program, microexperiments to test the responses of individual landlords and homeowners to a hypothetical program, and experiments at the neighborhood scale within larger housing markets), Rand and HUD agreed that the best way to learn about the effects of a full-scale program was to conduct one. None of the alternatives seemed likely to provide reliable and generally credible evidence about the effects of an actual program when so little was known about how eligibles would respond to the allowance offer, how they would communicate their housing demands in the open market, and how the suppliers of housing would respond to the resulting market signals.[5]

There were two obvious drawbacks to full-scale experimentation: its expense and the risks it entailed for the host communities. Considerations of cost led us to limit the experiment to two small metropolitan housing markets; risks were managed in two ways—by securing the informed consent of the host communities and by preparing contingency plans that included aborting the experiment after it was under way, if necessary to forestall or limit damage to the community.[6]

Methodologically, the limit on the number of sites was particularly vexing. In the Demand Experiment, the experimental treatment was an allowance offer to an individual household, whose behavioral responses would then be observed. In the Supply Experiment, the treatment was a housing allowance program "offered" to a community, whose aggregate (market) responses would then be observed. From the perspective of statistical inference, the Supply Experiment had a sample size of two. Furthermore, a little thought persuaded us that there was no practical way to identify an appropriate "control group" of sites that could be observed without treatment. However closely we matched the experimental sites with control sites, unpredictable events during the course of the experiment (a flood, the closing of a major industrial plant, or a municipal fiscal crisis) might invalidate the comparison. Comparably monitoring housing markets in a large control group of sites would be impossibly expensive.

In short, the model of the clinical trial was inappropriate for the Supply Experiment. Instead, we chose sites that differed sharply as to market characteristics likely to affect outcomes, and conducted identical allowance programs in each. From administrative records of the program, we could precisely measure the experimental stimulus (number of participants and their allowances) to local housing markets. By annually surveying the markets themselves, we could measure market outcomes (price and quantity of housing services consumed). However, we were dependent on analytical modeling rather than probability theory to distinguish the role of the measured stimulus in producing the measured outcomes, given uncontrollable nonprogram events in each site that could also affect housing markets.

From other essays in this volume and from the final reports of the Supply Experiment, the reader can judge how well we succeeded, as to both measurement and causal attribution. I judge that we established beyond controversy that the market stimulus inherent in a program of this type is much smaller than most observers expected, and for surprising and very important reasons. First, many who are eligible will not participate; second, most low-income families live in dwellings that can be easily and cheaply improved to meet program standards; and third, augmenting low incomes causes only a small increase in voluntary housing expenditures (i.e., beyond the expenditures needed to meet program standards). Further, I can think of no politically plausible variant of the allowance concept that would be likely to generate a substantially larger stimulus to local housing markets.

The measurement of market outcomes as regards housing prices was clouded by the instability of the unit of measurement. The experiment was conducted during a period of rapid national price inflation, led by escalating energy prices that especially affected housing. We established that rents and property values in the experimental sites approximately tracked regional and national indexes, and that the net operating return from rental properties was stable or diminishing during the period of rapid program growth (implying no short-run profits due to increased demand). Multivariate analysis of rent changes for individual dwellings indicates that participants paid a small premium when they brought a dwelling into the program; but if there was any spillover effect on nonparticipants' housing, it was too small to be detected in an inflationary environment (Rydell et al., 1982; see also Chapter 11).

As to neighborhood effects, program records enabled us to measure the direct effects—moves by participants, repairs to their dwellings—with precision, and our field surveys showed us that indexes of neighborhood quality, rents, and property values did not change in patterns that reflected the neighborhood concentration of enrollees or allowance payments. More important, it was clear that the direct program effects, when set against neighborhood aggregates, were too small to perturb neighborhood averages; only a large multiplier effect could have produced substantial neighborhood change (Hillestad and McDowell, 1982; see also Chapter 14).

In short, whatever its benefits to participants, the experimental allowance program did not measurably disturb the housing markets of Brown and St.

Joseph counties during the years of rapid program growth when market disturbances were most likely. That finding was important, because HUD-sponsored computer simulations of allowance programs, one using Brown and St. Joseph counties as examples, came to contrary conclusions (Barnett and Lowry, 1979).

However, the experiment was undertaken to provide guidance for a national program, and a sample of two small metropolitan areas does not provide the basis for statistical inference to other places.[7] Although statistical inference has many advantages as a mode of generalization, it is not the only valid form of inference. Understanding the logical structure of a process enables us to estimate how it would behave in contexts other than the experimental one. We did not, for example, have to launch a thousand rockets to the moon in order to program a trajectory that would reach the target.

As explained above, we observed the joint effects of the allowance program and other events on the housing markets of Brown and St. Joseph counties and found little evidence of program-induced market disturbance. We also explicitly modeled the effects of the allowance program in each site, abstracting from background price inflation and local population and income changes that might have affected actual market outcomes independently of the program. The structure of the model was suggested by our observations on program and market processes; some of its parameters were estimated from HASE data and some from national data gathered in the Annual Housing Survey. Initial conditions for the modeling exercise were those observed in our sites at baseline, and the program's market stimulus was given by the actual histories of participation in each site. The market effects of the program, as estimated by the model, are reasonably consistent with observed market outcomes, once allowance is made for background inflation (Rydell et al., 1982).

To help HUD with the generalization problem,[8] we devised a variant of this model that could subsist on the population and housing market data available from the Annual Housing Survey. HUD compiled the data and ran the model for a hypothetical allowance program conducted in a national sample of 20 metropolitan areas, varying the key parameters around the values estimated for the Supply Experiment. The results indicated that only in exceptional circumstances would an allowance program significantly perturb a local housing market.[9]

OTHER RESEARCH TOPICS

After the Supply Experiment was under way, it became apparent that its design offered opportunities for complementary research on issues originally assigned to the Demand and Administrative Agency experiments: the determinants of participation, effects on participants, and administrative effectiveness and efficiency. These studies were added to our agenda with only minor modifications of the data collection plan.

The Supply Experiment offered an unusual opportunity for participation analysis, in that our marketwide household surveys obtained enough data from respondents to determine their eligibility under program rules. Within the limits of sampling variability, we therefore had a solid base for the measurement of participation rates. Whereas the Demand Experiment individually invited a screened sample of eligible households to enroll, the Supply Experiment extended a general invitation (without time limit) to the public— a mode close to that of a permanent national program. Thus, one might expect the participation experience in the two experiments to differ. Because enrollment was open throughout the experiment, we were able to observe turnover (not just attrition). For all these reasons, HASE participation studies (Ellickson, 1981; Carter and Balch, 1981; Coleman, 1982; Wendt, 1982; Carter and Wendt, 1982) provide a valuable complement to those of the Demand Experiment, which focus on the effects of program variation.

With respect to effects on participants, the main advantage offered by the Supply Experiment was large samples. In the two sites combined, over 25,000 households enrolled and, of these, over 20,000 qualified for payments. We had complete dossiers on each case from the time of initial application. However, there were also disadvantages; an open enrollment program does not allow for a control group—households similar to the experimental subjects but not permitted to participate. Furthermore, there was only one allowance program design for the Supply Experiment; the effects of program variations could not be tested.

The control problem was handled analytically, by a Latin-square design (Mulford et al., 1982). From our baseline (preprogram) household surveys, we retrospectively identified households which later became allowance recipients. We compared their preprogram housing consumption with that of other baseline households, controlling on income and demographic characteristics. We found that, except for a small intercept shift, future recipients' consumption responded to the same factors in the same way as did the consumption of those who never joined the program. Taking account of that intercept shift, as well as of temporal shifts in other parameters, we were able to estimate how much housing all allowance recipients would have consumed absent the program. This analytical control method is less foolproof than using a contemporaneous control group as a benchmark, but it guards against the most prominent dangers of before-and-after comparisons.

The administrative studies (Kingsley and Schlegel, 1982; Kingsley et al., 1982; Tebbets, 1979; and Rizor, 1982) were based on detailed time-and-task records maintained by the HAOs under Rand's supervision, and on quality control programs for eligibility and housing certification. The former enabled us to estimate with unusual precision the cost per case of each step in administrative processing, and thereby to highlight opportunities for administrative change or program redesign that would save money without reducing program effectiveness; however, such variations were not systematically tried. The latter enabled us to estimate the incidence of errors in allowance entitlements and housing inspections and their fiscal and other consequences.

INCIDENTAL BENEFITS OF THE EXPERIMENT

In order to estimate program effects on the housing markets of our two sites, we compiled detailed time-series on key market variables and analyzed market structure and processes. Our observations led to some new insights into market processes and parameters that are both theoretically and practically important.

The annual surveys of residential properties conducted in Brown and St. Joseph counties were designed to measure changes in the characteristics of the housing inventory, its utilization, the cost of supplying housing services, and the prices charged for them. Our sample design yielded annual marketwide probability samples of households, dwellings, properties, and landlords; and time-series on specific properties, including their current owners and occupants. For each property in the sample, we compiled detailed annual accounts of both operating and capital expenses; for rental properties, the data cover both tenant and landlord outlays, as well as accounting for rental revenues and vacancy and collection losses (Neels, 1982a, 1982c). We know of no other marketwide survey that provides comparable financial detail.

From these data, we were able to estimate hedonic indexes for housing attributes (Barnett, 1979; Noland, 1980); the income elasticities of housing expenditures for both renters and owners (Mulford, 1979) and the elasticities of demand for specific housing attributes (Barnett and Noland, 1981); a four-factor (land, improvements, energy, building services) production function for housing services, including the elasticities of substitution between the factors (Neels, 1982b); the price elasticity of the rental occupancy rate (Rydell, 1982); and the determinants of housing repair and improvement policies (Helbers and McDowell, 1981).

The parameters we estimated are, of course, specific to our sites, and their generality remains to be confirmed by replication elsewhere. But the insights they suggest are powerful ones. Without going into detail, a few examples are in order:

- The cross-sectional income elasticity of housing demand is far below the long-run aggregate elasticity. In other words, cross-sectional variation of income about the mean has less effect on housing consumption than a long-run change in the average income of all households.

- The existing inventory of housing is flexible in response to demand changes. The output of housing services, as valued by the market, can be substantially increased or decreased by varying current inputs (energy, building services, repairs) without great loss of efficiency.
- In rental housing, rents vary surprisingly little with market condition. Imbalances between supply and demand tend to be reflected in vacancy rates rather than remedied by price changes. Property values, however, are quite sensitive to rental revenue, which reflects both price and vacancies.
- With respect to the production and consumption of housing services, submarkets are not salient; the flow prices of housing attributes are about the same throughout the market. Investment submarkets, however, are quite distinct; physically comparable properties in different neighborhoods may differ in market value by a factor of two for a long time.

DISAPPOINTMENTS

As one of the few who participated in the Supply Experiment from the beginning to end, I formed expectations about what might be accomplished, some of which were disappointed. Other participants and observers, with different expectations, doubtless were differently disappointed, but it seems worthwhile to call attention to a few aspects of our research whose yield seems to me less than it might have been.

My principal disappointment is that we were not able to exploit all the opportunities for useful research that were offered by the HASE data files. That outcome is less attributable to the topical limitations of our charter than to the time and expense entailed in converting raw data to clean, well-organized, well-documented research files. The HASE analysts "practiced" on early data from the allowance programs and the field surveys, and what they learned thereby greatly affected both the subsequent research agenda and the way data files were assembled and managed. But they had less than a year to operate on the full data sets before time and money ran out.

Fortunately, the data are preserved for others. Along with data from the other experiments, the HASE files—8 five-year files of program data and 32 files of survey data—and their documentation were deposited in HUD's Housing Research Data Center, where they will be accessible to the public.[10]

A more specific disappointment was the low yield of our research into residential mobility. How the allowance program affected the mobility of participants and the composition of neighborhood populations was a topic included in our initial research charter. Although our household surveys did not follow movers (the sample element was a dwelling whose current occupants were interviewed), we did obtain a five-year mobility retrospective on each household that entered the sample. Although the HAOs did not directly record moves as dated events, the approximate dates of moves by participants could be inferred from their housing evaluation records. Despite a large amount of data on movers and their circumstances before and after moving, we never developed a powerful model of residential mobility as an economic or social process.[11]

We were much more successful at modeling market adjustments to shifts in demand. As noted above, the data led us to some analytically powerful insights exploited in a series of theoretical and empirical papers, mostly by Rydell (1979a, 1979b, 1980, 1982). However, we never achieved micro-models of consumer and producer behavior that rigorously supported our macro-model, the parameters of which we estimated from HASE and AHS data. There were times when micro-macro integration seemed in reach; but each possibility faded under close scrutiny.

Finally, we contributed little to the theory of tenure choice. Nearly all our work follows the tradition of treating renters and homeowners as though they were different species. For me, this disappointment is mitigated by the observation that our data collection effort was not designed to serve the analysis of tenure choice; and further, that the separate species assumption was adequate for program analysis. But I had hoped for a wider model of consumer behavior than we achieved.

VALEDICTORY

Of the "social experiments" undertaken by the federal government in the 1960s and 1970s, the Supply Experiment was the largest in number of participants, longest in duration, most expensive, and operationally most complex. Nearly everyone who has paid attention to it believes important things were learned from it, but not everyone agrees that, on balance, it was worth the trouble and expense. That judgment surely should depend on the scientific and political consequences of the experiment, which cannot be fully evident at the moment of its completion, and may never be clearly attributable to it.

This book is one among several vehicles for placing the methods and findings of the EHAP experiments before the public for assimilation and application. As one who was present at the creation, I await the outcome with interest.

NOTES

1. The most detailed description of the two sites at baseline is given in Rand Corporation (1977: Sec. IV).

2. These cross-site averages conceal significant differences between Brown and St. Joseph counties. In the latter, incomes were lower and payments were higher. Rents for comparable dwellings were about the same in the two counties, though property values were much lower in St. Joseph County.

3. The administrative regulations governing the program were developed jointly by Rand

and HAO staffs and are documented in the *Housing Allowance Office Handbook* (Katagiri and Kingsley, 1980).

4. The following section is taken from the executive summary of the HASE final report (Lowry, 1982a). The findings are detailed in the full report (Lowry, 1983).

5. The history of the HASE experimental design can be traced through a series of reports first published in 1971-1973 but subsequently republished in the years indicated by the citations: Lowry et al. (1981); Lowry (1980b, 1980c, 1980d); HASE Staff (1980, 1981). The authoritative account of the final design is Lowry (1980b).

6. See Lowry (1980a). As it turned out, the experimental allowance program did not perturb housing markets in either site in ways that bothered local residents, so the contingency plans were never exercised.

7. This limitation, incidentally, applies also to social experiments more closely modeled on clinical trials. Those conducted to date have, for practical reasons, chosen their subjects in only a few places; there is no guarantee that similar subjects would behave identically in different local contexts, especially if the reasons for their observed behavior are not well understood.

8. Generalizing experimental findings to a national program was not part of Rand's charter for the Supply Experiment. Originally, that task was assigned to The Urban Institute.

9. The unpublished analysis was conducted in the spring of 1981 by Howard Hammerman, Office of Policy Development and Research, and is cited here with his permission. The underlying model of short-run market adjustment is presented in Rydell (1980).

10. The files are described in a three-volume *User's Guide to HASE Data* (Hansen et al., 1982).

11. We did, however, produce a useful study of housing search by renters who moved (McCarthy, 1979); it relates search techniques and outcomes to household characteristics.

22

Public Subsidies for Rental Housing Rehabilitation
A Productivity Analysis

F. Stevens Redburn

Rehabilitation subsidy programs are often undertaken by local governments to complement rent subsidies for lower-income households, where the supply of standard rental housing is inadequate. Rental rehabilitation programs are also used to help stabilize or revitalize neighborhoods where private investment in housing has been weak. In recent years, the number and variety of such programs has increased.

In 1983, the Department of Housing and Urban Development's Office of Policy Development and Research undertook an evaluation of the department's Rental Rehabilitation Demonstration, embodying a new approach to subsidizing the rehabilitation of privately owned rental properties. HUD's interest in rental rehabilitation was stimulated in part by the growing number and variety of local programs using public money to stimulate private rental property improvements. The evaluation was given greater immediacy by the department's proposal for a new rental rehabilitation grant program, modeled after the demonstration.

As research plans developed, the focus was broadened to include a look at rehabilitation under other federal programs. Other local programs, not involving federal funds, were also examined. By covering a wide range of subsidy mechanisms and other program variations, this broader comparative design

Author's Note: This research was designed and carried out by staff members of the Division of Policy Studies in HUD's Office of Policy Development and Research. In addition to the author, members of the study team included David W. Sears, Michael Rich, Lester Rubin, Marcia N. Hochman, Christopher Hewitt, Francetta J. White, Susan E. Clarke, and George Ferguson. The full report on this research has been published as *Rehabilitating Rental Housing: The Benefits and Costs of Alternative Approaches*, U.S. Department of Housing and Urban Development (Washington: December, 1984).

From F. Stevens Redburn, "Public Subsidies for Rental Housing Rehabilitation: A Productivity Analysis," original manuscript.

helped to place the demonstration results in perspective and to increase the generality of the study findings.

In September 1983, detailed information was collected by an in-house study team on 350 properties rehabilitated with public assistance in 18 communities that were part of the demonstration.[1]

In December 1983, as analysis of this information was under way, Congress authorized the new Rental Rehabilitation program—directed toward relatively moderate rehabilitation of lower-income occupied units in neighborhoods where rents can be expected to remain affordable to such households for at least five years. The new program, like the demonstration, encourages communities to leverage private rehabilitation investment by owners and lenders and to base rehabilitation subsidy levels on market rents rather than government-established rent levels.[2]

EXPERIENCE WITH RENTAL REHABILITATION

For some years now, housing rehabilitation has been regarded by many as a potentially more cost-effective alternative to new construction of low-cost housing. The apparent logic of a strategy to rehabilitate where possible, rather than to build a new structure, is that it is cheaper and faster to salvage the good parts and replace or repair the bad parts of an existing building than to construct an entirely new one. The attractiveness of this strategy is enhanced by its potential for indirectly stimulating private investment in other, nearby properties, thereby contributing to the stabilization or revitalization of entire neighborhoods.

Rental rehabilitation also is one way of addressing the housing problems of low-income people. In 1981, 15 percent of lower-income[3] renters in the United States occupied substandard units *and* paid excessive proportions of their income for rent.[4] Subsidies for rehabilitation can be used to reduce this number if, after rehabilitation, unit rents remain affordable to lower-income households or if these households receive federal rent assistance.[5]

In recent years, many communities have gained experience in designing and administering rental rehabilitation subsidy programs. Nearly all publicly subsidized rental rehabilitation has been carried out under five national programs: the demonstration; the Community Development Block Grant (CDBG) program; the Section 312 program; the Section 8 Moderate Rehabilitation program; and the Section 8 Substantial Rehabilitation program. All but the last of these were examined in this study; authority for the Section 8 Substantial Rehabilitation program was terminated with passage of the 1983 housing and community development legislation.[6]

Program Descriptions

Constraints imposed on the design and management of local rehabilitation efforts vary from one national program to another. By permitting only one method of financing, Section 312 is the most rigidly defined of the four programs studied. The Section 8 Moderate Rehabilitation program defines for localities the income group to be served and the methods to be followed in setting and subsidizing postrehabilitation rents. HUD's Rental Rehabilitation Demonstration allows localities broad discretion in the choice of financing technique, provided there is a substantial private contribution to the rehabilitation cost, but places some nonregulatory constraints on the neighborhoods where subsidies are to be used and on other aspects of the rehabilitation process. Other local programs using CDBG funds are constrained in their design and administration only by the general restrictions placed on all uses of Block Grant funds.

The Rental Rehabilitation Demonstration. Initiated in August 1981, the demonstration tests a new approach to publicly subsidized rehabilitation of privately owned rental housing. Communities are expected to provide rehabilitation subsidies only to the extent necessary to make each project financially feasible, with the majority of funds coming from the private side. The subsidy may be provided as a low-interest or deferred payment loan or as a forgiveable loan or grant, at the discretion of the locality.

Twenty-three cities and urban counties were selected to participate in the first round of the demonstration. Another 185 communities and 14 states joined the demonstration in August 1982.

Each participating local government used its available CDBG funds to finance the rehabilitation of properties and the administrative costs of operating the demonstration. A special allocation of Section 8 rental assistance certificates was made to each community to assist lower-income households residing in the properties to be rehabilitated, or tenants moving into rehabilitated units that were previously vacant.[7] Given that a principal feature of the demonstration is its separation of rehabilitation subsidies from rent subsidies, lower-income families residing in rehabilitated buildings may use the Section 8 certificate either to remain in the rehabilitated property or to move to other standard housing that rents within the local Fair Market Rent.[8]

The Section 312 Program. Under the Section 312 Rehabilitation Loan program, HUD provides direct below-market interest rate loans for the rehabilitation of residential properties.[9] Loans are restricted to properties located in CDBG target neighborhoods, Urban Homesteading neighborhoods, and certain categorical program areas such as Urban Renewal and Code Enforcement areas.

The maximum loan permitted on residential properties is $27,000 per unit. Until FY 1982, all loans carried an interest rate of 3 percent. Currently, only single-family loans made to owner-occupants carry the 3 percent rate. Investor-owned (i.e., rental) properties that employ private financing at least equal to the Section 312 loan amount receive a 5 percent interest rate. All other borrowers are given an interest rate of 11 percent.

Other rehabilitation programs funded under CDBG. The Block Grant program (enacted in 1974) provides grants to local governments and states to

carry out various community development activities. Although the nation;
objectives of the CDBG program require that funded activities benefit low- an
moderate-income persons, aid in the prevention or elimination of slums an
blight, and/or meet urgent community development needs, actual selection c
activities and priorities for spending the CDBG funds are determined locally.

Rehabilitation of housing (whether owner-occupied or rental) is an eligib!
use of CDBG funds and accounts for a large portion of CDBG-funded activitie
nationwide.[10] However, a November 1981 survey of CDBG spending i:
entitlement cities found that although 98 percent used some Block Grant fund
for rehabilitation of housing, only 50 percent did so for rehabilitation of investor
owned housing. A much smaller fraction could be said to have "extensive
experience with such efforts. At the same time, the surveyed communitie
estimated that 1.7 million of their private rental units were "in substandar(
condition suitable for rehabilitation" compared to 1.3 million homeowne.
units.[11] Because each grantee develops and implements a rehabilitation progran
suited to locally defined needs, the actual operation of rehabilitation program:
differs widely from locality to locality.

The Section 8 Moderate Rehabilitation Program. This program, establishec
in FY 1979, is operated by local Public Housing Agencies (PHAs). It provide:
rental assistance payments to property owners who lease units to lower-income
tenants of buildings rehabilitated to standards approved by the PHA. In mos!
cases, these standards are the Section 8 Existing program Housing Qualit}
standards; otherwise, they are local codes.

Subsidies are based on the difference between the gross rent (needed to cover
operating costs, debt service, and a predetermined return on investment) and the
tenant's contribution (set at 30 percent of its adjusted household income).[12]

Property owners are selected by the PHA to participate in the program and
are responsible for securing their own financing for the rehabilitation. The
program requires that a minimum of $1,000 per unit be spent for rehabilitation
and that all improvements and related costs be accomplished within the Fair
Market Rent limitations set for this program.

The 18 communities visited in this study were all first-round participants in the
Rental Rehabilitation Demonstration. In addition, nearly all had active Section
8 Moderate Rehabilitation and Section 312 programs between January 1981 and
September 1983, when data for the study were collected. Nine of the 18 had one
or more locally developed CDBG-funded rental rehabilitation programs—for a
total of 20 such programs—during this period. Also, four communities operated
a total of five programs that did not employ federal funds. Thus the 18
communities operated a total of 76 distinct rental rehabilitation programs; a
small sample of projects was drawn for study from each local program.[13]

ISSUES ADDRESSED BY THE RESEARCH

The research was designed to address several specific policy issues bearing on
these programs and not dealt with in previous evaluations of rehabilitation

ubsidy programs. The relatively few empirical studies of rental rehabilitation nat had been conducted prior to this one focused on cost comparisons between ubsidized rehabilitation and subsidized new construction for comparable low-ncome units.[14]

Rental rehabilitation programs are generally aimed at two goals. Some local rograms are aimed primarily at stabilizing or revitalizing neighborhoods hrough increased investment in the rental stock. Others are intended to help ower-income households obtain standard, affordable housing. Although the wo goals can conflict with each other, many programs seek to achieve both of hem simultaneously.

Relative to the first goal, greater benefits result where abandoned units are eturned to the stock and made standard or where units about to be lost due to evere deficiencies and inadequate operating income are rescued through timely ehabilitation. Relative to the second goal, greater benefits are achieved where ublic programs increase the supply of rental units occupied by lower-income iouseholds at rents they can afford. One issue concerning such programs is vhether and how the two goals can be reconciled.

A second set of questions concerns the relative value of alternative program lesigns—including whether the relatively flexible approach to structuring ubsidies and other features of the demonstration are a potential improvement over previously tried approaches.

A third set of questions concerns whether relatively moderate levels of rehabilitation (costing less than $15,000 per unit, for instance) can produce the desired benefits, in the form of new housing investment and increased low-income housing opportunities, at a rate of public expenditure below that of more substantial rehabilitation.

METHOD OF ANALYSIS

To address these and other evaluation questions, it is necessary (1) to measure the benefits of each rehabilitation project relative to the stated goals of most programs; (2) to calculate the net public cost of each project, including direct rehabilitation subsidy, any associated tax expenditures,[15] and any stream of rent subsidies subsequently provided to lower-income tenants; and (3) by combining these measures of benefits and public costs to estimate the relative productivity of projects grouped by national program, by level of rehabilitation, or by other characteristics.

The nature and extent of the benefits produced by rehabilitating a rental unit depend on the unit's status (occupancy, condition, etc.) prior to rehabilitation, its condition after rehabilitation, what happens to households who were living there before rehabilitation, who lives there afterward, and what they pay to rent the unit.

Benefits vary greatly from one rehabilitation project to another. In some cases, rehabilitation involves minor upgrading of an already occupied unit, the household remains after rehabilitation, and rents rise only slightly or not at all. In

other cases, rehabilitation involves major repairs and system replacement, th
restoring to standard condition units that are seriously deficient or ev
uninhabitable, and may lead to rents much higher than those charged prior
rehabilitation. Rent increases may or may not place these units out of reach
lower-income households, depending partly on whether rent assistance
available to these tenants.

Estimating the benefits produced by rental rehabilitation involves three step
(a) noting changes in the status of units produced by rehabilitation; (
examining changes in occupancy attributable to rehabilitation; and (c) noting th
extent to which lower-income households occupy rehabilitated units and ho
many of these are paying rents they can afford, either because the rents are lo
enough relative to their incomes or because they are receiving public re
assistance.

The cost to the public of subsidizing the rehabilitation of private rent
properties also varies widely and, in some cases, dramatically from project t
project. Obviously, some of the cost variation will reflect differences in th
condition of properties selected for subsidy and, therefore, the total expenditur
needed to restore them to standard condition. However, the public cost c
subsidizing rehabilitation also depends on the proportion of the financin
provided by the public sector, the terms under which it is provided, whethe
federal or local tax expenditures are generated by the project, and the extent c
any rent subsidies subsequently provided to households living in or initiall
moving from the rehabilitated properties.

More than one perspective on public cost is needed to reflect accurately th
nature of cost variations. The following are the principal per-unit measures o
public cost used in the analysis:

Rehabilitation subsidy cost: The discounted present value[16] of direct publi
subsidy, accounting for loan paybacks, plus the discounted present value o
the stream of tax expenditures associated with each project, per uni
rehabilitated.

Depth of rehabilitation subsidy: The ratio of rehabilitation subsidy cost (a
defined above) to the total rehabilitation expenditure (both public anc
private shares).

Rent subsidy cost: The discounted present value of rent subsidies paid o
behalf of subsidized lower-income households, estimated cumulatively a
the end of 1, 5, and 15 years—per rehabilitated unit.[17]

Total public cost: The sum of the rehabilitation subsidy cost and rent subsidy
cost, per rehabilitated unit—again, estimated at the end of 1, 5, and 1£
years.

Ratios of benefits to cost provide an indication of the relative productivity o
different rehabilitation efforts. Because both benefits and costs can appropriately be viewed from more than one perspective, several ratios are needed to fully
characterize the differences in productivity among programs or approaches.

ultiple regression analysis and other multivariate techniques have been used to erpret variations in productivity—especially to distinguish the influences of ogram design and administration, on the one hand, from the effects of the erent difficulty of the projects undertaken, on the other hand. Such analyses n produce a better understanding of what approaches to rental rehabilitation rk best, under given conditions, to achieve a desired result.

FINDINGS

Both the benefits and costs of rental rehabilitation efforts vary widely across e 18 communities—and from project to project within a community— imarily as a result of decisions made locally about the kinds of properties that ve been rehabilitated with public subsidies and the use that has been made of ction 8 rent subsidies to aid lower-income households.

ehabilitation Benefits

Benefits have been analyzed in relation to the two major goals of most local ograms.

Goal #1: Additions to the rental stock. When benefits are looked at in terms f additions to the rental stock, disregarding the kinds of households aided, the tent of benefits depends directly on the condition of properties selected for bsidy. By definition, units can be added to the stock, or saved from imminent ss, only where serious physical deficiencies are remedied by rehabilitation. reventing the loss of a unit that otherwise would soon be out of the stock ovides about the same benefit as returning a unit to the stock through habilitation.

In these 18 communities, on average, rental rehabilitation has added 37 units the stock and saved 38 from imminent loss for every 100 units rehabilitated. he other units that received subsidies would not have been lost to the stock but ere upgraded to local standards (22 percent) or were already standard (3 ercent).

Although properties in poorer condition may cost much more to rehabilitate han those in relatively good condition, they also produce more benefit as neasured by units added or saved. Moderate rehabilitation (costing between 5,000 and $15,000 per unit) has added or saved about 80 of every 100 units ehabilitated—a rate of benefit almost equal to that for substantial rehabilitation costing at least $15,000 per unit and often much more) and well above that for ight rehabilitation (costing $5,000 or less per unit).

Comparing the four national programs, the highest rate of benefit occurred in Section 312 projects, in which 90 percent of the units rehabilitated represented net additions to the rental stock (units added or saved). In the demonstration, where rehabilitation investments were lighter on average than in other programs, 50 units were added or saved per 100 rehabilitated. By this measure of benefit, Section 8 Moderate Rehabilitation (71 net additions per 100) and CDBG-funded projects (76 per 100) fall in the middle. However, the rate of benefits varies wid within each national program—from community to community and fr project to project.

Goal #2: Aiding lower-income households. Benefits to lower-income hou holds depend not only on whether the properties selected for assistance h; relatively severe deficiencies, but also on the extent to which rent subsid are provided or market rents remain low, so that units are affordable by low income households.

For every 100 units rehabilitated, 55 were subsequently occupied by low income households that would not have been available to such househo without the rehabilitation. However, some of the units were occupied unassisted lower-income tenants who paid over 30 percent of their income ; rent and utilities. As a result, the net increase in the *affordable* lower-inco: occupied rental stock due to the rehabilitation was 35 units for every ? rehabilitated. This number varies depending on the extent of rehabilitati investment. Moderate and substantial rehabilitation are about equal, havi added about one unit to the affordable lower-income rental stock for every t subsidized, but light rehabilitation added only one such unit for every fi rehabilitated.

Providing rent assistance following rehabilitation increases the rate at whi lower-income households benefit. In the Section 8 Moderate Rehabilitati program (where nearly all tenants are assisted), the rate of increase in t affordable lower-income stock was twice that of the demonstration (66 per 1· versus 34 per 100) and more than twice the rate produced by Section 312 (26 p 100) and CDBG-funded (22 per 100) projects. In projects where, after rehab itation, most households were assisted, 78 of every 100 rehabilitated un: represented a net gain in the affordable lower-income occupied rental supp But in projects where most postrehabilitation households were unassisted, on 14 of every 100 rehabilitated units constitute a gain in units affordably occupie by lower-income people.

Benefits are reduced or offset where households are forced to move as a resu of rehabilitation. In the 18 communities, 11 percent of prior tenants moved out ; connection with the rehabilitation; but some of these moves were voluntary. C prior occupants, 4 percent were recognized by local officials as official: displaced, making them eligible for various forms of relocation benefits. Thus tł actual rate of displacement was somewhere between 4 and 11 percent.

Because timely rehabilitation rescues many occupied units that woul otherwise soon be abandoned, it also avoids the displacement of man households. Taking into account the number of occupants of such units wh were displaced in connection with the rehabilitation, the number who avoide displacement due to rehabilitation is, nevertheless, much larger than the numbe displaced.

⸻ogram Costs

The cost to the public of a rehabilitation effort derives, as noted above, from ⸻ee forms of subsidy: direct subsidies (grants or loans) used to finance the ⸻abilitation;[18] indirect subsidies, especially reduced liability for federal income ⸻ or local property taxes, used in connection with some rehabilitation; and any ⸻t subsidies provided for eligible lower-income tenants of the rehabilitated ⸻operties.

The public cost of rehabilitation subsidies has been calculated for each project adjusting for the widely varying forms and terms of subsidy and subtracting ⸻ present dollar value of loan repayments to be made in the future. Projects ⸻re then compared in terms of the public cost of rehabilitation subsidy (direct ⸻bsidy plus tax benefits) and the total public cost of rehabilitation and rent ⸻bsidies combined. Because rent subsidies are paid over time, their cumulative ⸻st over periods of up to 15 years has been estimated for each project where they ⸻re provided.

Projecting to all projects carried out by these communities since 1980, $1 has ⸻en invested in rehabilitation from both public and private sources for every 53¢ ⸻e public sector spent on rehabilitation subsidies, including taxes foregone by ⸻e federal and local governments. It has cost the public an average of $10,700 to ⸻bsidize rehabilitation of a rental unit, of which 55 percent was in the form of ⸻rect subsidies and the remainder in tax benefits. Adding to this the cost of ⸻ction 8 rent assistance provided to 43 percent of the tenants in rehabilitated ⸻its, the total public cost under these programs averaged $12,500 for each ⸻habilitated unit.

Variation in program costs. The condition of properties selected for reha-⸻ilitation is the most important single influence on the public cost of ⸻habilitation subsidies. Where the cost of rehabilitation (both public and private ⸻ares) is higher, because of poorer property condition, the public contribution ⸻ the rehabilitation also tends to be higher. Costs also tend to be higher where ⸻roperties are older, where units are larger, and where projects take longer to ⸻omplete.

Apart from the nature of the project itself, the cost of subsidizing rental ⸻habilitation appears to be influenced by programmatic factors. Taking into ⸻ccount all other influences on the rehabilitation subsidy cost, these costs ⸻veraged about $3,000 lower per unit for properties improved under the ⸻emonstration or under other CDBG-funded programs than for properties ⸻habilitated under the other federal programs. Using a different method[19] of ⸻stimating the portion of the Section 8 Moderate Rehabilitation rent supplement ⸻evoted to rehabilitation subsidy, this difference remains but is reduced to about ⸻1,500 per unit. One possibility is that the greater flexibility in structuring ⸻ubsidies allowed under the demonstration and CDBG accounts for the ⸻ifference.

The public cost of subsidizing rehabilitation is less strongly influenced market conditions at a communitywide or neighborhood level than might ha been expected. Public expenditures tend to be lower, on average, in strong c markets, taking into account other influences on cost. However, the avera public cost of rehabilitation subsidies as a proportion of total rehabilitati expenditure is roughly the same in strong, moderate, and weak mark communities. And contrary to expectations, subsidy costs are somewhat high on average, in stronger market neighborhoods than in weaker mark neighborhoods.

Where a rental rehabilitation program is intended to improve housi opportunities for lower-income people, it is appropriate to consider re assistance as a component of public cost. Where more occupants of t rehabilitated units are assisted, this component of public cost is, of cours higher. In Section 8 Moderate Rehabilitation projects, nealy all postrehab. itation occupants were assisted; but under the demonstration only one-thi received aid and under the other two national (Section 312 and CDBG-funde programs, about one in seven was assisted.

Among the four national programs, as used in the study communities, t highest average public costs per unit (including rent assistance) were for Section Moderate Rehabilitation and CDBG-funded projects, reflecting both relative high rehabilitation subsidy costs in these programs and the large proportion assisted units in the former program. The average for these two programs w about $15,000 per rehabilitated unit—slightly higher than for Section 31 ($10,900) and about twice that averaged in the demonstration ($7,300).

Program Productivity

The productivity of a rehabilitation program or approach is defined as th dollars of public expenditure (including tax receipts foregone to stimulat rehabilitation) for every unit of benefit achieved. Higher productivity mean lower expenditures to achieve the same rate of benefit.

Two measures of productivity deserve special attention because they cor respond closely to the two often-stated objectives of local rental rehabilitatio programs:

- Where the emphasis is on increasing the supply of standard rental housing and not primarily on aiding lower-income households, then it is appropriat to judge productivity in terms of the rehabilitation subsidy required for eacl net addition to the rental stock.
- Where the objective is primarily to improve the housing for lower-incom households, then it is appropriate to judge productivity in terms of the combined public cost of rehabilitation and rent subsidies required for eacl unit added to the supply of affordable lower-income occupied renta housing.

A local rehabilitation effort that is more productive than average by one ndard may be less productive by the other. Some programs may, through a nbination of appropriate design and market conditions, achieve higher-than-erage productivity by both standards.

Standard #1: Additions to the rental stock. Productivity measured in terms net additions to the stock (units added or saved by rehabilitation) can be reased through careful selection of properties to receive subsidy. In these ms, light and moderate levels of rehabilitation were much more productive in e 18 study communities, typically, than was substantial rehabilitation. In ojects that received light rehabilitation, it cost the public $3,600 in rehabil-tion subsidy to add or save a rental unit. Moderate rehabilitation was mewhat less productive (costing $5,900 per unit of benefit) in these terms but is far more productive than substantial rehabilitation (which cost $18,600 per it of benefit). Evidence also suggests that productivity was higher when operties had serious physical deficiencies prior to rehabilitation but were still bitable, and in smaller properties. Thus where available, the ideal candidate r rehabilitation from this perspective would be a small structure in relatively or but not uninhabitable condition that can be made standard with a light or oderate level of investment.

Standard #2: Aiding lower-income households. Productivity measured as e total public cost (including 15 years of rent assistance) for every unit added to e affordable lower-income occupied stock is generally enhanced by the same oices that lead to higher productivity measured in terms of net additions to the ock. That is, the selection of smaller properties in relatively poor condition, but quiring light or moderate levels of investment to be made standard, was nerally the most efficient way of expanding the supply of affordable lower-come occupied housing in the 18 study communities.

Section 8 assistance was used to increase the number of such affordable units; ut it also added to public costs. The availability of Section 8 assistance may be rucial to ensuring that lower-income households occupy a particular rehabil-ated property. However, across all projects, the higher costs produced by such ssistance roughly offset the higher benefits thus achieved, other things equal, so hat productivity was unaffected. Also, although projects with higher propor-ions of Section 8 assisted tenants generally produced greater low-income enefit, this was primarily a function of their prerehabilitation condition and the evel of rehabilitation investment rather than the use of Section 8 assistance.

Under most market conditions, the expected trade-off between maximizing roductivity in terms of adding to the stock or maximizing productivity in terms f aiding lower-income households does not appear to be sharp or necessary. The esson to be learned from this is that by carefully selecting properties and eighborhoods, it is possible for most communities to use rental rehabilitation roductively to achieve both objectives simultaneously.

National programs and productivity. Evidence suggests that the four natio
programs are flexible enough to allow communities to address a range of hous
needs under varied market conditions. For instance, where a commun
specialized in rehabilitating one type of property (e.g., habitable structures)
typically used all national programs for this purpose. Of the 18 communities,
specialized in the rehabilitation of mostly habitable units; five rehabilita
mostly uninhabitable units; and seven selected a mix of habitable and un
habitable properties.

Given the flexibility of the national programs, communities appear able
fashion a productive approach to rental rehabilitation under any of them. F
this reason, and given the wide variations observed within national programs
both benefits and costs, comparing programs in terms of productivity averag
can be misleading. It is worth noting, however, that the Rental Rehabilitati
Demonstration, as used in these 18 communities, is, by a small margin, the mo
productive national program relative to net stock additions (units added
saved). Measuring productivity in terms of net additions to the affordab
low-income rental stock, the Section 8 Moderate Rehabilitation program a
the demonstration are, on average, about twice as productive as Section 312
local CDBG-funded programs. The latter programs expand the affordab
lower-income occupied rental supply at lower rates, on average, than t
demonstration and at a higher average cost per rehabilitated unit. Although cos
are higher under Section 8 Moderate Rehabilitation than under the demonstr
tion, so is the rate of low-income benefit. Exhibit A shows both productivi
averages for each of the national programs.

Wasted or unnecessary subsidies. Communities sometimes use subsidies in
manner that is less than optimal considering their stated objectives. Some spe
large amounts per unit to return uninhabitable structures to the rental stoc
when they might have achieved comparable gains by preventing the loss c
still-habitable units. Others emphasized light rehabilitation of units that wou
have continued as rental housing without rehabilitation, resulting in low pe
unit costs but achieving relatively minor improvements and adding no units t
the rental stock. And in some cases, public subsidies were used where none wa
needed to stimulate rehabilitation.

Where subsidized rehabilitation would have occurred without public subsid
the benefits of the rehabilitation cannot be ascribed to the subsidy. It is difficu
to determine whether or not public dollars were necessary to make a give
rehabilitation project financially feasible. However, where either local progra
officials or property owners indicated that some or all of the rehabilitation woul
have occurred without subsidy, this suggests that public funds may have merel
substituted for private investment. According to their subjective judgments, i
about 10 percent of the projects, rehabilitation would have occurred withou
subsidy; in another 16 percent, at least one-half of the rehabilitation would hav
occurred. These rates provide an estimate, probably conservative, of the exten

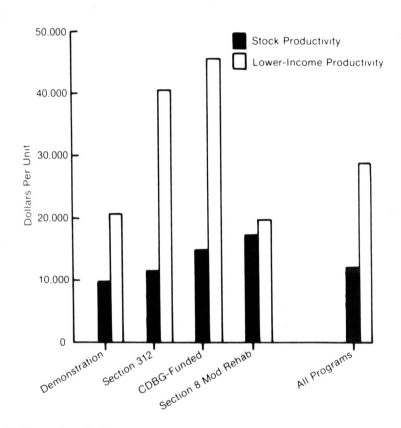

That is, stock productivity.

. That is, low-income productivity.

Using the alternate method of apportioning the Section 8 Moderate Rehabilitation subsidy, 1e cost of adding a unit to the stock is $12,332 rather than $17,358, as shown here.

xhibit A   Rehabilitation Subsidy Cost per Net Stock Addition[a] and Total Rehabilitation Subsidy and Rent Subsidy per Net Addition to the Affordable Low-Income Stock[b]

to which public funds were wasted in this manner on rehabilitation that would have occurred without subsidy.

Recognizing that such testimonial evidence of substitution is at best suggestive, using it as a basis for discounting benefits decreases the apparent productivity of local rental rehabilitation efforts by 22 percent relative to net stock changes and by 14 percent relative to low-income benefits.

The New Rental Rehabilitation Program

The newly adopted Rental Rehabilitation program builds on experie: gained in the Rental Rehabilitation Demonstration. It gives communities br(discretion in selecting properties and designing the financing and other rules t suited to local conditions. At the same time, it places restrictions on the size ε proportion of direct subsidy that can be provided from program funds. Al projects must be in neighborhoods where rents will remain affordable to low income households for an extended period; and a large proportion (70 percent more) of the households benefitting from a local program should have incon below 80 percent of the metropolitan area median income.

Based on results for projects that fit the profile of the new program, it see: likely to be highly productive relative to the principal objectives of most lo(programs. As a group, these projects are well above average in the efficiency w: which rehabilitation subsidies contribute to an increased rental supply, aver ing $7,100 of public expenditure for every unit added or saved compared $12,300 for all rehabilitation in the 18 communities. Relative to the seco measure of productivity, projects fitting the new program's profile are ag more productive than average, costing $22,000 in rehabilitation and re subsidies for each additional affordable lower-income occupied unit versus average $29,000 for all rehabilitation in the study communities. Thus t emphasis on relatively light rehabilitation subsidies and targeting to lowe income households and stable neighborhoods, combined with local discreti(over the terms of subsidy, appears to constitute a relatively productive approa(to rental rehabilitation.

CONCLUSIONS

This evaluation provides a new empirical basis for judgments about tl relative productivity of difference approaches to stimulating the rehabilitation (privately owned rental properties. In these 18 communities, rehabilitatio projects supported under the Rental Rehabilitation Demonstration and tl Section 8 Moderate Rehabilitation program have been about twice as pr(ductive, on average, in improving low-income housing opportunities as thos supported under Section 312 and CDBG. Also, rehabilitation efforts involvin relatively moderate levels of investment are, on average, more productiv (achieve benefits at a lower rate of public expenditure) than projects involvin more substantial rehabilitation. This is especially the case if productivity measured as the public cost (including rehabilitation and rent subsidies) of aidin lower-income households.

Perhaps as important as these substantive findings are the implications of th research for how such programs are actually designed and administered. Loca choices—concerning the kinds of properties to receive subsidy and the provisio of rent assistance to lower-income households—appear to be more importan in the formal structure of federal programs or market conditions in determining whether public funds are used productively to stimulate new investment in rental housing and to improve housing opportunities for lower-income people. Apparently the two distinct goals of most local rental rehabilitation programs—to stimulate private investment in rental housing and to aid lower-income households—can be achieved simultaneously under most market conditions through careful selection of properties to receive subsidy. There is evidence from past experience that the newly enacted Rental Rehabilitation program has the potential for being quite productive—again, provided localities make the proper choices in implementing the program. As communities undertake the new program, they can use this evaluation both to guide their thinking about how they choose projects that are consistent with their objectives and as a source of specific benchmarks against which to measure their own programs' productivity.

NOTES

1. Details on the research methodology are given in HUD (1984). The major information constraints on the analysis included the lack of direct physical inspections to determine property condition before and after rehabilitation and the lack of individual household information on income and other characteristics of occupants before and afterward.

2. This program is authorized by Section 301 of the Housing and Urban-Rural Recovery Act of 1983, P.L. 98-181.

3. "Lower-income" households are those whose annual incomes are below 80 percent of the median income for households of the same size in the same metropolitan area.

4. *1981 Annual Housing Survey*, U.S. Bureau of the Census and U.S. Department of Housing and Urban Development. This figure is based on an analysis of households earning less than $10,000 in 1980.

5. Rent assistance may be available in the form of Section 8 Vouchers or Certificates. See the *Federal Register*, Vol. 49, No. 135 (July 12, 1984) for current program rules.

6. The four examined programs are all designed to support varying levels of rehabilitation, whereas the Section 8 Substantial Rehabilitation program was not used for light or moderate rehabilitation.

7. Rent subsidies to lower-income tenants residing in properties rehabilitated under the demonstration have been provided under the Section 8 Existing Housing program on the basis of one unit (certificate) for each $5,000 of CDBG funds used for rehabilitation subsidies.

8. Fair Market Rents (FMRs) for the Section 8 Existing program are set by HUD for each metropolitan area at the level where 45 percent of the area's standard unassisted rental units that changed occupants in the past two years rent for less than that figure.

9. Section 312 was established by the Housing Act of 1964, 42 U.S.C. Section 1452b, to provide low-interest direct loans for rehabilitation of properties in Urban Renewal areas. Prior to 1979, Section 312 focused almost entirely on single-family loans. Since then, higher priority has been given to loans for multifamily properties and to improving housing for low- and moderate-income persons. Congress has appropriated no funds for Section 312 rehabilitation since FY 1981.

10. In entitlement cities, the rehabilitation of private property accounted for 28 percent of $2.1186 billion budgeted in FY 1982 for CDBG expenditures. No separate estimate of CDBG spending for rental rehabilitation is available. *Consolidated Annual Report to Congress on Community Development Programs*, U.S. Department of Housing and Urban Development (1983).

11. U.S. General Accounting Office, *Block Grants for Housing: A Study of Local Experien* and *Attitudes*, GAO/RCED-83-21 (December 13, 1982); and U.S.G.A.O., *Rental Rehabilitati* *with Limited Federal Involvement: Who is Doing it? At What Cost? Who Benefits?*, GAO/RCE 83-148 (July 11, 1983).

12. Fair Market Rents (FMRs) are used in the Section 8 Moderate Rehabilitation program to a ceiling on unit rents after rehabilitation. These FMRs are 120 percent of the FMRs published f the Section 8 Existing program.

13. Very few of these local programs are more than five years old. From January 1981 throu September 1983, nearly 3,800 rehabilitation projects (most involving a single property) had be completed under these programs, resulting in the rehabilitation of about 39,000 rental housing uni

14. See George Sternlieb and David Listokin, "Rehabilitation Versus Redevelopment: Co: Benefit Analyses," *Housing in the Seventies Working Papers 2, National Housing Review*, U. Department of Housing and Urban Development (Washington: 1976) 1033-1103.

15. Tax expenditures are revenues foregone due to special provisions of tax law intended reward particular forms of private investment.

16. Income received and expenditures to be made in the future are worth less, in today's dollar than present income and expenditures. Therefore, following standard practice for this kind analysis, future income and expenditures are discounted to their present values. The result is a true picture of the public costs of various forms of subsidy, all expressed in today's dollars. The assume discount rate is 12.5 percent annually, based on the long-term U.S. Treasury bond rate at the time th study was conducted.

17. Only 15-year cumulative costs are used in the reported computations.

18. In the Section 8 Moderate Rehabilitation program, in contrast to other programs, dire rehabilitation subsidies and rent subsidies are combined in a single rent supplement, which is paid t the property owner over a 15-year period. The portion of this supplement used to pay debt service o private rehabilitation loans can be considered a rehabilitation subsidy, except where noted below

19. The alternate method of apportioning rent supplements for Section 8 Moderate Rehabi itation projects treats as the rehabilitation subsidy that portion of the total subsidy that reimburse owners for costs over and above the local Section 8 Existing program Fair Market Rent. Under thi alternate assumption, the portion of the rent supplement considered a rehabilitation subsidy is ofte a much smaller fraction of the total.

23

The Pennsylvania Domiciliary Care Experiment
I. Impact on Quality of Life

Sylvia Sherwood and John N. Morris

Abstract: This paper reports findings concerning the impact on quality of life of a case management focused program of small board and care facilities serving aging, mental health, and mental retardation adult target populations—the Pennsylvania Domiciliary Care Program. Program participants from the counties in which the Domiciliary Care Program was initiated were matched with persons residing in similar counties without the program who were comparable on a large array of characteristics prior to program initiation. Conducted separately by target group, 10-month follow-up assessments provided the basis for determining impact. In general, the effects were positive, particularly with respect to meeting program quality of life goals (providing needed services, improving living conditions, increasing community integration, and reducing institutional days); the effects were more positive for the aging and mental health than for the mentally retarded target populations. (*Am J Public Health* 1983; 73:646–653.)

The population of at-risk individuals needing long-term care is substantial and increasing rapidly. It has been estimated that the potential demand for long-term care will increase from between 6.3 to 11.1 million in 1980 to between 7.4 and 12.5 million by 1985.[1,2] Current estimates are that: about 3 per cent of the population are mentally retarded;[3] about 12 per cent have mental disorders;[4] and, of the population age 65 and older, about 18 per cent have functional impairments sufficient to necessitate long-term supportive services.[5] Despite the increasing consideration given to alternatives in long-term care for all groups and deinstitutionalization efforts for the mental health and mental retardation target groups, institutional placement still constitutes a primary publicly supported service delivery mechanism.[6] At the same time, data indicate that many persons placed in such long-term care institutions could function in less sheltered community environments were they available.[7-9]

Small board and care facilities represent such an option. Unfortunately, little is known about the impact of such facilities on the quality of life of the residents or its cost/benefit implications. This paper reports measures of the impact on the quality of life of recipients of the Pennsylvania Domiciliary Care Program. A companion article presents cost/benefit findings for this program.[10]

Address reprint requests to Sylvia Sherwood, PhD, Director, Department of Social Gerontological Research, Hebrew Rehabilitation Center for Aged, 1200 Centre Street, Boston (Roslindale) MA 02131. Dr. Morris is Associate Director of the Department. This paper, submitted to the Journal August 31, 1982, was revised and accepted for publication December 29, 1982.
Editor's Note: See also related article p 645 and editorial p 638 this issue.

The Pennsylvania Domiciliary Care Experiment

The Pennsylvania Program was developed by state and regional staff of the interagency Domiciliary Care Task Force of the Pennsylvania Department of Public Welfare, with the following quality of life and cost saving goals in mind:*

- Meeting the service needs of the target populations (aging, physically impaired younger adults, mental health, and mental retardation clients);
- Having a positive impact on the living conditions of the target populations;
- Having a positive impact on integrating the target population into community life;
- Reducing institutionalization in a nursing home, state hospital, or other long term care institutional facility (encompassing both prevention and deinstitutionalization objectives); and
- Reducing costs of care; i.e., to be cost beneficial.

Although housed under the aegis of the Office of Aging, the program was planned and implemented as an integrated effort to serve the target populations of the offices of Aging, Mental Health and Mental Retardation, and Income Maintenance; the county agencies of these three offices were to contribute either in manpower or funds to the operation of the Domiciliary Care Program in their areas. The pilot phase was initiated in selected counties representing rural, mixed rural-urban, and urban areas; the program was begun in late 1976.

*The specification of these goals is based on a perusal of the minutes of the meetings and the resulting documents of the interagency Task Force.

Before the program was initiated, it was recognized by the program planners that a multi-faceted evaluation project accompanying the initial effort could provide valuable knowledge concerning its feasibility and impact. With the cooperation of the Pennsylvania Central Office of the Domiciliary Care Program, in July 1976, just prior to program implementation, an independent federally supported multi-faceted evaluation of the program was initiated by the Department of Social Gerontological Research of the Hebrew Rehabilitation Center for Aged in Boston. We report here the results of one part of this study.

Some of the features of the program and a summary of findings concerning applicants are presented first to serve as background for this and the companion article.[10]

The Domiciliary Care Program

The program offers supplementary payments for individuals (age 18 or older) residing in approved domiciliary care facilities who are financially eligible for Supplementary Security Income (SSI) and judged to be incapable of independent living in the community, but do not require services that can be obtained only in a nursing home or other long-term care institution (e.g., 24-hour medical supervision). Approved domiciliary care facilities include homes housing up to 13 clients in which personal care services, including 24-hour supervision, are offered by the proprietor in addition to the normal range of meals, laundry, and other needed household services. Facilities with three or less clients had to meet the program home criteria only; the larger homes had to meet the additional building and safety code regulations which apply to nursing and boarding homes. The vast majority of homes in the program were small homes with one to three clients. The only larger homes were group homes for the mentally retarded, functioning prior to the program, but housing program-eligible residents who became program clients.

Case Management and Home Approval/Monitoring Functions—Through contractual arrangements with local Area Agencies on Aging, local Domiciliary Care Placement Agencies were created and given responsibility for client assessment, placement, service coordination, and other case management functions as well as home/provider inspection, certification, and legal agreements. Staff were trained in the use of a standard assessment tool and home inspection criteria.** A complete reassessment of the client for functional eligibility and need for ancillary services and an inspection of the home were carried out annually.

The home providers were responsible for supervision within the home setting. Although the program organizes training sessions and provides back-up to the providers, the small home providers are generally not specifically trained as service professionals; in the few larger group homes for some of the mentally retarded target population, professional staff are responsible for the care of the residents.

The Financial Component—The area Income Maintenance Office is responsible for determining client financial

eligibility for the federally administered State optional plement for domiciliary care. From a combined state federal SSI payment, a fixed amount is paid to the propr of the domiciliary care home by each client. When program was first started in 1976, the state suppleme SSI payment to the client was $315 monthly, of which was paid by the client to the domiciliary care home prov During the period of data collection for this study, federal base increased as did the amounts paid to provider.

Applicants for Domiciliary Care—The majority adults applying for domiciliary care were referred by t respective target group agencies.*** Less than 10 per were difficult to place in one of the three groups to studied: Aging, Mental Health, and Mental Retardation a large extent, applicants not in these groups were physic impaired adults under age 65 referred by organizati dealing with the adult physically handicapped or by ph cians, or were self-referrals. In general, charac eristics these applicants so closely resembled those o: the ag client population that they were included with the ag group in the analyses.

Clinical assessments confirmed that the applicants w in need of the services provided by the Domiciliary C Program. In terms of prior living arrangements, a hig percentage of the mental health clients than of the aging mental retardation clients were institutionalized at the ti of application. There were also considerable areas of ov lap: almost one-half of the mental health and almost o fourth of the mental retardation referral populations we over 60 years of age; there was considerable overlap w respect to physical functioning and, to a lesser extent, intellectual functioning and emotional status. Over half the applicants in each of the target groups were female; or 3 per cent were currently married and living with spous only a minority in each of the target groups had childr living nearby, although there were significant differences per cent of the mental retardation group, 22 per cent of t mental health group, and 35 per cent of the aging clients h children nearby).

Domiciliary Care Homes/Providers—Based on inte views with domiciliary care providers, 91 per cent of hom were single family dwellings; 62 per cent had private be rooms for their clients, and an additional 18 per cent had mixture of private and shared bedrooms. The majority providers had at least a high school education. At applic tion, most providers did not work outside the home. Th median annual income (not including domiciliary care clie payments) was between $6,000 and $7,000. Thirteen per ce of the client applicant group and 30 per cent of the provide were Black (with almost all Black providers living in a urban area). There was an almost equal mixture of couple and single (the majority female and widowed) providers with the median age of the provider with primary responsi

---

** Available on request to authors.

*** Reports presenting empirical analyses concerning the appli cants and domiciliary care homes are available on request to th authors.

ty for care being 56 years. Thirteen per cent of the single
39 per cent of the married providers had children under
22 living with them. In addition, 27 per cent of the single
22 per cent of the married providers had other adults
ng in the household.

On the whole, relationships between the providers and
nts can be described as family-like. For example, in 82
cent of the homes the provider and clients address each
er by their first names, and 96 per cent of the providers
that their clients perceive their relationship in the home
resembling that of a family member or friend. Further-
re, a relatively low level of rules appears to be imposed
the clients; in virtually all cases the clients are free to fix
their rooms as they wish; there are no restrictions
garding where or when visitors are allowed; and, aside
m bedrooms, no rooms are out of bounds to clients.

About one-fifth of the providers report spending less
n four hours each day caring for their clients; 41 per cent
nd between four and eight hours, and 38 per cent report
ending more than eight hours each day. Homes rendered
following services: laundry (97 per cent); personal shop-
g (83 per cent); cleaning the client's room (80 per cent);
oviding transportation to social activities (77 per cent);
ndling money (65 per cent); and supervising or administer-
g medications (65 per cent). Other services rendered in
er 20 per cent of the homes include: assistance in groom-
g (49 per cent); bathing (37 per cent); dressing (26 per
nt); and preparing a special diet (21 per cent).

uality of Life Impact Evaluation

mple Construction

Individuals referred to the program (the potential Ex-
erimentals) were interviewed shortly after application but
ior to placement. On average, aging clients were placed
oner than mental health and mentally retarded clients.‡
dividuals in the target populations who resided in similar
eas of Pennsylvania in which a domiciliary care program
ad not been implemented (the potential Controls) were
terviewed at about the same time. These interviews consti-
ted the baseline or "pretest" data.

From these pools of potential Experimentals and Con-
ols, samples of Experimentals (placed clients) and Controls
ere constructed separately for each of the following
roups: aging (including physically impaired), mental health,
nd mental retardation, controlling as well for type of
esidence (community or institution) at pretest. For each
ub-category (e.g., "aging, institutionalized at pretest"), the
nal selection of Experimentals and Controls was based on a
omputer procedure entitled SIMRAN©.

For each sample, this procedure includes two stages: 1)
stablishing criteria for what is to be considered an accept-

able frequency matched sample of Experimentals and Controls; and 2) selecting the maximum acceptable impact
sample of Experimental and Control group subjects from the
two pools. The minimum criteria for inter-group comparability for acceptable samples is set by estimating what an
average random draw of Experimentals and Controls would
look like with respect to a large array of variables when the
combined potential Experimental and Control pools are
considered as a sample universe.‡‡ The second stage involves a large number of computer trials in which equal
numbers of Experimentals and Controls are selected, keeping, to the extent possible, the smallest potential pool intact
and randomly drawing samples from the larger of the potential pools of subjects. To be considered acceptable, the final
selection had to "look better" (e.g., have fewer significant
pretest differences between the selected samples of Experimentals and Controls) than the 50th percentile of the mod-
elled impact samples.‡‡‡ The final samples utilized in determining the effects on variables that did not specifically
require an interview with the sample member are shown in
Table 1.

Primarily because of deaths in the aging impact samples
(a little over 10 per cent, comparable for Experimentals and
Controls), posttest interviews, the source of data for a
number of the quality of life analyses, were not possible for
all of the sample members. Only sample members interviewed both at pretest and posttest were used in analyses
involving outcome variables derived from interview data.
While the aging institutional and community subsamples are
thus somewhat reduced for analyses of impact on such
quality of life outcome variables, these reduced subsamples
met the impact sample acceptability criteria. In general,
there was only slight attrition elsewhere. The reduced subsamples are also shown in Table 1.

Analytic Strategy

Four of the goals of the program involve quality of life
outcomes—provision of needed service, quality of living
conditions, integration into community life, and reducing
time spent in a long-term care facility. These outcomes plus
functional status (physical and psychological) constitute the
subject matter (outcome domains) of the analyses to be
presented.

Impact over a period of ten months was determined.
Differences found at the p ≤ .05 probability level were
considered to be statistically significant. Program impact in
all but one (reduced time in a long-term care facility) of these
five domains was measured by clinical assessment and

---

‡While the time it took to place applicants varied somewhat,
ase management program exposure for all applicants was initiated
hortly after application in all cases.
©Copyright 1980, JN Morris, CE Gutkin, CC Sherwood, S Sherwood, and S Morris.

‡‡In this study, 50 modeled random samples were generated
and computations completed for 47 variables for each of the aging
and mental health subgroups and, because of limited data, 34
variables for each of the mental retardation subgroups. The array of
variables included demographic, functional status, and pre-mea-
sures of outcome variables.

‡‡‡As is often the case, if no acceptable impact sample is found
within a preset number of such trials (100 in this study), extreme
outliers are excluded, the criteria reestablished using the reduced
sample universe, and the second stage is initiated once again.

TABLE 1—Samples Assessed by Residence at Pretest

	Experimentals			Controls		
	Total	Residence at Pretest		Total	Residence at Pretest	
		Community	Institution		Community	Institution
	N	N	N	N	N	N
Pretest Groups						
Aging	101	81	20	101	81	20
Mental Health	45	17	28	45	17	28
Mental Retardation	44	28	16	44	28	16
Pretest/Posttest Groups						
Aging	84	68	16	86	69	17
Mental Health	42	16	26	45	17	28
Mental Retardation	43	27	16	42	26	16

subject self-report data derived from pretest and posttest interviews with the Experimental and Control subjects.

Pretest/Posttest Comparisons—Results of clinical assessment of and interviews with the Experimental and Control samples were compared using analysis of variance techniques. Significant differences between the different groups considered as a whole were examined as well as interactions between Experimental-Control group outcome and residential setting at pretest. As might be expected from the sample construction techniques, for the overwhelming majority of variables for which significant differences at posttest were found, no pretest differences were found. For such variables, significant posttest differences were considered to be indicators of impact. There were a few outcome variables which appeared only on the posttest interview. Given the initial overall similarity between the Experimental and Control groups at pretest, a general assumption of pretest equivalency was made with respect to these variables, and significant posttest differences were also considered to be indicators of impact.

Pretest differences were found between Experimentals and Controls in one variable each for the mental retardation and aging samples. In the former case, the difference at pretest was in the opposite direction to that found at posttest, and impact is claimed. In the latter case, the difference at pretest was similar to that at posttest, and therefore no impact is claimed.

The operationalized quality of life measures were identical for the aging and mental health samples since the interview conducted was identical for these groups. For the mental retardation population, although clinical assessment measures were similar to those for the other two groups, it was neither possible nor appropriate to conduct the same type of interview. Thus many of the self-report outcome variables for the mental retardation group differ from those of the aging and mental health samples.

Operational definitions of the outcome variables include single items, scales based on self-report data, clinical assessments and observations made by the clinically trained interviewer and, in the case of the mental retardation sample, data collected from domiciliary or responsible agency staff.

All scales utilized had an alpha reliability of .50 higher. Inter-rater reliabilities (using an analysis of varian formula) for all clinical assessment outcome variables w .85 or higher, with most over .90. The single item self-rep items were among those used successfully in previous st ies and were found to be reliably obtained in this stu (almost 100 per cent agreement between interviewer a clinical trainer/supervisor prior to the completion of fi work training).

Data collected on days spent in a non-community s ting did not depend entirely on interviews with sam members. Although self-report data were utilized wh considered reliable, major sources of information includ interviews with facility staff and/or service providers (inclu ing informal supports), Domiciliary Care Program record interviews with Domiciliary Care Program officials, a hospital and social agency records.

Results

Meeting Service Needs

The impact of the program on meeting the service neec of the target population was based on clinical judgmene directly addressing this issue. Unmet needs in specif service areas* were assessed as well as a more globe measure assessing overall unmet needs. The global assess ment takes into consideration the overall level of service (including need for sheltered living arrangements) require by the subject in order to live at an adequate level in th community. It is considered the most important of th clinical assessments addressing this issue.

While there were some mixed results, on the whole th program had positive effects on meeting service needs, a illustrated in Table 2. Moreover, it is possible that th seeming negative transportation/recreation findings for the deinstitutionalized aging and mental health samples is a

---

*Transportation, recreation, escort service, counseling, advoc cacy.

_E 2—Significant Impact on Meeting Service Needs (Posttest Comparisons)

_ome Variable by Data _ce (Clinical Assessment or Self-Report)	Aging Exp. N = 84 X̄	Control N = 86 X̄	p	Mental Health Exp. N = 42 X̄	Control N = 43 X̄	p	Mental Retardation Exp. N = 43 X̄	Control N = 42 X̄	p	Comment re observed differences (p ≤ .05) in Impact by Place of Residence at Pretest
_al Assessments _erall Unmet Needs Summary Scale[1]	1.26	2.52	≤.001	1.05	3.47	≤.001	.81	2.55	≤.001	+ All groups more for Exp/Inst
_met Transportation/ Recreational Needs Scale[2]	.45	.60	n.s.	.46	.60	n.s.	.26	.29	n.s.	+ Aging and MH Exp/Comm − Aging and MH Exp/Inst
_nmet Counseling & Advocacy Needs[3]	.13	.20	n.s.	.07	.11	n.s.	.12	.14	n.s.	+ Aging Exp/Comm − Aging Exp/Inst

[1] Five point scale: 1 = no need, 5 = very high need.
[2] Four point scale: sum of 3 yes/no judgments, 0 = No unmet need.
[3] 0 = Needs met, 1 = Needs not met.

_ction of the frame of reference taken in these assess-_nts. Institutional residents are often confined to the _graphic area of the setting and, therefore, may not be _nsidered to have a need (met or unmet) for transportation _vices; the majority of Controls in the institutional sub-_up but only few of the Experimentals were still insti-_ionalized at posttest. This frame of reference may also _count for the mixed findings in the aging subsamples with _spect to Unmet Counseling and Advocacy needs; i.e., it _y have been assumed that advocacy needs are relevant _ly for community populations.

_proving Living Situations

In general, the program had a positive impact on the living situations for all three populations. Table 3 presents the findings. The one area of negative impact (for the mental health group) concerned access to medical facilities for the deinstitutionalized Experimentals. Persons in a state institution can be expected to have easier access to the type of medical services required.

Integration into Community Life

Despite some variability, the program had positive effects on integrating clients into community life, although more broadly for the mental health and aging than for the mental retardation group, as shown in Table 4. The two variables for which mixed outcomes were found for the mental health Experimentals pertained to contact with

_BLE 3—Significant Impact on Improving Living Situations (Posttest Comparisons)

_utcome Variable by Data Source (Clinical _sessment or Self-Report)	Aging Exp. N = 84 X̄	Control N = 86 X̄	p	Mental Health Exp. N = 42 X̄	Control N = 43 X̄	p	Mental Retardation Exp. N = 43 X̄	Control N = 42 X̄	p	Comment re observed differences (p ≤ .05) in Impact by Place of Residence at Pretest
_inical Assessments How well equipped is phys. environment[1]	1.43	1.81	≤.001	1.49	2.09	≤.01	1.24	1.92	≤.001	None
_elf-Report Good Place Scale[2]	4.70	4.88	n.s.	4.72	5.42	≤.05	4.39	4.80	n.s.	None
Relationship with people around[3]	2.84	2.68	≤.01	2.68	2.69	n.s.	2.98	2.85	n.s.	None
Feel about living situation[4]	1.15	1.36	≤.01	1.15	1.26	≤.001	N/A	N/A	N/A	+ Aging and MH mainly for Inst
Enough privacy[5]	1.07	1.13	n.s.	1.05	1.24	≤.05	1.05	1.14	n.s.	None
Environment Satisfaction Scale[6]	10.82	10.70	n.s.	10.80	9.69	≤.05	10.88	9.27	n.s.	+ MH = Inst
Location accessible to medical facilities[5]	1.89	1.82	n.s.	1.85	1.98	≤.01	2.00	1.83	n.s.	− MH = Mainly Inst
Gets to stores easily[5]	N/A	N/A	N/A	N/A	N/A	N/A	1.04	1.15	n.s.	+ MR/Inst

[1] Five point scale: 1 = very well equipped, 5 = dangerous.
[2] Responses to four questions scale: 4 = most favorable, 8 = least favorable.
[3] Three point scale: 3 = satisfactory, 1 = satisfactory.
[4] Three point scale: 1 = positive, 3 = negative.
[5] Two point scale: 1 = yes, 2 = no.
[6] Responses to four questions, scale: 12 = most favorable, 4 = least favorable.

TABLE 4—Significant Impact on Integration into Community Life (Posttest Comparisons)

Outcome Variable by Data Source (Clinical Assessment or Self-Report)	Aging Exp. N = 84 X̄	Control N = 86 X̄	p	Mental Health Exp. N = 42 X̄	Control N = 43 X̄	p	Mental Retardation Exp. N = 43 X̄	Control N = 42 X̄	p	Comment re observed differences (p ≤ .05) Impact by Place of Residence at Pretest
Clinical Assessments										
Involvement Scale[1]	22.32	22.02	n.s.	22.45	20.49	≤.01	21.98	22.79	n.s.	None
Extent of outside friends[2]	3.01	3.10	n.s.	2.98	3.33	≤.05	3.07	3.05	n.s.	+ Aging Inst
Extent of outside interests[2]	2.55	2.80	≤.01	2.29	2.71	≤.01	2.42	2.50	n.s.	None
Self-Report										
How often attend religious services[3]	2.77	2.65	n.s.	2.48	2.80	n.s.	3.56	3.34	n.s.	+ Aging & MR/Com − Aging & MR/Inst
Help Other People[4]	2.64	2.83	≤.05	2.53	2.64	n.s.	2.59	2.62	n.s.	− Aging more so for Inst
Contact with Friends Scale[1]	5.14	5.79	n.s.	5.32	4.68	n.s.	N/A	N/A	N/A	+ MH/Inst − MH/Comm
Visiting friends[5]	.51	.49	n.s.	.58	.57	n.s.	N/A	N/A	N/A	+ MH/Inst − MH/Comm
Participation in Clubs[5]	.32	.05	≤.01	.36	.05	≤.05	N/A	N/A	N/A	None
Takes rides[5]	.98	.68	≤.05	1.24	.64	≤.001	N/A	N/A	N/A	None
At least one person close[6]	1.21	1.24	n.s.	1.15	1.39	≤.01	1.16	1.17	n.s.	None
Interest in family visiting[7]	1.59	1.70	n.s.	1.68	1.60	n.s.	N/A	N/A	N/A	+ Aging/Inst − Aging/Comm
Interest in Clubs[7]	.53	.15	≤.001	.72	.19	≤.01	N/A	N/A	N/A	None
Interest in informal group activities[7]	.94	1.01	n.s.	1.35	.98 ·	≤.05	N/A	N/A	N/A	None
Interest in going for walks[7]	1.32	1.26	n.s.	1.83	1.50	≤.05	N/A	N/A	N/A	None
Interest in reading papers[7]	1.33	1.36	n.s.	1.44	1.48	n.s.	1.38	.95	≤.05	None
Desires more contact with friends[8]	5.14	5.79	n.s.	5.32	4.68	n.s.	.42	.07	≤.01	None

[1] Scale based on 0–3 score on each of 8 items, 24 = most positive.
[2] 4 = many, 1 = none.
[3] 7 = daily, 1 = never.
[4] 1 = not at all, 3 = a lot.
[5] 0 = several times a year or less, 2 = weekly or more.
[6] 1 = yes, 2 = no.
[7] 0 = not at all, 2 very interested.
[8] 0 = no, 1 = yes.

friends. Contrary to the positive findings for the deinstitutionalized mental health subgroup, persons placed into domiciliary care homes from another community setting may be losing contact with former friends which, as of a year later, was not counterbalanced by increased contacts in the new setting. On the other hand, there were positive effects for the mental health group with respect to having a confidante (at least one "close" person).

The lesser religious attendance of the subgroup of aging and mental retardation Experimentals placed from an institution as compared with their Controls may be a reflection of expanded interest in other areas of activity and community involvement. Many Controls were still institutionalized at posttest, and the ready availability of religious services in institutions may have contributed to their greater religious attendance.

Interestingly, an area of negative impact for the aging sample involved the helping role. It is possible that the home providers may be overprotective in the care they are giving to their elderly physically impaired clients.

Another area needing exploration concerns why the program had a positive effect on interest in family visiting for the deinstitutionalized aging sample but a negative impact on clients from a community setting at pretest. Other study analyses (not shown) found that eligible institutional applicants with children nearby were more likely to be placed in a domiciliary care facility than those without children nearby. This suggests that, while not willing to have their elderly parent live with them, these children did act as advocates for deinstitutionalization, possibly increasing the subject's interest in continued contact. No such relationship appeared for those placed from a community setting. One may also wonder whether the lesser interest in family visiting of aging community Experimentals reflects the fact that the domiciliary provider and members of the household are considered a substitute family.

TABLE 5—Impact Findings Concerning Physical and Psychological Functional Status (Posttest Comparisons)

Outcome Variable by Data Source (Clinical Assessment or Self-Report)	Aging Exp. N = 84 X̄	Aging Control N = 86 X̄	p	Mental Health Exp. N = 42 X̄	Mental Health Control N = 43 X̄	p	Mental Retardation Exp. N = 43 X̄	Mental Retardation Control N = 42 X̄	p	Comment re observed differences (p ≤ .05) in Impact by Place of Residence at Pretest
FUNCTIONAL STATUS:										
Clinical Assessments IADL (Community Survival Scale)[1]	14.20	13.93	n.s.	14.86	15.04	n.s.	12.12	13.60	≤.05	None
MR Staff Interview Data Subject Helps with Cooking[2]	N/A	N/A	N/A	N/A	N/A	N/A	1.88	1.57	≤.01	None
Subject Helps with Laundry[2]	N/A	N/A	N/A	N/A	N/A	N/A	1.76	1.45	≤.05	None
Self-Report Revised Rosow-Breslau Mobility Scale[3]	1.07	.87	n.s.	.31	.24	n.s.	.45	.17	≤.05	None
PSYCHOLOGICAL STATUS:										
Clinical Assessments Personal Adjustment[4]	2.30	2.10	n.s.	2.76	3.00	n.s.	2.26	2.57	≤.05	+ MH/Inst − MH/Comm
Emotional Health[5]	2.67	2.44	≤.05	2.83	2.36	≤.01	2.74	2.79	n.s.	None
Self-Report How the future looks[6]	2.34	2.76	≤.05	2.35	2.45	n.s.	1.78	1.56	n.s.	+ MH/Inst − MH/Comm

[1] 5 = poor survival skills, 20 = good survival skills (5 items scored 1–4).
[2] 1 = yes, 2 = no.
[3] 2 = good, 4 = poor (2 items scored 1–2).
[4] 1 = no neurosis, 5 = psychotic.
[5] 1 = very depressed, 3 = even mood.
[6] 1 = very optimistic, 5 = very pessimistic.

Functional Status (Physical and Psychological)

Table 5 summarizes the findings on physical and psychological functioning. While the program had no significant effect on physical functioning for the aging and mental health clients, negative effects were observed for the mental retardation clients, suggesting that the domiciliary care homes may be unnecessarily promoting dependence for this population. Although there was some variability in the results by living arrangement at pretest for the mental health clients, positive effects on psychological status were observed for all three groups on one or more variables.**

Impact on Reducing Institutional and Non-Community Days

As depicted in Table 6 and Figure 1, domiciliary care clients spent significantly fewer days in institutional settings during the impact period than did the Controls. The effects were more dramatic for the deinstitutionalized samples. There were substantial differences by group in the type of institutional days avoided: for the aging, nursing home utilization rates were lowered; for the mental health and mental retardation groups, mental health/mental retardation facility utilization rates were lowered.

**It should be noted that, in the case of the Revised Zung Depression Scale, significant differences in the opposite direction were found between the Experimentals and Controls at pretest; i.e., the Controls were better off at pretest than were the Experimentals.

An attempt also was made to estimate the impact of the Domiciliary Care Program on reducing non-community days over time. The impact period was separated into three equal segments.

For the aging there was an initial effect during months 1–3 and the same level of effect continued into months 4–6 and 7–9; Experimentals experienced about 1.2 days in the community for every one day spent in the community by Controls. For mental health and mental retardation samples the differences between Experimentals and Controls continued to escalate over time. For every one day that a mental

TABLE 6—Per Cent of Time Spent in a Non-Community Setting during Impact Period by Setting at Pretest

Group	Setting at Pretest Institutional %	Setting at Pretest Community %
Aging		
Experimentals	22	10
Controls	93	13
Mental Health		
Experimentals	34	1
Controls	76	15
Mental Retardation		
Experimentals	40	3
Controls	90	9

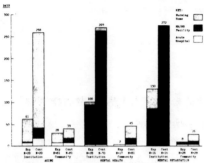

FIGURE 1—Average Number of Days In Hospital and Long-Term Care Settings

health sample Control spent in the community during months 1–3, the Experimentals spent 1.8 days. By months 7–9, this ratio had increased to 2.3. For the mental retardation sample the ratio during months 1–3 was 1.1, and by months 7–9 the ratio increased to 1.5. Data from other analyses (not shown) indicate that there were more difficulties in placing mental health and mental retardation applicants than in placing aging applicants within a short period of time. Nevertheless, as time went on the program's success in placing the mental health and mental retardation applicant populations increased.

Summary and Conclusions

In general, the effects were positive with respect to meeting the program's intended goals. They were most positive for the aging and mental health target groups. It is reasonable to hypothesize that many of the positive effects result from the client screening/case management procedures and the family-like nature of the domiciliary care homes. The family-like aspects of the environment may, however, be a factor in promoting excess dependent behavior on the part of some clients. If so, this would lead to a recommendation that provider training efforts focus more on promoting independence.

While the program was clearly a success with respect to deinstitutionalization, its effects were less impressive for clients entering the program from a community setting. Clinical studies have suggested that up to 60 per cent of the individuals who could be potentially deflected from entering a nursing home or similar facility would be appropriate for domiciliary care placement.[11,12] Clearly, the Pennsylvania Domiciliary intake from a community setting did not include many of these persons. Had the intake procedures concen-

trated more on clients about to enter a long-term care facility, the program might have had greater impact on preventing institutionalization.

The Domiciliary Care Program can be considered an important option in long-term care, particularly as a workable, less restrictive setting for eligible clients currently institutionalized in a long-term care facility. As will be seen in the companion article,[10] it is an economic option for deinstitutionalization as well.

REFERENCES

1. Congressional Budget Office: Long-Term Care: Actuarial Cost Estimates. Washington, DC, US Govt Printing Office, 1977.
2. US General Accounting Office: Entering a Nursing Home: Costly Implications for the Elderly. Washington, DC: GAO, 1979.
3. Mandelbaum A: Mental health and mental retardation. *In:* Encyclopedia of Social Work, 17th Issue. Board of Editors: JB Turner (Ed-in-Chief), R Morris, MN Ozawa, B Phillips, P Schreiber, BK Simon, and BN Saunders (Staff Editor-in-Chief). Washington, DC: National Association of Social Workers, 1977, Vol 2. pp 868–879.
4. US Department of Health, Education, and Welfare, Public Health Service, Office of the Assistant Secretary for Health: Health, United States. Hyattsville, MD: PHS, 1978.
5. Shanas E: Measuring the Home Health Needs of the Aged in Five Countries. J Gerontology 1971; 26:37–40.
6. US Department of Health, Education, and Welfare, Public Health Service, Office of the Assistant Secretary for Health: Health, United States. Hyattsville, MD: PHS, 1981.
7. Pfeiffer E: Introduction to the Conference Report. *In:* Pfeiffer E (ed): Alternatives to Institutional Care for Older Americans: Practice and Planning a Conference Report. Durham, NC: Duke University Center for the Study of Aging and Human Development, 1973.
8. Moroney RM, Kurtz NR: The evolution of long-term care institutions. *In:* Sherwood S (ed): Long-Term Care, A Handbook for Researchers, Planners, and Providers. New York: Spectrum Publications, 1975.
9. Sherwood S, Greer D, Morris JN, Mor V, & Associates: An Alternative in Long-Term Care: The Highland Heights Experiment. Cambridge, MA: Ballinger Publishing Company, 1981.
10. Ruchlin HS, Morris JN: Pennsylvania's Domiciliary Care Experiment: II. cost-benefit implications. Am J Public Health 1983; 73:654–660
11. Kahn KA, Hines W, Woodson AS, Burkham-Armstrong G: A multidisciplinary approach to assessing the quality of care in long-term care facilities. The Gerontologist 1977; 17:61–65.
12. Morris JN, Morris S, Sherwood S: Research findings regarding informal support system resiliency and the targeting of high risk elderly populations for formal agency support services. *In:* Granger CV, Gresham GE (eds): Functional Assessment in Rehabilitation Medicine. Baltimore: Waverly Press, 1983.

ACKNOWLEDGMENT

Findings reported are from a large scale evaluation study funded by Region III of the US Department of Health, Education, and Welfare (now the US Department of Health and Human Services), Contract #130-76-12, and carried out by the Department of Social Gerontological Research of the Hebrew Rehabilitation Center for Aged (HRCA), Boston, Massachusetts, with the collaboration of the Pennsylvania Central Office of the Domiciliary Care Program.

Pennsylvania's Domiciliary Care Experiment
II. Cost-Benefit Implications

Hirsch S. Ruchlin and John N. Morris

Abstract: A pilot program based on the substitu-tion of domiciliary care for traditional institutional care was established by the Commonwealth of Penn-sylvania to provide community-based care for individ-uals who could no longer live independently (aging, mentally retarded, mentally ill). To ascertain the cost saving potential of this program, 190 participants and a comparable pool of non-participants were followed for an average 10-month follow-up period. Within each subgroup, participants were disaggregated into two categories: those residing in a community setting at pretest, and those residing in an institutional setting. An analysis of medical care and social support service utilization profiles indicated that program savings ex-ceeded program cost for five of the six study subsam-ples; the one exception was the mental retardation cohort residing in a community setting at pretest. Net savings were greatest for the three subsamples resid-ing in an institutional setting at pretest. For all the subsamples, over 90 per cent of the program saving stemmed from a lower use of institutional placements. (*Am J Public Health* 1983; 73:654–660.)

Introduction

The increasing numbers of chronically ill, physically and mentally handicapped, and marginally adjusted adults in the population currently receive a disproportionate amount of their care in expensive and impersonal institutional set-tings, such as nursing homes, and chronic and acute hospi-tals. There is widespread agreement that such care is subop-timal, and efforts are underway to develop a variety of substitute community-based care systems. One such system, based on the use of domiciliary care, was developed and implemented on a pilot basis, by the Commonwealth of Pennsylvania in six counties during 1976–1977.* It was hypothesized that this program would improve the quality of life of the target population, and would lead to demonstrable cost-savings. The overall program description, evaluation design, and quality of life findings are reported in a compan-ion article in this issue of the Journal.[1] The research reported here focuses on the economic evaluation of this domiciliary care program.

Evaluation Methodology

Program Cost

Five program components were identified as the basis for estimating the operating costs of the domiciliary care program: 1) direct program management at the county level; 2) program management at the state level; 3) review team (i.e., advisory committee) program planning and supervision at the county level; 4) determination of client eligibility; and 5) direct client support by means of a Supplementary Securi-ty Income (SSI) supplement.

Program cost data were obtained by contacting state and county agency directors and asking them to provide their best estimate of agency cost that should be charged to the domiciliary care program.** At the county level, "in-kind" services were frequently provided by other agencies. In most cases, these services took the form of a staff person performing work directly related to the project. Where in-kind services were identified, estimates of their cost were made and included in the program cost statistic. Data on the cost of determining client eligibility were obtained for only one county (Allegheny) and, of necessity, were used as a

---

*Domiciliary care consists of a protected situation in the community which includes room, board, and personal services for individuals who cannot live independently yet do not require 24-hour institutional or nursing care.

Address reprint requests to Hirsch S. Ruchlin, PhD, Professor of Economics in Public Health, Department of Public Health, Cornell University Medical College, 1300 York Avenue, New York, NY 10021. Dr. Morris is Associate Director, Department of Social Gerontological Research, Hebrew Rehabilitation Center for Aged, Boston, MA. This paper, submitted to the Journal March 24, 1982, was revised and accepted for publication December 13, 1982.
Editor's Note: See also related article p 646 and editorial p 638 this issue.

**In obtaining personnel costs, instructions were given to include both wage and salary costs, and fringe benefit costs.

proxy for the remaining counties. Although cost data were accumulated for a four-year period (1976–1979), only 1979 data are reported here.***

Program Benefit

Program benefits were defined as the savings resulting from a reduced utilization of institutional and community support services over the 10-month impact period. Program benefit was quantitated by using a methodology initially proposed by Griffith.[2] This methodology involves a comparison of alternate cash-flow streams resulting from the use of different combinations of resources. It is well suited to the evaluation of programs that use a less expensive array of services or economize on expensive resources. Griffith used this technique to estimate the benefits of a home care program. It has also been used in evaluations of community versus institutional living and efforts to prevent the Wernicke-Korsakoff syndrome.[3,4]

Reduced utilization was ascertained by comparing the utilization profiles of a matched pool of experimental subjects and control clients.[1] Utilization data for individuals in both groups were obtained from detailed questionnaires completed by all study participants at posttest. Reported institutional utilization was verified by direct contact with these providers.

Six categories of institutional placement were identified as pertinent to the current study population: acute hospital days, mental health facility days, facility for the retarded days, skilled nursing facility days, intermediate care facility days, and rest home days.‡ In addition, data were gathered on days of placement in a domiciliary care facility and in a regular community setting.

Although utilization data were gathered from 1976 to 1979, cost per unit of utilization data were gathered for only one year, 1979. Thus the estimate of program benefit reflects 1979 cost patterns. The cost of a placement day in each institutional setting was obtained from the state Medicaid program. The cost of a day of community living was derived from data compiled by the Bureau of Labor Statistics on urban budgets for retired couples residing in the Philadelphia area.‡‡ The cost of a day of domiciliary care placement was determined by subtracting the special monthly provider

---

***As the domiciliary care pilot program was not fully operational until 1978, 1979 data are most representative of "steady state" operations.

‡Rest homes are county facilities which are not eligible for Medicaid payments. They provide the same level of service as domiciliary care facilities, but are much larger and as a result have an institutional rather than home-like environment.

‡‡All budget elements in the *lower* budget except medical care were utilized. Medical care was excluded as it was quantified separately in the study. Housing costs were utilized as reported. Food, personal care, other family consumption, and other items were divided by two and multiplied by 1.2. Transportation and clothing expenses were divided by two. The total estimated budget was then divided by 365 to obtain a daily cost estimate. This type of data is generated on a statewide basis, and for residents residing in the Philadelphia and Pittsburgh areas. The data series for the Philadelphia area was selected as most of the study participants resided in this geographic area.

supplement ($114) and the client's "pocket money" component ($45) from the 1979 monthly SSI payment received by domiciliary care residents ($341). The balance was annualized and then divided by 365 to obtain a daily cost.

Nine social and medical support services were identified as constituting the formal community support services used by the study sample: general and employment counseling, provision of meals, homemaker services, transportation, personal care, physician visits, visiting nurse care, therapy, and day care. Respondents indicated that four of these services—meals, homemaker care, transportation, and personal care—were also provided at no direct cost by relatives, friends, or neighbors on a volunteer basis. For the purpose of the current analysis, these services are designated as informal care services.

The cost of providing formal community social support services was obtained from the Pennsylvania Department of Aging. Medicare data were used to derive the cost of physician visits, and Medicaid data were used to obtain the cost of personal care, visiting nurse care, and therapy. State Department of Aging and Hebrew Rehabilitation Center for Aged clinical staff expertise were the basis for designating the assumed duration of each service. As services provided informally were, by and large, unskilled and rendered on a volunteer basis, the prevailing minimum wage ($2.90/hr) was used as the relevant cost statistic in estimating the economic value of informal care.

Sample Selection and Matching

As the pilot domiciliary care program was targeted at the elderly, and at individuals with mental health and mental retardation problems, it was decided to initially disaggregate study participants into these three categories. Within each of these categories, study participants were further disaggregated to reflect their residency status at pretest (i.e., community or institutional).

A computer program, SIMRAN[5,6] was used to select a comparable pool of experimental and control subjects for each of the six subsamples who were judged to be equivalent at pretest with regard to sociodemographic and medical/social characteristics.‡‡‡

Evaluation Findings

Program Cost

Total estimated annual program operating costs in 1979 were $2,007,775. As can be seen from the data presented in

---

‡‡‡The sample sizes reported in this article are slightly higher than those reported in the quality of life analysis.[1] In instances where subjects could not respond to self-reported questions or had died, procedures were employed to obtain service utilization data from alternate sources. Similar procedures could not be employed for the quality of life analysis, and some individuals were deleted from that aspect of the overall evaluation.

Where necessary, adjustments were made to ensure equal Experimental-Control exposure periods. That is, the utilization profile of the group with the shorter exposure period was inflated to an assumed utilization level that should have resulted from the longer exposure period experienced by the other group.

Table 1, 52 per cent of the total cost was accounted for by the direct domiciliary care supplement and 43 per cent of the cost was incurred for program management at the county level. During 1979, the average number of clients in placement was 758.3 yielding an average annual cost per client in placement of $2,647. This translates to an average daily cost per client in placement of $7.

The nature of the cost analysis did not permit the derivation of separate program cost estimates for the six study subsamples. Discussions with county and state officials indicated that program costs would not be expected to vary by subgroup (i.e., aging, mental health, and mental retardation) but would be about 10 per cent higher for those individuals residing in institutions at pretest than for those residing in the community due to higher client eligibility determination and placement costs. In recognition of this estimated cost differential, a cost per client placement day of $6.77 was used for individuals who at pretest were in a community setting, and $7.45 for those who, at pretest, were in an institutional setting.*

In the aggregate, 39,478 domiciliary care placement days were used during the 10-month impact period (Table 2). For each of the study subsamples, estimated program costs are spelled out in the Table.

Utilization Patterns and Program Benefit

Aging-Community Subsample—Differential utilization by Experimentals and Controls of the health-related and social support resources that constitute the basis for estimating program benefit is profiled in the left half of Table 3. Over the 10-month exposure period, a major difference in the use of institutional placement emerges for the mental health and mental retardation facility categories. As a result of their greater use of institutional care, the estimated total placement cost for this set of Controls was $154,023 more than that for the Experimentals.

Utilization of formal community support services by Controls exceeded that of Experimentals for five of the nine categories listed in Table 3. However, the magnitude of the differential in each case was relatively small, and total costs of community support service utilization by Controls were $25,544 higher than those of Experimentals.

Controls exhibited much greater use of two informal care services (meals preparation and homemaker care) than Experimentals but slightly less use of the remaining two, low cost, categories. The cost of total informal care use by Controls was $5,806 more than that of the Experimentals.

Summing across the three major resources categories yields a program benefit of $188,373. Eighty-two per cent of this benefit is attributable to lower placement costs, 15 per

cent to less expensive use of formal community support services, and 3 per cent to lower use of informal care.

Aging-Institutional Subsample—As can be seen from the data reported in the right half of Table 3, placement utilization differentials were greatest for skilled nursing and intermediate care facilities and for rest homes. As a result of their lower use of institutional care, Experimentals spent more time in community settings (4,467 days vs 295 days). Thus, the total cost of their placement equaled $92,349, as compared to $214,038 for Controls.

With one exception (therapy), Experimentals utilized more community support services than Controls. Sixty-nine per cent of the cost differential ($9,716) for community support services resulted from a greater use of day care. Experimentals also utilized more informal care services than Controls, primarily transportation assistance.

For this subsample, savings reaped from less costly placements far outweighed the more expensive use of community support care, yielding a saving (benefit) of $105,947.

Mental Health-Community Subsample—Comparable data for this subsample are reported in Table 4. In the aggregate, Experimentals generated $59,656 of health-related and social support resource while use of these resources by Controls cost $106,935. Eighty-nine per cent of the overall subsample saving of $47,279 was due to lower placement costs. Lower relative use of community support services accounted for 9 per cent of total subsample saving and lower use of informal care accounted for the remaining 2 per cent.

Mental Health-Institutional Subsample—Data for this group are reported in Table 4 and reflect similar findings. Savings resulting from less costly placement and community support services equaled $357,053. However, Controls utilized fewer informal care resources than Experimentals ($116 vs $525), thereby reducing the subsample saving to $356,644.

Mental Retardation-Community Subsample—Placement data reported in the left half of Table 5 indicate that Experimentals used 222 days of institutional care compared to 715 days used by Controls. The largest differentials

TABLE 1—Program Cost, Pennsylvania Domiciliary Care Pilot Program, 1979

Cost Component	Total Cost		Cost per Average Number of Clients in Placement
	Amount	Per Cent	
Program Management—County Level	$869,351	43.3	$1,146
Program Management—State Level	63,214	3.2	83
Review Team Planning/Supervision	8,663	0.4	11
Client Assessment	21,003	1.0	28
Domiciliary Care Supplement	1,045,544	52.1	1,379
TOTAL	$2,007,775	100.0	$2,647*

*Average Monthly Cost $221
Average Daily Cost $7

---

*The relative representation of both client groups in the overall sample is: community residence at pretest, 66 per cent, and institutional residence at pretest 34 per cent. Weighing the estimated program cost for each subgroup by its proportionate representation in the study sample yields a program cost per daily placement value of $7.00.

TABLE 2—Estimated Program Cost by Study Subsample, Pennsylvania Domiciliary Care Pilot Program, 1979

Study Subsample	Domiciliary Care Placement Days	Estimated Cost per Placement Day	Estimated Program Cost
Aging—Community	17,481	$6.77	$118,346
Aging—Institutional	3,692	7.45	27,505
Mental Health—Community	4,039	6.77	27,344
Mental Health—Institutional	4,712	7.45	35,104
Mental Retardation—Community	7,044	6.77	47,688
Mental Retardation—Institutional	2,510	7.45	18,700
TOTAL	39,478		$274,687

occurred in intermediate care facility and facility for the retarded utilization.

However, Experimentals used $57,546 of community support services compared to $27,245 for Controls. Most of this cost differential was accounted for by greater use of day care and therapy. Deducting this cost from the $46,643 saving generated by a less costly placement profile and recognizing the differential use of informal supports yields a total subsample program benefit of $18,243.

Mental Retardation-Institutional Subsample—Experimentals in this subsample utilized 2,093 days of institutional

placement while utilization by Controls equaled 4,683 days. All of the institutional care consumed by Controls was provided by mental health facilities and facilities for the retarded, while only 66 per cent of the 1,371 days of the institutional care used by Experimentals was provided by such facilities. The total placement cost for Experimentals was $243,627 less than that for Controls. Use of other services was relatively similar.

The total cost of all resources used by Experimentals was $169,791 compared to $410,735 for Controls, yielding a subsample saving (benefit) of $240,944.

TABLE 3—Estimated Program Savings, Pennsylvania Domiciliary Care Pilot Program, Aging Sample

Resource	Cost/Unit	Community Subsample				Institutional Subsample			
		Experimentals (N = 81)		Controls (N = 81)		Experimentals (N = 20)		Controls (N = 20)	
		Units	Cost	Units	Cost	Units	Cost	Units	Cost
PLACEMENT DAYS									
Acute Hospital	$216.62	579	$125,423	591	$128,022	171	$37,042	359	$77,767
Mental Health Facility	81.88	0	—	839	68,697	81	6,632	503	41,186
Facility for Retarded	84.21	0	—	211	17,768	0	—	0	—
Skilled Nursing Facility	26.00	1,222	31,772	825	21,450	362	9,412	1,515	39,390
Intermediate Care Facility	20.50	14	287	480	9,840	68	1,394	1,585	32,493
Rest Home	14.00	483	6,762	130	1,820	544	7,616	1,436	20,104
Community Residence	10.50	3,984	41,832	20,687	217,214	775	8,138	295	3,098
Domiciliary Care	5.99	17,481	104,712	0	—	3,692	22,115	0	—
Subtotals			$310,788		$464,811		$92,349		$214,038
COMMUNITY SUPPORT SERVICES									
Counseling (Visits)	8.76	143	$1,253	47	$412	0	—	0	—
Meal Preparation (Meals)	2.21	2,283	5,045	5,906	13,052	641	$1,417	91	$201
Homemaker (Hours)	6.54	64	419	3,028	19,803	0	—	0	—
Transportation (Hours)	4.40	3,434	15,110	3,584	15,769	727	3,199	146	642
Personal Care (Hours)	8.40	51	428	523	4,393	0	—	0	—
Medical Care (Visits)	15.00	651	9,765	408	6,120	103	1,545	4	60
Visiting Nurse Care (Hours)	21.00	117	2,457	99	2,079	1	21	0	—
Therapy (Hours)	21.00	300	6,300	543	11,403	0	—	41	861
Day Care (Half Days)	7.00	4,571	31,997	4,041	28,287	1,479	10,353	91	637
Subtotals			$72,774		$101,318		$16,535		$2,401
INFORMAL CARE									
Meal Preparation (Half Hour)	1.45	0	—	1,005	$1,457	0	—	0	—
Homemaker (Four Hours)	11.60	67	$777	457	5,301	35	$406	0	—
Transportation (One Hour)	2.90	599	1,737	543	1,575	100	290	159	$461
Personal Care (Half Hour)	1.45	651	944	642	931	947	1,373	0	—
Subtotals			$3,458		$9,264		$2,069		$461
TOTAL			$387,020		$575,393		$110,953		$216,900
SAVINGS			$188,373				$105,947		

TABLE 4—Estimated Program Savings, Pennsylvania Domiciliary Care Pilot Program, Mental Health Sample

Resource	Cost/Unit	Community Subsample				Institutional Subsample			
		Experimentals (N = 17)		Controls (N = 17)		Experimentals (N = 28)		Controls (N = 28)	
		Units	Cost	Units	Cost	Units	Cost	Units	Cost
PLACEMENT DAYS									
Acute Hospital	$216.62	37	$8,015	27	$5,849	35	$7,582	29	$6,282
Mental Health Facility	81.88	0	—	290	23,745	2,582	211,414	6,641	543,765
Facility for Retarded	84.21	0	—	0	—	62	5,221	271	22,821
Skilled Nursing Facility	26.00	0	—	108	2,808	0	—	0	—
Intermediate Care Facility	20.50	0	—	346	7,093	56	1,148	276	5,658
Rest Home	14.00	0	—	0	—	60	840	0	—
Community Residence	10.50	1,154	12,117	4,459	46,820	758	7,959	1,048	11,004
Domiciliary Care	5.99	4,039	24,194	0	—	4,712	28,225	0	—
Subtotals			$44,326		$86,315		$262,389		$589,530
COMMUNITY SUPPORT SERVICES									
Counseling (Visits)	8.76	210	$1,840	392	$3,434	323	$2,829	386	$3,381
Meal Preparation (Meals)	2.21	495	1,094	920	2,033	714	1,578	405	895
Homemaker (Hours)	6.54	0	—	113	739	0	—	26	170
Transportation (Hours)	4.40	986	4,338	36	158	1,519	6,684	1,182	5,201
Personal Care (Hours)	8.40	0	—	0	—	0	—	0	—
Medical Care (Visits)	15.00	126	1,890	114	1,710	216	3,240	30	450
Visiting Nurse Care (Hours)	21.00	34	714	63	1,323	0	—	4	84
Therapy (Hours)	21.00	0	—	0	—	176	3,696	1,955	41,055
Day Care (Half Days)	7.00	722	5,054	1,439	10,073	1,097	7,679	626	4,382
Subtotals			$14,930		$19,470		$25,706		$55,618
INFORMAL CARE									
Meal Preparation (Half Hour)	1.45	0	—	0	—	0	—	0	—
Homemaker (Four Hours)	11.60	0	—	13	$151	0	—	2	$23
Transportation (One Hour)	2.90	31	$90	330	957	181	$525	32	93
Personal Care (Half Hour)	1.45	214	310	29	42	0	—	0	—
Subtotals			$400		$1,150		$525		$116
TOTAL			$59,656		$106,935		$288,620		$645,264
SAVINGS				$47,279			$356,644		

Cost-Benefit Profile

Program savings generated and program costs incurred by each subsample are reported in the first two rows of Table 6, followed by four indicators of the domiciliary care program's economic efficacy: the benefit/cost ratio, net program saving, net saving per Experimental, and net daily saving per Experimental. Each of these evaluation statistics indicates that for five of the six subsamples the domiciliary care program saved more money than it cost. This is attested to by a benefit/cost ratio greater than one, and positive net program saving statistics. The one exception to this trend is the mental retardation-community subsample. For this client group, costs exceed benefits.

For each of the subsamples, individuals who resided in an institutional setting at pretest displayed much greater economic gains from the domiciliary care intervention than individuals who resided in the community.

Savings achieved by each of the subsamples for which a net benefit was reported were substantial. Even for the group with the lowest benefit-cost ratio, i.e., aging-community, benefits exceeded costs by 59 per cent, and annual net savings per Experimental equaled $1,077.**

**Annual net saving per Experimental = net saving per Experimental × 365.

Discussion

Our data generally support the hypothesis that Pennsylvania's pilot domiciliary care program would generate demonstrable cost savings. Had individuals in each of the six subsamples been aggregated into one large study sample, the analysis would have yielded a benefit/cost ratio of 3.5 and a net daily saving per Experimental of $12.07. If the sample disaggregation focused only on the types of clients served (i.e., aging, mental health, and mental retardation) and ignored residency status at pretest, one would also conclude that the intervention was cost-effective for all groups. It is only when the sample is further disaggregated by client residency at pretest that an unfavorable cost-benefit pattern emerges for one of the six subsamples—mental retardation-community.

Lower utilization of institutional placement emerges both as the dominant benefit element, accounting for over 90 per cent of the saving reported for each subsample, and as a major explanatory factor for the variation in the reported cost-benefit indices. Furthermore, the higher cost/benefit values exhibited by the three subsamples whose members were institutionalized at pretest is undoubtedly due to the ability of domiciliary care to effectively substitute for institutional care for individuals who cannot live independently but

TABLE 5—Estimated Program Savings, Pennsylvania Domiciliary Care Pilot Program, Mental Retardation Sample

		Community Subsample				Institutional Subsample			
		Experimentals (N = 28)		Controls (N = 28)		Experimentals (N = 16)		Controls (N = 16)	
Resource	Cost/Unit	Units	Cost	Units	Cost	Units	Cost	Units	Cost
PLACEMENT DAYS									
Acute Hospital	$216.62	83	$17,979	91	$19,712	0	—	0	—
Mental Health Facility	81.88	0	—	0	—	305	$24,973	1,817	$143,776
Facility for Retarded	84.21	139	11,705	264	22,231	1,066	89,768	2,866	241,346
Skilled Nursing Facility	26.00	0	—	75	1,950	196	5,096	0	—
Intermediate Care Facility	20.50	0	—	285	5,843	526	10,783	0	—
Rest Home	14.00	0	—	0	—	0	—	0	—
Community Residence	10.50	1,135	11,918	7,686	80,703	598	6,279	518	5,439
Domiciliary Care	5.99	7,044	42,194	0	—	2,510	15,035	0	—
Subtotals			$83,796		$130,439		$151,934		$395,561
COMMUNITY SUPPORT SERVICES									
Counseling (Visits)	8.76	294	$2,575	306	$2,681	9	79	0	—
Meal Preparation (Meals)	2.21	1,182	2,612	953	2,106	368	813	322	$712
Homemaker (Hours)	6.54	0	—	111	726	0	—	0	—
Transportation (Hours)	4.40	2,677	11,779	2,707	11,911	647	2,847	1,058	4,655
Personal Care (Hours)	8.40	0	—	0	—	0	—	0	—
Medical Care (Visits)	15.00	141	2,115	126	1,890	80	1,200	8	120
Visiting Nurse Care (Hours)	21.00	41	861	0	—	1	21	3	63
Therapy (Hours)	21.00	1,033	21,693	37	777	224	4,704	413	8,673
Day Care (Half Days)	7.00	2,273	15,911	1,022	7,154	1,132	7,924	0	—
Subtotals			$57,546		$27,245		$17,588		$14,223
INFORMAL CARE									
Meal Preparation (Half Hour)	1.45	0	—	0	. —	0	—	0	—
Homemaker (Four Hours)	11.60	0	—	0	—	0	—	77	$893
Transportation (One Hour)	2.90	19	$55	563	$1,633	85	$247	20	58
Personal Care (Half Hour)	1.45	0	—	223	323	15	22	0	—
Subtotals			$55		$1,956		$269		$951
TOTAL			$141,397		$159,640		$169,791		$410,735
SAVINGS			$18,243				$240,944		

do not require 24-hour institutional or nursing care. The domiciliary care program did not yield as great a saving when it was offered to clients residing in the community because the potential for generating a saving within this group is not as great.

Cost/benefit differences also emerge across subsamples when one controls for residency status at pretest. That is, among those clients residing in an institution at pretest, net saving was highest for the mental retardation group, followed by the mental health group, and the aging group. For individuals residing in a community setting at pretest, mental health clients displayed larger gains than aging clients, while mental retardation clients displayed no economic gains. As subsample members were exposed to the same intervention program, we attribute the reported difference across subsamples to the types of clients constituting the three groups.

The Pennsylvania domiciliary care experiment did not specifically attempt to deflect individuals who were active applicants to long-term care facilities. Community residents not applying for nursing home placement were also accepted into the program. A number of studies based on clinical assessments have hypothesized that domiciliary care could be an appropriate alternate living arrangement for many institutional applicants.[5,6] The efficacy of such a program had not been previously demonstrated. The data reported in

this article suggest that were such people to be successfully deflected, the savings would probably approximate those reported for the institutional subsamples.

With the exception of the aging-community group, the size of the remaining five subsamples is quite small. In such cases one cannot rule out small sample bias. In our opinion, such bias is less likely to exist with regard to savings from less expensive placements where the reported differences were large and significant. We are less confident, however, with regard to utilization differences associated with the other resources categories. Clearly, our findings must be viewed as tentative and we look to additional evaluations of the efficacy of domiciliary care to buttress the results reported here.

Differences in the reported net saving across subsamples highlight the importance of disaggregating the results of any program evaluation by pertinent client characteristics. It is becoming increasingly clear that some form of case management and service targeting is required to increase the likelihood that the anticipated savings of various alternatives to institutionalization actually materialize.[7,***] In the ab-

---

***Recognition of this fact underlies the recently initiated national channeling experiments funded by the US Department of Health and Human Services.

TABLE 6—Cost-Benefit Profile, Pennsylvania Domiciliary Care Pilot Program

	Aging Sample			Mental Health Sample			Mental Retardation Sample		
Statistic	Combined Sample	Community Subsample	Institutional Subsample	Combined Sample	Community Subsample	Institutional Subsample	Combined Sample	Community Subsample	Institutional Subsample
Program Saving	$294,320	$188,373	$105,947	$403,923	$47,279	$356,644	$259,187	$18,243	$240,944
Program Cost	$145,851	$118,346	$27,505	$62,448	27,344	$35,104	$66,388	$47,688	$18,700
Benefit/Cost Ratio	2.02	1.59	3.85	6.47	1.73	10.16	3.90	0.38	12.88
Net Program Saving	$148,469	$70,027	$78,442	$341,475	$19,935	$321,540	$192,799	$−29,445	$222,244
Total Number of Experimentals	101	81	20	45	17	28	44	28	16
Net Saving per Experimental	$1,470	$865	$3,992	$7,588	$1,173	$11,484	$4,382	$−1,052	$13,890
Impact Period (Days)	29,456	23,763	5,693	13,495	5,230	8,265	13,602	8,401	5,201
Net Daily Saving per Experimental	$5.04	$2.95	$13.78	$25.30	$3.81	$38.90	$14.17	$−3.51	$42.73

sence of such controls, services will all too often be provided to individuals who may not reap the maximum possible benefits.

Two additional implications for successful program planning and design emerge from the resource utilization patterns reported in this study. First, in exposing individuals to a new intervention, one should not expect an instantaneous and perfect adjustment. Indeed, Experimentals were not in a domiciliary care placement during the entire exposure period. While the time required to effect a placement is a partial explanation for this phenomenon, a more pertinent one is that some individuals had difficulty adjusting to a new service delivery model and first placements were not always successful. Although all Experimentals were able to ultimately achieve a successful placement, some had to undergo a "learning process" (i.e., an unsuccessful first placement). Second, despite a successful placement in domiciliary care facilities, Experimentals still required significant amounts of some community support services. For example, Experimentals in each of the three community subsamples utilized substantial amounts of day care services. On the other hand, they required very little homemaker assistance. This pattern results from the dual fact that clients included in the study were in need of support services to remain in a community setting, and that domiciliary care providers, being foster or group homes capable of accommodating only a few clients, could not be expected to provide the full range of required support services. Thus, provisions had to be made for the purchase of some services from external sources. Failure to recognize either of these points would have jeopardized the overall success of the program.

REFERENCES

1. Sherwood S, Morris JN: Pennsylvania's Domiciliary Care Experiment: 1. impact on quality of life. Am J Public Health 1983; 73:645–653.
2. Griffith JR: Quantitative Techniques for Hospital Planning and Control. Lexington, MA: D.C. Heath, 1972, pp 232–233.
3. Murphy JG, Datel WE: A cost-benefit analysis of community versus institutional living. Hosp Community Psychiatry 1976; 27:165–173.
4. Centerwall BS, Crequi MH: Prevention of the Wernicke-Korsakoff syndrome: a cost benefit analysis. N Engl J Med 1978; 229:285–289.
5. Morris JN, Sherwood S: A Program for Meeting the Needs of Nursing Home Applicants Who Have Intact Communication Skills: A Functional Typology of Applicants to Sixteen Nursing Homes in Metropolitan Minneapolis. Boston: Department of Social Gerontological Research, Hebrew Rehabilitation Center for Aged, December 1978 (mimeographed).
6. Sherwood S, Morris JN: Alternate Paths to Long Term Care. Final Report for AoA Grant No. 90-A-1066. Boston: Department of Social Gerontological Research, Hebrew Rehabilitation Center for Aged, 1982 (mimeographed).
7. Callahan JJ: How much, for what, and for whom? (editorial) Am J Public Health 1981; 71:987–988.

ACKNOWLEDGMENT

The research reported here was supported by HHS contract 130-76-12 to Sylvia Sherwood, PhD, Director, Department of Social Gerontological Research, Hebrew Rehabilitation Center for Aged, Boston, MA.

V

TRANSPORTATION

As both a requisite for commerce and a public good, transportation has been the subject of government policy in this country since the beginning of the nation. Issues of subsidies, regulation, and competition in transportation have been debated for more than 100 years. Thus the themes developed elsewhere throughout this volume concerning the impetus for government policy provided by the War on Poverty and Great Society programs is not so applicable with respect to transportation. No major experiments, demonstrations, or major policy changes comparable to the efforts in welfare reform, national health policy, or housing occurred during the period of interest that we can report on in these pages. Nonetheless, evaluation research in transportation is a rich and highly specialized field, and we found several excellent articles among which to choose.

We selected three disparate evaluation research studies on contemporary transportation issues. Topics include the impact of a new subway line on housing values, the impact of subsidies on the costs of urban mass transportation, and an evaluation of motor vehicle inspection. Though diverse in subject matter within the overall transportation field, the three papers all report on actual programs rather than on demonstrations or social experiments designed to inform the policy formation process; all are economic analyses based on secondary data sources; and all are impact evaluations of a public policy or public program in transportation. The latter two papers additionally assess the success of a public policy in achieving its objectives.

It is appropriate to follow the previous section on housing with this one on transportation because of the close links between the two fields, which together form much of the core of modern urban studies. The first selection provides an illustration of these linkages. One of the qualitative attributes of housing that will be reflected in its price is its proximity to other places—including work, schools, and shopping—that people frequent. To the extent people desire easy access to their workplace, schools, friends, shopping, and so on, the price of housing that more closely satisfies those desires will be greater than the price of housing that is farther from those destinations, other things being equal. Of course, proximity may be measured either in physical distance terms or in terms of travel time, hence the importance of transportation.

Vladimir Bajic's paper, in Chapter 24, examines the effect of an improvement in public transportation—the opening of a new subway line in metropolitan Toronto in 1978 that reduced commuting time—on the price of housing in the impact area. First, an econometric modal choice model is used to estimate the direct benefits from the improvement in transportation afforded by the new subway line; then hedonic price equations are used to measure the effect of the subway on housing prices. Findings are that the direct savings in commuting costs were capitalized into housing values.

The next selection, by Pucher, Markstedt, and Hirschman, is also concerned with urban public transportation (or "transit"). The issue, presented in Chapter 25, is the efficiency of governmental subsidies for urban transit, which have increased rapidly throughout the world since 1965. The authors consider the hypothesis that subsidies have actually exacerbated productivity and cost problems of urban mass transit in the United States. Using cross-sectional data for 1979 and 1980 obtained from several sources, the authors apply econometric techniques to examine the impact of government subsidies on productivity and costs of 212 urban bus systems. Findings suggest that higher government transit subsidies tend to increase transit costs by rewarding inefficiency. The authors offer several suggestions for improving transit subsidy policy.

In Chapter 26 we turn from issues of public transportation to regulation of private transportation. Peter Loeb and Benjamin Gilad's analysis is concerned with the efficacy and cost-effectiveness of state motor vehicle inspection programs. Using time-series data for New Jersey covering the period 1932-1979, the authors estimate an econometric model to assess the efficacy of inspection in reducing fatalities, injuries, and accidents. Findings suggest that motor vehicle inspection in New Jersey significantly reduces the number of highway fatalities and accidents, though no significant impact on injuries was found. In addition, a comparison of the costs associated with the New Jersey inspection program with the monetary value of a partial list of benefits suggested that the New Jersey program is also cost-effective.

24

The Effects of a New Subway Line on Housing Prices in Metropolitan Toronto

Vladimir Bajic

Summary. An analysis by means of using the estimation results of a modal choice model and the hedonic price regressions model is conducted in order to identify the effects of a subway line in Toronto on the values of housing units. The modal choice model is used for the estimation of the direct benefits from the improvement in transportation, and the hedonic price equations for the identification of subway effects on housing prices. Empirical results indicate that the direct savings in commuting costs have been capitalized into housing values.

1. Introduction

This paper examines the impact of the Spadina Subway line in Toronto on housing values. The analysis is conducted by means of the linkage of a modal choice model and housing price functions model. The need to utilize two different models stems from the fact that the direct benefits from the improvement in transportation (if capitalized into housing values) are reflected in the premium paid for housing in the impact area. The change in transportation is treated as a change in locational attributes that serve as proxies for accessibility to employment centres in the hedonic price functions. The value of such accessibility is estimated directly by the modal choice model. Such direct estimates permit identification of the current quasi-rents attributable to improved accessibility by means of the hedonic price functions models.

Recent empirical work on both modal choice and housing as a differentiated good is diverse and voluminous. In this study, we adopt the McFadden random utility model (McFadden (1974) and Domencich and McFadden (1975)) in order to identify the direct benefits from the opening of the subway.

The theoretical justification for using hedonic price functions has been provided by Rosen (1974). This last approach has been used by a multitude of researchers to test the importance of accessibility attributes (see Ball (1973) and Dewees (1976)), and the importance of externalities and neighbourhood characteristics. (Anderson and Crocker (1971), Mieszkowski and Saper (1977) and Schnare and Struyk (1976)).

In judging this study against past efforts, it is important to note that the approach used provides a method, first for careful measurement of at least direct benefits, i.e. savings in commuting time and second, provides a method for identifying the distribution of these benefits. In a policy evaluation context, the method used is of importance since it concentrates on the identification of the redistributional effects of a transportation investment which may be of critical importance in affecting political decisions.

We proceed as follows. In Section 2, we discuss the strategy for identifying the benefits and their impact on housing values. Section 3 discusses data and data sources. Section 4 deals with the estimation of the savings in commuting costs. Section 5 identifies the

The author is Assistant Professor of Economics, Saint Mary's University, Halifax, Nova Scotia, Canada.

Helpful comments have been received from John Bossons, Michael Denny, Donald Dewees, Mark Frankena, David Nowlan, and an anonymous referee. The author is however to be held responsible for remaining defects.

effects of the Spadina subway on housing values by estimating hedonic price functions for the impact and control areas. The total amount of capitalized benefits is deduced, and the findings compared with those arrived at by the estimation of modal choice model. Finally, Section 6 offers concluding observations on findings.

2. Identifying the Direct Benefits from the Improvement in Transportation and their Impact on Housing Values

Two modes are considered in the modal choice analysis: public transit and private auto mode. There is no need to analyse other modes, for these two are the only feasible alternatives available to most households in the sample. The values of time components of commuting trips are estimated by using the binary logit model. The logit estimator results from the adoption of the McFadden random utility model. Since the changes in time components of trips due to the improvement in transportation are given by the data, the direct current year savings in commuting costs are readily identifiable. The inelastic supply of housing is a necessary, but not sufficient condition for capitalization of these savings in the value of housing. The extent of capitalization depends on a set of explicit assumptions about an urban housing market, the supply and demand for housing, and tastes and incomes of the consumers. One should not, of course, assume that consumers' expectations are static and that they behave as though the present levels of benefits will be maintained forever. The assumption of non-static expectations is much more attractive. In this case the uncertainty is created by effects of future urban growth, long-run increases in the supply of housing due to the construction of major transportation facilities, shifts in employment patterns, changes in transportation technology and changes in the future level of congestion.[1]

Of course, these factors are interdependent and their effects cannot be taken into account separately. Their combined effect is reflected in shorter time horizons over which the benefits are projected and a somewhat higher rate of discount due to uncertainty. In addition, the expected future increases in land

rents due to the long-run increase in the housing stock (in the case of redevelopment at greater densities) are highly uncertain. Not only are the future paths of investment uncertain, but the adjustment costs in the Lucas-Treadway sense are increasing (Lucas (1967), and Treadway (1969)) as more and more capital is combined with the fixed quantity of land input in the impact area. In the same vein, the existing zoning by-laws and the scepticism over the net benefits from high-density development which prevails at different tiers of the municipal government (see Bossons (1978)) strongly indicate that redevelopment effects are likely to be very small.

In the case of the Spadina subway, supply and demand conditions are such that the number of commuters whose commuting costs would be reduced, given that they locate in the impact corridor is bigger than the number of residences in the corridor. Assuming non-identical households, the benefits from the improvement in transportation depend on household characteristics, foremost among these the level of income. Since the amount of capitalization depends on the valuations of the marginal consumer, the improvement in transportation results in an increase in the consumer surplus[2] for intramarginal consumers. This means that higher income households will be left with some consumer surplus, while most benefits accruing to lower income households will seep into land rents. The fact that we should expect a substantial capitalization indicates the relationship between the modal choice model and the hedonic price regressions model which will be used for the identification of capitalized benefits from housing price data.

In order to identify the effects of the subway, we assume that those demand and supply shifts which are not attributable to a change in transportation technology, are not different in the Spadina area from the rest of Metropolitan Toronto area. In other words, our procedure for identifying the incremental benefits from the subway consists of collecting data for a control sample (houses outside the impacted area) as well as in the area affected by the new subway. Two hedonic price regressions are separately estimated for each of the two samples: one before and one after the subway line was opened. The uniformity of demand changes over this time period may then be

[1] A detailed discussion of the effects of these factors is found in Mayer, Kain and Wohl (1965).
[2] We assume that there is little or no difference between the consumer's 'equivalent variation' and 'compensating variation'. Mishan (1971) is one of many authors who discusses these two alternative measures of consumer surplus.

aluated by testing for the equality between the two mples of changes in the parameters of the two gressions estimated for each sample. If the changes the implicit prices of attributes other than ccessibility are the same in both of the samples, the apitalized value of projected future benefits will be eflected in the increase in the consumer's evaluations f the particular housing location.

Data and Data Sources

his section is brief, since most comments on the data nd data sources are (together with explanatory haps) relegated to the Appendix.

The data used in the modal choice analysis were btained from the new homeowners survey. The nformation on commuting trips and socio-economic haracteristics refers to 385 households who urchased houses in 1978. Of these, 205 came from he Metropolitan Toronto (control) area and 180 rom the Spadina (impact) area. The selection of amples was dictated by the fact that the results will e incorporated into the hedonic price regressions model. Four samples of data on housing units (in all over 2000 dwellings) were taken from the population f houses sold in 1971 and 1978; data collected for hese units are used in the hedonic price functions analysis. Two of these refer to the control area and wo to the Spadina area. The first of the two samples or each area refers to 1971 (the year before the decision to build the subway was taken), and the second refers to 1978 (the year when the subway line was opened). We were able to obtain the data on almost all important structural and transportation characteristics for the hedonic price models. The only important characteristic on which data could not have been obtained was the age of the dwelling. All neighbourhood attributes are treated in the analysis as a single attribute. This was done by constructing location-specific dummy variables for nine homogeneous regions into which the Metropolitan Toronto area was divided. The parameters of the locational dummy variables include all unspecified neighbourhood quality effects not captured by structural and transportation access variables.

4. Identifying the Direct Benefits from the Opening of the Subway

In this section we estimate the direct benefits from the opening of the subway line. The modal choice model for the control and Spadina areas is used for the estimation of the values which commuters attach to different time components of trips. In this model we analysed trips to and from work. We decided to concentrate our efforts on only work trips for the following reason. First, in the case of work trips, reasonably accurate data can be developed for statistical estimation, given the fact that trip destination and frequency of travel are constrained for this type of trip. Second, most urban transportation pricing and investment policy is concerned with satisfying the demand for peak-hour trips. This reflects the importance of work trips, which in Toronto account for about 70 per cent of peak-hour person-trips, (Frankena (1979)). Third, it is likely that the variability of access to work (with trip travel and cost) across different locations within the metropolitan area is considerably greater than that of non-work trips, and so more important in affecting residential property values.

The best estimation results were obtained with the logit model. Since the individuals in our samples must choose between the use of a private auto as opposed to public transit, we are dealing with the model of binary choice. The model has the explicit form:

$$P = \frac{\exp\left(\beta_0 + \sum_{i=1}^{3} \beta_i z_{ij} + \sum_{k=1}^{4} \delta_k s_{kj}\right)}{1 + \exp\left(\beta_0 + \sum_{i=1}^{3} \beta_i z_{ij} + \sum_{k=1}^{4} \delta_k s_{kj}\right)}$$

$$= \frac{\exp(L(z))}{1 + \exp(L(z))} \tag{1}$$

where the variables are defined as follows:

P — Probability of choosing the auto mode.
Z_{1j} — Difference in money costs of auto travel and public transit trip.
Z_{2j} — Difference in auto and public transit in-vehicle times.
Z_{3j} — Difference in auto and public transit waiting plus walking times.[3]

---

[3] The preliminary analysis provided similar estimates for the parameters of walking and waiting times. A t-test on the equality of the two parameters indicated that the values were close enough to warrant the use of a specification where walking and waiting times will be equally weighted.

Table 1

Estimates for the Model for Work Trips

Explanatory Variables	CONTROL SAMPLE		SPADINA SAMPLE		POOLED SAMPLE	
	Parameter	t-value	Parameter	t-value	Parameter	t-value
S_1 — age	0.034	1.50	0.012	0.57	0.024	1.62[c]
S_2 — education	0.614	2.45[a]	0.422	1.87[c]	0.489	3.02[b]
S_3 — income	0.048	1.51	0.045	1.25	0.048	2.10[b]
S_4 — employment status	−0.205	−0.33	0.214	0.40	0.064	0.36
Z_1	−1.184	−3.88[a]	−0.851	−3.14[a]	−1.016	−5.14[a]
Z_2	−0.075	−4.82[a]	−0.049	−4.29[a]	−0.059	−6.51[a]
Z_3	−0.116	−4.03[a]	−0.091	−2.53[a]	−0.107	−4.95[a]
CONSTANT	−4.810	−2.50	−3.793	−2.08	−4.464	−3.48
$-2 \log \lambda$		126.50		147.26		277.21
Value of time — Z_2	$3.84		$3.48		$3.54	
Value of time — Z_3	$5.88		$6.42		$6.30	

a, b and c denote significance at the 1%, 2.5% and 5% level on a one-tailed test.

S_k is the vector of socio-economic characteristics of the individuals. S_1 refers to age, S_2 to education, S_3 to income and S_4 to employment status (S_4 is a dummy variable with the value of 1 for self-employed persons and 0 otherwise).

The results of the maximum likelihood estimation and the estimates of the values of time (obtained by comparing the magnitudes of the coefficients of the time components to the magnitude of the coefficient of the money cost variable) are presented in Table 1.

For the pooled sample, almost all parameters are significant. The exception is the variable employment status (S_4) which is insignificant. All the parameters also have the expected signs. The negative signs indicate that the individual is less likely to choose the auto-mode, as the money and time costs of the auto-mode increase relative to the public transit mode. As one would have expected, the results suggest that the weights for walking plus waiting and in-vehicle times in the hedonic price model should not be different for the control and Spadina samples.[4]

The obtained results are comparable to those generated by the value of time studies. In general, the results from the studies done by Beesley (1973), Quarmby (1967) and Domencich and McFadden (1975) indicate that on average, people at each income level value walking and waiting time two or three times as much as in-vehicle time. On the other hand, in-vehicle time per hour during the journey to work is valued at 20 to 50 per cent of the commuter's hourly wage rate. We estimate that the average wage rate for our sample is about $9.35 per hour,[5] which gives the estimated value of in-vehicle travel time per hour as about 37 per cent of the estimated average hourly wage rate.

Using the data from the new homeowners survey, we estimate that there is one commuter per owner-occupant household. The household decides whether to buy a certain house and how much to pay for it on the basis of the marginal number of commuters. Since this must be an integer, the data on the average number of trips per household suggest that the marginal number of commuters per household was one. In 1978 the average value of the subway time savings for the Spadina sample was 4.11 minutes.[6] Assuming 250 return work trips per year, the total amount of commuting time saved is 34 hours.

[4] Performing the likelihood ratio test, the hypothesis that the parameters of the two equations are the same is accepted at the 5 per cent significance level.
[5] The estimate of the hourly wage rate obtained should be taken as only an approximation, since we do not know the exact number of hours worked by each individual traveller. The average income of the heads of households in the pooled sample for 1978 is $19,460, and under the assumption that the working week is 40 hours, the average wage rate is about $9.35 per hour. The obtained wage rate looks a bit high, and one should bear in mind that our sample is comprised entirely of heads of households who purchased houses in 1978.
[6] The average decrease in in-vehicle time for Spadina locations is 4.7 minutes. This should be corrected for the increase in the walking plus waiting time of 0.33 minutes. The conversion factor for the walking plus waiting time into in-vehicle time is 1.78 (which is the ratio of the value of the walking plus waiting time to the value of in-vehicle time; see Table 1). Multiplying 0.33 by 1.78 and subtracting from 4.7 gives 4.11 minutes as a decrease in in-vehicle time.

multiplying this by $3.54 (from Table 1), we obtain $20 as yearly savings per household. The discussion in Section 2 indicated that one should expect the capitalization of benefits from the improvement in transportation into housing values. In the next section we identify the subway effect on the housing values and test whether the obtained value of the effect is consistent with the present value of the yearly savings per household.

The Identification of the Effects of the Subway Line on Housing Prices

It was pointed out in Section 2 that in order to estimate the overall impact of the new subway line on housing prices, we have to take into account changes in the prices of all housing attributes. In our attempt to control the effects of changes other than those due to the new subway line, we construct hedonic price indices for 1971 and 1978 for both the control and impact samples.

The best results were obtained by estimation of the following specification:[7]

$$\log P_j = \alpha + \sum_{i=1}^{6} P_{zi} \log Z_{ij} + \sum_{i=7}^{17} P_{zi}Z_{ij} + \sum_{k=1}^{8} P_{dk}D_{kj} + \varepsilon_j \qquad (2)$$

where P_{zi} and P_{dk} are the parameters to be estimated, and where:

P —House selling price, in thousands of dollars;[8]

Z_1 —Usable outdoor space (UOS) in hundreds of square feet;[9]

Z_2 —Floor area in hundreds of square feet;

Z_3 —Number of rooms;

Z_4 —Total commuting time using public transit from the house location to the five chosen destinations on the subway system (see Fig. 1 in the appendix). This variable is hereafter referred to as SUBTOT. The variable is constructed by summing the values of the walking plus waiting time (WWK) with the values of the public transit in-vehicle time (SUBTIME);[10]

Z_5 —Auto in-vehicle time in minutes from the house location to the intersection of Bay and King Streets in downtown Toronto (CBDTIME), weighted by the probability of choosing auto over public transit mode;

Z_6 —Composite, weighted (the procedure is analogous to that used in the computation of SUBTIME) auto in-vehicle time in minutes from the house location to five chosen interchanges on the Metropolitan Toronto expressway system (see Fig. 2). This variable is hereafter referred to as CARTIME;

Z_7 —Number of garage places;

Z_8 —1 if finished basement, 0 otherwise;

---

[7] First, we estimated the linear form, and a hybrid of semilog and linear models. In general, the obtained results were satisfactory, but further testing revealed that the models were heteroscedastic with respect to lot area and floor area attributes. The Goldfeld-Quandt F-test for the assumption of homoscedacticity of the variance of the disturbance term, applied to the specification (2) given in the text, gave computed F-statistics very close to unity (the critical F-value is 1.13 at the 5 per cent significance level, while the highest test F-value obtained was 1.08) which led to the acceptance of the null hypothesis. The specification (2) also had the lowest transformed residual sum of squares (see Theil (1971) pp. 544–545).

[8] The selling price of housing in 1971 has been corrected for the percentage increase in housing prices in Metropolitan Toronto between 1971 and 1978. The correction takes into account the overall effect of those factors which influenced the upward movement in housing prices.

[9] Usable outdoor space was computed by subtracting floor area, divided by the number of stories, from lot area. Since the floor area was obtained by summing areas in all rooms plus the kitchen (i.e. floor area does not include hallways, bathrooms, storage areas, etc), the value of UOS is slightly biased upward.

[10] The walking plus waiting time (WWK) part of the SUBTOT variable has been defined on the basis of the estimation results of the model from Section 4. Since there were no significant differences between a consumer's evaluations of waiting and walking time, the total amount of walking and waiting time from each house location, to the moment of boarding the transit vehicle was computed. The WWK variable was multiplied by 1.78, which is the ratio between the values of WWK time and in-vehicle time obtained from the results reported in Table 1. The SUBTIME part of the variable is the composite, weighted public transit in-vehicle time in minutes (using the subway and the feeder bus if necessary) from the house location to five chosen subway stations in the neighbourhood of the most important employment, consumption or transit centres (see Fig. 1). The weights are the probabilities that a resident from the minor planning district where the house is located would have a place of work in the boroughs where the five subway stations are located, and that he uses public transit in commuting. (The weights are computed on the basis of the 1971 employment data). The first set of weights is normalized to add up to unity and then corrected for the probability that public transit will be used. The final set of weights applied, therefore, does not add up to unity, since a good part of commuting goes to the auto mode.

Z_9 —1 if recreation room finished, 0 otherwise;
Z_{10} —1 if a two-storey building, 0 otherwise;
Z_{11} —Number of extras (this includes items such as: Broadloom, stove, refrigerator, curtains, washing machine, etc.);
Z_{12} —1 if house is in excellent or very good condition, 0 otherwise;
Z_{13} —Number of bathrooms;
Z_{14} —1 if house has private driveway, 0 otherwise;
Z_{15} —1 if house has private or mutual driveway, 0 otherwise;
Z_{16} —1 if house located within the city of Toronto boundaries and has a private driveway, 0 otherwise;
Z_{17} —1 if stone or brick house, 0 otherwise;
D_1 to   —Neighbourhood locational dummy variables for eight regions in Metropolitan Toronto defined as relatively homogeneous neighbourhoods (see Fig. 3).
D_8

The specification of model (2) requires some further explanation[11] (see also Bajic (1981)). The preliminary estimation failed to give a significant estimate of the coefficient of the public transit in-vehicle time variable (SUBTIME). The basic problem seems to arise because of interactions between the implicit price attached to the SUBTIME variable and the value of the walking and waiting time variable. To avoid this problem we used the SUBTOT variable obtained by summing the values of the walking and waiting time and SUBTIME.

To measure the effects of the subway, SUBTOT is the appropriate variable. The opening of the new subway line could not affect the variables CBDTIME and CARTIME, except through a reduction in auto congestion. It should be noted, however, that the savings from reduced congestion on auto routes should not be given any long run interpretation, because of the increase in the total amount of travel. In the extreme short run, one would expect that a shift of some motorists to a new transit line would reduce congestion levels on the streets. In the long run, this would lead to some additional motoring, either by previous subway riders or by those who had previously taken other routes and we might expect no impact on the private auto in-vehicle time. Therefore, the only transportation accessibility variable which

was affected is total public transit time. All components of this time have been affected by the opening the new subway line. After taking into accou changes in the values of other attributes, the effects the subway can be estimated by using the estimat values of the SUBTOT parameter and the savings total public transit time between 1971 and 1978.

To avoid possible specification bias caused omission of the age of the structure variable (due the lack of data), we made use of the fact th housing in the city of Toronto is older than t housing in the other boroughs of Metro. Any signi cant interactions between the city of Toron dummy variable with structural attributes wou indicate significant age effects. The estimatic showed, however, that all the interactions except o were insignificant. The parameters of (2) were al almost unaffected. This suggests that the omission the age variable does not substantially alter o results. The only significant interactive variab retained in the model was Z_{16}. This indicates that t geometry of a lot is important in the city, for t variable represents the percentage increase in t housing value if the house is located in the city c Toronto and has a private driveway.

Tables 2 and 3 present, in columns 1 and 2, t estimated parameters of the hedonic price model f 1971 and 1978 for both the impact and contr samples. The overall fits for both equations a good, and the signs of almost all the coefficients a as expected. Most of the estimates are statistical significant and give reasonable implicit prices for t attributes.

The question is posed now as to whether th changes in the implicit prices of attributes in th Spadina impact area were bigger than the corre sponding changes in the control sample. We start th analysis by testing for the homogeneity of the 197 and 1978 Spadina equations (see Table 2). The F-tes indicates that the hypothesis of the equality c parameters of the two equations should be re jected.[12] The same conclusion is reached for th Metropolitan Toronto equations. To answer th question as to whether the overall change (including the SUBTOT attribute) in the parameters of th Spadina equations was significantly different from the overall change in the parameters of the contro

[11] The fact that we do not know which mode was chosen forces us to include variables for both modes. This introduces som arbitrariness in our definition of access, which, given the availability data sets, is unavoidable.
[12] The computed F-value is 2.72 while the critical F-value at the 1 per cent significance level is 1.80.

Table 2

erage Housing Price as Predicted by the Spadina 1971 and 1978 Parameters

planatory Variables	1 $P_{z,71}(S)$	2 $P_{z,78}(S)$	3 $\bar{Z}_{s,78}$	4 $P_{z,71}(S)$ $\cdot \bar{Z}_{s,78}$	5 $P_{z,78}(S)$ $\cdot \bar{Z}_{s,78}$
— UOS	0.0870[a]	0.1123[a]	3.3390	0.2905	0.3750
— Floor area	0.2528[a]	0.3768[a]	2.1448	0.5422	0.8082
— Number of rooms	0.2249[a]	0.0475	1.8046	0.4059	0.0857
— SUBTOT	−0.1279[a]	−0.2284[a]	3.0042	−0.3842	−0.6862
— CBDTIME	−0.1315[a]	−0.0844[d]	2.6634	−0.3502	−0.2248
— CARTIME	−0.0947[a]	0.0173	2.9415	−0.2786	0.0509
— No. of garage places	0.0074	0.0140	0.8826	0.0065	0.0124
— Basement dummy	0.0293[d]	0.0082	0.8008	0.0235	0.0066
— Rec. room dummy	0.0483[a]	0.0490[a]	0.4675	0.0226	0.0229
— 2 storey dummy	−0.0213	−0.0431[b]	0.5325	−0.0113	−0.0230
— No. of extras	0.0199[a]	0.0179[a]	4.1237	0.0821	0.0738
— House condition dummy	0.1253[a]	0.1132[a]	0.6080	0.0762	0.0688
— No. of bathrooms	0.0569[a]	0.0047	1.7694	0.1007	0.0083
— Private driveway dummy	−0.0262[d]	0.0305[d]	0.4822	−0.0126	0.0147
— Driveway dummy (private or mutual)	0.0810[a]	0.0373	0.9015	0.0730	0.0336
— Interactive dummy	0.0828[b]	0.1709[a]	0.0377	0.0031	0.0064
— Stone or brick dummy	0.0493[a]	0.0250	0.8029	0.0396	0.0201
— Neighbourhood dummy	−0.0467	0.1626[c]	0.5304	−0.0248	0.0862
— Neighbourhood dummy	0.0792	0.2445[c]	0.0105	0.0008	0.0026
— Neighbourhood dummy	−0.0236	0.2050[b]	0.3103	−0.0073	0.0636
— Neighbourhood dummy	−0.0334	0.2123[b]	0.1384	−0.0046	0.0294
onstant	3.4519	3.2568	1	3.4519	3.2568
	$R^2 = 0.76$	$R^2 = 0.76$		4.0450	4.0921
	SE = 0.17	SE = 0.186			
	SS = 564	SS = 477			

hroughout this section a, b, c and d denote statistical significance at 1, 2.5, 5 and 10 percent level on a one-tailed test. R^2 is the oefficient of determination, S.E. stands for standard error of the estimate and S.S. for the sample size.

rea equations, we create an index, which uses as a ase a housing unit with the average of all housing haracteristics in the Spadina area in 1978. This verage housing unit is, then, priced at the implicit rices of characteristics obtained by the estimation of the 1971 and 1978 Spadina area equations. The lifference between the two predicted prices of the ame housing unit shows the extent of the overall changes in the parameters of the Spadina area equations. An analogous index is created for the control area equations. If the overall impact of the parameter shifts is the same in the two areas, we may conclude that the changes have been caused mainly by identical demand and supply factors interacting in the Metropolitan Toronto housing market. Since the changes in the control area housing market were not induced by changes in the transportation system, an overall change of an equal magnitude in the impact area would indicate that the change in the transportation system was not its source.

For each of the considered areas the null hypothesis is:

$$H_0 : P_{z,78}(j) * \bar{Z}_{j,78} - P_{z,71}(j) * \bar{Z}_{j,78} = 0 \quad (3)$$

and the alternative hypothesis is:

$$H_1 : P_{z,78}(j) * \bar{Z}_{j,78} - P_{z,71}(j) * \bar{Z}_{j,78} > 0$$

where $P_z\lambda(j)$ refers to the vectors of parameters estimated from the jth sample for year λ and $\bar{Z}_{j,78}$ is the vector of the average characteristics of the jth sample in 1978. For those attributes which have entered specification (2) in logarithmic form, the reported values (in columns 3, Tables 2 and 3) are the means of the natural logarithms of the attributes in question. The sums of columns 4 and 5 (in both tables) are the natural logarithms of the predicted prices of an average unit using the 1971 and 1978 parameters respectively. Taking the antilogarithms of the two sums (in each table), we find the differences indicate that the prices of the standard units

Table 3

Average Housing Price as Predicted by the Control Sample 1971 and 1978 Parameters

Explanatory Variables		1	2	3	4	5
		$P_{z,71}(C)$	$P_{z,78}(C)$	$Z_{c,78}$	$P_{z,71}(C)$ $\cdot Z_{c,71}$	$P_{z,78}(C)$ $\cdot Z_{c,78}$
Z_1	UOS	0.1157^a	0.1547^a	3.3155	0.3836	0.5129
Z_2	Floor area	0.2615^a	0.2847^a	2.1738	0.5684	0.6189
Z_3	Number of rooms	0.0113	0.0255	1.8469	0.0209	0.0471
Z_4	SUBTOT	-0.1256^a	-0.1602^a	3.1314	-0.3933	-0.5017
Z_5	CBDTIME	-0.0557^a	-0.0626^a	2.1963	-0.1223	-0.1375
Z_6	CARTIME	-0.0285	-0.0190	2.8304	-0.0807	-0.0538
Z_7	Number of garage places	0.0320^a	0.0509^a	0.8282	0.0265	0.0422
Z_8	Basement dummy	0.0082	0.0557^a	0.7710	0.0063	0.0429
Z_9	— Recreation room dummy	0.0298^d	0.0149	0.4540	0.0135	0.0068
Z_{10}	— 2-storey dummy	0.0353^d	0.0195	0.5971	0.0211	0.0116
Z_{11}	— Number of extras	0.0105^d	0.0156^a	4.1840	0.0439	0.0653
Z_{12}	— House condition dummy	0.1151^a	0.1009^a	0.6115	0.0704	0.0617
Z_{13}	— Number of bathrooms	0.0463^a	0.0174^d	1.6626	0.0770	0.0289
Z_{14}	— Private driveway dummy	0.0029	0.0746^a	0.5112	0.0015	0.0381
Z_{15}	— Driveway dummy (private or mutual)	0.1486^a	0.0296	0.8773	0.1304	0.0260
Z_{16}	— Interactive dummy	0.1434^a	-0.0612	0.0286	0.0041	-0.0018
Z_{17}	— Stone or brick dummy	0.0901^a	0.0675^a	0.7914	0.0713	0.0534
D_1	— Neighbourhood dummy	-0.0420	-0.0262	0.0634	-0.0027	-0.0017
D_2	— Neighbourhood dummy	-0.0689^d	-0.0562^d	0.1391	-0.0096	-0.0078
D_3	— Neighbourhood dummy	-0.0880^c	-0.0484	0.1595	-0.0140	-0.0077
D_4	— Neighbourhood dummy	-0.1845^a	-0.0100	0.3231	-0.0596	-0.0037
D_5	— Neighbourhood dummy	-0.1754^a	-0.0582	0.0634	-0.0111	-0.0037
D_6	— Neighbourhood dummy	-0.1101^d	-0.0180	0.0327	-0.0036	-0.0006
D_7	— Neighbourhood dummy	-0.1830^d	0.0535	0.0389	-0.0071	-0.0021
D_8	— Neighbourhood dummy	-0.0580	0.0642	0.1207	-0.0070	0.0077
Constant		3.3403	3.2662	1	3.3403	3.2662
		$R^2 = 0.63$	$R^2 = 0.75$		4.0682	4.1122
		SE = 0.205	SE = 0.172			
		SS = 488	SS = 489			

predicted by the 1971 parameters are $2,754 and $2,629 lower than the prices predicted by the 1978 parameters of the Spadina and control samples respectively. The obtained differences in predicted prices result from the overall changes in the parameters of the two areas between 1971 and 1978. The test for the assumption of equality of the two predicted prices for an average housing unit results in the rejection of the null hypotheses for both Spadina and control areas.[13]

Next, we test the null hypothesis that the two differences in predicted prices are equal. The calculated t-statistic is 0.38, which is insignificant at any conventional significance level.[14] The conclusion is that the overall change in the implicit prices in the impact area was not different from the overall change in the control area. This would indicate that the market forces behind these changes are the same. In conclusion, the overall shift in the implicit price in the Spadina corridor was not caused by the opening of the new subway line, for the same shift occurred in the rest of the Metropolitan Toronto where the impact of the subway would not have had any effect. In that case the impact of the subway due to the change in the implicit price of the SUBTOT attribute is rather small, and the main impact on housing values is identified as the direct impact due to the decrease in the SUBTOT time for the Spadina locations. The amount of capitalized savings in commuting time for an average housing unit from

[13] The calculated t-values are 4.23 for the Spadina area and 3.64 for the control area. Both values are highly significant. For this test see R. Pindyk and D. Rubinfield (1974) pp. 177–185.
[14] This finding is consistent with the results of the F-test for the homogeneity of the hedonic price equations in the two areas in 1978. The obtained F-value is 1.25, while the critical value at the 5 per cent significance level is 1.52.

e Spadina sample in 1978 can be readily obtained adjusting the hedonic price index (3) for the crease in commuting time. Taking into account e decrease in commuting time, we obtain the effect the subway on the market value of an average use in the Spadina area as $2,237. This is the erage amount of the savings in commuting costs r a single commuter per household, capitalized to housing values.[15]

Note also that the constant elasticity of the hous-g price with respect to the SUBTOT attribute plies that the market value of the savings in mmuting costs rises in proportion to what the arket price of the house would otherwise be. As ted previously in Section 2, this reflects an as-mption that the valuation of the time savings is roportional to income, and that house values are n average also proportional to incomes of occu-ants, reflecting an income elasticity of unity in ousehold demand for housing services.

One should expect that the total amount of avings to commuters is not too far removed from he total amount which has been capitalized into ousing values. However, we cannot compare the wo totals, since we do not know the distribution of he residence locations of the Spadina subway users. The only solution is to check whether the present alue of the yearly savings per household is consist-nt with the direct effect of the subway on housing alues (due to the decrease in commuting time). The nalysis in Section 4 gave $120 as the yearly savings er household. For different time horizons over which the savings are projected, the discount rates at which the present values of savings over the time horizon are equal to the estimated effect of the subway ($2,237) on the market value of an average house located in the Spadina area are as follows:

Length of Horizon	Real Discount Rate
∞	0.054
35	0.040
30	0.035
25	0.025
20	0.010

Of course, one should not expect that the savings in commuting time of the above magnitude will be realized over an indefinite period of time. (This case of non-static expectations is discussed in Section 2). For example, given that the period over which the savings in commuting costs are projected into the future is 35 years, and the real rate of discount is 4 per cent, the savings in commuting costs correspond to the calculated effect of the subway.

It would be useful to compare these findings with those of Dewees (1976), who examined the effects of the Bloor subway line on housing values in Toronto. The average travel time to the CBD for all com-muters in the areas studied by Dewees decreased by 0.067 hr. or 4.02 minutes which is very close to our results. However, the implicit price of travel time computed by using the site rent surface slope ob-tained by Dewees is too low (his highest estimate is $5,580 per hour, which would require a 17 per cent real rate of discount over 35 years to be consistent with the value of time assumed). This result seems to suggest that a substantial portion of the benefits did not seep into land rents, which is different from our conclusions. However, one could also argue that the simple distance variable used by Dewees failed to take into account the effects of the changes in the areas to the south and north of the Bloor corridor. The fact that not all of Dewees' results could have been explained by a monocentric city hypothesis offers further justification that more complex ac-cessibility variables should be used.

In summary, since the appropriate rate of discount is likely to be in the order of 4 per cent, our findings not only lend support to the degree of robustness of the models used for empirical investigations in this research, but also strongly suggest that the benefits to commuters from the opening of the subway have been capitalized into the values of those housing units located in proximity to the Spadina subway line.

6. Conclusions

The empirical analyses presented in this paper deal with two specific issues. The first concerns the identif-ication of the direct benefits from the improvement in transportation per owner-occupant household. The second concerns the formulation and testing of

[15] This is computed by taking the mean of the logarithms of the SUBTOT variable values in 1971 (this value is 3.171) instead of the 1978 value from Table 2. Keeping all other attributes and implicit prices unchanged, the sum of column 5, Table 2, decreases to 4.054. Taking the antilogarithms of this sum and the previous sum of the column 5, (4.0921) we find the difference gives the value of $2,237.

a model to investigate the effects of the subway on the price of housing.

The need to conduct the analysis by combining two different models stems from the fact that the benefits from an improvement in transportation (given certain demand and supply conditions) are reflected in the premium paid for housing. Using the obtained estimates of the values of different time components of the trips, actual trip frequencies on the new subway line, and the reduction in commuting time as defined by the relevant accessibility attributes from the hedonic price regressions model, we have identified the amount of direct savings in commuting costs from the improvement in transportation per owner-occupant household.

Comparing the present values of the savings from the subway (identified by the modal choice model) with the impact on an average private family house in the Spadina corridor (as identified by the hedonic price regressions model), we concluded that the direct savings from the improvement in transportation have been capitalized into the housing values, i.e. the savings in commuting costs which accrue to the commuters have been transferred to the home owners through the complex workings of the urban housing market.

Appendix

Data and Data Sources

The new-homeowners survey was undertaken in May 1979. The intention was to obtain the information on the basic socio-economic characteristics of commuters such as age, employment status, education, income in a normal year, number of children, and number of adults in the household. The rest of the questionnaire was designed to obtain information on the location of the work-place, method of transit, the location of the nearest available parking facility adjacent to work-place, and the amount charged for parking and walking time from parking place to the work destination. The transportation access variables for the two work trip alternatives are formulated in such a way as to allow use of the model to estimate the value of each time component of the trip separately.

The data for the hedonic price functions model were obtained from the Teela Sales Review and the Multiple Listing Service (MLS), published by the Toronto Real Estate Board (TREB). The data on

selling prices and almost all important structur characteristics were obtained from these sources.

A multitude of sources was used for the transport tion access variables. Data on subway times we obtained from: Toronto Transit Commissio Scheduled Service (1971) and (1978). The best au route between the two points was determined on t basis of speed and delay studies. The available spe and delay data were restricted to peak times onl which limits the selection of trips to peak-hour wor trips. Data on auto speeds on arterial roads we obtained from: Metro Toronto Traffic Contr Centre (1971) and (1979): 'Speed and Delay Pr gram for Main Arterial Roads in Metropolita Toronto'. Speeds on expressways were obtaine from: Metro Toronto Traffic Control Centre (197 and (1979): 'Speed and Delay Program for Metr politan Toronto Highways', and from: Urba Regional Transportation Planning Office (1971) an (1979): ROAD NETWORK (TARMS MODEL).

The transportation access variables for th hedonic price regressions model are as follows:

(1)   Walking time to the nearest subway station o feeder bus;
(2)   Waiting time for the feeder bus (or buses);
(3)   Bus in-vehicle time;
(4)   Driving time by car to the nearest expresswa interchange;
(5)   Driving time by car to the intersection of Ba and King Street in downtown Toronto;
(6)   Subway transit time between any pair of origin and destination stations on the Toronto subway system;
(7)   Auto in-vehicle time between any pair of origin and destination interchanges on the Metropolitan Toronto expressway system.

Naturally, not all destination stations on the subway and expressway system enter the model. After careful examination of the employment centres and areas in Metropolitan Toronto, we have chosen the five most important destinations on both transportation systems as subcentres. The chosen subway stations are: No. 5, No. 15, No. 31, No. 44, and No. 56, while the chosen interchanges are: No. 4, No. 12, No. 27, No. 32 and No. 44 (see Fig. 1, and Fig. 2, in Appendix).

All neighbourhood attributes are treated as a single attribute. This was done in the following way: the land-use maps of the Metropolitan Toronto area were examined and the whole area was divided into

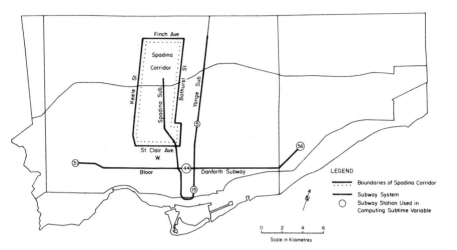

Fig. 1.   Spadina Corridor and Metropolitan Toronto Subway System.

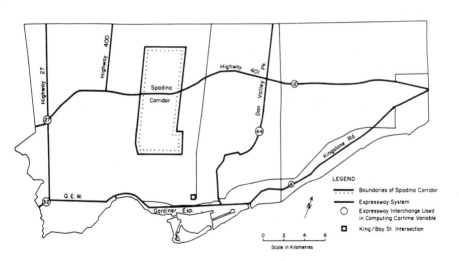

Fig. 2.   Spadina Corridor and Metropolitan Toronto Expressway System.

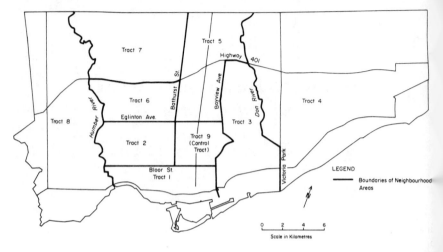

Fig. 3. Neighbourhood areas.

nine homogeneous regions. Location-specific dummy variables were constructed for eight of these regions (see Fig. 3 in Appendix). The last region, the area between Bathurst Street to the west, Bloor and Danforth Streets to the south, Eglinton Avenue to the north and Ramsey Road and the Don Valley Parkway to the east, was kept as the control area.

REFERENCES

ANDERSON, R. and CROCKER, T. (1971). 'Air Pollution and Residential Property Values.' *Urban Studies*, Vol. 8: 171–180.

BAJIC, V. (1981). 'Transportation System Changes and the Structure of Housing Prices: The Effect of a New Subway Line in Metropolitan Toronto.' Unpublished Ph.D. dissertation, University of Toronto, Toronto.

BALL, M. (1973). 'Recent Empirical Work on the Determinants of Relative House Prices'. *Urban Studies*, Vol. 10: 212–231.

BEESLEY, M. (1965). 'The Value of Time Spent in Travelling: Some New Evidence'. *Economica*, Vol. 32: 171–185.

BOSSONS, J. (1978), 'Reforming Planning in Ontario.' Discussion Paper Series, *Ontario Economic Council*. Toronto.

DOMENICH, T. and McFADDEN, D. (1975). *Urban Travel Demand: A Behavioural Analysis*, North-Holland/American Elsevier, New York.

DEWEES, D. (1976). 'The Effect of a Subway on Residential Property Values in Toronto.' *Journal of Urban Economics*, Vol. 3: 357–369.

FRANKENA, M. (1979). *Urban Transportation Economics*. Butterworths, Toronto, Canada.

LUCAS, R. (1967). 'Adjustment Costs and the Theory of Supply.' *Journal of Political Economy*, Vol. 75: 321–334.

McFADDEN, D. (1974). 'The Measurement of Urban Travel Demand.' *Journal of Public Economics*, Vol. 3: 303–328.

MEYER, J., KAIN, J. and WOHL, M. (1966). *The Urban Transportation Problem*, Harvard University Press, Cambridge, Mass.

MIESZKOWSKI, P. and SAPER, A. (1976). 'An Estimate of the Effect of Airport Noise on Property Values.' *Journal of Urban Economics*, Vol. 5: 425–440.

MISHAN, E. (1971), *Cost-Benefit Analysis*, Allen and Unwin, London.

PINDYCK, R. and RUBINFIELD, D. (1976). *Econometric Models and Economic Forecasts*, McGraw-Hill. Toronto.

QUARMBY, D. (1967). 'Choice of Travel Mode for the Journey to Work: Some Findings'. *Journal of Transport Economics and Policy*, Vol. 1: 273-314.

ROSEN, S. (1974). 'Hedonic Prices and Implicit Markets: Product Differentiation in Pure Competition'. *Journal of Political Economy*, Vol. 82: 34–55.

SCHNARE, A. and STRUYK, R. (1976). 'Segmentation in Urban Housing Markets'. *Journal of Urban Economics*, Vol. 3: 146–166.

THEIL, H. (1971). *Principles of Econometrics*, Wiley, New York.

TREADWAY, A. (1969). 'On Rational Entrepreneurial Behaviour and the Demand for Investment.' *Review of Economic Studies*, Vol. 36: 227–239.

25

Impacts of Subsidies on the Costs of Urban Public Transport

John Pucher, Anders Markstedt, and Ira Hirschman*

INTRODUCTION

Since 1965 subsidies to urban public transport (here called "transit") have increased rapidly throughout the world. In a study of transit finance in fifteen countries, Bly, Webster and Pounds (1980) reported large increases from 1965 to 1976 in the absolute amount of subsidies as well as in the percentage of costs covered by them. The growth of subsidies has been particularly striking in the United States. Though only $88 million in 1965 and $518 million in 1970, the combined capital and operating subsidy to transit exceeded $7.8 billion in 1980 (Pucher, 1980 and 1982). Passenger fares covered less than 42% of transit operating costs in the U.S. in 1980 (against 99% in 1965 and 86% in 1970) and did not contribute at all toward financing capital costs (Pucher, 1982).

Transit subsidies have long been controversial. For example, Meyer, Kain and Wohl (1965) rejected most arguments for subsidies, and therefore argued against proposed subsidy programmes in the U.S. In spite of early opposition, transit subsidies have burgeoned. The number of critics has grown as the results have been observed. Recent studies of subsidy impacts conclude that direct benefits to transit riders have been small relative to the increase in subsidy, and that the alleged environmental and secondary economic benefits are negligible or non-existent (Altshuler et al., 1981; Meyer and Gomez-Ibanez, 1981; Hilton, 1974; Hamer, 1976; Webber, 1976). Some critics—including former transit advocates—complain that subsidies have simply inflated costs instead of providing more, better, or cheaper service for transit riders (Altshuler et al., 1981; U.S. House of Representatives, 1981b; Bonnell, 1981). There is strong pressure in the Reagan Administration and in Congress to curtail the programme or at least to revise it so that subsidies would be more effective. (Executive Office of the President, 1981; U.S. General Accounting Office, 1979 and 1981).

This article examines the extent to which subsidies have worsened the productivity and cost problems of transit in the United States. It reviews nationwide aggregate trends in subsidies and then compares them with changes in productivity and cost

* John Pucher is Assistant Professor, Department of Urban Planning, Rutgers University, New Brunswick, New Jersey, U.S.A., and the other two authors are research assistants there. The preparation of this article was supported by the Urban Mass Transportation Administration, U.S. Department of Transportation, research grant no. UMTA–NJ–11–0011. The authors are indebted to Mr. Michael Kemp for a very helpful reviews and suggestions for improving the paper.

From John Pucher et al., "Impacts of Subsidies on the Costs of Urban Public Transport," *Journal of Transport Economics and Policy*, 1983, May, 155-176. Copyright 1983 by Journal of Transport Economics and Policy. Reprinted by permission.

TABLE 1

Trends in Transit Subsidies in the U.S. by Level of Government, 1970–1980

Type of Subsidy	1970	1975	1980
	$ million	$ million	$ million
Operating subsidies			
Federal	0 (0%)	408 (21%)	1,324 (30%)
State	30 (9%)	549 (29%)	992 (23%)
Local	288 (91%)	944 (50%)	2,062 (47%)
Total operating subsidy	318 (100%)	1,901 (100%)	4,378 (100%)
Capital subsidies			
Federal	133 (67%)	1,287 (80%)	2,787 (81%)[b]
State and local[a]	67 (33%)	322 (20%)	647 (19%)
Total capital subsidy	200 (100%)	1,609 (100%)	3,434 (100%)
Operating and capital subsidies			
Federal	133 (26%)	1,695 (48%)	4,111 (53%)
State and local	385 (74%)	1,815 (52%)	3,701 (47%)
Total subsidy	518 (100%)	3,510 (100%)	7,812 (100%)

Sources: Calculated on the basis of data in American Public Transit Association (1981a), Pucher (1980), Urban Mass Transportation Administration (1981a), and supplemental statistics collected by the author directly from the 26 largest transit systems in the U.S.
Commuter rail as well as rapid transit, streetcars, trolley buses, and motor buses are included in these statistics. The capital subsidy amounts do not include the special Congressional appropriations for the Washington subway system.
[a]The state and local portion of capital subsidy financing was estimated on the basis of statutory matching rates for different segments of the transit capital programme.
[b]The overall Federal matching rate for capital subsidies in 1980 exceeded 80% because of the 85% matching rate on Interstate Transfer funds.

indices. Next, multiple regression analysis on a pooled cross-section sample of 77 transit systems in 1979 and 135 systems in 1980 isolates the separate impacts of subsidies on costs, controlling for various other factors affecting costs. Recommendations are made for revisions in the subsidy programme that would encourage more efficient use of subsidy funds.

TRENDS IN SUBSIDIES

Subsidies to mass transit in the United States have increased rapidly since 1965. The total capital subsidy from all government levels then was $76 million, and the total operating subsidy only $14 million (Pucher, 1980). By 1970 the capital subsidy was $200 million, and the operating subsidy $318 million. Table 1 shows that from 1970 to 1980 subsidies increased more than 15-fold, exceeding $7.8 billion in 1980. Another striking trend evident in the table is the increased Federal role in transit finance. Federal assistance rose from $133 million in 1970 to $4.1 billion in 1980, from 26% to

3% of the total subsidy. State subsidies also increased substantially, but their relative importance has fallen since 1975.

Metropolitan regionwide taxes earmarked for transit have become increasingly widespread. Virtually no large city had adopted this financing mechanism by 1970. By 1980, however, 15 of the 26 largest U.S. metropolitan areas relied primarily on earmarked transit taxes for the local share of subsidy financing (Pucher, 1980). Of 101 cities surveyed in 1980 by the U.S. Conference of Mayors, 46 already had either state or local taxes dedicated for transit, and 21 had plans for implementing such taxes by 1982 (Gortmaker, 1981).

The natural results of these trends are as follows. First, capital projects are undertaken giving benefits that fall far short of total costs yet exceed local costs. Similarly, urban areas receiving relatively generous Federal operating assistance (50% in many cases) have initiated or maintained highly unprofitable routes and types of services that local officials would not have supported on their own. These effects have been compounded by the adoption of earmarked state and local taxes. Most of these arrangements rely on revenue-elastic sales taxes or income taxes. Especially during inflationary periods, they automatically yield growing tax revenues even if statutory rates remain constant. These dedicated funds have reduced local transit authorities' incentives to eliminate highly unprofitable services, to bargain for moderate settlements in wages and fringe benefits, and to increase productivity. Finally, no Federal or local subsidy programme has made funding contingent on performance standards, cost control, ridership gains, or the achievement of social, environmental, and economic goals. Few states have begun to tie subsidy payment to performance indicators. Even these have set aside only a small fraction of the state subsidy to do this.

The very design of transit subsidy programmes in the U.S. may, therefore, encourage inefficient use of subsidy funds. Subsequent sections of this article examine the extent to which they have encouraged escalation of costs.

TRENDS IN PRODUCTIVITY AND COSTS

Transit costs have increased rapidly over the past three decades, and productivity has fallen. But the rate of change has not been uniform throughout: costs have increased and productivity has fallen much faster when subsidy growth has been greatest. As Table 2 shows, the average annual rate of growth in operating cost per vehicle mile (in constant, inflation-adjusted dollars) was only 1.4% per year from 1950 to 1965. In contrast, cost per mile increased by an average of 4.1% per year during the rapid subsidy growth from 1965 to 1980, three times as fast. From 1965 to 1980, productivity—as measured by vehicle miles of service per transit employee—fell by 19%, from 13,800 miles per employee to only 11,200 (see Table 2). Miles per employee had *increased* by 10% over the 15–year period before.

These trends have not been the same for all portions of the industry. We could not obtain mode-by-mode breakdowns of trends over the entire 30-year period, but Table 3 disaggregates the transit operating and financial statistics for the crucial decade of the 1970s, when subsidies increased 15-fold in current dollars. Increases in operating expenses were larger for bus and commuter rail services than for rail rapid transit.

TABLE 2

Trends in Transit Productivity and Costs in the U.S., 1950–1980

Indicator	1950	1955	1960	1965	1970	1975	1980
Operating cost per vehicle mile							
Actual dollars[a]	0.46	0.56	0.64	0.72	1.06	1.89	3.1
1980 constant dollars[b]	1.38	1.56	1.65	1.71	2.07	2.63	3.1
Average annual rate of growth in operating cost per mile (% per year)[c]							
Unadjusted for inflation		4.0	2.7	2.4	8.0	12.3	10.5
Adjusted for inflation		2.5	1.1	0.7	4.0	5.0	3.4
Vehicle miles per employee per year (thousands)	12.5	12.4	13.7	13.8	13.6	12.5	11.2[d]

Source: Calculated on the basis of transit data in American Public Transit Association (1981a) an dollar deflation indices in the *Statistical Abstract of the U.S.* (Washington: U.S. Census Bureau, 1982). Only bus, rail rapid transit, trolley coach, and streetcar services are included in this table; commuter ra is excluded.

[a] Expressed in current dollars for each year, unadjusted for inflation.
[b] Expressed in constant, inflation-adjusted dollars.
[c] Calculated by fitting an exponential curve.
[d] For 1980 APTA reported 4,600 part-time workers and 184,700 full-time workers. For calculating th miles per employee in 1980, each part-time worker was counted as half a full-time worker; this yielded figure of 187,000 full-time workers.

Between 1970 and 1980, total operating costs increased by 287% for bus and streetcar service, by 228% for commuter rail service, and by 138% for rail rapid transit. These figures do not control for inflation or for changes in service. Inflation-adjusted operating costs per vehicle mile also increased considerably: by 73% for bus and streetcar and by 29% for rail rapid transit. Because of declining load factors, real cost escalation is slightly greater on a per-passenger basis: 75% for bus and streetcar, 74% for commuter rail, and 36% for rapid transit.

Perhaps the most striking of these operating and financial trends is the sharply increased unprofitability of bus and streetcar services relative to rail rapid transit and commuter rail. In 1970, bus services in aggregate in the U.S. covered all their operating costs from passenger fares, whereas rapid transit and commuter rail fares covered less than two-thirds of costs. By 1980, however, bus services covered only 39%, less than either of the other modes. This reversal stems both from the faster increase in bus costs—as noted above—and from the much slower increase in bus fares than in fares on the other modes. Between 1970 and 1980 average bus fares rose by only 33%, whereas rapid transit fares rose by 108%, and commuter rail fares by 139%. Thus the increase in operating subsidy was 62¢ per bus rider and 37¢ per rapid transit passenger. For commuter rail passengers it was even larger ($1.24), because of the greater average length of commuter rail trips.

The sudden escalation of operating deficits in bus service was due to two factors.

TABLE 3

*ends in U.S. Transit Operations and Finances for Different Modes, 1970–1980
(Statistics in millions, except for ratios)*

'atistic	Bus and Streetcar 1970	1975	1980	Rail Rapid Transit 1970	1975	1980	Commuter Rail 1970	1975	1980
	Modes								
Operating expense[a] ($)	1,303	2,500	5,049	613	1,085	1,458	297	571	973
Operating revenue ($)	1,323	1,483	1,957	384	491	717	188	283	436
Operating deficit ($)	−20	1,017	3,092	229	593	741	109	288	537
Operating revenue/ operating expense	1.02	0.59	0.39	0.63	0.45	0.49	0.63	0.50	0.45
Vehicle miles	1,476	1,567	1,710	407	423	385	n.a.	n.a.	164
Cost per vehicle mile ($)	0.88	1.60	2.95	1.51	2.57	3.79	n.a.	n.a.	5.93
Revenue passengers[b]	4,358	4,245	4,926	1,574	1,388	1,420	295	260	285
Cost per passenger ($)	0.30	0.59	1.02	0.39	0.78	1.03	1.01	2.20	3.41
Average fare[c] ($)	0.30	0.35	0.40	0.24	0.35	0.50	0.64	1.09	1.53
Operating subsidy per passenger ($)	0.00	0.24	0.62	0.15	0.43	0.52	0.37	1.11	1.88

ources: Calculated on the basis of data in American Public Transit Association (1981a), Pucher 1980), and supplemental statistics collected by the author directly from individual multi-modal transit ystems.
Excluding depreciation.
Also defined as linked passenger trips.
Average fare was calculated as the ratio of passenger revenue divided by revenue passengers, xcluding transfer passengers.

First, Federal operating subsidies per rider were much larger for all-bus systems in ow-density urban areas than for multi-modal systems in dense urban areas. Because he allocation formula for Federal operating subsidies is based primarily on population and population density, and not on ridership, transit-oriented cities with rail systems received substantially less subsidy than if the formula had distributed funds in proportion to ridership (Urban Mass Transportation Administration, 1976). Also, most rail rapid transit service is in older, declining urban areas, where the state and local governments have had the most severe budget crises. In those areas smaller Federal, state and local government operating subsidies led to larger fare increases and less service than on bus routes elsewhere. Second, bus transit is more labour-intensive than rail transit, so bus transit is more exposed to increasing labour costs and declining labour productivity, and has less opportunity to eliminate personnel through automation.

Capital costs increased rapidly for all transit modes. The price of a new standard-size bus rose five-fold from 1970 to 1980, from $33,000 to $153,000 (Urban Mass Transportation Administration, 1982b). Rail vehicle costs increased about three-fold over this period, though there were differences by size of vehicle. The price of smaller rapid transit cars, such as those used by the Chicago Transit Authority,

rose from $150,000 to almost $500,000. The price of larger cars, such as those used o
San Francisco's BART system and the Washington Metro, rose from $300,000 t
$825,000 (Urban Mass Transportation Administration, 1982b). Construction cost
for new rapid transit systems have also increased. The new Washington subway, fo
example, cost $90 million per mile to build, almost equal to the $89 million per mil
for the new Atlanta subway (U.S. House of Representatives, 1981a; Metropolita
Atlanta Rapid Transit Authority, 1981). The current extension to Boston's subway i
costing even more—$150 million per mile (U.S. House of Representatives, 1981b). I
contrast, San Francisco's rapid transit system, built in the late 1960s, cost $23 millio
per mile (Metropolitan Transportation Commission, 1980). From 1965 to 1980, rai
transit accounted for 76% of the nation's total cumulative capital subsidy to transit
but for only 27% of all transit ridership. Rail transit requires much more capita
subsidy per passenger than bus. Indeed, the capital subsidy per rail passenger trip ha
been nine times larger than the capital subsidy per bus trip (Urban Mas.
Transportation Administration, 1981a).

The question remains, however, whether increased subsidies have actually
encouraged increased costs, and thus whether the design of the subsidy programme i
responsible for its own ineffectiveness. As was evident from Tables 1 through 3, transi
cost increases in the U.S. have indeed been correlated with subsidy growth. During
periods of little or no subsidy (from 1950 to 1965) productivity increases and cost
increases were small. In contrast, productivity declined and cost increases were large
during periods of rapid subsidy growth (from 1965 to 1980). These trends are
consistent with the hypothesised adverse impact of the subsidy programme on costs.
Moreover, the bivariate regressions of Bly, Webster and Pounds (1980) reinforce this
impression. Examining changes in subsidies and costs from 1965 to 1976, they
estimated that, for every additional one per cent of operating costs covered by
subsidy, real unit costs rose by 0.4 to 0.6 per cent. Thus, for their time-series sample of
59 transit systems in seven countries—and national aggregate data from 15
countries—only about half of the real increase in subsidy was translated into lower
fares or additional service.

Factors beyond the control of the transit industry may have contributed to cost
escalation. In the econometric analysis which follows, a cross-section multiple
regression model is used to isolate the impacts of subsidies on costs by controlling for
other important cost determinants. Three different subsidy variables are employed to
determine the effects of earmarked transit taxes and subsidy grants from higher levels
of government.

MULTIPLE REGRESSION ANALYSIS

Past econometric analysis has focused almost exclusively on bus operating costs,
primarily to assess the extent of scale economies or diseconomies (Lee and Steedman,
1970; Wabe and Coles, 1975; Nelson, 1972; Miller, 1970; Mohring, 1972). Except for
the investigations of Bly, Webster and Pounds (1980) and Barnum and Gleason
(1979), the effect of subsidies on costs has been neglected. The analysis here is also
limited to bus costs, because the few rail transit systems in the U.S. yield few data. The
impacts of subsidies are explicitly incorporated in the regression model.

TABLE 4

Percentage Distribution of Transit Systems Included in the Regression Sample

us Fleet Size	%	*Percent Federal Subsidy*	%
Less than 100	49	Less than 25%	15
100–499	33	25%–44%	25
500 or more	17	45% or more	60

ost Per Hour		*Percent State Subsidy*	
Less than $20	21	Less than 10%	53
$20–$29	58	10%–24%	15
$30 or more	22	25% or more	32

Revenue/Cost Ratio		*Percent of State and Local Subsidy Dedicated*	
Less than 0.25	15	Less than 25%	55
0.25–0.49	69	25%–49%	8
0.50–0.74	16	50%–74%	8
0.75 or more	0	75% or more	30

Type of Management	%
Public	56
Private	44

Sample selection

The data base for the regression consisted of a pooled cross-section sample of 77 transit systems in 1979 and 135 systems in 1980. The systems were selected primarily because data were available for them. They included virtually all sizes and types of systems, types of urban areas, geographic locations, cost and service levels, fare policies, and, perhaps most important, institutional structures and subsidy financing arrangements. The percentage distribution of the sample along seven key dimensions is shown in Table 4. *All* the 40 largest transit systems in the U.S. were included in the data set. This greater proportional representation of the larger systems was felt to be justified because they account for 85% of total bus ridership in the U.S., and thus have far greater importance to the transit industry than the 1,014 smaller systems.

The necessary transit data were assembled from four sources: (1) mandatory financial and operating reports submitted by all Federally-subsidised systems to the Urban Mass Transportation Administration (1981b and 1982a); (2) voluntary financial and operating reports filed by member systems with the American Public Transit Association (1980 and 1981a); (3) annual reports published by most of the systems; and (4) supplemental, unpublished information obtained by the authors from all the systems. Use of this range of sources permitted cross-checking of statistical values and helped us to identify and revise inaccurate figures.

Theoretical considerations

Operating cost per bus hour was chosen as the dependent variable in the regression analysis, instead of cost per bus mile, in order to minimise the impact of travel speed which varies according to differences between cities in layout, density and traffic conditions—factors beyond the control of transit operators. Average speed of a bus system is also affected by routing decisions. For example, a system would appear to have lower costs per mile simply as a result of expanding express suburban service and curtailing local inner-city service. Using cost per hour alleviates these two problems. Vehicle hour statistics could not be obtained at the nationwide, aggregate level, but they were available for the individual systems included in the disaggregate econometric analysis which follows.

A number of factors were hypothesised to influence bus operating costs. These included the size and age of the bus fleet, the base hourly wage rate of bus drivers, transit worker productivity, type of management, and key aspects of the transit subsidy programme. In particular, it was expected that costs would be affected by the level of Federal operating subsidy, the level of state operating subsidy, and the proportion of state and local operating subsidies that was derived from taxes dedicated exclusively for transit. In addition, a dummy variable for the sample year was included to capture the effects of inflation and other cost increases from 1979 to 1980 that could not be explained by changes in the eight explanatory variables. The model was formally specified as follows:

$$COSTPH = f\,(FLTAGE,\ FLTSIZE,\ WAGE,\ PRODUCT,\ MANAGE,\\ FEDSUB,\ STSUB,\ DEDSUB,\ YEAR).$$

Definitions and descriptive statistics for each of the variables are contained in Table 5.

The relationships between bus operating costs and several of the explanatory variables are rather obvious. A transit system using old vehicles will probably experience more equipment failure and require greater maintenance expenditures than systems with new buses. Higher worker productivity—as measured by hours of bus service per employee—will lead to lower per-hour operating costs.[1] In contrast, higher hourly wage rates for bus drivers clearly lead to higher operating costs.[2]

The other variables require more consideration. The relation between unit costs and fleet size—an indicator of scale economies or diseconomies—is somewhat controversial. Most previous econometric studies, however, find either constant or slightly increasing unit costs as size system increases (Lee and Steedman, 1970; Wabe and Coles, 1975; Nelson, 1972; Miller, 1970). In the present study, informal examination of the data led to an expectation of diseconomies of scale, and thus a positive relation

---

[1] Bus hours of service per employee reflect the combined effects of worker performance, management effectiveness, and the quality of the capital stock.

[2] The hourly wage of bus drivers is not the only factor affecting a system's labour expenses. Fringe benefits, overtime arrangements, use of part-time workers, and non-driver wages are also important. Unfortunately, reliable data on these other factors were unavailable.

TABLE 5

Variable Definitions, Means, and Standard Deviations

riable Name	Definition	Mean	Standard Deviation
)STPH	Operating costs (nets of depreciation and taxes) per bus hour of service ($)	25.94	7.83
,TAGE	Average age of buses in fleet (years)	8.72	3.18
,TSIZE	Number of buses in fleet (natural logorithm)	4.89	1.30
AGE	Base hourly wage of bus drivers ($)	7.46	1.34
RODUCT	Bus hours of service per full-time equivalent transit employee (000)	1.06	0.22
EDSUB	Federal operating subsidies per bus hour of service ($)	6.19	2.34
TSUB	State operating subsidies per bus hour of service ($)	2.84	3.69
EDSUB	Dummy variable for dedicated state and local transit taxes (-1 if earmarked taxes accounted for 50% or more of state and local subsidies, 0 otherwise)	0.37	0.48
ARNINGS	Average monthly earnings of public employees in each metropolitan area ($)	1190.63	245.83
MODESPLT	Percentage of work trips in each urban area made by mass transit	6.05	6.02
PEAKING	Ratio of peak-hour buses in service to off-peak, mid-day buses in service	1.92	0.65
MANAGE	Dummy variable for private contract management ($= 1$ if private management, 0 otherwise	0.44	0.50
RESWAGE	Adjusted transit wage variable (residuals from the regression of wage on *FEDSUB, STSUB, DEDSUB, MANAGE, FLTAGE*, and *FLTSIZE*)	0.00	0.80
RESPRODUCT	Adjusted productivity variable (residuals from the regression of *PRODUCT* on *FEDSUB, STSUB, DEDSUB, MANAGE, FLTAGE*, and *FLTSIZE*)	0.00	0.20
YEAR	Dummy variable for year of observation ($=1$ if 1980, 0 if 1979)	0.64	0.48

between cost per bus-hour and number of vehicles. The form of the relation was four to be non-linear, with the rate of increase in unit costs declining as fleet size increase Consequently, the variable for fleet size was logarithmically transformed.

Of greatest interest in the model are the management and subsidy variables. It wa hypothesised that privately managed systems would be more efficiency-oriented tha publicly managed systems, and that private management facilitates lower cost Federal subsidy per hour and state subsidy per hour were included to capture the co: impacts of subsidies from higher levels of government. Both were expected t encourage higher costs, but differently. The Federal operating subsidy programme i structured as a matching grant, requiring a dollar of state or local subsidy for ever dollar of Federal subsidy, up to a specified maximum total Federal contribution that i different for each metropolitan area. State transit subsidies do not usually enta explicit matching provisions; they therefore represent simple lump-sum grants. Publi finance economists have long argued that matching grants from higher levels o government stimulate local government spending to a greater degree than non matching grants (Wilde, 1968; Oates, 1972; Gramlich and Galper, 1973). Becaus matching grants reduce the relative cost of the subsidised item, subsidy programme of this type have positive income and price effects on local government spending Empirical research in this area clearly demonstrates that matching grants lead to greater public expenditures than lump-sum grants (Inman, 1979).

Federal operating subsidies also differ from state subsidies because the maximun amount received by each area is determined by a formula based on population and population density, not according to a transit-related measure such as ridership, vehicl hours of service, or passenger revenues. So most low-density cities with little transi service receive the full 50% Federal match. In contrast, denser, transit-oriented urban areas receive a smaller proportion of their funding from Federal subsidies, because their total subsidy requirements are more than double the maximum Federal subsidy determined under the formula for their urban areas. Systems with high proportions of Federal aid are more likely to initiate costly and unprofitable services, because less of the cost is borne locally. Moreover, in spite of its statutory matching requirement, the Federal subsidy is likely to have the effect of a lump-sum grant for large systems in transit-oriented cities that have reached their Federal subsidy limit. At the margin, additional state and local subsidies attract no additional Federal subsidy for these systems. Thus the Federal subsidy probably acts as a matching grant only for systems in lower-density cities. Both by its matching effect and because of its higher proportion of the total subsidy, Federal subsidy encourages more cost escalation in lower-density cities.

Finally, local transit officials may be more politically accountable to state officials than to Federal officials for the way in which subsidies are spent. Local ta:payers share more directly and to a greater extent in the burden of state taxes channelled to transit subsidies; the link is much weaker for Federal taxes.

Each of these considerations suggests that Federal subsidies have a worse effect on transit costs than state subsidies. The Federal and state subsidy variables were included in the model to test this.

The third subsidy variable was the proportion of state and local subsidy funds derived from taxes dedicated for transit. This was included to test the notion, argued earlier, that they have reduced the incentive for cost control and improvement in oductivity by local transit authorities. Because most of the sampled transit systems d dedicated either very high or very low proportions of their state and local funding, is variable was specified as a 0–1 dummy variable, denoting systems above and low the 50% level.

The relationships between costs and subsidies described by the formal model stract from the complexities of transit finance and management. Many political and stitutional factors affect costs—and the degree to which costs are subsidised—but ey could not be incorporated. For example, a transit system's cost and subsidy levels e obviously affected by its organisational structure and the quality and motivation of s personnel; by the physical layout and climate of the city; by the fiscal capacity of e city and its propensity for public expenditures; and by the relative priorities given numerous alternative objectives for transit. Cost and subsidy levels are also affected y the degree of political opposition to either higher fares or increased taxes for bsidies, and by the social and economic consequences of strikes. Barnum and leason (1979) argue that wages will be higher where union strength is great, and here the political costs of higher transit fares exceed the political costs of higher taxes r subsidies. They were unable (as we are) to test this theory, because it is difficult to nd quantifiable proxies for these explanatory varables.

A less abstract but more complex depiction of the relationship between subsidy and ost would also reflect the joint determination of service levels, fares, subsidies and osts. It might be argued, for example, that higher unit costs result in larger operating eficits and thus create the need for more subsidies. Increased costs and deficits may lso motivate local and state officials to set aside earmarked revenue sourc for ransit. Higher costs, therefore, may be the cause as well as the result of i .eased ubsidies.

Again, subsidies probably affect costs indirectly through their impact on fares and services. It was noted earlier, for instance, that Federal matching formulas may cause higher costs by encouraging more expensive types of service. The indirect cost impact of subsidies through fares may take several forms. Higher subsidies make lower average fares possible. Concern of transit patrons for higher costs is almost certainly less than it would be if they were forced to pay a high proportion of cost increases through higher fares. Though taxpayers must bear the burden of those costs not borne by riders, political opposition to higher taxes may be less than to higher fares. The tax burden from financing subsidies is both more dispersed and less visible. Transit taxes for example, are often hidden within general-purpose tax structures. Moreover, Federal operating subsidies enable each urban area to shift elsewhere much of the tax burden of subsidising low fares.

In addition, the increasing availability of subsidies during the 1970s resulted in fare *structures* that exacerbated the cost problems of transit (Kirby, 1982; Wachs, 1981). Subsidies have permitted transit authorities to maintain or reinstate politically popular but inefficient flat fares instead of peak/off-peak and distance-based fares. This has encouraged riders to use transit at times of the day and over distances which have the highest marginal costs per trip.

It was impossible to estimate a comprehensive, multi-equation model incorporating all these interrelationships and institutional factors. Data limitations and insuperable statistical problems dictated the narrower, more focused approach described earlier. Despite this, the model produced interesting and useful empirical results.

TABLE 6

Multiple Regression of Operating Cost per Bus Hour

Dependent Variable	Independent Variable	Coefficient	t-statistic	Significance Level
COSTPH				
	PRODUCT	−15.065	−11.29	0.0001
	WAGE	1.896	5.78	0.0001
	FLTAGE	0.045	0.54	0.5890
	FLTSIZE	1.477	4.55	0.0001
	FEDSUB	0.293	2.39	0.0179
	STSUB	0.125	1.59	0.1131
	DEDSUB	1.483	2.45	0.0153
	MANAGE	−0.822	−1.47	0.1418
	YEAR	2.421	4.26	0.0001
	INTERCEPT	16.254	6.11	0.0001

Overall equation statistics:
$R^2 = 0.77$ F-statistic = 76.57   Std. Dev. = 3.81 $n = 212$

Regression results

The first version of the estimated equation for per-hour operating costs is reported in Table 6. As expected, the coefficient for fleet size is positive and statistically significant, indicating diseconomies of scale. The coefficient for fleet age is also positive, but it is small and statistically insignificant. This unexpectedly weak effect of fleet age is probably attributable to the recent introduction of the new, so-called "advanced-design", buses, which have experienced frequent breakdowns, high maintenance costs, and dramatic reductions in energy efficiency. The increase in costs from these new buses apparently offsets the hypothesised positive relation between fleet age and operating costs.

The estimated effect of transit wage rates on costs is positive and significant, whereas the impact of worker productivity is negative and significant. For every additional dollar in the base hourly wage of bus drivers, overall per-hour costs were $1.90 higher. This large coefficient reflects not only the direct effect of the base hourly wage on regular wage payments to drivers, but also the indirect effects of this key wage rate on overtime payments, premium payments (for split shifts and night work), and fringe benefits for drivers—as well as wage and salary payments to transit personnel other than drivers. The estimated effect of worker productivity was also in the expected direction: for every 10% decrease in worker productivity, per-hour costs were 6% higher.

Of greatest interest for this analysis, however, are the estimates for the management and subsidy variables. The coefficient for management—which is only significant at the 0.14 level—indicates that private management is associated with per-hour costs that are 82¢ lower. The coefficient for the dedicated subsidy variable is statistically

gnificant at the 0.02 level, and indicates that systems with more than half their state
ad local funding dedicated had costs that were $1.48 higher than systems with little
 no dedicated funding. The regression reported in Table 6 also provides evidence of
e particularly large increase in cost from Federal operating subsidies. Not only is the
ederal subsidy coefficient statistically more significant than the state subsidy
oefficient (0.02 against 0.11), but Federal subsidy is also estimated to have a greater
apact on per-hour costs (29¢ against 13¢).

The results support the hypothesis that Federal subsidies and dedicated state and
cal subsidies are cost-inflationary. Moreover, distortions arising from the original
odel specification were suspected of masking the full impacts of subsidies on costs.
ubsequent refinements in the model specifications dramatically improved the
erformance of these, as well as of several other explanatory variables.

In particular, one obvious problem with the equation as specified in Table 6 is the
kely multicollinearity between the wage and productivity variables and each of the
emaining explanatory variables.[3] Indeed, it might be expected that subsidies affect
osts *through* their impacts on transit wages and worker productivity, presumably by
ncouraging higher wages and lower productivity. Likewise, private management, fleet
ize, and fleet age may affect costs through their impacts on wages and/or
roductivity. The presence of all eight of these variables in the same equation may
esult in the wage and productivity variables siphoning off some of the effects on unit
osts of the other explanatory variables, thereby causing excessive standard errors for
hese variables and *t*-statistics that are too small.

To examine these effects, separate structural equations were estimated for wage
ates and worker productivity. In both equations the Federal, state, and dedicated
ubsidy variables are included as explanatory variables. Additional variables which
vere thought to influence hourly transit wages, and thus were included in that
egression equation, were the average monthly earnings for public employees in each
netropolitan area and the transit modal split for work trips in each area. Both
ariables were expected to have a positive influence on wage levels. Higher transit
nodal splits were assumed to increase the local bargaining power of transit unions.
verage earnings of public employees were viewed as a benchmark against which
ransit workers in each area gauged the fairness of their own wages. As is shown by
he regression results reported in Table 7, both modal split and earnings of public
mployees do indeed have highly significant impacts on transit wages. It is more
germane to the present discussion, however, that all three subsidy variables also have
oositive effects on wage rates. Of these three, the dedicated and state subsidy variables
nave the most statistically significant coefficients (at the 0.001 and 0.002 levels,

---

[3] Some multicollinearity *among* the three subsidy variables might also have been expected. For
xample, large Federal subsidies may evoke large state subsidies, because state subsidies can be used
ogether with local subsidies to match Federal funds. Alternatively, it may be that Federal subsidies are
nstead substituted for state subsidies—a countervailing, inverse relation which would offset positive
correlation. Multicollinearity between tax earmarking and the other two subsidy variables was also
suspected, because state and local tax earmarking may encourage higher absolute levels of state and
local subsidies. Yet the estimated correlation coefficients among the three subsidy variables were quite
low, suggesting that the multicollinearity was not serious. The correlation values were as follows: +0.04
between *DEDSUB* and *STSUB;* +0.11 between *DEDSUB* and *FEDSUB;* and +0.21 between *STSUB*
and *FEDSUB.*

TABLE 7

Multiple Regression of Transit Hourly Wage Rate

Dependent Variable	Independent Variable	Coefficient	t-statistic	Significance Level
WAGE				
	EARNINGS	0.002	7.36	0.0001
	MODESPLT	0.089	7.54	0.0001
	FEDSUB	0.060	1.92	0.0566
	STSUB	0.060	3.13	0.0020
	DEDSUB	0.524	3.51	0.0006
	YEAR	−0.225	−1.50	0.1348
	INTERCEPT	3.494	8.96	0.0001

Overall equation statistics:
$R^2 = 0.52$ F-statistic $= 36.86$ Std. Dev. $= 0.95$ $n = 212$

respectively), whereas the Federal subsidy variable is only significant at the 0.06
level. Nevertheless, the Federal coefficient is as large as the state coefficient (both 6¢
per hour).

The regression equation for the worker productivity variable is presented in Table 8.
In addition to the three subsidy variables, the equation covers type of management,
degree of service peaking, fleet size and fleet age. Private management probably
enhances productivity, whereas sharp differences in supply of service between time
periods almost certainly detract from worker productivity by leaving much of the
labour force idle during off-peak periods. It was also expected that fleet size and fleet
age might affect productivity, though in the case of fleet age it was not clear what the
direction of the net effect would be.

Table 8 shows that the private management and peaking variables have the
expected effects on productivity, and both variables are statistically significant (at the
0.01 and 0.001 levels, respectively). The Federal and state subsidy variables both have
the expected adverse impact on productivity, but Federal subsidy has three times as
much impact and is also much more statistically significant (at the 0.01 level vs. the
0.23 level). The dedicated subsidy variable is estimated to have an unexpected positive
effect on productivity. The coefficient has virtually no statistical significance, however,
and it is so small that the degree of impact is negligible.

The fleet size variable was estimated to have a significantly adverse effect on
productivity, as might be expected if bus operations are subject to diseconomies of
scale. The fleet age variable has a positive coefficient, but it is very small and
statistically insignificant. As in the aggregate cost equation, this result probably arises
from the confounding effects of the advanced-design buses.

Overall, the equations in Tables 7 and 8 indicate that both wage rates and worker
productivity are indeed significantly a function of the subsidy variables. Thus, it is
quite likely that if the direct effect of subsidies on costs were combined with their
indirect effects on costs—through the wage rate and productivity variables—the total

TABLE 8

Multiple Regression of Bus Hours of Service per Employee

Dependent Variable	Independent Variable	Coefficient	t-statistic	Significance Level
PRODUCT				
	MANAGE	0.072	2.51	0.0129
	PEAKING	−0.075	−3.33	0.0010
	FEDSUB	−0.015	−2.50	0.0131
	STSUB	−0.005	−1.21	0.2261
	DEDSUB	0.006	0.19	0.8461
	FLTSIZE	−0.043	−3.65	0.0003
	FLTAGE	0.001	0.32	0.7469
	YEAR	−0.001	−0.03	0.9768
	INTERCEPT	1.480	17.88	0.0001

Overall equation statistics:
$R^2 = 0.22$ F-statistic $= 7.14$ Std. Dev. $= 0.20$ $n = 212$

effect would be considerably greater than is shown in Table 6. Moreover, because wage rates and productivity are also affected by type of management and fleet size, the total impact of each of these two variables on costs would also be greater than their direct effects.

In an attempt to capture these total effects, the overall cost equation was re-estimated with modified versions of the wage and productivity variables. In particular, the estimated impacts of subsidies, management, fleet size, and fleet age were removed from the wage and productivity variables so that their transformations would include only that portion of the variation in wage rates and productivity that was *not* explained by variation in the other six explanatory variables. The procedure involved separately regressing wage rates and productivity on the six other variables, and using the residuals from these regressions as instrumental variables for wage rates and productivity in the overall cost equation (*RESWAGE* and *RESPRODUCT*, respectively). By construction, these instrumental variables are uncorrelated with the other six explanatory variables.

The results of the re-estimated cost equation are given in Table 9. With multicollinearity removed through the procedure described above, the impacts of subsidies, private mangement, and fleet size emerge dramatically. The estimated coefficients for these variables are not only much larger, but are much more statistically significant as well. A dollar of Federal subsidy is associated with hourly costs that are 62¢ higher, whereas a dollar of state subsidy is associated with costs that are 34¢ higher. Thus, state subsidies are still estimated to be only about half as cost-inflationary as Federal subsidies. Moreover, systems with more than half their state and local subsidies earmarked for transit had costs that were $2.38 per hour higher—when we controlled other factors affecting costs.

TABLE 9

Multiple Regression of Operating Costs per Bus Hour

Dependent Variable	Independent Variable	Coefficient	t-statistic	Significance Level
COSTPH				
	RESPRODUCT	−15.065	−11.29	0.0001
	RESWAGE	1.896	5.78	0.0001
	FLTAGE	0.062	0.74	0.4575
	FLTSIZE	3.675	17.06	0.0001
	FEDSUB	0.619	5.16	0.0001
	STSUB	0.338	4.55	0.0001
	DEDSUB	2.377	4.08	0.0001
	MANAGE	−1.722	−3.12	0.0021
	YEAR	3.068	5.50	0.0001
	INTERCEPT	0.553	0.35	0.7270

Overall equation statistics:
$R^2 = 0.77$ F-statistic = 76.57   Std. Dev. = 3.81 $n = 212$

The estimated effect of management also increases; after multicollinearity has been removed, private management is associated with costs per hour that are $1.72 less than for publicly managed systems. An increase in the estimated effect of fleet size suggests significantly larger diseconomies of scale than were evident from Table 6. The coefficient indicates, for example, that as fleet size increases from 100 to 500, hourly costs increase by 23% (other things being equal). Finally, the coefficient for fleet age increases slightly from its value in Table 6, but it remains statistically insignificant.

As a final refinement of the analysis, the same model was estimated separately for two subsets of the sample—those systems receiving the maximum 50% of their operating subsidy from the Federal government, and those receiving less than 50%.[4] The purpose of this disaggregation was to test the hypothesis that a dollar of Federal subsidy has a more cost-inflationary impact in low-density, auto-oriented areas, where the Federal subsidy covers a higher percentage of that deficit and has the full stimulative effect of a matching grant—in contrast to transit-oriented areas, where the Federal subsidy covers a lower percentage of the deficit and has the less stimulative effect of a lump-sum grant. Table 10 shows that the disaggregate regression results support this hypothesis. The Federal subsidy coefficient for the high-match sample is more than twice as large as for the low-match sample, and the high-match coefficient is more statistically significant. A dollar of Federal subsidy is associated with costs

---

[4] Because of the peculiar timing of Federal grants to each area and the idiosyncratic accounting procedures used by each transit system to apportion subsidies over time, some systems receiving the maximum Federal match reported slightly less than a 50% Federal match. Thus, in disaggregating the sample, 45% was used as the cutoff point instead of 50%

Table 10

Multiple Regressions of Per-Hour Operating Costs for Two Subsamples of Bus Systems

Equation A: Systems With Full Federal Match

Dependent Variable	Independent Variable	Coefficient	t-statistic	Significance Level
COSTPH				
	RESPRODUCT	−8.084	−7.90	0.0001
	RESWAGE	0.998	4.15	0.0001
	FLTAGE	0.078	1.48	0.1408
	FLTSIZE	2.081	10.88	0.0001
	FEDSUB	1.707	15.21	0.0001
	STSUB	0.040	0.53	0.5991
	DEDSUB	−0.652	−1.51	0.1341
	MANAGE	−0.414	−1.14	0.2559
	YEAR	1.258	3.32	0.0012
	INTERCEPT	0.678	0.57	0.5690

Overall equation statistics:
$R^2 = 0.83$ F-statistic = 66.31   Std. Dev. = 1.99 $n = 128$

Equation B: Systems With Less Than Full Federal Match

Dependent Variable	Independent Variables	Coefficient	t-statistic	Significance Level
COSTPH				
	RESPRODUCT	−18.913	−6.51	0.0001
	RESWAGE	2.682	4.12	0.0001
	FLTAGE	0.054	0.29	0.7751
	FLTSIZE	3.782	10.80	0.0001
	FEDSUB	0.653	2.96	0.0041
	STSUB	0.179	1.58	0.1194
	DEDSUB	2.594	2.33	0.0227
	MANAGE	−2.152	−1.85	0.0687
	YEAR	3.929	3.54	0.0007
	INTERCEPT	1.851	0.63	0.5313

Overall equation statistics:
$R^2 = 0.78$ F-statistic = 28.56   Std. Dev. = 4.67 $n = 84$

that are $1.71 higher in the high-match sample, but only 65¢ higher in the low-match sample. Clearly, aggregation of both groups of systems into the same sample conceals much of the differential impact of Federal and state subsidies. Indeed, the two disaggregate Federal subsidy coefficients in Table 10 are both larger than the aggregate Federal coefficient in Table 9. Conversely, the two disaggregate state subsidy coefficients are both smaller than the aggregate state coefficient.

The values of other variable coefficients in the model also vary somewhat between the two subsamples. Diseconomies of scale, for example, appear to be more pronounced in the low-match sample, which contains most of the largest transit systems. In addition, private management is estimated to have a more beneficial impact on costs in the low-match sample. A more surprising result is the opposite signs of the dedicated subsidy coefficient in the two equations. The expected positive effect on costs is found for the low-match subsample, but the dedicated coefficient actually negative for the high-match subsample, though it is not statistically significant. It is difficult to explain this result. It seems unlikely that tax earmarking has the estimated beneficial impact. Moreover, examination of the correlation matrix suggested that the anomalous result may have been produced by collinearity between the management and dedicated subsidy variables.

The main purpose of the disaggregation was to test the differential effects of Federal subsidies in high-match and in low-match cities. The results conform well to expectations. They also highlight the extraordinarily adverse cost impact of Federal subsidies overall. Even in the low-match sample, cost escalation associated with Federal subsidy dissipates about two-thirds of that subsidy. In high-match cities Federal subsidy is associated with cost increases so large that they fully consume not only the Federal subsidy itself, but 70% *more* than the Federal subsidy.

One final note on the regression results: pooling of the 1979 and 1980 datasets assumes that the same structural equation is appropriate for both years, and that the coefficients for the explanatory variables are approximately the same. To test the validity of pooling the data, separate sets of equations were estimated for each year. With the exception of the intercept term, which of course was different, the variable coefficients were virtually the same for the separate 1979 and 1980 regressions.

Limitations

As with any regression analysis, the results reported here must be interpreted with caution. It was noted earlier, for example, that costs and subsidies are jointly determined, as higher costs elicit more subsidies, which in turn induce higher costs. However, the multi-national time-series study by Bly, Webster and Pounds (1980) experimented with a number of different time-lag structures in their regressions and found that cost increases tended to *follow* subsidy increases, thus supporting the main hypothesis being examined here. Nevertheless, it seems likely that the reverse effect of costs on subsidies also occurs at least to some extent. Indeed, as suggested earlier, costs, subsidies, service levels and fares are all somewhat interdependent. The endogeneity of the subsidy and cost variables, in particular, may result in some positive simultaneous-equations bias to the subsidy coefficients (arising from the correlation of the subsidy variable with the error term in the cost equation).

To deal with these interrelationships, a two-stage least squares simultaneous equations model was attempted. Six separate but interdependent equations were timated for service levels, costs, fares and subsidies (Federal, state, and percentage dicated). Because of data limitations, however, no satisfactory instrumental riables could be estimated in the first stage that would permit statistically eaningful results in the second stage of the procedure.[5]

Another potential statistical problem was error in specification. For example, a mber of non-quantifiable political and institutional factors, such as union power, uld not be incorporated in the regression model. Assuming that costs varied directly th transit union strength and that union strength and subsidy levels were also sitively correlated, the estimated subsidy coefficient would be upwardly biased. owever, the presence of both worker productivity and wage variables in the gression model mitigates this problem. Much of the impact of transit unions on costs through their ability to influence wage rates and work rules governing productivity. onsequently, these two variables already capture a large part of the effect of labour nions on costs. The only direct cost impacts of labour unions not controlled for in the odel would be those arising from their ability to increase fringe benefits and premium ayments for overtime, night work, and split shifts. Thus the bias due to the omission f a union power variable is probably unimportant.

The several potential sources of statistical error do not appear to be so serious as to verturn the main finding. After controlling for other important variables affecting osts, we find that subsidies are very significantly correlated with higher costs per unit. his does not prove that subsidies cause higher costs, but it is certainly consistent with at hypothesis.

SUMMARY AND POLICY IMPLICATIONS

he preceding analysis suggests that transit subsidies have probably exacerbated 1creases in costs. During periods when subsidies have increased most, productivity as declined and costs have grown most rapidly. Moreover, when cost differences etween bus systems were examined by multiple regression, it was found that costs vere much higher for those systems that relied on large Federal and state subsidies nd dedicated state and local transit taxes.

These results suggest that transit operations should be monitored more carefully nd that subsidies should be related explicitly to output. Because most transit subsidy rogrammes in the United States simply cover costs—whatever they happen to e—without regard to any index of achievement of goals, there is not much incentive o use subsidies efficiently. Shifting the subsidy burden to the Federal government and armarking state and local taxes for transit have compounded the problem. Federal and tate subsidy programmes fail to reward efficient systems and penalise inefficient ones. nstead, distribution formulas—especially at the Federal level—arise from political

---

[5] As usual with two-stage least squares, the first stage required regressing each of the endogenous ariables in the model on all the exogenous variables in the six-equation system. These regressions roduce instrumental variables, which are substituted for the endogenous variables in the second stage of the procedure. Unfortunately, these estimated instrumental variables were very poorly correlated with their respective endogenous variables, and thus were inadequate substitutes.

bargains and have little relationship either to the transport needs of individual urb areas or to the performance of individual systems.

To survive, the transit subsidy programme must be improved. There are sever ways to improve it. One approach would be to alter Federal and state subsi formulas to reward those systems that raise productivity, attract new riders, enhance the quality of their service. This would tie the level of subsidy directly to t level of output, and, at the very least, would discourage unwarranted cost escalatio A limited version of this approach was implemented in Pennsylvania in 1978 (Mill 1980). Approximately a tenth of the state's operating subsidy is now set aside for bonus fund used to reward transit systems that achieve relatively slow growth in cos increased ridership and fare revenue per hour of service, and some state-determin standard for the revenue/expense ratio. The more criteria are satisfied, the larger is t subsidy bonus.

Another strategy would be to equalise Federal matching rates for the capital ar operating subsidy programmes to eliminate the present bias toward capital investmer This uniform rate might be set low to increase the proportion of costs directly releva to state and local decision makers. In addition, both subsidy programmes could k made open-ended to equalise the Federal proportion of the local transit subsidy in a metropolitan areas. The Federal government could then adjust the single matchir rate to reflect the total amount of the Federal transit budget in any given year. The proposed changes would certainly simplify the current programme, with its range c matching rates, complicated allocation formulas, and politically motivated distortion In combination, the modifications would in effect create a Federal transit block gran A subsidy system along these lines was recently endorsed by the Committee o Transportation and Public Works of the U.S. House of Representatives (1982), bt was not adopted by the Congress as a whole.

Transit subsidies will probably diminish, or grow much less rapidly, than in recer years. Failure to improve productivity will almost certainly lead to service cutback fare increases and ridership losses. Changes in the transit programme such as thos discussed above would help to alleviate the impact of retrenchment. Whether thes changes take the form of deregulation and reorganisation of the industry, or simply o a restructuring of the subsidy programme, the room for improvement is vas Adaptation to curtailed subsidy may be difficult, but it probably represents a uniqu opportunity to implement a more rational and more effective urban transport policy.

REFERENCES

Altshuler, A., J. Womack and J. Pucher (1981): *The Urban Transportation System: Politics and Polic Innovation.* M.I.T. Press, Cambridge, Mass.

American Public Transit Association (1980): *Transit Operating and Financial Reports.* Washington D.C.

American Public Transit Association (1981a): *Transit Fact Book.* Washington, D.C.

American Public Transit Association (1981b): *Transit Operating and Financial Reports.* Washington D.C.

Barnum, D., and J. Gleason (1979): *Measurung the Influence of Subsidies on Transit Efficiency an Effectiveness.* U.S. Department of Transportation, Urban Mass Transportation Administration Washington, D.C.

Bly, P. H., F. V. Webster and S. Pounds (1980): "Effects of Subsidies on Urban Public Transport" *Transportation,* Vol. 9, no. 4, pp. 311–331.

∎nnell, J. (1981): "Transit's Growing Fiscal Crisis". *Traffic Quarterly*, Vol. 35, no. 4, October, pp. 541–556.

∶ecutive Office of the President, Office of Management and Budget (1981): *Fiscal Year 1982 Budget Revisions: Additional Details on Budget Savings*. U.S. Government Printing Office, Washington, D.C., pp. 282–285.

∍rtmaker, L. (1981): *Transit Financing and the Cities*. U.S. Conference of Mayors, Washington, D.C.

⌐amlich, E., and H. Galper (1973): "State and Local Fiscal Behavior and Federal Grant Policy". In: *Brookings Papers on Economic Activity*. The Brookings Institution, Washington, D.C., pp. 15–58.

▪amer, A. (1976): *The Selling of Rail Rapid Transit*. Lexington-Heath Books, Lexington, MA.

▪lton, G. W. (1974): *Federal Transit Subsidies*. American Enterprise Institute, Washington, D.C.

man, R. (1979): "The Fiscal Performance of Local Government: An Interpretive Review". In: P. Mieszkowski and M. Straszheim (eds.): *Current Issues in Urban Economics*. Johns Hopkins University Press, Baltimore, MD., pp. 270–321.

irby, R. (1982): "Pricing Strategies for Public Transportation". *Journal of the American Planning Association*, Vol. 48, no. 3, summer, pp. 327–334.

∍e, N., and I. Steedman (1970): "Economies of Scale in Bus Transport". *Journal of Transport Economics and Policy*, Vol. 4, no. 1, pp. 15–28.

▪etropolitan Atlanta Rapid Transit Authority (1981): *Long-Range Capital Improvement Plan*. Atlanta, GA.

▪etropolitan Transportation Commission (1980): *BART in the San Francisco Bay Area: The Final Report of the BART Impact Program*. Berkeley, CA.

▪eyer, J., and J. Gomez-Ibanez (1981): *Autos, Transit, and Cities*. Harvard University Press, Cambridge, MA.

▪eyer, J., J. Kain and M. Wohl (1965): *The Urban Transportation Problem*. Harvard University Press, Cambridge, MA.

▪iller, D. (1970): "Differences among Cities, Differences among Firms, and Costs of Urban Bus Transport". *Journal of Industrial Economics*, Vol. 19, November, pp. 22–32.

▪iller, J. (1980): "The Use of Performance-Based Methodologies for the Allocation of Transit Operating Funds". *Traffic Quarterly*, Vol. 34, no. 4, October, pp. 555–574.

▪ohring, H. (1972): "Optimisation and Scale Economies in Urban Bus Transportation". *American Economic Review*, Vol. 60, September, pp. 591–604.

▪elson, G. (1972): *An Economic Model of Urban Bus Operations*. Institute for Defense Analyses, Washington, D.C.

)ates, W. (1972): *Fiscal Federalism*. Harcourt-Brace, New York.

▪ucher, J. (1980): "Transit Financing Trends in Large U.S. Metropolitan Areas". *Transportation Research Record*, no. 759, pp. 6–12.

▪ucher, J. (1982): "A Decade of Change for Mass Transit". *Transportation Research Record*, no. 858, November, pp. 48–57

J.S. General Accounting Office (1979): *Analysis of the Allocation Formula for Federal Mass Transit Subsidies*. Washington, D.C.

∪.S. General Accounting Office (1981): *Soaring Transit Subsidies Must be Controlled*. Washington, D.C.

∪.S. House of Representatives (1981a): *Metrorail Impacts on Washington Area Land Values*. Committee on Banking, Finance, and Urban Affairs, Washington, D.C.

∪.S. House of Representatives (1981b): *The Financial and Productivity Problems of Urban Public Transportation*. Committee on Transportation and Public Works, Washington, D.C.

▪.S. House of Representatives (1982): *The State of Public Transportation in the Nation and a Recommended New Block Grant Concept*. Committee on Transportation and Public Works, Washington, D.C.

▪Urban Mass Transportation Administration, Office of Policy Analysis (1976): *Transit Operating Performance and the Impact of the Section 5 Program*. U.S. Department of Transportation, Washington, D.C.

▪Urban Mass Transportation Administration, Office of Transit Assistance (1981a): *Capital Grants by Program, Urban Area, and Mode*. U.S. Department of Transportation, Washington, D.C.

Urban Mass Transportation Administration, Office of Transportation Management (1981b). *National Urban Mass Transportation Statistics*. U.S. Department of Transportation, Washington, D.C.; and the accompanying, much more detailed, computer tape.

Urban Mass Transportation Administration, Office of Technical Assistance (1982a): *National Url* *Mass Transportation Statistics*. U.S. Department of Transportation, Washington, D.C.; and accompanying, much more detailed, computer tape.

Urban Mass Transportation Administration, Office of Transit Assistance (1982b): *Summary of Trai Vehicle Costs*. U.S. Department of Transportation, Washington, D.C.

Wabe, J. S., and O. B. Coles (1975): "The Short and Long-Run Costs of Bus Transport in Urb Areas". *Journal of Transport Economics and Policy*, Vol. 9, no. 2, May, pp. 127–140.

Wachs, M. (1981): "Pricing Urban Transportation: A Critique of Current Policy". *Journal American Planning Association*, Vol. 47, no 3, pp. 243–251.

Webber, M. (1976): "The BART Experience: What have we Learned?" *The Public Interest*, Vol. fall, pp. 79–108.

Wilde, J. (1968): "The Expenditure Effects of Grants-in-Aid Programs". *National Tax Journal*, V 21, no. 3, pp. 340–348.

26

he Efficacy and Cost-Effectiveness of Vehicle Inspection
A State Specific Analysis Using Time Series Data

Peter D. Loeb and Benjamin Gilad*

I. INTRODUCTION

ost states in the United States have employed at one time or another a system f inspection of motor vehicles. The procedures used in inspections have varied om state to state as well as over time. However, almost since their inception, ere have been serious charges levelled against the efficacy and/or cost-ffectiveness of inspections in reducing fatalities, injuries and accidents.

Numerous studies have been conducted to evaluate motor vehicle inspection. hese studies, however, have mostly been plagued with statistical or method-logical problems which have made their conclusions far from definitive.

Only relatively recently has regression analysis been used, and then only on ne basis of cross-sectional data. Thus there have so far been no state-specific tudies which have used econometric techniques to test the efficacy of inspection.

The present study employs, for the first time, a time series analysis of the fficacy of inspection in reducing fatalities, injuries and accidents, using New ersey data. An econometric model is developed to evaluate inspection while ccounting for various socio-economic factors, as well as technology and driving-elated variables. The results of the econometric study are then used to evaluate partial benefit/cost analysis of the system of motor vehicle inspection.

Section II provides a short review of the literature in the area. Section III evelops an econometric model to evaluate motor vehicle inspection in New ersey, and Section IV presents a benefit/cost analysis of the system. Section V rovides a summary and some concluding comments.

*Rutgers University, New Brunswick, N. J. The authors are indebted to Barry Jackson and Karen Frank for comments and suggestions to an earlier draft. Karen Frank initiated an earlier eview of the literature. Thanks are due also to members of the New Jersey Division of Motor Vehicles who helped with data collection, to M. Dutta for comments, and to Diane Kurkewicz or research assistance, to Arnold Allentuch for continuous support of the project, and to Mary Armour and Edna Shepherd for secretarial assistance. A note of indebtedness is also due the ditor and an anonymous referee. This paper is based on the research results of a study commissioned by the State of New Jersey, Department of Law and Public Safety, Division of Motor Vehicles, under a grant provided to the New Jersey Institute of Technology.

II. VEHICLE INSPECTION AND HIGHWAY SAFETY – A REVIEW

Previous studies of vehicle inspection and highway safety can be divided in three categories: cross-sectional studies, experimental studies, and time ser studies. A review of these studies is presented below.

The cross-sectional studies reviewed (Mayer and Hoult (1963), Buxbau and Colton (1966), Fuchs and Leveson (1967) and Crain (1980)) made co parisons between states; they differed in the variables included and in t statistical techniques employed. The earliest study, by Mayer and Hoult, group states into four categories of inspection, ranging from mandatory state inspecti to no inspection, and compared death rates for each of these categories ove 12-year period from 1949 to 1958. The study found an inverse relation betwe accident death rates and the comprehensiveness of the inspection system. T Buxbaum and Colton study, using 1960 data with a slightly different definiti of the death rate and the inspection variables, found similar results. Buxbaum a Colton also included several additional variables not used by Mayer and Hou such as population, gasoline consumption per vehicle, number of vehicles, e After variable-by-variable comparisons, they still found lower accident rates f states with an inspection programme than for states without one.

The two other studies in this category employed econometric modellings wi cross-sectional data, which resulted in somewhat less favourable conclusio Fuchs and Leveson evaluated accident death rates with models using the followi independent variables: age of driver, education, median income, fuel consumptic per capita, population density, alcohol consumption per capita, serveral oth socio-economic variables, and a binary variable for inspection. When the inspe tion variable was the only independent variable, they found a significant negati effect on accident death rates. When more regressors were added to the mode the efficacy of motor vehicle inspection in reducing mortality rates was not stati tically significant. The study by Crain used 1974 data and similar socio-econom variables, and did not find a statistically significant effect of periodic inspectic on death rates, accident rates or non-fatal injury rates. However, Crain's stud employed five different measures of inspection, and his use of dummy variabl to account for type of inspection makes it difficult to interpret his results.

In an experimental study conducted by the U.S. Department of Transpor ation, NHTSA (1980), the accident rate of vehicles was observed over a 12-mont period. The vehicles were grouped into two samples: one consisted of vehicl that underwent (voluntary) inspection, and the other of non-inspected vehicle The two samples were matched for make, model and year of manufacture. Th results showed a statistically significant difference in accident rates, the inspecte vehicles having fewer accidents than the non-inspected ones. The results also hel when accident rates were adjusted for differences in age and sex. These result however, should be interepreted with caution, because the non-random samplin procedure used in the study may have biased the selection of drivers in the firs sample.

The time series studies conducted in the past have been basically a descriptiv comparison of accident rates before and after the introduction of inspectio programmes. These studies (State of Nebraska, Department of Motor Vehicle

974) and State of Alaska (1974)) compared the percentages before and after
introduction of an inspection programme of all fatal accidents in which
vehicle defects played a causative role. Both studies found a decline in these
percentages. No attempt was made to formalise the analysis, however, and the
circumstances of the accidents were not rigorously examined. Furthermore, the
analysis did not include factors other than inspection, and the sample space considered was quite small.

In summary, it seems that various studies of the efficacy of periodic inspection
reducing fatalities, injuries or accidents, give rise to mixed results and no
definitive conclusion. The more rigorous studies are cross-sectional only, and
somewhat limited in their conclusions. A systematic analysis using time series
data and econometric techniques provides a more definitive test for the efficacy
periodic inspection, and is more appropriate as a tool for policy decisions on
state by state basis.

III. TIME SERIES MODELS FOR EVALUATING MOTOR VEHICLE INSPECTION IN NEW JERSEY

General Model Specification

The previous econometric models, as stated above, were cross-sectional models as
opposed to time series models. As such they were not state specific. We propose
to evaluate the effect of motor vehicle inspection on reducing deaths, injuries and
accidents, using time series data for New Jersey. Consider, for expository
purposes, a model of the form:

$$D_t = \beta_1 + \beta_2 MVI_t + \sum_{i=3}^{k} \beta_i X_{it} + \epsilon_t \qquad (1)$$

where: D_t = a measure of deaths due to traffic accidents in year t
            MVI_t = a binary variable accounting for the existence or non-
                    existence of an inspection system in year t; $MVI=1$ for
                    the years an inspection system was in effect, and
                    $MVI=0$ otherwise.
       $X_i (i=3,...,k)$ = $k-2$ additional socio-economic variables which are
                    independent variables.

The ordinary least squares estimate of β_2 is an estimate of the effect of
inspection on mortality. We would expect that $\beta_2 < 0$ if inspection is efficacious.
Nonetheless, two-tail tests will be reported because they are more conservative.

Various alternative specifications of equations (1) will also be evaluated (for
example, natural log models), as was done both by Fuchs and Leveson (1967) and
by Crain (1980).

The time series model is state specific, but must account for changes in technology and the like occurring over time, which do not plague cross-sectional
studies. A time variable is included in the time series model as a proxy for
technological change.

The type of model specified in equation (1) can also be used to evaluate
injuries and accidents, which in turn may provide information on loss of property.

The Variables

Time series models were developed for fatalities, accidents and injuries. A pot tial list of independent variables was compiled, and data were collected for years 1929-1979 (unless otherwise noted). The final set of variables included measure of time (the Gregorian calendar year), maximum highway speed, gasol consumption, number of licenses revoked for drunken driving, per capita perso income, population (in thousands), number of motor vehicle registratio number of drivers licensed, vehicle mileage, GNP price deflator, a dummy varia for inspection, a dummy variable for the years of American involvement in Wo War II, a dummy variable for the year of the Great Depression, total number accidents reported, number of injuries (from 1932 to 1979), number of traf deaths and the death rate (per 100 million vehicle miles). A list of the variab and the sources of the data is given in the Appendix, which explains the proble encountered in the data and describes the techniques used to supply missi observations.

The time variable is a proxy for technological change over the years. Sin 1929 many engineering advances in automobiles, roads, lighting systems, et have been developed, and these may have contributed to a reduction in acciden fatalities and injuries. Technological change is difficult, if not impossible, measure. However, technological change progresses over time, so we use time a proxy for it.[1]

The maximum highway speed is expected to be directly proportional to deatl As highway speeds increase, an accident is more likely to be serious and to resu in a fatality than when speeds are lower. However, the higher maximum spee have been accompanied by the building of super highways and new designs access ramps. Thus, though accidents are more likely to be serious at high maximum highway speeds than at lower ones, there may indeed be few accidents.

Gasoline consumption is a measure of driving intensity. We would expect th to be positively related to the dependent variables (fatalities, injuries, accidents

The number of licences revoked for drunken driving is expected to be nega ively related to the dependent variable. As police arrest and courts punis drunken driving with greater rigour, one would expect to find not only th drunken drivers are evicted from our roads, but that a warning is issued t potential drivers who drink that there is a severe punishment for driving unde the influence. Both effects would be expected to reduce accidents, fatalities an injuries. Alternatively, we might observe increases in revocations as a result c increased fatalities (possibly reflecting a changing attitude of the courts).[2]

---

[1] Models incorporating time in quadratic and other nonlinear forms were also evaluated t allow for the possible non-steady progress of the effect of technology on fatalities. The resul are similar to those reported.

[2] Additionally, if increased revocations in the current period act as a deterrent to drunke driving, they may result (all else equal) in a reduction of revocations in a future period as fewe drunken drivers travel the roads. The revocations variable lagged one period was examined, a well as its current value, to account for a lagged effect of the deterring process of revocation: The lagged revocations variable was never significant, and so is not reported.

Per capita personal income is included in the model to account for the economic constraints on individuals to maintain their motor vehicles and/or to maintain a social/economic image. Individuals in higher income brackets can afford more modern and safer cars. Hence, as income per capita increases over time one might expect a reduction in the value of the dependent variables, all else equal. Additionally, income may be related to education, which in turn, is related to the skill of drivers. An increase in drivers' skill over time would result in reduction of fatalities. However, as incomes rise, individuals can afford to drive more readily. As more and more drivers enter the roadways, one might expect an increase in accidents, all else equal.

The population variable is expected to be positively correlated with accidents, fatalities and injuries. The larger the population, the greater the number of potential victims for automobile accidents.

The number of vehicles registered, drivers licensed, and vehicle mileage are measures of driving intensity and are expected to be positively related to the dependent variable. Only one of these three measures is included per model, since they are highly correlated with one another, and their contemporaneous linear inclusion in the model might lead to multicollinearity.

The GNP deflator was used to deflate the nominal income data to constant dollars, using 1972 as the base year.

A dummy variable (that is, a binary variable) was employed for measuring the effect of inspection. The binary variable takes the value of zero for years when inspection was not in practice (1929-1937) and the value of one for years when inspection was in force (1938-1979).[3] We expect, a priori, that inspection will have a negative effect on the dependent variable. Dummy variables for the years of American involvement in World War II and for the Great Depression years were investigated also. World War II had a drastic impact on the production of automobiles for domestic consumption. Furthermore, the war effort reduced the availability of gasoline for pleasure driving and reduced the number of potential drivers, as many men were in the armed forces. The dummy variable for the Great Depression takes into account the effect of massive economic turmoil on motor-vehicle-related accidents, injuries and fatalities.

The dependent variables of this study were based on data for: fatalities, number of accidents reported, number of injuries, and the death rate (per 100 million vehicle miles).

All these data, other than the GNP deflator, may be considered specific for New Jersey.

The independent variables will explain changes in the dependent variable over time. Inclusion of the relevant independent variables in a model designed to be structurally correct (with all classical assumptions upheld) will result in unbiased

---

[3] Additional dummy variables were employed to measure the influence of truck inspection and motorcycle inspection. Additionally, inspection was measured as the number of inspections per year (0-2). These variables do not add significantly to this study, and they are not included. Interested readers may obtain these results from the authors.

estimates. Hence, in the analysis which follows, it is assumed that the final mod
evaluated are properly specified, that is, that they conform with classical assum
tions.

Regression results on the fatality models – time series data

Ordinary Least Squares estimates were obtained for many variants of a measure
fatalities as a function of various independent variables. The OLS estimat
suffered from serial correlation and were corrected by a Cochrane-Orcutt pr
cedure.

Table 1 provides a list of definitions of variables, and Table 2 a set of regr
sions, using the level of fatalities as a function of various independent variables
It is interesting to note that the coefficient associated with the dummy variab
for inspection is always negative and significant. It is also of great interest that tł
absolute value of this coefficient is relatively stable across model specification
The R^2 figures indicate the percentage variation of fatalities, explained by tł
regressions as being between 0.9134 and 0.9332.

We have chosen equation 3 as the optimal model on the basis of the tra
itional criteria of: R^2, t-tests, signs of coefficients consistent with *a prio*
expectations, apparent avoidance of serial correlation, and containing variabl
suggested by theory. An additional criterion was to select the model indicatin
the most conservative effect of inspection.

Equation 3 suggests: (1) a significant reduction of fatalities over time –
measure of technology or technological change; (2) a significant positive influenc
of income on fatalities; (3) a significant positive influence of population o
fatalities; (4) a significant positive influence of registrations on fatalities; (5)
significant negative effect of inspection on fatalities; (6) a significant negativ
effect of the war years on fatalities. Thus the dummy variable for inspectio
indicates that fatalities are reduced by 304 deaths as a result of inspection. Thi
was the most conservative estimate obtained from the models in Table 2. Th
coefficient obtained is significantly different from zero at the 1% significanc
level.

In order to add additional confidence to the finding that inspection reduce
fatalities, a Chow-Test was preformed after homoscedasticity had been verifiec
by a Goldfeld-Quandt Test. The Chow-Test evaluates whether the coefficient.
in the model are stable over the entire period. If the universe from which w
sample changes over time, we would expect the estimated coefficients tc
reflect this. We therefore investigated whether a model using the first nin
observations (1929-1937) came from the same population as for the more
recent period (1938-1979). The Chow-Test as applied to equation 3 (devoid
of the dummy for inspection) rejects the hypothesis that the coefficients are
stable over time.

---

[4]The maximum speed variable, when included in the models, had estimated coefficients
which were not significant, so those results are not reported.

TABLE 1

Definitions of Variables

Symbol	Definition
T	Time (1929-1979)
RY_t	Real per capita personal income in year t, i.e., $$\frac{\text{per capita personal income }_t}{\text{GNP price deflator }_t}$$
DDR_t	Number of licences revoked for drunken driving in year t
POP_t	Population in year t
REG_t	Number of motor vehicles registered in year t
D	Dummy variable accounting for periods of inspection. The dummy variable takes on the value of one (1) for years in which inspection occurred and zero (0) otherwise.
$WW2$	Dummy variable accounting for direct American involvement in World War II. $WW2 = 1$ for years of American participation, 0 otherwise.
$GDEP$	Dummy variable denoting years of the Great Depression. $GDEP = 1$ during depression years, 0 otherwise.
$MILPDL$	Ratio of vehicle mileage to drivers licensed. This is a proxy for intensity of driving per potential driver.
$REGPDL$	Ratio of registrations to drivers licensed. This is a proxy of intensity of vehicle use.
$GASC$	Gasoline consumption (in gallons).

We also evaluated additional models having different dependent variables and structural forms. Models were estimated in terms of deaths per capita and deaths per 100 million vehicle miles, and natural log models with respect to deaths and deaths per capita where all non-binary variables were in natural log form. The results with regard to the dummy variable for inspection were consistently negative and significant. The magnitude of the coefficients associated with this dummy variable was stable for all variations of the model, by consistent measure

TABLE 2

Regression Results of the Determinants of Fatalities[a],[b]

Equation	Constant	T	RY	DDR	POP	REG	D	WW2	GDEP	MILPDL	R^2	F	DW
1	112779* (4.18)	−58.64* (−4.15)	0.18* (2.52)		0.33* (3.31)	0.00026** (2.48)	−316.61* (−4.19)	−158.93** (−2.26)	−93.45 (−1.25)		0.9321	82.32	2.1627
2	116294* (4.06)	−60.50* (−4.04)	0.18** (2.51)	0.0037 (0.87)	0.35* (3.22)	0.00024*** (2.13)	−316.70* (−4.16)	−156.09*** (−2.23)	−99.38 (−1.33)		0.9332	71.64	2.1745
3	99723* (4.09)	−51.90* (−4.06)	0.19* (2.75)		0.31* (3.23)	0.00021*** (2.16)	−303.93* (−4.02)	−168.55*** (−2.38)			0.9295	94.54	2.1439
4	67406.4 (1.90)	−34.44 (−1.87)	0.10 (1.44)			0.00036*** (2.21)	−381.42** (−4.92)	−173.02** (−2.53)	−76.14 (−1.00)		0.9220	84.72	2.0189
5	61483.1 (1.80)	−31.41 (−1.78)	0.12 (1.62)			0.00033*** (2.12)	−377.75* (−4.87)	−179.91** (−2.63)			0.9202	101.47	2.0235
6	76542.8* (3.34)	−40.07* (−3.32)	0.22* (3.00)		0.36* (3.60)		−373.32* (−4.89)	−160.58 (−1.86)	−19.71 (−0.27)	24050.1 (0.83)	0.9232	72.09	2.0568
7	87691.6* (3.60)	−45.89* (−3.58)	0.22* (3.00)	0.0059 (1.37)	0.40* (3.84)		−353.33 (−4.58)	−156.34 (−1.84)	−42.22 (−0.57)	20795.9 (0.72)	0.9265	64.64	2.0710
8	76339.4* (3.54)	−39.97* (−3.52)	0.22* (3.14)		0.36* (3.80)		−365.98* (−5.04)	−161.00 (−1.88)		25246.8 (0.88)	0.9230	85.96	2.0595
9	−3862.01 (−0.24)	2.35 (0.28)	0.10 (1.35)				−405.56* (−5.12)	−167.34*** (−2.05)		19670.4 (0.67)	0.9134	92.82	2.0090

[a] All models are estimated by the Cochrane-Orcutt procedure for the period 1929-1979.

[b] Numbers in parentheses indicate t-statistics associated with the estimated coefficients.

*, **, *** Indicate significance at the 99, 98 and 95% confidence intervals, respectively.

the dependent variable. However, the results reported in Table 2 for the level fatalities were, by and large, the most conservative estimates of the effect of pection.[5]

gression results on the injury models — time series data

.rious models were estimated in order to evaluate the influence of inspection on uries in New Jersey for the period 1932 to 1979. The results in general were at the coefficients associated with the inspection variable were negative, but not nificant (at the $\alpha = 0.05$ level).

Further, a few specifications resulted in positive coefficients. However, these re never significantly different from zero at reasonable α-levels.

No optimal model could be obtained for injuries while we used the same teria as for the fatality equations. If these criteria are modified, or if one is lling to accept a model based on a smaller sample, significant negative coef- cients result.

Several possible reasons must be postulated for the insignificant effect of spection on injuries. The inspection process may be efficacious in discovering d correcting major safety violations in vehicles, but not minor ones. Also, the spection process may serve as an educational device affecting drivers' *attitudes* wards the maintenance of vital safety factors in their vehicles, thereby reducing tal accidents.

egression results on the accident models — time series data

able 3 presents the regression results on the level of accidents. Except in the case f equations 2 and 3, we can reject the null hypothesis that the coefficient assoc- ted with D is equal to zero at the 0.02 or 0.01 level in favour of the two-tail ternative that the coefficient is not equal to zero. In the case of equations 2 nd 3, the null hypothesis that the coefficient is equal to zero can be rejected at e 0.05 level in favour of a one-tail alternative hypothesis that the coefficient is ss than zero.

Choice of an optimal model is more difficult in the case of accidents than in he case of fatalities. All models had R^2 statistics greater than 0.93, varying from .9371 to 0.9462. This indicates that the various models explained between 93.71 nd 94.62 per cent of the variation in the dependent variable.

The inclusion of *GASC* in the model resulted in the decline of the t-statistic ssociated with T (equation 1 vs 2). The correlation coefficient associated with T nd *GASC* is 0.979, indicating that multicollinearity may exist here. Equation 2 is hus omitted from the set of potential optimal models.

---

[5]The models for fatalities and accidents were evaluated without the dummy variable for nspection. As one would expect, the R^2 of the models including the dummy variable were lways higher than for the associated models without the dummy, all else equal. Furthermore, :he $\bar{R}^2$ was always higher for the models with the dummy variable than for those omitting it, ndicating a greater explanatory power of the models when the dummy variable is included.

TABLE 3

Regression Results of the Determinants of Accidents[a,b]

Equation	Constant	RY	POP	D	T	GASC	REGPDL	MILPDL	R^2/F	DW	Estimation Technique[c]
1	-8551570** (-2.46)	-5.31 (-0.53)	13.97 (0.90)	-37910.3** (-2.51)	4417.20*** (2.41)				0.9390 173.30	2.0659	CORC
2	-3157230 (-1.06)	-2.28 (-0.32)	3.73 (0.32)	-24290.1 (-1.78)	1630.74 (1.04)	0.05* (2.88)			0.9462 158.207	1.8279	OLS
3	-7403120*** (-2.22)	-9.40 (-0.95)	14.43 (1.00)	-29562.9 (-1.87)	3736.27*** (2.11)		215663 (1.46)		0.9416 142.00	1.9997	CORC
4	-7460360*** (-2.15)	-0.63 (-0.06)	11.59 (0.78)	-38755.7** (-2.65)	3829.25*** (2.09)			6103370 (1.13)	0.9407 139.49	2.0491	CORC
5	-9713040* (-5.13)	-2.20 (-0.22)		-46044.9* (-4.12)	5018.80* (5.00)			6585120 (1.24)	0.9398 175.74	2.0593	CORC
6	-10386300* (-18.18)			-47199.1* (-4.12)	5388.99* (18.25)				0.9371 349.91	2.0435	CORC
7	-7463350* (-2.73)		16.05 (1.09)	-36955.8** (-2.51)	3843.54** (2.67)				0.9387 234.65	2.0468	CORC

[a] All models are estimated for the period 1929-1979.

[b] Numbers in parentheses indicate t-statistics associated with the estimated coefficients.

[c] CORC indicates that the equation was estimated by the Cochrane-Orcutt procedure, and OLS indicates estimation by Ordinary Least Squares.

*, **, *** Indicate significance at the 99, 98 and 95% confidence intervals, respectively.

The coefficients associated with *REGPDL* and *MILPDL* were never signifi-
tly different from zero; therefore equations 3, 4 and 5 are dropped from
sideration.

Of the remaining equations (1, 6, 7), equation 6 has coefficients all of which
significantly different from zero at the 0.01 level. The inclusion of the pop-
tion variable in equation 7 reduces the absolute value of the estimated
fficients and *t*-statistics vis-a-vis equation 6. Since we expect population and
income to be important variables, their omission may result in biased
imates. Hence, equation 1 is chosen as the optimal model. The absolute value
the coefficient associated with *D* in equation 1 is slightly larger than that in
ation 7, and substantially smaller than that of equation 6. Hence, it provides
easonably conservative estimate of the impact of inspection on accidents (based
the equations evaluated), that is, a reduction of 37,910 accidents per year.

IV. COST AND BENEFITS ASSOCIATED WITH MOTOR VEHICLE INSPECTION IN NEW JERSEY – A PARTIAL ANALYSIS

ction III provided statistical evidence of the efficacy of motor vehicle inspec-
n. This is particularly noticeable in the consistent time series estimates on
duction of fatalities. The economic argument for periodic inspection, however,
ould be based on a benefit/cost analysis. This section applies the results of the
odel to a partial list of benefits and calculates a benefit/cost ratio. The analysis
performed with 1981 as a reference year.

nefits
eaths and injuries related to motor vehicles impose specific financial costs on
dividuals and society, including:
(1) Reduction of potential output of society due to deaths.
(2) Reduction of potential output of society while injured individuals are
    incapacitated.
(3) Cost of medical, legal and insurance services (which otherwise would not
    have been expended) rendered to the victims and families of victims of
    accidents.
(4) Property destroyed by accidents.
(5) Lost income of families and friends of accident victims while they are
    tending and ministering to the victims (or themselves) instead of using
    their energies in alternative production processes.
(6) Costs to society from pollution (air and noise) which may result in dis-
    eases as well as wasteful (inefficient) consumption of fuel.
(7) Costs of enforcement activities related to the investigation of accidents.
(8) Costs of activities of the Fatal Accident Review Board.
(9) Costs of internal motor vehicle administrative activities.
(10) Pain and suffering.

Some of the above costs are not measurable (for example, pain and suffering),

and some are not measured in various studies because of lack of data. Neverth
less, the avoidance of these costs through motor vehicle inspection amounts
benefits due to the inspection system.[6]

Costs
A partial list of costs associated with inspection includes:
(1) Direct cost of inspection.[7]
(2) Cost to the driver of spending time in having a vehicle inspected (inclu
ing travel time), as opposed to allocating that time to an alternati
endeavour (opportunity cost).
(3) Additional repairs which would not have been made if it were not f
inspection.
(4) Value of time expended in repairing the vehicle (including travel time
(5) Cost in time and direct payment for reinspection.

Calculation of benefits
1. Benefits due to avoidance of deaths
The present value of the income stream lost by victims of fatal accidents has bee
estimated by Hartunian, Smart and Thompson (1980), hereafter called HST. The
evaluate the present value of motor vehicle fatalities in 1975, using a 6 per cen
discount rate and adjusting for sex and age grouping.[8] Using their result, we calc
ulate that the average present value of forgone earnings is $160,640 per victim
We assume that the national average is representative of New Jersey.

2. Benefits due to avoidance of damage to property
The HST study does not provide estimates of damage to property. However, th
U. S. Department of Transportation, NHTSA (1976), estimates the average cos
of damage to property per accident in 1975 as $519 when the accident entaile
only damage to property. This figure includes: damage to the vehicle, insuranc

---

[6]The estimates of benefits due to inspection in this study pertain to avoidance of rea
resource costs and net output losses associated with accidents and fatalities. Jones-Lee (1976
has suggested that the total benefit associated with saving a life should include an additiona
element – the average value of human life in itself. This latter benefit is equivalent unde
certain conditions to the population average of the marginal value of a decrease in risk, both
direct and indirect (see Jones-Lee, section 5.IX). The estimated magnitude of this variable,
according to Jones-Lee, is several times larger than the figure based on real resource cost and
net output loss alone (p. 150). To this extent, our estimate is an underestimate of the true
benefits of inspection. We thank an anonymous referee who brought this point to our
attention.

[7]This cost includes the opportunity cost of the use of the inspection facility.

[8]See HST for definitions and assumptions. Their analysis takes into account the costs of
insurance administration and legal and court costs, as well as the traditional direct and indirect costs which they enumerate.

ministration, legal and court costs, police accident investigation, and traffic
lay. Fatalities and injuries also involve damage to property. Hence, the weighted
erage of costs would be higher than reported above. So $519 is a conservative
ure.

Furthermore, we find that, for the period 1974-1980, 63 per cent of all acci-
nts resulted in damage to property only.[9] Our regression results suggest that
cidents are reduced by 37,910. Assuming that 63 per cent of these accidents
ould have resulted in damage to property, we can estimate the value of property
mage avoided, keeping in mind that this figure underestimates the true cost to
ciety from property damage.

Table 4 provides the present value of selected accident costs in their nominal
75 terms as well as in their CPI-adjusted 1981 values. The total present value
ure comes to $103,467,670.

Given the list of potential benefits which were omitted, as denoted in Table 4,
is important that the reader be cognisant of the downward bias of this partial
nefit figure.

alculation of benefits based on alternative studies

wo additional estimates on 1975 accident costs were compiled by the National
afety Council (NSC) and the U. S. Department of Transportation, National
ighway Traffic Safety Administration (NHTSA). These estimates differ from the
TS study in methodology employed and benefits included. Hence, caution
hould be exercised in making comparisons across the studies.

Table 5 provides the results of these studies together with the 1981 up-date of
he figures by the consumer price index. It also provides the estimated present
alue of the selected benefits, based on the regression results of the previous
ection and the NSC and NHTSA estimates.

As can be seen from Tables 4 and 5, the estimates of benefits differ when dif-
erent studies are used to provide cost data on fatalities and property damage.

Calculation of Costs

. Cost of operating inspection facilities by State agencies (SE)

New Jersey's Division of Motor Vehicles reports an expenditure of $14,514,474
or 1981. We assume away problems associated with amortisation.[10] That this
ssumption is not heroic is indicated by U. S. Department of Transportation,
NHTSA (1975), where it was found that costs are dominated by operating
costs.[11]

---

[9]This estimate is based on the ratio of the number of accidents resulting in property damage
only to the total number of accidents. Data were provided by New Jersey DMV from *Department of Transportation Reports.*

[10]See Henn (1981) on this. New Jersey's DMV data do not include amortisation or rental
price of capital information directly.

[11]See U.S. Department of Transportation, NHTSA (1975), p. 22.

TABLE 4

Present Value (PV) of Benefits (partial list) *

Event	PV per event (1975)	PV per event (1981)[a]	Regression coefficient	Probability associated with coefficient† for PV calculation purposes	PV of event (1981)
	$	$			$
Fatalities[b]	160,640	271,454	304	1	82,522,016
Property damage[c]	519	877	37,910	0.63	20,945,654
Total					$103,467,670

*The following benefits were not included in the analysis because reliable data and/or models were not available:
  Reduction of fatalities and morbidity due to a reduction in air pollution.
  Reduction of property damage due to a reduction in accidents involving fatalities and injuries.
  Reduction of enforcement activities associated with accidents resulting in fatalities and injuries.
  Reduction of Fatal Accident Review Board activities.
  Reduction of internal motor vehicle administrative activities.
  Reduction in gasoline/fuel usage.
  Avoidance of pain and suffering.

†Property damage is evaluated from the regression on accidents and the estimate that 63% of all accidents involved property damage (only).

[a]Inflated by the CPI

[b]Based on HST (1980)

[c]Based on U.S. Department of T̲

Alternative Calculations of Present Value (PV) of Benefits *

Event	PV per event (1975)		PV per event (1981)[a]		Regression coefficient	Probability associated with coefficient for PV calculation purposes	Total PV of event	
	NSC	NHTSA	NSC	NHTSA			NSC	NHTSA
	$	$	$	$			$	$
Fatalities	110,000[b]	287,175[b]	185,881[b]	485,276[b]	304	1	56,507,824	147,523,904
Property damage†	570	519	963	877	37,910	0.63	22,999,618	20,945,654
Total							$79,507,442	$168,469,558

*The following benefits were not included in the analysis because reliable data and/or models were not available:
  Reduction of fatalities and morbidity due to a reduction in air pollution.
  Reduction in gasoline fuel usage.
  Reduction in internal motor vehicle administrative activities.
  Avoidance of pain and suffering.

† Property damage is evaluated using the regression on accidents and the estimate that 63% of all accidents involved property damage (only).

[a]Inflated via the CPI

[b]These figures include property damage, traffic delay, and accident investigation, which are not included in the HST estimates.

The Department of Environmental Protection reports another $600,000 expenditures devoted to inspection.[12] So the state expenditure for 1981 denot as SE was $15,114,474.

2. Opportunity cost associated with time spent bringing vehicles for inspectio (OCTR)

The opportunity cost associated with time expended bringing vehicles f inspection (that is, for travel) is estimated as:

$$OCTR = REG. \text{ x } TR \text{ x } WRATE$$

where: $OCTR$ = opportunity cost associated with travel time in 1981
    REG = number of cars inspected in 1981
    TR = average duration involved in travel time
    $WRATE$ = average wage rate[13]

Palmini and Rossi (1980) provide estimates of TR of 1.02 hours and $WRATE$ c $5.92 in 1977. Inflating the wage rate by the consumer price index results in wage rate of $8.88 for 1981. REG = 4,891,642 in 1981.[14] Hence,

$$OCTR = 4,891,642 \ (1.02)(\$8.88) = \$44,306,536$$

3. Opportunity cost associated with time spent waiting during the inspectio process (OCW)

The opportunity cost associated with waiting time may be calculated by th formula:

$$OCW = WT \text{ x } WRATE \text{ x } REG$$

where: WT = average waiting time = 9 minutes = 0.15 hours[15]
    OCW = 0.15($8.88)(4,891,642) = $6,515,667

4. Vehicle usage costs for the inspection process (VHC)

Vehicle usage costs are estimated as:

$$VHC = REG \text{ x } VC \text{ x } MI$$

where: REG = cars inspected
    VC = cost per mile of operating an automobile
    MI = average round trip to inspection station

VC and MI are reported by Palmini and Rossi (1980) as $0.18 per mile and 20 miles respectively. Hence,

$$VHC = 4,891,642 \text{ x } (0.18)(20) = \$17,609,911$$

---

[12]We are grateful to Mr. Daniel Cowperthwait of the New Jersey Department of Environ-mental Protection (DEP) for this information.

[13]If time expended for inspection purposes is leisure time, the cost figures presented over-estimate the true cost of inspection.

[14]Data from New Jersey's DMV.

[15]Data supplied by New Jersey's DMV.

epair Costs

epair costs and the associated benefits of repairs for items which, but for inspec-
on, would not have been repaired, are not included in this analysis, because
ere is no consensus of opinion on whether inspection increases or decreases
pair costs.[16]

verall costs

he overall costs are estimated as the sum of the above, that is:

		$
1.	*SE*	15,114,474
2.	*OCTR*	44,306,536
3.	*OCW*	6,515,667
4.	*VHC*	17,609,911
	Total cost (partial list)	83,546,588

Summary of costs and benefits – a partial analysis

On the basis of the HST estimates, our partial list of the benefits of inspection is
.103,467,670, as compared to a partial list of costs of inspection of $83,546,588
or 1981. The ratio of the benefits to costs is approximately 1.24. If the partial
ists of benefits and costs is representative of total benefits and costs, it appears
hat inspection is cost effective.

On the basis of the U. S. Department of Transportation, NHTSA estimates, our
partial list of benefits due to inspection is $168,469,558, and therefore the ratio
of benefits to costs is approximately 2.02. If the NSC estimate of benefits of
$79,507,442 is used, the ratio drops to approximately 0.95.

The benefit/cost ratio takes on values between 0.95 and 2.02 according to the
estimate of benefits. Since many benefits are not included in these estimates (for
example, benefits of reduction in pollution), it is most probable that a benefit/
cost ratio including the omitted benefits would be greater than 1. Furthermore,
the HTS procedure is well documented and methodologically elegant. This cannot
be readily said for the NSC and NHTSA reports. Therefore we have also more
confidence in the estimated benefit/cost ratio based on the HTS study.

V. CONCLUSIONS

This study has presented a wide array of findings concerning some of the benefits
and costs of motor vehicle inspection, with particular attention to the safety
benefits and costs of the motor vehicle inspection system in the State of New
Jersey.

---

[16]See U.S. Department of Transportation, NHTSA (1975), p. 14, and Program in Engineering and Public Affairs (1975), p. 90.

The study of the cost-effectiveness of the New Jersey inspection programm indicates that vehicle inspection in New Jersey significantly reduces the numb of highway fatalities. The time series regression analysis reported in Section I shows that vehicle inspection in New Jersey reduces highway fatalities by 3C deaths per year. This result is obtained when other changes that also might affe fatalities are taken into account in the analysis. Though inspection appears t make a significant reduction in the number of highway fatalities, the mode investigated do not show that it significantly reduces the number of highwa injuries. Finally, the analysis indicates that inspection in New Jersey significantl reduces the number of highway accidents by 37,910 accidents per year.

Previous research on the effects of vehicle inspection on highway safety wa reviewed in Section II. In general, the results of the earlier research do not sho' the kind of significant reductions in fatalities and accidents due to inspection tha are indicated by the findings from the present study. However, the earlier econo metric studies were based on cross-section data, as opposed to the time serie results reported here.

A calculation of most of the costs associated with the New Jersey inspectio programme, including the cost of operating the programme and costs incurred b drivers in undergoing inspection, resulted in a final figure of $83,546,588. A calc ulation of the partial list of benefits associated with the programme, as measure by the value of benefits connected with the avoidance of deaths and property damage, resulted in a final figure of $103,467,670 when the estimated figure from HST (1980) are used. The ratio of partial benefits to costs is approximately 1.24. This suggests that the New Jersey inspection system is cost-effective. I should be noted that the benefits measured in monetary terms are limited t those connected with the avoidance of deaths and property damage. Other bene fits that might accrue from vehicle inspection (such as reduction in pollution have not been included in the computation of the benefit/cost ratio. The value derived for that ratio is thus on the conservative side.

It would be interesting to determine, by using the methodology employed in this study, whether inspection would result in significant reductions in fatalities, injuries and accidents in other states. The difficulties associated with data collec tion should be weighed against the benefits of state-specific studies, especially during times of financial pressure when intensive efforts are being made to reduce the expenditures of state governments.

APPENDIX

Data Sources and Adjustments

We indicate below sources for series used in reported regressions.

Data on motor vehicle registrations, drivers licensed, vehicle mileage, traffic deaths, N. J. death rate per 100 million vehicle miles, and years when a state vehicle inspection was in force are found in New Jersey State Department of Law and Public Safety (1979).

Data on per capita personal income are from *Supplement to Survey of Current Business*, September 1956, for the years 1929-1947, and from U. S. Department of Commerce, Bureau of Economic Analysis, for the years 1948-1979.

Numbers of revocations for drunk driving were available for 1918-1958 from the annual reports of the New Jersey Division of Motor Vehicles, and for 1971-1981 from New Jersey Division of Motor Vehicles, Bureau of Driver Improvement. The data for missing years were estimated by means of a geometric mean to estimate growth rates when linear, exponential and moving average time series models had failed to extrapolate accurately.

Population data are from *Statistical Abstracts 1980*, U. S. Department of Commerce.

Data on gasoline consumption (1929-1950) are from annual reports of the N. J. Division of Motor Vehicles. For 1953-1979 the data were provided by the Division of Motor Vehicles. Missing data for the years 1951 and 1952 were estimated by evaluating the growth rate of the appropriate portion of the series.

Data on numbers of injuries (1932-1979) are from: New Jersey Division of Motor Vehicles Annual Reports and *Traffic Safety Service Summary of Motor Vehicle Traffic Accidents*; U. S. Department of Transportation, Bureau of Accident Records, *Summary of Vehicle Traffic Accidents*; and the N. J. Department of Motor Vehicles, Division of Traffic Control and Regulation.

Data on numbers of accidents reported are from the N. J. Division of Motor Vehicles, *Annual Reports (1916-1958), N. J. Traffic Accident Facts (1959-1966)*, and N. J. Department of Transportation Reports (1967-1980). Data were missing for the years 1930-1931 and 1952. The missing data for the earlier period were estimated from a geometric growth rate, and the 1952 observation was estimated as the mean of the values for 1951 and 1953.

The GNP deflator is from R. Gordon (1981) and the consumer price index from *Economic Report of the President, 1982*.

REFERENCES

Buxbaum, R. G., and T. Colton (1966): "Relationship of Motor Vehicle Inspection to Accident Mortality". *The Journal of the American Medical Association, 197*, 101-106.

Carnegie Institute of Technology: Program in Engineering and Public Affairs (1975): *An Assessment of Pennsylvania's Periodic Motor Vehicle Inspection System*. Carnegie Mellon University.

Crain, W. M. (1980): *Vehicle Safety Inspection Systems*. Washington, D. C.: American Enterprise Institute for Public Policy Research.

Economic Report of the President (1982): Washington, D. C.: U. S. Government Printing Office.

Fuchs, V. R., and I. Leveson (1967): "Motor Accident Mortality and Compulsory Inspection of Vehicles". *The Journal of the American Medical Association, 201*, 87-91.

Gordon, R. J. (1981): *Macroeconomics*. Boston, MA.: Little Brown.

Hartunian, N., C. Smart and M. Thompson (1980): "The Incidence and Economic Cost of Cancer, Motor Vehicle Injuries, Coronary Heart Disease, and Strokes: A Comparative Analysis". *American Journal of Public Health, 70*, 1249-1260.

Henn, W. (1981): *Justifications for Maintaining Vehicle Inspection*. Memo, New Jersey Division of Motor Vehicles, 20 November.

Jackson, B., Peter Loeb, and K. Frank (1982): *Comprehensive Analysis of New Jersey Motor Vehicle Inspection System.* A report submitted to the Department of Law and Public Safety, Division of Motor Vehicles, by New Jersey Institute of Technology, November.

Jones-Lee, M. W., (1976): *The Value of Life – An Economic Analysis.* Chicago: The University of Chicago Press.

Mayer, A. J., and T. F. Hoult (1963): *Motor Vehicle Inspection: A Report on Current Information, Measurement and Research.* Institute for Regional and Urban Studies, Wayne State University, 1963. Cited in AAA Foundation for Traffic Safety: *A Study of Motor Vehicle Inspection,* 1967, pp. 40-44.

National Safety Council (1981): *Accident Facts.* 1981 edition.

New Jersey State Department of Law and Public Safety, Division of Motor Vehicles: *Annual Reports,* various issues.

New Jersey State Department of Law and Public Safety, Division of Motor Vehicles (1979): *Margin of Safety: New Jersey's Roadway Safety Record.*

Palmini, D. J., and D. Rossi (1980): *Cost/Benefit of Air Pollution Controls in New Jersey. Part Four: The Cost of New Jersey Motor Vehicle Exhaust Emission Inspection and Maintenance Program.* Center for Coastal Environment Studies, Department of Agricultural Economics, Cook College, Rutgers.

State of Alaska (1974): *Periodic Motor Vehicle Inspection Survey,* Rommel Consultants. Cited in: United States Department of Transportation, National Highway Traffic Safety Administration: *Costs and Benefits of Motor Vehicle Inspection,* 1975.

State of Nebraska Department of Motor Vehicles (1974): *Status Report on Nebraska's Periodic Motor Vehicle Inspection Program.* Cited in: United States Department of Transportation National Highway Traffic Safety Administration: *Costs and Benefits of Motor Vehicle Inspection,* 1975.

United States Department of Commerce (1980): *Statistical Abstracts 1980.* Washington, D. C.: U. S. Government Printing Office.

United States Department of Transportation, National Highway Traffic Safety Administration (1975): *Costs and Benefits of Motor Vehicle Inspection.*

United States Department of Transportation, National Highway Traffic Safety Administration (1976): *1975 Societal Costs of Motor Vehicle Accidents.*

United States Department of Transportation, National Highway Traffic Safety Administration (1980): *The Effects of Automobile Inspections on Accident Rates.* HJS-805-401.

VI

CRIMINAL JUSTICE

In the late 1960s and early 1970s, as part of the nation's overall goal of improving life chances for the disadvantaged, there was considerable interest in trying to break what seemed to be an associated pattern of unemployment, crime, and poverty. The program interventions included efforts to improve youth employment, to divert juveniles from the prison system, and to help ex-offenders obtain jobs. The success of these programs is under considerable debate. Critics point to increasing crime and our overcrowded prisons as evidence that these programs have not worked. However, evaluation researchers continue to explore the efficacy of such efforts.

Chapter 27, by Osgood and Weichselbaum, presents new findings from a study of nine juvenile diversion programs in seven metropolitan areas throughout the United States. Much of the research on diversion programs has demonstrated that past programs have failed because they increase rather than decrease the reach of the justice system. That is, the clients in diversion programs tend to be youth who were arrested but would have been released anyway, or were never arrested but referred to diversion programs from outside the justice system. The findings from this evaluation support the utility of the concept of diversions if it is implemented properly.

In Chapter 28 Rhodes and Matsuba examine the sources of potential social discrimination in pretrial release programs in which defendants who are accused of criminal offenses are released from detention pending trial. The goals of the program are consistent with long-standing efforts to minimize the unintended negative consequences of the justice system. Interest in this strategy has also increased as overcrowding in jails and prisons has become a more widespread problem. Data were obtained from defendants in ten federal judicial districts. Multiple regression analysis is used to determine factors affecting judges' decisions regarding bail and factors associated with pretrial misconduct.

Chapter 29 by Sherman and Berk is a single-site evaluation of the deterrent effects of arrest for domestic assault. We selected this particular evaluation for inclusion because of its rigorous experimental outcomes design. Three interventions were evaluated in a randomized experiment. The outcome measure was rate of repeat incidents. The findings make a useful contribution to our understanding of deterrence. In brief, the evaluators concluded that in cases of domestic assault, the initial arrest and incarceration regardless of eventual judicial decision is enough to deter subsequent violations.

The final paper in this section, Chapter 30, is a review of what has been learned from evaluations of programs aimed at increasing employment opportunities for ex-offenders. Particular attention is given by Jacobs, McGahey, and Minion to a review of the impact of the Targeted Jobs Tax Credit, a program providing employers with tax deductions for hiring ex-offenders.

27

Juvenile Diversion
When Practice Matches Theory

D. Wayne Osgood and Hart F. Weichselbaum

Research has shown that most juvenile diversion programs are precluded from reaching their goals of reducing coercion, social control, and stigma because they serve populations that are not, in fact, diverted from the justice system. The present study addressed the issue of whether properly implemented diversion programs would meet these goals. The question was examined in terms of service providers' and clients' views about diversion and justice programs. The study included samples from nine diversion programs and associated justice agencies. Findings for both service providers and clients were quite consistent across sites in demonstrating that diversion programs do constitute a true alternative to services from justice agencies. The study also compared the views of clients to those of service providers. It was found that clients considered diversion programs more oriented to coercion and social control and less oriented to serving clients' needs. On the other hand, clients believed that service providers held more positive views about clients than was actually the case. The findings indicate that labeling processes differ among alternative societal responses to deviance, but also that youths may not be very sensitive to the negative opinions others hold about them. The import of the study for social policy is that diversion programs hold considerable promise for reducing coercion, social control, and perhaps stigma, if problems of implementation can be overcome.

Diversion programs have been the most popular of recent innovations in juvenile justice (Emey, 1982). It would be difficult to find a major city that has not had a diversion program of some sort. The idea of diverting offenders from formal dispositions in the justice system is an old one and is embodied in many basic practices of the juvenile justice

This research was conducted at the Behavioral Research Institute and funded by the National Institute of Juvenile Justice and Delinquency Prevention, grants 77-NI-99-0011, 77-JN-99-0009, and 78-JN-AX-0037. We are indebted to Martin Gold, Janis Jacobs, and Theodore Newcomb for their comments on an earlier draft of this article.

From D. Wayne Osgood and Hart F. Weichselbaum, "Juvenile Diversion: When Practice Matches Theory," *Journal of Research in Crime and Delinquency,* 1984, 21(1), 33-56. Copyright 1984 by Sage Publications, Inc.

system. The creation of diversion programs institutionalized this idea in that there came to be organizations specifically dedicated to diverting offenders and providing them with community-based services. The impetus for these programs came from the President's Commission on Law Enforcement and the Administration of Justice (1967). Diversion programs were one of the major strategies recommended by the commission for overcoming the shortcomings of the juvenile justice system, and this recommendation received considerable support from criminologists (for example, see Lemert, 1971; Polk and Kobrin, 1972).

It is clear that the popularity of juvenile diversion is waning, and there are far fewer juvenile diversion programs now than there were in the mid-1970s. The major federal initiatives that supported these programs have ended, and few programs have been able to enlist continuing local support, particularly given current economic constraints. Furthermore, the enthusiasm of the research community has been replaced by growing disenchantment (see Austin and Krisberg, 1981; Dunford, 1977; Klein, 1979; Lemert, 1981). Considering the resources that have been invested in juvenile diversion, a careful consideration of its strengths and weaknesses is in order before it is written off as a fad whose day has passed. The present article addresses a basic question about juvenile diversion that has received little attention: Do diversion programs provide their clients with a substantially different experience than they would receive through formal dispositions? Not only is this question of crucial importance to policy about diversion, it is also central to the criminological theorizing that justified the concept.

GOALS OF DIVERSION

The essential feature of diversion programs is their status as an alternative to formal dispositions in the juvenile justice system. The effectiveness of diversion programs at reaching their goals should result from this alternative status rather than from the nature of the services provided, such as whether youths are counseled, join in recreation, or receive school or job assistance. In fact, the full range of youth services appears under the aegis of both diversion programs and justice agencies, and there is little agreement about which services are most appropriate in either setting.

Assessing the merits of juvenile diversion is complex because of the variety of goals held by various proponents of the programs (as is probably true of most social programs). Palmer and Lewis (1980) provide a useful history of the commissions and governmental initiatives that led to the widespread adoption of diversion programs. They derive five goals that capture the most important expectations held for the programs; this list will serve as a useful framework for our discussion: (1) to reduce stigma, (2) to reduce coercion and social control, (3) to reduce recidivism (or, more broadly, to improve clients' social adjustment), (4) to provide services, and (5) to reduce the costs and improve the efficiency of the juvenile justice system.

The rise of juvenile diversion is in large part attributable to the popularity of labeling theory during the 1960s. Accordingly, the first three goals reflect labeling theory's concern that the unintended negative effects of involvement in the justice system may outweigh the benefits of any assistance that is offered. According to labeling theory (see Lemert, 1951, 1971), official reaction to deviance invokes stigma that sets an individual apart from others as a "deviant person." Furthermore, formal dispositions are likely to entail both coercion, by threatening sanctions in response to any lack of cooperation with officials, and social control, through placing the individual under strict rules of behavior. Such coercion and social control reinforce the message that the individual is not a normal person. They also make the individual subject to further official reactions for behavior that is acceptable from others (such as violating rules of probation). These processes can lead the individual to consider him- or herself a delinquent, which will lead to increased delinquency. Official reactions thereby become the cause of further delinquency.

The significance of labeling theory for juvenile justice goes beyond the validity of this assertion of a causal link between justice processing and recidivism. It is equally important that labeling theory highlighted stigma, coercion, and social control as unintended features of the justice system. Undoubtedly, many youth advocates beacame concerned with these issues in their own right, and they supported the idea of diversion simply because they considered such treatment inhumane.

The goal of providing services stands apart from labeling theory. The logic of the theory better lends itself to a hands-off approach than to any social service program (Schur, 1973). Nevertheless, many parties with an interest in juvenile justice are committed to delivering services, and from their perspectives diversion programs had special potentials. If service providers worked in community-based agencies they would not be obliged to act as agents of social control. Their time would be free to deliver more services, and the services might be more effective in a setting with less stigma, coercion, and social control.

The final goal is based on the assumption that the juvenile justice system is inefficient because it is overburdened. For example, probation officers have little chance of reducing recidivism if their caseloads are so large that they have little contact with most of their clients. Diversion programs would help by taking clients out of the system and reducing caseloads. This reduction could also be the basis of cost savings.

EVALUATION OF JUVENILE DIVERSION

There have been two types of research evaluating the success of diversion programs at reaching these goals. One type focuses on the impact of the program on its clients, usually in terms of recidivism. Though such research addresses only one of the five goals for diversion programs, this goal is likely to be of special importance in policy decisions, and it also has significant bearing on the validity of labeling theory. A review of this sizable body of research is beyond our present purposes. It is sufficient to note that the results are mixed, with some studies finding diversion programs superior to other alternatives (for example, see Baron et al., 1973; Davidson et al., 1977) and other studies finding no difference (see Dunford et al., 1981). Though the interpretation of these findings may be subject to debate, it is safe to say that they are not the major cause of the declining popularity of juvenile diversion. Even a skeptical view would allow that the programs are no worse than justice system alternatives in their impact on clients.

The second type of research about diversion concerns whether the programs have constituted true alternatives to processing through the justice system, and it is in this regard that criminologists have been most critical. As has been documented by Klein (1979), research shows that the client populations of most so-called diversion programs are not being "diverted" from formal dispositions in the justice system. Instead, they are youths who were arrested but would normally have been lectured and released, or they are youths who were never arrested but were referred to diversion programs from outside the justice system. Also, many diversion programs have failed to serve as alternatives because they were operated by justice system personnel (Rutherford and McDermott, 1976).

Most of the goals for diversion programs are predicated on the assumption that clients are offenders who are being removed from the justice system. Diversion programs cannot avoid the stigma, coercion, and social control of formal dispositions if their clients were never at risk of receiving those dispositions. The programs may actually increase these phenomena if they serve as extensions of the justice system and expand its clientele. Furthermore, diversion programs will fail to ease the burden of the justice system if they do not remove clients from its jurisdiction.

The essence of these criticisms is that the programs have failed precisely because they were *not diversion programs*. Given the prevalence of these problems of implementation, it is understandable that some authors are willing to write off diversion as an unworkable idea (Lemet, 1981; Austin and Krisberg, 1981). On the other hand, there is good evidence that some agencies have functioned as true diversion programs in that they delivered services in a community-based setting to youths who were diverted away from formal dispositions (Dunford et al., 1981). Though the problems of implementation may be serious, they are not necessarily insurmountable.

THE PRESENT STUDY

The glaring gap in our knowledge is whether properly implemented diversion programs would reduce stigma, coercion, and social control. If they do not, it would be well to give up on the idea of diversion and seek other means of reaching these goals. If they do, then diversion programs may merit further consideration. The present study is an attempt to shed light on this issue.

This topic is as important for criminological theory as it is for policy. The legacy of labeling theory is concern about negative connotations of even well-intended treatment for deviant individuals. Unfortunatley, this theoretical and humanitarian concern has not been matched by empirical research to establish which connotations follow from which possible responses to deviance. Without empirical investigations, applications of labeling theory to policy remain tenuous. Furthermore, such information is needed for the development of theory that goes beyond basic insights about labeling to an analysis of social processes involved in transmitting negative connotations to youths, their families, and the community at large.

The application of the labeling perspective to juvenile diversion rests on the perhaps simplistic assumption that stigma, coercion, and social control result from the formal affiliation of a service program with the justice system. It is, however, a leap of faith to presume that these problems will not exist for community-based programs dedicated to serving the same clientele. It seems quite possible that arrested youths might be labeled by being sent to any programs for delinquents, even if it is based in the community. It is in this regard that Cressey and McDermott (1973: 34) observed:

> So far as we know, no one has shown that the juvenile offender and his family perceived their handling as materially different under the auspices of a diversion unit than under a more traditional juvenile justice agency. The question is rarely formulated, let alone asked. It is probable that the juvenile does not discriminate as readily as the intake officer between such realities as counseling, informal probation, regular probation and coercion.

Nejelski (1976: 22) shares these concerns, arguing that the separation of diversion programs from the justice system may not be sufficient to alter the significance of participation in the eyes of clients, particularly with regard to coercion.

> The coercive power of the state and the court is always present in diversion. The child and his parents "agree" to enter a particular program "recommended" by some state official, because they can be ordered by a judge to accept this program or one that is substantially more unpleasant.

The present study attempts to determine if the connotations of participating in diversion programs differ from those of formal justice dispositions in accord with the goals of diversion. We do so by examining clients' and service providers' views. The connotations of participating in a program should be, at least in part, a function of service providers' views about their mission. If service providers at diversion programs view their work in the same way as their counterparts in the justice system, the significance of the programs for clients, their families, and the communities are likely to be the same as well.

It is essential to study both clients' and service providers' views about the programs because there is considerable potential for disagreement between the two parties. Wheeler et al.'s (1968) study of the sentencing practices of juvenile court judges offers a useful example. They found that judges who considered themselves more liberal and more concerned with rehabilitation gave harsher dispositions than judges who professed punishment and social control. It is doubtful that these liberal judges and the offenders who stood before them would have seen eye to eye about the emphasis on social control in those courtrooms.

Because of this potential for disagreement we will also compare clients' views about diversion programs with the views of service providers. Despite the prominence of these issues in labeling theory, we know very little about the dynamics between service providers' views about their work and their clients' interpretations of their treatment. A likely source of disagreement between these parties is the ambiguous relationship of diversion programs with the justice system. Even if diversion programs are autonomous agencies, they are necessarily dependent on the justice system for a client population. For service providers, the diversion program is defined in contrast to the juvenile justice system. Their mission is to provide an alternative. This contrast is likely to be less apparent to clients. For them, referral to a diversion program is part of the reaction by the justice system that began with apprehension. Thus the features said to be associated with services from justice agencies are likely to be attributed to diversion programs more by clients than by service providers.

The present study investigates client's and service providers' views about four issues: coercion, social control, concern with serving clients' needs, and service providers' opinions about clients. Reducing coercion and social control is one of the goals of diversion programs. Concern with serving client needs represents an important facet of the goal of delivering services. We have chosen to study service providers' opinions about clients and clients' beliefs about these opinions as an aspect of potential stigma located in the context of service delivery.

METHOD

Research Sites

In studying diversion, it is important that a variety of programs be considered rather than any single program or approach. Diversion programs vary in so many ways that a finding for any one may be quite irrelevant to others. Given our aims, we must also be selective about which programs we include. Though definitions of diversion are subject to debate, some standards are essential. It is clear that programs serving adjudicated delinquents do not qualify, nor do programs staffed by probation and police officers or programs to which clients are referred from outside the justice system.

The data presented here come from the national evaluation of the programs funded by the Diversion Initiative of the Office of Juvenile

Justice and Delinquency Prevention. The present study included nine diversion programs in seven metropolitan areas throughout the United States.[1] This set of programs constitutes an appropriate sample in several respects. The programs received adequate financial support, so they were not unfairly burdened by staff shortages or preoccupation with fund raising. They were also subject to stringent guidelines for client eligibility. Though the programs did not always fully adhere to these guidelines, they are among the better examples of programs that attempted to remove offenders from formal justice dispositions. Virtually all clients had been apprehended by the police. Only one program served status offenders, and even there status offenders were in the minority. None of the programs employed justice personnel as service providers.

The programs also represent a variety of approaches to diversion. Each program offered a range of youth services, including various forms of counseling, educational and vocational assistance, and recreation. Some programs employed their own staff to provide services, and others served a brokering role, arranging services from agencies with larger (and not necessarily delinquent) clienteles. The programs' statuses in relation to the justice system varied from administration by justice agencies to complete autonomy. Minority members (black or Hispanic) constituted at least 20% of each program's client population and virtually the entire populations of two programs. From 10% to 32% of the programs' populations were females. Finally, client populations ranged from solely first-time misdemeanants to solely repeat offenders, most of whom had been arrested one or more times for felony charges. Thus the sample of programs gives a good basis for generalizing to the majority of programs that satisfy an adequate definition of diversion.

Samples of Respondents

The design of the study calls for samples of four types of individuals: service providers at diversion programs, service providers at justice agencies, clients at diversion programs, and clients at justice agencies. The selection of the samples and methods of data collection are described below, followed by a discussion of sample losses.

An issue that arises in comparing diversion and justice programs is that service programs in the justice system are almost sure to serve a more delinquent client population. Inasmuch as diversion is considered a less severe disposition, it will be used for less serious cases. Such differences do not necessarily invalidate the comparisons of interest here, though they may. For our purposes, the important factor is whether the treatment of an individual client depends on his or her personal characteristics or on the characteristics of the program's entire client population. If program variables depend on the nature of the entire population, then all clients of a diversion program will benefit (or suffer) from attending a program with a less delinquent population. If program variables depend on characteristics of the individual, then there could appear to be differences between program, when, in fact, any given individual would receive the same treatment from either of them. Only in the latter case would differences in client populations confound our results.

It seems likely that the amount of emphasis programs place on coercion, social control, and serving clients' needs is constant within any program rather than tailored to individual clients. Service providers have not been allowed much flexibility on these issues in programs with which we are familiar. On the other hand, it would not be surprising if service providers' views about clients depended on individual characteristics.

If differences between programs were a function of individually tailored treatment for differing client populations. they would be eliminated by statistically controlling for individual characteristics. Such an analysis is quite feasible for clients' views about the programs. This approach is not applicable for the analysis of service providers' views because their responses concern the program rather than individual clients. Therefore, the findings for service providers must be interpreted in light of the effects of statistical controls in the analysis for clients.

Service Providers at Diversion Programs. All service providers who worked directly with diversion clients were considered eligible for the sample. Thus, for programs that brokered services, these individuals were actually employed by other agencies. They were asked to respond only with regard to their work with diversion clients.

The research staff contacted all service providers (diversion and justice) by mail and asked them to complete a brief questionnaire. At least two reminders were sent to any individuals who failed to respond. Data collection occurred 18 to 22 months after these programs began to accept clients.

Service Providers at Justice Agencies. Probation is the disposition in the juvenile justice system most comparable to receiving services from a diversion program. More informal dispositions do not usually involve services and more restrictive dispositions imply residential settings. Therefore, the probation officers who supervised caseloads in the jurisdictions served by the diversion programs were selected to serve as the comparison group for service providers at diversion programs. The selected samples included all officers who supervise probationers, except in Site B, where a random subsample was drawn. At Site B, probation services were rendered by a large group of volunteer probation officers. Probation officers at all other sites were full-time professionals. Data collection from justice and diversion personnel occurred simultaneously.

Clients at Diversion Programs. At four of the diversion programs (Sites A, B, and C, and Project 1 of Site G) data from diversion clients were gathered as part of a study of program impact. These data come from personal interviews conducted six months after referral to the program. Usually clients had completed their participation in the program by the time of the interview. The samples include all clients referred during the first ten to fourteen months of project operation. Only those respondents who indicated that they had actually received services from the program were included in the present analyses. This was necessary because the variables of interest concern the experience of participating in a program.

For the remaining five programs, only clients who received services were interviewed. All entered the progams during a six-month period that began six to ten months after the programs started serving clients. Again, clients were interviewed six months after their referral to the program. The samples selected were composed of either all referrals during the sampling period or a random subsample.

The research staff hired and trained the interviewers. Interviewers were instructed to make clear that they were not affiliated with the diversion programs and that responses were confidential. Respondents received $5.00 for participation.

Clients at Justice Agencies. Samples of justice clients were available for Sites A, B, and C as part of the study of the impact of diversion on clients. For the purposes of that study, these youths were randomly assigned to normal processing by the justice system rather than diversion, but this random assignment is of little consequence for the present study. Only youths who indicated that they had received services from a justice agency could be included in the present analyses, so random assignment did not necessarily mean that the samples of justice and diversion clients were comparable. The vast majority of justice clients were probationers; a few had been incarcerated. Data collection took the same form as for diversion clients at the three sites.

Sample Sizes. Table 1 presents the sizes of samples initially selected and of samples actually responding. Response rates were highest among service providers at diversion programs, probably because the agencies were obligated to cooperate with the researchers. Rates varied considerably within other categories. Though response rates were low in a few instances, there is little danger of losses biasing the results of the study, given the breadth of the sample of programs and the prevalence of high rates of response.

Measures

The five variables of interest in the study were measured by scales of four to eight items. The items were virtually identical for clients and service providers except for minor changes in wording (for instance, the term "you" for clients was replaced by "your clients" for staff). Respondents answered all items using a five-point scale ranging from "strongly agree" to "strongly disagree." Table 2 presents the means, standard deviations, and internal consistency reliabilities of these scales for service providers and clients. Descriptions of the variables and example items follow.

Coercion. High scores on coercion meant that clients had little choice about joining the program or continuing participation.

"Youth can choose to stop coming to this program whenever they want."

"Youth feel forced or pushed into this program."

Social Control. A social control orientation implies that the program has a punitive function, serves to monitor clients' activities, and attempts to enforce conforming behavior.

"Clients are sent to this program to pay for their crimes."

"Your clients know that you are keeping track of their behavior, even when they are away from your supervision."

Serving Needs. This variable reflects the program's emphasis on meeting the needs of clients.

TABLE 1: Sizes of Samples Selected and Responding

Site	Service Providers				Clients			
	Diversion		Justice		Diversion		Justice	
	Selected	Responding	Selected	Responding	Selected	Responding	Selected	Responding
A	13	11	30	28	– (212)	117 (180)	– (111)	31 (81)
B	43	38	40	18	– (299)	79 (169)	– (331)	25 (107)
C	14	14	18	13	– (244)	142 (176)	– (222)	28 (135)
D	21	21	15	9	49	39	–	–
E	22	22	38	19	49	40	–	–
F	18	15	16	11	52	40	–	–
G, Project 1	11	9	15	7	– (181)	24 (138)	–	–
G, Project 2	5	5	15	7	51	38	–	–
G, Project 3	9	9	15	7	43	31	–	–

NOTE: The three projects of Site G share a common sample of service providers from justice agencies. At sites A, B, C, and G, Project 1, clients included in the analysis come from a larger sample of respondents who had been referred to the diversion project or to juvenile court. The numbers in parentheses refer to those larger samples. Clients who stated that they had actually received services were retained for the analysis.

TABLE 2: Means, Standard Deviations, and Reliabilities of
the Measures of Views About Service Programs

Variable	Number of Items	Service Providers			Clients		
		Mean	S.D.	Reliability	Mean	S.D.	Reliability
Coercion	6	15.62	4.89	.79	16.12	3.94	.67
Social control	8	19.61	4.69	.70	20.97	5.26	.80
Serving needs	5	21.30	2.67	.75	18.88	2.87	.75
Clients viewed as delinquent	4	13.09	2.60	.73	10.02	2.81	.81
Clients viewed as emotionally disturbed	4	14.35	2.61	.74	9.42	2.61	.76

NOTE: The measure of reliability is Cronbach's alpha, which reflect the internal consistency of a scale.

"Youth workers are here to aid clients in making better lives for themselves."

"This agency provides clients with new opportunities."

Clients Viewed as Delinquent. This aspect of stigma concerns service providers' willingness to describe their clients in terms associated with delinquency.

"How much would you agree that the youth in your client population . . .

or

"How much would the staff at that agency agree that you . . . "

" . . . are bad kids?"

" . . . get into trouble?

Clients Viewed as Emotionally Disturbed.[2] Though this form of stigma is not normally discussed in rationales for diversion, it is worthy of our attention. The connotations of being seen as emotionally disturbed may be more debilitating than being considered delinquent, for the concept conveys an image of helplessness and lack of control over one's own fate.

"How much would you agree that the youth in your client population . . ."

" . . . need help emotionally?"

" . . . have a lot of personal problems?"

RESULTS

Comparisons Between Service Providers

Means for diversion and justice service providers on the five dependent variables appear in Table 3. For each variable, the two groups can be compared both within each site and across the entire set of nine sites. The statistic used for within-site comparisons was the t test, with individual respondents serving as the unit of analysis. In the comparisons across sites, each side was given equal weight, and the site became the unit of analysis. Because only one justice program served Site G, the three diversion programs were pooled (each receiving equal weight). Thus there were seven cases in the across-site comparisons.

An examination of Table 3 reveals a remarkable consistency in the results. For all of the dependent variables, the direction of difference between diversion and justice service providers is perfectly consistent across the nine sites. Furthermore, for each of the dependent variables the direction of difference implies that diversion programs offer a more benign context for service delivery. As can be seen in the bottom row of the table, the differences are statistically significant ($p < .05$) by t tests when sites are the unit of analysis. The differences are also significant by the nonparametric sign test ($p = .016$).

The most notable differences in service providers' views are that justice service providers characterize their programs as more coercive and more concerned with social control. Almost all within-site comparisons for these variables were significant, and the magnitude of the differences averaged more than a standard deviation.

Though the differences between the two program types are less striking for the remaining variables, they are still substantial. Service providers at diversion programs indicated greater concern with serving needs. They also described their clients as less delinquent and emotionally disturbed. Most within-site comparisons are significant for views about serving needs. This is not true for either dimension of views about clients. For those two variables the magnitude of the differences varies more widely across sites.

Comparisons Between Clients

We are able to compare the views of clients of diversion and justice programs only for the three sites at which there were samples of justice

TABLE 3: Means for Service Providers' Views About Diversion Programs and Justice Agencies

Site	Coercion		Social Control		Serving Needs		Clients Viewed as Delinquent		Clients Viewed as Emotionally Disturbed	
	Diversion	Justice	Diversion	Justice	Diversion	Justice	Diversion	Justice	Diversion	Justice
A	13.2	20.8***	20.1	24.2**	22.6	20.1**	13.9	14.0	13.0	15.0*
B	14.1	19.6***	17.6	21.4**	21.4	20.1	12.6	13.3	13.8	15.1*
C	14.9	19.6*	16.6	22.5**	22.0	19.8*	10.7	14.2***	11.5	14.9**
D	13.4	17.1*	17.5	19.7	22.6	21.6	14.0	14.9	14.0	15.6
E	12.4	18.4***	17.3	23.1***	23.0	21.2*	12.8	14.0	14.2	14.8
F	12.3	17.7**	15.4	22.2***	22.2	20.5	11.5	15.8***	13.9	14.5
G, Project 1	12.8	20.7***	17.3	23.4**	21.6	17.1**	12.2	14.6	13.2	15.9
G, Project 2	13.1	20.7***	17.0	23.4**	20.6	17.1*	13.0	14.6	14.3	15.9
G, Project 3	14.5	20.7***	18.9	23.4*	21.1	17.1*	12.6	14.6	13.8	15.9
Mean across sites	13.40	19.13***	17.46	22.36***	22.13	20.06**	12.59	14.40*	13.46	15.11**

NOTE: Significance levels are for t tests between diversion and justice means. For tests on the means across sites, each was treated as a single case.

*p < .05; **p < .01; ***p < .001; all tests two-tailed.

515

TABLE 4: Background Characteristics of Clients (percentages)

	Age			Sex		Ethnic Group		Prior Arrests		
	11-13	14-15	16-17	Male	Female	White	Minority	None	One	Two or More
Site A										
Diversion	28	38	34	84	16	32	68	44	26	30
Justice	18	54	28	93	7	25	75	32	32	36
Site B										
Diversion	22	32	46	90	10	39	61	60	24	16
Justice	13	38	49	83	17	33	67	33	33	33
Site C										
Diversion	19	45	36	66	34	61	39	83	12	5
Justice	22	44	34	59	41	78	22	74	11	15

clients. Table 4 presents comparisons of the two groups of clients on age, sex, ethnicity, and number of prior offenses.

Though clients wee randomly assigned between the two programs, the groups included in the analysis are not fully comparable. Clients of justice programs had more prior arrests at all three sites, though the differences are not dramatic. Differences occur because random assignment was to *referral* to the diversion program or juvenile court. As can be seen in Table 1, a substantial number of those referred to either program reported that they received no services during the six-month period. These respondents could not be included in the analysis because we are examining views about receiving services. If these views are a function of clients' characteristics, the comparisons might be biased.

Fortunately, a wide variety of information about these respondents was obtained at the time of referral. To take any prior differences into account, analysis of covariance was used to control for 20 variables in comparing clients of diversion and justice programs.[3] Though no statistical procedure can fully eliminate initial differences between groups, we can have more confidence in our conclusions if the results are consistent with and without the controls.

The comparisons between clients' views about the types of programs are presented in Table 5. Diversion programs again receive their strongest support for the dimensions of coercion and social control. Justice clients rated their programs higher on both these variables to a degree that is statistically significant at all three sites. The corrections for covariates have little effect on the magnitude of these differences.

At all three sites clients also felt that the diversion programs placed greater emphasis on serving clients' needs. The magnitude of the

TABLE 5: Means for Clients' Views About Diversion Programs and Justice Agencies

Site	Coercion		Social Control		Serving Needs		Clients Viewed as Delinquent		Clients Viewed as Emotionally Disturbed	
	Diversion	Justice	Diversion	Justice	Diversion	Justice	Diversion	Justice	Diversion	Justice
Uncorrected Means										
A	15.4	18.8***	20.6	25.4***	19.5	18.3***	10.2	10.9*	9.3	9.5
B	15.9	18.7***	20.6	25.0***	19.0	17.8	10.0	10.8	10.0	9.3
C	15.2	18.7**	19.3	23.0*	18.7	17.7	9.3	11.0*	8.7	8.8
Means Corrected for Covariates										
A	15.1	19.0***	20.3	25.7***	19.8	18.0**	10.6	10.4	9.5	9.3
B	15.7	19.0***	21.0	24.9**	18.9	18.0	9.8	10.9	9.8	9.5
C	15.8	18.2**	19.5	22.8**	18.4	17.8	9.3	11.1**	8.8	8.8

NOTE: Significance levels for raw means are from t tests between diversion and justice groups, and they are from analysis of covariance for means corrected for covariates.

*p < .05; **p < .01; ***p < .001.

differences was similar at the three sites, but only in Site A were the means (uncorrected and corrected) significantly different.

Results concerning clients' perceptions of being viewed as delinquent by service providers are more complex. Before correcting for covariates, at all three sites diversion programs are lower on this dimension than justice agencies, significantly so at Sites A and C. Correcting for covariates makes little difference for the means of Sites B and C, but this correction reverses the difference at Site A. Of all the comparisons between clients, this is the only instance in which the correction has a substantial effect. This result indicates that, at the time of referral, diversion and justice clients already differed on variables that predicted their perceptions about service providers' views.

It is also worth noting that at Site A there was negligible difference between diversion and justice *service providers* for viewing clients as delinquent (means of 13.9 and 14.0, respectively). Therefore, for this dimension we might expect diversion and justice clients to have more similar perceptions at this site than they would at other sites.

In all, the pattern of results is weaker for this variable than for others. Nevertheless, based on the evidence for Sites B and C and the weakness of the analysis for Site A, it appears that clients of most diversion programs would feel they were viewed as delinquent less than would clients of justice agencies.

There is no evidence of differences between the two groups of clients in their reports about service providers viewing them as emotionally disturbed. In no case do the groups differ significantly, and the means are quite similar, particularly after controlling for covariates.

The Role of Client Characteristics in Program Differences

As is shown in Table 5, statistical controls had little effect on the magnitude of differences between the two programs. This indicates that views about programs are not a function of the characteristics of individual clients being served. The consistency of this result for the three programs included in the analysis of clients' views supports generalizing this interpretation to the nine programs included in the analysis of service providers' views.

The only case in which the statistical controls altered a finding was for clients' perceptions about service providers viewing them as delinquent at Site A. This change actually brought the findings for clients at this site into agreement with those for service providers. Though clients at the

TABLE 6: Means for Service Providers' and Clients' Views About Diversion Programs

Site	Coercion		Social Control		Serving Needs		Clients Viewed as Delinquent		Clients Viewed as Emotionally Disturbed	
	Clients	Service Providers	Clients	Service Providers	Clients	Service Providers	Clients	Service Providers	Clients	Service Providers
A	15.4	13.2*	20.6	20.1	19.5	22.6***	10.2	13.9***	9.3	13.0***
B	15.9	14.1*	20.6	17.6***	19.0	21.4***	10.0	12.6***	10.0	13.8***
C	15.2	14.9	19.3	16.6*	18.7	22.0***	9.3	10.7	8.7	11.5*
D	15.0	13.4**	21.4	17.5***	19.8	22.6***	9.6	14.0***	9.6	14.0***
E	13.6	12.4	18.9	17.3	19.8	23.0***	9.5	12.8***	9.1	14.2***
F	13.5	12.3	19.9	15.4***	19.7	22.2*	10.6	11.5	8.8	13.9**
G, Project 1	15.3	12.8	21.3	17.3	19.9	21.6	9.8	12.2*	9.8	13.2**
G, Project 2	14.8	13.1*	21.2	17.0*	19.8	20.6	10.3	13.0*	10.8	14.3*
G, Project 3	16.4	14.5	23.0	18.9*	20.3	21.1	9.7	12.6*	10.1	13.8***
Mean across sites	15.01	13.41***	20.69	17.52***	19.61	21.90***	9.89	12.59***	9.58	13.52***

NOTE: Significance levels are for t tests between service provider and client means. For tests on the means across sites, each site was treated as a single case.

*p < .05; **p < .01; ***p < .001.

saw diversion and justice services as different. Both service providers and clients indicated that justice agencies placed greater emphasis on coercion and social control, and that diversion programs had a stronger orientation toward serving clients' needs. Service providers at diversion programs were also less prone to view their clients as delinquent, both by their own report and according to clients, but sites varied more widely in this regard than others. Only findings concerning clients being viewed as emotionally disturbed were equivocal. From the point of view of service providers, clients at diversion programs are less likely to be seen in this way, but there is no difference between the two types of agency from the point of view of clients.

The present findings are quite pertinent to labeling theory in that they demonstrate labeling processes to vary among alternative societal responses to deviance. In particular, we see that the formal affiliation of a service program with the justice system affects the connotations of participation. Even if diversion programs entail some degree of coercion and social control, it is substantially less than for formal dispositions.

The present study focuses on aspects of the labeling process that are located in the service setting itself, and in that limited domain the application of labeling theory to diversion is well supported. There are, however, many potential sources of stigma outside of the service setting. Therefore, our findings do not necessarily imply that diversion will reduce the likelihood of a delinquent and further delinquency, even if the causal assertions of labeling theory are valid. These relations merit further attention.

The comparison between client and service provider views about diversion yielded some unexpected findings. As was suspected, service providers held more positive opinions about the programs than did their clients. Clients felt the programs were more coercive, more oriented to social control, and less concerned with serving needs. We have no basis for determining whether client or service provider views are more accurate. Since clients reach the programs as a result of arrest, they may incorrectly presume that the programs serve a social control function and that sanctions would follow a lack of cooperation. This would also imply that service providers fail to allay such fears. It is equally possible that clients are correct, and service providers fail to realize how much power for coercion and social control is at their disposal. For example, service providers may fail to appreciate that giving a negative or even nonpositive report of client progress to the referring agency could mean that any rearrest would result in harsher dispositions.

Considering the above findings, we might guess that clients would presume service providers hold negative opinions about them. Quite the opposite was found. Service providers described their clients in much more negative terms than the clients thought they would. This might be seen as a success for the service providers, since diversion programs are intended to avoid stigma, and clients did not feel stigmatized by the service providers. Nevertheless, the findings probably represent a more general phenomenon since it appears that service providers and clients at justice agencies differ in the same way (see Tables 3 and 5). This finding seems to indicate that service providers and clients have different frames of reference for the judgments involved in such measures. Service providers expect most adolescents to be law abiding and find their clients deviant, yet the clients do not consider themselves exceptional. If this is true, one must wonder about the relevance of some central themes of labeling theory. Perhaps the self-images of youthful offenders are more resilient than had been suspected. Our pattern of findings is reminiscent of Sykes and Matza's (1957) conception of techniques of neutralization. They theorized that individuals who commit deviant acts are able to maintain a conventional self-image by finding personally adequate justifications for their behavior.

In conclusion, we believe that our findings make an important contribution to the debate about the role of diversion in juvenile justice. Other research has shown that most diversion programs fail at goals of reducing coercion and social control because they increase rather than decrease the reach of the justice system. We now see that, if diversion programs are used as an alternative rather than an addition to justice processing, these goals can be reached. Furthermore, diversion programs are characterized by a greater concern with serving their clients' needs, and they reduce at least one form of stigma. Of course, these benefits can be obtained only through the implementation of programs that match the theory behind diversion. The question that remains is whether there is enough commitment to these goals for that task to be accomplished.

NOTES

1. We will refer to the research sites by arbitrary letters. Eleven programs participated in the national evaluation. Two of the programs were not included in the present study because adequate samples of respondents could not be obtained. For a complete description of this study, see Dunford et al. (1981).

2. This dimension of stigma was suggested by Malcolm Klein, and our measure is adapted from one he provided us.

3. The variables used as covariates were as follows: number of prior arrests, age, sex, ethnicity, importance of conventional goals, commitment to parents, commitment to peers, normlessness, viewed as delinquent by others (friends, teachers, and family), viewed as emotionally disturbed by others, viewed as conforming by others, self-image as delinquent, self-image as emotionally disturbed, self-image as conforming, counter-labeling, social isolation, peers' disapproval of deviance, and self-reported delinquency (divided into serious, minor, and drug-related offenses).

REFERENCES

Austin, J. and B. Krisberg
    1981 "Wider, stronger and different nets: the dialectics of criminal justice reform." J. of Research in Crime and Delinquency 18: 165-196.

Baron, R., F. Feeney, and W. Thornton
    1973 "Preventing delinquency through diversion: the Sacramento County 601 Diversion Project." Federal Probation 37: 13-18.

Cressey, D. and R. McDermott
    1973 Diversion from the Juvenile Justice System. Ann Arbor, MI: National Assessment of Juvenile Corrections.

Davidson, W. S., E. Seidman, J. Rappaport, P. Berck, W. Rhodes, and J. Herring
    1977 "Diversion program for juvenile offenders." Social Work Research and Abstracts 14: 313-338.

Dunford, F.W.
    1977 "Police diversion: an illusion." Criminology 15: 335-352.

Dunford, F. W., D. W. Osgood, and H. F. Weichselbaum
    1981 National Evaluation of Diversion Projects: Final Report. Boulder, Co: Behavioral Research Institute. (National Criminal Justice Reference Service microfiche NCJ80830)

Empey, L. T.
    1982 American Delinquency: Its Meaning and Construction. Homewood, IL: Dorsey.

Klein, M. W.
    1979 "Deinstitutionalization and diversion of juvenile offenders: a litany of impediments," in N. Morris and M. Tonry (eds.) Crime and Justice: An Annual Review of Research, Vol. 1. Chicago: Univ. of Chicago Press.

Lemert, E. M.
    1951 Social Pathology. New York: McGraw-Hill.
    1971 Instead of Court: Diversion in Juvenile Justice. Rockville, MD: National Institute of Mental Health.
    1981 "Diversion in juvenile justice: what hath been wrought." J. of Research in Crime and Delinquency 18: 35-46.

Nejelski, P.
    1976 "Diversion: the promise and the danger." Crime and Delinquency 22: 393-410.

Palmer, T. and R. V. Lewis
　　1980　An Evaluation of Juvenile Diversion. Cambridge, MA: Oelgeschlager, Gunn &
　　　　　Han.
Polk, K. and S. Kobrin
　　1972　Delinquency Prevention Through Youth Development (DHEW Publication
　　　　　[SRS] 72-26013). Washington, DC: Government Printing Office.
President's Commission on Law Enforcement and the Administration of Justice
　　1967　Task Force Report: Juvenile Delinquency and Youth Crime. Washington, DC:
　　　　　Government Printing Office.
Rutherford, A. and R. McDermott
　　1976　Juvenile Diversion: Phase I Summary Report. Washington, DC: National
　　　　　Institute of Law Enforcement and Criminal Justice.
Schur, E. M.
　　1973　Radical Nonintervention: Rethinking the Delinquency Problem. Englewood
　　　　　Cliffs, NJ: Prentice-Hall.
Sykes, G. M. and D. Matza
　　1957　"Techniques of neutralization: a theory of delinquency." Amer. Soc. Rev. 22:
　　　　　664-670.
Wheeler, S., E. Bonacich, M. R. Cramer, and I. K. Zola
　　1968　"Agents of delinquency control: a comparative analysis," in S. Wheeler (ed.)
　　　　　Controlling Delinquents. New York: John Wiley.

28

Pretrial Release in Federal Courts
A Structural Model with Selectivity and Qualitative Dependent Variables

William Rhodes and Shelley Matsuba

Pretrial release is the legal process by which defendants who are accused of criminal offenses are released from detention pending trial. Evaluators are frequently concerned with the qualitative and quantitative importance of defendant and offense variables in the determination of which defendants gain release and, for those who are released, which defendants will engage in pretrial misconduct. This article presents a method for deriving unbiased parameter estimates, using maximum likelihood techniques in a structural equation paradigm, for the release decision and indicates how these techniques can be extended to the analysis of pretrial misconduct.

*T*he Eighth Amendment to the U.S. Constitution protects accused defendants by the dictate that "excessive bail shall not be required." In 1951, the Supreme Court decision in Stack v. Boyle defined "excessive bail" as anything greater than the amount that would guarantee the appearance of the accused at trial. The Federal Bail Reform Act of 1966 went a step further to ensure that the accused is not detained unjustifiably or discriminated against financially. The act mandates that all defendants (except capital offenders) be eligible for release.

As Landes (1974) has demonstrated, legality and reality may differ. Judges also seem to consider the potential for pretrial crime when setting bail conditions. Findings similar to Landes's, which pertained to New York City, have been reported in other settings (Bynum, 1977; Roth and Wice, 1980; Toborg, 1981; Stryker et al., 1983). These studies imply that judges do not adhere strictly to constitutional dictates and that some defendants may be financially discriminated against.

From William Rhodes and Shelley Matsuba, "Pretrial Release in Federal Courts: A Structural Model with Selectivity and Qualitative Dependent Variables," *Evaluation Review*, 1984, 8(5), 92-704. Copyright 1984 by Sage Publications, Inc.

Researchers have modeled pretrial release with single-equation models, which limit inference. This article provides a structural perspective. Judges appear to set bail conditional on the defendant's background, including social stability, criminal record, and the crime charged. Moreover, bail amounts differ across judicial districts. Once bail is set, defendants solicit funds to satisfy the judges' demands. Financial intermediaries—bondsmen, friends, and family—offer the requisite funds at prices that vary with the risk posed by the defendant as a borrower.

Several purposes motivated this study. First, assuring justice requires an understanding of criminal justice processing. A structural model advances this understanding. Second, pretrial misconduct is a major concern of criminal justice administrators, and several researchers have used regression analysis to predict its occurrence, arguably to inform the court when setting bail. These attempts suffer from potential selectivity bias (Heckman, 1979). A structural model of release on bail would be a first step toward overcoming this bias. Third, bail decision-making offers an opportunity to study a financial market for low-income, high-risk borrowers.

This study is primarily empirical. In the next section, we develop a sequential model of pretrial release and follow that with a discussion of estimation and identification. The third section presents a data review. Following this, in section four, findings are reported. The final section draws implications from the analysis.

THE MODEL AND ESTIMATION

Judges are assumed to act in the public interest. They set bail according to the perceived likelihood that a defendant will engage in pretrial misconduct, either by willfully failing to appear for scheduled court dates, or by engaging in pretrial crime, or both. Thus, bail varies with a defendant's background, especially his or her criminal record and social stability, and the charge, because these factors influence judicial perceptions of risk.

Judges do not minimize community risk by setting prohibitively high bail amounts, however. The Constitution prohibits excessive bail, and judicial opinion and an act of Congress strongly support release. In addition, jails have limited capacities to hold federal defendants pending trial.

Judicial interpretations of "excessive bail" likely vary across judicial districts, as do the capacities of jails. Thus, although all judges take risk into account when setting bail, similarly situated offenders who are accused of similar crimes will have different bail set in different courts.

A judge may set bail at zero, releasing the defendant on his own recognizance. Approximately two of every three federal defendants are released on recognizance; these represent the best risks in the view of the judges. Poorer risks are required to post bail as an incentive to appear for trial. Defendants who fail to appear may forfeit bail, with the loss borne by the bondsman or others who lent the defendant money. High bail amounts may prevent the worst risks from gaining release.

Let B represent the bail amount. Let B* represent a latent variable indicating perceived (by the judge) risk. Let X represent a vector of exogenous variables. Let D represent a vector of dummy variables coded 1 to denote the judicial district where bail is set and otherwise coded 0. The model representing the amount of bail can be written:

$$B^* = \alpha X + \delta D + u, \ u \sim N(0, \sigma u)$$
$$B = B^* \text{ if } B^* \geq 0$$

$$B = 0 \text{ otherwise.} \qquad [1]$$

Greek letters denote conformable vectors of parameters. The error term u is independent and normally distributed, with a variance of σ^2_u.

Loan markets exist. Lenders are assumed to act in their own interests to avoid lending large amounts to risky borrowers who are likely to abscond. Assuming capital markets are competitive, the availability of bail funds does not vary significantly across the country.

The cost of a loan is denoted Bs and is a function of the amount of bail required and the perceived (by the lender) risk posed by the defendant to the lender. Thus:

$$Bs = B^{\beta^0} \text{EXP}(\beta X + u_s), \ u_s \sim N(0, \sigma_s) \qquad [2]$$

Bs is a latent variable. EXP ( ) is interpreted as a "multiplier" that increases or decreases the cost of the loan contingent on the financial risk posed by the borrower and an error term u_s.

The defendant is willing to pay a maximum price for freedom. Assuming a utility function underlies the borrower's behavior, willingness to pay will be influenced by taste, social situations, and income.

Let the maximum payment be Bd; the demand for loans can be written:

$$Bd = EXP\ (\tau X + u_d),\quad u_d \sim N(0,\sigma_d) \tag{3}$$

where U_d is a random error term. Like Bs, the demand for loans is a latent variable.

The defendant posts bail if Bd $\geq$ Bs, and does not post bail otherwise. Formally:

$$P = 1\ if\ Bd \geq Bs$$

$$P = 0\ otherwise \tag{4}$$

Taking logarithms of (2) and (3) implies:

$$P = 1\ if\ e = u_d - u_s \geq \beta^0 \log B + (\beta - \tau)\ X = \beta^0 \log B + \Gamma X$$

$$P = 0\ otherwise \tag{5}$$

where P indicates that bail was posted.

The correlation between u and e is nonzero. This follows from interpreting u as unmeasured factors that make a defendant appear to a judge as more or less risky than the measurable attributes of the defendant's background indicate. The error term u_s can be given a similar interpretation with regard to the lender's perception. Thus, it is hypothesized that r, the correlation between u and e, is negative. Moreover, it will be assumed that u and e are distributed as bivariate normal with E(u) = 0, E(e) = 0.

ESTIMATION

The estimation of equation 1 is a straightforward application of the tobit model (Tobin, 1957; Amemiya, 1973). The likelihood function and first derivatives can be found in Maddala (1983). Estimation of equation 5 is more complicated. The likelihood function can be written:

$$L = \frac{\displaystyle\prod_{P=1}\Phi(-e/\sigma_e,\ -u/\sigma_u,\ r) \cdot \prod_{P=0}[1 - \Phi(-e/\sigma_e,\ -u/\sigma_u,\ r)]}{\displaystyle\prod\phi(-u/\sigma_u)}$$

where Φ denotes the bivariate normal distribution and ϕ is the univariate normal distribution. The likelihood can be simplified. The distribution of e conditional on u (known from the tobit estimates) is normal with:

$$E(e|u) = (\sigma_{ue}/\sigma_u^2) \cdot u$$

$$VAR(e|u) = \sigma_e^2 - \sigma_{ue}^2/\sigma_u^2$$

$$\begin{array}{cc} L = \Pi\phi(z) \cdot & \Pi[1 - \phi(z)] \\ P = 1 & P = 0 \end{array}$$

where:

$$Z = \frac{-\beta^0 \log \beta - \Gamma X - (\sigma_{ue}/\sigma_u^2) \cdot u}{\sqrt{\sigma_e^2 - \sigma_{ue}^2/\sigma_u^2}}$$

where σ_{ue} is the covariance between u and e, and σ_u^2 and σ_e^2 are the variances of u and e, respectively.

Questions arise regarding identification. First, equation 7 is basically a probit model. The Γ parameters are identifiable only to a scale factor. It will be assumed that $\sigma_e = 1$.

Second, the structural parameters β and τ cannot be identified without additional restrictions. Since $\Gamma = \beta - \tau$, a suitable restriction is that β_i or τ_i equals zero (i denotes a vector element), implying that a variable that influences the demand for loans does not influence the supply, or that a variable that influences the supply does not affect the demand. Restrictions will be advanced in the next section.

Third, some variables that affect the judicial decision to set bail do not influence either the demand for, or the supply of, bail funds. Otherwise, Γ cannot be identified. The judicial district variables satisfy this requirement.

An additional issue arises when fitting equation 5. Bail amount is endogenous; it is not independent of the error term e. Consequently, an instrument variable equal to the expected value of bail, given that bail was set, was used. The instrument was derived from the tobit model.

The likelihood function was maximized using a modified Gauss-Newton algorithm. Programs, which require BMDP software and IMSL subroutines, are available on request.

DATA

Data were available from a study sponsored by the Bureau of Justice Statistics to integrate 1979 criminal case disposition data across federal justice agencies. Assembly of this data file and data quality are described elsewhere (Forst et al., 1983). We elaborate here on one data source, however.

Experimental pretrial service agencies existed in ten federal judicial districts during 1979; other nonexperimental agencies existed in at least three other federal districts. These agencies interview accused offenders prior to bail hearings and report their findings to the judge. Interviewers probe the defendant's social stability (length of residence, marital ties, and so on), economic stability (employment history, income, and so on), criminal record (convictions, bail revocations, and so on) and drug use. Interviews with pretrial service agents indicate that verification was routine and reliability checks on redundant data items in other files indicate that data reliability was high.

Only 63% of the defendants in the reporting districts were interviewed. Several reasons for this include: (1) defendants may be released prior to the interview, (2) some defendants refuse to be interviewed, and (3) investigative agencies sometimes fail to notify interviewers of the defendant's arrest. Preliminary analysis indicated that substantive findings were not affected materially by selectivity. Thus, interviews are treated as random events.

FINDINGS

Table 1 defines variables used in the analysis. In Table 2, the first column lists variables used in each regression. The second column lists parameter estimates using tobit to regress bail amount on a set of variables that were significant in earlier regressions. The third column reports parameter estimates from the sequential tobit model, assuming u and e are distributed as bivariate normal. The final column reports parameter estimates when u and e are assumed independent. Asymptotic standard errors are reported in parentheses.

Bail amounts were found to vary across judicial districts. In five districts, the parameter estimates were between two and four standard deviations. Bail also varied with the charge. Eight high-frequency offenses were tested; five were statistically significant with four having t-values greater than 4.

TABLE 1

Variables Used in the Analysis

Variable	Definition
SEX	male = 1; female = 0
RACE	white = 1; other = 0
AGE	years, at time of arrest
MARITAL	married and common law = 1; other = 0
EDUCATION	education[a]
OFF-SEV	offense severity[a]
OFF-FIL	felony charged = 1; misdemeanor or petty offense = 0
DEP-SUP	number of dependents supported
TIME-RES	months at the same residence
TIME-JOB	months employed
GROSS-INC	income for last year, thousands
TIME-UN	months unemployed
ILLNESS	physical illness = 1; otherwise = 0
PSYCH-ILL	psychological treatment = 1; otherwise = 0
USE-OP	abuse of opiates = 1; otherwise = 0
USE-NON	abuse of drugs other than opiates = 1; otherwise = 0
USE-ALC	abuse of alcohol = 1; otherwise = 0
JUMP-BAIL	prior instance of failure to appear = 1; other = 0
PROB-REV	prior probation/parole revocation = 1; otherwise = 0
JUV-REC	evidence of a juvenile record = 1; otherwise = 0
FEL-CON	number of felony convictions
MIS-CON	number of misdemeanor convictions
IMPRISON	number of times imprisoned
SUPER	under probation/parole at time of offense = 1; otherwise = 0
PEND	on bail at time of offense = 1; otherwise = 0
AGGRAV	aggravating circumstances[a]
PUB-COUN	public or community defender = 1; otherwise = 0
PRV-COUN	private council = 1; otherwise = 0
D1-D11	district dummy variable[a]
BANKROB	dummy variable
THEFT	dummy variable
EMBEZZLE	dummy variable
FRAUD	dummy variable
FORGERY	dummy variable
DRUGS	dummy variable
IMMIGRATION	dummy variable
WEAPONS	dummy variable
LOG-BAIL	logarithm of the instrument variable (bail)
RHO	correlation between e and u

a. Education was coded one = eighth grade or less; two = eighth to eleventh grade or less; three = twelfth grade or vocational degree; four = thirteen to sixteen years; five = BA degree or higher.

Offense severity is a three-character code:

(1) Possible Sentence	(2) Type of Crime	(3) Fine
0 none	0 none	0 none
1 less than 1 year	1 moral terpitude	1 $1-99
2 1-2 years	2 property	2 $100-249
3 3-5 years	3 person	3 $250-499
4 6-10 years		4 $500-999
5 11-15 years		5 $1000-2499
6 16-25 years		6 $2500-4999
7 26 or more years		7 $5000-9999
8 life		8 $10,000-49,999
9 death		9 $50,000 or over

Aggravating circumstances include armed at arrest, resisted arrest, officer injured and victim injured. Twelve districts were included in the analysis. A thirteenth district had fewer than 100 defendants and was excluded.

TABLE 2
Regression Results

Variable	Bail Amount Set (tobit)		Posting of Bail (sequential tobit)		Posting of Bail (probit)	
CONSTANT	−478.02*	(78.09)	8.97*	(1.32)	6.76*	(1.57)
SEX	147.83*	(32.16)	−.36*	(.094)	−.25*	(.12)
RACE	−42.03*	(21.52)	.12*	(.054)	.058	(.065)
AGE			.0097*	(.0034)	.0071	(.0043)
MARITAL			.16*	(.060)	.20*	(.074)
EDUCATION			.091*	(.026)	.10*	(.031)
OFF-SEV	.27*	(.10)	.0002	(.0003)	.0007*	(.0004)
OFF-FIL	295.23*	(54.49)	−.073	(.22)	.32	(.27)
DEP-SUP			.0003	(.020)	.011	(.023)
TIME-RES	−1.51*	(.31)	.0043*	(.0009)	.0029*	(.0011)
TIME-JOB			−.21	(.94)	−.19	(1.05)
GROSS-IN			26.60*	(4.28)	29.00*	(5.04)
TIME-UN			−.0017*	(.0010)	−.0028*	(.0013)
ILLNESS			.074	(.068)	.13	(.086)
PSYCH-ILL			.12	(.16)	.28	(.20)
USE-OP			−.11	(.078)	−.065	(.099)
USE-NON			−.034	(.090)	.0048	(.10)
USE-ALC			−.17*	(.098)	−.11	(.13)
JUMP-BAIL			−.21*	(.082)	−.27*	(.10)
PROB-REV			−.13	(.082)	−.16	(.10)
JUV-REC			.015	(.069)	.043	(.084)
FEL-CON			.012	(.018)	.0074	(.021)
MIS-CON	−4.91	(4.64)	.014	(.0099)	.026*	(.013)
IMPRISON			−.039*	(.016)	−.066	(.020)
SUPER	91.40*	(29.52)	−.13*	(.074)	−.014	(.090)
PEND	128.83*	(25.07)	−.099	(.067)	.0056	(.082)
AGGRAV	231.61*	(49.26)	−.0055	(.14)	.14	(.16)
PUB-COUN	−45.94	(29.37)	−.014	(.064)	−.032	(.079)
PRV-COUN	−63.95*	(25.51)	.58*	(.070)	.58*	(.083)
D1	−47.91	(67.21)				
D2	−39.31	(69.34)				
D3	−90.35*	(42.85)				
D4	−208.01*	(41.91)				
D5	−57.05	(60.47)				
D6	33.62	(50.37)				
D7	−98.81*	(47.97)				
D8	−118.99*	(61.54)				
D9	−107.11*	(38.79)				
D10	81.64*	(36.33)				
D11	−13.26	(62.46)				
BANKROB	130.21*	(52.06)	−.071	(.13)	−.14	(.15)
THEFT	−214.73*	(45.01)	.32*	(.13)	.23	(.17)
EMBEZZLE	−388.30*	(83.30)	.43	(.40)	−.13	(.42)
FRAUD	−212.62*	(41.77)	.16	(.14)	.061	(.17)
FORGERY	−214.03*	(43.88)	.22*	(.12)	.042	(.15)
DRUGS	64.46	(47.60)	.46*	(.13)	.42*	(.15)
IMMIGRATN	118.83	(110.48)	−.36*	(.14)	−.094	(.17)
WEAPONS	−45.26	(57.55)	.45*	(.15)	.59*	(.19)
STD ERROR	347.35	(71.60)				
LOG-BAIL			−1.64*	(.26)	−1.41*	(.31)
RHO			−.65*	(.02)	0	−
NO. OF OBS.	2,016**		2,220		2,220	

*Asymptotic z-score in excess of 1.65.
**Denotes random sample from a population of 6,158.

Holding the district and offense constant, bail increased with offense seriousness, as measured by the potential sentence for the charge. Bail also increased if the charged offense was a felony rather than a misdemeanor or petty offense. In addition, bail was increased by aggravating circumstances, such as resisting arrest or possessing a weapon.

Finding that bail increased with offense seriousness is consistent with two explanations. First, defendants may be more likely to abscond if threatened with lengthy prison terms. High bail may be set either to prevent the release of these defendants or to impose a strong financial incentive for them to appear for court. Second, defendants accused of serious crimes may be seen as posing more serious threats to the community. High bail may be imposed as a preventative.

Most stability variables were not correlated with bail. The exception was time at the same residence. More telling, however, are variables that were excluded from the model because they were not statistically significant in earlier regressions. This set consisted of age, marital status, education, number of dependents supported, time employed, time unemployed, gross income, physical illness, psychological illness, abuse of narcotics, abuse of drugs other than narcotics, and abuse of alcohol. Defendants on probation or parole at the time of their federal arrests received higher bails than other defendants, as did defendants on bail pending trial for a separate charge. There was no statistically significant correlation between bail amount and probation revocations, number of felony or misdemeanor convictions, or number of incarceration terms.

The modest role played by stability and criminal record is curious, given that pretrial services agencies go to significant trouble to provide these data to judges. Yet bail amount is largely a function of the judicial district, the offense with which the defendant is charged, the seriousness of the offense, and recent evidence of misconduct while under supervision.

Two other findings are especially interesting because of the social significance of discrimination in the justice context. Men were forced to post higher bail amounts than were women, on average. Differential treatment of men is common in the criminal justice system (Blumstein et al., 1983).[1] Also, bail for nonwhite defendants was higher than for white defendants, although the t-value was only 1.96. The criminal justice literature regarding the importance of race is mixed, but it generally fails to show a strong effect associated with race (Blumstein et al., 1983; but see also Petersilia, 1983).

Turning to the second stage of the bail process, the assumption was made that neither the demand for freedom, nor the supply of bail, was associated with judicial districts. Thus, the district dummy variables did not enter these second-stage equations, an assumption that allowed the second-stage parameters to be identified. Column three presents findings.

One of the most important variables was the bail amount, which was highly significant (t = 6.3), despite being an instrument variable, indicating that the cost of borrowing increases with the amount of bail. Bail cost was a nonlinear function of bail (the coefficient equals –1.64); that is, the cost per dollar borrowed was greater for small amounts than for large amounts, perhaps because lenders imposed a fixed fee in addition to an interest charge for negotiating the loan.

To interpret the other parameters, it is necessary to make assumptions about whether β or τ is zero. Our arguments are impressionistic and tentative. Readers are invited to substitute their own.

If a defendant's desire to abscond is increased by the magnitude of his or her crime (because a severe penalty is anticipated), both β and τ would be positive and Γ would have an indeterminate sign. In fact, no strong correlation existed between posting bail and offense seriousness or the presence of aggravating circumstances. However, the offense mattered: Posting bail was least likely for immigration-law violators and most likely for drug-law and weapon-law violators. Immigration-law violators may be perceived as likely to abscond. Drug-law violators (mostly middle- and high-level dealers), and weapons-law violators to a lesser extent, may use profits from crime to gain release.

Defendants who jumped bail previously are less likely to post bail than are other defendants. Posting bail was less likely if the defendant was under supervision at the time of his or her instant federal arrest, but not if he was on bail. Posting bail decreased with the number of past terms of incarceration. Presumably, these effects can be attributed to the perceptions of risk by lenders, since the demand for bail is unlikely to be influenced strongly by past supervision; however, the probability of posting bail was not correlated with evidence of a juvenile record, the number of felony or misdemeanor convictions, or the use of drugs, except alcohol.

Social stability variables, which seemed to play little role in establishing the amount of bail, seem to indicate whether bail will be posted. Married defendants were most likely to post bail. Release increased with a defendant's education and the length of time at the same address. These findings are consistent with the presumed lesser risk posed by these defendants, but they also may reflect a willingness by these defendants to pay more for freedom.

A defendant's income is an important additional determinant of release. The demand for freedom may have a positive income elasticity, or lenders may consider higher income defendants to be better risks. Also, higher income defendants probably have access to more sources of funds, including savings. It is impossible to separate the supply and demand effects.

Three variables associated with discrimination are important. Men and women may exhibit different preferences for freedom, or they may pose different risks for lenders, or both. For whatever reason, men are less likely than women to post bail, which reinforces the preferential treatment given to women by the court at the time bail is set. The effect of race was also interesting: The results imply that nonwhites have disadvantageous access to pretrial release funds. Also, bail amounts did not vary with the defendants' ages, but the likelihood of posting bail did. Presuming that tastes for jail are invariant across age groups, older defendants have differential access to funds.

The final estimate to be discussed is that of the correlation between u and e. The correlation equals −.65 implying that omitted variables observed by judges and lenders are important in determining the amount of bail and, once bail is set, the availability of funds to the defendant. This high correlation points to the need for a structural model of bail.

The estimates in column four were found by constraining the correlation to equal zero and reestimating the second-stage regression. The constrained estimates differ from the unconstrained ones. Given the stronger theoretical justification for the estimation procedures used to derive the estimates in column three, these differences seem to indicate that single-equation methods may distort inferences about pretrial release in criminal courts.

DISCUSSION AND SUMMARY

The structural model of pretrial release described here indicates that bail decisions vary with judges' perceptions that the defendants will engage in pretrial misconduct. Bondsmen and other lenders post bail for detained defendants, but the cost to the defendant varies with the risk to the lender. Defendants seek loans for bail; the amount they are willing to pay varies with their incomes and their tastes for freedom. Statistical techniques were advanced for estimating the parameters associated with this model.

Findings tended to correspond to expectations. As the risk posed to the community increased, so too did the amount of bail. As risk to the lender increased, the likelihood of posting bail decreased. Defendant's income elasticity for freedom was positive.

Additional variables need to be introduced into the model and likelihood ratio techniques need to be used to test different structural models. We were not able to test these possibilities in this study. Nor were we able to test different distributional assumptions—including nonnormality and heteroscedasticity.

Several findings have significance for criminal justice administration. First, the market for bail funds seems to perform a sorting function. In general, defendants who threaten the community pose risk to lenders. Consequently, lenders provide an additional filter for the release of risky defendants.

It is an open question whether this second-stage filtering is socially desirable, which raises a second finding of social significance. Lenders seem to discriminate against men, nonwhites, and the young. Lenders may or may not have sexist, racist, and age-bias reasons for this discrimination. Young black men may, in fact, pose greater risks to lenders. Nevertheless, the question remains whether demands for substantive justice can tolerate such disparity in treatment.

A third finding is that the likelihood of posting bail increases with income, holding bail amount constant. Although the amount of bail set was found to be invariant with respect to income, the positive correlation between posting bail and income raises questions about whether financial discrimination exists in federal pretrial release practices, the Bail Reform Act notwithstanding.

One additional finding is of potential significance to future research about pretrial misconduct. The fact that the error terms u and e are so highly correlated implies that some residual risk factors, which are perceived both by judges and lenders, are unaccounted for by the data. If judges and lenders are accurate in their perceptions, the error term in a pretrial misconduct equation would be correlated with the error term in a pretrial release equation. Thus, the regressions in which pretrial misconduct is the dependent variable are subject to potentially severe bias unless this correlation is taken into account using techniques similar to those used in this study. Because past studies of pretrial misconduct have not taken such selectivity bias into account, conclusions from these past studies are subject to question.

NOTE

1. The defendant's sex may stand in for variables excluded from the model or variables (e.g., seriousness of the offense) that are measured with error. Men typically have more serious records than women; they probably commit more serious crimes. Although the correlation may, for this reason, be spurious, it is consistent with findings from other studies. Alternatively, pretrial detention facilities are not as readily available for women.

REFERENCES

AMEMIYA, T. (1973) "Regression analysis when the dependent variable is truncated normal." Econometrica 41: 997-1016.

BLUMSTEIN, A. et al. (1983) Research on Sentencing: The Search for Reform. Washington, DC: National Academy.

BYNUM, T. (1977) "An empirical exploration of the factors influencing release on recognizance." Ph.D. dissertation, Florida State University.

FORST, B. et al. (1983) Integrating Federal Justice Data: A Technical Report. Washington, DC: INSLAW.

HECKMAN, J. (1979) "Sample selection bias as a specification error." Econometrica 47: 153-161.

LANDES, W. M. (1974) "Legality and reality: some evidence on criminal procedure." J. of Legal Studies 2: 287-337.

MADDALA, G. S. (1983) Limited-Dependent and Qualitative Variables in Econometrics. Cambridge: Cambridge Univ. Press.

PETERSILIA, J. (1983) Racial Disparity in the Criminal Justice System. Santa Monica, CA: Rand Corp.

ROTH, J. A. and P. B. WICE. (1980) Pretrial Release and Misconduct in the District of Columbia. Washington, DC: INSLAW

STRYKER, R., I. NAGEL, and J. HAGEN (1983) "Methodological issues in criminal court research: pretrial release decision for federal defendant." Sociological Methods and Research 11: 469.

TOBIN, J. (1958) "Estimation of relationships for limited dependent variables." Econometrica 26: 273-285.

TOBORG, M. A. (1981) Pretrial Release: A National Evaluation of Practices and Outcomes. Washington, DC: National Institute of Justice.

William Rhodes has been Senior Economist at INSLAW, Inc. since 1977. Prior to that, he taught at the School of Criminology, Florida State University. He has a Ph.D. in economics (1974) from the University of Minnesota. His research interests include microeconomic theory, criminology, statistics, computer applications, and decision support for law firms and corporate legal departments.

Shelley Matsuba has been Research Analyst at INSLAW, Inc. since 1982. She previously worked at Resources for the Future analyzing energy issues in northeast Asia. Ms. Matsuba holds a B.A. in mathematics and economics from the University of Hawaii. She is currently conducting research on recidivism in a cohort of federal offenders.

three sites did not see the two types of programs as differing in viewing clients as emotionally disturbed, this is not a matter of a relationship between client characteristics and views about programs. Clients and service providers simply disagreed on this subject. There is strong support for concluding that there are true differences between the two types of programs for the remaining variables.

Comparisons Between
Service Providers and Clients

Results of comparisons between views of the service providers and clients at diversion programs are quite consistent across programs, as can be seen in Table 6. For each variable, differences between groups fall in the same direction at all sites. The across-size comparisons are all statistically significant by sign tests (p = .004) and by t tests (p < .001).

The differences between service providers' and clients' views of the programs form an intriguing pattern. Clients have less favorable views of the programs in terms of coercion, social control, and serving needs. They come closest to agreement on coercion, where the average difference is less than half a standard deviation and many of the within-site comparisons are not statistically significant. Nevertheless, clients describe programs as more coercive than do service providers. Clients disagree with service providers more markedly in reporting that the programs are more concerned with social control and less concerned with serving clients' needs.

The results for two variables concerning views about clients are even stronger, but in a seemingly opposite direction. Service providers held views about clients that were substantially more negative than clients' believed they would be. Almost all within-size comparisons were significant for both variables, and in most cases the means were more than a standard deviation apart.

DISCUSSION

A key assumption underlying the goals of juvenile diversion is that the experience of participating in a diversion program will differ substantially from that of receiving services through formal justice dispositions. The present study clearly demonstrates that, when programs match the theory behind diversion by serving youths who would normally have received formal dispositions, the assumption is justified. For the nine programs included in the study, respondents consistently

29

The Specific Deterrent Effects of Arrest for Domestic Assault*

Lawrence W. Sherman and Richard A. Berk

Sociologists since Durkheim ([1893] 1972:126) have speculated about how the punishment of individuals affects their behavior. Two bodies of literature, specific deterrence and labeling, have developed competing predictions (Thorsell and Klemke, 1972). Durkheim, for example, implicitly assumed with Bentham that the pains of punishment deter people from repeating the crimes for which they are punished, especially when punishment is certain, swift and severe. More recent work has fostered the ironic view that punishment often makes individuals more likely to commit crimes because of altered interactional structures, foreclosed legal opportunities and secondary deviance (Lemert,

1951, 1967; Schwartz and Skolnick, 1962; Becker, 1963).

Neither prediction can muster consistent empirical support. The few studies that allege effects generally employ weak designs in which it is difficult, if not impossible, to control plausibly for all important factors confounded with criminal justice sanctions and the rule-breaking behavior that may follow. Thus, some claim to show that punishment deters individuals punished (Clarke, 1966; F.B.I., 1967:34-44; Cohen and Stark, 1974:30; Kraut, 1976; Murray and Cox, 1979; McCord, 1983), while others claim to show that punishment increases their deviance (Gold and Williams, 1969; Shoham, 1974; Farrington, 1977; Klemke, 1978). Yet all of these studies suffer either methodological or conceptual flaws as tests of the effects of punishment (Zimring and Hawkins, 1973; Gibbs, 1975; Hirschi, 1975; Tittle, 1975), especially the confounding of incarceration with attempts to rehabilitate and the frequent failure to differentiate effects for different types of offenders and offenses (Lempert, 1981-1982).

Perhaps the strongest evidence to date comes from a randomized experiment conducted by Lincoln et al. (unpubl.). The experiment randomly assigned juveniles, who had already been apprehended, to four different treatments ranked in their formality: release; two types of diversion; and formal

* Direct all correspondence to: Lawrence W. Sherman, Police Foundation, 1909 K Street N.W., Washington, D.C. 20006.

This paper was supported by Grant #80-IJ-CX-0042 to the Police Foundation from the National Institute of Justice, Crime Control Theory Program. Points of view or opinions stated in this document do not necessarily represent the official position of the U.S Department of Justice, the Minneapolis Police Department, or the Police Foundation.

We wish to express our thanks to the Minneapolis Police Department and its Chief, Anthony V. Bouza, for their cooperation, and to Sarah Fenstermaker Berk, Peter H. Rossi, Albert J. Reiss, Jr., James Q. Wilson, Richard Lempert, and Charles Tittle for comments on an earlier draft of this paper.

From Lawrence W. Sherman and Richard A. Berk (with 42 Patrol Officers of the Minneapolis Police Department, Nancy Wester, Donileen Loseke, David Rauma, Debra Morrow, Amy Curtis, Kay Gamble, Roy Roberts, Phyllis Newton, and Gayle Gubman), "The Specific Deterrent Effects of Arrest for Domestic Assault," *American Sociological Review,* 1984, 49(April), 261-272. Copyright 1984 by the American Sociological Association. Reprinted by permission.

charging. The more formal and official the processing, the more frequent the repeat criminality over a two-year follow-up period. This study supports labeling theory for arrested juveniles, although it cannot isolate the labeling or deterrent effects of arrest per se.

In all likelihood, of course, punishment has not one effect, but many, varying across types of people and situations (Chambliss, 1967; Andenaes, 1971). As Lempert (1981–1982:523) argues, "it is only by attending to a range of such offenses that we will be able to develop a general theory of deterrence." The variables affecting the deterrability of juvenile delinquency, white-collar crime, armed robbery and domestic violence may be quite different. Careful accumulation of findings from different settings will help us differentiate the variables which are crime- or situation-specific and those which apply across settings.

In this spirit, we report here a study of the impact of punishment in a particular setting, for a particular offense, and for particular kinds of individuals. Over an eighteen-month period, police in Minneapolis applied one of three intervention strategies in incidents of misdemeanor domestic assault: arrest; ordering the offender from the premises; or some form of advice which could include mediation. The three interventions were assigned randomly to households, and a critical outcome was the rate of repeat incidents. The relative effect of arrest should hold special interest for the specific deterrence–labeling controversy.

POLICING DOMESTIC ASSAULTS

Police have been typically reluctant to make arrests for domestic violence (Berk and Loseke, 1981), as well as for a wide range of other kinds of offenses, unless victims demand an arrest, the suspect insults the officer, or other factors are present (Sherman, 1980). Parnas's (1972) qualitative observations of the Chicago police found four categories of police action in these situations: negotiating or otherwise "talking out" the dispute; threatening the disputants and then leaving; asking one of the parties to leave the premises; or (very rarely) making an arrest.

Similar patterns are found in many other cities. Surveys of battered women who tried to have their domestic assailants arrested report that arrest occurred in 10 percent (Roy, 1977:35) or 3 percent (see Langley and Levy, 1977:219) of the cases. Surveys of police agencies in Illinois (Illinois Law Enforcement Commission, 1978) and New York (Office of the Minority Leader, 1978) found explicit policies against arrest in the majority of the agencies surveyed. Despite the fact that violence is reported to be present in one-third (Bard and Zacker, 1974) to two-thirds (Black, 1980) of all domestic disturbances police respond to, police department data show arrests in only 5 percent of those disturbances in Oakland (Hart, n.d., cited in Meyer and Lorimer, 1977:21), 6 percent of those disturbances in a Colorado city (Patrick et al., n.d., cited in Meyer and Lorimer, 1977:21) and 6 percent in Los Angeles County (Emerson, 1979).

The best available evidence on the frequency of arrest is the observations from the Black and Reiss study of Boston, Washington and Chicago police in 1966 (Black, 1980:182). Police responding to disputes in those cities made arrests in 27 percent of violent felonies and 17 percent of the violent misdemeanors. Among married couples (Black, 1980:158), they made arrests in 26 percent of the cases, but tried to remove one of the parties in 38 percent of the cases.

An apparent preference of many police for separating the parties rather than arresting the offender has been attacked from two directions over the last fifteen years. The original critique came from clinical psychologists, who agreed that police should rarely make arrests (Potter, 1978:46; Fagin, 1978:123–24) in domestic assault cases, and argued that police should mediate the disputes responsible for the violence. A highly publicized demonstration project teaching police special counseling skills for family crisis intervention (Bard, 1970) failed to show a reduction in violence, but was interpreted as a success nonetheless. By 1977, a national survey of police agencies with 100 or more officers found that over 70 percent reported a family crisis intervention training program in operation. While it is not clear whether these programs reduced separation and increased mediation, a decline in arrests was noted for some (Wylie et al., 1976). Indeed, many sought explicitly to reduce the number of arrests (University of Rochester, 1974; Ketterman and Kravitz, 1978).

By the mid-1970s, police practices were criticized from the opposite direction by feminist groups. Just as psychologists succeeded in having many police agencies respond to domestic violence as "half social work and half police work," feminists began to argue that police put "too much emphasis on the social work aspect and not enough on the criminal" (Langley and Levy, 1977:218). Widely publicized lawsuits in New York and Oakland sought to compel police to make arrests in every case of domestic assault, and state legislatures were lobbied successfully to reduce the evidentiary requirements needed for police to make arrests for misdemeanor domestic assaults. Some legislatures are now considering statutes requiring police to make arrests in these cases.

The feminist critique was bolstered by a study (Police Foundation, 1976) showing that for 85 percent of a sample of spousal homicides, police had intervened at least once in the preceding two years. For 54 percent of the homicides, police had intervened five or more times. But it was impossible to determine from the cross-sectional data whether making more or fewer arrests would have reduced the homicide rate.

In sum, police officers confronting a domestic assault suspect facè at least three conflicting options, urged on them by different groups with different theories. The officers' colleagues might recommend forced separation as a means of achieving short-term peace. Alternatively, the officers' trainers might recommend mediation as a means of getting to the underlying cause of the "dispute" (in which both parties are implicitly assumed to be at fault). Finally, the local women's organizations may recommend that the officer protect the victim (whose "fault," if any, is legally irrelevant) and enforce the law to deter such acts in the future.

RESEARCH DESIGN

In response to these conflicting recommendations, the Police Foundation and the Minneapolis Police Department agreed to conduct a randomized experiment. The design called for random assignment of arrest, separation, and some form of advice which could include mediation at the officer's discretion. In addition, there was to be a six-month follow-up period to measure the frequency and seriousness of domestic violence after each police intervention. The advantages of randomized experiments are well known and need not be reviewed here (see, e.g., Cook and Campbell, 1979).

The design only applied to simple (misdemeanor) domestic assaults, where both the suspect and the victim were present when the police arrived. Thus, the experiment included only those cases in which police were empowered (but not required) to make arrests under a recently liberalized Minnesota state law; the police officer must have probable cause to believe that a cohabitant or spouse had assaulted the victim within the last four hours (but police need not have witnessed the assault). Cases of life-threatening or severe injury, usually labeled as a felony (aggravated assault), were excluded from the design for ethical reasons.

The design called for each officer to carry a pad of report forms, color coded for the three different police actions. Each time the officers

encountered a situation that fit the experiment s criteria, they were to take whatever action was indicated by the report form on the top of the pad. We numbered the forms and arranged them in random order for each officer. The integrity of the random assignment was to be monitored by research staff observers riding on patrol for a sample of evenings.

After police action was taken, the officer was to fill out a brief report and give it to the research staff for follow-up. As a further check on the randomization process, the staff logged in the reports in the order in which they were received and made sure that the sequence corresponded to the original assignment of treatments.

Anticipating something of the victims' background, a predominantly minority, female research staff was employed to contact the victims for a detailed face-to-face interview, to be followed by telephone follow-up interviews every two weeks for 24 weeks. The interviews were designed primarily to measure the frequency and seriousness of victimizations caused by the suspect after the police intervention.[1] The research staff also collected criminal justice reports that mentioned the suspect's name during the six-month follow-up period.

CONDUCT OF THE EXPERIMENT

As is common in field experiments, implementation of the research design entailed some slippage from the original plan. In order to gather data as quickly as possible, the experiment was originally located in the two Minneapolis precincts with the highest density of domestic violence crime reports and arrests. The 34 officers assigned to those areas were invited to a three-day planning meeting and asked to participate in the study for one year. All but one agreed. The conference also produced a draft order for the chief's signature specifying the rules of the experiment. These rules created several new situations to be excluded from the experiment, such as if a suspect attempted to assault police officers, a victim persistently demanded an arrest, or if both parties were injured. These additional exceptions, unfortunately, allowed for the possibility of differential attrition from the separation and mediation treatments. The im-

---

[1] The protocols were based heavily on instruments designed for an NIMH-funded study of spousal violence conducted by Richard A. Berk, Sarah Fenstermaker Berk, and Ann D. Witte (Center for Studies of Crime and Delinquency, Grant #MH-34616–01). A similar protocol was developed for the suspects, but only twenty-five of them agreed to be interviewed.

plications for internal validity are discussed later.

The experiment began on March 17, 1981, with the expectation that it would take about one year to produce about 300 cases (it ran until August 1, 1982, and produced 330 case reports.) The officers agreed to meet monthly with the project director (Sherman) and the project manager (Wester). By the third or fourth month, two facts became clear: (1) only about 15 to 20 officers were either coming to meetings or turning in cases; and (2) the rate at which the cases were turned in would make it difficult to complete the project in one year. By November, we decided to recruit more officers in order to obtain cases more rapidly. Eighteen additional officers joined the project, but like the original group, most of these officers only turned in one or two cases. Indeed, three of the original officers produced almost 28 percent of the cases, in part because they worked a particularly violent beat, and in part because they had a greater commitment to the study. Since the treatments were randomized by officer, this created no internal validity problem. However, it does raise construct validity problems to which we will later return.

There is little doubt that many of the officers occasionally failed to follow fully the experimental design. Some of the failures were due to forgetfulness, such as leaving the report pads at home or at the police station. Other failures derived from misunderstanding about whether the experiment applied in certain situations; application of the experimental rules under complex circumstances was sometimes confusing. Finally, from time to time there were situations that were simply not covered by the experiment's rules.

Whether any officers intentionally subverted the design is unclear. The plan to monitor randomization with ride-along observers broke down because of the unexpectedly low incidence of cases meeting the experimental criteria. The observers had to ride for many weeks before they observed an officer apply one of the treatments. We tried to solve this problem with "chase-alongs," in which the observers rode in their own car with a portable police radio and drove to the scene of any domestic call dispatched to any officer in the precinct. Even this method failed.

Thus, we are left with at least two disturbing possibilities. First, police officers anticipating (e.g., from the dispatch call) a particular kind of incident, and finding the upcoming experimental treatment inappropriate, may have occasionally decided to void the experiment. That is, they may have chosen to exclude certain cases in violation of the experimental design. This amounts to differential attrition, which is clearly a threat to internal validity. Note that if police officers blindly decided to exclude certain cases (e.g., because they did not feel like filling out the extra forms on a given day), all would be well for internal validity.

Second, since the recording officer's pad was supposed to govern the actions of each pair of officers, some officers may also have switched the assignment of driver and recording officer after deciding a case fit the study in order to obtain a treatment they wanted to apply. If the treatments were switched between driver and recorder, then the internal validity was again threatened. However, this was almost certainly uncommon because it was generally easier not to fill out a report at all than to switch.

Table 1 shows the degree to which the treatments were delivered as designed.[2] Ninety-nine percent of the suspects targeted for arrest actually were arrested, while only 78 percent of those to receive advice did, and only 73 percent of those to be sent out of the residence for eight hours were actually sent. One explanation for this pattern, consistent with the experimental guidelines, is that mediating and sending were more difficult ways for police to control the situation, with a greater likelihood that officers might resort to arrest as a fallback position. When the assigned treatment is arrest, there is no need for a fallback position. For example, some offenders may have refused to comply with an order to leave the premises.

Such differential attrition would potentially bias estimates of the relative effectiveness of arrest by removing uncooperative and difficult offenders from the mediation and separation treatments. Any deterrent effect could be underestimated and, in the extreme, artifactual support for deviance amplification could be found. That is, the arrest group would have too many "bad guys" *relative* to the other treatments.

We can be more systematic about other factors affecting the movement of cases away from the designed treatments. The three delivered treatments represent a polychotomous outcome amenable to multivariate statistical analysis. We applied a multinominal logit formulation (Amemiya, 1981:1516–19; Maddala, 1983:34–37), which showed that the designed treatment was the dominant cause of the treatment actually received (a finding suggested by Table 1). However, we also found that five other variables had a statistically sig-

---

[2] Sixteen cases were dropped because no treatment was applied or because the case did not belong in the study (i.e., a fight between a father and son).

Table 1. Designed and Delivered Police Treatments in Spousal Assault Cases

Designed Treatment	Delivered Treatment			
	Arrest	Advise	Separate	Total
Arrest	98.9%	0.0%	1.1%	29.3%
	(91)	(0)	(1)	(92)
Advise	17.6%	77.8%	4.6%	34.4%
	(19)	(84)	(5)	(108)
Separate	22.8%	4.4%	72.8%	36.3%
	(26)	(5)	(83)	(114)
Total	43.4%	28.3%	28.3%	100%
	(136)	(89)	(89)	(314)

nificant effect on "upgrading" the separation and advice treatments to arrests: whether police reported the suspect was rude; whether police reported the suspect tried to assault one (or both) of the police officers; whether police reported weapons were involved; whether the victim persistently demanded a citizen's arrest; and whether a restraining order was being violated. We found no evidence that the background or characteristics of the suspect or victim (e.g., race) affected the treatment received.

Overall, the logit model fit the data very well. For well over 80 percent of the cases, the model's predicted treatment was the same as the actual treatment (i.e., correct classifications), and minor alterations in the assignment threshold would have substantially improved matters. Moreover, a chi-square test on the residuals was not statistically significant (i.e., the observed and predicted treatments differed by no more than chance). In summary, we were able to model the assignment process with remarkable success simply by employing the rules of the experimental protocol (for more details, see Berk and Sherman, 1983).

We were less fortunate with the interviews of the victims; only 205 (of 330, counting the few repeat victims twice) could be located and initial interviews obtained, a 62 percent completion rate. Many of the victims simply could not be found, either for the initial interview or for follow-ups: they either left town, moved somewhere else or refused to answer the phone or doorbell. The research staff made up to 20 attempts to contact these victims, and often employed investigative techniques (asking friends and neighbors) to find them. Sometimes these methods worked, only to have the victim give an outright refusal or break one or more appointments to meet the interviewer at a "safe" location for the interview.

The response rate to the bi-weekly follow-up interviews was even lower than for the initial interview, as in much research on women crime victims. After the first interview, for which the victims were paid $20, there was a gradual falloff in completed interviews with

each successive wave, only 161 victims provided all 12 follow-up interviews over the six months, a completion rate of 49 percent. Whether paying for the follow-up interviews would have improved the response rate is unclear; it would have added over $40,000 to the cost of the research. When the telephone interviews yielded few reports of violence, we moved to conduct every fourth interview in person, which appeared to produce more reports of violence.

There is absolutely no evidence that the experimental treatment assigned to the offender affected the victim's decision to grant initial interviews. We estimated a binary logit equation for the dichotomous outcome: whether or not an initial interview was obtained. Regressors included the experimental treatments (with one necessarily excluded), race of the victim, race of the offender, and a number of attributes of the incident (from the police sheets). A joint test on the full set of regressors failed to reject the null hypothesis that all of the logit coefficients were zero. More important for our purposes, none of the t-values for the treatments was in excess of 1.64; indeed, none was greater than 1.0 in absolute value. In short, while the potential for sample selection bias (Heckman, 1979; Berk, 1983) certainly exists (and is considered later), that bias does not stem from obvious sources, particularly the treatments. This implies that we may well be able to meaningfully examine experimental effects for the subset of individuals from whom initial interviews were obtained. The same conclusions followed when the follow-up interviews were considered.

In sum, despite the practical difficulties of controlling an experiment and interviewing crime victims in an emotionally charged and violent social context, the experiment succeeded in producing a promising sample of 314 cases with complete official outcome measures and an apparently unbiased sample of responses from the victims in those cases.

RESULTS

The 205 completed initial interviews provide some sense of who the subjects are, although the data may not properly represent the characteristics of the full sample of 314. They show the now familiar pattern of domestic violence cases coming to police attention being disproportionately unmarried couples with lower than average educational levels, disproportionately minority and mixed race (black male, white female), and who were very likely to have had prior violent incidents with police intervention. The 60 percent suspect unemployment rate is strikingly high in a community

Table 2. Victim and Suspect Characteristics: Initial Interview Data and Police Sheets

A. Unemployment			
Victims	61%		
Suspects	60%		
B. Relationship of Suspect to Victim			
Divorced or separated husband		3%	
Unmarried male lover		45%	
Current husband		35%	
Wife or girlfriend		2%	
Son, brother, roommate, other		15%	
C. Prior Assaults and Police Involvement			
Victims assaulted by suspect, last six months		80%	
Police intervention in domestic dispute,			
last six months		60%	
Couple in Counseling Program		27%	
D. Prior Arrests of Male Suspects			
Ever Arrested For Any Offense		59%	
Ever Arested For Crime Against Person		31%	
Ever Arrested on Domestic Violence Statute		5%	
Ever Arrested On An Alcohol Offense		29%	
E. Mean Age			
Victims	30 years		
Suspects	32 years		
F. Education		Victims	Suspects
< high school		43%	42%
high school only		33%	36%
> high school		24%	22%
G. Race		Victims	Suspects
White		57%	45%
Black		23%	36%
Native American		18%	16%
Other		2%	3%

N = 205 (Those cases for which initial interviews were obtained)

with only about 5 percent of the workforce unemployed. The 59 percent prior arrest rate is also strikingly high, suggesting (with the 80 percent prior domestic assault rate) that the suspects generally are experienced lawbreakers who are accustomed to police interventions. But with the exception of the heavy representation of Native Americans (due to Minneapolis' unique proximity to many Indian reservations), the characteristics in Table 2 are probably close to those of domestic violence cases coming to police attention in other large U.S. cities.

Two kinds of outcome measures will be considered. One is a *police-recorded* "failure" of the offender to survive the six-month follow-up period without having police generate a written report on the suspect for domestic violence, either through an offense or an arrest report written by any officer in the department, or through a subsequent report to the project research staff of a randomized (or other) intervention by officers participating in the experiment. A second kind of measure comes from the *interviews with victims,* in which victims were asked if there had been a repeat incident with the same suspect, broadly defined to include an actual assault, threatened assault, or property damage.

The two kinds of outcomes were each formulated in two complementary ways: as a dummy variable (i.e., repeat incident or not) and as the amount of time elapsed from the treatment to either a failure or the end of the follow-up period. For each of the two outcomes, three analyses were performed: the first using a linear probability model; the second using a logit formulation; and the third using a proportional hazard approach. The dummy outcome was employed for the linear probability and logit analyses, while the time-to-failure was employed for the proportional hazard method.[3]

Given the randomization, we began in traditional analysis of variance fashion. The official measure of a repeat incident was regressed on the treatment received for the sub-

---

[3] In addition to the linear probability model, the logit and proportional hazard formulations can be expressed in forms such that the outcome is a probability (e.g., the probability of a new violent incident). However, three slightly different response functions are implied. We had no theoretical basis for selecting the proper response function, and consequently used all three. We expected that the substantive results could be essentially invariant across the three formulations.

Table 3. Experimental Results for Police Data

Variable	Linear		Logistic		Proportional Hazard Rate	
	Coef	t-value	Coef	t-value	Coef	t-value
Intercept (separate)	0.24	5.03*	-1.10	-4.09*	—	—
Arrest	-0.14	-2.21*	-1.02	-2.21*	-0.97	-2.28*
Advise	-0.05	-0.79	-0.31	-0.76	-0.32	-0.88
	F = 2.01		Chi-square = 5.19		Chi-square = 5.48	
	P = .07		P = .07		P = .06	
N = 314						

* p < .05, two-tailed test.

of 314 cases (out of 330) that fell within the definition of the experiment. Compared to the baseline treatment of separation, which had the highest recidivism rate in the police data, the arrest treatment reduced repeat occurrences by a statistically significant amount (t = -2.38). Twenty-six percent of those separated committed a repeat assault, compared to 13 percent of those arrested. The mediation treatment was statistically indistinguishable from the other two. To help put this in perspective, 18.2 percent of the households failed overall.

The apparent treatment effect for arrest in this conventional analysis was suggestive, but there was a danger of biased estimates from the "upgrading" of some separation and advise treatments. In response, we applied variations on the corrections recommended by Barnow et al. (1980: esp. 55). In brief, we inserted instrumental variables in place of the delivered treatments when the treatment effects were analyzed. These instruments, in turn, were constructed from the multinomial logit model described earlier.[4] Table 3 shows the results of the adjusted models. The first two columns report the results for the linear probability approach. Again, we find a statistically significant effect for arrest (t = -2.21). However, it is well known that the linear probability model will produce inefficient estimates of the regression coefficients and biased (and inconsistent) estimates of the standard errors. Significance tests, therefore, are suspect. Consequently, we also estimated a logit model, with pretty much the same result. At the mean of the endogenous variable (i.e., 18.2 percent), the logit coefficient for arrest translates into nearly the same effect (i.e., -.15) found with the linear probability model (t = -2.21).

One might still object that the use of a dummy variable outcome neglects right-hand

censoring. In brief, one cannot observe failures that occur after the end of the experimental period, so that biased (and inconsistent) results follow. Thus, we applied a proportional hazard analysis (Lawless, 1982: Ch. 7) that adjusts for right-hand censoring. In this model the time-to-failure dependent variable is transformed into (roughly) the probability at any given moment during the six-month follow-up period of a new offense occurring, given that no new offenses have yet been committed. The last two columns of Table 3 indicate that, again, an effect for arrest surfaces (t = -2.28). The coefficient of -0.97 implies that compared to the baseline of separation, those experiencing an arrest were less likely to commit a new battery by a multiplicative factor of .38 (i.e., e raised to the -0.97 power). If the earlier results are translated into comparable terms, the effects described by the proportional hazard formulation are the largest we have seen (see footnote 4). But the major message is that the arrest effect holds up under three different statistical methods based on slightly different response functions. Overall, the police data indicate that the separation treatment produces the highest recidivism, arrest produces the lowest, with the impact of "advise" (from doing nothing to mediation) indistinguishable from the other two effects.

Table 4 shows the results when self-report data are used. A "failure" is defined as a new assault, property destruction or a threatened assault. (Almost identical results follow from a definition including only a new assault.) These results suggest a different ordering of the effects, with arrest still producing the lowest recidivism rate (at 19%), but with advice producing the highest (37%).

Overall, 28.9 percent of the suspects in Table 4 "failed." Still, the results are much the same as found for the official failure measure. However, given the effective sample of 161, we are vulnerable to sample selection bias. In response, we applied Heckman's (1979) sample selection corrections. The results were virtually unchanged (and are therefore not reported).

---

[4] We did *not* simply use the conditional expectations of a multinomial logit model. We used an alternative procedure to capitalize on the initial random assignment. The details can be found in Berk and Sherman (1983).

Table 4. Experimental Results for Victim Report Data

	Linear		Logistic		Proportional Hazard Rate	
Variable	Coef	t-value	Coef	t-value	Coef	t-val
Intercept (advise)	0.37	5.54*	-0.53	-1.70	—	—
Arrest	-0.18	-2.00*	-0.94	-2.01*	-0.82	-2.0
Separate	-0.04	-0.35	-0.15	-0.10	-0.27	-0.0
	F = 2.31		Chi-square = 4.78		Chi-square = 4.3	
	P = .10		P = .09		P = .11	

N = 161 (Those cases for which *all* follow-up interviews were obtained)

* p < .05, two-tailed test.

An obvious rival hypothesis to the deterrent effect of arrest is that arrest incapacitates. If the arrested suspects spend a large portion of the next six months in jail, they would be expected to have lower recidivism rates. But the initial interview data show this is not the case: of those arrested, 43 percent were released within one day, 86 percent were released within one week, and only 14 percent were released after one week or had not yet been released at the time of the *initial* victim interview. Clearly, there was very little incapacitation, especially in the context of a six-month follow-up. Indeed, virtually all those arrested were released before the first follow-up interview. Nevertheless, we introduced the length of the initial stay in jail as a control variable. Consistent with expectations, the story was virtually unchanged.

Another perspective on the incapacitation issue can be obtained by looking at repeat violence which occurred shortly after the police intervened. If incapacitation were at work, a dramatic effect should be found in households experiencing arrest, especially compared to the households experiencing advice. Table 5 shows how quickly the couples were reunited, and of those reunited in one day, how many of them, according to the victim, began to argue or had physical violence again. It is apparent that *all* of the police interventions effectively stopped the violence for a 24-hour period after the couples were reunited. Even the renewed quarrels were few, at least with our relatively small sample size. Hence, there is again no evidence for an incapacitation effect. There is

also no evidence for the reverse: that arrest offenders would take it out on the victim wh the offender returned home.

DISCUSSION AND CONCLUSIONS

The experiment's results are subject to sever qualifications. One caution is that both kinds outcome measures have uncertain constru validity. The official measure no doubt n glects a large number of repeat incidents, part because many of them were not reporte and in part because police are sometimes r luctant to turn a family "dispute" into form police business. However, the key is whethe there is *differential* measurement error by th experimental treatments; an undercount ran domly distributed across the three treatment will not bias the estimated experimental effect (i.e., only the estimate of the intercept will b biased). It is hard to imagine that differentia undercounting would come solely from the ac tions of police, since most officers were no involved in the experiment and could not hav known what treatment had been delivered.

However, there might be differential under counting if offenders who were arrested wer less likely to remain on the scene after a nev assault. Having been burned once, they migh not wait around for a second opportunity. An police told us they were less likely during th follow-up period (and more generally) to re cord an incident if the offender was not pre sent. For example, there would be no arres forms since the offender was not available to arrest. If all we had were the official outcome

Table 5. Speed of Reunion and Recidivism by Police Action

	Time of Reunion				New Quarrel Within A Day	New Violence Within A Day
Police Action	Within One Day	More than One Day but Less Than One Week	Longer or No Return	(N)		
Arrested (and released)	38%	30%	32%	(N=76)	(2)	(1)
Separated	57%	31%	10%	(N=54)	(6)	(3)
Advised	—	—	—	(N=72)	(4)	(1)

N = 202 (Down from the 205 in Table 2 due to missing data)

asures, there would be no easy way to re-
e this possibility. Fortunately, the self-
port data are *not* vulnerable on these
unds, and the experimental effects are
und nevertheless.

It is also possible that the impact for arrest
und in the official outcome measure repre-
nts a reluctance of *victims* to call the police.
at is, for some victims, the arrest may have
en an undesirable intervention, and rather
an face the prospect of another arrest from a
w incident, these victims might decide not to
voke police sanctions. For example, the ar-
st may have cost the offender several days'
ork and put financial stress on the household.
r the offender may have threatened serious
olence if the victim ever called the police
ain. However, we can again observe that the
lf-report data would not have been vulnera-
e to such concerns, and the experimental ef-
cts were found nevertheless. The only way
e can see how the self-report data would fail
support the official data is if respondents in
ouseholds experiencing arrest became more
esitant to admit to *interviewers* that they had
en beaten a second time. Since there was no
ifferential response rate by treatment, this
ossibility seems unlikely. If the arrested sus-
ects had intimidated their victims more than
he other two treatment groups, it seems more
kely that such intimidation would have shown
p in noncooperation with the interviews than
n differential underreporting of violence in the
ourse of the interviews.

This is not to say that the self-report data are
lawless; indeed there is some reason to believe
hat there was undercounting of new incidents.
lowever, just as for the official data, unless
here is differential undercounting by the ex-
erimental treatments, all is well. We can think
f no good reasons why differential undercounting should materialize. In summary,
nternal validity looks rather sound.

The construct validity of the treatments is
more problematic. The advice and separation
nterventions have unclear content. Perhaps
"good" mediation, given consistently, would
fare better compared to arrest. The more general point is that the treatment effects for arrest
are only relative to the impact of the other
interventions. Should their content change, the
relative impact of arrest could change as well.

Likewise, we noted earlier that a few officers
accounted for a disproportionate number of the
cases. What we have been interpreting, therefore, as results from different intervention
strategies could reflect the special abilities of
certain officers to make arrest particularly effective relative to the other treatments. For
example, these officers may have been less
skilled in mediation techniques. However, we

re-estimated the models reported in Tables 3
and 4, including an interaction effect to capture the special contributions of our high-pro-
ductivity officers. The new variable was not
statistically significant, and the treatment effect for arrest remained.

Finally, Minneapolis is hardly representative
of all urban areas. The Minneapolis Police Department has many unusual characteristics,
and different jurisdictions might well keep suspects in custody for longer or shorter periods
of time. The message should be clear: external
validity will have to wait for replications.

Despite these qualifications, it is apparent
that we have found no support for the deviance
amplification point of view. The arrest intervention certainly did not make things worse
and may well have made things better. There
are, of course, many rejoinders. In particular,
over 80 percent of offenders had assaulted the
victims in the previous six months, and in over
60 percent of the households the police had
intervened during that interval. Almost 60 percent of the suspects had previously been arrested for something. Thus, the counterproductive consequences of police sanction, if
any, may for many offenders have already
been felt. In labeling theory terms, secondary
deviation may already have been established,
producing a ceiling for the amplification effects
of formal sanctioning. However, were this the
case, the arrest treatment probably should be
less effective in households experiencing recent police interventions. No such interaction
effects were found. In future analyses of these
data, however, we will inductively explore interactions with more sensitive measures of
police sanctioning and prior criminal histories
of the suspects.

There are, of course, many versions of
labeling theory. For those who theorize that a
metamorphosis of self occurs in response to
official sanctions over a long period of time,
our six-month follow-up is not a relevant test.
For those who argue that the development of a
criminal self-concept is particularly likely to
occur during a lengthy prison stay or extensive
contact with criminal justice officials, the dosage of labeling employed in this experiemnt is
not sufficient to falsify that hypothesis. What
this experiment does seem to falsify for this
particular offense is the broader conception of
labeling implicit in the prior research by Lincoln et al. (unpubl.), Farrington (1977) and
others: that for every possible increment of
criminal justice response to deviance, the more
increments (or the greater the formality)
applied to the labeled deviant, the greater the
likelihood of subsequent deviation. The absolute strength of the dosage is irrelevant to this
hypothesis, as long as some variation in dosage

is present. While the experiment does not falsify all possible "labeling theory" hypotheses, it does at least seem to falsify this one.

The apparent support for deterrence is perhaps more clear. While we certainly have no evidence that deterrence will work in general, we do have findings that swift imposition of a sanction of temporary incarceration may deter male offenders in domestic assault cases. And we have produced this evidence from an unusually strong research design based on random assignment to treatments. In short, criminal justice sanctions seem to matter for this offense in this setting with this group of experienced offenders.

A number of police implications follow. Perhaps most important, police have historically been reluctant to make arrests in domestic assault cases, in part fearing that an arrest could make the violence worse. Criminal justice sanctions weakly applied might be insufficient to deter and set the offender on a course of retribution. Our data indicate that such concerns are by and large groundless.

Police have also felt that making an arrest was a waste of their time: without the application of swift and severe sanctions by the courts, arrest and booking had no bite. Our results indicate that only three of the 136 arrested offenders were formally punished by fines or subsequent incarceration. This suggests that arrest and initial incarceration alone may produce a deterrent effect, regardless of how the courts treat such cases, and that arrest makes an independent contribution to the deterrence potential of the criminal justice system. Therefore, in jurisdictions that process domestic assault offenders in a manner similar to that employed in Minneapolis, we favor a *presumption* of arrest; an arrest should be made unless there are good, clear reasons why an arrest would be counterproductive. We do not, however, favor *requiring* arrests in all misdemeanor domestic assault cases. Even if our findings were replicated in a number of jurisdictions, there is a good chance that arrest works far better for some kinds of offenders than others and in some kinds of situations better than others.[5] We feel it best to leave police a loophole to capitalize on that variation. Equally important, it is widely recognized that discretion is inherent in police work. Simply to impose a requirement of arrest, irrespective of the features of the immediate situation, is to invite circumvention.

---

[5] Indeed, one of the major policy issues that could arise from further analysis of the interaction effects would be whether police discretion should be guided by either achieved or ascribed relevant suspect characteristics.

REFERENCES

Amemiya, Takeshi
1981 "Qualitative response models: a surve Journal of Economic Literature 19:14 1536.
Andenaes, Johannes
1971 "Deterrence and specific offenses." L versity of Chicago Law Review 39:537.
Bard, Morton
1970 "Training police as specialists in fam crisis intervention." Washington, D. U.S. Department of Justice.
Bard, Morton and Joseph Zacker
1974 "Assaultiveness and alcohol use in fam disputes—police perceptions." Crimin ogy 12:281–92.
Barnow, Burt S., Glen G. Cain and Arthur Goldberger
1980 "Issues in the analysis of selectivity bias Pp. 53–59 in Ernst W. Stromsdorfer a George Farkas (eds.), Evaluation Studi Review Annual, Volume 5. Beverly Hil Sage.
Becker, Howard
1963 The Outsiders. New York: Free Press.
Berk, Richard A.
1983 "An introduction to sample selection bias sociological data." American Sociologic Review, 48:386–98.
Berk, Richard A. and Lawrence W. Sherman
1983 "Police responses to family violence inc dents: an analysis of an experimental desig with incomplete randomization." Unpu lished manuscript, Department of Socio ogy, University of California at Barbara.
Berk, Sarah Fenstermaker and Donileen R. Losek
1981 "Handling family violence: situational d terminants of police arrest in domestic di turbances." Law and Society Revie 15:315–46.
Black, Donald
1980 The Manners and Customs of the Police New York: Academic Press.
Chambliss, William
1967 "Types of deviance and the effectiveness o legal sanctions." Wisconsin Law Reviev 1967:703–19.
Clarke, Ronald V. G.
1966 "Approved school boy absconders and cor poral punishment." British Journal o Criminology: 6:364–75.
Cohen, Lawrence E. and Rodney Stark
1974 "Discriminatory labeling and the five-finge discount." Journal of Research in Crime and Delinquency 11:25–39.
Cook, Thomas D. and Donald T. Campbell
1979 Quasi-Experimentation: Design and Analysis Issues for Field Settings. Chicago Rand McNally.
Durkheim, Emile
[1893] Selected Writings. Edited with an Intro-
1972 duction by Anthony Giddens. [Selection from Division of Labor in Society, 6th edition, 1960 (1893)] Cambridge: Cambridge University Press.
Emerson, Charles D.
1979 Family violence: a study by the Los

Angeles County Sheriff's Department Police Chief 46(6):48–50

_in_. James A
978 "The effects of police interpersonal communications skills on conflict resolution." Ph.D. Dissertation, Southern Illinois University Ann Arbor: University Microfilms.

rrington, David P.
977 "The effects of public labeling." British Journal of Criminology 17:112–25.

deral Bureau of Investigation
1967 Uniform Crime Reports. Washington, D.C.: U.S. Department of Justice.

_ld_, Martin and Jay Williams
1969 "National study of the aftermath of apprehension." Prospectus 3:3–11.

bbs, Jack P.
1975 Crime, Punishment and Deterrence. New York: Elsevier.

eckman, James
1979 "Sample selection bias as a specification error." Econometrica 45:153–61.

rschi, Travis
1975 "Labeling theory and juvenile delinquency: an assessment of the evidence." Pp. 181–203 in Walter R. Gove (ed.), The Labeling of Deviance. New York: Wiley.

inois Law Enforcement Commission
1978 "Report on technical assistance project—domestic violence survey." (Abstract). Washington, D.C.: National Criminal Justice Reference Service.

etterman, Thomas and Marjorie Kravitz
1978 Police Crisis Intervention: A Selected Bibliography. Washington, D.C.: National Criminal Justice Reference Service.

lemke, Lloyd W.
1978 "Does apprehension for shoplifting amplify or terminate shoplifting activity?" Law and Society Review 12:391–403.

raut, Robert E.
1976 "Deterrent and definitional influences on shoplifting." Social Problems 23:358–68.

angley, Richard and Roger C. Levy
1977 Wife Beating: The Silent Crisis. New York: E. P. Dutton.

awless, Jerald F.
1982 Statistical Models and Methods for Lifetime Data. New York: Wiley.

emert, Edwin M.
1951 Social Pathology. New York: McGraw-Hill.
1967 Human Deviance, Social Problems and Social Control. Englewood Cliffs, NJ: Prentice-Hall.

empert, Richard.
1981– "Organizing for deterrence: lessons from
1982 a study of child support." Law and Society Review 16:513–68.

Lincoln, Suzanne B., Malcolm W. Klein, Katherine S. Teilmann and Susan Labin
un-   "Control organizations and labeling theory:
publ. official versus self-reported delinquency." Unpublished manuscript, University of Southern California.

Maddala, G. S.
1983 Limited, Dependent and Qualitative Variables in Econometrics. Cambridge (Cambridge University Press

McCord, Joan
1983 "A longitudinal appraisal of criminal sanctions." Paper presented at the IXth International Congress on Criminology, Vienna, Austria, September.

Meyer, Jeanie Keeny and T. D. Lorimer
1977 Police Intervention Data and Domestic Violence: Exploratory Development and Validation of Prediction Models. Report prepared under grant #RO1MH27918 from National Institute of Mental Health. Kansas City, Mo., Police Department.

Murray, Charles A. and Louis A. Cox, Jr.
1979 Beyond Probation. Beverly Hills: Sage.

Office of the Minority Leader, State of New York
1978 Battered Women: Part I (Abstract). Washington, D.C.: National Criminal Justice Reference Service.

Parnas, Raymond I.
1972 "The police response to the domestic disturbance." Pp. 206–36 in Leon Radzinowicz and Marvin E. Wolfgang (eds.), The Criminal in the Arms of the Law. New York: Basic Books.

Police Foundation
1976 Domestic Violence and the Police: Studies in Detroit and Kansas City. Washington, D.C.: The Police Foundation.

Potter, Jane
1978 "The police and the battered wife: the search for understanding." Police Magazine 1:40–50.

Roy, Maria (ed.)
1977 Battered Women. New York: Van Nostrand Reinhold.

Schwartz, Richard and Jerome Skolnick
1962 "Two studies of legal stigma." Social Problems 10:133–42.

Sherman, Lawrence W.
1980 "Causes of police behavior: the current state of quantitative research." Journal of Research in Crime and Delinquency 17:69–100.

Shoham, S. Giora
1974 "Punishment and traffic offenses." Traffic Quarterly 28:61–73.

Thorsell, Bernard A. and Lloyd M. Klemke
1972 "The labeling process: reinforcement and deterrent." Law and Society Review 6:393–403.

Tittle, Charles
1975 "Labeling and crime: an empirical evaluation." Pp. 157–79 in Walter R. Gove (ed.), The Labeling of Deviance. New York: Wiley.

University of Rochester
1974 "FACIT—Family Conflict Intervention Team Experiment—Experimental Action Program." (Abstract). Washington, D.C.: National Criminal Justice Reference Service.

Wylie, P. B., L. F. Basinger, C. L. Heinecke and J. A. Reuckert
1976 "Approach to evaluating a police program

of family crisis interventions in sex demonstration cities—Final report." (Abstract). Washington, D.C.: National Criminal Justice Reference Service.

Zimring, Franklin E. and Gordon T. Hawkins
1973 Deterrence: The Legal Threat in Cri Control. Chicago: University of Chic Press.

30

Ex-Offender Employment, Recidivism, and Manpower Policy
CETA, TJTC, and Future Initiatives

James B. Jacobs, Richard McGahey, and Robert Minion

Over the past several decades, there have been many programs to reduce the continuing high level of ex-offender unemployment. These policies were often part of broader federal efforts to improve the labor market position of the disadvantaged. However, these traditional labor market policies have had disappointing outcomes, leading to dissatisfaction and skepticism about programs to alleviate ex-offender unemployment. This article reviews federal ex-offender employment initiatives with particular attention to the Targeted Jobs Tax Credit (TJTC), a program providing employers with tax deductions for hiring ex-offenders. Our analysis indicates that this credit (like other employment programs for ex-offenders) has had marginal impact at best. We suggest reasons why this is so, focusing on the specific problems of employing ex-offenders, and the general weaknesses of targeted employment strategies that rely on tax incentives. We conclude with some speculations about possible new directions for ex-offender employment programs.

INTRODUCTION

No problem in the crime and criminology domain is more intractable than the joblessness of high risk ex-offenders. The national rate of recidivism, variously estimated to be between 40 and 80% (Sutherland and Cressey, 1978; Waldo and Griswold, 1979), attests to the social cost of massive ex-offender unemployment. Although employment may not fully "cure" criminality, it is hard to imagine a sizeable reduction in serious crime without a substantial improvement in the employment

JAMES B. JACOBS: Professor of Law and Director, Center for Research in Crime and Justice, School of Law, New York University. **RICHARD McGAHEY:** Research

From James B. Jacobs et al., "Ex-Offender Employment, Recidivism, and Manpower Policy: CETA, TJTC, and Future Initiatives," *Crime & Delinquency,* 1984, 30(4), 485-506. Copyright 1984 by Sage Publications, Inc.

experiences of delinquents and ex-offenders. As two students of the problem have observed: "To continue to deny [ex-offenders] the opportunities to learn, to gain experience, and to make themselves useful as free and self-supporting members of society creates problems too costly and too disruptive for the nation to afford" (Coffey and Louis, 1979).

It is not surprising that the unemployment rate for ex-offenders is three times that of non-offenders (Tropin, 1977).[1] Such persons tend to have erratic connections to the world of work—spotty employment histories, low skill levels, lack of motivation, poor work discipline, convictions for violence and dishonesty, and drug and alcohol problems. It is little wonder that employers hesitate to hire ex-offenders even when they are assured that ex-offenders have skills and are subsidized. Combine these problems with high national unemployment—a sheer lack of jobs for all who want to work—and what is surprising is that any ex-offenders establish themselves in the labor market.

Policies to improve the employment of ex-convicts can either be specially designed, targeted, and funded, or established within general strategies for employing disadvantaged workers. Both elements are often found in existing programs, but employment programs covering ex-offenders are generally of the latter type.

Many initiatives in the 1960s and 1970s to improve ex-offender employment were part of broader efforts to improve the labor market opportunities of the disadvantaged. Liberal political leaders, policymakers, and social scientists reasoned that increased employment for ex-offenders would reduce this group's need for illegal income. Many employment programs promised to reduce future crime. This article reviews the history of federal efforts to employ ex-offenders, paying particular attention to the Targeted Jobs Tax Credit, which provides employers a tax deduction for hiring ex-offenders. Our analysis indicates that the effects of this credit (like other employment programs for ex-offenders) have been marginal at best. We suggest some reasons why this might be so, and discuss possible future initiatives to increase ex-offender employment.

Associate in the Urban Research Center at New York University. **ROBERT MINION:** in his second year at Stanford Law School.

Our thanks to Ronald Ehrenberg for comments on an earlier draft, to Susan Sheehan Wieler for research assistance, and to Yesmeen Sarkes and Linda Wheeler for manuscript preparation. Richard McGahey's work on this article was made possible in part by funds granted by the Charles H. Revson Foundation. The statements made and views expressed, however, are solely the responsibility of the authors.

FEDERAL INITIATIVES TO ENHANCE EX-OFFENDER EMPLOYMENT: MDTA AND CETA

Joblessness and crime are hardly new issues on the social agenda. Before the 1960s, policies that addressed the problem were formulated by charities, volunteer groups, and the occasional local government. This changed with the expansion of the American welfare state during the 1960s. "A quiet revolution of significant proportions took shape in the United States Department of Labor in the early 1960s with the introduction of experimental, demonstration, and research projects which focused on the criminal offender as a manpower resource" (Rovner-Pieczenik, 1973: 5). The Manpower Development Training Act of 1962 (MDTA) became the major vehicle for providing unemployed, disadvantaged groups such as ex-offenders with skills that would allow them to succeed in the labor market (Mangum, 1971). MDTA programs focused on job training and vocational counseling, aimed at increasing the unemployed individual's general literacy and specific work skills—in economists' jargon, their "human capital." Such programs were popular with the social welfare agencies that were created to administer these programs. These programs were also legitimized through tapping a long-standing American belief that education provides economic and social mobility.

MDTA was amended several times, each amendment making the original legislation more flexible in meeting the needs of different offender groups. However, job creation and federally funded public service employment remained outside the sphere of MDTA. (It was not until passage of the Economic Opportunity Act of 1964 that the federal government began to create jobs for certain categories of the unemployed.) By 1968, 251 MDTA-sponsored projects were aimed at improving job skills for offenders and ex-offenders, including work programs, and postrelease employment efforts (Daniels, 1975).

In reviewing these projects, the U.S. Department of Labor's Experimental Manpower Laboratory for Corrections (EMLC) concluded that inmate training could give offenders an employable skill. But such training did not ensure that offenders would have a greater chance of being hired or, if hired, of remaining employed. EMLC identified numerous barriers to the employment of released offenders, including employers' unwillingness "to forgive the criminal act or to see beyond the criminal label" (Rovner-Pieczenik, 1973: 11). From the employer's perspective, this bias was hardly irrational. Employers use a number of factors to predict job applicants' future behavior on and off the job. Their use of a criminal record as a predictor of reliability, honesty, and competency may be as rational as predictions based upon educational credentials.

In the late 1960s, the emphasis of national policy began to shift from job training programs to direct job placement. In 1970, the House Select Subcommittee on Labor concluded that the best method for reaching the economically disadvantaged offender was a job creation program. In the course of its hearings, the subcommittee found that ex-offender training programs generally did not lead to jobs for enrollees. Training allowances functioned as income transfers, and the inability to find or hold a job, after completion of the training, exacerbated enrollees' alienation from conventional life-styles. Advocates argued that direct job placement was the only way to assist trained ex-offenders in overcoming artificial barriers to employment (Torborg et al., n.d.).

The move toward creating jobs was not confined to ex-offender programs. The Comprehensive Employment and Training Act of 1973 (CETA), which replaced MDTA, set aside $250 million in fiscal 1974 and $500 million in fiscal 1975 for public service employment programs. Although CETA emphasized a national responsibility to meet the needs of offenders, CETA funds were dispensed by state and local block grant recipients who did not share the same goals and priorities (Bell et al., 1982). Federal agencies did not encourage local sponsors to serve clients, such as ex-offenders, with severe labor market disadvantages. This led to the "creaming" of eligible clients; the bulk of services went to those easiest to help.

Without special directions to allocate funds and services, local sponsors often ignored the needs of ex-offenders, a constituency with rather weak political influence. Funds expended on ex-offenders declined from $20 million in 1972 to $200,000 in 1977. In the 1978 reauthorization of CETA, Congress acted to reverse this trend, reaffirming the importance of ex-offender programs. "Financial assistance should be made available to conduct local programs to provide employment, training and related assistance and supportive services which will enable offenders to secure and retain meaningful employment" (Bell et al., 1982: 3). The amendments created new opportunities for offenders, including the provision of ex-offender services in new locations, and provided for the coordination of existing programs to reduce artificial employment barriers, such as occupational licensing restrictions.

The 1978 CETA amendments also reflected a growing interest in private sector solutions to social problems. CETA had been roundly criticized for producing make-work jobs that fattened municipal payrolls, while failing to lead to permanent private sector work for the disadvantaged. Title VII established Private Industry Councils to advise local CETA prime sponsors, thus increasing the policy role of the private sector. Congress intended that this private sector input would help CETA produce more effective training for all disadvantaged groups.[2] In the same session, they also passed a program directed at the private sector that specifically addressed problem groups such as ex-offenders: the Targeted Jobs Tax Credit.

THE TARGETED JOBS TAX CREDIT

Congress authorized the Targeted Jobs Tax Credit (TJTC) as part of the Revenue Act of 1978. It provided incentives for private corporations to hire the chronically unemployed. Rather than upgrading the unemployed person's work skills through human capital strategies, TJTC made an unemployed person's labor less expensive by subsidizing his wages. The strategy is inexpensive to administer, requires less bureaucracy, and is ideologically compatible with the anti-welfare state backlash of the late 1970s.

Congress aimed TJTC at groups whose unemployment problems did not seem responsive to macroeconomic growth or conventional training. Like all federal employment initiatives, TJTC was not designed solely to combat ex-offender joblessness, but represented a general attack on the predicament of the hard-core unemployed. In drafting TJTC, the House of Representatives' Ways and Means Committee concluded:

> The unemployment rate has declined sufficiently so that it is appropriate to focus employment incentives on those individuals who have high unemployment rates and on other groups with special employment needs. . . . The committee has designed a provision which should provide an incentive for private employers to hire individuals in seven target groups [U.S. Congress, 1978a].

However, ex-offenders were not one of the seven groups targeted by the original proposal.

The Senate Finance Committee (SFC) changed the House proposal and included ex-offenders as a target group. The SFC concurred with the House that unemployment had become increasingly concentrated among specific hard-to-reach groups and concluded that the existing New Jobs Credit (which allowed a tax credit for any new hiring) should be replaced by a targeted employment tax credit.

Why the SFC decided to include ex-offenders is something of a mystery. It was apparently not the result of lobbying by ex-offender groups and advocates. It may be that it simply struck Senator Russell Long, the committee's chairman, as a good idea. In his remarks at a Finance Committee meeting, Senator Long urged the committee to include ex-offenders:

> I think TJTC is a fine proposal. Let me just bring up one thing that concerns me about it. I attended the showing of "Born Again" at the Kennedy Center in which twenty or more men who are in prison were introduced. These men are religious people and they hope to rehabilitate themselves to become good citizens. One of these people made a speech there. He is doing fifteen years. He recited this beautiful old hymn, "Amazing Grace;" it was very touching. He indicated that he hopes that he is going to be able to do something for humanity, that he will be able to serve out his time and be a good citizen some day.
>
> When that man comes out of the penitentiary, he is going to find all doors are closed to him. . . . The result is that eighty percent of those people in those prisons are people who have been there before. When they come out, people will not hire them under any circumstances. I understand that, but somebody ought to try to give these people a break and give them a chance to go straight.
>
> These people are all too susceptible to being dragged into crime because they have no place else to go anyway. I would like to see them have the opportunity to be among the target groups that we are trying to find jobs for; otherwise, what we would find is that the poor things would just find their way back to jail again [Long, 1978].

No other senator or congressman spoke about the issue. The absence of any discussion or debate may be a tribute to Senator Long's interest and power. Without his involvement, ex-convicts may not have become a targeted group. This underscores just how tenuous is the national concern about ex-offenders' employment needs. (Of course, even without a special designation, some ex-offenders would have fallen into other targeted categories.)

The House-Senate Conference Committee ultimately drafted the bill which passed the 95th Congress as the Targeted Jobs Tax Credit (TJTC). It gave employers a federal tax credit for 50% of first-year wages and 25% of second-year wages, not to exceed $6000 per year, for employees falling within any of the seven following target groups: vocational rehabilitation referrals; economically disadvantaged youth; economically disadvantaged Vietnam-era veterans; Supplemental Security Income recipients; General Assistance recipients; youths participating in a cooperative education program; or economically disadvantaged ex-convicts. An ex-offender was any individual certified by a designated local agency as:

(1) a felon convicted under any statute of the United States or any state,
(2) a member of an economically disadvantaged family, and
(3) having a date of hire not more than five years after the last date on which such individual was convicted or released from prison.

In order to prevent employers from using subsidized targeted employees to displace nontargeted workers, the act provided that employers could claim no more than 30% of their aggregate Federal Unemployment Tax Act wages from the previous year. This restriction was deleted in the Reagan Administration's Economic Recovery Tax Act of 1981, as the number of employees hired under TJTC had not been large enough to substantially threaten nontargeted employees (ERTA, 1981).

The Economic Recovery Tax Act of 1981 restricted employers from claiming tax deductions for workers hired prior to the Act's passage who were later discovered to qualify for TJTC tax credits. Data collected from 24 states in 1980 had indicated that retroactive certifications comprised between 60 and 70% of all TJTC hires (Angrisani, 1981). Although retroactive certification may not have served the intended purpose of helping ex-offenders and other disadvantaged, unemployed individuals find jobs within the private sector, it may have provided an incentive for employers to retain targeted workers for the two-year life of the credit. Nonetheless, Congress amended TJTC in 1981 so that certification must be made before the employee begins work. The worker must either have been certified by a designated local agency or have requested in writing that the local agency provide a certification (TEFRA, 1982).[3]

The administrative apparatus of TJTC is quite simple. CETA sponsors, welfare offices, and job service agencies issue eligibility vouchers to qualifying individuals. The individual presents part of the voucher to a prospective employer. If the applicant is hired, the employer must provide the firm name, job title, starting date, wage, and Internal Revenue Service identification number to the Department of Labor's Job Service Division. That office subsequently sends the employer a certification form for each target employee; the form provides the necessary documentation for claiming the tax credit (U.S. Department of Labor, 1980).

EVALUATING TJTC

There is very little data on the effectiveness of the Targeted Jobs Tax Credit. The program was implemented haphazardly, and no comprehensive evaluation of its impact has been conducted. Data and records are handled differently in each locality and state, leading a 1981 study commissioned by the U.S. Department of Labor to conclude that "little can be made of the present statistics given the severe limits on the meanings of the numbers" (Cooper, 1981). As to whether or not TJTC has helped its clients find jobs, local agencies claim that they have no basis on which to make such an assessment.

A rigorous evaluation would compare the number of targeted employees hired under TJTC with an estimate of how many would have been hired without TJTC. Such a statistical model would compare employment of individuals in the targeted groups with the employment pattern of these same groups in the overall labor force. The lack of such evaluation limits what can be said about the specific impact of the credit.[4]

Statistics on the overall use of TJTC do not provide a basis for optimism about its impact. Table 1 shows the number of vouchers and certifications issued nationally for each fiscal half-year through the first half of fiscal 1982. Although 1,621,997 vouchers were issued for TJTC during this period, only 51.3% of those vouchers resulted in certifications of actual jobs. For the ex-offender group, the results were even lower. Of an estimated 117,233 certifications issued, only 30.6% resulted

TABLE 1

TJTC Vouchers and Certifications, Fiscal Half-Years 1979-1982, All Target Groups, and Ex-Offenders Only

Fiscal Half-year	All Target Groups			Ex-Offenders		
	Vouchers	Certifications	Certifications as a Percentage of Vouchers	Vouchers	Certifications	Certifications as a Percentage of Vouchers
Second-half 1979	89,527	37,020	41.4	6,918*	2,276	32.9
First-half 1980	256,600	158,513	61.8	23,055	6,005	26.0
Second-half 1980	270,815	110,201	40.7	21,943	6,764	30.8
First-half 1981	379,897	211,877	55.8	24,462	7,702	31.5
Second-half 1981	353,775	199,704	56.4	21,051	7,268	34.5
First-half 1982	271,383	114,813	42.3	19,804	5,871	29.6
Total	1,621,997	832,128	51.3	117,233	35,886	30.6

SOURCE: Employment and Training Administration, U.S. Department of Labor.
NOTE: TJTC = Targeted Jobs Tax Credit.
*Second-half 1979 voucher figure for ex-offenders is authors' estimate.

in certified jobs, with the ratio of certifications to vouchers in any fiscal half-year never rising above 34.5%.

TJTC had its greatest impact on youths and students. Table 2 shows different groups as a percentage of all TJTC hires. Economically disadvantaged youth and cooperative education students accounted for 84% of all hires; those specifically certified as ex-offenders only accounted for 4% of TJTC placements. Although some ex-offenders were undoubtedly members of the other certification groups, the data do suggest that ex-offenders did not benefit significantly from TJTC.

Furthermore, many of the job certifications shown in Table 1 were retroactive; that is, employers first hired the person, and then later discovered the person's eligibility for TJTC. In these cases, it certainly cannot be claimed that TJTC affected the hiring decision. According to Angrisani (1981), the Assistant Secretary for Employment and Training at the U.S. Department of Labor, the majority of TJTC hires probably would have occurred without the credit. Thus, TJTC has been even more limited in its impact than the numbers in Table 1 suggest. Why?

Several reasons have been advanced for TJTC's low use, but two recur: (1) a lack of publicity and inefficient administration and (2) insufficient subsidies. However, we believe that using targeted tax credits to foster employment, with the inadvertent stigmatizing of ex-offenders in this program, is inherently problematic as an ex-offender employment strategy.

Poor Publicity and Administration

In creating the Targeted Jobs Tax Credit, the House-Senate Conference Committee (U.S. Congress, 1978b) noted that:

> The credit can be effective only if the Department of Labor and the local employment and training agencies aggressively promote the credit and use it as a tool in finding jobs for members of the target groups.

But according to a series of reports by researchers at Ohio State University (1982) who studied employers' knowledge of the credit, TJTC suffered from a lack of publicity. Based on field interviews with administrators and employers at 25 sites across the nation, the researchers found that most employers' hiring practices were unaffected by TJTC. The researchers rated TJTC publicity as "high" if the sponsor

TABLE 2

Target Groups as a Percentage of All TJTC Hires

Economically disadvantaged youths and cooperative education students	84%
Vocational rehabilitation clients	5%
Ex-offenders	4%
Vietnam-era veterans	4%
General assistance recipients	2%
Supplemental security income recipients	1%
Total	100%

SOURCE: Employment and Training Administration, U.S. Department of Labor.
NOTE: TJTC = Targeted Jobs Tax Credit.

used at least three types of marketing techniques, including mass mailings, seminars, media advertising, and job development contracts; "medium" if the sponsor used one or two such techniques; and "low" if there was no marketing or publicity. None of the 25 sponsors rated high, 7 rated medium, and 18 rated low. Local CETA sponsors also felt that national publicity was inadequate. Also, many viewed TJTC credits as antithetical to what they considered their basic mission—the training of individuals for unsubsidized jobs. CETA sponsors did not define their clients as deficient workers and resisted the idea of subsidizing employers to hire clients.

The Wisconsin Health and Social Services Department (1980) found that lack of knowledge on the part of employers and job placement personnel explained, in part, the low use of TJTC. Many employers feared excessive paperwork, an increased risk of tax audit, and conflicts with affirmative action programs. A study by the Northeast-Midwest Institute (1980) criticized the national office of the Employment Service for insufficient TJTC publicity, which resulted in ineffective local placement efforts. The Ohio State, Wisconsin, and Northeast-Midwest Institute studies all recommended greater national publicity and funding to cover the administrative costs of local marketing and implementation of TJTC.

William Giery of the Foodservice and Lodging Institute (1981) made a broader attack on the federal implementation of TJTC. His study charged that the Department of Labor failed to implement its instructions and goals for state and local agencies:

Nobody at the state and local levels knew what to do; in several areas of the country the agencies responsible for certifying individuals had no idea of what a Targeted Jobs Tax Credit was. When they received certification forms, they had no idea of what they even were for and therefore were not certifying anyone as eligible. The Department of Labor did set up some organizational structures to deal with administering the program, but provided State Employment Security Agencies with no funds to carry out these responsibilities.

Neal Miller, a consultant on criminal justice issues, claimed that the Department of Labor had not done anything significant to advance TJTC or to educate potential applicants or employers about the program: "Nobody has taken up where the legislators left off and made a concentrated effort on behalf of the credit. It may be a good idea, but we may never really know it."[5] Fred Hufford, a placement specialist at Project LEEO (Liberation of Ex-Offenders through Employment Opportunities), a nonprofit agency that specializes in aiding former convicts find employment, claimed that for each TJTC employee, there are thousands of others who could benefit from the program if they knew about it, but that a lack of publicity and federal promotion has crippled the program (Washington Post, 1982).

Further Problems: Size of the Incentive and the Stigmatizing of Ex-Offenders

Although there were obvious inefficiencies in the administration and publicity of TJTC, these failures are probably not the principal reason for its lack of success. TJTC credits, which may seem generous to policymakers, do not attract employers for a variety of reasons. The size of the subsidy is small relative to potential employee problems, the needs of different firms for tax credits varies, and TJTC may have inadvertently stigmatized ex-offenders.

A TJTC subsidy is not large enough to induce many employers to overlook ex-offender problems such as a criminal record, poor work history, and drug or alcohol dependency. This is especially true at times of high unemployment when ex-offenders must compete with a sea of unskilled workers for a limited number of entry-level or dead-end, unskilled jobs. Employers who offer such jobs are overwhelmed with applicants, and modest subsidies will not put ex-offenders at the head of this queue. Although many specialists in offender unemployment see qualitative differences between offenders and others, it may be that offenders simply suffer from a larger quantitative number of labor market problems. As policy analyst Richard Tropp noted, it is possible that "all offender unemployment is explained by their being dispro-portionately young, unskilled, minority, and poorly located"(1978: 28).

In addition, ex-offenders are hampered by their criminal records. Employers, overwhelmed with applicants for entry-level and low-skilled jobs, and lacking clear criteria to turn down many applicants, may use this stigma as a reason for rejecting ex-offenders. Indeed, one major problem with TJTC is that ex-offenders themselves do not want to reveal to employers that they have been approved for a voucher on the basis of their criminal records. Although offenders were not required to reveal to employers the basis for their eligibility, employers wanted to know why the job applicant was eligible for a tax credit, thus creating pressure to reveal the criminal record.

Ironically, the effort to help ex-offenders through designation for a special tax credit may have hurt them by waving a red flag in front of employers. It may have been better for ex-offenders to qualify for TJTC based on some other criterion than a stigmatizing criminal record. However, all targeted tax credits potentially stigmatize the chronically hard-to-employ groups whom they aim to assist.

It is too much to expect that modest tax incentives alone can surmount ex-offender employment problems that range from human capital deficiencies to artificial employment barriers to the sheer lack of jobs. At some price and at some subsidy, chronically unemployed ex-offenders would hypothetically become economically attractive to certain employers, unless other disadvantaged job seekers are similarly subsidized. However, a subsidy just for ex-offenders is politically inconceivable. Even if it materialized, it may not be effective, as subsidies like TJTC are generally not effective for large-scale job creation.

*Windfalls From Tax Subsidies and
the Real World of Small Business*

The major impact of subsidies like TJTC is probably the creation of windfall tax relief for selected private employers, whose hiring decisions probably are not affected by the tax subsidies. (A windfall occurs when taxes are reduced for something the taxpayer would have done without the reduction.) According to researchers at Brandeis University:

A large number of TJTC certifications are the result of employers claiming credits on behalf of workers hired independently of TJTC, and . . . only a moderate share of employers report using TJTC to increase overall or target group employment [Center for Employment and Income Studies, 1982b: 12].

In this regard, TJTC does not operate differently for ex-offenders than for other disadvantaged groups. In the late 1970s, the federal Youth Incentive Entitlement Pilot Project (YIEPP) conducted an experimental wage subsidy program to increase youth employment. They offered employers a subsidy ranging from 50 to 100% of the minimum wage: only 5% of the employers contacted were lured by the 50% subsidy, and only 18% by the 100% subsidy. Remarkably, fewer than one out of five firms was willing to hire a program participant, even with a 100% wage subsidy (Center for Employment and Income Studies, 1982a). The reasons most often given by nonparticipating employers were lack of work for additional employees (48.3%) and a need for higher skilled workers (21.1%). Only 3.4% of the employers cited a general dislike for government subsidy programs.

Employer disinterest in subsidized workers is also seen in New York City's experience with TJTC. According to the city's Department of Employment, from January 1979 to May 1981, fewer than 6,400 workers were awarded TJTC credits, at a time when the city estimated that over one million city residents were eligible for CETA. Fewer than one-tenth of one percent of city firms made extensive use of the credit. One-third of the TJTC-certified jobs paid less than the minimum wage, and an unspecified but "large number" of certifications were retroactive (issued after the hiring took place), suggesting that many of the disadvantaged persons eventually certified would have been hired with or without TJTC (Radison, 1982). This lack of interest is found in many other tax incentive programs. Although program proponents typically make extravagant claims about the impact of tax credits like TJTC, research suggests that most private hiring decisions are barely affected by tax credits.[6]

Tax incentives also fail to address the particular needs of small businesses which have proportionately more unskilled jobs and thus have the potential to be a major source of employment for the disadvantaged. Small businesses do not benefit from tax reductions on business income. According to economist Robert Eisner (1981), approximately 40% of firms with assets under $5 million earn no taxable income. Most firms in their early years do not have taxable income. They would require refundable tax credits, similar to a negative income tax for businesses, that would allow them to "cash in" tax voucher credits and improve their cash flow.

Such a policy is politically unlikely and probably undesirable. Legislators prefer TJTC-type credits because of their invisibility, or at least obscurity, to taxpayers. Unlike direct dollar subsidies and outlays, tax credits seem to be cost-free. In reality this is an illusion; other taxpayers pick up the tab. However, refundable credits mean direct public payments to businesses, rather than the hidden revenue transfer provided by TJTC-type tax reductions.

Extensive refundable credits for support of small businesses may also be undesirable. Small firms are more likely to offer low-paying, less secure jobs. They are less able to withstand swings in business cycles, less likely to be unionized or to provide benefits such as medical care, and less likely to offer promotions and on-the-job training. Refundable credits to small businesses would generally subsidize labor intensive jobs with low pay, less stability, and fewer opportunities to upgrade skills.

In summary, TJTC's record is not a cause for optimism for two reasons: the program stigmatizes ex-offenders in an effort to aid them and tax credits like TJTC fail to produce many new jobs for disadvantaged workers, whether or not they are ex-offenders.

Some general reforms of TJTC may make it more efficient. For example, economist John Bishop of the Institute for Research on Poverty has suggested that: (1) employers be allowed to conduct their own certifications, subject to public audit, (2) programs like TJTC be better publicized, and (3) eligibility for the credit not be contingent on social stigma, but be made more generally available to referrals from public employment agencies. As Bishop (1981) notes, "a subsidy for tax credits for employing stigmatized target groups will not attract the participation of many employers." Although these suggestions would improve TJTC, the powerful combination of ex-offender employment deficiencies and the sheer lack of jobs for many disadvantaged individuals does not make us optimistic about TJTC's potential to produce a substantial employment effect.

NEW DIRECTIONS FOR EX-OFFENDER EMPLOYMENT

What other special efforts may be made to improve employment opportunities for ex-offenders? Preferential treatment of ex-offenders over other high unemployment groups is not socially acceptable, much less politically feasible. Efforts to improve postrelease job placement could be redoubled, but the same impediments are quickly encountered. Where would a constituency in support of ex-offenders come from? Special job finding and placement assistance for ex-offenders at a time of high general unemployment in urban and minority labor markets would be attacked as "rewarding criminals." And why would employers knowingly prefer ex-offenders to other job applicants?

Can the existing institutions of the criminal justice system be used more effectively? Again, post mortems of MDTA and other programs are not encouraging. Many efforts have been made to improve vocational training in prisons and jails, but there are enormous, if not insurmountable, barriers to success. Steele and Jacobs (1975, 1977) have analyzed the complexities and confusion of goals in prison operations that tend to cripple programs such as job training. Access to prisons with better programs is often used by administrators as a means to reward and punish inmate behavior. Routinely, prisoners are assigned to institutions for security reasons and not according to the individual prisoner's vocational needs. Inmates often participate in programs to obtain transfer to less onerous institutions or to gain earlier release by parole boards. It is extremely difficult to attract talented vocational instructors to work in prisons: the pay, working conditions, interference from administrators, and quality of students and facilities are inferior to other institutions.

Of course, improved economic conditions and job creation in urban ghettos would go some distance in improving the prospects of ex-offenders, along with all other distressed workers. Job training alone cannot remedy the joblessness produced by the the structural labor market conditions that face many ex-offenders upon release. Jobs are increasingly available in office and service sectors located in downtown cores or suburbs, not in the poor urban neighborhoods to which many ex-offenders return. More community-based economic development may increase work options for ex-offenders. Cities could encourage new manufacturing and warehousing operations to locate in these neighborhoods, providing direct employment in their firms and collateral jobs in support services such as lunch counters, security patrols, and retail sales. Without some mix of direct public jobs and increased private employment in these poor neighborhoods, ex-offenders will likely remain at the end of the employment queue.

Parole officers may serve as brokers to community job efforts and may take a more active role in directing ex-offenders to training and job tax credit programs. It is imperative that a "blind" institutional mechanism be designed to implement the program, as the direct referral from a parole agency could stigmatize the ex-offender.

We are not optimistic about this option. Calls for improved job placement efforts by parole officers are second in frequency only to calls for more effective job training inside prisons. At a time when prison populations and parole caseloads are high and resources scarce, there is little reason to think that parole officers will become more effective job brokers; if anything, the situation is likely to get worse.

Options for the Future

Two recent efforts hold some promise for improving ex-offender employment, at least in the short run. The first is the Transitional Aid to Released Prisoners (TARP) program, which provides released prisoners with unemployment insurance to aid their transition from incarceration to work. Rossi et al. (1980) found that the program, which paid offenders whether they actively sought jobs or not, discouraged job seeking. But the researchers also found that the program did reduce criminal behavior. They felt that the program could be redesigned to increase the incentives to find work while retaining the crime reduction benefits. Although we are skeptical about these claims (McGahey, 1982), the tentative program results seem more promising than other strategies. Hence, our qualified endorsement for further experimentation with TARP-like efforts.

The second promising initiative is the Vera Institute of Justice's Neighborhood Work Program (NWP). Since its inception in November of 1978, NWP has provided recently released jail and prison inmates a maximum of 28 hours of work per week for up to six months. NWP pays slightly above the minimum wage for jobs such as demolition or repair of city-owned buildings in New York's poorer neighborhoods. The only eligibility requirement is that an applicant must have been released from incarceration within the last 30 days and be at least 18 years of age. The program employs over 300 workers at any one time, and has had to turn away at least as many people as it has accepted. NWP has employed over 7,500 ex-offenders, 95% of them men, 80% black, 15% Hispanic, and 5%

white and other (Neighborhood Work Project, 1983). As yet, no research has been done regarding NWP's impact on recidivism.

NWP is unique in that it is funded through fee-for-service performance contracts with local governments. The majority of released prisoners are from state and local institutions, and locally based programs are more likely to be responsive to labor market conditions and political tensions. NWP currently has a service contract with New York City's Department of Housing Preservation and Development that provides most of its four million dollar annual budget; another small contract is held with the Public Development Corporation of New York. NWP crews have worked on over 1700 construction projects for over 100 clients, primarily New York City community groups.[7] Although still funded by public monies, payment on a fee-for-service basis frees NWP somewhat from the accusation that it rewards ex-convicts at the expense of other impoverished groups. Such a funding arrangement also requires NWP to perform useful work to obtain contract renewals.

The fee-for-service approach seems promising. Private employers may make similar arrangements with a pledge to employ ex-offenders as a condition of the contract, or with contract performance standards adjusted in consideration for hiring the disadvantaged. "First source" agreements could be used whereby private sector recipients of development aid pledge to interview or hire public employment service clients as their first source of new hires. The development aid is made contingent on living up to the "first source" agreement (Van Horn and Ford, 1983). A similar approach would be for public agencies to make fee-for-service contracts with the condition that employers hire designated groups of distressed workers, such as ex-offenders.

There is no guarantee that these initiatives will improve the employment opportunities of ex-offenders. Although research on postprogram effects of NWP is just beginning, other employment programs have found that participants return to their previous poor labor market positions once they leave the program. But we are persuaded that programs like TJTC have been of little use, and that such targeted wage subsidies are unlikely to be of much help to ex-offenders. Programs to revitalize urban economies through direct public job creation and public-private cooperation remain an untested possibility in solving the broad employment problems of ex-offenders and others. Experimental efforts like TARP or NWP hold some promise for short run integration of ex-offenders into the labor market; given the current lack of promising program options, these short run programs should be explored further.

NOTES

1. This estimate is probably low considering that many ex-offenders are not included in the Bureau of Labor Statistics' category of the civilian workforce because they are no longer actively looking for employment.

2. From a strong advisory role under CETA, private sector participation has come to dominate federal employment and training planning in the Reagan Administration's Job Training Partnership Act (JTPA), an omnibus replacement for CETA enacted in 1983. This interest in the private sector is part of a cycle in employment and training initiatives that focuses alternatively on government employment, the private sector, and schools as the solution to employment problems of the disadvantaged. If the number of recent research reports on school quality is any indication, we now seem to be entering a schooling phase.

3. In 1982, amendments to TJTC added one new target group and made some clerical updates, but made no significant changes affecting ex-offenders except for the two-year extension of the credit.

4. According to a telephone interview with Burman Skrable, Office of Strategic Planning and Policy Development, U.S. Department of Labor, National Employment and Training Administration (September 28, 1982), the Department of Labor did plan an evaluation for spring 1981, but tabled the study pending the administration's consideration of terminating the credit. With the extension of TJTC through 1984, the Department had rescheduled an evaluation (to be contracted to an independent agency).

5. Telephone interview with Neal Miller, February 15, 1982.

6. See McGahey (1983), for a more extended discussion of the problems with tax incentive schemes for job creation.

7. Telephone conversation with Joe Stillman, Director, Neighborhood Work Project, January 27, 1984.

REFERENCES

Angrisani, A.
    1981   Testimony before the U.S. Senate Finance Committee, Subcommittee on Economic Growth, Employment and Revenue Sharing, April 3, 1981.
Bell, L., C. N. Louis, M. Johnson, E. Cohen, and P. O. Brien-Reynolds
    1982   An Assessment of the Offender Planning Grant Program: Final Report of the American Bar Association Division of Public Service Activities (Vol. 1) Washington, DC: U.S. Department of Labor.
Bishop, I.
    1981   "An examination of U.S. experience with employment subsidies." Testimony

before the U.S. Senate Finance Subcommittee Hearings on the Targeted Jobs Tax Credit, April 3, 1981.

Center for Employment and Income Studies

1982a "Private sector involvement: lessons from YIEPP," in Youth Programs. Waltham, MA: Brandeis University.

1982b "The Targeted Jobs Tax Credit (TJTC): the 1979-1981 experience and the future outlook," in Youth Programs. Waltham, MA: Brandeis University.

Coffey, O. and C. N. Louis

1979   "Unemployment, crime, and the local jail." Corrections Today 41, 2: 36-39.

Cooper, M.

1981   Testimony on the Targeted Jobs Tax Credit before the U.S. Senate Finance Committee, Subcommittee on Economic Growth, Employment, and Revenue Sharing, April 3, 1981.

Daniels, D.

1975   "Evolution of manpower legislation." Labor Law J. 26, 6: 328.

Economic Recovery Tax Act of 1981 (ERTA)

1981   Public Law number 97-34, Section 261

Eisner, R. J.

1981   Testimony at the Joint Hearing on Economic Programs to Stimulate Employment in the Small Business Sector before the U.S. House Education and Labor Subcommittee on Labor Standards and the House Small Business Subcommittee on SBA and SBIC Authority, Minority Enterprise, and General Small Business Problems, April 29, 1981.

Giery, W. G.

1981   Testimony on the Targeted Jobs Tax Credit before the U. S. Senate Finance Committee Subcommittee on Economic Growth, Employment, and Revenue Sharing, April 3, 1981

Long, R.

1978   Statement before the U.S. Finance Committee's Discussion on the Targeted Jobs Tax Credit, 95th Congress, Second Session, September 26, 1978.

Mangum, G. L.

1971   "Manpower research and manpower policy," in A Review of Industrial Relations Research (Vol. II). Madison, WI: Industrial Relations Research Assn.

McGahey, R.

1982   "Review of Money, Work, and Crime." Crime and Delinquency 28, 1: 137-139.

1983   "Whatever happened to enterprise zones?" New York Affairs 7, 4: 45-62.

Neighborhood Work Project

1983   Getting the Job Done. New York: Vera Institute of Justice.

Northeast-Midwest Institute

1980   Putting the Targeted Jobs Tax Credit Back to Work. Unpublished paper.

Ohio State University

1982   The Implementation of the Targeted Jobs Tax Credit: Final Reports of the Mershon Center CETA Study. Columbus: Ohio State Univ. Press.

Radison, W.

1982   The Targeted Jobs Tax Credit in New York City. Unpublished report, New York City Department of Employment.

Rossi, P., R. A. Berk, and K. J. Lenihan

1980   Money, Work, and Crime: Experimental Evidence. New York: Academic.

Rovner-Pieczenik, R.
   1973   A Review of Manpower Research and Development in the Correctional Field
          (1963-1973). Washington, DC: U.S. Department of Labor, Manpower
          Research Monograph 28.
Steele, E. H. and J. Jacobs
   1975   "A theory of prison systems." Crime and Delinquency 21, 2: 149-162.
   1977   "Untangling minimum security: concepts, realities, and implications for correc-
          tional systems." J. of Research in Crime and Delinquency 14, 1: 68-83.
Sutherland, E. H. and D. R. Cressey
   1978   Principles of Criminology. New York: J. B. Lippincott.
Tax Equity and Fiscal Responsibility Act of 1982 (TEFRA)
   1982   Public Law Number 97-248, Section 233.
Toborg, M. A., L. Center, R. H. Milkman, and D. W. Davis
   n.d.   The Transition from Prison to Employment: An Assessment of Community-
          Based Assistance Programs. Washington, DC: Law Enforcement Assistance
          Administration, National Institute of Law Enforcement.
Tropin, L. A.
   1977   Testimony before the U.S. House Judiciary Subcommittee on Crime, Septem-
          ber 27, 1977.
Tropp, R. A.
   1978   "Suggested policy initiatives for employment and crime problems," in L.
          Leiberg (ed.) Crime and Employment Issues. Washington, DC: American
          University Law School. Institute for Advanced Studies in Justice.
U.S. Congress
   1978a House Report 95-1445 on H.R. 13511, 95th Congress, Second Session.
   1978b U.S. House-Senate Conference Comparison on H.R. 13511, 95th Congress,
          Second Session.
U.S. Department of Labor
   1980   "Hire more workers, pay less taxes." Employment and Training Administra-
          tion, Document Number 0-331-973.
Van Horn, C., D. Ford, and R. Beauregard
   1983   A Final Report on the Targeted Jobs Demonstration Program. New Brunswick,
          NJ: Rutgers State University of New Jersey.
Waldo, G. and D. Griswold
   1979   "Issues in the measurement of recidivism." Commissioned paper for the
          National Academy of Sciences Panel on Research and Rehabilitation Tech-
          niques.
Washington Post
   1982   "Employers applaud tax credit program to aid unemployed," January 21, 1982.
Wisconsin Department of Health and Social Services
   1980   A Report of the Wage Bill Subsidies Research Project, Phase I. Division of
          Policy and Budget, Office of Client Employment Programs.

VII

METHODOLOGICAL ISSUES
IN EVALUATION STUDIES

Evaluation research is the systematic application of social research procedures in assessing the conceptualization and design, implementation, and utility of social intervention programs. . . . Evaluation research involves the use of social research methodologies to judge and to improve the planning, monitoring, effectiveness, and efficacy of health, education, welfare, and other human service programs. (Rossi & Freeman, 1982)

As Rossi and Freeman aptly describe, evaluation is a highly applied field of social science research concerned with the development, implementation, and improvement of practical, real-world programs. In fulfilling these immediate objectives, however, evaluation researchers have also contributed significantly to the state of the art of their craft and, more generally, to social science theory and techniques.

The six chapters that make up this section are representative of a rich and diverse body of work that appeared during the period covered by this volume. It was difficult to choose only a few from many excellent publications. We chose the selections that follow not only because we felt them to be worthy of review but also because they provide a sense of the broad spectrum of current work in the areas of evaluation methodology and design.

Chapter 31 is a treatise by Larry Orr on changes in the design of demonstration projects that have facilitated evaluation of program effects. In demonstrations, as contrasted with experiments, the treatment is administered by regular program agency staff rather than by an organization under the direct control of the evaluating organization. In the early 1970s, Orr argues, demonstrations were limited to providing "at best . . . a qualitative feel for the consequences of [a] single program variant . . . and some idea of the administrative feasibility of the program." Since that time, the utility of demonstrations for evaluation purposes has been enhanced by the use of principles of social experimentation, most notably that of random assignment to treatment and control groups. Problems of evaluating demonstrations and some advantages of demonstrations over social experiments are also discussed.

Chapter 32, by Orley Ashenfelter, is a highly technical piece of evaluation research directed toward solving a practical matter of program design: that of estimating the expected program participation rate. The case considered is that of programs in which eligibility is determined by individuals' or families' incomes. The simplest approach would use data on income distributions alone to estimate the subset of the relevant population with incomes at or below the proposed program cutoff. But these estimates will underestimate program participation to the extent that workers who normally have incomes above the cutoff reduce their labor supply to make themselves eligible for the program. And they will overestimate participation if some eligible families or individuals choose not to participate. Ashenfelter addresses these issues through an econometric analysis using data from the Seattle-Denver Income Maintenance Experiment. Findings suggest that both sources of potential bias have minimal effects on program participation rates and that the simple estimates are likely to be adequate.

Chapter 33 offer a provocative examination by Anne Schneider and Robert Darcy of the normative implications of the ways significance tests are used and interpreted in evaluation research. Most evaluation researchers take the position that their task is to measure the impact of a policy on some relevant outcome, and they reserve to policymakers the role of forming normative, political, or philosophical judgments concerning policy impact or effectiveness. However, evaluators often make normative decisions unintentionally through the use of the traditional .05 statistical significance level when the number of observations is small. Other problems that may cause evaluators to miss detecting significant policy impacts through use of standard statistical tests are also discussed. The authors propose that the one-tailed test be used more frequently and that evaluators consider using alternatives to the standard .05 convention when appropriate. Other solutions are offered to improve the design of evaluations to permit researchers to identify meaningful policy impacts through conventional statistical methods.

Much of evaluation research entails analysis of primary data, collected expressly for the purposes of the evaluation. This volume thus would be incomplete without at least one contribution on survey methodology. Chapter 34, by Berk, Wilensky, and Cohen, provides such a selection in the form of an evaluation of procedures used in the 1977-1978 National Medical Care Expenditure Survey (NMCES), "one of the most ambitious data-collection efforts ever conducted by a federal health agency." The NMCES achieved high response rates at considerable cost. The authors discuss reasons for nonresponse and approaches for obtaining high response rates in the NMCES and imputation procedures for partial responses. They suggest that high response rates may not always merit the cost of achieving them and advise researchers to consider the costs and benefits of obtaining high response rates. Other topics include the NMCES approaches to ensure data reliability, use of proxy respondents, and consumers' lack of accurate information on the details of their own health insurance coverage.

In the last two chapters in this section, we turn to the methods of meta-analysis, or research synthesis. Chapter 35 addresses the issue of how to select the primary research studies to be included in a synthesis of the research literature on a given subject or issue. Authors Fred Bryant and Paul Wortman pose the question, "Should meta-analysis abandon critical judgments about the quality of primary research and include all available studies in data syntheses, or should they exclude flawed studies that suffer from threats to validity?" The conclusion of their analysis, which provides useful guidelines for the meta-analyst, is that it depends on the range of experimental rigor within the particular research literature and the analyst's own priorities regarding internal and external validity. The discussion focuses particular attention on the problems encountered when a literature is based largely on quasi-experiments, which is frequently the case in evaluation research.

Bryant and Wortman recommend the secondary analysis of meta-analytic databases toward the end of refining the methods of meta-analysis. An example of such a secondary meta-analysis is provided in Chapter 36. Prioleau, Murdock, and Brody's reanalysis concerns the effectiveness of psychotherapy compared with a placebo treatment. The issue arises again of which primary research studies should be included in the research synthesis. The original meta-analysis, based on 520 primary studies, seemed to provide definitive evidence of the effectiveness of psychotherapy. However, Prioleau et al.'s examination of a subset of 32 studies included in the original meta-analysis found no evidence that the benefits of psychotherapy are greater than those for placebo treatment.

REFERENCE

Rossi, P. H., & Freeman, H. E. (1982). *Evaluation: A systematic approach* (2nd ed.). Beverly Hills, CA: Sage.

31

Using Experimental Methods to Evaluate Demonstration Projects

Larry L. Orr

It is important from the outset to distinguish experimentation from the related, but distinctly different, concept of "demonstration." . . . What I shall call "demonstrations" typically involve little or no controlled variation of policy parameters. A uniform treatment is applied to a specified group or geographic area, often without even an attempt to define a comparable control group. Thus, it is difficult to test hypotheses rigorously in a demonstration; at best, one gets a qualitative feel for the consequences of the single program variant applied, and some idea of the administrative feasibility of the program [Orr et al., 1971: 47-48].

One of the clearest and perhaps most important legacies of the social experiments of the 1970s is that this characterization (Orr et al., 1971) of demonstrations is no longer accurate. In the twelve years since it was written, there has come to be a widely shared presumption if not that every demonstration will have a randomly selected control group, at least the burden of proof is on those that do not. Thus while no major social experiments comparable to the income maintenance, health insurance, and housing allowance experiments have been initiated since the mid-1970s, the fundamental principle of experimentation—random assignment—has been incorporated in a variety of program innovations in employment, welfare, health, and long-term care policy. At this year's meetings of the American Public Health Association, for example, one session included representatives of five different demonstration projects, all of which involved randomly assigned control groups.

At the time the social experiments were being fielded, the government was funding a variety of evaluations of demonstrations and ongoing programs based

Author's Note: The author is affiliated with Abt Associates, Inc., Washington, D.C. This paper was presented at the 96th Annual Meeting of the American Economic Association, San Francisco, December 1983.

on nonexperimental methodologies. In many cases, the results were disappointingly ambiguous and unreliable. It became clear by the mid-1970s that the use of nonrandom comparison groups—the strongest and most widely used the nonexperimental approaches—often yielded misleading or uninterpretable results. The Office of Economic Opportunity and the Labor Department, for example, sponsored a series of evaluations of manpower programs throughout the late 1960s and 1970s that, in the end, still left considerable uncertainty about the effects of these programs on the earnings and employment of recipients. One of the best of these, the 1977-1978 Job Corps evaluation, was based on a carefully selected comparison group of nonparticipants in areas without Job Corps centers. When the data were analyzed, it was discovered that 50 percent of the females in the comparison group had children, whereas only 23 percent of the females in the Job Corps member group had children (Mallar et al., 1980: 39-40). Such a wide disparity in an easily observable variable must raise serious concern about the comparability of the two groups in other, unobservable dimensions.

Similar problems afflicted many of the other nonexperimental evaluations of the period. The analysis of the $20 million Continuous Longitudinal Manpower Survey attempted to use comparison groups drawn from the Current Population Survey. More than a dozen comparison groups were formed, using different selection methodologies; each gave different estimates of program impact, with the result that only broad ranges of effects could be presented with any confidence (Westat Inc., 1981). In the late 1970s, the Labor Department funded a demonstration of employment services for dislocated workers from three plants in Michigan; the evaluation, being conducted by Abt Associates, is based on the experiences of workers in these three plants and those in four comparison plants in the same area. As compared with the mean outcomes for workers in the comparison plants, it appears that the demonstration had a significant positive effect in one of the demonstration plants, a significant negative effect in a second, and little or no effect in the third. Because of differences in the two groups of plants (and the small number of plants involved), it is unclear whether these outcomes reflect real differences in program effects or are merely artifacts of the sample of plants chosen.

Experiences like these—and many others could be cited—have led the government to search for a stronger methodology for evaluating public programs. The most obvious model is that provided by the social experiments.

The growing acceptance of random assignment as the norm for evaluating demonstration projects has blurred the distinction between experiments and demonstrations that seemed so obvious in 1971. In principle, almost any social policy that could be tested in an experiment can be implemented as a demonstration and, given random assignment, evaluated with equal rigor and precision. A demonstration with a randomly assigned control group is, in that sense, an experiment. Nevertheless, the two modes of research continue to be viewed as distinctly different, and in at least one fundamental respect they are: In demonstrations, the treatment is typically administered by the staff of regular

rogram agencies, rather than by an organization under the direct control of the
valuating organization. In contrast to the tight control of treatment adminis-
ation exercised by the researchers in charge of the income maintenance and
ealth insurance experiments, the evaluators of demonstrations play a much
ore passive, third-party role of observation, data collection, and analysis, with
ttle direct control over program operations.

This operational distinction has important implications for the design and
nalysis of demonstration evaluations. The first section of this chapter describes
n ongoing demonstration evaluation, the AFDC Homemaker-Home Health
ide Demonstration Evaluation being conducted by Abt Associates, which can
e considered typical of this new breed of evaluations. The last two sections turn
o a discussion of the problems that have arisen in this and other evaluations as a
irect result of program operators' primary role in the field component of the
olicy to be tested and, finally, the unique advantages and opportunities that
emonstrations afford as a method of testing public policies.

THE AFDC HOMEMAKER-HEALTH AIDE
DEMONSTRATION EVALUATION

AFDC Homemaker-Home Health Aide Demonstrations sponsored by the
U.S. Health Care Financing Administration are being conducted in selected
ocalities in seven states.[1] In each, up to 300 AFDC recipients will be trained as
homemaker-home health aides each year of the three-year demonstration.
Following the four-eight-week training course, each aide will be employed in a
subsidized position for one year—providing home care to aged, disabled, and
other functionally impaired individuals who, without such care, would be likely
to require residential care in nursing homes or hospitals. It is anticipated that
approximately 3000 clients will be served in each state over the course of the
demonstration.

The objectives of the demonstrations are twofold. First, provision of training
and subsidized employment is intended to increase the long-run employment and
earnings of AFDC recipients and thereby reduce welfare costs and dependence.
Second, provision of home care services to functionally impaired clients is
intended to prevent or delay institutionalization, for which a large share of the
cost is likely to be borne by public programs.

The demonstrations are being evaluated by Abt Associates Inc. (AAI). The
main focus of the evaluation is on the costs and benefits of the two demonstration
program components: training and service delivery. The benefits of the training
component will be measured primarily in terms of increased earnings and
reduced benefits from public welfare programs (AFDC, Medicaid, and Food
Stamps). On the client side, benefits will include reductions in the cost of
institutional and other medical care as well as in benefits from public programs
(SSI and Food Stamps). In both cases, benefits will be assessed from the
viewpoint of the participant and the program agency as well as from the

viewpoint of society as a whole. Due to data limitations, however, some pure private costs and benefits will not be measured.

To serve as a valid basis for comparison with participant outcomes, contr groups of aides and service clients are being randomly selected at the point enrollment into the demonstrations. The selection and assignment process is follows. Program intake workers receive referrals of potential clients from variety of sources (home care agencies, hospitals, nursing homes, social servi agencies, etc.); AFDC receipients volunteer for training in response to writte announcements, personal contacts by caseworkers, and mass media advertisin Demonstration staff in the various sites use a variety of methods to scree referrals and applicants for eligibility and appropriateness. Trainee applican are typically given a group orientation and a personal interview; client referra are screened on the basis of initial information provided by the referral sourc and are then interviewed in person, using an assessment form developed by AA After all eligibility and screening criteria are applied by demonstration staff, th names of those selected are telephoned to evaluation staff at AAI, who randoml assign each potential trainee or client to treatment or control status (in equa numbers) and inform demonstration staff of the assignment. Demonstratio staff, in turn, inform the individuals whether they have been selected to receiv training or home care services. In most cases, those assigned to the treatmen group are then scheduled to start training or receiving services within one o two weeks.

Data for the evaluation analyses will be drawn from a variety of sources:

- the client assessment instrument completed for all treatment and contro clients prior to assignment;
- a self-administered questionnaire completed by potential trainees prior to assignment;
- a series of monthly tracking forms that document the progress of, and services received by, members of both treatment groups throughout thei participation in the demonstration;
- telephone follow-up interviews with service clients and controls six and twelve months after enrollment;
- telephone follow-up interviews with trainees and controls late in third year of the demonstration;
- follow-up assessments of 200 service clients and 200 controls in each state, conducted in person during the third year, using the same instrument as at baseline; and
- benefit records drawn from state AFDC, Medicaid, and Food Stamp program information systems, and the Federal Medicare record system.

Development of data collection instruments is the responsibility of AAI. State demonstration staff trained by AAI perform the actual collection of all data except the follow-up interviews, which are conducted directly by AAI staff. It is anticipated that complete data will be collected for 500 trainees and 500 controls,

us 1150 home care clients and 1150 controls in each state. In addition, data will
e extracted from program records for all demonstration participants who
ceive benefits from the four public programs in question.

The analytic framework is a relatively straightforward comparison of mean
utcomes for the treatment and control groups, contolling for a number of
aseline characteristics. For some outcomes, such as nursing home admissions,
ore sophisticated analytic techniques like hazard rate models may be used.
eparate analyses will be performed for each state for all outcomes except the
hysical functioning measures taken from the follow-up assessment. In addition,
limited amount of analysis of pooled data from all seven states will be
onducted.

THE UNIQUE PROBLEMS OF
EVALUATING DEMONSTRATIONS

As noted above, the defining characteristic of demonstrations is that the
reatment is administered by regular program staff who are not under the direct
ontrol of the evaluator. This characteristic gives rise to certain problems and
constraints on the evaluation that are not present in experiments where the
esearcher has direct control over the implementation of the treatment.

Limitations on the Number of Treatments

The most obvious limitation of demonstrations is that, in most cases, the
number of distinct treatments tested is small. Whereas the income maintenance
experiments tested as many as 47 distinct treatments,[2] demonstrations typically
involve at most 5 or 6 different treatments, and often have only 1 or 2. This
reflects very real constraints on the number of different program variants that
can realistically be implemented in the context of a real-world program agency,
especially where the treatment involves direct, in-person delivery of services,
rather than simply financial transactions as in the income maintenance and
health insurance experiments. Regular program staff in social service agencies
are trained and conditioned to provide all appropriate services at their disposal
to all eligible applicants. Faced with a choice between maintaining the
experimental design by denying certain services to an otherwise eligible applicant
or giving that applicant the services he or she "needs," program staff are very
likely, consciously or unconsciously, to opt for meeting the applicant's needs.
Even if there is no conscious subversion of the design, distinctions among groups
eligible for different services are likely simply to get lost in the press of getting on
with the main mission of the agency: providing services.[3]

This problem can be avoided by segregating agency staff according to
treatment. However, staff size, normal agency operating procedures, and/or
the nature of the treatment itself (e.g., minimum class sizes for training courses)
are likely to place severe limits on the number of separate service delivery units
that can be created within a single agency.

These operational considerations are compounded by considerations sample sizes necessary for proper evaluation. In most demonstrations, the treatments do not lend themselves naturally to characterization by a small number of continuous, quantifiable policy parameters, such as guarantees, tax rates, or coinsurance rates. Thus the evaluator is driven to analysis of variance comparisons of means in estimating program effects. For any given sample size or budget, the precision of such estimates declines rapidly as the number of treatments increases.

The disadvantage of this mode of analysis, of course, is that the results are not very robust to changes in the specification of the treatments and, therefore, not very generalizable to the broader range of policy options. Unlike the income maintenance and health insurance experiments, where estimated response functions can be used to predict the effects of guarantees or coinsurance rates not actually tested, demonstration evaluations typically can tell us very little about program configurations not tested. This is a serious problem, because policy interest in specific program options can shift rather rapidly; an evaluation that takes four or five years to complete runs a serious risk of providing results on a program configuration that is obsolete, even though there may still be strong policy interest in program variants of the same general type.

Although this problem is unavoidable in most instances by the nature of the policy process, judicious application of prior information in the design of the demonstration may help to increase the utility and generalizability of the final results of the evaluation. Suppose, for example, that 15 different major program variants can be identified, of which only four can be tested in the demonstration. If the likely effects of the 15 options can be rank-ordered a priori, then the options to be tested can be chosen to provide upper and lower bounds on the effects of those not tested. In the example just posed, testing the options ranked first, fifth, tenth, and fifteenth in terms of likely effects would not only span the policy space but would also allow one to bracket the effects of those options not tested. In effect, this approach amounts to creating a "judgmental response surface." The efficacy of this approach depends crucially on the demonstration designer's ability to identify the full range of policy options and to rank-order their effects a priori. Still, in those cases where program variants cannot be characterized with continuous quantitative variables and a true response surface estimated, this approach at least allows the use of whatever prior information exists in designing the demonstration; and the rank-ordering of the estimated effects of the options tested provides a crude test of the accuracy of the prior ranking of the full range of options.

Control Group Contamination

A related, but conceptually distinct problem in evaluating demonstrations with randomly selected control groups is the risk that the results will be biased by control group contamination. Again, this danger arises because the treatment is administered by a regular program operating agency. In most cases, such agencies also provide similar nondemonstration services for which control group members may be eligible. For example, WIN staff serving as intake workers in the training component of the AFDC Homemaker-Home Health Aide Demonstrations can also provide employment counseling, job search assistance, nondemonstration training, and other employment services to AFDC recipients, as well as refer them to a variety of other employment and social service agencies. On the client side of that demonstration, health agencies routinely provide elderly and disabled individuals a wide range of services that may prevent or delay institutionalization; in some states, these services include home care financed by other funding sources.

It is not, of course, necessary or desirable that control group members receive *no* services from public programs. For a valid comparison of the demonstration treatment with the status quo, however, they should receive only those services that they would have received in the absence of the demonstration. Control group members may receive services that they would not have received in the absence of the demonstration for several reasons. First, program staff may favor control group members over other, equally eligible applicants for the limited supply of services available in order to compensate them for having been rejected by the demonstration. Even if such compensatory behavior does not occur, the outreach activities of the demonstration are likely to bring individuals who would not otherwise have sought public services into contact with the program; some of them are likely to receive regular program services as a result. Second, in situations where there is excess demand for nondemonstration services, the provision of demonstration services to the treatment group reduces excess demand for nondemonstration services, making it easier for controls to receive services.[4]

I know of no way to correct for such bias analytically. Once the outcomes of the controls have been affected by the existence of the demonstration, there is no way to infer from data on the controls themselves what would have happened in its absence. And any approach that attempts to adjust observed outcomes for the controls by using data on nonparticipants really comes down to replacing the randomly selected control group with a nonrandom comparison group.

Even the direction of the bias is not always clear. In the AFDC Homemaker-Home Health Aide Demonstrations, for example, providing controls more home care than they would have otherwise received will tend to reduce their use of institutional care. But at the same time, reduced use of institutional care by treatment group members will shorten nursing home waiting lists, making it easier for controls to gain admission. The net effect of these offsetting biases is impossible to predict a priori.

This is evidently a situation in which an ounce (or several) of operational prevention is worth a pound of econometric cure. If the bias cannot be corrected analytically, great care must be taken in the administration of the demonstration to prevent or minimize its occurrence. The general rule for demonstration intake staff must be that once controls are identified and informed that they have not

been selected for demonstration services, they should be returned to the situatic
in which the demonstration initially found them. For referrals from oth
agencies, this means informing the referral agency and turning over respons
bility for any further action on the control's behalf to that agency. For sel
referrals, it means informing the control and initiating no further action on his c
her behalf. In no case should intake staff refer the control to any other source c
services; in all cases, it should be made clear to applicants that nonselection fc
demonstration services does not affect the individual's eligibility for othe
services.

A number of organization and administrative steps can be taken to facilitat
the application of this general principle. Most important, intake staff should b
as organizationally separate from regular program staff as possible. Ideally, th
specific individuals responsible for demonstration intake should not also hav
responsibility for regular program services. Stringent control of communication
and documents is also important. Controls should be informed by letter, rathe
than in person, to avoid inadvertent referrals and to be sure that they are clearl
informed of their continuing rights to other services. The letter to controls shoulc
include a phone number for questions and complaints, but the person who take
these calls should be trained in how to respond to them. Lists of control grour
members should be destroyed or removed from local program offices, as shoulc
all copies of any baseline instruments or application forms completed by or for
controls; if available to local staff, these can provide a convenient source of
prescreened applicants for nondemonstration services. Access to all documents
relating to controls should be restricted to the absolute minimum number of local
staff members.

By working closely with state and local demonstration staff, we have managed
to achieve surprisingly good cooperation with these types of safeguards in the
AFDC Homemaker-Home Health Aide Demonstrations. We have even had a
good deal of success in educating demonstration staff as to why these precautions
are necessary—on a number of occasions, we have received inquiries from state
and local staff asking whether a particular operational procedure would
contaminate the control group. In the end, of course, we can never really know
how successful our efforts have been; that is the nature of the problem.

As this discussion makes clear, the validity of the evaluation requires that the
evaluator be intimately involved in the operational details of the demonstration—just as the researchers were in the social experiments. Evaluators cannot
adopt (or be relegated to) the position of neutral, outside observers. My own view
is that in most programmatic settings control group contamination is the greatest
single threat to the integrity of randomized demonstration evaluations.

Resistance to Random Assignment

A third important way in which the central role of program staff in
demonstrations complicates the application of experimental design principles is
that it requires the evaluator to explain and defend the use of random assignment

nd, in particular, the use of a control group. The orientation of program
perators to service provision, rather than to research, almost invariably leads
em to feel that random assignment is at best a burdensome nuisance, and at
'orst an unethical denial of services to needy, eligible individuals in the control
roup. Addressing these concerns can take an enormous amount of time and
ffort in a project like the AFDC Homemaker-Home Health Aide Demon-
tration, where we are dealing with the program staffs of seven different states
nd over 100 local training and service delivery agencies. Nevertheless, it is
mportant that these concerns be addressed as fully and forthrightly as possible.
Quite aside from the initial problem of gaining acceptance of random assignment, it is important that demonstration staff understand why random
assignment is necessary. Grudging acceptance of an imposed design will result in
problems ranging from careless intake and assignment procedures to outright
sabotage of the design. Lack of understanding of the function of the control
group is likely to lead to control group contamination through inadvertent (and
largely undetectable) actions at the local level. In short, demonstration staff at all
levels must be "sold" on the concept of random assignment.

The fundamental concern about random assignment most widely shared by
program operators is that it involves an unethical denial of services to needy
controls. We have found that the most effective (and accurate) response to this
concern is to point out that the funds and/or slots available to the demonstration
are limited and that services to eligible individuals in the aggregate are not
reduced by random assignment; random assignment can be viewed simply as a
method of allocating those limited services among applicants. In fact, random
drawings or lotteries are often used as a fair method of allocating scarce resources
in similar situations. It is also useful to stress the fact that program operators are
free to apply any screening and selection procedures they wish (consistent with
overall demonstration rules and guidelines) prior to random assignment, to
ensure that demonstration services go only to those most in need of them.

A closely related concern is that demonstration staff will be subjected to a
barrage of emotional appeals and angry complaints from controls who feel that
they have been unfairly denied the services they need. Such appeals and
complaints undeniably occur in any demonstration with random assignment of
controls. In our experience, however, they are much less frequent than program
operators expect or fear.[5] And most of those who do question the necessity or
fairness of their assignment as controls seem to accept a rational explanation of
the nature of the demonstration as a research project that can serve only a limited
number of people, the fundamental even-handedness of assignment by random
drawing, and the importance of collecting information from people who do not
receive demonstration services (i.e., controls) to help policymakers decide
whether such services should be made available on a wider scale. Nevertheless,
the evaluator has little standing to reassure program operators before the fact
that their concerns in this regard are exaggerated. An approach that we have used
in several states, and found to be quite effective in calming such fears, is to invite a

state or local program staff member who has had experience with random assignment in some other demonstration to meet with the demonstration staff and candidly discuss that experience. As demonstrations with random assignment become more common, this technique will be increasingly applicable.

Finally, program staff frequently express a variety of complaints about the added burden and intrusion on normal operating procedures entailed in random assignment and data collection for the evaluation. We have tried very hard to keep these aspects of the evaluation as nonintrusive as possible—for example, we guarantee assignment of applicants on the same day they are telephoned to us, to avoid delays in service delivery. Still, at a minimum, program staff are required to screen and select twice as many eligible applicants as they would normally have to, in order to provide for the control group, and to collect more extensive information about participants than they would in a regular program. Aside from making a conscientious effort to ensure that the evaluation's burden on demonstration staff is in fact the minimum necessary, the only really honest response to these complaints is the one given by a county program staffer whom we invited to speak to the demonstration staff in one of our states about his experience in another demonstration: Local staff have to accept from the outset that this is a research project, not a service delivery program, and as such it involves a good deal of added burden. If they are unwilling to accept that burden, they should simply opt out. That message is, of course, better received coming from a peer than coming from the evaluators themselves. In this particular case, nobody got up and left the room.

THE ADVANTAGES OF DEMONSTRATIONS OVER SOCIAL EXPERIMENTS

Although the central involvement of regular program staff in demonstrations unavoidably presents certain problems that are largely absent in social experiments, it also creates certain advantages and opportunities to obtain useful knowledge about the programs tested.

From the standpoint of government research managers and policymakers, demonstration evaluations have two distinct advantages. First, the costs allocated to government research and evaluation budgets are substantially smaller, given that service delivery costs are usually charged to the regular program budget. Thus whereas the full cost of the AFDC Homemaker-Home Health Aide Demonstrations will exceed those of the largest social experiments, the portion of that cost allocable to the sponsoring agency's evaluation budget will be only about one-tenth the cost of the Health Insurance Experiment. For better or worse, I am convinced that this disparity is largely responsible for the government's marked preference in recent years for randomized demonstrations over randomized experiments.

The second advantage of demonstrations from the government's point of view is more substantive. Precisely because of the "real-world" administration of emonstrations, their outcomes tend to have more face validity among olicymakers. Social experiments are viewed as somewhat artificial and herefore prone to yield results that would not be replicated if the same policy vere implemented by regular program staff.

From an analytic viewpoint, real-world administration also offers the opportunity to observe the kinds of bureaucratic and administrative difficulties hat are likely to arise in the implementation of the program. These range from urf battles and political problems to the technical and procedural problems of leveloping forms and paper flow or hiring the kinds of staff required to run the orogram. Very little can be learned about these issues in a social experiment set up outside the regular program bureaucracy. Of course, it is not always clear that the problems encountered and solutions developed in a demonstration project are directly generalizable to a full-scale program, but at least the demonstration provides a dry run prior to full-scale implementation. If the demonstration is mounted in a number of different sites, one can at least have some confidence that most of the generic types of operational problems that can be expected will be confronted, a variety of solutions considered and/or tried, and, perhaps, some general lessons emerge.

Given the current state of the art of "implementation analysis" or "process analysis," the role of the evaluator with respect to these operational issues is appropriately the rather modest one of systematically describing and documenting problems and attempted solutions. None of the social sciences has yet developed a sufficiently rigorous theoretical understanding of the internal dynamics of program bureaucracies to support an organizational analysis with any reliable predictive power. Nevertheless, systematic description and documentation of the planning and implementation of the demonstration in a case study mode can provide extremely useful information to policymakers and program operators involved in later attempts to implement the same or similar programs. At a minimum, such case studies can call attention to potential problems and solutions that might otherwise be overlooked. They can also provide useful guidance for the development of implementation schedules and procedures, and serve to codify a cross-section of views and interpretations of knowledgeable local program staff about operational issues. For operations staff, the "story" of the demonstration may well be as useful as the quantitative statistical estimates of outcomes.

A final analytic advantage afforded by demonstrations that is not available in social experiments is that of observing and analyzing the outreach and selection process associated with the program. In many cases, there is at least as much uncertainty about how many and what kinds of people will participate in a new program as there is about the behavioral responses of participants. As anyone who has attempted to provide realistic budget projections for a new program knows, different assumptions or estimates of participation rates can have an enormous effect on estimates of program costs.

In principle, outreach and selection, and therefore program participation, are susceptible to rigorous, quantitative analysis. The problems revolve around collection of the data required to support such analysis. It is often conceptually difficult and/or inordinately expensive to define and collect data on eligible nonparticipants in the broader population from which participants are drawn. The approach taken in the evaluation of the Employment Opportunity Pilot Projects, for example, was to conduct personal interviews with a random sample of 30,000 households in the demonstration and comparison sites. This survey alone cost over $8 million.

A much less ambitious approach was initially proposed in the AFDC Homemaker-Home Health Aide Demonstration Evaluation. Because the eligibility and screening criteria for those demonstrations are highly judgmental,[6] it seemed clear that we could not identify nonparticipating eligibles in the population at large without replicating the entire demonstration intake process for a random sample of the population. We therefore proposed instead to collect data, largely from program records, on a random sample of applicants and referrals to the demonstration in order to analyze the screening process used to select participants from this population. Ultimately that approach was rejected, at least for the home care clients, primarily because of the difficulty of obtaining informed consent from individuals whose only contact with the demonstration was over the telephone or through a referral agency not directly involved in the demonstration. For service clients, then, this evaluation—like most other demonstration evaluations—will be restricted to analysis of program impacts on those actually selected for participation. We still hope to be able to obtain some data on nonparticipating AFDC recipients (where the target population of eligibles is more clearly defined) in order to do some analysis or participation in the demonstration.

CONCLUDING REMARKS

Over the past 10 years, the use of randomly selected treatment and control groups in the evaluation of demonstrations of program innovations has gained growing acceptance. In my view this is directly traceable to the large-scale social experiments of the 1970s, which demonstrated the methodological superiority of random assignment over other available methods of measuring the effects of experimental programs. Moreover, given the continuing pressures on government research managers both to produce reliable evidence on the effects of proposed policies and to hold down at least the nominal costs of research and evaluation activities, I expect this trend to persist for the foreseeable future.

As I have indicated in this chapter, even with random assignment there are substantial difficulties involved in deriving valid, generalizable results from demonstration evaluations. These difficulties arise precisely from the fundamental difference between a demonstration with random assignment and a social xperiment: implementation of the treatment by regular program agencies, ather than by an organization under the direct control of the researchers. Without minimizing the importance of these problems and limitations, it is also rue that demonstrations afford the opportunity to investigate certain questions hat cannot be pursued in an experiment divorced from regular program perations. I hope that the experimental research community will be as maginative, energetic, and successful in devising methods of overcoming these roblems and exploiting these opportunities as it was in the development of the methodology embodied in the social experiments.

NOTES

1. Arkansas, Kentucky, New Jersey, New York, Ohio, South Carolina, and Texas are participating in the demonstration.
2. The Seattle-Denver Experiment included 11 NIT-only plans, 3 counseling/training-only plans, and 33 plans formed by the interaction of the NIT and counseling/training variants. See U.S. Department of Health and Human Services (1983).
3. In some demonstrations, where the service provided is primarily informational, merely having members of different treatment groups come into contact in the same building raises a significant risk of blurring the distinction among treatments.
4. Both of these forms of control group contamination are examples of what Burtless has labeled "queueing bias": The first changes the order and/or the composition of the queue for services; the second shortens the queue.
5. One piece of evidence of this acceptance on the part of controls is that only about 2 percent of the controls contacted in our client follow-up survey have refused to be interviewed.
6. For example, intake staff must decide whether the applicant could be "reasonably anticipated to require institutional care in the absence of demonstration services."

REFERENCES

MILLAR, C. et al. (1980) Evaluation of the Economic Impact of the Job Corps Program: Second Follow-Up Report. Princeton, NJ: Mathematica Policy Research.
ORR, L. L., R. G. HOLLISTER, and M. J. LEFCOWITZ [eds.] (1971) Income Maintenance. Chicago: Markaham.
U.S. Department of Health and Human Services, Office of Income Security Policy (1983) Overview of Seattle-Denver Income Maintenance Experiment Final Report. Washington, DC: Government Printing Office. (May)
Westat Inc. (1981) Continuous Longitudinal Manpower Survey: Net Impact Report No. 1. Washington, DC: U.S. Department of Labor.

32

Determining Participation in
Income-Tested Social Programs

Orley Ashenfelter*

Estimates of the number of participants to expect in income-tested social programs may be made from data on income distributions alone. These simple estimates will be biased if the social program induces incentive effects or if some eligible participants do not pursue their application for benefits. This article brings these issues together and sets out a statistical framework for testing whether the simple estimates are likely to be adequate in practice. The data used for the empirical work come from the Seattle and Denver Income Maintenance Experiments, the largest of several similar experiments thus far undertaken. The results imply that the simple estimates of program participation may be adequate if a program of the experimental type investigated here is implemented nationally.

KEY WORDS: Discrete choice models; Social experiments; Probit model.

1. INTRODUCTION

The overall costs of government welfare programs are determined both by the benefits received per participant and by the number of participants. In most social programs, individuals or families may participate in the receipt of benefits only if their income falls below a cutoff level specified by Congress or by the program's operators. Estimating the extent of program participation for different levels of income eligibility is thus an important factor in public discussions of the initiation and modification of these social programs.

At first blush it might seem that determining the extent of program participation is a straightforward statistical problem. The number of program participants could simply be estimated as the number of families or individuals in the relevant population with incomes at or below the proposed program cutoff income. The data required to produce these estimates are nothing more than a random sample of the incomes of the relevant population and the associated cumulative income distribution function. More generous social programs, which are those with higher income cutoffs determining eligibility, would naturally be expected to have a greater number of participants.

There are two potential difficulties with this approach to estimating program participation. First, some workers who would normally have incomes in excess of the program income cutoff may reduce their labor supply to make themselves eligible for program participation. To the extent that these incentive effects exist, estimates of program participation based on simple cumulative income distributions will systematically understate actual participation. For a given level of program generosity, however, the size of these incentive effects will vary with the implicit tax rate in the social program. The key to identifying these incentive effects is therefore to isolate the effects on program participation of variations in implicit social program tax rates that are independent of program generosity. Doing this requires data that contain variations in both program generosity *and* program tax rates. Estimating the size of these incentive effects is of considerable practical importance because they provide an indication of how and to what extent simple tabulations of the cumulative income distribution will understate program participation.

Second, estimates of the actual participation in existing U.S. welfare programs often indicate that many families who are eligible on the basis of their income do not participate. This raises the possibility that the incidence of information, reporting, or other unobserved nonpecuniary costs are a significant deterrent to actual program participation. The key to identifying the presence of these deterrent costs is the ability to compare actual program participation against the participation predicted for a group whose income distribution would otherwise have been identical to that of the participants. In an experimental setting the natural place to obtain these data is from a comparison of treatment and control groups. Estimating the size of these nonpecuniary participation effects is of considerable practical importance because they provide an indication of how and to what extent simple tabulations of the cumulative income distribution will *overstate* program participation.

The purpose of this article is to bring these three issues together in such a way that they may be explored empirically. The data used for this purpose are probably the best that will be available for some time and come from

* Orley Ashenfelter is Professor, Department of Economics, Princeton University, Princeton, NJ 08544. The author is grateful to the editor and two referees for helpful comments; to Robert Moffitt, John Pencavel, and Philip Robins for helpful discussions; and to Mark Plant for skillful assistance. Financial support for this research was provided in part by the Department of Health and Human Services through a contract with SRI International.

Seattle and Denver Income Maintenance Experiments, the largest of several similar experiments thus far undertaken. The empirical strategy is to construct a statistical framework that treats the cross-sectional heterogeneity of incomes as an inevitable determinant of some correlation between program generosity and program participation, but that allows the data to confirm the further presence or absence of both economic incentives and unobserved nonpecuniary participation costs. The basic goal is to set out a convenient and tractable scheme for organizing the relevant data that nests all of the relevant hypotheses to be tested.

The first section of the article is expository and sets out the basic issues as clearly as possible. The natural focus is on the characteristics of families that make them eligible for benefits without changing their labor supply and how to distinguish these families from those that do change their behavior. Inevitably, the elementary empirical analysis it contains is instructive, but too simple.

The second section contains a correct but nevertheless easily implemented statistical framework based on a convenient specification of a model of labor supply. The empirical results are contained in the third section, and the conclusion contains a discussion of the further research that these results suggest may be useful.

2. ELEMENTARY DETERMINANTS OF PROGRAM PARTICIPATION

2.1 Eligibility for Experimental Families

In a negative income tax program, families receive an income guarantee of G dollars and face a tax rate of t on their nonwelfare income (y). If they claim it, they therefore receive a subsidy (D) of $D = G - ty$ dollars as long as their income (y) is less than G/t. If family income y is greater than the quantity G/t, the family cannot receive a subsidy. The income cutoff G/t is called the *breakeven income* for the program. Families with incomes below the breakeven are said to be eligible for program participation, whereas families with higher incomes are not eligible.

Suppose at the outset that families do not control their incomes, but that incomes differ among families. Suppose also that there are no unobserved nonpecuniary costs of program participation such as "welfare stigma." In this situation families whose incomes fall below the breakeven income would then choose to receive a subsidy, whereas other families would be ineligible for the program. The only economic behavior involved in this prediction is the trivial assumption that more is preferred to less.

To make things concrete suppose that the logarithm of income (henceforth called *log income*) is normal with mean μ and standard deviation σ. Under the assumptions just stated, the fraction of families eligible for benefits will be identical to the fraction who participate in the program (P) and will be

$$P = F [\ln G/t - \mu)/\sigma] \qquad (2.1)$$

where F indicates the value of the cumulative standardized normal distribution function. Now suppose several groups are randomly selected from the pool whose log income is normally distributed and that these groups are offered negative income tax plans with varying income guarantees and tax rates. This is a stylized description of the Seattle and Denver Income Maintenance Experiments. Equation (2.1) then describes a series of points relating the participation fraction (P) and the log of the breakeven of the offered plan. There are two observations to make about this relationship. First, higher income guarantees (G) and lower tax rates (t) are associated with greater participation. This relationship is purely mechanical in the sense that it merely reflects increased eligibility for program benefits as the breakeven of the plan increases and the program becomes more generous. Moreover, in this simple setup the elasticity of program participation across groups with respect to the program guarantee is equal but opposite in sign to the elasticity of program participation with respect to the tax rate. A regression of program participation on G and t does not, therefore, establish anything more than the fact that families offered programs with high breakevens are more likely to be eligible for program benefits even if they do not change their behavior.

Second, a plot of the participation fraction P against the log of the breakeven reveals the parameters of the log income distribution and can be used both to estimate those parameters and to test the normality assumption. Table 1 contains data from the Seattle/Denver experiments to illustrate this point. Column 1 lists the fraction of families initially offered a negative income tax program who received more than a nominal payment during any quarter of the second year of the experiment. The data are classified by the breakeven of the program offered to the experimental family. Since some of the programs have similar breakeven levels, I have aggregated those that were similar when it equalized cell sizes. All experimental families received at least $60 per quarter independently of their incomes as compensation for various administrative obligations. The number of families in the numerator of the participation fraction is the number of families receiving more than this nominal payment in at least one calendar quarter of the second year of the experiment. Families that drop out of the program are therefore included in the data as nonparticipants, and this classification is an enormous advantage for this analysis. After all, attrition is logically equivalent to nonparticipation and Pencavel and West (1978) have shown that it is highly correlated with the program breakeven to which a family is assigned. As one can see from Table 1, the participation proportion increases with the breakeven of the program, as expected. (There are several definitions of program breakeven that might be used for this analysis, but I have simply used the ratio of the nominal program income guarantee to the nominal tax rate as the breakeven throughout.)

Unfortunately, because of the setup of the Seattle/Den-

Table 1. Data on Experimental and Control Families in the Second Year of the Seattle/Denver Income Maintenance Experiment

Program Earnings Breakeven for Experimental Families $	The Proportion of Experimental Families Participating in the Receipt of Payments		Income Ordinate for Control Families $	The Cumulative Earnings Distribution for Control Group Families	
	Unadjusted for Truncation (1)	Adjusted for Truncation (2)		Unadjusted for Truncation (3)	Adjusted for Truncation (4)
5,430–6,850	.328	.29	6,850	.315	.28
7,366–7,600	.319	.29	7,600	.383	.34
8,000	.521	.45	8,000	.433	.39
8,001–8,821	.558	.48	8,821	.527	.46
9,600	.673	.57	9,600	.609	.53
11,200	.734	.64	11,200	.774	.66

ver experiments the participation proportions in Table 1 are not estimates of the cumulative values of the normal distribution given by (2.1). In these experiments, as in others, families were initially screened on the basis of their pre-experimental incomes before being assigned to an experimental program. To account for the truncation of the income distribution on the basis of pre-experimental incomes I have also reported the adjusted participation proportion in column 2 of Table 1. (The method of adjustment is contained in Appendix A.) The actual participation proportions observed in the sample are upward biased estimates of the participation proportions that would be observed in a national negative income tax program, because the experimental sample overrepresents families with low incomes in the pre-experimental year and incomes are positively correlated in subsequent years.

The dashed line in Figure 1 is a plot on normal probability paper of the adjusted participation fractions against the log of the breakeven for the six groups listed in Table 1. Although there is clearly considerable variation, these points do roughly coincide with a straight line and are not strong evidence against the normality assumption.

2.2 Control Families

The design of the Seattle/Denver negative income tax experiments also includes provision for a control group

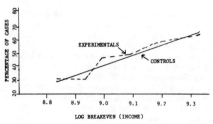

Figure 1. Cumulative Income Distribution (contols) and Probit Function (experimentals).

of randomly selected families. A natural question arises as to what use the data from this group are for the analysis of program participation. The answer is that these data provide independent evidence on both the form of the cumulative distribution function of log income and the values of the parameters of that distribution.

To continue, suppose that the log incomes of control families are also normal with mean μ and standard deviation σ. The fraction of control families with log incomes below a value R is then

$$P = F\left[(R - \mu)/\sigma\right] \quad (2.2)$$

Choosing $R = \ln G/t$ gives a relationship between the values of the empirical cumulative distribution function of log income and the values of R among the control families that should be the same as the relationship between the participation fraction and the program breakeven among the experimental families. The unadjusted points on the cumulative income distribution for the control group are listed in column 3 of Table 1. The ordinates were selected to correspond with the six program breakevens for the experimentals. The numbers listed in column 3 are simple, distribution-free estimates of the actual participation fractions in column 1 that ignore both incentive and nonpecuniary deterrent effects in the determination of participation. Most (but not all) of these estimates seem reasonably accurate. In essence, improving on these benchmark estimates provides the basic challenge for any statistical model of participation.

As with the experimental families, the control families are selected in the Seattle/Denver experiments so as to overrepresent low income families and this requires an adjustment of the observed cumulative proportions $\hat{P}$. The adjustment method for the control families is identical to that made for the experimental families. These adjusted proportions in column 4 of Table 1 are also plotted in Figure 1. As one can see from Figure 1, the estimated points of the cumulative distribution of log incomes for the control families do closely coincide with a straight line. This suggests that the normality assumption is reasonable. Moreover, the position of this line is close, but by no means identical, to the position of the similar relationship for experimental families. This suggests that the data for both control and experimental families are useful for the analysis of program participation, and that systematic labor supply behavior or the presence of non-pecuniary participation costs may partly account for the difference between the positions of the two lines in Figure 1.

2.3 Labor Supply Behavior and Participation

The analysis so far has emphasized the mechanical determinants of program participation by treating the family's income as exogenous. The spirit of the analysis of labor supply, however, is that by choosing their hours of work family members may manipulate their income so as to become eligible for negative income tax payments. To determine how many families will engage in this behavior it is necessary to recognize that a negative income tax offers a change, both harmful and beneficial, in the opportunity set that a family faces. The harmful aspect is the decrease in the wage rate from w to $(1 - t)w$ that a family member faces, but the beneficial aspect is the increase in the guaranteed (unearned) income level of G that the family now has. The family that is offered the opportunity to participate in a negative income tax program presumably will do so if the harmful effect of participating is outweighed by the beneficial effect. It is shown to a second-order approximation in Appendix B that all families whose earned incomes would have fallen below the quantity

$$y^0 = (G/t)(1 - .5et)^{-1} \qquad (2.3)$$

will perceive the net benefits of program participation to be greater than the net costs. In equation (2.3), e is the elasticity of labor supply and is assumed to be constant for purposes of estimation. The relaxation of this assumption could be easily handled by working out a third- or higher-order approximation to family behavior, and it would merely introduce powers of t into (2.3). As it stands, (2.3) demonstrates the intuitive proposition that the choice of program participation will vary from what it would be if there were no incentive effects to the extent that the labor supply elasticity (e) differs from zero. If $e = 0$, labor supply is insensitive to tax rates and participation is determined as if incomes were exogenously determined. The larger e is, the greater participation is, and the more sensitive participation is to variations in the tax rate.

It is a straightforward matter to use the criterion of (2.3) as the basis for a simple econometric model of participation. First, for reasonable values of e and t, the logarithm of (2.3) is

$$\ln y^0 \approx \ln G/t + .5et. \qquad (2.4)$$

Second, assume that however families determine their earnings in a given period, $\ln(y)$ is normal with mean μ and standard deviation σ. If the earned income that would be received in the absence of program participation, $\ln y$, turns out to be less than $\ln y^0$ in any period the family

will choose to make itself eligible for program participation. The fraction of families that do choose participation when offered a program with breakeven G/t and tax rate t is thus

$$P = F[(\ln y^0 - \mu)/\sigma]$$
$$= F[(\ln G/t + .5et - \mu)/\sigma]. \qquad (2.5)$$

Equation (2.5) neatly separates the mechanical from the behavioral aspects of program participation. From (2.1), one finds that the mechanical component of participation is $F[(\ln G/t - \mu)/\sigma]$. This is the participation that would be expected if incomes were exogenously determined, or if $e = 0$. The participation induced by a change in labor supply behavior is thus the difference between (2.5) and (2.1): $F[(\ln G/t + .5et - \mu)/\sigma] - F[(\ln G/t - \mu)\sigma]$.

2.4 Nonpecuniary Costs of Participation

A natural way to investigate the effect of nonpecuniary participation costs or inclinations toward program participation is to assume that each family behaves as if these were of a dollar quantity Q. The condition for participation in the program for the family is then that $\ln y < \ln y^0 + Q$. If $Q < 0$, the family has a distaste for participation, while if $Q > 0$, the family feels otherwise. Suppose that these inclinations are normally distributed and independent of $\ln y$ with mean μ^* and standard deviation σ^*. (Assuming $\ln y$ and Q are independent has no quantitative content here, since a correlation between Q and $\ln y$ would change the definition of $\hat{\sigma}$ in (2.6) by merely the subtraction of twice the covariance between $\ln y$ and Q. There would be no change in the form of (2.6), however.) The fraction of families that will choose participation, when offered a program with breakeven G/t and tax rate t, is then just the fraction for which $\ln y - Q < \ln y^0$, and is simply

$$P = F[(\ln y^0 - (\mu - \mu^*))/(\sigma^2 + \sigma^{*2})^{1/2}]$$
$$= F[(\ln G/t + .5et - (\mu - \mu^*))/\hat{\sigma}], \qquad (2.6)$$

where $\hat{\sigma} \equiv (\sigma^2 + \sigma^{*2})^{1/2}$. The difference between (2.5) and (2.6) is the amount by which program participation differs from what would be the case if there were no nonpecuniary participation costs or tastes. It seems plausible that the parameters of the distribution of these costs or tastes would differ according to the type of program and the manner of its administration, and (2.6) shows just how these differences will affect program participation.

Equation (2.6) leads naturally to a simple probit estimation scheme using the data on the experimental group. Not all of the parameters in (2.6) can be estimated from these experimental data alone, however. The importance of the data from a randomly selected control group is that they may be used to estimate μ and σ; using those estimates, one can then estimate μ^* and σ^* to test the importance of nonpecuniary participation costs as determinants of program participation. As a result, all of the parameters in (2.6) may be identified. After all, the observed distribution of log earnings for the experimental group does not provide data to estimate μ and σ by simple methods because it is contaminated by any experimental effects that exists.

It is now clear why the analysis whose results are pictured in Figure 1 is too simple. Equation (2.6) indicates that the dashed line portraying the fractional participation of the experimental group may differ from the solid line indicating the cumulative distribution of the log earnings of the control group for two different reasons. On one hand, the level and/or slopes of these lines may differ because of the presence of nonpecuniary program participation costs. On the other hand, in the absence of these costs the dashed line should lie above the solid line so long as $e \neq 0$, and the size of any systematic difference should depend on the tax rate in the negative income tax programs. We turn next to a simple estimation scheme for sorting out these effects.

3. STATISTICAL FRAMEWORK

3.1 Likelihood of the Experimental Sample

Equation (2.6) gives the probability of observing a participant and leads directly to the likelihood of the experimental sample. Two preliminary issues require some discussion, however. First, as we have observed, the experimental families offered participation in the Seattle and Denver Income Maintenance Experiments were screened on the basis of their pre-experimental incomes. Assuming that the joint distribution of pre-experimental and experimental log earnings is bivariate normal, however, implies that the conditional log earnings distribution during the experimental period is normal with mean linear in pre-experimental log earnings. It follows that (2.6) applies directly with the understanding that μ in that equation is replaced by a linear function of pre-experimental earnings. Thus, the truncation of the sample on the basis of pre-experimental earnings may be handled by simply including an additional regressor and taking some care in the interpretation of the parameters μ and σ. (The precise interpretation is given in Appendix A.) Second, it is natural to suppose that μ and μ^* in equation (2.6) are not constants, but instead vary across individuals with a (row) vector of variables X_i'. This also causes no problem for the interpretation of (2.6) as $\mu - \mu^*$ may simply be replaced in (2.6) by putting $\mu = X_i'\beta$ and $\mu^* = X_i'\beta^*$, so that $\mu - \mu^* = X_i'(\beta - \beta^*)$, where β and β^* are vectors of coefficients. It should be understood that because of the pre-experimental screening on income, the vector X_i must contain, at a minimum, the value of pre-experimental income, but it may contain other variables as well. Since a primary concern is to obtain a consistent estimator for the parameters e and $\hat{\sigma}$ in (2.6), it is most important to include variables in the vector X_i that may be correlated with the assignment of families to the various programs.

It follows that if the first n experimentals participate and the next m do not, the (log) likelihood of the observed sample is

$$\mathscr{L}^1 = \sum_{i=1}^{n} \ln F_i + \sum_{i=n+1}^{n+m} \ln (1 - F_i), \qquad (3.1)$$

where $F_i = F[(\ln G/t_i + .5et_i - X_i' (\beta - \beta^*)/\hat{\sigma}]$. This is nothing more than the (log) likelihood function for a simple probit analysis. Indeed, the only difference between this analysis and a simple probit analysis is that here the parameter $\hat{\sigma}$ is identified because of the structure of the model. It follows that estimates of the parameter $1/\hat{\sigma}$ may be taken as the probit coefficient on $\ln G/t_i$ and that the coefficients e and $\beta - \beta^*$ are simple functions of the ratios of these probit coefficients. Standard computing routines may thus be used.

An important message of this analysis is that the presence of economic incentives to program participation may be identified from data on an experimental group alone because of variation in the tax rates t_i. On the other hand, the correlates or presence of nonpecuniary program participation costs cannot be identified from experimental data alone. Regressions of program participation on the variables X_i cannot distinguish whether a variable influences participation because it is a determinant of the conditional mean of the earnings distribution or because it is a determinant of the conditional mean of the distribution of nonpecuniary participation costs.

3.2 Likelihood of the Control Sample

The value of the control sample is that it provides information on μ and σ, or, equivalently, β and σ, and this information identifies β^* and σ^* as well. The (log) likelihood function for the control sample is equivalent to the conventional setup for a regression function and is

$$\mathscr{L}^2 = \sum \ln f_i/\sigma, \qquad (3.2)$$

where $f_i = f[(\ln y_i - X_i'\beta)/\sigma]$ and f indicates the unit normal density function. The regression estimates of β and σ that result from the maximization of (3.2), taken with the probit estimates of $\beta - \beta^*$ and $\hat{\sigma}$ that result from the maximization of (3.1), then identify all of the parameters in this model.

The form of the likelihood functions (3.1) and (3.2) suggests an important test of this model. If there are no nonpecuniary participation costs, or if they are uncorrelated with the variables in X_i, then $\hat{\sigma} = \sigma$ or $\beta - \beta^* = \beta$. In this case the combined (log) likelihood of the experimental and control samples taken together is

$$= \mathscr{L}^1 + \mathscr{L}^2$$

$$= \sum_{i=1}^{n} \ln F_i + \sum_{i=n+1}^{n+m} \ln (1 - F_i)$$

$$+ \sum_{i=n+m+1}^{n+m+r} \ln f_i/\sigma, \qquad (3.3)$$

where r indicates the number of control observations and $F_i = F[(\ln G/t_i + .5et_i - X_i'\beta)/\sigma]$. By examining the omponents of (3.3) it is clear that the parameters β and are common to all parts of the likelihood function. It s a relatively straightforward matter to maximize (3.3) with respect to these parameters and e by numerical methods and to compare the maximized value of (3.3) against the sum of the unconstrained values of (3.1) and 3.2) by a likelihood ratio test. The economic significance of this test is that the null hypothesis that $β - β^* = β$ and $σ = \hat{σ}$ is consistent with a model in which program participation is not influenced by "welfare stigma" or other nonpecuniary participation costs. If this null hypothesis is accepted it offers the opportunity of pooling the data from the control and experimental groups so as to increase the efficiency of the estimation of the effect of economic incentives on program participation by increasing the precision with which the parameter e may be estimated. If this null hypothesis is rejected, however, then these nonpecuniary participation costs must be judged important determinants of program participation and this raises questions about whether the results ought to be generalized to other populations without further investigation.

4. EMPIRICAL RESULTS

An important message from (2.5) is that it should be fitted to data on groups that come from homogeneous populations. Particularly, groups with differences in mean earnings may be pooled using dummy variables to account for these differences, but this is not sufficient to handle differences in variances because the value of σ affects every coefficient in (2.5).

As a preliminary effort, therefore, the data for the control group were stratified by location of experiment (Seattle or Denver) and the variance in log earnings was calculated for the separate parts of the control group. The ratio of these variances (Denver/Seattle) was 1.006 and clearly did not justify stratification. A similar calculation comparing the variance in log earnings for Chicanos and others also indicated no necessity for stratification, but the same variance ratio comparing whites to blacks was 1.27 and clearly was significantly different from unity at conventional test levels. Since the variance in the log earnings of whites is significantly larger than for blacks, it follows that σ in equation (2.5) differs for these two groups and that special care must be taken in pooling the data for them. As a consequence, the first set of results reported in the following subsections is for white families, who constitute about two-thirds of the sample.

4.1 Results for White Families

Column 1 of Table 2 contains estimates of the parameters σ and β obtained by maximizing (3.2). This is nothing more than a regression of log earnings on the variables indicated and the estimate of $1/σ$ is nothing more than the reciprocal of the estimated standard deviation of the regression disturbances. The variables in the vector X are a constant, pre-experimental log earnings, a dummy var-

Table 2. Estimates of the Determinants of Payment Receipt for White and Chicano Two-Parent Families (estimated standard errors in parentheses)

	Controls (Regression)	Experimentals (Probit)	Combined	Combined
	(1)	(2)	(3)	(4)
Estimates of:				
$1/σ$ (or $1/\hat{σ}$)	1.332	1.562	1.328	1.351
	(.038)	(.187)	(.036)	(.037)
e	—	.232	.134	.190
		(.295)	(.278)	(.314)
Coefficient of:				
Pre-Experimental	.395	.187	.309	.421
Earnings	(.046)	(.046)	(.035)	(.043)
3-Year Treatment	—	.108	.134	.118
		(.067)	(.057)	(.076)
Denver Location	.004	-.102	-.050	-.039
	(.061)	(.065)	(.047)	(.048)
E0	-.383	-.224	-.352	-.339
	(.243)	(.269)	(.193)	(.189)
E1	-.085	.130	.163	.021
	(.539)	(.376)	(.343)	(.335)
E2	-.467	-.155	-.361	-.343
	(.145)	(.156)	(.115)	(.113)
E3	-.242	-.011	-.141	-.128
	(.101)	(.099)	(.074)	(.074)
E4	-.061	.079	-.006	.003
	(.081)	(.087)	(.068)	(.061)
E6	.033	.122	.061	.061
	(.086)	(.103)	(.070)	(.069)
Constant	5.493	7.295	6.220	5.243
	(.432)	(.312)		(.385)
Pre-Experimental Earnings*				.171
				(.037)
Constant*				7.420
				(.471)
Log-Likelihood	-701.7	-479.5	-1193.5	-1184.7
Number of Observations	624	800	1424	1424

NOTE: Coefficients with a star are for experimentals.

iable indicating location, a dummy variable indicating whether the experimental family was offered a three- or five-year treatment, and a set of dummy variables indicating a family's predicted income level. These latter variables were assigned values prior to the experiment based on pre-experimental data and were used for the purpose of assignment to the 11 different negative income tax programs with various combinations of income guarantee (G) and tax rate (t). (Families within predicted income groups were assigned randomly to the various negative income tax programs. Predicted income was defined by a procedure explained in Keeley, et al. 1978.) As one can see from Table 2, most of these variables have very little explanatory power except for pre-experimental earnings.

Column 2 of Table 2 contains the estimates of $1/\hat{σ}$, $β - β^*$, and e obtained by the maximization of (3.1). This is nothing more than the fit of a probit equation to the explanation of participant status among the experimental group. As with the control group, the X variables other than pre-experimental earnings have very little explanatory power in this equation. The log of the breakeven, on the other hand, is a powerful predictor of participant status. As the data in Table 1 also indicate, it follows that the major determinant of participant status is the generosity of the negative income tax plan that an experimental family was offered. The estimate of the compensated substitution elasticity, c, is around .2, which is certainly consistent with the other experimental and cross-sectional evidence available, but it is very poorly determined and has an estimated standard error of around .3. (See the summary of other experimental and cross-section results in Ashenfelter (1978), and the results in Keeley, et al. 1978, for example.) This implies that the tax rate in the experimental plan has only a poorly determined effect on the family's participant status.

There is also very little evidence from the comparison of the estimates of $1/\sigma$ and $1/\hat{\sigma}$ in columns 1 and 2 of Table 2 that "welfare stigma" is at work in these data. Although the estimate of $1/\hat{\sigma}$ from the data for experimentals is larger than the estimate of $1/\sigma$ for controls, these estimates are clearly not significantly different. This lends remarkable support for the basic model of (2.5), especially when one recognizes that the results in column 2 are derived from observed dichotomous behavior that is based on a sample completely independent from that used to obtain the estimates in column 1 of Table 2.

The most efficient estimator of e may be that obtained from the combined evidence from the experimental and control groups and these results from the maximization of the combined likelihood function (3.3) are contained in column 3 of Table 2. (Maximization was carried out by Standard numerical methods by first using an algorithm due to Davidon and to Fletcher and Powell and then by an algorithm due to Goldfeld, Quandt, and Trotter. A standard reference for these methods is Goldfeld and Quandt (1972).) Although the estimated standard error of the estimate of e does decline slightly, the estimate of e does also. In neither case would the estimate of e be judged significantly different from zero at conventional test levels. Again, there is little evidence of a well-determined effect of the tax rate on participant status.

It is, of course, possible to test whether it is sensible to combine the data for controls and experimentals by contrasting the maximized likelihood in column 3 against the sum of the maximized likelihoods in columns 1 and 2. This gives an estimated test statistic (twice the difference between the unconstrained and constrained likelihood values) of 24.6 to be compared against the tabulated χ^2 distribution with 10 degrees of freedom. This comparison implies that the constraints would be rejected at the .01 significance level, but not at the .005 level. A comparison of the coefficients in columns 1 and 2 of Table 2 makes it clear why the constraints are rejected: The constants and coefficients of pre-experimental earnings are very different in the experimental and control samples. The difference in constants is perhaps not very surprising since the assignment to experimental and control status was based, in part, on estimates of permanent income. It follows that experimental and control families may very well have been drawn from populations with different mean earnings levels. The difference in coeffi-

cients on pre-experimental earnings might likewise reflect differences in the correlation coefficient between earnings in adjacent periods between the two groups and could also be a result of the method of assignment to experimental and control group status.

The results in column 4 of Table 2 combine the data on controls and experimentals, but allow the constants and coefficients on pre-experimental earnings to be different for the control and experimental groups. The χ^2 statistic comparing the sum of the likelihoods in columns 1 and 2 against the likelihood in column 4 now falls to 7.0 and would not be judged statistically significant at even the .10 level. Although the model in column 4 has a plausible a priori basis and obviously provides a satisfactory fit to the data, it is derived after an examination of the results in columns 1 through 3 of Table 2 and may simply be a case of overfitting. It should be made clear, therefore, that the model reflects the following fact in the data: Participant status is less highly (negatively) correlated with pre-experimental earnings than would have been predicted on the basis of data from the control group only. An alternative explanation, therefore, is that "welfare stigma" is significantly negatively correlated with pre-experimental earnings. Still, as the comparison of the likelihood values in columns 3 and 4 indicates, this modification does very little to improve the predictions of participant status, so that the results in column 3 are perhaps still the most useful summary of the data.

4.2 Results for Black Families

Column 1 of Table 3 contains the results for black families from the maximization of the combined likelihood function (3.3). As expected, the estimate of $1/\sigma$ is larger for black families than for white families, indicating the smaller variance in the log earnings of black families. The estimates of e and the coefficients on pre-experimental earnings are very similar for black and white families, however. It seemed useful, therefore, to combine the data

Table 3. Additional Estimates* of the Determinants of the Receipt of Payments in a Negative Income Tax Experiment
(Estimated Standard Errors in Parentheses)

	Black Families	All Families
Estimates of:		
$1/\sigma$ for Blacks	1.521	1.491
	(.060)	(.060)
$1/\sigma$ for Whites	—	1.332
		(.037)
$1/\sigma$	—	—
e	.132	.165
	(.349)	(.242)
Coefficient of Pre-Experimental Earnings	.323	.316
	(.053)	(.030)
Log-Likelihood	−562.7	−1768.6
Number of Observations	695	2119

* Other variables included in these equations whose coefficients are not reported are a dummy variable for the Denver site, the normal income variables, and a dummy indicating participation in a 3-year treatment.

n both black and white families, duly allowing the estimates of $1/\sigma$ to differ between the two groups, to increase the precision of the estimate of the compensated labor supply elasticity e. These estimates for the full sample of 2,119 families are contained in column 2 of Table 3. As one can see from the table, the estimated standard error of the estimate of e is at its lowest there, although the estimate of e is still so imprecise that it would not be judged to be significantly different from zero in this table either.

5. CONCLUSION

The advantages of the econometric framework set out here for analysis of the discrete choice of participation in a negative income tax program are considerable. First, the purely mechanical fact that a more generous program will inevitably lead to greater receipt of program benefits is neatly separated from the behavioral responses the program may induce. The former behavior implies nothing more than that a family eligible for an income transfer will take it, while the latter emphasizes the importance of estimating the labor supply effects that are the traditional objects of study by economists. Second, the estimation of the parameters necessary for predicting the extent of participation or receipt of benefits is straightforward and can be carried out with familiar computational methods. At an empirical level, the results from the Seattle/Denver Income Maintenance Experiment suggest that differences in participation across negative income tax plans are due primarily to differences in program breakevens or generosity. Tax rate variations have only small additional effects on participation, although estimates of elasticities of labor supply are certainly consistent with previous research. Perhaps most important, the empirical results also suggest that in this experiment the receipt of benefits was not affected by welfare stigma or other nonpecuniary program participation costs. Taken with the weak tax rate effects in the data, this fact provides considerable evidence of the value of simple program participation estimates such as those in columns 3 and 4 of Table 1 that are based on simple uncontaminated estimates of the income distribution.

The analysis also opens up a considerable agenda for further research. First, it is natural to consider combining the discrete choice model of participation with an analysis of the actual labor supply responses of program participants. Program participation is clearly a choice variable and the analysis here provides one potential method for treating participation and labor supply response as jointly determined endogenous variables. Whether models that force a common economic structure to explain both the participation and hours variables are useful empirically is a matter that can be subject to test in further research. Likewise, the analysis can be generalized to deal with intertemporal choice and the time pattern of participation in a negative income tax program. Results of such an application are reported by Plant (1982), who works out a specialized multivariate probit analysis like (2.5) that emphasizes both the serial correlation in the stochastic determination of low earnings and the role of labor supply elasticities.

Finally, the analysis provides a simple scheme for building the information from experiments into the simulation of the aggregate determination of program enrollment. Such projections must use information on the characteristics of the relevant aggregate population, and (2.6) shows just how estimates of the parameters of the appropriate group's earnings distribution can be used for this purpose. The same methods could well have wide applicability to any situation where discrete choices are possible, ranging from block pricing for electricity to food or housing purchases under alternative subsidy arrangements.

APPENDIX A: ADJUSTMENT FOR INCOME TRUNCATION

The adjustment of the participation fractions reported in column 1 of Table 1 (for the fact that a truncated income distribution was being sampled) was accomplished as follows. Write the joint cumulative distribution function of experimental and pre-experimental log incomes as $F(\ln \bar{y}_2, \ln y_1)$. The right side of (2.1) is then $F(\ln G/t, \infty)$, the marginal cumulative distribution function of experimental income evaluated at the log of the breakeven. Assuming that the log of the truncation point is T, the unadjusted participation fractions in Table 1 are estimates of $\hat{P} = F(\ln G/t, T)/F(\infty, T)$. These may be converted to estimates of the adjusted participation fraction

$$P = F(\ln G/t, \infty) = F(\infty, T)\hat{P}$$
$$+ [F(\ln G/t, \infty) - F(\ln G/t, T)],$$

if estimates of $F(\infty, T)$ and $F(\ln G/t, \infty) - F(\ln G/t, T)$ are available. To calculate these, it is necessary to estimate μ_2, μ_1, σ_2, σ_1, and ρ, the means and standard deviations of the untruncated log incomes in the experimental and pre-experimental years and the correlation (ρ) between them. The estimates of these parameters from the control group sample using a straightforward maximum likelihood scheme are $\hat{\mu}_2 = 8.993$, $\hat{\mu}_1 = 8.990$, $\hat{\sigma}_2 = .840$, $\hat{\sigma}_1 = .925$, $\hat{\rho} = .413$. These lead to an estimate of .72 for $F(\infty, T)$ and estimates of $F(\ln G/t, \infty) - F(\ln G/t, T)$ for the six breakeven incomes of Table 1 of .057, .063, .077, .081, .090, and .107.

In the probit and regression analyses described in subsections 3.1 and 3.2, the joint normality of $\ln y_1$ and $\ln y_2$ implies that the conditional distribution of $\ln y_2$ will be linear in $\ln y_1$. The parameters μ and σ in Equation (2.5), using the above notation, may then be interpreted as

$$\mu = [\mu_2 - (\sigma_2/\sigma_1)\sigma\mu_1] + (\sigma_2/\sigma_1)\rho \ln (y_1),$$

where $\ln (y_1)$ is the logarithm of earnings in the pre-experimental period, and $\sigma^2 = \sigma_2^2 (1 - \rho^2)$.

APPENDIX B: ECONOMIC DETERMINANTS OF PROGRAM PARTICIPATION

The classical model of labor supply assumes that a worker chooses to consume goods (x) and leisure (l) as if maximizing a quasi-concave utility function $u(l, x)$ subject to the budget constraint $x = wh + z$, where w is the wage rate, h is hours at work (total time minus l), and z is income received independently of work. This maximization problem leads to the demand functions $l = l(w, z)$ and $x = x(w, z)$ that indicate the most desirable consumption levels for any given values of w and z. The maximized or indirect utility level $\hat{u} = u(l(w, z), x(w, z)) = v(w, z)$ indicates how a worker's welfare varies as w and z vary. The inverse function $z = v^{-1}(w, \hat{u})$ therefore gives the minimum unearned income required by a worker with wage rate w to reach the utility level $\hat{u}$. The function $E(w, \hat{u})$ is called an excess expenditure function, and its properties and uses in this context are explored by Ashenfelter (1978,1980) and by Deaton and Muellbauer (1980). This function is a particularly convenient representation of family behavior for determining whether a family's welfare will be increased by participation in a social program. If the family participates in the program, it needs unearned income of $E[(1 - t) w, \hat{u}]$ to reach the utility level $\hat{u}$, while it needs unearned income of only $E(w, \hat{u})$ to reach the same utility level if it remains a nonparticipant. On the other hand, as a participant, the family obtains an increase in its unearned income of G dollars. Clearly, the family will choose to participate in the program if $E[(1 - t)w, \hat{u}] - E(w, \hat{u}) < G$, that is, if the extra unearned income needed to compensate the family for the damaging effects of the tax rate is less than the extra unearned income actually transferred to the family as a result of the program.

A natural procedure is to approximate the difference $E[(1 - t)w, \hat{u}] - E(w, \hat{u})$ by a second-order Taylor series around the nonparticipant equilibrium. Using the properties of the excess-expenditure function in which $\partial E/\partial w = -h$, where h is nonparticipant hours of work, and in which $\partial^2 E/\partial w^2 = -s$, where $s > 0$ is the compensated or utility-constant derivative of the labor supply function, we then have

$$E[(1 - t)w, \hat{u}] - E(w, \hat{u})$$

$$\approx \frac{\partial E}{\partial w}(-tw) + \frac{1}{2}\left(\frac{\partial^2 E}{\partial w^2}\right)(-tw)^2$$

$$= htw - \tfrac{1}{2}s(tw)^2.$$

A family will choose to participate and receive a subsidy if

$$D + \tfrac{1}{2}s(tw)^2 > 0. \qquad (A.1)$$

Since $s > 0$, it follows immediately that any family eligible

for a positive subsidy on the basis of its nonparticipant hours decision $(D = G - twh > 0)$ will participate, but also that some families above the breakeven will too. Even though these latter families will have lower total incomes as a result of their choice to participate, their decline in consumption of goods is more than compensated by the increased leisure they consume.

The earned income level below which a family will choose to participate may be called the *opting-in income level* and is obtained by converting (A.1) into an equality and solving for

$$y^o = wh^o = (G/t)(1 - .5te)^{-1}, \qquad (A.2)$$

where $e = s(w/h)$ is the compensated elasticity of labor supply. Equation (A.2) demonstrates that the choice of program participation varies from what it would be when total income and labor supply cannot be controlled by the family.

Several economists have observed that the assumption used in the empirical analysis in the text that e is a constant implies an excess expenditure function of the form $E = f(\hat{u}) - g(\hat{u})w^{1+e}$. For this particular constant-elasticity function

$$y^o = (1 + e)G/[1 - (1 - t)^{1+e}], \qquad (A.3)$$

which differs from (A.2). This demonstrates that (A.2) is only an approximation. It is nevertheless a good approximation as long as e and t are small. For example, with $e < .6$ and $t < .9$ the ratio of (A.2) to (A.3) is never larger than 1.06. Despite this, it may be of interest to future researchers to replace (A.2) with (A.3) to see what effect this has on the results. Doing this will, of course, introduce nonlinearities into the estimation of the probit function (2.5).

[*Received September 1981. Revised January 1983.*]

REFERENCES

ASHENFELTER, O. (1978), "The Labor Supply Response of Wage Earners," in *Welfare in Rural Areas: The North Caroline-Iowa Income Maintenance Experiment*, eds. J.L. Palmer and J.A. Pechman, Brookings Institution, Washington, D.C., 109–138, 131–137.

—— (1980), "Unemployment as Disequilibrium in a Model of Aggregate Labor Supply," *Econometrica*, 48, 547–564.

DEATON, A., and MUELLBAUER, J. (1980), *Economics and Consumer Behavior*, New York: Cambridge University Press.

GOLDFELD, S., and QUANDT, R. (1972), *Nonlinear Methods in Econometrics*, Amsterdam: North-Holland Publishing Company.

KEELEY, M.C., ROBINS, P., SPEIGELMAN, R., and WEST, R. (1978), "The Estimation of Labor Supply Models Using Experimental Data," *The American Economic Review*, 68, 873–887.

PENCAVEL, J., and WEST, R. (1978), "Attrition and the Labor Supply Effects of the Seattle and Denver Income Maintenance Experiments," Menlo Park: SRI International.

PLANT, M.W. (1982), "An Empirical Analysis of Welfare Dependency," Discussion Paper No. 237, Los Angeles: University of California, Department of Economics.

33

Policy Implications of Using Significance Tests in Evaluation Research

Anne L. Schneider and Robert E. Darcy

Significance tests have certain normative implications that are not commonly recognized and present serious complications for evaluation research. One of the conclusions reached in this article is that evaluators often make normative decisions, albeit unintentionally, when they use the traditional .05 significance level in studies with small numbers of cases. Another conclusion, however, is that evaluators cannot abandon significance tests, but should use and interpret them differently than in conventional social science research.

*E*valuators generally contend that it is their task to measure the impact of a policy on society or to elucidate some other empirical information concerning its operation, and that it is the role of others to make appropriate normative, political, and philosophical judgments when they are called for.[1] This distinction between technical or statistical judgments on the one hand and normative, political, or philosophical judgments on the other is a comfortable one for evaluators as it relieves them of responsibility for determining whether the policy serves the public interest.[2] By insuring that normative, political, or philosophical decisions are not within the scope of the study, evaluators are also relieved of the responsibility for judging the net social value of policies which benefit some groups, but which impose burdens on others. Thus, evaluators can focus on making technical decisions and scientific judgments according to established disciplinary conventions.

It may be theoretically possible to do policy research in which normative and scientific judgments are independent and separable from

From Anne L. Schneider and Robert E. Darcy, "Policy Implications of Using Significance Tests in Evaluation Research," *Evaluation Review,* 1984, 8(4), 573-582. Copyright 1984 by Sage Publications, Inc.

political ones but this is far from typical. Instead, there is a subtle but strong interplay between the two types of judgment.

The purpose of this article is to examine the normative implications of applying significance tests in evaluation research. One of our conclusions is that evaluators often make normative decisions, albeit unintentionally, and should modify the use and interpretation of significance tests to better fit the needs of policy-oriented evaluations.

PROBLEMS IN THE USE OF SIGNIFICANCE TESTS

Evaluation often requires causal analysis of a policy or program, using either field experimental designs or quasi-experimental approaches. Typically, analysis has been carried out by evaluators in the same manner commonly used in social science research (Cronbach, 1980; Cook and Campbell, 1979). When using multivariate models, for example, the partial regression coefficient between the policy variable (the independent variable) and the dependent variable is used to judge the strength of a relationship when other factors are controlled. A significance test is usually conducted on the partial regression coefficient (and sometimes the entire model, although this is more common in traditional social science research than in evaluation research). If the coefficient is not statistically significant (usually at the .05 level), it is assumed that the policy had no impact on the social condition measured by the dependent variable.

Normative, political, or philosophical criteria are applied only after determining the statistical significance. Thus, the test of significance serves as a screening device for subsequent decisions. This approach to the use of significance tests often establishes, by default, the amount of impact a policy must have on society if it is to be considered effective or successful by policymakers. When the study includes a sizable number of cases, the implication is well-known within the evaluation community and generally is referred to as the problem of "statistical vs. substantive" significance (see Riecken and Boruch, 1974). With a large sample, a tiny policy effect could be statistically significant but of no substantive value.[3]

Most evaluators would agree that this situation presents no real problems because the actual amount of impact can be reported, along with the observed significance level, and the policymakers can make the judgment of whether the size of the effect is great enough to conclude that the policy serves the public interest. Alternatively, one could argue that the evaluator needs to make clear whether the results are trivial or not. In doing so, the evaluator must go beyond normal scientific and statistical considerations to assess the normative and political dimensions of concern to decision-makers.

Serious problems arise in evaluation research, however, when the sample is small. With a small number of cases, policy impacts of considerable importance can be statistically insignificant—certainly at the .05 or .01 levels.

If the impact is not large enough to achieve statistical significance, evaluators often follow the tradition of social scientists and conclude that the policy had no effect. Considerations of statistical power (i.e., the probability that the study would detect a true effect, if one actually existed) are rare.[4] It is often assumed that statistical significance is determined by whether or not there is actually an impact to be detected. The outcome of significance tests, however, is determined by at least seven factors, and actual impact is only one of these. These elements are:

(1) Actual strength of impact
(2) Number of cases used in the study
(3) Variation among cases on relevant variables
(4) The complexity of the analysis (degrees of freedom)
(5) The appropriateness of the statistical measures and tests used
(6) The hypotheses tested
(7) The significance level chosen

All things being equal, stronger policy impacts are more likely to test as significant than weaker impacts. A weak policy impact is not the same as no policy impact, however.

The fewer the cases upon which the evaluation is based the less likely an impact will be detected. This is well known, yet examples abound in the criminal justice area of designs with too few cases to detect policy effects. A famous experimental study of police patrolling in Kansas City, for instance, was designed in such a way that if the level of victimization dropped to zero, the effect would not have been great enough to be statistically significant at the .05 level (Kelling, 1972).

Interrupted time series designs sometimes suffer from low statistical power because the number of cases (i.e., time points) is often low (Wilson, 1982). Field experiments also may have low statistical power because of the difficulty in generating enough cases in the "trickle through" designs commonly employed (Medler et al., 1981).

The problem is especially acute in criminal justice research because even a small decrease in crime rates or recidivism rates, for example, is viewed as politically relevant. The goals established by congress for the Law Enforcement Assistance Administration (LEAA), for instance, were to reduce crime by five percent in two years and by twenty percent in five years. A five percent change in crime rates is quite low given the normal variability in these data across time or geographic areas. Even a twenty percent change over a five-year aggregated time period would be difficult to detect because of the limited number of available time periods.

Another often overlooked factor that influences the probability of detecting a true effect is the amount of variation present in the dependent variable. The more variation originally present, the less likely an impact will be detected as significant. Conversely, true policy impacts are more likely to be unambiguously observed in cases that are otherwise homogeneous on relevant variables.

Complex statistical analyses, involving many independent and control variables, are less likely to identify a true policy impact, all other things being equal. In fact, a researcher can always assure insignificant findings for the policy variable by introducing enough control variables to exceed the analyzability of even a large number of cases. Complex statistical analyses are especially needed when there is a large amount of variation in the dependent variable that is not associated with the relevant policy. Thus, the problem of excessive variability in the criterion variable and the commonly used solution (a complex multivariate analysis) may both reduce the probability of identifying a true policy effect when one actually exists.

A fifth issue in attempting to find true policy impacts involves the choice of statistics. Different statistical tests do not measure the same things even though the findings are often verbalized the same way: "the policy had a significant impact" or "the policy did not have a significant impact." The simple correlation coefficient, for example, measures the extent to which the data fit a linear model. An insignificant correlation can mean either that there is no relationship or that there is a relationship but that it is not linear (assuming other aspects of the analysis such as number of cases, etc., are sufficient).

If it is appropriate to specify a one-tailed hypothesis, the evaluator stands a better chance of detecting an effect than when a two-tailed hypothesis is used. Hardly anyone discusses the issues involved in specifying one- or two-tailed tests anymore and, instead, rely on standard statistical analysis packages for this decision. It is not always clear, for example, from a printout whether "significance" or "sig," or "probability" or "prob" represent a two- or a one-tailed test. An effect rejected as not significant by a printout may turn out to be rejected through a two-tailed test. It seems reasonable to argue that one-tailed tests are almost always appropriate in evaluation research. The smallest amount of research should be able to indicate the intended direction of effects and, should the effect actually be in the opposite direction, little is lost because negative effects can be noted impressively enough from a policy standpoint, without the benefit of a significance test.

The final issue, and the one of greatest concern in this article, is the level of significance chosen for the test. Fisher suggested the .05 significance level as reasonable for the type of work he was doing (1970). Fisher's concern was scientific generalization, and the .05 level was designed to create a bias in favor of the null hypothesis. With a .05 significance level, the evidence against the null hypothesis must be overwhelming before it is rejected in favor of some theory concerning the source of an effect.

Another approach, that of Neyman and Pearson (1970) and Wald (1970), reaches the same conclusion although their purposes are different. This latter approach focuses on the test as a procedure that will be performed continuously over time. The .05 significance level insures that the null hypothesis will incorrectly be rejected only five percent of the time. This reasoning is valid for testing in industrial processes, for example, where the same tests are continuously repeated.

Neither of these situations are faced by the social scientist or policy evaluator. First, why create a bias in favor of the null hypothesis? Next, why must this bias be enormous? In the Fisherian pursuit of pure science or the Neyman-Pearson-Wald industrial decision, the quality control process and normative and political stakes are quite obscure, if present at all. This is not true in the social sciences or in public policy analysis. Can evaluators actually make a case for an enormous bias favoring "no policy effect" out of the normative and political background of the policy? Perhaps they could in some instances, but to do so as a normal part of the scientific process is to adopt an extremely status quo (and usually conservative) stance.

Several researchers have urged an alternative to the standard .05 convention and suggest that a case can be made for a .10, a .20, and even a .35 significance level under these circumstances.[5] Nagel and Neef (1979), argue that the investigator should calculate the costs and benefits of each type of error and, on that basis, establish the level of significance to be used.

POTENTIAL SOLUTIONS

The argument presented above is that judgments regarding the net social value of a policy should be based on the magnitude of the policy's impact (and/or the distribution of the effects). The implication is that tests of significance should not be used to preclude normative, political, or philosophical judgments. Several different solutions have been used in criminal justice evaluations.

Power analysis is perhaps the most commonly recommended solution to the problem of failing to detect true policy effects in evaluation research (Cohen, 1977; Cook and Campbell, 1979). This approach was used in a recently completed national evaluation of juvenile restitution programs.[6] The evaluators estimated the smallest policy-relevant effect as being a five percent difference in recidivism rates between or among groups involved in the different experimental conditions. They then sought to continue random assignment into groups until the probability of detecting an effect as small as five percent (if it actually occurred) was .80 (Schneider and Schneider, 1982). This approach requires an estimate of the smallest nontrivial impact (that is, the smallest effect that would be worthwhile to detect) and information about the true sampling distribution (Blalock, 1972).

A second strategy is to design the study with sufficient cases so that if a difference in the amount established as the policy or program goal is observed in the study, the difference will be statistically significant at the desired significance level (Schneider et al., 1978). This strategy has an obvious common sense appeal and is especially useful when specific quantitative levels of achievement have been set. It seems only reasonable that a researcher would design a study so that if the program's stated goals are achieved, the results will be statistically significant.

Another variant of this approach would be to take the results observed in the study and substitute values for t (which would be significant at .05 or some other level), the actual sample size, and the standard error to solve for the difference. This reveals the minimum difference that the test could detect at the selected significance level. If this value is smaller than the minimum policy-relevant effect, the study is adequate, otherwise, it is not.

A third approach, used by Berk (1977), is to test a null hypothesis of no difference, but also to test the quantitative goal of the project as the null hypothesis. It is possible that the investigator may not reject the null hypothesis of no effect, but also wouldn't be able to reject the null hypothesis of an impact equivalent to the stated goal. The concept of null hypothesis is often defined as the hypothesis of no difference but it was originally the nullifying hypothesis that could include any difference (Bakan, 1970).

All three of these solutions require that the evaluator know in advance the amount of impact that will be considered large enough to be relevant to policymakers. Only by knowing or estimating the smallest nontrivial effect is it possible to design a study that has a reasonable probability of detecting that effect. Thus, the argument has come full circle. Evaluators may wish to avoid the normative, political, or philosophical judgments of whether a policy effect is substantial enough to serve the public interest, but it may be necessary to estimate the smallest nontrivial impact in order to design the study.

One additional approach to the issue should not go unnoticed: the use of confidence intervals rather than statistical tests of significance. In this approach the evaluator does not have to make any explicit statement about the presence or absence of an effect but, instead, can report the range of impacts that are within some specified confidence interval. Therein, however, lies the problem because the policymaker's judgment regarding the true impact will be strongly influenced by the size of the range which, in turn, depends on whether the chosen interval was .95, .90. or.80, and so forth. Nevertheless, the use of confidence intervals is clearly called for in many studies.

A fifth solution is to abandon tests of significance entirely, especially if the evaluator has population data or nonrandom samples, and simply report the actual observed impact. This procedure has its drawbacks. Evaluators need to offer decision-makers some way of judging whether the observed effects were produced by the policy being studied or whether it was a chance observation.

It is essential that evaluators provide information on the probability that an apparent impact, whether in a sample or a population, could have been produced by chance or by some other variable rather than by the policy of interest. In this sense, chance refers to any kind of random process or randomly selected variable. Chance is a rival hypothesis: an alternative explanation that might account for the observed patterns in the data (Campbell and Stanley, 1963; Winch and Campbell, 1970).

Thus, significance tests clearly have a role in evaluation research because they guide decisions about whether apparent impacts were produced by the policy of interest or by chance. It follows, then, that the investigator should report the magnitude of impact, such as a partial regression coefficient, the significance level (regardless of its value), and the power of the test (the probability of detecting an impact equivalent to the smallest nontrivial effect). If the smallest nontrivial effect is not known, the evaluator could report the probability of detecting effects of varying sizes.

This interpretation of significance tests in the context of evaluation research raises several new issues. Perhaps most critical is whether conventional approaches to significance testing actually measure the probability that observed patterns in the data are produced by chance rather than by the policy of interest. We did not attempt to resolve that issue in this article, but a limited Monte Carlo test of whether significance tests are good approximations of tests for random processes demonstrated that they are.[7]

Interpreting significance tests as the likelihood that random processes, rather than the policy, produced certain observed effects clearly invites reexamination of the traditional .05 level. Many policymakers would not require a .95 level of certainty regarding true versus chance effects. In some instances, policymakers may be willing to continue support of a program that apparently produced a nontrivial impact even if there was a substantial probability (e.g., 30 or 40 percent) that the effect was a chance occurrence. Hence, a sixth solution—and the one proposed here—is that evaluators become accustomed to reporting the impact of the policy, the probability that an impact of this magnitude was produced by chance (i.e., the actual, observed level of significance), and the probability that an effect large enough to be relevant would have been detected if it had, in fact, existed (the power of the test).

One critical point, however, needs to be reiterated: evaluators cannot entirely ignore the question of how much impact a policy should have if it is to be judged an effective policy, that is, one that serves the public interest, because knowledge of this type is needed to design the study.

NOTES

1. Evaluation includes many different types of research activity other than impact analysis, but the major focus of this article is directed toward quantitative evaluation, especially impact assessments that rely on causal analysis.

2. The problem of developing a normative standard to judge public policies is an old one but the fundamental philosophical issues have largely been ignored by most evaluators (see Havemen and Margolis, 1983, however, as a major exception). In economics, these issues are associated with the field of welfare economics (which basically contends that there are ways of applying normative standards to public policies, but they disagree on what these are), and in political science the issues are discussed by the public choice theorists and political philosophers. See Pitkin, 1972, chapters 10 and 11, for a more critical view.

3. When the number of cases analyzed is very large, almost any relationship will be significant. Meehl (1970), for example, reports finding 91% pairwise associations among 45 miscellaneous variables significant in a sample of 55,000 high school seniors.

4. There are exceptions, of course, and within the past five years considerable efforts have been made by some evaluation methodologists (such as Nagel, 1979 and Cook and Campbell, 1979) to bring this problem to the attention of the evaluation community.

5. See the collection of articles in Morrison and Henkel (1970), especially Rozeboom, Skipper, Guenther and Nass, and Labovitz.

6. This national restitution evaluation was funded by the National Institute of Juvenile Justice and Delinquency Prevention. The study was conducted by Peter R. Schneider and Anne L. Schneider at the Institute of Policy Evaluation (see Schneider and Schneider, 1982).

7. These results are available from the authors.

REFERENCES

BAKAN, D. (1970) "The test of significance in psychological research," pp. 231-251 in D. E. Morrison and R. E. Henkel (eds.) The Significance Test Controversy. Chicago: Aldine.

BERK, R. A. and P. H. ROSSI (1977) "Doing good or worse evaluation research politically re-examined." Social Problems 23: 337-349.

BLALOCK, H. M., Jr. (1972) Social Statistics. New York: McGraw-Hill.

CAMPBELL, D. T. and J. C. STANLEY (1963) Experimental and Quasi-Experimental Designs for Research on Teaching. Chicago: Rand McNally.

COHEN, J. (1977) "Statistical Power Analysis for the Behavioral Sciences." New York: Academic.

COOK, T. D. and D. T. CAMPBELL (1979) "Quasi-Experimentation: Design and Analysis Issues for Field Settings." Chicago: Rand McNally.

CRONBACH, L. J. (1982) Designing Evaluations of Educational and Social Programs. San Francisco: Jossey-Bass.

———(1980) Toward Reform of Program Evaluation. San Francisco: Jossey-Bass.

DANIELS, M. and R. DARCY (1983) "Notes of the use and interpretation of discriminate analysis." Amer. J. of Pol. Sci. 27: 359-380.

FISHER, R. A. (1970) The Design of Experiments. London: Oliver and Boyd.

GOLD, D. (1970) "Comment on 'a critique of tests of significance,' " pp. 107-108 in D. E. Morrison and R. E. Henkel (eds.) The Significance Test Controversy. Chicago: Aldine.

HAGOOD, J. (1970) "The notion of a hypothetical universe," pp. 65-78 in D. E. Morrison and H. E. Henkel (eds.) The Significance Test Controversy. Chicago: Aldine.

HAVEMAN, R. H. and J. MARGOLIS (1983) Public Expenditure and Policy Analysis. Boston: Houghton Mifflin.

KELLING, G. (1972) The Kansas City Preventive Patrol Experiment. Washington, DC: The Police Foundation.

MEDLER, J. F., P. R. SCHNEIDER, and A. L. SCHNEIDER (1981) "Statistical power analysis and experimental field research: some examples from the National Juvenile Restitution Evalution." Evaluation Rev. 5, 6: 834-850.

MEEHL, P. E. (1970) "Theory testing in psychology and physics: a methodological paradox," pp. 252-266 in D. E. Morrison and R. E. Henkel (eds.) The Significance Test Controversy. Chicago: Aldine.

MEIER, K. J. and J. L. BRUDNEY (1981) Applied Statistics for Public Administration. Boston: Duxbury.

MORRISON, D. E. and R. E. HENKEL (1970) The Significance Test Controversy. Chicago: Aldine.

NAGEL, S. S. and M. NEEF (1979) Policy Analysis in Social Science Research. Beverly Hills, CA: Sage.

NEYMAN, J. and E. S. PEARSON (1970) "On the problem of the most efficient tests of statistical hypothesis," in D. E. Morrison and R. E. Henkel (eds.) The Significance Test Controversy. Chicago: Aldine.

PITKIN, H. F. (1972) Wittgenstein and Justice. Berkeley, CA: Univ. of California Press.

RIECKEN, H. W. and R. F. BORUCH (1974) Social Experimentation. New York: Academic.

SCHNEIDER, A., P. SCHNEIDER, L. A. WILSON, and W. GRIFFITH (1978) Handbook of Research for Criminal Justice Evaluators. Washington, DC: Government Printing Office.

SCHNEIDER, P. R. and A. L. SCHNEIDER (1982) The National Evaluation of Juvenile Restitution Programs: A Proposal. Eugene, OR: Institute of Policy Analysis.

WALD, A. (1970) Selected Papers in Statistics and Probability. New York: McGraw-Hill.

WELCH, S. and J. C. COMER (1983) Quantitative Methods for Public Administration. Homewood, IL: Dorsey.

WILSON, M. (1982) "Power analysis: comparisons of ARIMA and ANCOVA time series analysis. Ph.D. dissertation. University of Oregon.

WINCH, R. F. and D. T. CAMPBELL (1970) "Proof? No evidence? Yes. The significance of tests of significance," in D. E. Morrison and R. E. Henkel (eds.) The Significance Test Controversy. Chicago: Aldine.

Anne L. Schneider is an Associate Professor of Political Science and Director of Research for the College of Arts and Sciences at Oklahoma State University. She has conducted numerous evaluations in the areas of juvenile and criminal justice.

Robert E. Darcy is an Associate Professor of Political Science at Oklahoma State University. His research interests include statistics, women in politics, and the develoment of mathematical models of legislative turnover.

34

Methodological Issues in Health Surveys
An Evaluation of Procedures Used in the National Medical Care Expenditure Survey

Marc L. Berk, Gail R. Wilensky, and Steven B. Cohen

The National Medical Care Expenditure Survey (NMCES) is one of the most comprehensive health surveys ever conducted by the federal government. NMCES used a series of procedures designed to increase the quality and accuracy of the data. Since many of these procedures are expensive and time-consuming, often survey researchers must choose between alternative bias reducing strategies. This article presents findings from a series of methodological studies conducted to evaluate issues such as response bias, organizational effects, the effect of improved response rates, and the usefulness of surveys of medical providers and health insurers to supplement the data collected in a household health survey. The results of these investigations should prove useful in the design of future surveys.

*I*n recent years government agencies, legislative bodies, health professionals, and others concerned with the formulation of national policy, have demanded increasingly detailed data about health care use and expenditures. The collection of such data poses numerous problems to the survey researcher. Achieving high response rates on

AUTHORS' NOTE: *An earlier version of this article was presented at the Annual Meeting of the American Statistical Association, Cincinnati, Ohio, 1982.*

The views expressed in this article are those of the authors and no official endorsement of either the National Center for Health Services Research, the Department of Health and Human Services, or Project Hope is intended or should be inferred. We would like to thank Judith Kasper and Daniel Walden for their suggestions and advice.

From Marc L. Berk et al., "Methodological Issues in Health Surveys: An Evaluation of Procedures Used in the National Medical Care Expenditure Survey," *Evaluation Review,* 1984, 8(3), 307-326.

both household surveys and surveys of physicians can be difficult. Those respondents who do participate may be reluctant to report sensitive information such as income or the presence and treatment of stigmatizing medical conditions. The collection of health-expenditure data offers a particularly formidable challenge since a large proportion of medical care is paid for by third-party payers. Respondents therefore are often unaware of the actual cost of service.

The National Medical Care Expenditure Survey (NMCES) was designed to provide a comprehensive picture of how health services are used and paid for in the United States. NMCES is one of the most ambitious data-collection efforts ever conducted by a federal health agency. The survey employed a series of methodological procedures and innovations that were used to increase the accuracy and completeness of the data. In this article, we describe the major findings from a series of studies that were conducted to evaluate methodological issues encountered during the NMCES.

Data for the survey were obtained in three complementary stages. First a household survey of 14,000 randomly selected households in the noninstitutionalized population were interviewed over an 18-month period during 1977 and 1978. Five interviews plus a brief clean-up interview were conducted to collect health care use and expenditure data for 1977. Respondents were asked to provide detailed data about episodes of disability, visits to various types of medical providers, charges and sources of payment relating to these providers, health insurance coverage, medical-condition data and some basic economic and demographic characteristics. For the second through fifth interviews, respondents received a computerized summary of use and expenditure information reported in the previous interview. They were to review this information and make any needed additions or corrections. Although respondents are generally knowledgeable about their health expenses and their own direct payments to medical providers, concern has been raised about the accuracy of their reporting of third-party payments, medical diagnoses, and the specific provisions of their health insurance policies. At the conclusion of the household survey, therefore, supplementary surveys were conducted with the physicians and health care facilities providing care to household members during 1977, and with employers and insurance companies responsible for their insurance coverage.

The design of the NMCES provides a unique opportunity to assess the reliability of estimates obtained in a household health survey. This article begins by discussing some of the research on nonresponse that has been conducted using NMCES data. We then discuss problems of data reliability, focusing particular attention on the relationship among estimates obtained on the household questionnaire, the computer-generated summary, and the verification surveys of medical providers, employers, and health insurance companies. Other methodological issues examined as part of the NMCES also are addressed. The purpose of this article is not to provide the detailed results of these investigations but rather to discuss some general methodological issues raised by NMCES, as well as to present an overview of some of our findings.

NONRESPONSE

The NMCES was able to achieve high response rates on both the household survey as well as the surveys of medical providers. About 92% of all eligible respondents completed the first round of interviewing while the Physicians' Practice Survey obtained a response rate of 74%. The causes and consequences of nonresponse were examined in four analyses of nonresponse issues. These include two descriptive studies that examine the reasons for nonresponse in the household and medical provider surveys. The implications of this nonresponse are further examined in two studies that focus on the analytical consequences of survey nonresponse. One study explores the issue of survey attrition on panel surveys and compares three alternative procedures for imputing estimates to those who provided data for only a portion of the time they were eligible to respond. The other nonresponse investigation examines the issues of response rates on physician surveys. NMCES achieved a high response rate on the Physicians' Practice Survey but only after a considerable expenditure of time and money. We therefore examine whether the estimates obtained at the conclusion of the survey differ significantly from those that would have been obtained if we had terminated data-collection efforts earlier.

REASONS FOR NONRESPONSE

The difficulty of maintaining adequate response rates presents a major problem for health service researchers. Concern about privacy and the confidentiality of survey data may be contributing factors in the decision not to participate. In addition, government-sponsored health surveys may encounter additional opposition by people who are distrustful of government in general or who oppose federal health policies and perceive noncompliance as a possible method of protest. The problem of obtaining adequate participation levels is especially difficult when conducting surveys with physicians. The American Medical Association has noted the growing annoyance of physicians who are asked to participate in social surveys (Martin, 1974) and has itself seen a steady decline in the response rate obtained in its Periodic Survey of Physicians from 80% in 1966 to 49% in 1977 (Goodman and Jensen, 1981).

The NMCES household-nonresponse study conducted by Meyers and Oliver (1978) was derived from noninterview report forms completed by field interviews whenever the first round interview could not be completed. Nonresponse forms were also completed whenever a physician refused to participate in the Physicians' Practice Survey (PPS). An eligible respondent included anyone in the noninstitutionalized civilian population although data about children were generally obtained from adult household members. The response rate for the PPS was about 74%. The results presented here are based on the reasons for nonparticipation cited on the 985 nonresponse forms completed in the household survey and the 811 forms obtained during the PPS.

Meyers and Oliver (1978) concluded that reasons for nonparticipation in the household survey were seldom ideological. About 12% of the nonresponders expressed concerns about privacy while 5.5% expressed resentment of government. Almost 16%, however, claimed that they did not have time to participate and over 27% cited a general lack of interest. About 11% of nonresponders had a general antipathy to surveys while about 3% had a specific antagonism to NMCES. About 23% mentioned other reasons while 24% of nonresponders refused for unspecified reasons. These totals exceed 100% because some respondents mentioned more than one reason.

The Physicians' Practice Survey consisted of a single 15-minute telephone interview in which the physician was asked questions relating to the characateristics of his or her practice setting, as well as some basic demographic data. Berk and Meyers (1980) found that despite the relatively low-response burden associated with the survey, 34.6% of those declining to participate cited a lack of time while about 39% stated that they lacked interest in the survey. About 19% mentioned a general antipathy to surveys while 3.3% noted a specific antagonism to the PPS. About 7% stated a desire to protect privacy. As in the case of the

TABLE 1
Respondents' Reasons for Refusal to Participate in NMCES

	Percentage of Respondents Mentioning Reason	
Reasons	Physicians' Practice Survey	NMCES Household Survey
No time to participate	34.6	15.8
Not interested	39.3	27.5
Antipathy to surveys in general	19.0	10.7
Antagonism to this survey	3.3	3.1
Hostility to government	7.1	5.5
Desire to protect privacy	7.3	11.9
Other	7.0	22.7
Unspecified refusal	13.5	23.9
	131.2[a]	121.1[a]
	(N = 811)	(N = 985)

SOURCE: Data are from Meyers and Oliver (1978) and Berk and Meyers (1980).
a. Total percentage greater than 100 because respondents could give more than one reason.

household survey, hostility to government was only rarely mentioned as a reason for refusing to participate in the household portion of NMCES. We suspected that this reason might be more important in a survey of physicians since federal health care policies are more salient to this population, but only about 7% of the physicians cited this as a refusal reason. This estimate, however, may be conservative since resentment against the government may be masked in other reasons given such as "not interested," "lack of time," or "unspecified."

Our findings indicate that the key to obtaining high-response rates lies in convincing respondents that the survey merits an expenditure of their time. "Lack of time" was one of the most often mentioned reasons for nonparticipation in both the Physicians' Practice Survey and the household survey. While it may be true that some people mentioned a "lack to time" to avoid a discussion of more serious ideological objections, the time element was cited often enough to convince us that it represents one of the most serious obstacles to survey participation. This is true for both the national household survey as well as for a more specialized survey of physicians. We suggest, therefore, that increased attention be focused on sensitizing interviewers to the perceived burden of survey participation.

PARTIAL NONRESPONSE IN THE NMCES

In addition to the traditional form of complete nonresponse encountered for individuals, approximately 11% of all responding survey participants provided data for only a partial period of the time in which they were eligible to respond. This problem of partial nonresponse is not limited or unique to the NMCES but characteristic of national panel surveys in general. To allow for the derivation of national estimates of relevant health parameters from NMCES data with a minimal level of nonresponse bias, it was necessary to derive an appropriate imputation strategy for the partial respondents—one that would adjust their data to the entire period in which they were eligible to participate in the survey. Prior to implementing the imputation strategies, the demographic composition of the partial-participant population was compared to those providing data for the entire period in which they were eligible to respond. Partial respondents were less likely to be married and more likely to be nonwhite, in poor health, and residing in an SMSA.

Three alternative imputation strategies were considered for implementation using prescribed medicine data from the National Medical Care Expenditure Survey (Cohen, 1982a). They included a weighted adjustment to the partial data, the use of only the data from participants with complete information, and a substitution of data from complete respondents who matched the partials on key demographic characteristics. To determine the optimal strategy, a controlled experiment was conducted by artificially creating partial data for respondents with complete information (those providing data for the entire period were eligible to respond), and then adjusting the synthetically derived partial data by each of the three imputation strategies.

The estimates of the expenditure and utilization measures expressed in terms of population means and derived by the strategy that used a weighted adjustment to partial data, were consistent with the estimates derived from complete data. The only noticeable deviation in all comparisons with actual data occurred for distributional estimates on prescribed medicine utilization. Consistent estimates also were obtained by the second strategy that considered the partial respondents as total nonrespondents. This method inflated the data of complete respondents by a standard nonresponse adjustment.

The third strategy, which required a substitution of data from similar individuals to correct for partial nonresponse, was optimal in terms of precision and satisfaction of underlying assumptions of homogeneity inherent in the matching of the partial respondents with their "complete" counterparts. However, when time and cost were factored in, the advantages of this method of imputation were less obvious. Although the linkage between partial and complete respondents with similar characteristics was a one-time operation, data (for the relevant time period in which the "partial" individual was eligible to respond but did not) had to be derived for the linked-complete respondent and transferred for each time-dependent variable of interest—a rather massive undertaking.

Since the proportion of partial respondents relative to the entire sample is small in NMCES, an imputation strategy that is straightforward in its derivation, is directly applicable to a diverse set of time-dependent analysis measures, includes partial respondents in all analyses, and allows for the derivation of statistically valid estimates of utilization and expenditure measures expressed in terms of population means and totals, has formidable advantages. The use of the direct-weighted adjustment imputation strategy represents such an approach and serves as an adopted method.

THE EFFECT OF INCREASED RESPONSE RATE ON PPS ESTIMATES

Many survey researchers assume that low response rates are indicative of a biased sample and some studies have demonstrated significant differences between the respondent and nonrespondent populations. Studies of physicians, however, suggest that nonrespondents and respondents are similar on most important characteristics (Berk et al., 1981; Goodman and Jensen, 1981; Kasper, 1983; Loft, 1980; Harkins, 1981). Even when minor differences are found between the characteristics of responding and nonresponding physicians, however, it cannot be inferred that a higher response rate would reduce bias. Since a 100% response rate is never a realistic option, the real issue is not whether nonrespondents differ from respondents, but rather whether the estimates obtained at the conclusion of the survey differ significantly from those that would be obtained if the survey had a shorter field period. Thus, the consequences of accepting a lower response rate can better be examined by comparing the cumulative estimates that would be obtained if the survey were stopped at various points in time.

Previous comparisons of early and late responders have failed to produce a consensus about the usefulness of high response rates. Koenig et al. (1977), Goudy (1978), and Robins (1963) found relatively small differences between early and late responders while Pavelko and

Lutterman (1973) and Hawkins (1977) found much larger effects. None of these studies, however, considered physicians. Nor did any of the 28 surveys discussed by Leslie (1972) in his review of the literature. Since an increasing number of surveys target the physician population, it is particulary appropriate to examine their response patterns and the consequences of efforts to improve the response rate. Berk (1983) examines whether or not single-variable estimates would have been different if the survey field period had lasted four months instead of the actual six months.

The addition of late responders to the sample does not appear to have a substantial effect on most estimates of key demographic variables. Fourteen key variables pertaining to the characteristics of physicians and their practices were examined. These include physician's age, board certification status, income, sex, country of training, specialty, number of doctors in practice, percent of patients on Medicaid, hours worked per week, weeks worked per year, fee for initial visit, and average wait for a new patient before first appointment. A comparison of the estimates obtained after four months of the field period with those obtained at the conclusion of the survey shows that only three of the fourteen estimates for key provider and practice characteristics changed by more than 5% and only one estimate (number of doctors in practice) changed by more than 10%. Seven of the estimates changed by less than 1% during the last two months of the survey. If the survey had ended after a four-month field period, the final survey results would have underestimated the average number of physicians associated with a practice. This, however, is the only large difference. Moreover, using traditional methods of quality, cumulative estimates also indicate that data quality may have been higher during the earlier stages of the survey. In particular, there was a substantial decrease during the later months in the percent of cases that could be completed by interviewing the physician directly instead of through the use of a proxy.

These data then show that most estimates obtained from early responders closely approximate those made at the conclusion of the field period. Furthermore, the closeness persists when the analysis is extended to multivariate relationships. To test whether similar estimates would be produced if the survey had terminated earlier, two regression equations were estimated to predict physician's income. Annual income was selected as the dependent variable because economic surveys of physicians are frequently designed to study the impact of various factors on physicians' earnings. Thirteen other physician and practice characteristics were used as independent variables. The final regression equation produced from a survey with a 74% response rate was very similar to the regression estimates that would have been produced if the survey terminated after 4 months when the response rate was 49%. Board certification, practice size, weeks and hours practiced, percent of patients on Medicaid, average fee, and physician specialty were all found to be significant predictors of income on both equations while the other five variables were found to be significant in neither. Thus, the equation that would have been produced after 4 months yielded the exact same set of predictors as that produced at the end of the field period. In addition, the difference in R^2 was negligible going from. 10 after 4 months to .09 at the survey's conclusion. The results of this analysis indicate that it may not always be necessary to obtain high response rates on physician surveys. It is therefore suggested that health service researchers consider the relative costs and benefits of high response rates. Relaxing the requirement of high response rates will result in considerable cost savings, and will not necessarily produce biased estimates. These findings, however, are only applicable to surveys such as the PPS, which focused on basic demographic data and data about practice costs. Inferences, cannot be made about other types of surveys that examine physicians' attitudes or modes of treatment.

ISSUES OF DATA RELIABILITY AND VALIDITY

While missing data represents a serious problem to survey researchers, the reliability and validity of data that was collected is of equal concern. The NMCES used several methodological innovations to insure data reliability. During each round of interviews, respondents were asked to report the diagnosis, total charge, and sources of payment for each inpatient hospital stay, medical provider visit, dental visit, prescription drug, or purchase of eyeglasses or other medical equipment. In addition, respondents were asked to provide information about their health insurance coverage. Data on health care use and expenditures were updated each round through the use of a computerized summary of the information reported in the previous interview. Respondents were asked to review this information and make any needed additions or corrections.

In particular, the summary was expected to allow respondents a means to provide more complete charge and payment data at a later date if it was unknown at the time of the interview. All respondents were asked to complete the summary. Approximately 32% of household survey respondents were also included in the medical provider survey. The medical provider survey (MPS) was a record check or verification procedure to obtain expenditure and diagnostic data from physicians and hospitals who treated a sample of household respondents during the year. Thus, for each person in the household survey, the data obtained from the questionnaire was checked in a subsequent interview through the summary mechanism, and, in about a third of the cases, subjected to verification through the MPS. In addition, household data on health insurance coverage was verified through the Health Insurance/Employer Survey (HIES) that collected, for each private health insurance plan reported in the household survey, data from employers, insurance carriers, or other insuring organizations.

THE RELATIONSHIP BETWEEN HOUSEHOLD SUMMARY AND MEDICAL PROVIDER ESTIMATES

A comparison of expenditure data among the household questionnaire, summary, and medical provider survey (MPS), revealed disagreements concerning the occurrence of specific types of health care events and their characteristics (Kasper, 1983). The overall mean estimates from each data source, however, were generally similar. The investigation contains a comprehensive discussion of the difficulties in analyzing data from multiple sources with reference to the work of Marquis (1980), Andersen et al. (1979), and others.

Comparison between the household questionnaire and summary showed that only rarely did the charge reported on the questionnaire differ from that recorded on the summary (see Table 2). Charges were identical for 87.9% of the hospital stays and 92.8% of the physician visits. There was, however, greater disagreement over the source of payment for each hospital stay or physician visit. In about 30% of all cases, the questionnaire and summary disagreed as to whether the source of payment for a hospital stay was the family. Similarly, in about 26% of the physician visits, source of payment data on the questionnaire was not consistent with information on the summary.

When the summary is compared to the estimates obtained from the medical provider survey, there was substantial agreement between mean charges for both hospital stays and physician visits (see Table 3). The average stay for a hospital event was $1239 in the summary data and $1302 on the MPS, representing a difference of $63 in the mean charge estimates. There was no statistical difference between the summary and

TABLE 2

Comparison of Charges Between Household Questionnaire and Summary

		Hospital Stays		Physician Visits	
		N	%	N	%
Charges					
Questionnaire charge and summary charge are same		2,562	87.9	82,858	92.8
Questionnaire charge exceeds summary charge		229	7.8	3,798	4.3
Questionnaire charge is less than summary		123	4.2	2,615	2.9
Source of Payment					
Questionnaire	*Summary*				
not family	not family	3,379	55.2	43,657	26.1
family	not family	244	4.0	24,432	14.6
not family	family	1,542	25.2	19,736	11.8
family	family	951	15.5	79,615	47.5

SOURCE: Data are from Kasper (1984).

MPS estimates of physician visits, with an average charge of $26 reported in the summary compared to $28 reported in the MPS. The difference between MPS and household estimates for both types of events was greatest for persons in the low-income group. With regard to source of payment, the MPS data indicated lower levels of family and private insurance payments and somewhat higher levels of Medicaid—and for hospital stays—Medicare payment.

One of the major goals of the summary in NMCES was to reduce the level of missing expenditure information by providing a mechanism to update this data. It appears to have served this purpose for a substantial number of cases. However, one-quarter to one-third of hospital and physician charges remained missing at the end of the survey period. One probable explanation for some of this missing data is the association, demonstrated in this article, between Medicaid as a source of payment and the inability to report charge data. This suggests that if a summary-type instrument is used, it might be targeted to persons with missing data for whom Medicaid is not a payer. Alternative procedures such as a medical provider verification survey are more useful for the Medicaid

TABLE 3

Estimates of Mean Charges and Payment for Hospital Stays and Physician Visits
from Summary and Medical Provider Survey

	Summary $	Medical Provider Survey (MPS) $
Mean Charge		
Hospital stay	1239	1302
family income		
$12,000 or less	1351	1415
$12,000-19,999	1108	1158
$20,000 or more	1238	1266
Physician visit	26	28
family income		
$12,000 or less	25	33
$12,000-19,999	25	23
$20,000 or more	27	25

Source of Payment	Family		Private Insurance		Medicaid		Medicare		Other	
	Summary	MPS	Summary	MPS	Summary	MPS	Summary	MPS	Summary	MPS
Hospital stay	17.8	10.1	57.5	48.3	2.9	8.7	10.7	17.2	3.2	5.5
family income										
$12,000 or less	21.8	10.6	37.8	28.8	5.9	14.9	20.8	30.6	4.0	3.6
$12,000-19,999	16.1	9.9	66.5	61.9	1.7	5.9	7.0	9.0	2.2	4.8
$20,000 or more	15.1	9.6	66.7	64.7	1.0	2.2	3.9	4.8	3.2	8.9
Physician visits	67.4	63.0	20.9	8.6	1.4	6.7	5.4	3.2	1.9	6.3
family income										
$12,000 or less	67.2	51.8	12.2	5.3	3.5	14.0	10.9	6.6	2.0	6.2
$12,000-19,999	69.0	69.1	22.6	10.0	0.7	3.0	3.6	1.2	1.6	6.6
$20,000 or more	66.2	70.5	26.7	10.8	0.0	1.7	2.3	1.2	2.0	6.1

SOURCE: Data are from Kasper (1984).

population. Changes in initially reported charge data and removal of visits or stays from the summary were infrequent and cannot conclusively be demonstrated to have improved data quality.

Several issues are discussed in this analysis with regard to medical provider surveys for record check purposes. Overall, comparisons between household and MPS data indicated mean charge data for the total population; across age and income classes were quite similar and surprisingly stable across different data sources. There were indications, however, that there may be more variation in charges for stays with certain types of payers. The analysis suggested that household respondents may be a better source of information about who ultimately paid for physician care than physicians themselves. However, there are some major areas of disagreement with regard to family and Medicaid payers for hospital care that are not easily resolved for one side or the other.

COMPARISON OF DATA FROM HOUSEHOLD SURVEY AND HEALTH INSURANCE/EMPLOYER SURVEY

A major goal of the NMCES was to measure the depth and breadth of insurance coverage in the United States accurately. There was concern, however, that respondents might not necessarily be knowledgeable about the provisions of their policies. Moreover, some people might even misreport whether or not they were offered coverage through their place of employment. Supplementary surveys were therefore developed to provide verification of the data collected in the household survey.

During the second round of interviewing a Health Insurance Supplement was administered in order to collect data about the health insurance coverage of household respondents for specific benefits. Employers and health companies also were asked to provide supplementary information about the people who reported that they were covered by private health insurance in the household survey (the Health Insurance/Employer Survey, HIES). In addition, an Uninsured Validation Survey (UVS) was used to collect additional data from employers about people who were employed but who reported that they were not covered by employer-related insurance. This survey was used to provide confirmation that such people were not covered, and, when it was found that they were covered, to collect information about their benefits.

An analysis by Walden et al. (1982) compared household data with information obtained from employers and insurers. Their findings showed that most people do know whether or not they are covered by private health insurance; only 1.2% of those who claimed to have private insurance were not covered by any private health plan according to the HIES survey. Similarly, only 3.7% of those who said they were not covered were found to have health insurance in the UVS. Weighted comparisons of HIES/UVS estimates with household estimates reveal no differences in the national estimates of the percent of the population covered by private health insurance. There was no difference in the HIES and household survey estimates by race, age, sex, or education of family head. Persons in families with a total income of less than $12,000 however, were more likely to be classified as covered in the household survey than in the HIES. In this category, almost 14% of those claiming to have private health insurance did not have the coverage confirmed in the verification survey.

Although household respondents generally had accurate perceptions of whether or not they had insurance, they appear to be less knowledgeable about what benefits are actually included in their policies. In most cases respondents underestimated their coverage. About 66% of respondents believe that they are covered for ambulatory x-rays and diagnostic tests but HIES estimates indicate that over 87% had this coverage. Only about 27% of household respondents claimed to be covered for inpatient mental health services but estimates from HIES indicate that over 76% had such coverage. Similarly HIES shows that 80.5% are covered for ambulatory physician visits but only 42.4% reported this coverage on the household survey. Large differences were also observed between household and HIES estimates for coverage of prescription drugs and nursing homes.

Results of the HIES, then, indicate that data on who is covered by private health insurance coverage can be obtained accurately from a household survey. If it is necessary, however, to obtain data on the specific benefits covered in the policy, the use of a verification survey is highly desirable. In fact, if the sole concern of the investigation is to determine extent of coverage, a survey of insurance providers may be sufficient. The advantage of the design used in NMCES, however, is that it allows the analyst to relate data on coverage with population characteristics and health care utilization patterns.

OTHER NMCES STUDIES

Several other methodological inquiries have been conducted as part of the NMCES. These studies are concerned with issues such as organizational effects and the use of proxies in both household and physician studies.

The survey design of the NMCES combines two independently drawn national samples of households—one by the Research Triangle Institute (RTI) and one by the National Opinion Research Center (NORC). It was assumed that since the structures of both national area samples were similar, they were thereby compatible and would allow for the derivation of statistically equivalent, unbiased, national estimates of relevant health parameters.

Findings reported by Cohen (1982c) show that the data obtained by RTI and NORC yield statistically equivalent age-race-sex population estimates. Equivalent distributional estimates of demographic measures such as region, family income, and marital status also were found. There was also a consistent observation of a nonsignificant data-collection organization effect when testing for differences in alternative health indices.

Some research has also been completed on the use of proxies in the collection of NMCES data. It has been reported in earlier studies that self-respondents score higher on measures of illness and disability (Kovar and Wright, 1973; Haase and Wilson, 1972) than do respondents for whom a household proxy reports. By allowing a household proxy to provide information on other family members, however, survey costs are greatly reduced. Moreover, it has been suggested (Haase and Wilson, 1972) that the higher scores of self-respondents on illness measures may reflect higher underlying rates of morbidity and are therefore not necessarily indicative of reporting bias. Since NMCES obtained supplementary diagnostic data in the medical provider survey, we are able to examine this possibility. An analysis by Berk et al. (1982) suggests that for certain types of highly threatening and stigmatizing conditions, underlying health levels are in fact higher in the self-respondent population; therefore, the lower rates of illness reported by proxies to provide information about the treatment for stigmatizing conditions of other family members appears to be appropriate.

NMCES also used proxy respondents in the Physicians' Practice Survey. Interviewers were instructed to interview the physician directly whenever possible. When necessary, however, it was permissible to conduct the interview with a knowledgeable proxy such as a nurse or receptionist designated by the physician. On the income question only about half of the proxies were willing or able to provide data compared to 15% of the physicians who declined to answer the question. The findings suggest that whenever possible, interviews should be conducted directly with the physician. With the exception of income, however, item nonresponse rates for proxies were generally low, even if slightly higher than those obtained from physicians. The use of proxies, then, appears to be advisable whenever a direct interview with the physician is not possible.

CONCLUSION

The complex survey design employed in NMCES allows a unique opportunity to examine the usefulness of a wide range of survey procedures. NMCES used a series of procedures to increase the quality and accuracy of the data. Many of these procedures are expensive and time consuming and survey researchers must often choose between alternative bias-reducing strategies. Many of the procedures used in NMCES proved to be cost-effective and sufficiently furthered survey objectives. The usefulness of other procedures is less obvious. While the PPS component of the survey achieved a relatively high response rate, accepting a lower response rate probably would not have had a major effect on survey estimates. The data examined thus far indicates that the use of proxies does not increase bias on the reporting of stigmatizing conditions and has only a moderate negative effect on the quality of data obtained from physicians. Since the use of proxies is cost-effective, such a strategy should be considered for the collection of certain types of data when the respondent is not directly available. Future surveys to verify actual insurance coverage are probably not necessary since most respondents accurately report this information. A survey to confirm data on the actual provisions of these policies, however, does appear to be very important—despite the cost. The value of the computer-generated summary was not convincing for the population as a whole, although it might be useful if targeted for certain population groups. Similarly, with respect to expenditure data, the Medical Provider Survey appears to be more useful for the poor, the elderly, and those with hospitalizations, than it is for the rest of the population.

Additional studies are currently in progress and will consider sampling problems as well as issues pertaining to interviewer effects. Results of the NMCES methodological studies should facilitate the development of cost-effective strategies for collecting data in future health surveys.

REFERENCES

ANDERSON, R., J. KASPER, M. R. FRANKEL, and ASSOC. (1979) Total Survey Error: Applications to Improve Health Surveys. San Francisco: Jossey-Bass.

BERK, M. L. (1983) "The effect of improved response rates on estimates obtained from a survey of physicians," pp. 527-532 in Proceedings of the Social Statistics Section. Rockville, MD: American Statistical Association.

———and S MEYERS (1980) "Reasons for nonresponse on the physicians practice survey," pp. 202-204 in Proceedings of the Social Statistics Section. Rockville, MD: American Statistical Association.

BERK, M. L., M. HORGAN, and S. MEYERS (1982) "The reporting of stigmatizing health conditions: a comparison of proxy and self reporting," pp. 506-510 in Proceedings of the Social Statistics Section. Rockville, MD: American Statistical Association.

BERK, M. L., S. B. COHEN, and S. M. MEYERS (1981) "The usefulness of proxy reporting in an economic survey of physicians," pp. 671-673 in Proceeding of the Survey Research Section. Rockville, MD: American Statistical Association.

BONHAM, C. and L. CORDER (1981) National Medical Care Expenditure Survey: Household Instruments Reports. Rockville, MD: National Center for Health Statistics and Health Services Research.

COHEN, S. B. (1982a) "An analysis of alternative imputation strategies for individuals with partial data in the national medical care expenditure survey." Rev. of Public Data Use 10: 153-165.

———(1982b) "Family unit analysis in the national medical care expenditure survey," in Proceedings of the Survey Research Section. Rockville, MD: American Statistical Association.

———(1982c) "Estimated data collection organization effect in the national medical care expenditure survey." Amer. Statistician 36: 337-341.

———NMCES Estimation and Sampling Variance in the Household Survey, DHHS publication No. (PHS) 81-3281. Rockville, MD: National Center for Health Services Research.

FLEISHMAN, E. and M. L. BERK (1981) "Survey of interviewer attitudes toward selected methodological issues in the national medical care expenditure survey," pp. 249-256 in Seymour Sudman (ed.) Health Survey Research Methods, Proceedings of the Third Biennial Conference. Rockville, MD: National Center for Health Services.

GOODMAN, L. and L. JENSEN (1981) "Economic surveys of medical practice: AMA's periodic survey of physicians, 1966-1978," in Seymour Sudman (ed.) Health Survey Research Methods. Proceedings of the Third Biennial Conference. Rockville, MD: National Center for Health Services.

GOUDY, W. (1978) "Interim response to a mail questionnaire: impacts on variable relationships." Soc. Q. (Spring): 253-265.

HAASE, K. W. and R. W. WILSON (1972) "The study design of an experiment to measure the effects of using proxies resources in the national health interview survey," in Proceedings of the Social Statistics Section. Rockville, MD: American Statistical Association.

HARKINS, E. (1981) "An evaluation of the reliability of data gathered from three primary care medical specialties using a self-administered log diary," pp. 38-53 in Seymour Sudman (ed.) Health Survey Research Methods, Proceedings of the Third Biennial Conference. Rockville, MD: National Center for Health Services.

HAWKINS, D. (1977) "Nonresponse in Detroit area study surveys: a ten year analysis." Chapel Hill: Univ. of North Carolina, Institute for Research in Social Science.

KASPER, J. (1984) "Comparisons of three data sources from the national medical care expenditure survey," in Charles Cannell (ed.) Proceedings of the Fourth Conference on Health Survey Research Methods. Rockville, MD: National Center for Health Services Research.

KOENIG, D., G. MARTIN, and L. SEILER (1977) "Response rates and quality of data: a reexamination of the mail questionnaire." Canadian Rev. of Sociology and Anthropology (November): 432-438.

KOVAR, M. G. and R. A. WRIGHT (1973) "An experiment with alternate respondent rules in the national health interview survey" pp. 311-316 in Proceedings of the Social Statistics Section. Rockville, MD: American Statistical Association.

LESLIE, L. (1972) "Are high response rates essential to valid surveys." Social Sci. Research (September) 323-334.

LOFT, J. (1980) "Methodology of the national ambulatory medical survey," pp. 68-78 in Seymour Sudman (ed.) Health Survey Research Methods, Proceedings of the Third Biennial Conference. Rockville, MD: National Center for Health Services Research.

MARQUIS, K. H. (1980) Hospital Stay Response Error Estimates for the Health Insurance Study's Dayton Baseline Survey, R-2555 HEW. Santa Monica, CA: Rand.

MARTIN, B. (1974) Don't Survey Physicians! Chicago: American Medical Association.

MEYERS, S. M. and J. D. OLIVER (1978) "Privacy and hostility toward government as reasons for nonresponse in the national medical care expenditure survey," pp. 509-513 in Proceedings of the Social Statistics Section. Rockville, MD: American Statistical Association.

PAVALKO, R. and K. LUTTERMAN (1973) "Characteristics of willing and reluctant respondents." Pacific Sociological Rev. (October) 463-476.

POE, G. and D. C. WALDEN (1984) "A comparison of estimates of out-of-pocket expenditures for health services obtained from the national health interview survey family expense supplement and the national medical care expenditure survey household survey" in Charles Cannell (ed.) Proceedings of the Fourth Conference on Health Survey Research Methods. Rockville, MD: National Center for Health Services Research.

ROBINS, L. (1963) "The reluctant respondent." Public Opinion Q. (Summer): 276-286.

WALDEN, D. C., C. M. HORGAN, and G. L. CAFFERATA (1984) "Consumers knowledge of their health insurance coverage" in Charles Cannell (ed.) Proceedings of the Fourth Annual Conference on Health Survey Research Methods. Rockville, MD: National Center for Health Services Research.

WILENSKY, GAIL R. (1981) "Some methodological issues raised by the national medical care expenditure survey," pp. 260-264 in Seymour Sudman (ed.) Health

Survey Research Methods, Proceedings of the Third Biennial Conference. Rockville, MD: National Center for Health Services Research.

Marc L. Berk is a Senior Sociologist at the National Center for Health Services Research. His areas of interest include medical sociology and survey methods. He has recently published articles on physician manpower, the role of Medicaid, and methodological issues in physician surveys.

Gail R. Wilensky is Vice President of the Domestic Division of Project Hope where she also serves as Director of the Center for Health Information Research and Analyses. She was formerly a Senior Research Manager at the National Center for Health Services Research and has published widely on the distribution and financing of health care services and other issues relating to health economics.

Steven B. Cohen is Senior Statistician at the National Center for Health Services Research and Associate Professorial Lecturer at George Washington University. His major areas of interest are in complex survey sampling, small area estimation, and applied statistics, and his publications include numerous articles in the field of survey research.

35

Methodological Issues in the Meta-Analysis of Quasi-Experiments

Fred B. Bryant and Paul M. Wortman

Locate all available studies on a topic . . . eliminate from consideration studies with severe methodological inadequacies. Results from these studies are likely to be more misleading than helpful.
Mansfield and Busse, 1977, p. 3

It's bad advice to eliminate virtually any studies on strictly methodological grounds.
Glass, 1978, p. 3

How should meta-analysts proceed when deciding which evidence to include in a synthesis of the research literature on a given subject or issue? The two epigraphs to this chapter represent diametrically opposed viewpoints on this

The authors thank Craig King for his assistance in the research synthesis of desegregation studies, Judy Savage for typing the manuscript, and Linda Perloff for helpful comments on an earlier version of this chapter. The research reported in this chapter was supported by grant NIE–G–79–0128 from the National Institute of Education.

From Fred B. Bryant and Paul W. Wortman, "Methodological Issues in the Meta-Analysis of Quasi-Experiments," pp. 5-24 in *Issues in Data Synthesis* edited by William H. Yeaton and Paul M. Wortman. New Directions for Program Evaluation, No. 24. Copyright 1984 by Jossey-Bass Inc., Publishers. Reprinted by permission.

issue. Should meta-analysts abandon critical judgments about the quality of primary research and include all available studies in data syntheses, or should they exclude flawed studies that suffer from threats to validity?

Such questions become especially important when the research literature of interest is largely quasi-experimental. In contrast to traditional literatures, in which most studies are randomized true experiments, much evaluation research involves nonrandomized quasi-experiments, which have methodological weaknesses (Cook and Campbell, 1979; Rossi and Williams, 1972). Indeed, in some cases the evidence that they provide can hardly be considered valid. Thus, quasi-experiments represent a particularly problematic area for the debate about selectivity in the choice of evidence for research synthesis.

In this chapter, we argue that meta-analysts need to address two issues when considering studies for inclusion: the range of experimental rigor within the particular research literature and their own priorities regarding internal and external validity. In some content areas, there may be enough randomized true experiments with which those of poorer quality can be compared (Wortman and Yeaton, 1983). In these cases, the meta-analyst may be justified in including all studies, regardless of their methodological quality. However, in content areas where all studies are nonrandomized quasi-experiments, there may be no high-quality baseline with which poorer-quality studies can be compared. In these cases, if enough studies are available, the meta-analyst can exclude studies with severe methodological flaws and include only studies of relatively high quality. Further, the unavoidable trade-offs between methodological rigor and representativeness force investigators who favor external validity to be more inclusive in choosing evidence and investigators who favor internal validity to be more selective.

In this chapter, we examine two sets of decisions, one regarding relevance, the other regarding acceptability, that meta-analysts must make when evaluating evidence for inclusion in research syntheses. For each set of decisions, we analyze the issues raised by the validity of primary studies. We illustrate our analysis with examples drawn from a recent research synthesis of quasi-experiments on school desegregation and black student achievement (Wortman and Bryant, forthcoming). Next, we consider the consequences of decisions to exclude studies in the context of our synthesis of desegregation research. We then explore how different criteria for the selection and analysis of evidence can yield different meta-analytic conclusions. Last, we discuss ways of resolving the inevitable disagreements that will arise among meta-analysts.

Criteria for Evaluation of Research Studies

Two different sets of decisions must be made when evaluating research evidence for inclusion in research syntheses. First, we must decide whether a given study is relevant to the questions of interest in the research synthesis. Second, we must decide which of the studies deemed relevant should be included in the research synthesis. One way of understanding these two sets of decisions is to consider them in terms of Cook and Campbell's (1979) four types of validity: construct validity, external validity, statistical conclusion validity, and internal validity. As Wortman (1983) notes, the first set of decisions is largely an issue of construct and external validity, whereas the second set of decisions focuses primarily on statistical conclusion and internal validity. The following section describes this selection procedure.

Decisions Regarding Relevance

Construct Validity. Construct validity concerns the degree to which the treatments and outcome measures of a particular study accurately represent the relevant underlying constructs (Cook and Campbell, 1979). We can judge a study to be irrelevant on grounds of low construct validity if its independent or dependent variables involve constructs that differ from those specified in the meta-analytic research question. Thus, in our synthesis of the desegregation literature (Wortman and Bryant, forthcoming), we formulated the following research question: What are the effects of U.S. public school desegregation on the achievement (that is, general, reading, or mathematics test scores) of black students bused to previously all-white schools? To compute effect size, we decided to use the traditional meta-analysis formula (Cohen, 1977; Glass, 1976) whereby the posttest mean of the segregated group was subtracted from the posttest mean of the desegregated group and the resulting difference was divided by the posttest standard deviation of the segregated group.

On close reading, some of the studies that investigated treatments labeled *desegregation* or outcomes labeled *achievement* operationalized these constructs in invalid ways. With respect to the construct validity of treatment, we decided to ignore studies in which interventions did not involve racial desegregation, such as studies of bus transportation per se (for example, Davies, 1969). We also rejected studies that compared untreated control groups of all-black classrooms with "desegregated" classrooms in which most students were actually black (for example, Akin, 1977), since such treatments did not represent racial desegregation (Armor, 1972).

With respect to the construct validity of outcome measures, we decided to ignore studies in which outcomes were not measured by standardized tests of math, reading, or general achievement. Thus, we excluded studies using IQ scores (for example, Moorehead, 1972), grade point averages (for example, Hayden, 1976), dropout rates (for example, Felice and Richardson, 1976), and unstandardized tests (for example, Geiger, 1968). We also rejected studies that aggregated achievement test scores across all participating ethnic minorities (for example, Purl and Dawson, 1973), since ethnically heterogenous scores did not specifically measure black students' achievement.

Judgments regarding the relevance of a given study's constructs are fundamental when choosing evidence for inclusion in research syntheses. All meta-analysts use construct validity criteria to some extent in selecting their data base. If we are overly inclusive, we run the risk of compiling a hodge-podge of information from which meaningful conclusions cannot be drawn (Gallo, 1978). Indeed, as Cook and Leviton (1980) have noted, it would be poor practice not to exclude studies that are irrelevant on theoretical grounds.

However, our restrictiveness in judging the relevance of study constructs depends on the specificity of our research question (Wortman, 1983). If we have formulated a highly detailed research question that specifies a precise set of critical constructs, then we will have to be fairly restrictive in selecting relevant studies. In contrast, if our research question is relatively general and if it encompasses a relatively wide range of constructs, then we can be relatively permissive in selecting relevant studies. Thus, meta-analysts with narrow research questions typically draw conclusions of fairly limited representativeness (Cooper, 1982).

External Validity. External validity concerns the degree to which the settings, populations, or time periods involved in a particular study restrict the generalizability of its results (Campbell and Stanley, 1966; Cook and Campbell, 1979). We can judge a given study to be irrelevant on grounds of low external validity if its setting, research population, or historical period diverges from those specified in the meta-analytic research question. Thus, because of the specific nature of our research question, we decided to ignore studies that occurred in settings other than U.S. public schools, such as private schools (for example, Gardner and others, 1970), kindergartens (for example, Dawson, 1973), or schools outside the United States (for example, Dunlop and others, 1958). We also decided to ignore studies that involved only desegregated populations other than blacks, such as white students (for example, Cypert, 1971) and Hispanic children (for example, Mahard and Crain, 1980). In addition, we excluded studies that occurred before the 1954 Supreme Court decision (for example, Crowley, 1932) that made desegregation a public policy issue.

Another limitation to the generalizability of a study's results is created by failure to report when and where the experimental treatment occurred. Thus, we excluded studies that did not report the dates or locations of desegregation interventions (for example, Morrison, 1972), because such omissions prevented us from making judgments about their relevance to our specific research question.

Another strategy for handling cases of insufficient reporting is to contact the original researcher and request the missing information (Cordray and Orwin, 1983). However, this approach goes beyond meta-analysis of primary research toward a form of secondary analysis, and in practice it may be relatively inefficient. For example, in a meta-analysis of research on cognitive gender differences, Hyde (1981) wrote letters requesting unreported statistics to the authors of eighteen different studies. She received seven responses, and only two provided the information that she had requested. Bias may also be operating, such that those who respond may be systematically different from those who do not. While it may be easier for primary researchers to provide information about dates and locations than it is to furnish unreported statistics, rates of response to requests for additional information of any kind are notoriously low. Bryant and Wortman (1978) analyze this problem in some detail.

If the meta-analyst decides to contact primary investigators to obtain missing information, he or she must avoid being selective in choosing which studies to pursue, because the researcher's own prejudices can bias the process of requesting unreported information. In order not to introduce such bias, the meta-analyst who decides to pursue incomplete reports should request information for all studies that lack necessary details, not just for those whose findings support the meta-analyst's hypothesis or political viewpoint. In our research synthesis of desegregation studies (Wortman and Bryant, forthcoming) the funding agency—the National Institute of Education—convened a panel of experts with contrasting attitudes on busing to evaluate our methods and findings. Several panel members suggested that we request missing information from primary researchers. Interestingly, some opponents of busing suggested contacting only authors whose findings were negative. In fact, the panel only contacted the author of one study, whose findings were negative, to obtain missing information.

As with judgments of relevance concerning construct validity, the degree to which meta-analysts must consider the relevance of a study's settings, populations, and dates of conduct varies with the specificity of their research question (Bryant, 1983). Meta-analysts who formulate highly detailed research questions that specify precise treatment locales, target populations, or chronological periods must be relatively restrictive in selecting relevant studies. Meta-analysts who formulate relatively general research questions can be more inclusive in selecting relevant evidence. As a result, investigators with narrower research questions will exclude as irrelevant many studies that investigators with broader research questions will include. Again, selectivity limits the generalizablity of conclusions drawn from research syntheses (Cooper, 1982). Although the formulation of the research question itself is in principle the major determinant in selecting the evidence for meta-analysis, such other factors as cost, convenience, and comparability of dependent variables can make the selection process somewhat more interactive.

Decisions Regarding Acceptability

After selecting relevant studies for research synthesis, we may decide that some studies seem more appropriate for inclusion than others. While it can be relatively easy to justify the exclusion of studies that we deem to be irrelevant to our research question, disagreements can arise if we wish to reject some relevant studies as unacceptable for research synthesis. In this section, we will examine such decisions about acceptability in light of the statistical conclusion validity and internal validity described by Cook and Campbell (1979).

Statistical Conclusion Validity. Statistical conclusion validity concerns the degree to which valid inferences can be drawn from the statistical analyses performed in a particular study (Cook and Campbell, 1979). We may judge a given study to be unacceptable on grounds of low statistical conclusion validity if it lacks the necessary descriptive statistics for evaluation and coding, or if it involves only statistical comparisons other than those specified in the meta-analytic research question. Thus, in our synthesis of desegregation research, we decided to exclude summary statements that lacked statistical information (for example, Beers and Reardon, 1974) as well as nonempirical literature reviews (for example, Weinberg, 1977). Moreover, some of the relevant empirical studies provided us with insufficient information to derive necessary means, standard deviations, or sample sizes for meta-analysis (for example, Calhoun, 1978). As with nonempirical reports that lacked data, these studies, too, had to be excluded from our meta-analysis. As an alternative, we could have contacted the authors of these studies to request unreported statistics. However, since this strategy goes beyond the normal role of meta-analysis and since it is not likely to be successful, we chose not to do so.

Other relevant studies provided sufficient information, but they suffered from flaws that invalidated their statistical comparisons, such as very inadequate sample sizes (for example, Teele, 1973) and inappropriate use of statistical tests (for example, Phillips and Bianchi, 1975) where the raw data are unavailable. Because inferential statistics are misleading in such cases (Cook and Campbell, 1979), we decided to reject these studies. Mansfield and Busse (1977) also have argued that studies involving very small sample sizes should be eliminated to avoid capitalizing on chance (Gilbert and others, 1977).

Another threat to statistical conclusion validity that we considered when judging relevant studies for acceptability involved random heterogeneity in the sample of respondents (Cook and Campbell, 1979). For instance, several relevant desegregation studies globally combined data across different grade levels to test for treatment effects (for example, Lemke, 1979). Because this approach allows variations in the age of students and in the duration of the treatment to influence statistical conclusions, we decided to reject these studies. We also ignored desegregation studies that reported only statistical comparisons across ethnicity; that is, we rejected studies that compared black students' test scores with white students' test scores (for example, Merchant, 1969), because we considered such comparisons to be statistically invalid assessments of black students' achievement. Including them could have threatened the construct validity of the meta-analytic statistic.

As with judgments about the relevance of a given study's constructs, judgments regarding the acceptability of a given study's statistical comparisons are unavoidable when choosing studies for meta-analysis. Studies that provide no statistical information and studies that make irrelevant comparisons must necessarily be discarded. For example, nonempirical investigations provide no outcome data, and thus they are unacceptable as evidence in meta-analysis. Studies involving only inappropriate comparisons must also be rejected in order to preserve the validity of meta-analytic conclusions.

In contrast to judgments of relevance concerning construct and external validity, however, judgments regarding the acceptability of a study's statistical comparisons are relatively independent of the specificity of the research question. Whether the research question is specific or general, certain rules of valid statistical inference must be maintained when selecting appropriate evidence. Clearly, the absence of appropriate statistical information or of tables containing raw data necessitates exclusion, no matter what the research question is. Similarly, although decisions to reject particular statistical comparisons can be more clear-cut when the research question is very specific, some types of comparisons are always irrelevant. Because judgments of acceptability based on statistical conclusion validity are required to some extent in order to assure valid results, they represent a necessary restriction in the representativeness of meta-analytic conclusions. In some cases, the lack of appropriate statistical information can be overcome by contacting the original authors (Wortman and Bryant, forthcoming). The limitations of this procedure have already been noted.

Internal Validity. Internal validity concerns the degree to which valid causal inferences can be drawn from the methodology used in a particular study (Campbell and Stanley, 1966; Cook and Campbell, 1979). By far the most controversial decisions regarding the acceptability of relevant studies concern studies whose methodology prevents valid causal inferences (Wortman, 1983). On the one hand, Glass (1976, 1977, 1978) and his colleagues (Glass and others, 1981; Glass and Smith, 1978) have repeatedly argued that meta-analysts should not exclude studies on the basis of methodological quality. They maintain that all available studies on a topic should be included and that the effects of design quality should be examined a posteriori. On the other hand, critics of meta-analysis (Eysenck, 1978; Mansfield and Busse, 1977) have argued that studies with methodological weaknesses should be discarded in favor of studies with high design quality. These authors maintain that the conclusions that we can draw from a research synthesis are only as valid as the evidence on which it is based (Eysenck, 1978).

Proponents of the traditional all-inclusive approach argue that the influence of design quality on treatment effects is essentially an empirical issue that is best examined by combining all available studies across the full range of methodological rigor (Glass, 1978; Glass and Smith, 1978), and they recommend including all studies even when most are methodologically weak (Glass, 1977). This viewpoint assumes a type of strategic combination argument (Staines, 1974)—that flawed studies can be combined because their weaknesses when pooled will cancel out each other and yield a coherent, unbiased result (Wortman and Bryant, forthcoming). However, when all studies share a common bias, this all-inclusive approach can be misleading. Research synthesis may not be able to detect bias that operates predominantly in one direction (Cook and Leviton, 1980; Wortman, 1983), and if it does detect bias, it may not be able to correct it. Without well-designed studies that can be used as a baseline for comparison, it is impossible to determine how methodological quality affects results (Jackson, 1980). Thus, rather than canceling each other out, shared sources of bias can simply create one large, biased set of evidence.

The research literature on school desegregation exemplifies this problem. Research on desegregation is almost exclusively quasi-experimental, and its methodology is extremely uneven in quality. Indeed, desegregation studies generally share the same major sources of bias. For example, treatment and control groups are usually self-selected, so that desegregated students typically begin with higher initial achievement test scores (Wortman and Bryant, forthcoming). In the absence of well-designed studies that can be used as a standard of comparison, it is difficult to use traditional meta-analytic procedures to adjust effect size for this selection bias. In the few cases for which pretest data are available, it may be possible to remove much of the selection bias from the posttest results with nontraditional techniques (Wortman and Bryant, forthcoming).

For this reason, we decided to reject relevant desegregation studies that suffered from threats to their internal validity and to consider only a relatively pure subset of studies for research synthesis. For example, we excluded cross sectional surveys of students in schools distributed across a wide geographical area (for example, McPartland, 1969). Because these nonexperimental research designs rarely permit control of factors that can influence academic achievement independently of school desegregation, we believe that they are inherently weak and that they have little use for program evaluation and policy development.

We also rejected studies that lacked adequate nondesegregated control group data. In these cases, comparison groups consisted of district or statewide test norms (for example, Purl and Dawson, 1973), cohort data from a different historical period (for example, Prichard, 1969), or "segregated" students who had in fact experienced some form of desegregation (for example, Sacramento City Unified School District, 1971). Such comparisons constitute invalid tests of desegregation in which inadequate experimental controls are likely to produce artifactual achievement differences. We also excluded studies that used different achievement tests for segregated and desegregated students (for example, Danahy, 1971). These studies suffer from instrumentation threats (Campbell and Stanley, 1966; Cook and Campbell, 1979) of differential test reliability that can either produce spurious treatment effects or mask true effects.

In constrast to the literature on school desegregation, research literatures that contain a relatively large portion of high-quality evidence can afford the meta-analyst the luxury of integrating the full range of available studies. Traditional experimental literatures usually contain at least some studies of high methodological quality with which poorer-quality studies can be compared (Wortman and Yeaton, 1983). The all-inclusive approach can be justified in these cases, since the meta-analyst possesses an absolute, high-quality baseline against which the effects of bias can be assessed.

The preceding discussion suggests that it would be shortsighted to recommend either the all-inclusive or the methodologically selective approach for all research syntheses. Whether the meta-analyst should be inclusive or selective depends on the range of experimental rigor in the particular research literature. Content areas that contain well-designed true experiments may offer a sufficient number of high-quality studies with which the studies of poorer quality can be compared. In contrast, in content areas that contain only quasi-experiments there may not be enough studies of high methodological quality to afford the meta-analyst a standard of comparison. Thus, he or she may be forced to exclude the studies with severe flaws in order to obtain a set of higher-quality evidence for research synthesis.

Effects of Decisions to Exclude Studies

Final Samples

As already noted, we decided to exclude studies from our synthesis of the desegregation literature (Wortman and Bryant, forthcoming) that were irrelevant to our research question. Of the 157 studies retrieved, close reading revealed that 46 (29 percent) were irrelevant because of inappropriate constructs, settings, populations, historical periods, statistical comparisons, or research designs. After eliminating these studies, we were left with a total of 111 studies (71 percent) that appropriately addressed issues of interest to our research synthesis. From the relevant studies, we eliminated those that were unacceptably flawed. Of the 111 studies deemed relevant, 80 (72 percent) were judged to be unacceptable for research synthesis because of excessive threats to their statistical conclusion or internal validity. This left a sample of thirty-one methodologically pure studies for our analyses. Thus, we judged that only 20 percent of the studies that we retrieved and 28 percent of the studies that we deemed relevant were acceptable for research synthesis.

Comparing Acceptable and Unacceptable Studies

When validity criteria are used to exclude some portion of relevant studies, a question naturally arises as to the comparability of acceptable and unacceptable studies. Do the acceptable and unacceptable differ systematically in some other respects besides methodological quality? Is a form of confirmatory bias (Lord and others, 1979; Mahoney, 1977) operating so that the studies that are accepted tend more to confirm the investigator's expectations and beliefs than the rejected studies do? Regardless of their nature, any differences between accepted and rejected studies represent limits on the generalizability of research conclusions that meta-analysts should identify and acknowledge (Cooper, 1982). Table 1 summarizes some of the differences between the studies that we accepted and rejected for our research synthesis.

Characteristics of the Desegregation Intervention. Desegregation interventions in the accepted studies were more likely to be voluntary or de facto plans in New England or Middle Atlantic states that involved cross-district busing of black students from urban schools to other urban or to suburban schools. Desegregation interventions in rejected studies were more likely to be mandatory plans in South Atlantic states that involved intradistrict busing of black students from suburban schools to other suburban schools. Accepted studies used fewer sending and receiving schools, had smaller percentages of blacks in desegregated groups, and had larger differences in the percentage of blacks between segregated and desegregated groups than rejected studies did.

Table 1. Summary of Selected Chi Square Analyses Comparing Accepted and Rejected Studies

Variable	Accepted Studies	Rejected Studies
Type of Desegregation Plan [a]		
Mandatory *(N = 88)*	9.6%	43.1%
Voluntary *(N = 157)*	71.2%	45.9%
De facto *(N = 40)*	19.2%	11.0%
Types of Sending and Receiving Schools [b]		
Urban–urban *(N = 187)*	74.7%	62.0%
Urban–suburban *(N = 38)*	22.0%	9.4%
Rural–rural *(N = 6)*	0.0%	3.1%
Suburban–suburban *(N = 18)*	3.3%	25.5%
Geographical Location of Study [a,c]		
New England *(N = 26)*	14.2%	5.2%
Middle Atlantic *(N = 45)*	27.4%	7.5%
East North Central *(N = 87)*	22.6%	29.6%
West North Central *(N = 7)*	0.0%	3.3%
South Atlantic *(N = 54)*	6.6%	22.1%
East South Central *(N = 8)*	1.9%	2.8%
West South Central *(N = 45)*	15.0%	13.6%
Mountain *(N = 7)*	1.9%	2.3%
Pacific *(N = 40)*	10.4%	13.6%
Type of Research Design [a]		
One-group pretest-posttest *(N = 71)*	17.0%	28.5%
Pretest-posttest nonequivalent control group *(N = 144)*	57.5%	44.6%

Table 1. Summary of Selected Chi Square Analyses
Comparing Accepted and Rejected Studies (cont'd.)

Variable	Accepted Studies	Rejected Studies
Type of Research Design [a] (continued)		
Static group comparison ($N = 70$)	18.9%	26.9%
Randomized study ($N = 7$)	6.6%	0.0%
Method of Forming Control Group [a]		
Random sampling ($N = 50$)	26.0%	13.1%
Matching ($N = 51$)	30.0%	11.5%
National norms ($N = 19$)	0.0%	10.4%
Historical data ($N = 37$)	0.0%	20.2%
Predicted score ($N = 11$)	0.0%	6.0%
Subjects as own control ($N = 71$)	14.0%	31.1%
Full universe ($N = 44$)	30.0%	7.7%
Type of Publication [a]		
Technical report ($N = 161$)	41.5%	51.1%
Article or book ($N = 53$)	3.8%	21.4%
Dissertation or thesis ($N = 121$)	54.7%	27.5%
Type of Outcome [d]		
Reading Achievement		
Positive effect ($N = 86$)	34.6%	42.5%
Zero effect ($N = 85$)	51.9%	36.2%
Negative effect ($N = 41$)	13.5%	21.3%
Math Achievement		
Positive effect ($N = 69$)	48.6%	40.0%
Zero effect ($N = 62$)	42.8%	36.2%
Negative effect ($N = 34$)	8.6%	23.8%
General Achievement [b]		
Positive effect ($N = 25$)	37.5%	40.7%
Zero effect ($N = 18$)	62.5%	24.1%
Negative effect ($N = 19$)	0.0%	35.2%

Note: The analyses summarized here used cases—separate comparisons of a treatment and a control group—within each study as the unit of analysis. On the average, there were 3.05 cases per study, with accepted studies providing 3.42 cases and rejected studies providing 2.90 cases. Using the study as the unit of analysis did not change the interpretation of these results.
[a] $p < .01$
[b] $p < .05$
[c] This coding scheme is based on the U.S. Census Bureau categorization of states into regions.
[d] This vote-counting (Light and Smith, 1971) categorization of overall results is based on the conclusions drawn by the authors of the studies subjected to meta-analysis. We also attempted to categorize each study's outcomes according to our own judgment of the conclusions that were justified. However, this strategy led us to code the vast majority of reading, mathematics, and general achievement outcomes as not ascertainable because of the threats to validity. For this reason, we have only reported the results of comparisons using the authors' conclusions.

Characteristics of the Study. Accepted studies were more likely to involve pretest-posttest nonequivalent control group designs and smaller comparison groups. Rejected studies were more likely to involve one-group pretest-posttest designs and larger control groups formed by using black students before desegregation, national norms, or historical data. Compared with the two-group designs, the weaker one-group quasi-experiments were generally confounded by such threats to internal validity as selection, maturation, and mortality (Campbell and Stanley, 1966; Cook and Campbell, 1979), which are associated with inflated estimates of effect size in desegregation research (Wortman and Bryant, forthcoming).

In addition, we were more likely to accept dissertations and theses and to reject articles and books. Studies published in professional journals or books often lacked the information necessary to extract an effect size or to make judgments about construct, external, statistical conclusion, or internal validity. In contrast, the typical dissertation or thesis contained highly detailed information specifying operations, methods, sampling procedures, and statistical comparisons. Consequently, we were more likely to find a level of detail sufficient for coding among dissertations and theses than among articles and books. We also found that studies published in journals and books had larger effect sizes than unpublished studies did. This publication bias has been noted by other meta-analysts (for example, Smith, 1980) across a variety of content areas. This suggests that retrieval techniques that rely only on published reports may overestimate effect size (Bryant, 1983; Cooper, 1982).

Historical Differences. On the average, accepted studies were conducted at an earlier point in history than the rejected studies were. The year of the pretest and posttest, the year in which the desegregation intervention began, and the date on which the report was made public were earlier for accepted studies than they were for rejected studies. On the average, the rejected studies were conducted in the late 1960s, and the accepted studies were conducted earlier in the 1960s.

These historical differences between accepted and rejected studies help to explain the differences in desegregation interventions and study characteristics just noted. School districts in New England or Middle Atlantic states tended to implement desegregation plans of their own volition early in the 1960s. These voluntary interventions typically involved fewer sending and receiving schools and the percentages of blacks in the desegregated groups were typically smaller. Because voluntary plans could be implemented in some segregated schools and not in others, separate control groups of nonbused black students could be formed from all-black schools. In these cases, the strong comparison group or nonequivalent control group design (Campbell and Stanley, 1966) could be used to evaluate the intervention. Since this design suffers from fewer threats to internal validity than others do, we were more likely to include studies that used it in our research synthesis.

In contrast, it was not until the late 1960s that school districts in the

South were ordered by courts to implement mandatory desegregation plans. These forced-busing interventions typically involved more sending and receiving schools, and the percentages of blacks in the desegregated groups were typically larger. Because the court-ordered plans generally required desegregating every all-black classroom in the school district, groups of non-bused black students rarely remained to serve as separate control groups. In these cases, one-group pretest-posttest designs or historical controls were the only methodological recourse available. And, as mentioned earlier, these weak designs suffer from substantial threats to internal validity, which made us more likely to exclude the studies that used them from our research synthesis. Differences in the characteristics of accepted and rejected studies thus appear to be logical offshoots of the historical development of school desegregation.

Differences in Outcomes. Another crucial question raised in comparing the accepted and rejected studies is this: Did the two sets of studies find different effects? Although we ignored study results when judging threats to validity, the critical observer may still wonder whether we unintentionally produced systematic differences between study outcomes when selecting among studies for high-quality evidence. Unfortunately, many of the studies that we rejected failed to provide necessary statistical information, so we could not directly compare effect sizes for the two sets of studies. However, we were able to use a rough vote-counting method (Light and Smith, 1971) to categorize the direction of reported effects and to compare frequencies of outcomes for accepted and rejected studies. The "type of outcome" section in Table 1 presents the results of these vote-counting analyses for each type of achievement test.

Although math and reading achievement tests showed no significant differences, accepted studies were more likely to find no effects, and rejected studies were more likely to find negative effects, for general achievement tests. This finding indicates that slight systematic biases in general achievement outcomes may exist between the two sets of studies. Obviously, this crude ordinal categorization is not precise enough to allow us to distinguish differences in the magnitude of effects.

Experimental Rigor Versus Representativeness

It is clear from these comparative analyses that the final sample of studies included in our research synthesis was not representative of the entire body of evidence. In selecting only evidence of relatively high methodological quality, we compiled a set of studies that differed systematically from the set of studies that we rejected. Thus, we made a conscious choice between two sets of priorities—maximizing the validity of causal inferences and maximizing the generalizability of research conclusions. We chose to place more weight on internal validity than on external validity.

Because these two sets of priorities tend to be mutually exclusive (Cook and Campbell, 1979), researchers must usually sacrifice one objective in gaining the other. That is, they must typically make a trade-off between unequivocal results whose generalizability is limited and equivocal results that are widely generalizable. Consequently, the reseacher's scientific priorities largely determine the researcher's decision to be more selective or more inclusive in choosing evidence for research synthesis. Researchers who consider external validity to be more important (Cronbach and others, 1980) will favor the all-inclusive approach. Researchers who consider internal validity to be more important (Campbell and Stanley, 1966) will favor the methodologically selective approach. We opted to be more selective, because we believe that internal validity is a sine qua non in experimentation.

Yet, even when external validity takes priority in research synthesis, the specific types of generalizations that the researcher wishes to make will influence his or her selectivity when choosing evidence. Those who wish to generalize across a variety of settings, populations, or historical periods will be more inclusive. Those who wish to generalize to specific settings, populations, or historical periods will be more selective (Cook and Campbell, 1979). Thus, the range of evidence that the researcher selects depends not only on his or her scientific priorities but also on the purposes of the research synthesis.

The Limits of Selectivity

But, just how far should selectivity go? We excluded 80 percent of the studies that we retrieved for our research synthesis, so that our final sample contained thirty-one studies. It is easy to imagine instances in which the selective meta-analyst is left with even fewer acceptable studies (Berk and Chalmers, 1981). As restrictions on the number of studies selected for inclusion increase, research synthesis at some point ceases to be a quantitative integration of an entire body of evidence as in meta-analysis, and becomes just a rigorous, systematic literature review.

What is the minimum number of studies that a research synthesis should include? This question may best be addressed by considering meta-analysis as analogous to primary research (Saxe, 1983). Primary researchers impose entry criteria for the admission of subjects into studies and data analyses. In much the same way, we have argued, meta-analysts must use criteria for admitting studies into research syntheses. To select relevant evidence, studies should be evaluated for their contruct and external validity. To select acceptable evidence, studies should be evaluated for their statistical conclusion and internal validity. To extend the analogy, just as the primary researcher must determine the minimum number of subjects to include in primary research, so must the meta-analyst determine the number of studies to include in research synthesis. In making such decisions, primary researchers use statistical power analysis (Cohen, 1977) to specify minimum sample size as a function of the effect size under investigation. Required sample size increases as effect size decreases. Analogously, meta-analysts can use power curves (Feldt and Mahmoud, 1958) to determine the minimum number of studies or outcomes that must be included, given the expected magnitude of effects. Research literatures in which effects are relatively small will thus require a relatively large minimum number of studies, while literatures in which effects are relatively large will require a relatively small minimum number of studies.

The Inevitability of Disagreement

Although individual meta-analysts may use the same criteria to select evidence for research synthesis, they may make different subjective judgments that in turn yield different meta-analytic conclusions (Bryant, 1983). For example, the panel of experts convened by NIE to review our work on studies of school desegregation essentially agreed with the set of threats to validity that we used in selecting evidence. However, in performing their own independent research syntheses, individual panel members tended to obtain slightly different estimates of the average effect size. These estimates ranged from about + .04 to + .30. Although panel members agreed that desegregation had no negative effects on black student achievement, they disagreed on the size of the positive effects; opponents of busing found the smallest positive effects, while proponents of busing found the largest effects.

These disagreements about average effect size can be traced to three different types of decisions that meta-analysts must make. First, disagreements can arise from decisions about the studies to include in research synthesis. Different sets of primary studies can yield different meta-analytic results (Bryant, 1983; Cooper, 1982).

Second, disagreements can arise from decisions about the comparisons to consider within a given study. Choices about which comparison group or which comparison between treatment and control groups to use can cause estimates of effect size to vary. Indeed, NIE panel members often selected only those comparisons within a particular study that supported their own ideological viewpoint.

Third, disagreements can arise from decisions about the type of data analysis to perform. Different analysis strategies can yield different meta-analytic results. For example, one NIE panel member decided to adjust effect sizes for differences in the ages of the children involved, whereas others computed a traditional estimate of effect size (Cohen, 1977; Glass, 1976). However, a number of alternatives are available. We could reduce bias in our estimates of effect size by using the pooled within-group standard deviation as a denominator (Hedges, 1981), by weighting for sample size (Hedges, 1982), or by adjusting for unreliability in measures (Hunter and others, 1982); we could correct posttest effect sizes for any pretest differences between treatment and control groups (Wortman and Bryant, forthcoming); we could use significance levels from the primary studies to quantify treatment effects (Rosenthal 1980); or we could use vote-counting methods to categorize results (Light and Smith, 1971). Each technique could yield different results.

Because research synthesis will always entail subjective judgments on the part of the meta-analyst, disagreements among individual meta-analyst are unavoidable. We thus return full circle to the point from which we began. First, we confronted inconsistencies in the findings of primary studies. Then we considered meta-analysis as a means of resolving these inconsistencies. Now, we find that research syntheses themselves can reach different findings.

Recommendations

How should we respond to the inevitability of disagreement? Perhaps the best way of addressing this issue is to consider the analogy between meta-analysis and primary research. To help resolve contradictions among primary researchers, Campbell (1971, 1979) has suggested that investigators should make their data publicly available for secondary analysis by others. This practice would allow independent researchers with different theoretical and methodological perspectives to examine the same set of evidence, as the NIE panel did for our study. If their results converge, then our confidence in the overall conclusions increases. For the NIE panel, for example, the results form a kind of confidence interval that "brackets" (Wortman and others, 1978) a positive effect. If their results diverge, then we can pinpoint sources of disagreement by comparing different researchers' decisions about the cases to include, the statistical comparisons to make, and the types of analyses to perform. However, such pinpointing is possible only if both primary and meta-analytic data are publicly available.

Perhaps applying Campbell's notions about primary research to research synthesis would help to resolve the inevitable disagreements among meta-analysts. If meta-analytic data bases are archived and made publicly available, then investigators with different perspectives can synthesize exactly the same sets of evidence. If they were to do so, we could identify sources of disagreement among meta-analysts and explore the consequences of decisions about which studies to include, which comparisons within studies to consider, and which types of analyses to perform. For example, Smith and Glass's (1977) meta-analysis of psychotherapy outcome studies has been reanalyzed by Landman and Dawes (1982), who adjusted effect sizes for nonindependence and replicated the original findings on a random subset of the original studies. Even more recently, Orwin and Cordray (1983) resynthesized the same literature, selecting a stratified random sample of studies from Smith and Glass's bibliography and correcting for unreliability. This most recent reanalysis, however, obtained different results. Because the literature in question is widely accessible, all three meta-analyses were able to use a comparable data base. And because each investigation made public its criterion for selecting studies and for selecting comparisons within studies, all three meta-analyses used similar comparisons between experimental and control groups. Thus, we can conclude that differences in the type of analysis performed account for the discrepant conclusions.

The public availability of meta-analytic data sets will be especially critical for research literatures that contain a high proportion of inaccessible fugitive studies, as is the case for research on school desegregation. These data bases must include copies of the original research reports and codebooks. They should also identify the studies that were excluded as well as the criteria used in accepting and rejecting studies. By making our desegregation data base available to other investigators, we hope to promote meta-synthesis — that is, the cumulation and comparison of conclusions drawn from independent meta-analyses of the same research literature. Only by comparing results across different research syntheses that use different criteria to select and evaluate evidence can we ultimately converge on the underlying truth.

References

Akin, J. P. "A Study of the Relationship of Racial Integration to Reading Achievement in Grades 2, 3, and 5 in Alexandria, Virginia, City Public Schools." Unpublished doctoral dissertation, George Washington University, 1977. (ED 159 265)

Armor, D. J. "The Evidence on Busing." *The Public Interest,* 1972, *28,* 90–126.

Beers, J. S., and Reardon, F. J. "Racial Balancing in Harrisburg: Achievement and Attitudinal Changes." *Integrated Education,* 1974, *12* (5), 35–38.

Berk, A. A., and Chalmers, T. C. "Cost and Efficacy of the Substitution of Ambulatory for Inpatient Care." *New England Journal of Medicine,* 1981, *304* (7), 393–397.

Bryant, F. B. "Issues in Omitting Studies from Research Syntheses." Paper presented in the 1983 Joint Meeting of the Evaluation Research Society and Evaluation Network, Chicago, October 1983.

Bryant, F. B., and Wortman, P. M. "Secondary Analysis: The Case for Data Archives." *American Psychologist,* 1978, *33,* 381–387.

Calhoun, P. C. "A Study of the Effects of the Forced Desegregation Pairing of a Low-Socioeconomic-Status White Elementary School on Achievement, Social Interaction, and Enrollment." Unpublished doctoral dissertation, Georgia State University, 1978.

Campbell, D. T. "Reforms as Experiments." *Urban Affairs Quarterly,* 1971, *7,* 133–171.

Campbell, D. T. "Degrees of Freedom and the Case Study." In T. D. Cook and C. S. Reichardt (Eds.), *Qualitative and Quantitative Methods in Evaluation Research.* Beverly Hills, Calif.: Sage, 1979.

Campbell, D. T., and Stanley, J. C. *Experimental and Quasi-Experimental Designs for Research.* Chicago: Rand McNally, 1966.

Cohen, J. *Statistical Power Analysis for the Behavioral Sciences.* (Rev. ed.) New York: Academic Press, 1977.

Cook, T. D., and Campbell, D. T. *Quasi-Experimentation: Design and Analysis Issues for Field Settings.* Chicago: Rand McNally, 1979.

Cook, T. D., and Leviton, L. C. "Reviewing the Literature: A Comparison of Traditional Methods with Meta-Analysis." *Journal of Personality,* 1980, *48* (4), 449–472.

Cooper, H. M. "Scientific Guidelines for Conducting Integrative Research Reviews." *Review of Educational Research,* 1982, *52* (2), 291–302.

Cordray, D. S., and Orwin, R. G. "Improving the Quality of Evidence: Interconnections Among Primary Evaluation, Secondary Analysis, and Quantitative Synthesis." In R. J. Light (Ed.), *Evaluation Studies Review Annual.* Vol. 8. Beverly Hills, Calif.: Sage, 1983.

Cronbach, L. J., Ambron, S. R., Dornbusch, S. M., Hess, R. D., Hornik, R. C., Phillips, D. C., Walker, D. F., and Weiner, S. S. *Toward Reform of Program Evaluation: Aims, Methods, and Institutional Arrangements.* San Francisco: Jossey-Bass, 1980.

Crowley, M. R. "Cincinnati's Experiment in Negro Education: A Comparative Study of the Segregated and Mixed School." *Journal of Negro Education,* 1932, *1,* 25-33.

Cypert, K. E. "The Immediate Effects of Classroom Integration on the Academic Progress, Self-Concept, and Racial Attitudes of Elementary White Students." Unpublished doctoral dissertation, North Texas State University, 1971.

Danahy, A. H. "A Study of the Effects of Busing on the Achievement, Attendance, Attitudes, and Social Choices of Negro Inner-City Children." Unpublished doctoral dissertation, University of Minnesota, 1971.

Davies, E. A., Jr. "A Comparative Study of the Academic Achievement of Transported and Nontransported Pupils at Holly Hill Elementary School, Holly Hill, Florida." Unpublished master's thesis, Stetson University, 1969.

Lawson, J. A. *A Longitudinal Cross Sectional Study of Achievement of Black and Spanish-Surnamed Students in Desegregated Elementary and Secondary Schools.* Riverside Unified School District, 1973. (ED 086 770)

Dunlop, G. M., Harper, R. J. C., and Hunka, S. "The Influence of Transporting Children to Centralized Schools upon Achievement and Attendance." *Educational Administration and Supervision,* 1958, *44,* 191-198.

Eysenck, H. J. "An Exercise in Mega-Silliness." *American Psychologist,* 1978, *33,* 517.

Feldt, L. S., and Mahmoud, M. W. "Power Function Charts for Specification of Sample Size in Analysis of Variance." *Psychometrika,* 1958, *23,* 335-353.

Felice, L. G., and Richardson, R. L. *The Effects of Busing and School Desegregation on Majority and Minority Student Dropout Rates: An Evaluation of School Socioeconomic Composition and Teachers' Expectations.* Waco, Texas: Baylor University Press, 1976.

Gallo, P. S., Jr. "Meta-Analysis—A Mixed Metaphor?" *American Psychologist,* 1978, *33,* 515-517.

Gardner, B. B., Wright, B. D., and Dee, R. *The Effect of Busing Black Ghetto Children into White Suburban Schools.* Chicago: Catholic School Board, 1970. (ED 048 389)

Geiger, G. O. "Effects of Desegregation on Classroom Achievement." Unpublished doctoral dissertation, University of South Carolina, 1968.

Gilbert, J. P., McPeek, B., and Mosteller, F. "Progress in Surgery and Anesthesia: Benefits and Risks of Innovative Therapy." In J. P. Bunker, B. A. Barnes, and F. Mosteller (Eds.), *Costs, Risks, and Benefits of Surgery.* New York: Oxford University Press, 1977.

Glass, G. V. "Primary, Secondary, and Meta-Analysis of Research." *Educational Researcher,* 1976, *5,* 3-8.

Glass, G. V. "Integrating Findings: The Meta-Analysis of Research." In L. S. Shulman (Ed.), *Review of Research in Education.* Vol. 5. Itasca, Ill.: Peacock, 1977.

Glass, G. V. "Reply to Mansfield and Busse." *Educational Researcher,* 1978, *7,* 3.

Glass, G. V., McGaw, B., and Smith, M. L. *Meta-Analysis in Social Research.* Beverly Hills, Calif.: Sage, 1981.

Glass, G. V., and Smith, M. L. "Reply to Eysenck." *American Psychologist,* 1978, *33,* 517.

Hayden, J. E. "An Analysis of the Grade Point Averages of Black Bused and Nonbused Students at a Desegregated High School." Unpublished doctoral dissertation, University of Louisville, 1976.

Hedges, L. V. "Distribution Theory for Glass's Estimator of Effect Size and Related Estimators." *Journal of Educational Statistics*, 1981, *6*, 107–128.

Hedges, L. V. "Estimation of Effect Size from a Series of Independent Experiments." *Psychological Bulletin*, 1982, *92*, 490–499.

Hunter, J. E., Schmidt, F. L., and Jackson, G. *Meta-Analysis: Cumulating Research Findings Across Studies*. Beverly Hills, Calif.: Sage, 1982.

Hyde, J. S. "How Large Are Cognitive Gender Differences? A Meta-Analysis Using W^2 and *d*." *American Psychologist*, 1981, *36*, 892–901.

Jackson, G. B. "Methods for Integrative Reviews." *Review of Educational Research*, 1980, *50*, 438–460.

Landman, J. T., and Dawes, R. "Psychotherapy Outcome: Smith and Glass's Conclusions Stand Up Under Scrutiny." *American Psychologist*, 1982, *37* (5), 504–516.

Lemke, E. A. "The Effects of Busing on the Achievement of White and Black Students." *Educational Studies*, 1979, *9*, 401–405.

Light, R. J., and Smith, P. V. "Accumulating Evidence: Procedures for Resolving Contradictions Among Different Research Studies." *Harvard Educational Review*, 1971, *41*, 429–471.

Lord, C., Ross, L., and Leper, M. "Biased Assimilation and Attitude Polarizations: The Effects of Prior Theories on Subsequently Considered Evidence." *Journal of Personality and Social Psychology*, 1979, *37*, 2098–2109.

McPartland, J. "The Relative Influence of School and of Classroom Desegregation on the Academic Achievement of Ninth-Grade Negro Students." *Journal of Social Issues*, 1969, *25* (3), 93–102.

Mahard, R. E., and Crain, R. L. "High School Racial Composition and the Academic Achievement and College Attendance of Hispanic Students." Paper presented at the annual American Sociological Association meetings, New York, August 1980.

Mahoney, M. "Publication Prejudices: An Experimental Study of Confirmatory Bias in the Peer Review System." *Cognitive Therapy and Research*, 1977, *1*, 161–175.

Mansfield, R. S., and Busse, T. V. "Meta-Analysis of Research: A Rejoinder to Glass." *Educational Researcher*, 1977, *6*, 3.

Merchant, J. N. "A Comparative Study of the Academic Achievement of Selected Negro and White Students in Desegregated Classrooms." Unpublished doctoral dissertation, East Texas State University, 1969.

Moorehead, N. F. "The Effects of School Integration on Intelligence Test Scores of Negro Children." Unpublished doctoral dissertation, Mississippi State University, 1972.

Morrison, G. A., Jr. "An Analysis of Academic Achievement Trends for Anglo American, Mexican American, and Negro American Students in a Desegregated School Environment." Unpublished doctoral dissertation, University of Houston, 1972.

Orwin, R. G., and Cordray, D. S. "The Effects of Deficient Reporting on Meta-Analysis: A Conceptual Framework and Reanalysis." Unpublished manuscript, Northwestern University, 1983.

Phillips, L. W., and Bianchi, U. "Desegregation, Reading Achievement, and Problem Behavior in Two Elementary Schools." *Urban Education*, 1975, *11* (4), 325–329.

Prichard, P. N. "Effects of Desegregation on Student Success in the Chapel Hill School." *Integrated Education*, 1969, *7*, 33–38.

Purl, M. C., and Dawson, J. A. *The Achievement of Students in Primary Grades After Seven Years of Desegregation*. Riverside, Calif.: Riverside Unified School District, 1973.

Rosenthal, R. "Summarizing Significance Levels." In R. Rosenthal (Ed.), *Quantitative Assessment of Research Domains*. New Directions for Methodology of Social and Behavioral Sciences, no. 5. San Francisco: Jossey-Bass, 1980.

Rossi, P. H., and Williams, W. *Evaluating Social Programs*. New York: Seminar Press, 1972.

Sacramento City Unified School District. *Focus on Reading and Math, 1970–1971: A Evaluation Report on a Program of Compensatory Education (ESEA Title 1).* Sacramento Calif.: Sacramento City Unified School District, 1971.

Saxe, L. "Meta-analysis." Paper presented at the annual meeting of the American Public Health Association Convention, Dallas, November 1983.

Smith, M. L. "Publication Bias and Meta-Analysis." *Evaluation in Education,* 1980, *4,* 22–24.

Smith, M. L., and Glass, G. V. "Meta-Analysis of Psychotherapy Outcome Studies." *American Psychologist,* 1977, *32,* 752–760.

Staines, G. L. "The Strategic Combination Argument." In W. Leinfellner and E. Kohler (Eds.), *Developments in the Methodology of Social Science.* Dordecht, Holland: Reidel, 1974.

Teele, J. E. *Evaluating School Busing: A Case Study of Boston's Operation Exodus.* New York: Praeger, 1973.

Weinberg, M. *Minority Students: A Research Appraisal.* Washington, D.C.: U.S. Department of Health, Education, and Welfare and National Institute of Education, 1977.

Wortman, P. M. "Evaluation Research: A Methodological Perspective." *Annual Review of Psychology,* 1983, *34,* 223–260.

Wortman, P. M., and Bryant, F. B. "School Desegregation and Black Student Achievement: An Integrative Review." *Sociological Methods & Research,* forthcoming.

Wortman, P. M., Reichardt, C. S., and St. Pierre, R. G. "The First Year of the Education Voucher Demonstration: A Secondary Analysis of Student Achievement Test Scores." *Evaluation Quarterly,* 1978, *2,* 193–214.

Wortman, P. M., and Yeaton, W. H. "Synthesis of Results in Controlled Trials of Coronary Artery Bypass Graft Surgery." In R. J. Light (Ed.), *Evaluation Studies Review Annual.* Vol. 8. Beverly Hills, Calif.: Sage, 1983.

Fred B. Bryant is assistant professor of social psychology at Loyola University of Chicago. His research interests include meta-analysis of quasi-experimental literatures and selection of appropriate evidence.

Paul M. Wortman is director of the Methodology and Evaluation Research Program in the Institute for Social Research and professor in the School of Public Health at the University of Michigan-Ann Arbor. His current research interests include research synthesis methods and medical technology assessment.

36

An Analysis of Psychotherapy Versus Placebo Studies

Leslie Prioleau, Martha Murdock, and Nathan Brody

Abstract: Smith, Glass, and Miller (1980) have reported a meta-analysis of over 500 studies comparing some form of psychological therapy with a control condition. They report that when averaged over all dependent measures of outcome, psychological therapy is .85 standard deviations better than the control treatment. We examined the subset of studies included in the Smith et al. meta-analysis that contained a psychotherapy and a placebo treatment. The median of the mean effect sizes for these 32 studies was .15. There was a nonsignificant inverse relationship between mean outcome and the following: sample size, duration of therapy, use of measures of outcome other than undisguised self-report, measurement of outcome at follow-up, and use of real patients rather than subjects solicited for the purposes of participation in a research study. A qualitative analysis of the studies in terms of the type of patient involved indicates that those using psychiatric outpatients had essentially zero effect sizes and that none using psychiatric inpatients provide convincing evidence for psychotherapeutic effectiveness. The only studies clearly demonstrating significant effects of psychotherapy were the ones that did not use real patients. For the most part, these studies involved small samples of subjects and brief treatments, occasionally described in quasibehavioristic language. It was concluded that for real patients there is no evidence that the benefits of psychotherapy are greater than those of placebo treatment.

Keywords: meta-analysis; methodology; outcome research; placebo; psychotherapy

Eysenck's well-known (1952) paper is the first of a long series of studies dealing with the question of the effectiveness of psychotherapy. Eysenck argued that many patients recover spontaneously and that the changes following psychotherapy do not exceed the spontaneous recovery rate. Eysenck has reviewed literature on psychotherapy outcome on other occasions and has continued to argue that the studies suggest that psychotherapy is an ineffective treatment (see, e.g., Eysenck 1966). Other reviewers, more favorably disposed to psychotherapy, have argued that Eysenck distorted the data and dealt with a biased sample. Meltzoff and Kornreich (1970), for example, reviewed a larger body of work dealing with psychotherapy outcomes and argued that the better-designed studies tended to provide stronger evidence for the benefits of psychotherapy and that there was an ample body of convincing evidence suggesting that psychotherapy was an effective treatment.

Smith, Glass, and Miller (1980) have attempted to resolve the controversy surrounding the effectiveness of psychotherapy by using the statistical procedure of meta-analysis as a technique for reviewing systematically a substantial – and, they claim, unbiased – portion of the literature dealing with the effectiveness of psychotherapy. They analyzed all the data they could find comparing psychotherapy or behavior therapy and a control group. For each dependent variable included in

each of the studies surveyed they computed a measure of effect size defined as the difference between the mean of the therapy group and the mean of the control group, divided by the standard deviation of the control group. They conclude that the mean effect size of psychological therapies is .85, indicating that when averaged over all measures in all studies, the outcome of psychological therapy is superior to that of nontreatment in control groups.

Smith et al.'s (1980) analyses appear to provide definitive evidence in favor of the effectiveness of psychological therapies. However, we felt that the research analyzed by Smith et al. should be subjected to further analyses. We had some reservations about the use of meta-analytic procedures for a body of literature as diverse as that summarized by Smith et al. (1980) (see Eysenck 1978; Strahan 1978). [See also Rosenthal & Rubin: "Interpersonal Expectancy Effects" *BBS* 1 (3) 1978.] While meta-analysis may be appropriate for summarizing the results of investigations using the same dependent variable with similar subject populations, it is questionable whether the method should be extended to the analysis of research using grossly different patient populations being subjected to grossly different methods of therapy where the outcomes are assessed using different dependent variables. Accordingly, we have tried to look in somewhat greater detail at a subset of the studies used by Smith et al. (1980) and we have tried to supplement a meta-analysis by a more traditional examination of individual studies.

The procedures used by Smith et al. (1980) in their meta-analysis may not have been ideal. In particular, these researchers performed a meta-analysis using dependent variables as their unit of measure. This procedure, in effect, weights a study by the number of dependent variables included in the analysis. Given the degree of variability across studies, we feel that it is more appropriate to use the study itself as a unit of analysis. Accordingly, we present, separately, effect size measures for each dependent variable included within a study and we obtain a mean effect size for each one (see Landman & Dawes 1982 for a comparable reanalysis of a subset of the studies used by Smith et al. 1980).

In order to permit us to examine this body of literature in greater depth we have focused on the subset of studies reported by Smith et al. (1980) using psychotherapy rather than behavior therapy. Although psychotherapy and behavior therapy may no longer be as theoretically distinct as they once were, the techniques, patients, and methods of assessment of the outcomes of therapy used in the research literature for these two broad classes of therapeutic treatments are still somewhat different. Our decision to limit the scope of our analyses to research on psychotherapy was done in part for theoretical reasons and in part in order to permit us to examine a subset of studies in somewhat greater detail.

Finally, we restricted our analysis to those studies that included a placebo treatment. We believe that placebo treatments provide a more appropriate control group for assessing psychotherapeutic outcome than the more usual wait-list controls. Wait-list controls may lead to outcomes that are more negative than would have occurred merely through the passage of time. Individuals who seek therapeutic services and who are placed in a wait-list control group may be disappointed. In addition, such individuals may be experiencing an unintended reverse placebo effect. In being told they are being placed on a wait list, they are in effect told that they should not expect to improve since no therapeutic intervention will be provided for them. Since there is no appropriate control for a wait-list control group, there is no way of testing this notion. Whether wait-list controls are appropriate or not, it is relevant to inquire whether the benefits of psychotherapy exceed changes attributable to placebo expectations. Smith et al. (1980) deal with this issue only in passing. They indicate that the majority of placebo-controlled studies are in the behavior-therapy rather than psychotherapy outcome literature. They assert that psychological treatments are approximately twice as effective as placebo treatments, and accordingly they expect that a comparison of psychotherapy against placebo would yield an effect size of approximately .42 standard deviations. We will focus on this comparison in our analysis.

We had several reasons for focusing on the comparison of psychotherapy treatments and placebo treatments. First, as a general principle, the comparison of treatment with some type of placebo control is a standard research design. The comparison is justified, since there is abundant evidence that individuals who believe they are receiving a treatment will improve as a result of the belief they are in treatment, even if there is no other theoretical reason for the treatment to be efficacious (see Shapiro & Morris 1978).

Second, we were aware of a study by Brill, Koegler, Epstein & Forgy (1964) which provided evidence that the psychotherapy effect was equivalent to the placebo effect. Brill et al. (1964) randomly assigned psychiatric outpatients to one of several groups: a psychotherapy group that received 20 sessions of psychoanalytically oriented psychotherapy administered by psychiatric residents; a wait-list control group; a pill-placebo group that received chemically inert pills combined with occasional brief visits to psychiatrists (primarily to check on their response to medication, which was administered in a double blind design); and groups that received psychoactive drugs. Several outcome measures were used to assess therapeutic effects including the MMPI (Minnesota Multiphasic Personality Inventory), therapist and patient ratings, independent reports by a social worker, and rating from a relative, spouse, or friend. Brill et al. report that for all measures the patients who received treatment were improved relative to the patients who were assigned to the wait-list control group. However there were no significant differences among the various forms of treatment, including the placebo treatment. Brill et al. (1964) examine the effectiveness of psychoanalytically oriented psychotherapy of somewhat longer duration than is characteristic of many outcome studies, have a sample size exceeding that which is typical in outcome research (30 patients in each of several conditions), and use real patients. They provide evidence for the proposition that the effects of psychotherapy are equivalent to the effects of a relatively minimal placebo, which is essentially equivalent to knowledge that one is in treatment.

There are several limitations to the Brill et al. (1964) study. There was a high dropout rate; although the range of dependent variables used to assess outcomes was moderately varied, there were no behavioral measures used; and the therapy was administered by relatively inexperienced therapists. We wanted to see whether the corpus of about 500 studies included in the Smith et al. (1980) reviews would yield data that contradicted or supported the results obtained by Brill et al. (1964).

Third, an analysis of the differences between psychotherapy and placebo treatments may have implications for the provision of psychological treatment. If, for example, psychotherapy is no more effective than pill placebos, it may be cheaper and simpler to provide patients with pill placebos administered by general practitioners rather than long and relatively expensive treatment by trained psychotherapists. Our example should not be construed as advocacy of any form of treatment. Rather, we use the example as an illustration of the proposition that the results of an analysis of outcome research comparing psychotherapy to placebo treatments may have consequences for the design of treatment programs.

Fourth, there are results in the literature which are at least suggestive of the possibility that the outcomes of psychotherapy may, in part, be attributable to the influence of placebos. These include the following:

A. Duration of treatment is unrelated to the magnitude of therapeutic effect, according to Smith et al. (1980). If quite brief treatment and extended treatment produce outcomes of similar magnitude, one is led to elieve that the activities engaged in by the therapist are relevant to the outcomes of treatment.

B. There is a body of research which suggests that xperience and training in psychotherapy are unrelated o the magnitude of the psychotherapeutic effect (see Durlak 1979). Presumably, professional training would ead a therapist to engage in therapeutically relevant ctivities in a more accomplished manner. If the competence acquired by the therapist is unrelated to therapeutic outcome then it is possible that the activities of the therapist are not the cause of the changes in the patient.

C. Strupp (1973) and Bergin and Lambert (1978), among others, have suggested that some of the variance in outcome of psychotherapy is attributable to the characteristics of the patient. Patients who are articulate and intelligent and inclined to interpret their problems as being of psychological origin are said to have a higher probability of favorable outcome than patients without these characteristics. If there are patient characteristics that can predict the outcomes of psychotherapy, it is at least possible that these effects occur autonomously. That is, certain patients have the ability to change either as a result of their personality characteristics or the environmental circumstances in which they find themselves, or both, and a sufficient condition for the change is the knowledge that one is receiving some form of therapy. Thus it is possible that the activities of the therapist are irrelevant to the actual changes that occur.

D. Strupp (1977) and Bergin and Lambert (1978) have suggested that in a small minority of patients psychotherapy may produce adverse outcomes. While the general effect of placebo treatment is beneficial, placebo effects have also been found on occasion to produce reverse effects. Duncan and Laird (1980), for example, have suggested that individuals who are self-attentive are more likely to experience reverse placebo effects. Such individuals may become aware of the fact that a placebo has not dramatically altered their condition even though they were told it would be beneficial, and as a result they infer that their problems are more severe than they had thought. Thus placebo effects could, in principle, account for a possible deterioration effect in a minority of patients as a result of psychotherapy.

We do not mean to imply that we accept any of these conclusions about the results of outcome research on psychotherapy. We merely wish to indicate that a number of the conclusions which responsible reviewers have drawn from their examination of outcome studies are at least compatible with the assertion that part or all of the psychotherapy effect is attributable to the effects of placebos.

We have used the term "placebo" without an explicit definition. We consider a treatment a placebo treatment if the patient is led to believe that the treatment is efficacious and the treatment does not contain any other therapeutic components. Such a treatment defines an ideal case of a placebo. An operational procedure that comes close to meeting this idealized definition is the provision of a chemically inert pill to a patient combined with the assertion by a professional therapist that the pill will be an effective treatment. There are several variables that can, at least on speculative grounds, influence the effectiveness of this type of treatment. The patient must believe the assertion made by the therapist, and if the therapist harbors doubt about the effectiveness of chemically inert medications (or, in the case of a double blind study, of psychoactive drugs) for the treatment of psychological problems, the therapist may in subtle ways communicate these doubts to the patient and the effectiveness of the placebo may be mitigated. Moreover, the beliefs of the patient with respect to the potential efficacy of pill medications for the treatment of psychological problems may influence the effectiveness of such placebo treatments. Finally, in an actual experimental situation pill placebos may be accompanied by several other quasitherapeutic elements. For example, in the Brill et al. (1964) study, patients who received drug treatments including placebo were seen by resident psychiatrists for 15 minutes or less weekly, biweekly, or monthly. The sessions were brief in order to decrease the probability of psychotherapeutically relevant exchanges, and the residents were instructed to focus on the drug reactions of the patients. Despite these strictures, there is no way of knowing the extent to which these conditions were adhered to in a large-scale study with several therapists. It is conceivable, as Brill and his colleagues note, that some brief psychotherapeutically relevant interchanges may have occurred on occasion.

The problem of the comparison of psychotherapy with placebo treatments is complicated by the fact that many placebo treatments include a variety of elements in addition to an attempt to manipulate the belief that one is receiving an efficacious treatment. Some studies have used placebo treatments that include discussion groups in which a therapist explicitly attempts to steer the groups' conversation toward topics that are assumed to be irrelevant to the psychological problems which led the patients to be selected for psychotherapy. Such a placebo treatment attempts to control for such features of psychotherapy as duration of treatment, meeting with fellow-patients, and having an opportunity to engage in conversation in a quasitherapeutic setting. Presumably the treatment is construed as a placebo in the belief that discussions that do not focus on specific problems are not therapeutically efficacious. But this belief may be no more than an act of faith. It may well be that the essential features of psychotherapy which account for its therapeutic effectiveness are well reproduced by this type of placebo treatment. Grünbaum (1981) has stressed the importance of theoretical assertions as a basis for ascertaining the placebogenic status of a particular form of treatment. However, since our understanding of the nature of the processes that induce change is imperfect (if not downright lacking), our attempts to distinguish between placebo treatments and treatments that reproduce several features of psychotherapy may involve imprecise theoretical and empirical distinctions. Although we prefer minimal placebo treatments we are restricted to the available research literature. We will accordingly consider as a placebo treatment any procedure so described by an investigator where we are informed or able to infer that the possibility of therapeutic benefits is conveyed to the patient. In addition, we require either implicit or explicit evidence that the authors have a theoretical rationale for the assertion that the placebo treatment omits features of psychotherapy which are essential for therapeutic effectiveness.

While the reader may feel that the variability of

placebo treatments renders a comparison between placebo and psychotherapeutic treatments vexed, it should be noted that there may be considerable variability among wait-list control treatments. Duration of wait-list assignment may be a critical variable. The extent to which the assignment to a wait-list control is accompanied by preliminary assessment procedures, the kinds of information conveyed to the patient about the potential harm involved in the wait period, and the availability of psychotherapeutic services during the wait period in the event of an emergency may have a considerable influence on the changes that may occur among patients during their time on the wait list. For example, Sloan, Staples, Cristol, Yorkston, and Whipple (1975) explain their failure to find therapeutic improvement relative to their wait-list control group on follow-up as follows: The psychological assessment that preceded assignment to the wait list group, combined with the information conveyed by the researchers that wait-listed patients could receive therapeutic treatment in an emergency were sufficient to create therapeutic benefits in the wait-list control subjects that eventually matched the alleged benefits of psychotherapy and behavior therapy. Thus wait-list control conditions may vary considerably, and the comparison of such controls with psychotherapeutic treatments may involve the comparison of two forms of treatment, each variable across different investigations. Thus the comparison between psychotherapy and wait-list control treatments may raise as many theoretical problems as the comparison between psychotherapy and placebo treatments.

Method

We were able to locate and read in either original or abstract form 513 of the 520 studies included in the psychotherapy and drug meta-analyses included in Smith et al. (1980). Of the 513, we selected for analysis only the small subset that included both a psychotherapy treatment and a placebo treatment. The distinction between psychotherapy and behavior therapy was not problematic for the great majority of studies analyzed (for a more comprehensive treatment of this issue see Murdock 1982; Prioleau 1982). We classified as psychotherapy a number of the studies using such techniques as rational emotive therapy and even social learning therapy described in rather traditional behavioristic language, whenever we were able to infer from the description of the therapist's activities that he was required to engage in a process of exploration and clarification of the emotional experiences of the patient. In addition to classifying a study as containing a psychotherapy treatment, we looked for evidence that there was an attempt to foster and develop an emotional relationship between the therapist and the patient.

We judged that 40 of the 513 studies contained both a psychotherapy and a placebo treatment. From these 40 we discarded 8, either on the grounds that they were so seriously flawed as to render any comparison unjustified or because even with a number of ad hoc assumptions it was not possible to compute measures of effect size.

We computed a measure of effect size for each of the dependent variables included in the remaining 32 stud-

ies. Effect size was defined as the difference between the psychotherapy group mean and the placebo group mean divided by the pooled standard deviation for psychotherapy and placebo groups. If pretreatment scores existed for a measure, we obtained the difference between the pre- and posttreatment score, subtracted the comparable difference score for placebo treatment groups, and divided the difference between the change scores by the pooled standard deviation of the change scores. When such standard deviations were not available or could not be calculated or inferred from the statistics presented, we assumed that the correlation between pre- and posttreatment scores was .5, and we adjusted the posttreatment standard deviation to obtain an estimate of the standard deviation of the change scores. If a variable was presented in terms of nominal scale measurement (e.g., percentage of improvement), we dummy coded the variables, calculated r, and converted r into a measure expressed in terms of standard deviation units. If standard deviations were not reported, we attempted to derive them from available statistics. Where the author indicated that there were no differences between therapy and placebo treatments and data were not presented, we assumed that the effect size was zero. (For a general discussion of obtaining measures of effect size, see Cohen 1969; and for a discussion of inferring effect size measures from limited data presentations, see Smith et al. 1980.) We adjusted our effect size indices such that positive scores indicated that the psychotherapy group did better on a particular measure than the placebo group. We obtained a mean effect size for each study by taking the mean of the separate effect sizes.

We have departed from the procedures used by Smith et al. (1980) in the calculation of effect sizes in three respects. First, the numerator of the fraction we use to define effect size is defined as the difference between psychotherapy and placebo treatments rather than as the difference between psychotherapy and a control group. Second, Smith et al. (1980) use as a denominator of the fraction the standard deviation of the control group, whereas we use a pooled standard deviation. The use of the standard deviation of the control group yields the advantage of permitting one to define mean differences between two or more therapy treatments in a single study against a common base line. We chose to use a pooled standard deviation because we found that for a majority of studies included here, separate standard deviations were not available and accordingly we were forced to estimate standard deviations from such statistics as t and F. Such a procedure permits one to obtain only a pooled standard deviation rather than a separate estimate for the control and treatment group. Since we were forced to use pooled estimates for some of our calculations, it seemed to us to be more consistent to use pooled estimates for all our calculations. Smith et al. (1980) report that they found no difference in variability of control group and therapy outcomes. If a comparable result holds for the studies we examined, the decision to use pooled estimates should not appreciably influence our estimates of effect size, although it might influence an estimate in a particular set of data. Third, for the subset of studies in which data on the standard deviation of change scores were not provided, we arbitrarily assumed that the correlation between pretest and posttest scores was .5. Smith et al.

980) used a variable value to estimate corrections de-
nding on the nature of the outcome variables used and
.e duration of time intervening between pretest and
osttest. We felt that for many of the measures used we
ere not in a position to make an informed guess about
.e value of the test–retest correlation. The value of .5
as at the upper end of the range of correlations used by
mith et al. (1980). It seemed to us to be somewhat less
rbitrary to use a standard value rather than a variable
ne. In any case, this arbitrary correction was used in
wer than one-third of our calculations and is probably
ot a major source of influence in the magnitude of effect
izes.

Results

Table 1 presents a description of the 32 studies included
n our analysis and includes the calculations of mean effect
izes for each. The mean values are corrected for the
sampling bias of effect sizes (see Hedges 1981). The
corrected distribution of mean effect sizes is skewed to
the right. The modal category of a grouped frequency
distribution with an interval of .20 occurs at an effect size
value of .00. The median effect size is .15 and the mean
is .42. The distribution includes one extreme value. This
study, in which virtually all of the children given psychotherapy and none of the children in the placebo treatment
are reported as having improved, has an effect size 1.54
standard deviations higher than any other.

It is apparent that there is considerable diversity in
magnitude of outcome in these studies. We attempted to
define characteristics that might be related to the measure of effect size. We analyzed the following variables:
(1) duration of treatment, (2) sample size, (3) the use of
real patients as opposed to subjects solicited by the
investigators, and (4) the nature of the outcome measure
used.

Duration of therapy was correlated −.24 (n.s.) with
effect size. Thus the nonsignificant trend is for the benefits of therapy relative to placebo to decrease as the
duration of treatment increases. The correlation between
sample size and effect size was −.21 (n.s.). Sample size
was inversely related to therapeutic effects. The mean
effect size for the eight studies using patients was .35
(median = .08) and the mean effect size for the studies
using solicited subjects was .44 (median = .16). A t test
comparing these means yields a value of .36 (n.s.).

We assigned each dependent variable to one of six
categories (see Table 1). We obtained a mean effect size
for the category of undisguised self-report measures and a
mean effect size measure for all other measures used in
each study. We compared these means in a subset of 19
studies, which permitted us to obtain within the same
study a mean effect size for one or more outcomes of
undisguised self-reports and one or more measures of any
other type. The mean of the means for undisguised self-
reports was .43 and the mean of the means for all other
measures was .17. A matched group t test had a value of
1.58 (n.s.).

Six of the studies included in Table 1 reported follow-
up data. We calculated that there were minimal changes
during follow-up in mean effect sizes for three of these
studies: Schwartz and Dubitzky (1967), Gillan and Rach-

man (1974), and DiLoreto (1971). Two showed declines
of .23 and .61 in mean effect size (Paul 1964 and Hedquist & Weinhold 1970, respectively), and one (Jarmon
1972) showed a gain in effect size of .22. These data
indicate that for this small subset of studies there is no
tendency for the benefits of psychotherapy relative to
placebo to increase during a follow-up period.

Discussion

Our estimate of a mean effect size of .42 is exactly in
agreement with the magnitude of the psychotherapy
effect size relative to placebo treatments estimated by
Smith et al. (1980). Quite apart from the central tendency
of effect size in these studies, the trends in the characteristics of studies that are related to measures of effect
size, albeit weakly, do not support an intuitive model,
which suggests that the effects of therapy are more
powerful than the effects of placebo treatments. Assume
that the effects of psychotherapy are strong and that the
effects of placebo are weak and emphemeral. One might
argue on intuitive grounds that placebo effects would
decline more than therapy through time and hence would
be less likely to be equivalent to therapy where outcomes
are assessed after long durations of therapy and at follow-
up investigation. Moreover, one might expect ephemeral
and perhaps misguided beliefs in the benefits of placebo
to be most strongly present for undisguised self-report
measures. In addition, one would expect real patients to
be more likely to benefit from the effects of a powerful
treatment than solicited subjects, on the assumption that
the former group are more disturbed than the latter. Our
data are consistent in their bearing on this set of crude
intuitions – in all respects our findings contradict these
expectations. Our data suggest that as we examine these
studies in a more critical manner and examine their
implications for the benefits of psychotherapy, we are led
to assume that the benefits of therapy relative to placebo
treatments become vanishingly small.

It is possible to supplement the quantitative analysis of
these studies by a somewhat more traditional analysis of
their descriptive properties. And given the diversity of
measures, therapies, and subjects included in these investigations, there is some question whether attempts to
relate quantitative indices of effect size to other variables
is entirely legitimate. After examining this set of studies
we have concluded that the most informative classification is derived from an analysis of the types of patients
included. It is possible to organize these studies into four
subclasses as defined by the type of patient receiving
therapy. The first sub-class, which we consider the most
crucial for an evaluation of psychotherapy outcome research, is defined as studies of outpatients, in which the
patient population seeks psychological services and is not
institutionalized. The three studies included in this group
all deal with patients who may be described as neurotics.
In addition to the Brill et al. (1964) study, which we have
already described in the introduction and which we
calculate to have an effect size of .07, Lorr, McNair,
and Weinstein (1963) reported a similar investigation
using a pill placebo treatment for psychiatric outpatients.
The duration of treatment was brief (four sessions), and
only two measures were used to assess outcome (global

Table 1. *Description of design, placebo, dependent measures, and effect sizes of studies in the analysis*

Author and year	Type of therapy	Subjects	N[a]	Contact hours	Therapists	Placebo description	Dependent measures[b]	Estimated effect sizes[c]	Remarks
Winkler et al. (1965)	Rogerian	Underachieving elementary school students	60	7	M.A. level	Listened to records and stories	(2) CA test of personality (6) GPA	−.55 .11 −.22	
Bruyere (1975)	Group client-centered	Disruptive junior high school students	48	16	School counselors	Group problem solving	(1) Self-concept (5) Conduct GPA Behavior scale Ratings of disruptive classroom behavior	−.64 −.09 .00 + −.18	Data for effect size computation n/a for last measure
Schwartz and Dubitzky (1967)	Group therapy	Moderate smokers	72	12	Psychologists	Pill placebo	(6) Cessation of smoking	−.13	
Orlov (1972)	Group Rogerian	Maladjusted middle school students	40	15	Psychologists	Reading and discussion Books	(5) Sociometric test Rating scale Classroom behavior Improvement rating by teacher (6) GPA	.00 .00 .00 −.30 −.21 −.10	
Bruce (1971)	Group client-centered	Vocational rehabilitation clients	20	12	Psychology graduate student	Social group functions	(1) Index of adjustment (5) Job performance evaluation	.89 −1.06 −.09	
Gillan and Rachman (1974)	Group insight rational therapy	Multiphobic outpatients	24	15	Psychiatrists Psychologist	Muscle relaxation training; phobic hierarchy no relaxation training	(1) Anxiety scale (2) EPI (4) Therapist rating phobia & depression (5) Rating phobia & depression; external rater (6) Behavioral avoidance test Skin conductance	−.46 .00 .19 −.24 .00 .00 −.09(−.07)	
Matthews (1972)	Group reality therapy	Maladjusted elementary school children	221	15	Elementary school teachers	Language arts classes	(2) CPI (5) Problem behavior rating (6) Reading	−.11 .18 −.18 −.04	
Jarmon (1972)	Group rational emotive therapy	Speech-anxious college students	41	3	Psychology graduate students	Group discussion of neutral topics; reading RET book	(1) Fear survey schedule Confidence as a speaker Social anxiety Fear of evaluation Irrational ideas Fear rating (5) Speech anxiety rating Speech disruptions	−.31 −.16 .34 .07 −.18 .25 −.24 −.23 −.01	
Shapiro and Knapp (1971)	Group ego therapy	High-anxious college students	42	14	No information	Group discussion of general topics	(1) Personal integration Response bias Anxiety level	.00 .00 .00 .00	
Coche and Douglas (1977)	Group problem-solving training	Adult psychiatric inpatients	46	8	No information	Group play reading	(1) Adjective checklist (2) Minimult Means-ends problem-solving	.26 .01 −.11 .05	
Desrats (1975)	Group Rogerian	Institutionalized adolescent orphans	39	25	Counselors with "limited counseling experience"	Viewed films and study lessons	(1) Self-esteem (2) CPI (5) Behavior rating (6) GPA Adjustment tally	.00 .00 .00 .28 .00 .06	
Brill et al. (1964)	Psychoanalytic	Adult outpatients	60	20+	Psychiatric residents	Pill placebo	(1) Patient rating (2) MMPI (4) Therapist rating Global evaluation	.05 −.12 .10 .00	S.D. estimate ⅙ of range

Table 1. *(cont.)*

Author and year	Type of therapy	Subjects	N[a]	Contact hours	Therapists	Placebo description	Dependent measures[b]	Estimated effect sizes[c]	Remarks
							(5) Relative rating	−.12	
							Social worker rating	.38	
								.07	
Herman (1972)	Humanistic counseling (group and individual)	High-anxious junior high school students with reading problems	40	4.5	Junior high school counselors	"Bull" session	(1) MAS	.74	
							(5) Anxiety rating	−.08	
							(6) Reading test	−.42	
								.08	
Lorr et al. (1963)	Individual therapy	Adult outpatients	50	4	Psychiatrists, psychologists, and social workers	Pill placebo	(1) Global improvement	.19	
							(3) Global improvement	.00	
								.10	
Rosentover (1974)	Group counseling	Underachieving high school students	63	7	Education graduate student	Heard speakers, viewed films, limited discussion	(2) Minnesota Counseling Inventory	.00	
							(6) GPA	.23	
								.12	
Warner (1969)	Group verbal and model reinforcement	Alienated junior high school students	102	4.5	Three high school counselors	Group discussion	(1) Alienation	.56	
							Anxiety	−.06	
							Self-concept	.11	
							(6) GPA	−.15	
								.12	
Paul (1964)	Individual insight therapy	College students with speech performance anxiety	30	5	Psychologists	Pill placebo and boring task	(1) Anxiety	.22	
							(3) Global rating	.40	
							(5) Anxiety	.69	
							(6) Pulse rate	−.03	
							Palmar sweat	−.37	
								.18(.17)	
West (1969)	Group client-centered	Disruptive elementary school children with learning difficulty	16	10	Psychology graduate students	Read, played with puzzles, or sat quietly under supervision of counselor. No verbal interchange	(1) Self-esteem	.29	
							(2) Draw-a-Person	−.01	
							Apperception Test	−.27	
							(5) Sociometric	.69	
							(6) WISC	.16	
								.17(.16)	
Rehm and Marston (1968)	Nonspecific group	High-anxious college students	16	2.5	Psychology graduate students	General group discussion	(1) Fear of opposite sex	1.13	
							Situation test	.50	
							Fear survey	−.07	
							Anxiety scale	−.54	
							Adjective list	.16	
							(5) Situation anxiety	.07	
								.21(.19)	
Paykel et al. (1975)	Individual supportive	Clinically depressed inpatients	34	36	Psychiatric social workers	Pill placebo	(1) Psychic and somatic complaints	.00	
							(4) Psychiatric rating	.00	
							Interview for depression	.00	
							Depression scale	.00	
							(3) Psychiatric evaluation	.79	
							(3) Relapse rate	.32	
							(5) Social adjustment	.78	
								.27(.26)	
Alper and Kranzler (1970)	Individual client-centered therapy	Disruptive elementary school children	18	10	Graduate students in counseling	Read and discuss stories	(2) Self social symbols	−.10	
							(5) "Out of seat" behavior	1.26	
							Sociometric test	−.12	
								+.34(.32)	
Trexler and Karst (1972)	Group rational emotive therapy	Speech-anxious college students	22	4	Psychology graduate student	Relaxation training	(1) Irrational beliefs test	1.37	
							Anxiety scale	1.03	
							Confidence as a speaker	1.10	
							(5) Behavior checklist	.41	
							Overall estimate of anxiety	.25	
							(6) Finger sweat print	.26	
								.39(.36)	

(continued)

Table 1. (cont.)

Author and year	Type of therapy	Subjects	N[a]	Contact hours	Therapists	Placebo description	Dependent measures[b]	Estimated effect sizes[c]	Remarks
Lester (1973)	Individual relationship counseling	High-anxious junior high school students	13	3	Graduate student in counseling	Guided discussion of current events	(1) Test anxiety Global self-report	.00 1.18 .59(.55)	
Coche and Flick (1975)	Group problem-solving training	Psychiatric inpatients	64	8	No information	Group play reading with discussion	(2) Means-ends problem-solving procedure	.69 .69	f
Hogan and Kirchner (1968)	Individual eclectic therapy	Snake-phobic college students	20	.75	No information	Bibliotherapy	(6) Ability to lift snake	.74 .74(.71)	
DiLoreto (1971)	Group client-centered and rational emotive therapy	High-anxious college students	60	9	Psychology graduate students	Group discussion over lunch focused on academic topics	(1) Interpersonal anxiety S-R inventory of anxiousness Trait anxiety Social desirability (5) Checklist of interpersonal anxiety	.37 .86 1.17 .50 1.25 .82	d
Grande (1975)	Group rational emotive therapy	High-anxious college students	34	4.5	Three graduate students and one undergraduate	Relaxation training via tape	(1) Interpersonal anxiety MAS Fear survey (5) Interpersonal anxiety Behavior rating	1.32 1.21 1.09 .50 .74 .97(.95)	
Meichenbaum et al. (1972)	Individual and group rational emotive therapy	High-anxious college students	24	8	Psychologists	Group discussion	(1) Checklist for anxiety Anxiety differential (5) Performance anxiety (6) Duration of silences Number of "ah" statements	1.34 .42 .57 2.00 1.02 .98(.95)	d
Hedquist and Weinhold (1970)	Group social learning	Anxious college students	30	6	Psychology graduate students	Group discussion	(1) Assertive behaviors	1.22 1.22(1.19)	
House (1970)	Group non-directive play therapy	Unpopular elementary school children	24	10	Education graduate student	Reading group	(1) Self-concept and motivation inventory (5) Sociometric test	2.50 .70 1.60(1.55)	
Roessler et al. (1977)	Group counseling	Physical rehabilitation clients	43	10	Rehabilitation counselor	Personal hygiene training	(1) Self-scale Facility outcome measure Goal attainment scale	.80 .84 3.40 1.68(1.65)	f
Platt (1970)	Group Adlerian	Disruptive elementary school children	24	5	No information	Listened to records and studied	(5) Rating by parents Rating by teachers	3.80 2.80 3.30(3.19)	Ratings were not "blind"

[a]Only the number of subjects in the psychotherapy and placebo treatments are included.   [b]The number in parentheses refers to type of dependent measure according to the following code: 1 = undisguised self-report; 2 = disguised self-report; 3 = global report by therapist; 4 = rating of independent behavior by therapist; 5 = rating of independent behavior by others; 6 = independent behavior.   [c]Numbers in parentheses indicate mean effect size corrected for sampling bias.   [d]Study used two types of psychotherapy and one placebo group. Information on number of subjects and effect size is pooled across both comparisons.   [e]Study used one psychotherapy group and two types of placebo. Information on number of subjects and effect size is pooled across both comparisons.   [f]Study used real patients.

ratings by therapists and patients). However, unlike in the Brill et al. (1964) study, the therapists were described as being experienced. We calculate the effect size of Lorr et al. (1963) to be .10. The last study in this group, Gillan and Rachman (1974), provides a significant amount of therapy to a small number of patients, all multiphobic.

Psychotherapy was administered by experienced therapists who are described as believing that psychotherapy is the treatment of choice for this condition. Two placebo treatments were used: relaxation training without an attempt to pair the relaxation response with the phobic stimulus and a placebo condition in which the phobic hierarchy was presented without relaxation training. Several outcome measures were used, including behavioral and psychophysiological measures. We calculate the effect size of this study to be negative, −.07.

An additional study reported by McLean and Hakstian (1979) was not included in our formal analysis since it was published too late to appear in the Smith et al. (1980) analysis. However, it is relatively well designed and does buttress the conclusions suggested by the three studies we review in the category of psychiatric outpatients. McLean and Hakstian report data for 37 clinically depressed outpatients who received 8–12 hours of insight-oriented psychotherapy from licensed psychologists and psychiatrists; one group of therapists had at least 2–4 years of experience and the other 5 years or more. Psychotherapy was the treatment of choice for these professionals. The experience of the therapist was unrelated to outcome and accordingly this variable was dropped from the analysis. Outcome was assessed by the use of 10 self-report measures derived from analyses of questionnaire data. A number of outcome measures were adjusted for relevant covariates. The placebo treatment was administered to 38 randomly assigned patients who received 10 hours of muscle relaxation therapy. Subjects were informed that the muscle relaxation treatment was therapeutically relevant, although McLean and Hakstian assert that they consider the variable as a placebo since there is no compelling rationale for the view that treatment of depression by muscle relaxation is therapeutically efficacious. At the end of therapy, in a comparison of the patients assigned to the psychotherapy and the placebo treatment group there was no appreciable difference on any outcome measure, although a group of subjects randomly assigned to a behavior therapy treatment condition were discernibly improved relative to the relaxation therapy patients. The relaxation therapy patients had slightly better outcomes than the psychotherapy patients. We calculate the effect size to be negative (−.11). Three months after the termination of psychotherapy there was again no discernible difference in outcome. The effect size was negative (−.08).

In a number of ways, McLean and Hakstian's is a well-designed study. It uses well-trained psychotherapists with a commitment to the virtues of psychotherapy; it includes a well-defined patient group and a follow-up. It has perhaps two limitations. There is exclusive reliance on questionnaire and self-report data (although arguably the instruments used are well standardized and have some validity for the particular target population). And it is conceivable that the placebo treatment might include a number of complex aspects (e.g., following instructions, etc.) that extend beyond the pure case of an expectancy manipulation. However, if considered in conjunction with the results of the three other studies of outpatients, this study appears to buttress the view that psychotherapy does not lead to outcomes that are more favorable than those attained by placebo treatment for outpatients.

A second subset of studies deals with institutionalized patients. There are four in this group. Desrats (1975) deals with institutionalized adolescents given counseling by relatively untrained counselors and has an effect size of .06. Paykel, DiMascio, Haskell, and Prusoff (1975) deal with clinically depressed inpatients and use a pill placebo treatment. We calculate an effect size of .26 for

this study. In this group, only Coche and Flick (1975) report a substantial positive effect size. It is a study of outcome among psychiatric inpatients who are given group problem-solving training. For a single measure of group problem solving, which may or may not be contaminated by the therapeutic procedures followed, we calculate an effect size of .69. However, in a study designed in part to be a replication of Coche and Flick's (1975) work, Coche and Douglas (1977) report a failure to replicate their earlier findings. For a somewhat more extended set of outcome measures used in this study, we calculate an effect size of .05. Thus the results of the only study using psychiatric inpatients with a substantial positive effect size is nonreplicable.

The third class of studies deals with students in school. One of these, Bruyere (1975), deals with students attending a special school for disruptive junior high school pupils. Bruyere's study has a negative effect size. School counseling did not lead to positive outcomes on a variety of measures. There are 21 additional studies in this group, all dealing with therapy provided to solicited subjects: groups of students who are nominated or selected for therapy because they have an extreme score on some measure. Clearly, such subjects are not representative of the patients who seek therapeutic services. Six of these studies have relatively positive effect sizes ranging from .74 to 3.19. This subset, with relatively large positive effect sizes, may be characterized collectively (with exceptions that can be noted by an examination of Table 1) as studies in which relatively brief therapy is provided to relatively small groups of subjects. Three of the six involve rational emotive therapy and one involves group social learning therapy. Therefore, these studies deal with quasibehavioristic forms of treatment.

Our last group of studies is somewhat heterogeneous, consisting of those that do not fit into the preceding three groups. One study in this group, Schwartz and Dubitzky (1967), which has a negative effect size, deals with group therapy as a treatment for smokers who wish to stop smoking. Another with a negative effect size involves vocational rehabilitation clients. The final study in this group, Roessler, Cook, and Lillard (1977), is of the effectiveness of group counseling for physical rehabilitation clients. The effect size is 1.65 and it is the study we calculate to have the largest effect size among those that do not deal with solicited subjects. The outcome measures consist solely of undisguised self-reports, and the authors note that they do not know whether the optimism of their clients will be reflected in their actual behavior.

Concluding Speculations

One can distinguish between two propositions: (1) In the research literature surveyed, psychotherapy has been found to produce changes in real patients that are equivalent to those produced by placebo treatments. (2) In general, psychotherapy produces changes in patients that are equivalent to those produced by placebo treatments. Proposition 1 is limited in its range of application to the studies we review and does not attempt to imply anything about what is true of psychotherapy in general. Yet, clearly, the goal of outcome research in psychotherapy is to discover what is true about psychotherapy and not to discover what is true about a particular body of research, which may be flawed. Accordingly, in what follows we shall speculate about the possible truth of proposition 2. Any psychotherapy outcome study has as its variables, therapists, patients, types of therapy, and measures of outcomes. Let us consider the potential limitations of the studies we have reviewed from the perspective of the several variables that jointly define an outcome study.

Some therapists may be able to produce beneficial effects through treatment. For a variety of reasons we are not sanguine about the possibility that variations among therapists is a major or important source of variance in outcome research. If the true size of the psychotherapy effect relative to placebo treatment is .0 then any allocation of main effect variance to individual differences among therapists would imply that some therapists consistently make their patients worse. The existence of individual differences among therapists as a major source of variance in outcome for diverse patients is of little practical relevance unless some way can be found of communicating to potential patients information about the competence of therapists. Since competence to produce changes among patients appears to be unrelated to professional training, it is hard to see how it could be practically determined. In addition, it is likely that some (and perhaps a major part) of the variance in outcome is not associated with a consistent effect of therapists but is best described as interaction variance in which certain therapists may have a higher likelihood of success with some types of patients. Finally, it should be noted that the hypothesis of individual differences in therapists' ability consistently to produce beneficial changes in their patients is testable in any study in which outcomes are obtained for several therapists each treating several patients. With such a design one could obtain a measure of the consistency of therapeutic outcome as a function of individual differences among therapists.

Certain types of therapy may have effect sizes that exceed those of placebo treatments. Clearly, the 32 studies we reviewed do not contain an exhaustive range of therapies. For example, rational emotive therapy appears to produce positive effect sizes in some of the work we review. However, none of the data we examined involved this type of therapy with true patients: nor was family therapy examined. It could be that some forms of therapy are more effective than placebo treatments and, similarly, there may exist certain types of patients who consistently benefit from psychotherapy. Obviously, we would be rash to deny such a possibility. However, it should be noted that such reviewers as Bergin and Lambert (1978) and Smith et al. (1980) have suggested that differences in outcome among types of therapy are minimal.

The weakest aspect of outcome research involves the measures used to assess change. It is possible that psychoterapy produces beneficial changes which exceed those attributable to minimal placebo treatments, but that the available outcome measures are too crude to detect such differences. Perhaps the major respect in which outcome research could be improved would be through the use of a wider range of dependent variables with more power to detect (possibly subtle) differences. None of the studies we examined used individually tailored measures of out-

come in which one specifies at the start of treatment the kinds of changes that would indicate therapeutic progress for each patient. While it is certainly true that researchers could use a more extended and imaginative set of outcome measures than are characteristically used, there is no guarantee that such measures would increase the likelihood of demonstrating positive effects of psychotherapy. Recall that in the studies we examined the largest effects of psychotherapy relative to placebo were obtained for measures we would consider as biased and theoretically primitive: undisguised self-reports. One possible explanation of this result is that such measures are construed in part as a representation of the believability of the placebogenic component of therapy. If some patients prefer psychotherapy to, say, relaxation training as a method of treatment, then they may come to believe psychotherapy to be the more powerful treatment; they would accordingly report greater benefits from psychotherapy than from relaxation treatment. Undisguised self-report measures suggesting that psychotherapy is more beneficial than placebo may be attributable to psychotherapy's being a more believable placebo treatment than most actual placebo treatments. It would be useful to include a measure of the expectations for therapeutic improvement at the start of therapy for subjects assigned to various placebo and therapy treatments. Such a measure might relate to outcome measures.

Apart from the occasional use of psychophysiological measures, the studies we have reviewed have rarely relied on laboratory procedures to define outcomes. Although laboratory measures might yield positive results, there could be questions as to their ecological validity and their relation to significant actions and judgments in the everyday life of the patient.

We recognize that our speculations about the potential for demonstrating significant effects of psychotherapy relative to placebos are just that – speculations. On the basis of the available data we see no reason to believe that subsequent research using better research procedures and investigating other types of therapy administered to other types of patients will yield clear-cut indications that psychotherapy is more beneficial than placebo treatment. Thirty years after Eysenck (1952) first raised the issue of the effectiveness of psychotherapy, twenty-eight years after Meehl (1955) called for the use of placebo controls in psychotherapy, eighteen years after Brill et al. (1964) demonstrated in a reasonably well-done study that the psychotherapy effect may be equivalent to the placebo effect, and after about 500 outcome studies have been reviewed – we are still not aware of a single convincing demonstration that the benefits of psychotherapy exceed those of placebos for real patients. Such a study would have to show that psychotherapy administered to real patients yields improvements relative to placebo on a variety of measures and that these improvements endure over time. We believe that securing such data should be viewed as an urgent task by those who practice or advocate the use of psychotherapy. Given the absence of convincing contradictory data, and considering the partial support (at least) that the available research literature provides, we regard it as likely that the benefits of psychotherapy do not exceed those of placebo in real patients. That is, our conclusion may not only be valid when its range of application is restricted to a limited set of studies but may also be true of psychotherapy in general.

References

Alper, T. B. & Kranzler, G. D. (1970) A comparison of the effectiveness of behavioral and client-centered approaches for the behavior problems of elementary school children. *Elementary School Guidance and Counseling* 5:35–43. [taLP]

Andrews, G., Guitar, B. & Howie, P. (1980) Meta-analysis of the effects of stuttering treatment. *Journal of Speech and Hearing Disorders* 45:287–307. [GA]

Andrews, G. & Harvey, R. (1981a) Does psychotherapy benefit neurotic patients? A reanalysis of the Smith, Glass, and Miller data. *Archives of General Psychiatry* 38:1203–8. [GA, NBr, RPG]
   (1981b) Regression to the mean in pretreatment measures of stuttering severity. *Journal of Speech and Hearing Disorders* 46:204–7. [GA]

Andrews, G., MacMahon, S. W., Austin, A. & Byrne, D. B. (1982) Hypertension: A comparison of drug and nondrug treatments. *British Medical Journal* 284:1523–26. [GA]

Baer, D. M. & Stolz, S. B. (1978) A description of the Erhard seminars training (est) in the terms of behavior analysis. *Behaviorism* 6:45–70. [JDF]

Bandura, A. (1977) Self-efficacy: Toward a unifying theory of behavioral change. *Psychological Review* 84:191–215. [EE]
   (1978) The self system in reciprocal determinism. *American Psychologist* 33:344–58. [EE]

Barber, T. X. (1969) *Hypnosis: A scientific approach.* Van Nostrand-Reinhold. [JMF]

Barber, T. X., Spanos, N. P. & Chaves, J. F. (1974) *Hypnotism: Imagination and human potentialities.* Pergamon. [JMF]

Bergin, A. E. & Lambert, M. J. (1978) The evaluation of therapeutic outcomes. In: *Handbook of psychotherapy and behavior change: An empirical analysis,* ed. S. L. Garfield & A. E. Bergin, pp. 139–89. Wiley. [taLP, TLR]

Bootzin, R. R. & Lick, J. R. (1979) Expectancies in therapy research: Interpretive artifact or mediating mechanism? *Journal of Consulting and Clinical Psychology* 47:852–55. [DSC]

Brill, N. Q., Koegler, R. R., Epstein, L. J. & Forgy, E. W. (1964) Controlled study of psychiatric outpatient treatment. *Archives of General Psychiatry* 10:581–95. [GA, RPG, tarLP]

Brody, N. (1983) *Human motivation: Commentary on goal-directed action.* New York: Academic Press. [rNB]

Bruce, J. (1971) The effects of group counseling on selected vocational rehabilitation clients. Ph.D. dissertation, Florida State University. [taLP]

Bruyere, D. H. (1975) The effects of client centered and behavioral group counseling on classroom behavior and self concept of junior high school students who exhibited disruptive classroom behavior. Ph.D. dissertation, University of Oregon. [DSC, taLP]

Catanese, R. A., Rosenthal, T. L. & Kelley, J. E. (1978) Strange bedfellows: Reward, punishment, and impersonal distraction strategies in treating dysphoria. *Cognitive Therapy and Research* 3:229–305. [TLR]

Cattell, R. B. & Kline, P. (1977) *The scientific analysis of personality and motivation.* Academic Press. [PK]

Chertok, L. N. & Fontaine, M. (1963) Psychosomatics in Veterinary Medicine. *Journal of Psychosomatic Research* 7:229–35. [TAS]

Coche, E. & Douglas, A. A. (1977) Therapeutic effects of problem-solving training and play-reading groups. *Journal of Clinical Psychology* 33:820–27. [GVG, taLP]

Coche, E. & Flick, A. (1975) Problem-solving training groups for hospitalized patients. *Journal of Psychology* 91:19–29. [GVG, taLP]

Cohen, J. (1969) *Statistical power analysis for the behavioral sciences.* Academic Press. [taLP]

Comas-Díaz, L. (1981) Effects of cognitive and behavioral group treatment on the depressive symptomatology of Puerto Rican women. *Journal of Consulting and Clinical Psychology* 49:627–32. [GVG, taLP]

Conley, J. J. (1982) Longitudinal consistency of adult personality: Neuroticism and social introversion-extroversion over forty-five years. Unpublished manuscript, Wesleyan University, Department of Psychology. [rNB]

Cook, T. D. & Leviton, L. C. (1980) Reviewing the literature: A comparison of traditional methods with meta-analysis. *Journal of Personality* 48:449–72. [DAS]

Cordray, D. S. & Orwin, R. G. (1983) Facilitating the quality of research: Interconnections among primary research, secondary analysis and quantitative synthesis. In: *Evaluation studies review annual,* ed. R. Light. Sage Publications (in press). [DSC]

Desrats, R. G. (1975) The effects of developmental and modeling group counseling on adolescents in childcare institutions. Ph.D. dissertation, Lehigh University. [taLP]

DiLoreto, A. O. (1971) *Comparative psychology.* Aldine-Atherton. [JDF, taLP, DAS]

Dohrenwend, B. P., Oksenberg, L., Shrout, P. E., Dohrenwend, B. S. & Cook, D. (1982) What brief psychiatric screening scales measure. In: *Proceedings of the Third Biennial Conference on Health Survey Research Methods, May, 1979,* ed. S. Sudman. National Center for Health Services Statistics, in press. [JDF]

Duncan, J. W. & Laird, J. D. (1980) Positive and reverse placebo effects as a function of differences in cues used in self-perception. *Journal of Personality and Social Psychology* 39:1024–36. [taLP]

Durlac, J. A. (1979) Comparative effectiveness of paraprofessional and professional helpers. *Psychological Bulletin* 86:80–92. [tarLP]

Eysenck, H. J. (1952) The effects of psychotherapy: An evaluation. *Journal of Consulting Psychology* 16:319–24. [HJE, taLP]
   (1966) *The effects of psychotherapy.* International Science Press. [taLP, DAS]
   (1978) An exercise in mega-silliness. *American Psychologist* 33:517. [taLP]
   (in press a) Meta-analysis: An abuse of research integration. *Journal of Special Education.* [HJE]
   (in press b) Special review: The benefits of psychotherapy. A battlefield revisited. *Behaviour Research and Therapy.* [rNB, HJE]

Fish, J. M. (1973) *Placebo therapy.* Jossey-Bass. [JMF]

Fisher, S. & Greenberg, R. P. (1977) *The scientific credibility of Freud's theories and therapy.* Basic Books. [RPG]

Foster, G. (1971) *Enquiry into the practice and effects of scientology.* H.M.S.O. [MS]

Frank, J. D. (1973) *Persuasion and healing: A comparative study of psychotherapy.* Rev. ed. Johns Hopkins Press. [JMF]
   (1974) Therapeutic components of psychotherapy. *Journal of Nervous and Mental Disease* 159:325–42. [MNE]
   (1978) Expectation and therapeutic outcome – the placebo effect and the role induction interview. In: *Effective ingredients of successful psychotherapy,* ed. J. D. Frank, R. Hoehn-Saric, S. D. Imber, B. L. Liberman & A. R. Stone, pp. 1–34. Ballinger/Mazel. [JDF]

Garfield, S. L. (1980) Psychotherapy: A 40-year appraisal. *American Psychologist* 36:174–83. [SLG]
   (in press) The effectiveness of psychotherapy: The perennial controversy. *Professional Psychology.* [SLG]

Gillan, P. & Rachman, S. (1974) An experimental investigation of desensitization and phobic patients. *British Journal of Psychology* 124:392–401. [GA, EE, SLG, tarLP, TLR]

Gist, R. & Stolz, S. B. (1982) Mental health promotion and the media: Community response to the Kansas City hotel disaster. *American Psychologist* 37:1136–39. [BM]

Glass, G. V. & Kliegl, R. M. (1982) An apology for research integration in the study of psychotherapy. *Journal of Consulting and Clinical Psychology* 50 (in press). [GVG]

Grande, L. M. (1975) A comparison of rational-emotive therapy, attention placebo and no-treatment groups in the reduction of interpersonal anxiety. Ph.D. dissertation, Arizona State University. [JDF, taLP, TLR]

Greenberg, R. P. & Staller, J. (1981) On personal therapy for therapists. *American Journal of Psychiatry* 138:1467–71. [RPG]

Grünbaum, A. (1981) The placebo concept. *Behavior Research and Therapy* 19:157–67. [MNE, tarLP]

Haley, J. (1977) *Uncommon therapy: The psychiatric techniques of Milton H. Erickson.* Norton. [taLP]

Hedges, L. V. (1981) Distribution theory for Glass's estimator of effect size and related estimators. *Journal of Educational Statistics* 6:107–28. [LVH, taLP, RR]
   (1982a) Estimation of effect size from a series of independent experiments. *Psychological Bulletin* 92:490–99. [LVH, RR]
   (1982b) Fitting categorical models to effect sizes from a series of experiments. *Journal of Educational Statistics* 7:119–37. [LVH]

Hedquist, F. S. & Weinhold, B. K. (1970) Behavioral group counseling with socially anxious and unassertive college students. *Journal of Counseling Psychology* 17:237–42. [taLP]

Herman, B. (1972) An investigation to determine the relationship of anxiety and reading disability and to study the effects of group and individual counseling on reading improvement. Ph.D. dissertation, University of New Mexico. [taLP]

Hogan, D. (1980) *The regulation of psychotherapists,* vol. 1. Ballinger. [MS]

Hogan, R. A. & Kirchner, J. H. (1968) Implosive, eclectic, verbal and bibliotherapies in the treatment of fears of snakes. *Behavior Research and Therapy* 6:167–71. [taLP]

House, R. M. (1970) The effects of nondirective group play therapy upon the sociometric status and self-concept of selected second grade children. Ph.D. dissertation, Oregon State University. [LVH, taLP]

Janov, A. (1970) *Primal therapy: The cure for neurosis.* Putnam. [JDF]

Jarmon, D. D. (1972) Differential effectiveness of rational-emotive therapy, bibliotherapy and attention-placebo in the treatment of speech anxiety. Ph.D. dissertation. Southern Illinois University. [SLG, taLP]

Jong, E. (1977) *How to save your own life.* Secker & Warburg. [GA]

Kahneman, D., Slovic, P. & Tversky, A. (1982) *Judgment under uncertainty: Heuristics and biases.* Cambridge University Press. [rNB]

Kandel, E. R. (1979) Psychotherapy and the single synapse: The impact of psychiatric thought on neurobiologic research. *New England Journal of Medicine* 301:1028–37. [JDF]

Kazdin, A. E. (1980) *Research design in clinical psychology.* Harper & Row. [AEK, GTW]

Kazdin, A. E. & Wilson, G. T. (1978) *Evaluation of behavior therapy: Issues, evidence and research strategies.* Ballinger. [GTW]

Kazrin, A., Durac, J. & Agteros, T. (1979) Meta-analysis: a new method for evaluating therapy outcome. *Behaviour Research and Therapy* 17:397–99. [GA]

Kiesler, D. J. (1966) Some myths of psychotherapy research and the search for a paradigm. *Psychological Bulletin* 65:110–36. [PK, GTW]

Kirsch, I. & Henry, D. (1977) Extinction versus credibility in the desensitization of test anxiety. *Journal of Consulting and Clinical Psychology* 45:1052–59. [TLR]

Klein, D. F. (1981) Anxiety misconceptualized. In: *Anxiety, new research and changing concepts,* ed. D. F. Klein & J. G. Rabkin, pp. 235–63. Raven Press. [JDF]

Kline, P. (1981) *Fact and fantasy in Freudian theroy.* 2nd ed. Methuen. [PK]

Landman, J. T. & Dawes, R. M. (1982) Psychotherapy outcome: Smith and Glass' conclusions stand up under scrutiny. *American Psychologist* 37:504–16. [GA, RPG, SLG, taLP, RR]

Lester, B. G. (1973) A comparison of relationship counseling and relationship counseling combined with modified systematic desensitization in reducing test anxiety in middle school pupils. Ph.D. dissertation, University of Virginia. [taLP]

Lick, J. R. & Bootzin, R. R. (1975) Expectancy factors in the treatment of fear: Methodological and theoretical issues. *Psychological Bulletin* 82:917–31. [DSC]

London, P. & Klerman, G. L. (1982) Evaluating psychotherapy. *American Journal of Psychiatry* 139:709–17. [BM]

Lorr, M., McNair, D. M. & Weinstein, G. J. (1963) Early effects of chlordiazepoxide (Librium) used with psychotherapy. *Journal of Psychiatric Research* 1:257–70. [GA, MNE, RPG, taLP]

Luborsky, L., Chandler, M., Auerbach, A. H., Cohen, J. & Bachrach, H. M. Factors influencing the outcome of psychotherapy: A review of quantitative research. *Psychological Bulletin* 75:145–85. [RPG]

Luborsky, L., Mintz, J., Auerbach, A., Christoph, P., Bachrach, H., Todd, T., Johnson, M., Cohen, M. & O'Brien, C. (1980) Predicting the outcome of psychotherapy: Findings of the Penn psychotherapy project. *Archives of General Psychiatry* 37:471–81. [HD]

Lykken, D. T. (1982) Research with twins: The concept of emergenesis. *Psychophysiology* 19:361–373. [rNB]

Maher, B. A. (1981) Mandatory insurance coverage for psychotherapy: A tax on the subscriber and a subsidy to the practitioner. *Clinical Psychologist* 1:9–12. [BM]

Malan, D. (1959) On assessing the results in psychotherapy. *British Journal of Medical Psychology* 32:86–105. [PK]

Marks, I. (1981) Behavioral treatment and drugs in anxiety symptoms. In: *Anxiety, new research and changing concepts,* ed. D. F. Klein & J. G. Rabkin, pp. 265–89. Raven Press. [JDF]

Matthews, D. B. (1972) The effects of reality therapy on reported self-concept, social adjustment, reading achievement, and discipline of fourth and fifth grades in two elementary schools. Ph.D. dissertation, University of Southern California. [taLP]

McGlynn, F. D., Kinjo, K. & Doherty, G. (1978) Effects of cue-controlled relaxation, a placebo treatment, and no treatment on changes in self-reported test anxiety among college students. *Journal of Clinical Psychology* 34:707–14. [TLR]

McLean, P. D. & Hakstian, A. R. (1979) Clinical depression: Comparative efficacy of outpatient treatments. *Journal of Consulting and Clinical Psychology* 47:818–36. [GA, rNB, MNE, GVG, taLP]

Meehl, P. E. (1955) Psychotherapy. *Annual Review of Psychology* 6:357–79. [taLP]

Meichenbaum, D. H., Gilmore, J. B. & Fedoravicious. (1972) Group insight versus group desensitization in treating speech anxiety. In: *Psychotherapy 1971,* ed. J. D. Matarazzo, pp. 513–23. Aldine-Atherton. [JDF, taLP]

Meltzoff, J. & Kornreich, M. (1970) *Research in psychotherapy.* Aldine-Atherton. [SLG, taLP]

Milgram, S. (1974) *Obedience to authority.* Harper and Row. [rNB]

Miller, J. (1978) *The body in question.* Random House. [TAS]

Morgan, R., Luborsky, L., Crits-Christoph, P., Curtis, H. & Solomon, J. (1982) Predicting the outcomes of psychotherapy by the Penn helping alliance rating method. *Archives of General Psychiatry* 39:397–402. [HD]

Mountcastle, V. B. (1975) The view from within: Pathways to the study of perception. *Johns Hopkins Medical Journal* 136:109–31. [JDF]

Murdock, M. N. (1982) A meta-analysis of psychotherapy outcome research: "Sentence first – verdict afterwards?" Honors thesis, Wesleyan University. [taLP]

Nisbett, R. E. & Wilson, T. DeC. (1977) Telling more than we can know: Verbal reports on mental processes. *Psychological Review* 84:231–259. [rNB]

Orlov, L. (1972) An experimental study of the effects of group counseling with behavior problem children at the elementary school level. Ph.D. dissertation, The Catholic University of America. [taLP]

Parloff, M. B. (1979) Can psychotherapy research guide the policymaker? *American Psychologist* 34:296–306. [MS]

(1980) Psychotherapy and research: An anaclitic depression. *Psychiatry* 43:279–93. [JDF]

(1982) Psychotherapy research evidence and reimbursement decisions: Bambi meets Godzilla. *American Journal of Psychiatry* 139:718–27. [BM]

Parloff, M. B., Waskow, I. E. & Wolfe, B. E. (1978) Research on therapist variables in relation to process and outcome. In: *Handbook of psychotherapy and behavior change,* ed. S. L. Garfield & A. E. Bergin, pp. 233–82. Wiley. [RPG]

Paul, G. L. (1964) Effects of insight, desensitization and attention-placebo treatment of anxiety: An approach to outcome research in psychotherapy. Ph.D. dissertation, University of Illinois. [GA, taLP, DPS, GTW]

Paul, G. (1969) Outcome of systematic desensitization. II. Controlled investigations of individual treatment, technique variations and current status. In: *Behavior therapy: Appraisal and status,* ed. C. M. Franks. McGraw-Hill. [EE]

Paykel, E., DiMascio, A., Haskell, D. & Prusoff, B. (1975) Effects of maintenance amitriptyline and psychotherapy on symptoms of depression. *Psychological Medicine* 5:67–77. [GA, taLP]

Platt, J. M. (1970) Efficacy of the Adlerian model in elementary school counseling. Ph.D. dissertation, University of Arizona. [taLP, LVH]

Presby, S. (1978) Overly broad categories obscure important differences. *American Psychologist* 33:514–15. [LVH]

Prioleau, L. A. (1982) A meta-analysis of psychotherapy outcome research: "Sentence first – verdict afterwards?" Master's thesis, Wesleyan University. [taLP]

Quality Assurance Project. (1982) A treatment outline for agoraphobia. *Australian and New Zealand Journal of Psychiatry* 16:25–33. [GA]

Rachman, S. & Wilson, G. T. (1980). *The effects of psychological therapy.* Pergamon Press. [rNB, EE, HJE, SLG, GTW]

Rehm, L. P. & Marston, A. R. (1968) Reduction of social anxiety through modification of self-reinforcement: An investigation therapy technique. *Journal of Consulting and Clinical Psychology* 32:5. [taLP]

Roessler, R., Cook, D. & Lillard, D. (1977) Effects of systematic and group counseling on work adjustment clients. *Journal of Consulting Psychology* 24:313–17. [LVH, taLP]

Rosen, D. (1977) A primal primer for psychotherapists. *American Journal of Psychiatry* 134:46. [JDF]

Rosenthal, R. (1978) Combining results of independent studies. *Psychological Bulletin* 85:185–93. [RR]

(1983) Assessing the statistical and social importance of the effects of psychotherapy. *Journal of Consulting and Clinical Psychology* 51:4–13. [RR]

Rosenthal, R. & Rubin, D. B. (1978) Interpersonal expectancy effects: The first 345 studies. *Behavioral and Brain Sciences* 3:377–415. [RR]

(1982a) Comparing effect sizes of independent studies. *Psychological Bulletin* 92:500–4. [LVH, RR]

(1982b) Further meta-analytic procedures for assessing cognitive gender differences. *Journal of Educational Psychology* 74:708–12. [RR]

(1982c) A simple, general purpose display of magnitude of experimental effect. *Journal of Educational Psychology* 74:166–69. [RR]

Rosenthal, T. L. (1980) Social cueing processes. In: *Progress in behavior modification,* vol. 10, ed. M. Hersen, R. M. Eisler & P. M. Miller, pp. 111–46. Academic Press. [TLR]

Rosentover, I. (1974) Group counseling of the underachieving high school student as related to self-image and academic success. Ph.D. dissertation, Rutgers University.   [taLP]

Rush, A. J., Beck, A. T., Kovacs, M. & Hollon, S. (1977) Comparative effects of cognitive therapy and pharmacotherapy in the treatment of depressed outpatients. *Cognitive Therapy and Research* 1:17–37.   [JDF]

Russell, M. A. H., Armstrong, E. & Patel, U. A. (1976) Temporal contiguity in electric aversion therapy for smoking. *Behaviour Research and Therapy* 14:103–23.   [TLR]

Schwartz, J. L. & Dubitzky, M. (1967) Clinical reduction of smoking. *Addictions* 14:35–44.   [taLP]

Sebeok, T. A. (1981) *The play of musement*. Indiana University Press.   [TAS]

Shapiro, A. K. & Morris, L. A. (1978) Placebo effects in medical and psychological therapies. In: *Handbook of psychotherapy and behavior change: An empirical analysis*, ed. S. L. Garfield & A. E. Bergin, pp. 396–410. Wiley.   [taLP]

Shapiro, D. A. (1981) Comparative credibility of treatment rationales: Three tests of expectancy theory. *British Journal of Clinical Psychology* 21:111–22.   [DAS]

Shapiro, D. A. & Shapiro, D. (1981) Meta-analysis of comparative therapy outcome studies. *MRC/SSRC Social and Applied Psychology Memo No. 438*, Department of Psychology, University of Sheffield.   [GA]

(1982a) Meta-analysis of comparative therapy outcome research: A critical appraisal. *Behavioural Psychotherapy* 10:4–25.   [PK, DAS]

(1982d) Meta-analysis of comparative therapy outcome research: A reply to Wilson. *Behavioural Psychotherapy* 10:307–10.   [PK]

(1982c) Meta-analysis of comparative therapy outcome research: A replication and refinement. *Psychological Bulletin* 92:581–604.   [rNB, DAS]

(1982b) Comparative therapy outcome research: Methodological implications of meta-analysis. *Journal of Consulting and Clinical Psychology*, in press.   [DAS]

(in press) Meta-analysis of comparative therapy outcome studies: A replication and refinement. *Psychological Bulletin*.   [SLG]

Shapiro, S. B. & Knapp, D. M. (1971) The effect of ego experience on personality integration. *Psychotherapy: Theory, Research and Practice* 8:208–12.   [taLP]

Shepherd, M. (1979) Psychoanalysis, psychotherapy, and health services. *British Medical Journal* 2:1557–59.   [MS]

(1980) The statutory registration of psychotherapists? *Bulletin of the Royal College of Psychiatrists* November, pp. 166–69.   [MS]

Sloane, R. B., Staples, F. R., Cristol, A. H., Yorkston, N. J. & Whipple, K. (1970) *Psychotherapy versus behavior therapy*. Harvard University Press.   [EE, JDF, tarLP]

Smith, M. L. & Glass, G. V. (1977) Meta-analysis of psychotherapy outcome studies. *American Psychologist* 32:752–60.   [SLG, AEK]

Smith, M. L., Glass, G. V. & Miller, T. I. (1980) *The benefits of psychotherapy*. Johns Hopkins University Press.   [GA, rNB, DSC, HD,
HJE, MNE, JDF, GVG, RPG, SLG, AEK, PK, BM, trLP, RR, TLR, DAS, GTW]

Strahan, R. F. (1978) Six ways of looking at an elephant. *American Psychologist* 33:693.   [taLP]

Strube, M. J. & Hartmann, D. P. (1982) A critical appraisal of meta-analysis. *British Journal of Clinical Psychology* 21:129–39.   [DAS]

Strupp, H. (1973) *Psychotherapy: Clinical research and theoretical issues*. Aronson.   [taLP]

(1977) *Psychotherapy for better or worse. The problem of negative effects*. Aronson.   [taLP]

Strupp, H. H. & Hadley, S. W. (1979) Specific vs. nonspecific factors in psychotherapy. *Archives of General Psychiatry* 36:1125–36.   [rNB, GTW]

Time (1979) Psychiatry on the couch. 2 April, p. 74.   [MS]

Trexler, L. D. & Karst, T. O. (1972) Rational-emotive therapy, placebo, and no-treatment effects on public-speaking anxiety. *Journal of Abnormal Psychology* 79:60–67.   [JDF, taLP]

Vanden Bos, G. & Pino, C. (1980) Research on the outcome of psychotherapy. In: *Psychotherapy: Practice, research, policy*, ed. G. Vanden Bos. Sage Publications.   [EE]

Warner, R. (1969) An investigation of the effectiveness of verbal reinforcement and model reinforcement counseling on alienated high school students. Ph.D. dissertation, State University of New York – Buffalo.   [DSC, taLP]

Weissman, M. M., Klerman, G. O., Prusoff, B. A. et al. (1981) Depressed outpatients. *Archives of General Psychiatry* 38:51–55.   [GA, rNB]

Weissman, M. M., Prusoff, B. A., DiMascio, A. et al. (1979) The efficacy of drugs and psychotherapy in the treatment of acute depressive episodes. *American Journal of Psychiatry* 136:555–58.   [GA, rNB]

West, W. B. (1969) An investigation of the significance of client-centered play therapy as a counseling technique. Ph.D. dissertation, North Texas State University.   [taLP, DPS]

Wilson, G. T. (1982) How useful is meta-analysis in evaluating the effects of different psychological therapies? *Behavioural Psychotherapy* 10:221–31.   [PK, DAS]

Wilson, G. T. & Rachman, S. (1982) Meta-analysis and the evaluation of psychotherapy outcome: Limitations and liabilities. *Journal of Consulting and Clinical Psychology*, in press.   [GTW]

Winkler, R. C., Teigland, J. J., Munger, P. F. & Kranzler, G. D. (1965) The effects of selected counseling and remedial techniques on underachieving elementary school students. *Journal of Counseling Psychology* 12:384.   [taLP]

Zeiss, A. M., Lewinsohn, P. N. & Munoz, R. F. (1979) Nonspecific improvement effects in depression using interpersonal skill training, pleasant activity schedules, or cognitive training. *Journal of Consulting and Clinical Psychology* 47:427–39.   [TLR]

VIII

EVALUATION STUDIES:
IMPLICATIONS FOR PUBLIC POLICY

Over the past two decades, substantial progress has been made in the development of the art and science of evaluation research. However, the relationship between evaluation research and policy formulation is far from clear. Experimental programs that are rigorously evaluated are subjected to a level of critical examination rarely imposed on existing programs. Not surprisingly, such examination is likely to reveal undesirable program effects that might not otherwise be detected. Moreover, even when positive results are confirmed, often program impact falls short of expectations, which dampens enthusiasm for continuing the program.

In addition, evaluation research takes time and the policy process does not stand still. Too often the treatment tested is of little interest by the time the research is completed, and the findings are of limited value in assessing current policy options.

These issues are the subject of this final section. Burtless and Haveman in Chapter 37 examine policy lessons from three labor market experiments: the Seattle-Denver Income Maintenance Experiment, the National Supported Work Demonstration, and the Employment Opportunity Pilot Project.

In Chapter 38 Himmelstein and Woolhandler illustrate how the relative cost-effectiveness of an intervention may appear radically different depending on the alternative with which it is compared. The authors compare findings from a randomized clinical trial of the effectiveness of a particular drug in preventing premature death with the Health Insurance Study of the impact of free care on the prevention of death. The drug trial was widely interpreted as supporting the adoption of the new therapy, although cost-effectiveness was not evaluated. The trial of free medical care is widely thought to suggest that broad insurance coverage is not cost-effective. The authors point out, however, that if the same criteria for cost-effectiveness are applied to both clinical trials, free care is significantly more cost-effective than the widely heralded drug intervention in preventing death. The purpose of the paper is to demonstrate that the selection of options for evaluation and cost-effectiveness comparisons involves many implied value judgments.

Usually evaluations focus on a single program and its impact. However, as Lewis illustrates in Chapter 39, a change in one large social program is likely to affect other programs as well. The Lewis paper examines how congressional modifications in the AFDC program created substantial changes in the financial incentives for families to choose publicly subsidized day care over private day care, even though subsidized day care is more expensive for the government. Sometimes the unintended consequences of programs are of greater policy significance than those that were planned.

The final chapter in the volume is a broad analysis of the contributions of evaluation research over the past two decades. Nathan proposes a typology of evaluation studies that is useful in gauging what has been learned from two decades of evaluation research, and suggests how future evaluations might be improved.

37

Policy Lessons from Three Labor Market Experiments

Gary Burtless and Robert H. Haveman

Social experimentation began in earnest when the New Jersey negative income tax experiment was launched in 1967. For the next 14 years, government agencies and philanthropic organizations sponsored a wide variety of experiments and demonstrations involving innovations in social policy; none were more important than those concerning the controversial income support-work issue. In this paper we consider three of the most important social policy experiments: the Seattle-Denver Income Maintenance Experiment, the National Supported Work Demonstration, and the Employment Opportunity Pilot Project. These projects have yielded findings of broad significance to social policy, though the significance of their findings is only dimly perceived by policymakers and interested scholars. Our purpose in this review is to briefly describe the experiments and state the main policy conclusions that can be drawn from them. In our final section, we will discuss some conclusions about the effects and value of social experiments in general.

From Gary Burtless and Robert H. Haveman, "Policy Lessons from Three Labor Market Experiments," pp. 105-133 in *Employment and Training R&D: Lessons Learned and Future Directions,* edited by R. Thayne Robson, 1984. Copyright 1984 by the W.E. Upjohn Institute for Employment Research, Kalamazoo, Michigan. Reprinted by permission.

The Seattle-Denver Experiment

The Seattle-Denver experiment was the largest and most comprehensive of the Negative Income Tax (NIT) experiments. It was begun in Seattle in 1970 and in Denver in 1971 under contracts between the States of Washington and Colorado and the U.S. Department of Health, Education, and Welfare. The experiment was administered by Mathematica, a research organization that had already gained valuable administrative experience running the New Jersey experiment. The Stanford Research Institute designed the experiment and was given major responsibility for evaluating it. There is no doubt that the Seattle-Denver experiment was the best run of the NIT experiments, and it was the most thoroughly studied.

Approximately 4800 families were enrolled in the experiment, and families assigned to experimental NIT plans were potentially eligible for payments for a period of either three or five years.[1] To be eligible for enrollment, families had to contain at least one ablebodied, nonaged adult. If only a single adult was present, the family was also required to have one or more dependent children. The sample enrolled in the experiment consisted of lower- and middle-income black, white, and Hispanic families with either one or two parents present. While participation was restricted to residents of Seattle and Denver, families could continue to participate if they moved out of those cities.

The experiment had two main goals, both of which were reflected in its rather elaborate design. The first was to determine the effect of alternative NIT plans on the work behavior of the poor. The second was to test the feasibility and effectiveness of educational vouchers aimed at low-income workers.

The idea behind a negative income tax is fairly well-known and will not be discussed in detail here. In its simplest form, a NIT offers a guaranteed monthly or annual income to a family that has no other income of its own. This amount varies depending on the number of persons in the family and was systematically varied in the experiment to measure the impact of higher or lower income support levels. If a family receives income from nonexperimental sources, such as wage earnings, interest, or public transfers, the monthly NIT payment is reduced in proportion to the amount of other income received. As income from other sources rises, the NIT payment is reduced by an amount determined by the program's tax (or benefit reduction) rate. The tax rate was also systematically varied in the experiment. When income from other sources is sufficiently high that the benefit reduction exactly offsets the income guarantee—at a point known as the break-even—payments under a NIT cease. A NIT's break-even level is algebraically determined by its guarantee and tax rate. As the guarantee level rises, the break-even also rises; as the tax rate rises, the break-even level declines.

Both theory and common sense suggest that the transfer scheme just described will affect work effort. Those who receive payments will have more income, so the necessity for earned income falls. Because payments are reduced as earned income rises, the reward for work is also affected. Under a benefit reduction rate of 70 percent, for example, a recipient who earns an additional dollar loses $0.70 in NIT benefits, and the net increase in income is only $0.30. The Seattle-Denver experiment tested 11 NIT plans with income guarantees ranging from slightly below to about 40 percent above the poverty threshold and tax rates ranging from about 50 to 70 percent. With this range of tested guarantees and tax rates, the designers hoped to detect the impact of a meaningful array of plans. In retrospect, we can criticize the designers for their conservative assessment of the meaningful range of tax rates. The policy debate since 1977, and especially since 1981, has shown that tax rates in excess of 90 percent or even 100 percent are well within the policy-relevant range.

The random assignment of families or individuals to alternative treatments—or no treatment at all—is what gives social experimentation its unique advantage as a tool for policy analysis. With only a few modest and believable statistical assumptions, it is possible for the analyst of experimental data to establish a definite cause-and-effect relationship between treatment variations and observed outcomes. The direction and precise magnitude of the relationship can be established with known levels of statistical confidence. In the case of the Seattle-Denver experiment, families were randomly assigned to 1 out of the 11 tested NIT plans or to control status. A family enrolled in one of the NIT plans was eligible to receive NIT grants if its income was below the plan's break-even. A family in the control group was not eligible to receive these experimental transfers but could continue to receive any nonexperimental transfers for which it remained eligible. The effect of the NIT plans on work behavior can be reliably determined simply by statistically comparing the work effort of individuals enrolled in the various plans and in the control group.

The work-effort findings from the Seattle-Denver experiment have been summarized in a final report recently issued by the Department of Health and Human Services. Briefly, the report shows that the tested NIT plans caused substantial reductions in labor market activity, particularly for persons enrolled in longer duration (5-year) plans and for women. By "substantial" we mean that prime-aged men reduced their annual hours of work by 9 or 10 percent; that their spouses reduced annual hours by 17 to 20 percent; and that women heading single-parent families reduced annual hours by more than 20 percent—perhaps by as much as 28 to 32 percent.[2] These reported work reductions are large enough to cause alarm among conservatives already opposed to a NIT and even among centrists with no strong opinions about the desirability of a NIT.

Taken by themselves, however, the work reductions just reported have almost nothing to tell us about the desirability or feasibility of enacting a NIT. The work reductions appear to be fairly substantial, but the work disincentive provided by the tested plans was also quite substantial, larger in fact than that which would be provided under most proposed NIT plans. The Seattle-Denver plans tested an average income guarantee of 115 percent of the poverty threshold and a marginal tax averaging only about 50 percent. In addition, the experiment provided rebates for state, federal, and FICA taxes on earned income. About 80 percent of enrolled families faced a break-even level that was more than one-and-a-half times the poverty threshold, and 50 percent faced a break-even more than twice the poverty level (that is, above $19,600 for a family of four in 1982 dollars). By contrast, the combined income guarantee provided by AFDC and food stamps is now below the poverty level in most states, and the *break-even* level for AFDC is below the poverty level in all but 15 states.[3]

Even so, the labor supply findings from Seattle-Denver were considered sufficiently important to affect the welfare reform proposals submitted by the Carter Administration.[4] The reason was quite simple. The results showed quite convincingly that the work incentive provided by a NIT's low marginal tax rate was more than offset by the work disincentive effects caused by higher overall transfers. For example, simulations based upon the Seattle-Denver results demonstrated that replacement of the current welfare and food stamp programs with a national NIT that has a guarantee equal to three-quarters of the poverty line and a marginal tax rate of 50 percent would reduce aggregate labor supply in two-parent families by about 1 percent. Labor supply in two-parent families with annual incomes below $5,000 would be reduced by more than 8 percent.[5] Although we do not find these estimates discouraging by themselves, they contain an implication that is dispiriting to policymakers who wish to simultaneously support incomes and increase the self-reliance of needy families. According to the Seattle-Denver estimates, under the NIT plan just described it would cost the government $1.79 in transfer outlays to raise the net income of poor two-parent families by $1.00. In other words, 44 percent of the net program costs of the NIT would be "consumed" by breadwinners in the form of leisure. (The net program cost of the NIT is the amount by which NIT transfers exceed those now paid under the welfare and food stamp programs.)

Another important—though at first glance, per-verse—result from the experiment was that lowering work incentives in transfer programs by raising their marginal tax rates (holding the guarantee constant) serves to *increase* aggregate work effort. For example, if the tax rate in the NIT just described were raised from 50 to 70 percent, the Seattle-Denver results indicated that aggregate work effort would rise by 1 percent.[6] The result is attributable to the fact that while increases in marginal tax rates may indeed reduce the work effort of continued transfer recipients, that effect is more than outweighed by the *increases* in work effort that occur among those who lose benefits altogether. (Recall that a rise in the marginal tax rate with a constant guarantee causes a fall in the break-even and hence a reduction in the number of transfer recipients.)

If one's sole objective is to increase work effort, the recent increases in AFDC tax rates might conceivably be justified by findings of the Seattle-Denver experiment.[7] This conclusion, however, rests on the premise that the main objective of transfer policy is to encourage work effort. In fact, the primary objective of a NIT is to protect the living standards of people who would otherwise be destitute, and to do so in an equitable and efficient way. The contribution of the NIT program to this objective, it should be noted, has received only slight attention in the hundreds of research reports filed on the NIT experiments. This in spite of the fact that the tested NIT plans were potentially quite effective in attaining that goal. Nevertheless, the Seattle-Denver experiment has played the useful role of overturning the notion, especially popular among economists and idealistic reformers, that lower marginal tax rates are automatically associated with a greater stimulus to work.

The second objective of the experiment was to test the effectiveness of issuing education and training vouchers to low-income breadwinners. Families in the experiment were randomly assigned to one of three employment-training programs or to control status.[8] All three of the labor market programs provided a structured course of manpower counseling to help participants decide on an appropriate strategy of employment, education, and training. This course was voluntary, informational in content, and non-directive (that is, participants were not encouraged to pursue any particular course of action). One of the tested programs offered no service beyond this counseling. The other two offered subsidies to pay for some or all of the direct costs of schooling or training.[9] Two levels of voucher subsidy were tested. In the more generous plan, 100 percent of direct training costs were reimbursed by the experiment. In the other plan, only 50 percent of costs were reimbursed. Participants could use their vouchers to pay for any education or training they chose, so long as it was at least tangentially related to improving their future job prospects.

The purpose of the vouchers was to encourage eligible breadwinners to invest in worthwhile training and education, which according to human capital theory should have improved participants' employability and future earnings. Participation in the program was reasonably high. About one-

fifth of family heads in two-parent families used the 50 percent vouchers, and over one-third used the 100 percent
vouchers. About one-third of single mothers eligible for the
50 percent vouchers used them, as did nearly one-half of
those eligible for the 100 percent vouchers. Not surprisingly,
much of the subsidy went to pay for schooling that would
have been obtained in the absence of the program. Most of
the subsidies paid for attendance in formal academic programs, such as those run by community colleges, rather than
for technical training. The more generous subsidy program
succeeded in encouraging extra investment in formal schooling, with the rise averaging about one-half an academic
quarter among men eligible for the subsidies and about one
to one-and-one-half extra quarters among eligible women.[10]

The interesting finding from this experiment is the complete lack of evidence that the increased investment in
schooling by participants led to any pay-off in the job
market. On the contrary, persons eligible for vouchers—in
comparison to control-group members—suffered short term
reductions in wage rates, earnings, and employment during
the initial phase of their eligibility. And they never showed
consistent earnings gains over the entire 6-year span for
which information is available, a period which includes a
fairly lengthy spell in which participants had completed their
schooling.[11] One explanation for this result is that the
vouchers induced significant short term reductions in work
effort and work intensity by subsidizing an alternative use of
time—enrollment in formal schooling. After the training was
completed, participants' earnings failed to rise above the
level observed in the control group because of the amount
and character of extra schooling obtained. The amount of
extra schooling was on average very small, and it was apparently not particularly relevant to the participants' labor
market situation. A second explanation concerns the effect
of a rather poor and generally deteriorating labor market on

the earnings potential of those who reduce (or cease) their work in order to obtain additional schooling. In such a labor market, the returns to work experience and job-keeping may be in excess of those to increased schooling. It is difficult to make training pay off if there are few jobs available.

Employment and training programs for the poor are sometimes criticized for being too rigid, too bureaucratic, too paternalistic, and too insensitive to the special needs of different clients. The experimental test of manpower vouchers in Seattle and Denver shows that completely decentralized decisionmaking, an approach often advocated by economists, may not be an effective substitute for our present arrangements, at least in the face of low labor demand. When given the resources and freedom to choose their own training strategy, low-income breadwinners appear to be no better at selecting a winning strategy than are the administrators and training specialists who now run training and employment programs.

The National Supported Work Demonstration

The 1970's commitment to assist hard-to-employ workers in finding jobs is perhaps best illustrated by the Supported Work Program. The program was a research and demonstration program, rather than a comprehensive employment program. It began in 1975 and was, from its inception, scheduled to last five years. Its basic objective was to provide individuals who had severe employment problems with work experience of about one year. The work experience was provided under conditions of gradually increasing demands, close supervision, and work in association with a crew of peers. The guiding principle of the demonstration was that ". . . by participating in the program, a significant number of people who are severely handicapped for employment may be able to join the labor force and do productive work, cease engaging in socially destructive or dependent behavior, and become self-supporting members of society."[12]

Four groups of employment-handicapped workers were eligible for the program: female long term recipients of AFDC, convicts recently released from prison, former drug addicts, and young school dropouts who often had a delinquency record. Fifteen sites were chosen for the program. While each site was given responsibility for defining the type of work on which it would focus and the source of local funds on which it would draw, the entire program had a common research-evaluation emphasis. Hence, a variety of factors were standardized across the 15 sites. These included the basic program design of low supervisor-participant ratios, steadily increasing standards of attendance, punctuality, and productivity, crew work and peer group support, and common eligibility criteria, wage rates, and employment duration. Like the Seattle-Denver experiment, the Supported Work Demonstration used a rigorous experimental design involving the random assignment of applicants to experimental (participant) and control (nonparticipant comparison) groups. We can therefore place substantial confidence in the demonstration's findings.

Over its 5-year life, the demonstration provided services to over 10,000 persons, although at any point in time the number of participants at any site was limited to 300. The evaluation of the demonstration was based on interviews with 3,214 participants and 3,402 controls. Each person in the research sample was interviewed prior to participation and given up to four additional interviews at 9-month intervals.

The participants suffered severe employment handicaps. Fewer than one-third had graduated from high school, most were black or Hispanic, fewer than one-quarter were married, the number weeks worked in the year prior to enrollment averaged six or seven, and (except for the female welfare group) arrest rates ranged from 54 to 100 percent. The work provided varied across sites, but included home rehabilitation, recapping tires, building furniture, and operating day care centers. Some program outputs were sold in the market in order to raise revenues for the program.

The program performance of the four enrolled groups varied considerably. Supported Work proved most effective in preparing the welfare women who had least work experience for gainful employment. It also had a significant impact on the ex-addict group. For the ex-offender group, the results were marginal and not statistically significant, while no long term positive results were found for the group of young dropouts. Overall, the participants in the program stayed an average of 6.7 months, even though the goal of the demonstration was about 12 months of participation. Thirty percent of the participants were fired because of poor performance; an equivalent number, however, moved on to full-time regular jobs. (The successful transition rate improved steadily over the course of the program.) About 10 percent of the participants (25 percent of the long term welfare women) had to be released after 12 months of participation, because their maximum permissible program stay had been attained. The average cost to the public per recipient was $5,740, but because most participants stayed in the program less than one year, the average cost per service year was over $10,000. This cost declined steadily over the five years of the demonstration and is about the same as the service-year cost in another targeted training program, Job Corps.

The program had a variety of impacts on its participants in areas ranging from drug use and criminal activity to employment behavior and welfare dependency. The AFDC group showed the most consistently positive response to the demonstration. In this group, participation was associated with increases in employment rate, hours worked, and earnings, both during and after the period of program participation. In addition, there was a significant reduction in welfare dependency as well as reduction in the average amount of food stamps and other transfers received. The welfare women helped most by Supported Work tended to be older (between 36 and 44), to be less educated, to have been on welfare for a longer period, and to have little or no prior work experience. At least the last three of these effects would have been difficult to predict prior to the program, and indeed are somewhat surprising.

Among ex-addicts the demonstration raised employment and reduced criminal activity, but failed to have a statistically significant impact on drug use. The main impact on criminal activity seems to have been concentrated in the first 18 months after enrollment in the demonstration. The demonstration's effect on employment probably persisted for longer than that. Ex-convicts in the demonstration do not seem to have been helped as much as the two groups just mentioned. The demonstration did not affect employment, welfare dependence, drug use, or criminal activity after participation ended. Similarly, the youth enrollees were not helped much, if at all, by the program. In this case, however, the evaluators found evidence that the target group was probably more employable than originally believed. At some time during the period of the study, between 80 and 90 percent of youth dropouts in the control group held a job. This level far exceeds the rate of the other three control groups studied, indicating that the youth group was less disadvantaged than the other target groups enrolled.

The Manpower Demonstration Research Corporation and Mathematica conducted a very careful benefit-cost evaluation of the demonstration. They computed the benefits and costs of the program from three different perspectives—that of program participants, that of taxpayers, and that of society as a whole (participants and taxpayers). The social benefits include the output produced by workers in the program, increases in their post-program earnings, reductions in criminal activities, and savings from reduced participation in other public employment, training, or drug treatment programs. The social costs include all program operating costs (excluding transfer payments, however, because these are simply a redistribution of income). The benefit-cost tabulations were based on extrapolations over the typical working life of the participants, with benefits assumed to decay at a rate of 50 percent every five years except among AFDC mothers where no decay rate in benefits is assumed.

The benefit-cost analysis showed that the demonstration had considerable net social payoff for the welfare mothers enrolled, primarily due to the long term earnings gains assumed and the value of the output from the demonstration jobs. Benefits also exceeded costs for the ex-addicts, in large part because of the reduction in socially destructive behavior (i.e., crime) and the gains in employment and earnings. For ex-convicts the results were less conclusive. The net benefit of the program may have been positive or negative depending on the assumptions used to value the benefits of the program. Not surprisingly in view of the estimated impact of the demonstration on youths, the program's cost was found to outweigh its benefits for the youth dropout group.

Because of the very specific nature of the treatment tested in the Supported Work Demonstration, it is difficult to draw broad policy conclusions from its results. The finding that the Supported Work approach had its greatest payoff in the case of AFDC mothers is consistent with a few other findings from the last decade of research on training and employment programs. Some of the studies of the Continuous Longitudinal Manpower Survey (CLMS) have also concluded that disadvantaged women helped by CETA appear to obtain the greatest program benefit. Similarly, in the Seattle-Denver experiment, the only group to show a positive impact from the counseling program (as distinct from the voucher program) was the sample of unmarried women with children. Also, as we shall see below, the Employment Opportunity Pilot Project appeared to have a more consistently and significantly positive effect on unmarried women than on other groups served. It would thus appear that single mothers are more susceptible to being helped by public training and employment efforts than other groups of hard-to-employ workers.

The Employment Opportunity Pilot Project

The history of the Employment Opportunity Pilot Project—or EOPP—was a tumultuous one, marked by shifting objectives and premature cancellation. It is said that we learn from our mistakes. If this were true, EOPP should have been one of the most richly informative demonstrations ever undertaken. The project was begun by the Carter Administration in order to estimate participation rates and potential effects of a guaranteed jobs program similar to that proposed in Carter's welfare reform package. Alarmed by the work effort reductions estimated in the Seattle-Denver experiment, the Administration was determined to limit the work disincentive effects of its welfare proposal by requiring certain welfare recipients to accept public service employment (PSE) if they were unable to obtain unsubsidized jobs. The President's welfare reform efforts were twice rebuffed by Congress, but his PSE proposals were treated more sympathetically. In 1978 Congress permitted the Department of Labor to set up a 14-site pilot test of a guaranteed jobs program.

Even before the first EOPP enrollments took place in 1979, the basic objectives of the demonstration had already been modified. This was due in part to the Administration's evolving objectives in reforming welfare and CETA. In addition to simply providing a test of the guaranteed jobs concept, which was expected to be very expensive, the architects of EOPP also hoped to test new approaches to job finding among the hard-core unemployed. If applicants for PSE jobs could be required to participate in intensive and structured programs of job finding, and if those programs turned out to be successful, the "demand" for PSE job slots, and hence the cost of PSE, could be limited.

At the time the demonstration began in 1979, its objective was to determine whether a program that provided a combination of ". . . job search assistance and subsidized employment and training could succeed in increasing the employment and, hence, reducing the welfare dependence of adults in low-income families with children. The program, targeted primarily toward families that were receiving AFDC, provided participants with intensive job search assistance and support services, such as child care and transportation assistance. Participants who were unsuccessful at finding an unsubsidized job after a prescribed period of active search were offered a subsidized job or training."[13]

When President Reagan took office in 1981, the goals of the program, or at least the focus of the program evaluation, shifted once again. The new Administration wished to abolish public service jobs, not to pilot test a program that guaranteed them. It emphatically signaled this goal by ending enrollments into EOPP's PSE jobs program, sharply curtailing enrollment in other components of the EOPP program, and prematurely terminating the entire project in October 1981, less than two-and-one-half years after operations began in 1979. Mathematica, the prime research contractor for the project, was directed to discover the impact, if any, of EOPP's job search assistance program and to provide a cost-benefit analysis of that program.

The implementation of EOPP and its evaluation were seriously harmed by these shifts in program objective. The original research and implementation design of EOPP was sensible for a pilot test of a guaranteed jobs program. However, it was extremely deficient for evaluating alternative approaches to job search assistance, the goal emphasized in the final evaluation contract. The available control group was ill-suited to examining job search assistance. To evaluate a guaranteed jobs program it is necessary to conduct saturation demonstrations under a variety of local labor market conditions. By saturation demonstrations we mean that the program had to be offered on an unlimited basis to all income-eligible families in a particular community. Saturation was required in order to determine participation rates in a well-publicized program and, equally important, to see whether such a program would seriously disrupt local labor markets by driving down the available supply of labor for unsubsidized employment. To see how local labor market conditions were affected by EOPP, it was necessary to obtain a basis for comparison. Mathematica and DOL officials selected 14 comparison sites to be used as a "control group" for the 14 pilot sites in the demonstration. (Because "control sites" were selected, EOPP might arguably be called an experiment rather than a demonstration project. However, eligibility for treatment was not randomly assigned to individuals except in Dayton and Philadelphia, and hence the project was probably closer to an ordinary demonstration than to a formal social experiment.) This strategy required massive amounts of household interviewing in both pilot and comparison sites.

Only a small proportion of these household interviews would have been needed for an adequate assessment of the job search assistance program by itself. Moreover, the experimental and control groups should have been randomly selected from the eligible population in the pilot sites. Indeed, for testing job search assistance, an experimental design involving at most a few thousand participants and controls in selected labor market environments is all that would have been required. Neither saturation, nor multiple control sites, nor massive interviewing would have been necessary.

EOPP was adminstered by the state and local officials (prime sponsors) responsible for administering local CETA programs. The competence and commitment of local administrators thus varied considerably. The prime sponsors were responsible for publicizing the availability of EOPP services, identifying, recruiting, and determining the technical eligibility of potential clients, providing support services like child care for enrolled participants, establishing and administering a structured program of job search assistance, and providing public service jobs, work experience slots, and classroom and on-the-job training opportunities for clients unable to obtain unsubsidized employment. The broad character of program responsibilities and the potential for administrative discretion at each point are noteworthy, and they threaten the reliability of evaluation findings. We simply cannot be confident about the exact nature of the treatment as delivered in the field.

EOPP tested self-directed job search methods that are quite distinct from the job referral and job development techniques usually used in the Employment Service or CETA. Clients were taught effective methods of job search and encouraged to follow a rigorous and structured routine in looking for employment. People who could not find unsubsidized jobs in five to eight weeks were offered a subsidized employment or training position, which could last up to one year before workers or trainees were recycled through the job search assistance program. Workers in PSE jobs and OJT training positions were paid regular wages, while those in work experience or classroom training slots were given a weekly training stipend.

To be eligible for EOPP job search assistance, applicants had to be adult members of families that included one or more children and that either received AFDC or had income below 70 percent of BLS's Lower Living Standard. To be eligibile for subsidized employment or training, individuals were required to complete the job search phase of the program without obtaining unsubsidized employment and, in addition, be the family's primary earner and either receive AFDC or have low enough income to qualify for AFDC. In most sites the program was aimed primarily at adult AFDC recipients.

Mathematica's evaluation of EOPP covers only 10 of the 14 communities involved in the demonstration. In those ten communities it is estimated that over 190,000 adults were eligible for EOPP services at some point during the demonstration.[14] However, of that total only 120,000 were eligible for the full range of EOPP services, including subsidized employment and training. Only 21,000—or 18 percent—of those fully eligible chose to enroll in EOPP. An additional 2,000 adults eligible only for job search assistance also enrolled in the program.[15] Of those individuals who filled out the forms to enroll, only about 62 percent remained in the program long enough to receive some job search assistance. One-third of the people receiving job search help obtained an unsubsidized job. Only 4,100—or 17 percent of enrollees—remained with the program long enough to receive subsidized employment or training, of which approximately two-thirds were assigned to PSE jobs.[16] Thus, of the 120,000 potential participants in EOPP's "guaranteed jobs" program, fewer than 3 percent actually obtained PSE jobs.

The striking feature of these statistics is the very small proportion of program eligibles who actually received program services, especially very expensive services like subsidized jobs and training. This suggests that a guaranteed public jobs program aimed at the welfare-eligible poor would be considerably less expensive than anticipated by the Carter Administration, which expected a much higher participation rate. On the other hand, the program would also be much less successful than expected in reducing welfare dependence, since only a small percentage of AFDC recipients would apparently be forced to participate in such a program.[17] In part the low participation rate in the jobs program was attributable to uncertain guidelines from the Labor Department, poor program administration at the local level, normal start-up problems, and a lack of publicity for the program. Even with these problems it was astonishing to program operators that so small a proportion of obviously eligible people chose to enroll. Among AFDC recipients who were mandatory participants in the WIN program (and thus likely to be ready to hold a job), only one-third enrolled in EOPP, and the availability of EOPP was widely advertised among that group.[18] Among nonrecipients of AFDC who were eligible for EOPP PSE jobs, only 8 percent enrolled in the EOPP program.[19]

In view of the apparently generous offer provided by the program, this studied indifference to EOPP is interesting. Of course, it is possible to keep enthusiasm for public jobs down by erecting enough bureaucratic hurdles—a complex and lengthy application process, mandatory participation in a job search program, and potentially lengthy delays before assignment to a PSE job. Nonetheless, it appears that the attractiveness of a temporary PSE job paying between one and two times the minimum wage is not nearly as great as sometimes assumed. Even though EOPP provided a highly imperfect test, the administration of the demonstration was probably not perceptibly inferior to what would be provided in an on-going program. The local administrators of the program were after all the same people responsible for administering CETA and are probably now running training and referral programs under JTPA. If there is any future consideration of a guaranteed jobs program for welfare recipients, EOPP has taught us that both the costs and benefits will be considerably below what was expected in the mid-1970s.

What of the other objectives of the project? The evaluation contractor concluded that the job search assistance program run by EOPP was probably effective in helping participants find jobs. Enrollees in the job search assistance program increased the amount and effectiveness of their search efforts. In comparison to unemployed workers in the target population who did not enroll in EOPP, participants spent nearly twice as many hours a week searching for a job, contacted about four times as many potential employers, and filed approximately 75 percent more formal job applications.[20] As mentioned earlier, about one-third of enrollees receiving job search help landed an unsubsidized job. Although it is unclear how much of an improvement is indicated by this placement rate, Mathematica concluded that for the largest group of enrollees—single mothers—EOPP probably raised the employment rate by 10 to 12 percentage points and raised the probability of *unsubsidized* employment by 7 to 9 percentage points.[21]

Because EOPP was so poorly designed to measure the effectiveness of job search assistance, Mathematica could not determine the fraction of the employment gain that was due solely to the job search plans tested. Nor were the researchers able to reliably measure the impact of EOPP on the other groups served—married women and men with dependent children. Mathematica could detect no impact of the program on welfare dependency, a surprising finding in view of the population served by EOPP, which consisted overwhelmingly of public assistance recipients. Because EOPP and its evaluation were terminated with unseemly haste in 1981, we will never know whether the employment gains registered by EOPP participants were temporary or long-lasting. Nor can we ascertain whether welfare dependency was eventually affected by the program. Because of the limitations described above, Mathematica was unable to perform a benefit-cost analysis of the job search program alone, although the analysts did conclude that the EOPP project's overall social benefits probably exceeded its social costs. Based on our reading of the evidence, it appears that a modest and comparatively inexpensive program to help low-income breadwinners search for work may reduce spells of unemployment and raise the fraction of time spent working. Even though it is doubtful that this kind of help will change many workers' lives or radically change the nature of jobs they obtain, the help is nonetheless worthwhile, and it comes at relatively low cost.

Before concluding this discussion of EOPP, we should also note that some of the pilot sites tested variants of the basic self-directed job search model. One of the most interesting variants was tested in Dayton, Ohio where wage-subsidy vouchers were distributed to a randomly selected subgroup of enrollees in the job search classes. The vouchers were simply certificates provided to participants to help them in their search for work. Participants were encouraged to alert potential employers of their vouchered status. If a vouchered job seeker was hired by a qualified employer, the employer could claim a subsidy for a fraction of the wages paid to the newly hired worker. The subsidy was payable either in the form of a tax credit or a direct check payment to the employer. It was worth up to $4,500 over a 2-year period.

In effect, the vouchered workers were "on sale." Employers, however, appeared to regard these workers as damaged goods. In comparison to unvouchered participants in the EOPP program, vouchered job seekers were significantly less likely to obtain employment during their 5- or 8-week job search period. Although this experiment is limited in many ways, and the research on it was discontinued too early to be definitive, the findings are intriguing. The basic result appears to show that a targeted wage voucher may hurt rather than help a job seeker's chances of employment. It should thus come as no surprise that our nation's two most important wage subsidy programs—the WIN and Targeted Jobs tax credits—are so little used. Because the stigma associated with these programs may outweigh their tax advantages to employers, the unemployed may be reluctant to use them and employers may be less likely to hire job seekers who offer them.

A Moral and Some Lessons

Social experiments have primarily been tools of social scientists seeking guidance for effective policy reform or innovation, but their conclusions have often been very pessimistic for those wishing to change public policy. According to the Foreword of the New Jersey Income Maintenance Experiment final report, the decision to undertake that experiment was based on the ". . . rapid spread of the belief, especially among economists, that negative income taxation was an idea whose time had come."[22] After the New Jersey Experiment began, two Presidents—Nixon and Carter—proposed variants of a federal negative income tax, but in neither case was the cause of the proposal advanced by findings from the experiments. In fact, the high price tag of the proposed Carter plan, which certainly harmed its chances of enactment, was estimated using interim results from the Seattle-Denver experiment.

Because of the rigor with which experiments are designed and evaluated there may be a bias toward reaching pessimistic conclusions about policies that are experimentally tested. The tested program is subject to critical examination of a type that is rarely imposed on existing programs. Such an examination is likely to reveal undesirable or even pernicious side-effects of a policy that might not otherwise be detected. Consider, for example, the earned income tax credit. Under this apparently benign provision of the tax code, refundable tax credits are provided to low-wage workers who have dependents. The purpose of the credit is to encourage work effort. If this policy were systematically evaluated using the methods applied to social experiments, the credit might be shown to reduce work effort or encourage family dissolution as the NIT was found to do. Indeed, the credit increases work disincentives because it increases marginal tax rates for more workers than are eligible for a subsidy on marginal work. If these effects were found to occur, and if they were widely publicized, the credit could be politically doomed. However, such effects are unlikely to be investigated because of the program's uncontroversial nature.

Numerous other examples could be mentioned. Do subsidized student loans stimulate increases in education? If they do, is the added investment in education worth its social and private cost? Do business tax reductions and other state-local subsidy programs to attract new business achieve their goals? Such programs could conceivably reduce or delay local investment projects if businesses delayed their decisions as a result of their efforts to attract subsidy support.

If an experimentally tested program fails to achieve its intended purpose, or if it has disagreeable consequences, those facts can be demonstrated with statistical rigor. Even more disturbing, if the program fails to achieve spectacular positive results, the degree to which it falls short of perfection can be measured precisely and then used as an argument against its implementation. If on the other hand an on-going program does not achieve its objectives or does harm, its failure may remain unsuspected, or at least unproved.

As an empirical fact, politically divisive policies are the ones most likely to be subject to rigorous experimentation—negative income taxation, housing vouchers for the poor, national health insurance, and labor market assistance to low-income workers. Programs aiding the able-bodied poor are among those with the weakest popular mandate, and hence their reform will nearly always inspire deep controversy. It is unclear whether experimentation *per se* can shed much light on the main points at issue—the demands of equity, the nature of a fair distribution, and the limit of society's obligation to help those who are at least partly able to help themselves. Our experience in the last fifteen years has taught us that large-scale social experiments can be relied on to teach us something of value about the policy in question, but what we are taught can seldom be relied on to aid the cause of reforming or improving policy. Since society is not even-handed in subjecting programs for the poor and nonpoor to experimental investigation, we should not be surprised that experimental scrutiny has been less than kind to programs for the poor. There is a moral here, and it is illustrated in the three experiments we have considered: if you advocate a particular policy reform or innovation, do not press to have it tested.

Beyond this political economy moral, are there lessons for research or evaluation that can be gleaned from the experiments? One such lesson concerns the costs and benefits of large-scale social experimentation relative to nonexperimental social research. Clearly, the research costs of social experimentation are enormous. For the three experiments reviewed here, the costs of program administration (including experimental transfers, stipends, and wages) and evaluation exceeded $200 million. The potential benefits in terms of additions to knowledge may also be substantial, especially when it is recognized that obtaining reliable information about human behavior is usually a slow process. However, if the opportunity cost of any proposed experiment is a reduction in nonexperimental research costing the same amount of money, the expected findings would have to be extremely valuable for the benefits of an experiment to exceed its cost. Of course, this conclusion is weaker if the opportunity cost of the resources used for experimentation is low. This would be the case, for example, for resources that are diverted from some activity with low social value.

In view of the high cost of experiments, it is appropriate to subject proposals for future experiments to a test that includes the following questions:

1. Have adequate models of the behavior which the experimental treatment is designed to affect been developed and tested on existing bodies of data?

2. Can the experiment and its evaluation meet high standards of basic research? That is, can problems of time horizon, contamination, Hawthorne effects, replicability, and extrapolation of results to a national program be handled adequately in the experimental design or in the evaluation of experimental results?

3. Can the experiment provide evidence about a social policy that cannot be obtained using less expensive, nonexperimental methods? Alternatively, can the experiment provide findings that are sufficiently more reliable or statistically precise to justify the added cost of the research?

4. How important are the potential research findings about experimental outcomes? Are they crucial in determining whether the tested treatment is a good or bad policy?

5. Can the experiment permit tests and evaluation of the operational feasibility of social policy measures and yield evidence on the effectiveness of alternative administrative arrangements of such programs?

6. Can the experimental findings be validly generalized to infer the consequences of policies not specifically tested in the experiment?

The number of potential social experiments that can pass the test implied by these questions is not likely to be large. This conclusion is strengthened by our review of the findings of the three experiments. While the evidence on behavioral responses is more reliable than is likely to be obtained from nonexperimental research, its value, in terms of added knowledge per dollar of cost, was not uniquely high except in the case of the tested NIT plans. For the training and employment experiments, including the one run as part of the Seattle-Denver experiment, the programs tested were so specific in nature that it is difficult to extrapolate the findings except to other programs that are run exactly as they were. (For EOPP, even this may be impossible because the tested treatments are essentially nonreplicable.)

The NIT experiment was more valuable for two reasons. Its findings were considerably more reliable and statistically precise than any that had been obtained in the preceding 10 years of nonexperimental research. Moreover, its findings are useful in evaluating tax and welfare policies in addition to those actually tested in Seattle-Denver, in part because there is a well-developed theory for assessing labor supply responses to tax rates and guarantees.

But the exception represented by the Seattle-Denver experiment is rare. Many conceivable experiments in the field of employment and training must concentrate on testing "black box" treatments. Supported Work and the job club model tested in EOPP both represent this kind of treatment. There is no well-established theory, as existed in the case of the NIT experiments, that permits us to predict whether and how these particular approaches will affect participants. Nor can we predict from experimental findings the effect of similar—but not identical—policy options. This lack of knowledge regarding the process by which treatment affects performance limits the applicability of the findings. In the case of both Supported Work and EOPP, the treatment tested was of little interest by the time the research was completed, and the findings, in turn, were of limited value in assessing policy options then being considered.

Black box experiments can be valuable in employment and training research if they are relatively inexpensive but rigorous and if there is systematic variation in the treatments which are tested. Investing large sums of money to test a single approach is likely to be a serious error except under very unusual conditions. To justify its high cost, a social experiment must offer the prospect of valuable additions to knowledge about human behavior. In light of the moral mentioned above, the benefits of an experiment will seldom include basic reforms to policy.

NOTES

1. A very small number of families were enrolled in experimental plans lasting up to 20 years.

2. Office of Income Security Policy, U.S. Department of Health and Human Services, *Overview of the Seattle-Denver Income Maintenance Experiment Final Report,* Government Printing Office, Washington, DC, 1983, pp. 13-16. The higher estimate of the impact on women heading single-parent families is based on the responses of women in the 5-year group during the fourth and fifth experimental years. Remaining estimates are based on reported responses of enrollees in both the 3- and 5-year groups during the second and third experimental years.

3. Ibid., p. 6.

4. See Henry Aaron and John Todd, "The Use of Income Maintenance Experiment Findings in Public Policy, 1977-78." *Industrial Relations Research Association Proceedings,* 1979, pp. 46-56.

5. Implementing a NIT program for single-parent families, given the combination of existing transfer programs, is difficult. Because of the widely varying AFDC benefit levels across states, it is difficult to select a NIT guarantee level that is low enough to be affordable, but high enough so that only a small fraction of families in the high-benefit states receive a NIT payment that is no lower than their current benefit. A national NIT plan with a guarantee equal to three-quarters of the poverty line would increase labor supply among single mothers, not because of the work incentive embodied in a low tax rate, but because transfer benefits would be slashed for so many mothers in states currently paying high benefits.

6. This result as well as those reported in the preceding paragraph are from Philip K. Robins and Richard W. West, "Labor Supply Response," in *Final Report of the Seattle-Denver Income Maintenance Experiment*, vol. I, *Design and Results*, U.S. Department of Health and Human Services, Government Printing Office, pp. 180-87.

7. Strictly speaking, the experiment provided no evidence about the impact of raising marginal tax rates to 100 percent. Within the range of tax rates tested in the experiment, however, higher tax rates appear to be associated with higher aggregate labor supply. See Ibid., p. 182.

8. Assignments to the employment-training programs were conducted in such a way that analysts were able to reliably distinguish the separate impacts of those programs and the tested NIT plans.

9. Reimbursable (or direct) expenses included costs for tuition, books, transportation, and child care.

10. Note that this was the impact on program *eligibles;* the impact on program *participants* was of course much greater. The 50 percent subsidy also encouraged some extra schooling, but the increases were smaller. See Bureau of Social Science Research, *Vouchering Manpower Services: Past Experiences and Their Implications for Future Programs*, Bureau of Social Science Research report to the National Commission on Employment Policy, Washington, DC, 1982, p. 20.

11. Ibid., p. 29.

12. This quote as well as much of the material for this section is drawn from Manpower Demonstration Research Corporation, *Summary and the Findings of the National Supported Work Demonstration*, Ballinger Publishing Co., Cambridge, MA, 1980.

13. Mathematica Policy Research, *Final Report: Employment Opportunity Pilot Project: Analysis of Program Impacts*, MPR, Princeton, NJ, p. 1.

14. Ibid., p. 20.

15. Ibid., p. 22.

16. Ibid., pp. 27, 105 and 116.

17. We should emphasize that the low participation of welfare recipients in the demonstration was partly attributable to poor enforcement of job search requirements in local welfare departments. If the job search/PSE jobs and welfare programs were more tightly coordinated, the costs and hence potential benefits of an EOPP-type program might have been greater.

18. Mathematica Policy Research, *Final Report,* p. 22. Many mandatory participants in WIN are in fact required to participate in an activity like EOPP as a condition for continued receipt of welfare benefits.

19. Ibid., p. 22.

20. Ibid., p. 108.

21. Ibid., p. 3. A small percentage of enrollees obtained employment in EOPP's own jobs program. For that reason the gains in unsubsidized employment were smaller than those in all forms of employment.

22. David Kershaw and Jerilyn Fair, *The New Jersey Income Maintenance Experiment,* Volume I, *Operations, Surveys, and Administration,* Academic Press, New York, 1976, p. xi.

38

Free Care, Cholestyramine, and Health Policy

David U. Himmelstein and Steffie Woolhandler

OVER the past decade the efficacy and cost of medical interventions have been subject to increasing scrutiny with quantitative techniques, such as the randomized controlled trial and cost-effectiveness analysis. Such studies provide invaluable guidance for the clinician choosing from a limited range of options in caring for an individual patient. However, in the field of health policy myriad competing programs, services, institutions, and interests must be weighed. Unfortunately, quantitative methods are virtually always used to compare two, or at most a few, alternative strategies. Since the relative cost effectiveness of an intervention may appear radically different depending on the alternative with which it is compared, the decision about which options to consider is critical.

The basis for the decision to examine some alternatives while excluding others is rarely made explicit and is subject to considerable bias. The tendency for such a bias to reflect the prevailing wisdom and status quo is of particular concern. Unpopular alternatives may be subject to the most stringent comparisons, with radical innovations totally excluded from consideration. In contrast, practices that are less controversial or enjoy the support of powerful constituencies may be evaluated for efficacy but not cost or even accepted without evaluation. Thus, the usefulness of universal free medical care, if considered at all, may be measured against that of childhood immunization rather

From David U. Himmelstein and Steffie Woolhandler, "Free Care, Cholestyramine, and Health Policy." Reprinted by permission of *The New England Journal of Medicine*, Vol. 311 (December 6), pp. 1511-1514, 1984. Copyright 1984 by the Massachusetts Medical Society.

than executive stress testing; the efficacy of new drugs is scrutinized, but their cost effectiveness is rarely considered; and the burgeoning administrative apparatus of health care escapes evaluation altogether. To illustrate the pitfalls of health-policy conclusions based on narrow comparisons, we have juxtaposed cost-effectiveness analyses of two recent studies of medical-intervention strategies. One trial was widely interpreted as supporting the adoption of a new therapy, although cost effectiveness was not evaluated. The other trial has been cited as providing evidence that the intervention studied is not cost effective and should be discontinued. Our comparative analysis illustrates that such isolated conclusions may be misleading.

A TALE OF TWO STUDIES

The publication of the results of the Lipid Research Clinics Coronary Primary Prevention Trial[1] was widely hailed as a landmark in efforts to prevent coronary heart disease. Newspapers carried front-page stories on this breakthrough,[2] and many authorities agreed with the study's authors that the trial

leaves little doubt of the benefit of cholestyramine therapy. . . .The trial's implications . . . could and should be extended to other age groups and women and . . . to others with more modest elevations of serum cholesterol levels. The benefits that could be expected from cholestyramine treatment are considerable.[1]

Six weeks earlier the findings of the Rand Health Insurance Experiment[3,4] were published with equal fanfare. This study examined the relative costs and effects on health of a variety of health-insurance plans, including one offering complete coverage at no cost and several plans requiring copayments. Free health care led to a substantial increase in the use and cost of services and slightly diminished the risk of early death for people at high risk. The authors of the report concluded, "These mortality reductions in and of themselves are not sufficient to justify free care for all adults." Both the authors and an accompanying editorial[5] urged caution in interpreting and extrapolating these findings, though they concurred that in the study population free care conferred small benefits for a high cost. Newspapers, policy makers, and even the authors when interviewed by the lay press were less cautious in drawing conclusions.[6-8] The study was taken as virtual proof that health-care costs could be contained by charging patients more for care, with few or no adverse health consequences. Even the organ of the American Public Health Association, an organization that advocates creation of a national health service to provide universal free medical care, proclaimed in a headline, "Health Does Not Seem Improved When Care Is Free."[9]

These two randomized trials provide an interesting contrast. The Lipid Research Trial proves that a therapy is efficacious, whereas the Rand Study throws into question the wisdom of social policies that insulate the patient from the costs of care. But are the results of the two studies really so different? Is cholestyramine a more cost-effective intervention than free health care?

COSTS AND EFFECTS: THE LIPID RESEARCH TRIAL AND THE RAND EXPERIMENT

The Lipid Research Trial screened over 480,000 men to identify 3806 who had plasma cholesterol levels above the 95th percentile despite a lipid-lowering diet and who were free of other lipid disorders, coronary heart disease, and other illnesses. The 3806 participants were randomly assigned to two groups; one received six packets of cholestyramine per day, and the other a placebo. After an average follow-up of 7.4 years the cholestyramine group had three fewer deaths overall (68 vs. 71) and 12 fewer deaths due to definite or suspected coronary heart disease (32 vs. 44). If definite or suspected nonfatal myocardial infarction is included with deaths from coronary heart disease, the cholestyramine group had 34 fewer events associated with coronary heart disease.

Although these benefits of cholestyramine therapy were carefully considered in the report of the trial, the costs were not analyzed. Satisfactory cost estimates are difficult to obtain, since the costs of a trial are unlikely to reflect those in routine clinical practice, costs attributable to physician visits and laboratory tests for cholesterol screening and follow-up of patients given cholestyramine are unknown, and possible savings due to decreased rates of coronary bypass surgery and other medical care are likewise uncertain. However, the cost of cholestyramine alone is considerable. The wholesale cost of 50 packets[10] is $37.71, the mean retail price at six pharmacies we surveyed is $42.50, and the average cost of a one-year supply is $1,861.50 (6 packets per day × 365 days × $0.85 per packet). The cost of cholestyramine per myocardial infarction or death prevented ranges from $775,600 to $9,307,500 (Table 1).

How do these costs compare with the costs of reducing the risk of early death in the Rand Experiment? Free care reduced the risk of dying for the sickest 25 per cent of the relatively healthy study population by 21 per cent, as compared with high-risk individuals enrolled in the various cost-sharing insurance plans. For 50-year-old men, the group comparable to participants in the Lipid Research Trial, this would represent a reduction of 2.1 deaths per 1000 men per year. The risk of nonfatal events associated with coronary heart disease would presumably also be reduced, but the magnitude of this reduction has not been reported.

The total cost of care for those in the free-care group exceeded costs for those in copayment groups by 24 to 49 per cent, depending on the amount of copayment. This difference amounted to between $82 and $142 per person per year at the time of the study. However, per capita health-care costs have increased by approximately 230 per cent since that time. Accounting for health-care cost inflation, the excess expense attributable to free care would be between $189 ($82 × 2.3)

Table 1. Cost of Preventing a Death or Myocardial Infarction: Free Care versus Cholestyramine.

INTERVENTION	ANNUAL COST OF INTERVENTION PER 1000 PEOPLE ($)	ADVERSE OUTCOME PREVENTED*	NO. OF ADVERSE OUTCOMES PREVENTED PER 1000 PEOPLE PER YEAR	COST PER ADVERSE OUTCOME PREVENTED ($) †
Cholestyramine	1,861,500	Death from any cause	0.2	9,307,500
Cholestyramine	1,861,500	Death from CHD	0.9	2,068,300
Cholestyramine	1,861,500	CHD death or nonfatal MI	2.4	775,600
Free care for high-risk 50-year-old men	189,000 −327,000	Death	2.1	90,000 −155,700
Free care for all 50-year-old men	189,000 −327,000	Death	0.5	378,000 −654,000
Free care for all people	189,000 −327,000	Death	0.45	420,000 −726,700

*MI denotes myocardial infarction, and CHD coronary heart disease.
†Annual cost of intervention per 1000 people ÷ no. of adverse outcomes prevented per 1000 people per year.

and $327 ($142 × 2.3) per person per year in 1984 dollars. Thus, the cost per life saved by a strategy of free care for generally healthy 50-year-old men ranges from $90,000 to $654,000, depending on two factors: whether free care is given to all men or only the 25 per cent at highest risk, and the alternative insurance plan used as a basis for comparison (Table 1). Since a policy of free care would be unlikely to apply only to 50-year-old men, we also calculated the cost per life saved by universal, "cradle to grave" free care, which ranges from $420,000 to $726,700 (Table 1). This calculation is based on the 1982 U.S. death rate of 857.6 per 100,000 population[11] and the assumption that the relative risk and cost changes for all age groups would (on average) be similar to those reported by the Rand Experiment.

DISCUSSION

The above analyses suggest that free care is between 3 and 100 times as cost-effective as cholestyramine therapy in preventing death. We have probably underestimated the cost advantage of free care over cholestyramine for several reasons. Our analysis excludes nondrug costs of cholestyramine therapy, such as extra physician visits and laboratory tests, although such costs are likely to be substantial. The Lipid Research Trial included only men with cholesterol levels above the 95th percentile, whereas our calculations based on the Rand data pertain to lower-risk persons as well. Cholestyramine therapy in lower-risk persons (which would be virtually certain to occur) would undoubtedly produce smaller benefits and, hence, considerably higher costs per life saved or coronary-heart-disease event prevented. We conservatively assumed that lower-risk patients would receive no benefit from free care. Long-term changes in health-care costs and patients' earnings due to decreased rates of cardiovascular disease were also excluded but would probably be similar with cholestyramine therapy and free care,

since risk reductions were roughly equal. Although widespread adoption of cholestyramine therapy might decrease drug costs by encouraging bulk manufacture or the introduction of a generic formulation, the savings would probably not be large enough to alter our findings substantially and would probably be equalled by a decrease in administrative costs attendant on the introduction of a system of universal free care. Finally, side effects and subjective benefits of the two interventions were not considered and would almost certainly favor free care.

The perception that the Lipid Research Trial represents a breakthrough in prevention and the Rand Experiment demonstrates the relative ineffectiveness of unfettered access to medical care appears unwarranted and may be due to unrecognized bias. The Lipid Research Trial is the culmination of a decades-long search for confirmation of a widely believed hypothesis. Its therapeutic strategy conforms closely to a model for intervention that is familiar to physicians and lucrative for drug manufacturers. Since this expensive therapy would presumably be unavailable to the 30 million uninsured poor in our country (barring a major expansion of Medicaid or the issuance of cholestyramine vouchers to poor people with hypercholesterolemia), it would perpetuate the status quo of inequalities in health and health care, as well as the prevailing bias favoring individual medical interventions over population-based preventive strategies. The Rand Experiment was carried out in response to the growing clamor for control of health-care costs. Its findings were reported at a time of Medicaid cutbacks, increasing Medicare copayments, a rising tide favoring cuts in private insurance benefits, and a swelling of the ranks of the uninsured. The results of this trial have been widely interpreted as supporting this status quo of increasing inequality in access to care based on ability to pay.

In this context it seems somehow natural to compare free care to highly cost-effective interventions such as blood-pressure screening, as was done by the Rand researchers. In contrast, cholestyramine was not subjected to cost comparisons; the demonstration of benefit was sufficient. Countless other components of our health-care system have never even been examined for efficacy. Thus, the cost effectiveness of health administrators, billing computers, and the advertising of drugs and medical supplies remain outside the domain of evaluation.

In some respects the decision to make free medical care available or prescribe cholestyramine are dissimilar. The extent of health-insurance coverage is a result of health policies largely beyond the control of the clinician, whereas clinical decisions are the province of individual physicians and patients. Yet in many ways the two situations are analogous. For a high-risk patient, prescriptions for cholestyramine or free care appear approximately equally efficacious in preventing death. Indeed, both seem to exert their beneficial effects through similar mechanisms of risk-factor reduction. Each would increase the cost and improve the quality of health care. Although it may be unthinkable to tell a patient that he cannot have an efficacious drug because the cost is too high, it is only a quirk of our current reimbursement system that makes it more acceptable to force him to curtail his use of medical services for the same reason.

The resources available for health care are vast but finite. Ultimately, those who determine health policy must weigh the value of a $100,000 computer program to maximize diagnosis-related-group (DRG) reimbursement against the value of 2000 free visits for patients who cannot afford a $50 clinic fee or that of cholestyramine therapy for 54 people. Current policies implicitly influence such decisions by fostering administrative hypertrophy, allowing unlimited interventions for the well insured, and constraining the resources available for the less fortunate. Alternative policies would have different health and cost consequences that should be analyzed, made explicit, and publicly debated. Perhaps the American people and their physicians would choose to condemn 30 people to early deaths for lack of free care so that 3 well-insured patients could take cholestyramine and live or a hospital might maximize its DRG income. We doubt it.

Our intent is not to denigrate the achievement of the Lipid Research Trial, which has at last shown that lowering cholesterol decreases the risk of coronary heart disease and which may pave the way for more broadly applicable interventions such as changes in diet. Nor are we indifferent to the problems of skyrocketing costs. Rather, our purpose is to demonstrate that the selection of options for evaluation and cost-effectiveness comparison involves many implicit value judgments. In facing painful decisions about containment of health-care costs the facets of the health-care system excluded from rigorous evaluation and comparison may be as important as the results of the evaluations that are carried out. We cannot afford to spare sacred cows.

The Cambridge Hospital
Cambridge, MA 02139   David U. Himmelstein, M.D.

Boston University
  School of Public Health   Steffie Woolhandler,
Boston, MA 02118   M.D., M.P.H.

References

1. Lipid Research Clinics Program. The Lipid Research Clinics Coronary Primary Prevention Trial results: I. Reduction in the incidence of coronary heart disease. JAMA 1984; 251:351-64.
2. Boffey PM. Study backs cutting cholesterol to curb heart disease risk. New York Times. January 13, 1984:1,10.
3. Brook RH, Ware JE Jr, Rogers WH, et al. Does free care improve adults' health?: results from a randomized controlled trial. N Engl J Med 1983; 309:1426-34.
4. Newhouse JP, Manning WG, Morris CN, et al. Some interim results from a controlled trial of cost sharing in health insurance. N Engl J Med 1981; 305:1501-7.
5. Relman AS. The Rand Health Insurance Study: is cost sharing dangerous to your health? N Engl J Med 1983; 309:1453.
6. Macrae N. Health care international. The Economist. April 28, 1984: 17-33.
7. Little link found between cost of care and health. Boston Globe. December 8, 1983:22.
8. Brazda JF, ed. Briefly this week. Washington Report on Medicine and Health. December 19, 1983; 37:4.
9. Health does not seem improved when medical care is free. The Nation's Health 1984; January:1,6.
10. Red book — drug topics 1984. Oradell, N.J.: Medical Economics Co, 1984.
11. Health, United States 1983. Hyattsville, Md.: National Center for Health Statistics, 1983. (DHHS publication no. (PHS)84-1232).

39

The Day Care Triangle
Unexpected Outcomes When Programs Interact

Gordon H. Lewis

Abstract

The day care policy of the United States is generated effectively by interactions among tax law, food stamps, Aid to Families with Dependent Children, and block grants for social services. These various programs are administered or controlled by different departments, different branches, and different levels of government. As a result, it is difficult to know what effect a change in one program will have on the overall system that determines de facto policy. Congressional changes to the AFDC program, for example, created large changes in the financial incentives for families to choose publicly subsidized day care over private day care, even though subsidized day care is more expensive for the government. By the nature of these changes, it is clear that they were unforeseen and unintended.

Making public policy, according to most textbook prescriptions, requires a careful weighing of benefits and costs. Executing any such policy effectively requires a thorough understanding of the incentives and disincentives that affect the main participants. In many areas of public policy, however, it is not easy to respond to such maxims. A number of different levels of government have a hand in setting policy; and a number of different programs operate jointly to provide results. Moreover, all of the entities whose activities affect the outcome march to different music, responding to different constituencies and different goals; the interactions between the multiple programs, therefore, are largely uncontrolled and the consequences often unintended.

Nor are such situations mere aberrations; they describe most areas involving social benefit programs, from day care and energy rebates to pensions and unemployment. The implications of the existence of these multiple interactions can be profound, a fact well illustrated by the case of subsidized day care.

Title XX of the Social Security Act specifies that, up to a given

From Gordon H. Lewis, "The Day Care Triangle: Unexpected Outcomes When Programs Interact," *Journal of Policy Analysis and Management*, 1983, 2(4), 531-547. Copyright 1983 by the Association for Public Policy Analysis and Management. Reprinted by permission of John Wiley & Sons, Inc.

ceiling specified for each state, 75% of the cost of various social services provided or purchased by state governments will be reimbursed by the federal government. Because day care is one of the allowable services, one might suppose that the benefits and costs of subsidized day care would be determined mainly by the characteristics of the program developed by each state. But day care is also indirectly subsidized through Aid to Families with Dependent Children (AFDC), food stamps, and the federal tax laws; as a consequence, who gets what, and who pays what, is determined by the choices made by the families and by the interactions among these programs.

Our study of the day care program of the state of Pennsylvania during 1981 and 1982 demonstrates that changes in the state's program in 1982 were far less important in determining the financial outcomes to the various participants than the changes in other programs, notably AFDC, administered quite independently of the day care program. To appreciate the extent of these interactions between the various programs, we begin with the situation as it existed early in 1981, before the changes were made.

THE INTERACTIVE MAZE, 1981

The Family's Viewpoint

In May 1981, according to a survey of day care providers in the Pittsburgh metropolitan area, the average cost of full-time day care in private centers was about $45 per child per week. At that time, day care centers that received Title XX subsidies, which we shall also refer to as "public" day care centers, were required not to charge more than $26 per child per week.

From the viewpoint of the paying parents, the relative financial merits of the two forms of day care seemed perfectly clear. But a simple comparison of the parent's out-of-pocket expenses did not tell the whole story. As previously indicated, three other federal programs, in one way or another, had a direct effect on day care costs, whether private or public:

- Under the AFDC program, the grant to any recipient was affected directly by work-related day care expenses incurred by the recipient; in determining the size of the grant, such day care expenses could be deducted from the recipient's income, thereby effectively increasing the size of the ADFC grant.

- In the food stamp program a similar deduction was given. Work-related day care expenses (up to a limit of $35 per month) could be deducted from the recipient's income, thereby effectively increasing the size of the food stamp benefit.

- In the calculation of federal income taxes, the law permitted a credit for dependent care expenses, with a maximum credit of $400.

Further complicating matters was the fact that these three programs affected one another: Federal tax withholdings were deductible from earned income in determining the AFDC grant, and the AFDC grant had to be included with other income when calculating food stamp benefits.

Figure 1 shows schematically how the various factors interacted to determine the net income of a low-income family with day care expenses. As the diagram indicates, day care expenses had a direct, positive effect on net income by increasing AFDC, food stamps, and the dependent care tax credit; but these had various effects on one another and ultimately on the net income of the family. Figure 1 suggests why the simple, first-order consideration of day care costs would not have begun to capture the full ramifications of day care expenses to the family.

A thorough analysis requires that one incorporate the various interactions among these programs. The present analysis uses a computer package specially designed for such analyses. That package, which is briefly described in Appendix A, allows the analyst not only to explore the complex interactions for different classes of recipients, but also to analyze the consequences that would ensue from changes in the programs.

The exact nature of the various interactions is determined in part by the regulations of each state. Here, as a demonstration of the importance of those interactions, we present the results of analysis based on the Pennsylvania program in 1981, for a hypothetical household consisting of a single parent with one child who needs day care when the parent is working.

In 1981, as was noted earlier, the cost of private day care in the Pittsburgh area was $45 per child per week. Those that were eligible to use Title XX day care centers paid an amount that was determined by family income; families earning less than 65% of the state's median income for a family of that size got day care services free; those with incomes in a range between 65% and 115% of the state's median income paid fees ranging from $2 to $26 per week, on a schedule that rose by $2 for each five-point interval in the range; those with higher incomes were ineligible. If there was already one child in the day care center, the cost for each additional child from the same family was one-half the amount for the first child.

As indicated in Figure 1, the principal programs interacting with the day care program were AFDC, food stamps, medicaid, and the dependent care tax credit. The specific assumptions used in defining the effects of each of these programs are too detailed for

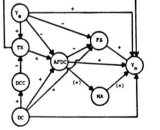

AFDC	Aid to Families with Dependent Children
DC	Day care expenses
DCC	Dependent care tax credit
FS	Food stamps
MA	Medicaid
TX	Taxes, state and federal
Y_e	Earned income
Y_n	Net income

presentation in full although they may be obtained by writing the author. Some of the most important assumptions, however, are presented briefly in Appendix B.

Figure 2 shows the direct charges for private and public day care as a function of annual earned income, before taking into account any of the indirect effects. The sloping portion of the charges for private care (the upper line) reflects the assumption that persons earning less than $6,700 per year were working part-time and therefore received only part-time care for their children in day care centers. The charges shown for public day care reflect the fact, mentioned earlier, that the costs of public day care increased in a step function, according to the recipient's income. Under the rules prevailing in 1981, a two-person family with income in excess of $15,447 was not eligible to use a Title XX day care center because that income exceeded 115% of the state's median income for that size family.

We pointed out earlier that the decision of any family whether to use private day care facilities or the seemingly less costly Title XX facilities would affect how much the family received under AFDC, food stamps, and medicaid, as well as the size of its federal income tax credit for dependent care expenses. For the private day care alternative and the Title XX alternative, the amount that our hypothetical family would have received under each of these programs is shown in Table 1, the figures being presented separately for various income levels.

For families with earnings under $3,350, there was no financial difference between using private day care and using public day

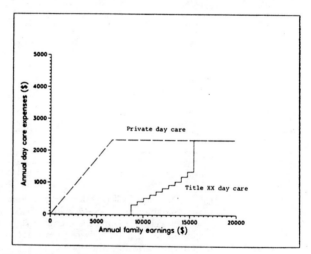

Figure 2. Annual day care expenses of hypothetical family as a function of earned income, 1981.

Table 1. Benefits received by a hypothetical family from various programs as a result of choosing private day care or Title XX day care.

Annual earnings	AFDC benefits with		Food stamp benefits with	
	Private day care	Title XX day care	Private day care	Title XX day care
0.00	3144.00	3144.00	1324.80	1324.80
3349.99	2910.27	2910.27	590.93	590.93
3350.00	2910.27	1740.27	590.92	941.92
4000.00	2818.35	1421.33	462.50	881.60
5000.00	2774.94	1028.67	235.52	759.40
6000.00	2773.52	678.00	0.00	621.90
7000.00	2619.33	279.33	0.00	441.30
8000.00	2228.67	0.00	0.00	207.00
9000.00	1848.00	0.00	0.00	0.00
10000.00	1477.33	0.00	0.00	0.00
11000.00	1118.67	0.00	0.00	0.00
12000.00	788.00	0.00	0.00	0.00
13000.00	457.33	0.00	0.00	0.00
14000.00	130.67	0.00	0.00	0.00
15000.00	0.00	0.00	0.00	0.00
16000.00	0.00	0.00	0.00	0.00

Annual earnings	Medicaid benefits with		Income tax credit with	
	Private day care	Title XX day care	Private day care	Title XX day care
0.00	910.00	910.00	0.00	0.00
3349.99	910.00	910.00	0.00	0.00
3350.00	910.00	910.00	0.00	0.00
4000.00	910.00	910.00	0.00	0.00
5000.00	910.00	910.00	98.00	0.00
6000.00	910.00	910.00	238.00	0.00
7000.00	910.00	910.00	390.00	0.00
8000.00	910.00	0.00	400.00	0.00
9000.00	910.00	0.00	400.00	62.40
10000.00	910.00	0.00	400.00	83.20
11000.00	910.00	0.00	400.00	124.80
12000.00	910.00	0.00	400.00	145.60
13000.00	910.00	0.00	400.00	187.20
14000.00	910.00	0.00	400.00	208.00
15000.00	0.00	0.00	400.00	270.40
16000.00	0.00	0.00	400.00	400.00

care; this result follows from the fact that a parent working less than half-time was not eligible for Title XX day care. At the $3,350 level, however, the outcomes begin to diverge. At the $8,000 level, the family using private day care was still receiving AFDC benefits amounting to $2,229; but the family using a Title XX center was deemed to have sufficient available income so that it was no longer eligible for AFDC.

Those differences had effects that were felt in the benefits received under other programs as well. As Table 1 shows, families using Title XX day care continued to receive food stamps at higher income levels than families using private day care; that result came about because AFDC benefits were counted as income in the food stamp program, so that the higher day care expenses, which were reimbursed through AFDC, caused the food stamp benefits to be reduced. The effect on medicaid is even more striking. The family that chose private day care, having greatly extended the earnings range under which it was eligible for AFDC, thereby extended the range in which it was eligible for medicaid.

The net effect on our hypothetical family of its choice between private day care and Title XX day care is obtained by adding up all the relevant components: the family's out-of-pocket costs of the day care it chose, the benefits it received from various programs that were affected by its choice, and the size of its income tax credit. The difference between the family's net income under private day care and its net income under Title XX day care is a measure of the financial incentive to the family to choose a particular type of day care.

Figure 3 portrays the direction and size of the incentive for our hypothetical family as a function of the family's annual income. In Figure 3, positive values indicate that the family benefited by choosing private day care over Title XX day care; negative values indicate that the family benefited by choosing the Title XX option.

The message of Figure 3 is quite clear. For families with incomes between $3,350 and $7,224, Title XX day care was the better

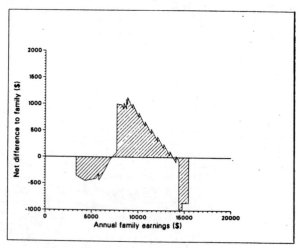

Figure 3. Net difference to hypothetical family, day care minus Title XX day care, 1981.

choice, by amounts up to $451 annually, depending on the family's income level. For families with income levels between $7,224 and $13,784, the situation was reversed, with private day care bestowing higher benefits up to $1,125. Finally, if a family earned between $14,185 and $15,447, Title XX day care once again became the better choice, generating annual gains up to $983.

The computer program that was used for calculating these effects also readily identifies the underlying elements that determine these results. Over all, a few fundamental factors stand out. At income levels between $3,350 and $7,224, the family was eligible for AFDC and medicaid, whether it chose private day care or Title XX day care; by choosing Title XX day care, however, the family saved on its out-of-pocket costs. At income levels from $7,724 to $13,784, the higher out-of-pocket costs of private day care served to keep the family eligible for AFDC and medicaid, a result that more than offset the higher payments for private day care facilities. At income levels between $14,421 and $15,447, where AFDC and medicaid were no longer available in either case, the lower out-of-pocket costs of Title XX day care again became the controlling factor.

The Government's Viewpoint The family's choice between private day care and Title XX day care has complex effects not only upon its own income but also upon the fiscal position of the federal and state governments. Moreover, inasmuch as the cost of different programs is distributed differently between federal and state governments, these effects are not the same for the various programs. The subsidies for Title XX day care centers are a mixture of 75% federal and 25% state money. In the case of AFDC and medicaid, at least in Pennsylvania, the federal government pays approximately 50% of the program costs; in the case of food stamps and the dependent care tax credit, the federal government bears all the cost.

Figuring the costs to the state of Pennsylvania of the family's choice between private day care and Title XX day care, therefore, required tracing the costs in all the various programs affected— not only the state's portion of the Title XX program itself, but also the state's portion of the AFDC and medicaid programs. The state's portion of the Title XX program was calculated using the 1981 Pennsylvania regulations, which allowed Title XX day care centers to receive a maximum amount of $3,948 per year for each nonpaying, preschool child. If our hypothetical family with one child had an annual income of $10,000, a Title XX center which served that child would be entitled to receive $520 directly from the family, leaving a subsidy of $3,428—to be shared on a 75–25 basis between the federal government and the state. Adding that element of the state's cost to the attendant effects on its expenditures for AFDC and medicaid, one obtains the total impact of the family's choice upon the state's expenditures.

Figure 4 shows the net difference in costs to the state resulting from the family's choice between private day care and Title XX day care. Since these are costs rather than benefits, we reversed the calculation used in Figure 3, subtracting the cost of private day care from the cost of public day care; accordingly, when the difference carries a positive value, it indicates that the state was better off if the family utilized private day care, while a negative result indicates that the state was better off if the family used Title XX day care.

As Figure 4 shows, for families at most levels of income, the state was better off if the family used Title XX day care. Although the state was obliged to subsidize those families, its share of the Title XX subsidy was only 25%; for most of the income range shown in Figure 4, those subsidies cost the state less than the savings it incurred in the AFDC and medicaid programs. If the family earned more than $12,432, however, the advantage to the state was reversed. Here the factor that produced these effects was not the termination of benefits from a particular program, but rather the offsetting of expenses under the two conditions. When the family had earned income of $12,432, the state's portion of the costs of subsidized day care if the family used Title XX day care was exactly equal to the state's portion of the costs of AFDC and medicaid if the family used private day care.

The impact of our hypothetical family's choice upon the federal government required yet another set of calculations, whose results are shown in Figure 5. The obvious feature of Figure 5 is that if our hypothetical family was eligible for Title XX day care—that is, if it had income between $3,350 and $15,447—the federal government was always better off if the family chose private day care. The

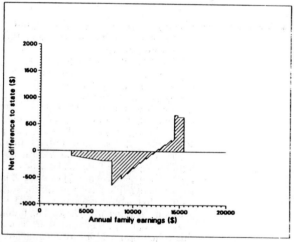

Figure 4. Net difference in cost to state, Title XX minus private day care, 1981.

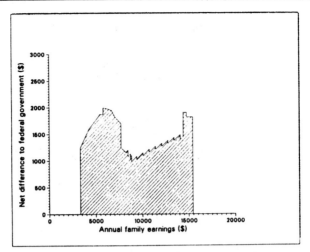

Figure 5. Net difference in cost to federal government, Title XX minus private day care, 1981.

second striking feature is the magnitude of the difference. For families earning as little as $5,960 the federal government was $1,991 better off if the family chose private rather than public day care; and the difference was never less than $1,000 at any income level.

The Overall Evaluation Looking at the interests of the family, the state, and the federal government simultaneously under the conditions of 1981, some significant patterns are clear. The state was almost always better off if the family used a public day care center, and the federal government was overwhelmingly better off if the family used a private day care center. Low-income families and the state had a strong common interest in encouraging Title XX centers. Higher-income families and the federal government shared a strong common interest in the use of private day care facilities.

On the other hand, if one looks at the problem from the standpoint of the total dollars involved, a different picture emerges. The costs to the federal government associated with families' choosing Title XX facilities were very large relative to the costs of private day care. They were so large indeed that the federal government could have paid off the state and the families with the money that would have been saved by abolishing the Title XX program, leaving all parties—including the federal government itself—better off financially than they were before. What is more, this conclusion held for all income levels, including the lowest.

Of course, the possibility of abolishing the Title XX day care program would have promptly run up against one practical difficulty: The money received by the state from the federal government under Title XX came as part of a block grant, which covered many services. To abolish the day care program and leave all parties at least as well off would have required a number of different steps: adding restrictions on the state's use of Title XX funds, reducing the block grant by the amount of money saved, and redistributing the saved funds to each of the parties in a pattern that would offset the Title XX losses. In principle such restrictions and transfers were possible, although they would have created a more restrictive rather than a less restrictive block grant program and therefore run counter to the current administration's philosophy concerning block grants. In any event, the changes that actually occurred in the day care program during and after 1981 took an entirely different direction.

FEDERAL CHANGES, 1981   Early in 1981 the administration asked Congress to make a large number of changes to AFDC, including a proposal that working AFDC parents be allowed a maximum reimbursement of $50 per child per month for day care expenses. In August of that year, as part of the Omnibus Budget Reconciliation Act, Congress passed most of the proposed changes, but not before raising the day care ceiling to $160 per child per month. In so doing Congress no doubt thought that it had protected families needing day care.

Predictably, there were outcries from a number of sources complaining about various features of the new provisions. There was little protest, however, over the imposition of the ceiling on day care expenses or over the implicit effects of the other changes upon day care. Because the $160 per month ceiling was fairly high, those interested in day care probably did not feel that day care was threatened. As we shall see, however, the various changes were to have a large impact on the financial outcomes for individual families, for the state, and for the federal government.

Figure 6 portrays the incentives for our hypothetical family, after the amendments went into effect, in choosing between private day care and Title XX day care. Figure 6 is therefore the postamendment parallel of Figure 3; and as in Figure 3, positive values show that the family would benefit by choosing private day care over Title XX day care, while negative values indicate the reverse. As the figure shows the overwhelming effect of the changes in federal law is to make it financially advantageous to the family to place the child in a public day care center. This is so because typically the family is eliminated from AFDC at relatively low levels of earnings—in the case of our hypothetical family in Pennsylvania, if the parent earns more than $4,287. Once the family loses AFDC support, no penalty is attached to its using a Title XX day care center.

The effect of the federal changes on the state is shown in Figure 7. Again, there is a marked change in the financial outcomes.

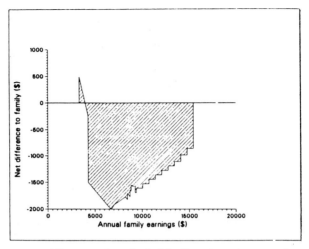

Figure 6. Net difference to hypothetical family, private day care minus Title XX day care, after 1981 amendments.

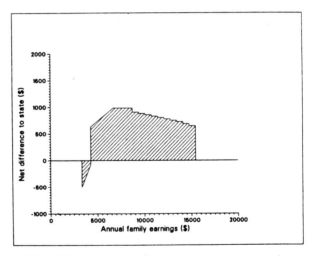

Figure 7. Net difference in cost to state, Title XX minus private day care, after 1981 amendments.

Whereas previously the state was usually better off if the family chose public day care, now the state is almost always better off if the family chooses private day care. Once again, it is the loss of AFDC support that accounts for the change; once the family is ineligible for such support, its use of Title XX centers is a cost to the state that is not offset by savings in AFDC and medicaid.

Finally, Figure 8 shows the results for the federal government itself after the amendments went into force. Although the general shape of the function is somewhat different from the function displayed in Figure 5, both functions are always positive. In both situations, therefore, the federal government is better off if the family chooses private day care. Nevertheless, although the amendments increase the advantage to the federal government when the family uses private day care facilities, one must be careful in interpreting that result. The increased advantage to the federal government of the family choosing private day care is not because there has been any change in the cost of Title XX day care, but rather because there has been a reduction in cost for the federal government due to the reduction or elimination of payments for AFDC and medicaid.

While the advantage to the federal government is now larger than before if the family chooses private day care, reexamination of Figure 6 reminds us that there is almost no advantage to the family to choose private day care. The reasonable conclusion is that from a financial perspective families will prefer public day care, and the federal contribution to public day care is substantial.

These results underline the crucial importance of tracing out the

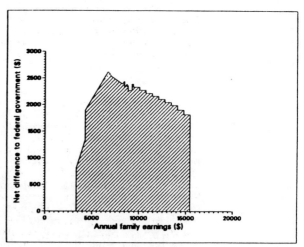

Figure 8. Net difference in cost to federal government, Title XX minus private day care, after 1981 amendments.

second-order effects of program interactions. In this instance, the principal parties appear to have been misled because they failed to take these factors into account. As the federal administration set about reducing AFDC benefits, they apparently ignored that they were substantially increasing the incentive to use public day care, which would result in increased demands on federal monies, and increased demands for patently more expensive forms of day care. At the same time, private day care providers appeared to have less than an adequate understanding of the implications of the AFDC changes for their programs.

CHANGES BY THE STATE, 1982

The interactive nature of policymaking in the day care area was illustrated again when the Pennsylvania Department of Public Welfare made changes to the subsidized day care program in July 1982.

The state redefined the fee schedule, with a new minimum fee for low-income families and a reduced maximum fee for higher-income families; it lowered the maximum reimbursement to $3,400 for fiscal year 1982–1983; and it defined gross income for the program to include AFDC grants. In addition, a family that is eligible for AFDC is now required to pay the provider's rate for day care, up to the maximum that it can recoup from AFDC. At the same time, the state changed the upper limit for eligibility from 115% of the state's median income to 90% of a different income standard, the U.S. Bureau of Labor Statistics' so-called intermediate standard.

Unlike the changes made by the federal government in 1981, these changes did generate reactions from day care providers and others associated with day care. Concern was expressed that the quality of subsidized day care would decline and that the new programs would prove difficult to implement. The present question, however, is what effect these changes had upon the incentives for a family to choose one type of day care over another and on the consequent effects on federal and state costs.

Figure 9 shows our hypothetical family's situation after the provisions were put in effect. The shape of the function in Figure 9 is quite similar to the function in Figure 6, the situation that existed after the federal changes of 1981. But with predictable differences: The small advantage of private day care for low-income families that had previously existed now disappears, because for a family that is eligible for AFDC the parent now effectively pays the private day care rate; the maximum advantage of public day care is less than before because the fee schedule for lower-income families has been increased; and the maximum income at which the family is eligible for subsidized day care has now been lowered slightly, from $15,447 under the prior regulations to $14,159. Nevertheless, the similarity of Figure 6 and Figure 9 illustrates how little effect the state's changes in the subsidized day care program actually had on the incentives for families to choose one form of day care over the other.

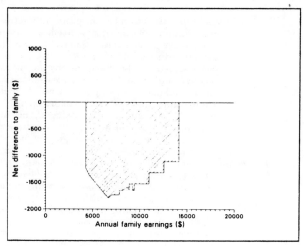

Figure 9. Net difference to hypothetical family, private day care minus Title XX day care, after 1982 changes by state.

The position of the state and that of the federal government also are somewhat altered by the amendments, but the changes are not large enough to require extended comment. It should be noted, however, that the major effect is felt by the federal government, whose total cost in subsidizing day care is reduced because of the state's reduction of the maximum reimbursement.

CONCLUSIONS As policy analysts have observed from time immemorial, things are not always what they seem. The actions of the federal government were more important in affecting the day care program than those of the state, but the actions of the federal government that really mattered were those related to AFDC, not to the day care program directly. Cosmetically, the federal government's amendments in 1981 were not especially threatening to the day care program, inasmuch as they contained fairly generous provisions for child care, but changes in the formula for income eligibility in AFDC had a substantial effect on the incentives for families to choose private day care over Title XX day care. The state, on the other hand, appeared to some observers to be substantially reducing program eligibility when it changed the upper-income limit from 115% of the state median income to 90% of the BLS intermediate standard; but in fact the reduction was less than it appeared, because of the simultaneous shift in the applicable standard.

Although it is trite to observe that the outcome of policy is a result of the actions of all its participants, the present case also illustrates how readily the point is overlooked in practice. In cutting back on AFDC, the federal government increased the attractiveness of public day care to families, even though the cost of subsidized day care is greater than the cost of AFDC and other benefits combined. If the federal government did not suffer from these changes it was only because Title XX funds are capped, whereas AFDC funds and medicaid are not; accordingly, the federal government's losses were limited. Meanwhile, because the state made changes of its own which essentially reinforce the changes made by the federal government, the state and federal governments increased the incentives for families to choose public day care over private day care, a result probably not intended.

We have focused on three specific lessons from the changes that have occurred in subsidized day care, but there is another lesson which is sufficiently general that it pervades the entire analysis: the necessity of analyzing entire systems of programs. The fact that programs interact is not a new point; it has been made by many observers and analysts. Yet the Congress and other policymaking bodies routinely receive analyses of single programs even when it is known that there are important interactions between the program in question and other programs. With the technology increasingly available to explore these interactions systematically, good policy analysis will demand that such interactions be analyzed and understood. To do less would be to remain entangled in the thicket of multiple-program interactions.

The author wishes to express appreciation to the Department of Health and Welfare, Canada, for making MAPSIT available, to Carnegie–Mellon University for providing computer time for the analysis, to Denise DiPasquale and Rick Morrison for comments, and to John Mercer, Heidi Todd, and William Vandivier.

APPENDIX A
The Computer Package

The analysis presented in this article utilizes MAPSIT, a computer package designed for the analysis of systems consisting of interdependent, piecewise-linear functions. Like various microsimulation models (for example, TRIM and DYNASIM), MAPSIT operates on a microanalytic basis. Unlike the standard microsimulation models, however, MAPSIT allows the analyst to model many different types of systems, is not dependent on a data base, and might be thought of as a microaccounting package rather than a behavioral model. Readers wishing further information about MAPSIT should consult Richard J. Morrison and Gordon H. Lewis, *Income Transfer Analysis* (Pittsburgh, PA: School of Urban and Public Affairs, Carnegie–Mellon University, 1982).

APPENDIX B
Basic Assumptions

The following notes provide information about major assumptions used in this analysis. Further detail can be found in the listings of the MAPSIT models, available from the author.

Day Care and Employment Several programs require assumptions about day care and employment. In AFDC, food stamps, and the federal tax credit, the only day care expenses that are "reimbursable" are those that are incurred in order for the parent to work, and Title XX day care is restricted to persons working at least 20 hours per week. We assume that anyone earning at least $6,700 per year, the amount earned working full-time (40 hours per week for 50 weeks) at the minumum wage ($3.35) in 1981, is working "full-time" and eligible to claim full-time day care costs. We assume that those earning less than $6,700 are working part-time at the minimum wage, and the fraction of full-time day care that they can claim is equal to the fraction of the minimum full-time earnings ($6,700) that they receive. Thus, someone earning $3,350 is assumed to be working half-time and could claim only half-time day care expenses.

Throughout the analysis we assume that the child needs day care in order for the parent to work; we ignore the case of children who do not need day care even though the parent is working and the case of children who need day care (for example, severely disabled children) even when the parent is not working.

Subsidized Day Care, 1982 In the regulations established by the Pennsylvania Department of Public Welfare in 1982, the fee to be charged for Title XX day care depends on gross income, including AFDC. But computation of the amount to be received from AFDC presumes that one already knows the amount of the day care expenses. It is not clear how the circularity induced by this regulation is intended to be worked out. In the present analysis we have assumed that the parent was paying the maximum deductible private day care. This maximizes the AFDC benefit, which in turn maximizes the fee charged for public day care. If one ignores day care expenses in computing AFDC and then computes the fee to be paid for public day care, the result is a lower day care charge and a lower termination point for AFDC.

Medicaid Medicaid eligibility is extended automatically to those eligible for certain federal income maintenance programs, among them AFDC. Thus, if the family's earnings qualify it for AFDC, we assume that the AFDC recipient unit is also receiving medicaid. In 1971 medicaid costs for AFDC recipients in Illinois averaged $222 per person.[1] When updated by the ratio of the April 1980 CPI for medical services to the March 1971 CPI for medical services (2.05), the estimated medicaid reimbursement is $455 per person per year.

Although we recognize the controversy concerning the treatment of in-kind benefits as if they were cash payments, in the present analysis we have taken the average reimbursement cost as the value of medicaid to the family. If one assumes that the value of medicaid to the family is less than the reimbursement cost, different numerical values result, but most of the basic conclusions remain the same. For example, if medicaid were valued at full cost ($455) at zero income, but valued at only 80% of that ($364) at incomes of $10,000 or above, the three major segments of Figure 3 would remain. The function would be unchanged from $0 to $7,724 of earnings, because the family is eligible for medicaid whether in private or Title XX day care, but the maximum net advantage of private day care above $7,724 would be only $964 rather than $1,125, and the crossover point, where Title XX day care was again preferred, would occur at $12,731 rather than at $13,784.

Whatever one's judgment may be concerning the value of medicaid benefits to recipients, it is appropriate to treat the actual costs of medicaid at face value for the state and federal government, which must make the actual payments to the vendors.

Taxes Taxes are modeled using the Internal Revenue Service regulations for tax year 1981, utilizing schedule Z for heads of household. In order to focus on the effects of the changes in AFDC and in subsidized day care, we retained the 1981 federal tax structure for the subsequent analyses. In calculating the amount of tax withheld, which was needed for the calculation of AFDC benefits in 1981, we used net taxes payable (that is, after the dependent tax credit) to avoid the necessity of an end-of-year AFDC reconciliation. This is equivalent to assuming that the person anticipated the tax credit and adjusted withholdings to produce a net tax due of zero at the end of the year.

GORDON H. LEWIS is an Associate Professor in the School of Urban and Public Affairs, Carnegie–Mellon University.

NOTES 1. Hausman, L., "Cumulative tax rates in alternative income maintenance systems," in *Integrating Income Maintenance Programs*, I. Lurie, Ed. (New York: Academic, 1975).

40

The Missing Link in Applied Social Science

Richard P. Nathan

One of the by-products of the sixties and the Great Society was the creation of the public policy research industry. It was well fed and grew large. Now, like the social programs of the same period, it is on a reduced—some would say, starvation—diet. There is growing skepticism about the contribution of social science research in the field of domestic policy. Conservatives generally do not like social science research, yet they often use the results to raise sharp questions about social programs. Liberals who generally like and support social science research are increasingly skeptical about its results and applications.

In a December 1983 radio address, President Reagan said, "There is no question that many well-intentioned Great Society type programs contributed to family break-ups, welfare dependency and a large increase in births out of wedlock." Although the President's radio address did not specify the sources for these unquestionable conclusions, most social scientists who work on domestic policy issues have a pretty good idea of the history and studies to which the president's comments refer.

My main point is that despite the negativism of the current period, there is reason to have a hopeful view of prospects for applied social science. The key to this brighter future is large, interdisciplinary evaluation and demonstration studies that link quantitative and qualitative research techniques. I begin this argument with an organizational scheme for distinguishing three approaches to applied social science. Some policy research is *analytical*, i.e., research on social and economic conditions and how they have evolved and can be understood. Other studies examine how particular programs work, *evaluation* studies. Others are *demonstration* studies to test new approaches to social problems. Different people do research; their interests and disciplinary predilections vary as shown in the diagram.

At research centers and schools of public policy,

analytical studies are often seen as "defining the problem." The presumption is that policy analysts can then test (using simulations and demonstrations) various alternative "solutions." There are serious difficulties with this problem-solution metaphor. Social scientists who specialize in domestic policy studies, not surprisingly, tend to believe in government. While they may not admit to it, or even think very hard about it, there often is a subtle liberal bias in an approach in which domestic policy analysts call attention to a problem and then proceed to study ways of solving it. Social scientists who do applied research should avoid this progovernment bias.

It is useful to subdivide analytical studies into two subcategories—general studies covering a broad functional area and relying on secondary data, and specific and more focused analytical studies that frequently involve the collection of original data.

General analytical policy studies burgeoned in the mid-sixties. The most notable demonstration of this was the planning-programming-budgeting (PPB) system created in typical grandiose fashion by Lyndon Johnson when he ordered, in August 1965, the entire federal government to adopt the PPB system. Other examples of general policy analysis by social scientists emerged outside of government. A prominent example is the work done in the Brookings Institution budget books, the annual *Setting National Priorities* volumes begun in 1970. The Brookings model of an annual volume of essays by knowledgeable, conscientiously objective analysts became a new genre for policy researchers with similar volumes published by the American Enterprise Institute, the Hoover Institute, the Heritage Foundation, the Urban Institute, etc. This motif has been adopted so widely that it is now old hat. There are only so many ways one can write an essay on current health, welfare, environmental, job-related, urban, and education issues. After a while these books lose their attention-getting value. When the Brookings budget volumes first came out, they were the

From Richard P. Nathan, "The Missing Link in Applied Social Science." Published by permission of Transaction from SOCIETY, Vol. 22, No. 2, pp. 71-77 copyright © 1985 by Transaction.

subject of large press conferences and extensive media coverage. Now, fourteen volumes later, they have much less impact. Considerable time and energy are devoted to general policy analyses by social scientists. Some of these resources could be more productively devoted to other types of policy studies.

Specific policy analysis studies, the second subtype under analytical studies, range from "cubicilized" social science (one social scientist, one discipline, one terminal, one article) to larger empirical studies involving original data collection. My concern applies to studies in this group that have a highly theoretical focus and little relevance to real-world conditions.

Domestic policy studies that are "Analytical/Qualitative" constitute an empty cell for modern social science. No self-respecting practitioner would claim that he or she does qualitative analytical work. The emphasis is on rigorous proof in Cartesian fashion. (Descartes was a mathematician.) Qualities that cannot be defined and measured have little standing. Fortunately, in recent years there has been an increase in the writing of academic social scientists who are challenging this "scientism" in the social sciences. In economics, Donald N. McCloskey argues convincingly that the behavior of economists differs markedly from their "official methodology." McCloskey, in a 1983 article in the *Journal of Economic Literature*, says that, despite the fact that the official methodology of economics is what he calls the "modernist view,"

> Economists in fact argue on wider grounds, and should. Their genuine, workaday rhetoric, the way they argue inside their heads or their seminar rooms, diverges from the official rhetoric. Economists should become more self-conscious about their rhetoric, because they will then better know why they agree to disagee, and will find it less easy to dismiss contrary arguments on merely methodological grounds.

I tie this point to my framework by noting that a great deal of what is regarded as general analytical writing by social scientists, in reality, is highly qualitative. Although the Analytical/Qualitative category may suggest to some readers the work of advocates and polemicists, honest reflection about current practice would result in classifying much of what purports to be systematic analytical policy writing as essentially qualitative. It describes and interprets conditions rather than subjecting propositions to systematic tests of their validity. This is expressed by the wavy line in the diagram.

It is the second category in my framework—evaluation studies—that brings us to the consideration of the "immutable boundary" area of social science. The war

TYPES OF STUDIES AND THE "IMMUTABLE BOUNDARY" BETWEEN THEM

Type of Study	Quantitative (Crunchers)		Qualitative (Noncrunchers)
Analytical Studies (assessments of conditions)	Type 1		Type 2
Evaluation Studies (assessments of policy changes that have occurred)	Type 3	IMMUTABLE BOUNDARY	Type 4
Demonstration Studies (assessments of policy changes that are proposed for wider application)	Type 5		Type 6

between the crunchers (quantitatively oriented) and case studiers (qualitatively oriented) has produced a no-man's land of intellectual and professional danger. Battles occur between disciplines and within disciplines. I discuss two main categories of evaluation studies—quantitative and qualitative.

Einstein once said, "I have little patience with scientists who take a board of wood, look for its thinnest part, and drill a great number of holes where the drilling is easy." Demographic and economic variables are used in many social science evaluations in ways that the drilling is easiest. Political and institutional variables, because they cannot be measured, are left out or treated cavalierly. Fortunately, there are social scientists who are concerned about this problem.

In a brilliant work published in 1977, *The Moon and the Ghetto: An Essay on Public Policy Analysis*, Richard Nelson reviewed the three main traditions of policy analysis—economic, organizational, and research and development—and came to a conclusion that has important implications for evaluation studies. Nelson found all three traditions wanting and said that domestic policy research, when it is at its best, indicates the need for, and often the best approach to, institutional change. He called for evaluation research in the social sciences that includes both analytics and institutional knowledge and blends the two in creative ways. Nelson was not the first person to call for such linkages. In the 1930s, University of Wisconsin economist John R. Commons stressed the importance of understanding institutions in the public sector. Commons described governmental institutions as "collective action in control of individual action." In *Collective Action* he wrote:

> Public programs and policies cannot be evaluated in terms of the logical consequences of isolated assumptions.... they must be judged by the practical consequences of their operations. This requires a subtle balancing of many parts.... it means continuous attention to the resolution of conflicts.... it requires that analysis must come to focus upon judgments which evaluate the parts in relation to the whole and take account of the strategy and timeliness of action.

Quantitative evaluation studies often use strong mathematical techniques to assess the effects of small treatments with weak data. This approach is inexpensive. Such studies can be conducted by individual researchers on a personal computer. There often is no cost for data collection and for field investigation. This kind of research inspired Wassily Leontief's famous letter to the editors of *Science* magazine in 1982 complaining about academic economics. Leontief said, "the king is naked.... no one dares to speak up." His point was that government statistics are too weak to be used for high-powered research. "Page after page of prof⋅ ·sional economic journals are filled with mathematical formulations leading the reader from sets of more or less plausible but entirely arbitrary assumptions to precisely stated but irrelevant theoretical conclusions."

Good examples of the limits of quantitative evaluation studies are described by Henry Aaron in *Economic Effects of Social Security*. After reviewing the literature, Aaron states that, depending on the assumptions adopted about the employment behavior of workers, one can reach diametrical conclusions about the economic effects of social security.

> Reputable economists may be found who argue that social security has decreased savings, increased savings, or had no perceptible effect. Similarly, economists may be found who hold that social security has increased labor supply, reduced it, left it unchanged, or caused offsetting changes in labor supply by workers of different ages. It is safe to say at this time no major issue concerning the effect of social security on economic behavior has been settled to the satisfaction of a dominant majority of analysts.

Similar examples can be found in the literature on poverty. Comedian Flip Wilson used to do a brassy "Geraldine" skit impersonating a woman. One line was, "What you see is what you get!" Many poverty researchers get what they see because of the behavioral assumptions they start out with.

Abraham Kaplan in his seminal book on methods in the behavioral sciences, *The Conduct of Inquiry*, wrote about what he called "the law of instrument."

> Give a small boy a hammer, and he will find that everything he encounters needs pounding. It comes as no particular surprise to discover that a scientist formulates problems in a way which requires for their solution just those techniques in which he himself is especially skilled.

Kaplan also maintains, "The fragmentation of a science into 'schools' is by no means unknown even in as rigorous a discipline as mathematics." Then the punch line: "What is striking in behavioral science is how unsympathetic and even how hostile to one another such scholars often are." This is a war zone. The tragedy of war is that both sides get hurt.

I use the term *qualitative* in a way that is conservative from the point of view of my argument. Qualitative research is defined to include studies that use numbers (dollars spent, people served, types of recipients and programs) as well as words (big, small, new, old). The main distinction between studies under this heading and studies classified as quantitative is that in qualitative studies researchers do not use conventional statistical tests of probability to establish (or at least infer) causality and proof.

The bulk of the research I have done, beginning a dozen years ago—"field network evaluation studies"—comes under this heading. This research consists of similarly structured case studies conducted by a group of economists and political scientists to study the effects of major changes in the domestic policies of the United States national government. The federal programs we have studied using this approach are general revenue sharing, the community development .block grant (CDBG), the Comprehensive Employment and Training Act (CETA) public service jobs program, and, most recently, the Reagan administration cuts in federal aid programs. In all of these studies, we have been interested in impact issues. Among the issues studied are: (1) substitution in the case of revenue sharing; (2) incidence for CDBG; (3) displacement for the CETA jobs program; and (4) replacement for the 1981 cuts in grants-in-aid.

These impact issues are often the same as those that are the focus of quantitative evaluation studies. Among the principal research questions asked for the major programs we have studied are:

- Revenue sharing: To what extent were revenue sharing funds used on a substitutive basis to allow the recipient jurisdictions to cut taxes?
- Community development block grant: What proportion of CDBG funds benefited the poor?
- CETA job-creation program: To what extent were CETA job-creation funds used to displace state and local funds, thereby supporting positions that would have been funded in the absence of this aid?
- The Reagan cuts: To what extent have state and local governments "ratified" the cuts, i.e., passed along the reductions in the form of reduced services? To what extent have they "replaced" the cuts out of their own revenues?

In these studies, we have modeled the counterfactual in that most powerful of all computers, the human brain. Field researchers observe the way in which the jurisdictions they are studying are affected by specific federal policy changes compared to what they (the field researchers) have determined would have occurred in the absence of the policy change being evaluated. Each study began when the new federal policy was adopted and has involved a representative sample of state and local governments.

Our focus is on the effects of the policy changes studied on the sample governments and the people they serve. We have studied four main types of effects— fiscal, programmatic, incidence, and institutional. In some instances, we have had opportunities to change field researchers, to duplicate field observations, and to estimate the range of confidence the field researchers

have in their impact assessments, but we have not used statistical techniques in the conventional way to assign probabilities to the results obtained.

Despite the lack of statistical tests of significance, field studies came up with what many politicians and government and interest group officials have regarded as straightforward, credible results. One accomplishment of the study we conducted of the revenue sharing program, for example, was to clear the air on the so-called fungibility issue. We argued that the U.S. Treasury Department data on how shared revenue was used (based on self-administered reports by state and local officials) were not useful, but harmful, because funds can be moved around so easily that these official accounts data can be totally misleading. You have to wrestle with the concept of substitution to make sense out of the use of revenue sharing funds. This wrestling match has to be waged at the local level, with researchers on the scene using local records and budget data and interviewing local officials. No central data are available from the U.S. Bureau of the Census or budget or agency sources providing uniform and detailed information that can be used to answer crucial questions at the national level— questions about the stimulative versus the substitutive impact of federal revenue sharing funds. All of the researchers in the field network for the Brookings Institution study of revenue sharing were using the same conceptual apparatus to study substitution under revenue sharing.

The field researchers not only presented their best judgments as to the impact of revenue sharing, they also indicated why, in their view, a particular state or local government responded as it did to the new program. The field evaluation study of the revenue sharing program produced a number of interesting findings. One, for example, was that fiscally and economically distressed local jurisdictions tended to use their shared revenue for what we classified as substitution in some cases and "program maintenance" (that is, maintaining programs that would otherwise have been cut or eliminated) in others. Whatever you call it, it spelled "relief" for these distressed jurisdictions. The liberal argument against revenue sharing changed as a result of this clearer dialogue on the substitution issue.

One of the researchers involved in these field network studies, Steve B. Steib, an economist at the University of Tulsa, made the following point about the linkage between quantitative and qualitative studies in research such as ours.

> What we need to do is to have qualitative studies provide the understanding upon which formal modeling can be done. Qualitative research should be used to provide hypotheses, lists of important variables, and tentative conclusions. Quantitative researchers can then subject it to the falsification criteria.

We have applied Steib's point in our research on the effects of major changes in federal grant-in-aid policies. In two of our studies, after we had finished the field analysis, we used nationally available statistical data and regression techniques to analyze and "check" some of our key findings. We call these *complementary* studies. The rationale for this combined approach is that you are not likely to know how to use statistical data (for example, U.S. Census of Government data) to study the impact of revenue sharing—i.e., to model the counterfactual and study the program's effects—unless and until you have done field analysis.

Several field researchers (notably Charles F. Adams, Jr., Dan Crippen, Robert F. Cook, Arthur Maurice, V. Lane Rawlins, and Michael Wiseman) collaborated on complementary statistical and field studies of the revenue

Conservatives generally do not like social science research, yet they often use the results to raise sharp questions about social programs.

sharing and CETA jobs programs on a basis that used the lessons and insights from the field analyses to devise a better "mousetrap" for econometric analysis. The findings of these complementary studies were quite similar to what we found in the field evaluations.

The work done in this way on the displacement effect of the CETA public service jobs program provides an interesting example. Previous econometric studies on the actual and potential effects of federally aided public service job-creation programs had come to the conclusion that eventually all or nearly all of these federal aid funds become substitutive. That is, the recipient state and local jurisdictions eventually use all of this aid to employ workers who would have been employed anyway. We found a very much lower displacement rate (around 20 to 25 percent) both in our field study and in the statistical study linked to the field evaluation. We then went back and identified the assumptions used in the econometric models that caused the difference. We found the assumptions involved to be a result of a lack of understanding of governmental institutions and processes on the part of those conducting the econometric studies. Greater power was obtained by linking institutional and statistical studies.

Some may say we were foolish to take the risk of doing linked field network and statistical evaluation studies, or that we must have done it in ways that are

suspect, but the record is out there to be read. I believe it reflects useful learning and modest, but real, methodological advances; it required operating in that dangerous boundary area between quantitative and qualitative studies. Similar points need to be made about my final category—demonstration studies.

I use the term *demonstration* to refer to research projects in which a treatment is administered for the purpose of assessing its impact and learning about its costs and benefits. Evaluation and demonstration studies are closely related. A demonstration is a more elaborate study (sometimes with a randomly selected control group) that tests a program or program idea. An evaluation study, on the other hand, assesses on ongoing program; it may use comparison sites, but it does not use a randomly selected control group.

To illustrate, I use the work of the Manpower Demonstration Research Corporation (MDRC), a ten-year old nonprofit research corporation located in New York City, which conducts national demonstration studies of job and training programs focused on "underclass" groups.

In 1973, a group of policy experts assembled by Mitchell Sviridoff, then vice president of the Ford Foundation, addressed the challenge of how to conduct a large-scale demonstration study with random assignment to test the "supported work" approach to aiding underclass groups. Supported work is a job-focused "treatment" characterized by graduated stress and peer-group support to help very disadvantaged persons enter the labor market. Although Sviridoff originally recruited us as an advisory committee, we soon found that it would be necessary to become incorporated in Delaware in order to serve as the intermediary corporation to receive funds from several government agencies and foundations to conduct the supported work demonstration. Over 10,000 people participated in the treatment and control groups for this demonstration, divided into four groups—female welfare family heads, ex-offenders, ex-addicts, and problem youths. The strongest positive finding of this first demonstration study by MDRC was that the supported work program significantly helped the aid to families with dependent children (AFDC) group; it did not aid the other three target groups. The MDRC experience with this demonstration encouraged us to undertake other similar studies.

The corporation's newest demonstration is its work/welfare demonstration initiated in 1982 to test the efficacy of the work provisions in the Omnibus Budget Reconciliation Act of 1981, including the administration's "workfare" approach to welfare reform. This Reagan initiative involves a fundamental shift in concept from welfare to workfare for the heads of families under the AFDC program.

In a typical state program, qualified AFDC family heads in this demonstration are initially assigned to an intensive job-search program. If the job-search phase is unsuccessful for a particular recipient, it is then followed by mandatory assignment to a low-skilled public service job, usually for three months, often renewable for another three months. Participants usually work for the number of hours each week that equals their welfare grant divided by the minimum wage (e.g., about three days per week). Other qualified welfare family heads in the test areas are randomly assigned to a control group whose members do not receive intensive job-search assistance and are not assigned to a mandatory public service job. To date, we have found, based on interviews with participants at a random sample of worksites, that

---

Liberals who generally like and support social science research are increasingly skeptical about its results and applications.

---

both participants and controls want public service jobs and believe that it is "fair" to require welfare recipients to work. Other studies have made similar findings.

Consistent with the point I attributed to Commons and Nelson about the need to take institutional factors into account in policy research, the design for the MDRC work/welfare project includes both process and impact studies. We are interested in the welfare system. How could the welfare system be changed in a way that would reduce welfare dependency and enhance the public credibility and acceptability of these transfer payments? In this case, the research target has been chosen on a basis that views the role of research as a potential institutional change agent in an area where basic systems changes are widely felt to be needed.

This demonstration is being conducted with large enough samples in several states so that we can compare the way the programs and systems work or do not work in each of the states. Process or institutional data collection and analysis are a critical element of the overall research design. The MDRC staff for process analysis, along with on-site contract researchers, is collecting uniform information on the way these programs work—including, the participants, the jobs provided, the experience of participants on the job, the type of work involved, the structure and management of the job-search and job programs.

In short, we have designed and are executing this demonstration so that we can take full advantage of the variation among the states in a way that will enable us to go beyond what has been done previously—in a way that

effectively links impact and process research. This study has other attributes that build on past experience with demonstrations. We are cutting costs (the supported work demonstration was expensive) by using administrative reporting data in the research. The hope and expectation for this demonstration is that we will learn about welfare both in behavioral and institutional terms on a basis that will provide valuable lessons for public policy.

Although the first large-scale demonstration conducted by MDRC—the supported work demonstration—produced useful findings, several caveats need to be entered about this demonstration. Large interdisciplinary studies can be most successful if two conditions are met, conditions that were only partially met in the case of the supported work demonstration. The conditions involve research design and strategy. We should have done more in the design of the supported work demonstration to link the process and impact analysis. The second important lesson of the supported work demonstration involves the selection of the research subject. In this case, the subject of study (the supported work program) was a New York City program developed by the Vera Institute that as it turned out did not have sufficiently deep roots in Washington and around the country.

To sharpen this point, it is my opinion that the subjects of large interdisciplinary demonstrations have to be very carefully selected with the goal uppermost in mind that "success" could attract enough political support to cause dissemination and replication. The supported work demonstration (highly successful for welfare mothers) has influenced state and local policy and the literature, but it involved a relatively high-cost program that because of its cost has not been as widely adopted as some of its advocates would have liked. We hope that the current MDRC work/welfare demonstration will have wider applicability because the basic idea involved has deep and broad public support. This depends on the results of the demonstration.

I do not have much to say about the final category in the typology I present—viz., "Demonstration/Qualitative" studies. It makes me think of Woody Allen and the expression, "So what else is new?" This reference may be too obscure. The point is that the idea of conducting "demonstrations" to learn about new programs and approaches has been abused for a long time. It has often been used as an excuse for inexpensive, politically focused programs that are not at all serious about anything even resembling research. You can call this a qualitative demonstration if you like. I would not do so.

My essential argument is that more emphasis should be placed by social scientists interested in applied research on evaluation and demonstration studies that operate in the critical boundary area between quantitative and qualitative research. The subjects for these studies should be carefully chosen, with major attention given to their potential for replication. Subjects should be selected to focus on systems on a basis so that applied social science has a potential for being an institutional change agent.

The task of bringing about such a shift in applied social science ultimately falls on the shoulders of the foundations and government agencies that support such research. Skillful strategies on their part could have a big payoff. Large applied research projects could be organized to enable researchers to carve out pieces of the analysis. Ideally such research designs would involve coordinated, individually authored articles and books suitable for review and assessment on a basis consistent with the standards of the academic social science departments that award advanced degrees and tenure.

Although I believe it is possible to be creative in these terms without being radical, the terrain is difficult and the job of achieving institutional change for social science would not be an easy one. There is reason to hope that, in the process of trying to move in this direction, research funders would attract talented social scientists to applied work, promote a better balance between theoretical and applied work and cause greater emphasis to be placed on empiricism, realism, and opportunities for replication.

Grand Academy of Lagado

At the end of *Gulliver's Travels*, Jonathan Swift has a wonderful piece of satire, meant to apply to the British Royal Academy, that has an eerie relevance for modern social science. He describes a voyage to Laputa and a visit to its major metropolis, Lagado. Everything in the kingdom of Laputa is in a state of disrepair and decay. Meanwhile, experts in the Grand Academy of Lagado are at work on projects so that "all the fruits of the earth shall come to maturity, at whatever season we think fit to

chuse, and encrease an hundred fold more than they do at present: with inumerable other happy proposals."

The author visits the Grand Academy, and among the academicians he meets there, my favorite is a man "with meagre aspect, with sooty hands and face; his hair and beard long, ragged and singed in several places." The author explains that this academician "had been eight years upon a project for extracting sunbeams out of cucumbers; which were to be put into vials, hermetically sealed, and let out to warm the air, in raw inclement summers."

The moral of this story for social scientists is that we need to get out of our laboratories and give more attention to real-world conditions. I believe social scientists interested in applied research need to give more attention to institutions and especially to the link between institutional change and behavioral change. It is not enough to study impacts if we do not have a deep understanding of the real-world nature of the programs and activities of government that produce or do not produce the impacts being studied. The analogy is not perfect, but more than a knowledge of cucumbers is necessary to an understanding of the wonder and power of sunshine!□

Richard P. Nathan is professor of public and international affairs at Princeton University and directs the university's Urban and Regional Research Center. He has been a federal government official and currently serves as chairman of the board of directors of the Manpower Demonstration Research Corporation. His books include The Administrative Presidency *and, with Fred C. Doolittle and Associates,* The Consequences of Cuts: The Effects of the Reagan Domestic Program on State and Local Governments.

41

Evaluation Research and Public Policy
Lessons from the National Hospice Study

Linda H. Aiken

The national hospice demonstration is a rare instance of the application of scientific methods to test the efficacy and costs of a new government health insurance benefit prior to its enactment. The demonstration sought to respond to congressional concerns about whether a new hospice benefit under Medicare would be politically and professionally acceptable, feasible to implement, and affordable. The unique contribution of this demonstration to public policy, however, is its explicit intent to test scientifically the relative efficacy of hospice care compared to conventional medical treatment for terminally ill cancer patients. It sets a precedent in suggesting to Congress that independent assessments of the impact of new health insurance benefits on patients and families are feasible and useful.

The controversy about how to provide more effective and humane care for terminally ill patients was stimulated by three developments: the increasing sophistication of technologies that can sustain life in situations formerly considered hopeless; the public's perception that medical care was becoming increasingly depersonalized; and the rapid growth of hospices as alternative sites of care.

The public policy debate focused on cost implications of paying for hospice services and encouraging the growth of new health care institutions when many hospitals were partially empty. Some believed that hospices would reduce

Author's Note: The ideas contained in this paper are those of the author. No endorsement by The Robert Wood Johnson Foundation is intended or should be inferred.

Editor's Note: Readers are referred to Chapter 7 by David S. Greer et al. for more information on the National Hospice Study.

expenditures for dying patients, and a number of small studies provided supporting evidence (Aiken and Marx, 1982). Skeptics, however, pointed out that every health insurance benefit expansion has resulted in substantially higher costs than originally anticipated. Medicare's End-Stage Renal Disease Program, for example, was estimated by it sponsors in 1972 to eventually cost up to $110 million a year. By 1983, costs had already reached $1.8 billion and are expected to be $4.6 billion by 1995 (Rettig, 1980).

At the patient care level, debate concerned the appropriate mix of medical interventions and psychological and social support. Hospices provide a supportive environment for the terminally ill at home or in special homelike settings with minimal professional "interference." But many physicians and even some hospice proponents, such as Sylvia Lack (1978), the medical director of the New Haven Hospice who came to the United States from St. Christopher's Hospice in London, feared that patients cared for at home in this country would become isolated from effective medical care and suffer unnecessarily from vomiting, pain, and other symptoms that can be controlled by appropriate medical interventions.[1]

The sponsors of the national hospice demonstration and its evaluation were interested in two deceptively simple questions that are at the heart of the hospice policy debate: Is there any evidence that widespread access to hospices will adversely affect the functioning and quality of life of the terminally ill and their families; and is there any reason to believe that insurance coverage for hospice care will be substantially more costly than existing benefits?

The findings (Greer et al., forthcoming [see Chapter 7 in this volume]) suggest that the answers to both questions are reassuring. The terminally ill and their families appear to fare equally well in hospices and conventional arrangements; both groups seem satisfied with their choice of treatment setting; and there is no evidence that hospice care is substantially more costly. It may even have some cost savings.

Beyond these general conclusions, the evaluation of the hospice demonstration provides a wealth of information on the clinical trajectory of terminally ill patients, the responses of families, and the variations in services provided for the terminally ill in different settings. These data should prove to be useful to clinicians in both hospices and conventional medical settings in suggesting new clinical management strategies for the terminally ill that warrant additional study. The findings also have a number of important implications for the future organization and reimbursement of services for the terminally ill.

The evaluation confirmed that hospices provide a different constellation of services to the terminally ill than is the case in the conventional care system: less diagnostic testing, less aggressive cancer therapy, and more social services. Substantial differences were also documented between home-based hospices without inpatient units of their own and hospital-based or freestanding hospices with inpatient beds. Two-thirds of patients in home-based hospices died at home compared with 27 percent of patients in hospices with inpatient facilities, and 13 percent of conventional care patients. The families of hospice patients were more satisfied with the place of death, although overall satisfaction with choice of setting was high for all families.

Hospices with inpatient units appeared to achieve better pain control, possibly as a result of more liberal use of analgesics, and their patients had fewer symptoms such as nausea and dyspnea than either conventional settings or home-based hospices. General functional performance and quality of life followed a similar pattern for patients in all settings. Family members had fewer adjustment problems in the postmortem period than had been expected on the basis of previous research, and no significant differences were found between hospice and nonhospice families.

In the demonstration, savings for both types of hospices were found when costs were compared to conventional care settings. The most substantial savings were achieved by hospices without inpatient beds. Whether savings will be realized on a national basis, however, depends on a number of factors, including the extent to which hospices develop their own inpatient services. The savings achieved by hospices were greatest in the final weeks before death and narrowed as length of hospice stay increased. Hence, earlier referrals to hospices as a result of wider acceptance of the hospice concept by physicians and families may offset, to some extent, the savings found in the demonstration where average length of stay was relatively short. Extending hospice benefits to patients without family caregivers, to for-profit organizations, and to terminally ill patients with diagnoses other than cancer would all have an unknown effect on costs.

The National Hospice Study is not without limitations that deserve discussion. The strongest research design to test the efficacy of hospice care would have been a clinical experiment with random assignment of patients to home-based and hospital-based hospices and a control group that received standard care in the conventional medical care system. An experimental design would have permitted a level of standardization of the intervention that was not possible to achieve in this demonstration. Moreover, randomization would have permitted a higher level of confidence that differences observed between groups were the result of different patterns of care rather than the special characteristics of patients who selected different care settings. Although it has become the norm in academic centers to conduct clinical studies using random assignment, in community studies involving practicing physicians, community institutions, and patient advocacy groups the randomization of patients is still not an accepted practice. Neither Congress nor the Executive Branch was willing to mandate randomization of Medicare benefits in the national hospice demonstration.

Given that patients in the National Hospice Study were not randomized, the evaluators had to attempt to control statistically for differences in the types of patients choosing both kinds of hospices and conventional care. Patients in the conventional care sample were significantly younger and had more functional impairment upon admission to the study than patients in the hospice sample. The researchers used multiple regression techniques to control statistically for these and other differences, but the degree to which statistical techniques can serve to standardize groups is uncertain.

It is reassuring, however, that a single-site randomized trial of hospice care at a Veterans' Administration facility reported very similar findings to the National Hospice Study (Kane et al., 1984 [Chapter 8 in this volume], 1985). The hospice, in this case, had an inpatient unit and a home care program. Outcome measures included the measurement of pain, depression, anxiety, functional status, patient satisfaction, and costs. The satisfaction of both patients and their families was greater in the hospice group, but other outcomes did not differ significantly. The superior symptom control documented in hospital-based hospices in the national evaluation was not found in the randomized trial. The randomized trial also found little difference in cost between hospice and conventional care, a finding that is not substantially different from the national demonstration.

It has been argued that a true test of the efficacy of hospice care would focus on the very best model hospices (Mount and Scott, 1983). From a policy perspective, however, it is equally important to understand how the health care system will respond to a new insurance benefit, what kinds and how many institutions will participate, and how many and what kinds of people choose hospice care when payment policies are altered. This information is best gleaned from demonstrations and explains, in part, why the government, in recent years, has preferred demonstrations over experiments with "model" programs (Orr, 1985 [Chapter 31 in this volume]). The results of a "real-world" test tend to have greater face validity among policymakers and offer opportunities to observe and correct implementation problems before enactment of the new benefit.

The development of social and clinical measures of quality of life and function in terminally ill people is a relatively new area of scientific inquiry, one that is particularly difficult. Although the evaluators used state-of-the-art measures that had been extensively tested in other studies, social science simply may not yet be able to measure adequately the benefits that the terminally ill and their families derive from hospice care. Given this possible limitation, the study was not able to document substantially superior outcomes for hospice patients. From a policy perspective, however, the solid evidence that patients fared as well in hospices as in conventional settings is likely to be seen as a sufficient basis on which to support a new hospice benefit in a pluralistic system that values personal choice.

Household circumstances of the terminally ill vary substantially, and the ability of family members to provide support and assistance may better match some treatment settings than others. The evaluation documented the substantial investments made by spouses and adult children in hospice settings, particularly in home-based hospices. A hospice benefit provides a broader range of choice that allows families to fit better the pattern of care to their special needs. The hospice demonstration shows that choice can be offered without adverse consequences for patients and without necessarily resulting in substantially higher costs.

The failure of Congress to wait for the results of the congressionally mandated National Hospice Study before enacting the new hospice benefit reflects the unique pressures and priorities of the political process. Clearly, using research in the implementation of public policy is a sensitive and difficult challenge. It is hard to generate sufficient government support for a large-scale demonstration unless pressures for enactment of legislation are building. Once a benefit is offered even on a limited demonstration basis, political pressures to enact the legislation grow rapidly, making it increasingly difficult to delay the political decision.

If evaluation research is to play a meaningful role in future congressional decisions, the research community must continue to pursue strategies to complete good studies faster and Congress must place a higher value on having the results of evaluations before decisions are made. There is, of course, no guarantee that political actors, given their own ideologies and political needs, will translate the results of studies directly into legislative actions. But the information and understanding that result from such careful investigations inform the thinking and policy alternatives considered over time and contribute to a process of adjustment and readjustment of benefit structures.

In this issue of the *Journal of Chronic Diseases*, the major findings of the National Hospice Study are being disseminated to the scientific community and others. Many believe the new Medicare hospice benefit is more restrictive than the hospice evaluation suggested was necessary. Many hospices have found the new benefit unrealistic and do not participate (Subcommittee on Health, 1985). The availability of these results will allow all interested parties to examine the findings of the evaluation in relation to the new hospice benefit and make their own determinations as to what an appropriate benefit would be given the evaluation findings. It seems likely that although the hospice evaluation was not used very extensively to design the original benefit, the findings will influence the congressional debate in 1986 when the benefit must be reconsidered. It is through this process of knowledge and understanding, pressures from interested professional and patient advocacy groups, and political debate that we can ultimately arrive at a benefit structure fitting to the needs of dying patients and their families, and also consistent with the nation's agenda to contain rising health care costs.

NOTE

1. For a view of the potential adverse consequences of hospices, see Gibson (1984).

REFERENCES

AIKEN, L. H. and M. MARX (1982) "Hospices: perspectives on the public policy debate." American Psychologist 37, 11: 1271-1279.
GIBSON, D. E. (1984) "Hospice: morality and economists." The Gerontologist 24, 1: 4-8.

GREER, D. S., V. MOR, J. N. MORRIS, S. SHERWOOD, D. KIDDER, and H. BIRNBAUM (forthcoming) "An alternative in terminal care: results of the National Hospice Study." Journal of Chronic Diseases.

KANE, R. L., S. J. KLEIN, L. BERNSTEIN, R. ROGHENBERG, and J. WALES (1985) "Hospice role in alleviating the emotional stress of terminal patients and their families." Medical Care 23, 3: 189-197.

KANE, R. L., J. WALES, J. BERNSTEIN, A. LEIBOWITZ, and S. KAPLAN (1984) "A randomised controlled trial of hospice care." The Lancet 1: 890-894.

LACK, S. (1978) "Characteristics of a hospice program of care," in G. W. Davidson (ed.) The Hospice: Development and Administration. Washington, DC: Hemisphere.

MOUNT, B. M. and J. F. SCOTT (1983) "Whither hospice evaluation." Journal of Chronic Diseases 36, 11: 731-736.

ORR, L. L. (1985) "Using experimental methods to evaluate demonstration projects," in L. L. Aiken and B. H. Kehrer (eds.) Evaluation Studies Review Annual Volume 10. Beverly Hills, CA: Sage.

RETTIG, R. A. (1980) "The politics of health cost containment: end-stage renal disease." Bulletin of the New York Academy of Medicine 56: 115-138.

Subcommittee on Health, Committee on Finance, U.S. Senate (1985) Implementation of the Medicare Hospice Benefit (September 17, 1984). Washington, DC: Government Printing Office.